Mastering™
Microsoft® SQL Server™ 2005

Mastering™

Microsoft® SQL Server™ 2005

Mike Gunderloy

Joseph L. Jorden

David W. Tschanz

Wiley Publishing, Inc.

Acquisitions and Development Editor: Thomas Cirtin
Technical Editor: Rick Tempestini
Production Editor: Vanessa Nuttry
Copy Editors: Cheryl Hauser, Tiffany Taylor
Production Manager: Tim Tate
Vice President & Executive Group Publisher: Richard Swadley
Vice President and Executive Publisher: Joseph B. Wikert
Vice President and Publisher: Neil Edde
Book Designers: Maureen Forys, Happenstance Typo-O-Rama; Judy Fung
Compositor: Craig Woods, Happenstance Type-O-Rama
Proofreader: Nancy Riddiough
Indexer: Ted Laux
Cover Design: Design Site
Cover Illustration: Jack T. Myers, Design Site

ISBN-13: 978-0-7821-4380-5
ISBN-10: 0-7821-4380-6

For general information on our other products and services or to obtain technical support, please contact our Customer Care Department within the U.S. at (800) 762-2974, outside the U.S. at (317) 572-3993 or fax (317) 572-4002.

Wiley also publishes its books in a variety of electronic formats. Some content that appears in print may not be available in electronic books.

Manufactured in the United States of America

10 9 8 7 6 5 4 3 2 1

For all my online blog buddies.
—M. G.

For all of my family and friends, but especially my wife, Rachelle.
—J. L. J.

To Karl and Eric — Sons I can't help being proud of
—D. W. T.

Acknowledgments

This book, like the database that it covers, has been percolating for a long time. After Sybex published *Mastering SQL Server 2000*, Joe Jorden and I had to take a break before we could contemplate writing more about our favorite database. But after a few years, it became obvious that Microsoft wasn't standing still, and that a new version of SQL Server was in the works. At that point we started trading e-mails with our editor at Sybex every few months, trying to figure out when the new version would come out. Along the way we decided to invite David Tschanz to join the writing team, switched editors, watched our publisher merge with Wiley, lived through numerous revisions to the product, and installed far too many beta versions. It's definitely not been a dull five years!

Being a revision, this book still reflects our original editorial team: Melanie Spiller, Denise Santoro-Lincoln, Ronn Jost, Kylie Johnston, and Acey Bunch. Now it's also had the benefit of a new group of editors: Tom Cirtin, Rachel Gunn, Tiffany Taylor, and Rick Tempestini. With all these helping hands, and the immense amount of work that my co-authors have done, this book is definitely a team effort. Still, I'm well aware that SQL Server 2005 is a large and complex product, and despite our best efforts we probably made a few mistakes. If any of these slipped by, blame me, not the editors.

Too many people have had a hand in my database education for me to thank them all. Some are on the Access and SQL Server teams at Microsoft; some are former business partners or clients; some are co-authors; many are just helpful developers out on the Internet. To everyone who's helped me think about databases over the past decade or two, thanks.

But one group of people needs to be singled out for special thanks: my family. My wife understands what I'm doing in front of the computer all day long, my kids don't, but they all tolerate that fact. Dana Jones provides love, support, lunches, and pretty much anything else I could ask, and helps with farm work, meals, technical support, homeschooling, and everything else that makes up our crazy lives together. Adam, Kayla, and Thomas provide a large number of smiles, hugs, and general chaos. Some day they'll understand that papa needs the royalties to pay for that new pair of shoes.

—Mike Gunderloy

Five short years ago, Mike and I completed the Herculean task of writing *Mastering SQL Server 2000*. Then, after taking a much needed break from writing and getting back to my developing roots I was ready to hit the books again, so Mike and I teamed up with David and off we went.

This time was a bit easier though because the groundwork had already been laid, and all of the people that performed the original work are still deserving of thanks. So Melanie Spiller, Denise Santoro-Lincoln, Ronn Jost, Kylie Johnston, and Acey Bunch, thanks for all your hard work. And special thanks to all of the people that made this project a success: Tom Cirtin, Rachel Gunn, Tiffany Taylor, Rick Tempestini, and of course Microsoft for making such an excellent product.

And where would I be without my friends and family? Many of them deserve special thanks for supporting me and telling me how cool it is that I wrote a book (even if they don't quite understand what it's about). First, my family: Mary (a.k.a. Mom), Buddy, and Shelly Jorden and Janet, Colin and Leian McBroom, thanks to all of you. There are also personal friends who tried to help keep me sane through all of this (sorry it didn't work everyone): Zerick Campbell and I have had many good times together, and with his new wife, Tanya, and the boys, Jostin and Brenton, it just keeps getting better. Timothy, Rebecca and Aiden Calunod; rum balls, what else need I say? Thanks to Dan Rosman, and the entire IT department at Jelly Belly for taking me on and Sue Hernandez for making my job that much easier. Most important though, thanks to my wife, Rachelle Jorden, for letting me take the time to write yet another book. Finally, thanks to all of you for reading this work; may it serve you well.

—Joseph L. Jorden

This is a big book. And it required the help and assistance of a large number of people, so I have a number of people to say thanks to.

First I want to thank Mike Gunderloy for inviting me to be a part of this project. I've known Mike as an editor for several years and have always been delighted and appreciative of his assistance, support and encouragement. I also want to thank Joe Jorden for his help and invaluable input. If there are two finer co-authors, I don't know who they are and I doubt they exist.

I also want to thank Tom Cirtin, Sybex acquisition and development editor, for his role in helping this book become a reality and Rachel Gunn for keeping track of all the moving bits and pieces while keeping a sharp eye on the deadlines. Microsoft needs to be thanked for turning out an incredibly rich and subtle product. I think we'll all spend a long time plumbing the depths of SQL Server 2005.

There are a number of personal friends, colleagues and family who have supported me through this book and some of the trials that came up during it. I'd like to mention my father, Alfred Tschanz, who encouraged me to keep writing as have the rest of my family—Cyndy, Karl and Eric Tschanz. I've also had tremendous support from colleagues, associates and friends who have either encouraged me, kept me sane, or been patient when I wrote book chapters instead of doing other things. All of them were necessary and each of them contributed directly or indirectly in making sure the product was my best: Khalid G. Al-Buainain, Salah Al-Dughaither, Bob Miller, Ahmed Ghanim, Jacqueline Mullen, Aisha Alireza, Emad Al-Dughaither, Paul Sauser, Rob Lebow, John Bischoff, Dick Doughty, Everett Richardson, Mike Flynn and Nadia El-Awady. Lastly, I also need to thank Dr. Eric T. McWilliams of SAMSO and Dr. Fuad Abdul Khader of the Bahrain Defence Forces without whose skills I could not have finished this book.

—David W. Tschanz

Contents at a Glance

Contents

Introduction

The first release of Microsoft SQL Server, back in 1988 (in conjunction with Ashton-Tate and Sybase), was a wimp of a database. Other database servers kicked sand in its face.

Microsoft SQL Server 2005, by contrast, isn't going to be bullied by anyone. At the end of a nearly two decades of development, it's ready to do some sand-kicking of its own. Consider these raw numbers:

- Maximum database size roughly 1,000,000 terabytes. To put that in perspective, you could store 100 megabytes each about every man, woman, child, and dog on the planet in a single SQL Server database (if you could afford the disk space!).
- Up to 16 simultaneous instances of SQL Server can run on a single computer. This is a great help if you're trying to run a complex Internet site, for example.
- Support for up to 64 processors in a single instance (if you're running the Enterprise edition of SQL Server 2005 on a computer equipped with an operating system that supports 64 processors).
- Support for as much physical RAM as your operating system allows you to install. With the 64-bit version of SQL Server 2005, that currently means 1TB of RAM on Windows Server 2003, Datacenter x64 Edition, but you can expect that limit to rise in the future (if you can afford to purchase that much RAM!)

The bottom line is clear: SQL Server 2005 is ready to play in the big leagues. As of this writing, the beta version of SQL Server 2005 running on a high end HP system holds the record in the industry-standard TPC-C benchmark with over one million transactions per minute—at a cost 35% less per transaction than that of Oracle's best result.

However, there's more to this product than just large numbers. Consider some of the other new features in this version of SQL Server:

- Support for writing stored procedures, triggers, and user-defined functions in .NET languages
- A native XML data type
- Service Broker, a new technology for reliable distributed applications in SQL Server
- Completely revamped management and development tools
- Integrated Reporting Services including an end-user Report Builder

The list goes on from there. You'll meet all of these technologies, and many more, later in this book. If you've worked with SQL Server in the past, you're in for a treat with the new version. If this is your first SQL Server experience, we think you'll be impressed with the depth and range of this enterprise-level database server.

How This Book Is Organized

We've designed this book to be a reference for the user new to SQL Server or the experienced user who might want to see what's new in this version. Our emphasis is on getting up and running quickly, whether you're a database administrator, a developer, or an end user. Because SQL Server 2005 was designed for the Windows interface, we emphasize using the graphical tools whenever they make sense. Of course, when the command line or the T-SQL programming language is superior, we don't hesitate to tell you so. We haven't tried to cover everything in every corner of the product. That would take a book five times as large as this one. Instead, we've provided the essential information that you need when you're getting oriented and starting to use SQL Server to manage your data.

The book is divided into six parts:

Part 1 (Chapters 1–4) will quickly introduce you to the major concepts in database technology and to SQL Server itself. You'll definitely want to start here if you're new to SQL Server.

Part 2 (Chapters 5–8) covers the Transact-SQL programming language, from the simple SELECT statement to advanced concepts including cursors and distributed cursors. Transact-SQL is at the heart of much SQL development, and understanding it is essential if you want to make efficient use of your data.

Part 3 (Chapters 9–15) digs into the core components of SQL Server in more depth. Here you'll learn how to use SQL Server Management Studio to ride herd on your data, and see how tables, views, stored procedures, and other SQL Server objects work together with your data.

Part 4 (Chapters 16–18) looks at administering SQL Server. This is where you'll need to read carefully if you're responsible for keeping a SQL Server installation running smoothly. We cover all the basic administrative tasks, from performing backups to scheduling automatic jobs to setting security.

Part 5 (Chapters 19–22) is for developers. We cover the most important of the "alphabet soup" technologies for working with SQL Server (.NET, SMO, RMO, and SSIS).

Part 6 (Chapters 23–30) covers a mix of advanced topics, including locking, optimization, replication, Analysis Services, Notification Services, Reporting Services, Service Broker, and troubleshooting. This section of the book will give you an idea of some of the more advanced capabilities of SQL Server and provide a springboard from which you can investigate further.

How to Contact the Authors

This book was written in 2004 and 2005 using various beta versions of SQL Server 2005. Although we've tried to make it as accurate as possible, inevitably there will be differences between what we were using and the version that finally ships. There will be updates, service packs, and release versions that change this software. If something strikes you as odd, or you find an error in the book, please drop us a line via e-mail. Our e-mail addresses are `MikeG1@larkfarm.com`, `jljorden@comcast.net`, and `dtschanz@sahara.com.sa`, and we're always happy to hear from our readers.

Part 1

Introducing SQL Server

In this section:

Chapter 1

Introduction to SQL Server 2005

Welcome to SQL Server 2005. In this book, we'll help you learn the basics of SQL Server and advance to more complex skills. You won't learn *everything* about Microsoft's flagship database here: It's a huge set of programs that can take years, if not decades, to learn fully. However, we'll show you how to get up and running quickly and how to handle typical everyday tasks of keeping your data safe, secure, and available to your users.

SQL Server 2005 isn't just an upgrade of SQL Server. Originally planned for 2003, the two extra years of work on Yukon (Microsoft's development code name for SQL Server 2005) have resulted in a product that is so different and so much better than its predecessor as to make you think the only things the two version have in common are similar names and use of SQL.

This isn't just hype or a marketing device. Microsoft has overhauled nearly every aspect of SQL Server. What we have today is a product that is more fully integrated, flexible, and extensible than any relational database product.

Before we dig deep into the details of SQL Server, we want to introduce you to the product. You may be a budding database administrator (DBA), anxious to manage a database for others to use; you may be a developer, ready to write code that will extract information from a server someone else is maintaining; or you may be a regular user who just needs to see some data and doesn't have time to wait for the IT department to build an application.

Whoever you are, *Mastering SQL Server 2005* has something for you. In this chapter, we'll talk briefly about the ways you'll probably work with SQL Server 2005, whether you're a DBA, a developer, or a user. Users in particular should review these pages even if you don't expect to ever write a line of code or manage a database. By knowing what *can* be done with SQL Server 2005, you'll be in a much better position to discuss with your IT people the sort of solutions and assistance you need. You may even discover that SQL Server 2005 can help you solve that problem you've been having with your data.

In this introductory chapter, we'll also look briefly at most of the new enhancements in SQL Server 2005. Of course, we can't highlight all the features or all the changes in SQL Server 2005, but we can show you enough to make you as excited about this database management system as we are.

The Editions of SQL Server 2005

Because SQL Server 2005 is used by a vast audience of different people—businesses, school, government agencies, and so on, all of whom have different needs as well diverse requirements—it comes in different editions. Each targets a group based on creating a good match to the unique performance, runtime, and price requirements of organizations and individuals. The five editions of SQL Server 2005 are as follows:

- Microsoft SQL Server 2005 Enterprise Edition
- Microsoft SQL Server 2005 Standard Edition

- Microsoft SQL Server 2005 Workgroup Edition
- Microsoft SQL Server 2005 Developer Edition
- Microsoft SQL Server 2005 Express Edition

The most common editions used are the Enterprise, Standard, and Workgroup editions as these work best in production server environments.

SQL Server 2005 Enterprise Edition (32-bit and 64-bit) This edition comes in 32- and 64-bit varieties. It's the ideal edition if you need to have a SQL Server 2005 that can scale to limitless size while supporting enterprise-sized online transaction processing (OLTP), highly complex data analysis, data warehousing systems, and websites.

In simplest terms, Enterprise Edition has all the bells and whistles and is beautifully suited to provide comprehensive Business Intelligence and analytics capabilities. It includes high-availability features such as failover clustering and database mirroring. It's ideal for large organizations or situations with the need for a SQL Server 2005 that can handle complex situations.

SQL Server 2005 Standard Edition (32-bit and 64-bit) Standard Edition includes the essential functionality needed for e-commerce, data warehousing, and line-of-business solutions without some advanced features such as Advanced Data Transforms, Data-Driven Subscriptions, and DataFlow Integration using Integration Services. Standard Edition is best suited for the small- to medium-sized organization that needs a complete data-management and analysis platform without many of the advanced features found in Enterprise Edition.

SQL Server 2005 Workgroup Edition (32-bit only) Workgroup Edition is the data-management solution for small organizations that need a database with no limits on size or number of users. It includes only the core database features of the product line (it doesn't include Analysis Services or Integration Services, for example). It's intended as an entry-level database that's easy to manage.

SQL Server 2005 Developer Edition (32-bit and 64-bit) Developer Edition has all the features of Enterprise Edition. However, it's licensed for use only as a development and test system, not as a production server. This edition is good choice for people or organizations who build and test applications but don't want to pay for Enterprise Edition.

SQL Server 2005 Express Edition (32-bit only) SQL Server Express is a free database that's easy to use and simple to manage. It comes without many of the features of other editions, including Management Studio, Notification Services, Analysis Service, Integration Services, and Report Builder, to name only a few. SQL Server Express can function as the client database or as a basic server database. It's a good option when all you need is a stripped-down version of SQL Server 2005, typically among low-end server users (such as small businesses), nonprofessional developers building web applications, and hobbyists building client applications. For more information about Express Edition, see *Mastering SQL Server 2005 Express Edition* by Mike Gunderloy and Susan Harkins (Sybex, 2006).

For more information on the differences in the various editions of SQL Server 2005, visit the SQL Server section of the Microsoft website at `http://www.microsoft.com/sql/2005/productinfo/sql2005features.mspx`.

Administering SQL Server

One of the key elements built into SQL Server 2005 is a high degree of integration between the development side and the management side. Microsoft designers worked to break down silos between the two groups and to make it possible to work together.

If you have experience with SQL Server 2000, the first thing you'll notice is that the Enterprise Manager has been completely revamped into SQL Server Management Studio, which performs most of the functions of Enterprise Manager along with many new ones.

We'll take a few moments to look at how you use this interface to administer data and services as well as to keep track of what's happening on your server. This will be a short visit, though. Management Studio is covered again briefly in Chapter 3. In addition, all of Chapter 9 is devoted to this important tool.

Opening SQL Server Management Studio

To launch Management Studio, choose Programs ➤ Microsoft SQL Server ➤ SQL Server Management Studio from the Windows Start menu. Management Studio is installed when you install SQL Server 2005. When it opens, you're asked to connect to a SQL Server instance. As soon as you connect, the SQL Server instance will appear in Object Explorer.

From here, you can expand a treeview to drill down from servers to databases to objects and inspect individual objects in a list view. Figure 1.1 shows how Management Studio might look after you drill down a few levels. In this case, we're examining the tables in the AdventureWorks database on a server named GARAK in the default server group.

NOTE The AdventureWorks database comes with SQL Server 2005. In many cases throughout the book, we use AdventureWorks as a good generic example of a database. We also use the AdventureWorks sample database or create examples that you can emulate for your own database needs.

FIGURE 1.1
SQL Server Management Studio

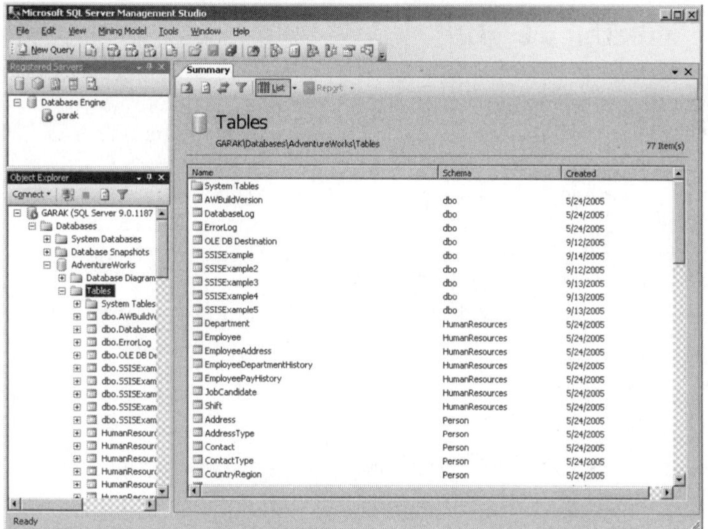

Even if you don't know anything about Management Studio, you'll appreciate the wide list of objects that can be manipulated using this interface:

Databases	Alerts
Database diagrams	Operators
Tables	Jobs
Views	Backups
Stored procedures	Process information
Users	Database maintenance plans
Roles	SQL Server logs
Rules	Replication
Defaults	Logins
User-defined datatypes	Server roles
User-defined functions	Performance Analyzer
Full-text catalogs	Analysis services cubes
Integration Services packages	Linked servers
Metadata Services packages	Remote servers
Data Transformation Services metadata	Notification services subscriptions
Credentials	Shared schedules

And that's just a sample! You'll learn about most of these objects in coming chapters.

Creating a Login

If you're a DBA, one of your main tasks is managing security on your SQL Server. We'll discuss security in much more detail in Chapter 18, but for now, let's look at one part of the picture: creating a login. A SQL Server login is a necessary part of making your SQL Server data available to a Windows user on your network.

There are several ways to create a new login. The easiest technique is to use the Logins folder under the Security folder in Management Studio. Open Object Explorer, expand the server instance, and then expand the Security Folder. Right-click the Login folder, and select New Login. The Login - New property window opens (see Figure 1.2).

In the top part of the pane, you select the authentication mode. SQL Server can use two different methods to verify that a user is who they claim to be:

- Windows Authentication compares the user with their credentials in the Windows 2000/2003 user database.
- SQL Server Authentication prompts the user for a password that's evaluated by SQL Server itself.

In most cases, you should choose Windows Authentication—your users won't have to supply a separate password for SQL Server, and you won't have two sets of passwords to audit and coordinate. You might want SQL Server accounts, though, for operations such as accessing a database over the Internet. Also, you should be aware that Windows Authentication is available only if this copy of SQL Server is running on Windows 2000 or Windows 2003.

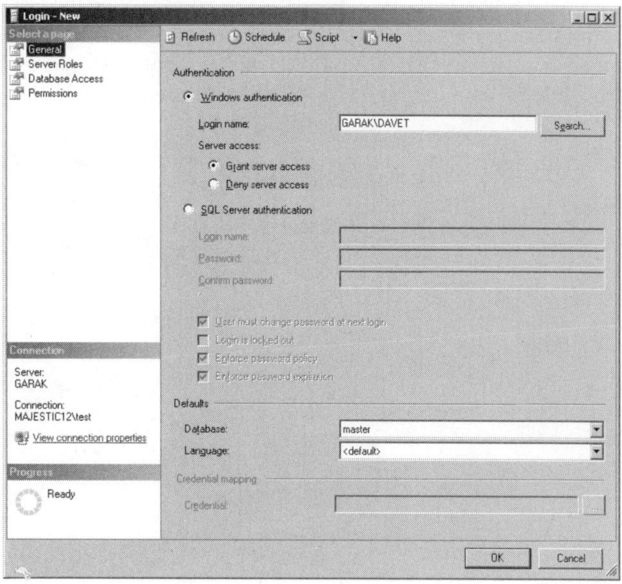

FIGURE 1.2
Login - New window, General page

In the Login Name text box, you specify the Windows user for whom you want to create a login (assuming that you chose Windows Authentication mode). You can type in the domain and username manually or search for the user by clicking the Search button.

In the Server Access section, you can either grant a user access to your server or deny a user all access to your server. As a general rule, you should deny access to everyone who doesn't explicitly need to get to the data on your server. There's no point in having idle hands rifling through your database.

Now, click Server Roles in the left-hand pane to open the Server Roles page, as shown in Figure 1.3. Here you can select which server-wide security privileges this user should have.

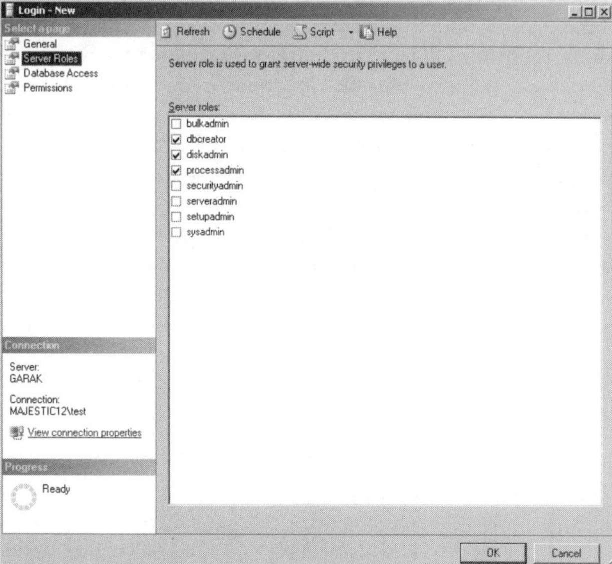

FIGURE 1.3
Login - New window, Server Roles page

Select Database Access in the left-hand pane to open the Database Access page shown in Figure 1.4, and select what databases will be accessible to the specified login. If you don't choose any databases, the user can log in but can't do anything. If you want to set specific permissions, select Permissions in the left-hand pane, and select and set specific permissions.

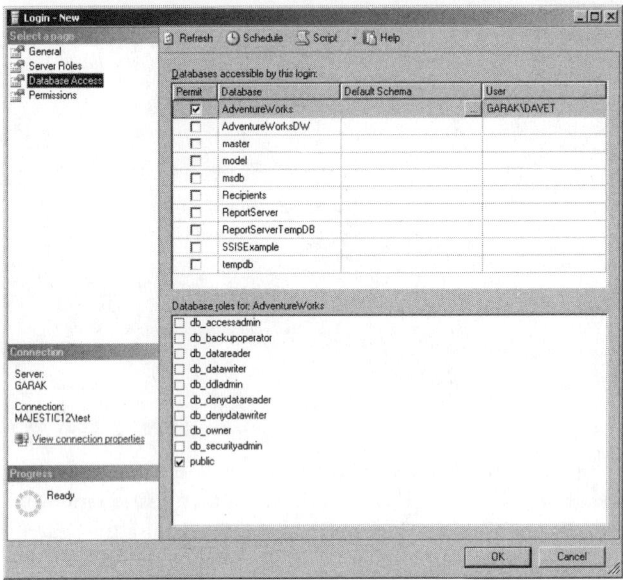

FIGURE 1.4
Login - New window, Database Access page

If all is well, click OK to create the login. That's all there is to it!

Using the Configuration Manager

Another task you may be called on to perform is to change the way a SQL Server instance starts or make an adjustment to the SQL Server configuration. To do these sorts of tasks, you use a different server tool: the SQL Server Configuration Manager. To launch the SQL Server Configuration Manager, click Windows Start ➤ Programs ➤ Microsoft SQL Server ➤ Configuration Tools ➤ SQL Server Configuration Manager.

The SQL Server Configuration Manager opens as a Microsoft Management Console (MMC) snap-in. As you can see in Figure 1.5, it includes a number of trees.

Let's use SQL Server Configuration Manager to set SQL Server to start automatically. Select SQL Server 2005 Services. Next, in the Details pane, right-click the name of the SQL Server instance you want to start automatically, and then click Properties.

In the SQL Server Properties dialog box, click the Service tab, and set Start Mode to Automatic as shown in Figure 1.6. (Because this is the default value, it should already be set to Automatic.) Click OK, and then close SQL Server Configuration Manager.

Viewing Current Activity

At times, you may want to know what's going on in your database. You can get a quick overview through Management Studio by selecting the Activity Monitor node in the Management section of Object Explorer. Right-click, and select View Processes from the pop-up menu to open the Activity Monitor Process Info page. Figure 1.7 shows typical activity on a lightly loaded server.

You may find a process running here that you don't recognize. If so, double-clicking the process lets you see the last set of T-SQL commands that were submitted by that particular process. If you're still in the dark, you can send a message from Enterprise Manager directly to the user or computer from which the process originated.

Other nodes within Management Studio allow you to easily view current locks and detect deadlock situations that may be harming performance.

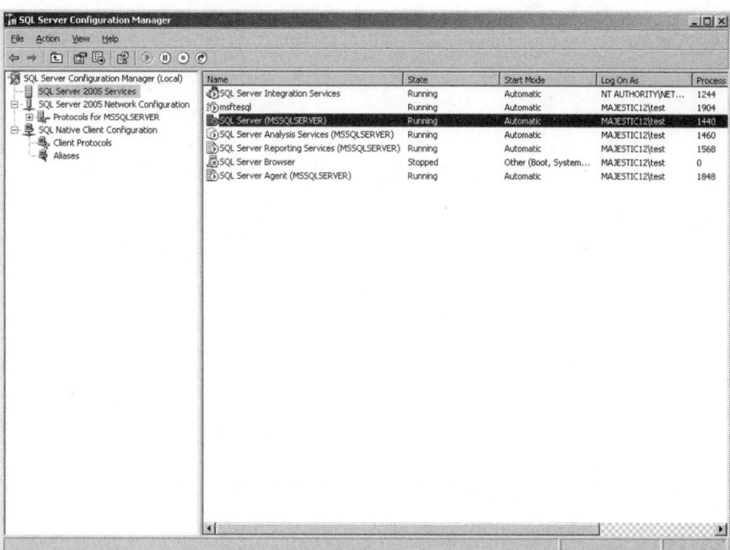

FIGURE 1.5
SQL Server Configuration Manager

FIGURE 1.6
Setting Start Mode to Automatic

FIGURE 1.7
Viewing current activity

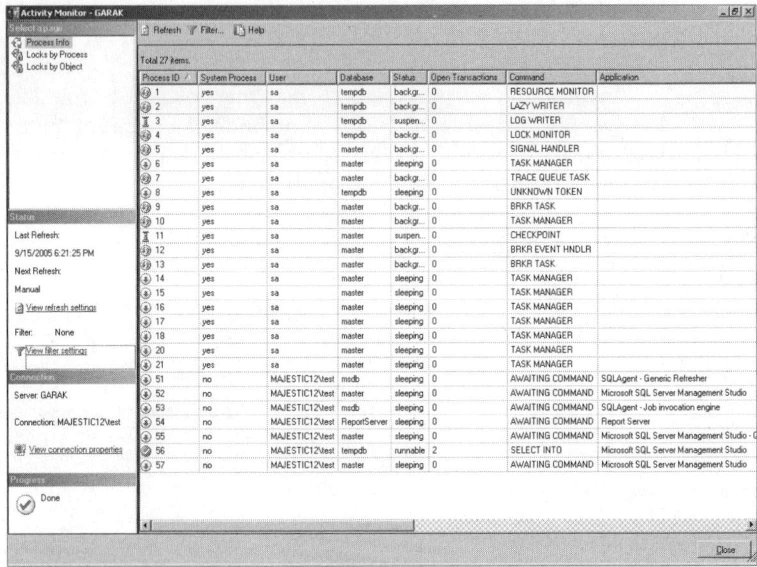

Development Tools

If you're a developer, you'll be less concerned with the design and maintenance of your database than with what you can do with it. SQL Server 2005 ships with a variety of tools for developers, including ActiveX Data Objects (ADO), SQL-DMO, SQL-NS, Integration Services, Analysis Services, and Bulk Copy Program (BCP). You'll learn about many of these in Parts 5 and 6 of this book, so we won't cover them in detail here. For now, we'll concentrate on one tool, Business Intelligence Development Studio (BIDS) and give you an overview of how much simpler design and development have become.

Business Intelligence Development Studio

Business Intelligence Development Studio (BIDS) is the SQL Server 2005 studio environment for developing Business Intelligence solutions including cubes, data sources, data source views, reports, and Integration Services packages.

To open BIDS, click Windows Start ➢ Programs ➢ Microsoft SQL Server ➢ SQL Server Business Intelligence Development Studio. You'll be using BIDS to work on projects, so click File ➢ New ➢ Project to open the New Project window, shown in Figure 1.8.

Note that there are six projects or wizards covering three different technologies to choose from: Analysis Services Project, Import Analysis Services 9.0 Database, Integration Services Project, Report Server Project Wizard, Report Model Project, and Report Server Project.

For now, let's look at a the AdventureWorks Sample Reports in BIDS, as shown in Figure 1.9. (If you want, you can open the project yourself— assuming you've installed the sample— by clicking Open ➢ Project Solution then navigating to `C:\Program Files\Microsoft SQL Server\90\SamplesReporting Services\Report Samples\AdventureWorks Sample Reports\ AdventureWorks Sample Reports.sln` and then selecting the Sales Order Detail.rdl item in the Reports folder.)

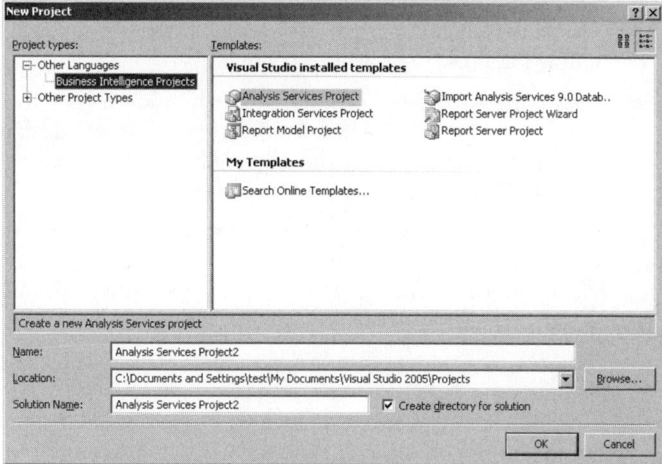

FIGURE 1.8
BIDS New Project window

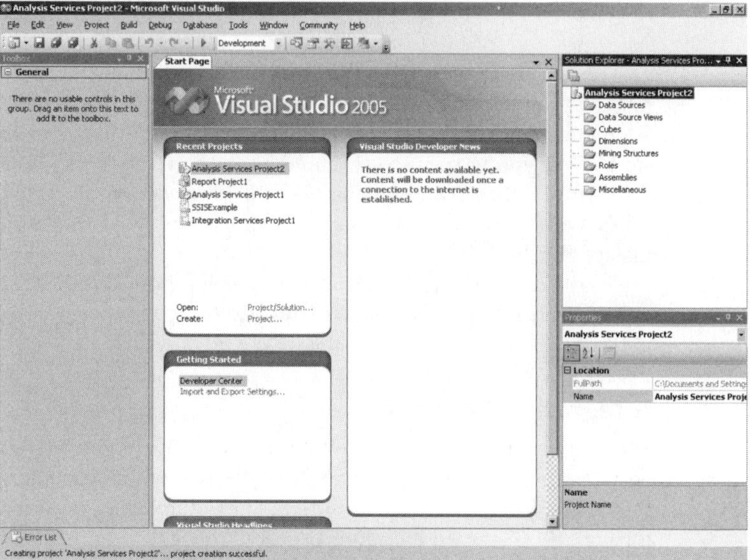

FIGURE 1.9
Sample Project in Business Intelligence Development Studio

As you can see, the BIDS project consists of four main windows:

Designer window The Designer window, which appears as the central pane with Toolbox to the left and the Solution Explorer and Properties panes to the right, provides a graphical view of an object and is used to create and modify Business Intelligence objects. Each of the three SQL Server 2005 Business Intelligence components has a designer tailored to it. For example, the Integration Services Package Designer provides the design surfaces to create Integration Services packages, and the Report Designer does the same when you create and preview reports. Some object types, such as data source views, are available to all Business Intelligence projects, and Data Source View Designer is included in all project types. The designers provide a code view and a design view of an object.

Solution Explorer Solution Explorer provides you with an organized view of your project and associated files as well as easy access to the commands relevant to them. A toolbar in this window offers commonly used commands for the item you highlight in the list.

Properties window The Properties window is used to view and change the design-time properties and events of selected objects in editors and designers. This window displays different types of editing fields including edit boxes, drop-down lists, and links to custom editor dialog boxes. Properties shown in gray are read-only.

Toolbox window This window shows a variety of items for use in Business Intelligence projects. The tabs and items available from the Toolbox change, depending on the designer or editor currently in use. The Toolbox always displays the General tab. Additional tabs may display depending on the project type.

BIDS also includes other windows for viewing search results and error and output information. Windows and their contents change depending on the type of project you're working on.

All BIDS projects are developed within a *solution*. A solution is a server-independent container that can include multiple Integration Services projects as well as Analysis Services and report projects.

You'll learn more about BIDS and its use as a powerful development tool in Chapters 22, 26, and 28 when we cover Integration Services, Analysis Services, and Reporting Services.

New and Improved

A great deal has changed in SQL Server 2005, and although you may be familiar with earlier versions, what you've seen so far should be enough to convince you that things in SQL Server are very different. The depth and flexibility of the product as reflected in the new Management Studio and BIDS should be enough to convince you that knowledge of SQL Server 2000 isn't enough to truly master SQL Server 2005.

To attempt to list and explain every change, new feature, and enhancement in SQL Server 2005 would likely take another book. In the next few pages, we'll introduce those that you're likely to see in the components you'll probably make the most use of.

Integration Services

SQL Server Integration Services (SSIS) is virtually a complete redo of the old Data Transformations Services, as you'll see in Chapter 22. With such wholesale changes, we can touch on only a few of them here. Key differences include the introduction of graphical tools, such as the SSIS Designer through BIDS (shown in Figure 1.10) and the SQL Server Import and Export Wizard; increased extensibility by using custom tasks, sources, destinations, and transformations; and changes to the architecture.

Data flow and control flow have been separated into two distinct engines—the Integration Services runtime engine and the Integration Services data flow engine. This separation provides better control of package execution, increases the visibility of data transformations, and enhances the extensibility of Integration Services by simplifying the creation and implementation of custom tasks and transformations.

Support for the Microsoft .NET Framework makes it easier to create custom Integration Services tasks, transformations, and data adapters.

FIGURE 1.10
Integration Services Package Designer

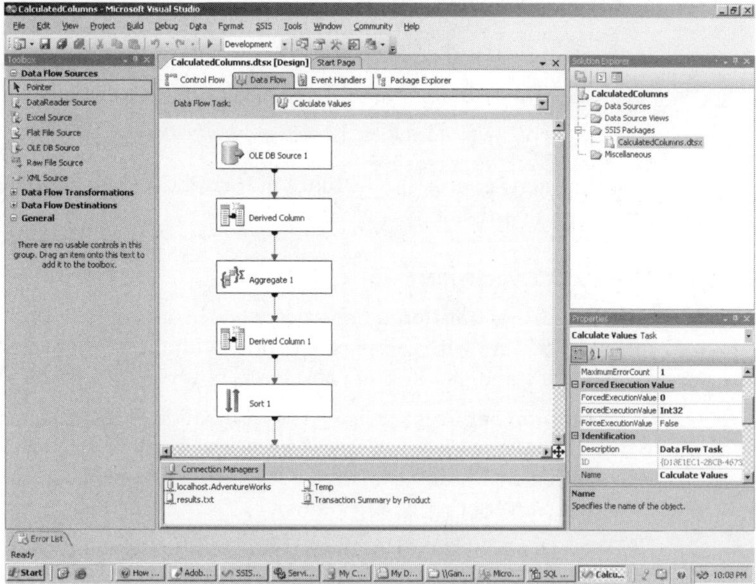

NEW TASKS

The following new tasks have been added:

- The WMI Data Reader task for querying Windows Management Instrumentation (WMI) data
- The WMI Event Watcher task for listening to WMI events
- The File System task for performing operations on files and folders in the file system
- The Web Service task for accessing web services
- The XML task for working with XML documents
- The Analysis Services Execute DDL task for running DDL scripts
- The Data Mining Query task for querying data mining models

NEW DATA SOURCES AND DESTINATIONS

SSIS now uses the following new sources and destinations in addition to the SQL Server, OLE DB, and flat file sources and destinations:

- Data Mining Query destination
- DataReader source and destination
- Dimension Processing destination
- Partition Processing destination
- Raw File source and destination

- Recordset destination
- SQL Server Mobile destination
- The Data Mining Model Training destination
- XML source

Integration Services also includes the Script Component for simplified development of custom sources and destinations.

New Data Transformations

There are 20 new transformations, described in detail in Chapter 22, making it easier for developers to build packages with complex data flow without writing any code.

Managing and monitoring packages is now easier with the following new tools:

Integration Services service The Integration Services service is a new Microsoft Windows service that manages package storage and displays a hierarchical view of saved packages in Management Studio. The service supports packages stored in the msdb database in an instance of SQL Server or in the file system.

DTUTIL The `dtutil` command-line utility lets you copy, delete, move, and sign packages stored in the msdb database, in an instance of SQL Server, or in the file system.

Running packages list This tool displays a list of running packages in Management Studio.

Package logging options SSIS includes multiple logging providers, a logging schema from which you can choose the type of information to log, and a flexible logging model that supports logging configuration at the package level and the task level.

Package restart capability Checkpoints can be set to let you restart a package from the failed task instead of having to rerun the whole package.

Security features New security features include:

- Roles can be used for packages in the msdb database in an instance of SQL Server.
- Packages can be encrypted with various levels of encryption to protect sensitive data.
- Packages can now be digitally signed.

New and updated Integration Services wizards Integration Services includes a set of new and updated wizards that help you accomplish complex tasks such as deploying, importing, and exporting packages or migrating SQL Server 2000 Data Transformation Services (DTS) packages from the SQL Server 2000 format to SQL Server 2005, as well as other tasks as listed in Table 1.1.

Table 1.1: Integration Services Wizards

Wizard	Description
SQL Server Import and Export Wizard	Creates packages that copy data between a source and a destination
Package Configuration Wizard	Creates configurations that can be deployed with packages

TABLE 1.1: Integration Services Wizards *(CONTINUED)*

WIZARD	DESCRIPTION
Package Installer Wizard	Deploys packages and updated package configurations
Package Migration Wizard	Migrates SQL Server 2000 DTS packages to SQL Server 2005 Integration Services packages

Replication

Replication is the process of copying and distributing data and database objects from one database to another and then synchronizing between databases to maintain consistency. Without a good replication modality in place, you'll get in trouble sooner or later if more than one person is accessing the database, or if more than one copy of it exists.

Take this simple example: Imagine you have a database of all your DVDs on your home network. You copy the database onto your laptop and go on vacation. Three days into the vacation, you buy more DVDs and enter them into the database on your laptop. However, what you don't know is that the day after you left, your son purchased a new DVD and added it to the database at home. You return home and copy the laptop database over to your home database. It's now "updated" with the most recent files. Unfortunately, it's wrong, because you've erased all entries except those made by you. DVDs are one thing—imagine what it would be like if those were your financial records, or a company's inventory database. If you didn't have replication, then eventually drift would occur; instead of one database, you'd have many, each containing slightly different data.

Using replication, you can distribute data to different locations and to remote or mobile users over local and wide area networks, dial-up connections, wireless connections, and the Internet.

Recognizing the important role replication plays in good database health, several new features and enhancements have been added in SQL Server 2005. As you'll see in Chapter 25, a number of enhancements make keeping databases properly synchronized and replicated much easier, even with non-SQL Server 2005 databases:

Simplified user interface The New Publication Wizard has 40 percent fewer pages than its SQL Server 2000 counterpart.

The Push Subscription Wizard and Pull Subscription Wizard are combined into the New Subscription Wizard, which provides a convenient way to create multiple subscriptions with different properties.

Replication Monitor has been completely redesigned (see Figure 1.11).

Improved replication between different types of databases You can now publish from Oracle databases to SQL Server 2005. In addition, you can now publish data to Oracle and IBM DB2, using snapshot and transactional replication.

Replication Management Objects (RMO) RMO is a Microsoft .NET library that provides a set of common language runtime classes for configuring, managing, and scripting replication, and for synchronizing Subscribers. This means programs can work on individual classes, such as the publication or subscription class, without traversing from top-level classes.

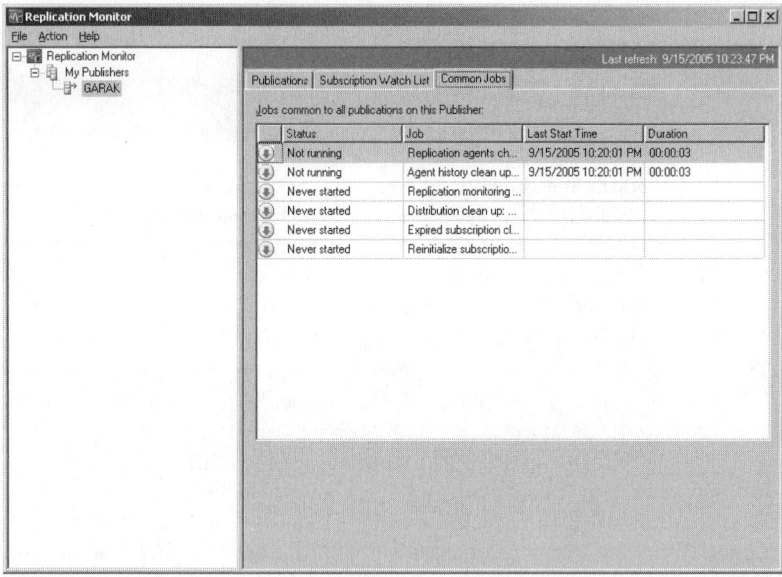

FIGURE 1.11 Replication Monitor has been completely redesigned for SQL Server 2005

Business logic handlers for merge replication The business logic handler framework allows you to write a managed code assembly that is called during the merge synchronization. This means that if a salesperson enters an order from a handheld device, the inventory can be checked during synchronization, and the salesperson can be notified if the product is sold out.

Changes to transactional replication

- Peer-to-peer transactional replication
- Ability to initialize a transactional subscription from a backup
- Ability to modify call formats for transactional articles without reinitializing
- Increased number of columns allowed in transactional publications
- Tracer tokens for transactional publications
- Default use of concurrent snapshots by transactional publications

Other enhancements In addition to those already listed, SQL Server 2005 adds the following features to its replication capabilities:

- Improved identity range management
- Parallel snapshot preparation
- Resumable snapshot delivery
- Improved monitoring statistics for merge subscriptions
- Improvements to snapshots for merge publications with parameterized filters
- Declarative ordering for articles in merge publications
- Conditional delete processing for articles in merge publications
- Replication of schema changes

- Replication of logical records
- Improved error messages

Analysis Services

Many changes have been made to Analysis Services, sometimes still referred to as *business analytics*. As you'll see in Chapter 26, the topic of Analysis Services is vast.

Building on its beginnings in SQL Server 2000, Microsoft SQL Server 2005 Analysis Services (SSAS) provides additional support for Business Intelligence, delivering increased scalability, availability, and security to Business Intelligence solutions while making them easier to create, deploy, and manage. Many new features, and improvements to existing features, have been added to Analysis Services as shown in the following tables.

SSAS comes with a number of new and advanced designers, as described in Table 1.2

TABLE 1.2: New and Improved SSAS Designers

DESIGNER	DESCRIPTION
Cube Designer	Now provides support for dimension usage, translation, MDX scripting, and Key Performance Indicator (KPI) functions
Data Mining Model Designer	Used for defining, viewing, and testing mining structures and mining models in BIDS
Data Source View Designer	Provides a simple, diagram-based environment for defining the tables and relationships in a Data Source view on which to base Analysis Services objects
Dimension Designer	Enhanced to provide support for attribute-based dimension definitions, user-defined and attribute hierarchies, translations, and dimension writeback

New and improved wizards make many SSAS tasks much simpler to perform for users, developers, and DBAs. Table 1.3 summarizes these wizards.

TABLE 1.3: New and Improved SSAS Wizards

WIZARD	DESCRIPTION
Business Intelligence Wizard	Provides advanced Business Intelligence features, such as currency conversion, account intelligence, time intelligence, and dimension writeback support.
Cube Wizard	Walks you through the steps of designing and prototyping a cube. Provides several enhancements, including autobuild technology, to analyze and determine dimensions and hierarchies intelligently and to measure groups from the tables and relationships of the underlying data source (see Figure 1.12).
Data Mining Model Wizard	Creates new mining structures based on either relational or multidimensional data that can be modified later by using the Data Mining Designer.

TABLE 1.3: New and Improved SSAS Wizards *(CONTINUED)*

WIZARD	DESCRIPTION
Data Source View Wizard	Quickly and automatically retrieves the relational schema of a data source and constructs tables and relationships on which Analysis Services objects, such as dimensions and cubes, can be based.
Dimension Wizard	Adds slowly changing dimension support, dimension writeback, account intelligence, and time intelligence to the design of database dimensions in Analysis Services.
Migration Wizard	Migrates databases from previous versions of Analysis Services to an instance of SSAS.
Schema Generation Wizard	Allows you to create relational schemas based on existing Analysis Services objects. Can be used to define your dimensions and cubes first and then design a Data Source view based on your dimensions and cubes. The Data Source view can be used to create and populate a relational database specifically to support your Business Intelligence solution.

FIGURE 1.12
Cube Wizard

SSAS' Analysis Services service has been beefed up and expanded to include the changes and enhancements described in Table 1.4.

TABLE 1.4: SSAS Changes and Improvements

FEATURE	DESCRIPTION
Failover clustering	Support for 8-node failover clusters on 32-bit systems and 4-node clusters on 64-bit systems.
Language and collation support	Support for language and collation settings at both the instance level and the database level.
Multi-instance support	Ability to install up to 50 instances of the Analysis Services service from Microsoft SQL Server 2005 Enterprise Edition on one computer. Up to 16 instances of the Analysis Services service can be installed from other editions of SQL Server 2005.
Orphan fact table rows	Ability to use settings for each hierarchy in a dimension to determine how to handle orphan fact table rows.
Proactive caching	Used to increase the performance of dimensions, partitions, and aggregations.
Processing support	Additional flexibility, including direct support of parallel processing.
Scripting support	Ability to script databases and subordinate objects by using the Analysis Services Scripting Language (ASSL).
XML support	Full implementation of the XML for Analysis (XMLA) 1.1 specification.

Table 1.5 shows the SSAS management enhancements and new features available in SQL Server 2005.

TABLE 1.5: SSAS Management Enhancements

FEATURE	DESCRIPTION
Deployment engine	Analysis Services now includes its own engine for deploying Analysis Services projects and solutions.
Security	Analysis Services provides increased security features, including better access control, encryption, and monitoring tools.
SQL Server Profiler integration	Analysis Services now supports SQL Server Profiler for monitoring and capturing any events that are generated by an instance of Analysis Services for future analysis or playback.

SSAS includes the cube, dimension, and data-mining enhancements and new features shown in Table 1.6.

TABLE 1.6: SSAS Cube, Dimension, and Data-Mining Enhancements

TOPIC	ITEM	DESCRIPTION
Cube	Key Performance Indicators	KPIs are customizable business metrics used by companies to track performance and improve performance.
Cube	Multiple fact tables	Multiple fact tables within a single cube are supported through the use of measure groups.
Cube	Perspectives	New perspectives let you define a viewable subset of the cube and can provide a focused, business-specific or application-specific viewpoint on a cube.
Cube	Semi-additive measures	Semi-additive measures enable aggregation for an account dimension to be set by account. Business users can then set up cubes that reflect a company's account structure without writing custom rollup formulas.
Dimensions	Attributes	Dimensions are now based on attributes, which correspond to the columns in the tables of a dimension. Each attribute contains the members of a dimension table column.
Dimensions	Linked measure groups and dimensions	Data from different data sources can be used by linking a cube to a measure group in another cube that is stored either in the same database or in a different database on an instance of SSAS. You can also link a cube to a dimension in another database.
Dimensions	Multiple hierarchies	Multiple hierarchies are supported in a single dimension.
Dimensions	Simplified dimension types	Two dimension types, standard and linked, replace the four dimension varieties in SQL Server 2000 Analysis Services.
Data mining	Microsoft Association Algorithm	This algorithm builds rules that describe which items are most likely to appear together in a transaction.
Data mining	Microsoft Linear Regression Algorithm	This algorithm provides linear regression support.
Data mining	Microsoft Logistic Regression Algorithm	This algorithm provides logistic regression support.
Data mining	Microsoft Naive Bayes Algorithm	This algorithm is used to explore data between input columns and predictable columns and discover the relationships between them.

TABLE 1.6: SSAS Cube, Dimension, and Data-Mining Enhancements *(CONTINUED)*

TOPIC	ITEM	DESCRIPTION
Data mining	Microsoft Neural Network Algorithm	This algorithm creates classification and regression mining models by constructing a multilayer perceptron network of neurons. Ideal for nonlinear models.
Data mining	Microsoft Sequence Clustering Algorithm	This algorithm identifies clusters of similarly ordered events in a sequence that can be used to predict the likely ordering of events in a sequence based on known characteristics.
Data mining	Microsoft Time Series Algorithm	This algorithm analyzes time-related data, such as monthly sales data or yearly profits, for patterns to use to predict values for future time steps.

Other changes to cubes, dimensions, and data mining include the following:

- Data and metadata are now loaded into memory only when needed, allowing dimensions of virtually unlimited size.
- Several tasks have been added to SSIS that can be used to create a complete data-mining solution.
- Member group requirements for dimensions have been eliminated.
- Support is now provided for
  - Fact dimensions through Fact Dimensions Relationships
  - Many-to-many relationships between fact tables and dimension tables by using association tables
  - Reference dimensions through the use of Reference Dimension Relationships, in which a reference dimension is indirectly coupled to a measure group by another dimension
  - Role Playing Dimension Relationships, which express multiple relationships between a dimension table and a fact table as a single dimension.

Developers and programmers will be pleased to see that they have not been forgotten. SSAS introduces the development enhancements and new features summarized in Table 1.8.

TABLE 1.7: SSAS Development Changes and improvements

FEATURE	DESCRIPTION
ADOMD.NET	Formerly part of the SQL Server 2000 ADOMD.NET SDK, ADOMD.NET is now fully integrated into SSAS.
Analysis Management Objects (AMO)	AMO replaces the Decision Support Objects (DSO) object model.

TABLE 1.7: SSAS Development Changes and improvements *(CONTINUED)*

FEATURE	DESCRIPTION
Microsoft .NET Framework support	SSAS is now fully integrated with the Microsoft .NET Framework.
Multidimensional Expressions enhancements	Multidimensional Expressions (MDX) language has added support for scripting, scope and context control, and enhanced subcube manipulation.
Persisted calculations	The results of calculated members or calculated cells of cubes can now be persisted and managed in a separate cache for each cube.
Stored procedures	SSAS provides more extensibility and programmability in stored procedures, external routines in programming languages such as C#, C++, or Visual Basic that you can use to extend SSAS functionality.

Notification Services

Notification Services is a new platform for developing and deploying applications that generate and send notifications. Notification Services can send timely, personalized messages to thousands or millions of subscribers using a wide variety of devices. For example, you can use Notification Services to send a text message to a cell phone about a stock price when a certain price is reached.

Notification Services 2.0 was a downloadable component of SQL Server 2000 and was released in 2002. In SQL Server 2005, Notification Services is integrated into SQL Server.

For DBAs, the main advantage is that Notification Services is now fully integrated into Management Studio. Using Object Explorer, you can perform most of the tasks you previously needed to do at the command prompt using the `NSCONTROL` utility. You can start and stop instances of Notification Services.

If you're a developer, you can use Management Studio as your XML and T-SQL editor for a Notification Services instance. You can easily edit your instance configuration file (ICF), application definition files (ADFs), and T-SQL scripts for managing security or administering the instance, and you can then deploy the instance using Object Explorer.

In Notification Services 2.0, an application developer defined the complete T-SQL action for generating notifications, and subscribers could only provide parameters for the action. Now Notification Services has a new type of action, the *condition action*. Subscribers can now fully define their own subscriptions over the data set.

SQL Server Notification Services has a new management API, `Microsoft.SqlServer.Management.Nmo`. You can use this API to develop and manage Notification Services instances and applications.

Notification Services has added a new standard event provider to gather event data from SSAS databases using MDX queries.

The following views have been added or modified to simplify application development and troubleshooting:

- *<EventClassName>*—One of these is created for each event class defined in an application. When you write event-driven (not scheduled) notification generation queries, you typically select events from this view. Now you also can insert event data into this view.
- *<NotificationClassName>*—One of these is created for each notification class. You can use this view to review notifications generated by your application.

Notification Services now provides three views for viewing and managing subscriber and subscription data:

- NSSubscriberView lists all of the subscribers for an instance of Notification Services. You can use this view to manage subscriber data.
- NSSubscriberDeviceView lists all of the subscriber devices for an instance of Notification Services. You can use this view to manage subscriber device data.
- NS*SubscriptionClassName*View lists all the subscriptions for a subscription class. You can use this view to manage basic event-driven subscriptions but not scheduled or condition-based subscriptions.

You'll learn a lot more about Notification Services in Chapter 27.

Reporting Services

If there is one technology that will be heavily used by everyone who accesses a SQL Server 2005 instance, then the strongest candidate is Reporting Services.

Having well programmed, beautifully managed, exquisitely replicated, exceptionally developed, and brilliantly analyzed data means absolutely nothing if you can't get it out of the database in a form that anyone can use. For most users, reporting is still the heart of database management.

SQL Server 2000 didn't originally ship with a Reporting Services component. However, in 2002, under growing pressure from the SQL Server community, Microsoft released Reporting Services as a free add-on that was downloaded by hundreds of thousands of people.

Although there have been many improvements to Reporting Services, without a doubt those with the most far-reaching impact are the new Report Builder, the new Model Builder, and very enhanced Report Designer, which is fully integrated with BIDS:

Report Builder Report Builder may prove to be the hottest addition in SQL Server 2005. Designed to be used by end users without extensive technical knowledge, it's used from a web-based interface to generate ad hoc reports. Report Builder can be accessed through a URL or from Report Manager.

Model Builder A new type of project, Report Model, has been added. Report Models are used by Report Builder to generate ad hoc reports. You create a model using Model Designer in BIDS. Model Designer has several wizards to help you specify data sources and data views and generate models.

Report Designer The new Report Designer runs in BIDS and contains a number of changes and improvements from its predecessor:

- Expression Editor now includes functions for authors as well as Intellisense features.
- You can now specify data sources dynamically, permitting you to switch data sources at runtime based on conditions you specify in the expression.
- A new Analysis Services Query Designer helps you create MDX queries.
- A new data-processing extension allows you to build reports from data generated by an SSIS package.

Report functionality SQL Server 2005 Reporting Services includes several improvements in report functionality of particular benefit to users:

- Interactive sorting in reports
- Ability to print multipage reports
- Ability to use multivalued parameters

Reporting Services Configuration Tool This new tool runs from the Start menu on the computer that hosts the report server. It can be used to configure a report server to create and use a report server database on a remote SQL Server instance, among other things, as you can see in Figure 1.13. You can also use this tool to specify accounts for the Microsoft Windows and web services, virtual directories, and e-mail delivery. Deploying multiple report servers on cluster nodes (previously known as a *report server web farm*) is now handled exclusively through the Configuration Tool or through configuration scripts.

This is of course only the tip of the iceberg, as you'll see when you learn more about Reporting Services in Chapter 28.

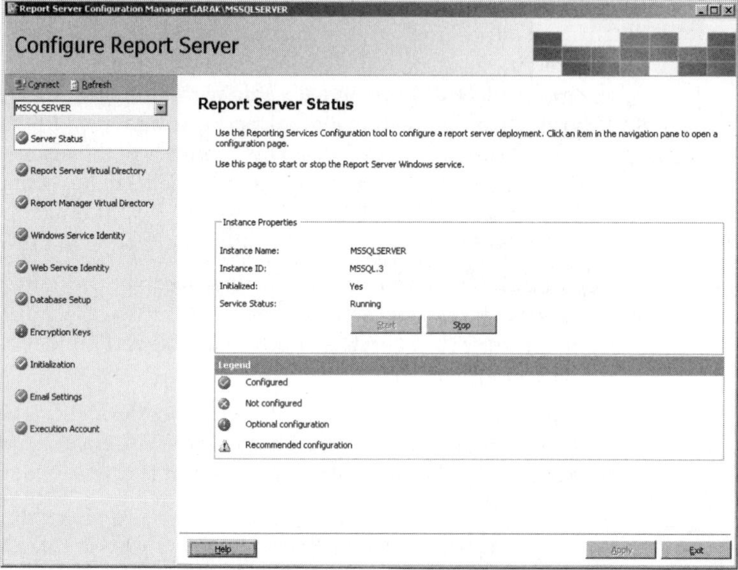

FIGURE 1.13
Reporting Services Configuration Tool

Service Broker

SQL Server 2005 introduces a completely new technology called Service Broker. The role of Service Broker is to aid in the building of database-intensive distributed applications that are secure, reliable, and scalable.

Part of the database engine, Service Broker provides facilities for storing message queues in SQL Server databases. In addition, Service Broker provides new T-SQL statements used by applications to send and receive messages. Each message is part of a *dialog*: a reliable, persistent communication channel between two participants.

Other things that Service Broker brings to SQL Server 2005 are as follows:

- An asynchronous programming model that allows database applications to perform tasks as resources become available
- Reliable messaging between SQL Server instances using TCP/IP
- A consistent programming model that can be used for messages whether they're within the same instance or between many instances, improving the ability to scale up or scale down by applications

Because Service Broker is elegantly designed to implement messaging within the SQL Server database engine, message queues are part of SQL Server databases and can take advantage of the performance capabilities of the database engine. In addition, Service Broker automatically handles issues such as message ordering and grouping, and a built-in locking capability allows only one reader at a time to read messages in a conversation group.

Finally, Service Broker stores message queues as part of the database. Hence, they are backed up and restored when the database is. Database security features can be used to secure applications. Similarly, messaging operations become an integral part of any transaction that includes database data, meaning there is no need to manage distributed transactions as you would have to do if the message queue were managed by a service separate from the database engine.

Service Broker is discussed in Chapter 29.

Summary

SQL Server isn't everything to everybody, but in the current release, it certainly has something for almost every computer user. The range of SQL Server goes from simple customer databases intended for a single user all the way to terabytes (a *terabyte* is one trillion characters) of data in cases such as Microsoft's TerraServer (`http://www.terraserver.microsoft.com`).

In the rest of this book, you'll learn about various aspects of SQL Server:

- Part 1 will teach you basic SQL Server and database concepts.
- Part 2 will teach you Transact-SQL.
- Part 3 examines the basic SQL Server objects and Management Studio.
- Part 4 covers administrative tasks.
- Part 5 reviews the developer tools that ship with SQL Server.
- Part 7 introduces some advanced topics and new technologies.

We hope that what you've read in this chapter has whetted your appetite for more. The next chapter will introduce you to some basic database concepts.

Chapter 2

Overview of Database Concepts

Before we get started with Microsoft SQL Server, we want to step back for a few moments and discuss the basic ideas of database technology. Depending on your experience, you might already know everything in this chapter, in which case you can just skim it to make sure the terminology we use is the terminology you're familiar with. On the other hand, if you've never worked with a database before, this will be your introduction to the basic concepts of the subject. What's stored in a database, anyhow? What can you do with a database? We'll try to answer those questions here in a very broad fashion. You might want to read this chapter now to get an overview and then refer back to it as necessary to refresh your memory about the big picture when you read the details later in the book.

All the concepts in this chapter will be discussed later in the book in the context of SQL Server. For example, one of the first things we'll introduce in this chapter is the notion of a database table. All of Chapter 11 is devoted to tables as implemented by SQL Server. So while you read the current chapter, if you want to know the mechanics of working with a particular piece of your database, you can follow the references forward to the specific chapters. For now, we'll start with a general overview.

Databases

A *database* is a place to store data. Suppose you're running a small business and you want to store all the data that pertains to that business. Your data isn't just a big heap of disparate facts (or at least, it shouldn't be a big heap if you want to be able to find things). The facts are naturally organized into a hierarchy.

For example, consider a single fact: A particular employee of your company was hired on October 17, 1993. By placing that fact together with other facts, you can organize your database at four levels:

- The hire date of the employee
- All the important facts about that employee
- All the important facts about all employees
- All the important facts about your entire business

In database terms, you refer to these four levels of organization by four special terms:

- The *field* holds an individual fact, in this case the hire date of the employee.
- The *record* holds all facts about an entity, in this case the facts about the employee.
- The *table* holds all facts about a group of similar entities, such as all the employees.
- The *database* holds all facts about all the entities in a connected whole, such as the business

Strictly speaking, if a database allows for storing records, fields, and tables, that's all it needs to keep track of. Some simple databases go no further than this. However, many database manufacturers add storage for additional things. Microsoft SQL Server in particular stores many items in the database other than data. As you read through this chapter, you'll encounter these other things (such as views or stored procedures), which are collectively called *database objects*. But first, you should know more about types of databases. Specifically, you'll frequently run across three topics in the database world:

- File-server versus client-server databases
- Relational databases
- OLTP versus OLAP databases

NOTE For more information on the mechanics of creating and managing SQL Server databases, refer to Chapter 10.

File-Server and Client-Server Databases

One important distinction is that between *file-server* and *client-server* databases. These two terms refer to fundamentally different ways of working with data.

In a file-server database, the data is stored in a file, and individual users of the data take what they need directly from the file. When there is a change to be made, the application opens the file and writes new data. When existing data is needed for display, the application opens the file and reads the data. If a database has 20 different users, all 20 users are reading from and writing to the same file.

In a client-server database, by contrast, the data is stored in a file, but all access to the file is controlled by a single master program (the *server*). When an application wants to make use of existing data, this application (the *client*) sends a request to the server. The server finds the proper data and sends it back. When an application wants to write new data to the database, it sends the data to the server, which does the actual writing. Only a single program reads from and writes to the data files.

Typically, databases aimed at a single-user desktop (such as Microsoft Access and Microsoft FoxPro) are file-server databases. Databases that are aimed at departmental, company, or enterprise users (such as Oracle, Sybase, or Microsoft SQL Server) are client-server databases. Client-server databases have several important advantages in large-scale use, including the following:

- Because only a single program is reading and writing data, there is less chance of accidental changes or crashes destroying vital data.
- The single server program can act as a gatekeeper for all clients, making the creation and enforcement of a security policy easier.
- Because only requests and results flow across the wire, client-server databases make more efficient use of network bandwidth than file-server databases.
- Because all the reading and writing is done by a single computer, it's easier to increase database performance by upgrading that one computer.
- Client-server databases tend to offer features that protect your data, such as logging transactions and recovery from disk or network errors. Strictly speaking, these features could be offered by file-server databases as well, but in practice, they're found only in the more expensive client-server market.

Relational Databases

A *relational database* stores your data in multiple places called *tables*, while also keeping track of how those tables are related to one another. Sometimes you'll see the term *RDBMS*, which stands for Relational Database Management System, used for a relational database.

For example, consider a database that's used to keep track of students in a college. You might want to collect information about students, courses, and instructors. Data about each of these subjects would be stored in separate individual tables, which would have names:

- Students
- Courses
- Instructors

In addition, the RDBMS would keep track of the facts relating these tables to each other. For example, each student could be enrolled in one or more courses, and each instructor could teach one or more courses.

NOTE SQL Server is a relational database.

OLTP and OLAP Databases

Another important distinction is that between *online transaction processing* (OLTP) and *online analytical processing* (OLAP) databases. The distinction isn't as clear-cut as that between file-server and client-server. In fact, most databases are used as both OLTP and OLAP products during their lifetime.

OLTP refers to a usage pattern involving rapid insertion, deletion, and updating of data. This is typical of many applications. For example, suppose you're running a travel agency and have 20 agents all updating a database of customer trip information. This is a typical OLTP application. The ability to quickly locate and change data is of paramount importance to avoid the database becoming a bottleneck for the entire operation.

On the other hand, suppose you're the manager of the travel agency. You might be interested in seeing summary information from many bookings. Perhaps there's a pattern indicating that women travel more often to Greece and men more often to Spain; knowing this could enable you to better target your advertising to appropriate periodicals. Such analysis, involving summaries of all or most of the data in a database, is the hallmark of OLAP applications.

It's very difficult for a server to be efficient for both OLTP and OLAP applications. The data structures that are appropriate for fast updating are suboptimal for aggregate querying. Microsoft solves this problem by shipping two servers together. The first, Microsoft SQL Server 2005, is mainly an OLTP server. It can perform summary queries, but it's not optimized for them. That's the job of the second program, Microsoft SQL Server 2005 Analysis Services: It ships with every copy of SQL Server 2005 Enterprise, Developer or Standard Edition and is designed to build efficient structures for OLAP applications to use.

NOTE You'll learn more about Microsoft SQL Server 2005 Analysis Services in Chapter 26.

Transaction Logs

Another feature commonly found in client-server databases is the *transaction log*. This is a separate file (or other distinct storage area) where the database server keeps track of the operations it's performing. For example, suppose you add a new record to a table. Before it adds the record to the table, the database server makes an entry in the transaction log that says, essentially, "About to add this record to the table," along with the data from the record. Only after the transaction log entry has been saved does the server actually save the change to the database.

Transaction logs are an important part of protecting your data. By keeping track of operations in a log, the database server makes it possible to recover from a wide range of disasters. For example, suppose the hard drive that stores your database fails. If you've kept backups, and if the transaction log is stored on a separate hard drive (both worthwhile and intelligent precautions), you can easily recover the data by first restoring the backup and then telling the server to reapply all the changes that were noted in the transaction log after the backup was made.

Tables

Tables are the objects that actually store your data. One of the basic guidelines for databases is that each table should store information on a particular entity. This is what's known as a *normalization* rule. You'll learn much more about normalization in Chapter 4.

Figure 2.1 shows a table of information about employees. In this particular case, the table is stored on a Microsoft SQL Server, and the screenshot was taken inside SQL Server Management Studio, one of the utilities that ships as a part of SQL Server (you'll learn more about SQL Server Management Studio in Chapter 9).

Much of the work you do with a database will revolve around tables. Every database supports these four basic operations:

- Adding information to a table
- Updating information that already exists in a table
- Deleting information from a table
- Viewing information contained in a table

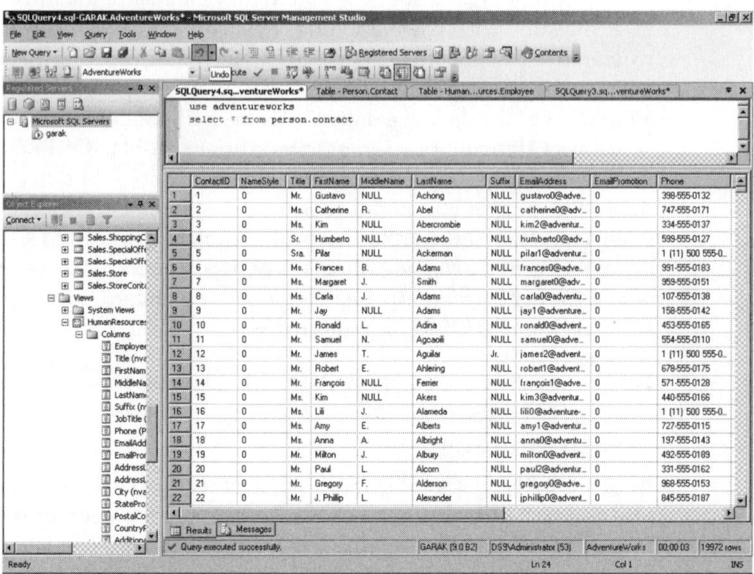

FIGURE 2.1
A table about contacts

Generally speaking, you'll perform these operations by executing SQL statements. SQL stands for Structured Query Language, a standard computer language for working with the contents of a database. You'll learn more about SQL later in this chapter and throughout this book.

Records, Fields, and Values

Every table is made up of records and fields. A *record* is all the information about one of the entities within a table. A *field* is a particular piece of information stored in a table. For example, referring back to Figure 2.1, the first record is all the information for the contact named Gustavo Achong, Contact ID 1. Some of this information is listed in the figure; the rest is off to the right and not visible. On the other hand, there's also the ContactID field, which has the values 1 through 22 visible for the records in this table (there are more further down the table, out of view).

Depending on what you're doing, it's sometimes convenient to manipulate records, and sometimes fields. For example, if you wanted to know everything stored in a database about a particular employee, you'd retrieve that employee's record from the appropriate table. However, if you wanted to know the e-mail addresses of all your contacts, you'd need to inspect the contents of the EmailAddress field for all records in the same table.

WARNING Note the ambiguous nature of the term *field*. Sometimes it refers to an individual piece of information; sometimes it refers to every piece of similar information within a table. When the meaning isn't clear from context, we'll refer to these as a *field in a record* and a *field in a table* if it's necessary to differentiate between them.

When you inspect a particular field in a particular record, you see the *value* of that field in that record. For example, the value of the first field in the first record in this table is the number 1.

Rows and Columns

You'll also find records and fields referred to as table *rows* and *columns*. It's easy to see why this is if you look at Figure 2.1. Database tables are traditionally displayed on a grid, with the fields running across and the records running down. So, you might refer to the row in the table for Gustavo Achong, or the column containing information on last names. The terms are equivalent, and there's seldom a reason for preferring one set to the other. The SQL Server documentation usually uses *row* and *column*, but much general database literature is written in terms of records and fields instead.

Null Values

As we mentioned, a value is the actual data stored in a particular field of a particular record. But what happens when there is no data? Consider, for example, a database that records contact information. One of the things that you'd like to keep track of is the middle name for each contact, for formal invitations, monograms on promotional material and gifts, and the like. However, some contacts don't have middle names, or perhaps they have one but you don't know it. Figure 2.2 shows a SQL Server table illustrating this. The highlighted contact, Kim Akers, doesn't have information stored for her middle name in this database.

As you can see in the figure, the answer to this problem is something displayed as NULL. This is SQL Server's way of displaying a null value. A *null value* represents the absence of information. You can think of it as a placeholder value in a table; it's the database's way of telling you that it doesn't know what data belongs in that field.

FIGURE 2.2
Contact with no middle name

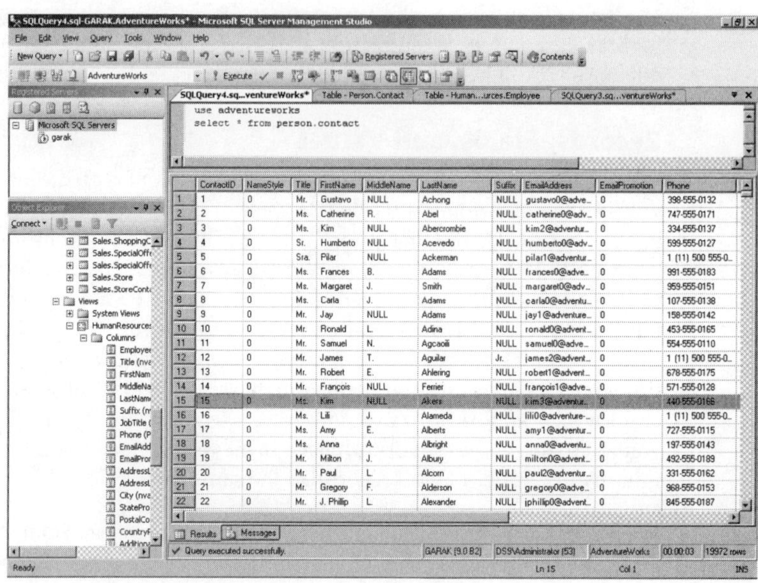

Because nulls represent missing information, they cause what is sometimes called *null propagation.* If you use a field with a null value in a calculation, the result will always be null. For example, you might calculate a line item total by multiplying quantity times unit price. If the quantity for a particular record is null, the answer will also be null. If you don't know how many you're buying, you can't know what the total cost will be, either.

Field Properties

Not all fields are created equal. That's obvious if you stop to think about it for a moment: Phone numbers look different from birth dates, which in turn look different from last names. A full-featured database such as SQL Server lets you capture these differences by specifying *field properties.*

Figure 2.3 shows a different way of looking at the Person.Contact table in a SQL Server database. This view shows the *schema* information for the table, rather than the data that the table contains. The schema of a database is a way of referring to all the design information that constrains what can be stored in that database.

This view shows the four most important properties for each field in the table:

- Column name
- Datatype
- Allow nulls

NOTE **For the currently selected field (LastName in the figure, indicated by the arrow to its left), the view shows additional properties at the bottom of the dialog box. You'll learn more about these properties, and others, in Chapter 11.**

The column name of a field (or column) provides a way to refer to that field in the table. Generally speaking, you'll want to assign meaningful names to your fields, as was done in this example.

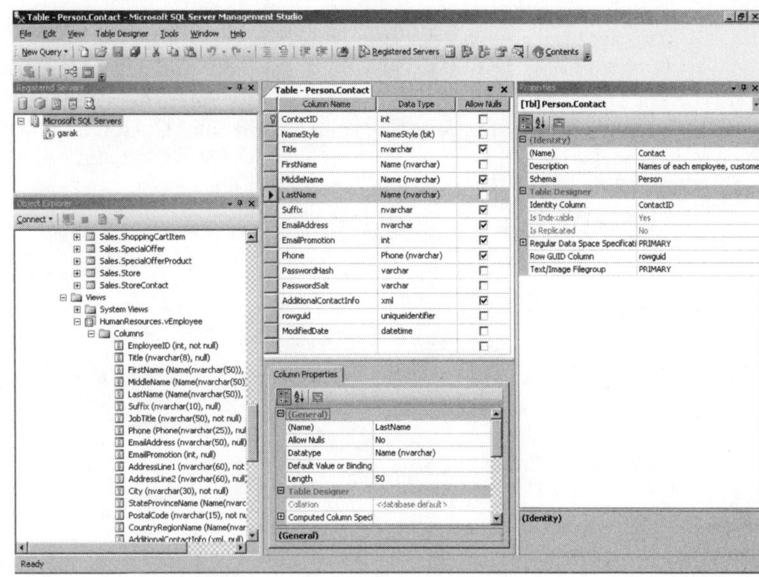

FIGURE 2.3
Design view of the Person.Contact table

The datatype for a field constrains the data that can be stored in that field. The LastName field holds data of the type nvarchar. That's a SQL Server datatype that refers to Unicode data of varying length, stored as characters. Other datatypes include int (for integers), datetime (for date or time information), and binary (for information such as pictures).

The length property for a field specifies the maximum amount of data that you can store in that field.

The allow nulls property for a field shows whether null values are allowed in that field. If a field doesn't allow nulls, you must supply a non-null value for that field in each record before you can save the record.

By using field properties to distinguish one field from another, you help keep your database neat and orderly. That's one of the things that distinguishes databases from spreadsheets: With a database, you can use field properties to set rules that the database automatically enforces, so the data you store actually makes sense.

Keys and Relationships

Looking again at Figure 2.3, you'll see a little key symbol to the left of the ContactID column. It indicates that this column is the primary key for this table. A *primary key* is a piece of unique identifying information that lets you find a particular record within a table. No two records in the same table can have the same value in the primary key field. A primary key might be made up of a single field (as in this case) or multiple fields. For example, suppose you have a table of students with fields for first name and last name. There might be many students with the first name of Mary, and many students with the last name of Jones, but only one Mary Jones. If all the students had unique names, you could choose the combination of first name and last name as the primary key for this table.

Sometimes you'll find a good primary key contained within the data of a table. For example, if you're tracking craters on the moon, you'll discover that no two craters have the same name, in which case you can use the crater name as the primary key. This is called a *natural key*. In other cases, you'll have to add something to the data to provide a primary key. For instance, if you're creating a database of newspapers, you'll find many newspapers named *The Post*. In this case, you can assign each newspaper an arbitrary number and store that number in a field named NewspaperID. This is called a *synthetic key*.

In addition to primary keys, there's another important type of key in database theory: the *foreign key*. The purpose of a foreign key is to allow you to match up records from two or more tables. For example, look at the Sales.Salesperson and Sales.Customer tables in Figure 2.4.

FIGURE 2.4
Using keys to relate two tables

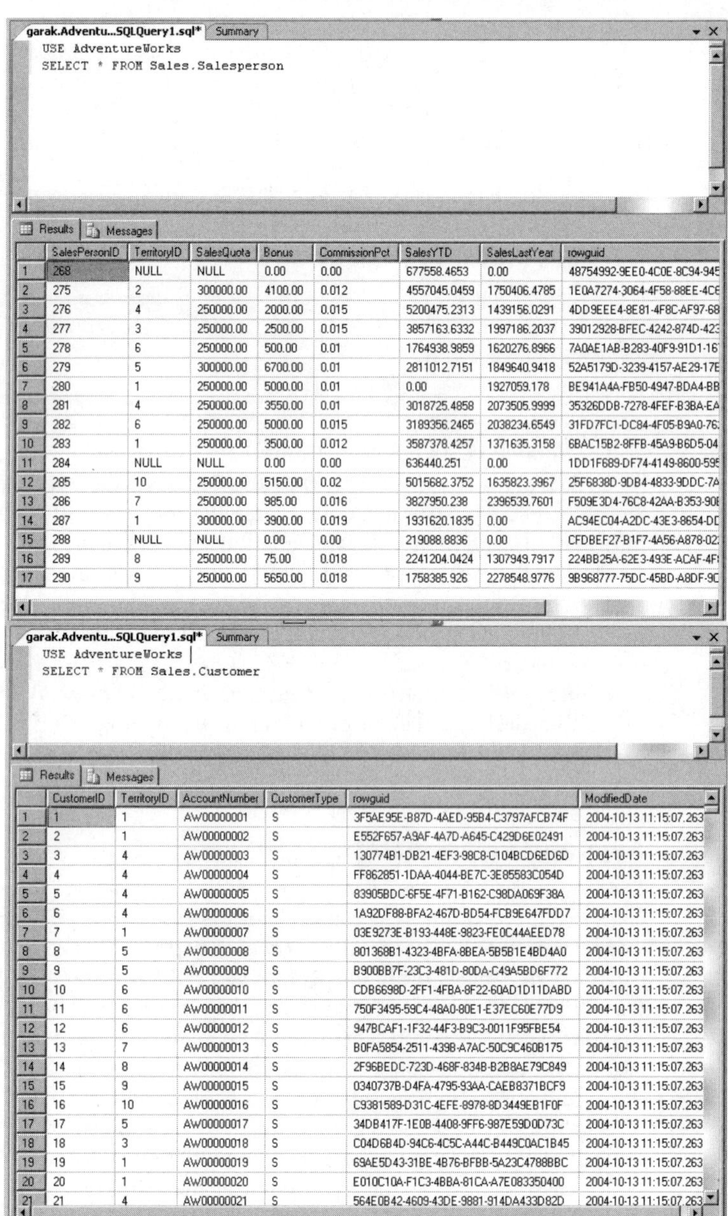

	SalesPersonID	TerritoryID	SalesQuota	Bonus	CommissionPct	SalesYTD	SalesLastYear	rowguid
1	268	NULL	NULL	0.00	0.00	677558.4653	0.00	48754992-9EE0-4C0E-8C94-945
2	275	2	300000.00	4100.00	0.012	4557045.0459	1750406.4785	1E0A7274-3064-4F58-88EE-4C6
3	276	4	250000.00	2000.00	0.015	5200475.2313	1439156.0291	4DD9EEE4-8E81-4F8C-AF97-68
4	277	3	250000.00	2500.00	0.015	3857163.6332	1997186.2037	39012928-BFEC-4242-874D-42
5	278	6	250000.00	500.00	0.01	1764938.9859	1620276.8966	7A0AE1AB-B283-40F9-91D1-16
6	279	5	300000.00	6700.00	0.01	2811012.7151	1849640.9418	52A5179D-3239-4157-AE29-17E
7	280	1	250000.00	5000.00	0.01	0.00	1927059.178	BE941A4A-FB50-4947-BDA4-BB
8	281	4	250000.00	3550.00	0.01	3018725.4858	2073505.9999	35326DDB-7278-4FEF-B3BA-EA
9	282	6	250000.00	5000.00	0.015	3189356.2465	2038234.6549	31FD7FC1-DC84-4F05-B9A0-76
10	283	1	250000.00	3500.00	0.012	3587378.4257	1371635.3158	6BAC15B2-8FFB-45A9-B6D5-04
11	284	NULL	NULL	0.00	0.00	636440.251	0.00	1DD1F689-DF74-4149-8600-59
12	285	10	250000.00	5150.00	0.02	5015682.3752	1635823.3967	25F6838D-9DB4-4833-9DDC-7A
13	286	7	250000.00	985.00	0.016	3827950.238	2396539.7601	F509E3D4-76C8-42AA-B353-90
14	287	1	300000.00	3900.00	0.019	1931620.1835	0.00	AC94EC04-A2DC-43E3-8654-DD
15	288	NULL	NULL	0.00	0.00	219088.8836	0.00	CFDBEF27-B1F7-4A56-A878-02
16	289	8	250000.00	75.00	0.018	2241204.0424	1307949.7917	224BB25A-62E3-493E-ACAF-4F
17	290	9	250000.00	5650.00	0.018	1758385.926	2278548.9776	9B968777-75DC-45BD-A8DF-9C

	CustomerID	TerritoryID	AccountNumber	CustomerType	rowguid	ModifiedDate
1	1	1	AW00000001	S	3F5AE95E-B87D-4AED-95B4-C3797AFCB74F	2004-10-13 11:15:07.263
2	2	1	AW00000002	S	E552F657-A9AF-4A7D-A645-C429D6E02491	2004-10-13 11:15:07.263
3	3	4	AW00000003	S	130774B1-DB21-4EF3-98C8-C104BCD6ED6D	2004-10-13 11:15:07.263
4	4	4	AW00000004	S	FF862851-1DAA-4044-BE7C-3E85583C054D	2004-10-13 11:15:07.263
5	5	4	AW00000005	S	83905BDC-6F5E-4F71-B162-C98DA069F38A	2004-10-13 11:15:07.263
6	6	4	AW00000006	S	1A92DF88-BFA2-467D-BD54-FCB9E647FDD7	2004-10-13 11:15:07.263
7	7	1	AW00000007	S	03E9273E-B193-448E-9823-FE0C44AEED78	2004-10-13 11:15:07.263
8	8	5	AW00000008	S	801368B1-4323-4BFA-8BEA-5B5B1E4BD4A0	2004-10-13 11:15:07.263
9	9	5	AW00000009	S	B900BB7F-23C3-481D-80DA-C49A5BD6F772	2004-10-13 11:15:07.263
10	10	6	AW00000010	S	CDB6698D-2FF1-4FBA-8F22-60AD1D11DABD	2004-10-13 11:15:07.263
11	11	6	AW00000011	S	750F3495-59C4-48A0-80E1-E37EC60E77D9	2004-10-13 11:15:07.263
12	12	6	AW00000012	S	947BCAF1-1F32-44F3-B9C3-0011F95FBE54	2004-10-13 11:15:07.263
13	13	7	AW00000013	S	B0FA5854-2511-439B-A7AC-50C9C460B175	2004-10-13 11:15:07.263
14	14	8	AW00000014	S	2F96BEDC-723D-468F-834B-B2B8AE79C849	2004-10-13 11:15:07.263
15	15	9	AW00000015	S	0340737B-D4FA-4795-93AA-CAEB8371BCF9	2004-10-13 11:15:07.263
16	16	10	AW00000016	S	C9381589-D31C-4EFE-8978-8D3449EB1F0F	2004-10-13 11:15:07.263
17	17	5	AW00000017	S	34DB417F-1E0B-4408-9FF6-987E59D0D73C	2004-10-13 11:15:07.263
18	18	3	AW00000018	S	C04D6B4D-94C6-4C5C-A44C-B449C0AC1B45	2004-10-13 11:15:07.263
19	19	1	AW00000019	S	69AE5D43-31BE-4B76-BFBB-5A23C4788BBC	2004-10-13 11:15:07.263
20	20	1	AW00000020	S	E010C10A-F1C3-4BBA-81CA-A7E083350400	2004-10-13 11:15:07.263
21	21	4	AW00000021	S	564E0B42-4609-43DE-9881-914DA433D82D	2004-10-13 11:15:07.263

In the Sales.Salesperson table, the primary key is the field named SalesPersonID, which has a unique value for each of the 17 salespersons. In the Sales.Customer table, the primary key is the field CustomerID, which has a unique value for each customer. However, notice that the Sales.Customer table also contains a field named SalesPersonID and that the values in this field are drawn from the Sales.Salesperson table. For example, the order that has the value 20 in the CustomerID field has the value 283 in the SalesPersonID field, which is also the value in the SalesPersonID field of one of the records in the Sales.Salesperson table.

We say that SalesPersonID in the Sales.Customer table is a *foreign key*. Its purpose is to allow you to find the sales person for a particular customer. In database terms, this is referred to as a *relationship* between the two tables; the Orders table and the Customers table are related through their primary key–foreign key connection.

NOTE You'll learn about keys and relationships in more depth in Chapter 4.

Indexes and Constraints

Other features of tables can limit the data placed in the table. Two of these are *indexes* and *constraints.*

An index on a table is conceptually very similar to an index in a book. An index in a book provides a way to locate individual pages quickly. An index on a table provides a way to locate individual records quickly. With a table index, you choose which field or fields to index. For example, you could index a table of employees by EmployeeID, which would make locating individual employees very fast once you knew the value of the EmployeeID field. You could also index the same table by the combination of FirstName and LastName, to make it easier to locate records when you knew both the first and the last name of the employee.

Indexes can be *unique* or *nonunique.* A unique index serves to limit the data placed within the table. For example, if you created a unique index on a field named VendorNumber, no two records in the table could share the same vendor number; the database wouldn't allow you to save a record with a vendor number that duplicated that of an existing record.

Indexes can also be *clustered* or *nonclustered.* This term refers to the physical storage order of the table. If you create a clustered index on the CustomerID field of the Customers table, the records are stored on disk in order of CustomerID. This makes creating a list of customers in order of CustomerID faster; but it can make it slower to add records to the Customers table, because existing records may need to be shuffled around to create room.

TIP Although a table can have many indexes, it can have only one clustered index.

SQL Server offers another type of index called a *full-text index*. Unlike regular indexes, which are stored with the table that they index, full-text indexes are stored in special objects called *catalogs*. Full-text indexes aren't updated automatically, you need to do something to make them happen. They can be updated by running a special indexing job on the server, or you can configure them to be updated automatically when the table is changed. However, full-text indexes offer special types of searching that are less precise than those supported by regular indexes. When you're using a regular index to locate a record, you must supply exactly the value that was placed in the index. When you're using a full-text index, you can search in a more natural fashion. For example, a full-text index could be used to search for records where any of the following conditions are true:

- The record contains the word *connect.*
- The record contains the word *connect* or any of its forms such as *connecting* or *connects.*

- The record contains both the word *connect* and the word *network* in any order.
- The record contains the word *connect* but not the word *disconnect.*
- The record contains the word *connect* within three words of the word *network.*

Constraints are rules that apply to the data in a table. For example, you might have the rule that the unit price of all products must be greater than one dollar when the products are entered. You could enforce this rule by creating a constraint on the Products table:

```
([UnitPrice] >= 1)
```

Any attempt to add or edit a record that breaks this constraint would be rejected by the database server.

NOTE Constraints are covered in Chapter 11, and Chapter 12 is devoted to indexes.

Rules and Defaults

Two other objects that you'll find associated with tables in some databases are rules and defaults. A *rule* is an expression that can be evaluated as being either True or False when applied to the value of a particular field. For example, a rule might assert that the value of a field is between 0 and 100. If this rule were associated with a particular field, you'd be prohibited by the server from entering values outside of that range into that field.

A *default* is a separate object that specifies a single value—for example, 0. By associating the default with a column in a table, you make the default value of that column in new records added to that table equal to the value of the default.

Although SQL Server supports both rules and defaults, it does so only for compatibility with older versions of the software. For new development, rules have been replaced by constraints, and defaults have been replaced by the default value property of fields. Because they're obsolete, we won't cover rules and defaults in this book.

Views

Although all the data in your database is stored in tables, tables often don't present that data the way you'd like to see it. Consider a database with Customer, Employee, Order, and Order Detail tables, for example. Looking at a table can get you all the information about every customer or every order. However, you might like to do some other things with this information:

- Create an invoice with a total price for a particular order
- See all customers grouped by country
- List employees with their birth dates but not their other information

To perform tasks like these, databases provide a tool object called the *view.* A view behaves very much like a table; it contains records and fields that can be displayed as rows and columns, and it allows you to retrieve the value of a particular field in a particular record. However, unlike a table, a view doesn't store any data. Rather, it stores instructions to the database server, telling it how to retrieve that data. When you open a view, the server executes those instructions and creates a *virtual table* from the view. This virtual table exists only as long as you're working with it; it's never stored on the hard drive.

SQL

The instructions to create a view are written in a language called *Structured Query Language* (SQL). There is a standard (promulgated by the American National Standards Institute) called ANSI SQL or, sometimes, SQL-92 (from the year when the last widespread revisions to the standard were accepted). As is the case with most standards, individual database vendors make their own extensions and changes when they create a product. Microsoft SQL Server's version of SQL is called Transact-SQL, sometimes abbreviated T-SQL.

You'll learn about SQL in Part 2 of this book (Chapters 5 through 8). However, we'll give you a few examples here, so you can get a brief taste of the language in advance. Views are created by using `CREATE VIEW` statements. Each `CREATE VIEW` statement has a its heart a SQL statement that starts with the `SELECT` keyword. For example, the view in Figure 2.5 was created by executing the following select query:

```
SELECT EmployeeID, Gender, MaritalStatus, Title FROM HumanResources.Employee
```

NOTE This figure and the next several were taken from a tool called SQL Server Management Studio, which allows you to interactively test SQL statements to see the results they return. By convention, SQL keywords are shown in all capital letters in SQL statements. However, the server will understand them whether they're capitalized or not.

You can read SQL statements as if they were English and get most or all of their sense. In this case, the statement instructs SQL Server to select the contents of the EmployeeID, Gender, MaritalStatus and Title fields from the HumanResources.Employee table and display them. As you can see, the other fields aren't even displayed. This has two benefits. First, because it's delivering less data to the screen, the server can deliver the data more quickly. Second, by eliminating extraneous fields, the view enables the user to concentrate only on the desired data.

FIGURE 2.5
A simple select query

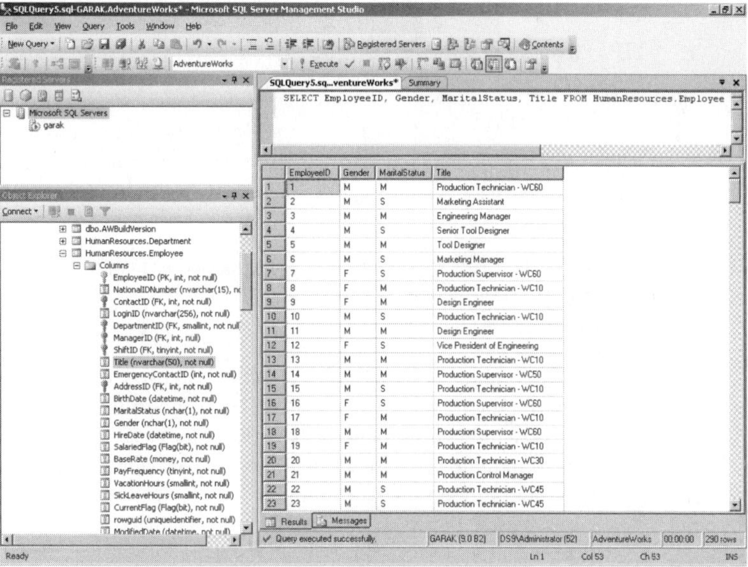

You can also use a view to eliminate extraneous records. Perhaps you're interested only in the employees who have base pay rates higher than $25.00 per hour. In that case, you can add the `WHERE` keyword (producing a *where clause*) to the SQL statement that defined the view, to retrieve the more specific set of records:

```
SELECT EmployeeID, Gender, MaritalStatus, Title FROM HumanResources.Employee
WHERE BaseRate > 25
```

This statement produces the more specific results shown in Figure 2.6.

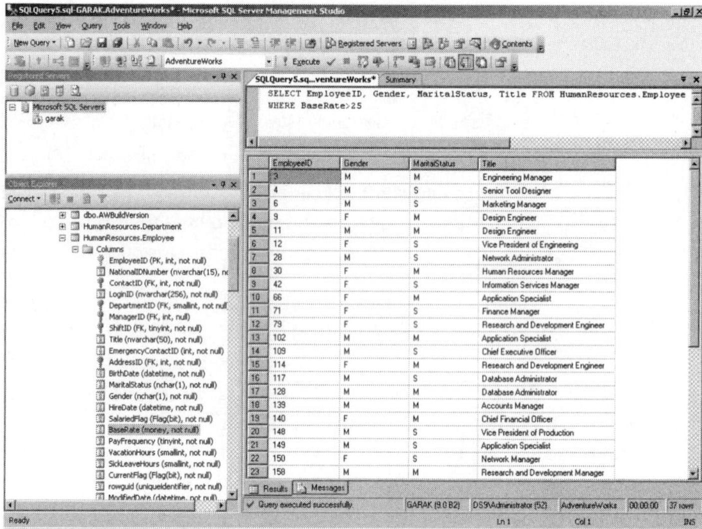

FIGURE 2.6
A view with a where clause

TIP It doesn't matter whether SQL statements are presented to the server on one line or many. In general, you can add tabs, spaces, and carriage returns as you'd like to make SQL statements more readable.

You can also use a view to group information. For example, you might like to count the number of employees in each job title. You can do that with the following SQL statement, whose results are shown in Figure 2.7:

```
SELECT Title, Count(EmployeeID) AS TitleCount
FROM HumanResources.Employee
GROUP BY Title
```

To look up data in more than one table, you must perform a *join* in the where clause of the SQL statement. As the name suggests, a join combines the output from two tables by specifying the columns that are to be joined between tables. Figure 2.8 shows how you can combine data from the Sales.Customer table and the Sales.Store table using the CustomerID field column. This view is produced by the following SQL statement:

```
SELECT Name, SalesPersonID, AccountNumber, CustomerType
FROM Sales.Customer
JOIN Sales.Store ON Sales.Customer.CustomerID=Sales.Store.CustomerID
ORDER BY Name
```

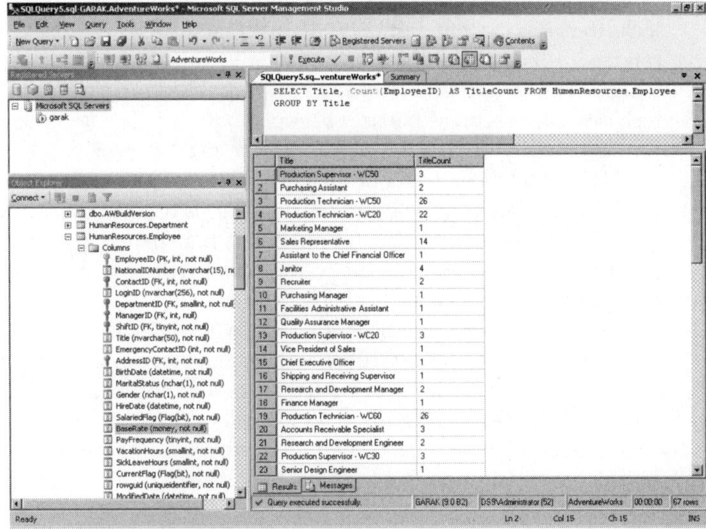

FIGURE 2.7
A select query with grouping

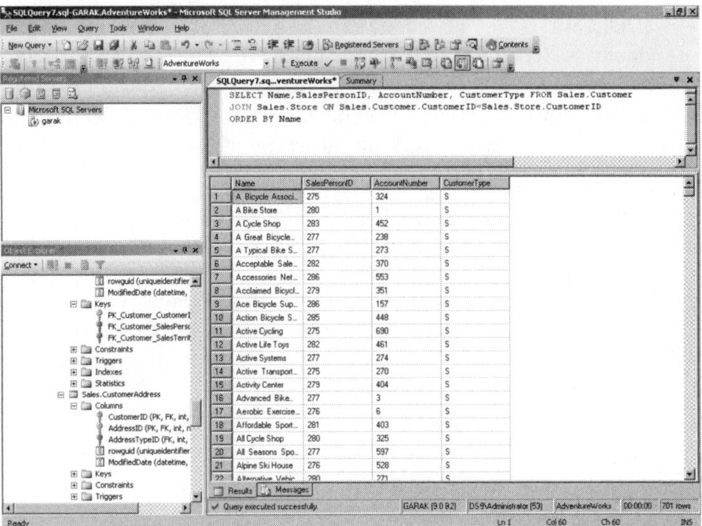

FIGURE 2.8
Complex view combining information from two tables

SQL statements can do more than just select data for presentation. They can also insert new data in a table (using the INSERT keyword), remove data from a table (using the DELETE keyword), and modify existing data (using the UPDATE keyword), among many other things. SQL statements that modify data are called *action queries*. You'll learn more about action queries in Chapter 7.

Locking

Databases that allow multiple users to modify data must have some mechanism to ensure that those modifications stay consistent. Most databases (including SQL Server) use *locking* for this purpose.

The basic idea of locking is that sometimes a user needs exclusive access to a table, so the server locks the table for that particular user. When the user is done working with the table, the lock is released, which makes the data in the table available to other users again.

Locking is often classed into *pessimistic locking* and *optimistic locking*. With pessimistic locking, a lock is taken as soon as the user begins modifying data and released when the user is completely finished modifying data. This ensures that no other user can change the data while the first user is modifying that data. With optimistic locking, on the other hand, the lock is taken only when the modifications are complete and the database is ready to write them to the table. Optimistic locks typically lock other users out for much less time than do pessimistic locks.

Optimistic locking raises the possibility of write conflicts. Suppose two different users choose to modify the same record, and both choose to use optimistic locking. The second user may finish their work and write modifications back to the database while the first user is still working. Then, when the first user goes to write their changes, they're not changing the data that they thought they were changing. Most databases detect this situation and allow the user or the application developer to decide whether their changes should overwrite those made by the other user.

SQL Server has a rich and complex system of locks, designed to lock resources as rarely as possible while still protecting your data. You'll learn more about SQL Server data in Chapter 23.

DDL and DML

When you're learning about the SQL language, you'll find references to *Data Definition Language* (DDL) and *Data Manipulation Language* (DML). DDL is concerned with creating new objects in the database, whereas DML is concerned with using existing objects. All the `SELECT` statements you saw earlier in this chapter are DML statements; they all manipulate data in existing tables.

The simplest of the DDL statements is the `CREATE TABLE` statement. For example, you can create a new table named Cust with this statement:

```
CREATE TABLE Cust
(CustID int NOT NULL,
  CustName varchar(50) NOT NULL)
```

This statement creates a table with two columns. The first column is named CustID and uses the int datatype. The second column is named CustName and uses the varchar datatype with a maximum length of 50 characters. Neither one of these fields accepts null values.

You're likely to use a good deal more DML than DDL in most databases, because objects need to be created only once, although they'll be used many times. You'll find some discussion of common DDL statements in Chapters 10 through 15, where we discuss the basic database objects in more depth.

Query Plan

Suppose you have to locate some information in a long and complex book. You might choose to flip through the pages one by one, looking for the information. Or you might use the index to find the correct page, or the table of contents to find the correct section, and then search from there.

Similarly, database servers have many ways to locate information in a table. They can look at each record in order looking for the requested information. Alternatively, they can use an index to quickly find a requested record, or perhaps a binary search to locate a group of records and then search only those records sequentially.

When you save a view, the database server also saves information on how it will find the records for this view. This additional information is called the *query plan* for the view. By computing this plan at the time the view is saved, rather than when it's executed, the server can typically deliver results more quickly when they're called for.

SQL Server offers tools for both inspecting and modifying query plans. You can use Management Studio (discussed in Chapter 9) to view the query plan that SQL Server has developed for any given view. You can also use *query hints* (special clauses in the SQL statement defining the view) to instruct the server to use a different query plan than it would otherwise choose. Query hints provide a powerful mechanism for fine-tuning the performance of queries and are discussed in Chapter 8.

Stored Procedures

SQL statements are also the basis of *stored procedures.* SQL is a complete programming language. Not only does it include data-oriented statements (such as the `SELECT` statement you saw in the previous section), but it also includes control structures such as `IF...THEN` and looping, procedure declarations, return values, and so on. Thus it makes sense that you can write entire procedures in SQL and store them on a database server.

Stored procedures can accept input values or simply be called by name if they don't require any inputs. They can return no information, a single return value, or multiple values in output parameters. They can even return entire virtual tables, making them similar to views. In fact, you can create a stored procedure that executes any SQL statement you've used for a view.

SQL Server parses stored procedures when they're stored and stores them in an optimized form. Thus stored procedures can provide a way to execute SQL code more quickly than it could be executed if it were all being sent from the client. In addition, stored procedures can be invoked by name, which saves the client from needing to send all the SQL statements involved to the server.

You'll see this theme many times in this book. The less information you send from client to server, or from server to client, the more efficient your application will be.

Stored procedures are created with a T-SQL `CREATE PROCEDURE` statement. For example, you can create a simple stored procedure to return a particular customer's information with the following statement:

```
CREATE PROCEDURE GetName
@LName char(50)
AS
SELECT * FROM Person.Contact
WHERE LastName = @Lname
```

Here, `@custid` @Lname is an input parameter to the stored procedure. The stored procedure returns the results of the `SELECT` statement to the calling application. You can call this stored procedure with the following `EXECUTE` statement:

```
EXECUTE GetName 'Achong'
```

Figure 2.9 shows the result of executing this statement.

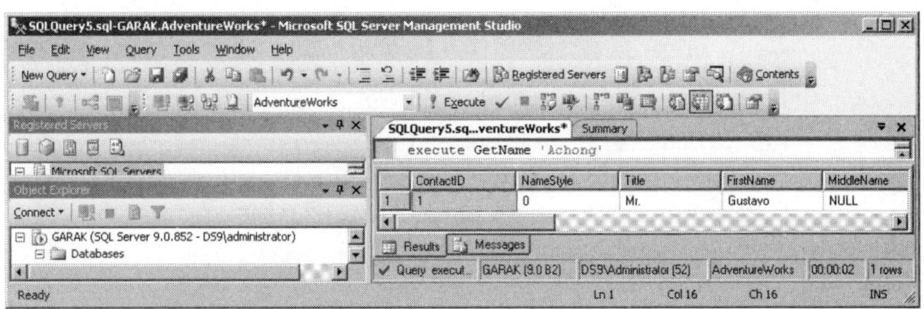

FIGURE 2.9 Retrieving results with a stored procedure

Stored procedures are defined with the same T-SQL language that is used to define views. However, stored procedures are more flexible than views. Stored procedures can display records in a particular order, return more than one set of records, and even perform database operations (such as starting backups) that aren't associated with records at all.

Triggers and Event Notifications

Triggers are a special type of stored procedure. Instead of being executed by the user, triggers are executed by the database server when certain operations are performed on a table:

- An *insert trigger* runs whenever a new record is inserted in a table.
- A *delete trigger* runs whenever an existing record is deleted from a table.
- An *update trigger* runs whenever an existing record in a table is changed.

Triggers are useful whenever you'd like to have the database automatically react to user actions. For example, when a record is deleted from a working table, perhaps you'd like to keep a copy in a separate archive table to preserve an audit trail. You can do this by creating a delete trigger on the first table. During the deletion, this trigger will be invoked, at which time it will have full access to all the deleted data and can copy it elsewhere.

Triggers can also be used as a more sophisticated and flexible form of constraint. A constraint is limited to dealing with the information in a single table, whereas a trigger potentially has access to the entire database. Suppose you want to allow new orders only from customers who have no outstanding delinquent invoices. You can write an insert trigger that uses a view on the Invoices table to determine whether this order should be accepted.

Some products support only a single trigger of each type on a table; others (including SQL Server) allow you to have multiple insert, update, and delete triggers all on the same table. SQL Server also supports *instead-of triggers*, which fire instead of, rather than in addition to, the action that called them. Instead-of triggers make it easy to prevent data deletion, for example.

SQL Server 2005 has gone beyond the traditional triggers and expanded them to include other operations such as changes to the schema of the database or database server. *DDL triggers* can, as the name implies, be fired for DDL operations like `CREATE`, `ALTER`, and `DROP`. They're a means of enforcing development rules and standards for objects in a database and preventing accidental drops, and they can aid other activities including object check-in/check-out, versioning, and log management. DDL triggers are also useful in auditing and logging.

Event notifications are a new feature in SQL Server 2005. They're similar to triggers, but the actual notification doesn't execute any code. Instead, information about the event is posted to a SQL Server Service Broker (SSB) service and is placed on a message queue from which it can be read by another process. Another key difference between triggers and event notifications is that event notifications respond to trace events in addition to DDL and DML statements. The principal value of event notifications is their value as enterprise auditing tools.

Transactions

Powerful database servers (including Microsoft SQL Server) support grouping operations into *transactions*. You can think of a transaction as an indivisible unit of change in your database. Each transaction is something that must be either finished entirely or discarded completely; a transaction can't remain partially finished indefinitely.

For example, consider a database that tracks bank accounts and the amounts in those accounts. Suppose you want to move money from a checking account to a savings account. This involves two operations:

- Lowering the balance in the checking account
- Increasing the balance in the savings account

If either one of those operations fails, neither operation should be performed. Otherwise, either the bank or the customer will be unhappy. The two operations together make up a single transaction that must succeed or fail as a unit.

Transactions are supported through mechanisms called *commitment* and *rollback*. First, you notify the server that you're beginning a transaction. Then, you perform the individual operations that make up the transaction. If an error occurs in any of these individual operations, you notify the server that it should *roll back* the entire transaction. Doing so causes the server to throw away all the work that's already been done and return the database to the state it was in before the transaction started. If all the operations are completed successfully, you notify the server that it should *commit* the transaction. It then stores all the changes made by the individual operations, making them a permanent part of the database.

SQL Server also supports *distributed transactions*. These are transactions in which the different operations are performed on different database servers but still committed or rolled back as a unit.

NOTE You'll learn more about transactions in Chapter 8.

System Stored Procedures

Most databases that support stored procedures, among them SQL Server, come with some stored procedures already written. These stored procedures perform common tasks and have already been optimized by the database designers. *System stored procedures* perform operations such as these:

- Listing all the users logged on to a server
- Listing all the tables or views in a database
- Adding objects such as operators or subscribers to a server
- Configuring the server
- Deleting jobs that are no longer needed
- Showing help on database objects and operations
- Sending e-mail directly from a database
- Managing security for objects

If you're a database administrator, you'll find that having a thorough knowledge of system stored procedures will make it vastly easier for you to manage a server or group of servers. We'll discuss some of the more important system stored procedures in Chapter 14.

Ownership and Security

Database servers manage access to your data. In some cases, this means handing that data out to anyone who asks. However, most servers (among them Microsoft SQL Server) contain a security model that lets you protect sensitive data.

In the case of SQL Server, the security model depends on interactions between several entities:

- Logins
- Users
- Roles
- Owners
- Permissions

Logins are the accounts through which users connect to SQL Server. SQL Server offers two different ways to authenticate that users are who they say they are. The older method is through a username and password stored with SQL Server itself. More recently, SQL Server security has been integrated with Windows NT security. This allows your users to log on once, when they connect to the server, and then not worry about supplying separate credentials to SQL Server.

Although logins are a concept that spans the entire database server, *users* refer to identities within a specific database. Each login might map to different users in different databases. Within a database, your user identity controls what you can do.

Roles allow you to collect users into groups for easier management. By using roles, you can identify the actions that, for example, members of the accounting department should be able to perform. Then you can handle the individual members of that department by assigning them to the role. This can be a great time-saver if there are many users in a particular database. SQL Server also includes some built-in roles for administrative tasks such as database backups.

Every object (table, view, stored procedure, and so on) in a database has an *owner*. The owner of an object is by default the user who created the object, and they're the only one who can use it. Owners can grant *permissions* to other users. Permissions on an object control what you can do with that object. For example, you might have the permission to read data through a view but not permission to change that same data.

Owners are a part of the full naming scheme for SQL Server objects. So far, we've been referring to objects by a simple name such as *Person.Contact*. However, the full name of an object has four parts:

```
server.database.owner.object
```

So, for example, if the Person.Contact table was created by the dbo user in the AdventureWorks database on a server named Garak, the full name of the object would be as follows:

```
Garak.AdventureWorks.dbo.Person.Contact
```

Depending on the circumstances, you can usually omit the additional pieces from the name and just use the simple name to refer to the object. However, when an object is in a database other than the current database, or when the name is ambiguous, you'll need the full name.

Jobs, Alerts, and Operators

As database servers increase in complexity, the need to manage them grows also. SQL Server in particular provides a framework of *jobs, alerts,* and *operators* to help automate both routine operations and response to unusual conditions.

A *job* is a set of steps that SQL Server can perform. Tasks can include the execution of T-SQL statements, Windows commands, executable programs, or ActiveX scripts. Jobs can be run on demand from the console, on a periodic schedule, or in response to other conditions. Jobs can also contain conditional logic to handle the failure of individual tasks.

Jobs are most useful to automate routine database operations. For example, a job to do database maintenance might check the integrity of data and back up the data to tape each night on a regular schedule.

Alerts are automatic responses to error conditions. SQL Server raises an error in certain circumstances—for example, if a disk gets full while writing data. By associating an alert with this particular event, you can cause a job to be run in response.

Operators are identified by e-mail addresses. SQL Server can be configured to notify operators by e-mail or page if an alert occurs.

NOTE You'll learn more about these and other administrative features of SQL Server in Chapters 16 through 18.

Replication

With the broadening presence and role of internetworks of computer systems over the past decade, new database capabilities have become increasingly important. A critical one is *replication.* The basic idea behind replication is to make identical data available in multiple locations at more or less the same time.

Why is this important? Consider a company that has two branch offices, each with 20 users, connected by a single slow and expensive leased telephone line (or an unreliable Internet connection). If you install a database server at one office, all the users at the other office will have to send data requests over the slow, expensive, or unreliable line. With replication, you install a database server at each office and use replication to synchronize the contents of the two servers. Users always retrieve data from their local server, and traffic across the problematic line is limited to that which the servers use to stay in synchronization with one another.

Replication involves *publishers, distributors,* and *subscribers.* A publisher is a database that makes information available. The information is composed of *articles* (tables or views drawn from specific tables), which are organized into *publications* (groups of articles). A distributor is a database whose job it is to collect publications and make them available to other databases. These other databases are the subscribers: They take the information from a distributor and use it to update their own copy of a database.

It's also possible to set up a two-way relationship, in which case each database is both a publisher and a subscriber. Doing so allows you to keep two copies of a database synchronized even if changes are being made to both copies. In this case, the databases must be aware of the possibility of *conflicts.* A conflict occurs when the same record is updated in two copies of the same table at the same time. A process called *conflict resolution* is used to determine which information is preserved in this case.

Subscriptions can be grouped into *push subscriptions* and *pull subscriptions.* In a push subscription, the publishing database determines the schedule that it will use to make updates available to subscribers. In a pull subscription, the subscribers determine the schedule that they will use to request updates from the publisher.

Replication can be *homogeneous* or *heterogeneous.* In homogeneous replication, all the databases involved are managed by the same product. In heterogeneous replication, multiple database products are involved. For example, one common heterogeneous replication scheme in the Microsoft world is to replicate data from SQL Server to Microsoft Access.

SQL Server supports a variety of replication methods and topologies. You can use default or custom conflict resolution, and you can choose when and how to synchronize data among replicated servers. You'll find the details of replication covered in Chapter 25.

Summary

In this chapter, you learned the basic concepts and terminology of databases. Although this book as a whole is focused on Microsoft SQL Server, this terminology will help you engage in sensible discussion about any full-featured database. Now that you have the background for orientation, it's time to dig into the architecture that Microsoft SQL Server uses to implement these basic concepts.

Chapter 3

Overview of SQL Server

Once you have SQL Server installed and running, you need to know how to use the programs that come with it. If you examine the SQL Server 2005 group on the Start menu, you'll see a number of programs used with SQL Server. In the first part of this chapter, we'll look at what those programs are for and how to use them.

It's probably safe to say that you've installed SQL Server to store data, so you'll need to understand the structure of databases. This chapter will examine the various parts of a database and their purposes. You'll also need to understand how those databases are stored on disk, so we'll examine the structures used for data storage. Some of the topics you'll find in this chapter are as follows:

- How to use the programs installed with SQL Server
  - SQL Server Books Online
  - SQL Computer Manager
  - SQL Profiler
  - SQLCMD
  - SQLCMD Bulk Copy Program (BCP)
  - SQL Server Management Studio
- Application programming interfaces (APIs)
- The parts of a database
  - Tables, views, stored procedures, user-defined datatypes, and user-defined functions
  - Database user accounts and database roles
  - Rules, constraints, and defaults
  - Full-text catalogs
  - XML and SQL Server
- SQL Server storage concepts
  - Pages and extents

Programs Installed with SQL Server

To work with this product effectively, you'll need to understand the tools at your disposal. If you look at the Microsoft SQL Server 2005 program group on the Start menu, you'll see the programs that have been designed to help you work. The first of these programs is SQL Server Books Online.

SQL Server Books Online

Over the years, SQL Server Books Online has undergone a series of improvements that have taken it from the lowly and forgotten tool it once was to the troubleshooting behemoth it is today. In this new iteration, SQL Server Books Online connects you to a wealth of information about SQL Server both locally and on the Internet, so you're sure to find answers to your questions.

You can access SQL Server Books Online by opening the Microsoft SQL Server 2005 menu from the Programs group on your Start menu. After you open the program, a welcome screen will greet you on the right—you'll see a contents pane on the left from which you can perform searches and access data.

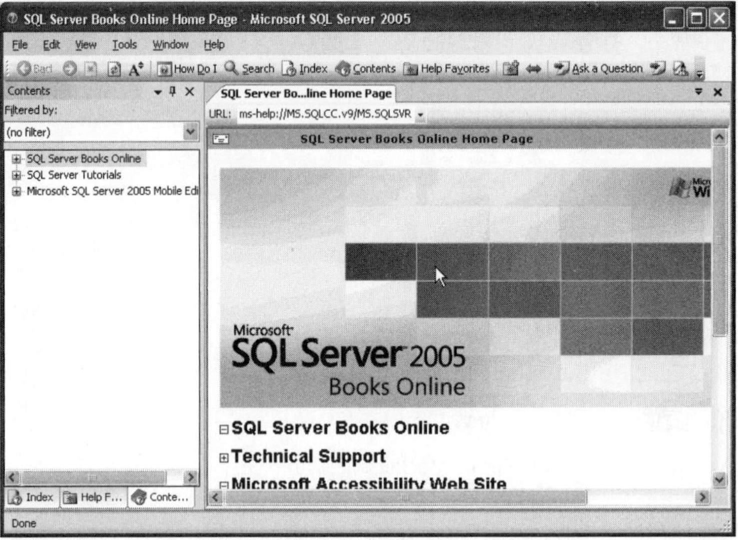

From the opening screen, you can read any of the topics listed on the contents pane, or you can go to the index pane to see an indexed list of subjects (like at the back of a book) and pick a topic from there. If you don't see the topic you need, click the Search button on the toolbar.

Virtually any question you may have about SQL Server can be answered by researching in SQL Server Books Online. For example, suppose that you need help developing summary reports of your data. On the toolbar, click the Search button; you'll be presented with a search page in the contents pane. In the Search For text box, enter **summarizing data**, and click the Search button. In the contents pane, you'll see a list of available subjects in the left column and a summary of online help sources in the right column. The first topic listed should be titled Summarizing Data. After you read this topic, let's say you notice that `CUBE` and `ROLLUP` are used for summarizing data. Because these topics are hyperlinks, you can click one and jump right to the new topic.

TIP The first time you perform a search you may be asked whether you would like to use online or local help as your primary help source. It is best to have a broadband Internet connection if you want to use online help as your primary source.

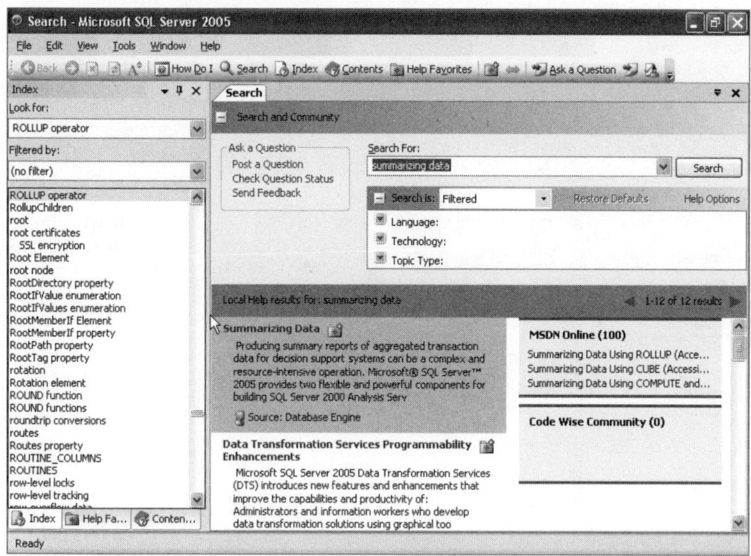

Once you locate Summarizing Data Using CUBE, you probably want to make that topic easier to find for future reference by using the Favorites tab. To add this topic to your list of favorites, click the Add To Help Favorites button on the toolbar or right-click anywhere on the topic in the contents pane and select Add To Help Favorites. Now, if you look at the Favorites tab, you'll see your topic listed under Help Favorites. You can also add searches to the Favorites tab by clicking the Add To Help Favorites toolbar button while on the search screen.

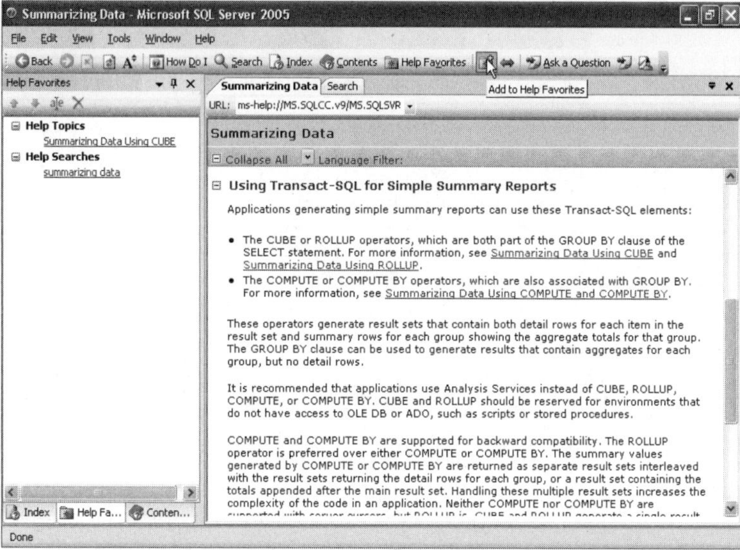

If you know exactly what you're looking for, you can use the Index tab. If, for instance, you need a definition of the ntext datatype, you need only select *ntext data type* from the list on the Index tab to see a definition.

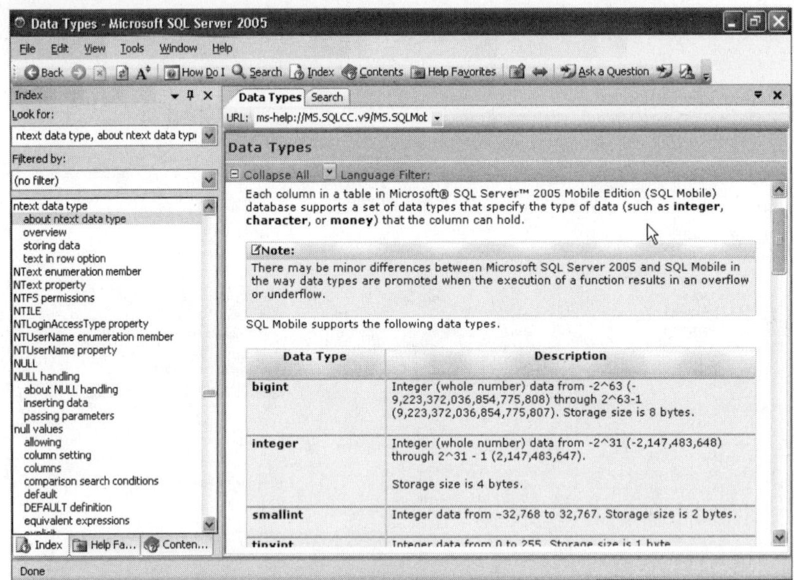

The Contents tab contains a broad spectrum of information that you can peruse to get general ideas about SQL Server. A good example is the *Database Engine* section. Under this section, you'll find several other topics dealing with the database engine in general, such as *Using XML in SQL Server* and *Administering the Database*. You could just as easily search for these topics on the Index or Search tab, if you knew these subjects were covered. This tab can help you get to know SQL Server for the first time.

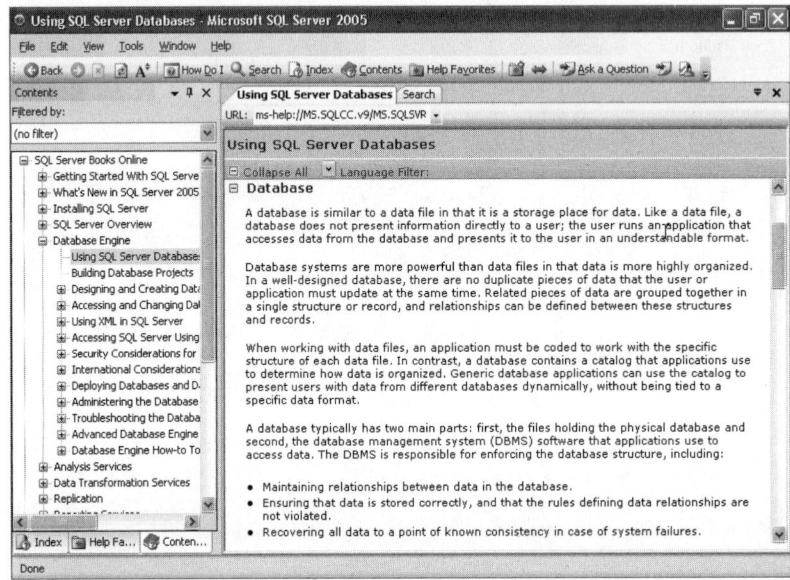

There is also a handy new How Do I button on the toolbar. When you first click this button, a simple screen will open, asking you to select a default How Do I page from a list. Once you've select the default page, you can click the How Do I button at any time, and you'll be taken directly to a list of topically arranged answers. For example, if you need to know how to administer a database, you can click How Do I and select Database Engine under Administration, which will take you to a list of topics on the subject of database engine administration.

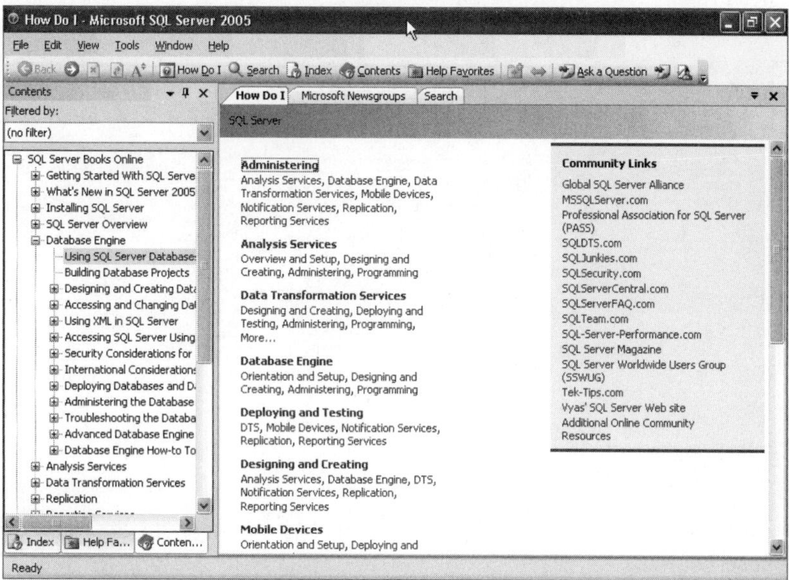

SQL Configuration Manager

The SQL Configuration Manager provides basic configuration services for your server. Using this tool, you can configure the services on the machine as well as the client and server network protocols. Let's look at the services first.

NOTE In previous versions, SQL Computer Manager had three separate tools: Client Network Utility, Server Network Utility, and Services Manager.

SQL Server 2005 Services

When you expand Services, you'll see a list of categories that contain one or more services installed on your server:

DTS Server This service is used to author, publish and manage reports that you create using your databases. These reports can be viewed and managed over a web-based interface.

msftesql This service creates and maintains full-text search indexes. These indexes allow users to perform faster searches on fields of the text datatype. For more about full-text searching, see Chapter 8, "Topics in Advanced Transact-SQL."

Analysis Server If you installed Analysis Services on your server, you'll see this category. Analysis Services is a powerful tool for data mining and analysis. This is an advanced topic that we'll discuss in Chapter 26, "Analysis Services."

SQL Agent This service, which controls automation, will be discussed in detail in Chapter 17, "Automating Administration." SQL Agent executes tasks (such as backing up a database) and sends e-mail in the event of a problem.

SQL Server This service is the heart of SQL Server, because it performs such functions as executing queries, managing access to data, and allocating system resources (such as RAM and CPU).

SQL Browser This service listens for incoming requests for SQL Server resources on the network and provides information about the SQL Server instances installed on the server.

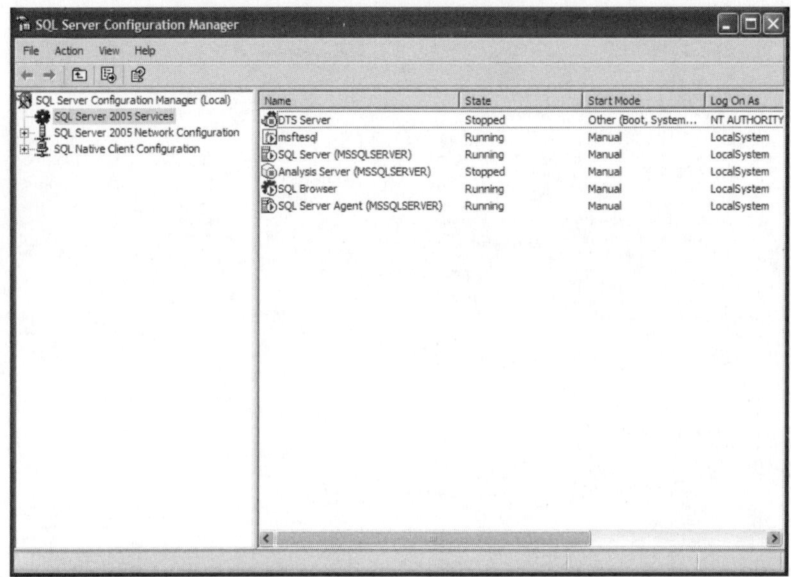

When you select one of these categories, a list of all the related services appears in the right pane. Right-click the service you want to manage (or use the Action menu on the menu bar), and you'll be able to start, stop, or pause the service. Or, you can select Properties to modify the service's configuration properties. For instance, you can change the username and password of the service account or the start mode for the service.

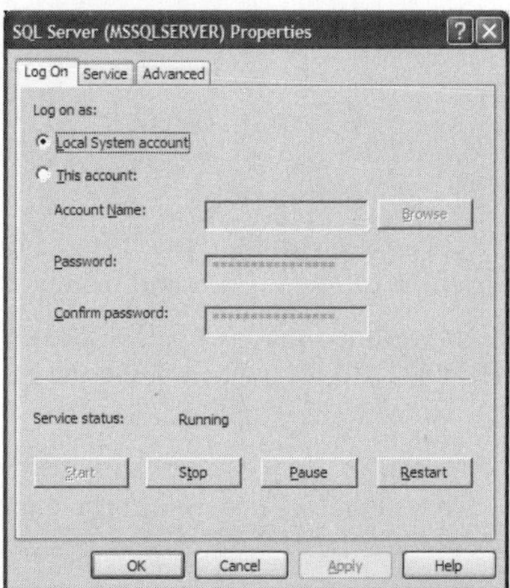

SQL Server 2005 Server Network Configuration

For a client to communicate with a SQL Server over the network, both of them must be running a common network library. The Server Network Configuration tool shows you which network libraries are installed on the server and allows you to configure those libraries.

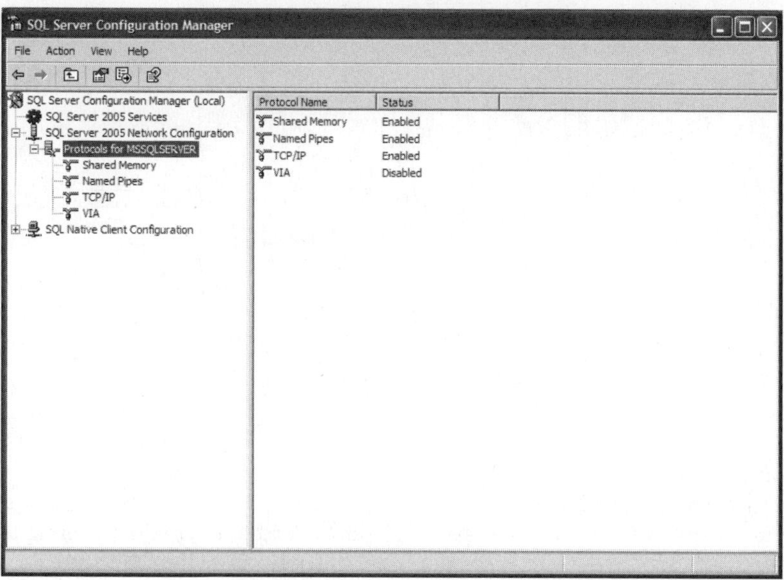

When you expand Protocols For MSSQLSERVER, you'll see a list of the protocols that are available for the server to listen on. To configure the properties for one of the libraries, right-click the library and select Properties. Each protocol has its own set of properties to configure.

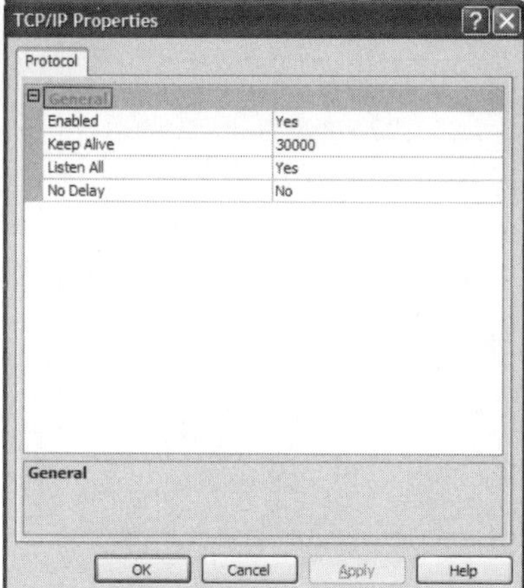

Click Tcp, and you'll see separate listings for each network adapter in the contents pane. This means you can disable Tcp on some adapters and enable the protocol on others. Or you can use the special IPAll adapter setting and configure Tcp settings for all of your adapters as a single unit. To configure the adapter settings individually, right-click the adapter and bring up the properties.

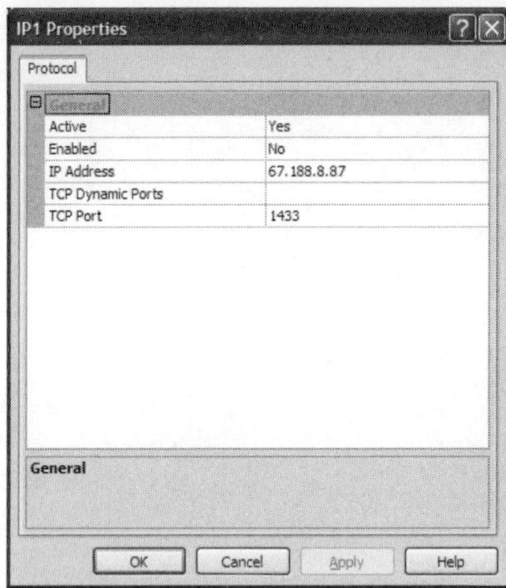

You can also configure encryption properties for all the protocols on the server. Right-click the Properties For MSSQLSERVER node in the left pane, and select properties, and a dialog box with two tabs opens. The Flags tab has only one option: Force Encryption. Enabling this flag tells SQL Server to send and accept encrypted data over the network using the Secure Sockets Layer (SSL). On the Certificate tab, you can select the certificate that your system will use to encrypt and decrypt your data.

SQL Native Client Configuration

The SQL Native Client Configuration tool is the counterpart to the Server Network Configuration tool. It's used to configure the protocols that the client uses to communicate with the server. When you expand SQL Native Client Configuration, you'll see only two choices: Client Protocols and Aliases.

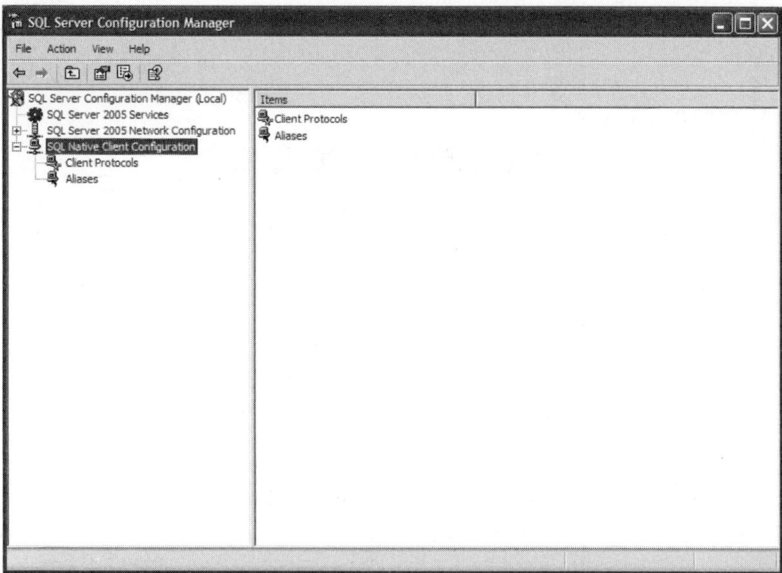

Select Client Protocols, and a list of available protocols appears in the contents pane. As in the Server Network Configuration utility, you can configure each protocol by right-clicking it and selecting Properties.

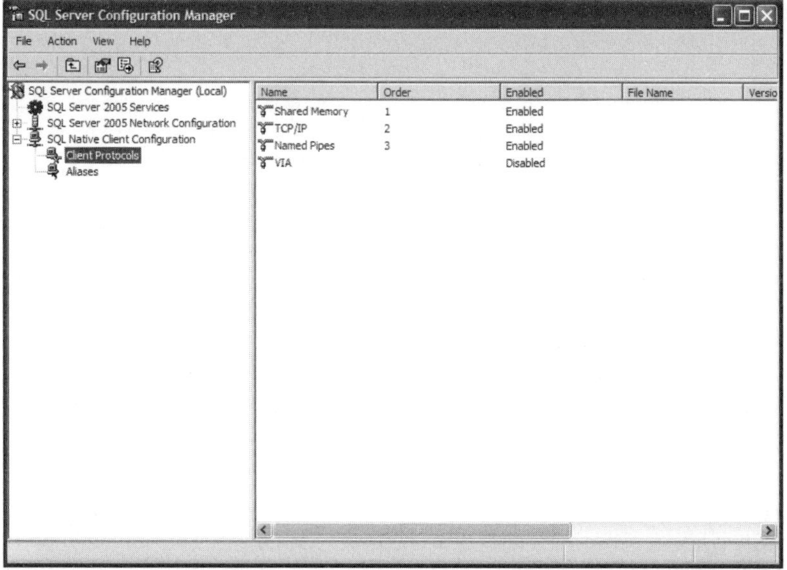

One big difference is that each of the client protocols has an order number: Shared Memory is 1, TCP/IP is 2, and Named Pipes is 3. This is the order in which your client will try to connect to the server; the client first tries Shared Memory, then TCP/IP, and then Named Pipes. If you're running the client and server on the same computer, this is the best order; but if you're using TCP/IP, you should change the order so that TCP/IP is 1. To change the order, right-click Client Protocols and select Properties. You'll see a list of disabled protocols on the left and a list of enabled protocols on the right. You can enable a protocol by selecting it in the Disabled Protocols list and clicking Enable; conversely, you can disable a protocol by selecting it in the Enabled Protocols list and clicking Disable. To change the order of enabled protocols, select the protocol you want to move, and click Move Up or Move Down.

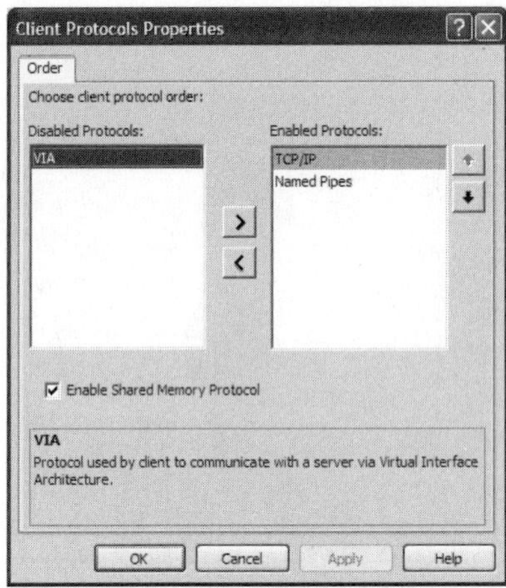

The Aliases tab is a little more involved. Many companies have several SQL Servers running concurrently, and each of those servers has different settings. For example, one SQL Server may be running the TCP/IP net-library configured to listen on port 1433, and another server may be configured to listen on TCP port 37337 (which is usually done for security purposes). Other servers may have different configurations for the various clients to be able to connect properly. If this is the case in your company, you need to create server aliases for each of the servers in your organization that isn't set to the defaults for the network library.

For example, on each of the clients, the administrator must create an alias for the server that is using port 37337. You need an alias because it isn't the default port, but the clients can connect to the server by listening on port 1433 without any further modification. Port 1433 is the default port for the TCP/IP net-library. In essence, the alias is like a profile of settings that your clients use to connect to the servers on your network.

To connect to a server named Accounting that is listening on port 65000 using the TCP/IP net-library, for instance, you right-click Aliases and click New Alias. When the Add Configuration dialog box pops up, add the setting to connect to the Accounting server and set the port number to 65000. Doing so creates the server alias, and the client can connect until an administrator manually deletes the connection.

SQL Profiler

Once you've successfully designed and deployed your databases, and your users are accessing them on a regular basis for inserting, updating, and deleting data, you need to monitor the server to make sure it's running the way it's supposed to. You need to know such things as how fast the server is

running, what sort of data the users are accessing, and whether anyone is trying to hack into your server. In the SQL Server 2005 group in the Programs group on the Start menu, you'll find SQL Profiler, a powerful monitoring tool that can show you all this information and a great deal more.

Using SQL Profiler involves setting up event-monitoring protocols called *traces*. An event is anything that happens to a running system, such as a failed or successful login, a query being properly routed and the results retrieved, or a report being run. You can design each trace to look at specific aspects of the system, which you'll get a chance to do in Chapter 26 ("Analysis Services"). By monitoring events, you can tell how the system is being used and whether anything needs tweaking for greater efficiency.

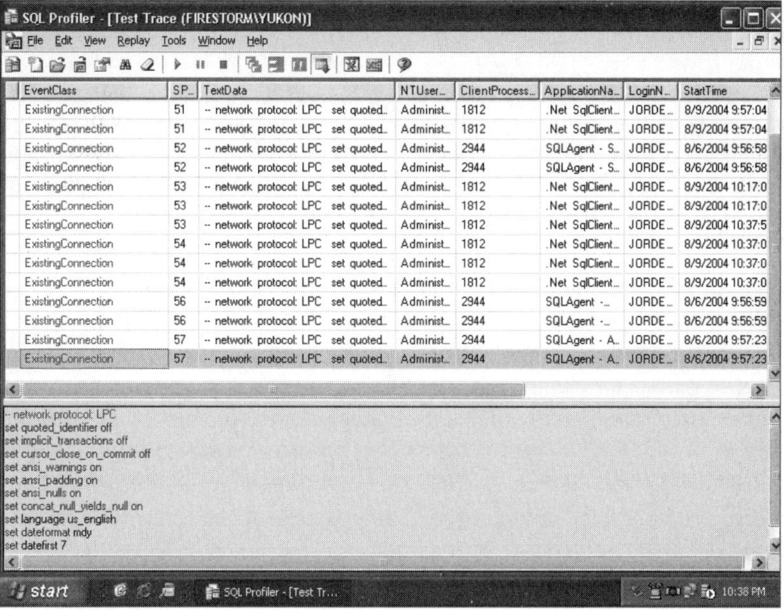

SQLCMD

SQLCMD is a command-line tool that executes Transact-SQL code and displays the results, just like the query tool in SQL Server Management Studio. Aside from the fact that SQL Server Management Studio is graphical and SQLCMD is a command-line tool, there is only one small difference between the two: SQLCMD doesn't have the ability to analyze queries and display statistics on speed of execution. Other than that, the two tools perform much the same function. This begs the question, "Why should I use SQLCMD if I have SQL Server Management Studio?" The answer is scheduling.

Suppose you have a sales manager who needs to see daily figures on sales. Because you can't schedule SQL Server Management Studio to run a command automatically, you would need to teach the manager how to execute a query in SQL Server Management Studio so that he could manually extract the data every night. Not many managers have this kind of time on their hands, though. Another method you could consider is creating a job to automate the task. A *job* is a series of steps that can be executed automatically by SQL Server. One of those steps could be the query that extracts the data your manager needs, but there is no way to get that data from a job to the manager. SQLCMD can be used to run the query and save the data to a text file. The command can also be scheduled (using such tools as the Windows `AT` command or a SQL Server job) to run automatically. The manager can then read the text file whenever he wants.

NOTE SQLCMD runs in one of two modes: *interactive* or *batch*. Interactive mode functions much like SQL Server Management Studio in that it allows you to enter commands at a prompt. When you finish, you type `EXIT`. Batch mode sends a single command to the server and returns a result set. Batch mode is used for automation.

You can use several arguments to control the behavior of the SQLCMD program. All of them are case-sensitive, which means that an uppercase *E* means something entirely different than a lowercase *e*. The arguments that you can use are listed here:

***-U* login_id** To send queries to a SQL Server, you must gain access by logging in. There are two ways to log in. One way is by using a trusted connection, which means that SQL Server trusts Windows to verify your username and password. The second way is by establishing a nontrusted connection, which means that SQL Server must verify your username and password. The `-U login_id` parameter tells SQL Server which user to log you in as using a nontrusted connection. Therefore, if you want to log in as a user named Bob, the `-U` parameter would look as follows: `-U bob`.

***-P* password** This parameter specifies the case-sensitive password to be used in conjunction with the `-U` parameter. If you're logging in as Bob and your password is *doughnut*, the `-P` parameter looks as follows: `-Pdoughnut`.

-E This parameter specifies a trusted connection, where SQL Server trusts Windows to verify your username and password. No username or password needs to be entered, because SQLCMD detects the username and password you used to log on to your computer and uses that information to log you in to SQL Server. This is the default connection type.

***-S* server_name[\instance_name]** This parameter specifies the name of the server that you want to connect to in order to perform queries. The `-S london` parameter, for example, connects you to a server named london.

-L[c] If you can't remember the name of the server you want to connect to in order to query, the `-L` parameter detects all the SQL Servers on the network and displays a list. The optional `c` parameter specifies *clean* output, which means the `Servers:` header isn't displayed and leading spaces are removed from the server names.

-e This parameter repeats (or *echo*s) the commands you type. If you enter a query, for example, it's repeated on the first line of the result set.

***-p*[1]** This parameter prints performance statistics about the query executed. It displays execution time, extracted records per second, and network packet size. If the optional 1 parameter is specified, then the output is displayed as a series of colon-separated values that can be imported into a table or spreadsheet.

***-d* db_name** This parameter sets the database with which you'll be working. If you want to query one of the tables in the pubs database, for example, this parameter is `-dpubs`.

***-Q*"query"** This parameter executes the query enclosed in quotation marks and immediately exits the SQLCMD program. Note that queries must be encased in double quotes.

***-q*"query"** This parameter also executes the query in quotes, but it doesn't exit SQLCMD after execution. Once the query is finished, you remain in interactive mode.

***-c* cmd_end** Ordinarily, when you're working in interactive mode, you must enter the word `GO` on a line by itself to tell SQLCMD that you've finished entering code and it should be executed now. This is called a *command terminator*. Using this parameter, you can set a different command terminator.

***-h* headers** By default, the names of the columns in the result set are printed only once, at the top of the result set. If this isn't enough, you can use the `-h` command to print the header more often. The `-h5` parameter reprints the names of the columns (the headers) every five lines.

***-V* level** This parameter limits the severity level of errors that SQLCMD reports on. If an error occurs that's lower than the option specified by the `-V` parameter, then it isn't reported, and the command continues to run.

***-v var*="value"** Use this option to pass variables to the T-SQL batch you're running. Enclose the value of the variable in quotes if the value contains characters.

-W This option removes trailing spaces from a column.

***-w* column_width** By default, 80 characters are displayed on a single line of output. The `-w` parameter changes that to more or fewer characters. For example, `-w70` displays only 70 characters on a line of output.

***-s* col_separator** By default, columns on the screen are separated by a blank space. Because this format may be difficult for some people to read, you can change the separator using the `-s` parameter. For instance, `-s>` separates your columns from one another using the > symbol.

***-t* timeout** If a command fails while it's running (for example, the SQL Server goes down), the command will run indefinitely by default. To change that behavior, you can specify a timeout parameter. For example, `-t5` instructs SQLCMD to time out after waiting 5 seconds for a response.

***-m* error_level** SQL Server recognizes several levels of error severity, from 1 to 25; 1 is the lowest (reserved by SQL Server), 10 is informational (something happened, but it's not too bad), and 25 is the highest (your server is having a stroke). The `-m` parameter tells SQLCMD which levels to display: For instance, `-m10` displays all level-10 errors and higher, but nothing lower.

-I In interactive mode, you ordinarily place strings of text inside single quotes (`' '`). With this option set, you can encase text strings in double quotes instead (`" "`).

-r {0|1} Not all error messages are printed to the screen, but you can use this parameter to redirect them to the screen. The parameter `-r0` displays error messages of 17 or higher, and `-r1` displays all messages on the screen.

***-H* wksta_name** With this parameter, you can specify the name of the computer from which you're connecting. The default is the computer name. However, if you're on a Windows machine that has both a computer name (used by other Microsoft machines) and a hostname (used by Unix machines and other TCP/IP hosts), you can instruct SQLCMD to connect as your hostname rather than your machine name.

-R Various settings control the process of converting currency, date, and time values into character data to be displayed on the screen. The `-R` setting instructs SQLCMD to use the client settings rather than the server settings to perform this conversion.

***-i* input_file** SQL Server can accept a text file as an input parameter if you use the `-i` parameter. This means you can enter all your settings and your query in a text file (using something like Notepad); then, instead of entering the information on the command line every time, you can specify an input file.

***-o* output_file** This parameter copies the result set to a text file, as opposed to the screen (which is the default). The `-oc:\output.txt` parameter, for instance, copies the result set from your query to a file named `output.txt`.

-u This parameter is used in conjunction with the `-o` parameter to specify that the output file should be stored as Unicode data rather than ASCII (the standard character set that displays 256 characters). It's useful for companies that store data in multiple languages.

***-a* packet_size** This parameter specifies the amount of data (in kilobytes) that SQL Server sends to or receives from SQLCMD at a time, called a *packet* of data. The default size is 512KB, which works fine for most transfers; but if you're performing a bulk insert of data from a large text file into a table, you may want to increase the size to 8192 (Microsoft recommends this value based on their testing).

-b This parameter instructs SQLCMD to exit to DOS and return a DOS error level of 1 when a problem arises. DOS error levels can be used in batch files for troubleshooting.

***-l* timeout** This parameter specifies the amount of time that SQLCMD waits for a login to be verified. If this parameter isn't specified, SQLCMD waits indefinitely. The default is 8 seconds.

-? This parameter displays a list of all the available switches to be used with SQLCMD.

-A This option logs in to SQL Server using a Dedicated Administrator Connection, which is a special connection used to troubleshoot servers.

-*X*[*1*] This command disables the `ED` and `!!` commands, which can be potentially dangerous to your system. If the optional `1` parameter isn't used, then the disabled commands are still recognized and SQLCMD displays an error and continues. If the `1` parameter is specified, then SQLCMD recognizes the disabled commands, displays an error, and exits.

-*f* <codepage> | *i:*<codepage>[,*o:*<codepage>] This parameter specifies the input and output codepages.

-*k*[*1*|*2*] This parameter removes all control characters (such as tab and new line) from the output while still preserving column formatting. If the `1` parameter is specified, then the control characters are replaced by a single space. If 2 is used, then consecutive control characters are replaced by a single space.

-*y* display_width This parameter limits the number of characters that are returned for large variable datatypes. If the display width is 0, then the output isn't truncated. The datatypes that this truncates are as follows:

- Varchar(max)
- Nvarchar(max)
- Varbinary(max)
- Xml
- User-defined datatypes

-*Y* display_width This parameter limits the number of characters returned for these datatypes:

- Char
- Nchar
- Varchar(n)
- Nvarchar(n)
- Sql_variant

Fortunately, you don't need to specify every parameter listed here to make SQLCMD work. Let's look at using SQLCMD to run a query and save the results to a text file:

1. To get to the command prompt, click Start button, select Programs, and click the Command Prompt icon.
2. To execute a query with SQLCMD, type the following command at the command prompt:

```
SQLCMD -S server_name -d AdventureWorks -Q "select * from Purchasing.Vendor"
-U sa -P password
-ooutput.txt
```

3. Open output.txt with a text editor such as Edit. The result set should display all the records in the Purchasing.Vendor table in the AdventureWorks database.

Another command-line tool that may come in handy is BCP, the Bulk Copy Program.

Bulk Copy Program (BCP)

Once you've created databases in SQL Server, you'll need to fill them with data. A popular way to do this is by importing text files into your tables. If you opt for this route, you can use the Bulk Copy Program (BCP), which is a command-line tool designed solely for the purpose of importing and exporting text files to and from tables at the rate of about 2000 rows per second (for you Trekkies, that's about Warp 9.9). This program is still here to provide backward compatibility and is being replaced by faster methods of import, such as the Bulk Import Transact-SQL command. This command will be discussed in more detail in Chapter 14, "Stored Procedures."

SQL Server Management Studio

Many of the administrative tasks you perform with SQL Server are accomplished using SQL Server Management Studio. Using this tool, you can create databases and all of their associated objects (tables, views, and so on). You can execute collections of Transact-SQL statements (referred to as *queries*). You can perform maintenance tasks such as database backups and restorations. Server and database security can be maintained from this tool, error logs can be viewed, and much more. When you first open SQL Server Management Studio, the window looks like Figure 3.1.

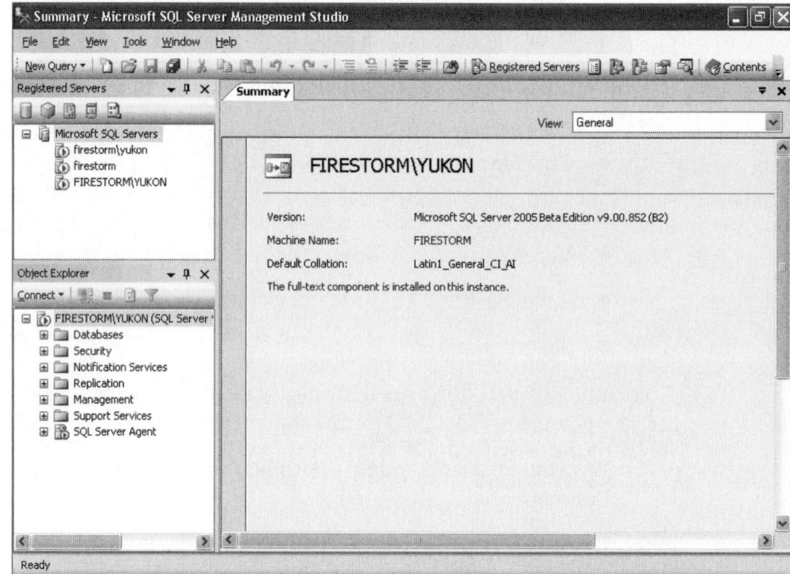

FIGURE 3.1
SQL Server Management Studio is used for many administrative tasks.

TIP The old Query Analyzer tool that you may have used in previous versions of SQL Server has been incorporated into SQL Server Management Studio, so you won't see it as a separate tool now.

By default, SQL Server Management Studio has three panes: the contents pane on the right and the Object Explorer and Registered Servers panes on the left. The Registered Servers pane functions in much the same way it did in SQL Server 2000; you can register a server so it's easier to connect to and manage in future sessions.

After you've connected to a server, you'll see a list of available objects in the Object Explorer pane. Some common objects you should see on a SQL Server are Databases, Security, Management, Support Services, Replication, and SQL Server Agent. If you're connected to an Analysis Server, then you'll see an Analysis Services category in the Object Explorer; the same is true for Reporting Services or other applications that plug into SQL Server Management Studio.

By clicking the + icons next to the container objects in the Object Explorer pane, you can drill down to greater levels of detail. You can examine the contents pane to see the objects contained in the container objects. For example, if you click the + icon next to Databases, click the + icon next to AdventureWorks, expand Tables, expand HumanResources.Department, and then select Columns, you'll see a summary of all the columns in the HumanResources.Department table, as shown in Figure 3.2.

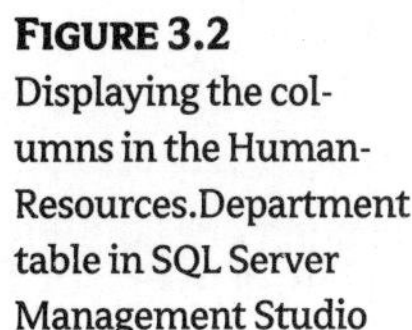

FIGURE 3.2
Displaying the columns in the HumanResources.Department table in SQL Server Management Studio

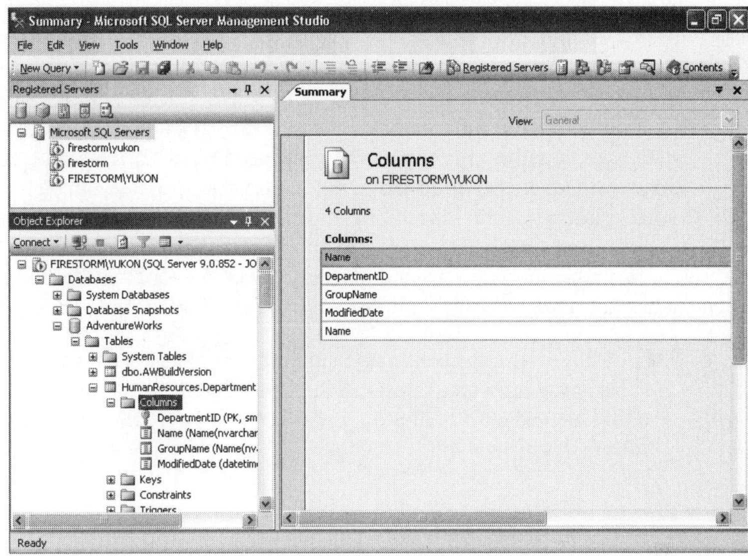

As we journey through the rest of this book, you'll be exposed to SQL Server Management Studio on an ongoing basis and will gain a great deal of experience with it. Let's take a look at some of the more advanced tools available with SQL Server 2005, the Application Programming Interfaces.

NOTE For more information on the capabilities of SQL Server Management Studio, see Chapter 9, "Using SQL Server Management Studio."

Application Programming Interfaces

All database servers offer one or more *application programming interfaces* (APIs). An API is a way to communicate with the database server to tell it to perform useful work. We've already mentioned one of the most important SQL Server APIs: the T-SQL programming language. However, SQL Server is a flexible server that supports many more APIs. Among them are the following:

- OLE DB/ActiveX Data Objects
- SQL Management Objects
- SQL Namespace
- Data Transformation Services

OLE DB is a Microsoft-developed standard API for retrieving data from a wide variety of data sources. This includes not just databases, but also file systems and even e-mail stores. *ActiveX Data Objects* (ADO) is an object library that works with OLE DB. Object libraries make it more convenient to write applications that work with an API by abstracting the API into a series of self-contained objects. You'll learn more about ADO in Chapter 20, "ADO.NET and SQL Server."

SQL Management Objects (SMO) is an API that can be used to programmatically perform administration and configuration tasks on SQL Server. For example, you can use SMO to create new tables, list existing views, or launch database backups. SMO is an object-oriented API that allows control of nearly every facet of SQL Server applications. We'll cover SMO in Chapter 21, "SMO and RMO Programming."

SQL Namespace (SQL-NS) is another API that exposes some of the administrative functionality of SQL Server. Unlike SQL-DMO, though, SQL-NS exposes the user-interface elements of the server. For example, you can use SQL-NS to launch any of the wizards that SQL Server supplies to create new objects. You'll learn about SQL-NS in Chapter 21, "SMO and RMO Programming."

Finally, *Data Transformation Services* (DTS) gives you programmatic control over SQL Server's data warehousing capabilities. You can use DTS to move data from one data source to another, across homogeneous or heterogeneous servers. The data can be transformed when it's moved, and you can use a built-in scheduling engine to perform these operations on a regular basis. We'll cover DTS in Chapter 22, "Data Transformation Services."

Now that you have a general overview of the tools available to you, you need to understand what you'll be creating with those tools. Let's look at the various parts of a database.

TIP **SQL Server also continues to support several legacy APIs that were important in earlier versions of the software. These include Open Database Connectivity (ODBC), Open Data Services (ODS), Embedded SQL (E-SQL), and DB Library for C (DB-Lib). We won't be covering these legacy APIs in this book.**

Parts of a Database

As Microsoft describes it, a *database* is an object that contains tables and other objects that are combined to facilitate data retrieval. In essence that is true, but you can think of a database as being more like a toolbox. If you own any number of tools, you probably don't just have them scattered about your property. If you did, you'd have no way of finding them when you needed them. Rather, you put them all in a toolbox. Your wrenches go in the wrench drawer, screwdrivers in the screwdriver drawer, and so on. When your tools are organized that way, you know exactly where to look when you want a particular tool.

A database is like a toolbox in that it's useless by itself, but when you fill it with other objects (tables, views, and so on), it serves a purpose by keeping those objects organized. Now when you want data, you know exactly where to go to get it. If, for instance, you want accounting data, you go to the Accounting database and dig through the accounting tables to find your data.

Because a database is primarily a conglomeration of objects, you need to understand those objects before you can successfully use a database. Let's look at some of those now, starting with tables.

Tables

Tables are the objects in the database that actually store the data. Because all other objects in the database depend on their existence, tables can be considered the building blocks of the database. The data stored in tables is organized further into fields and rows. A *field* is a vertical element in the table and contains information of the same type, such as last name or zip code. Fields are organized into columns. A *record* is a horizontal element and contains information that spans all the fields in the table within a single row. One record in an employee database, for example, might contain the last name, first name, address, Social Security number, and hire date of a single employee. A *spreadsheet*, such as that shown in Figure 3.3, will help you visualize fields and records.

Each of the fields in a table can contain only one type of data, such as character or numeric data. This aspect of the field is referred to as the column's *datatype*. In the example presented in Figure 3.3, you'll notice that the Address column has a datatype of Char(30), which means that this column holds 30 characters. If any numbers are stored here, you won't be able to perform any mathematical functions on them (such as adding or subtracting) without first converting the values stored in the field to numeric data.

FIGURE 3.3
Tables are organized into fields and records.

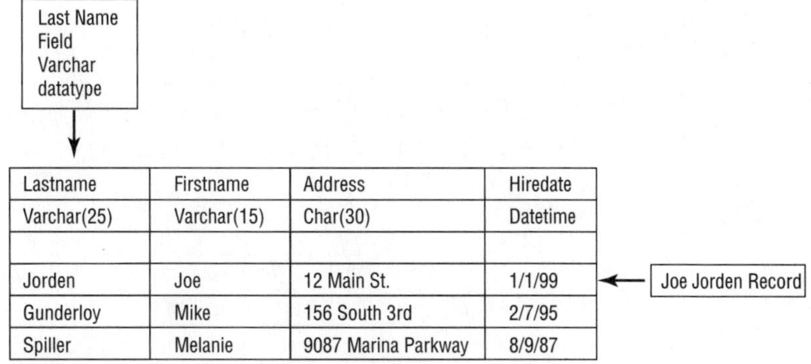

Once you've created tables in your database (which we'll discuss in more detail in Chapter 11, "Tables"), you can start creating other objects that depend on them, such as views and stored procedures.

Views

Much like tables, *views* consist of fields and records. Unlike tables, views don't contain any data. Views are always based on tables and are used to provide a different perspective of the data stored in those tables. For example, suppose you have a human resources database that contains employee names, addresses, phone numbers, Social Security numbers, and pay rates. The names, addresses, and phone numbers are usually public information, but the Social Security numbers and pay rates aren't meant for the general populace. You can secure this data so that only authorized people can see it by creating a view that doesn't contain the latter two columns and setting permissions on the table and view. This way, only people with the proper authority can read from the table itself, and everyone else can read from the view. You can use the view method to store the data only once (in the table) but still have two ways of looking at it. Figure 3.4 will help you visualize this.

FIGURE 3.4
Views can display select fields from a single table.

Lastname	Firstname	Address
Jorden	Joe	12 Main St.
Gunderloy	Mike	156 South 3rd
Spiller	Melanie	9087 Marina Parkway

Lastname	Firstname	Address	SSN	Payrate
Jorden	Joe	12 Main St.	555-66-7777	1.00
Gunderloy	Mike	156 South 3rd	666-77-8888	1.00
Spiller	Melanie	9087 Marina Parkway	888-99-0000	1.00

Another valuable service provided by views is the ability to combine data from two or more separate tables into one easy-to-read format. For instance, suppose you have two tables, one that contains customer information such as name, address, and so on, and a second table that contains information about what those customers have ordered from you. If you want to see your customers' names, addresses, and order details, you can create a view that combines the two tables and presents the data all at once, rather than execute two separate queries; see Figure 3.5.

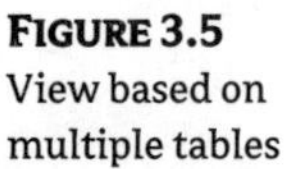
FIGURE 3.5
View based on multiple tables

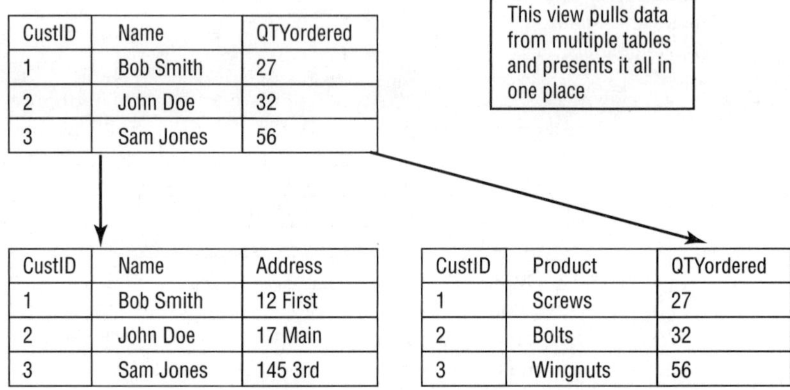

This view pulls data from multiple tables and presents it all in one place
CustID | Name | QTYordered
1 | Bob Smith | 27
2 | John Doe | 32
3 | Sam Jones | 56
CustID | Name | Address
1 | Bob Smith | 12 First
2 | John Doe | 17 Main
3 | Sam Jones | 145 3rd
CustID | Product | QTYordered
1 | Screws | 27
2 | Bolts | 32
3 | Wingnuts | 56

TIP Why not just store the data in the format you'd like to view it in later? The organization that makes the most sense to human beings may not make the most sense for quick and error-free data storage and retrieval. The name for this notion is *normalization*, and you can read much more about it in Chapter 4, "Database Design and Normalization."

Stored Procedures

You already know that data is stored in tables and that you need to execute queries to read the data in the tables. But where should those queries be stored? One place to store them is in a database on the server. Such stored queries are called *stored procedures*. You can also store the queries in the code on the client machines, or you can let users generate queries themselves using Query Analyzer; these are called *ad hoc queries*. Stored procedures are generally preferred because of the problems that are inherent with the spontaneity of ad hoc queries.

The first problem with ad hoc queries is that all your users will be performing queries to get the data from the tables, all those queries will be traversing the network, and all will cause network traffic. If every query contains several lines of text, you can imagine the havoc that will be wreaked on your bandwidth.

Another problem caused by ad hoc queries is that they can slow SQL Server. When an ad hoc query is sent to SQL Server the first time, it can't be executed right away; it must first be compiled. To compile a query, SQL Server must read the query and figure out the fastest way to execute it by comparing the query to the available indexes. The process of compiling takes system resources (such as CPU time and RAM) and slows the system.

NOTE To accelerate query processing, SQL Server uses *indexes*. Indexes speed up data access by keeping a list of all the values in one or more fields of a table and pointers to where the records that contain those values are located. Indexes are discussed in detail in Chapter 12, "Indexing."

An interesting fact about users is that most of them want to see the same data as everyone else, which means that all your users are sending the same queries to the SQL Server over the network. Instead of having each user send the same query many separate times over the network, you can store the query on the server and have users send a simple command to have SQL Server run the stored procedure. This way, instead of sending several lines of text over the network and wasting bandwidth, your users send a one-line command: `execute` *`stored_procedure`*. These stored procedures are also precompiled, which means you're saving system resources as well.

NOTE For a detailed discussion, please see Chapter 14, "Stored Procedures."

Diagrams

When you looked at the tables container in the AdventureWorks database earlier in this chapter, chances are that you did not find it very easy to look at. That is a natural reaction for most people: People don't like staring at long lists trying to find what they need. That is why there are database diagrams.

A *database diagram* is a graphical representation of a database that shows all of the objects in the database and how they relate to one another. Using a diagram, you can change table structure (for example, adding fields), relate them to other tables, and even create new indexes for them (all of which are discussed later). Without these diagrams, you would need to find each object individually in its own container and try to work with each separately, a mind-numbing task indeed. The following graphic shows what a diagram of the AdventureWorks database might look like (the actual diagram is huge so we can only show you part of it).

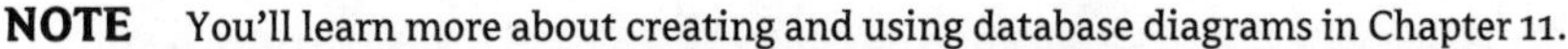

NOTE You'll learn more about creating and using database diagrams in Chapter 11.

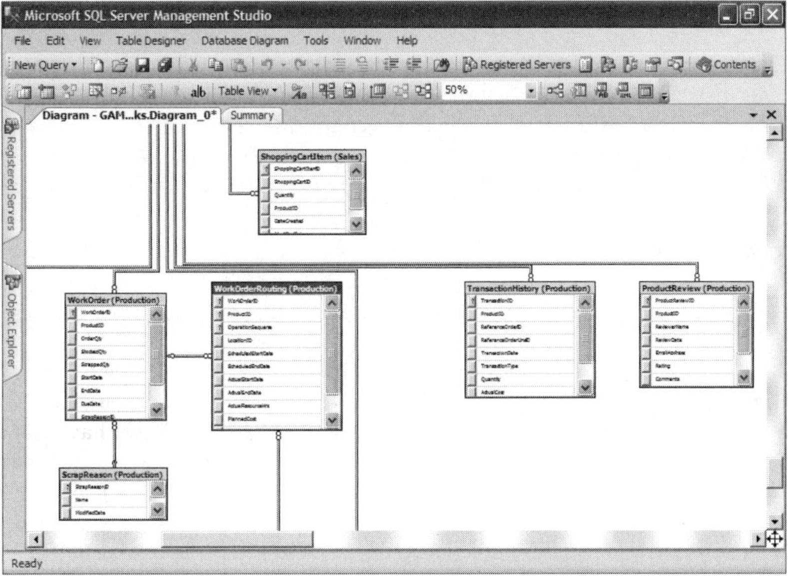

Database User Accounts

As we mentioned earlier, most companies store data that isn't meant for the general populace of the company. Not everyone is privy to pay rates and Social Security numbers, for instance. You can keep prying eyes out of places they don't belong with database user accounts.

To access SQL Server, users must have a *login account*. There are two types of login accounts that you can give your users: *standard* and *integrated*. An integrated account is also referred to as a *trusted connection*, because with this type of login, SQL Server trusts Windows to verify the username and password. This type of login can be used only for Microsoft Windows clients. Standard accounts don't trust Windows to verify account information and therefore are useful for clients that don't have a Windows account, such as Macintosh or Unix clients. Either type of login account lets your users access SQL Server as a whole but not the individual databases.

To give users access to individual databases, you must create a database user account for them in each database where they require access. For example, suppose you have a user named Bob who requires access to the Accounting database but isn't allowed to access the Sales database for any reason. To grant Bob access to the Accounting database, you can create a database user account in the Accounting database. This database user account lets Bob access the Accounting database. Because you don't want Bob to access the Sales database, you don't create a database user account for him in the Sales database; he won't be able to get in without it. This is just an overview, of course. Security is discussed at length in Chapter 18, "Security and SQL Server 2005."

Database Roles

Many large companies have thousands of users, assigned organizationally into various departments. Each of the people in the various departments requires access to the same segments of information. For instance, accounting personnel all need access to the accounting data, sales personnel need access to the sales data, and so on. There are two ways to give users the access they need. The first way is to create user accounts for each and every one of the users (which you have to do anyway) and then individually grant permissions to each user. The second and much easier way is to create the user accounts and assign the accounts to roles in the database.

A *role* is a predefined set of permissions to which you can add users. Once a user is a member of a role, they inherit the permissions of that role, and you need not individually assign them permissions. For example, if everyone in your accounting department needs to be able to read data from the accounting tables, you can assign the individual users' accounts to a role that already has the appropriate permission—and *voila*, they can read the data.

System Datatypes

As we discussed earlier, each of the fields in a table can contain only data of a certain type referred to as the *datatype*. SQL Server has several built-in datatypes, including the following:

bit This can contain only a 1 or a 0 as a value (or null which is no value). It's very useful as a status bit—on/off, yes/no, true/false.

int This can contain integer (or whole number) data from -2^{31} (–2,147,483,648) through $2^{31} - 1$ (2,147,483,647). It takes 4 bytes of hard-disk space to store and is useful for storing large numbers that you'll use in mathematical functions.

bigint This datatype includes integer data from -2^{63} (–9,223,372,036,854,775,808) through $2^{63} - 1$ (9,223,372,036,854,775,807). It takes 8 bytes of hard-disk space to store and is useful for extremely large numbers that won't fit in an int type field.

smallint This datatype includes integer data from -2^{15} (–32,768) through $2^{15} - 1$ (32,767). It takes 2 bytes of hard-disk space to store and is useful for slightly smaller numbers than you would store in an int type field, because smallint takes less space than int.

tinyint This datatype includes integer data from 0 through 255. It takes 1 byte of space on the disk and is limited in usefulness since it stores values only up to 255. Tinyint may be useful for something like a product-type code when you have fewer than 255 products.

decimal This datatype includes fixed-precision and scale-numeric data from $-10^{38} - 1$ through $10^{38} - 1$ (for comparison, this is a 1 with 38 zeros following it). It uses two parameters: precision and scale. *Precision* is the total count of digits that can be stored in the field, and *scale* is the number of digits that can be stored to the right of the decimal point. Thus, if you have a precision of 5 and a scale of 2, your field has the format 111.22. This type should be used when you're storing partial numbers (numbers with a decimal point).

numeric This is a synonym for *decimal*—they're one and the same.

money This datatype includes monetary data values from -2^{63} (–922,337,203,685,477.5808) through $2^{63}-1$ (922,337,203,685,477.5807), with accuracy to a ten-thousandth of a monetary unit. It takes 8 bytes of hard-disk space to store and is useful for storing sums of money larger than 214,748.3647.

smallmoney This datatype includes monetary data values from –214,748.3648 through 214,748.3647, with accuracy to a ten-thousandth of a monetary unit. It takes 4 bytes of space and is useful for storing smaller sums of money than would be stored in a money type field.

float This datatype includes floating precision number data from –1.79E + 38 through 1.79E + 38. Some numbers don't end after the decimal point—pi is a fine example. For such numbers, you must approximate the end, which is what float does. For example, if you set a datatype of float(2), pi will be stored as 3.14, with only two numbers after the decimal point.

real This datatype includes floating precision number data from –3.40E + 38 through 3.40E + 38. This is a quick way of saying float(24)—it's a floating type with 24 numbers represented after the decimal point.

datetime This datatype includes date and time data from January 1, 1753, to December 31, 9999, with values rounded to increments of .000, .003 or .007 seconds. This takes 8 bytes of space on the hard disk and should be used when you need to track very specific dates and times.

smalldatetime This datatype includes date and time data from January 1, 1900, through June 6, 2079, with an accuracy of 1 minute. It takes only 4 bytes of disk space and should be used for less specific dates and times than would be stored in datetime.

timestamp This is used to stamp a record with the time when the record is inserted and every time it's updated thereafter. This datatype is useful for tracking changes to your data.

uniqueidentifier The `NEWID()` function is used to create globally unique identifiers that might appear as follows: 6F9619FF-8B86-D011-B42D-00C04FC964FF. These unique numbers can be stored in the uniqueidentifier type field; they may be useful for creating tracking numbers or serial numbers that have no possible way of being duplicated.

char This datatype includes fixed-length, non-Unicode character data with a maximum length of 8000 characters. It's useful for character data that will always be the same length, such as a State field, which will contain only two characters in every record. This uses the same amount of space on disk no matter how many characters are actually stored in the field. For example, char(5) always uses 5 bytes of space, even if only two characters are stored in the field.

varchar This datatype includes variable-length, non-Unicode data with a maximum of 8000 characters. It's useful when the data won't always be the same length, such as in a first-name field where each name has a different number of characters. This uses less disk space when there are fewer characters in the field. For example, if you have a field of varchar(20), but you're storing a name with only 10 characters, the field will take up only 10 bytes of space, not 20. This field will accept a maximum of 20 characters.

varchar(max) This is just like the varchar datatype; but with a size of (max) specified, the datatype can hold $2^{31}-1$ (2,147,483,67) bytes of data.

nchar This datatype includes fixed-length, Unicode data with a maximum length of 4000 characters. Like all Unicode datatypes, it's useful for storing small amounts of text that will be read by clients that use different languages (i.e. some using Spanish and some using German).

nvarchar This datatype includes variable-length, Unicode data with a maximum length of 4000 characters. It's the same as nchar except that nvarchar uses less disk space when there are fewer characters.

nvarchar(max) This is just like nvarchar; but when the (max) size is specified, the datatype holds 2^{31} –1 (2,147,483,67) bytes of data.

binary This datatype includes fixed-length, binary data with a maximum length of 8000 bytes. It's interpreted as a string of bits (for example, 11011001011) and is useful for storing anything that looks better in binary or hexadecimal shorthand, such as a security identifier.

varbinary This datatype includes variable-length, binary data with a maximum length of 8000 bytes. It's just like binary, except that varbinary uses less hard-disk space when fewer bits are stored in the field.

varbinary(max) This has the same attributes as the varbinary datatype; but when the (max) size is declared, the datatype can hold 2^{31} –1 (2,147,483,67) bytes of data. This is very useful for storing binary objects like JPEG image files or Word documents.

xml This datatype is used to store entire XML documents or fragments (a document that is missing the top-level element).

identity This isn't actually a datatype, but it serves an important role. It's a property, usually used in conjunction with the int datatype, and it's used to increment the value of the column each time a new record is inserted. For example, the first record in the table would have an identity value of 1, and the next would be 2, then 3, and so on.

sql_variant Like identity this isn't an actual datatype per se, but it actually lets you store values of different datatypes. The only values it cannot store are; varchar(max), nvarchar(max), text, image, sql_variant, varbinary(max), xml, ntext, timestamp, or user-defined datatypes.

NOTE The text, ntext, and image datatypes have been deprecated in this version of SQL Server. You should replace these with varchar(max), nvarchar(max), or varbinary(max).

NOTE You may have noticed that some of these datatypes are used to contain Unicode data. *Unicode* is a character set that can display and store 65,536 different characters, whereas a standard character set can store and display only 256 different characters. This is because a standard character set uses only 1 byte (8 bits) to store a character, and Unicode uses 2 bytes (16 bits). Unicode is very useful for international companies that use data stored in many different languages.

With these built-in datatypes, you must specify all the associated parameters every time you use them. For example, if you want to add a phone number column to several tables, you must create a column with a datatype of character(10) in each table. Then you need to create a constraint on each one that disallows letters and symbols, because those aren't allowed in phone numbers. (If you're concerned about the hyphen and parentheses in the phone number, don't be. These can be displayed to your end user without storing them in the database.) An easier way is to create your own user-defined datatype that already has these parameters defined. Then, rather than creating columns with the character datatype and supplying parameters each time, you create a column and assign it the new phone number datatype.

NOTE There's more information on using datatypes in Chapter 11.

User-Defined Functions

A *function* is a grouping of Transact-SQL statements that can be reused. SQL Server has a large number of built-in functions, but these may not meet all your needs. For this reason, SQL Server gives you the ability to create your own functions, called *user-defined functions*, to perform any tasks you may require. A good example is a function that multiplies two numbers; the code to create such a function looks as follows:

```
CREATE FUNCTION Multiply
' Input parameters to be multiplied
  (@First int, @Second int)
RETURNS int 'Results of multiplication
AS
BEGIN
  RETURN (@First * @Second)
END
```

To call this new function and have it multiply 2 times 3, you execute the following (returning a result of 6):

```
Table_name.Multiply(2,3)
```

NOTE User-defined functions are discussed in more detail in Chapter 5, "Transact-SQL Overview and Basics." SQL Server 2005 also lets you create user-defined functions with one of the .NET languages such as C#. You can read more about that capability in Chapter 19, "Integrating SQL Server with Microsoft .NET."

Rules and Constraints

In some instances, it may not be enough to restrict a field to a datatype. For example, what if you have a field designed to store the state in which someone lives? It's a character-type field limited to storing two characters, which works fine except for one small problem: If one of your users entered *XZ* as a state, SQL Server would accept it, because it's a character value. By using *constraints*, you can have SQL Server check the data that is being entered against a list of acceptable values (the constraints); when SQL Server encounters XZ, which isn't a valid state abbreviation, it will reject the update.

Rules perform the same function as constraints, but they're primarily used for backward compatibility. Rules have one advantage over constraints: You can bind rules to a datatype, whereas constraints are bound only to columns. This means that you can create your own datatype and, with a rule, tell SQL Server what data to accept on the column to which that datatype is applied.

For example, assume that you have a company database with several tables: one for employee information, one for manager information, and one for customer information. Each of these tables needs to have a field that is constrained to accept only valid phone numbers. You must define the constraint on each phone number field in each of the tables—you'll define the same constraint three times. Using a rule, you enter the code only once and bind the rule to a user-defined datatype (a datatype that you've made up yourself). Now, whenever you apply your new user-defined datatype to a field in a table, it's automatically restricted by the rule.

Defaults

Defaults are used to fill in data that the user forgets to enter. A good time to use these is when most of the values in one of the fields in your table will be the same for every record. For example, if you have a table of employee information that has a state of residence field, and all your employees live in California, you can use a default to fill in the state field automatically. Every time a user enters a new employee record or modifies an existing one, the state field will be filled in with CA automatically, saving your users some typing time. There are two types of defaults for you to choose from:

Object defaults *Object defaults* are defined when you create your table, usually in the table designer. Object defaults are defined on a column in a table and affect only that column. If you define an object default on a state field in a customer information table, for example, only that state field in the customer table will be affected; no other field in any other table will have a defined default.

Definition defaults *Definition defaults* are bound to user-defined datatypes. This means you can define the default once and bind it to a datatype (possibly named *state*). Then, every time you create a field, in any table, of the state datatype, it will automatically have the correct definition default.

Object defaults are best used when you have defaults for each table but the value to be filled in is different. For instance, if your employees all live in California and most of your customers are in Arizona, you need separate defaults for each table. If, however, your customers and employees are all in California, can could use a definition default, bind it to a datatype (probably the state), and apply it to both tables.

Full-Text Catalogs

One of SQL Server 2005's nicest features is the full-text search functionality. Full-text search is designed to plow through pages and pages of text looking for phrases or words that are in proximity to each other. For example, you could perform a full-text search on a text-type column looking for *SQL* and *book* in close proximity to each other, and one of the results returned could be *Mastering Microsoft SQL Server 2005, a great new book from Sybex.* Notice that SQL and book are very close to one another in the same sentence. You'll learn how to create these queries in Chapter 6, "Select Queries."

If you want to run full-text catalog queries, you must first create a *full-text index*. This is a special index that indexes only text-type columns when looking for words that might be used in a query. Such indexes aren't part of the database, because they're stored in their own files on disk, but they're administered through the database.

Let's create a full-text search catalog here:

1. Open SQL Server Management Studio, expand Databases in the Object Explorer, expand AdventureWorks, expand Storage, right-click Full-Text Catalogs, and select New Full-Text Catalog.
2. On the New Full-Text Catalog screen, enter the following information:
   - Full-Text Catalog Name: Test
   - Catalog Location: c:\temp
   - Filegroup: <default>
   - Owner: dbo

Also select Set As Default Catalog.

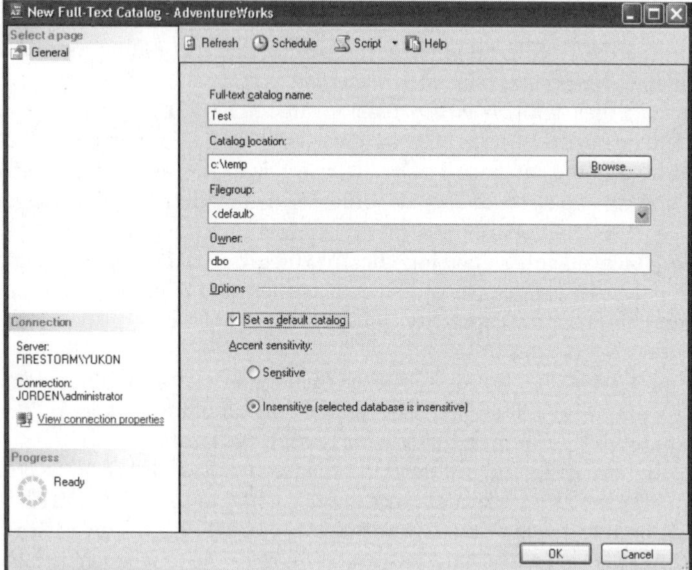

3. Click OK to create the catalog.

XML and SQL Server

SQL Server 2005 is tightly integrated with XML, much more so than any of its predecessors. With this new version, you now have an xml datatype, which allows you to store XML documents or fragments in a column all their own. XML datatype columns can be typed based on a schema; then they will only store documents that match the schema. They can also be untyped so they can store any type of document.

Why store XML data in a table? Why not just store the data in tables without the XML markup? There are several good reasons to consider storing XML data in tables:

- You may want to use the tools available with SQL Server to administer and manage your XML data.
- You may want to store, share, query, and modify your XML data using the efficient tools that SQL Server gives you.
- You may want interoperability between SQL Server databases and XML data in your applications.
- You may want the server to guarantee that your data is well-formed and possibly to validate that data against a schema.
- You may need to index your XML data for faster query processing.
- You may need ADO.NET, SOAP, and OLE DB access to the same data, which can be accomplished using XML.

Now that you have a better understanding of some of the things SQL Server stores in a database, you should know how it stores them. Let's peer into the depths of SQL Server's storage.

SQL Server Storage Concepts

Just like any data saved on a computer, the databases that you create with SQL Server must be stored on the hard disk. SQL Server uses three different types of files to store databases on disk: *primary data files*, *secondary data files*, and *transaction log files*.

Primary data files, with an `.MDF` extension, are the first files created in a database and can contain user-defined objects, such as tables and views, as well as system tables that SQL Server requires for keeping track of the database. If the database gets too big and you run out of room on your first hard disk, you can create secondary data files, with an `.NDF` extension, on separate physical hard disks to give your database more room.

Secondary files can be grouped together into filegroups. *Filegroups* are logical groupings of files, meaning that the files can be on any disk in the system and SQL Server will still see them as belonging together. This grouping capability comes in handy for very large databases (VLDBs), which are gigabytes or even terabytes in size.

For the purpose of illustration, suppose you have a database that is several hundred gigabytes in size and contains several tables. Users read from half of these tables quite a bit and write to the other half quite a bit. Assuming that you have multiple hard disks, you can create secondary files on two of your hard disks and put them in a filegroup called READ. Next, create two more secondary files on different hard disks and place them in a filegroup called WRITE. Now, when you want to create a new table that is primarily for reading, you can specifically instruct SQL Server to place it on the READ filegroup. The WRITE group will never be touched. You have, to a small degree, load-balanced the system, because some hard disks are dedicated to reading and others to writing. Of course, using filegroups is more complex than this in the real world, but you get the picture.

The third type of file is transaction log files. Transaction log files use an `.LDF` extension and don't contain any objects such as tables or views. To understand transaction log files, it's best to know a little about how SQL Server writes data to disk.

When a user wants to make changes to data in your table, SQL Server doesn't write that change directly to the data file. Instead, SQL Server extracts the data to be modified from the data file and places it in memory. Once the data is in memory, the user can make changes. Every now and then (about every 5 minutes), SQL Server takes all the changes that are sitting in memory and writes them to the transaction log file. Then, after the changes are written to the transaction log, SQL Server writes the changes to the database file. This is called a *write-ahead* log, because SQL Server writes to the log before it writes to the database.

"Why do we want to do this?" you may ask. There are two reasons, the first of which is speed. Memory is about 100 times faster than hard disk, so if you pull the data off the disk and make all the changes in memory, the changes occur about 100 times faster than they would if you wrote directly to disk. The second reason you'll want to use transaction logs is for recoverability. Suppose you backed up your data last night around 10 P.M. and your hard disk containing the data crashed at 11 A.M. the next day. You would lose all your changes since last night at 10 P.M. if you wrote to only the data file. Because you've recorded the changes to the data in the transaction log file (which should be on a separate disk), you can recover all your data right up to the minute of the crash. The transaction log stores data and data changes in real time and acts as a sort of preliminary backup.

Now, try to imagine the inside of these database files. Think what would happen if they had no order or organization—if SQL Server wrote data wherever it found the space. It would take forever for SQL Server to find your data when you asked for it, and the entire server would be slow as a result. To keep this from happening, SQL Server has even smaller levels of data storage inside your data files that you don't see, called *pages* and *extents* (as shown in Figure 3.6).

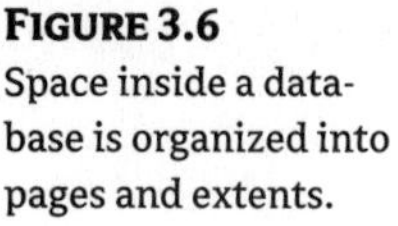

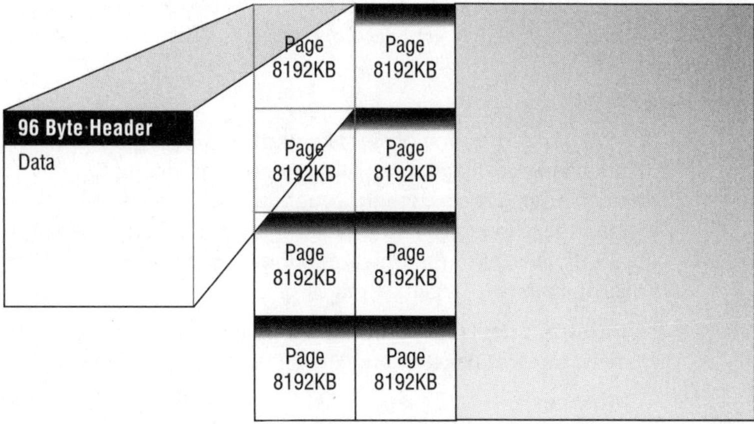

FIGURE 3.6
Space inside a database is organized into pages and extents.

Pages

Pages are the smallest unit of storage in a SQL Server data file. Pages are 8192 bytes each and start off with a 96-byte header. This means that each page can hold 8096 bytes of data. There are several types of pages, each one holding a different type of data:

Data This type of page contains most of the data that you enter into your tables. The only data entered by users that isn't stored in a data page is text and image data, because text and image data are usually large and warrant their own pages.

Global Allocation Map When a table requires more space inside the data file where it resides, SQL Server doesn't just allocate one page at a time. It allocates eight contiguous pages, called an *extent*. The Global Allocation Map (GAM) page type is used to keep track of which extents are allocated and which are still available.

Index Indexes are used to accelerate data access by keeping a list of all the values in a single field (or a combination of multiple fields) in the table and associating those values with a record number. Indexes are stored separately from data in their own page type.

Index Allocation Map Although the GAM pages keep track of which extents are in use, they don't keep track of the purpose for which the extents are being used. The Index Allocation Map (IAM) pages are used to keep track of what an extent is being used for—specifically, to which table or index the extent has been allocated.

Page Free Space This isn't an empty page, as the name may suggest. It's a special type used to keep track of free space on all the other pages in the database. Each Page Free Space page can keep track of the free space on up to 8000 other pages. That way, SQL Server knows which pages have free space when new data needs to be inserted.

Text/image The char(max), varchar(max), and varbinary(max) datatypes are designed to hold rather large objects, up to 2GB. Large objects such as pictures and large documents are difficult to retrieve when they're stored in a field in one of your tables because SQL Server returns the entire object when queried for it. To break the large, unwieldy objects into smaller, more manageable chunks, char(max), varchar(max), and varbinary(max) datatypes are stored in their own pages. This way, when you request SQL Server to return an image or a large document, it can return small chunks of the document at a time rather than the whole thing all at once.

NOTE Transaction logs aren't organized into pages or extents. They contain a list of transactions that have modified your data, organized on a first-come, first-served basis.

Extents

An *extent* is a collection of eight contiguous pages used to keep the database from becoming fragmented. *Fragmentation* means that pages that belong together, usually belonging to the same table or index, are scattered throughout the database file. To avoid fragmentation, SQL Server assigns space to tables and indexes in extents. That way, at least eight of the pages should be physically next to one another, making them easier for SQL Server to locate. SQL Server uses two types of extents to organize pages:

Uniform extents These are entirely owned by a single object. For example, if a single table owns all eight pages of an extent, it's considered uniform.

Mixed extents These are used for objects that are too small to fill eight pages by themselves. In that instance, SQL Server divvies up the pages in the extent to multiple objects.

Figure 3.7 shows the difference between uniform and mixed extents.

FIGURE 3.7 SQL Server uses uniform and mixed extents to further organize space inside the data files.

Uniform Extent

Table 1	Table 1
Table 1	Table 1
Table 1	Table 1
Table 1	Table 1

Mixed Extent

Table 2	Table 2
Table 2	Table 3
Table 3	Index 1
Index 1	Index 1

Summary

This chapter contains a lot of information. We started by looking at each of the programs that come with SQL Server and what those programs can do for you:

SQL Server Books Online This is a compilation of documents and tutorials that can be used to answer many of your questions regarding SQL Server.

SQL Computer Manager Use the SQL Computer Manager to configure the services installed on your server as well as the client and server network protocols and libraries used for client-server communication.

SQL Profiler This tool is used to monitor events that happen on the database engine, such as a failed login or a completed query.

Query Analyzer You use this tool to execute Transact-SQL code and display the results. It can also analyze queries to help you optimize them.

SQLCMD This tool is used to execute Transact-SQL code, but SQLCMD works at the command line.

Bulk Copy Program (BCP) Use BCP to import text files into tables and export data from tables to text files.

SQL Server Management Studio Most of your day-to-day administrative duties will be performed through SQL Server Management Studio tool—activities such as backups and restorations, security maintenance, and so on. You can also use this tool to run queries against you databases.

After discussing the various programs that you'll be using to work with SQL Server, we discussed the objects that make up a database:

Tables The building blocks of the database, tables are the structures that contain data. Tables are divided into fields and records.

Views Views are used to display the data contained in tables in different formats. They're useful for displaying only a portion of a table or displaying data from multiple tables simultaneously.

Stored procedures These are queries that are stored on the server as opposed to on the client. They run faster than queries stored on the client and don't traverse the network, thus saving bandwidth.

Database diagrams These make database administration easier by creating a graphical view of the entire database and how all of the tables inside relate to one another.

Database user accounts These are used to grant users access to a database after they have logged in to SQL Server with their login account.

Database roles Database roles control what access your users have to data and objects in the database.

System datatypes Microsoft has given you a variety of datatypes that you can use to store data in table columns and memory variables.

Rules and constraints Rules and constraints are designed to limit what your users can insert into a field.

Defaults Defaults are used to fill in information that users forget or that is repetitive.

Full-text catalogs These special indexes are used to accelerate access to large character fields such as varchar(max) and nvarchar(max).

XML You can store XML data in columns of the xml datatype, which has several advantages over storing it on disk as a file. XML data can be index, queried, and accessed much more efficiently when it's stored in a table than when it's stored on disk.

Finally, you learned about the files that make up a database and how those files are organized:

Database files Up to three files make up a database:

- The primary data file is the first file created in the database and is used to store the system tables as well as user data.
- Secondary data files are used to expand the database onto additional physical hard disks and contain user data.
- Transaction log files keep track of all user transactions that modify data so that in the event of a disaster, your data can be recovered right up to the time of the crash.

Pages The smallest unit of storage in a data file is the 8KB page. There are several types of pages:

Data Except for text, ntext, and image data, this type of page contains all your user data.

Global Allocation Map (GAM) The GAM page type keeps track of which extents are allocated and which are still available.

Index This type of page stores only index information.

Index Allocation Map (IAM) The IAM pages keep track of what an extent is being used for—specifically, to which table or index the extent has been allocated.

Page Free Space This keeps track of free space on all the other pages in the database.

Text/image This type of page contains only text, ntext, and image data.

Extents Extents are blocks of eight contiguous pages that help keep the space inside the data files defragmented. There are two types of extents:

- Uniform extents are owned entirely by a single object.
- Mixed extents are owned by multiple objects that aren't large enough to warrant an extent of their own.

Armed with this knowledge, you're ready to move on to the more advanced topic of database design.

Chapter 4

Database Design and Normalization

If you've worked in other areas of software development, the idea of design might conjure up images of decomposing an application into basic functions, writing code for those functions, and creating a user interface that enables users to work with the application. Although all of those activities are important in developing full-blown SQL Server applications, database development demands an additional level of design. Before you can design the part of the application that the user will see, you must design the logical organization of the data that the database will store.

The technical name for the process of designing an optimal organization for your data is *normalization*. In this chapter, you'll learn the basic concepts of normalization. You'll also see the tools that SQL Server provides to implement these concepts. Later in the book, you'll learn exactly how to use these tools as you develop your databases.

What Is Normalization?

Normalization is the process of taking all the data that will be stored in a particular database and separating it into tables. Unless you're going to keep all your data in a single table (probably not the best idea), this is a decision-making process. By defining a number of normal forms (ways in which tables can be structured), normalization helps you come up with an efficient storage structure.

Efficient in this case doesn't mean *of minimum size*. Rather, as you'll see when you learn about the various normal forms, efficiency refers to structuring the database so that data stays organized and changes are easy to make without side effects. Minimizing storage size is sometimes a product of normalization, but it's not the main goal.

Key Concepts of Normalization

Normalization is mainly for preserving the integrity of your data. No matter what operations are performed in your database, it should be as difficult as possible to insert or create meaningless data. Normalization recognizes four types of integrity:

- Entity integrity
- Domain integrity
- Referential integrity
- User-defined integrity

In this section, we'll discuss these four types of integrity and take a brief look at the SQL Server tools that are available to enforce them.

ENTITY INTEGRITY

An *entity* is a single object or concept from the real world. A database stores information about entities. Entities can have physical existence (for example, a book could be an entity) or conceptual existence (for instance, a company). Entities can even be events, such as an appointment to see a doctor. One of the steps toward organizing the data in a database is to identify the entities with which the database is concerned.

The basic idea of *entity integrity* is that you must be able to uniquely identify each entity that you store in a database. This helps to prevent conflicts or redundant information. An entity within the database is a representation of any real-world entity that you choose to store in the database. This might be as follows:

- An object, such as a product your company sells
- A subject, such as a customer or vendor with which your company deals
- An event, such as the sale of a product to a customer

For example, suppose you're developing a database to track the livestock on a farm and their feeds. Entities in this database might include:

- The various types of animals
- The various types of feeds
- The various suppliers of those feeds
- The dates the feeds have most recently been delivered to the farm

There is an art to identifying entities. Entities occupy a middle level of detail between the smallest facts you need to store and the larger groups of similar entities. Consider for a moment all the animals on a small farm. You could look at these animals on various levels of detail. From the largest to the smallest facts, you might think about:

- All the animals as a single group
- All the animals of the same species (all ducks, all pigs) as a group
- An individual animal (one particular cow)
- A fact about an animal (the color of the cow)

Which of these things is an entity depends in large part on what you need to do with the data. In general, you want to identify as entities those things that you're most likely to work with as a unit; since all the information about an entity will be stored together, it's often convenient to retrieve that information as a single operation.

Sometimes you can make the decision about what to call an entity by thinking about the sorts of questions you want to be able to answer. If the questions are, "How many of each species do we have on this farm?" and "How much feed did all the cows eat last month?" you might decide that the entity is all the animals of a particular species. On the other hand, if the more likely questions are, "When was this particular cow born?" and "How much feed did that chicken get in May?" the entity is a single animal.

Once you've decided on an entity identity, there are two additional steps to take. First, you need to identify the facts that describe this entity. If you choose a single animal as the entity, the facts could be as follows:

- Name of the animal
- Breed of the animal
- Birth date of the animal
- Sex of the animal
- Color of the animal

Second, you need to identify the group of similar entities that are all described by the same set of facts. In this case, that would be all the animals on the farm. Each animal has a name, a breed, a birth date, and so on.

Figure 4.1 shows how this logical organization corresponds to the basic database concepts you learned in Chapter 2. The entity corresponds to a row or record in a table. The fact corresponds to the column or field in a table. The group of similar entities makes up a table. Each entity has a value for each particular field. The set of those values defines everything you know about the entity.

FIGURE 4.1
Organizing informa- [illegible] tabase

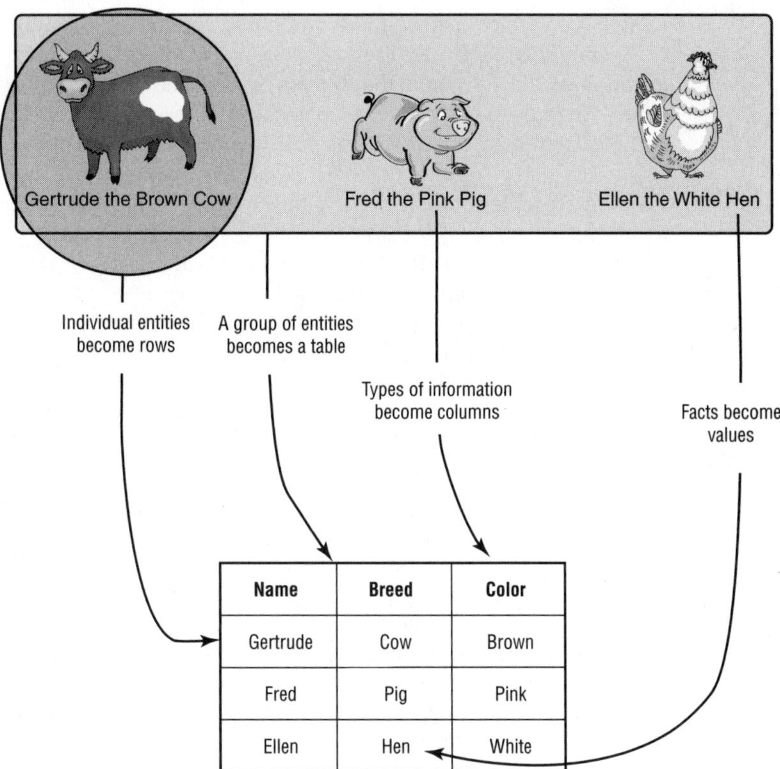

Each entity stored in a database needs to have a *primary key*, which consists of a unique characteristic or set of characteristics that distinguish it from other entities of the same type. For example, if you have a list of all the animals on the farm, you might choose to use the animal's name or a number that matches a tag or brand as the primary key for that list.

If you can locate a single column that serves to identify records in a table, you've found a *simple primary key*. If it takes a combination of columns to do this, the table is said to have a *composite primary key*. For example, think about a table containing all the animals on a farm. Suppose you have just four animals:

- A sheep named Fred
- A cow named Bossy
- A duck named Mildred
- A horse named Danny

In this case, you might choose to define a table with columns for breed and name. In the data for these four animals, you could use either the breed or the name as a simple primary key; there are no duplicated values in either column. But would either one be a good choice? Probably not, if you're ever going to buy new animals. If you bought a cow named Millie, for example, you'd have two cows—the breed would no longer work as a primary key. If you bought a cat named Fred, though, you'd have two animals named Fred—the name wouldn't work as a primary key. In this case, it might be best to use the composite of the two columns as a primary key. Then you could add all the sheep you like, or all the animals named Herman you like, without having two records in the table with the same primary key. In general, choosing a primary key requires consideration not just of the current data, but of possible future data as well.

As you're developing a database *schema* (a set of tables with interrelationships) to represent your real-world problem, you'll create a table to store each entity and a field (or group of fields) to store the primary key for each entity.

Why is it so important to identify a unique primary key for each record? Because the primary key is the main "handle" that the database server uses to grab the information in which you're interested. By identifying a primary key, you're telling the server which information you want to work with at the moment. If primary keys weren't unique, the database wouldn't know which record to give back to you. Primary keys are the primary mechanism that the database uses to enforce entity integrity, which is the basis of being able to retrieve the information that you inserted into a database.

One final distinction that you'll sometimes run across in the database literature is the difference between a natural primary key and a surrogate primary key. Sometimes there just isn't a good primary key in the data that you're given. Suppose, for example, that you own 200 chickens and haven't bothered to give them names. You still need a way to tell those chickens apart in the database. You could do this by assigning a number to each chicken: Chicken 1, Chicken 2, and so on (perhaps by using numbered bands on the chickens' legs). In this case, you'd have created a primary key where none existed before. That's a surrogate primary key. A natural primary key, in contrast, is one that exists in the data itself.

Once you've identified the key fields for your tables, you can use a variety of SQL Server features to enforce entity integrity. You can create a unique index on the field, as discussed in Chapter 12, "Indexing," to prevent users from entering duplicate key values. You can also use `PRIMARY KEY` or `UNIQUE KEY` constraints, or the identity property, to enforce entity integrity. These features are discussed later in this chapter.

DOMAIN INTEGRITY

The purpose of entity integrity is to make it possible to retrieve the information that you store in a database. *Domain integrity*, on the other hand, enforces restrictions on the information that you store in the database. You can think of the domain as the set of business rules that govern the allowable data in each column of a table. For any given piece of data—for example, the animal's name or the feed supplier in the farm database—some domain of values is valid for each entry in that field.

At the simplest level, the datatype assigned to the column enforces domain integrity. For example, you won't be able to enter text in a domain that is defined using a numeric datatype. The more you can do to limit the data that can be entered into the field to its domain, the higher your chance of keeping bad data from entering your database.

Domain integrity rules also specify which data is absolutely necessary for the database to function properly. For example, consider the database of farm animals. If one of the jobs of this database is to tell you what to feed each animal, then knowing the breed of each animal is crucial to the proper functioning of the database. In this case, you'd say that breed is a *required field* in the Animal table. You must enter data in all the required fields of a record before that record can be stored. In addition, of course, all fields in the record must conform to the other domain integrity rules.

NOTE When a database is storing a record, it must store something in each field, even if the field isn't required. SQL Server (like most other database products) can store a special value called *null*. Null is a placeholder for unknown data: It's not equal to anything else, not even another null. As you're considering the domain integrity rules for your database, you should think about the special case of whether a column should allow nulls, or whether to require users to enter a value when they create a new record. SQL Server uses the `NOT NULL` clause in a `CREATE TABLE` statement to specify that a particular column should not accept null values. If you do specify `NOT NULL` on a field, you won't be able to save the record until a value for that column is supplied.

SQL Server provides a variety of tools for enforcing domain integrity. These include:

- Datatypes
- User-defined datatypes
- `DEFAULT` constraints
- `CHECK` constraints
- Rules
- `FOREIGN KEY` constraints

You'll learn about these tools in Chapter 11, "Tables," which will teach you the details of creating tables.

REFERENTIAL INTEGRITY

If you think about the farm database, you'll notice that there are some columns whose acceptable values are defined in terms of columns in other tables. For example, suppose you're keeping track of the breeds of animals on the farm and what those animals are fed. In particular, suppose each animal has several possible types of feed, as shown in Table 4.1.

TABLE 4.1: Animal Breeds and Feeds

BREED	FEEDS
Horse	Pasture, Sweet Feed, Apples
Llama	Purina Llama Feed, Llama Lite, Llama Power
Goat	Hi-Pro

You could capture the information shown in Table 4.1 in a database by creating two tables, one of animal breeds and a second table of feeds. You also know that there's a connection between these two tables; for each feed, you can identify an animal who eats that feed. You could capture this information by including the name of the breed in the feed table, as a pointer back to the breed table (which could also contain information other than the breed name). You might end up with the Breed table shown in Table 4.2 and the Feed table shown in Table 4.3.

TABLE 4.2: Breed

BREED	LEGS	COVERING
Horse	4	Hair
Llama	4	Wool
Goat	4	Hair

TABLE 4.3: Feed

BREED	FEED
Horse	Pasture
Horse	Sweet Feed
Horse	Apples
Llama	Purina Llama Feed
Llama	Llama Lite
Llama	Llama Power
Goat	Hi-Pro

If your database contained these two tables, you could answer questions that concerned both breeds and feeds. For example, you could determine the number of legs of the breed that eats Hi-Pro. You'd do this by noting that the Breed column in the Feed table for the Hi-Pro row contains the value Goat, and then look at the Goat row in the Breed table. The two tables are then said to be *related* by the shared column (the Breed column, in this case).

The purpose of *referential integrity* is to make sure that related rows in a pair of tables stay related even when you make changes to the data. When a database enforces referential integrity, it prevents some actions on the part of database users. To preserve referential integrity between the Breed and Feed tables in this example, the database must constrain, or limit, a number of possible database actions:

- The user can't add a Feed for a Breed that hasn't been entered yet. This rule makes sure that the database can always answer breed-related questions about particular feeds.
- The user can't change the Breed name for an existing row in the Breed table. If the database allowed the user to break this rule, it would be possible to orphan a row in the Feed table so that it no longer referred to a row in the Breed table.
- The user can't delete a Breed that has rows in the Feed table. Again, this rule is necessary to prevent orphaned rows in the Feed table.

These rules aren't as arbitrary as they might seem at first glance. The basic idea is that no matter what actions you perform in the database, you always have to be able to match each Feed to a corresponding Breed. Referential integrity states that there are immutable relationships between tables in your database that need to be enforced.

SQL Server provides several tools for maintaining referential integrity:

- `FOREIGN KEY` constraints
- `CHECK` constraints
- Triggers and stored procedures

You'll learn more about these tools in Chapter 12.

User-Defined Integrity

Entity integrity, domain integrity, and referential integrity are all formal database concepts. You'll find these types of integrity available in every database. Although a particular database may not make use of the domain integrity tools offered by SQL Server or use referential integrity to constrain the data shared by a pair of tables, the support for those types of integrity is built in.

User-defined integrity encompasses all other business rules that don't fit neatly into one of these concepts. For example, you might know that any animal that is normally pastured must also have a backup feed for times when no pasture is available. Such a rule can't be expressed through other types of integrity rules and can be implemented only using triggers, rules, or stored procedures saved in the database, or through logic implemented in whatever client program you use to retrieve and manipulate data from the database. For example, if you always worked with the data in the farm database using a client program written in Visual Basic, that program could contain the business rules for enforcing user-defined integrity.

In most cases, you'll do best to keep user-defined integrity rules on the server with the rest of the database, because you can use many different clients to access the data stored by SQL Server. These range from the simple tools supplied with SQL Server (such as SQL Server Management Studio, which you'll meet in Chapter 5, "Transact-SQL Overview and Basics") to custom applications written in Microsoft Access, Visual Basic .NET, C#, or another programming language. If you place business rules on the client side, you'll have to duplicate and maintain them in every client application. If you place them on the server, you'll have only one copy of the rules to maintain no matter how many client applications you use to manipulate the data.

First Normal Form

Now that you understand the different types of data integrity, we can examine the normal forms. Each normal form is characterized by rules about how data should be organized. The various normal forms are referred to by numbers: First Normal Form, Second Normal Form, and so on. Each builds on the previous set of rules, so that data that is in Third Normal Form, for example, is automatically in First and Second Normal Forms as well.

The easiest way to understand the process of normalization is to work through an example. Let's take the example of the farm animal database we've been discussing. Table 4.4 shows some sample data that you might like to keep in this database.

TABLE 4.4: Raw Data for Normalization

NAME	BREED	FEED	SUPPLIER
Danny	Horse	Pasture	Jones, Endicott
Danny	Horse	Sweet Feed	Grange, Colfax
Tango	Llama	Pasture	Jones, Endicott
Tango	Llama	Purina Llama Feed	Grange, Colfax
Scotty	Llama	Pasture	Jones, Endicott
Scotty	Llama	Purina Llama Feed	Grange, Colfax
Genghis	Goat	Hi-Pro	Costco, Spokane

Although this table contains the data you want to track, it isn't normalized. In the next few sections, we'll look at some of the specific problems with this arrangement of data and normalize it.

NOTE On a real farm, of course, there would be a lot more data to track than this. You'd probably want to keep track of purchases, have a way to add new animals and remove existing ones, use multiple suppliers for a single type of feed, and so on. However, if you understand the normalization rules in this simple example, you'll be able to apply them to more complex situations as well.

Defining First Normal Form

The rules for First Normal Form are simple: Each field in a table must contain only a single type of data, and each piece of data must be stored in only one place. This requirement is sometimes phrased as a requirement for *atomic data:* that is, each field is indivisible, like a classical atom. First Normal Form is commonly violated two ways in unnormalized database designs. First, related data may be lumped into a single field. For example, the Supplier field in Table 4.4 includes both the supplier's name and the city in which they're located. In this case, getting to First Normal Form would mean breaking this field into two separate fields (Name and City).

The other common violation of First Normal Form is the repeating field. For example, suppose you're creating a database to track invoice information. You might define an Invoice table with fields such as Quantity1, Part1, Amount1, Quantity2, Part2, Amount2, Quantity3, Part3, and Amount3. A structure such as this runs into problems because it isn't flexible enough, wastes space, and is an inefficient structure for quickly retrieving data once it's entered. For example, if you need only a single line on a particular invoice, you're wasting space with all the empty columns. If you need four lines, you'd have to create extra columns because there's nowhere to put the fourth one. You can solve this problem temporarily by entering multiple rows in the table, but the real solution is to break out a separate InvoiceLine table and use referential integrity to relate it back to the main Invoice table.

As with the other normalization rules, putting a database into First Normal Form is a matter of judgment. You must consider not just the formal arrangement of your data, but also the business scenarios for which you'll use it. Think about people's names, for example. If you use just the name as a customer identifier and almost never get repeat business or need to find a particular customer, you can probably get by with a single Name field. However, the moment you need to sort people alphabetically by last name or search for a particular person by last name, you'll find it necessary to have FirstName and LastName fields. The business requirements in this case dictate that a single Name field isn't atomic, whereas in other circumstances, such as storing a company name, it can be.

Table 4.5 shows the sample farm data in First Normal Form. Each column in the table contains only a single type of information, and there's only one column for each type of information. To create this table, we started with Table 4.4 and broke the Supplier column into two separate columns, one for each of the types of information that we want to store in that column.

TABLE 4.5: Data in First Normal Form

NAME*	BREED	FEED*	SUPPLIERNAME	SUPPLIERCITY
Danny	Horse	Pasture	Jones	Endicott
Danny	Horse	Sweet Feed	Grange	Colfax
Tango	Llama	Pasture	Jones	Endicott
Tango	Llama	Purina Llama Feed	Grange	Colfax
Scotty	Llama	Pasture	Jones	Endicott
Scotty	Llama	Purina Llama Feed	Grange	Colfax
Genghis	Goat	Hi-Pro	Costco	Spokane

There are still problems with this format for storing the table. You'll note that in the table contains repeated information (for example, Purina Llama Feed always comes from the Grange in Colfax). What if you started buying Llama Feed from a different supplier? You'd need to update two rows in the table to make the change. Worse, if you accidentally missed one of the rows, your data would be in an inconsistent state. This sort of repeated information is a sure sign that you're not yet finished normalizing your data.

Identifying a Primary Key

You'll notice that the Name and Feed columns in Table 4.5 are marked by asterisks in their headings. These fields make up the primary key for that version of the table. If you know the value of these two columns, you can determine the value of every other column in the same row. Put another way, no two rows in the table have exactly the same values in those columns. The uniqueness of the primary key fields ensures entity integrity in this table.

Choosing primary keys is an art. You need to know how to identify possible primary keys and how to choose the best one.

CANDIDATE KEYS

Any set of columns that could be used as a primary key in a table is referred to as a *candidate key.* In Table 4.5, any of these sets of columns are candidate keys:

- Name, Feed
- Name, Breed, Feed
- Name, Feed, SupplierName

There are plenty of other choices for candidate keys. In general, any moderately complex table is likely to have more than one candidate key. Out of all the possible candidate keys, it's your job as database designer to choose the best primary key.

CHOOSING A GOOD PRIMARY KEY

In deciding which candidate key to use as a primary key, you should consider these factors:

Stability If the value in the column is likely to change, it won't make a good primary key. That's because when you relate tables together, you're making the assumption that you can always track the relation later by looking at the primary key values.

Minimality The fewer columns in the primary key, the better. A primary key of Name and Feed is superior to one of Name, Breed, and Feed. Adding the extra column doesn't make the key more unique; it merely makes operations involving the primary key slower.

Familiarity If the users of your database are accustomed to a particular identifier for a type of entity, it makes a good primary key. For example, you might use a part number to identify rows in a table of parts.

SURROGATE KEYS

Sometimes the natural data of a table doesn't include a particularly good key. Suppose, for example, you have a table of the customers for your product, including Name, Phone Number, and Address. None of these fields are especially stable. People move around, change their phone numbers, and even change their names.

In such a situation, you should consider creating a surrogate key for the table and using that surrogate key as the primary key. A *surrogate key* is a unique identifier for rows in a table that's not ordinarily part of the table's data. In the case of a customer table, for example, you might assign every customer a unique customer number and then use that customer number (a surrogate key) as the primary key for the table.

Second Normal Form

To achieve Second Normal Form, you must make sure that your tables are in First Normal Form and that they each contain data about one and only one entity. Operationally, you can check this by making sure that you can identify a primary key for every table and that all non-key fields depend on the primary key, and not on other fields in the table.

Some violations of Second Normal Form are easy to spot. For example, in an invoicing database, you might decide to put both customers and suppliers in a single BusinessParty table, because they share the same fields (Name, Address, City, State, and so on). However, this structure would violate Second Normal Form, which requires separate Customer and Supplier tables. More important, if you didn't separate these tables, you'd find certain fundamental operations very hard to implement. For example, you might want to present your users with an easy way to select the supplier for an invoice from a list of all suppliers in the database. How could you do this if customers and suppliers were all muddled up in a single table?

When a table has a composite primary key, violations of Second Normal Form can be harder to spot. For example, in Table 4.5, you might think it's okay to include the SupplierName field in the single table, because it depends on the Feed column. However, it doesn't depend on the entire primary key, only part of it. A simple test of this is that different rows with the same value in the first column (Name) of the primary key can have different values in the SupplierName column. This is a clue that to put this table in Second Normal Form, it will have to be broken into multiple tables.

In fact, we can normalize our example to Second Normal Form only by breaking it into two tables, which are shown in Tables 4.6 and 4.7.

TABLE 4.6: Animal Table in Second Normal Form

NAME*	BREED
Danny	Horse
Tango	Llama
Scotty	Llama
Genghis	Goat

TABLE 4.7: Feed Table in Second Normal Form

BREED*	FEED*	SUPPLIERNAME	SUPPLIERCITY
Horse	Pasture	Jones	Endicott
Horse	Sweet Feed	Grange	Colfax
Llama	Pasture	Jones	Endicott
Llama	Purina Llama Feed	Grange	Colfax
Goat	Hi-Pro	CostCo	Spokane

You can see that all the information from the original table is still present in the new tables. In fact, some of it (the breed names) is now repeated. Normalizing your data won't necessarily minimize its storage space. Rather, the point of normalization is to maximize the usefulness of the data by organizing it in an efficient fashion.

Foreign Keys and Relations

When you break a table into two tables, as we've done in this example, you need to know how those tables can be combined to re-create the original data. In this case, you can do that by matching the Breed column from the Animal table with the Breed column from the Feed table. Breed is part of the primary key in the Feed table. The corresponding field in the other table is referred to as a *foreign key*. By identifying a foreign key and its corresponding primary key, you can tell the database server about the referential integrity to be maintained between the two tables.

The relationship between a primary key and a foreign key can take one of several forms. It can be one-to-many, as in this example, where one breed can be matched to more than one row in the Animal table; that is, there can be more than one animal of a single breed. It can be one-to-one, where precisely one row in each table matches one row in the other. Or it can be many-to-many, where multiple matches are possible (imagine a table of physicians and a table of patients, each of whom might see many physicians).

TIP **To implement a many-to-many relation in SQL Server, you need to use an intermediate joining table to break the relation into two one-to-many relations. For example, if our farmer bought each type of feed from multiple suppliers, they might use a table of purchases to indicate the relation, where one supplier might have many sales, and one feed might also be a part of many sales.**

Third Normal Form

The rules for Third Normal Form are that the database must be in Second Normal Form and that all non-key fields must directly depend on the primary key. The most obvious violations of Third Normal Form are calculated fields. If you design an Invoice table that includes Quantity, Price, and TotalPrice fields (with TotalPrice being Quantity multiplied by Price), you've violated Third Normal Form. You can derive the total price any time you need it by knowing the Quantity and Price values for the record. Storing it requires you to make multiple changes to keep the record self-consistent any time you must change one of these fields.

Third Normal Form also helps you see that some tables need to be split into multiple pieces. For example, in the Second Normal Form of the animal feed example, if a supplier moved to a different city, you'd need to make changes to more than one row of the Feed table. This is an inefficient and potentially error-prone process. You're better off moving the list of suppliers and cities to its own table. Tables 4.8, 4.9, and 4.10 show the animal feed database in Third Normal Form.

Another way to think about Third Normal Form is that it's concerned with making each table contain information about only one thing. In the Second Normal Form version of these tables, the Feed table contained both facts about feeds and facts about suppliers. Now the supplier facts are in their own table. There is still a SupplierName field in the Feed table, because you still need to be able to trace the relationships between the tables and preserve referential integrity. Also, you can use the Breed field in the Animal table and the Breed field in the Feed table to trace the relationships between animals and feeds. For example, llamas eat pasture and llama feed.

TABLE 4.8: Animal Table in Third Normal Form

NAME*	BREED
Danny	Horse
Tango	Llama
Scotty	Llama
Genghis	Goat

TABLE 4.9: Feed Table in Third Normal Form

BREED*	FEED*	SUPPLIERNAME
Horse	Pasture	Jones
Horse	Sweet Feed	Grange
Llama	Pasture	Jones
Llama	Purina Llama Feed	Grange
Goat	Hi-Pro	CostCo

TABLE 4.10: SupplierCity Table in Third Normal Form

SUPPLIER*	CITY
Jones	Endicott
Grange	Colfax
CostCo	Spokane

Boyce-Codd Normal Form

There's still one problem with the feed tables in Third Normal Form. Although the SupplierName field in the Feed table does depend on the primary key of the table (that is, knowing the Breed and Feed, you can deduce the SupplierName), the field depends on only a part of that key. So if you decide to buy a type of feed from a different supplier, you might need to fix multiple rows of the table.

Boyce-Codd Normal Form (BCNF) adds the restriction that every column not in the primary key must depend on the entire primary key. This isn't the case in Table 4.9 (in the previous section), because the Supplier depends only on the Feed column. Once again, the problem can be remedied by splitting the tables further. Tables 4.11 through 4.14 show the example feed database in BCNF.

TABLE 4.11: Animal Table in BCNF

NAME*	BREED
Danny	Horse
Tango	Llama
Scotty	Llama
Genghis	Goat

TABLE 4.12: Feed Table in BCNF

BREED*	FEED*
Horse	Pasture
Horse	Sweet Feed
Llama	Pasture
Llama	Purina Llama Feed
Goat	Hi-Pro

TABLE 4.13: FeedSupplier Table in BCNF

FEED*	SUPPLIER
Pasture	Jones
Sweet Feed	Grange
Purina Llama Feed	Grange
Hi-Pro	CostCo

TABLE 4.14: SupplierCity Table in BCNF

SUPPLIER*	CITY
Jones	Endicott
Grange	Colfax
CostCo	Spokane

If you examine these tables and think about the sorts of information you might like to change in the database, you can see that any potential change will affect only one row of a table at a time. This is the end result of normalization: a set of tables that can be updated easily without the need to change more than one piece of data at a time to make the updates.

Advanced Normalization

It's worth mentioning that BCNF isn't the end of the road for normalization. Database researchers have identified additional normal forms, including Fourth Normal Form and Fifth Normal Form. For most everyday databases, though, putting your tables into BCNF should be sufficient. In fact, if your database is relatively straightforward, it may already be in Fifth Normal Form when you design it in BCNF. If the database is complex enough to be subject to the problems that lead to Fourth and Fifth Normal Forms, you might want to consult someone who does a lot of normalization for guidance.

Fourth Normal Form

Fourth Normal Form addresses the issues that arise when there are dependencies of sets of entities. For example, suppose you're designing tables for a database used by a college math department to track course assignments. There might be a set of books used in each course and a set of teachers who teach each course. One approach would be to create a single table as shown in Table 4.15.

TABLE 4.15: Example Table Not in Fourth Normal Form

TEACHER*	COURSE*	TEXT*
George	Algebra	Fundamentals of Algebra
George	Algebra	Advanced Algebra
Phyllis	Algebra	Fundamentals of Algebra
Phyllis	Algebra	Advanced Algebra
Ethel	Geometry	Plato's Solids
Ethel	Geometry	Mickey Does Geometry
Adam	Geometry	Plato's Solids
Adam	Geometry	Mickey Does Geometry

This table is in Third Normal Form, but it still suffers from a problem when you try to insert a new teacher for an existing course with multiple texts. For example, if you added another teacher for the Geometry course, you'd have to add two rows to the table, one for each text used in the course.

In this case, the table contains what is called a *multivalued dependency*. The course doesn't determine the teacher uniquely, but it does determine a set of teachers. The same applies to the relation between course and text—the course doesn't determine the text, but it does determine a set of texts.

To obtain Fourth Normal Form, you can break this single table into two tables, one for each relation implied in the first table. These two tables are shown in Tables 4.16 and 4.17.

TABLE 4.16: CourseTeacher Table in Fourth Normal Form

COURSE*	TEACHER*
Algebra	George
Algebra	Phyllis
Geometry	Ethel
Geometry	Adam

TABLE 4.17: CourseText Table in Fourth Normal Form

COURSE*	TEXT*
Algebra	Fundamentals of Algebra
Algebra	Advanced Algebra
Geometry	Plato's Solids
Geometry	Mickey Does Geometry

Now you can assign a new teacher to a course, or a new text to a course, with only a single insertion operation. Further, you retain the flexibility to have one teacher teach multiple courses, which would not be the case if you used Teacher as the primary key in the CourseTeacher table.

Fifth Normal Form

Fifth Normal Form addresses an issue where a table can't be decomposed into two tables without losing information, but it can be decomposed into more than two tables. Examples that demonstrate this tend to be highly artificial and difficult to understand, so we won't try to give one here. The important thing is to know that Fifth Normal Form is mainly an academic notion, not one of practical database design. It's hard to find such dependencies in any real database, and the inefficiencies they produce aren't large in practice. In other words, it's not really worth knowing more than this about Fifth Normal Form.

Denormalization

Just as normalization is the process of arranging data in a fashion that allows you to make changes without redundancy, *denormalization* is the process of deliberately introducing redundancy to your data. Theoretically, of course, you should never denormalize data. However, in the real world, things aren't that simple. Sometimes it may be necessary to denormalize data in the interest of performance. An overnormalized database can be slow on a network due to the number of joins that have to be performed to retrieve data from multiple tables. For instance, in the Farms database, suppose you need to know all the cities where you purchased food for a particular animal. That will require retrieving information from all the tables in the database.

TIP When you're forced to denormalize data for performance, make sure you document your decision, so that another developer doesn't think you simply made a mistake.

Although it's not possible to tell you exactly how (or whether) to denormalize tables in all circumstances, we can offer some guidance. If your normalized data model produces tables with multipart primary keys—particularly if those keys include four or more columns and are used in joins with other tables—you should consider denormalizing the data by introducing arbitrary surrogate keys. Identity columns, combined with `UNIQUE` constraints, provide a convenient means for creating these surrogate keys. You can then add arbitrary foreign keys to tables that join back to the main table and enforce the join on the surrogate keys, instead. Doing so often provides a substantial performance benefit, because SQL Server can resolve the relationships faster between tables if those relationships are represented in a single field.

If producing calculated values such as maximum historic prices involves complex queries with many joins, you should consider denormalizing the data by adding calculated columns to your tables to hold these values. SQL Server supports defining calculated columns as part of a table (for more details, see Chapter 11).

If your database contains extremely large tables, you should consider denormalizing the data by creating multiple redundant tables. You may do this either by column or by row. For example, if an Employees table contains many columns, and some of these (such as hire date) are very infrequently used, it may help performance to move the less frequently used columns to a separate table. By reducing the volume of data in the main table, you can make it faster to access this data. If the Employees table is worldwide, and most queries require information about employees from only one region, you can speed up the queries by creating separate tables for each region.

If data is no longer live and is being used for archiving or is otherwise read-only, denormalizing by storing calculated values in fields can make certain queries run faster. In this case, you might also consider using Microsoft Analysis Server to store the nonlive data for fast analysis. We'll talk about Analysis Server in Chapter 26, "Analysis Services."

TIP If you split a table into multiple tables by row, you can still query all the data by using the Transact-SQL `UNION` operator. You'll learn about the `UNION` operator in Chapter 6, "Select Queries."

If queries on a single table frequently use only one column from a second table, consider including a copy of that single field in the first table. For example, you might choose to include the SupplierCity field in the Feed table, even though the table already includes the SupplierName, because you always print your shopping list organized by the city where each feed store is located. In this case, of course, you'll need to write code to ensure that the SupplierCity field is updated every time the SupplierName is changed. This code might take the form of a stored procedure that is used to update supplier information.

WARNING Remember that you should never denormalize your data without a specific business reason for the denormalization. Careless denormalization can ruin the integrity of your data and lead to slower performance as well—if you denormalize too far, you'll end up including many extra fields in each table, and it takes time to move that extra data from one place in your application to another.

Making the Trade-offs

So, given a list of rules for normalization and a set of ideas for denormalization, how do you make the trade-offs between the two? Although it's impossible to give a cookbook recipe for coming up with the perfect database, here's a strategy that's worked well for many people in practice:

1. Inspect the data to be stored in your database. Be sure you talk to end users at this point to get a sense of what they really need to know. Don't just ask about what they think needs to be stored, ask what they need to do with the data. Often this last step reveals additional data that needs to be stored.
2. Normalize the database design to BCNF.
3. Armed with the BCNF design of the database, review the list of operations that users wish to perform with the data. Make sure that there's enough data to perform each of these operations. Also make sure that none of the operations require multiple simultaneous rows to be updated in the same table (a sign that you haven't completely normalized the database).
4. Implement the BCNF version of the database. Build the necessary user interface to allow users to work with the data.
5. Deploy a pilot version of the application.
6. During the pilot program, collect information using SQL Server Profiler on all operations performed.
7. Use the SQL Server Profiler information to tune the indexes in your database. Inspect the SQL Server Profiler information to identify bottlenecks. SQL Profiler was covered in Chapter 3, "Overview of SQL Server," and you'll learn about index tuning in Chapter 24, "Monitoring and Optimizing SQL Server 2005."
8. Interview users to identify any operations during which the database isn't performing quickly enough.
9. Use the information from steps 7 and 8 to selectively denormalize the database.
10. Repeat steps 5 through 9 until the database delivers adequate performance.

TIP If you must maintain the design of a large database with many tables, or if you're frequently involved in database design projects, you may find a third-party design product to be helpful. These products allow you to concentrate on the logical design of the database and automatically produce the physical design to match. Tools in this category include Computer Associates' AllFusion ERwin Data Modeler (`http://www3.ca.com/Solutions/Product.asp?ID=260`) and Microsoft Visio Professional (`www.microsoft.com/office/visio/prodinfo/default.mspx`).

Tools for Normalization in SQL Server

SQL Server supplies a number of tools that help you maintain your database in a normalized form. These tools help make sure that only sensible data is inserted in tables and that only sensible changes can be made. Any time you can enforce normalization directly at the server, you don't have to write application code to do so. This is a big win for most databases.

In this section, we'll look briefly at these tools:

- Identity columns
- Constraints
- Declarative referential integrity
- Triggers

All of these tools are covered in more detail later in the book, but let's get the big picture before we dig into the details.

Identity Columns

A simple tool for enforcing entity integrity is the identity column. An *identity column* is a column in a table for which SQL Server automatically supplies values. By default, the first value is 1, and each succeeding value is one more than the previous value, but both the starting value (the seed) and the increment can be specified by the database designer.

An identity column provides a handy way to include a surrogate key in a table's design. Surrogate keys often lead to enhanced database linking by relating tables on small numeric columns rather than more natural textual data.

NOTE You'll learn how to create identity columns in Chapter 11.

Constraints

SQL Server uses constraints to enforce limitations on the data that can be entered into a particular column in a table. *Constraints* are rules that govern what data is acceptable for a particular column in a table. You can use `UNIQUE`, `DEFAULT`, and `CHECK` constraints to enforce entity, domain, and user-defined integrity. In addition, SQL Server uses `PRIMARY KEY` and `FOREIGN KEY` constraints to implement referential integrity. These two types of constraints are discussed in their own section later in this chapter.

Chapter 11 shows you how to create constraints when you're building tables in your own databases.

TIP If a constraint is violated, the command that caused the violation is terminated and has no effect. However, if this command is part of a batch transaction, the transaction will continue. If statements in a transaction may violate constraints, you should check the value of the `@@ERROR` global variable and execute a `ROLLBACK TRANSACTION` statement if the `@@ERROR` variable isn't equal to zero. Chapter 8, "Topics in Advanced Transact-SQL," has more information on using transactions in SQL Server.

UNIQUE Constraints

A `UNIQUE` constraint specifies that all values in a given column must be unique; that is, the column must have a different value in every row in the table. A table can have multiple `UNIQUE` constraints, in which case they must all be satisfied for every row. `UNIQUE` constraints bring entity integrity to a table because they guarantee that every row is different. Any table that has a primary key consisting of a single column should also have a `UNIQUE` constraint applied to this column. If you're using SQL Server's declarative referential integrity (DRI), SQL Server will automatically create a unique index on this column for you.

WARNING If you've used Microsoft Access, you might expect a SQL Server identity column to automatically enforce entity integrity, but this isn't the case. You can insert duplicate values into an identity column. To enforce entity integrity, you should also apply a `UNIQUE` constraint to the column.

DEFAULT CONSTRAINTS

A `DEFAULT` constraint gives you a way to supply a default value for a column in any table. That is, the constraint provides the value that will be stored with new rows in the data when the value for the column isn't otherwise specified. `DEFAULT` constraints can help enforce domain integrity by providing reasonable values for new records. They also help with some user-defined integrity problems: For example, all new customers might start with an account balance of zero.

CHECK CONSTRAINTS

A `CHECK` constraint allows you to control the data entered into a particular column by evaluating an expression. The expression must return a Boolean value. If the return value is False, the constraint has been violated, and the command that caused the violation is terminated. `CHECK` constraints are useful for setting limits on acceptable data to enforce domain integrity, as well as for enforcing more complex user-defined integrity rules.

Declarative Referential Integrity (DRI)

Declarative referential integrity (DRI) is a process that allows you to notify SQL Server of the referential integrity between tables and to have the server automatically enforce these relationships. Prior to the implementation of DRI, keeping referential integrity enforced required writing trigger code for every table to perform appropriate actions under developer control. Now that SQL Server can do this automatically, performance has improved, and the developer has more time to work on other parts of the application.

NOTE A *trigger* is a bit of code that causes one action to initiate another. You can read more about triggers in Chapters 14 ("Stored Procedures") and 15 ("Triggers").

As with other integrity support, DRI is implemented using constraints on tables. Two types of constraints are used: `PRIMARY KEY` and `FOREIGN KEY`. We'll look at each of these in turn. `PRIMARY` and `FOREIGN KEY` constraints are covered in detail in Chapter 11.

PRIMARY KEYS

In SQL Server databases, the primary key of a table performs two duties. First, because it's guaranteed to be unique on every record, it enforces entity integrity. Second, it serves as an anchor for referential integrity relationships from other tables.

FOREIGN KEYS

Foreign keys, in conjunction with primary keys, provide the other half of SQL Server's implementation of referential integrity. A *foreign key* is a copy of the primary key in the parent table that is inserted in the child table to create a relationship between the two. Just like primary keys, foreign keys are implemented with `CONSTRAINT` clauses. Unlike with primary keys, a single table can have multiple foreign keys.

TIP The datatypes and sizes of columns in a foreign key must match exactly the corresponding columns in the primary key.

Cascading Referential Integrity

SQL Server 2000 was the first version to offer *cascading referential integrity*. This is a feature that, while still preserving referential integrity between tables, allows a wider range of operations than would otherwise be possible.

To see the effect of cascading, consider a related pair of tables, Customers and Orders. In the Customers table, the primary key is CustomerID. In the Orders table, the primary key is OrderID, and there's also a CustomerID column that is a foreign key relating to the Customers table. So, you might have a customer whose CustomerID is A4511 and then multiple rows in the Orders table, each of which has A4511 as the CustomerID value and a unique value in the OrderID column.

In a strict referential integrity situation, you're limited in what you can do with the record in the Customers table. In particular, you can't change the value in the CustomerID column, because doing so would leave orders that didn't refer to a customer. You also can't delete a row from the Customers table if that customer has orders, because doing so would also leave orphaned records in the Orders table. Either of these operations would break the referential integrity between the two tables.

You can implement two types of cascading to get around these problems:

- If a relationship between tables is defined to include *cascading updates,* then when the value of a primary key in the parent table is changed, the value of the foreign-key column in all related records in the child table is changed to match.
- If a relationship between tables is defined to include *cascading deletes,* then when a record is deleted from the parent table, all corresponding records from the child table are also deleted.

WARNING Just because you can define relationships to use cascading updates and cascading deletes doesn't mean you should always do this. If the primary key of a table truly is invariant, for example, there's no point in defining cascading updates. If you need at all times to be able to retrieve historical information from a database, even if a record becomes inactive, you won't want to use cascading deletes.

In SQL Server 2005, you define cascading updates and deletes using the optional `CASCADE` keyword when you're using the `ALTER TABLE` or `CREATE TABLE` statement to create a foreign key. You'll learn more about these keywords in Chapter 11.

Triggers

Triggers are pieces of Transact-SQL code that can be run when something happens to a table:

- An *update trigger* runs whenever one or more rows are updated.
- A *delete trigger* runs whenever one or more rows are deleted.
- An *insert trigger* runs whenever one or more rows are added.

Triggers can be as complex as necessary, so they're an ideal tool for enforcing business rules and user-defined integrity. Triggers can run in addition to the operation that caused them to fire, or instead of that operation. You'll learn about triggers in Chapter 15.

TIP In versions prior to SQL Server 2000, triggers were necessary to create relationships that supported cascades. Now that SQL Server DRI supports cascading, you should use DRI for all relationships between tables and save triggers for more complex situations.

Summary

This chapter has introduced you to the basics of database normalization, which is a key component of design. If you get interested in the topic, a lot more information is available in books dedicated specifically to that subject. However, for most everyday purposes, normalizing your data to BCNF is sufficient. You should also consider the recommendations in this chapter for optimizing and denormalizing your database as necessary.

You've also been introduced to some of the tools that SQL Server supplies for enforcing normalization within a database. You'll learn much more about those tools in the coming chapters. First, though, it's time to learn about the language used within SQL Server itself: Transact-SQL.

Part 2

Transact-SQL

In this section:

- **Chapter 5: Transact-SQL Overview and Basics**
- **Chapter 6: SELECT Queries**
- **Chapter 7: Action Queries**
- **Chapter 8: Topics in Advanced Transact-SQL**

Chapter 5

Transact-SQL Overview and Basics

Now that you've had a broad overview of SQL Server and the process of database design, it's time to learn how to work within SQL Server databases. SQL, as you probably already know, stands for Structured Query Language. In this chapter, we'll begin teaching you how to use this language within your own applications. Transact-SQL is a large topic, and detailing it will take up a large portion of this book. In addition to the introduction in this chapter, you'll find significant SQL content in these other chapters:

- Chapters 6 and 7 will introduce you to some common SQL queries.
- Chapter 8 covers some advanced SQL topics.
- Chapter 10 will show you how to use SQL to construct database objects.

What Is Transact-SQL?

Transact-SQL is Microsoft's implementation of the standard Structured Query Language (SQL). Sometimes called T-SQL, but usually just called SQL (at least by developers who work with Microsoft products), this language implements a standardized way to ask questions of databases. However, it's important to understand that this standard really isn't all that much of a standard. Although there is in theory a standardized SQL, in practice the picture is much more complex.

ANSI SQL

The official promulgator of the SQL standard is the American National Standards Institute (ANSI). ANSI is a body that brings together committees to standardize everything from practices for installing plumbing to computer languages. Among the products of these efforts is the standard for SQL. The current standard is usually called SQL-92 because it was finalized in 1992. A more recent version of the standard, sometimes called SQL3 or SQL-99, was finalized a few years ago. There's a long road between standard and products; you're unlikely to be affected by SQL3 for several years yet.

TIP If you want to investigate the ANSI standard further, you can visit ANSI's website at `www.ansi.org`. However, you'll find that all of the ANSI standards are copyrighted, and none of them are available online. A full copy of the ANSI SQL standard will cost you hundreds of dollars.

SQL Dialects

Just because there's a standard on paper doesn't mean that there's a standard in practice. If every vendor of a database product supported exactly the same SQL, life would be easier for developers but much harder for marketers. So it is that every real database product diverges from the standard to a greater or lesser extent. Some features are implemented differently than the standard specifies.

Other features are completely nonstandard, vendor-specific extensions to the language. To make matters more complex, SQL-92 isn't one standard, but several, since there are various defined levels of conformance with the standard.

So, is SQL Server 2005 ANSI SQL-92 compliant? That proves to be a surprisingly hard question to answer. Up until 1996, the National Institute of Standards and Technology had an official program to test databases for compliance with FIPS-127, a federal standard that included SQL-92. At that time, SQL Server was compliant with the entry level of the standard. Since then, the federal testing program has been discontinued, and SQL Server has been revised twice.

The bottom line for you, as a developer working with SQL Server, is that most basic SQL is the same from product to product. What you learn by knowing the SQL implemented by SQL Server is close enough to ANSI SQL-92 to give you a head start if you ever move to a different product.

SQL Configuration Options

Over the years, SQL Server has moved more and more into compliance with SQL-92. This has posed some problems for database administrators who depended on nonstandard features in previous versions. So, SQL Server provides several mechanisms for adjusting the behavior of its SQL in certain circumstances. These mechanisms—the `SET` statement, the `sp_dboption` stored procedure, and the `sp_dbcmptlevel` stored procedure—can be important tools if you're trying to use an application written for an older version of SQL Server.

Using *SET* for ANSI Compatibility

The SET statement is one of the workhorses of the SQL language. You can use SET in SQL scripts to alter a wide range of server behaviors. In particular, SET can be used to change some defaults in SQL Server's processing to adhere to the SQL-92 standard.

Let's start with one of the possible SET statements having to do with ANSI compatibility:

```
SET ANSI_WARNINGS ON
SET ANSI_WARNINGS OFF
```

As you might guess, the first form of this statement turns on certain warning messages required by the ANSI standard, and the second form turns off the same warnings. More compactly, we can define the syntax of the `SET ANSI_WARNINGS` statement as follows:

```
SET ANSI_WARNINGS {ON|OFF}
```

Here, the curly braces indicate that you must choose one of the options separated by vertical bars inside the braces. You'll learn more about reading this sort of T-SQL syntax diagram in a few pages.

When you set the `ANSI_WARNINGS` option on, any statement that causes a divide-by-zero error or an overflow error is rolled back (undone) and generates a warning message. Any aggregate statement that includes a null value (for example, an attempt to print the sum of a column that contains nulls) also generates a warning message. When you set the `ANSI_WARNINGS` option off, none of these events generate a warning or a rollback.

Because this chapter is the first time that we cover any SQL statement in depth, let's take a moment and learn how to follow along. The easiest tool to use for SQL testing is SQL Server Management Studio, which you can launch from the Start menu by choosing Programs ➢ Microsoft SQL Server 2005 ➢ SQL Server Management Studio. When you launch SQL Server Management Studio, you need to supply the name of your SQL Server as well as valid authentication information. Once you've done this, the summary page for the server appears, along with several other windows. One of these is the Object Explorer window, which provides a treeview of the structure of the SQL Server and its contents. Expand the treeview to see the databases on the server, and then right-click on a database (we suggest using the AdventureWorks sample database) and select New Query. A new query window appears. You can type SQL in the query window and then click the Execute button on the SQL Editor toolbar or press F5 to see the results.

NOTE More information about using SQL Server Management Studio to execute queries appears later in this chapter, in the section "Executing T-SQL." You'll learn more about SQL Server Management Studio's other capabilities in Chapter 9, "Using SQL Server Management Studio."

Figure 5.1 shows the process of testing some SQL in SQL Server Management Studio. The upper pane contains a set of SQL statements to be executed. There are 11 different statements in this example:

- The `CREATE TABLE` creates a new table.
- The `INSERT` statements insert some test data into the table.
- The `PRINT` statements echo output to the results pane.
- The `SET` statements toggle ANSI warnings.
- The `SELECT` statements are used to retrieve data. `SELECT` is discussed extensively in Chapter 6, "*SELECT* Queries."

The lower pane shows the results of running the set of SQL statements (usually called a *SQL script*) in the upper pane. In this case, you can see that with warnings on, the `SELECT` statement warns the user that the aggregate function encountered a null value, while with warnings off, this warning is suppressed.

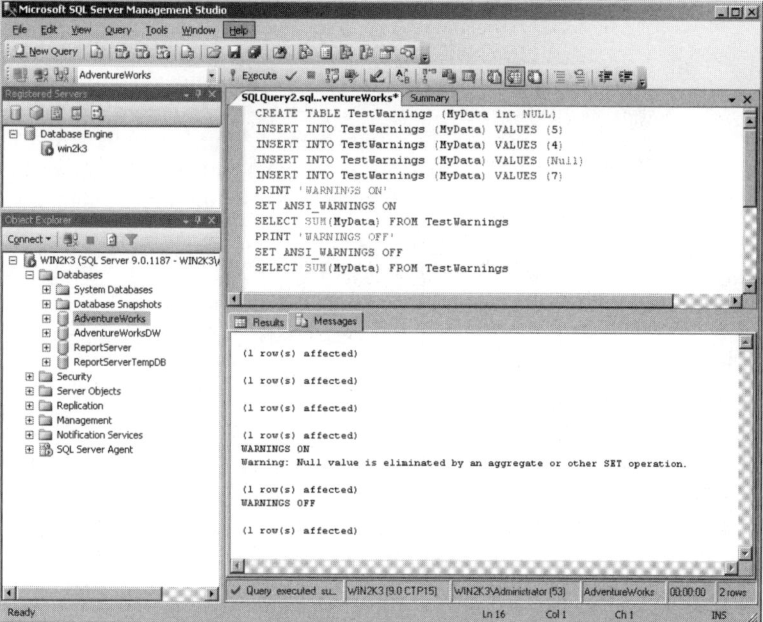

FIGURE 5.1
Testing `SET ANSI_WARNINGS` with SQL Server Management Studio

The sp_dboption stored procedure, discussed in the next section, can also be used to set ANSI warnings on or off. If SET ANSI_WARNINGS is on, it takes precedence over the sp_dboption setting.

Now that you've seen how to execute simple SQL statements, let's look at the other eight variations of the SET statement having to do with ANSI compliance:

SET ANSI_PADDING {ON | OFF} This statement controls what happens with trailing blanks or trailing zeros when inserting values into fixed- or variable-length columns. Table 5.1 shows the effects of this option.

TABLE 5.1: Effect of SET ANSI_PADDING

DATATYPE	SET ANSI_PADDING ON	SET ANSI_PADDING OFF
char(n) NOT NULL	Pads with trailing blanks to the size of the column	Pads with trailing blanks to the size of the column
binary(n) NOT NULL	Pads with trailing zeros to the size of the column	Pads with trailing zeros to the size of the column
char(n) NULL	Pads with trailing blanks to the size of the column	Trims all trailing blanks
binary(n) NULL	Pads with trailing zeros to the size of the column	Trims all trailing zeros
varchar(n)	Doesn't trim or pad values	Trims trailing blanks, but doesn't pad
varbinary(n)	Doesn't trim or pad values	Trims trailing zeros, but doesn't pad

SET ANSI_NULLS {ON | OFF} This statement controls whether you can use the equality operator to test for null. Older versions of SQL Server allowed you to use, for example, WHERE ColumnName=Null to see whether a column contained null values. This is a violation of the ANSI standard, which (properly) considers null to be a completely unknown value, not equal to anything else. Setting ANSI nulls on causes all comparisons with null to return null.

SET ANSI_NULL_DFLT_ON {ON | OFF} This statement controls whether columns created with the CREATE TABLE or ALTER TABLE statement should be automatically set to allow nulls (if this option is on, they allow nulls).

SET ANSI_NULL_DFLT_OFF {ON | OFF} This statement also controls whether columns created with the CREATE TABLE or ALTER TABLE statement should be automatically set to allow nulls (if this option is on, they allow nulls).

WARNING Only one of ANSI_NULL_DFLT_ON and ANSI_NULL_DFLT_OFF can be set to ON at a time. If they're both set to OFF, the corresponding sp_dboption setting is used instead. The simplest way to keep this straight is to always use explicit NULL or NOT NULL when using the CREATE TABLE statement and not depend on any of these settings.

SET CONTEXT_INFO {binary | @binary_var} This statement can be used to associate 128 bits of binary information with a particular connection to the database. The session can later retrieve this information by looking at the context_info column in the master.dbo.sysprocesses table.

SET CURSOR_CLOSE_ON_COMMIT {ON | OFF} This statement controls what happens to open cursors when you commit a change on that cursor. If this option is set on, the cursor is automatically closed. (You'll learn more about cursors in Chapter 8, "Topics in Advanced Transact-SQL.") The ANSI default is `SET CURSOR_CLOSE_ON_COMMIT ON`.

SET IMPLICIT_TRANSACTIONS {ON | OFF} This statement causes certain SQL statements (including `CREATE`, `SELECT`, `INSERT`, and `UPDATE`) to automatically start transactions whenever they're executed, if this setting is on (which is the ANSI standard). If you set this on, you need to explicitly commit or roll back all such statements. You'll probably never want to turn on this option.

SET QUOTED_IDENTIFIER {ON | OFF} This statement, if set on, causes SQL Server to follow the ANSI rules for quoting identifiers (names of things). Setting this on allows you to use SQL Server reserved words as the names of objects by surrounding them in double quotation marks.

TIP Although you *could* create a table named, for example, SELECT, this is almost certainly a bad idea. Your code will be less confusing if you stick to sensible identifiers that aren't reserved words.

SET ANSI_DEFAULTS {ON | OFF} This statement is equivalent to a collection of other settings and provides a handy way to force SQL Server to full ANSI compatibility. It's a combination of the following:

- `SET ANSI_NULLS ON`
- `SET ANSI_NULL_DFLT_ON ON`
- `SET ANSI_PADDING ON`
- `SET ANSI_WARNINGS ON`
- `SET CURSOR_CLOSE_ON_COMMIT ON`
- `SET IMPLICIT_TRANSACTIONS ON`
- `SET QUOTED_IDENTIFIER ON`

TIP For the most part, the default behavior with SQL Server is `SET ANSI_DEFAULTS ON` followed by `SET CURSOR_CLOSE_ON_COMMIT OFF` and `SET IMPLICIT_TRANSACTIONS OFF`. This is the set of choices made by the SQL Server ODBC driver and the SQL Server OLE DB provider when they connect to the server. Because all the built-in tools (such as SQL Server Management Studio) use the SQL Server OLE DB provider, this is the behavior you're most likely to see. In the examples in this book, we'll assume this default environment unless stated otherwise. It's also a good set of defaults to use in your own work with SQL Server.

Using *ALTER DATABASE* to Change Options

In SQL Server 2005, you can also make permanent changes to the defaults that you set with the SET statement (and many others) by using the `ALTER DATABASE` statement. This is the most complex SQL Statement you've seen yet, and here's just part of its syntax:

```
ALTER DATABASE database_name
SET
{SINGLE_USER|RESTRICTED_USER|MULTI_USER} |
{OFFLINE|ONLINE|EMERGENCY} |
(READONLY|READWRITE) |
```

```
{READ_ONLY|READ_WRITE} |
CURSOR_CLOSE_ON_COMMIT {ON|OFF} |
CURSOR_DEFAULT {LOCAL|GLOBAL} |
AUTO_CLOSE {ON|OFF} |
AUTO_CREATE_STATISTICS {ON|OFF} |
AUTO_SHRINK {ON|OFF} |
AUTO_UPDATE_STATISTICS {ON|OFF} |
AUTO_UPDATE_STATISTICS_ASYNC {ON|OFF} |
ANSI_NULL_DEFAULT {ON|OFF} |
ANSI_NULLS {ON|OFF} |
ANSI_PADDING {ON|OFF} |
ANSI_WARNINGS {ON|OFF} |
ARITHABORT {ON|OFF} |
CONCAT_NULL_YIELDS_NULL {ON|OFF} |
NUMERIC_ROUNDABORT {ON|OFF} |
QUOTED_IDENTIFIERS {ON|OFF} |
RECURSIVE_TRIGGERS {ON|OFF} |
RECOVERY {FULL|BULK_LOGGED|SIMPLE} |
PAGE_VERIFY {CHECKSUM|TORN_PAGE_DETECTION|NONE}[,...n]
```

As you can see, ALTER DATABASE includes most of the capabilities of the SET statement and a good deal more. When you make a change with ALTER DATABASE, though, the change is permanent (at least, until you use ALTER DATABASE again to reverse the change). Only database owners, creators, and system administrators are allowed to execute the ALTER DATABASE statement.

Here are some details about what the various options of this statement do:

- SINGLE_USER puts the database into single-user mode. This allows only one user at a time to access the database; everyone else is locked out. RESTRICTED_USER allows only members of the db_owner, dbcreator, and sysadmin roles to use the database (see Chapter 18, "Security and SQL Server 2005" for more information about roles). MULTI_USER returns the database to its normal operating state.
- OFFLINE can be used to put the database entirely offline and inaccessible. ONLINE reverses this state and makes the database available again. EMERGENCY puts the database in a special read-only state where it can be accessed only by members of the sysadmin role.
- READ_ONLY prohibits all changes to the database. Users can read data but can't write it. The exception is the master database. If master is placed in READ_ONLY mode, the system administrator can still make changes (which is a good thing, or they wouldn't be able to turn off this flag). READ_WRITE, of course, returns the database to normal.
- CURSOR_CLOSE_ON_COMMIT has the same effect as the corresponding SET statement.
- CURSOR_DEFAULT LOCAL causes cursors to be local to the stored procedure that creates them by default. CURSOR_DEFAULT GLOBAL causes cursors to default to being global in scope.
- AUTO_CLOSE ON causes the database to be cleanly closed whenever the last user exits.
- AUTO_CREATE_STATISTICS ON tells SQL Server to build any statistics needed by a query whenever that query is optimized.
- AUTO_SHRINK ON tells SQL Server that it's OK to shrink this database if it doesn't need all the space allocated to it (for example, if a large amount of data has been deleted).

- AUTO_UPDATE_STATISTICS ON tells SQL Server to update statistics during optimization if necessary.
- AUTO_UPDATE_STATISTICS_ASYNC ON lets queries compile while fresh statistics are still being generated.
- ANSI_NULL_DEFAULT, ANSI_NULLS, ANSI_PADDING, ANSI_WARNINGS, and QUOTED_IDENTIFIERS perform the same functions as the corresponding SET statements, but on a permanent basis.
- ARITHABORT ON tells SQL Server to terminate a query if an overflow or divide-by-zero error happens during query processing.
- CONCAT_NULL_YIELDS_NULL ON causes any string concatenation operation involving a null to return a null.
- NUMERIC_ROUNDABORT tells SQL Server to terminate a query if any loss of precision occurs in a query expression.
- RECURSIVE_TRIGGERS tells SQL Server to use the results of triggers to trigger other triggers.
- RECOVERY FULL causes SQL Server to log enough information to be robust in the case of any media failure. RECOVERY BULK_LOGGED causes SQL Server to compress log information for certain bulk operations such as SELECT INTO. RECOVERY SIMPLE saves the least amount of log space while still allowing you to recover from all common failures.
- PAGE_VERIFY tells SQL Server which strategy to use to detect corrupt data caused by disk I/O failures. PAGE_VERIFY CHECKSUM stores a checksum on disk with each page. PAGE_VERIFY TORN_PAGE_DETECTION uses a single bit to mark pages that have been successfully written. PAGE_VERIFY NONE turns off all page verification. We recommend that you avoid the PAGE_VERIFY NONE setting.

The *sp_dboption* Stored Procedure

SQL Server includes dozens of system stored procedures. These are chunks of SQL code that are already built into the server. Most of them operate on the system tables, and you can't really get at their internal workings. You can treat them as just more SQL commands.

The sp_dboption stored procedure can be used for setting database options, just like ALTER DATABASE. Some of these options affect ANSI compatibility, and some don't. Formally, the syntax of this stored procedure is as follows:

```
sp_dboption [[@dbname=] 'database_name']
 [, [@optname=] 'option_name']
 [, [@optvalue=] 'option_value']
```

In this syntax diagram, square brackets indicate optional items, and italics indicate variables that you need to replace when running the stored procedure. Table 5.2 lists the full set of available option names for this stored procedure. Many of these aren't ANSI compatibility options, but they're included for completeness. Of course, the *database_name* variable indicates the database in which you're setting the option in, and *option_value* can be true, false, on, or off.

For example, Figure 5.2 shows how you could use sp_dboption in SQL Server Management Studio to make changes to ANSI compatibility options for a database. The EXEC keyword tells SQL Server to run a stored procedure. These changes are persistent, unlike changes made with SET (which last only for the current session).

TABLE 5.2: Options for sp_dboption

OPTION	EFFECT IF SET ON
auto create statistics	Any statistics needed for optimization are created during optimization if necessary.
auto update statistics	Any statistics needed for optimization are updated during optimization if necessary.
autoclose	The database is shut down when the last user exits.
autoshrink	The database is periodically checked for free space and shrunk if possible.
ANSI null default	CREATE TABLE follows ANSI rules for defaults.
ANSI nulls	Comparisons to null yield null.
ANSI warnings	Warnings are issued for divide-by-zero, overflow, and nulls in aggregates.
arithabort	The batch terminates on overflow or divide-by-zero errors.
concat null yields null	Concatenating a string with a null returns a null.
cursor close on commit	Open cursors are closed when changes are committed.
dbo use only	Only the database owner can work with the database.
default to local cursor	Cursor definitions default to LOCAL.
merge publish	The database can be used for merge replication.
numeric roundabort	An error is generated when an operation causes a loss of precision.
offline	The database is offline (unavailable).
published	The database can be used for replication.
quoted identifier	Identifiers can be quoted with double quotes.
read only	No changes can be written to the database.
recursive triggers	Triggers can cause other triggers to fire.
select into/bulkcopy	SELECT INTO and fast bulkcopy operations are allowed.
single user	Only one user at a time can use the database.
subscribed	The database can be subscribed for replication.
torn page detection	Incomplete data pages are automatically detected.
trunc. log on chkpt.	The transaction log is truncated each time a system checkpoint occurs.

FIGURE 5.2
Using sp_dboption

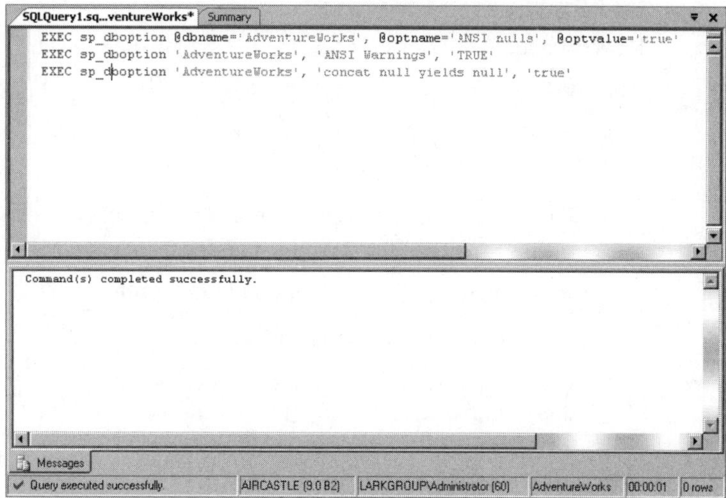

WARNING The sp_dboption stored procedure is officially considered obsolete in SQL Server 2005, because everything that it can do can now be done by the native SQL ALTER DATABASE statement. We've included this section because you're likely to encounter sp_dboption in existing databases. If you want this functionality in new databases, you should use ALTER DATABASE instead.

THE *SP_DBCMPTLEVEL* STORED PROCEDURE

The other system stored procedure that can have a substantial impact on the behavior of the server is sp_dbcmptlevel:

```
sp_dbcmptlevel [[@dbname=] 'database_name']
  [,[@new_cmptlevel=] version]
```

The *version* parameter can be set to 90, 80, or 70. The purpose of sp_dbcmptlevel is to make SQL Server behave as if it were a previous version of itself. That is, if you execute

```
sp_dbcmptlevel 'AdventureWorks', 80
```

the AdventureWorks database will behave as if it's running on SQL Server 2000 instead of SQL Server 2005.

Changing the compatibility level changes a lot of things, from which identifiers are treated as reserved words to the behavior of certain queries. Refer to SQL Server Books Online if you'd like to see the whole list.

TIP You should limit the use of sp_dbcmptlevel to applications that you're migrating from a previous version of SQL Server. There's no cause to use it with new applications.

T-SQL Syntax and Conventions

Now that you've seen a few examples of T-SQL syntax, it's time for a more formal introduction to the conventions used in syntax diagrams. In this section, we'll introduce the syntax that we'll use in defining SQL statements throughout this book and also look at the rules for naming SQL Server objects.

Reading Syntax Diagrams

Here's the full set of rules for reading the syntax diagrams of T-SQL statements:

- Words in UPPERCASE are SQL keywords, to be typed exactly as shown.
- Words in *italics* are variables that you need to replace with object names or values when you type the statement.
- The vertical-bar character (`|`) separates choices. You need to pick one and only one of a set of options separated by vertical bars.
- Square brackets (`[]`) surround optional syntax items.
- Curly braces (`{}`) surround required syntax items.
- `[,...n]` means that the immediately preceding syntax item can be repeated one or more times, with instances separated by commas.
- `[ ...n]` means that the immediately preceding syntax item can be repeated one or more times, with instances separated by spaces.
- Labels can be used to make a complex piece of SQL Server syntax more readable by deferring the explanation of certain items. Labels are surrounded by chevrons (<>) when they occur and are surrounded by chevrons and followed by `::=` where they're defined.

As an example, here's a small part of the SELECT statement syntax illustrating several of these conventions:

```
SELECT [ALL|DISTINCT]
 <select_list>
<select_list>::=
 {*
  |{table_name|view_name|table_alias}.*
  |{column_name|expression|$IDENTITY|$ROWGUID}
  |udt_column_name {.|::} {{property_name|field_name}|
   method_name(argument [,...n])}
    [[AS] column_alias]
  |column_alias=expression
 } [,...n]
```

You can see that the `SELECT` statement starts with the required `SELECT` keyword, followed optionally by either an `ALL` or a `DISTINCT` keyword (but not both), and then by a `select_list`. The `select_list` is defined as a star character, a table name, a view name, or a table alias followed by a star, a column name, an expression, the `IDENTITYCOL` or the `ROWGUID` keyword, a user-defined datatype column name, or a Common Language Runtime (CLR) expression, which may be followed by a column alias (optionally prefixed by the AS keyword), or a column alias/expression pair separated by the equals sign. The parts of the `select_list` can be repeated more than once.

As you can see, the syntax diagram is much easier to read and understand than the corresponding verbal explanation.

Valid Identifiers

An *identifier* in SQL Server is the name of an object. This might be a table name, a view name, a column name, a username, or many other things. A set of rules defines what a valid identifier looks like:

- The first character can be a letter from the Unicode character set. This includes the standard U.S. English a–z and A–Z characters as well as foreign letters.
- The first character can also be an underscore (_), at sign (@), or pound sign (#). Identifiers starting with an at sign can be used only for local variables. Identifiers starting with a pound sign can be used only for a temporary table or procedure. Identifiers starting with two pound signs can be used only for global temporary objects.
- Identifiers can be up to 128 characters long, except the names of local temporary tables, which can be up to only 116 characters long.
- Characters after the first character can be Unicode letters, decimal numbers, or the @, $, _, and # symbols.
- Identifiers can't be a SQL Server reserved word, in either upper- or lowercase.
- Identifiers can't contain embedded spaces or special characters other than those specified in this list.

Although these rules define valid identifiers, you're not limited to using valid identifiers for objects in SQL Server. Practically speaking, you can use any Unicode string up to 128 characters long to name an object. However, if the string isn't a valid identifier, you need to quote it, using either square brackets or quotation marks.

For example, the string *New Customers* isn't a valid SQL Server identifier, because it contains a space. So, the following would not be a valid SQL statement:

```
SELECT * FROM New Customers
```

However, you can quote the table name to make the statement valid in either of the following forms:

```
SELECT * FROM "New Customers"
SELECT * FROM [New Customers]
```

NOTE **Because the setting of the QUOTED_IDENTIFIER option can affect the interpretation of quotation marks, we'll use square brackets for quoting in this book, and we recommend that you do the same in your code.**

Referring to Objects

The identifier for an object isn't the only way to refer to an object. In fact, there are four possible parts to an object name:

- The name of the server containing the object
- The name of the database containing the object
- The name of the owner of the object
- The identifier of the object

For example, suppose that a server named MOOCOW contains a database named AdventureWorks that contains an object named Sales that's owned by a user named dbo. The fully qualified name of this object would be as follows:

```
MOOCOW.AdventureWorks.dbo.Sales
```

You can also omit all or part of this information. You can omit intermediate information that's not necessary to uniquely identify the object, and you can omit leading information if it's the same as that of the database where the reference is made. So, depending on circumstances, any of the following might also be an identifier for this object:

```
MOOCOW.AdventureWorks..Sales
MOOCOW..dbo.Sales
MOOCOW...Sales
AdventureWorks.dbo.Sales
AdventureWorks..Sales
dbo.Sales
Sales
```

Note that leading periods are always omitted, but intermediate periods are never omitted.

Reserved Words

SQL Server reserves a number of keywords for its own use. For example, you can't name an object SELECT (unless you use quoted identifiers), because SQL Server uses the SELECT keyword in the SELECT statement. The SQL Server Books Online contains an extensive list of reserved words (search Books Online for the topic *Reserved Keywords (Transact-SQL)* to see the entire list).

You can use SQL Server Management Studio to check whether a particular word is a keyword. Figure 5.3 shows how you can do this with a SELECT statement. The first statement tells SQL Server to select the constant 1 and report it using the alias Foo. The second and third statements try the same thing but with the alias WHERE. Because WHERE is a reserved word, the second statement fails; but the third statement (using quoted identifiers) succeeds.

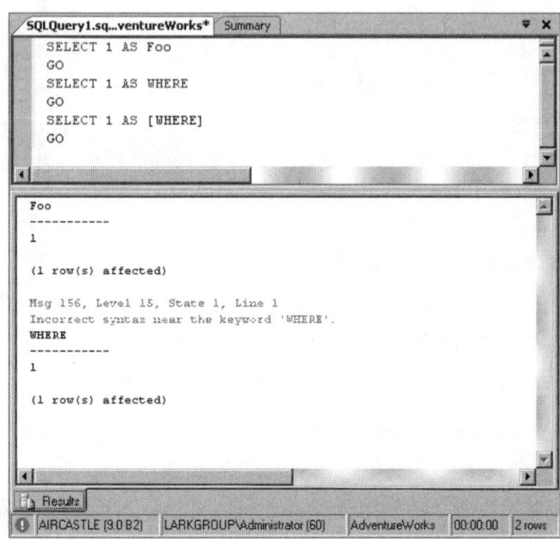

FIGURE 5.3
Checking for a reserved word using SQL Server Management Studio

The GO keyword tells SQL Server Management Studio to execute the statements to that point as a single batch. If you try to run all three statements without the intervening GO keywords, the entire batch will fail because of the syntax error in the second line.

Datatypes

One of the building blocks of T-SQL is the notion of *datatypes*. Each kind of data you store in a SQL Server table (numbers, character strings, images, and so on) is defined by its datatype. For the most part, you'll be using datatypes defined by SQL Server itself. It's also possible to define your own datatypes. You'll learn about these user-defined datatypes in Chapter 11, "Tables."

In this section, we'll discuss the various datatypes supplied by SQL Server, including both the keywords used to refer to them and the type of data that they can store.

Integers

SQL Server supplies five different datatypes for storing exact integer numbers: bit, tinyint, smallint, int, and bigint. These five types are distinguished by the range of values they can hold:

TIP In general, you should choose the smallest type that will hold the data with which you expect to deal. All other things being equal, operations on smaller datatypes are faster than operations on larger datatypes.

bit A column of the bit datatype can store 1, 0, or null. Null is a special value used to indicate that a value is unknown. SQL Server will combine multiple bit fields into bytes to save storage space if possible.

tinyint A column of the tinyint datatype can store 0 through 255, or null.

smallint A column of the smallint datatype can store –32,768 through 32,767, or null.

int A column of the int datatype can store -2^{31} through $2^{31} - 1$, or null. This gives an int column a range of –2,147,483,648 through 2,147,483,647.

bigint A column of the bigint datatype can store -2^{63} through $2^{63} - 1$, or null. This gives a bigint column a range of –9,223,372,036,854,775,808 through 9,223,372,036,854,775,807.

Text

SQL Server supplies four different datatypes that can hold textual data: char, varchar, nchar, and nvarchar. For these datatypes, you must specify a length as well as the datatype when you're defining a column. For example, you might speak of a char(10) column—one that will hold 10 characters:

char A column of the char datatype holds a fixed number of non-Unicode characters. That is, a char(30) column, for example, will always store 30 characters, even if you assign a string of less than 30 characters to the column. The maximum size for a char column is 8000 characters.

varchar A column of the varchar datatype holds a variable number of non-Unicode characters. That is, a varchar(30) column, for example, will store up to 30 characters. The maximum size for a varchar column is 8000 characters. You can also use the special form varchar(max), which will store up to 2^{31} characters.

nchar A column of the nchar datatype holds a fixed number of Unicode characters. That is, an nchar(30) column, for example, will always store 30 characters, even if you assign a string of less than 30 characters to the column. Because nchar columns use the Unicode character set, they're capable of storing a much wider range of characters than regular char columns. However, because each Unicode character requires two bytes of storage, the maximum size of an nchar column is 4000 characters.

nvarchar A column of the nvarchar datatype holds a variable number of Unicode characters. That is, an nvarchar(30) column, for example, will store up to 30 characters. Because nvarchar columns use the Unicode character set, they're capable of storing a much wider range of characters than regular varchar columns. The maximum size for an nvarchar column is 4000 characters. You can also use the special form nvarchar(max), which will store up to 2^{30} characters.

TIP For variable data, varchar and nvarchar provide more efficient storage than char and nchar. For data that's likely to be all the same size, char and nchar are faster than varchar and nvarchar. You should reserve varchar(max) and nvarchar(max) for data that will be longer than 8000 characters. In general, you should use the Unicode datatypes (nchar, nvarchar, and nvarchar(max)) only if there's a chance that the data will contain special characters.

NOTE Previous versions of SQL Server includes the text and ntext datatypes for long character data. These have been superseded by the varchar(max) and nvarchar(max) datatypes.

Decimal

SQL Server supplies a single datatype for handling exact floating-point numbers without rounding, although that datatype has two names: decimal or numeric:

decimal or numeric When you're defining a decimal or numeric column, you must specify both the precision and the scale:

- The *precision* of the datatype is the total number of decimal digits that can be stored.
- The *scale* of the datatype is the number of decimal digits that can be stored to the right of the decimal point.

For example, a column defined as decimal(5,3) could store numbers such as 12.345.

The maximum precision of a decimal column by default is 38. The maximum scale of a column is the precision for that column.

NOTE *Numeric* is an exact synonym for *decimal*, as far as datatypes in SQL Server go.

Money

SQL Server provides two native datatypes for storing monetary data: smallmoney and money. They differ in the maximum size of the data that they can store:

smallmoney A column defined using the smallmoney datatype can store values from –214,748.3648 through 214,748.3647. Data stored in a smallmoney column is always stored with precisely four digits to the right of the decimal point.

money A column defined using the money datatype can store values from –922,337,203,685,477.5808 through 922,337,203,685,477.5807. Data stored in a money column is always stored with precisely four digits to the right of the decimal point.

Floating Point

SQL Server supplies two datatypes for floating-point data. Unlike with the decimal datatype, information stored in a floating-point datatype may be rounded if it can't be represented accurately in the binary arithmetic that SQL Server uses internally:

float A column of the float datatype can store data from -1.79×10^{308} to 1.79×10^{308}, if the column is defined with the maximum possible precision. When defining a column of the float datatype, you specify the number of bits used to store the number and thus the precision. This may range from 1 through 53. So, float(53) is the most precise possible floating-point storage (and correspondingly uses the most storage space).

real In SQL Server, real is a synonym for float(24). A column of the real datatype can store data from roughly -3.4×10^{38} through 3.4×10^{38}.

Date

SQL Server supplies two different datatypes for date storage: smalldatetime and datetime. They differ in the range of dates and the accuracy that they use for storing those dates:

smalldatetime A column defined with the smalldatetime datatype can hold dates from January 1, 1900, through June 6, 2079, with accuracy to 1 minute.

datetime A column defined with the datetime datatype can hold dates from January 1, 1753, through December 31, 9999, with accuracy to 3.33 milliseconds.

Binary Data

SQL Server provides two datatypes for storing arbitrary binary data: binary and varbinary.

binary A binary column can hold up to 8000 bytes of binary data. It's defined with a size—for example, binary(100). Binary columns are padded so that they always store exactly the number of bytes the column is defined to hold.

varbinary A varbinary column holds variable-length binary data up to the specified size. For example, a varbinary(12) column could hold any number from 0 to 12 bytes of data. The varbinary datatype is limited to 8000 bytes of data. The varbinary(max) datatype can hold up to 2^{31} bytes of data.

NOTE Previous versions of SQL Server include the image datatype for long binary data. This has been superseded by the varbinary(max) datatype.

Special-Purpose Datatypes

SQL Server also provides six special-purpose native datatypes: cursor, sql_variant, table, timestamp, uniqueidentifier, and xml:

cursor The cursor datatype is the only one of the native SQL Server datatypes that can't be used to define a column in a table. Instead, it's used as the datatype for the output of a stored procedure or SQL statement that returns a pointer to a set of records. You'll learn more about cursors in Chapter 8.

sql_variant The sql_variant datatype is a wildcard datatype that can hold any other datatype except varchar(max), nvarchar(max), timestamp, and sql_variant. For example, a column defined as sql_variant could hold integers in some rows of a table and varchar data in other rows of the same table. Like variants in other languages (such as Visual C++ or Visual Basic), variants in SQL take up extra storage space and are slower to process than the simple datatypes they can contain, so you should use them only if you absolutely need the flexibility they provide.

table The table datatype is used for temporary storage of a result set during a function, stored procedure, or batch. You can't define a column in a saved table as the table datatype. However, if you need to keep track of a selection of data during a batch, table datatypes can be useful. Here's a small batch of T-SQL statements that demonstrates (as a purely artificial example) the use of this datatype:

```
DECLARE @T1 TABLE
    (PK int PRIMARY KEY, Col2 varchar(3))
INSERT INTO @T1 VALUES (2, 'xxx')
INSERT INTO @T1 VALUES (4, 'yyy')
SELECT * FROM T1
```

These statements create a variable of the table datatype named T1, insert two rows into this temporary table, and then select all the rows from the table. If you run this batch of statements in SQL Server Management Studio, you'll see that it prints out both rows from the table.

timestamp A timestamp column is an 8-byte binary column that holds a unique value generated by SQL Server. Any table can have only one timestamp column. The value in a timestamp column for a row of data is automatically updated by SQL Server whenever there's a change to any date in that row. This makes timestamps useful for detecting whether another user has changed data while you're working with it.

uniqueidentifier A column defined with the uniqueidentifier datatype can store a single globally unique identifier (GUID). Within SQL Server, you can generate GUIDs with the NEWID function. GUIDs are guaranteed to be unique. You'll never see the same GUID generated twice, even in different databases on different computers.

xml The xml datatype is new in SQL Server 2005. It's designed to store an entire XML document. This datatype provides advanced functionality, such as searching via XQuery syntax. If your application manipulates XML, the xml datatype will be a much better fit than the nvarchar(max) datatype in most cases.

Synonyms for Datatypes

The ANSI standard specifies some names that should be recognized for datatypes. SQL Server recognizes these names as synonyms for built-in datatypes. These names can be used interchangeably with the native names for the datatypes. Table 5.3 lists the available datatype synonyms.

TABLE 5.3: Datatype Synonyms

ANSI DATATYPE	SQL SERVER EQUIVALENT
binary varying	varbinary
char varying	varchar
character	char(1)
character(n)	char(n)

TABLE 5.3: Datatype Synonyms *(CONTINUED)*

ANSI DATATYPE	SQL SERVER EQUIVALENT
character varying	varchar(1)
character varying(n)	varchar(n)
dec	decimal
double precision	float
integer	int
national char(n)	nchar(n)
national character(n)	nchar(n)
national char varying(n)	nvarchar(n)
national character varying(n)	nvarchar(n)
national text	ntext
rowversion	timestamp

Operators

The SQL language supports a number of operators. An *operator* is a symbol that causes an operation to be performed. For example, + is the addition operator. Generally speaking, you can use SQL operators together with object names, constants, and variables wherever an expression is allowed.

Available Operators

Table 5.4 lists the operators that are implemented in T-SQL.

TABLE 5.4: T-SQL Operators

OPERATOR	MEANING
+	Addition
-	Subtraction
*	Multiplication
/	Division
%	Modulus (for example, 13%3=1—the remainder when 13 is divided by 3)
=	Assignment

TABLE 5.4: T-SQL Operators *(CONTINUED)*

OPERATOR	MEANING
&	Bitwise AND
|	Bitwise OR
^	Bitwise XOR
=	Equality comparison
>	Greater than
<	Less than
>=	Greater than or equal to
<=	Less than or equal to
<>	Not equal to
!=	Not equal to
!>	Not greater than
!<	Not less than
ALL	True if every one of a set of comparisons is true
AND	True if two Boolean expressions are true
ANY	True if any one of a set of comparisons is true
BETWEEN	True if an operand is within a range
EXISTS	True if a subquery contains any rows
IN	True if an operand is in a list
LIKE	True if an operand matches a pattern
NOT	Reverses the value of other Boolean operators
OR	True if either of a pair of Boolean expressions is true
SOME	True if some of a set of comparisons are true
+	String concatenation
+	Positive number
-	Negative number
~	Ones complement

Operator Precedence and Grouping

You can construct complex expressions in T-SQL. In an expression involving multiple operators, the operators are evaluated in order of their *precedence*. Operators are split into precedence groups: All operators in a higher group are evaluated left to right before any operators in a lower group are evaluated. The precedence groups are as follows (from higher to lower):

- Positive, negative, and ones complement (+, -, ~)
- `*`, `/`, `%`
- + (addition or concatenation), `-`, `&`
- = (comparison), >, <, >=, <=, <>, `!=`, `!>`, `!<`
- `^`, `|`
- `NOT`
- `AND`
- `ALL`, `ANY`, `BETWEEN`, `IN`, `LIKE`, `OR`, `SOME`
- = (assignment)

You can use parentheses to force a different order of evaluation or make the order of evaluation in a complicated expression clearer to the reader. For example, although you can use the rules to determine how 3+5*4 will evaluate, it's easier to just write 3+(5*4) and remove any doubt.

Wildcards

The `LIKE` operator is used to compare a character string to a pattern. These patterns can include wildcards, which are special characters that match particular patterns of characters in the original character string. Table 5.5 shows the T-SQL wildcards.

TABLE 5.5: T-SQL Wildcards

PATTERN	MEANING
`%`	Any string of zero or more characters
`_`	Any single character
`[a-d]`	Any character within the range of *a* to *d*, inclusive
`[aef]`	A single character—*a*, *e*, or *f*
`[^a-d]`	Any single character except those in the range of *a* to *d*, inclusive
`[^aef]`	Any single character except *a*, *e*, or *f*

Variables

SQL Server supports two types of variables in T-SQL. First, there are global variables that the system defines and maintains for you. Second, there are local variables that you can create to hold intermediate results. In this section, we'll introduce the system global variables and then show you how to create and use your own local variables.

System Global Variables

SQL Server's global variables are all prefixed with two @ signs. You can retrieve the value of any of these variables with a simple SELECT query, as shown in Figure 5.4. In this case, we've used the @@CONNECTIONS global variable to retrieve the number of connections made to the SQL Server since it was started.

FIGURE 5.4
Retrieving the value of a global variable

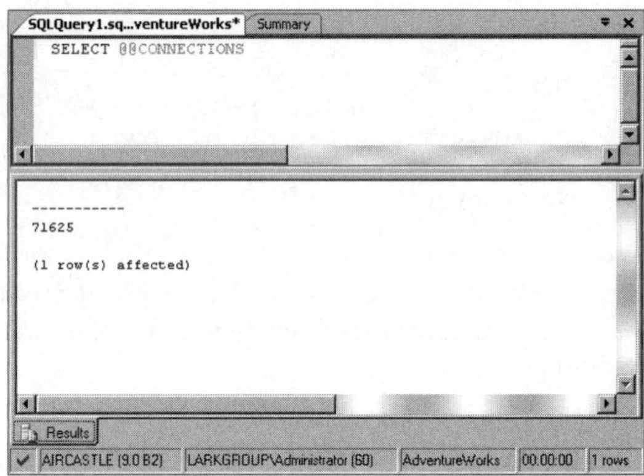

Table 5.6 lists all the SQL Server system global variables.

TABLE 5.6: Global Variables

VARIABLE	MEANING
@@CONNECTIONS	Number of connections made to the server since it was last started
@@CPU_BUSY	Number of milliseconds the system has been processing since SQL Server was started
@@CURSOR_ROWS	Number of rows in the most recently opened cursor
@@DATEFIRST	The current value of the SET DATEFIRST parameter, which controls the day that's considered to be the first day of the week
@@DBTS	Last used timestamp value
@@ERROR	Error number of the last T-SQL error
@@FETCH_STATUS	Zero if the last FETCH operation was successful; –1 or –2 if there was an error
@@IDENTITY	Last inserted identity value

TABLE 5.6: Global Variables *(CONTINUED)*

VARIABLE	MEANING
@@IDLE	Number of milliseconds that the server has been idle since it was last started
@@IO_BUSY	Number of milliseconds that the server has been active with input and output since it was last started
@@LANGID	Language ID of the language currently in use
@@LANGUAGE	Name of the language currently in use
@@LOCK_TIMEOUT	Number of milliseconds until locks time out in the current session
@@MAX_CONNECTIONS	Maximum number of concurrent connections that can be made to this server
@@MAX_PRECISION	Maximum precision for decimal or numeric datatypes
@@NESTLEVEL	Nesting level of the currently executing stored procedure
@@OPTIONS	A bitmapped value indicating the status of a number of options
@@PACK_RECEIVED	Number of packets received from the network by the server since it was last started
@@PACK_SENT	Number of packets sent to the network by the server since it was last started
@@PACKET_ERRORS	Number of network errors since the server was last started
@@PROCID	Stored procedure ID of the currently executing procedure
@@REMSERVER	Name of the server from which a stored procedure is being run
@@ROWCOUNT	Number of rows affected by the most recent SQL statement
@@SERVERNAME	Name of the local server
@@SERVICENAME	Name of the SQL Server service on this computer
@@SPID	Server process ID of the current process
@@TEXTSIZE	Current value from SET TEXTSIZE, which specifies the maximum number of bytes to return from a text or image column to a SELECT statement
@@TIMETICKS	Number of microseconds per tick on the current computer
@@TOTAL_ERRORS	Number of disk read and write failures since the server was last started
@@TOTAL_READ	Number of disk reads since the server was last started
@@TOTAL_WRITE	Number of disk writes since the server was last started
@@TRANCOUNT	Number of transactions open on the current connection
@@VERSION	Version information for SQL Server

TIP The `@@VERSION` variable is useful for telling what service packs have been applied to a server, because it changes every time a service pack is applied.

Local Variables

Like almost any other programming language, T-SQL allows you to create and use local variables for temporary storage while you're running a batch of SQL statements.

To create a local variable, you use the `DECLARE` statement, which has the following syntax:

```
DECLARE
{@local_variable data_type|
  @cursor_variable CURSOR
} [,...n]
```

NOTE For information on cursor variables, see Chapter 8.

All local variable names must start with an at sign (`@`). For example, to create a local variable to hold up to 16 characters of Unicode data, you could use the following statement:

```
DECLARE @user_name varchar(16)
```

To assign a value to a local variable, you can use either the SET statement or the SELECT statement:

```
SET @local_variable = expression
SELECT @local_variable = expression [,...n]
```

NOTE More clauses are available in both `SET` and `SELECT`; however, the forms shown here are the only ones you need to assign values to local variables.

SET and SELECT are equivalent in this context, so you can choose the one that looks best or reads most easily to you.

Once a local variable has been declared and contains data, you can use it anywhere that a value is required. For example, you might use it in a `WHERE` clause. Figure 5.5 shows a SQL batch that declares a local variable, places a value in it, and then uses this value to help retrieve records from a table.

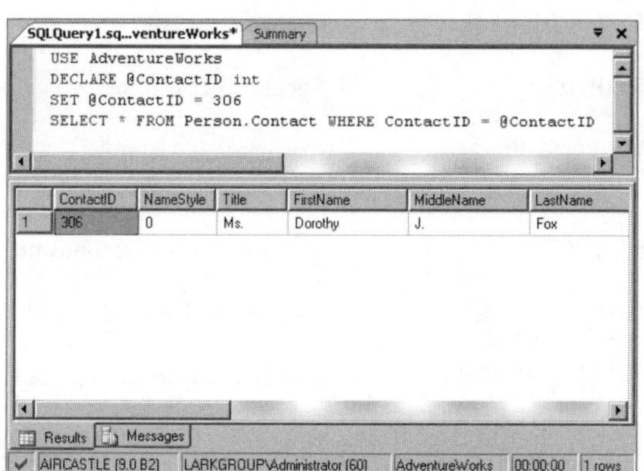

FIGURE 5.5
Using a local variable

Functions

The T-SQL language also includes a large number of functions. These functions can be useful when you're calculating or otherwise manipulating data. Broadly speaking, there are four classes of T-SQL functions:

- Rowset functions can be used in place of table names in SQL. You'll learn more about rowset functions in Chapter 8.
- Aggregate functions calculate a single number (for example, a sum or a standard deviation) from all the values in a column. You'll learn more about aggregate functions in Chapter 6.
- Window functions operate on the results of a `FROM` clause. They divide these results into a set of partitions and then apply an aggregate function separately to each partition. You'll learn more about window functions in Chapter 6.
- Scalar functions operate on zero, one, or more values and return a single value. These are the functions that you can use in expressions. The remainder of this section is devoted to the scalar functions.

SQL Server implements dozens of functions. Table 5.7 lists the categories of functions that SQL Server makes available. We won't cover all of these functions in detail. Instead, we'll demonstrate the use of a few of the more useful functions in this section. You can find the complete list of SQL Server functions by searching for *Functions* in the Transact-SQL reference in SQL Server Books Online.

TABLE 5.7: SQL Server Function Categories

CATEGORY	CONTAINS
Configuration functions	Functions that return information about the current configuration of the server
Cursor functions	Functions that return information about cursors
Date and time functions	Functions for manipulating dates and times
Mathematical functions	Functions for performing mathematical calculations
Metadata functions	Functions to return information about database objects
Security functions	Functions related to users and roles
String functions	Functions for manipulating textual data
System functions	Functions for low-level object manipulation
System statistical functions	Functions that return statistical information about the server's activity
Text and image functions	Functions that operate on large (text and image datatypes) columns

Generating GUIDs

As a simple example of a function, consider NEWID. This function takes no arguments, and it returns a GUID. A GUID, as we mentioned earlier in the discussion of the uniqueidentifier datatype, is a globally unique identifier. These numbers are generated from a complex formula that includes hardware characteristics of the computer, a random seed, and date and time information—the net result being that GUIDs are truly unique, across computers and across time.

Figure 5.6 shows how you might use the NEWID function. The SQL batch shown first declares a local variable using the uniqueidentifier datatype and then uses the NEWID function to assign a value to that variable. Finally, the batch prints out the variable's new value.

FIGURE 5.6
Using the NEWID function

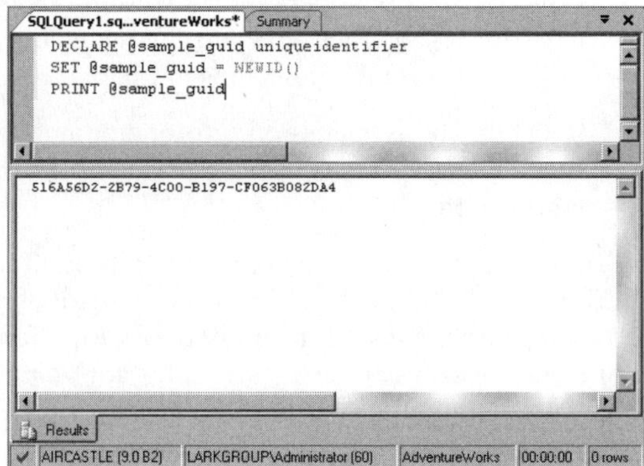

NOTE Of course, if you run this same SQL batch on your computer, you'll get a slightly different result, because the NEWID function generates a different GUID every time it's run.

String Functions

SQL Server supports almost two dozen functions for manipulating strings of characters. We'll look at just a few of the most useful ones here:

- The LEFT function selects characters from the left end of a string. So, for example, `LEFT('abcdefg', 4)` returns the string *abcd*.
- The LEN function returns the length of a character string.
- The LOWER function converts a string to lowercase.
- The LTRIM function removes leading blanks from a string.
- The REPLACE function replaces instances of a string with another string. For example, `REPLACE('abc', 'b', 'e')` returns the string *aec*.
- The RIGHT function selects characters from the right end of a string.
- The RTRIM function removes trailing blanks.
- The SOUNDEX function returns the Soundex code for a string. Soundex codes are designed so that two names that sound alike return identical codes.

- The SUBSTRING function returns a specified number of characters starting at a specified point in a string. For example, SUBSTRING('abcde', 2, 3) returns the string *bcd*.
- The UPPER function converts a string to uppercase.

Figure 5.7 demonstrates some of these functions within SQL Server Management.

FIGURE 5.7
Examples of some string functions

NOTE Note the use of the + operator to concatenate strings in the example shown for SOUNDEX.

Date and Time Functions

SQL Server supplies nine functions for manipulating date and time values. Several of these functions take a datepart argument specifying with what granularity of time they're operating. Table 5.8 lists the possible settings for datepart.

TABLE 5.8: SQL Server datepart Constants

CONSTANT	MEANING
yy or yyyy	Year
qq or q	Quarter
mm or m	Month
wk or ww	Week
dw or w	Weekday
dy or y	Day of year (1 to 366)

TABLE 5.8: SQL Server `datepart` Constants *(CONTINUED)*

CONSTANT	MEANING
dd or d	Day
hh	Hour
mi or n	Minute
ss or s	Second
ms	Millisecond

For example, the DATEADD function takes as arguments a datepart, a quantity, and a date. It returns the result of adding the given quantity of the given datepart to the given date. Thus, to add three days to the current date, you could use the following expression:

```
PRINT DATEADD(d, 3, GETDATE())
```

WARNING The `datepart` constants aren't strings and thus should not be enclosed in single quotes.

Here's the full list of available date and time functions:

- DATEADD adds time to a date.
- DATEDIFF reports the number of dateparts between two dates.
- DATENAME extracts textual names (for example, *February* or *Tuesday*) from a date.
- DATEPART returns the specified datepart from a specified date.
- DAY returns the day from a date.
- GETDATE returns the current date and time.
- GETUTCDATE returns the current date and time translated to UTC time.
- MONTH returns the month from a date.
- YEAR returns the year from a date.

Mathematical Functions

SQL Server supplies almost two dozen mathematical functions for manipulating integer and floating-point values. These functions include all the common functions that you'd naturally expect to find in any programming language. Table 5.9 lists the available mathematical functions.

TIP SQL Server uses radians to measure angles for trigonometric functions.

TABLE 5.9: Mathematical Functions in T-SQL

FUNCTION	MEANING
ABS	Absolute value
ACOS	Arccosine
ASIN	Arcsine
ATAN	Arctangent
ATN2	Arctangent of the angle defined by two angles
CEILING	Smallest integer greater than the expression
COS	Cosine
COT	Cotangent
DEGREES	Converts radians to degrees
EXP	Exponential
FLOOR	Largest integer smaller than the expression
LOG	Base 2 logarithm
LOG10	Base 10 logarithm
PI	The constant pi
POWER	Exponentiation operator
RADIANS	Converts degrees to radians
RAND	Random number generator
ROUND	Rounds floating-point numbers by precision
SIGN	Sign of the expression
SIN	Sine
SQRT	Square root
SQUARE	Square
TAN	Tangent

System and Metadata Functions

System and metadata functions return internal information about SQL Server and the data it's storing. Most of these functions are pretty obscure or useful only in specialized circumstances; you can find a full list in the T-SQL help in Books Online. However, you might find a few of the following functions useful in your databases:

- The CONVERT function converts one type of data to another (for example, integer to character).
- The CURRENT_USER function returns the name of the current user (the one running the SQL batch).
- The ISDATE function tells you whether its input represents a valid date.
- The ISNULL function replaces any null value with a specified replacement value.
- The ISNUMERIC function tells you whether its input is a number.

Figure 5.8 demonstrates the use of these functions in SQL Server Management.

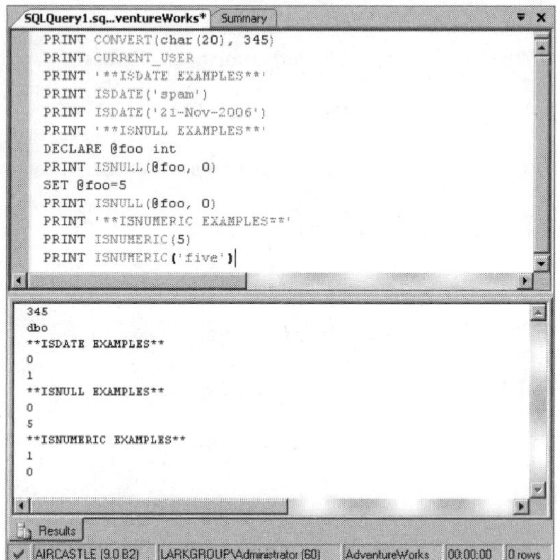

FIGURE 5.8
Some useful system functions

User-Defined Functions

SQL Server 2005 also allows you to define your own functions for use anywhere you can use the system-defined functions. To do this, you use the CREATE FUNCTION statement:

```
CREATE FUNCTION [schema_name].function_name
(
 [{@parameter_name data_type [=default_value]} [,...n]]
)
RETURNS data_type
[AS]
{BEGIN function_body END}
```

NOTE This definition has been simplified somewhat. In particular, we've omitted the clauses you'd use to return a table from a user-defined function. See Books Online for more details.

For example, you could define a function named TwoTimes in the following way:

```
CREATE FUNCTION TwoTimes
(@input int=0)
RETURNS int
AS
BEGIN
 RETURN 2 * @input
END
```

After it's been created, you could call this function as part of a SELECT statement:

```
SELECT SalesOrderID, dbo.TwoTimes(OrderQty) AS Extra
FROM sales.SalesOrderDetail
```

Figure 5.9 shows the result set from this query. Note that you need to specify the schema of the function (by default, the creating user—in this case, dbo, the owner of the database) when you call the function, even if you don't specify the owner when you create the function.

NOTE You'll learn more about the SELECT statement in Chapter 6.

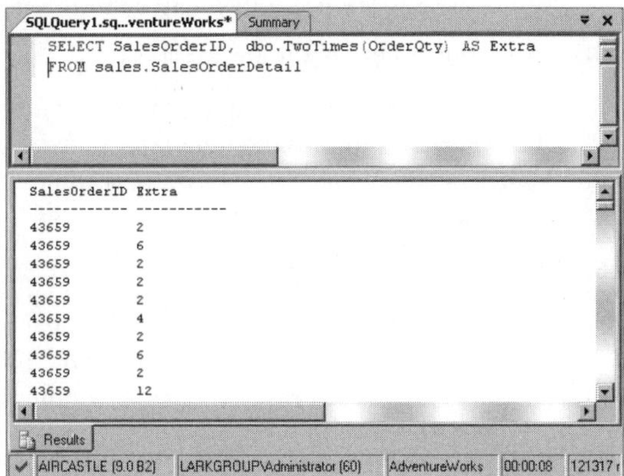

FIGURE 5.9
Calling a user-defined function

NOTE SQL Server 2005 adds a new type of function, the CLR function, which lets you call code compiled with the .NET Common Language Runtime. You'll learn about these functions in Chapter 19, "Integrating SQL Server with Microsoft .NET."

Executing T-SQL

So far, the few examples we've shown for executing SQL have all used SQL Server Management Studio. In this section, we'll look at SQL Server Management Studio in more detail. Then we'll consider two alternatives for executing SQL: the command line OSQL and SQLCMD utilities.

Using SQL Server Management Studio

In addition to executing queries, SQL Server Management Studio offers some functionality to make it both easier to use and more powerful. In this section, you'll learn how to create, save, and retrieve queries; how to view results in several formats; and how to view the *execution plan* of a query, which is a list of the actions that SQL Server will undertake to deliver the results of the query. You'll also learn how to create views and stored procedures.

CREATING A QUERY

You've already learned how to create a query to test arbitrary SQL statements, but let's review the steps here:

1. Launch SQL Server Management Studio from the Start menu by choosing Programs ➤ Microsoft SQL Server 2005 ➤ SQL Server Management Studio.
2. Choose the SQL Server that you want to connect to from the combo box. This box shows servers with which you've recently connected. To see other servers on your network, select the <Browse for more…> entry from the combo box. You can also use the special name (local) to connect to a server on the computer that you're using.
3. Either select Windows Authentication in the Authentication combo box, or select SQL Server Authentication and supply your SQL Server username and password. If you don't know how to log on, try Windows Authentication first, before you call your database administrator. We recommend this option for all new installations of SQL Server.
4. Click Connect to log on to the server.
5. The SQL Server Management Studio user interface appears. Expand the treeview in the Object Explorer to find the database that you'd like to work with. Right-click the database, and select New Query to create a new query window. Type in as many SQL statements as you'd like to execute.
6. Click the Execute toolbar button or press F5 to see the results.

You can also use the New Query button on the toolbar to open additional query windows. SQL Server Management Studio will let you open an almost unlimited number of windows, so you don't have to lose one set of results to try something else.

SAVING A QUERY

SQL Server Management Studio lets you save SQL batches for later. This is useful for complex queries that you might want to run again in the future. It's also useful if you need to keep track of versions of a SQL batch during development; you can save the SQL batch and use a source code control tool such as Visual Sourcesafe to store it. For example, you might have a query that gives you aggregate sales results by joining half a dozen tables from your sales database. Once you've perfected the query, you'll want to save it so you don't have to type in the complex SQL code again the next time you want to see current results.

To save a query, choose File ➤ Save from the SQL Server Management Studio menu or click the Save button. SQL Server Management Studio will suggest a default filename, but you can use any name you'd like. By default, Query Analyzer uses `.SQL` as an extension for queries.

OPENING A SAVED QUERY

To open a previously saved query, choose File ➢ Open ➢ File from the SQL Server Management Studio menu or click the Open button. Browse to the query you want to open, and click OK. The query will be displayed in the current query window, and you'll be able to execute it immediately.

VIEWING RESULTS

Management Studio lets you view results in two formats. The first format, Results to Text, is the format that we've used for most of the examples so far in this chapter. This format is most useful for queries that return only a bit of information.

The other format shows results in a grid. This is useful if the query returns a set of records. Figure 5.10 shows a set of results in a Management Studio grid.

FIGURE 5.10
Viewing results in a grid

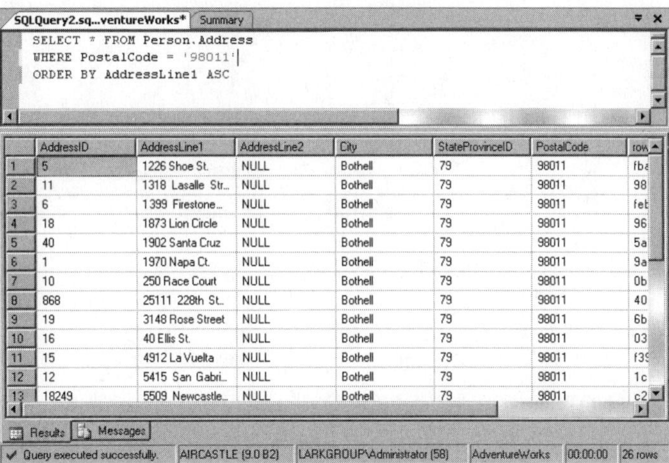

To switch from one format to the other, choose the Execute Mode drop-down toolbar button, or select Query ➢ Results To ➢ Results to Text or Query ➢ Results To ➢ Results To Grid from the SQL Server Management Studio menus.

TIP As you can see in Figure 5.10, white space is generally not significant in the T-SQL language. You can insert new lines, spaces, and tabs to make your SQL statements more readable. SQL Server doesn't care if you spread a query over multiple lines.

You can also select Query ➢ Results To ➢ Results To File to save the results instead of seeing them immediately on-screen.

VIEWING THE EXECUTION PLAN

SQL Server Management Studio can also show you the estimated execution plan for any query. The execution plan is the set of steps that SQL Server uses to execute the query. This information is useful because each step shows its estimated relative cost (in time). You can use this tool to locate bottlenecks in your applications and to help you change slow queries to make them faster. To see the execution plan for a query, select Query ➢ Display Estimated Execution Plan or use the Ctrl+L shortcut.

Figure 5.11 shows the execution plan for a query. Each step is represented by an icon. If you make the mouse hover over an icon, you'll see detailed information for that step.

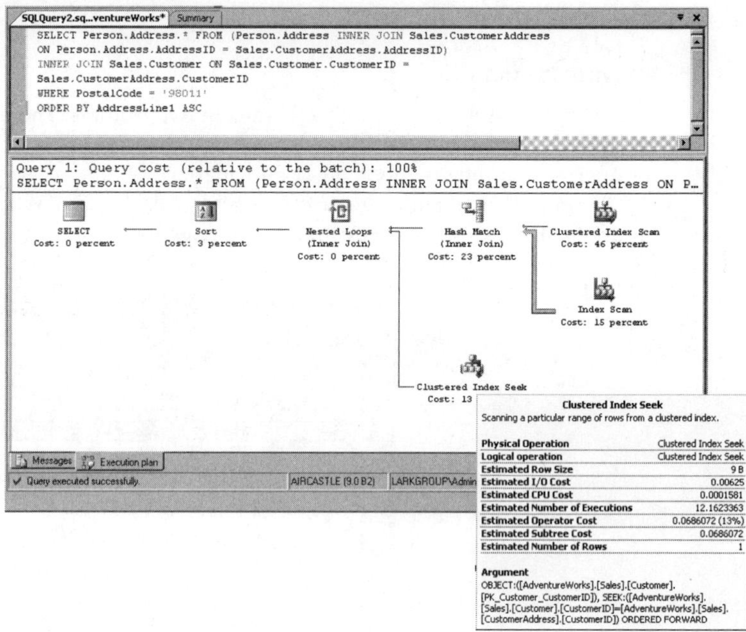

FIGURE 5.11
Viewing a query's execution plan

NOTE There's more information on using execution plans to optimize queries in Chapter 24, "Monitoring and Optimizing SQL Server 2005."

Creating a View

A *view* is a SQL Server SELECT statement that's been saved in a database. You can use a view to retrieve data from one or more tables, and to summarize, sort, or filter this data. You'll learn more about views in Chapter 13, "Views." Until then, here's how you can create a very simple view within SQL Server Management Studio:

1. Drill down to the Views node in the treeview for the database you want to query.
2. Right-click the Views node, and select New View.
3. Assign a name to the view in the upper pane of the view editor.
4. Enter the SQL statement for the view in the lower pane of the view editor.
5. Click the Save button to create the view. Note that this actually creates a database object, not an external file like the saved query you created earlier.

Figure 5.12 shows a simple view in SQL Server Management Studio.

FIGURE 5.12
A SQL Server view

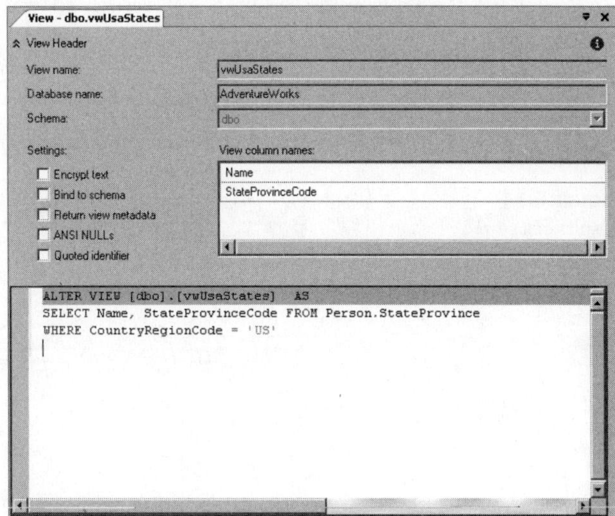

The view designer consists of two panes:

- The header pane shows metadata about the view.
- The SQL pane shows the SQL statement that the view is creating.

Changes in either of these panes are reflected in the other pane. For example, if you add a new field in the SQL pane, that field will appear in the header pane when you save the view.

CREATING A STORED PROCEDURE

You can also create a stored procedure to execute arbitrary SQL statements using SQL Server Management Studio. Unlike a view, a stored procedure can contain multiple SQL statements; in that way, it's similar to the queries you've seen in SQL Server Management Studio. You'll learn more about stored procedures in Chapter 14, "Stored Procedures."

To create and execute a simple stored procedure, follow these steps:

1. Navigate to the Stored Procedures node in the treeview for the database you want to query. It's a child of the Programmability node.
2. Right-click the node, and select New Stored Procedure.
3. Assign a name to the stored procedure in the upper pane of the view editor.
4. Type the SQL statements that make up the stored procedure. Click the Check Syntax toolbar button if you'd like to verify that your SQL code is correct. Figure 5.13 shows this step of defining the stored procedure.

FIGURE 5.13
Defining a stored procedure

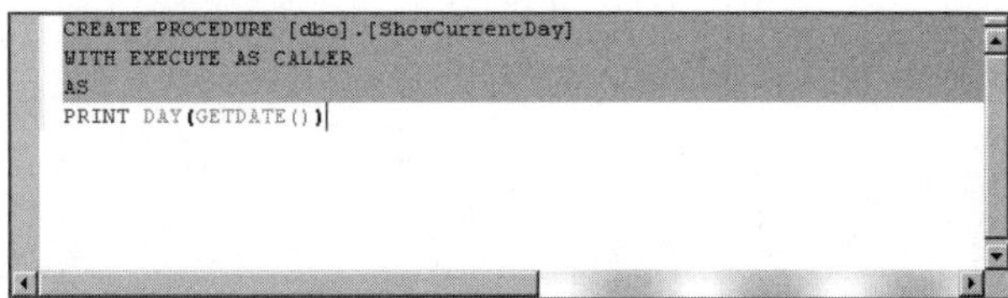

5. Click the Save button to save the stored procedure.
6. Open a new query window in the database where you created the stored procedure.
7. Type the name of the stored procedure into the query window, and execute it.

Figure 5.14 shows the results of executing the stored procedure that you just defined.

FIGURE 5.14
Results of a stored procedure

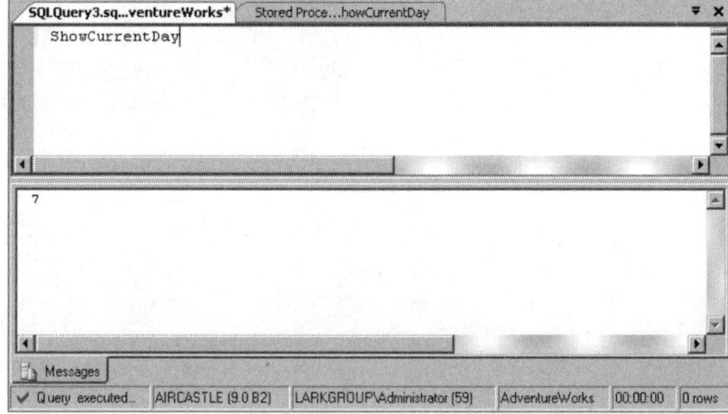

Using Command-Line Utilities

You may sometimes want to see the results of a SQL statement without any of the overhead of a graphical tool. In those cases, you can use one of the command-line utilities—`OSQL` or `SQLCMD`—to execute your SQL statement. Both tools take input as text and deliver their results to the command prompt. If you're already familiar with OSQL, feel free to keep using it; if you're learning a command line tool for the first time, we suggest starting with SQLCMD.

USING *OSQL*

Figure 5.15 shows the use of `OSQL` to retrieve the results of a query in the AdventureWorks database. Here, the `-d` argument tells `OSQL` the name of the database, the `-Q` argument contains the SQL statement to execute, and the `-E` argument specifies that `OSQL` should use Windows integrated security.

FIGURE 5.15
Using `OSQL`

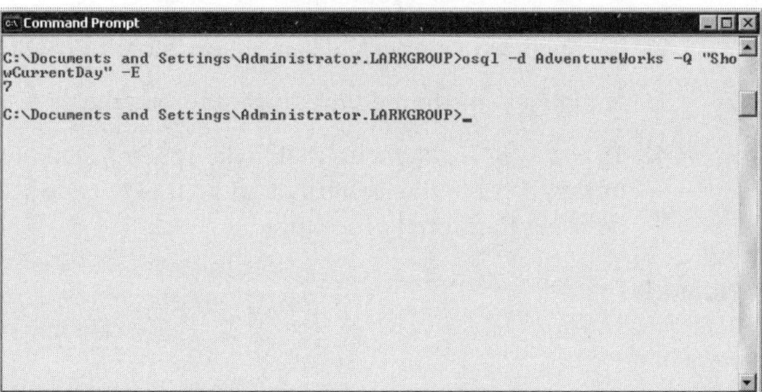

OSQL is a powerful utility, if you can remember all of its command-line options. As you can see in this example, if an option requires more information, it's supplied immediately after the argument. Table 5.10 lists all the arguments that you can use with OSQL.

TABLE 5.10: OSQL Arguments

ARGUMENT	MEANING
-a *packet_size*	Specifies the packet size to use when talking to the server. If you're sending a very long batch, you may wish to increase this from the default size of 512.
-b	Aborts the batch and returns a DOS ERRORLEVEL when an error occurs.
-c *command_terminator*	Specifies an end-of-batch marker. By default, this is GO.
-d *database*	Uses the specified database.
-D *datasourcename*	Uses the specified ODBC Data Source Name (DSN) to connect to a database. The DSN must point to a SQL Server database.
-e	Echoes input to output.
-E	Uses Windows NT integrated security.
-h *rows*	Sets the number of rows to print before repeating column headers.
-H *workstation*	Sets the workstation name to use when communicating with the server.
-I *input_file*	Designates a file containing SQL statements to execute.
-I	Sets QUOTED_IDENTIFIER ON.
-l *timeout*	Sets the number of seconds to wait for a login to complete.
-L	Lists known servers.
-m *error_level*	Sets the minimum severity error to display.
-n	Specifies that input lines aren't numbered.
-o *output_file*	Designates a file to create or overwrite with results.
-O	Disables new features so OSQL acts like the defunct ISQL utility.
-p	Prints performance statistics when the query is completed.
-P *password*	Sets the SQL Server password.
-R	Uses local client settings when displaying numbers, dates, and currency.
-q *"query"*	Executes the supplied query, but doesn't exit OSQL.
-Q *"query"*	Executes the supplied query, and immediately exits OSQL.

TABLE 5.10: OSQL Arguments *(CONTINUED)*

ARGUMENT	MEANING
`-r0`	Sends error messages to the screen even when piping results to a file.
`-s` *`separator`*	Sets a separator character to use between columns. By default, this is a blank space.
`-S` *`server`*	Sets the server with which to connect. If this isn't supplied, OSQL uses the local server.
`-t` *`timeout`*	Sets the number of seconds to wait for results before aborting a batch.
`-u`	Displays results in Unicode.
`-U` *`login_id`*	Designates the SQL Server login ID.
`-w` *`width`*	Sets the number of columns to print before wrapping output.
`-?`	Displays a syntax summary.

WARNING OSQL arguments are case-sensitive.

USING *SQLCMD*

OSQL has been around for several versions. SQL Server 2005 includes a newer utility, SQLCMD, which is destined to replace OSQL. Although there's no need to stop using OSQL if you're already familiar with it, SQLCMD is the way of the future; you should learn how to use it for new work.

Figure 5.16 shows the use of SQLCMD to retrieve the results of a query in the AdventureWorks database. Here, the -d argument tells SQLCMD the name of the database, the -Q argument contains the SQL statement to execute, and the -E argument specifies that SQLCMD should use Windows integrated security.

FIGURE 5.16
Using SQLCMD

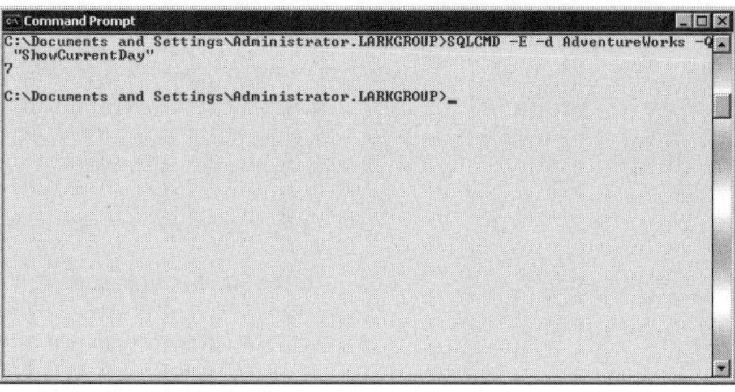

Like OSQL, SQLCMD can be customized through many command-line arguments. Table 5.11 lists all the arguments you can use with SQLCMD.

TABLE 5.11: SQLCMD Arguments

ARGUMENT	MEANING
-a *packet_size*	Specifies the packet size to use when talking to the server. If you're sending a very long batch, you may wish to increase this from the default size of 512.
-A	Logs in with a Dedicated Administrator Connection (DAC) for troubleshooting.
-b	Aborts the batch, and returns a DOS ERRORLEVEL when an error occurs.
-c *command_terminator*	Specifies an end-of-batch marker. By default, this is GO.
-d *database*	Uses the specified database.
-e	Echoes input to output.
-E	Uses Windows NT integrated security.
-f *<codepage>*	Specifies a codepage for both input and output.
-h *rows*	Sets the number of rows to print before repeating column headers.
-H *workstation*	Sets the workstation name to use when communicating with the server.
-i *input_file*	Designates a file containing SQL statements to execute.
-I	Sets QUOTED_IDENTIFIER ON.
-k	Removes control characters from the output.
-l *timeout*	Sets the number of seconds to wait for a login to complete.
-L	Lists known servers.
-m *error_level*	Sets the minimum severity error to display.
-o *output_file*	Designates a file to create or overwrite with results.
-p	Prints performance statistics when the query is completed.
-P *password*	Sets the SQL Server password.
-q *"query"*	Executes the supplied query, but doesn't exit SQLCMD.
-Q *"query"*	Executes the supplied query, and immediately exits SQLCMD.
-r0	Sends error messages to the screen even when piping results to a file.

TABLE 5.11: SQLCMD Arguments *(CONTINUED)*

ARGUMENT	MEANING
`-R`	Uses local client settings when displaying numbers, dates, and currency.
`-s` *`separator`*	Sets a separator character to use between columns. By default, this is a blank space.
`-S` *`server`*	Sets the server with which to connect. If this isn't supplied, `SQLCMD` uses the local server.
`-t` *`timeout`*	Sets the number of seconds to wait for results before aborting a batch.
`-u`	Displays results in Unicode.
`-U` *`login_id`*	Designates the SQL Server login ID.
`-v` *`var="value"`*	Create a variable that can be used in the script.
`-V`	Sets the minimum security level for error reporting.
`-w` *`width`*	Sets the number of columns to print before wrapping output.
`-W`	Removes trailing spaces from a column.
`-X`	Disables commands that can compromise system security when run from a batch file.
`-y, -Y`	Limits the number of characters used for wide columns.
`-?`	Displays a syntax summary.

WARNING SQLCMD arguments are case-sensitive.

The `SQLCMD` utility uses the .NET OLEDB provider to do its work, whereas `OSQL` uses older libraries. This may occasionally result in different results from the two utilities.

Summary

This chapter has introduced you to the basics of the Transact-SQL programming language, which is the native language of SQL Server. You learned about SQL standards and compatibility, and how to configure SQL Server for various levels of compatibility. You've also seen T-SQL datatypes and functions, as well as some of the tools that will let you execute T-SQL batches.

Now it's time to move on to the most important statement in the SQL language, the `SELECT` statement. The `SELECT` statement is used to retrieve data from database tables, and it's both complex and flexible. You'll learn about this powerful statement in the next chapter.

Chapter 6

SELECT Queries

You now have the knowledge you need to create databases and fill them with data, but that knowledge is useless without the ability to pull that data back out in a meaningful fashion, a fashion that is well-organized and easy to read. To do this, you must understand the SELECT statement and its various options.

In this chapter, we'll discuss the various ways that you can get your data from one or more tables by using joins. We'll also look at how to limit the data that is returned by using the WHERE clause. Once you have the data you want, we'll show you how to organize it by using such clauses as GROUP BY, HAVING, TOP *N*, ROLLUP, CUBE, and OVER.

After SELECT queries are mastered, we'll move into Full-Text Search, a marvelous tool for searching through massive amounts of text with accuracy. We'll also show you how to make all this happen when the data spans more than one server by using linked server queries. Finally, we'll look at the new XML querying capabilities in SQL Server 2005. So hold on, it's going to be quite a ride.

Using Basic *SELECT* Queries

As we already mentioned, SELECT queries are the primary method for reading the data that is stored in your tables. These queries can be very complex (as you'll soon see) or very simple. The simplest of SELECT queries is one that pulls all the data out of a table and displays it in no particular order. In fact, let's take a gander at such a query—the following example displays all the records in the Person.Contact table of the AdventureWorks database, which is a test database that comes with SQL Server and contains information about production and sales in a hypothetical company:

1. Open SQL Server Management Studio in the Microsoft SQL Server 2005 group in Programs on the Start menu.
2. Connect using Windows Authentication.
3. Click the New Query toolbar button on the Standard toolbar, and select New SQL Server Query from the drop-down list that the button displays.
4. Type the following code:

```
USE AdventureWorks
SELECT * FROM Person.Contact
```

TIP All the table names in the AdventureWorks database contain a period as part of their name. Thus Person.Contact is the name of a single table. To be more precise, Person is the schema and Contact is the name of the table, but you may find it simpler to think of Person.Contact as the full name of the table.

5. Click the Execute toolbar button on the SQL Editor toolbar or press F5 to execute. You should see the results shown in Figure 6.1.

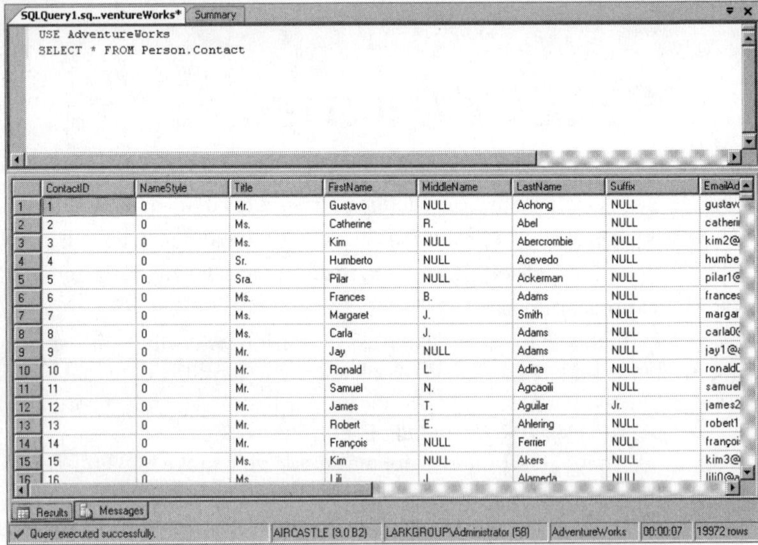

FIGURE 6.1
`SELECT * FROM Person.Contact` is a basic SELECT query.

NOTE Throughout this chapter, we'll be querying the AdventureWorks databases. This database was created by Microsoft expressly for you to experiment with and test out your SQL skill set. You'll need to do a full installation of SQL Server to get the sample databases; they're not included in the default installation.

This query returns every single record and every single column from the Person.Contact table. That would be fine if you really needed to see all this information, but that is seldom the case. It's recommended that you don't use such queries regularly because they cause SQL Server to perform a table scan. A *table scan* occurs when SQL Server must read every record of your table to return a result set, which can create a strain on your server. It's much better to limit the information returned by the SELECT query to just the data you need to see. The first bit of information to limit is the number of columns that are returned in your result set. The next set of steps shows you how to limit the number of columns that are returned by a SELECT query by adding a list of columns to the query:

1. Open another new SQL Server query window, or reuse the one that you already have open.
2. Enter the following code:

```
USE AdventureWorks
SELECT FirstName, LastName, Phone
FROM Person.Contact
```

3. Click the Execute toolbar button or press F5 to execute. You should see the results shown in Figure 6.2.

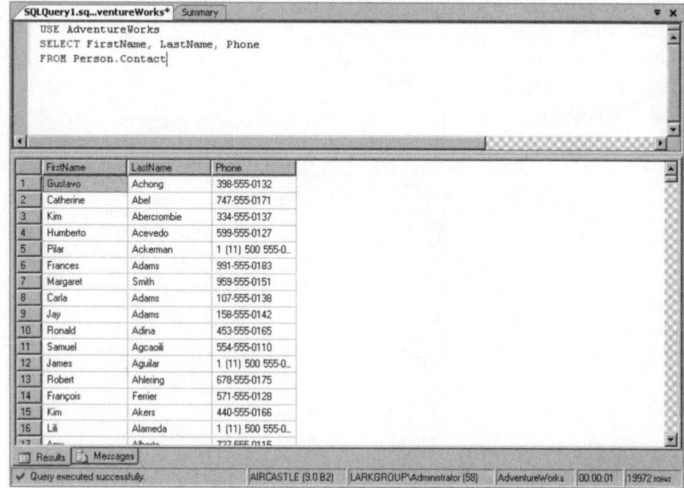

FIGURE 6.2
Limiting the columns returned by SELECT can make your result sets easier to read.

Compare the result set from Figure 6.2 with the result set in Figure 6.1, and notice the difference. This time you listed the columns that you wanted to see: FirstName, LastName, and Phone. Because you supplied a list of columns, the SELECT statement returned only the information from the columns listed. Now you're making progress, but you still have too much information because you're still retrieving every record in the table—nearly 20,000 of them! You can limit the number of records that are returned by employing the `WHERE` clause.

NOTE You can also limit the number of records with the `TABLESAMPLE` clause. This clause allows you to return a random selection of records from the result set, and it's most useful for testing your work without waiting for large result sets. For example, you can get back a random 10 rows with `SELECT * FROM Person.Contact TABLESAMPLE (10 ROWS)` or a random 10 percent of the results with `SELECT * FROM Person.Contact TABLESAMPLE (10 PERCENT)`.

Limiting Records with the *WHERE* Clause

Now that you know how to limit the number of columns returned by the `SELECT` query, you need to learn how to limit the number of records returned; you probably don't need to see all of them. By using the `WHERE` clause with a `SELECT` query, you can restrict the number of records that are returned by instructing SQL to return only records that meet certain criteria. For example, suppose that you want to see only contacts with a last name of White. By using the `WHERE` clause, you can instruct SQL to return only those records. Let's try that clause here:

1. Open another new SQL Server query window, or reuse the one that you already have open.
2. Enter the following code:

```
USE AdventureWorks
SELECT FirstName, LastName, Phone
FROM Person.Contact
WHERE LastName = 'White'
```

3. Click the Execute toolbar button or press F5 to execute. You should see the results shown in Figure 6.3.

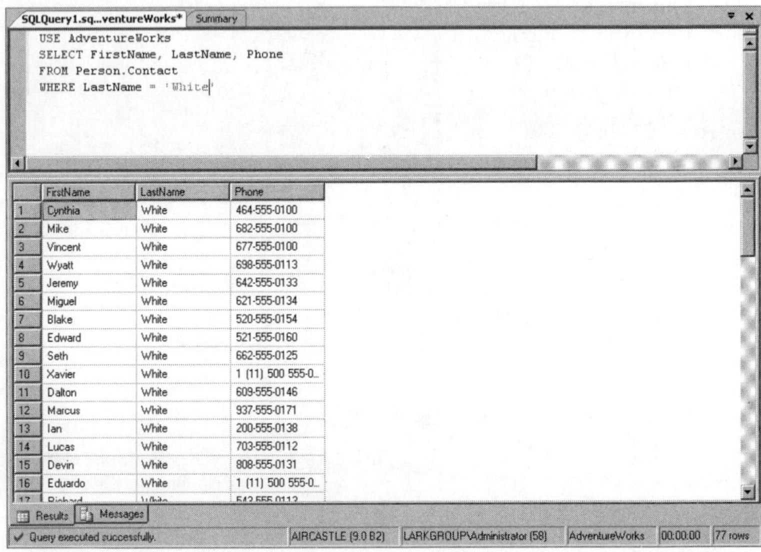

FIGURE 6.3
Use the WHERE clause to limit the number of records returned by a SELECT query.

You should have only the 77 records in the result set shown in Figure 6.3, the records in which `LastName = 'White'`. By using the WHERE clause, you restricted the number of records to only the records you wanted to see. Now let's get a little fancier with the WHERE clause. This time, you're going to find everyone except the Whites:

1. Open another new SQL Server query window, or reuse the one that you already have open.
2. Enter the following code:

```
USE AdventureWorks
SELECT FirstName, LastName, Phone
FROM Person.Contact
WHERE LastName <> 'White'
```

3. Click the Execute toolbar button or press F5 to execute. You should see the results shown in Figure 6.4.

Scroll through that result set (as shown in Figure 6.4), and see whether you can find anyone with a last name of White. They're not there, are they? That is because you threw in the <> operator, which means *not equal*. Essentially, you told SQL Server to return every record where the LastName field was not equal to White, and that is exactly what happened.

What if you need to base your query on more than one column? Suppose, for instance, that you need to find Brandon Foster, but you have more than one contact with the last name of Foster in the database. If you base your search on only the last-name column, you'll return all the Fosters in the database, which isn't a very clean solution. If you need to base your query on more than one column (first and last name, for example), you need to use the AND clause. In the next example, you'll first verify that there is more than one Foster in the database by basing your search on a single column (LastName) and then narrow the search by searching on two columns (FirstName and LastName) using the AND clause:

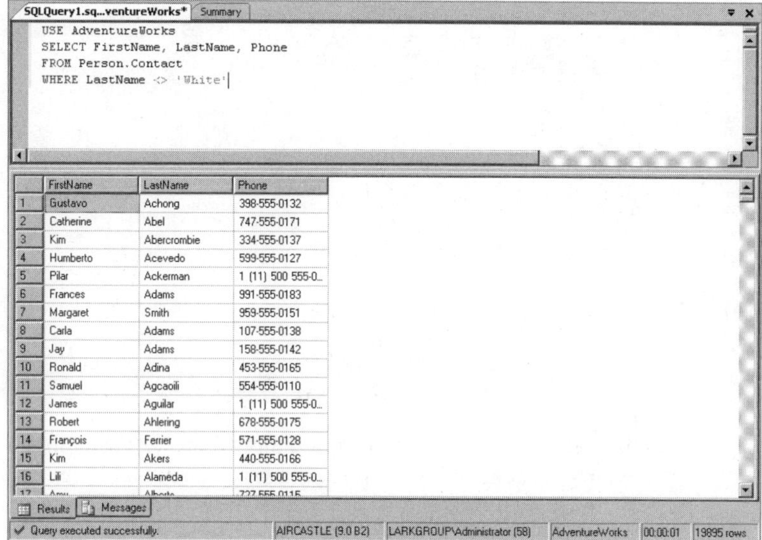

FIGURE 6.4
The <> (not equal) operator with the WHERE clause can be used to further refine a SELECT query.

1. Open another new SQL Server query window, or reuse the one that you already have open.
2. Enter the following code:

```
USE AdventureWorks
SELECT FirstName, LastName, Phone
FROM Person.Contact
WHERE LastName = 'Foster'
```

3. Click the Execute toolbar button or press F5 to execute—notice that you get 113 records in the result set.
4. Execute the following code to restrict the result set even further:

```
USE AdventureWorks
SELECT FirstName, LastName, Phone
FROM Person.Contact
WHERE LastName = 'Foster' AND FirstName = 'Brandon'
```

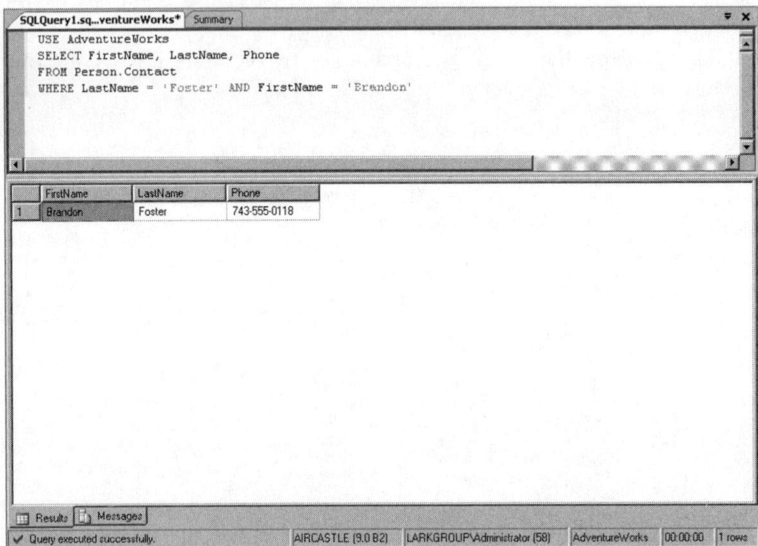

In the first query listed, you found more than one Foster in the database. Because you were interested in only Brandon, you were able to screen out all of the unwanted records by combining the first- and last-name columns in your search by using the `AND` clause. But wait, it gets better.

How many times have you forgotten the exact spelling of someone's last name? That happens to most of us and can cause problems with querying. Because the operators you've been working with thus far (<> and =) require exact spelling for the search criteria, you'd need to remember the exact spelling. If you can't remember the exact spelling, but you can remember small sections (starts with *St*, for instance), you can use the `LIKE` operator to fill in the blanks.

The `LIKE` operator works with wildcard characters that are used to fill in the characters that you don't remember. The % wildcard character can be used to fill in any number of characters and can be used anywhere in the clause. For example, if you use the % wildcard at the front (`%st`), your query will retrieve any values that end in *ST*, no matter how many characters are in front of the *ST*. You can also place the wildcards at the front and back (`%st%`) and return values that have *ST* anywhere in them. You also have the underscore (_) character, which is used to replace a single character in the value. For instance, if you search for ST_, your query will return *STY* and *STU*, but not *STIE*: The latter has four characters, and you're specifically searching for three character values starting with *ST*.

In the following example, you'll specifically search for anything that begins with *ST* to demonstrate the power of the `LIKE` operator:

1. Open another new SQL Server query window, or reuse the one that you already have open.
2. Enter the following code:

```
USE AdventureWorks
SELECT FirstName, LastName, Phone
FROM Person.Contact
WHERE LastName LIKE 'ST%'
```

3. Click the Execute toolbar button or press F5 to execute—notice that you get 141 records in the result set (see Figure 6.5).

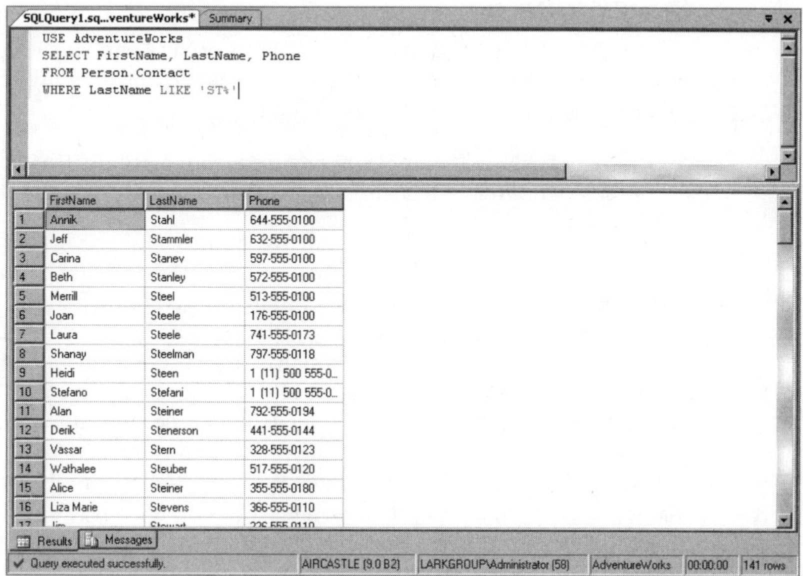

FIGURE 6.5
Use the LIKE operator when you can't remember the spelling of a word.

When you look at the result set, as shown in Figure 6.5, notice that many records were returned. All the names in the LastName field of the result set start with *ST* because you used the LIKE operator to return anyone whose last name starts with *ST*; the rest of the characters (represented by the % symbol) in the value could be anything else.

You now know how to read data from a single table at a time. Because most databases are made up of several tables, you also need to know how to pull data out of more than one table at a time and turn the subsequent result set into something meaningful. To work this miracle, you must understand joins.

Using Joins

Databases usually consist of more than one table, with these tables related in some way. A good example might be a human resources database in which you have a salary table, an employee information table, a sick days and vacation days table, and so on. In such a database, you may need to pull information from more than one table at a time so that the result set makes sense. If you want to know, for example, which employees have used more than 15 sick days, you need information from the sick days table and the employee information table in the same result set. A situation like this calls for the use of *joins*, which are used to extract data from more than one table at a time and display the information in a single result set. There are several types of joins, the simplest of which is the INNER JOIN.

NOTE If you're wondering why you don't just store all your information in a single table and retrieve it that way, you may want to read Chapter 4 ("Database Design and Normalization"), which discusses the need to break down your data as much as possible—a concept called *normalization*.

NOTE The AdventureWorks sample database includes nearly 70 tables.

INNER JOINs

An INNER JOIN (referred to also as a JOIN) is used as part of a SELECT statement to return a single result set from multiple tables. The JOIN is used to link (or join) tables on a common column and return records that match in those columns.

NOTE An INNER JOIN can also be referred to as an EQUI-JOIN because it returns an equal number of records from each table in the JOIN. For simplicity's sake, we'll refer to these as JOINs.

The AdventureWorks database demonstrates why you need to use joins. The HumanResources.Employee table in the AdventureWorks database contains the accumulated vacation hours for each employee (in the VacationHours column) and the ID of the employee's department (in the DepartmentID column). The HumanResources.Department table contains information on the departments in the company, such as department name and the department group name. If you need to see the amount of vacation accumulated for each department, you can use a standard SELECT query to return the records from the HumanResources.Employee table and count them by DepartmentID. Then you need to extract all the records from the HumanResources.Department table to match the DepartmentID in the first result set to the department name contained in the HumanResources.Department table, which is time-consuming and messy.

Because you want to see the department name in the result set instead of a cryptic department number, you need to join the HumanResources.Employee table to the HumanResources.Department table where the department names are kept. By joining these two tables on the DepartmentID column, you'll be able to return only records that have a match between the two tables. This means that if a department in the HumanResources.Department table doesn't show up in the HumanResources.Employee table (because no employees are assigned to that department), the department won't appear in the result set. Not only that, but you'll see the department names instead of the department ID. Take a look:

1. If it's not already open, open SQL Server Management Studio, and log in with Windows Authentication.

2. Execute the following query to return data from the HumanResources.Employee and HumanResources.Department tables:

```
USE AdventureWorks
SELECT HumanResources.Employee.VacationHours,
  HumanResources.Employee.LoginID,
  HumanResources.Department.Name
FROM HumanResources.Employee
INNER JOIN HumanResources.Department
ON HumanResources.Employee.DepartmentID =
HumanResources.Department.DepartmentID
```

3. You should see the results shown in Figure 6.6.

Looking through the result set in Figure 6.6, notice that you extracted all the records in the HumanResources.Employee table that had a matching record in the HumanResources.Department table based on the DepartmentID column. This means that SQL Server looked at the DepartmentID column of each record in the HumanResources.Employee table and compared it to the DepartmentID column of the HumanResources.Department table. When SQL Server found a match between the two, the record was added to the result set. For example, the first employee in the Production department has 21 accumulated vacation hours. If a department didn't have any employees, it wouldn't have a record in the

HumanResources.Employee table and therefore wouldn't be displayed in the result set, because only records that match between the tables are shown. If you need to see a listing of every department, whether it has employees or not, you need to use an `OUTER JOIN`.

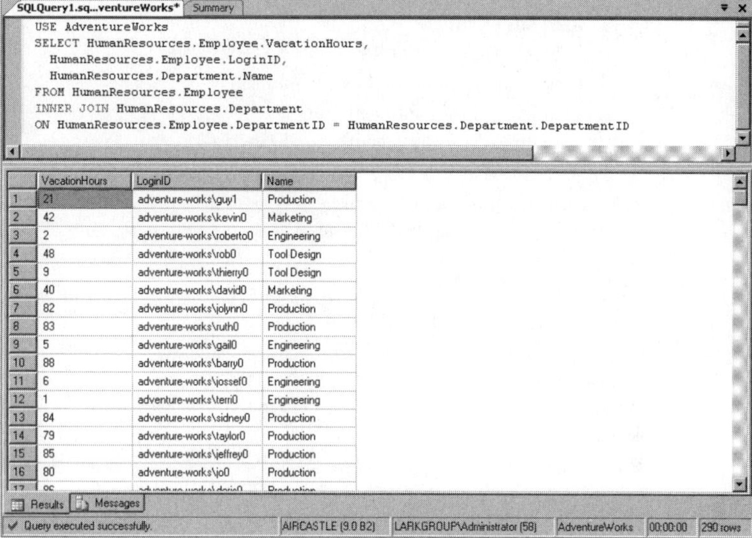

FIGURE 6.6
Joining two tables can make result sets easier to read.

OUTER JOINs

There are three types of `OUTER JOINs`. You use a `RIGHT OUTER JOIN` (usually shortened to `RIGHT JOIN`) if you need to see all the records from the table on the right-most side of the `JOIN` clause, whether or not they have a matching record in the left table. To see all the records in the left-most table, regardless of whether they match records in the right-most table, you use a `LEFT OUTER JOIN` (or `LEFT JOIN`). If you need to see all the records from both the left and the right tables, whether or not they have a corresponding record in the other table, you use a `FULL OUTER JOIN` (or `OUTER JOIN`). In the previous example, to see a listing of all the departments, whether or not they have employees with vacation time, you need to use a `RIGHT JOIN`, which returns of the records from the table on the right of the `JOIN` clause. Let's demonstrate by running the same query as last time, but this time displaying all the departments in the HumanResources.Department table regardless of whether they have any employees:

1. Add the `RIGHT JOIN` to the query from the last exercise so it looks as follows:

```
USE AdventureWorks
SELECT HumanResources.Employee.VacationHours,
  HumanResources.Employee.LoginID,
  HumanResources.Department.Name
FROM HumanResources.Employee
RIGHT JOIN HumanResources.Department
ON HumanResources.Employee.DepartmentID =
HumanResources.Department.DepartmentID
```

2. At first glance, it looks like nothing's changed (if you run the query, you'll still get 290 rows back). So, add a record to the HumanResources.Department table without adding a matching record to the HumanResources.Employees table, by executing the following in a new query window:

```
USE AdventureWorks
INSERT INTO HumanResources.Department
(Name, GroupName, ModifiedDate)
VALUES ('Loss Prevention',
'Inventory Management', GETDATE())
```

3. Execute the query from step 1 again, and notice the Loss Prevention department. You should see it in the result set, as shown in Figure 6.7.

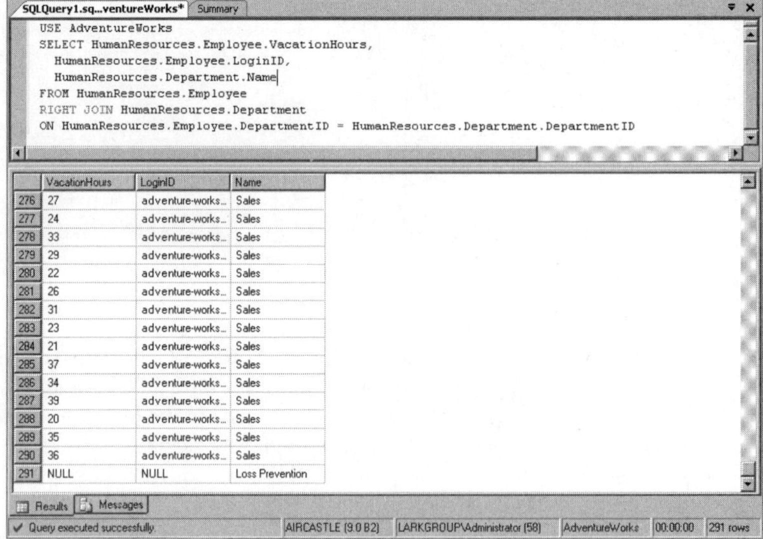

FIGURE 6.7
Using a `RIGHT JOIN` displays all the records from the table on the right of the `JOIN` clause.

NOTE For a complete discussion of the `INSERT` statement, please refer to Chapter 7, "Action Queries."

In the query from step 1, you should not notice a change, because all the departments in the HumanResources.Department table have matching records in the HumanResources.Employee table. That is why you add the Loss Prevention record in step 2; it has no matching record in the HumanResources.Employee table, meaning that the Loss Prevention department has no employees. After you add the new record to the HumanResources.Department table and run the query again, you should see Loss Prevention appear with null values in the VacationHours and LoginID columns. Those null values mean that there are no matching records in the left table (HumanResources.Employee), but the records from the right table (HumanResources.Department) were returned anyway.

So far, you've seen only department names associated with LoginIDs, such as adventure-works\guy1 working in Production. Although it's helpful to see the LoginID, it would be much more helpful to see the department name and the employee name (instead of a LoginID). To get the names of the employees as well as the names of the departments where they work, you need to involve the table where the employee names are stored, and that means adding another join.

Joining Multiple Tables

In this next query, we want to see the names of the employees as well as the names of the departments where those employees work. To display employee names instead of their cryptic IDs, you need to access the Person.Contact table where the employee names are stored. Because the HumanResources.Employee table has a ContactID column and the Person.Contact table has a matching ContactID column, you can join the two tables on the ContactID column. To get the department name, you'll join the HumanResources.Employee table and the HumanResources.Department table on the DepartmentID column again. With these JOINs in place, you should see the names of the employees followed by the names of the departments and the amount of accumulated vacation time for each employee:

1. In SQL Server Management Studio, execute the following query to join the three tables:

```
USE AdventureWorks
SELECT Person.Contact.FirstName, Person.Contact.LastName,
  HumanResources.Department.Name,
  HumanResources.Employee.VacationHours
FROM HumanResources.Employee
INNER JOIN HumanResources.Department
ON HumanResources.Employee.DepartmentID =
HumanResources.Department.DepartmentID
INNER JOIN Person.Contact
ON HumanResources.Employee.ContactID = Person.Contact.ContactID
```

2. You should see the result set shown in Figure 6.8.

Notice what the second JOIN did? The nondescript LoginIDs you saw before have been replaced by employee names, making the result set much easier to read. You still have a problem, though: All of the result sets you've looked at so far have been random—there is no order to them—so it's hard to find a specific record. Let's now look at some methods for lending order to your result sets so that they read more like an organized report instead of a random jumble of information.

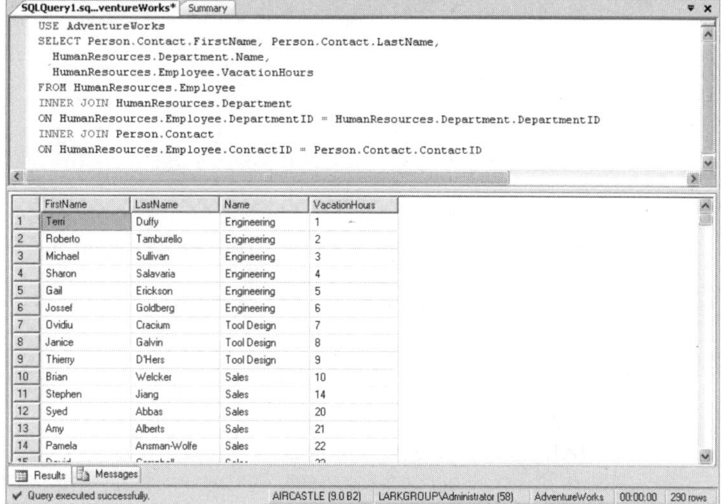

FIGURE 6.8
Joining more than two tables can further refine your queries.

Turning Result Sets into Reports

If you've ever been to a wedding, funeral, or fancy party, you've probably seen a guest book in which everyone signs their name. To find a specific name in that guest book, you have to search every single line of every page. A default result set from SQL Server works the same way: It has no order, so you're forced to look through every line of the result set to find a specific record. This is tedious, but unlike the guest book from the party, you can organize the result set so that it's easier to read. There are several tools at your disposal to accomplish this organization, starting with `ORDER BY`.

WARNING You may notice apparent order in some result sets even without `ORDER BY`. Any such order is a side effect of the way that SQL Server processed the particular query, and such behavior isn't guaranteed to stay dependable from release to release. Always use `ORDER BY` if you want to ensure a particular order.

Using *ORDER BY*

`ORDER BY` does exactly what its name implies: It organizes your result set on the column(s) that you specify. Using the last example of departments, employees, and vacation hours, you probably noticed that there was no real order to the result set. Using `ORDER BY`, you can organize the result set based on the department name or the number of vacation hours, or even by the employee's first name. To demonstrate how this works, organize the result set from the previous queries based on which employee has the most accumulated vacation time by using `ORDER BY` on the HumanResources.Employee table's VacationHours column:

1. If you aren't in SQL Server Management Studio, open it and log in using Windows Authentication.
2. Execute the following query, and notice that the result set is random:

```
USE AdventureWorks
SELECT Person.Contact.FirstName, Person.Contact.LastName,
  HumanResources.Department.Name,
  HumanResources.Employee.VacationHours
FROM HumanResources.Employee
INNER JOIN HumanResources.Department
ON HumanResources.Employee.DepartmentID =
HumanResources.Department.DepartmentID
INNER JOIN Person.Contact
ON HumanResources.Employee.ContactID = Person.Contact.ContactID
```

3. Add the `ORDER BY` clause on the end, and look at the results (as shown in Figure 6.9):

```
USE AdventureWorks
SELECT Person.Contact.FirstName, Person.Contact.LastName,
  HumanResources.Department.Name,
  HumanResources.Employee.VacationHours
FROM HumanResources.Employee
INNER JOIN HumanResources.Department
ON HumanResources.Employee.DepartmentID =
HumanResources.Department.DepartmentID
INNER JOIN Person.Contact
ON HumanResources.Employee.ContactID = Person.Contact.ContactID
ORDER BY HumanResources.Employee.VacationHours
```

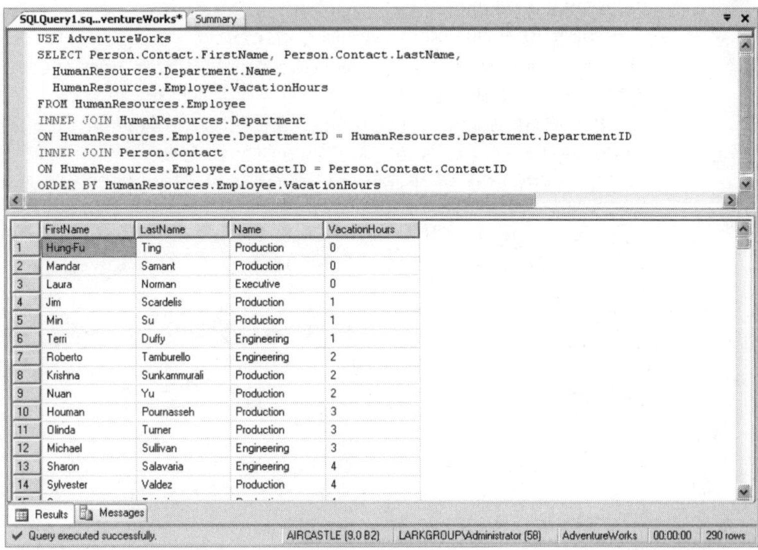

FIGURE 6.9
Using ORDER BY can bring organization to your result sets.

Notice that the result set in Figure 6.9 is now organized, with the lowest values in the VacationHours column at the top of the result set. If it's more useful to you to see the highest numbers at the top of the list instead of the lowest, use the DESC clause (short for *DESCending*) with ORDER BY to reverse the order of the result set. With DESC, higher numbers, such as 100, are at the top of the list, and lower numbers, such as 1, are at the bottom. The letter *Z* is at the top, and *A* is at the bottom. Overall, you'll see higher values at the top of the result set instead of lower ones. The DESC clause is used at the end of the ORDER BY clause, as shown here:

```
USE AdventureWorks
SELECT Person.Contact.FirstName, Person.Contact.LastName,
  HumanResources.Department.Name,
  HumanResources.Employee.VacationHours
FROM HumanResources.Employee
INNER JOIN HumanResources.Department
ON HumanResources.Employee.DepartmentID = HumanResources.Department.DepartmentID
INNER JOIN Person.Contact
ON HumanResources.Employee.ContactID = Person.Contact.ContactID
ORDER BY HumanResources.Employee.VacationHours DESC
```

NOTE There's also a corresponding ASC clause, to force an ascending sort, but because this is the default you never need to specify ASC.

As mentioned, you can use the ORDER BY clause with more than one column to make your results even easier to read. For example, if you want to see the higher quantities of vacation hours first, organized by department, you can enter the following:

```
USE AdventureWorks
SELECT Person.Contact.FirstName, Person.Contact.LastName,
  HumanResources.Department.Name,
  HumanResources.Employee.VacationHours
```

```
FROM HumanResources.Employee
INNER JOIN HumanResources.Department
ON HumanResources.Employee.DepartmentID = HumanResources.Department.DepartmentID
INNER JOIN Person.Contact
ON HumanResources.Employee.ContactID = Person.Contact.ContactID
ORDER BY HumanResources.Department.Name,
  HumanResources.Employee.VacationHours DESC
```

Notice in Figure 6.10 that the departments are listed in alphabetical order, and the vacation hours in each department are listed from highest to lowest.

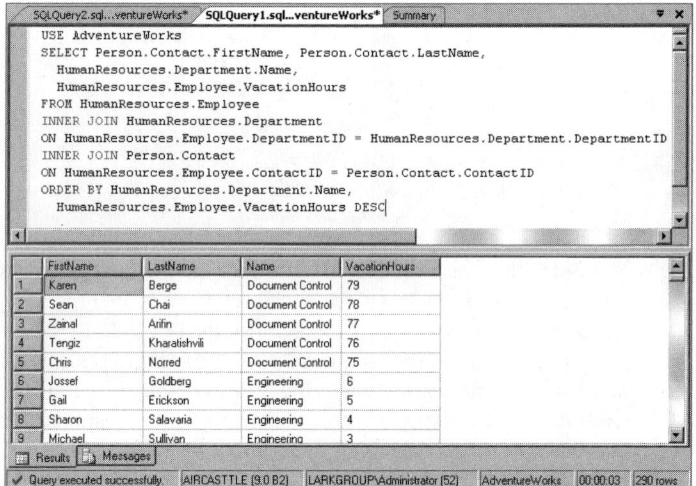

FIGURE 6.10
ORDER BY can be used on more than one column.

ORDER BY can be a powerful ally in the fight against disorder, but it still may not be enough. Many reports require summaries as well as order. Using HAVING and GROUP BY can provide these summaries. In the next section, you'll see how to use these clauses.

Using *GROUP BY* and *HAVING*

Quite often, it's desirable not only to organize your reports in an alphabetical or numeric order but also to see summary information with the report. In your queries so far, you've seen the number of vacation hours for each employee and organized that report based on who has the most hours. You would have to use GROUP BY if you needed to know the total number of vacation hours for each department. GROUP BY gives you that summary at the end of the report when it's used in conjunction with an aggregate function. *Aggregate functions* provide a summary value of some sort, such as an average or total of all the values in a column.

To get a better understanding of what GROUP BY does, let's look at an example. In this query, you'll provide a summary of the number of accumulated vacation hours for each department by grouping on the department name:

1. Open SQL Server Management Studio, if you aren't already there, and log in using Windows Authentication.

2. Execute the following query, and notice that there is no easy way to tell how many hours are charged to each department:

```
USE AdventureWorks
SELECT HumanResources.Department.Name,
  HumanResources.Employee.VacationHours
  AS TotalVacation
FROM HumanResources.Employee
INNER JOIN HumanResources.Department
ON HumanResources.Employee.DepartmentID =
HumanResources.Department.DepartmentID
```

3. Add the SUM function and GROUP BY clause to organize the result set. You should see the same results as those in Figure 6.11:

```
USE AdventureWorks
SELECT HumanResources.Department.Name,
  SUM(HumanResources.Employee.VacationHours)
  AS TotalVacation
FROM HumanResources.Employee
INNER JOIN HumanResources.Department
ON HumanResources.Employee.DepartmentID =
HumanResources.Department.DepartmentID
GROUP BY HumanResources.Department.Name
```

In the first query, you select the department names and the number of vacation hours using a column alias (TotalVacation) to refer to the VacationHours column. Like a nickname, a *column alias* (introduced by the AS keyword) is just a means to reference a column using a different name; it's the easiest way to reference long column names or *summarized columns* (columns on which you've used an aggregate function). This first query has no real order, so in the second query, you made some changes.

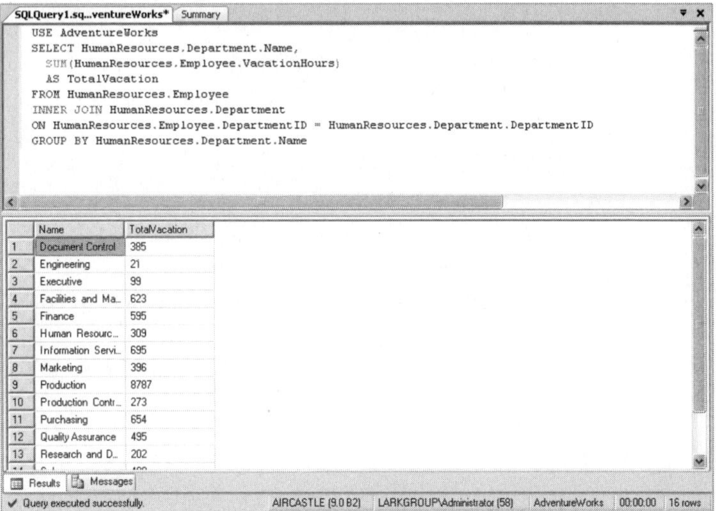

FIGURE 6.11 GROUP BY is used to give summary information with a result set.

First, you used the aggregate function SUM to add the values in the VacationHours column. If you left it alone, SUM would add every value in the entire column; but you only wanted it to add the values for each department and give a summary of how many hours are charged to each department, which is why you added GROUP BY. By using GROUP BY, you made sure the values were added for each individual department and reported back. You can think of this as creating a pigeonhole for each department, sorting the records into those pigeonholes, and then taking a sum of the records in each pigeonhole in turn. Now you know how many hours belong to each department. For instance, Marketing has 396 vacation hours, total. However, what if you're interested only in departments with more than 500 vacation hours outstanding? That is where the HAVING clause comes in.

HAVING works a great deal like the WHERE clause you used earlier, but the big difference is that HAVING can use aggregate functions, and WHERE can't. This means you can tell the SELECT query to add up all the values in a column and then, with the HAVING clause, display only those summarized values that have the value in which you're interested. Let's use an example to explain. Here you'll use HAVING to generate a result set of all departments with more than 500 vacation hours:

1. Let's prove that a WHERE clause can't use aggregate functions. In SQL Server Management Studio, try to execute the following code, and notice the error:

```
USE AdventureWorks
SELECT HumanResources.Department.Name,
  SUM(HumanResources.Employee.VacationHours)
  AS TotalVacation
FROM HumanResources.Employee
INNER JOIN HumanResources.Department
ON HumanResources.Employee.DepartmentID =
HumanResources.Department.DepartmentID
WHERE SUM(HumanResources.Employee.VacationHours) > 500
GROUP BY HumanResources.Department.Name
```

2. Change your code to use the HAVING clause, and execute it:

```
USE AdventureWorks
SELECT HumanResources.Department.Name,
  SUM(HumanResources.Employee.VacationHours)
  AS TotalVacation
FROM HumanResources.Employee
INNER JOIN HumanResources.Department
ON HumanResources.Employee.DepartmentID =
HumanResources.Department.DepartmentID
GROUP BY HumanResources.Department.Name
HAVING SUM(HumanResources.Employee.VacationHours) > 500
```

Notice that you get all departments that have over 500 vacation hours, as shown in Figure 6.12.

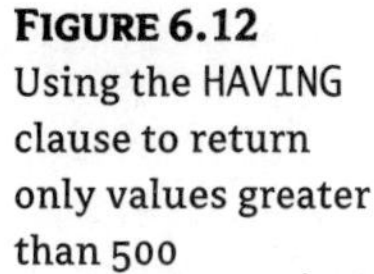

FIGURE 6.12
Using the HAVING clause to return only values greater than 500

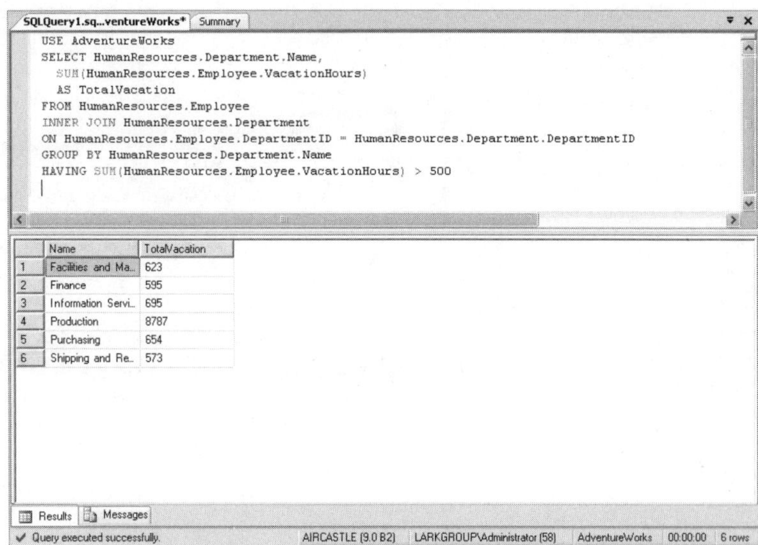

3. Let's see how WHERE and HAVING can work together by restricting your query even further with a WHERE clause. Notice that only records for Finance and Production are returned (as shown in Figure 6.13):

```
USE AdventureWorks
SELECT HumanResources.Department.Name,
  SUM(HumanResources.Employee.VacationHours)
  AS TotalVacation
FROM HumanResources.Employee
INNER JOIN HumanResources.Department
ON HumanResources.Employee.DepartmentID =
HumanResources.Department.DepartmentID
WHERE HumanResources.Department.Name IN ('Finance', 'Production')
GROUP BY HumanResources.Department.Name
HAVING SUM(HumanResources.Employee.VacationHours) > 500
```

Notice what you did with this last series of steps. First, you proved beyond a shadow of a doubt that the WHERE clause can't use aggregate functions and therefore can't be used to display summarized information.

Next, you invoked HAVING, with its ability to use aggregate functions, to limit what was returned with the GROUP BY clause. Specifically, you instructed the HAVING clause to scan what the GROUP BY clause returned and filter out everything that had a value lower than 500 in the TotalVacation column.

Finally, you combined the powers of WHERE and HAVING. You limited what the SELECT portion of the statement returned by using WHERE. Then, using HAVING, you were able to further restrict what GROUP BY returned.

FIGURE 6.13
Combining HAVING and WHERE

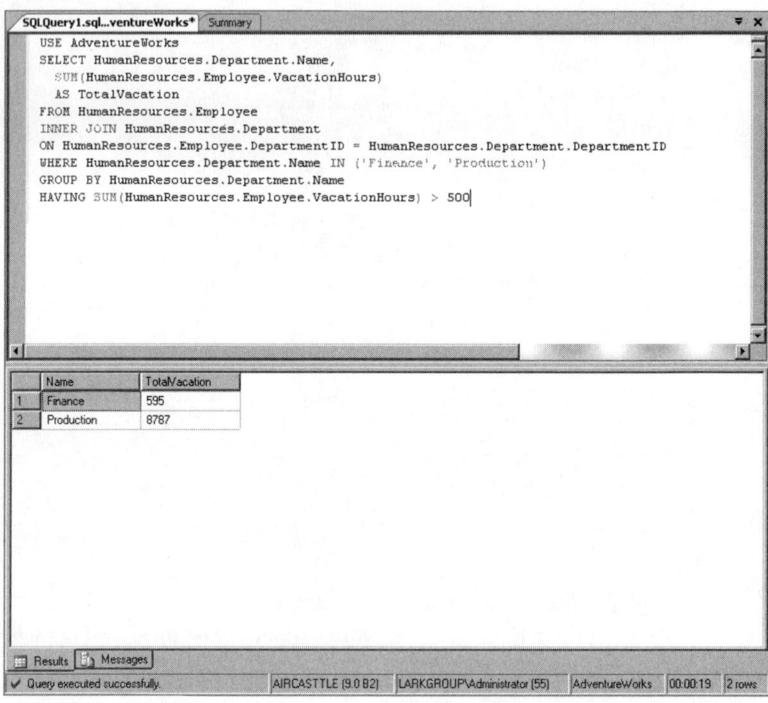

These clauses can be powerful tools for reporting purposes, but you may need even more. Many times, you may require detailed information in your reports rather than just summaries, which is why we have ROLLUP and CUBE.

Using *ROLLUP*

In the queries you've been using so far, you've seen summary information telling you how many total vacation hours each department has accumulated. Many times, though, it's helpful to see not only the summary of hours, but also detailed information about exactly how many hours have been accumulated by each employee. Then you'll know that the Finance department has 595 hours total set aside, and you can see a breakout telling you what makes up that 595-hour total. To get such detail in your reports, you need to use ROLLUP, which is specially designed to give details as well as summary information. Look at the following series of steps, and notice the level of detail as you use ROLLUP:

1. In SQL Server Management Studio, execute the following code to get summary information on hours. Notice that there is no detail:

```
USE AdventureWorks
SELECT HumanResources.Department.Name,
  SUM(HumanResources.Employee.VacationHours)
  AS TotalVacation
FROM HumanResources.Employee
INNER JOIN HumanResources.Department
```

```
ON HumanResources.Employee.DepartmentID =
HumanResources.Department.DepartmentID
GROUP BY HumanResources.Department.Name
ORDER BY HumanResources.Department.Name
```

2. Add detail to your report by adding `ROLLUP`. Notice the extra rows in the result set, as shown in Figure 6.14:

```
USE AdventureWorks
SELECT HumanResources.Department.Name,
  Person.Contact.LastName,
  SUM(HumanResources.Employee.VacationHours)
  AS TotalVacation
FROM HumanResources.Employee
INNER JOIN HumanResources.Department
ON HumanResources.Employee.DepartmentID =
HumanResources.Department.DepartmentID
INNER JOIN Person.Contact
ON HumanResources.Employee.ContactID = Person.Contact.ContactID
GROUP BY HumanResources.Department.Name, Person.Contact.LastName
WITH ROLLUP
ORDER BY HumanResources.Department.Name, Person.Contact.LastName
```

Looking at the result set in Figure 6.14, you'll notice that the first row of the result set has NULL values for the Name and LastName columns and a value of 14678 for the TotalVacation column. That first row is a grand total for all departments, meaning that all departments have a total of 14,678 accumulated vacation hours combined.

FIGURE 6.14
ROLLUP displays detailed information with your summary.

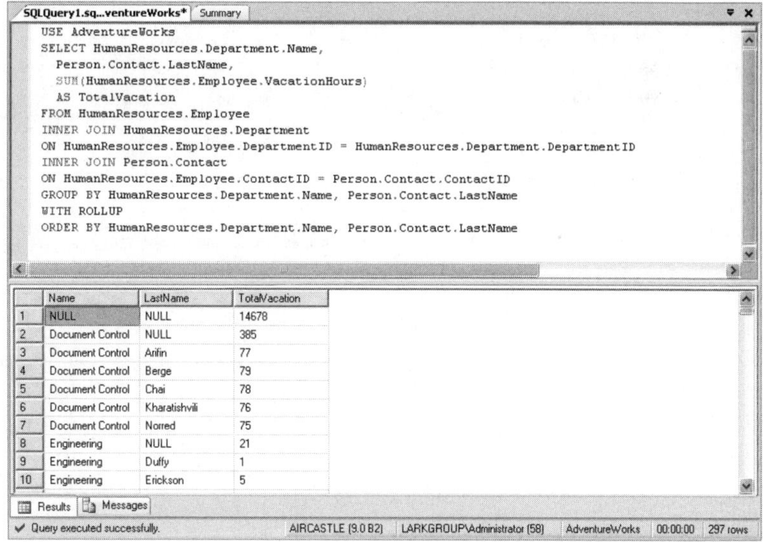

Just below the grand total, notice Document Control in the Name column, NULL in the LastName column, and 385 in the TotalVacation column. This row is summary information for Document Control, meaning that Document Control has accumulated 385 hours total.

Just below the summary information for Document Control, you start running into the detailed information about employees in the Document Control department. Notice that Arifin has accumulated 77 hours and Berge 79 hours, for example. As you traverse the list, you should notice that each department has a summary row at the top (signified by a NULL value in the Name column) and detailed information lower in the list. If you require still more detail, you can use CUBE.

Using *CUBE* and *GROUPING*

Suppose that you need to see the total number of hours for all departments, the total number of hours for each department, and the total hours for each employee regardless of department. In an instance such as this, you need to use CUBE. The CUBE operator is designed to give you summary information on every possible column combination in the result set. To get a better idea of what this means, execute the following code in SQL Server Management Studio (also see Figure 6.15):

```
USE AdventureWorks
SELECT HumanResources.Department.Name,
  Person.Contact.LastName,
  SUM(HumanResources.Employee.VacationHours)
  AS TotalVacation
FROM HumanResources.Employee
INNER JOIN HumanResources.Department
ON HumanResources.Employee.DepartmentID = HumanResources.Department.DepartmentID
INNER JOIN Person.Contact
ON HumanResources.Employee.ContactID = Person.Contact.ContactID
GROUP BY HumanResources.Department.Name, Person.Contact.LastName
WITH CUBE
ORDER BY HumanResources.Department.Name, Person.Contact.LastName
```

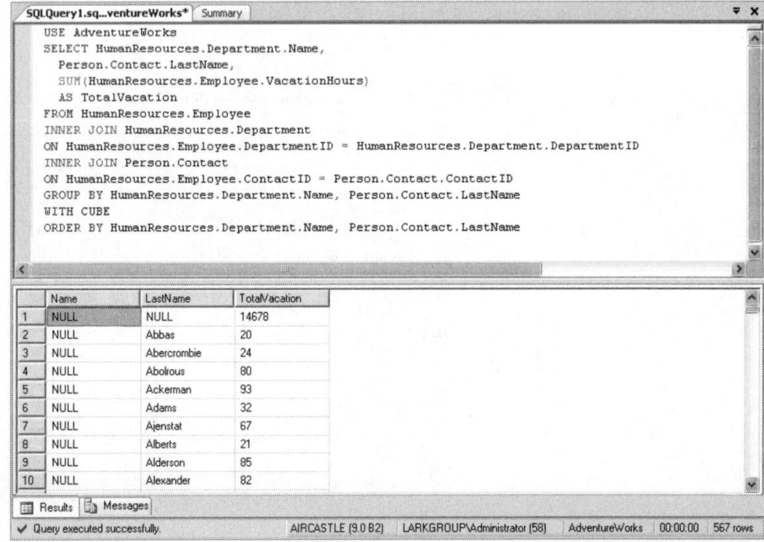

FIGURE 6.15
Using CUBE to display summary information on every possible column combination

Look at all those extra records in the result set (as shown in Figure 6.15). The top record, with NULL in the first two columns and 14678 in TotalVacation, is the grand total for all employees and departments, just like it was with ROLLUP. The big difference is that you have more summaries now. Look at the second row in the result set—the one that has NULL in the first column, Abbas in the second column, and 20 in TotalVacation. That row is a summary of how many hours have been allotted to any employee with the last name Abbas in any department.

Those extra summaries at the top can come in very handy when you need the detailed information—but it's a little difficult to tell which is summary and which is detailed information at first glance. GROUPING can make this task easier. The GROUPING operator, when used with either CUBE or ROLLUP, is used to insert extra columns to indicate whether the preceding column is a detail (a value of zero) or a summary (a value of one). Executing the following code should help you visualize this a little better (also see Figure 6.16):

```
USE AdventureWorks
SELECT HumanResources.Department.Name,
  GROUPING(HumanResources.Department.Name),
  Person.Contact.LastName,
  GROUPING(Person.Contact.LastName),
  SUM(HumanResources.Employee.VacationHours)
  AS TotalVacation
FROM HumanResources.Employee
INNER JOIN HumanResources.Department
ON HumanResources.Employee.DepartmentID = HumanResources.Department.DepartmentID
INNER JOIN Person.Contact
ON HumanResources.Employee.ContactID = Person.Contact.ContactID
GROUP BY HumanResources.Department.Name, Person.Contact.LastName
WITH CUBE
ORDER BY HumanResources.Department.Name, Person.Contact.LastName
```

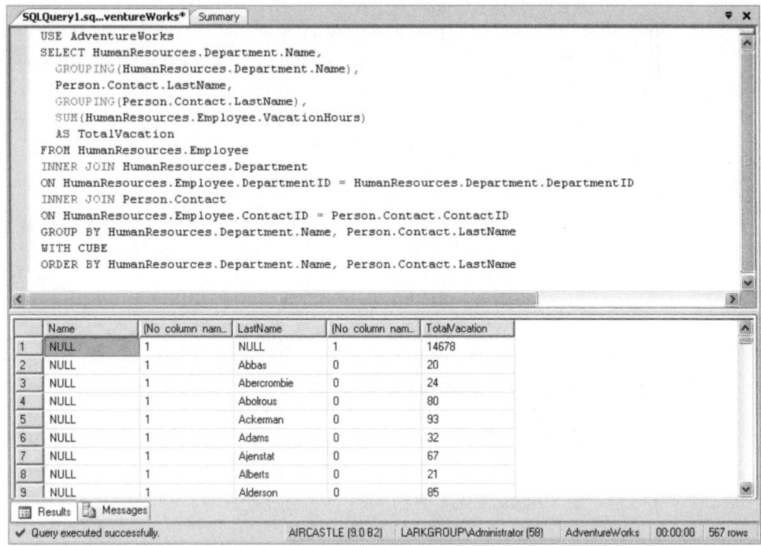

FIGURE 6.16
Using GROUPING to differentiate between detailed and summary information in your result set

The result set shown in Figure 6.16 includes two extra columns full of ones and zeros. The ones indicate summary information, and the zeros represent detailed information. Look at the top row in the result set, and notice that the second and fourth columns both contain ones. This means that the first and third columns contain summary information. The second row has a one in the second column and a zero in the fourth column, which tells you that this is a summary of the third column—that is, the total number of hours for Abbas.

It's easy to see that GROUPING, when combined with either ROLLUP or CUBE, can get you detailed reports. The only drawback is that these reports can be difficult to decipher, especially if you keep forgetting which value means detail and which means summary. In some cases, you may be able to extract the information that you need with a much simpler tool, the TOP *N* query.

NOTE For more powerful CUBE calculation abilities, including the ability to rearrange grouping levels on the fly, you should investigate SQL Server Analysis Services. You'll learn more about this in Chapter 26.

NOTE In addition to ROLLUP and CUBE, you can also use COMPUTE and COMPUTE BY to create result sets with summaries. These keywords produce summaries at the bottom of the result set, rather than interleaved. However, because they aren't ANSI compliant, Microsoft is discouraging the use of these keywords. You can read more in SQL Server Books Online.

Using *TOP N* and *TOP N%*

A common request from sales departments is a report that displays the top percentage of sellers in the company so that bonuses can be handed out. Another common need is to see the top percentage of products that are being sold so that inventory can be kept up. Perhaps the human resources department needs to see the top percentage of employees who use up all their sick days. All these reports could be generated with clauses and statements such as GROUP BY and HAVING, but then you'd see all the records involved, not just the top percentage of those records. If you're looking for only, say, the top 5 percent of something, or the top 5 values, you need to use the TOP *N* clause.

The *N* in TOP *N* is a placeholder for a number. When you replace it with a 5, for example, you can retrieve the top 5 of whatever you're looking for. Alternatively, you can use 5 percent to retrieve the top 5 percent of the records, however many records that comes to. TOP *N* by itself provides no organization, though; it simply looks through the tables and pulls out whatever it can find. That is why you should combine TOP *N* with ORDER BY. When you organize the result set with ORDER BY, you can see a real representation of the top percentage of what you need. Look at the following example, which retrieves the top 10 most popular products sold by AdventureWorks (also see Figure 6.17):

1. If you aren't in SQL Server Management Studio, open it, and log in using Windows Authentication.

2. Execute the following:

```
USE AdventureWorks
SELECT TOP 10 Production.Product.Name,
  SUM(Sales.SalesOrderDetail.OrderQty)
FROM Production.Product
INNER JOIN Sales.SalesOrderDetail
ON Production.Product.ProductID =
  Sales.SalesOrderDetail.ProductID
GROUP BY Production.Product.Name
ORDER BY SUM(Sales.SalesOrderDetail.OrderQty) DESC
```

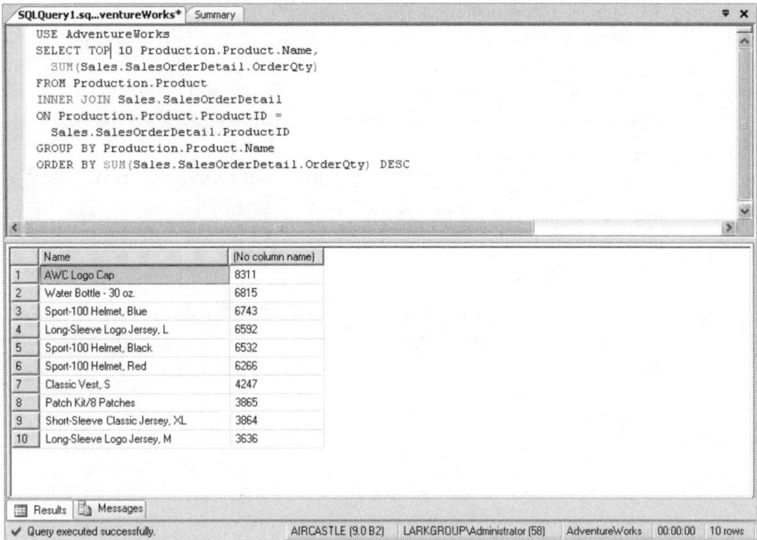

FIGURE 6.17
Use TOP N to return the top records from a query.

Notice in the result set from this query, as shown in Figure 6.17, that you now know the top 10 of all products sold based on quantity. You have to throw DESC (descending order) into the clause, because without it, you'll see the lowest 10—the lowest numbers show up at the top of the result set by default, so SQL Server will start at one and worked its way up. To get the top 10 percent instead of the top 10, modify the TOP clause slightly:

```
USE AdventureWorks
SELECT TOP 10 PERCENT Production.Product.Name,
  SUM(Sales.SalesOrderDetail.OrderQty)
FROM Production.Product
INNER JOIN Sales.SalesOrderDetail
ON Production.Product.ProductID =
  Sales.SalesOrderDetail.ProductID
GROUP BY Production.Product.Name
ORDER BY SUM(Sales.SalesOrderDetail.OrderQty) DESC
```

There is just one small potential problem with the TOP 10 query. Notice that the last record in the result set shows that 3,636 long-sleeve logo jerseys have been sold. The problem is that other products might also have sold the same amount. If there is a tie with the last value in the result set, SQL Server doesn't show it. You asked for 10 records, you got 10 records. If you want to see ties with the last value in the result set, you need to use the WITH TIES clause, as follows:

```
USE AdventureWorks
SELECT TOP 10 WITH TIES Production.Product.Name,
  SUM(Sales.SalesOrderDetail.OrderQty)
FROM Production.Product
INNER JOIN Sales.SalesOrderDetail
ON Production.Product.ProductID =
  Sales.SalesOrderDetail.ProductID
GROUP BY Production.Product.Name
ORDER BY SUM(Sales.SalesOrderDetail.OrderQty) DESC
```

NOTE In this particular example, WITH TIES has no effect because there's not a tie for the tenth position.

Using WITH TIES, you see every record that has the same value as the last record of the result set. This is an excellent way to give a quick report on the top percentage of a quantity without leaving out the last-place contestants.

You might also want to know just where in a set of rows a particular record lies. That's the purpose of the OVER clause, which is new with SQL Server 2005.

Using *OVER*

Suppose you want to sort the orders made by a particular customer by quantity, and then number the rows. You could do this by hand, of course, but now there's an easier way: You can use the RANK function together with the OVER clause:

1. If you aren't in SQL Server Management Studio, open it, and log in using Windows Authentication.
2. Execute the following (Figure 6.18 shows the results):

```
USE AdventureWorks
SELECT Sales.SalesOrderHeader.CustomerID,
  Production.Product.Name,
  Sales.SalesOrderDetail.OrderQty,
  RANK() OVER (PARTITION BY Sales.SalesOrderHeader.CustomerID
    ORDER BY Sales.SalesOrderDetail.OrderQty DESC) as Rank
FROM Production.Product
INNER JOIN Sales.SalesOrderDetail
ON Production.Product.ProductID =
  Sales.SalesOrderDetail.ProductID
INNER JOIN Sales.SalesOrderHeader
ON Sales.SalesOrderDetail.SalesOrderID =
  Sales.SalesOrderHeader.SalesOrderID
WHERE Sales.SalesOrderHeader.CustomerID = 697
ORDER BY OrderQty DESC
```

The RANK function is used to generate ranking numbers for a result set. For each row, it returns the number of rows that are higher in the result set. The OVER clause tells SQL server how to partition the result set for ranking purposes. In this case, you tell it to do the ranking for each customer separately and to use OrderQty to generate the ranks. In Figure 6.18, we used a WHERE clause to limit the results to records for a single customer, so that you can see clearly what's going on. For example, the most popular product (Full-Finger Gloves, L) is given a rank of 1 for this customer. Notice that two products have a rank of 5, because they're tied on quantity; the next product has a rank of 7 because there are 6 products ahead of it.

Figure 6.19 shows the same query without the WHERE clause.

Now the result set includes all customers, but the rank for each customer is calculated separately. For example, the Classic Vest is given rank 1 for customer 302, even though other rows are higher in the overall result set, because it's the highest row for that particular customer.

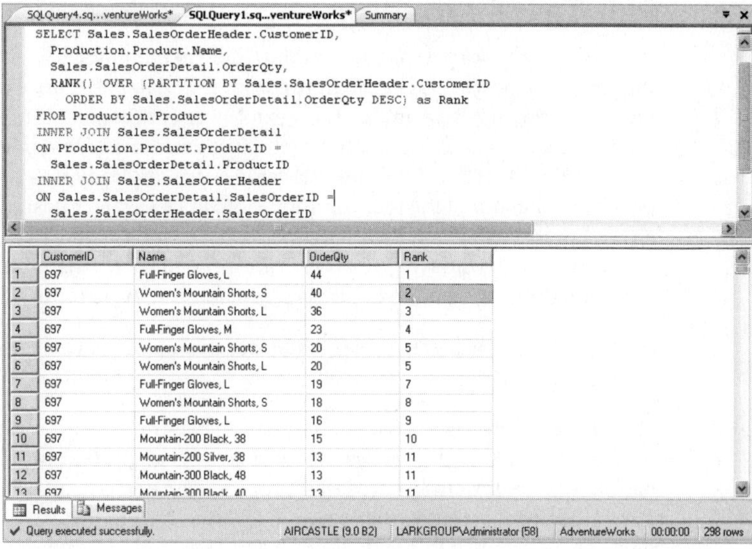

FIGURE 6.18
Using RANK and OVER to display the rank for results

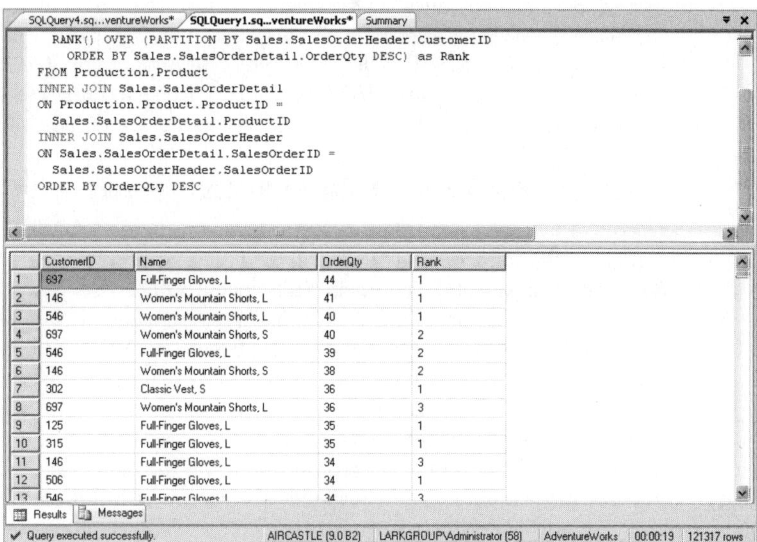

FIGURE 6.19
Using RANK and OVER with a partitioned result set

These SELECT queries and all the various associated clauses can get you almost any data that you require from your database in a variety of formats, but they still have a limitation. SELECT queries don't work well with columns of the text datatype, because these columns can contain huge amounts of text. If you need to find something in a text column, you need Full-Text Search capability.

Full-Text Searching

People generally stored small amounts of data in their tables when databases first came into use. As time went on, however, people figured out that databases are excellent containers for all sorts of data, including massive amounts of text. Many companies store entire libraries of corporate documents in their databases. To store such large amounts of text in a database, the text datatype was formulated. When this datatype first came out, everybody was still using standard SELECT queries to pull the data out of the text columns, but SELECT wasn't designed to handle such large amounts of text. For instance, if you want to find a phrase somewhere in the text column, SELECT can't do it. Or if you want to find two words that are close to each other in the text, SELECT falls short. That is why something else had to be devised, something more robust. Enter Full-Text Search.

TIP In this version of SQL Server, text has been replaced by varchar(max), but the same principles continue to apply.

Full-Text Search is a completely separate program that runs as a service. Windows supplies a service called the Microsoft Search Service (MSSearch) that can be used to index all sorts of information from most of the Microsoft server (or even non-Microsoft) products. For example, Full-Text Search can index an entire mailbox in Exchange 2003 to make it easier to find text in your mail messages. To accomplish this task, Full-Text Search runs as a separate service in the background from which the server products can request data.

SQL Server 2005 builds on the MSSearch service by installing its own service, MSFTESQL. The MSFTESQL service is automatically installed with SQL Server; it supplies SQL Server–specific searching services. MSFTESQL is completely independent of MSSearch, so changes to the MSSearch service don't affect SQL Server full-text searching. Thus, when you perform one of these full-text searches, you're telling SQL Server to make a request of the MSFTESQL service.

Installing and Configuring Full-Text Search

Of course, before you can start using the awesome power of Full-Text Search, you need to install and configure it. The easiest way to install the Full-Text Search engine is to perform a custom install and select it as one of the components to install. Otherwise, you can use the Add Or Remove Programs applet in Control Panel to add it to your SQL Server installation.

After the short task of installation has been completed, you're ready to configure Full-Text Search for use. The first thing you need to do is create a full-text index. Full-text indexes are created with SQL Server tools, such as SQL Server Management Studio, but they're maintained by the MSFTESQL service and stored on the disk as files separate from the database. To keep the full-text indexes organized, they're stored in catalogs in the database. You can create as many catalogs as you like in your databases to organize your indexes, but these catalogs can't span databases.

When a full-text index is first created, it's useless. Because these indexes are maintained by the MSFTESQL service, you must specifically instruct the service to fill the index with information about the text fields that you want to search. This filling of the full-text indexes is called *populating* the index. As your data changes over time, you'll need to tell the search service to rebuild your full-text indexes to match your data—a process called *repopulating*.

In the following steps, you'll create a catalog and index for the Production.ProductDescription table in the AdventureWorks database. We chose this table because it has a varchar column with some lengthy text. Here's how to create the index and catalog:

1. If you're not already in SQL Server Management Studio, log in using Windows Authentication. Then, run this query to create the catalog for the AdventureWorks database:

```
USE AdventureWorks
CREATE FULLTEXT CATALOG AdventureWorks_FullText
```

2. Expand the Object Explorer tree, and locate the Production.ProductDescription table. Right-click the table, and select Full-Text Index ➤ Define Full-Text Index.

3. On the first screen of the Full-Text Indexing Wizard, click Next.

4. Each table on which you create a full-text index must already have a unique index associated with it in order for full-text to work. In this instance, select the default PK_Product Description_ProductDescriptionID index, and click Next.

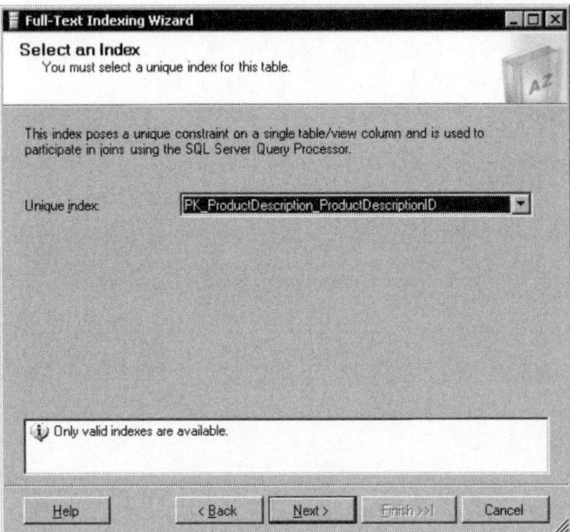

5. On the next screen, you're asked which column you want to full-text index. Because Description is your varchar column, select it by checking the box next to it. You can also specify a language to be used when determining word roots. Click Next.

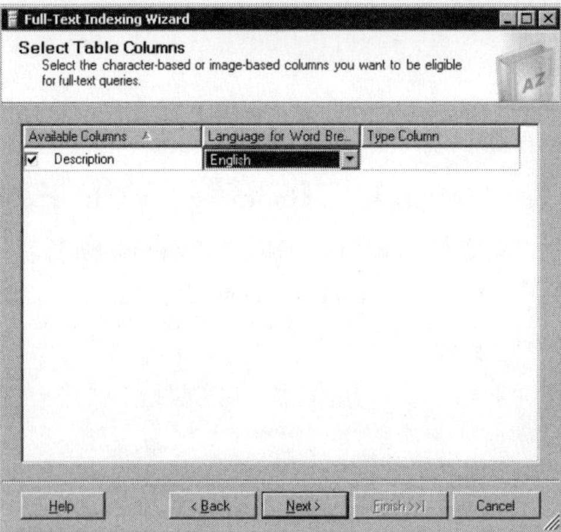

6. On the next screen, you can choose between automatic and manual change tracking. This controls whether the index will be updated for you whenever the data changes, or whether you need to repopulate it manually. Choose the default Automatic setting, and click Next.

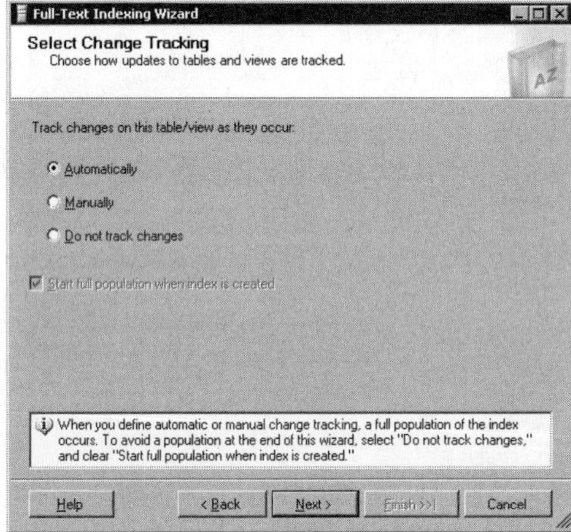

7. On the next screen, you're asked in which catalog you would like to store this new index. Select the AdventureWorks_FullText catalog, and click Next. If you hadn't already created the catalog using SQL, you could create it here.

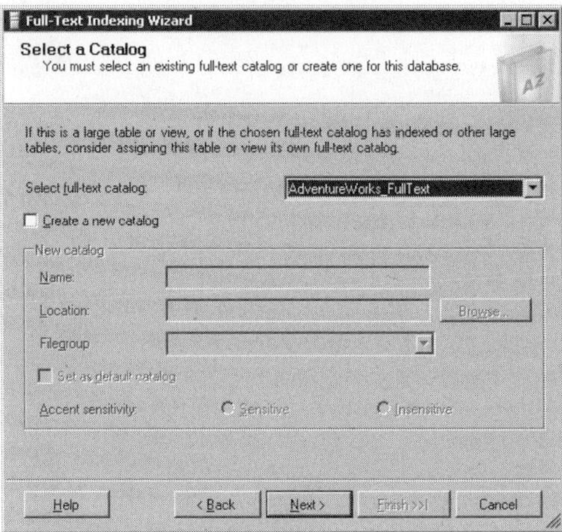

8. On the next screen, you're asked to create a schedule for automatically repopulating the full-text index. If your data is frequently updated, you'll want to do this more often, maybe once a day. If it's read more often than it's changed, you should repopulate less frequently. You can schedule population for a single table or an entire catalog at a time. In this case, set repopulation to happen just once for the entire catalog by clicking the New Catalog Schedule button.

9. In the New Full-Text Indexing Catalog Schedule dialog box, enter **Populate AdventureWorks**. Change the Schedule Type to Recurring, and click OK.

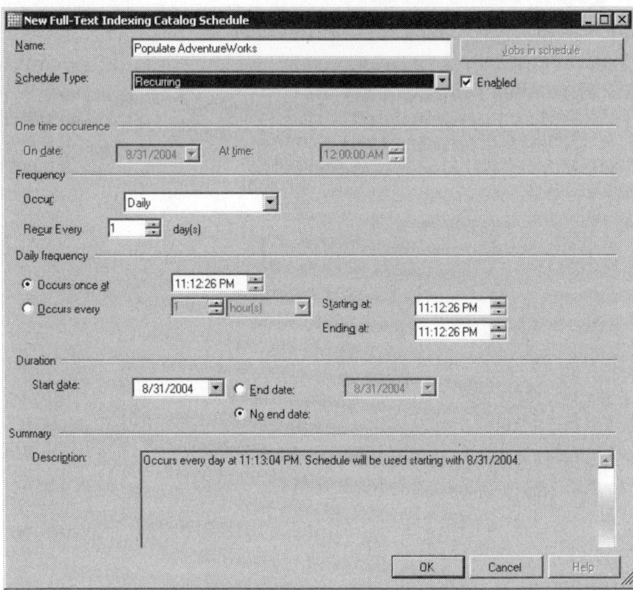

10. When you're taken back to the Full-Text Indexing Wizard, click Next.

11. On the final screen of the wizard, you're given a summary of the choices you've made. Click Finish to create the index.

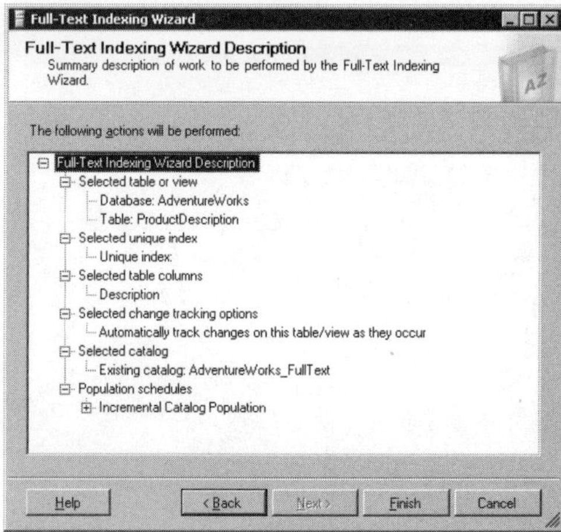

To use your new full-text index, you'll need to populate it for the first time. To do so, right-click the Production.ProductDescription table in Object Browser again, and select Full-Text Index ➤ Start Full Population. SQL Server will display a progress dialog box while it creates the index for the first time.

With a new, fully populated full-text index in place, you're ready to unleash the power of the full-text search. To do that, you need to know how to modify your `SELECT` query to work with the MSFTESQL service that scans your new index. Let's look at some new clauses for full-text search.

Performing Full-Text Searches

The nice thing about performing a full-text search is that you already know how to do it, or at least you're very close. Full-text searches are just `SELECT` queries that use full-text operators. Four operators are used to search a full-text index:

CONTAINS* and *CONTAINSTABLE These can be used to get exact or not-so-exact words or phrases from text columns. Not-so-exact means that if you look for *cook*, you can also find *cooks*, *cooked*, *cooking*, and so on.

FREETEXT* and *FREETEXTTABLE These are less precise than `CONTAINS`; they return the meaning of phrases in the search string. For example, if you search for the string "SQL is a database server", you'll receive results containing the words *SQL*, *database*, *server*, and any derivative thereof.

The difference between `CONTAINS`/`FREETEXT` and `CONTAINSTABLE`/`FREETEXTTABLE` is that the latter don't return a normal result set. Instead, they create a new table for you to search through. These operators are generally used in complex queries that require you to join the original table with the newly created table that came from the `CONTAINSTABLE`/`FREETEXTTABLE` query.

To see how to use the `CONTAINS`/`FREETEXT` operators, let's execute some queries:

1. Open SQL Server Management Studio, and log in using Windows Authentication.

2. Execute the following query:

```
USE AdventureWorks
SELECT DESCRIPTION FROM Production.ProductDescription
WHERE CONTAINS (Description, 'Aluminum')
```

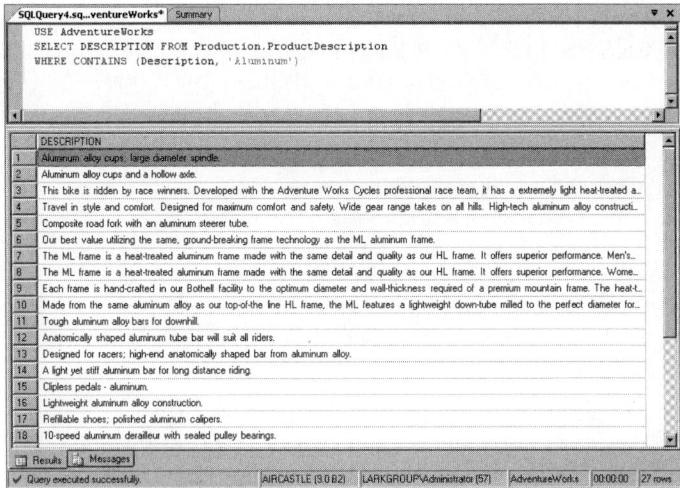

3. In the result set, notice that each record returned contains the word *Aluminum*. Now execute the following code to test FREETEXT:

```
USE AdventureWorks
SELECT DESCRIPTION FROM Production.ProductDescription
WHERE FREETEXT (Description, 'Aluminum wheels')
```

4. In the result set, notice that each record contains either *Aluminum* or *wheels* in some form.

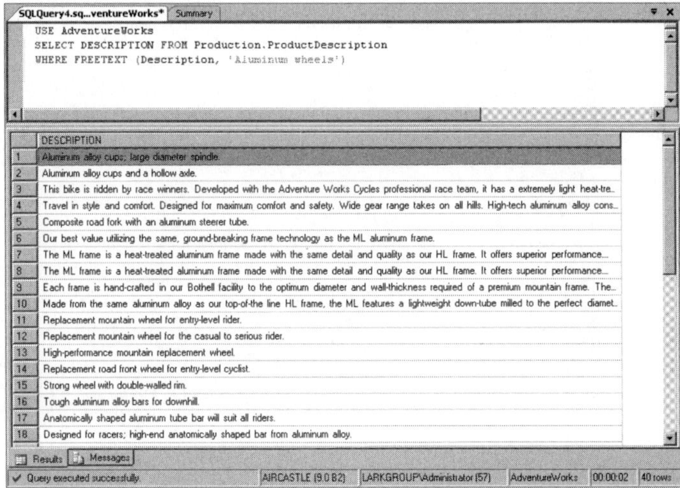

The FREETEXTTABLE and CONTAINSTABLE operators function quite a bit differently from their counterparts. These two operators look through the full-text indexes and create a brand-new table with two columns: key and rank. The key column tells you the record number of the record that matches your query; so, if record number 3 in the queried table matches your query, the key column would contain the value 3. The rank column tells you how closely the record matches your query: 1000 indicates an exact match, and 1 indicates a low chance of a match. You can use the new table that is created by FREETEXTTABLE in a JOIN to see how closely each record in your table matches your query. For example, if you want to know which of the company's products feature mountain wheels, you can use the following query (also see Figure 6.20):

```
USE AdventureWorks
SELECT new.[key], new.rank,
Production.ProductDescription.Description
FROM Production.ProductDescription
INNER JOIN
FREETEXTTABLE(Production.ProductDescription, Description,
  'mountain wheels') AS new
ON Production.ProductDescription.ProductDescriptionID = new.[key]
ORDER BY new.rank DESC
```

Let's examine the result set that comes from this query, as displayed in Figure 6.20. First you told SQL to select the key and rank columns from the table that the FREETEXTTABLE operator creates. The key column tells you the primary key of the matching record, and the rank column tells you how closely that record matches. Look at the first record: The key is 686, which means that the primary key is 686. The rank column value is 243—this is the highest matching record in the table. Now read the Description column, and notice that it has the phrase *mountain wheel*. As you proceed through the result set, the records are worse and worse matches for the search phrase.

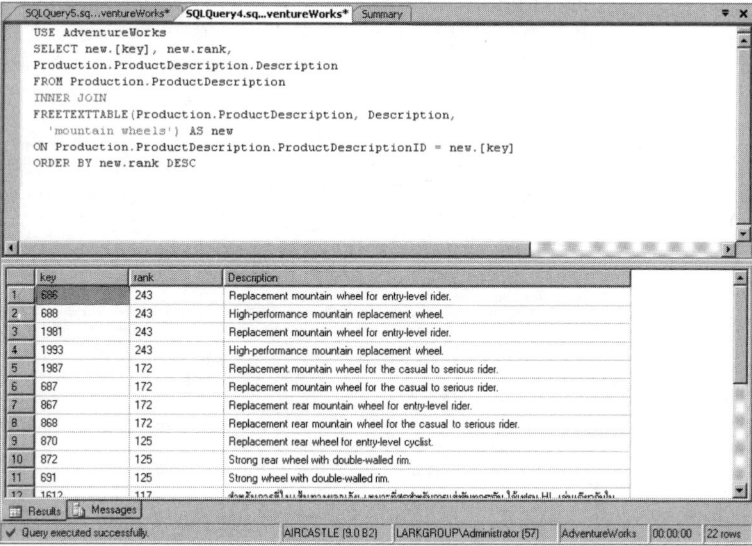

FIGURE 6.20
FREETEXTTABLE generates a new table with a rank column.

TIP You can use other tricks with full-text searches, including looking for inflectional word forms and words near other words. See the SQL Server Books Online topic "Full-Text Search Queries" for details.

These full-text search queries can be very powerful tools for locating data in large text columns, but they're valueless if you don't maintain them. Let's see what it takes to administer your new-found indexes.

Administering Full-Text Search

There isn't a lot of work involved in administering Full-Text Search. The most important thing to remember is the repopulation of the full-text indexes, and that can be scheduled when you first create the catalog. However, if you underestimate the frequency of data updates, you may need to change that schedule. To change the repopulation schedule, right-click the indexed table in Object Browser and select Full-Text Index, Properties. The Schedule tab of the Properties dialog box allows you to modify existing schedules or create new ones.

If you've just made a massive number of changes (such as a bulk insert) to a table, you may not have time to wait for the scheduled repopulation of the index. You can force repopulation by right-clicking the table and selecting Full-Text Index, and then selecting either Full or Incremental Population. A full population rebuilds the entire full-text index, and an incremental population updates only the changes to the index since the last repopulation.

The only other administrative activity you need to engage in for Full-Text Search is backing up the indexes themselves. Although full-text indexes are managed through Enterprise Manager, they aren't actually part of the SQL Server database structure. In fact, they're stored outside of SQL Server in a separate directory, which is managed by the MSFTESQL service. To back up these indexes, you need to remember to stop the MSFTESQL service and perform a full backup of the database containing the index. SQL Server automatically includes the index files in the backup.

Using all the tools we have discussed thus far, you can get any data you want out of your server. However, many companies have data spread across many servers. To access that multiserver data, you need to link your servers and perform linked server queries.

Linked Server Queries

A growing number of companies have more than one server from which they need to extract data to formulate reports. With the queries you've seen thus far, this task would be very difficult, because all of these `SELECT` queries are designed to work with only one server at a time. To get data from multiple servers with standard query methods, you would need to execute `SELECT` queries on each server and then manually try to combine the results into something meaningful. To ease the process of getting result sets that comprise data from multiple servers, there are *linked server queries* (also known as *distributed* or *heterogeneous* queries).

When you perform a query using SQL Server Management Studio, you're asked to log in every time. The process of linking servers allows one SQL Server to log in to another database server, just the way you log in with Management Studio. This allows SQL Server to perform queries on the remote server on behalf of the end user. The database server in question doesn't even have to be SQL Server, which means that you can query an Access or Oracle database with this type of query. Two different types of linked server queries are at your disposal: *ad hoc* and *permanent*.

If you're going to use a particular linked server query infrequently, you should use ad hoc linked server queries. The ad hoc queries don't take up space in your database, and they're simple to write. The code to perform an ad hoc linked server query involves using the `OPENROWSET` command. OPENROWSET creates a new temporary table from a foreign database that can be searched by a standard SELECT statement. The syntax for OPENROWSET is as follows:

```
OPENROWSET('provider_name','data_source','user_name','password',object)
```

For example, code to run an ad hoc query against the Access version of Northwind looks as follows:

```
SELECT Access.*
FROM OPENROWSET('Microsoft.Jet.OLEDB.4.0',
'c:\MSOffice\Access\Samples\northwind.mdb';'admin';'mypwd', Orders) AS Access
GO
```

This code signifies that you've selected all records from the Orders table of the Microsoft Access version of the Northwind database.

If you need to execute a linked server query on a more frequent basis, OPENROWSET won't work for you. For frequent linked server queries, you need to permanently link your server with the sp_addlinkedserver stored procedure. This stored procedure lets the local server (where the user logs on) log on to the remote server and stay logged on. With OPENROWSET, the link is disconnected every time the query is finished. To link a SQL Server named Washington, for example, you can use the following:

```
sp_addlinkedserver 'Washington', 'SQL Server'
```

To query the AdventureWorks database on the Washington SQL Server machine, all you need to do is add the server name to your SELECT query, as follows:

```
SELECT * FROM Washington.AdventureWorks..HumanResources.Employee
```

Linking to a non-SQL server is also easy—it just requires a little more typing. Here's how to link to the Northwind database on an Access machine named Marketing on a more permanent basis:

```
sp_addlinkedserver 'Marketing','Microsoft.Jet.OLEDB.4.0', 'OLE DB Provider for
Jet', 'C:\MSOffice\Access\Samples\Northwind.mdb'
```

To query the newly linked Access database, all you need to do is use the following:

```
SELECT * FROM Marketing.Northwind..Employees
```

XML Queries

In the years since SQL Server 2000 was released, another type of data has become increasingly important in data processing applications of all sorts: XML data. As you learned in Chapter 5, "Transact-SQL Overview and Basics," SQL Server 2005 includes a native xml datatype. A column with this datatype can store an entire XML document.

Along with this storage, SQL Server supports a new way to get data out of XML documents placed in xml columns. By using XQuery expressions, you can retrieve a specified part of a stored XML document, rather than the whole thing (as a simple SELECT statement would retrieve). To do this, you use the xml.query function.

For example, the Production.ProductModel table in the AdventureWorks sample database contains an xml column named Instructions. This column can optionally hold an XML document containing assembly instructions for the product. Figure 6.21 shows one of these documents, extracted to a disk file.

FIGURE 6.21
XML document stored in an xml column

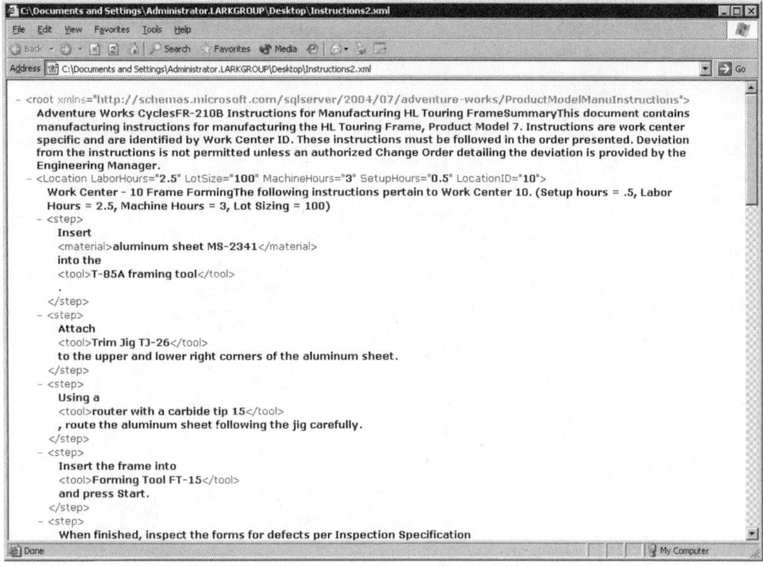

Because this document contains both data and metadata (in the form of XML tags), it's possible to extract any desired piece with a proper XQuery expression. This SQL Server query uses XQuery to pull out and format the first two steps in the instructions:

```
USE AdventureWorks
SELECT Instructions.query('
 declare namespace AWMI="http://schemas.microsoft.com/sqlserver/2004/07/
➥ adventure-works/ProductModelManuInstructions";
 for $Inst in /AWMI:root
 return
     (
     <step1> {string(($Inst/AWMI:Location[@LocationID =
➥ 10]/AWMI:step[1])[1]) } </step1>,
     <step2> {string(($Inst/AWMI:Location[@LocationID =
➥ 10]/AWMI:step[2])[1]) } </step2>
     )
') AS x
FROM Production.ProductModel
WHERE ProductModelID=7
```

Figure 6.22 shows the result of running this query.

NOTE XQuery is a very complex language, and the details of XQuery expressions are beyond the scope of this book. For an introduction to XQuery, see XML.com's article "What Is XQuery?" (http://www.xml.com/pub/a/2002/10/16/xquery.html) and for more details investigate the W3C's XQuery page at http://www.w3.org/XML/Query/.

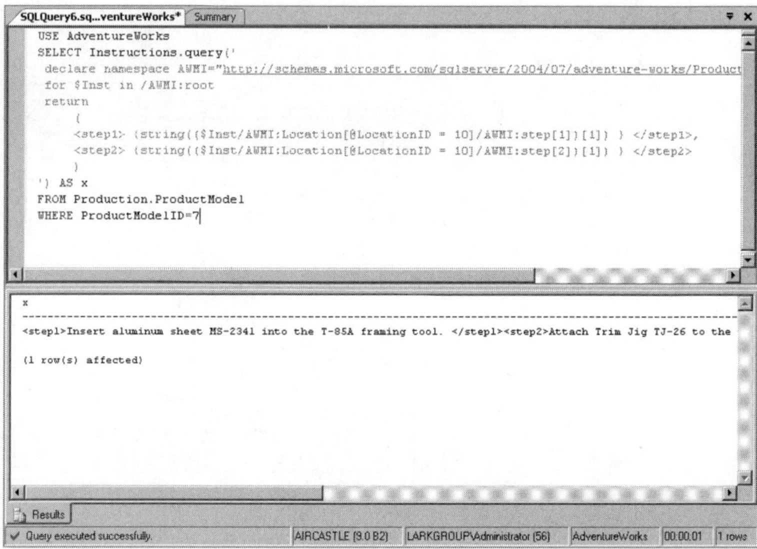

FIGURE 6.22
Using XQuery within SQL Server

Summary

That was a lot of information—but rest assured that you'll use everything you've read here at some point in your illustrious career as a SQL Server guru. The first thing you learned here was how to use a basic SELECT query to retrieve data from a single table in your database. After examining the result sets from the basic queries, you discovered that there is just too much information displayed, so you learned how to use WHERE to limit what is returned in the result set.

Next, because most databases contain more than one table, you learned how to use joins to combine the information from multiple tables in a single result set.

Then, you figured out that the result sets aren't in any particular order when they're displayed, so you learned how to bestow organization upon them using the ORDER BY clause.

Even with ORDER BY, though, your result sets still didn't look enough like reports to be easily read, so you went through the process of adding summary and detailed information using GROUP BY with the HAVING, ROLLUP, and CUBE operators.

After that, you learned the proper use of TOP *N* to retrieve the top percentage of a group of values, such as the top 5 percent of salespeople in a company. Finally, RANK and OVER let you calculate rankings on a subset of a result set.

Afterward, you found that Full-Text Search can greatly enhance SELECT queries by allowing you to find words or phrases in your text fields.

You also discovered the value of the linked server query, which allows you to access data from more than one server at a time during the same query. Finally, you saw some of the power of XQuery for retrieving information from xml columns.

With SELECT queries under your belt, you're ready to move on to action queries.

Chapter 7

Action Queries

As you saw in Chapter 6, SELECT queries allow you to retrieve the data from your database in a flexible manner. However, there's more to using a database than just retrieving existing data. You need to be able to perform three other fundamental operations:

- Deleting existing data from tables
- Making changes to existing data in tables
- Inserting new data in tables

Fortunately, the T-SQL language provides a mechanism to accomplish all of these tasks. That mechanism is the action query, and in this chapter, you'll learn how to construct and use action queries to perform these three fundamental operations.

What Are Action Queries?

Action queries are SQL statements that modify one or more records in an existing table. These statements include:

- DELETE statements, which can delete individual records or every record in a table
- TRUNCATE TABLE statements, which delete every record in a table
- UPDATE statements, which can make changes to one or more columns within one or more records in a table
- INSERT statements, which can insert one or more rows into an existing table
- SELECT INTO statements, which can create an entire new table from existing data

In the rest of this chapter, we'll explain the syntax of each of these five types of statements and show how you can use them in your own applications.

NOTE Action queries work on existing tables. To create a new table, you can use a CREATE TABLE statement; to completely destroy a table, you use a DROP TABLE statement. You'll learn about creating and dropping tables in Chapter 11, "Tables."

Delete Queries

You can use two different statements to delete records from an existing table. DELETE statements are the more flexible of the two and allow you to specify exactly which records you wish to delete. When you want to delete every record in a table, you'll find that TRUNCATE TABLE is faster and uses fewer system resources.

Syntax of *DELETE*

The DELETE statement has a number of options, but the basic syntax is fairly straightforward:

```
DELETE
[FROM]
{
 table_name [WITH (table_hint [...n]])
 | view_name
 | OPENQUERY | OPENROWSET | OPENDATASOURCE
}
[FROM table_source]
[WHERE search_conditions]
[OPTION query_hints]
```

Taken piece by piece, here's what's in a DELETE statement:

- The DELETE keyword identifies the statement.
- The optional FROM keyword can be used if you think it makes the SQL more understandable.
- You have to specify either a table name, a view name, or the results of an OPENQUERY, OPENROWSET, or OPENDATASOUCE function as the source for the rows to delete. OPENQUERY, OPENROWSET, and OPENDATASOURCE are discussed in Chapter 8, "Topics in Advanced Transact-SQL."
- The optional WITH clause can be used to provide optimizer hints for the table. Optimizer hints are also discussed in Chapter 8.
- The FROM clause has the same syntax and options as the FROM clause in a SELECT statement, which you've already seen in Chapter 6.
- The WHERE clause has the same syntax and options as the WHERE clause in a SELECT statement.
- The OPTION clause can be used to provide further hints, which are also discussed in Chapter 8.

Overall, the DELETE statement is very similar to the SELECT statement. In fact, as long as a SELECT statement doesn't contain any aggregate functions, you can create a DELETE statement to delete the corresponding rows by replacing the SELECT keyword with the DELETE keyword and removing any explicit column names from the SELECT clause.

Limitations of *DELETE*

If a DELETE statement uses a view rather than a table as the source for the rows to be deleted, that view must be updateable. *Updateable* views have no aggregate functions or calculated columns. In addition, a view in a DELETE statement must contain precisely one table in its FROM clause (the FROM clause used to create the view, not the FROM clause in the DELETE statement).

NOTE For more on updateable views, see Chapter 13, "Views."

If you omit the WHERE clause from a DELETE statement, the statement will delete all the rows in the target table. If you include a WHERE clause, the statement deletes only the rows that the WHERE clause selects.

A DELETE statement can't remove rows from a table on the nullable side of an outer join. For example, consider a DELETE statement with the following FROM clause:

```
FROM Person.Contact LEFT JOIN Sales.SalesOrderHeader ON
Person.Contact.ContactID = Sales.SalesOrderHeader.SalesOrderID
```

In this case, the Sales.SalesOrderHeader table is nullable. That is, the columns from that table will contain null values for rows corresponding to contacts who have not placed an order. In this case, the DELETE statement can't be used to delete rows from the Sales.SalesOrderHeader table, only from the Person.Contact table.

If a DELETE statement attempts to violate a trigger or a referential integrity constraint, the statement will fail. Even if only one row from a set of rows being deleted violates the constraint, the statement is cancelled, SQL Server returns an error, and no rows are deleted.

If you execute a DELETE statement on a table that has an INSTEAD OF DELETE trigger defined, the DELETE statement itself won't be executed. Instead, the actions in the trigger will be executed for each row in the table that would have been deleted. You'll learn about triggers in Chapter 15, "Using Triggers."

Examples of *DELETE*

The simplest possible DELETE statement deletes all the rows from the target table. To experiment safely, we'll use the SELECT INTO statement (covered later in this chapter) to make a copy of the Person.Contact table, and work with the copy:

```
SELECT * INTO Person.ContactCopy FROM Person.Contact
DELETE Person.ContactCopy
DROP TABLE Person.ContactCopy
```

If you run these statements, you'll see these messages from SQL Server:

```
(19972 row(s) affected)
(19972 row(s) affected)
```

The first message records SQL Server creating the Person.ContactCopy table, and the second comes from SQL Server deleting all 19,972 rows from the new table.

NOTE The DROP TABLE statement removes the temporary copy of the table when you're done running these statements so that you can make a fresh copy for the next example.

Optionally, if you'd like the SQL statement to be a bit more readable, you can include the FROM keyword:

```
SELECT * INTO Person.ContactCopy FROM Person.Contact
DELETE FROM Person.ContactCopy
DROP TABLE Person.ContactCopy
```

To delete a single row, you need to include a WHERE clause that specifies that particular row:

```
SELECT * INTO Person.ContactCopy FROM Person.Contact
DELETE Person.ContactCopy
WHERE ContactID = 1
DROP TABLE Person.ContactCopy
```

Or, with a less restrictive WHERE clause, you can delete multiple rows, but less than the entire table:

```
SELECT * INTO Person.ContactCopy FROM Person.Contact
DELETE Person.ContactCopy
WHERE LastName LIKE 'Whit%'
DROP TABLE Person.ContactCopy
```

TIP To check that a DELETE statement will delete the rows you intend it to delete, you might want to use SQL Server Management Studio to examine the results of the corresponding SELECT statement (`SELECT * FROM Person.Contact WHERE LastName LIKE 'Whit%'` in the previous case).

You can also delete rows from one table based on rows from another table by using the second FROM clause. Consider the case where you have contacts and orders joined on a common ContactID field. In this case, you can delete all the orders for contacts who are in the 206 area code with the following statement:

```
SELECT * INTO Person.ContactCopy FROM Person.Contact
SELECT * INTO Sales.SalesOrderHeaderCopy
FROM Sales.SalesOrderHeader
DELETE FROM Sales.SalesOrderHeaderCopy
FROM Person.ContactCopy INNER JOIN Sales.SalesOrderHeaderCopy
ON Person.ContactCopy.ContactID = Sales.SalesOrderHeaderCopy.ContactID
WHERE Person.ContactCopy.Phone LIKE '206%'
DROP TABLE Sales.SalesOrderHeaderCopy
DROP TABLE Person.ContactCopy
```

TIP In this case, the corresponding SELECT statement retrieves only the data from the Sales .SalesOrderHeader table: `SELECT Sales.SalesOrderHeader.* FROM Person.Contact INNER JOIN Sales.SalesOrderHeader ON Person.Contact.ContactID = Sales .SalesOrderHeader.ContactID WHERE Person.Contact.Phone LIKE '206%'`.

You can also use a subquery as the table you're deleting from (a *subquery* is a SELECT query embedded in another query). For example, consider the problem of deleting the first 10 entries in a table, alphabetically sorted. You can do that with the following statement:

```
SELECT * INTO Person.ContactCopy FROM Person.Contact
DELETE Person.ContactCopy
FROM (SELECT TOP 10 * FROM Person.ContactCopy
ORDER BY au_LastName) AS t1
WHERE Person.ContactCopy.ContactID = t1.ContactID
DROP TABLE Person.ContactCopy
```

Here the SELECT statement inside the parentheses is a subquery that gives the basic set of rows for the DELETE statement to operate on. The result of this subquery is aliased as t1, and the WHERE clause specifies how to match rows from t1 to the permanent authors table. The DELETE clause then automatically deletes all the matching rows.

Finally, consider the problem of deleting all the contacts who don't have any orders. You can do this by using a LEFT JOIN and putting a condition on the Orders table:

```
SELECT * INTO Person.ContactCopy FROM Person.Contact
DELETE Person.ContactCopy
```

```
FROM Person.ContactCopy LEFT JOIN Sales.SalesOrderHeader ON
Person.ContactCopy.ContactID = Sales.SalesOrderHeader.ContactID
WHERE Sales.SalesOrderHeader.ContactID IS NULL
DROP TABLE Person.ContactCopy
```

This works because the LEFT JOIN creates rows for every contact and fills the columns from the Sales.SalesOrderHeader table with null values for any contact who has no information in the joined table.

Syntax of *TRUNCATE TABLE*

The other statement you can use to delete rows is TRUNCATE TABLE. The syntax of TRUNCATE TABLE is just about as simple as you can get:

```
TRUNCATE TABLE table_name
```

That's it. Functionally, TRUNCATE TABLE is the equivalent of a DELETE statement on a single table with no WHERE clause. However, TRUNCATE TABLE is more efficient if what you want to do is get rid of all the data in a table, because the DELETE statement removes rows one at a time and makes individual entries in the transaction log for each row. By contract, the TRUNCATE TABLE statement removes all the rows by deallocating the data pages assigned to the table, and only these deallocations are recorded in the transaction log.

WARNING **Because TRUNCATE TABLE is an unlogged statement, you must make a full backup after using it to ensure that your database can be restored without data loss if there is any problem.**

Limitations of *TRUNCATE TABLE*

When you use TRUNCATE TABLE to delete all the rows from a table that has an Identity column, the identity counter is reset, so that the next row added gets the initial seed value for this column. If you want to preserve the counter, so the next row added gets the next available value that hasn't yet been assigned, you should use a DELETE statement instead of a TRUNCATE TABLE statement.

You can't use TRUNCATE TABLE to delete rows from a table that's referenced by a foreign-key constraint from another table. Again, you must use a DELETE statement in this case.

Deletions made via TRUNCATE TABLE won't activate delete triggers on the table. In some cases, this is a way to get around a limitation of the DELETE statement, but you must be cautious: If you're expecting a delete trigger to take some automatic cleanup or logging action when rows are deleted, you must avoid TRUNCATE TABLE.

If a table is part of a view and the view is indexed, you can't use TRUNCATE TABLE on that table. If you try, you'll get error message 3729 ("Could not TRUNCATE TABLE 'tablename'. It is being referenced by object 'viewname'.").

Example of *TRUNCATE TABLE*

To remove all the data from a table named Person.Contact, execute the following:

```
TRUNCATE TABLE Person.Contact
```

WARNING **If you try this statement, be sure you're trying it on data you can afford to lose. All rows will be deleted from the table without any warning.**

Update Queries

In most databases, the data stored in tables isn't static. Sure, some data (such as a list of U.S. state names) rarely or never changes. However, other data (such as customer address information) is more dynamic. The UPDATE statement provides you with the means to change any or all of the data contained in a table. You can write an UPDATE statement in such a way that it affects only a single field in a single row, or more broadly so that it calculates changes in a column for every row in a table—or even so that it makes changes to multiple columns in every row.

In addition to the UPDATE statement, there are two specialized statements for dealing with large values stored in text, ntext, or image columns. The WRITETEXT statement replaces a value in one of these columns with an entirely new value, whereas the UPDATETEXT statement can make a change to part of such a column. The WRITETEXT and UPDATETEXT statements are *deprecated*—that is, they will be removed entirely in some future version of the product, and Microsoft discourages their use now. Instead of using these statements and text, ntext, or binary columns, you should use a standard UPDATE statement with varchar(max), nvarchar(max), or varbinary(max) columns. We won't cover WRITETEXT or UPDATETEXT; details are in Books Online if you're working with a legacy application that uses these statements.

Syntax of *UPDATE*

The UPDATE statement has a fairly complex syntax. Here are the most common clauses:

```
UPDATE
{
 table_name [WITH (table_hint [...n])]
 | view_name
 | OPENQUERY | OPENROWSET
}
SET
{
 column_name = {expression | DEFAULT | NULL}
 | @variable = expression
 | @variable = column = expression
 | column_name { .WRITE (expression , @Offset , @Length)
} [,...n]
{
 [FROM {table_source} [,...n]]
 [WHERE search_condition]
}
[OPTION (query_hint [,...n])]
```

Here's some information about the various pieces of the UPDATE statement:

- The UPDATE keyword identifies the statement.
- You have to specify either a table name, a view name, or the results of an OPENQUERY or OPENROWSET function as the source for the rows to delete. OPENQUERY and OPENROWSET are discussed in Chapter 8.

- The optional WITH clause can be used to provide optimizer hints for the table. Optimizer hints are also discussed in Chapter 8.
- The SET keyword introduces the changes to make.
- You can set a column equal to an expression, to its default value, or to null.
- You can also set a local variable equal to an expression.
- You can combine setting a local variable and a column to the same expression.
- You can use the .WRITE clause to modify part of a varchar(max), nvarchar(max), or varbinary(max) column at a specified offset and length.
- You can also set multiple columns in a single SET clause.
- The FROM clause has the same syntax and options as the FROM clause in a SELECT statement, which you've already seen in Chapter 6.
- The WHERE clause has the same syntax and options as the WHERE clause in a SELECT statement.
- The OPTION clause can be used to provide further hints, which are also discussed in Chapter 8.

Limitations of *UPDATE*

If you're using an UPDATE statement to update through a view, the view must be updateable (of course). In addition, the UPDATE statement can affect only one of the tables in the view.

You can't use an UPDATE statement to update the view in an Identity column. If you need to update an Identity column, you'll need to use DELETE to remove the current row and then INSERT to insert the changed data as a new row.

You can only use an expression that returns a single value in an UPDATE statement.

If you use the SET *@variable = column = expression* form of the SET clause, both the variable and the column are set equal to the results of the expression. This differs from SET *@variable = column = expression* = expression (which would set the variable to the preupdate value of the column). In general, if the SET clause contains multiple actions, these actions are evaluated from left to right.

In general, if the UPDATE would violate a constraint on the table, whether that's an actual constraint, a rule, the nullability rules for a column, or the datatype setting for the column, the UPDATE statement is cancelled and an error is returned. If the UPDATE would have updated multiple rows, no changes are made, even if only a single row would violate the constraint.

If an expression in an UPDATE statement generates an arithmetic error (for example, divide by zero), the update isn't performed, and an error is returned. In addition, such errors cancel the remainder of any batch containing the UPDATE statement.

UPDATE statements are logged, which means that all their data is written to the transaction log. However, an exception is made for the use of the .WRITE clause, which results in only minimal logging.

If an UPDATE statement that contains columns and variables updates multiple rows, the variables will contain the values for only one of the updated rows (and it's not defined which row will supply this value).

If an UPDATE statement affects rows in a table that has an INSTEAD OF UPDATE trigger, the statements in the trigger are executed instead of the changes in the UPDATE statement.

Examples of *UPDATE*

The simplest use of UPDATE is to make a single change that affects every row of a table. For example, you can change the price of every book listed in the Production.Product table to $20.00 with the following statement:

```
UPDATE Production.Product
SET ListPrice = 20.00
```

WARNING If you execute this statement in the AdventureWorks database, you'll change data. For a technique that allows you to experiment with updates without altering data, see the following sidebar, "Updating within Transactions."

More commonly, you'll want to limit your updates to a few rows. The following statement affects all products whose names begin with the letter *s:*

```
UPDATE Production.Product
SET ListPrice = 20.00
WHERE Name LIKE 's%'
```

Updating within Transactions

When you're learning SQL, it's useful to be able to experiment with the UPDATE and DELETE statements without actually altering data. You can do this by using transactions. You'll learn about transactions in depth in Chapter 8; but basically, a *transaction* is a SQL Server unit of work. You can tell SQL Server when to start this unit of work with the BEGIN TRANSACTION statement. When you're done with the work, you can tell SQL Server either to go ahead and finish the job with the COMMIT TRANSACTION statement or to throw away the work with the ROLLBACK TRANSACTION statement. You can think of ROLLBACK TRANSACTION as an "undo" that affects everything since the most recent BEGIN TRANSACTION statement.

For example, here's how you might use this technique in practice to experiment with an UPDATE statement in the AdventureWorks database:

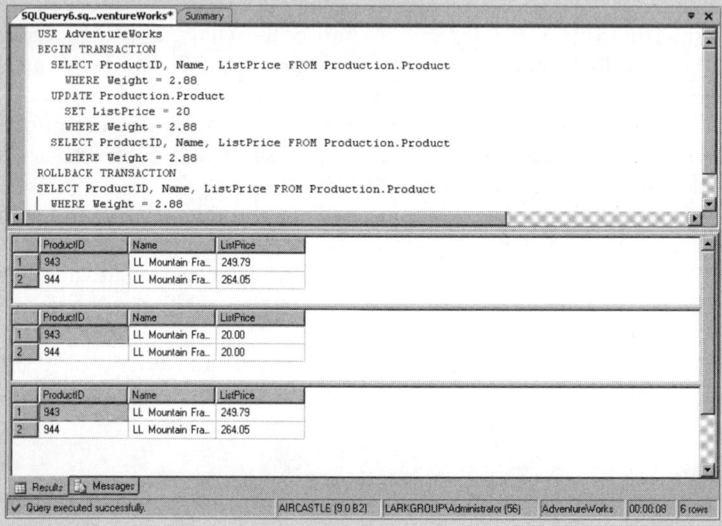

This set of SQL statements performs the following steps:

1. The BEGIN TRANSACTION statement tells SQL Server to start a unit of work.
2. The first SELECT statement retrieves two records before they're changed.
3. The UPDATE statement makes changes to those two records.
4. The second SELECT statement retrieves the two records and shows that they've changed.
5. The ROLLBACK TRANSACTION statement tells SQL Server to throw away all the work it's done since the BEGIN TRANSACTION statement.
6. The final SELECT statement shows that the two records have reverted to their original contents.

Here's the complete output from this batch. You can see that the changes made by the UPDATE statement were temporary:

```
ProductID   Name                                               ListPrice
----------- -------------------------------------------------- ---------------------
943         LL Mountain Frame - Black, 40                      249.79
944         LL Mountain Frame - Silver, 40                     264.05

(2 row(s) affected)


(2 row(s) affected)
ProductID   Name                                               ListPrice
----------- -------------------------------------------------- --------------------
-
943         LL Mountain Frame - Black, 40                      20.00
944         LL Mountain Frame - Silver, 40                     20.00

(2 row(s) affected)

ProductID   Name                                               ListPrice
----------- -------------------------------------------------- --------------------
-
943         LL Mountain Frame - Black, 40                      249.79
944         LL Mountain Frame - Silver, 40                     264.05

(2 row(s) affected)
```

If you use this technique, you should be sure to roll back every transaction you begin, to avoid leaving extra locks on tables when you're done.

Even more precisely, this statement updates only the single product with the specified ProductID:

```
UPDATE Production.Product
SET ListPrice = 20.00
WHERE ProductID = 327
```

You can also update more than one column at a time by separating the updates with commas:

```
UPDATE Production.Product
SET ListPrice = 20.00, ProductNumber = 'LI-5800a'
WHERE ProductID = 418
```

Note that you don't repeat the UPDATE or SET keyword to update multiple columns.

Updating through a view is just as easy as updating through a query. Here's an example using the Sales.vStore view that's included in the AdventureWorks sample database. This view brings together information from half a dozen tables. In this case, the UPDATE statement finds all contacts with the title Owner and changes only those rows:

```
UPDATE Sales.vStore
SET ContactType = 'President'
WHERE ContactType = 'Owner'
```

Of course, you can do more complex things than setting a column equal to a simple value. You can set a column equal to the results of an expression, including an expression that refers to columns. For example, here's how you could raise the price of every product by 10 percent:

```
UPDATE Production.Product
SET ListPrice = ListPrice * 1.1
```

When SQL Server sees a word that's not a keyword (such as *ListPrice* in this example), SQL Server tries to identify it as the name of a SQL Server object. Here, because the UPDATE statement works on the Production.Product table, it's clear to SQL Server that there's only one such object, the ListPrice column in the table.

You can use the special DEFAULT keyword to set a column equal to its default value:

```
UPDATE Production.Product
SET Size = DEFAULT
```

NOTE If a column is *nullable* (that is, if null values can be entered in a column) and has no explicit default value, setting it to DEFAULT has the effect of setting it to Null. If a column is not nullable and has no explicit default value, setting it to DEFAULT results in SQL Server error 515: "Cannot insert the value NULL into column *column_name*, table *table_name;* column does not allow nulls. UPDATE fails. The statement has been terminated."

To explicitly set a nullable column to Null, you can use the NULL keyword:

```
UPDATE Production.Product
SET Size = NULL
```

NOTE Even though this statement appears to contain an *equals null* construction, it's not affected by the ANSI Nulls setting: This is a use of the equals operator for assignment rather than for comparison.

You can also use the UPDATE statement to assign values to local variables. For example, the following batch creates a local variable, assigns it a value, and prints the result:

```
USE AdventureWorks
DECLARE @Name nvarchar(50)
UPDATE Production.Product
  SET @Name = 'Fake'
PRINT @Name
```

Figure 7.1 shows the results of running this batch.

FIGURE 7.1
Using UPDATE with a local variable

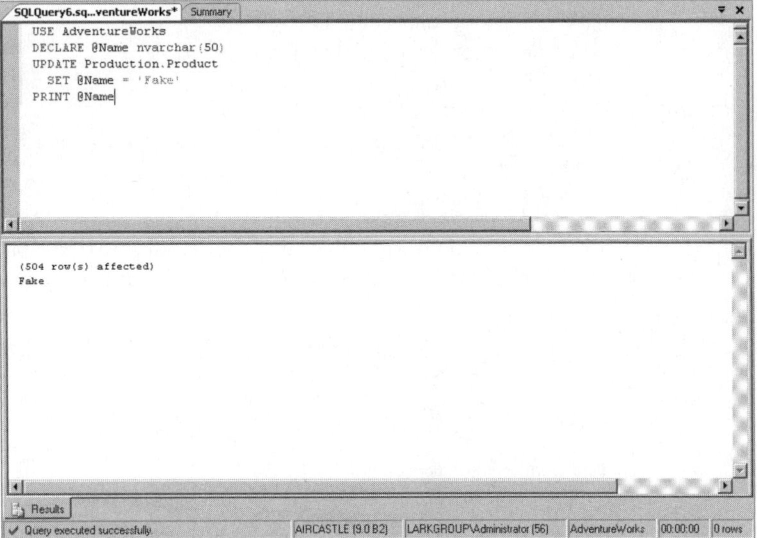

Note that SQL Server processed all 504 rows in the table in this case, even though the UPDATE statement didn't change any of the data stored in the table. To make the update more efficient, you can add a WHERE clause that selects a single record:

```
USE AdventureWorks
DECLARE @Name nvarchar(50)
UPDATE Production.Product
  SET @Name = 'Fake'
  WHERE ProductID = 418
PRINT @Name
```

You might think you can make the process even more efficient by selecting zero records from the table. For example, you can try the following statement:

```
USE AdventureWorks
DECLARE @Name nvarchar(50)
UPDATE Production.Product
  SET @Name = 'Fake'
  WHERE ProductID IS NULL
PRINT @Name
```

However, if the UPDATE doesn't select any rows, it won't set the local variable (try it in Query Analyzer and see for yourself).

TIP To put a value in a local variable without reference to a table, use the SET statement, as discussed in Chapter 5, "Transact-SQL Overview and Basics."

You can also simultaneously update a row in a table and put the result in a local variable. Consider the following example, shown in Figure 7.2:

```
USE AdventureWorks
BEGIN TRANSACTION
DECLARE @newprice money
UPDATE Production.Product
 SET @newprice = ListPrice = ListPrice * 1.1
 WHERE ProductID = 741
PRINT @newprice
SELECT ProductID, ListPrice FROM Production.Product
 WHERE ProductID = 741
ROLLBACK TRANSACTION
```

As you can see, both `@newprice` and the actual row in the table have the same value after running the UPDATE statement. The PRINT statement prints the contents of the variable to the screen.

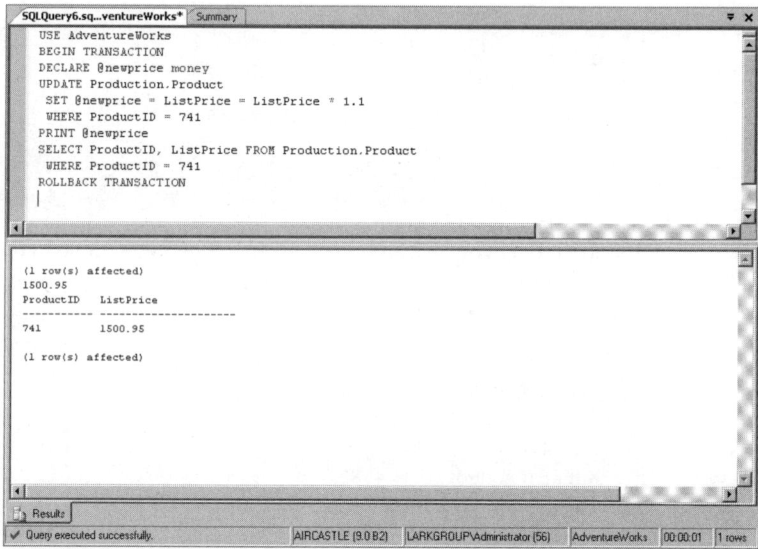

FIGURE 7.2 Updating a row and a variable simultaneously

If you split the previous statement to use a pair of assignments in the SET clause, you may get unexpected results. Figure 7.3 shows that the result is to get the old value into the local variable and the new value into the column. This shows that the changes in a multicolumn UPDATE are processed in the same order that they appear in the SET clause.

```
USE AdventureWorks
BEGIN TRANSACTION
DECLARE @newprice money
```

```
UPDATE Production.Product
 SET @newprice = ListPrice, ListPrice = ListPrice * 1.1
 WHERE ProductID = 741
PRINT @newprice
SELECT ProductID, ListPrice FROM Production.Product
 WHERE ProductID = 741
ROLLBACK TRANSACTION
```

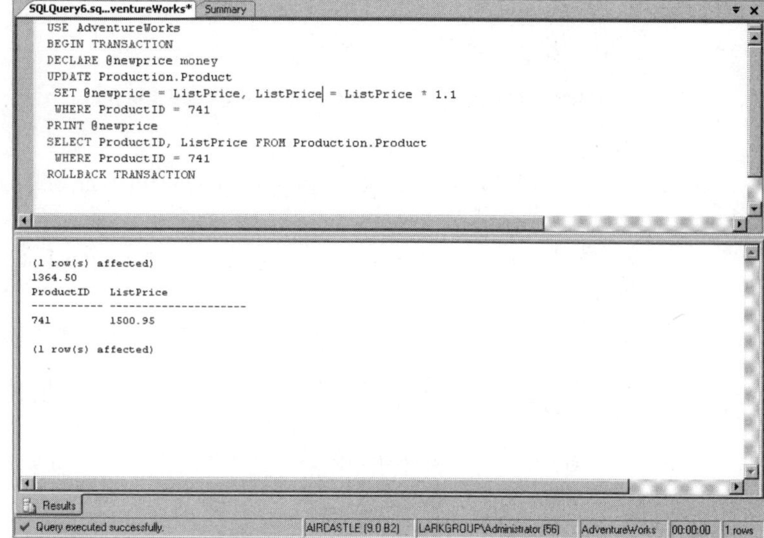

FIGURE 7.3
Unexpected results when trying to update a row and a variable

Insert Queries

Insert queries are designed to insert new rows of data in a table. These queries use the T-SQL INSERT statement.

Syntax of *INSERT*

The INSERT statement is generally simpler than the DELETE and UPDATE statements, which you've already seen:

```
INSERT [INTO]
{
 table_name [WITH (table_hint [...n])]
 | view_name
 | OPENQUERY | OPENROWSET
}
{
 [(column_list)]
 {
  VALUES
```

```
        ( { DEFAULT | NULL
          | expression }[,...n] )
        | derived_table
        | execute_statement
      }
    }
    | DEFAULT VALUES
```

This breaks down as follows:

- The INSERT and optional INTO keywords introduce the statement. INTO is used strictly to enhance readability.
- The *table_name* argument supplies the target table.
- Optionally, you can include table hints.
- You can also specify a *view_name* or the results of an OPENQUERY or OPENROWSET function as the target of the insertion.
- The *column_list* is an optional comma-delimited list of columns that will receive the inserted data.
- Values to insert can be supplied by the DEFAULT or NULL keyword, by expressions.
- Alternatively, you can use a SELECT statement to create a *derived_table*, which will be the source of the insert.
- Or, you can use an *execute_statement* with a stored procedure or a SQL batch to create the data to be inserted.
- The DEFAULT VALUES clause uses the table's default for every column in the new row.

An INSERT statement can insert multiple rows of data if you use a derived table or the results of an execute_statement to supply the data to be inserted.

Limitations of *INSERT*

Of course, if you're inserting data via a view instead of via a table, the view must be updateable. In addition, you can insert data into one of the base tables that a view references through only a single INSERT statement.

If you don't supply a column list, the INSERT statement will attempt to insert values into every column in the table, in the order that the values are supplied. With or without a column list, INSERT works only if SQL Server can determine what value to insert in every column in the table. This means that for every column, at least one of the following is true:

- The INSERT statement supplies a value.
- The column is an IDENTITY column.
- The column has a default value.
- The column has the timestamp datatype.
- The column is nullable.

If you want to insert a particular value in an IDENTITY column, the SET IDENTITY_INSERT option must be ON for the table, and you must supply that value explicitly in the INSERT statement.

If you supply the DEFAULT keyword and a column doesn't have a default, a Null is inserted if the column is nullable. Otherwise, the INSERT statement causes an error, and no data is inserted.

If you're inserting data into a table with a uniqueidentifier column, you can use the NEWID() function to supply a new, unique value for that column.

If a table has an INSTEAD OF INSERT trigger, the code in the trigger will be executed instead of any INSERT statement that attempts to put rows into that table.

Examples of *INSERT*

The simplest situation for INSERT is a table that has default values for every column. There's no such table in the AdventureWorks database, so we'll create one to experiment with:

```
USE AdventureWorks
CREATE TABLE Person.Preferences (
  PreferenceID int IDENTITY(1, 1) NOT NULL,
  Name nvarchar(50) NULL,
  Value nvarchar(50) NULL)
```

TIP For information on the CREATE TABLE statement, see Chapter 11.

This table has a column with the IDENTITY property, and every other column is nullable. So, you can insert a row into this table by specifying the DEFAULT VALUES clause:

```
INSERT INTO Person.Preferences
 DEFAULT VALUES
```

Of course, if you'd like, you can also supply values for a set of columns when you do the insert:

```
INSERT INTO Person.Preferences
 (Name, Value)
 VALUES ('Connection', 'Fast')
```

You need not list columns in the same order that they appear in the table, as long as you match the column list and the value list. For example, the following statement would insert the same row as the previous statement:

```
INSERT INTO Person.Preferences
 (Value, Name)
 VALUES ( 'Fast', 'Connection')
```

When you're inserting to a table that has an IDENTITY column, you can't ordinarily specify the value for that column. However, by using SET IDENTITY_INSERT first, you can specify a value for an IDENTITY column:

```
SET IDENTITY_INSERT Person.Preferences ON
INSERT INTO Person.Preferences
 (PreferenceID, Name, Value)
 VALUES (17285, 'Details', 'Show All')
```

If you're inserting values into every column, you can omit the column list. However, doing so makes the statement more confusing, and we recommend that you always include a default column list. Note that this isn't an option if the table contains an IDENTITY column.

You can also insert the results of a SELECT statement. For example, you might want to clone a location in the AdventureWorks sample database:

```
INSERT INTO Production.Location
 ('NewName', CostRate, Availability)
 SELECT Name, CostRate, Availability
  FROM Production.Location
  WHERE Production.Location.LocationID = 5
```

Note that this works only because the LocationID column is an IDENTITY column. When the duplicate information is inserted, SQL Server automatically creates a new value for that column.

Syntax of *SELECT INTO*

You're already familiar with the syntax of the basic SELECT statement from the previous chapter. SELECT INTO is a variant of the simple SELECT statement. Schematically, it looks as follows:

```
SELECT select_list
INTO new_table_name
FROM table_source
[WHERE condition]
[GROUP BY expression]
HAVING condition]
[ORDER BY expression]
```

Most of the SELECT INTO statement is identical to the SELECT statement. In particular, you can refer to Chapter 6 for the details of the SELECT, FROM, WHERE, GROUP BY, HAVING, and ORDER BY clauses.

The key new element is the INTO clause. You can specify a table name here (using any valid SQL Server identifier), and executing the SELECT INTO statement will create this table. The table will have one column for each column in the results of the SELECT statement. The name and datatypes of these columns will be the same as those for the corresponding columns in the SELECT list.

In other words, SELECT INTO takes the results of a SELECT statement and transforms those results into a permanent table.

TIP Tables created with SELECT INTO don't have indexes, primary keys, foreign keys, default values, or triggers. If you require any of these features in a table, you should create the table with CREATE TABLE and then use an INSERT statement to fill the table with data. That's usually easier than creating the table with SELECT INTO and then fixing the other features with an ALTER TABLE statement.

You can also use SELECT INTO to create a temporary table. To do this, make sure the first character of the table name is a pound sign (#). Temporary tables are useful when you're working with SQL in the midst of a long trigger or stored procedure and need to keep track of information for the duration of the procedure. SQL Server automatically removes temporary tables when you're done using them.

Limitations of *SELECT INTO*

Whether a SELECT INTO statement is completely safe depends on the recovery option that's currently in effect for the database. SQL Server 2005 allows a database to use one of three different recovery models:

- Full
- Bulk-logged
- Simple

You can set the recovery model for a database using the ALTER DATABASE function, as you learned in Chapter 5. By default, every new database uses the same recovery model as the model database at the time the new database was created. The model database defaults to the Full recovery model.

These recovery models differ in how much log space they require and in how much exposure you have to data loss in case of hardware failure.

Under the Full recovery model, no work can be lost to a damaged data file (a damaged log file can require repeating all work since the last log backup). You can also recover the database to any arbitrary point in time. This capability lets you reverse the results of a user error, for example.

Under the Bulk-logged recovery model, database performance is improved for bulk operations (these include SELECT INTO, BULK INSERT, CREATE INDEX, BCP, WRITETEXT, and UPDATETEXT). However, this improvement comes at a cost: If a damaged data file included changes made by bulk operations, those changes must be redone. With this logging model, you can recover the database to the state it was in at the end of any backup.

Under the Simple recovery model, performance is improved further, and log file size is minimized. However, in case of damage to any data file, all changes since the most recent database or differential backup are lost.

SELECT INTO statements are logged when a database is using the Full recovery model, are partially logged under the Bulk-logged model, and aren't logged at all under the Simple model.

Unless you're having a serious performance problem, we recommend using the Full recovery model with all databases.

NOTE You can't execute a SELECT INTO statement in the middle of a transaction.

Examples of *SELECT INTO*

One good use of SELECT INTO is to create a temporary table on which to experiment. For example, you can make an exact copy of the Person.Contact table in the AdventureWorks database with the following statement:

```
SELECT *
INTO [copy_of_Person.Contact]
FROM Person.Contact
```

If you run this statement in SQL Server Management Studio, you'll get a message stating that 19972 rows were affected. These are the rows that were copied to the new table. You can verify this by executing the following statement:

```
SELECT *
FROM [copy_of_Person.Contact]
```

You can also use SELECT INTO to make a temporary table for later use. For example, you might want to select all the rows from the view named Purchasing.vVendor where the vendor is in Bellevue and later display those rows sorted by last name. You can do that with the following batch:

```
USE AdventureWorks
SELECT *
INTO #temp_vv
FROM Purchasing.vVendor
WHERE City = 'Bellevue'
GO
SELECT *
FROM #temp_vv
ORDER BY LastName
GO
```

Figure 7.4 shows the result of executing this query batch.

FIGURE 7.4
Using SELECT INTO to create a temporary table

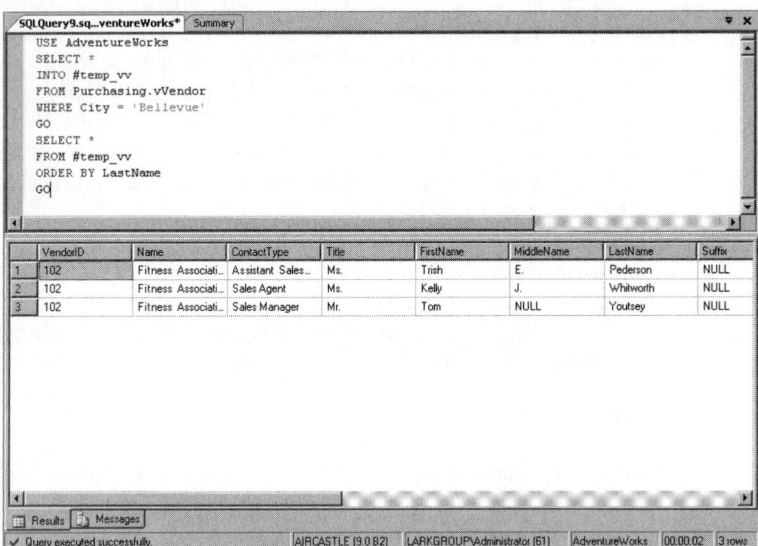

Of course, you can also create this same result set with the following statement:

```
SELECT *
FROM Purchasing.vVendor
WHERE City = 'Bellevue'
ORDER BY LastName
```

Using SELECT INTO with temporary tables is useful when you're reducing a very large data set into a smaller set that you want to analyze extensively. If you have 1,000,000 rows of data, for example, and you want to display a subset of 400 rows sorted three different ways, you can use a SELECT INTO to create a temporary table with just the 400 rows and then perform the rest of the work with the temporary table.

Summary

SQL Server provides methods to delete, update, and insert data as part of its T-SQL programming language. These methods include:

- The `DELETE` and `TRUNCATE TABLE` statements to remove data
- The `UPDATE` statement to update data
- The `INSERT INTO` statement to add new data
- The `SELECT INTO` statement to create new tables

With these tools, you can keep your database up to date, making sure that current results are always available to the `SELECT` statement discussed in Chapter 6. Now that you've seen the four basic operations in T-SQL, it's time to move on to more advanced topics in the next chapter.

Chapter 8

Topics in Advanced Transact-SQL

Just like any other full-featured programming language, T-SQL has more features than it's possible to do justice to in a brief introduction. In this chapter, we're going to introduce some of the more advanced features of T-SQL.

We've chosen these features of T-SQL because they can be very powerful and useful, but they certainly don't exhaust the feature set of the language. You'll learn more about other features of T-SQL elsewhere in the book (for example, Chapter 18, "Security and SQL Server 2005," will mention the security features of T-SQL), but for exhaustive coverage, you'll need to refer to Books Online.

Transactions

Before we discuss the T-SQL language support for transactions, we'll review just what transactions are in the first place. After you understand the basic principles of transactions, we'll cover both local and distributed transactions.

What Are Transactions?

The idea of a *transaction* is one of the core concepts of modern database theory. The simplest way to think of a transaction is as a unit of work. If you think in analogies, transactions are the quarks of a database: the fundamental particles that can't be split into something smaller.

For example, updating a row in a table through an UPDATE query is treated as a single transaction by SQL Server. Suppose you execute the following query:

```
UPDATE Production.Product
  SET SafetyStockLevel = 1000,
    ReorderPoint = 10
  WHERE ProductID = 321
```

When you run this query, SQL Server assumes that your intention is to make both changes (the change to the SafetyStockLevel column and the change to the ReorderPoint column) as a single action. Suppose that there was a constraint on the ReorderPoint column that prevented any reorder point from being less than 50. In that case, neither the update to the SafetyStockLevel column nor the update to the ReorderPoint column would be performed. Because they're both in the same UPDATE statement, SQL Server treats these two updates as part of a single transaction.

If you'd like to have the two updates considered independently, you can rewrite this as two statements:

```
USE AdventureWorks ;
UPDATE Production.Product
  SET SafetyStockLevel = 1000
```

```
  WHERE ProductID = 321
UPDATE Production.Product
  SET ReorderPoint = 10
  WHERE ProductID = 321
```

With this rewrite, the update to the SafetyStockLevel column can be made even if the update to the ReorderPoint column fails.

As you'll see in a few pages, you can also use T-SQL statements to create transactions that span multiple statements. For example, you can execute the following batch:

```
DECLARE @SSL_err int, @RP_err int
BEGIN TRANSACTION
UPDATE Production.Product
  SET SafetyStockLevel = 1000
  WHERE ProductID = 321
 SET @SS_err = @@ERROR
UPDATE Production.Product
  SET ReorderPoint = 10
  WHERE ProductID = 321
 SET @RP_err = @@ERROR
 IF @SS_err = 0 AND @RP_err = 0
  COMMIT TRANSACTION
 ELSE
  ROLLBACK TRANSACTION
```

The `BEGIN TRANSACTION` statement tells SQL Server that it should consider everything up to the next `COMMIT TRANSACTION` or `ROLLBACK TRANSACTION` statement as a single transaction. If SQL Server sees a `COMMIT TRANSACTION` statement, it saves all the work since the most recent `BEGIN TRANSACTION` statement to the database; if SQL Server sees a `ROLLBACK TRANSACTION`, it throws this work away instead.

The ACID Properties

Formally, we say that transactions are identified by the ACID properties. ACID is an acronym for four properties:

- Atomicity
- Consistency
- Isolation
- Durability

Atomicity

Atomicity is a fancy way to refer to the concept of a transaction being a unit of work. When a transaction is over, either all of the work within the transaction has been performed in the database or none of it has been performed. You'll never find a database in a state where only part of a transaction has been performed.

CONSISTENCY

When a transaction is committed or rolled back, everything must be left in a *consistent* state. This means that none of the operations within the transaction can violate any of the constraints or rules of the database. If any part of the transaction would leave the database in an inconsistent state, the transaction can't be committed.

ISOLATION

If two transactions are in progress at once (for example, two users at different computers might be modifying the same table), the transactions can't see each other. Each transaction is *isolated* from the other. When a transaction goes to read data from the database, the transaction finds everything either in the state it was in before other transactions were started or in the state it becomes after they're committed. A transaction never sees an intermediate state in another transaction.

NOTE Although in theory one transaction can never see state in another transaction, in practice SQL Server lets you modify this by choosing an isolation level.

Because transactions are isolated from one another, you're guaranteed to get the same results if you start with a fresh copy of the database and execute all the operations over again in the same order you did the first time. This is why a database can be restored from a backup and a transaction log.

NOTE For more discussion of restoring databases, see Chapter 16, "Basic Administrative Tasks."

DURABILITY

Finally, once a transaction has been committed, it *endures*. The work performed by a transaction is saved permanently. If you commit a transaction and the computer later crashes, the results of the transaction will still be present after a reboot.

Using Transactions

Transact-SQL uses four statements to manage transactions:

- `BEGIN TRANSACTION`
- `COMMIT TRANSACTION`
- `ROLLBACK TRANSACTION`
- `SAVE TRANSACTION`

In addition, two global variables are useful in transaction processing:

- `@@ERROR`
- `@@TRANCOUNT`

In this section, you'll see the syntax of these statements and learn how to use transactional processing within T-SQL batches.

BEGIN TRANSACTION

The BEGIN TRANSACTION statement is used to tell SQL Server to start a new transaction:

```
BEGIN [TRAN | TRANSACTION] [transaction_name | @name_variable]
 [WITH MARK ['description']]
```

- You can use BEGIN, BEGIN TRAN or BEGIN TRANSACTION as the basic statement. Many people prefer one of the shorter forms, but we find the long form to be more readable.
- Supplying a literal transaction name, or the name of a variable that in turn contains a transaction name, lets you refer to this transaction by name when you commit it or roll it back.
- The WITH MARK clause inserts a place marker in the transaction log for the database, using the supplied description plus the current time as an identifier. This allows you to use the RESTORE command to restore the database to either the state just before the transaction or the state just after the transaction when you're recovering from a problem. The description of a place marker may be 255 characters long if you're working with Unicode names, or 510 characters long if you're working with ANSI names.

WARNING **Although transaction names conform to the normal rules for SQL Server identifiers, names longer than 32 characters aren't allowed.**

Transactions can be nested. That is, you can issue a BEGIN TRANSACTION statement and then issue another BEGIN TRANSACTION statement before you either commit or roll back the pending transaction. This nests the second transaction within the first transaction. The rule is that you must commit or roll back the inner transaction before the outer transaction. That is, a COMMIT TRANSACTION or ROLLBACK TRANSACTION statement refers to the most recent BEGIN TRANSACTION statement.

Committing a nested transaction doesn't write the changes from that transaction permanently to the database; it merely makes them available to the outer transaction. Suppose you have the following SQL batch:

```
BEGIN TRANSACTION
UPDATE Production.Product
  SET SafetyStockLevel = 1000
  WHERE ProductID = 321
  BEGIN TRANSACTION
  UPDATE Production.Product
    SET ReorderPoint = 10
    WHERE ProductID = 321
  COMMIT TRANSACTION
ROLLBACK TRANSACTION
```

In this case, the COMMIT TRANSACTION statement tells SQL Server that you're finished with the second transaction you started. However, the ROLLBACK TRANSACTION then rolls back all the work since the first BEGIN TRANSACTION, including the inner nested transaction.

Although transaction names appear to offer increased readability for your code, they interact poorly with nested transactions. In fact, you can refer to a transaction by name only if it's the outermost transaction in a batch. Our recommendation is to avoid naming transactions if you plan to ever nest transactions.

COMMIT TRANSACTION

The syntax of COMMIT TRANSACTION is very similar to that of BEGIN TRANSACTION. There's also an alternative statement with the same purpose:

```
COMMIT [TRAN | TRANSACTION] [transaction_name | @name_variable]
COMMIT [WORK]
```

When you issue a COMMIT TRANSACTION statement, the most recent transaction you started is marked as ready to commit. When you commit the outermost in a series of nested transactions, the changes are written back to the database. Of course, if only one transaction is open, the changes are written immediately.

It's your responsibility to make sure you've made all the changes you want before issuing a COMMIT TRANSACTION statement. Once a transaction has been committed, it can't be rolled back.

Although you can use a name in the COMMIT TRANSACTION statement, SQL Server makes no attempt to match this to a name in a BEGIN TRANSACTION statement. The name is purely for your convenience in making your code more readable.

COMMIT, with or without the optional keyword WORK, is exactly synonymous to COMMIT TRANSACTION with no transaction name. This form of the statement is ANSI SQL-92 compatible.

ROLLBACK TRANSACTION

ROLLBACK TRANSACTION also comes in two forms:

```
ROLLBACK [TRAN | TRANSACTION]
 [transaction_name |
 @name_variable |
 savepoint_name |
 @savepoint_variable]
ROLLBACK [WORK]
```

ROLLBACK TRANSACTION throws away all changes since the most recent BEGIN TRANSACTION. Again, you can supply a transaction name as either a constant or a variable, but SQL Server ignores this name.

You can also roll back part of a transaction by supplying a savepoint name. We'll talk about savepoints in the next section. If a transaction is a *distributed* transaction (one that affects databases on multiple servers), you can't roll back to a savepoint.

ROLLBACK, with or without the optional WORK keyword, is the SQL-92 compliant form of the statement. However, in this form, you can't roll back only one of a set of nested transactions. ROLLBACK WORK always rolls back to the outermost (first) transaction in a batch.

WARNING **ROLLBACK WORK rolls back all nested transactions and sets @@TRANCOUNT to zero.**

If you call ROLLBACK TRANSACTION as part of a trigger, subsequent SQL statements in the same batch aren't executed. On the other hand, if you call ROLLBACK TRANSACTION in a stored procedure, subsequent SQL statements in the same batch are executed.

SAVE TRANSACTION

The SAVE TRANSACTION statement lets you partially commit a transaction while still being able to roll back the rest of the transaction:

```
SAVE [TRAN | TRANSACTION] {savepoint_name | @savepoint_variable}
```

Note that when you issue SAVE TRANSACTION, you must name it. This name provides a reference point for a subsequent COMMIT TRANSACTION or ROLLBACK TRANSACTION statement.

An example will make the use of SAVE TRANSACTION more clear. Consider the following T-SQL batch:

```
BEGIN TRANSACTION
  UPDATE Production.Product
    SET SafetyStockLevel = 1000
    WHERE ProductID = 321
  SAVE TRANSACTION SSsaved
  UPDATE Production.Product
    SET ReorderPoint = 10
    WHERE ProductID = 321
  ROLLBACK TRANSACTION SSsaved
COMMIT TRANSACTION
```

In this case, the ROLLBACK TRANSACTION statement removes the effects of the update to the ReorderPoint column, while leaving the update to the SafetyStockLevel column ready to be committed. Then the COMMIT TRANSACTION statement commits the part of the transaction that wasn't rolled back (in this case, the change to the SafetyStockLevel column).

@@TRANCOUNT

The @@TRANCOUNT system global variable tells you the number of nested transactions that are currently pending. If no transactions are pending, this variable contains zero. This is useful for determining whether a trigger, for example, is executing in the middle of a transaction already started by a T-SQL batch.

@@ERROR

The @@ERROR system global variable holds the most recent error number from any T-SQL statement. Whenever a statement is executed that doesn't cause an error, this variable contains zero. That is, it's reset to zero every time you successfully execute a statement. So, if you want to check at some later point whether a statement has caused an error, you need to save the value of @@ERROR to a local variable.

A Transaction Example

Let's end this section with a more complex T-SQL batch that illustrates the transaction-processing statements:

```
DECLARE @SS_err int, @RP_err int
BEGIN TRANSACTION
 UPDATE Production.Product
  SET SafetyStockLevel = 1000
  WHERE ProductID = 321
 SET @SS_err = @@ERROR
 SAVE TRANSACTION SSsaved
 UPDATE Production.Product
  SET ReorderPoint = 10
  WHERE ProductID = 321
 SET @RP_err = @@ERROR
 IF @RP_err <> 0
```

```
    ROLLBACK TRANSACTION SSsaved
  IF @SS_err = 0 AND @RP_err = 0
   BEGIN
    COMMIT TRANSACTION
    PRINT 'Changes were successful'
   END
  ELSE
   ROLLBACK TRANSACTION
```

Here's a blow-by-blow account of this batch:

1. The DECLARE statement sets up two local variables.
2. The BEGIN TRANSACTION statement starts a transaction.
3. The first UPDATE statement makes a change to the SafetyStockLevel column.
4. The first SET statement is used to save the value of @@ERROR so that you can check later whether the first UPDATE statement was successful. Note that this statement must immediately follow the UPDATE statement.
5. The SAVE TRANSACTION statement sets a savepoint.
6. The second UPDATE statement makes a change to the ReorderPoint column.
7. The second SET statement is used to save the value of @@ERROR so you can tell whether the second UPDATE statement succeeded.
8. If there was an error on the second UPDATE statement, the first ROLLBACK TRANSACTION statement undoes the transaction back to the savepoint.
9. If there are no errors at all, the transaction is committed, and a message is printed. Note the use of BEGIN and END to group two T-SQL statements into one logical statement. This is necessary because by default, the IF statement refers only to the following statement.
10. If there are any errors, the second ROLLBACK TRANSACTION statement undoes all of the work.

Distributed Transactions

So far, we've been discussing local transactions: those that make changes in a single database. SQL Server also supports distributed transactions: transactions that make changes to data stored in more than one database. These databases need not be SQL Server databases; they can be databases on other linked servers.

NOTE For more information on linked servers, see Chapter 6.

A distributed transaction can be managed in code using exactly the same SQL statements as you'd use for a local transaction. However, when you issue a COMMIT TRANSACTION on a distributed transaction, SQL Server automatically invokes a protocol called *two-phase commit* (sometimes referred to as *2PC*). In the first phase, SQL Server asks every database involved to prepare the transaction. The individual databases verify that they can commit the transaction and set aside all the resources necessary to do so. The second phase starts only if every involved database tells SQL Server that it's OK to commit the transaction. In this phase, SQL Server tells every involved database to commit the transaction. If any of the databases involved are unable to commit the transaction, SQL Server tells all the databases to roll back the transaction instead.

MICROSOFT DTC

Distributed transactions are managed by a SQL Server component called the *Distributed Transaction Coordinator (DTC)*. This is a separate service that's installed at the same time as SQL Server. If you're going to use distributed transactions, you should set this service to autostart. Figure 8.1 shows this service selected in the Services administration tool.

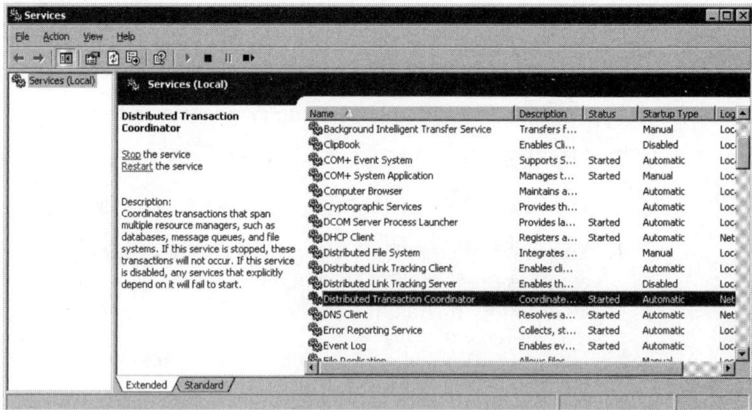

FIGURE 8.1
Checking the status of the Microsoft DTC service

BEGIN DISTRIBUTED TRANSACTION

You can tell SQL Server explicitly to start a distributed transaction with the `BEGIN DISTRIBUTED TRANSACTION` statement:

```
BEGIN DISTRIBUTED TRAN[SACTION]
 [transaction_name | @name_variable]
```

The only difference between this statement and the regular `BEGIN TRANSACTION` statement is the inclusion of the `DISTRIBUTED` keyword.

Local transactions are automatically escalated to distributed transactions if you change data on a remote server during the transaction. For example, if you execute an `INSERT`, `UPDATE`, or `DELETE` statement on a remote server, or call a remote stored procedure, while you're in the midst of a transaction, that transaction will become a distributed transaction.

Transaction Tips

Transactions consume resources on the server. In particular, when you change data within a transaction, that data must be locked to ensure that it's available if you commit the transaction. So, in general, you need to make transactions efficient to avoid causing problems for other users. Here are a few points to consider:

- Don't do anything that requires user interaction within a transaction, because this can cause locks to be held for a long time while the application is waiting for the user.
- Don't start transactions for a single SQL statement.
- Change as little data as possible when in a transaction.

- Don't start a transaction while the user is browsing through data. Wait until they're actually ready to change the data.
- Keep transactions as short as possible.

Rowset Functions

Rowset functions are functions that return an object that can be used in place of a table in another SQL statement. For example, as you saw in Chapter 7 ("Action Queries"), some rowset functions can be used to provide the rows to be inserted with an INSERT statement. There are six rowset functions in SQL Server 2005:

- CONTAINSTABLE
- FREETEXTTABLE
- OPENQUERY
- OPENROWSET
- OPENDATASOURCE
- OPENXML

CONTAINSTABLE

The CONTAINSTABLE statement lets you construct a virtual table from the results of a complex full-text search. This statement's syntax is a bit more complicated than that of most of the statements we've examined so far:

```
CONTAINSTABLE (table_name, {column_name | (column_list) | *},
 '<search_condition>' [ , LANGUAGE language_term] [,top_n])

<search_condition>::=
{
 <generation_term> |
 <prefix_term> |
 <proximity_term> |
 <simple_term> |
 <weighted_term>
}
| {(<search_condition>)
 {( AND | & ) | ( AND NOT | &! ) | ( OR | | )}
 <search_condition> [...n]
 }

<simple_term> ::=
word | "phrase"

<prefix_term> ::=
{"word*" | "phrase*"}
```

```
<generation_term> ::=
FORMSOF((INFLECTIONAL | THESAURUS), <simple_term> [,...n])

<proximity_term> ::=
{<simple_term> | <prefix_term> }
{{NEAR | ~} {<simple_term> | <prefix_term>}} [...n]

<weighted_term> ::=
ISABOUT (
{{
  <generation_term> |
  <prefix_term> |
  <proximity_term> |
  <simple_term>
 }
[WEIGHT (weight_value)]
} [,...n])
```

TIP You can use CONTAINSTABLE only on a table that's been enabled for full-text indexing. For more on full-text indexing, see Chapter 6.

If you work carefully through that syntax, you'll see that the basic idea of CONTAINSTABLE is to allow you to do a *fuzzy* search, which returns items that might not match entirely. Some further syntactical notes:

- Using the asterisk (*) to specify columns tells CONTAINSTABLE to search all columns that have been registered for full-text searching, which may not be all the columns in the table.
- Weight values are numbers between zero and one that specify how important each match is considered to be in the final virtual table.
- You can limit the number of results returned by specifying an integer in the *top_n* parameter. This is useful when you're searching a very large source table and want to see only the most important matches.

The CONTAINSTABLE statement returns a virtual table containing two columns, always named KEY and RANK. For example, consider the following statement:

```
SELECT * FROM
CONTAINSTABLE(Production.ProductDescription, Description,
'ISABOUT(titanium WEIGHT(.8), aluminum WEIGHT(.2))')
```

Assuming that you've enabled the Production.ProductDescription table in the AdventureWorks sample database for full-text searching on the Description column, this statement returns the results shown in Figure 8.2. The ISABOUT search condition here specifies that results containing the word *titanium* should be rated as more important than those containing the word *aluminum*.

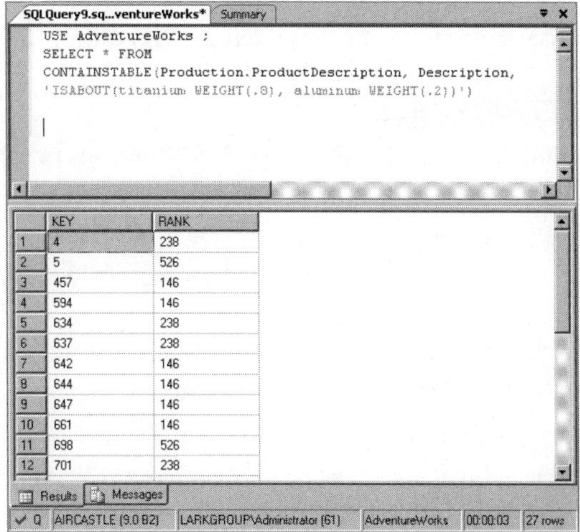

FIGURE 8.2
Using `CONTAINSTABLE` to generate a virtual table

The `KEY` column always contains values from the column that you identified as the primary key to the full-text indexing service. To make this statement more useful, you'll probably want to use this column to join back to the original table. It also helps to add an `ORDER BY` clause so that the highest-ranked products are listed first. Figure 8.3 shows the results of the following statement:

```
SELECT * FROM
CONTAINSTABLE(Production.ProductDescription, Description,
'ISABOUT(titanium WEIGHT(.8), aluminum WEIGHT(.2))')
AS C
INNER JOIN Production.ProductDescription
ON Production.ProductDescription.ProductDescriptionID =
C.[KEY]
ORDER BY C.RANK DESC
```

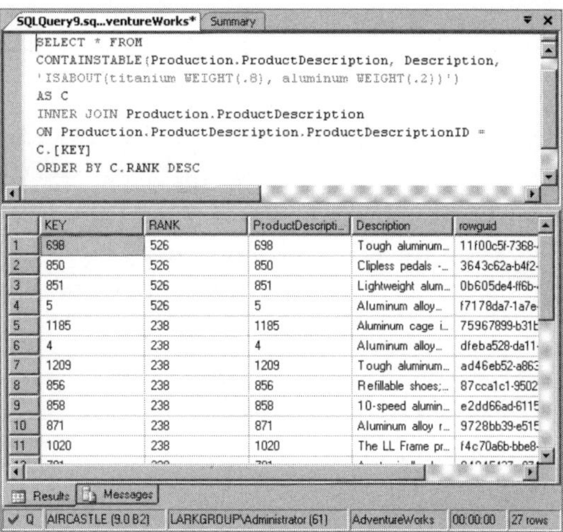

FIGURE 8.3
Using `CONTAINSTABLE` joined to the original search table

NOTE The virtual table needs to be aliased to be included in a join, and you must include the square brackets around the joining name because KEY is a SQL Server keyword.

FREETEXTTABLE

Like CONTAINSTABLE, FREETEXTTABLE generates a virtual table based on full-text indexing information. However, the syntax of FREETEXTTABLE is a good deal simpler:

```
FREETEXTTABLE (table_name, {column_name | (column_list) *},
 'freetext' [, LANGUAGE language_term ] [,top_n])
```

TIP You can use FREETEXTTABLE only on a table that's been enabled for full-text indexing. For more on full-text indexing, see Chapter 6.

You can think of FREETEXTTABLE as being like a black-box version of CONTAINSTABLE. Internally, SQL Server breaks the freetext string into words, assigns a weight to each word, and then looks for similar words. For example, the following statement can be used to retrieve items whose description looks somehow similar to *aluminum wheels:*

```
SELECT ProductDescriptionID, Description, RANK FROM
FREETEXTTABLE(Production.ProductDescription, Description,
'aluminum wheels')
AS C
INNER JOIN Production.ProductDescription
ON Production.ProductDescription.ProductDescriptionID =
C.[KEY]
ORDER BY C.RANK DESC
```

Just like CONTAINSTABLE, FREETEXTTABLE returns a virtual table with KEY and RANK columns. Figure 8.4 shows the result of this particular statement.

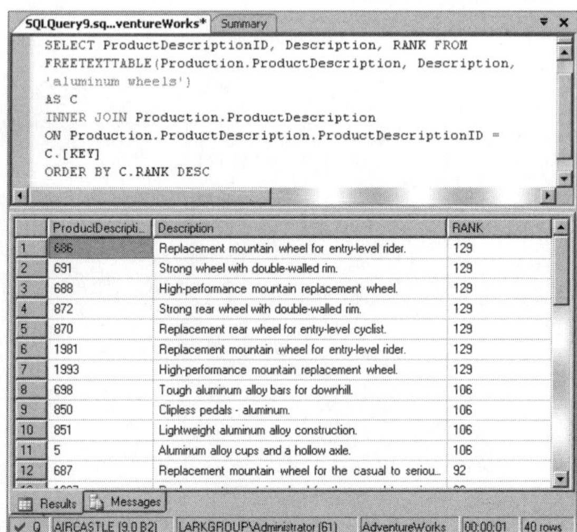

	ProductDescripti...	Description	RANK
1	686	Replacement mountain wheel for entry-level rider.	129
2	691	Strong wheel with double-walled rim.	129
3	688	High-performance mountain replacement wheel.	129
4	872	Strong rear wheel with double-walled rim.	129
5	870	Replacement rear wheel for entry-level cyclist.	129
6	1981	Replacement mountain wheel for entry-level rider.	129
7	1993	High-performance mountain replacement wheel.	129
8	698	Tough aluminum alloy bars for downhill.	106
9	850	Clipless pedals - aluminum.	106
10	851	Lightweight aluminum alloy construction.	106
11	5	Aluminum alloy cups and a hollow axle.	106
12	687	Replacement mountain wheel for the casual to seriou...	92

FIGURE 8.4
Using FREETEXTTABLE to locate products

TIP FREETEXTTABLE is probably more useful than CONTAINSTABLE when the search term is being input by a user, who might not understand the exact syntax SQL Server uses for full-text searches.

OPENQUERY

The OPENQUERY statement lets you use any query (SQL statement that returns rows) on a linked server to return a virtual table. The syntax of OPENQUERY is as follows:

```
OPENQUERY(linked_server, 'query')
```

NOTE For more information on creating linked servers, see Chapter 6.

Figure 8.5 shows in SQL Server Management Studio that the Aircastle server knows about a linked server named Sandcastle, which is also a Microsoft SQL Server. If you connected to the Sandcastle server directly, you could run a query like the following:

```
SELECT *
FROM AdventureWorks.Person.Contact
```

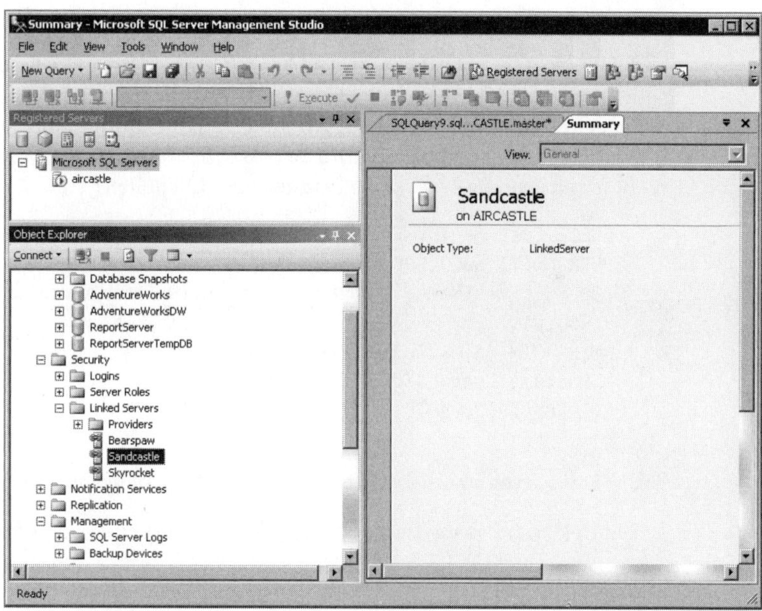

FIGURE 8.5 Inspecting properties for a linked server

This query would return all of the rows in the Contact table from the Person schema in the AdventureWorks database. So far, there's no need for OPENQUERY. However, suppose you want to join the Person.Contact table from the Sandcastle server to the Sales.Individual table from the Aircastle server. In this case, you might connect to the Aircastle server and run the following statement instead:

```
SELECT CustomerID, FirstName, LastName FROM
OPENQUERY(Sandcastle, 'SELECT FirstName, LastName, ContactID
➥ FROM AdventureWorks.Person.Contact')
```

```
AS Contact
INNER JOIN Sales.Individual
ON Contact.ContactID = Sales.Individual.ContactID
ORDER BY CustomerID
```

Note that a query that retrieves the records in the context of the Sandcastle server has been incorporated as one of the parameters of the OPENQUERY statement.

OPENQUERY is the easiest tool you can use to perform distributed queries using SQL Server. By using OPENQUERY, you can join any number of tables from different data sources. These data sources don't even need to be SQL Server tables; as long as they're data sources that you can represent as linked servers (basically, any data source that you have an OLE DB provider to connect with), you can use them with OPENQUERY.

OPENROWSET

OPENROWSET also provides a way to use data from a different server in a SQL Server statement. In the case of OPENROWSET, you supply the information needed to connect via OLE DB directly. Here are the essential options for OPENROWSET (refer to Books Online for more advanced options):

```
OPENROWSET ('provider_name',
 'datasource';'user_id';'password',
 'query')
```

OPENROWSET is useful when you haven't already created a linked server for a particular data source. Instead of using a linked server name, this statement takes the necessary information to connect to a data source via OLE DB directly. For example, suppose that the Sandcastle server has a user named sa with the password Sql#1. In that case, you can use the following OPENROWSET statement to retrieve the exact same results as the OPENQUERY statement in the previous section:

```
SELECT CustomerID, FirstName, LastName FROM
OPENROWSET('SQLOLEDB', 'Sandcastle';'sa';'99Schema@',
 'SELECT FirstName, LastName, ContactID FROM AdventureWorks.Person.Contact')
AS Contact
INNER JOIN Sales.Individual
ON Contact.ContactID = Sales.Individual.ContactID
ORDER BY CustomerID
```

TIP Some of the arguments in OPENROWSET are separated by semicolons instead of commas.

Figure 8.6 shows the results of running this particular statement.

OPENDATASOURCE

The OPENDATASOURCE statement provides a more flexible way (compared to OPENROWSET) to make a temporary connection to an OLE DB data source. It does this by taking an entire OLE DB connection string as one of its parameters:

```
OPENDATASOURCE(provider_name, connection_string)
```

OPENDATASOURCE is more flexible than OPENROWSET in that OPENDATASOURCE can be used in place of a linked server name, so it need not refer to any particular database or table on the other server. You can use OPENDATASOURCE to refer to any table.

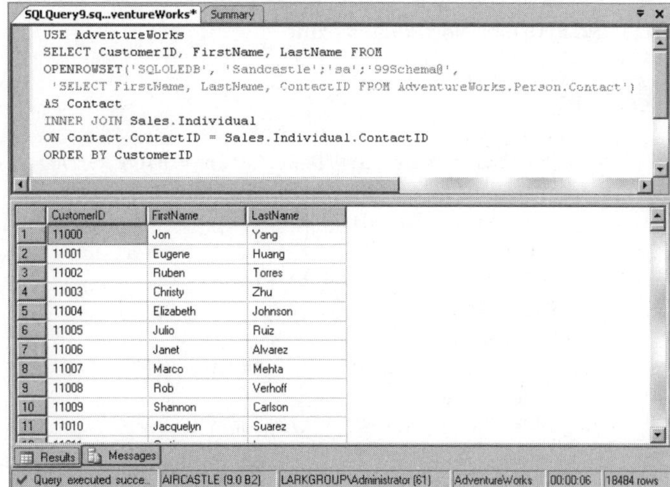

	CustomerID	FirstName	LastName
1	11000	Jon	Yang
2	11001	Eugene	Huang
3	11002	Ruben	Torres
4	11003	Christy	Zhu
5	11004	Elizabeth	Johnson
6	11005	Julio	Ruiz
7	11006	Janet	Alvarez
8	11007	Marco	Mehta
9	11008	Rob	Verhoff
10	11009	Shannon	Carlson
11	11010	Jacquelyn	Suarez

FIGURE 8.6
Using OPENROWSET

For example, you could perform the same query that was shown in the OPENROWSET example with the following OPENDATASOURCE statement:

```
SELECT CustomerID, FirstName, LastName FROM
OPENDATASOURCE('SQLOLEDB',
 'Data Source=Sandcastle;User ID=sa;Password=Sql#1'
 ).Adventureworks.Person.Contact
AS Contact
INNER JOIN Sales.Individual
ON Contact.ContactID = Sales.Individual.ContactID
ORDER BY CustomerID
```

TIP OPENROWSET **and** OPENDATASOURCE **should be used only for data sources that you need to query on an infrequent basis. If you need to regularly connect to a particular data source, it's more efficient to use a linked server for that connection.**

OPENXML

You already know that SQL Server 2005 brings XML features into the database server. With OPENXML, you can treat a set of nodes within an XML file as a rowset source, just like a table or a view. To do so, you need to specify the document, supply an XPath expression for selecting nodes, and specify the column mapping between the XML and the final rowset.

UNDERSTANDING XPATH

Before you can understand the syntax of OPENXML, you need to understand the basics of XPath. XPath isn't itself an XML standard (that is, an XPath expression isn't a well-formed XML document); rather, it's a language for talking *about* XML. By writing an appropriate XPath expression, you can select particular elements or attributes within an XML document. To make this more concrete, we'll use the XML document shown in Listing 8.1.

LISTING 8.1: NewProducts.xml

```
<?xml version="1.0" ?>
<ROOT>
  <NewProduct>
    <ProductID Status="New" Rating="High">10001</ProductID>
    <Name>Tiny Little Screws</Name>
    <ProductNumber>TLS</ProductNumber>
    <Color>Silver</Color>
    <InitialStock>5000</InitialStock>
  </NewProduct>
  <NewProduct>
    <ProductID Status="New" Rating="Medium">10002</ProductID>
    <Name>Grommets</Name>
    <ProductNumber>GS-42</ProductNumber>
    <Color>Bronze</Color>
    <InitialStock>2500</InitialStock>
  </NewProduct>
  <NewProduct>
    <ProductID Status="Restock" Rating="High">10003</ProductID>
    <Name>Silvery shoes</Name>
    <ProductNumber>SS-14A</ProductNumber>
    <Color>Silver</Color>
    <InitialStock>27</InitialStock>
  </NewProduct>
  <NewProduct>
    <ProductID Status="Restock" Rating="Low">10004</ProductID>
    <Name>Flying wingnuts</Name>
    <ProductNumber>FWN</ProductNumber>
    <Color>Black</Color>
    <InitialStock>1000</InitialStock>
  </NewProduct>
  <NewProduct>
    <ProductID Status="New" Rating="High">10005</ProductID>
    <Name>Winged helmet</Name>
    <ProductNumber>WH-001</ProductNumber>
    <Color>Red</Color>
    <InitialStock>50</InitialStock>
  </NewProduct>
</ROOT>
```

As you can see, this file stores information about five new products that we might like to work with in conjunction with the AdventureWorks database. Some of the information, such as the color of each product, is stored in XML elements. Other information, such as the status of the product, is stored in attributes of the ProductID element.

To understand XPath, it's helpful to think of an XML file as a tree of information. In the case of the `NewProducts.xml` file, the tree starts with the `ROOT` element, which contains `NewProduct` elements, and so on. Two parts of the XPath syntax are of interest for our purposes: identifying elements, and identifying attributes. These are the parts of an XML file that OPENXML can work with. The full XPath specification is much more comprehensive than this. For details, refer to the W3C XPath recommendation at www.w3.org/TR/XPath.html.

To identify a set of elements using XPath, you use the path down the tree structure to those elements, separating tags by forward slashes. For example, this XPath expression selects all the NewProduct elements in the NewProducts.xml file:

```
/ROOT/NewProduct
```

Similarly, this XPath expression selects all the InitialStock elements:

```
/ROOT/NewProduct/InitialStock
```

XPath expressions select a set of elements, not a single element. This makes them roughly analogous, in this case, to fields in a table or view.

The XPath specification allows the use of a single forward slash to specify the root of the entire XML document. SQL Server doesn't allow this in the XPath that it uses. You need to specify the root element by name. This will be ROOT in some cases, but an XML document can have any name for the root element. You need to use the name of the first element in the file, directly after the XML declaration.

To identify a set of attributes, you trace the path down the tree to the attributes, just as you do with elements. The only difference is that attribute names must be prefixed with an @ character. For example, this XPath expression selects all the Status attributes in the NewProducts.xml file:

```
/ROOT/NewProduct/ProductID/@Status
```

XPath also offers a predicate language to allow you to specify smaller groups of nodes or even individual nodes in the XML tree. You might think of this as a filtering capability similar to a SQL WHERE clause. One thing you can do is to specify the exact value of the node you'd like to work with. To find all ProductID nodes with the value 10001, you can use the following XPath expression:

```
/ROOT/NewProduct/ProductID[.="10001"]
```

Here, the dot (.) operator stands for the current node. You can also filter using values of elements or attributes within the current node. For example, to find NewProduct nodes where the Color element has the value Silver, you can use this expression:

```
/ROOT/NewProduct[Color="Silver"]
```

To find ProductID elements with a Rating attribute having the value Low, use this expression:

```
/ROOT/NewProduct/ProductID[@Rating="Low"]
```

There is no forward slash between an element and a filtering expression in XPath.

You can also use operators and Boolean expressions within filtering specifications. For example, you might want to find products where the InitialStock amount is between 10 and 100:

```
/ROOT/NewProduct[InitialStock>=10 and InitialStock<=100]
```

The full XPath specification includes operators for such things as finding ancestors, descendants, and siblings of a particular node in the XML tree. We won't be using any of these operators, and you're unlikely to need them when you're learning OPENXML.

OPENXML Syntax

Now that you've seen how XPath works, it's time to consider the Transact-SQL `OPENXML` statement. `OPENXML` works in concert with two stored procedures: `sp_xml_preparedocument` and `sp_xml_removedocument`. The first of these converts an XML document represented as a string of text into a tree and stores it in SQL Server's memory. The second removes such a parsed version of an XML document from the SQL Server memory when you're done with it.

The syntax for `sp_xml_preparedocument` is as follows:

```
sp_xml_preparedocument hdoc OUTPUT
  [, xmltext]
  [, xpath_namespaces]
```

This stored procedure has three parameters:

- *`hdoc`* is an integer variable that contains a returned document handle. You need this document handle for the calls to `OPENXML` and `sp_xml_removedocument`; it identifies the particular XML document to SQL Server.
- *`xmltext`* is the text of the XML document to be parsed by the procedure.
- *`xpath_namespaces`* lets you specify a namespace to define additional information about the XML document. You're unlikely to need this optional parameter.

`sp_xml_preparedocument` uses the MSXML parser to do its job, and it allots a large part of the SQL Server total memory setting to this task. It's important to remember to call `sp_xml_removedocument` to free this memory when you're done with it:

```
sp_xml_removedocument hdoc
```

In this stored procedure, the single parameter is the document handle that was originally retrieved from `sp_xml_preparedocument`.

Between the calls to `sp_xml_preparedocument` and `sp_xml_removedocument`, you can use `OPENXML` to retrieve data from the document. Here, at last, is the syntax of `OPENXML`:

```
OPENXML(idoc, rowpattern, [flags])
  [WITH (SchemaDeclaration | TableName)]
```

The parameters of `OPENXML` are as follows:

- *`idoc`* is a document handle returned by `sp_xml_preparedocument`.
- *`rowpattern`* is an XPath expression that indicates the nodes that should be treated as rows in the resulting rowset.
- *`flags`* is a value that specifies how to process the XML into columns. Table 8.1 shows the possible values for this parameter.
- *`SchemaDeclaration`* specifies the column mapping between the XML and the resulting rowset. We'll discuss this parameter in more detail later in this section.
- *`TableName`* is the name of an existing table that has the structure of the rowset that should be created.

TABLE 8.1: *flags* Values for OPENXML

VALUE	MEANING
0 (default)	Attribute-centric mapping
1	Attribute-centric mapping
2	Element-centric mapping
8	Add to any of the other values to discard data that won't fit in a column rather than saving it in a metaproperty

If you omit the optional WITH clause, then the results are returned in *edge table* format. An edge table provides a full description of all the nodes that are at the edge of the XML parse tree. Table 8.2 lists the columns that are returned in edge table format.

TABLE 8.2: Edge Table Format

COLUMN	MEANING
id	Unique identifier of this node
parentid	Identifier of the parent of this node
nodetype	1 for an element, 2 for an attribute, 3 for text
localname	Name of the node
prefix	Namespace prefix for the node
namespaceuri	Namespace URI for the node
datatype	Datatype of the node
prev	Identifier of the previous sibling of the node
text	Node content in text form

Although the edge table completely describes the XML, it isn't very useful as a rowset if you want to work with the data rather than examine its schema. In most cases, you'll want to use the WITH clause to supply a schema definition. A schema definition is a string of fields for the output rowset in this format:

```
ColName ColType [ColPattern | MetaProperty]
  [, ColName ColType [ColPattern | MetaProperty]...]
```

A schema definition uses these four parameters:

- *ColName* is the name to use for the output column in the rowset.
- *ColType* is the data type of the column.

- *ColPattern* is an XPath expression that describes the data to map in relation to the *rowpattern* parameter of the OPENXML statement.
- *MetaProperty* is a name of an OPENXML metaproperty. Metaproperties allow you to use information such as the namespace of the nodes in the output rowset. Refer to SQL Server Books Online for more information about OPENXML metaproperties.

OPENXML EXAMPLES

The simplest OPENXML query retrieves the information from the XML file in edge table format:

```
DECLARE @idoc int
DECLARE @doc varchar(2000)
SET @doc ='
<?xml version="1.0" ?>
<ROOT>
  <NewProduct>
    <ProductID Status="New" Rating="High">10001</ProductID>
    <Name>Tiny Little Screws</Name>
    <ProductNumber>TLS</ProductNumber>
    <Color>Silver</Color>
    <InitialStock>5000</InitialStock>
  </NewProduct>
  <NewProduct>
    <ProductID Status="New" Rating="Medium">10002</ProductID>
    <Name>Grommets</Name>
    <ProductNumber>GS-42</ProductNumber>
    <Color>Bronze</Color>
    <InitialStock>2500</InitialStock>
  </NewProduct>
  <NewProduct>
    <ProductID Status="Restock" Rating="High">10003</ProductID>
    <Name>Silvery shoes</Name>
    <ProductNumber>SS-14A</ProductNumber>
    <Color>Silver</Color>
    <InitialStock>27</InitialStock>
  </NewProduct>
  <NewProduct>
    <ProductID Status="Restock" Rating="Low">10004</ProductID>
    <Name>Flying wingnuts</Name>
    <ProductNumber>FWN</ProductNumber>
    <Color>Black</Color>
    <InitialStock>1000</InitialStock>
  </NewProduct>
  <NewProduct>
    <ProductID Status="New" Rating="High">10005</ProductID>
    <Name>Winged helmet</Name>
    <ProductNumber>WH-001</ProductNumber>
    <Color>Red</Color>
    <InitialStock>50</InitialStock>
  </NewProduct>
```

```
</ROOT> '
EXEC sp_xml_preparedocument @idoc OUTPUT, @doc
SELECT *
FROM OPENXML (@idoc, '/ROOT')
EXEC sp_xml_removedocument @idoc
```

This may look like a lot of SQL, but most of it is setup and teardown. First, we place the XML document into a variable. Then we use `sp_xml_preparedocument` to parse it into memory, where it can be read by `OPENXML`. Finally, we use `sp_xml_removedocument` to free the memory. In the rest of the examples, we'll omit the setup and teardown steps and just show you the `OPENXML` statement. Figure 8.7 shows the results of running this query.

FIGURE 8.7
`NewProducts.xml` in edge table format

	id	parentid	nodetype	localname	prefix	namespaceuri	datatype	prev
1	0	NULL	1	ROOT	NULL	NULL	NULL	1
2	4	0	1	NewProduct	NULL	NULL	NULL	NULL
3	5	4	1	ProductID	NULL	NULL	NULL	NULL
4	6	5	2	Status	NULL	NULL	NULL	NULL
5	49	6	3	#text	NULL	NULL	NULL	NULL
6	7	5	2	Rating	NULL	NULL	NULL	NULL
7	50	7	3	#text	NULL	NULL	NULL	NULL
8	8	5	3	#text	NULL	NULL	NULL	NULL
9	9	4	1	Name	NULL	NULL	NULL	5
10	51	9	3	#text	NULL	NULL	NULL	NULL
11	10	4	1	ProductNumber	NULL	NULL	NULL	9
12	52	10	3	#text	NULL	NULL	NULL	NULL
13	11	4	1	Color	NULL	NULL	NULL	10
14	53	11	3	#text	NULL	NULL	NULL	NULL
15	12	4	1	InitialStock	NULL	NULL	NULL	11
16	54	12	3	#text	NULL	NULL	NULL	NULL
17	13	0	1	NewProduct	NULL	NULL	NULL	4
18	14	13	1	ProductID	NULL	NULL	NULL	NULL
19	15	14	2	Status	NULL	NULL	NULL	NULL
20	55	15	3	#text	NULL	NULL	NULL	NULL
21	16	14	2	Rating	NULL	NULL	NULL	NULL
22	56	16	3	#text	NULL	NULL	NULL	NULL
23	17	14	3	#text	NULL	NULL	NULL	NULL

Results | Messages

To retrieve a recordset with `ProductID` and `Name` information, you can use this query:

```
SELECT * FROM OPENXML(@iDoc, '/ROOT/NewProduct', 2)
  WITH (ProductID varchar(5), Name varchar(32))
```

As you can see, there's no need to supply the `ColPattern` parameter in the `WITH` clause if the column names in the rowset are the same as the tag names in the XML document. Also note the use of 2 as a flag value. If you omit this, you'll still get a recordset with five rows; but all the values will be empty, because `OPENXML` will be looking for attributes with the names `ProductID` and `Name` rather than elements. If you want to retrieve attributes, use 3 for the flag value instead. Figure 8.8 shows the results of running this query.

FIGURE 8.8
XML data as a rowset

	ProductID	Name
1	10001	Tiny Little Screws
2	10002	Grommets
3	10003	Silvery shoes
4	10004	Flying wingnuts
5	10005	Winged helmet

Results | Messages

Cursors

Traditionally, SQL provides a set-oriented look for your data. For example, when you execute a SELECT statement, it returns a set of rows. This set is all one thing, not a selection of individual rows. Although this is a useful view for many traditional batch-processing applications, it's less appealing for interactive applications where a user might want to work with rows one at a time.

SQL Server's solution to this problem is to introduce cursors. If you've worked with recordsets in a product such as Access or Visual Basic, you can understand cursors as a server-side recordset. A *cursor* is a set of rows together with a pointer that identifies a current row. T-SQL provides statements that let you move the pointer and work with the current row. In the remainder of this section, you'll learn about the following statements:

- DECLARE CURSOR
- OPEN
- FETCH
- CLOSE
- DEALLOCATE

WARNING Cursors are often slower than traditional set-based SQL approaches to retrieving data. You should only resort to cursors when you've exhausted other ways of solving your query problems.

DECLARE CURSOR

The DECLARE CURSOR statement is used to set aside storage for a cursor and to set the basic properties of the cursor. There are two different forms of the DECLARE CURSOR statement. The first form is the ANSI standard DECLARE CURSOR:

```
DECLARE cursor_name [INSENSITIVE][SCROLL] CURSOR
 FOR select_statement
 [FOR {READ ONLY | UPDATE [OF column_name [,...n]]}]
```

In this form of the DECLARE CURSOR statement:

- The DECLARE and CURSOR keywords are required to declare a cursor.
- The *cursor_name* is an arbitrary SQL identifier that will identify this cursor in subsequent T-SQL statements.
- INSENSITIVE tells SQL Server to establish a temporary table just for this cursor. Modifications that other users make while the cursor is open won't be reflected in the cursor's data, and you won't be able to make any modifications through the cursor.
- SCROLL specifies that all of the options of the FETCH statement should be supported. If you omit SCROLL, only FETCH NEXT is supported.
- The *select_statement* argument is a standard T-SQL SELECT statement that supplies the rows for the cursor. This statement can't use the COMPUTE, COMPUTE BY, FOR BROWSE, or INTO options.
- READ ONLY prevents any updates through the cursor. By default, the cursor allows updating (unless it was opened with the INSENSITIVE option).

- UPDATE specifies explicitly that the cursor should allow updating. If you use UPDATE OF with a list of column names, only data in those columns can be updated.

There's also an extended form of DECLARE CURSOR that is *not* ANSI SQL compatible:

```
DECLARE cursor_name CURSOR
 [LOCAL | GLOBAL]
 [FORWARD_ONLY | SCROLL]
 [STATIC | KEYSET | DYNAMIC | FAST_FORWARD]
 [READ_ONLY | SCROLL_LOCKS | OPTIMISTIC]
 [TYPE_WARNING]
 FOR select_statement
 [FOR UPDATE [OF column_name [,...n]]]
```

In this form of the DECLARE CURSOR statement:

- The DECLARE and CURSOR keywords are required to declare a cursor.
- The *cursor_name* is an arbitrary SQL identifier that will identify this cursor in subsequent T-SQL statements.
- The LOCAL keyword limits the use of the cursor to the batch, stored procedure, or trigger where it was created.
- The GLOBAL keyword makes the cursor available to any statement on the current connection.
- FORWARD_ONLY specifies that only the NEXT option of the FETCH statement is supported.
- SCROLL specifies that all the options of the FETCH statement should be supported. If you specify SCROLL, you can't specify FAST_FORWARD.
- STATIC causes the cursor to return a set of rows that reflects the state of the database when the cursor is opened and that is never updated. You can't make changes through a static cursor.
- KEYSET specifies that the cursor should be updateable, both by the connection and by other users. However, new rows added by other users won't be reflected in the cursor.
- DYNAMIC specifies that the cursor should be fully updateable and that it should reflect new rows.
- READ_ONLY specifies that the cursor should be read-only.
- SCROLL_LOCKS specifies that updates or deletions made through the cursor should always succeed. SQL Server ensures this by locking the rows as soon as they're read into the cursor.
- OPTIMISTIC uses optimistic locking when you attempt to change a row through the cursor.
- TYPE_WARNING tells SQL Server to send a warning if the selected cursor options can't all be fulfilled.
- The *select_statement* argument is a standard T-SQL SELECT statement that supplies the rows for the cursor. This statement can't use the COMPUTE, COMPUTE BY, FOR BROWSE, or INTO options.
- FOR UPDATE specifies explicitly that the cursor should allow updating. If you use UPDATE OF with a list of column names, only data in those columns can be updated.

OPEN and *@@CURSOR_ROWS*

The OPEN statement is used to populate a cursor with the records to which it refers:

```
OPEN {{[GLOBAL] cursor_name} | cursor_variable_name}
```

You must use the GLOBAL keyword if you're referring to a cursor declared with the GLOBAL keyword. You can use either the name of a cursor directly or the name of a cursor variable (one declared with the DECLARE statement and set equal to a cursor with the SET statement).

Of course, the cursor must be declared before you issue the OPEN statement.

If the cursor was declared with the INSENSITIVE or STATIC keyword, the OPEN statement creates a temporary table in the tempdb database to hold the records. If the cursor was declared with the KEYSET keyword, the OPEN statement creates a temporary table in the tempdb database to hold the keys. You don't need to worry about these tables; SQL Server will delete them when the cursor is closed.

Once a cursor has been opened, you can use the @@CURSOR_ROWS global variable to retrieve the number of rows in this cursor. For example, consider the following T-SQL batch:

```
DECLARE contact_cursor CURSOR
 LOCAL SCROLL STATIC
 FOR
  SELECT * FROM Person.Contact
OPEN contact_cursor
PRINT @@CURSOR_ROWS
```

As you can see in Figure 8.9, the PRINT statement shows that all 19,972 rows of the Person .Contact table are in the cursor.

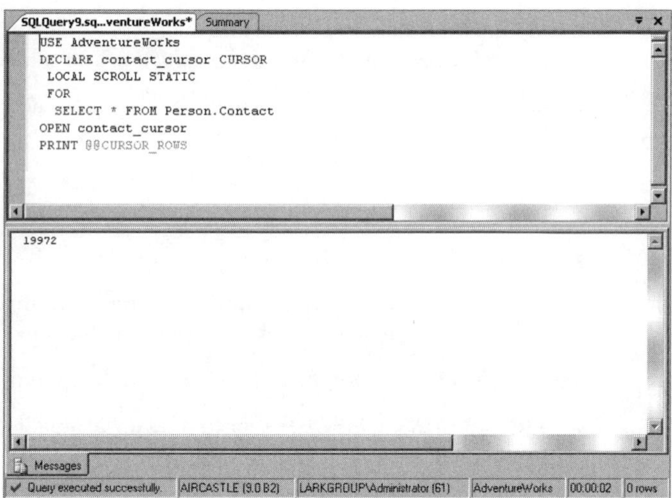

FIGURE 8.9 Counting rows in a cursor

WARNING The @@CURSOR_ROWS variable always refers to the most recently opened cursor. You may want to store the value of this variable directly after the OPEN statement so that you can refer to it later.

You need to be a bit cautious about using @@CURSOR_ROWS, because under some circumstances, it won't reflect the actual number of rows in the cursor. That's because SQL Server might decide to fetch data into the cursor asynchronously, so that processing can continue while the cursor is still being populated.

SQL Server will fill a cursor asynchronously if the cursor is declared with the STATIC or KEYSET parameter and SQL Server estimates that the number of rows will be greater than a certain threshold value. You can set this value with the sp_configure system stored procedure; the name of the option is *cursor threshold*. By default, the value is set to –1, which tells SQL Server to always populate cursors synchronously.

NOTE See Chapter 14, "Stored Procedures," for more information on sp_configure.

Depending on the circumstances, @@CURSOR_ROWS may return one of the following values:

- A negative number indicates that the cursor is being populated asynchronously and shows the number of rows retrieved so far. The value –57, for example, indicates that the cursor has 57 rows, but that SQL Server hasn't finished populating the cursor.
- The value –1 is a special case that's always returned for dynamic cursors. Because other users can be adding or deleting data, SQL Server can't be sure about the number of rows in a dynamic cursor or whether it's fully populated.
- Zero indicates that there isn't an open cursor.
- A positive number indicates that the cursor is fully populated with that number of rows.

FETCH and *@@FETCH_STATUS*

The FETCH statement is used to retrieve data from a cursor to variables so that you can work with the data. This statement has a number of options:

```
FETCH
[[ NEXT | PRIOR | FIRST | LAST
  | ABSOLUTE {n | @n_variable}
  | RELATIVE {n | @n_variable}
 ]
 FROM
]
{{[GLOBAL] cursor_name} | @cursor_variable_name}
[INTO @variable_name [,...n]]
```

If you keep in mind that a cursor is a set of records with a pointer to a particular record, it's pretty easy to understand the FETCH statement. FETCH is used to move the record pointer:

- NEXT is the default option and fetches the next row in the cursor. If FETCH NEXT is the first statement issued, it fetches the first row from the cursor.
- PRIOR fetches the previous row in the cursor.
- FIRST fetches the first row in the cursor.
- LAST fetches the last row in the cursor.

- ABSOLUTE fetches the particular record specified. For example, ABSOLUTE 5 fetches the fifth record. If you use a variable to hold the number, the variable must be of type int, smallint, or tinyint.
- RELATIVE fetches a record ahead or behind the current record by the specified amount. For example, RELATIVE 5 fetches the record five past the current record, and RELATIVE –5 fetches the record five before the current record. If you use a variable to hold the number, the variable must be of type int, smallint, or tinyint.
- INTO lets you specify variables that will hold the fetched data. You must supply enough variables to hold all the columns from the cursor. The variables will be filled in column order, and the datatypes must match those in the cursor or be datatypes that can be implicitly converted from those in the cursor.

Not all FETCH options are supported by all cursors, depending on how the cursor was declared. Here are the rules:

- If the cursor was declared with SQL-92 syntax without SCROLL, only NEXT is supported.
- If the cursor was declared with SQL-92 syntax with SCROLL, all options are supported.
- If the cursor was declared with SQL Server syntax with FORWARD_ONLY or FAST_FORWARD, only NEXT is supported.
- If the cursor was declared with SQL Server syntax with DYNAMIC SCROLL, all options except ABSOLUTE are supported.
- If the cursor was declared with SQL Server syntax and doesn't fall into one of the previous two categories, all options are supported.

The @@FETCH_STATUS global variable contains information about the most recent FETCH operation. If the value is zero, the fetch was successful. If the value isn't zero, the FETCH statement failed for some reason.

As a simple example of FETCH, here's how you might print some data from the first row of a cursor:

```
DECLARE @FirstName nvarchar(50), @LastName nvarchar(50)
DECLARE contact_cursor CURSOR
 LOCAL SCROLL STATIC
 FOR
  SELECT FirstName, LastName FROM Person.Contact
OPEN contact_cursor
FETCH NEXT FROM contact_cursor
 INTO @FirstName, @LastName
PRINT @FirstName + ' ' + @LastName
```

More often, you'll want to do something that moves through an entire cursor. You can do this by using the @@FETCH_STATUS variable with the WHILE statement. We haven't discussed the WHILE statement yet, but it's similar to WHILE in most other programming languages. It performs the next statement repeatedly as long as some condition is true. Figure 8.10 shows an example of using FETCH to retrieve multiple rows by executing the following T-SQL batch:

```
DECLARE @FirstName nvarchar(50), @LastName nvarchar(50)
DECLARE contact_cursor CURSOR
 LOCAL SCROLL STATIC
 FOR
```

```
  SELECT FirstName, LastName FROM Person.Contact
OPEN contact_cursor
FETCH NEXT FROM contact_cursor
 INTO @FirstName, @LastName
PRINT @FirstName + ' ' + @LastName
WHILE @@FETCH_STATUS = 0
 BEGIN
  FETCH NEXT FROM contact_cursor
   INTO @FirstName, @LastName
  PRINT @FirstName + ' ' + @LastName
 END
```

FIGURE 8.10 Fetching multiple rows of data with a WHILE loop

CLOSE

The CLOSE statement is the reverse of the OPEN statement. Its syntax is similar to that of OPEN:

```
CLOSE {{[GLOBAL] cursor_name} | cursor_variable_name}
```

When you're done with the data in a cursor, you should execute a CLOSE statement. This frees up the rows that are being held in the cursor, but it doesn't destroy the cursor itself. The cursor could be reopened by executing the OPEN statement again. While a cursor is closed, of course, you can't execute a FETCH statement on it.

DEALLOCATE

The DEALLOCATE statement is the reverse of the DECLARE CURSOR statement:

```
DEALLOCATE {{[GLOBAL] cursor_name} | cursor_variable_name}
```

When you're done with a cursor, you should use DEALLOCATE to destroy the cursor data structures and remove the name from the SQL Server namespace.

A Cursor Example

By now, you know enough T-SQL to understand quite complex examples. Consider the following batch:

```
DECLARE @departmentid int, @name nvarchar(50)
DECLARE @nemployees int
DECLARE department_cursor CURSOR
 LOCAL SCROLL STATIC
 FOR
  SELECT DepartmentID, Name
  FROM HumanResources.Department
OPEN department_cursor
PRINT 'Results for ' + CAST(@@CURSOR_ROWS AS varchar) +
  ' departments'
Print '------------'
FETCH NEXT FROM department_cursor
 INTO @departmentid, @name
SELECT @nemployees = (
 SELECT COUNT(*) FROM HumanResources.EmployeeDepartmentHistory
  WHERE DepartmentID = @departmentid)
PRINT @name + ' has ' +
 CAST(@nemployees AS varchar) + ' employees'
WHILE @@FETCH_STATUS = 0
 BEGIN
  FETCH NEXT FROM department_cursor
   INTO @departmentid, @name
  SELECT @nemployees = (
   SELECT COUNT(*) FROM HumanResources.EmployeeDepartmentHistory
   WHERE DepartmentID = @departmentid)
  PRINT @name + ' has ' +
   CAST(@nemployees AS varchar) + ' employees'
 END
CLOSE department_cursor
DEALLOCATE department_cursor
```

Let's look at the statements in this batch, step by step:

- The first DECLARE statement sets aside storage for two variables.
- The second DECLARE statement sets aside storage for one more variable.
- The third DECLARE statement declares a static cursor to hold information from two columns in the HumanResources.Department table.
- The OPEN statement gets the rows that the cursor declares.
- The first PRINT statement uses the @@CURSOR_ROWS global variable to print the number of records in the cursor. Note the use of the CAST statement to convert this numeric value to character format before the value is concatenated with other strings.

- The first FETCH NEXT statement gets the first row from the cursor.
- The SELECT statement uses some of the data from the cursor together with the COUNT function to count the rows in the HumanResources. EmployeeDepartmentHistory table for the first department.
- The PRINT statement formats the selected data for the user.
- The WHILE statement tells SQL Server to continue until it has exhausted the cursor.
- The BEGIN statement marks the start of the statements controlled by the WHILE statement.
- The FETCH NEXT, SELECT, and PRINT statements within the WHILE loop tell SQL Server to continue fetching rows and printing the results.
- The END statement marks the end of the statements controlled by the WHILE statement.
- The CLOSE statement removes the records from the cursor.
- The DEALLOCATE statement removes the cursor from memory.

Can you visualize the results of running this batch of T-SQL statements? You can refer to Figure 8.11 to confirm your results.

FIGURE 8.11
Running a batch in SQL Server Management Studio

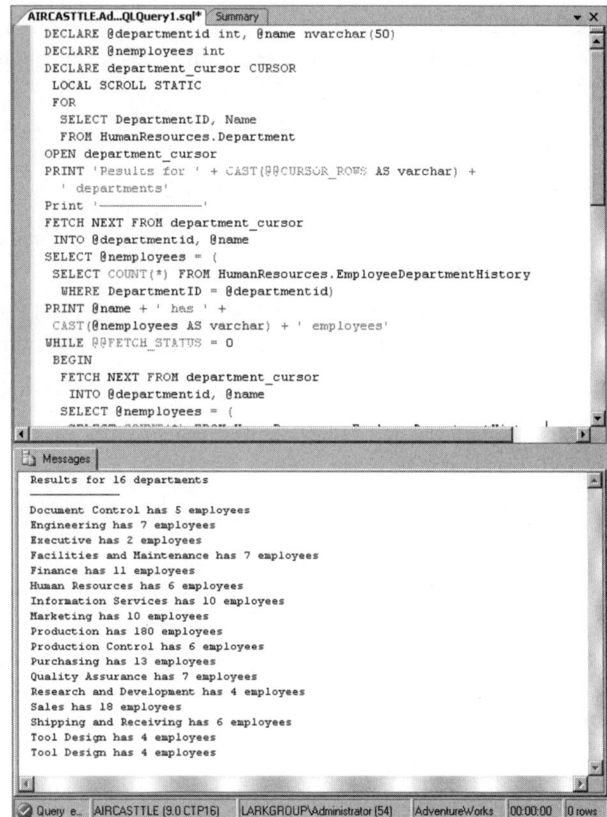

Using the System Tables and Information Schema Views

There will be times when you need to retrieve metadata from SQL Server. *Metadata* is data about data. For example, the data in your database might include

- Customer names
- Order dates
- Employee numbers

By contrast, the metadata for the same database might include

- Table names
- Login names
- Column sizes

Metadata tends to be most useful to database administrators and application developers, rather than to end users. SQL Server provides several tools for retrieving metadata. In this section, we'll introduce you to two of those tools: the system tables and the information schema views.

What's in the System Tables?

In a word, everything. The *system tables* are a set of tables that SQL Server uses to track information about users, databases, tables, replication tasks, and so on. If SQL Server knows about a piece of information, it's more than likely stored in a system table.

System tables break down into seven groups:

- The master database contains a set of tables with information on databases, logins, servers, and other systemwide information.
- Each database contains a set of tables with information on objects, indexes, columns, and other database-specific information.
- The msdb database contains a set of tables used by SQLServerAgent to store information about alerts, jobs, and the other items that Agent manages.
- The msdb database also contains a set of tables with backup and restore information.
- The master database contains a set of tables with systemwide replication information such as the names of publishing and subscribing servers.
- The distribution database contains a set of tables with information on replication schedules and transactions.
- Each database that participates in replication contains a set of tables with information on the replicated objects within that database.

All told, there are nearly 200 system tables. Of these, the ones that you're most likely to be interested in are in the first two groups: those that describe databases and the information that they contain, as well as the overall system information. Table 8.3 lists these tables.

TABLE 8.3: Important System Tables

NAME	LOCATION	CONTAINS
sysaltfiles	master	Files used to hold databases
syscacheobjects	master	Objects currently cached
syscharsets	master	Character sets and sort orders
sysconfigures	master	Configuration options
syscurconfigs	master	Current configuration options
sysdatabases	master	Databases on the server
sysdevices	master	Database devices (now obsolete)
syslanguages	master	Languages
syslockinfo	master	Current lock information
syslogins	master	Login accounts
sysmessages	master	System error and warning messages
sysoledbusers	master	Login information for linked servers
sysperfinfo	master	Performance counters
sysprocesses	master	Processes
sysremotelogins	master	Remote login accounts
sysservers	master	Linked servers
syscolumns	Each database	Columns
syscomments	Each database	Comments on objects
sysconstraints	Each database	Constraints
sysdepends	Each database	Dependency information
sysfilegroups	Each database	Filegroups
sysfiles	Each database	Files
sysforeignkeys	Each database	Foreign-key constraints
sysfulltextcatalogs	Each database	Full-text catalogs
sysindexes	Each database	Indexes
sysindexkeys	Each database	Columns in indexes

TABLE 8.3: Important System Tables *(CONTINUED)*

Name	Location	Contains
sysmembers	Each database	Members of roles
sysobjects	Each database	All database objects
syspermissions	Each database	Permissions
sysprotects	Each database	Permissions for roles
sysreferences	Each database	Columns for foreign keys
systypes	Each database	User-defined datatypes
sysusers	Each database	Users

Of course, each of these tables has a number of columns containing the information it holds. We could list each of these columns here, but that would be a waste of paper, because the information is readily available in Books Online. You can find this information by opening the following series of books in the Books Online contents pane:

SQL Server Language Reference
Transact-SQL Reference
System Tables

Figure 8.12 shows a sample definition of one of the system tables from Books Online.

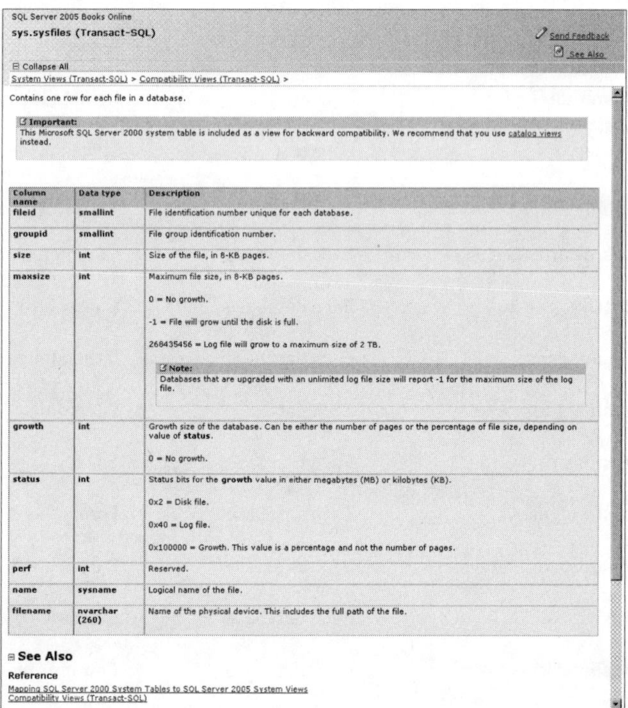

SQL Server 2005 Books Online

sys.sysfiles (Transact-SQL)

Send Feedback
See Also

Collapse All

System Views (Transact-SQL) > Compatibility Views (Transact-SQL) >

Contains one row for each file in a database.

Important:
This Microsoft SQL Server 2000 system table is included as a view for backward compatibility. We recommend that you use catalog views instead.

Column name	Data type	Description
fileid	**smallint**	File identification number unique for each database.
groupid	**smallint**	File group identification number.
size	**int**	Size of the file, in 8-KB pages.
maxsize	**int**	Maximum file size, in 8-KB pages. 0 = No growth. -1 = File will grow until the disk is full. 268435456 = Log file will grow to a maximum size of 2 TB. **Note:** Databases that are upgraded with an unlimited log file size will report -1 for the maximum size of the log file.
growth	**int**	Growth size of the database. Can be either the number of pages or the percentage of file size, depending on value of **status**. 0 = No growth.
status	**int**	Status bits for the **growth** value in either megabytes (MB) or kilobytes (KB). 0x2 = Disk file. 0x40 = Log file. 0x100000 = Growth. This value is a percentage and not the number of pages.
perf	**int**	Reserved.
name	**sysname**	Logical name of the file.
filename	**nvarchar (260)**	Name of the physical device. This includes the full path of the file.

See Also

Reference

Mapping SQL Server 2000 System Tables to SQL Server 2005 System Views
Compatibility Views (Transact-SQL)

FIGURE 8.12 Definition of the sysfiles table

Sample System Table Queries

Although almost everybody does it, retrieving information from the system tables isn't a supported way of dealing with SQL Server.

WARNING It's important enough to make the point again: Querying the system tables isn't supported. Microsoft can and does change the information stored in these tables from release to release. If you depend on information from the system tables, it's up to you to figure out how to fix any problems caused by upgrading.

Nevertheless, querying the system tables is so prevalent and so simple that we're going to show you a few examples. These examples all worked on SQL Server 2005; if you're using a later version, you might have to modify any or all of these examples to make them work.

WARNING Under no circumstances should you add, delete, or update information in the system tables.

As one simple example, it's possible to get an idea of which physical devices SQL Server is using by retrieving information from the sysdatabases table:

```
USE master
SELECT name, filename
FROM sysdatabases
```

As you can see in Figure 8.13, this gives you the locations of the primary file for each database.

FIGURE 8.13 Retrieving primary filenames from sysdatabases

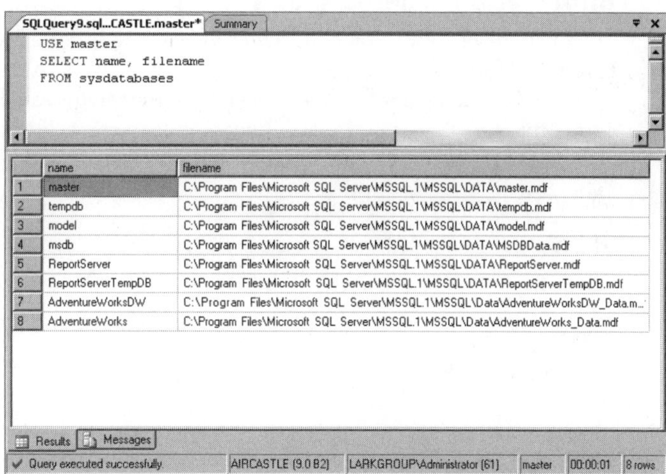

If you'd like more information, you can retrieve the names of all the files used by any particular database by querying the sysfiles table in that particular database:

```
SELECT name, filename
FROM sysfiles
```

To see which users are running the largest number of processes on your server, you might summarize some of the information in sysprocesses:

```
SELECT loginame,
COUNT(loginame) AS processcount
FROM sysprocesses
GROUP BY loginame
ORDER BY processcount DESC
```

Or, if you'd like a list of all the tables in a database, you can get the information from sysobjects within that database:

```
SELECT * FROM sysobjects
WHERE xtype = 'U'
ORDER BY name
```

Again, although querying the system tables can be a very fast way to obtain information, it's a dangerous way, because it's not supported. If possible, you should consider alternatives to querying the system tables. Depending on what information you're after, these alternatives include:

- Information schema views (discussed in the next section)
- System stored procedures (discussed in Chapter 14)
- SMO (discussed in Chapter 21, "SMO and RMO Programming")

Information Schema Views

You can think of the information schema views as a supported way to retrieve information from the system tables. Although the system tables may change from release to release, the information schema views will continue to return the same information in the same columns. These views conform to the part of the SQL-92 standard that defines ways to retrieve metadata from different databases.

SQL Server defines 20 information schema views in each database. These views are listed in Table 8.4.

TABLE 8.4: Information Schema Views

VIEW	CONTAINS
CHECK_CONSTRAINTS	Check constraints
COLUMN_DOMAIN_USAGE	Columns based on user-defined datatypes
COLUMN_PRIVILEGES	Column-level security
COLUMNS	Columns
CONSTRAINT_COLUMN_USAGE	Columns with defined constraints
CONSTRAINT_TABLE_USAGE	Tables with defined constraints
DOMAIN_CONSTRAINTS	User-defined datatypes

TABLE 8.4: Information Schema Views *(CONTINUED)*

VIEW	CONTAINS
DOMAINS	User-defined datatypes
KEY_COLUMN_USAGE	Columns with primary or foreign keys
PARAMETERS	Parameters for stored procedures and user-defined functions
REFERENTIAL_CONSTRAINTS	Foreign keys
ROUTINES	Stored procedures and functions
ROUTINE_COLUMNS	Columns from stored procedures and functions
SCHEMATA	Databases
TABLE_CONSTRAINTS	Table constraints
TABLE_PRIVILEGES	Table-level security
TABLES	Tables
VIEW_COLUMN_USAGE	Columns included in views
VIEW_TABLE_USAGE	Tables included in views
VIEWS	Views

You'll find complete definitions of each of these views in Books Online in the *Information Schema Views* topic. You can use the SELECT statement to retrieve information from these views. You need to identify these views as belonging to the INFORMATION_SCHEMA user. For example, to get a list of all the tables in the current database using one of these views, you can execute the following query:

```
SELECT * FROM
INFORMATION_SCHEMA.TABLES
```

Optimizer Hints

When you create a SQL Server stored procedure, the server creates an execution plan for that stored procedure. The *execution plan* is a list of the steps that SQL Server will take to get the results of the stored procedure. This plan is based on statistical information that the server maintains about things such as the number of rows in each table, the number of unique indexes in each table, and so on. Based on this information, SQL Server decides what strategy is likely to be the fastest and uses that strategy for the execution plan. SQL Server also comes up with execution plans on the fly when you execute SELECT statements and other ad-hoc queries.

This optimization system is based on probability. SQL Server doesn't run each query to decide what will be the most efficient strategy. Rather, it relies on its best guess. Sometimes, this guess might be wrong. In those cases, you can use optimizer hints to instruct the server how you'd like it to carry out the steps involved in resolving a view.

In this section, we'll look at the available optimizer hints and their effects. Of course, you shouldn't use this technique unless you have a situation where you can make your queries faster by using hints. You'll find more information on optimizing queries, including how to tell when you need to use hints, in Chapter 24 ("Monitoring and Optimizing SQL Server 2005").

The optimizer supports the use of three types of hints:

- Table hints
- Join hints
- Query hints

We'll discuss each of these types in turn. For information on which SQL statements can use optimizer hints, refer back to Chapters 6 and 7.

Table Hints

Table hints tell the optimizer how to retrieve data from a table, and can be used almost anywhere that you specify a tablename. Most of these hints are ways of fine-tuning the locking behavior of the table. You'll learn more about locking in Chapter 23. There are 16 table hints in all:

- `INDEX` specifies which index to use. If a table has a clustered index, `INDEX(0)` forces a scan on the clustered index. If a table doesn't have a clustered index, `INDEX(0)` forces a table scan. `INDEX(n)` or `INDEX(name)` forces the use of the index with the corresponding number or name.
- `FASTFIRSTROW` optimizes for retrieving the first row, rather than all rows, of the result.
- `HOLDLOCK` holds locks until the current transaction has been completed instead of releasing them as soon as SQL Server is done with a particular table.
- `NOLOCK` specifies that read rows should not be locked, which may result in data that's being rolled back being erroneously read.
- `PAGLOCK` forces shared page locks in place of individual shared locks or shared table locks.
- `READCOMMITTED` forces shared locks while the data is being read. The `READ_COMMITTED_SNAPSHOT` database option overrides this setting.
- `READCOMMITTEDLOCK` forces shared locks while the data is being read, regardless of the `READ_COMMITTED_SNAPSHOT` database option.
- `READPAST` specifies that locked rows should be skipped in a table scan.
- `READUNCOMMITTED` is the same as `NOLOCK`.
- `REPEATABLEREAD` forces exclusive locks while the data is being read.
- `ROWLOCK` specifies that row-level instead of page-level locks should be used.
- `SERIALIZABLE` is the same as `HOLDLOCK`.
- `TABLOCK` specifies that table-level locking should be used.
- `TABLOCKX` specifies that exclusive table-level locking should be used.
- `UPDLOCK` specifies that update locks instead of shared locks should be used.
- `XLOCK` specifies that exclusive locks should be taken and held until the end of any containing transaction.

Join Hints

Join hints are used to force a particular joining strategy between tables, and are used in JOIN clauses. There are four available join hints:

- LOOP specifies that a loop join should be used.
- HASH specifies that a hash join should be used.
- MERGE specifies that a merge join should be used.
- REMOTE specifies that a join should be performed by the remote server rather than the local server when tables from two different servers are being joined.

Of these, the one that's most likely to be useful is REMOTE. If you're joining a large remote table to a small local table, the REMOTE hint can vastly increase performance.

Query Hints

Query hints apply to an entire query. There are 15 hints you can specify here:

- HASH GROUP specifies that aggregations in a GROUP BY or COMPUTE clause should be computed by hashing.
- ORDER GROUP specifies that aggregations in a GROUP BY or COMPUTE clause should be computed by ordering.
- MERGE UNION specifies that unions should be computed by merging.
- HASH UNION specifies that unions should be computed by hashing.
- CONCAT UNION specifies that unions should be computed by concatenation.
- FAST *n* specifies that the query should be optimized to return the first *n* rows.
- FORCE ORDER preserves the join order from the query into the optimization process.
- MAXDOP *n* specifies the maximum number of processors to use when executing a parallelized query.
- OPTIMIZE FOR (@*variable name* = *literal constant*) specifies a value to use for a local variable when optimizing the query.
- RECOMPILE prevents SQL Server from caching executing plans.
- ROBUST PLAN forces a query plan that will work with the widest possible row size.
- KEEP PLAN prevents a query from generating a new plan when a table has new data added.
- KEEPFIXED PLAN prevents a query from generating a new plan due to statistics or index changes.
- EXPAND VIEW specifies that any indexed views should be replaced with their underlying definitions.
- MAXRECURSION *n* specifies the maximum levels of recursion that will be allowed during query execution.

View Hints

View hints tell the optimizer how to deal with an indexed view. There are two view hints:

- `INDEX` specifies which index to use. `INDEX(0)` forces a clustered index scan. `INDEX(`*n*`)` or `INDEX(`*name*`)` forces the use of the index with the corresponding number or name.
- `NOEXPAND` tells the optimizer to treat the view like a table with a clustered index rather than expanding it and optimizing the parts.

Summary

The last four chapters have provided you with an introduction to the Transact-SQL language used for working with data stored on SQL Server. In this chapter, you learned some of the more advanced skills for using T-SQL:

- Working with transactions
- Using rowset functions
- Using cursors
- Retrieving metadata
- Using optimizer hints

At this point, you should know enough T-SQL to handle most of your querying needs. Now it's time to look at SQL Server from a different standpoint, by considering the objects that SQL Server stores rather than the data that those objects hold. In the next chapter, we'll start with a look at SQL Server Management Studio.

Part 3

Digging into SQL Server

In this section:

Chapter 9

Using SQL Server Management Studio

In response to many user requests (and complaints), Microsoft reengineered the way you manage and administer tasks in SQL Server 2005. Whether this is your first exposure to SQL Server or you're an old hand at it, you'll quickly notice that a single, consolidated tool—SQL Server Management Studio—allows you to access nearly all of the management functions in SQL Server. Management Studio now combines the formerly fragmented Analysis Manager, Enterprise Manager, and Query Analyzer applications into a unified interface resembling the Visual Studio 2005 model. You can also manage notification services, replication, reporting services, earlier versions, and SQL Server Mobile Edition through the Management Studio interface. In other words, if you're a database administrator, Management Studio is where you'll spend nearly all of your time. This is an extremely rich and powerful application, and you should become very familiar with it.

In this chapter, you'll get an overview of using Management Studio. We'll start by discussing the general framework that holds the Management Studio. Then we'll look at the objects and tasks within Management Studio, particularly those in Registered Servers, Object Explorer, Template Explorer, and Solution Explorer.

Introducing SQL Server Management Studio

To launch Management Studio, click Start ➢ All Programs ➢Microsoft SQL Server 2005 ➢ Management Studio (see Figure 9.1). Note that the default view consists of three windows: Registered Servers, Object Explorer, and Summary (we have also opened some of the nodes and folders in Figure 9.1, for illustration purposes).

If you're familiar with Visual Studio (VS), the layout and feel of Management Studio is very similar. The VS interface is slowly becoming the environment of choice in Microsoft development applications. This is primarily because the design allows for a high degree of articulation and granularity while at the same maximizing visibility. You'll find that the tool windows in Management Studio are highly customizable and can be configured to maximize development and/or management workspace.

Through some simple customization, you can readily access the tools and windows you use frequently as well as control how much space you want to allocate to different information and tasks. There are a variety of ways to increase your editing space without impacting the functioning of Management Studio:

- All the windows can be moved to different locations.
- Most windows can be undocked and dragged out of the Management Studio frame—a valuable attribute when you're using more than one monitor.

- All the windows have an Auto Hide feature that lets you reduce the window to a tab within a bar on the border of the main Management Studio window. When you place the cursor over one of these tabs, the underlying window reveals itself. (You can toggle Auto Hide for a window by clicking the Auto Hide button, represented by a pushpin, in the upper-right corner of the window. You can also choose Window ➤ Auto Hide All.)
- You can configure some components in either tabbed mode (components appear as tabs in the same docking location) or multiple document interface (MDI) mode (each document has its own window). To configure this feature, choose Tools ➤ Options ➤ Environment ➤ General and then select either the Tabbed or MDI radio button. The default setting is Tabbed documents.

FIGURE 9.1
Default view of Management Studio

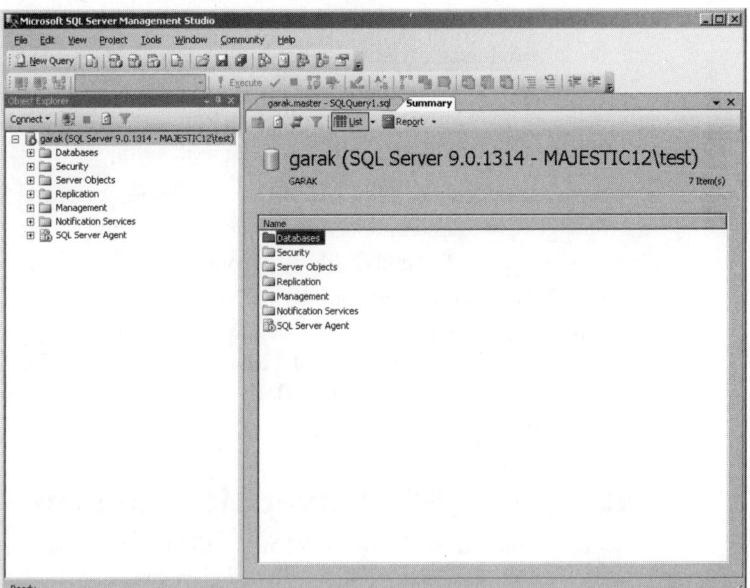

One other feature worth mentioning is that even though we'll be discussing them separately, the tools in Management Studio were designed to work together. For instance, you can register a server with Object Explorer or open a SQL Editor window while connected to a specific database from Object Explorer. This intertwining of access and functions makes Management Studio a very powerful tool.

Finally, as should be obvious, Management Studio doesn't need to be installed on the same computer as SQL Server itself. In fact, often you'll probably want to install a copy on your database administrator's workstation, because Management Studio is designed to allow you to administer any number of servers from a single location.

With all that said, let's walk through the key windows of Management Studio.

The Registered Servers Window

The Registered Servers window is one of the three windows (along with Object Explorer and Summary) usually available by default when you first open Management Studio. Registered Servers lets you organize servers that you access frequently. You can also use it to organize servers into server groups for ease of access and identification. The icons shown in Table 9.1 indicate server types.

NOTE If the Registered Servers window doesn't appear, you can add it by choosing View ➤ Registered Servers.

You can perform a number of different tasks from this window to access or manage servers and their connections. To connect to a registered server, right-click the server and choose Connect ➤ Object Explorer. You are then prompted to log on to the server.

If you're creating a new server registration, there is no wizard per se; you right-click Microsoft SQL Servers and choose New ➤ Server Registration. In the New Server Registration dialog box, click the General tab. In the Server Name text box, type the name of the server you wish to register. You can either accept the default Windows Authentication or click SQL Server Authentication and complete the Login and Password boxes. The Registered Server Name text box is automatically completed with the name from the Server Name box (you can change the name if you wish). You can also (optionally) provide connection properties information and/or change network settings such as the protocol or packet size, through the settings under the Connection Properties tab. Other settings allow you to set the connection and script execution timeout values (they may or may not be available, depending on the server type being registered). You can also opt to encrypt the connection.

TABLE 9.1: Registered Servers Icons

SYMBOL	TYPE
	Database Engine
	Analysis Services Server
	Reporting Services Server
	SQL Server Mobile
	Integration Services Server

You can edit or modify the connection information for a server at any time by right-clicking a server and choosing Properties to open the Edit Server Registration Properties dialog (Figure 9.2). Here you can perform any of the following operations:

- Switch the authentication type from Windows to SQL Server or vice versa
- Change the SQL Server username and password
- Replace the registered server name with a new name and optional description

- Select the name of the database for the connection
- Choose which network protocol to use
- Specify the network packet size
- Enter connection and execution timeouts
- Choose whether to encrypt the connection

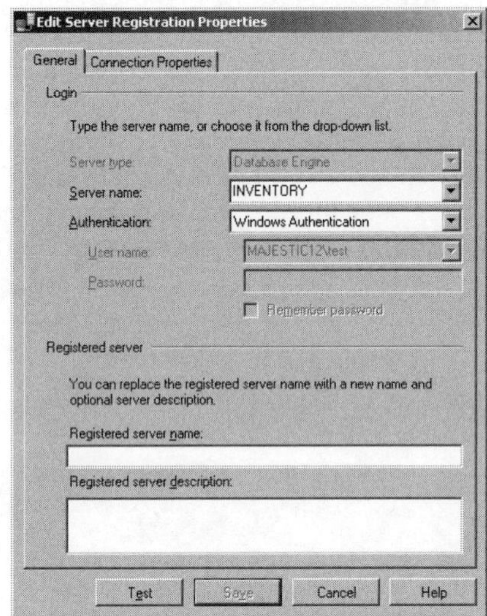

FIGURE 9.2
Edit Server Registration Properties window

Importing previously saved registered server information (from another server) gives you a way to create a standard user interface on multiple servers. To import registered server information, choose the server type on the Registered Servers toolbar. The server type must be the same as the registered server export file type. After that, it's a simple process to right-click a server or server group and select Import. In the Import Registered Servers dialog box, select the file you want to import, and then click OK. You'll need to click the location in the registered servers tree where you want to place the imported server or server group. If you're importing a server to a server group and the group has a server by that name you'll receive a message asking you if you want to overwrite the already existing server. If you opt to overwrite the server or server group, that node will be replaced by the new imported registered server information.

You can rename a server or server group by right-clicking it and selecting Rename.

Deleting or removing a server or server group is also easy. Right-click the server or server group, and select Delete. Click Yes in the Delete Confirmation window to confirm your choice.

Server Groups

SQL Server 2000 introduced the concept of server groups as a convenient way to organize a large number of servers into manageable groups for administrative purposes. Because server groups are purely an administrative convenience, they have no bearing on the actual operation of the server. The real benefit is organizational. They also provide a way for you to rename servers that might have cryptic names. For example, a server called DHA_SQL_EDHA0552_NF04 can be placed in the Material Supplies Server Group and renamed Pipeline Components. Server groups can be nested, meaning you can create a server group within another server group.

Figure 9.3 shows an organization with three SQL Server groups:

- The Production server group includes the INVENTORY and SALES servers.
- The Financials server group includes the ACCOUNTING server.
- The Medical server group includes the PHARMACY, SUPPLIES, and ACCOUNTING servers.

Note that because server groups are entirely administrative, it's possible (as we did here) to place a SQL Server in more than one group (to make it easier to find, for instance, or to match the preferred nomenclature of a group).

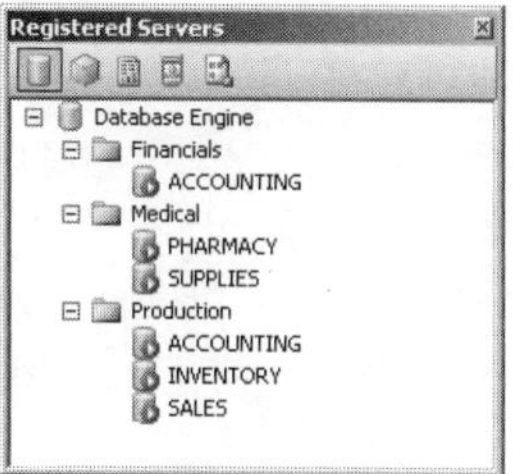

FIGURE 9.3
SQL Server groups and SQL Servers

CREATING A SERVER GROUP

Creating a server group is simple:

1. In the Registered Servers window, select the server type on the Registered Servers toolbar.
2. Right-click a server or a server group, and choose New ➤ Server Group.
3. In the resulting New Server Group dialog box, shown in Figure 9.4, type a unique name for the server group in the Group Name text box.
4. In the Group Description text box, you can type a descriptive name for the server group—for example, **Medical**.
5. In the Select A Location For The New Server Group box, click a location for the group.
6. Click Save.

You can also create a new server group while you're registering a server, by clicking New Group and then completing the New Group dialog box.

NOTE The Microsoft SQL Servers node in the treeview isn't a SQL Server group.

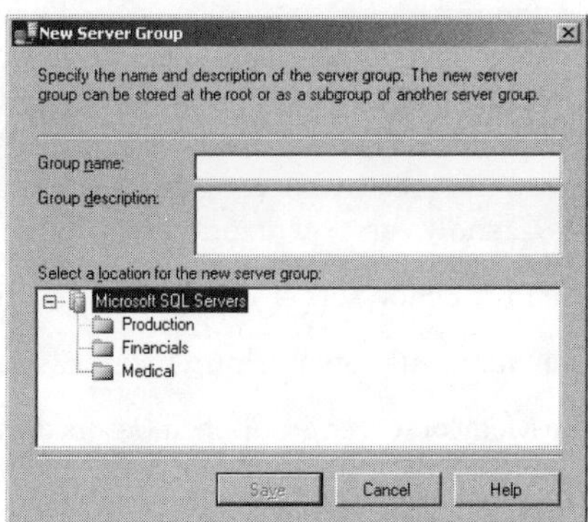

FIGURE 9.4
Creating a new SQL Server group

To rename a SQL Server group, right-click the group in Management Studio, and choose Rename.

MANAGING SERVERS IN A GROUP

Once you've created a server group, you'll want to work with the servers within the group.

There are three ways to add a server to a group:

- The easiest is to right-click a server group and choose New ➤ Server Registration to open the New Server Registration window The new server is placed in the server group from which you started the process.
- Right-click the server group, and select Import to open the Import Registered Servers dialog. The imported server is placed at the top level by default.
- Right-click a server, and select Move To. In the resulting Move Server Registration dialog box, shown in Figure 9.5, select the server group (either top-level or subgroup) or the root node to move the server to.

To remove a server from a SQL Server group, right-click the server name and choose Delete. Management Studio will ask for confirmation that you really want to remove the selected server.

WARNING Once you've deleted a server from the Registered Servers window, you must run the create process outlined earlier to reinstate it. Remember that since server groups are an administrative tool, all you have removed is the listing—you haven't removed the server itself from the computer.

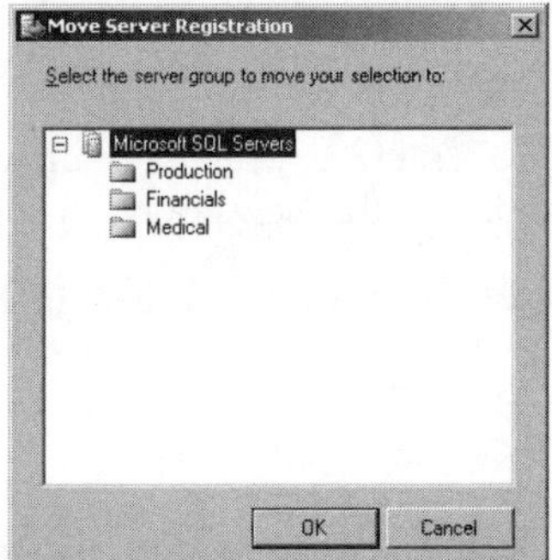

FIGURE 9.5
Move Server Registration dialog box

SERVER ICONS

Management Studio uses icons in its tree views to indicate the current state of each server. Table 9.2 lists these icons and their interpretation.

Management Studio collects this information by polling each server. You can control whether this polling is done and how often each server is polled by utilizing the properties box in Object Explorer, as you'll see in the next section.

TABLE 9.2: Management Studio Icons

ICON	MEANING
	Server is running normally.
	Server is stopped.
	Server is paused.
	Server can't be contacted.

The Object Explorer Window

Another of the three default windows that opens with Management Studio is Object Explorer. If you don't see Object Explorer, you can open it via View ➤ Object Explorer.

Object Explorer connects to SQL Server instances, analysis servers, DTS servers, report servers, and SQL Server Mobile Edition. For users of SQL Server 2005, Object Explorer has a familiar, although certainly not exact, resemblance to the older Microsoft Management Console. The capabilities of Object Explorer will vary depending on the type of server, but they include development features for databases and management features for all server types. In this chapter, we'll focus on the features associated with SQL Server instances, dealing with variations related to the other server type in the appropriate chapters.

Connecting to a Server Using Object Explorer

Click Connect on the Object Explorer toolbar, and choose the type of server from the drop-down list. The Connect To Server dialog box opens, as shown in Figure 9.6. To connect, you must provide at least the name of the server and the correct authentication information. You can also configure additional options by clicking the Options button in the Connect To Server dialog box. (The Connect To Server dialog box retains the last used settings. Any new connections will also use these settings.)

FIGURE 9.6
Connect To Server dialog box

Clicking the Options button opens a two-tabbed dialog box. The Login tab lets you do the following:

- Display the server type
- Select the server
- Choose either Windows or SQL Server authentication
- Specify the login and password for SQL Server authentication

Under the Connection Properties tab (Figure 9.7) you can do the following:

- Use Connect To Database to choose from the available databases on the server that you have permission to view
- Select the network protocol from Shared Memory, TCP/IP, or Named Pipes
- Select the network packet size, and configure the size if you want to change the default value of 4096 bytes
- Set the connection timeout
- Set the execution timeout in seconds (the default setting [0] means that execution will never time out)

Object Explorer contains a small menu that lets you choose from among the options listed in Table 9.3.

TABLE 9.3: Management Studio Object Explorer Icons

OBJECT	DESCRIPTION
Connect ▾	Connects to server type
	Disconnects from the active server

TABLE 9.3: Management Studio Object Explorer Icons *(CONTINUED)*

OBJECT	DESCRIPTION
	Stop (only displays as red when process being run)
	Refreshes the list of objects in a folder
	Filters the list of objects (grayed out when items can't be filtered)

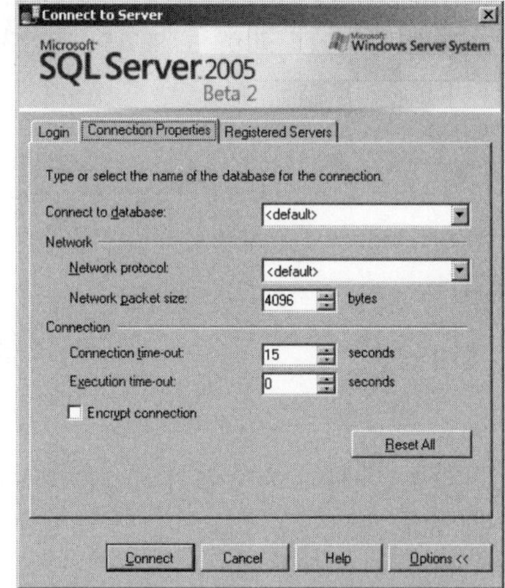

FIGURE 9.7 Connection Properties tab

Folder Structure and Usage

Object Explorer uses a tree structure to group information into folders for each server. In this section, we'll look at what's in that treeview and the contents of those folders for each server.

But first, some general housekeeping and navigation tips. To expand or collapse a folder, click the plus sign or double-click the folder. Usually you'll expand folders for more details. Management Studio is designed so that you can right-click folders or objects to perform common tasks.

The first time you expand a folder, Object Explorer queries the server for information to populate the tree. While Object Explorer is populating the tree, you can click Stop to halt the process. Any actions you take, such as filtering, apply only to the portion of the folder that was populated, unless you refresh the folder to start populating the tree again.

In order to save system resources, the folders in the Object Explorer tree don't automatically refresh their list of contents. To refresh the list of objects within a folder, right-click the folder, and then click Refresh; or click the Refresh button on the Object Explorer menu.

NOTE Object Explorer can display a total of 65,536 objects. If you exceed that number of objects, you won't be able to view additional objects. In that case, you should close unused nodes or apply filtering to reduce the number of open objects.

Object Explorer lets you filter the object list to reduce the size of the displayed components for ease of use or to reduce unwanted clutter. For example, you may want to find a specific database user or view only the most recently created tables in lists that contain hundreds of objects. To use the filter feature, click the folder you want to filter, such as Tables or Views, and then click the Filter button to open the Filter Settings dialog box. Alternatively, you can right-click and select Filter. You can filter the list by name, creation date, and (sometimes) schema, and provide additional filtering operators like Starts With, Contains, and Between. Note that not all folders can be filtered.

The Object Explorer tree contains folders that separate objects first by their object type and then by their schema, as the default arrangement. You can use the Schema button on the toolbar to modify the presentation mode to separate first by schema and then by object type. This option, which is also available from View ➤ Arrange Objects By, affects all of Object Explorer.

Nodes in Object Explorer

Each SQL Server in Object Explorer contains the following nodes:

- Databases
- Security
- Server Objects
- Replication
- Management
- Notification Services

In addition, SQL Server Agent (dealt with later in this chapter) is also present. Different folder structures exist for other server instances. For example, Analysis Server contains only Database and Assemblies folders.

Summary Page

At each level in Object Explorer, Management Studio shows information, and in some instances makes available reports, for each object selected in Object Explorer through the Summary page. If the list of objects is large, the Summary page may take longer to process the information.

There are two views of the Summary page. The Details view presents several categories of information of interest for each object type. The List view presents a simple list of the objects in the selected node or folder of Object Explorer.

The Summary Window is open by default, but can also be accessed by going to the View ➤ Summary. Alternatively you can select the Summary button on the Standard toolbar. The Summary page opens, if it is not already open, and comes to the front if it is open in the background.

The Summary page can also be used to access a set of predefined reports created by SQL Server 2005 Reporting Services (SSRS). Clicking the arrow on the Report button shows the list of reports, if any, that are available. When selected, the reports open in Summary page window as show in Figure 9.8.

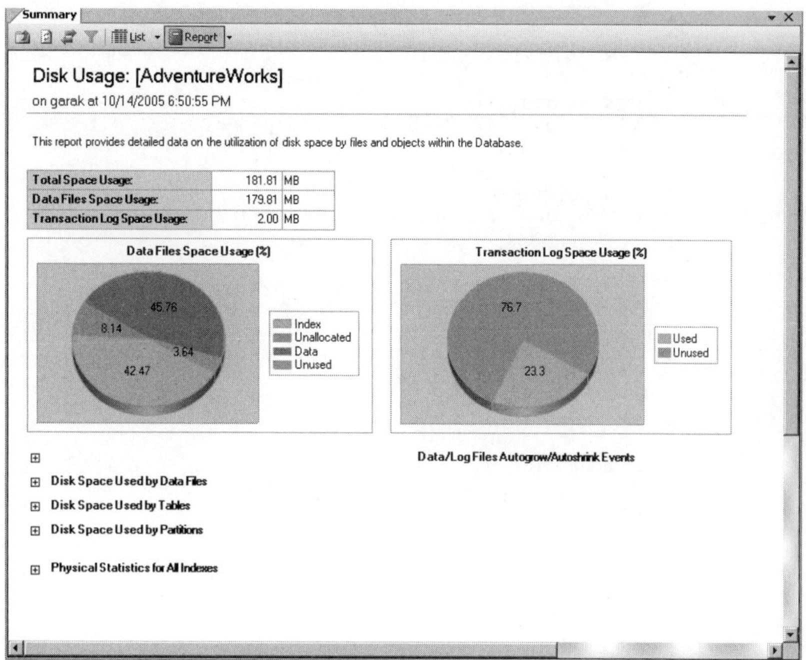

FIGURE 9.8
Summary window showing disk usage report on Adventure-works database

The Databases Node

This node contains the System Databases folder, the Database Snapshot folder, and user databases. The user databases have folders for each type of object they contain, including the following (see Figure 9.9):

- Tables
- Views
- Synonyms
- Programmability
    - Stored Procedures
    - Functions
    - Database Triggers
    - Assemblies
    - Types
    - Rules
    - Defaults

- Service Broker
  - Message Types
  - Contracts
  - Queues
  - Services
  - Routes
  - Remote Service Binding
- Storage
  - Full Text Catalogs
  - Partition Schemes
  - Partition Functions
- Security
  - Users
  - Roles
  - Schemas
  - Asymmetric Keys
  - Certificates
  - Symmetric Keys

Databases

If you right-click the database name you're presented with a menu that includes these options:

- New Database…
- New Query
- Script Database As
- Tasks
  - Detach
  - Take Offline
  - Bring Online
  - Shrink
  - Back-up
  - Restore

- Mirror
- Ship Transaction Logs
- Generate Scripts
- Import Data…
- Export Data…
- Copy Database
- Import or Export Data through the Data Transformation Services Import/Export Wizard
- Rename
- Delete

- Refresh

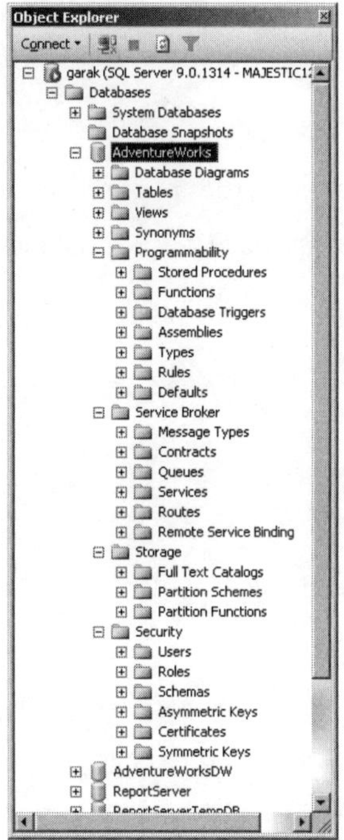

FIGURE 9.9
Typical Databases folder within Management Studio

The Properties page (Figure 9.10) consists of seven subpages: General, Files, Filegroups, Options, Permissions, Extended Properties, Mirroring, and Transaction Log Shipping.

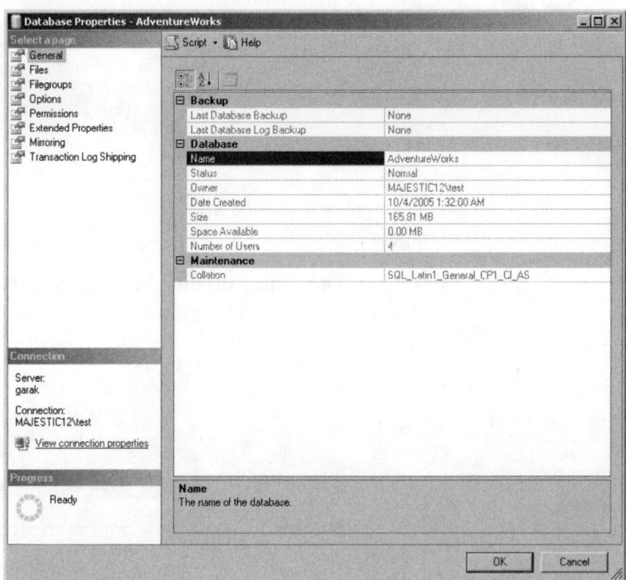

FIGURE 9.10 Database Properties page

The General properties page shows basic information, including the following:

- Dates of last database and database log backups
- Database name
- Status
- Owner
- Date created
- Size
- Space available
- Number of users
- Collation

From the Files Properties page you can view or modify the following:

- Database name
- Owner
- Whether to enable or disable full-text indexing
- Database files for the associated database
  - Logical Name
  - File Type

    - Filegroup
    - Initial size (MB)
    - Autogrowth options
    - Path
    - Filename
- You can also add a file to or remove a file from the database.

The Filegroups properties page lets you add a new filegroup to the selected database.

The Options Properties page contains a number of modifiable settings related to the database. These include:

- Collation
- Recovery model
- Compatibility level
- Automatic settings for closing, creating statistics, shrinking, and updating statistics
- Cursor behavior
- ANSI settings
- Page verification methods during recovery
- Database state
- Other miscellaneous settings

Clicking the Permissions Properties button opens a page where you can set user and group permissions for the table.

On the Extended Properties page, you can view, change, or delete the associated extended properties for the object (consisting of a name/value pair of metadata associated with the object). Page contents include the following:

- Database name
- Collation used for the selected database
- Properties window where you can view, create, or change the extended properties
- Delete button

The Mirroring properties page can be used to configure database mirroring and to pause or end the database mirroring session. You can also use this page to launch the Configure Database Mirroring Security Wizard.The Transaction Log Shipping properties page allows you to configure the database as a primary database in a log shipping configuration if desired. Once enabled, you can configure transaction log backup configurations, secondary databases, and whether or not tp monitors a server instance. You can only make a database the primary database in a log shipping configuration if it uses the full or bulk-logged recovery model.

Database Diagrams

A database diagram is a visual portrayal of a database. You can create a database diagram by right-clicking on the Database Diagram folder and selecting New Database Diagram from the pop-up menu. Figure 9.11 shows a typical database diagram.

Right-clicking on a specific database diagram, allows you to

- ◆ Create a new database diagram
- ◆ Modify the database diagram
- ◆ Rename the database diagram
- ◆ Delete the diagram
- ◆ Refresh the view

Tables

Selecting a Tables folder under a database file presents a different Summary sheet listing all the tables in the database, as shown in Figure 9.12. By default each table is listed alphabetically by schema and by name within schema along with its date of creation. You can sort tables in the Summary window by clicking on the headings, Name, Schema, or Created. In Figure 9.13, tables are sorted by table name.

FIGURE 9.11
Database diagram

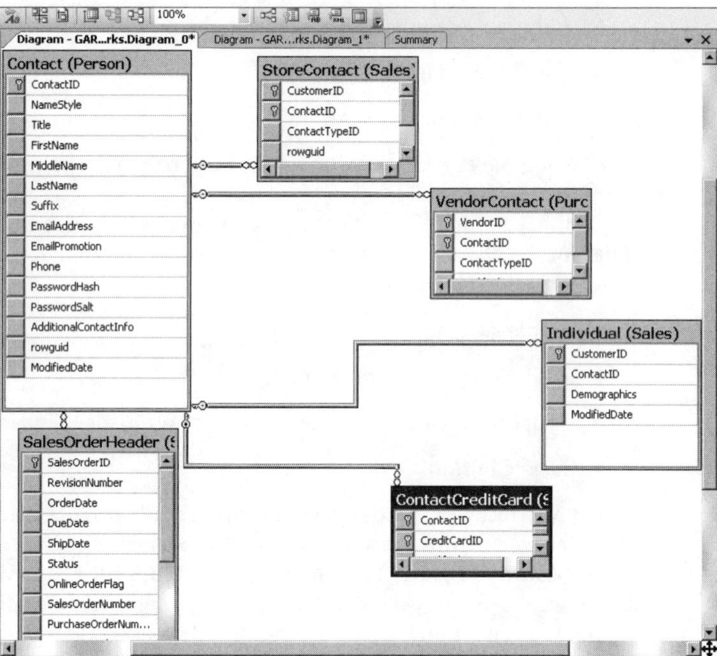

If you right-click the main Tables folder, you can choose to create a new table. You can also apply or remove filtering and refresh the view.

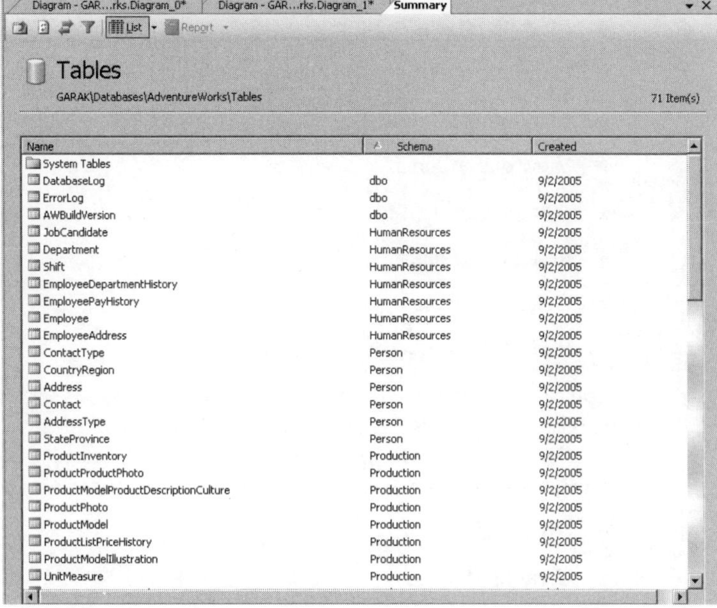

FIGURE 9.12
Summary sheet view of tables in a database sorted by schema

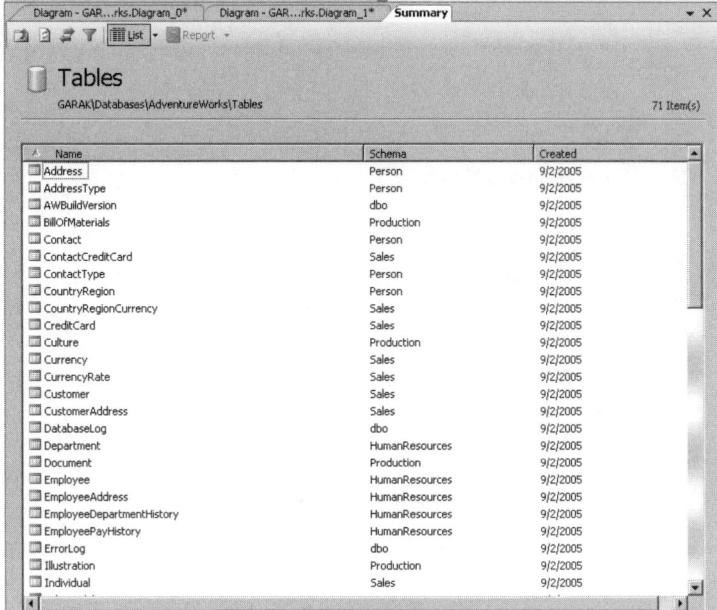

FIGURE 9.13
Tables view sorted by name

Right-clicking a specific table, such as HumanResources.Department, gives you the option to perform basic table operations:

- Create a new table
- Modify the existing table
- Open the table
- Script the table
- View dependencies
- Add or modify a full-text index to the table
- Rename the table
- Delete the table
- Refresh the table contents

You can also open the Properties sheet for the table, as shown in Figure 9.14 for the Department table. Three properties pages are available via the left pane: General, Permissions, and Extended Properties. This pane also provides information regarding the connection and progress status.

The General properties page gives basic information including the following:

- ANSI NULLs
- Creation date
- Data disk space
- Database
- Filegroup
- Index disk space
- Name
- Partition scheme
- Quoted identifier
- Row count
- Schema
- Server
- Whether the table is a system object
- Whether the table is partitioned
- Whether the table is replicated
- Text filegroup
- User

Note that you can't change these settings; you can only view them from the Properties sheet.

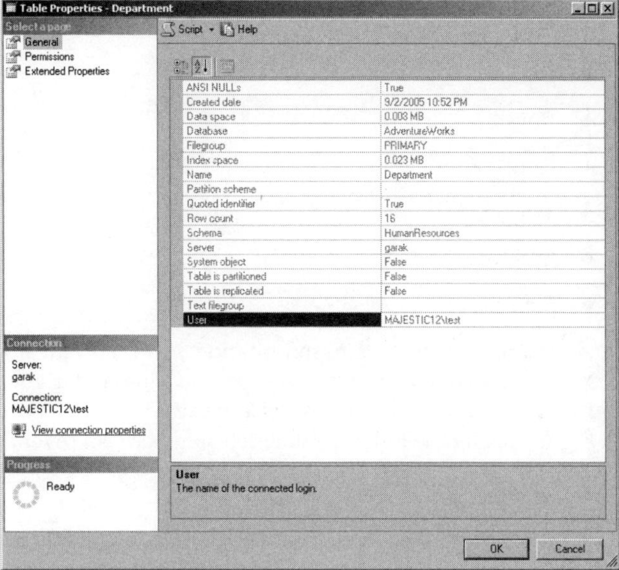

FIGURE 9.14
Table Properties dialog box

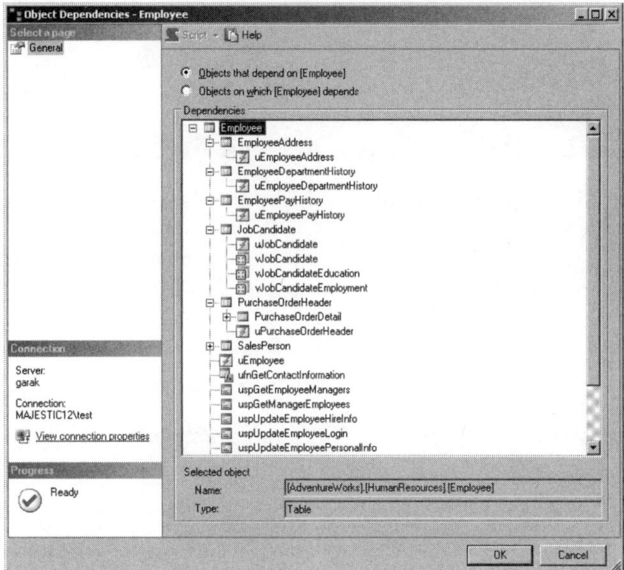

FIGURE 9.15
Object Dependencies dialog box

The Permissions properties page lets you set user and group permissions for the table. The Extended Properties page is identical to the Database Properties page.

Right-clicking a specific table, for example HumanResources.Employee in the Adventure Works database and selecting the View Dependencies menu selection opens the Object Dependencies dialog box shown in Figure 9.15. This dialog is particularly useful if you're considering modifying an object. It tells you which objects the selected table depends on and which objects depend on the selected table.

Double-clicking a specific table—HumanResources.Department, in the example shown in Figure 9.16—opens another set of folders:

- Columns
- Keys
- Constraints
- Triggers
- Indexes
- Statistics

Each of these in turn contains information for the specific instance of the object.

You can create new columns, keys, constraints, and triggers by right-clicking the specific folder and selecting New. You can also refresh each of these.

Right-clicking the Indexes folder lets you perform several tasks:

- Create a new index
- Rebuild all
- Reorganize all
- Disable all
- Filter
- Refresh

NOTE Indexing is covered in greater detail in Chapter 12.

Right-clicking the Statistics folder allows you to create new statistics using the Properties sheet or delete all statistics.

Each individual item under a folder can be right-clicked. Doing so opens a menu giving you the opportunity to select one of the actions listed in Table 9.4.

TABLE 9.4: Actions That Can Be Performed on Individual Table Components*

COLUMN	KEY	CONSTRAINTS	TRIGGERS	INDEXES	STATISTICS
New	Script As	Script As	New	New	New
Modify	Modify	Rename	Modify	Script As	Script As
Rename	Rename	Delete	Script As	Rebuild	Delete
Delete	Delete	Refresh	View Dependencies	Reorganize	Refresh
Refresh	Refresh		Enable	Disable	Properties

TABLE 9.4: Actions That Can Be Performed on Individual Table Components* *(CONTINUED)*

COLUMN	KEY	CONSTRAINTS	TRIGGERS	INDEXES	STATISTICS
Properties			Disable	Rename	
			Delete	Delete	
			Refresh	Refresh	
				Properties	

*Actions relate to that specific component type. For example, New in the Key column means New Key; Script As in the Indexes column means Script Index As, and so on.

As you can see, you can rename, delete, or refresh most components by right-clicking the object. You can also create new components (except keys and constraints) and use Script As to launch the Query Editor for all components except columns. Only triggers provide the option to view dependencies by right-clicking an instance.

Columns, keys, and triggers can be modified by right-clicking. To modify a column, right-click an individual column (for example, Name under Human Resources.Department in Figure 9.16), and then select Modify. A new window opens instead of the summary sheet (Figure 9.17), where you can change the various properties for either the specific column you clicked or any other column in the same table by selecting a different one in the list above the properties list.

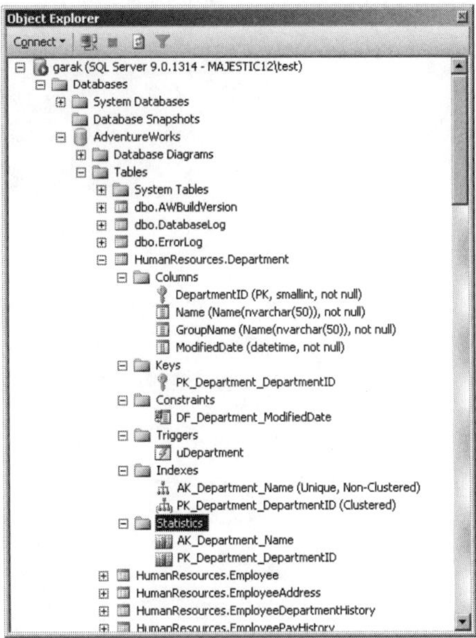

FIGURE 9.16
Expanded Tables folder showing components

You can also view the Properties sheet for columns, indexes, and statistics. For example, right-clicking the Name column under HumanResources.Department and then selecting Properties opens the Column Properties sheet, as shown in Figure 9.18. The General properties page lets you view a number of the column properties. To change them, however, you need to use the Modify Column option when right-clicking the specific column. The Extended Properties sheet is also available. Similar sheets open when you right-click properties for individual indexes and statistics.

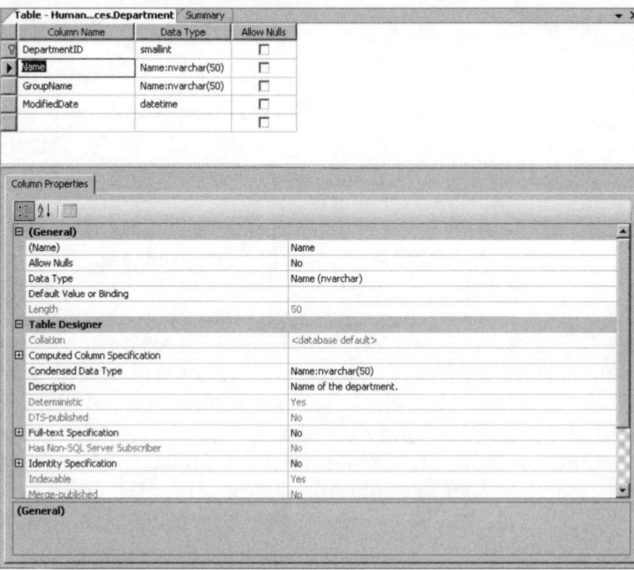

FIGURE 9.17 Modify column properties

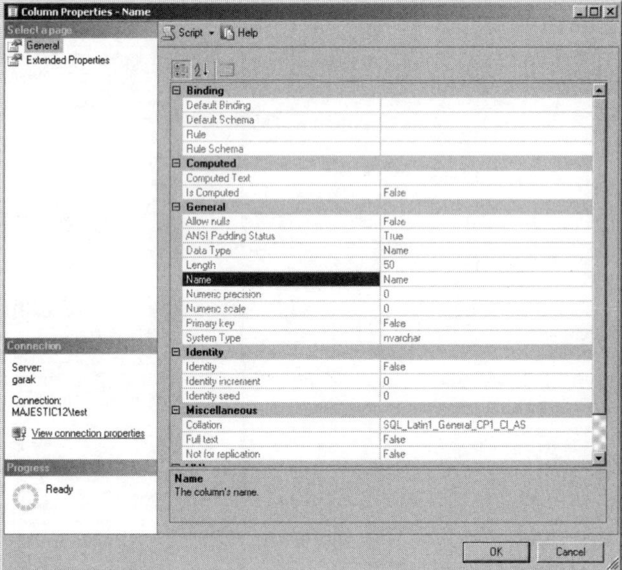

FIGURE 9.18 Column Properties page

Views

If you select the Views folder for a database in Management Studio, the right pane displays a list of all the views in the current database and the date created. Figure 9.19 shows this list for the AdventureWorks database. System views can be located in the System Views folder. As you should anticipate by now, right-clicking the Views folder provides you with the option to create a new view, filter the object list, and refresh the object list.

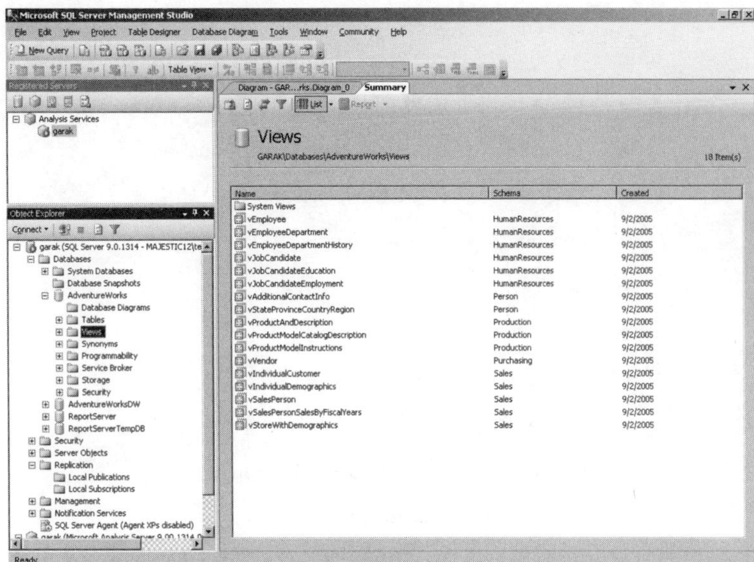

FIGURE 9.19
Views summary in Management Studio

Each individual user view consists of a set of four subfolders: Columns, Triggers, Indexes, and Statistics. Right-clicking any of these lets you create new instances of that type. Right-clicking a specific view provides you with a menu to perform the follow basic operations:

- Create a new view
- Modify an existing view
- Open the view
- Generate SQL scripts (via Script View As)
- View dependencies
- Manage full-text indexes
- Rename
- Delete
- Refresh
- Open the Properties sheet to view the general properties, set permissions, and view/modify extended properties

NOTE Views will be reviewed in greater detail in Chapter 13.

Synonyms

A *synonym* is a database object that does the following:

- Provides an alternate name for another database object, called the *base object*, which can exist on a local or remote server
- Provides an abstraction layer that minimizes the impact of changes made to the name or location of a base object

A synonym belongs to a schema, and as is true for other objects in a schema, its name must be unique. Synonyms can be created for the following objects:

- Assembly (CLR) stored procedures
- Assembly (CLR) table-valued functions
- Assembly (CLR) scalar functions
- Aggregate (CLR) functions
- Replication-filter procedures
- Extended stored procedures
- SQL scalar functions
- SQL table-valued functions
- SQL inlined-tabled-valued functions
- SQL stored procedures
- Views
- Tables (user-defined and including local and global temporary tables)

To create a new synonym, right-click the Synonyms folder to open the New Synonym properties page. Here, as shown in Figure 9.20, you can specify the following:

- Synonym name
- Synonym schema
- Server name
- Database name
- Schema
- Object type
- Object name

Figure 9.20 shows how to create a new synonym, MyContacts, that references the AdventureWorks database's Person.Contact table. You can use the Permissions tab to set permissions as well as access the Extended Properties page.

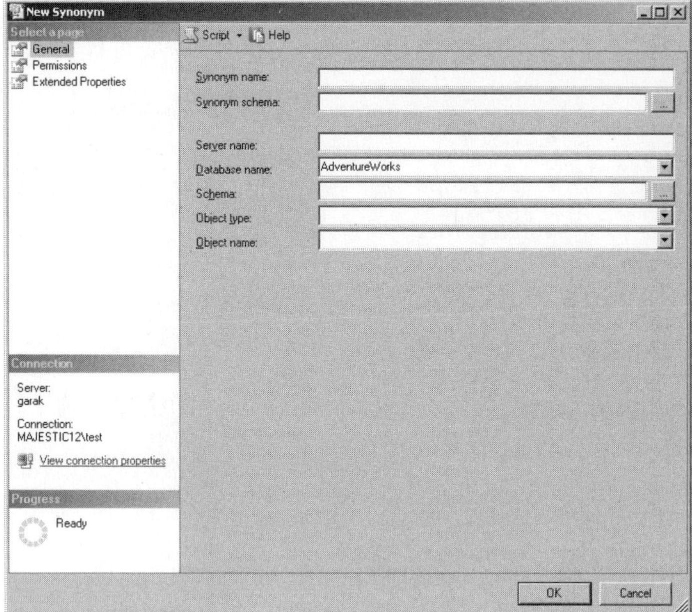

FIGURE 9.20
New Synonym properties page

Right-clicking a specific synonym allows you to do the following:

- Create a new synonym
- Generate SQL script
- Delete
- Refresh
- Access the Properties sheet

Programmability

This folder is a placeholder for a series of subfolders related to programming in SQL Server:

Stored Procedures As you should expect by now, when you select the Stored Procedures folder in Management Studio, a list of all the stored procedures in the current database, including the date of creation, appears in the Summary window. Figure 9.21 shows this list for the AdventureWorks database.

You can right-click the Stored Procedures folder to create a new stored procedure, filter the current object list, or refresh the list.

Right-clicking a specific stored procedure allows you to do the following:

- Create a new stored procedure
- Modify a stored procedure
- Execute the stored procedure

- Generate SQL scripts
- View dependencies
- Rename
- Delete
- Refresh
- Properties

NOTE You'll learn more about stored procedures in Chapter 14.

FIGURE 9.21
Stored Procedures in Management Studio

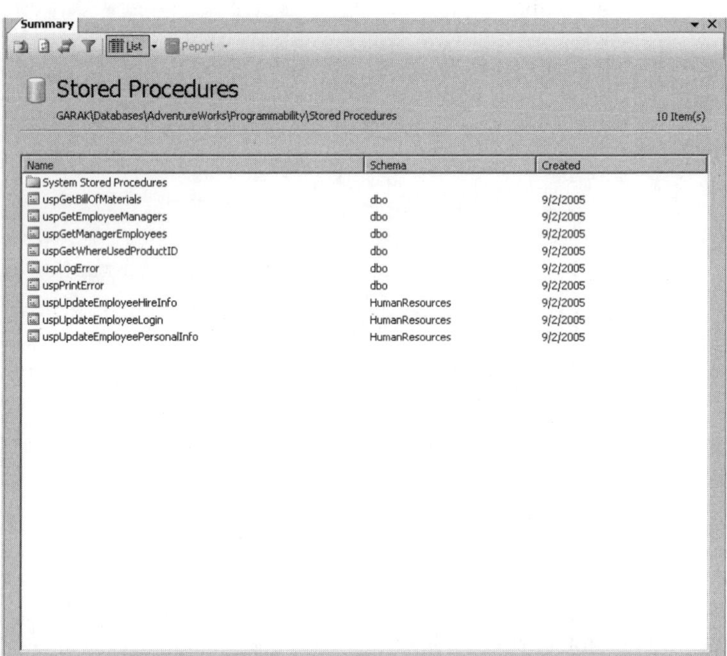

Functions The Functions folder and its subfolders—Table-Valued Functions, Scalar-Valued Functions, and System Functions—contain functions that perform operations on and return values, objects, and setting in SQL Server 2005. As you would expect, right-clicking subfolders provides you the opportunity to create new functions or filter or refresh the objects list. Right-clicking individual functions in the Table-Valued or Scalar-Valued Functions folders allows you to do the following:

- Create new functions
- Modify existing functions

- Generate SQL script
- View dependencies
- Rename
- Delete
- Refresh
- View the Properties sheet

Database Triggers Clicking a Database Triggers folder shows you all the database triggers in the current database. If none are present, then the folder is empty.

Assemblies This folder contains the assemblies in the current database. Managed code must be written and compiled into a .NET assembly in order to create objects. Typically, developers use Visual Studio.NET to formulate a new class library project and compile it into a DLL assembly. It's then loaded using the T-SQL `CREATE ASSEMBLY` command. You can also create an assembly by right-clicking the Assemblies folder in Analysis Server and selecting New Assembly.

Types This folder is composed of four subfolders: System Data Type, User-Defined Data Types, User-Defined Types, and XML Schema Collections.

When you click the User-Defined Data Types folder, Management Studio shows you all the user-defined datatypes in the current database. You can think of user-defined datatypes as aliases for system datatypes. Figure 9.22 shows the user-defined datatypes in the Adventure-Works database.

You can right-click the User-Defined Data Types folder to create a new user-defined datatype or refresh the existing folder view. Right-clicking a specific user-defined datatype opens a menu that allows you to do the following:

- Create a new user-defined datatype
- Generate SQL script
- View dependencies
- Rename the datatype
- Delete the datatype
- Refresh the datatype
- Open the datatype properties sheet

NOTE You'll learn more about user-defined datatypes in Chapter 11.

The XML schema collection is a metadata entity that is similar to a table in a database. Schemas are imported into the XML schema collection object when created using the `CREATE XML SCHEMA COLLECTION` statement. You can use the XML schema collection to type XML variables, parameters, and columns. Right-clicking a specific XML schema collection lets you generate SQL script, view dependencies, delete, or refresh.

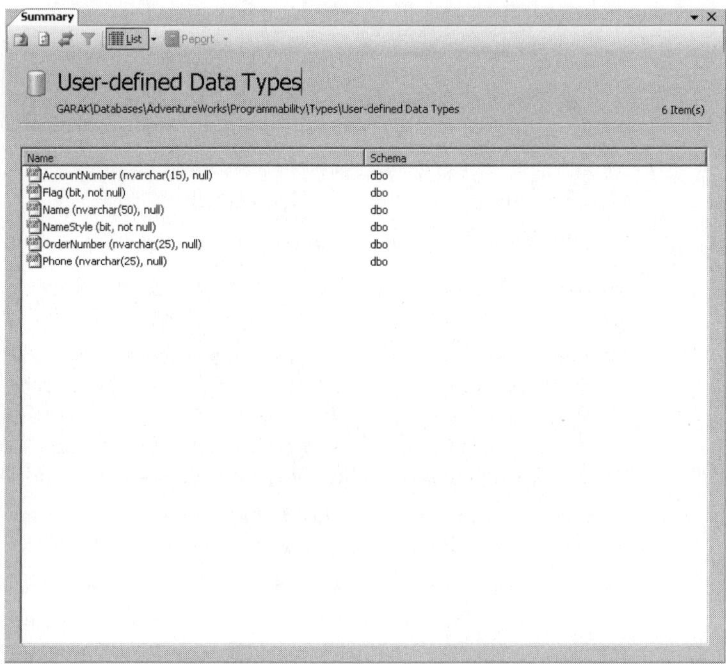

FIGURE 9.22 User-defined datatypes

Rules Clicking a Rules folder shows you all the rules in the current database. *Rules* are conditions expressed in T-SQL syntax (for example, `@salary < 20000`) that can be used to limit the data contained in columns of a table.

NOTE You usually won't find any rules in SQL Server 2000 or 2005 databases. Rules are now considered to be obsolete and have been largely replaced by constraints.

Defaults When you click a Defaults folder, the Summary window of Management Studio shows you all the defaults in the current database. A *default* is a default value that can be attached to one or more table columns for use when a value isn't explicitly supplied for that column in a new row of the table.

TIP Like rules, defaults are largely obsolete. For the most part, you should use default constraints instead of defaults in your database designs. There's further information on defaults in Chapter 4, "Database Design and Normalization."

Service Broker

Service Broker is a new technology introduced in SQL Server 2005. It's intended to make it easier for database developers to build secure, reliable, scalable applications. Its principal function is to provide queuing and reliable messaging as part of the Database Engine.

The Service Broker folder consists of six subfolders:

- Message Types
- Contracts

- Queues
- Services
- RoutesRemote Service Binding

Right-clicking individual instances lets you generate SQL script and delete and refresh each object.

NOTE Service Broker is discussed in full in Chapter 29.

Storage

The Storage folder consists of three subfolders: Full Text Catalogs, Partition Schemes, and Partition Functions.

Right-clicking the Full-Text Catalogs folder lets you create a new full-text catalog, delete one, or refresh the object tree. Clicking an individual full-text catalog allows you to do the following:

- Create a new full-text catalog
- Generate SQL script
- Rebuild
- Delete
- Refresh
- Open the Properties sheet

From the Properties sheet of an existing full-text catalog, you can view general settings, assign table/view objects to the catalog, and select eligible columns, as well as schedule when the full-text catalog is populated.

The Partition Schemes folder stores the partition schemes used for storing the tables, when any are used. These describe the way that data is mapped to file groups. If no partition schemes are used in the database, the folder isn't populated. The Partition Functions folder contains the objects representing all the partition functions implemented by the partition schemes. If none exist, the folder isn't populated.

Security

The Security folder consists of six subfolders: Users, Roles, Schemas, Asymmetric Keys, Certificates, and Symmetric keys. The contents of these folders relate to the current database, not the entire server:

Users If you click a Users node, you'll see a list of all the users for the current database, as shown in Figure 9.23. Users are specific to a database (unlike logins, which apply to entire servers) and are the basis for permissions within that database.

You can create new users by right-clicking the Users folder, as well as filter and refresh the folder objects. Right-clicking an individual user contained within the folder allows you to create a new user, generate SQL script, delete the user, or refresh the user. You can also open the Properties sheet (Figure 9.24) and use it to specify owned schemas and database role membership. In addition, you can specify the login name and default user.

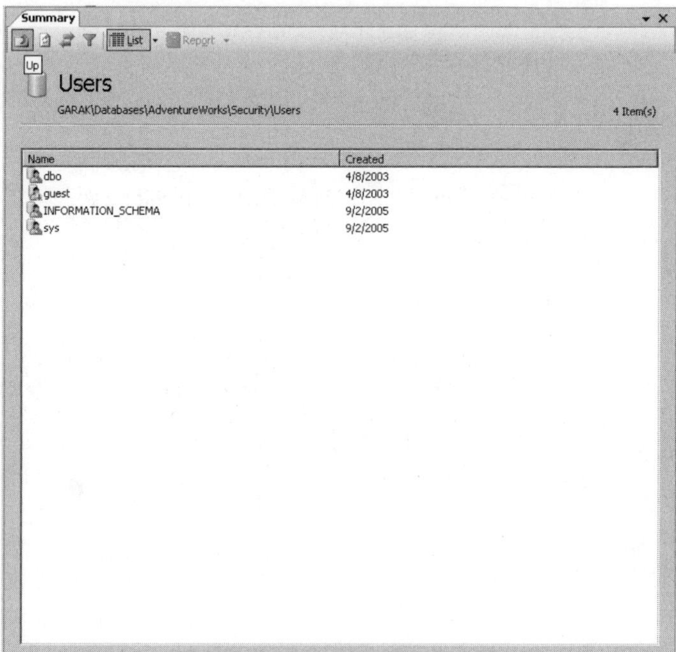

FIGURE 9.23 User list in Management Studio

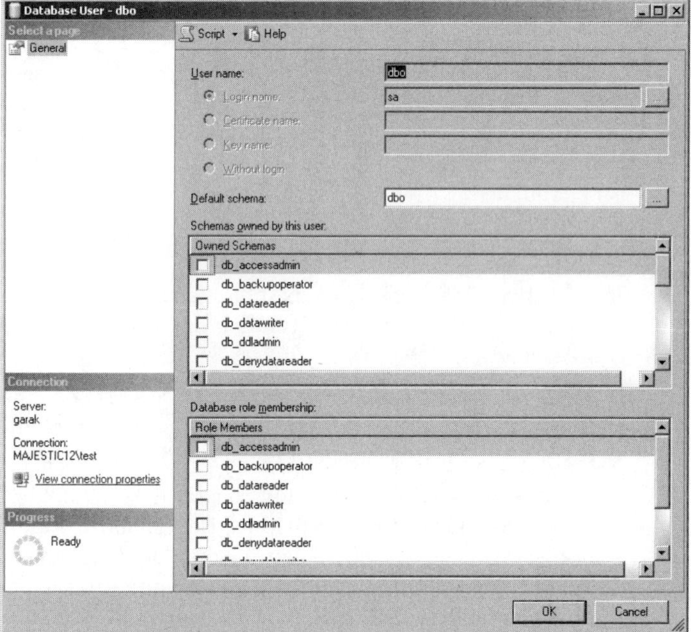

FIGURE 9.24 Database User Properties sheet

Roles Roles allow you to manage permissions for groups of users rather than for individual users. The Roles folder consists of two subfolders, since there are two types of roles: Database Roles contain SQL Server users, and Application Roles are designed for client-side validation of the user's identity. Clicking either subfolder shows you a list of all the roles in the current database in the Summary window, as shown in Figure 9.25 for Database Roles in the AdventureWorks database.

By right-clicking the Roles folder, you can create either a new database or an application role. Right-clicking a specific subfolder enables you to create a new role of that type. Choosing New launches an empty property sheet (Figure 9.26). You can use this to create a new role and specify all pertinent settings. For an existing role, you can use this page to view or modify role properties. This page is accessed in two ways: by right-clicking Database Roles (or Application Roles) in Object Explorer and clicking New Database (or Application) Role, or by right-clicking an existing role and clicking Properties. In the latter case, some of the options aren't editable.

FIGURE 9.25
Database Roles list in Management Studio

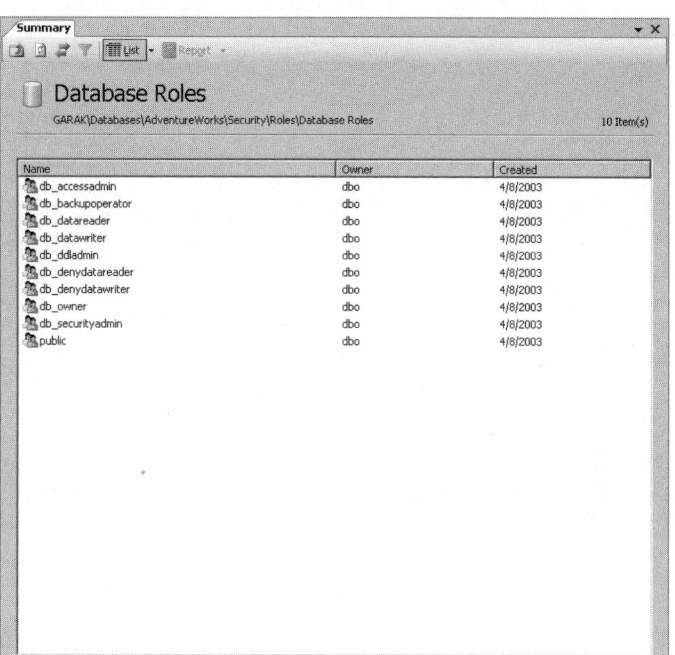

NOTE You'll learn more about roles in Chapter 18, "Security and SQL Server 2005."

Schemas Schemas contain database objects like tables, views, stored procedures, and so on. This folder contains all the schemas associated with the database. Right-clicking the Schemas folder lets you create a new schema. Right-clicking an existing schema enables you to create a new schema, generate SQL script, or delete or refresh the schema. Selecting Properties opens the same sheet as when you create a new schema, but some options (such as the schema name) aren't editable. You can also set permissions and extended properties.

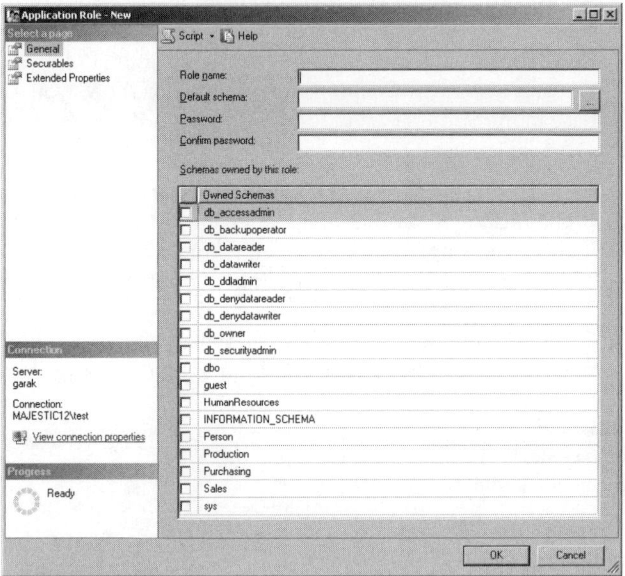

FIGURE 9.26
New Application Role Properties sheet

Asymmetric Keys The Asymmetric Keys folder contains the asymmetric keys associated with the particular database. If the database has no associated asymmetric keys, the folder is empty.

Certificates The Certificates folder contains the certificates associated with the particular database. If the database has no associated certificate, the folder is empty.

Symmetric Keys The Symmetric Keys folder contains the symmetric keys associate with the particular database. If the database has no associated symmetric keys, the folder is empty.

The Security Node

The server Security node (not be confused with the database Security folder) contains settings that effect the entire server, not just the particular database. There are three subfolders: Logins, Server Roles, and Credentials.

LOGINS

Logins provide the security context for the users on SQL Server. When you click the Logins folder, Management Studio displays a list of all the logins known to the current server. Right-clicking the main Logins folder lets you create a new log-in or filter or refresh the objects list. When you create a new login, you're directed to a blank Properties sheet.

Opening the Properties sheet for an existing login (by right-clicking the login and selecting Properties) shows you (and in some cases allows you to modify) the following:

- The login name
- Whether the login is permitted or denied access to the server
- The default database for the login
- The default language for the login
- The database role

- Server roles
- Which databases are accessible by the login
- Securables (formerly called permissions)

Right-clicking an existing login lets you create a new login, generate SQL script, delete the login, or refresh it.

SERVER ROLES

Server *roles* are built-in sets of permissions that SQL Server supplies. For example, there's a Server Administrator role that allows its members to configure server-wide settings. When you click the Server Roles folder, Management Studio displays all the server roles on that server.

Right-clicking a server role allows you to manage membership by adding or removing logins from the server role.

NOTE Unlike most other objects displayed in Management Studio, you can't create or delete server roles.

CREDENTIALS

A credential is a record containing the authentication information needed to connect to a resource outside of SQL Server. Most credentials consist of a Windows login name and password. On Windows 2003 Server and above, the password may not be required. When you click the Credential folder, Management Studio displays all the credentials on that server.

After creating a credential, you can use the Login Properties to map it to a login. A single credential can be mapped to multiple SQL Server logins. But a SQL Server login can be mapped to only one credential. Right-clicking a credential allows you to manage the credential through the Properties page, as well as create new credentials or delete the current one.

Server Objects Node

The Server Objects Node contains settings related to the server, as well as system wide objects. There are four subfolders: Backup Devices, Endpoints, Linked Servers, and Triggers.

BACKUP DEVICES

When you click the Backup Devices folder, Management Studio displays information about all backup devices known to the current server. (A *backup device* is a tape drive or a disk file that can be used to hold a backup copy of a database.)

From the Backup folder, you can create and delete backup devices, as well as create an actual backup job to run immediately or on a scheduled basis. Right-clicking either the Backup Devices folder or an individual backup device lets you start a backup job.

ENDPOINTS

The Endpoint folder provides a collection point for reviewing of four types of HTTP endpoints

- Database mirroring
- Service Broker
- SOAP
- TSQL

LINKED SERVERS

Linked servers are servers that Management Studio knows about but that aren't necessarily Microsoft SQL Servers. A linked server might be an Oracle database or a Microsoft Access database, for example. You can link to any database that can be accessed via an OLE DB provider.

The Linked Servers folder in Object Explorer contains one folder for each server linked to the current server. Each server node in turn contains a Tables node. When you click a Tables node, it displays all the tables on that linked server.

A separate Providers folder allows you to select and configure individual providers settings that are then applied to all linked servers that use this provider.

NOTE Linked servers are primarily used in T-SQL statements. You can't manage a linked server with Management Studio.

TRIGGERS

This folder contains server-scoped DDL triggers. As you have seen above, database-scoped DDL triggers appear in the Database Triggers subfolder of the Programmability folder of the corresponding database.

NOTE Triggers are discussed in more detail in Chapter 15, "Using Triggers."

The Replication Node

The Replication folder provides a central location to organize and administer publications and subscriptions, and to implement and administer a complete replication environment across your enterprise.

The node consists of two subfolders: Local Publications and Local Subscriptions.

By right-clicking the Replication node, you can perform the following tasks:

- Launch the Configure Distribution Wizard
- Launch the Replication Monitor
- Generate Scripts
- Update Replication Passwords
- Create New Publications, Oracle Publications, and Subscriptions by launching wizards
- Refresh

LOCAL PUBLICATIONS FOLDER

Right-clicking the Local Publications folder allows you to launch the New Publication Wizard and the New Oracle Publication Wizard.

New Publication/ NewOracle Publication Wizards These wizards let you configure the following:

- The publication database
- The type of publication to create (snapshot, transactional, transactional with updatable subscriptions, or merge)
- Which data and database objects to include in the publication

- Static row filters and column filters for all types of publications, and parameterized row filters and join filters for merge publications
- The snapshot agent schedule
- A name and description for the publication

The same menu that provides access to the publication wizards allows you to

- Launch Replication Monitor
- Generate scripts
- Launch the Configure Distribution Wizard
- Refresh the folder

If you right-click a specific publication, you can launch the New Subscriptions Wizard, launch the New Publication Wizard, launch Replication monitor, generate scripts, reinitialize all subscriptions, view the status of the Snapshot Agent, delete, refresh, or open the Properties sheet shown in Figure 9.27.

FIGURE 9.27 Example of the Publication Properties sheet

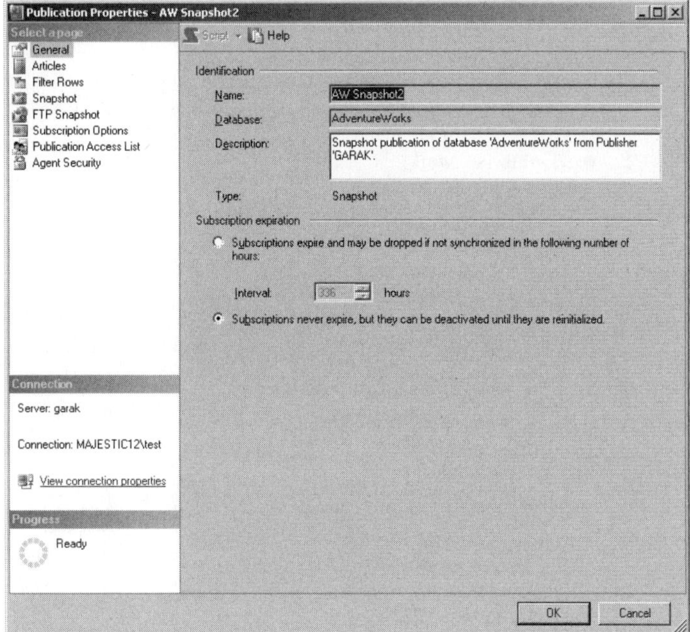

LOCAL SUBSCRIPTIONS FOLDER

Right-clicking the Local Subscriptions folder opens a menu from which you can launch the New Subscription Wizard, which lets you specify the following.

- The publication to which you want to subscribe
- Where the distribution agent or merge agent should run

- Which subscribers receive published data
- The subscription database that will receive the published data at each subscriber
- Whether the subscription should be initialized and, if so, when
- Agent schedules for how frequently updates are propagated to the subscriber
- Additional information based on publication settings

NOTE Replication is covered in greater detail in Chapter 25, "Replication."

The Management Node

Each SQL Server in Management Studio contains a Management node. This folder provides access to traditional database administrator information, including the following:

- Maintenance Plans
- SQL Server logs
- Activity Monitor, including
  - Process information
  - Locks by process
  - Locks by object
- Database Mail
- Distributed Transaction Coordinator
- Full Text Search
- Legacy Folder

Figure 9.28 shows this portion of the Management Studio tree in Object Explorer.

FIGURE 9.28
Management Node treeview

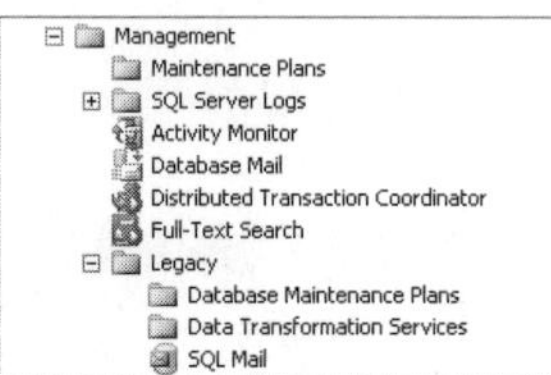

MAINTENANCE PLANS FOLDER

When you click the Maintenance Plans folder, Object Explorer shows you all the database maintenance plans that are stored on the current server. A database maintenance plan contains a schedule for operations such as checking database integrity, shrinking bloated files, and backing up databases. Typically, you create a maintenance plan to order a workflow and keep your database performing well. Right-clicking the Maintenance Plans folder or a specific maintenance plan lets you create a new maintenance plan in Design view. Alternatively, you can launch the Maintenance Plan

Wizard to create core maintenance plans. Generally, you'll find that creating maintenance plans manually allows much more flexibility of workflow.

From a Database Maintenance Plans node, you can not only create a maintenance plan or launch the Maintenance Plan Wizard; you can also delete or refresh a maintenance plan and view the history of the plan, which tells you when it was most recently executed and provides details about the activities it carried out. Finally you can modify the plan.

NOTE Chapter 16, "Basic Administrative Tasks" contains more information about database maintenance.

SQL Server Logs

The SQL Server Logs folder for a server contains nodes for the current activity log and for the six most recent activity logs before that. Whenever you start SQL Server, it begins writing events to the SQL Server log. A subset of these events can also be found in the Application event log (the same one found in Event Viewer).

When you select one of the individual log nodes and either double-click or right-click and select View SQL Server Log, Management Studio opens the Log File Viewer. On the left side, you can select the logs you wish to view; the right pane shows the individual log entries, as shown in Figure 9.29. For each entry, Management Studio displays the date, the source of the entry, the message it contains, the log type, the log, and the log source.

NOTE You'll learn more about interpreting SQL Server logs in Chapter 16.

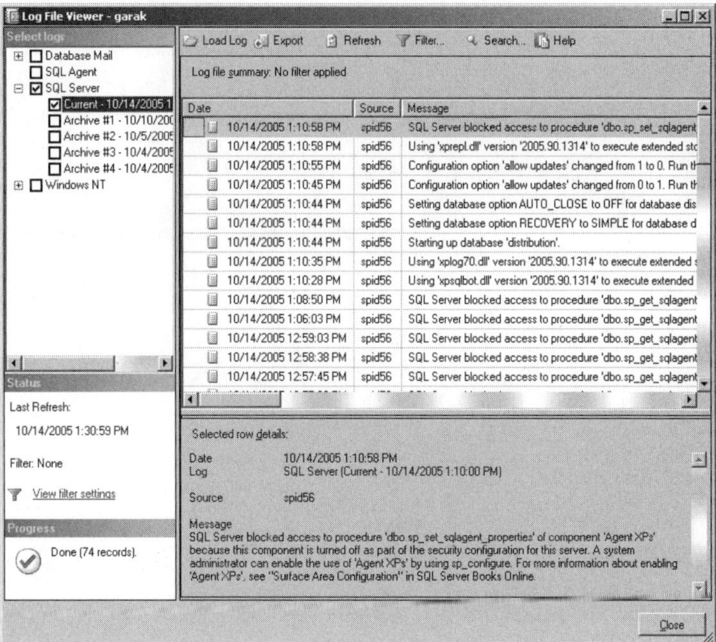

FIGURE 9.29 Entries in a SQL Server Log File Viewer

Activity Monitor

Activity Monitor can be used to analyze server performance, view user connections, and resolve deadlocks. You can also apply filters to restrict the display to items of interest as well as change the refresh rate to watch activity as it occurs. There are three pages in Activity Monitor: Process Info, Locks by Process, and Locks by Object.

For each process, the Process Info page (see Figure 9.31) shows the following:

- Process ID (this is the unique ID that SQL Server assigns to each process when it's started—also known as a spid)
- System Process
- User
- Database
- Status
- Open Transactions
- Command
- Application
- Wait Time
- Wait Type
- Resource
- CPU
- Physical IO
- Memory Usage
- Login Time
- Last Batch
- Host
- Net Library
- Net Address
- Blocked By
- Blocking
- Execution Context ID (a unique ID for each of the subthreads operating on behalf of a single process)

Double-clicking a process lets you see the most recent SQL batch submitted by that process. You can also kill the process from the same windows.

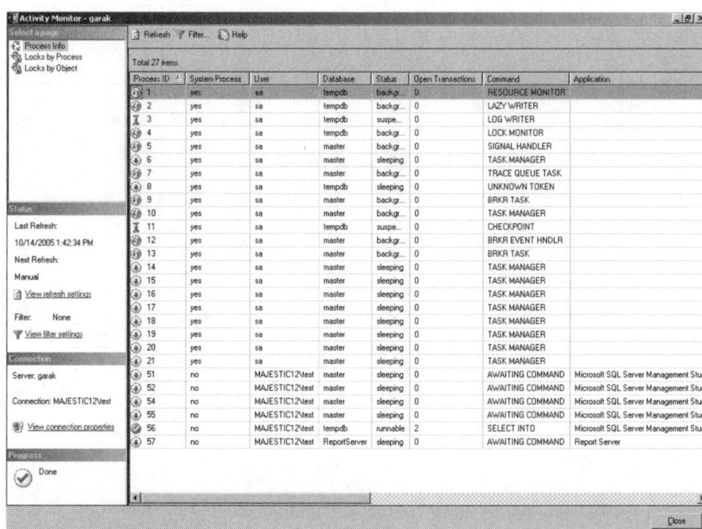

FIGURE 9.30
Process Info page

The Locks By Process page contains one entry for each process running on the server. The following information is displayed about each lock:

- Object
- Type
- Subtype
- Object ID
- Description
- Request Mode
- Request Type
- Request Status
- Owner Type
- Owner ID
- Owner GUID
- Database
- Process ID
- Context
- Batch ID

The Locks By Object page contains information about locks belonging to specific objects. The following information is displayed about each lock:

- Content
- Batch ID
- Type
- Subtype
- Object ID
- Description
- Request Mode
- Request Type
- Request Status
- Owner Type
- Owner ID
- Owner GUID
- Database
- Object

NOTE You'll learn more about locking in Chapter 23.

Database Mail

New to SQL Server 2005, Database Mail is designed to allow database applications to send e-mail messages to users. The messages can contain query results and can also include files from any resource on your network. Database Mail is not active by default. To use Database Mail, you must explicitly enable Database Mail, typically by using the Database Mail Configuration Wizard.

Right-clicking the Database Mail node in Object Explorer and selecting Configure Database Mail launches the Database Mail Configuration Wizard, which performs these tasks:

- Sets up Database Mail
- Installs or uninstalls Database Mail objects in a database
- Manages Database Mail accounts and profiles
- Manages profile security
- Views or changes system parameters

The Set Up SQLiMail option guides you through all the tasks required to set up SQLiMail for the first time. Additional options allow you to perform other setup and maintenance tasks, as shown in Figure 9.31.

You can also launch the SQLiMail Configuration Wizard by double-clicking the node.

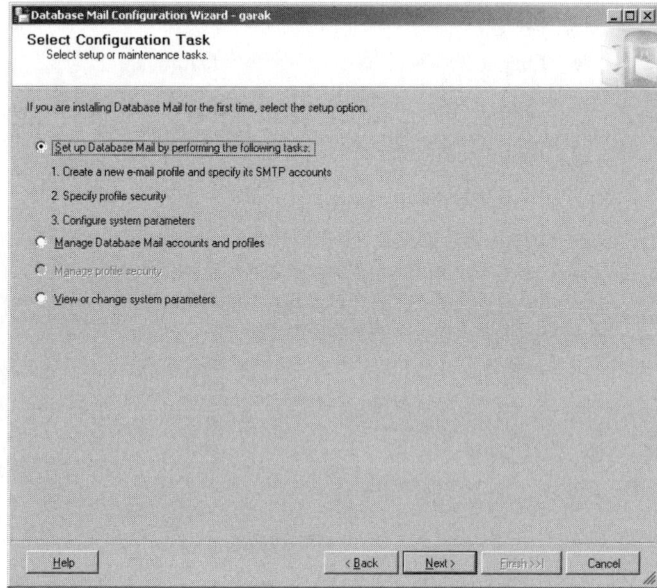

FIGURE 9.31
Database Mail Configuration Wizard's Select Configuration Task page

NOTE You'll learn more about Database Mail in Chapter 17, "Automating Administration."

DISTRIBUTED TRANSACTION COORDINATOR

The Distributed Transaction Coordinator service is responsible for managing transactions that involve multiple databases. There's more information about distributed transactions in Chapter 8, "Topics in Advanced Transact-SQL" and Chapter 22, "Integration Services."

FULL-TEXT SEARCH

The Full-Text Search service handles full-text searching. This icon appears only if indexing is enabled on the current server. Full-text searching is covered in detail in Chapter 6, "*SELECT* Queries."

LEGACY

If you have been working with SQL Server in earlier version, this folder allows you to successfully keep track of and manage three key classes of activities: database maintenance plans, DTS packages, and SQL Mail.

Database Maintenance Plans

This folder allows you to work with Database Maintenance plans that were developed for previous versions of SQL Server.

Data Transformation Services

This folder allows you to manage the various Data Transformation Services packages you may have created in SQL Server 200 and want to use with SQL Server 2005. By right-clicking this folder you can:

- Open SQL Server 2000 Data Transformation Packages
- Import a DTS 2000 Package
- Launch the Package Migration Wizard

You'll learn more about how Data Transformation Services packages from SQL Server 200 are dealt with by SQL Server 2005 in Chapter 22, "Integration Services."

SQL Mail

The SQL Mail service provides an interface to Microsoft Exchange electronic mail for SQL Server. You'll learn about SQL Mail in Chapter 17, "Automating Administration."

The Notification Services Folder

As the name implies, *notification services* are services that transmit notifications to the interested entities, depending on what they wish to be notified about. Most notifications are based on data changes or additions; hence notification services can also be described as services that check whether an event has occurred on specified data, check to see if there is a subscription about it, and send the notification.

Notification Services will be examined in Chapter 27, but you need to be familiar with some basic terms. An *event* is any action that affects the specified data. A *subscriber* is an entity that wishes to be notified when an event occurs. A *subscription* is a request by a subscriber that describes when he wants to be notified and what he wants to be notified about. (For example, a subscriber may want to know when the price of oil exceeds $50 per barrel.) *Notification* is any mode/channel of communication by which a subscriber is notified of an event to which she has a subscription. E-mail and data files are examples.

Right-clicking the Notification Services folder opens a shortcut menu that lets you create a new notification services instance, unregister an instance, list versions of notification services and instances, and refresh the folder contents.

Selecting New Notification Services Instance opens the New Notification Services Instance dialog, as shown in Figure 9.32. To create a new instance, select the instance configuration file and then add or modify parameter values. You can also set encryption options from the Encryption page. Once an instance is created, it appears in the Notification Services folder.

Right-clicking an individual instance opens a shortcut menu from which you can provide a number of key tasks. You can enable or disable the instance, start or stop the instance, refresh it, or open the Properties sheet. An additional menu item, Tasks, allows you to export the instance to the code editor, registering (creating) an `NS$`*`instance`* Windows service. You can also unregister the instance with the effect of removing the instances form the Registry and deleting any associated Windows service and performance objects that might exist. You can also update, upgrade, or delete the instance.

Opening the Instance Properties windows allows you to open one of four pages: Applications, Subscribers, Encryption, and Windows Services. On the Applications page, you can enable or disable associated components such as subscriptions, event providers, generators, and distributors. The Subscribers page lets you enable or disable subscribers. You can enable or disable encryption on the Encryption page. On the Windows Services page, you can stop or start the instance-related service, if you have enabled one.

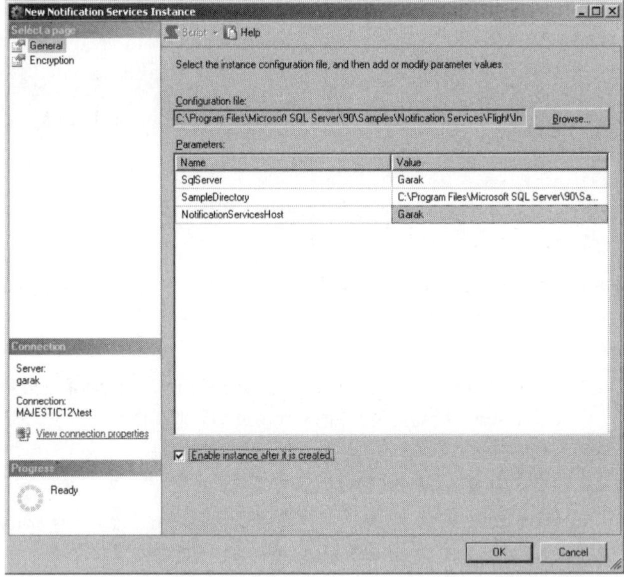

FIGURE 9.32
Creating a new notification services instance

SQL Server Agent

The SQL Server Agent node is displayed only to members of the sysadmin role. This node is basically a container for objects managed by the SQL Server Agent service. SQL Server Agent is a separate component of SQL Server that's responsible for managing alerts, jobs, and operators, and there are nodes of the tree underneath the SQL Server Agent node for each of these objects.

By right-clicking the SQL Server Agent node, you can start, restart, and stop the SQL Server Agent service, or create a new operator, job, schedule, or alert. You can also view the SQL Server Agent error log (as well as the other logs in the Log File Viewer), view history, make this a master or target server for multiserver administration, manage job categories, refresh the objects, or open the Properties sheet.

The SQL Server Agent node contains five folders: Jobs, Job Activity Monitors, Alerts, Operators, Proxies, and SQL Server Agent Error Logs.

JOBS

When you open the Jobs folder, Object Explorer shows a list of all jobs on the server (a list of all jobs is also shown in the Summary window when you select the Jobs folder). A *job* is a set of actions that SQL Server Agent can run in response to alerts or on a schedule.

Right-clicking the Jobs folder opens a shortcut menu that lets you create a new job, manage schedules, manage job categories, view the job history, filter, or refresh. Right-clicking a specific job allows you to do the following:

- Create a new job
- Start the job
- Stop the job
- Script the job as
- View the job history

- Enable/disable the job
- Rename the job
- Delete the job
- Refresh
- Open the job properties sheet

Job Activity Monitor

This tool allows you to view the current activity and status of SQL Server Agents Job. Use Filter to limit the jobs displayed and click on the column headers to sort the grid.

To modify a job, double-click the job to open the Job Properties dialog box. Right-click a job in the grid to start it running all job steps, start at a particular job step, disable or enable the job, refresh the job, delete the job, view the history of the job, or view the properties of the job.

Alerts

When you click the Alerts folder, Object Explorer shows a list of all alerts configured on the current server in the Summary window as well as all the individual alerts in treeview. An *alert* is a condition that SQL Server Agent can respond to (for example, an error of a particular severity), together with an action SQL Server Agent should take if the alert's condition occurs (for example, running a particular job).

By right-clicking the Alerts folder, you can create a new alert, enable all alerts, disable all alerts, and refresh the objects list. The shortcut menu for an individual alert lets you create a new alert, generate SQL script, enable or disable the individual alert, rename, delete, refresh, or open the Properties sheet. Double-clicking an alert opens the Properties sheet for that alert.

Operators

When you click the Operators folder, Object Explorer shows you a list of all operators for the current server in the Summary window. An *operator* is a user who should be notified in the case of certain alerts.

Right-clicking the Operators folder lets you create new operators and refresh the list. The shortcut menu for an individual operator lets you create a new operator, generate SQL script, rename, delete, refresh, or open the Properties sheet. Double-clicking an operator also opens the Properties sheet for that operator. In the Properties sheet are three pages:

- General displays the notification methods and the pager schedule defined for the operator.
- Notifications lists those the operator receives.
- History shows the most recent notification attempts.

Proxies

When you click the Proxies folder, Object Explorer shows you a list of all the proxies, grouped for the current server in the Summary window. A *proxy* is a means of providing SQL Server Agent with the security credentials of a Windows user. A proxy can be associated with one or more subsystems, allowing the job step that uses it access to the specified subsystem as if it were supplying the user's credentials.

Right-clicking the Proxies folder lets you create a new proxy or refresh the list. Right-clicking a specific proxy opens the shortcut menu and lets you create or delete a proxy, generate SQL script, refresh, or open the Properties sheet. Double-clicking the proxy also opens the Properties sheet. You can select from three pages: General, Principals, and References.

Error Logs

The SQL Server Agent Errors Logs folder contains nodes for the current activity log and for the nine most recent activity logs before that.

When you select one of the individual log nodes and either double-click or right-click and select View Agent Log, Management Studio opens the Log File Viewer. In the left pane, you can select the logs you wish to view; the right pane shows the individual log entries, as shown in Figure 9.33. For each entry, Management Studio displays the date, the message it contains, the log type, and the log source.

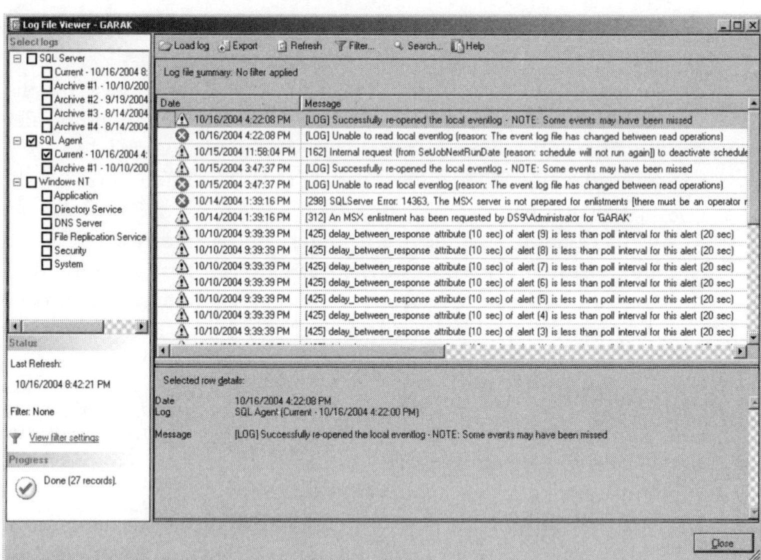

FIGURE 9.33
SQL Server Agent Error Log in Log File Viewer

NOTE The SQL Server Agent error log contains only errors directly related to the SQL Server Agent service, not to the operation of SQL Server as a whole. For convenience, the Log File Viewer also contains error logs for SQL Server and Windows NT server.

NOTE For more information about alerts, operators, jobs, and proxies, see Chapter 17.

Other Server Types

In addition to the plain vanilla SQL Server, Object Explorer can connect to other types of server instances: Analysis servers, Integration Services servers, Report servers, and SQL Server Mobile Edition. Each has a different arrangement of folders, depending on type.

ANALYSIS SERVER

An Analysis Server instance contains only two folders:

- Databases, which contains the Analysis Services databases. You can use Management Studio to manage existing databases; create new roles and database assemblies; and process cubes, dimensions, and mining structures.
- Assemblies, which contains the server assemblies. You can create, delete, or modify assemblies in this folder.

NOTE Analysis Services is covered in Chapter 26, "Integration Services."

INTEGRATION SERVICES (SSIS) SERVER

Integration Services Server contains two folders:

- Running Packages, which contains opened and running SSIS packages. You use the Business Intelligence Development Studio environment to create SSIS packages.
- Stored Packages, which hold links to all DTS packages stored on the file system or in MSDB.

NOTE Data Transformation Services is covered in depth in Chapter 22.

REPORT SERVER

You can use Management Studio to manage one or more report servers within a single workspace. Each report server is represented as a node in an object hierarchy. Reporting Services is covered in detail in Chapter 28, "Reporting Services."

SQL SERVER MOBILE

SQL Server Mobile Edition contains a restricted set of the usual SQL Server nodes: Tables, Views, Programmability, and Replication.

SQL Server Actions

Before we leave Object Explorer, we should mention the shortcut menu. By right-clicking the SQL Server instance, you can perform the following actions:

- Connect to the server
- Disconnect the server
- Register the server as well as create or add the server to an existing server group
- Open a new Query window
- Start, stop, restart, pause, or resume the Server Service
- Refresh
- Open the server's Properties sheet, which consists of 9 pages:
  - General
  - Memory

- Processors
- Security (including authentication method, login auditing, and the service account logins and proxy accounts)
- Connections
- Database Settings
- Advanced Settings
- Permissions

NOTE The Properties sheet will differ depending on the server type.

Template Explorer

Template Explorer is a newly introduced feature in SQL Server 2005. Essentially, it's a collection of folders containing templates. *Templates* are standardized files containing SQL scripts that you can use to create objects in the database. Microsoft SQL Server 2005 comes with a number of different templates that are installed by default in the `C:\Program Files\Microsoft SQL Server\90\Tools\Binn\VSShell\Common7\IDE\sqlworkbenchnewitems` directory.

To open Template Explorer, choose View ➢ Template Explorer or press Ctrl+Alt+T.

Templates are available for solutions, projects, and various types of code editors. They're also available to create objects such as databases, tables, views, indexes, stored procedures, triggers, statistics, and functions. In addition, there are templates that help you to manage your server by creating extended properties, linked servers, logins, roles, users, and templates for Analysis Services and SQL Server Mobile Edition.

You can open a template from the File menu or from Template Explorer. To open a template from Template Explorer, Choose View ➢ Template Explorer. A new window opens, as shown in Figure 9.34. Note that the Template Explorer window includes a small pane below the folder list containing the three most recently used templates.

Template Explorer contains shortcuts for three server types: SQL Server, Analysis Server, and Mobile Server. Each type of server has different folders associated with it by default.

The following folders are included in the SQL Server Templates folder:

- Aggregate
- Assembly
- Backup
- Certificate
- Database
- Database Mail
- Database Trigger
- Default
- Earlier Versions
- Endpoint
- Event Notification
- Partition Function
- Partition Scheme
- Recursive Queries
- Restore
- Role
- Rule
- Service Broker
- SQL Trace
- Statistics
- Stored Procedure
- Synonym

- Extended Property
- Full Text
- Function
- Index
- Linked Server
- Login
- Notification Server
- Table
- Trigger
- User
- User-Defined Data Type
- User Defined Type
- View
- XML Schema Collection

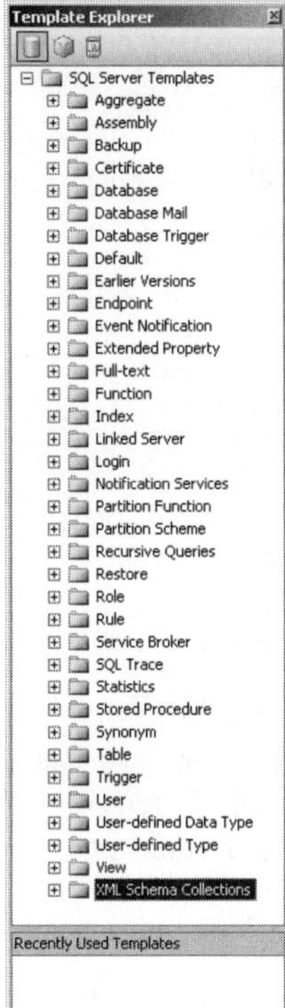

FIGURE 9.34
Template Explorer

The Analysis Server folder contains the following folders:

- DMX
- MDX
- XMLA

Subfolders in the SQL Mobile Templates folder are as follows:

- Database
- Index
- Table

Right-clicking any of the three server root folders, any subfolder, or any template lets you create a new folder or template, launch a search, cut, copy, paste, delete, or open the Properties sheet. Right-clicking a specific template also makes available the Edit function on the shortcut menu. Double-clicking a template opens it in the appropriate code editor

You can create a new custom template in Template Explorer as follows:

1. Right-click a folder, subfolder, or template; click New; and then select Template.
2. Right-click the new template, and select Edit.
3. When you're prompted to connect to SQL Server (this is optional), click Connect.
4. In the subsequent windows, use Query Editor to create the script.
5. Right-click the Template tab, and click Save *<template name>*.

As you'll see, there are a number of alternative methods to create new queries (for example, by choosing File ➤ New Query or by selecting New Query from the menu bar). You can make any query into a template as follows:

1. Create the script.
2. Choose File ➤ Save *<window name>* As, which opens the Save File As dialog box.
3. In the Save In box, navigate to the template directory, which by default is `C:\Program Files\Microsoft SQL Server\90\Tools\Binn\VSShell\Common7\IDE\sqlworkbenchnewitems\`, and then to any appropriate subfolder.
4. In the File Name box, type the name you want for the template, using the `SQL` extension in the format `<file name>.sql`.
5. Click Save.

Solution Explorer

Solution Explorer is another new feature of SQL Server 2005. This tool allows you to view and manage items and perform item-management tasks in a solution or a project. Solution Explorer also provides access to Management Studio editors so you can work on the items contained within a script project.

NOTE Solution Explorer isn't opened by default. To open it, choose View ➤ Solution Explorer or press Ctrl+Alt+L.

Management Studio provides two containers—projects and solutions—for managing database projects such as scripts, queries, data connections, and files. The objects these containers hold are referred to as *items*. Solution Explorer is structured to group scripts and connections in script projects.

Solutions

A *solution* includes one or more projects, plus any individual files and metadata that define the whole solution as opposed to a particular project within the solution. A complex database application can require multiple solutions.

Solutions and projects, by forming containers for information, can be used to do the following:

- Enforce source control on queries and/or scripts
- Manage settings for the solution as a whole
- Manage settings for individual projects

Solutions allow you to take a more systematic approach to administration and management of project files, scripts, and connections. You can organize the bits and pieces in any fashion that makes sense for the tasks you're trying to complete. For example, you can add items that are useful to multiple projects in the solution or to the solution without referencing the item in each project. In addition, you can access and work on files and other items that are independent of solutions or projects. You can also work on related items that apply to a particular project and control source files.

Creating a New Solution

You create a new solution by first creating a new project:

1. Choose File ➤ New ➤ Project to open the New Project window.
2. You're given a choice of three script types: SQL Server Scripts, Analysis Server Scripts, and SQL Mobile Scripts. In this example, select SQL Server Scripts.
3. In the top Name Box, enter **Sample Project One**.
4. Accept the default location.
5. Make sure Create New Solution appears in the Solution box, as shown in Figure 9.35.
6. In the bottom Name box, enter **Sample Solution One**.
7. Click OK. The Solution Explorer window opens, as shown in Figure 9.36, displaying Sample Solution One and Sample Project One.

Management Studio stores the definition for a solution in two files: the solution definition file and a solution user options file. The solution definition file (`.sqlsln`) holds the metadata as well as the list of projects associated with the solution. User-defined options are stored in the solution user options (`.sqlsuo`) file.

NOTE Management Studio doesn't support Visual Studio or Business Intelligence Development Studio solutions or projects.

FIGURE 9.35
Creating a new solution and project in Management Studio

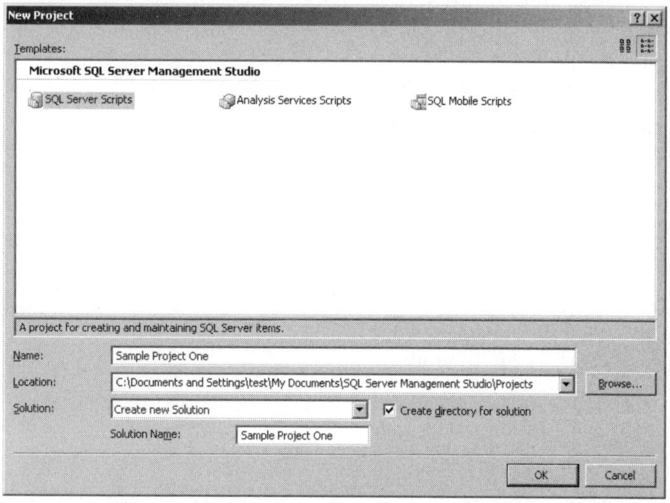

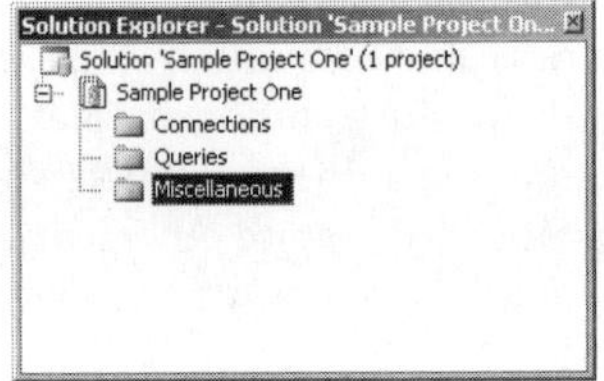

FIGURE 9.36
Sample Solution One treeview

Projects

Every solution has one or more *projects*. A project is a container holding related files and other items, such as data connection information, relating to a specific activity you're working on. You can specify which project or projects (if any) run when you start Management Studio (*startup projects*) through the Solution Property pages accessed when you right-click the Solution and select Set StartUp Projects. Alternatively, you can choose Project ➤ Set StartUp Projects when pointing to a solution, or Project ➤ Set As StartUp Project when pointing to a specific project.

Right-clicking a project allows you access to a shortcut menu from which can create new items or add existing items. If you add a new item—for example, an existing template such as Create Database—Solution Explorer places it in the correct folder and adds any additional files (such as the connection) if they aren't already present (see Figure 9.37). You can also save, cut (and paste), remove a project from the solution, or open the Properties sheet. The Properties sheet allows you to view a variety of configuration and other settings.

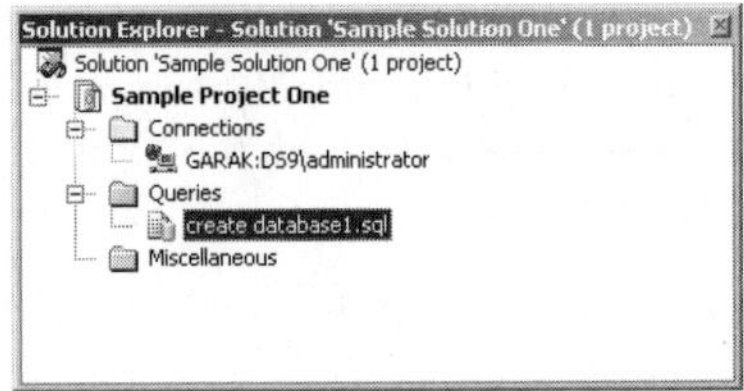

FIGURE 9.37
Solution Explorer, showing connections and queries populating the project

If you right-click the Connections folder, you can create a new connection or view the Connection folder's Properties sheet. Right-clicking a specific connection lets you create a new query, remove the connection, or open the Properties sheet. In the Properties sheet, you view and, in some cases, modify the following:

- Authentication methods
- Date created
- Execution timeout
- Initial database
- IsDisposed
- Login timeout
- Protocol to use

- Server to connect to
- Type
- User

Right-clicking the Queries folder opens a shortcut menu that lets you create a new query or open the Properties sheet. Right-clicking an individual query enables you to open, cut, copy, remove, rename, or open the query Properties sheet.

Right-clicking the Miscellaneous folder enables you to open the Properties sheet. Miscellaneous files are those that aren't created from Solution Explorer. They're held in the Miscellaneous folder until you move them into a project.

NOTE **Note that clicking any of these items in a solution or project in SQL Server, Analysis Server, or SQL Server Mobile Edition will open the same shortcut menus regardless of server type.**

Moving Items

You can move queries and miscellaneous files between projects in Solution Explorer. Connections can't be moved. To move an item, select it in Solution Explorer. From the menu bar, choose Edit ➢ Cut. Select the destination folder, and then choose Edit ➢ Paste.

Alternatively, you can drag and drop the items within Solution Explorer. Occasionally, if you drag queries between projects, they may be classified as miscellaneous in the target project. Also note that moving a connected query doesn't move the connection to the target, meaning the query loses its connection when it's moved.

External Tools

You can launch any Microsoft Windows or Windows .NET application from Management Studio by adding external applications such as Notepad to the Tools menu, as shown in Figure 9.38. To add an external tool to the Tools menu, perform the following procedure:

1. Choose Tools ➢ External Tools.
2. In the Title box, type the name as you want it to appear on the menu bar. (Hint: If you put an ampersand [&] before a letter in the name of the tool, you can use that letter as an accelerator key.) For example, &Notepad displays Notepad on the Tools menu and makes the letter N into an accelerator key
3. In the Command windows, enter the path to the executable file.
4. In the Arguments box, specify any value you want passed to the tool, or command-line switches if appropriate.
5. In the Initial Directory box, specify the tool's working directory.
6. Set the following options, when available: Use Output Windows, Prompt For Arguments, and Close On Exit.
7. Click OK. The new program is added to the Tools menu.

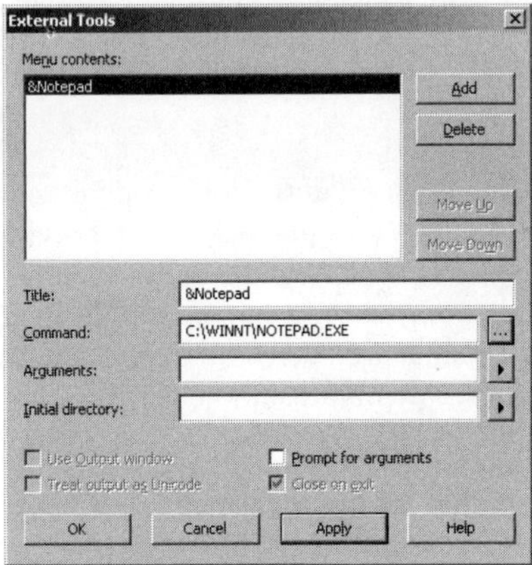

FIGURE 9.38
Adding Notepad to the Tools menu using the External Tools window

Summary

In this chapter, we have introduced you to the immensely rich and powerful Management Studio. Styled on the look of Visual Studio, this is the central master control system for all SQL Server operations. As you've seen, you can perform many common SQL Server operations without ever leaving the SQL Server Enterprise Manager window.

In addition to displaying information about SQL Server objects and operations, Management Studio is lavish in the various ways it provides you to perform basic tasks. Nearly everything you need to do can be accomplished through shortcuts menus in Object Explorer, Template Explorer, Solution Explorer, and Registered Servers. You also learned how to add external tools so that you can easily access other applications such as Notepad.

Now it's time to look at the objects within Management Studio more closely. In the next chapter, we'll start with databases.

Chapter 10

Databases

We're going to go out on a limb here and assume that you own stuff—clothes, food, VCRs, tools, and so on. Most people keep the stuff they own in their homes, but where? Do you just randomly throw your stuff in your house and hope you can find it again later? Of course not—you store your belongings in containers, such as cabinets or dressers, so that you can find your belongings when you need them. Now go one step further: Do you keep all your stuff in the same container? Imagine the chaos that would ensue if you kept your tools, food, and clothes in the same cabinet—you wouldn't be able to find anything when you needed it. These principles hold true with SQL Server.

The stuff you own in SQL Server includes things such as tables, views, stored procedures, and other objects. Much like with your clothes, food, and tools, you need containers to store those objects in; with SQL Server, those containers are databases. Again, go one step further: Do you want to keep all your objects in the same database? Definitely not. Just like storing all your personal belongings in the same cabinet, you would have a terrible time sorting out the data if it was all in one database. That is why you need to have more than one database, each dedicated to a specific task, such as an accounting database to hold all of the accounting objects and data, or a Sales database for the sales objects and data.

It makes sense, then, that before you start creating objects, such as tables and views, you must create the database that will contain those objects. That is what this chapter deals with: creating, configuring, and administrating databases. We'll start by reviewing the basics of how a database works.

Database Basics

As with anything, you need to understand the basics before you can jump into the more advanced topics—this is especially true with databases. As we mentioned in Chapter 3, "Overview of SQL Server," a *database* is a series of files on your hard disk. These files are just space that has been preallocated on the hard disk for storing other SQL Server objects, such as tables and views. These files on the hard disk can be one of three types: primary data files, secondary data files, or transaction log files.

The *primary data file* (with an `.MDF` extension) is the first file created for the database. This file can be used to store two types of objects: user and system objects. *User objects* are such things as tables, views, stored procedures, and the like that are used to modify or store information that has been input by a user. *System tables* contain information that SQL Server needs to keep your database functioning, such as table names, index locations, database user accounts, and information about other system objects. The system tables must reside in the primary data file, but the user information and other objects can be moved to secondary data files.

When you run out of room on the hard disk that contains the primary data file, you can create a *secondary data file* (with an `.NDF` extension) on a separate hard disk. Once you have created the secondary file, you can use it to store user data, such as tables, indexes, and views, but not system objects (those reside only in the primary data file).

The third type of file requires a little more explanation than the data files. The *transaction log file* functions much like a constant online backup by storing transactions. A *transaction* is a group of data-modification commands (for example, `INSERT`, `UPDATE`, and `DELETE`) that is contained in a `BEGIN TRAN...COMMIT` block and executed as a unit, meaning that all the commands in the transaction are applied to the database or none of them are. SQL Server understands two types of transactions: implicit and explicit. An *implicit* transaction occurs when you send a data-modification command to SQL Server without specifically encasing it in a `BEGIN TRAN...COMMIT` block; in this case, SQL Server will add the block for you. An *explicit* transaction occurs when you specifically type the `BEGIN TRAN` and `COMMIT` statements at the beginning and end of your statement block. A typical explicit transaction might look as follows:

```
BEGIN TRAN
  INSERT RECORD
  DELETE RECORD
COMMIT TRAN
```

SQL Server sees the `INSERT` and `DELETE` commands as a single unit of modification. Either they both happen or neither happens—or, in SQL Server terminology, they're either rolled forward or rolled back. The `DELETE` can't happen without the `INSERT` and vice versa. Every command in SQL Server that modifies data is considered a transaction, each having `BEGIN` and `COMMIT` statements, whether or not you put them there (if you don't add the `BEGIN` and `COMMIT`, SQL Server will).

You might expect each of these transactions to be written directly to the database file, but that isn't the case. When a user tries to modify a record in a database, SQL Server locates the data page (pages are discussed in Chapter 3) in the database that contains the record to be changed. Once located, the page in question is loaded into memory—specifically, it's loaded into a special area of memory called the *data cache*, which SQL Server uses to store data that is to be modified. All the changes to the page are now made in memory (or random access memory [RAM]), because RAM is about 100 times faster than hard disk, and speed is of the essence.

NOTE As discussed in Chapter 3, a *page* is 8KB and is the smallest unit of storage in a SQL Server database.

Leaving those changed records in RAM is a bad idea, though, because RAM is considered *volatile*, which means that the contents of RAM are erased every time the computer loses power. If the machine were to lose power, you would lose all the changes in the data cache. So rather than leaving those changes at the mercy of RAM, SQL Server writes the changes made in the data cache to the transaction log at the same time. Now you have a copy of the data in RAM and on the hard disk in the transaction log file. If the server were to lose power now, all the changes stored in the data cache would be erased, but you could still recover them from the transaction log. In that sense, the transaction log is like a constant online backup of the data cache.

So why not just write all the changes from data cache directly to the database file? Why put the transaction log in the middle? Imagine what would happen to your database if your server were to crash right in the middle of writing changes from memory to the data file if there were no transaction log. The transaction would be partially written to disk, and the original transaction would be erased from memory with no hope of recovery. However, because the transaction is written to the transaction log first, if the server crashes, the original transaction is preserved, and partial transactions aren't written to the database.

If a crash occurs, SQL Server reads the transaction logs for each database, looking for completed transactions that haven't been applied to the data file. If SQL Server finds any, it rolls them forward, writing them to the data file. Any uncompleted transactions (a `BEGIN TRAN` with no corresponding `COMMIT`) are rolled back or deleted from the transaction log. This way, you can recover your databases right up to the minute of a crash.

Because of the benefits that you gain from transaction logs, they're required for each database—you can't have a primary data file without a transaction log. The transaction log file (with an `.LDF` extension) should be placed on a different physical hard disk than the data file. If the hard disk with the data file crashes, you still have the transaction log file and the last good backup to re-create the data file on a new hard disk. The transaction log file should be approximately 10 to 25 percent of the size of the data files to accommodate the transactions made during the day. If your users don't make many modifications to the data, you can go with a smaller transaction log (10 percent being the minimum), whereas if your users are constantly modifying the data, you should make the transaction log file larger (maybe even up to 30 percent).

TIP **SQL Server doesn't enforce the MDF, NDF, and LDF extensions for the three files types, but they're considered good form for naming your files.**

NOTE **Because all the changes are written to the transaction log before they're written to the data file, the transaction log is referred to as a *write-ahead* log.**

Now that you know how these files work, you need to know how big to make them. Let's look at capacity planning.

Planning for Capacity

Perhaps you've heard the old adage *waste not, want not.* That rings true regarding hard-disk space on your SQL Server. Because databases are files that are stored on your hard disk, you can actually waste hard-disk space if you make them too big. If you make your database files too small, though, SQL Server will have to expand the database file, or you may need to create a secondary data file to accommodate the extra data—a process that can slow down users. Neither of these options is very appealing, so you need to find a happy balance between too big and too small, which requires a little math. Here are the general steps to estimate the size of your database:

1. Calculate the record size of the table in question. You get this by adding the size of each column in the table.
2. Divide 8092 by the row size from step 1, and round down to the nearest number. The figure 8092 is the actual amount of data a single data page can hold, and you round down because a row can't be split across pages.
3. Divide the number of rows you expect to have by the result from step 2. This will tell you how many data pages will be used for your table.
4. Multiply the result from step 3 by 8192—the size of a data page in bytes. This will tell you exactly how many bytes your table will take on the disk.

In Chapter 11, "Tables," you'll learn how to plan a database—deciding what tables to put in it, what datatypes to use, and how big the fields in the tables should be—so we'll forego that discussion here. In this section, we'll assume that the planning phase is complete and create a Sales database containing three tables: one for customer information, one for product information, and one for order detail information. To calculate the size of your new database, let's apply the following steps to the customers table to discern how big it will be with 10,000 records:

1. Assuming you have already planned your database, add together all the field sizes in the customers table. Remember that nvarchar takes twice the space you assign it so nvarchar(20) is actually 40 bytes. Here is the table layout (you should get 235 bytes):

Custid	int (note: this is 4 bytes of storage)
Fname	nvarchar(20)
Lname	nvarchar(20)
Address	nvarchar(50)
City	nvarchar(20)
State	char(2)
Zip	char(9)

2. Divide 8092 by 235, and round down to the nearest number to find out how many of these rows can fit on a single data page. You must round down in every case because a row can't span a page. The answer should be 34.
3. Divide 10,000 (the estimated number of rows in the table) by the number of rows on a page (34), and round up to the nearest number. You round up here because a partial row will be moved to a whole new page—there is no such thing as a partial page of storage. The answer should be 294.
4. Multiply 294 (the number of pages required to hold 10,000 records) by 8192 (the size of a page on disk). This should be 2,408,448 bytes.

So, with 10,000 records, the customers table in your Sales database would require approximately 2.4MB of hard-disk space. By repeating these steps for each table in the database, you can figure out approximately how much space to allocate to the database when you first create it.

With the math out of the way, you're ready to start creating a database.

Creating Databases

We discussed earlier that a database comprises at least two files: the primary data file (with an `.MDF` extension) and the transaction log file (with an `.LDF` extension). You may also need secondary data files if the hard disk that contains the primary data file fills up, but we'll discuss those later in this chapter.

To get started with the database, you only need to create the primary data file and transaction log file. There are two different ways to go about it:

- Graphically, with SQL Server Management Studio
- Via Transact-SQL code

We'll look at each method here, starting with the SQL Server Management Studio.

TIP New databases are actually copies of the Model database, because Model has all the system objects necessary for any database to function. This means that if you want any standard objects in all your databases (for example, a database user account), if you add the object to the Model database, the object will automatically exist in all new databases.

Creating Databases with SQL Server Management Studio

The easiest way to create a database in SQL Server is through SQL Server Management Studio. To help you get the feel of using SQL Server Management Studio for creating databases, we'll use this next series of steps to create a Sales database that can later be filled with tables, views, and other objects for a sales department:

1. Open SQL Server Management Studio from the SQL Server 2005 group in Programs on the Start menu, and connect using Windows Authentication.
2. Expand your server in the Object Explorer pane, and then expand the Databases icon.
3. Right-click Databases, and select New Database.
4. In the left pane, you'll see the Select A Page list. Make sure you're on the General page, and fill in the following information:

   Database name: Sales

   Owner: sa

   Collation: *<server default>*

   Recovery Model: Full
5. In the Database Files list, you should see two rows: one for the data file and another for the log file. Change the initial size of the data file to **10**.
6. Click the ellipsis button in the Autogrowth column for the data file, click the Restricted File Growth radio button, and change the maximum size to **20**. If you left this set to Unrestricted File Growth, the data file could fill the entire hard drive, which could make your computer crash if the data file was on the same hard disk as other programs (such as the Windows operating system).

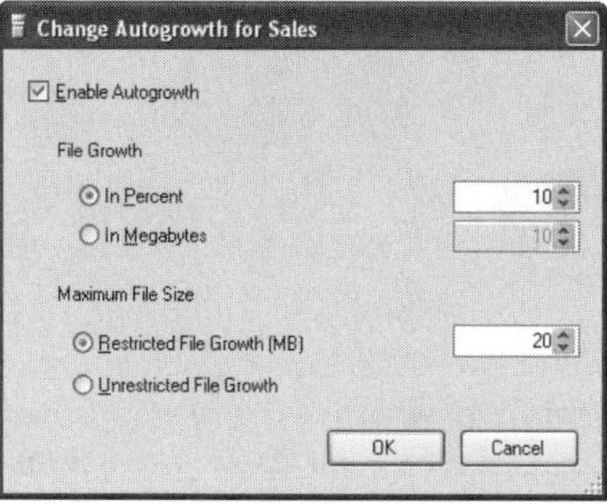

7. Click the ellipsis button in the Autogrowth column for the log file, click the Restricted File Growth radio button, change the maximum size to **2**, and change the File Growth to 10 percent.

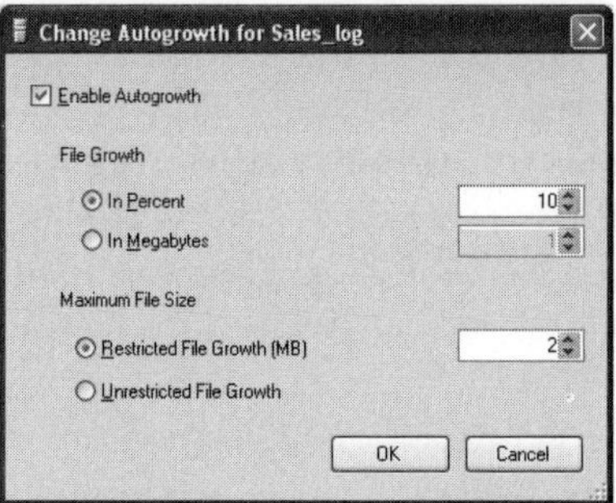

8. If you leave Use full-text indexing checked then your general page should look like Figure 10.1.
9. Click OK to create the new database.
10. You should now see your new database in Object Explorer in SQL Server Management Studio. Click the new Sales database to view its properties.

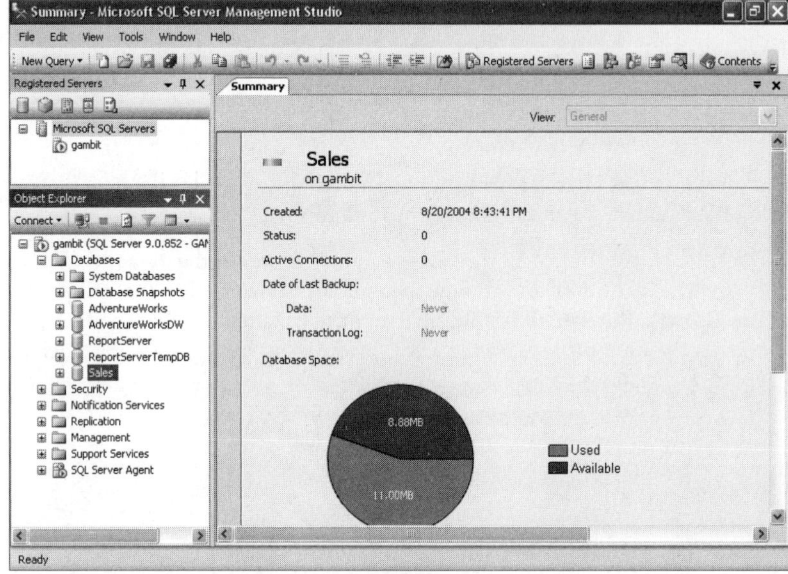

TIP When you create a new object in SQL Server, you may not see it in Object Explorer right away. Right-clicking the level just above where your new object should be and selecting Refresh forces SQL Server to reread the system tables and display any new objects in your database.

The Sales database is now ready to be filled with other objects (for example, tables or views), and it didn't take long to create. But what happened behind the scenes? You'll see that as you go through the next method for creating a database: using Transact-SQL.

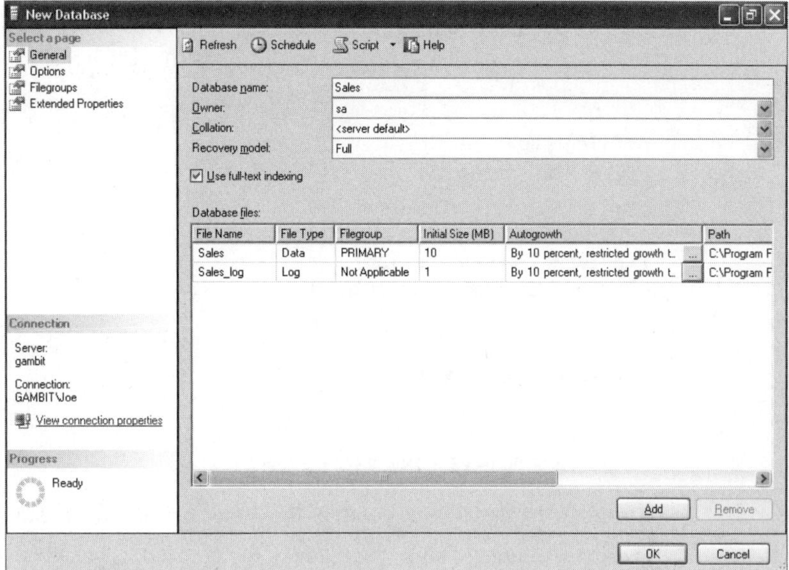

FIGURE 10.1 The completed General page

Creating Databases with Transact-SQL

Although using SQL Server Management Studio is an effective and easy way to create a database, you may not always have it available to you. For instance, suppose you're a developer, and you have written a custom database application. Your installation program needs to create the necessary databases for your application. SQL Server Management Studio won't work in this scenario, so you need to know how to create the database using T-SQL (a shortened form of Transact-SQL). The syntax for the CREATE DATABASE statement looks as follows:

```
CREATE DATABASE database_name
    [ ON
        [ <filespec> [ ,...n ] ]
        [ , <filegroup> [ ,...n ] ]
    ]
[
    [ LOG ON { <filespec> [ ,...n ] } ]
    [ COLLATE collation_name ]
    [ FOR { ATTACH [ WITH <service_broker_option> ]
        | ATTACH_REBUILD_LOG } ]
    [ WITH <external_access_option> ]
]
[;]

<filespec> ::=
[ PRIMARY ]
(
    [ NAME = logical_file_name , ]
    FILENAME = 'os_file_name'
```

```
        [ , SIZE = size [ KB | MB | GB | TB ] ]
        [ , MAXSIZE = { max_size [ KB | MB | GB | TB ] | UNLIMITED } ]
        [ , FILEGROWTH = growth_increment [ KB | MB | % ] ]
) [ ,...n ]

<filegroup> ::=
FILEGROUP filegroup_name
    <filespec> [ ,...n ]

<external_access_option> ::=
    DB_CHAINING { ON | OFF }
  | TRUSTWORTHY { ON | OFF }

<service_broker_option> ::=
    ENABLE_BROKER
  | NEW_BROKER
  | ERROR_BROKER_CONVERSATIONS
```

Here's an explanation for each of the items in this syntax listing:

database_name This is the name of the new database, which can be up to 128 characters.

ON This option specifies the filegroup on which to create a data file. A *filegroup* is a logical grouping of secondary data files that can be used to control placement of user objects (such as tables and indexes). The PRIMARY option that comes after the ON argument is used to specify the PRIMARY filegroup, which is the default for all files created and the only filegroup that can contain the primary data file.

PRIMARY This option specifies that the associated <filespec> list defines the primary files. The primary files contain the logical start of the database and all the required system tables.

LOG ON This specifies where the log files are to be created and their size. If LOG ON isn't specified, SQL Server creates a log file that is 25 percent of the size of all data files, that has a system-generated name, and that is placed in the same directory as the data files. It's best to use LOG ON to place the transaction log file on a separate physical hard disk from the data files so that, in the event of a system crash, you can access all the transactions that occurred before the disaster.

COLLATE **collation_name** This specifies the default collation for the database, which can be either a Windows or SQL Server collation name.

FOR ATTACH Use this option to create a database by attaching an existing set of database files. To successfully attach a database, you'll need the .mdf file and all the .ndf files; if there are multiple data and log files, make sure you have them all, or this command won't succeed.

FOR ATTACH_REBUILD_LOG You can use this option to create a database by attaching an existing set of database files, but with this option you don't need all the log files. This command is useful if you want to keep a read-only copy of a database on another server for reporting purposes. Using this option you don't need to copy over all the transaction log files (.ndf) but you do need all the data files (.mdf) available.

NAME This option specifies the logical name of the database, which will be used to reference the database in Transact-SQL code. This option isn't required when FOR ATTACH is used.

FILENAME This is the name and path of the database file as it's stored on the hard disk. This must be a local directory (not over the network) and can't be compressed.

SIZE This is the initial size of the data files. It can be specified in MB or KB. If you don't provide a size for a primary data file, SQL Server generates a file that is the same size as the Model system database. If a size isn't provided for a secondary file, SQL Server automatically makes it 1MB.

MAXSIZE This is the maximum size that the database is allowed to reach automatically. This can also be in MB or KB; or you can specify `UNLIMITED`, thus instructing SQL Server to expand the data file to fill the entire hard disk.

UNLIMITED This option specifies that the file being defined can grow until the disk is full. This isn't recommended unless the file is on a dedicated disk.

FILEGROWTH This is the increment in which to expand the file. It's specified in either MB, KB, or percent (%). If none of these symbols are used, MB is assumed.

FILEGROUP This specifies the logical name for the filegroup on which the file is being created.

DB_CHAINING {ON | OFF} If a user selects data from a view, the view must access underlying tables. The link between the view and the tables is called an *ownership chain*. If this option is turned `ON`, then the database can be the source or target of an ownership chain; if the option is `OFF`, then the database can't be involved in a chain.

TRUSTWORTHY {ON | OFF} When this option is set to `ON`, database modules that use an impersonation context are allowed to access resources outside of the database. Only members of the sysadmin fixed server role can set this option.

ENABLE_BROKER This option specifies that the Service Broker is enabled for this database.

NEW_BROKER This creates a new service_broker_guid in sys.databases and in the restored database.

ERROR_BROKER_CONVERSATIONS This option ends all conversations with an error that indicates a copy of the broker has been created.

Use the following steps to create a database with T-SQL code (we'll use this to test dropping databases later in this chapter):

1. Open SQL Server Management Studio, and log in using Windows Authentication.
2. Choose File ➤ New ➤ New SQL Server Query.
3. To create a 10MB database named DoomedDB on the C drive with a 2MB log file, execute the following code (note that you should replace the `C:\` with the drive on which you installed SQL Server):

```
CREATE DATABASE DoomedDB
ON PRIMARY
(name = DoomedDB,
 filename = 'c:\Program Files\Microsoft SQL
Server\MSSQL.1\MSSQL\data\DoomedDB.mdf',
 size = 10MB,
 maxsize = 15MB,
 filegrowth = 1MB)
LOG ON
(name = DoomedLog,
 filename = 'c:\Program Files\Microsoft SQL Server\
MSSQL.1\MSSQL\data\DoomedLog.ldf',
```

```
size = 2MB,
maxsize = 3MB,
filegrowth = 10%)
```

4. In the results pane (at the bottom) in the query window, you should see a message stating that the command completed successfully. To verify that this database has been created, expand your server in Object Explorer and then expand Databases. You should see DoomedDB in the list of available databases.

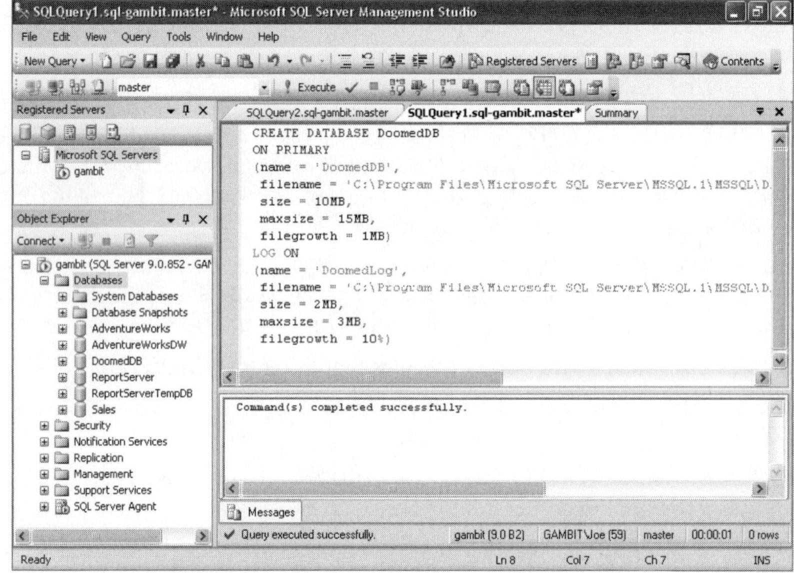

Now that your database is created, you can make a few configuration changes to modify the way the database works.

Modifying Databases

As noted earlier, new databases are copies of the Model database. This means that all new databases have a standard set of options that control their behavior. These options may need to be changed according to the function of the database.

Not only do you need to change the options that control the database, you may need to change the size of the database as well, expanding it or shrinking it. If you expand the database, you may need to expand it to another physical hard disk, which means adding secondary data files or transaction log files to the database. These secondary files may need to be added to filegroups so that you have better control over object placement.

In this section, we'll discuss what actions may be necessary to make your databases behave the way you need them to, how to change the size of the database, and how to add files and filegroups.

Setting Database Options

If you have ever bought a new car or at least watched commercials for new cars, you know that cars come with options. Options on a car include items like a fancy radio and anti-lock brakes—things that wouldn't ordinarily come with a floor-model car. Such options make the car behave differently. SQL Server databases also have options that you can set to make the database behave differently. Before you jump in and start using your database, you may want to consider setting some of those options.

Most of these database options can be set using SQL Server Management Studio. If you right-click one of your databases, select Properties, and then select the Options page, you'll see the window shown in Figure 10.2.

FIGURE 10.2
The Options tab

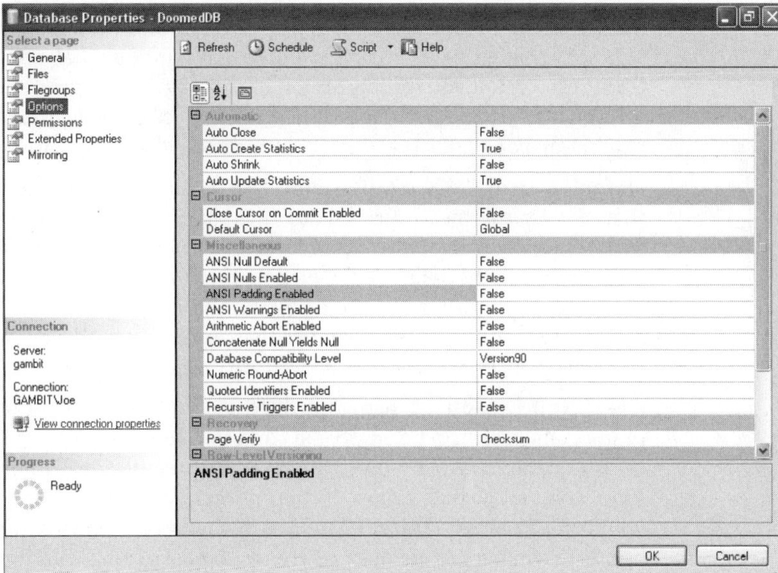

Here is a list of what those options are for and when you should use each one:

Auto Close When a user connects to a database, it must be opened. When a database is open, it consumes system resources such as RAM and CPU time. If this option is set to True, it closes the database when the last user disconnects from it. Because there isn't usually an abundance of available resources on a desktop system, the default for this option in the Express Edition is set to True. That way, a database will be closed when it isn't in use. On all other versions, this option is set to False because users would be opening and closing the database all day and night, which would slow down your system.

Auto Create Statistics When you send a query to the database server, the query is intercepted by the query optimizer, whose sole purpose is to find the fastest way to return a result set. It does this by reading statistics about each of the columns mentioned in your SELECT statement (these statistics are based on the number of values in the column you're selecting from that are unique and the number of duplicates). If this option is set to True, SQL Server automatically creates statistics for any column that is part of an index. If this option is set to False, you must create your own statistics. Again, it's best to leave this turned on until you understand SQL Server well enough to outsmart the query optimizer.

Auto Shrink SQL Server periodically scans your databases to see whether they contain more than 25 percent free space; if so, SQL Server can automatically reduce the size of your database so that it contains only 25 percent free space. If this option is set to True (the default in the Desktop

Edition), autoshrink can occur; if this option is set to False (the default in all other editions), autoshrink doesn't occur. It's best to leave this option set to the default since the autoshrink process can consume system resources on a server, and you don't want to waste disk space on a desktop. We'll discuss how to manually shrink databases on a server shortly.

Auto Update Statistics Setting this option to True instructs SQL Server to automatically update your statistics from time to time. If this is set to False, you must update the statistics manually. Uncheck this option if you're low on system resources (such as RAM or CPU time). You can create a database maintenance plan that will accomplish this task on a scheduled basis later.

Cursor Close On Commit Enabled You can think of a cursor as a subset of a result set. Cursors return single rows of data at a time and therefore make data retrieval faster in the case of a large result set. If you set this option to True, cursors are closed as soon as transactions are committed. It's better to leave this option set to False so that cursors stay open until all data modifications are complete. The cursor can then be closed manually.

Default Cursor When this option is set to Local, any cursor created is local to the procedure that called it; this means that if you execute a stored procedure (a prewritten query stored on the SQL Server) that creates a cursor, only that stored procedure can use that cursor. If this option is set to Global (the default), any other procedure used by the same connection can use the cursor that was created. Therefore, if Joe executes a stored procedure that creates a cursor, any other procedure that Joe executes can use that cursor when this option is set to Global. If this option is set to Local, only the stored procedure that created the cursor could reference it.

ANSI Null Default When you create a table in SQL Server, you can specify whether the columns in the table can be empty—a condition referred to as *null*. If you don't specify nullability on your columns when you create or modify a table, and if this option is set to False, your column won't allow null values. If this option is set to True, and you don't specify nullability on your columns when you create or modify a table, then your columns will accept null values. This option is a matter of personal preference; if most of your columns should not contain null values, you should leave this option set to False—the default setting.

ANSI Nulls Enabled When this option is set to True, any comparison made with a null value yields an answer of null. If this option is set to False, comparisons of non-Unicode data with null values yield False, and null-to-null comparisons yield True. This option is set to False by default.

ANSI Padding Enabled This setting controls the way a column stores values that are shorter than the defined size of the column. If this is set to True then columns of type char(*n*) NOT NULL, char(*n*) NULL, char(*n*) NULL, and binary(*n*) NULL are padded to the length of the column; and columns of type varchar(n) and varbinary(n) aren't padded and trailing data isn't trimmed. If this is set to OFF, then columns of type char(*n*) NOT NULL and char(*n*) NULL are padded to the length of the column, and columns of type char(*n*) NULL, binary(*n*) NULL, varchar(n), and varbinary(n) aren't padded and trailing data is trimmed.

ANSI Warnings Enabled You know that it isn't possible to divide anything by zero, but the computer has to be told. If this option is set to False and you try to divide by zero or use a null value in a mathematical equation, your answer will be null, and you'll see no error. If this option is set to True, you'll receive a warning. This option is set to False by default.

Arithmetic Abort Enabled This option tells SQL Server what to do in the event of an overflow or divide-by-zero arithmetic error. If this option is set to True, then the entire query or transaction is rolled back. If this is set to False, then the query or transaction continues to execute and a warning message is displayed.

Concatenate Null Yields Null String concatenation combines multiple strings into one string by using a + operator. For example, *Hello my name + is Joe* would return *Hello my name is Joe* as one string. If this option is set to True and you try to concatenate *Hello my name* + null, you'll get null. If this option is False and you try to concatenate *Hello my name* + null, you'll get *Hello my name.* This option is False by default.

Database Compatibility Level This option is designed to force your database to behave like one in an earlier version of SQL Server. This is useful for older applications that haven't yet been updated to function with SQL Server 2005. You'll notice four settings here: Version65, Version70, Version80, and Version90, each forcing compatibility with a specific version of SQL Server. Some examples are as follows:

- In Version65 compatibility mode, a `SELECT` statement that has a `GROUP BY clause` but no `ORDER BY` clause is sorted by the columns listed in the `GROUP BY` clause. In Version70 compatibility mode, no sorting takes place without the `ORDER BY` clause.
- In Version65 mode, table aliases can be used in the `SET` clause of an `UPDATE` statement. The Version70 mode doesn't allow table aliases in `UPDATE` statements—you must use the table name specified immediately after the `UPDATE` statement.
- In Version65 mode, when you're creating or altering a table with a bit datatype column, if you don't specify nullability of the column, it's set to `NOT NULL` (meaning that it won't accept null values). In Version70 mode, the nullability of bit columns is set by the current session setting.
- In Version 65 mode, you can't use the `ALTER COLUMN` clause on `ALTER TABLE`. In Version70 mode, this is perfectly acceptable.
- In Version65 mode, if a trigger is saved without the `WITH APPEND` option, any existing trigger of the same type is overwritten. In Version70 mode, the `WITH APPEND` option is assumed; any trigger you create is automatically appended to any existing trigger, rather than erasing it.
- In Version65 mode, when a batch or procedure contains an invalid object name, a warning is issued when the batch is compiled, letting you know that a referenced object doesn't exist. The Version70 mode uses deferred resolution, which means that SQL Server doesn't look for the referenced object until the batch is actually run. Deferred resolution allows you to create a batch or procedure and then create the objects it references later.
- In Version65 mode, an empty string ('') is interpreted as a single blank character, which means that `DATALENGTH` returns a value because it's counting the number of spaces in the string. In Version70 mode, a blank string ('') is interpreted as blank, not as a space, so `DATALENGTH` doesn't count the blank string as a character.
- In Version65 mode, the `CHARINDEX` and `PATINDEX` functions return `NULL` only when both required parameters are null values. In Version70 mode, these commands return `NULL` when any of these parameters are set to `NULL`.
- In Version65 mode, if you reference a text- or image-type column in the inserted or deleted tables, you receive a null value in return. In Version70 mode, references to text and image columns in the inserted and deleted tables aren't allowed.
- In Version65 mode, the concatenation of null-yields-null-value is off by default, which means that if you try to combine a value with a null, you receive an empty string in

return. In Version70 mode, the concatenation of null-yields-null is on by default, meaning that if you combine a value with a null, you receive NULL in return.

- In Version65 mode, you can use SELECT statements in the VALUES list of an INSERT statement. In Version70 mode, SELECT statements aren't allowed in the VALUES list of the INSERT statement.
- In Version80 mode, if a passthrough query against a remote datasource returns columns with duplicate names, they're ignored unless they're specifically named in the query. In Version90 mode, an error is raised in this situation.
- In Version80 mode, character string and varbinary constants with a size larger than 8000 are treated as text, ntext, or image datatypes. In Version90 mode, they're treated as varchar(max), nvarchar(max), or varbinary(max).
- In Version80 mode, the WITH keyword is optional when you're using locking hints in the FROM clause of a SELECT statement. In Version90 mode, the WITH keyword is required.
- In Version80 mode, when you're selecting data from multiple tables that have columns with duplicate names, ambiguities are ignored. In Version90 mode, they aren't ignored, and an error is raised.
- In Version80 mode, comparisons between numeric datatypes are done by converting the type with the lowest precedence to the type with the highest precedence, so both values are compared as the same type. In Version90 mode, numeric types are compared without conversion.
- In Version80 mode, metadata functions truncate input longer than 4000 characters. In Version90 mode, these functions raise an error if the truncation would result in the loss of nonspace characters.
- In Version80 mode, the UNION of a variable-length column and a fixed-length column returns a fixed-length column. In Version90 mode, a variable-length column is produced.

Each version mode also has its own set of reserved keywords:

Version90: PIVOT, UNPIVOT, TABLESAMPLE

Version80: COLLATE, FUNCTION, OPENXML

Version70: BACKUP, CONTAINS, CONTAINSTABLE, DENY, FREETEXT, FREETEXTTABLE, PERCENT, RESTORE, ROWGUIDCOL, TOP

Version65: AUTHORIZATION, CASCADE, CROSS, DISTRIBUTED, ESCAPE, FULL, INNER, JOIN, LEFT, OUTER, PRIVILEGES, RESTRICT, RIGHT, SCHEMA, WORK

Numeric Round-Abort This specifies how the database handles rounding errors. If it's set to True, then an error is generated when there is a loss of precision in an expression. If it's set to False, then no error is generated, and the value is rounded to the precision of the column or variable containing the result.

Quoted Identifiers Enabled If you're going to use spaces in a table name (such as Order Details in the Northwind database) or use reserved keywords (such as check or public), you ordinarily need to encase them in square brackets ([ ]). If this option is set to True, you can use double quotation marks (" ") as well.

Recursive Triggers Enabled Triggers are watchdogs for your tables. They can be defined to fire (activate) whenever someone inserts, updates, or deletes data, to make certain that your complex business logic is applied. For example, if you have a database with one table for managers and another for employees, you can create a `DELETE` trigger on the managers table to ensure that you aren't trying to delete a manager with employees underneath them without first assigning another manager to the employees. When set to True, this option allows triggers to fire other triggers. For example, suppose a user updates an orders table, which fires a trigger on a customers table. The trigger from the customers table can update the orders table. If this option is set to True, the original trigger (on the orders table) fires again; if this option is set to False, the original trigger doesn't fire again. This option is for very complex logic and should be used only when you fully understand all your triggers and tables.

Page Verify In the event of a hardware or power failure, SQL Server may not be able to finish writing data to disk. This is known as a *disk I/O* error, and it leads to corrupt databases. The Page Verify option gives you three settings to control how SQL Server recovers from such a problem:

Checksum The default option, Checksum tells SQL Server to create a checksum value for the entire data page and store it in the page header when the page is written to disk. When the page is later read from the disk, the checksum value is recalculated and compared to the value stored in the page header. If the two match, then the page is good; if they don't, then the page is bad. This option catches the most page errors.

TornPageDetection This instructs SQL Server to write a reversed bit in the page header for each 512-byte sector in the page when it's written to disk. If the bit is in the wrong state when the page is subsequently read from disk, then the page is bad. You should consider using this option when disk I/O errors are primarily caused by torn pages.

None This option specifies that no action is taken when pages are written to or read from disk.

Row-Level Versioning When this option is set to True, SQL Server makes a copy of each modified row in the tempdb database. This allows you to use the new snapshot isolation level, read committed isolation level, multiple active result sets, and index operations that support the `ONLINE` option. If this option is set to False, then you can't use any of these new options. Use this judiciously, because it increases the resources required for all data modifications in the database.

Database Read-Only Exactly as its name suggests, this option makes a database read-only—no writing can occur. There are a few notable side effects. First, read-only databases are skipped during autorecovery, a process at system startup that verifies that all committed transactions have been written to all databases. Second, SQL Server places locks on data that is being read in a standard database so users don't try to modify data that is being read by other users. However, since no writing can occur on a read-only database, no locks are placed on the data, which can accelerate data access. So, read-only is a good option to set on databases that don't change often, such as an archive database or a decision-support database.

Database State This noneditable field shows you the status of the database. The common values are as follows:

Emergency The database has been set to Emergency mode by a system administrator for troubleshooting purposes. In this mode, the database is read-only, logging is disabled, and only administrators can access the database.

Inaccessible The server that houses this database has been switched off or is inaccessible over the network.

Normal Everybody's favorite value, Normal means that everything is running smoothly.

Offline The database was shut down gracefully and can't be modified.

Suspect There is a problem with the database. It will need to be checked and probably restored from a backup.

Restrict Access This option lets you control which users can access a database. There are three options:

Multiple This setting allows all users that have the proper permissions to access the database. Multiple is the default setting.

Single As the name implies, Single allows only one user at a time to connect to the database. That one user could be anybody, but since you're the one setting the option, it should be you. You should set this option just before restoring or renaming a database, since you don't want anyone (including other members in the db_owner role) trying to use the database during these activities.

Restricted There is a special group in each database called db_owner whose members have administrative control over the database of which they're members. Dbcreator is another special group with privileges inside a database. Sysadmin is a special group that has administrative control over every database on the server. When this option is set to Restricted, only members of these three groups can access the database. People already using the database aren't disconnected, but as soon as they exit, they can't come back in. Use this option during initial database development or when you need to change the structure of one of the objects in the database, such as adding a column to a table.

NOTE A few of these options deal with Unicode data, which stores characters using 2 bytes (or 16 bits) instead of the standard single byte (8 bits). This allows you to store 65,536 different characters in Unicode as opposed to the 256 characters that you get with the standard ANSI character set.

Now that you know how to modify your database to behave the way you want it to, you're ready to start filling it with data. Once your users begin working with the database, you may need to resize it. Let's look at how to do that next.

Changing Database Size

Once you put your database in production and your users start filling it with data, you'll eventually need to resize the database—making it bigger if it turns out to be very popular, or smaller if it isn't used as much as anticipated. Let's look at how to expand the original database file first.

Expanding a Data File

If the database you created turns out to be more popular than you expected and your users are constantly adding data to it, you may need to increase the size of the database. Of course, the easiest way to do this is to allow the database to automatically grow, like you did with the `MAXSIZE` and `FILEGROWTH` options on the Sales database. However, when the database hits the size restriction you set for it, you may need to expand it still further. There are two ways to accomplish this: by increasing the size of the existing data file or by adding secondary data files.

To increase the size of the Sales database, use the following steps:

1. Open SQL Server Management Studio, expand Databases under your server in Object Explorer, right-click the Sales database, and select Properties.
2. In the Select A Page column, select the Files page.
3. In the Initial Size column of the Sales data file row (the file of type Data), enter **15**.
4. In the Initial Size column of the Sales_log log file row (the file of type Log), enter **3**.
5. Click the ellipsis button in the Autogrowth column of the Sales_log row, and change the Maximum file size to **4**.

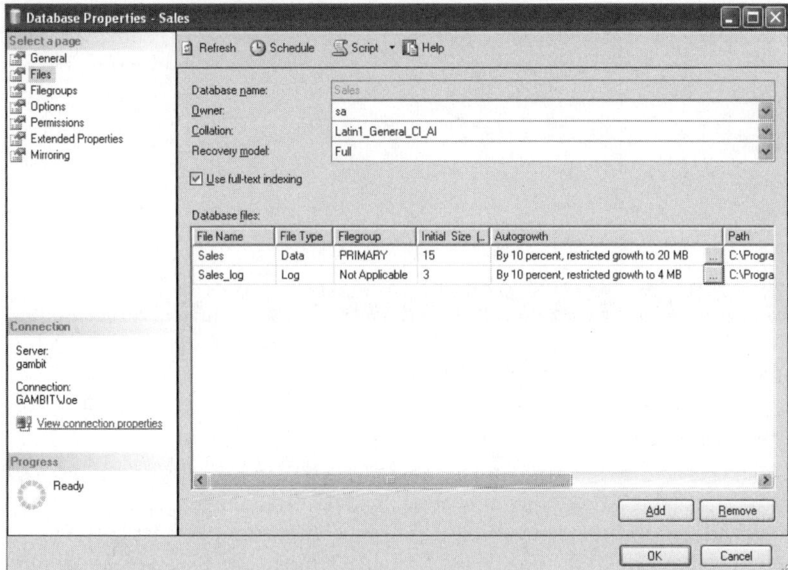

6. Click OK to change the size of the database.

Adding Secondary Data and Transaction Log Files

If your hard disk is too full to accommodate a larger data file, you may need to add a secondary data file on another hard disk. In this example, you'll add a secondary data file to the DoomedDB database:

1. While still in SQL Server Management Studio, right-click DoomedDB and select Properties.
2. Select the Files page, and click the Add button at the bottom of the Database Files list box. This will add a third row to the list box.
3. In the new row, enter **doomed_data2** in the File Name column. The rest of the fields are filled in for you.
4. Click the Add button again to add another new row.

5. In the new row, enter **doomed_log2** in the File Name column, and change the file type to Log.

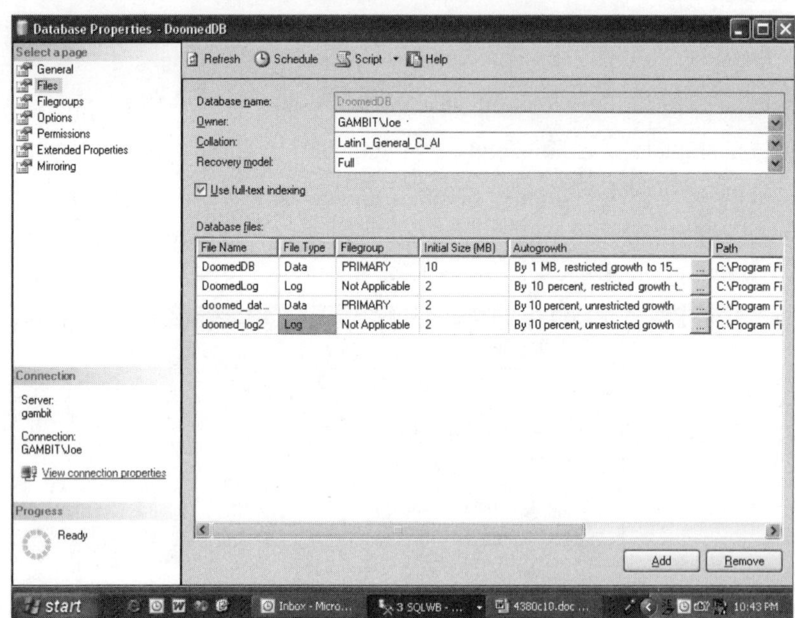

6. Click OK to add the secondary data and log files.

ADDING FILEGROUPS

Once you have created some secondary data files, you can logically group them together into a filegroup to help manage disk-space allocation. By default, all the data files you create are placed in the PRIMARY filegroup, so when you create an object (for example, a table or a view), that object can be created on any one of the files in the PRIMARY filegroup. If you create different filegroups, though, you can specifically tell SQL Server where to place your new objects.

For example, suppose that you have a Sales database with several tables—some are primarily for reading from, some are mainly for writing to. If all these tables are placed in the same filegroup, you have no control over the file in which they're placed. If you place a secondary data file on a separate physical hard disk (for example, disk D) and place another secondary data file on another physical hard disk (disk E, perhaps), you can place each of these data files in its own filegroup, which will give you control over where objects are created. Place the first secondary data file in a filegroup by itself named READ, and place the second secondary data file in its own filegroup named WRITE. Now, when you create a table that is primarily meant to be read from, you can tell SQL Server to create it on the file in the READ group, and you can place tables that are meant to be written to in the WRITE filegroup. The configuration would look like that shown in Figure 10.3.

FIGURE 10.3
Filegroups can be used to allocate disk space more efficiently.

C: Drive

D: Drive

E: Drive

Let's create a secondary data file for the DoomedDB database and place that secondary file in a filegroup called DoomedFG1 using the following steps:

1. Open SQL Server Management Studio by selecting it from the SQL Server 2005 group in Programs on the Start menu.
2. In Object Explorer, expand your server and then Databases.
3. Right-click the DoomedDB database, and select Properties.
4. Select the Filegroups page, and click the Add button at the bottom of the page.
5. In the Name column, enter **DoomedFG1**.

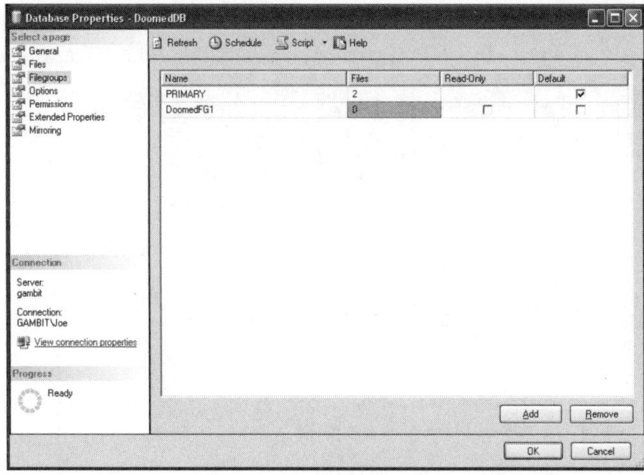

6. Select the Files page, and click the Add button at the bottom of the Database Files list box.
7. In the new row, enter **doomed_data3** in the File Name column.
8. In the Filegroup column, select DoomedFG1.

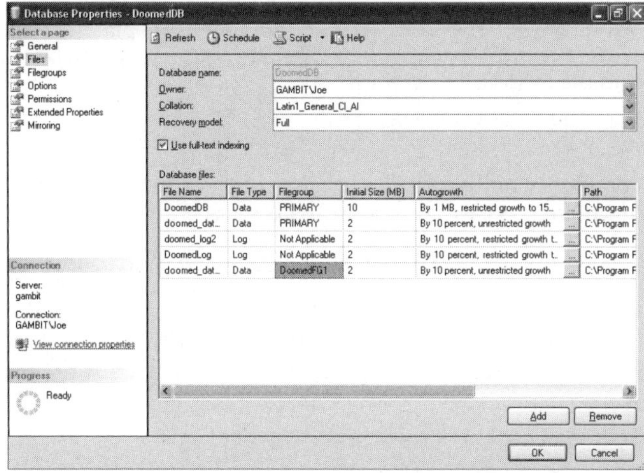

9. Click OK.

With this new filegroup in place, you can instruct SQL Server to create objects on the new filegroup, thus controlling disk-space allocation.

Now that you know how to enlarge your databases, let's learn how to shrink them.

Shrinking the Data Files

If your database doesn't turn out to be as popular as you had originally anticipated, or if it loses its usefulness over time, you may need to shrink the size of the database. The following steps will shrink the Sales database back down to size:

1. In SQL Server Management Studio, right-click the Sales database, point to Tasks, and then select Shrink Database.
2. In the Shrink Database dialog box, you're asked to reorganize the data files, shrink them, and subsequently schedule this to happen later. Select the defaults, and click OK.

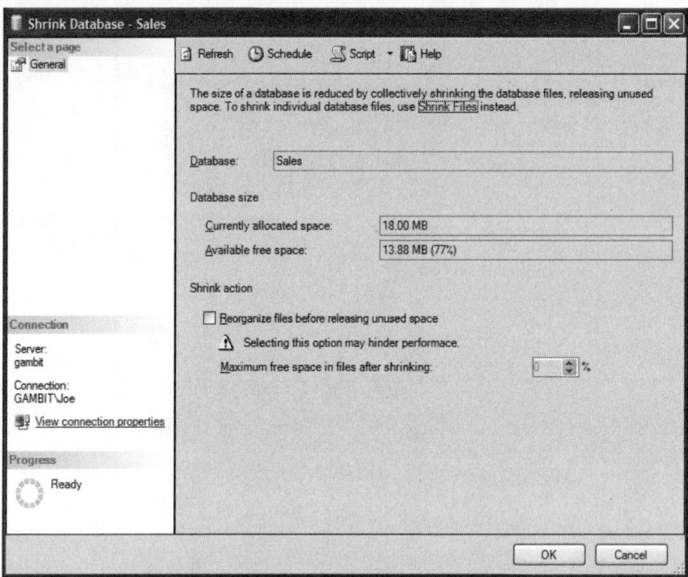

It's really just that simple to shrink a database.

Deleting a Database

If your database has completely outlived its usefulness, you may want to delete it altogether to make room for more useful data. Here's how to drop DoomedDB:

1. In SQL Server Management Studio, right-click DoomedDB, and choose Delete.
2. In the Delete Object dialog box, leave the option to delete backup and restore history selected; this will free up space in the msdb database, where the history is stored. You should also select the Close Existing Connections check box to disconnect users from the database.

3. Wave goodbye, and click the OK button to confirm the deletion.

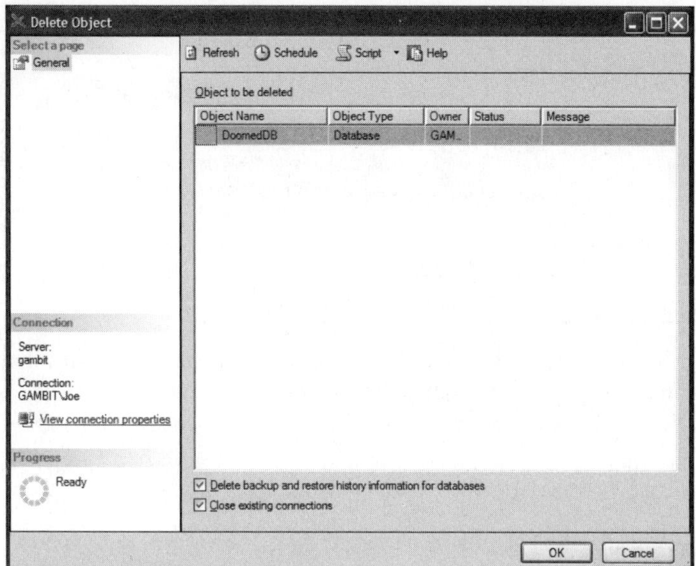

You have now successfully dropped the DoomedDB database and all the files that went with it. Any of the primary, secondary, and log files that formed the database have been deleted from the hard disk.

WARNING Deletion is a permanent action, so make certain you're really done with the database before you get rid of it.

Database Snapshots

The database snapshot is a new feature in SQL Server 2005. Simply put, a *snapshot* is a picture of a database at a given point in time. It may help to think of it like a real snapshot. When you take a picture of someone, the image in the photograph looks exactly like the person you're taking a picture of at the time you took the picture. But what happens if the person in the picture gets a haircut a week later? Does the snapshot you took change to reflect the person's new coif? That would be pretty cool, but snapshots don't work that way—once you take a picture of someone, it's always the same image of that person at that point in time.

A database snapshot is the same way; it's an image of a database as it existed at the point in time the snapshot was taken. You could technically accomplish this functionality in previous versions of SQL Server by making a backup of your database and restoring it to a standby server, but that takes up a lot of resources. Database snapshots are nowhere near as resource intensive because they work much more efficiently.

When it's first created, a database snapshot is an empty shell containing pointers back to the original database pages. This means that when someone reads data from a new snapshot, they're actually reading data from the original database. Things get interesting when modifications are made to the original database, though. Just before a modification is written to the original data page, the page is copied to the snapshot file. That way, the original page still exists; so when users query a snapshot, they see the data as it existed before the modification. Figure 10.4 will help you visualize the process.

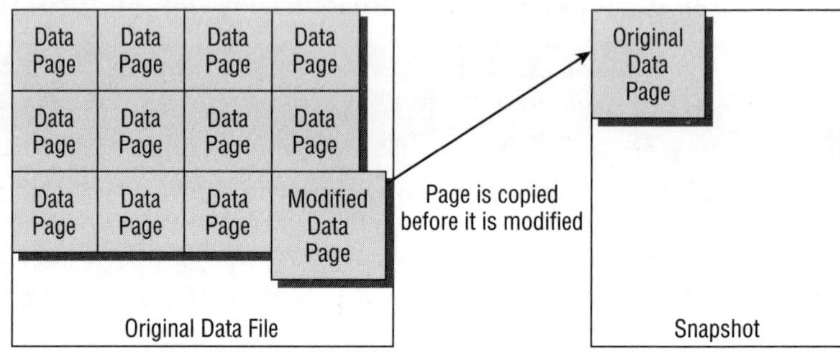

FIGURE 10.4
Data pages are copied from the original database file to the snapshot file before modifications are written to disk.

Snapshots can be used for a variety of reasons:

- They're an excellent choice for archiving historical data that you still need access to. For example, you may create a snapshot of a financial database every quarter; then at the end of the year you can access the quarterly snapshots to generate a year-end report.
- They can be used to revert to an older copy of a database in the event of a user error or lost data.
- They can increase performance when they're used to generate reports, because while you're reading from the snapshot, your users can continue writing to the original database without waiting for you to finish reading first.

You create snapshots using the `CREATE DATABASE` statement. Here is the syntax:

```
CREATE DATABASE database_snapshot_name
    ON
    (
        NAME = logical_file_name,
        FILENAME = 'os_file_name'
    ) [ ,...n ]
    AS SNAPSHOT OF source_database_name
[;]
```

Notice the differences between creating a database and a snapshot. First is the `AS SNAPSHOT OF` clause, which tells SQL Server to create a snapshot. Also, there is no `LOG ON` clause: A snapshot is read-only, so no log is required. You also need to remember that the `NAME` clause here refers to the name of the original data file.

Let's create a snapshot of the Sales database:

1. Open SQL Server Management Studio, and log in using Windows Authentication.
2. Choose File ➤ New ➤ SQL Server Query.
3. To create a snapshot of Sales on the C drive, execute the following code (note that you should replace the `C:\` with the drive on which you installed SQL Server):

```
CREATE DATABASE Sales_Snapshot
ON
(
   name = Sales,
```

```
    filename = 'c:\Program Files\Microsoft SQL Server\MSSQL.1\MSSQL\data\Sales_
shapshot.mdf'
)
as snapshot of sales
```

4. In the results pane (on the bottom) in the query window, you should see a message stating that the command completed successfully.

5. To verify that the snapshot has been created, expand your server in Object Explorer and then expand Database Snapshots. You should see Sales_Snapshot in the list of available snapshots.

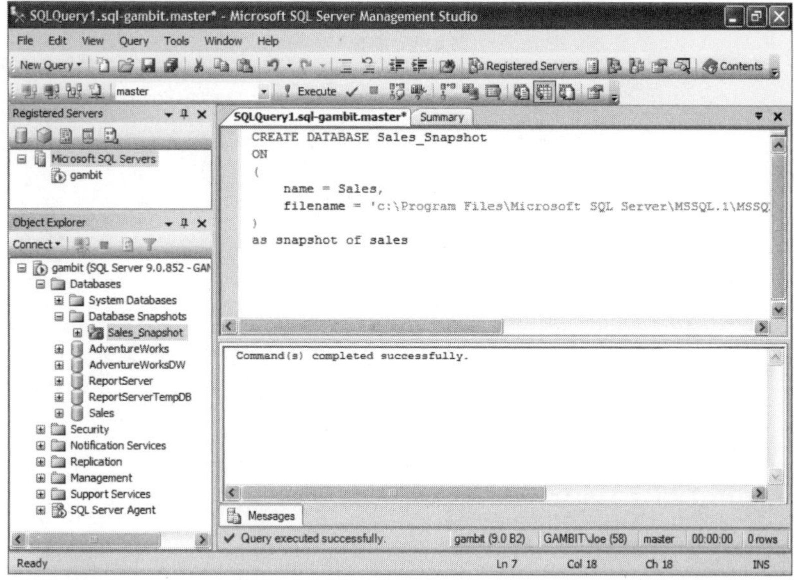

Summary

The very building block of SQL Server—the database itself—is now at your command, and that took quite a bit of learning. First you learned that a database is a container for other objects, such as tables and views, and that without databases to contain all these objects, your data would be a hopeless mess.

You learned that databases consist of up to three types of files: primary data files, secondary data files, and transaction log files. The primary data files are used to store user data and system objects that SQL Server needs to access your database. The secondary data files store only user information and are used to expand your database across multiple physical hard disks. The transaction log files are used for up-to-the-minute recoverability by keeping track of all data modifications made on the system before they're written to the data files.

Because your databases may have more or less data than you originally anticipated, you learned how to change their size by expanding and shrinking them. You also learned how to add extra files to the database in case your hard disk runs out of space. In addition, secondary data files can be logically grouped together into filegroups to better allocate disk space.

Next, in case your database outlives its usefulness, you learned how to delete it entirely and free up hard-disk space for more important data. Finally, you learned about database snapshots, why you should consider using them, and how to create them.

Now that you know how to create and size your databases properly, you're ready to start filling the databases with objects. In the next chapter, let's start by creating tables.

Chapter 11

Tables

In the last chapter, we compared a database to a cabinet in your house, which you might use to store your possessions. To expand a bit on that analogy, suppose we're talking about storing your tools: wrenches, screws, pliers, and so on. Would you keep all your tools in the same drawer of your toolbox? Probably not. You most likely keep your tools in separate drawers in the toolbox—pliers in the pliers drawer, screws in the fasteners drawer, and so forth.

Your data is like the tools in this analogy—you don't want to just dump it all in one drawer, so to speak, which is why your toolbox (the database) has several drawers for holding data. These drawers are tables. Inside the database, you have several tables that are used to hold the various types of data you need to store. Just like you have a fasteners drawer for screws and a pliers drawer for pliers in your toolbox, you would have a Customers table for your customer data and a separate Products table for product information.

In this chapter, we'll discuss tables. We'll look at all the parts of a table and then show how to create them. Finally, we'll hash out some methods of restricting the data that your users will be allowed to put in your tables, so you can keep your data neat and tidy. Finally, we'll simplify table maintenance through the use of database diagrams.

Before you can create any tables in your database, though, you must plan how they will look and function. Our first section deals with just that—planning tables.

Planning Tables

Tables are the objects in the database that you use to hold all your data. As shown in Figure 11.1, tables are made up of two basic objects, fields and records:

Fields Fields contain a certain type of information such as last name or zip code. They're also referred to as *columns*.

Records A record is a group of related fields containing information about a single entity (such as a person) that spans all the fields. Records are also referred to as *rows*.

FIGURE 11.1
Tables are made up of fields and records.

The Fname Field

Fname	Lname	Address	Address	State	Zip
Varchar(20)	Varchar(20)	Varchar(50)	Varchar(50)	Char(2)	Char(5)
Tom	Smith	111 Main	New York	NY	11101
Janet	McBroom	715 3rd	Phoenix	AZ	85034
Shane	Travis	816 Star	Chicago	IL	21563
John	Thomas	3035 1st	Sacramento	CA	94305

Fname has a datatype of Varchar(20)

The "Shane Travis" record, number 3

Actual Records

You should grab a piece of paper and a pencil for the first phase of creating your tables, because it's much easier to create them when you can see them drawn in front of you, rather than trying to remember all the details involved. The first thing to decide is what fields should be in your table.

If you're creating a customer table, for example, you may want it to contain each customer's first and last names, address, phone and fax numbers, and customer ID number. When you create these fields, it's best to make them as specific as possible. Instead of creating a name field for customers' first and last names, for instance, you should create a first-name field and a last-name field. This will make it easier to search your database for a specific customer later, because you need to search only on last name instead of first and last name combined. The same holds true for the address—separate it into street address, city, state, and zip code fields. This will make it easier to find customers who live in certain cities or zip codes, or even to find a specific customer based on address alone. Once you have defined the most specific fields possible, you're ready to pick datatypes for your fields.

Built-in Datatypes

Each field in a table has a specific datatype, which restricts the type of data that can be inserted. For example, if you create a field with a datatype of int (short for integer, which is a whole number [a number with no decimal point]), you won't be able to store characters (A–Z) or symbols (such as %, *, #) in that field because SQL Server allows only numbers to be stored in int type fields. In Figure 11.1, you can see the datatypes listed in the second row (note that datatypes don't show up as a record—it's done this way in the figure merely for readability). You'll notice that all the fields in this table are either char or varchar (short for character and variable character, respectively), which means you can store characters in these fields as well as symbols and numbers. However, if numbers are stored in these fields, you won't be able to perform mathematical functions on them because SQL Server sees them as characters, not numbers. The following is a list of all the datatypes and their limitations:

bit This can contain only a 1 or a 0 as a value (or null which is no value). It's very useful as a status bit—on/off, yes/no, true/false.

int This can contain integer (or whole number) data from -2^{31} (–2,147,483,648) through $2^{31} - 1$ (2,147,483,647). It takes 4 bytes of hard-disk space to store and is useful for storing large numbers that you'll use in mathematical functions.

bigint This datatype includes integer data from -2^{63} (–9,223,372,036,854,775,808) through $2^{63} - 1$ (9,223,372,036,854,775,807). It takes 8 bytes of hard-disk space to store and is useful for extremely large numbers that won't fit in an int type field.

smallint This datatype includes integer data from -2^{15} (–32,768) through $2^{15} - 1$ (32,767). It takes 2 bytes of hard-disk space to store and is useful for slightly smaller numbers than you would store in an int type field, because smallint takes less space than int.

tinyint This datatype includes integer data from 0 through 255. It takes 1 byte of space on the disk and is limited in usefulness since it stores values only up to 255. Tinyint may be useful for something like a product-type code when you have fewer than 255 products.

decimal This datatype includes fixed-precision and scale-numeric data from $-10^{38} - 1$ through $10^{38} - 1$ (for comparison, this is a 1 with 38 zeros following it). It uses two parameters: precision and scale. *Precision* is the total count of digits that can be stored in the field, and *scale* is the number of digits that can be stored to the right of the decimal point. Thus, if you have a precision of 5 and a scale of 2, your field has the format 111.22. This type should be used when you're storing partial numbers (numbers with a decimal point).

numeric This is a synonym for *decimal*—they're one and the same.

money This datatype includes monetary data values from -2^{63} (–922,337,203,685,477.5808) through $2^{63} - 1$ (922,337,203,685,477.5807), with accuracy to a ten-thousandth of a monetary unit. It takes 8 bytes of hard-disk space to store and is useful for storing sums of money larger than 214,748.3647.

smallmoney This datatype includes monetary data values from –214,748.3648 through 214,748.3647, with accuracy to a ten-thousandth of a monetary unit. It takes 4 bytes of space and is useful for storing smaller sums of money than would be stored in a money type field.

float This datatype includes floating precision number data from –1.79E + 38 through 1.79E + 38. Some numbers don't end after the decimal point—pi is a fine example. For such numbers, you must approximate the end, which is what float does. For example, if you set a datatype of float(2), pi will be stored as 3.14, with only two numbers after the decimal point.

real This datatype includes floating precision number data from –3.40E + 38 through 3.40E + 38. This is a quick way of saying float(24)—it's a floating type with 24 numbers represented after the decimal point.

datetime This datatype includes date and time data from January 1, 1753, to December 31, 9999, with values rounded to increments of .000, .003 or .007 seconds. This takes 8 bytes of space on the hard disk and should be used when you need to track very specific dates and times.

smalldatetime This datatype includes date and time data from January 1, 1900, through June 6, 2079, with an accuracy of 1 minute. It takes only 4 bytes of disk space and should be used for less specific dates and times than would be stored in datetime.

timestamp This is used to stamp a record with the time when the record is inserted and every time it's updated thereafter. This datatype is useful for tracking changes to your data.

uniqueidentifier The `NEWID()` function is used to create globally unique identifiers that might appear as follows: 6F9619FF-8B86-D011-B42D-00C04FC964FF. These unique numbers can be stored in the uniqueidentifier type field; they may be useful for creating tracking numbers or serial numbers that have no possible way of being duplicated.

char This datatype includes fixed-length, non-Unicode character data with a maximum length of 8000 characters. It's useful for character data that will always be the same length, such as a State field, which will contain only two characters in every record. This uses the same amount of space on disk no matter how many characters are actually stored in the field. For example, char(5) always uses 5 bytes of space, even if only two characters are stored in the field.

varchar This datatype includes variable-length, non-Unicode data with a maximum of 8000 characters. It's useful when the data won't always be the same length, such as in a first-name field where each name has a different number of characters. This uses less disk space when there are fewer characters in the field. For example, if you have a field of varchar(20), but you're storing a name with only 10 characters, the field will take up only 10 bytes of space, not 20. This field will accept a maximum of 20 characters.

varchar(max) This is just like the varchar datatype; but with a size of (max) specified, the datatype can hold $2^{31} - 1$ (2,147,483,67) bytes of data.

nchar This datatype includes fixed-length, Unicode data with a maximum length of 4000 characters. Like all Unicode datatypes, it's useful for storing small amounts of text that will be read by clients that use different languages (i.e. some using Spanish and some using German).

nvarchar This datatype includes variable-length, Unicode data with a maximum length of 4000 characters. It's the same as nchar except that nvarchar uses less disk space when there are fewer characters.

nvarchar(max) This is just like nvarchar; but when the (max) size is specified, the datatype holds $2^{31}-1$ (2,147,483,67) bytes of data.

binary This datatype includes fixed-length, binary data with a maximum length of 8000 bytes. It's interpreted as a string of bits (for example, 11011001011) and is useful for storing anything that looks better in binary or hexadecimal shorthand, such as a security identifier.

varbinary This datatype includes variable-length, binary data with a maximum length of 8000 bytes. It's just like binary, except that varbinary uses less hard-disk space when fewer bits are stored in the field.

varbinary(max) This has the same attributes as the varbinary datatype; but when the (max) size is declared, the datatype can hold $2^{31}-1$ (2,147,483,67) bytes of data. This is very useful for storing binary objects like JPEG image files or Word documents.

xml This datatype is used to store entire XML documents or fragments (a document that is missing the top-level element).

identity This isn't actually a datatype, but it serves an important role. It's a property, usually used in conjunction with the int datatype, and it's used to increment the value of the column each time a new record is inserted. For example, the first record in the table would have an identity value of 1, and the next would be 2, then 3, and so on.

sql_variant Like identity this isn't an actual datatype per se, but it actually lets you store values of different datatypes. The only values it cannot store are; varchar(max), nvarchar(max), text, image, sql_variant, varbinary(max), xml, ntext, timestamp, or user-defined datatypes.

TIP The text, ntext, and image datatypes have been deprecated in this version of SQL Server. You should replace these with varchar(max), nvarchar(max), and varbinary(max).

NOTE A number of these datatypes deal with Unicode data, which is used to store up to 65,536 different characters, as opposed to the standard ANSI character sets, which store 256 characters.

When you're adding these datatypes, you must specify any required parameters. For example, if you're creating a field to hold state abbreviations, you need to specify char(2) and then the appropriate constraints (discussed later in this chapter) to ensure that users enter only valid state abbreviations. Finally, you include a default that will add data to the fields if your users forget.

User-defined Datatypes

If you're constantly creating tables that require a State field, you can create a datatype of your own based on the char datatype with all the parameters prespecified, including any necessary constraints and defaults. Datatypes that you design and implement yourself are called *user-defined datatypes* even though they're always based on a system datatype. To show you how it's done, let's create a State datatype that you can use in your Customers table later:

TIP In this exercise we will be using the Sales database created in Chapter 10.

1. Open SQL Server Management Studio by selecting it from the SQL Server 2005 group in Programs on the Start menu, and connect using Windows Authentication.
2. In Object Explorer, expand Databases ➤ Sales ➤ Programmability ➤ Types.
3. Right-click User-Defined Datatypes, and select New User-Defined Datatype.
4. In the Name text box, enter **State**.
5. In the Data Type drop-down list, select nchar.
6. In the Length text box, enter **2**.
7. Leave Allow Nulls unchecked (because you require this field to contain data).
8. In the Bindings section, leave Rule and Default set to None, and click OK.

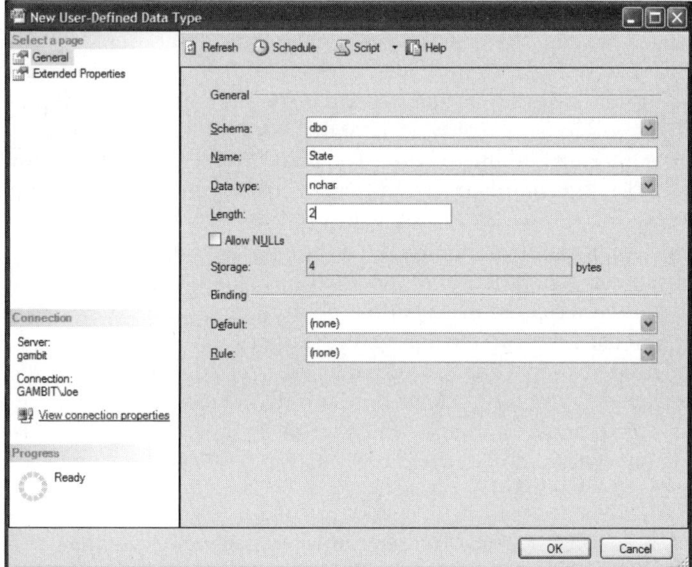

Computed Columns

Along with user-defined datatypes, you can create computed columns. These are special columns that don't contain any data of their own, but display the output of an expression performed on data in other columns of the table. For example, in the AdventureWorks sample database, the TotalDue column of the Sales.SalesOrderHeader table is a computed column. It contains no data of its own but displays the values of Subtotal + TaxAmt + Freight columns as a single value.

TABLE AND CURSOR DATATYPES

There are two other datatypes that you can't assign to a column: table and cursor. These two datatypes can only be used as variables:

Cursor Queries in SQL Server return a complete set of rows for an application to work with. Sometimes the application can't work with the resulting set of rows as a whole, so it requests a *cursor*, which is a subset of the original recordset with some added features (such as the ability to move back and forth between records, or positioning on a specific row). The cursor datatype allows you to return a cursor from a stored procedure. You can also store a cursor in a variable. However, you can't store a cursor in a table using this datatype.

Table This datatype is used to return tables from stored procedures or to store tables in variables for later processing. You can't use this datatype to store a table in a column of another table, however.

Partitioning Tables

Tables in SQL Server can range from very small, having only a single record, to extremely huge, with millions of records. These large tables can be difficult for users to work with simply because of their sheer size. To make them smaller without losing any data, you can *partition* your tables.

Partitioning tables works just like it sounds: You cut tables into multiple sections that can be stored and accessed independently without the users' knowledge. Suppose you have a table that contains order information, and the table has about 50 million rows. That may seem like a big table, but such a size isn't uncommon. To partition this table, you first need to decide on a partition column and a range of values for the column. In a table of order data, you probably have an order date column, which is an excellent candidate. The range can be any value you like; but since you want to make the most current orders easily accessible, you may want to set the range at anything older than a year. Now you can use the partition column and range to create a partition function, which SQL Server will use to spread the data across the partitions.

Next you need to decide where to keep the partitioned data physically; this is called the *partition schema*. You can keep archived data on one hard disk and current data on another disk by storing the partitions in separate filegroups, which can be assigned to different disks.

Once you have planned your partitions, you can create partitioned tables using the CREATE TABLE function that we'll discuss shortly.

TIP The TransactionHistory and TransactionHistoryArchive tables in the AdventureWorks database are partitioned on the ModifiedDate field.

The hard part of creating anything is the planning stage, so congratulations on getting through it. With everything written down on paper, you're ready to start creating your tables.

Creating Tables

In Chapter 10, "Databases," you created a Sales database. In this section, you'll create three tables in that Sales database. The first table, cleverly named *Customers*, will store customer information such as name, address, customer ID, and so on. The next table, which you'll call *Orders*, will contain order detail information such as an order number, product ID, and quantity ordered. Finally, the *Products* table will contain such product information as the name of the product, the product ID, and whether the product is in stock. Tables 11.1, 11.2, and 11.3 provide a list (on paper, just as it should be) of the properties of all three tables.

TABLE 11.1: Customers Table Fields

FIELD NAME	DATATYPE	CONTAINS
CustID	int, Identity	A unique number for each customer that can be referenced in other tables
Fname	Nvarchar(20)	The customer's first name
Lname	Nvarchar(20)	The customer's last name
Address	Nvarchar(50)	The customer's street address
City	Nvarchar(20)	The city where the customer lives
State	State	The state where the customer lives (you created this user-defined datatype earlier in the chapter)
Zip	Nchar(5)	The customer's zip code
Phone	Nchar(10)	The customer's phone number without hyphens or parentheses (to save space, those will be displayed but not stored)

TABLE 11.2: Orders Table Fields

FIELD NAME	DATATYPE	CONTAINS
CustID	int	References the customer number stored in the Customers table so you don't need to duplicate the customer information for each order placed
ProdID	int	References the Products table so you don't need to duplicate product information
Qty	int	The amount of product sold for an order
OrdDate	Smalldatetime	The date and time the order was placed

TABLE 11.3: Products Table Fields

FIELD NAME	DATATYPE	CONTAINS
ProdID	int, Identity	A unique ID number for each product that can be referenced in other tables to avoid data duplication
Description	Nvarchar(100)	A brief text description of the product
InStock	int	The amount of product in stock

Tables can be created both graphically (using SQL Server Management Studio) and via Transact-SQL code (T-SQL). Because the graphic method is easiest, we'll focus on that in this next series of steps, where you begin creating your tables:

1. Open SQL Server Management Studio. In Object Explorer, expand your server ➢ Databases ➢ Sales.
2. Right-click the Tables icon, and select New Table to open the table designer.
3. In the first row, under Column Name, enter **ProdID**.
4. Just to the right of that, under Data Type, select Int.
5. Make certain that Allow Nulls isn't checked. The field can be completely void of data if this option is checked, and you don't want that here.
6. In the bottom half of the screen, under Column Properties, in the Table Designer section, expand Identity Specification and change (Is Identity) to Yes.
7. Just under ProdID, in the second row under Column Name, enter **Description**.
8. Just to the right of that, under Data Type, enter **nvarchar**.
9. Under Column Properties, in the General section, change the Length setting to **100**.
10. Make certain that Allow Nulls is cleared.
11. Under Column Name in the third row, enter **InStock**.
12. Under Data Type, select Int.
13. Uncheck Allow Nulls.

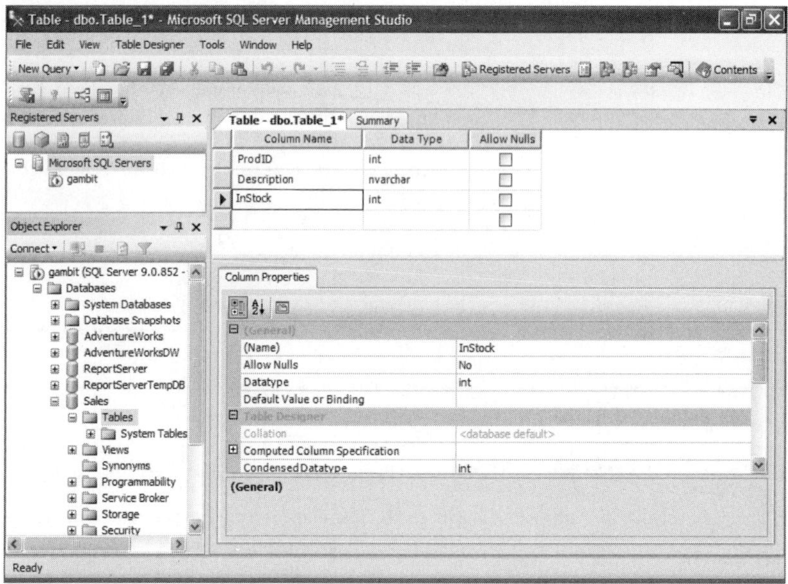

14. Click the Save button on the left side of the toolbar (it looks like a floppy disk).

15. In the Choose Name box that pops up, enter **Products**.

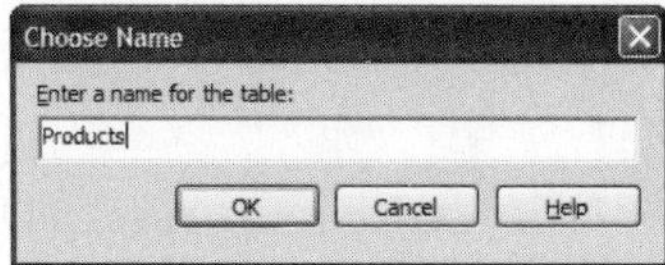

16. Close the table designer screen by clicking the X in the upper-right corner of the window.

With the Products table in place, you're ready to create the Customers table:

1. Right-click the Tables icon, and select New Table to open the table designer.
2. In the first row, under Column Name, enter **CustID**.
3. Under Data Type, select Int.
4. Make certain that Allow Nulls isn't checked.
5. Under Column Properties, in the Table Designer section, expand Identity Specification and change (Is Identity) to Yes.
6. Just under CustID, in the second row under Column Name, enter **Fname**.
7. Just to the right of that, under Data Type, enter **nvarchar**.
8. Under Column Properties, in the General section, change the Length setting to **20**.
9. Make certain Allow Nulls is unchecked.
10. Using the parameters displayed earlier, fill in the information for the remaining columns (remember to select the new State datatype for the State field). Don't allow nulls in any of the fields.

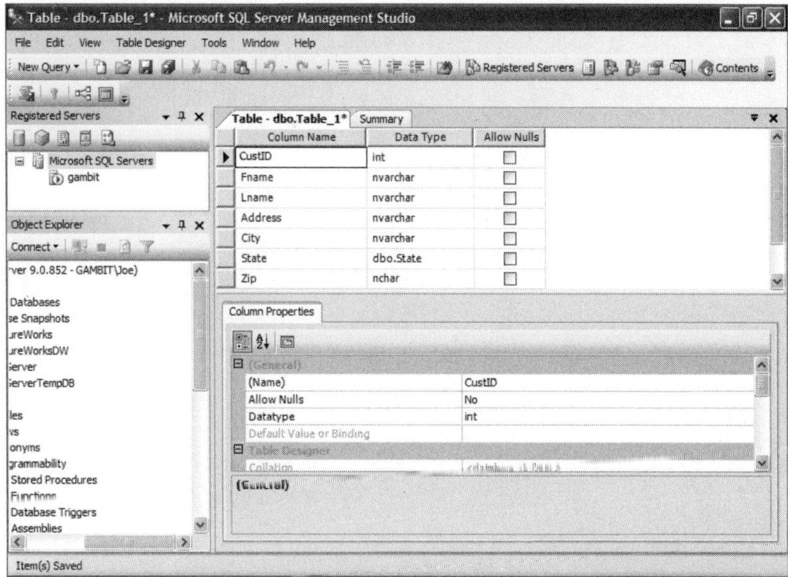

11. Click the Save button.
12. In the Choose Name box that pops up, enter **Customers**.
13. Close the table designer screen.

Now let's follow the same steps to create the Orders table:

1. Right-click the Tables icon, and select New Table to open the table designer.
2. In the first row, under Column Name, enter **CustID**.
3. Under Data Type, select Int.
4. Make certain that Allow Nulls isn't checked.
5. This won't be an identity column like it was in the Customers table, so don't make any changes to the Identity Specification settings.
6. Just under CustID, in the second row under Column Name, enter **ProdID** with a datatype of int. Don't change the Identity Specification settings. Don't allow null values.
7. Just below ProdID, create a field named Qty with a datatype of int that doesn't allow nulls.
8. Create a column named OrdDate with a datatype of smalldatetime. Don't allow null values.

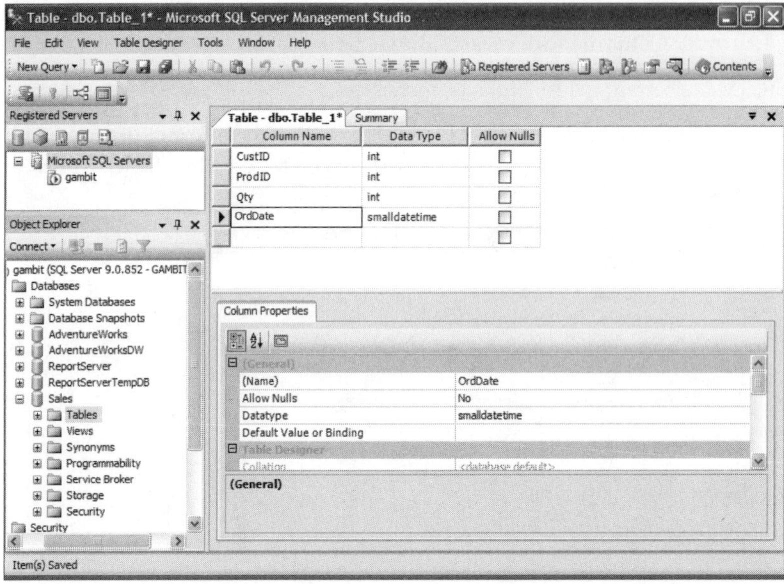

9. Click the Save button.
10. In the Choose Name box that pops up, enter **Orders**.
11. Close the table designer screen.

To verify that all three of your tables exist, expand Tables under the Sales database—you should see the three tables you created (you may need to right-click the Tables icon and select Refresh to see the tables).

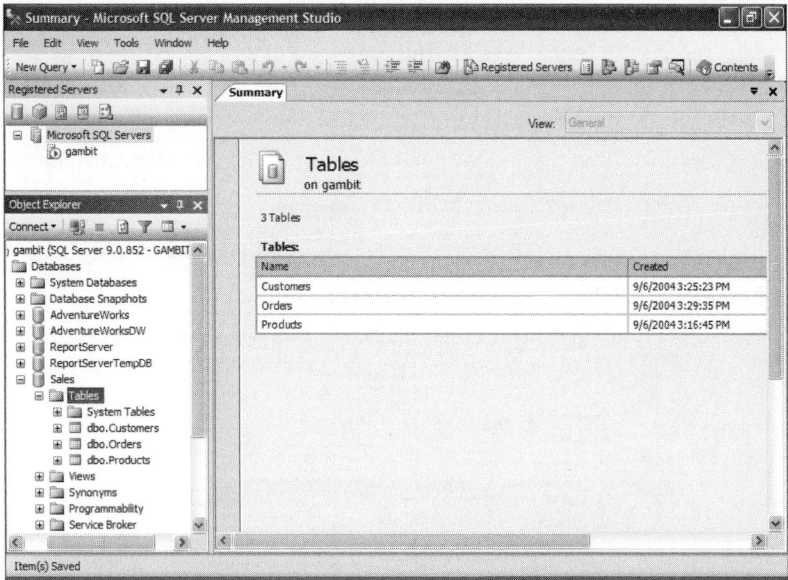

With all three of these tables in place, you're almost ready to unleash the users. Before you can allow the users to start working with the tables, though, you must further restrict what they can enter.

Restricting the Data

When you first create a table, it's wide open to your users. It's true that they can't violate datatype restrictions by entering characters in an int type field and the like, but that is really the only restriction. The process of restricting the data your users can enter in your tables is referred to as *enforcing data integrity*. There are three kinds of data integrity: *domain*, *entity*, and *referential*. Let's first see how you can restrict your users via domain integrity.

Enforcing Domain Integrity

It's safe to say that you don't want your users entering whatever they feel like in your tables. For example, you probably don't want your users to enter XZ for a state abbreviation in a State field (because XZ isn't a valid abbreviation), nor do you want them entering numbers for someone's first name. You need to restrict what your users can enter in your fields—or, as we say, you need to enforce *domain integrity*. This type of integrity can be enforced using check constraints or default constraints.

USING CHECK CONSTRAINTS

A *check constraint* is a Transact-SQL statement that is linked to a field. Check constraints are used to restrict the data that is accepted in the field even if the data is of the correct datatype. For example, the zip field in the Customers table is the nchar datatype, which means that it could technically accept letters. This can be a problem, because in the USA there are no zip codes with letters (zip codes with letters are generally referred to as postal codes); so, you need to keep users from entering letters in the zip field. Here is how to create the check constraint that will accomplish this:

1. In Object Explorer, expand the Sales database ➤ Tables ➤ dbo.Customers.
2. Right-click Constraints, and click New Constraint.
3. In the New Constraint dialog box, enter **CK_Zip** in the (Name) text box.
4. In the Description text box, enter **Check for valid zip codes**.
5. To create a constraint that will accept only five numbers that can be zero through nine, type the following code in the Expression text box:

```
(zip like '[0-9][0-9][0-9][0-9][0-9]')
```

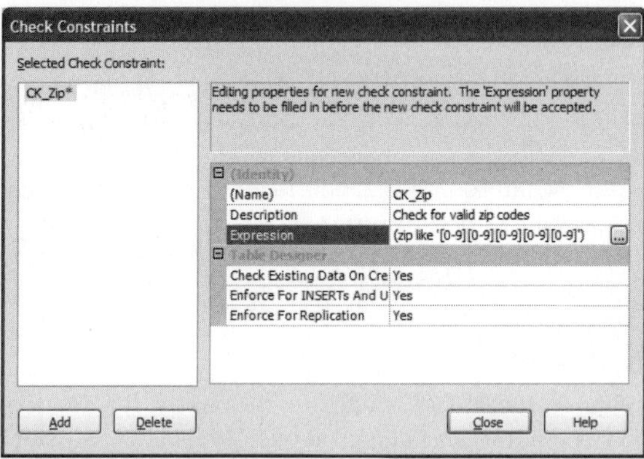

6. Click Close.
7. Click the Save button at the top left of the toolbar.
8. Close the table designer (which was opened when you started to create the constraint).

To test the new constraint you just created, let's enter some new records into the table by using the INSERT statement you learned about earlier. Here are the steps:

1. In SQL Server Management Studio, click the New Query button and select New SQL Server Query. Connect with Windows Authentication if requested.

2. Type the following code into the query window:

```
USE sales
INSERT customers
VALUES ('Gary','McKee','111 Main','Palm Springs','CA','94312',' 7605551212')
```

3. Click the Execute button just above the query window to execute the query, and notice the successful results.

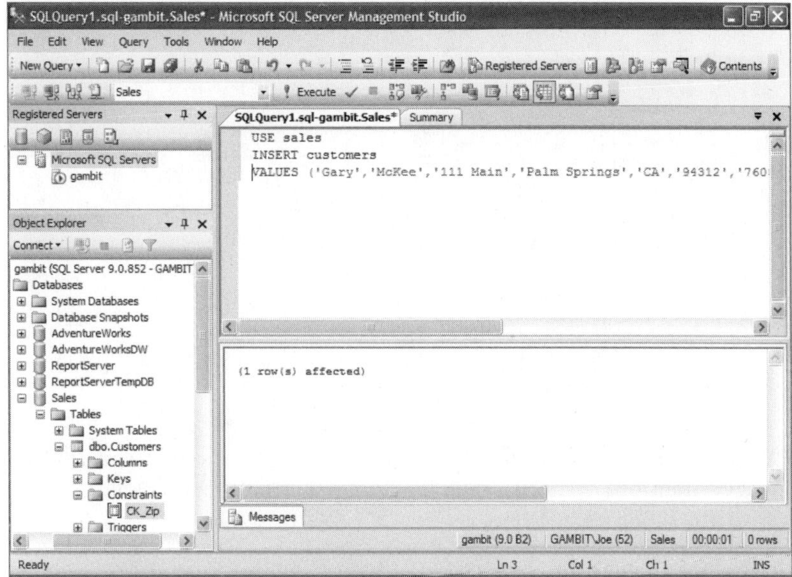

4. To see the new record, select Query ➢ New Query With Current Connection (or press Ctrl+Q).

5. Enter and execute the following code:

```
SELECT * FROM customers
```

6. Notice that the record now exists with a CustID of 1 (because of the identity property discussed earlier, which automatically added the number for you).

7. To test the check constraint by adding characters in the zip field, select Query ➢ New Query With Current Connection.

8. In the query window, enter the following code, and note the letters in the zip code field:

```
USE sales
INSERT customers
VALUES ('Amanda','Smith','817 3rd','Chicago','IL','AAB1C','8015551212')
```

9. Notice in the results pane that the query violated a constraint and so failed.

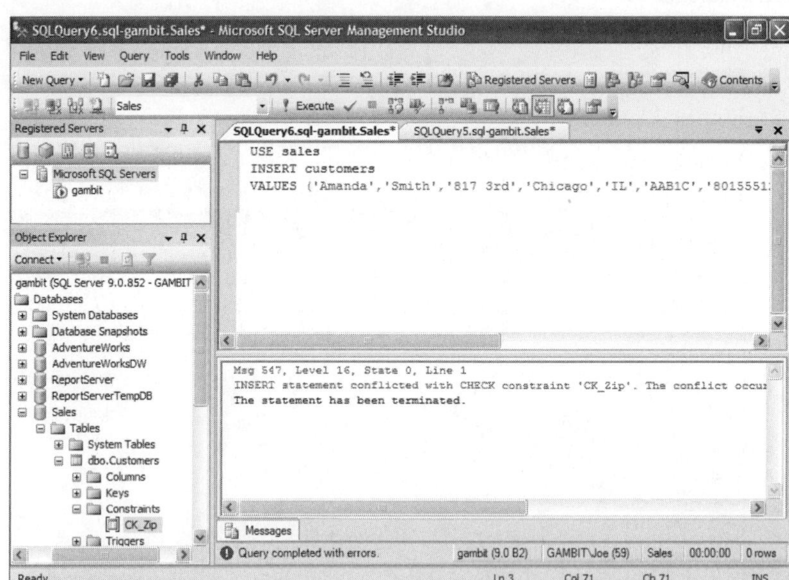

TIP You may have used *rules* in the past to do the work of check constraints. Rules are slated to be removed from future versions of SQL Server, so you should convert all your existing rules to check constraints.

It's easy to see how the check constraint can be a powerful ally against entering wrong data—all you need to do is figure out what data belongs in your column and create a constraint instructing SQL Server not to accept anything else. Check constraints serve no purpose if your users simply forget to enter data in a column, though—that is what default constraints are for.

Using Default Constraints

If users leave fields blank by not including them in the `INSERT` or `UPDATE` statement that they used to add or modify a record, *default constraints* are used to fill in those fields. There are two types of defaults: object and definition. *Object defaults* are defined when you create your table; they affect only the column on which they're defined. *Definition defaults* are created separately from tables and are designed to be bound to a user-defined datatype (just like the rule we discussed earlier). Either type of default can be a big time-saver in a data-entry department if you use it correctly.

For example, suppose that most of your clientele live in California and that your data-entry people must type **CA** for every new customer they enter. That may not seem like much work, but if you have a sizable customer base, those two characters can add up to a lot of typing. By using a default constraint, your users can leave the State field intentionally blank, and SQL Server will fill it in. To demonstrate the capabilities of the default constraint, let's create a definition default on the Customers table:

1. Open SQL Server Management Studio. In Object Explorer, expand your server ➤ Databases ➤ Sales ➤ Tables ➤ dbo.Customers ➤ Columns.
2. Right-click the State column, and click Modify Column.
3. In the bottom half of the screen, in the Default Value Or Binding text box, type **'CA'** (with the single quotes). Note that SQL Server will place this inside single quotes for you.

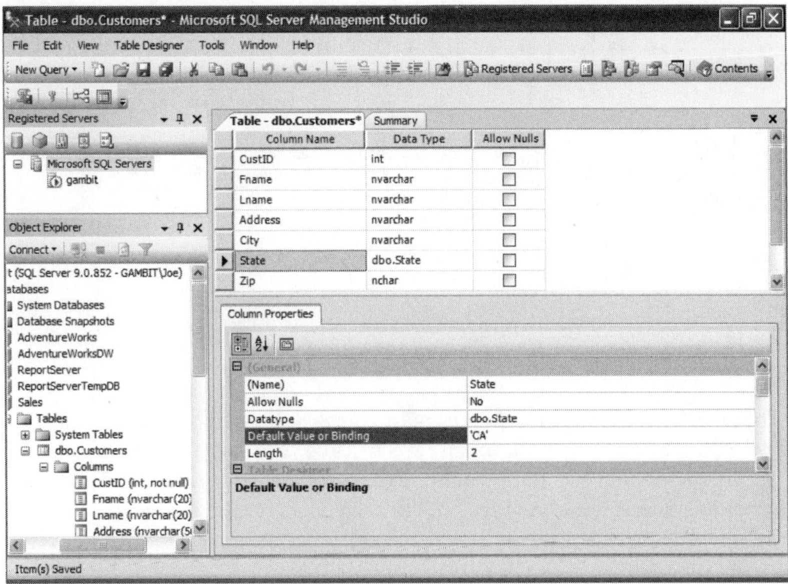

4. Click the Save button, and exit the table designer.
5. To test the default, click the New Query button in SQL Server Management Studio. Select New SQL Server Query, and connect with Windows Authentication if requested.
6. Enter and execute the following code:

```
USE sales
INSERT customers (fname, lname, address, city, zip, phone)
VALUES ('Tom','Smith','609 Georgia','Fresno','33405','5105551212')
```

7. To verify that CA was entered into the State field, select Query ➤ New Query With Current Connection.
8. Enter and execute the following code:

```
SELECT * FROM customers
```

9. Notice that the Tom Smith record has CA in the State field, as shown in the following graphic.

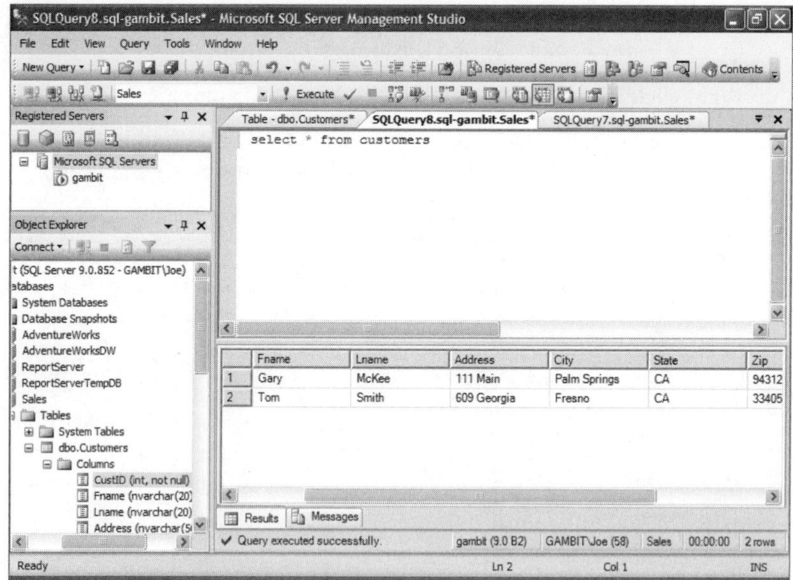

That is all there is to enforcing domain integrity—controlling what your users can enter into your fields. You can use check constraints to force your users to enter the proper data, and default constraints will fill in any data that your users forget. However, there are still two more types of integrity to enforce. Next we'll see how to keep users from entering duplicate records by enforcing entity integrity.

Enforcing Entity Integrity

Ensuring that each of the records in your tables is unique in some way and that no record is accidentally duplicated is referred to as enforcing *entity integrity*. Why do you need to be sure that there are no duplicate records in your tables? Imagine what would happen if a customer were accidentally entered twice in your Customers table, thus duplicating the data. You would have one customer with two different IDs, making it very difficult to decide which one to bill for orders. Or, worse yet, suppose that someone accidentally entered two customers with the same ID. This could cause big problems when making sales or generating reports, because you wouldn't know which customer actually bought what—they would both show up as the same customer. You can avoid such a mess by enforcing entity integrity. There are two ways to enforce entity integrity—the first is with a primary key.

Using Primary Keys

A *primary key* is used to ensure that each of the records in your table is unique in some way. It does this by creating a special type of index called a *unique index*. An index is ordinarily used to speed up access to data by reading all the values in a column and keeping an organized list of where the record that contains that value is located in the table. A unique index not only generates that list, but it also doesn't allow duplicate values to be stored in the index. If a user tries to enter a duplicate value in the indexed field, the unique index will return an error, and the data modification will fail.

Suppose, for instance, that you have defined the CustID field in the Customers table as a primary key and that you have a customer with ID 1 already in the table. If one of your users were to try to create another customer with ID 1, they would receive an error, and the update would be rejected because CustID 1 is already listed in the primary key's unique index. Of course this is just for example: Your CustID field has the identity property set, which automatically assigns a number with each new record inserted and won't allow you to enter a number of your own design.

NOTE **When a column can be used as a unique identifier for a row (such as an identity column), it's referred to as a *surrogate* or *candidate key*.**

The primary key should be made of a column (or columns) that contains unique values. This makes an identity column the perfect candidate for becoming a primary key, because the values contained therein are unique by definition. If you don't have an identity column, make sure you choose a column, or combination of columns, in which each value is unique. Since you have an identity column in the Customers table, let's use it to create a primary key:

1. Open SQL Server Management Studio by selecting it from the SQL Server 2005 group in Programs on your Start menu, and connect using Windows Authentication.
2. In Object Explorer, expand Databases ➢ Sales ➢ Tables.
3. Right-click the Customers table, and select Modify Table.
4. In the table designer screen, right-click CustID under Column Name, and select Set Primary Key.
5. Notice that just to the left of the CustID field is a small key icon denoting that this is the primary key.

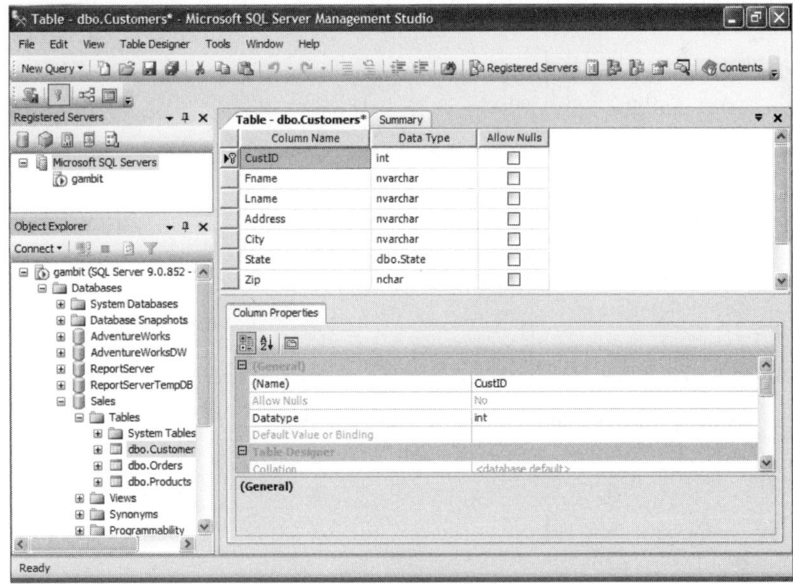

6. When you click the Save icon on the toolbar, SQL Server creates the unique index, which ensures that no duplicate values can be entered in the CustID field.
7. Close the table designer.

TIP When a column has mostly unique values, it's said to have *high selectivity*. When a column has several duplicate values, it's said to have *low selectivity*. Therefore the primary key field must have high selectivity (entirely unique values).

That procedure was fairly simple, but suppose that you need to maintain entity integrity separately on more than one column. Perhaps you have an Employees table with an EmployeeID field that has been set as the primary key, but you also have a Social Security Number field on which you need to enforce entity integrity. Because you can have only one primary key per table, you would need to create a unique constraint to enforce such entity integrity.

Using Unique Constraints

There are two major differences between primary key constraints and unique constraints. The first is that primary keys are used with foreign keys to enforce referential integrity (which we'll discuss a little later in this chapter), and unique keys aren't. The second difference is that unique constraints allow null (blank) values to be inserted in the field, whereas primary keys don't allow null values. Aside from that, they serve the same purpose—to ensure that unique data is inserted in a field.

You should use a unique constraint when you need to ensure that no duplicate values can be added to a field that isn't part of your primary key. A good example of a field that might require a unique constraint is a Social Security Number field, because all the values contained therein need to be unique; yet there would most likely be a separate employee ID field that would be used as the primary key. Because you don't have a perfect candidate for a unique constraint in your tables, you'll come as close as you can by creating a unique constraint on the Phone field:

1. In SQL Server Management Studio, click the New Query button, and select New SQL Server query. Connect with Windows Authentication if requested.
2. Select Sales in the database drop-down list on the toolbar.
3. Enter and execute the following code:

```
ALTER TABLE customers
ADD CONSTRAINT CK_Phone
UNIQUE (Phone)
```

4. Right-click the Sales database in Object Explorer, and select Refresh.
5. Expand Sales ➢ Tables ➢ Customers ➢ Keys.

6. Notice that your new unique constraint is listed under Keys with the primary key you created earlier.

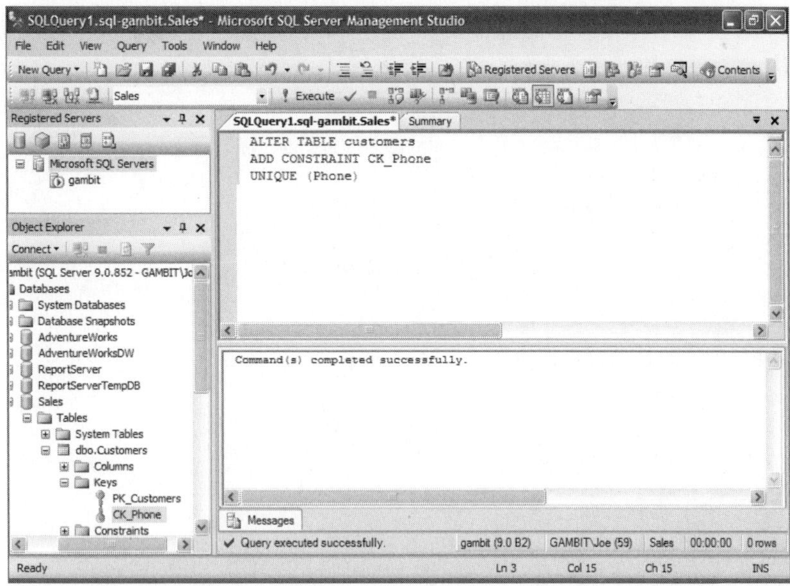

Now you can test the unique constraint by trying to add some duplicate phone numbers through Query Analyzer using some INSERT statements:

1. Choose Query ➢ New Query With Current Connection.
2. Enter and execute the following code to add a new record to the Customers table:

```
USE sales
INSERT customers
VALUES ('Shane','Travis','806 Star','Phoenix','AZ','85202','6021112222')
```

3. Choose Query ➢ New Query With Current Connection, and try entering another customer with the same phone number by entering and executing the following:

```
USE sales
INSERT customers
VALUES ('Janet','McBroom','5403 Western','Tempe','AZ','85103','6021112222')
```

4. Notice that this fails, with a message that the UNIQUE_KEY constraint was violated by the duplicate phone number.

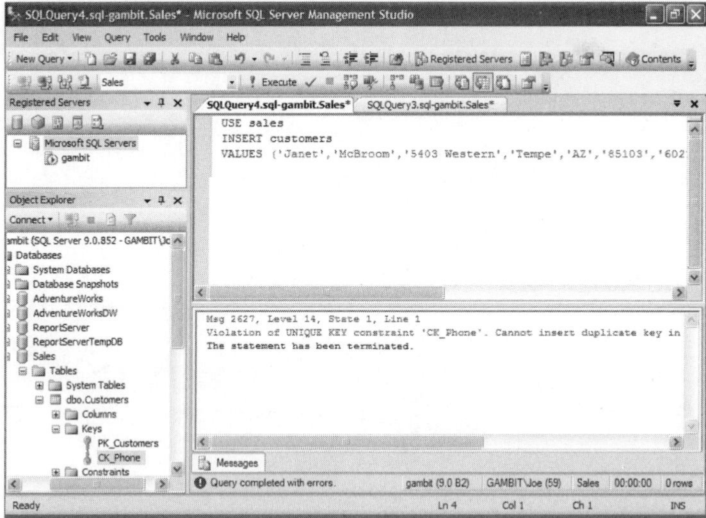

You now know how to protect the data that is entered in your tables by enforcing domain and entity integrity, but there is still one more area of integrity to consider. You need to know how to protect related data that is stored in separate tables by enforcing referential integrity.

Enforcing Referential Integrity

You have three tables in your Sales database right now: one for customer data, one for product data, and one for order data. Each of these tables contains data that is affected by what is stored in one of your other tables. For instance, the Orders table is affected by the Customers table in that you should not create an order for a customer that doesn't exist in your Customers table. The Orders table is also affected by the Products table in that you don't want to create an order for a product that doesn't exist. To make sure that a customer exists in your Customers table before you sell them something, or to avoid selling nonexistent products, you need to enforce *referential integrity*.

Enforcing referential integrity does just what its name implies: Data in one table that refers to data in another table is protected from improper updating. In SQL Server terminology, the process of enforcing referential integrity is called *declarative referential integrity (DRI)*, and it's accomplished by linking the primary key of one of your tables to a foreign key in another table. Let's see what foreign keys do and how to create them.

Using Foreign Keys

A *foreign key* is used in combination with a primary key to relate two tables on a common column. You could, for example, relate the Orders table and the Customers table on the CustID column that they have in common. If you use the CustID field in the Customers table as the primary key (which you already have), you can use the CustID field in the Orders table as the foreign key that relates the two tables. Now, unless you enable cascading referential integrity (which we'll discuss shortly), you won't be able to add a record to the Orders table if there is no matching record in the Customers table. Not only that—you can't delete a record in the Customers table if there are matching records in the Orders table, because you don't want to have orders out there with no customer information.

Before you see how this works, it's probably best to show you exactly what happens without referential integrity being enforced:

1. If you're still in SQL Server Management Studio, click the New Query button, and select New SQL Server Query. Connect with Windows Authentication if requested.
2. To insert a record with a customer ID, product ID, quantity, and current date (as reported by the `GETDATE()` function) in the Orders table, enter and execute the following code:

```
USE sales
INSERT orders
VALUES (999,5,57,getdate())
```

3. Notice in the preceding step that you were successful even though there is no customer in the Customers table with an ID of 999.
4. To remove the erroneous records, enter and execute the following code (note that this is a potentially dangerous command, because it deletes all records from a table):

```
truncate table orders
```

Now that you have proven that you can enter an order for a nonexistent customer, you need to protect your database against that. To do so, you'll create a foreign key on the CustID field of the Orders table that relates to the CustID field of the Customers table (which is the primary key of the Customers table). With this relationship in place, your data will be protected across your tables. Let's create that relationship:

1. Open SQL Server Management Studio. In Object Explorer, expand your server ➤ Databases ➤ Sales ➤ Tables ➤ Orders.
2. Right-click Keys, and select New Key.
3. In the (Name) box, enter **FK_Customers_Orders**.
4. In the Description box, enter **Relate tables on CustID**.
5. Click the box next to Tables And Columns Specification, and click the ellipsis button in the box.
6. Select Customers from the Primary Key Table drop-down list.
7. Select CustID from both drop-down list boxes in the grid, as shown in this graphic:

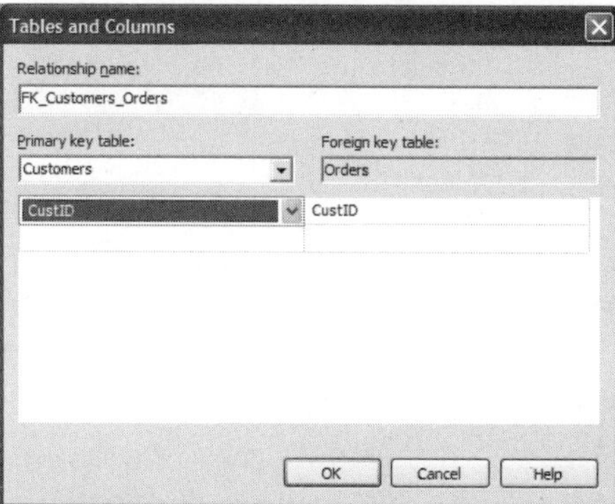

8. Click OK. The Foreign Key Relationship dialog should look like this:

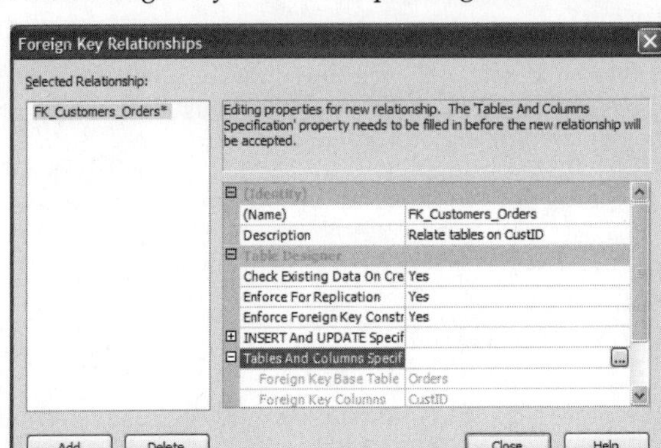

9. Click Close to create your key.
10. Click the Save button to save your table, and click Yes in the Save dialog box.
11. In Object Explorer, right-click Keys under the Orders table, and select Refresh.
12. Expand Keys, and notice your new key.

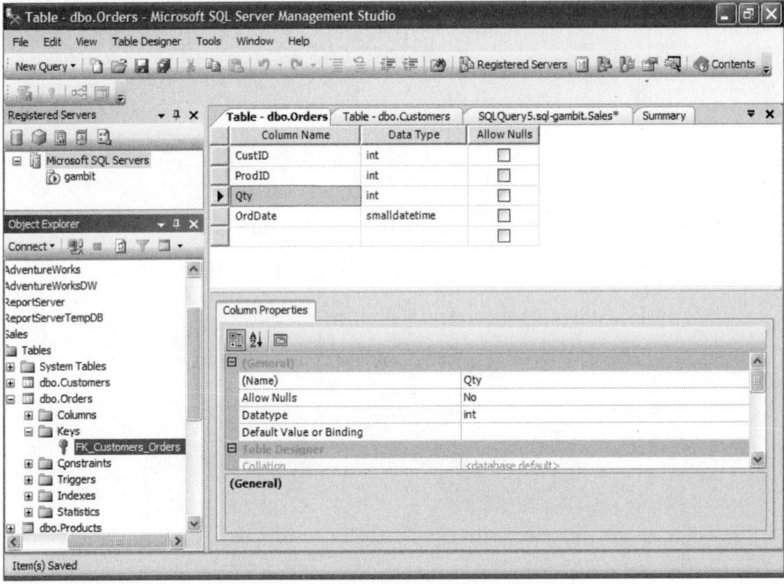

We'll test that new relationship in just a moment—you're probably wondering what those options at the bottom of the dialog box were for, though. We'll discuss the `INSERT` and `UPDATE` specifications a little later in this chapter, but here are descriptions for three of them:

Check Existing Data On Creation Or Re-Enabling The first option instructs SQL Server to verify that all the existing data in both tables fits the constraint parameters. If it doesn't, you'll receive a warning instructing you to fix it.

Enable Relationship For Replication Replication is used for copying databases from one server to another. This option enables the relationship to be copied via replication to another server along with the primary- and foreign-key tables.

Enforce Foreign Key Constraint If you find that you no longer need the relationship you have created, you can uncheck this box to disable it while leaving the relationship in place. This way, you don't need to completely re-create the relationship if you need it again later.

Now you're ready to test the new relationship. Here you'll try to add some records to the Orders table that have no corresponding record in the Customers table; then you'll try to delete a record from the Customers table that references a record in the Orders table:

1. Try to add the same record as in the last set of steps in SQL Server Management Studio:

```
USE sales
INSERT orders
VALUES (999,5,57,getdate())
```

2. Notice that the addition failed because there is no customer with ID 999 in the Customers table.

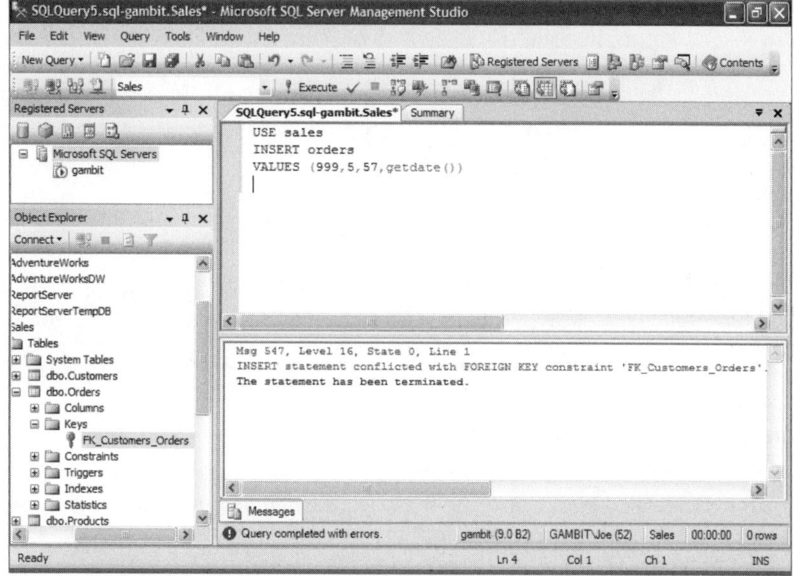

3. To make very sure that this is working, add a record to the Orders table that has a matching customer number by executing the following code in a new query window:

```
USE sales
INSERT orders
VALUES (1,5,57,getdate())
```

4. Notice that the previous code was successful because customer 1 exists.
5. Now that you have a matching record in the Orders table, try to delete customer 1 from the Customers table:

```
USE sales
DELETE from customers
WHERE custid = 1
```

You can see how the records in related tables are protected from improper updates. Users can't add a record to a foreign-key table without a corresponding record in the primary-key table, and primary-key records can't be deleted if they have matching foreign-key records. But wait, it gets even better: You have the option to use cascading referential integrity.

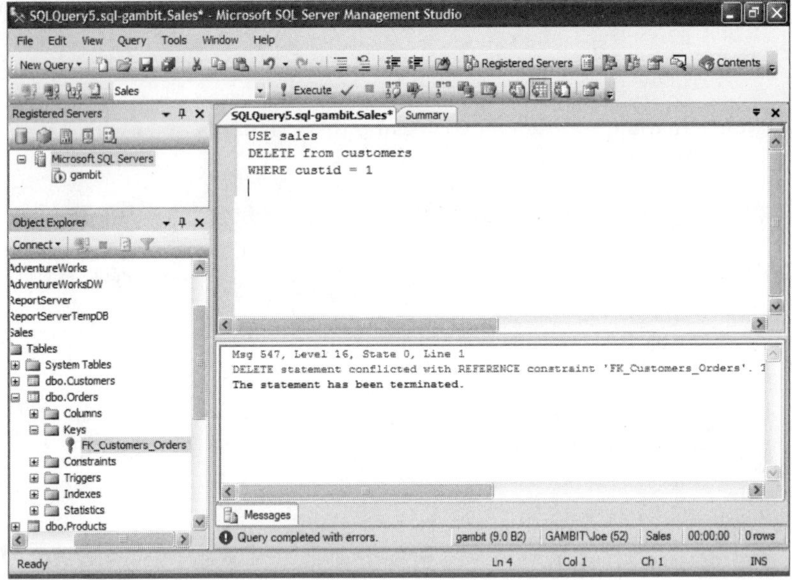

USING CASCADING REFERENTIAL INTEGRITY

You just saw that the default behavior for a relationship is to prevent the addition or deletion of records in the related tables based on the existence of matching records. A record in a primary key can't be deleted if there are corresponding records in the foreign-key table, for example. You can change this behavior, however, by using *cascading referential integrity*.

You probably noticed the INSERT and UPDATE Specifications option in the Foreign Key Relationships dialog box. It has two suboptions, Delete Rule and Update Rule, which control the behavior of cascading referential integrity. Both of these options have four possible settings, as described in Table 11.4.

Let's give this a try to demonstrate how it works. First, you need to disable the identity property of the CustID field in the Customers table—you can't manually assign a value to a field with an identity property assigned to it, and you need to do that for a full test of cascading referential integrity.

Once that process is finished, you'll set both cascade options on your relationship and test the cascade capabilities:

1. Open SQL Server Management Studio and expand your server ➢ Databases ➢ Sales ➢ Tables.
2. Right-click the Customers table, and select Modify Table.
3. Click the CustID field. In the bottom half of the screen, expand Identity Specification, and set the (Is Identity) property to No.
4. Click the Save button, and click Yes in the Save dialog box.
5. Right-click the CustID field, and select Relationships.
6. Expand INSERT And UPDATE Specifications, and set Delete Rule and Update Rule to Cascade.

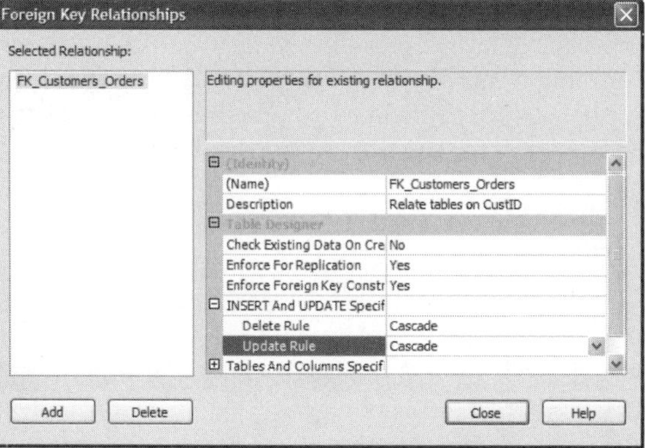

7. Click Close.
8. Click the Save icon on the toolbar, and click Yes in the Save dialog box.
9. Close the table designer window.

TABLE 11.4: INSERT and UPDATE Specification Settings

ACTION	DELETE RULE	UPDATE RULE
No Action	You can't delete a row in a primary table that is referenced by a row in a foreign table.	You can't insert a row in a foreign table that doesn't have a matching row in the primary table.
Cascade	If you delete a row in a primary table that is referenced by a row in a foreign table, then the foreign row is also deleted.	If you update a key value in a primary table, that value is updated in all rows of the foreign table.
Set NULL	If you delete a row in a primary table that is referenced by a row in a foreign table, then the values of the columns that form the foreign key are set to NULL.	If you update a row in a primary table that is referenced by a row in a foreign table, then the values of the columns that form the foreign key are set to NULL.

TABLE 11.4: INSERT and UPDATE Specification Settings *(CONTINUED)*

ACTION	DELETE RULE	UPDATE RULE
Set Default	If you delete a row in a primary table that is referenced by a row in a foreign table, then the values of the columns that form the foreign key are set to their default value. All the columns in the foreign key must have a default value for this to work.	If you update a row in a primary table that is referenced by a row in a foreign table, then the values of the columns that form the foreign key are set to their default value. All the columns in the foreign key must have a default value for this to work.

Now that you have enabled cascading referential integrity between the Customers and Orders tables, you're ready to test it:

1. Click the New Query button, and select New SQL Server Query. Connect with Windows Authentication if requested.
2. Verify the existing records in the Customers and Orders tables by entering and executing the following code (note that both lines are executed at the same time). You should see three customers and one order for CustID 1 in the result sets:

```
USE Sales
select * from customers
select * from orders
```

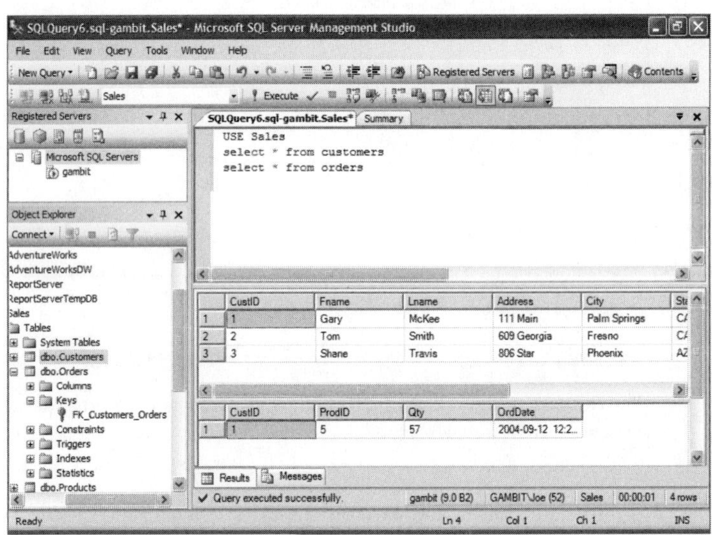

3. To test the cascaded update feature, enter and execute the following code:

```
UPDATE customers
SET custid = 5
WHERE custid = 1
```

4. Enter and execute the code from step 2 again. Notice that CustID 1 has been changed to 5 in the Customers and Orders tables.

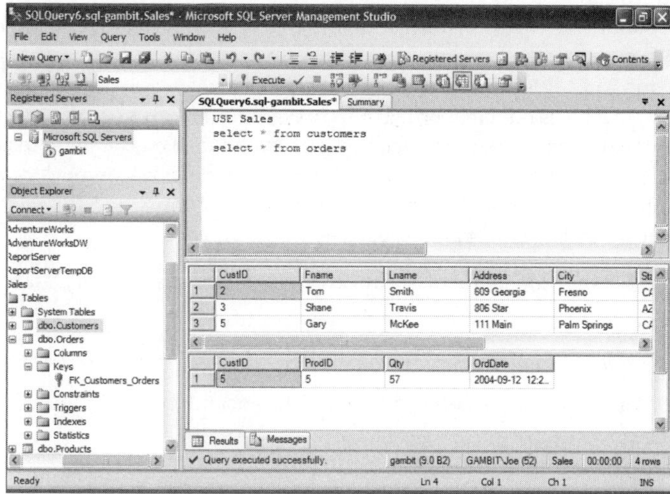

5. To test the cascaded delete feature, enter and execute the following code to delete customer 5:

```
USE Sales
DELETE from customers
WHERE custid = 5
```

6. Enter and execute the code from step 2 again. Notice that the customer 5 record has been deleted from the Customers table along with the matching records from the Orders table.

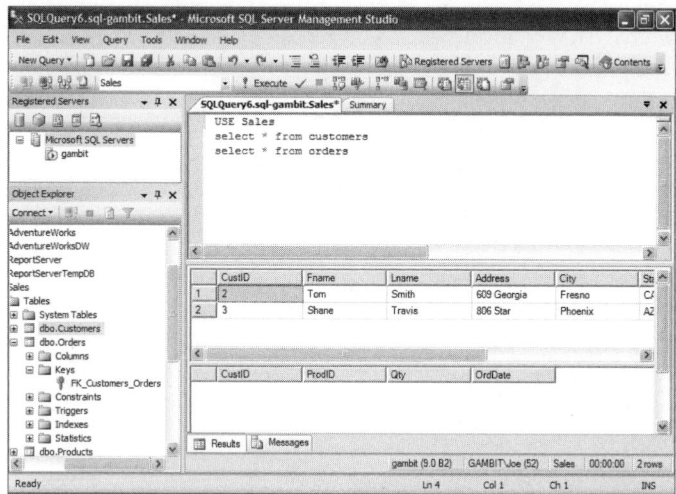

You now know how to declare referential integrity that both denies and cascades updates. In fact, you know how to restrict any data that a user may try to enter in your tables.

Using Database Diagrams

Everything you have done up to this point has been graphical, meaning that you have been able to use Enterprise Manager to do everything rather than using Transact-SQL code. That is good, but it could be better. Remember the foreign-key relationship that you created a few pages back? It would have been easier if you could've actually seen the tables and maybe used drag and drop to create the relationship. You can use database diagrams to do this and a great deal more. In fact, quite a few of your database management activities can be performed using a database diagram.

A *database diagram* is a picture of the database. Specifically, it is a graphic depiction of the schema (whole or partial) of the database, showing the tables and columns, and the relationships between them. Let's create a database diagram here to see what it is capable of:

1. Open SQL Server Management Studio and expand your server ➤ Databases ➤ Sales ➤ Tables.
2. Right-Click Database Diagrams under the Sales database and click New Database Diagram.
3. In the Add Table dialog, select Customers, Orders and Products and click Add.

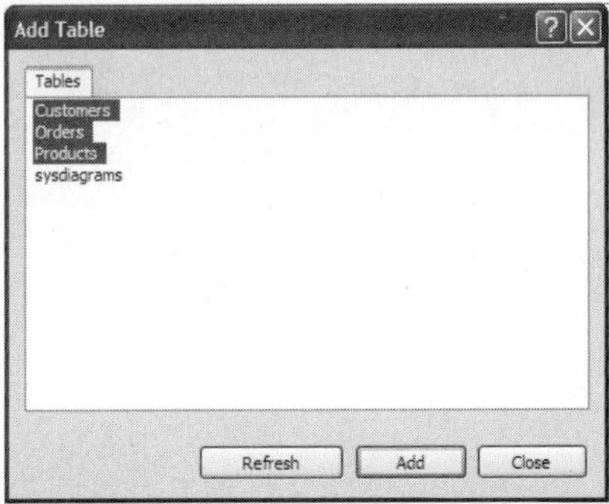

4. After the tables have been added click Close and you will see your database diagram (the one in the image has been altered so you can see the whole thing). Notice the foreign-key relationship you created earlier as well as the primary key on the customers table.

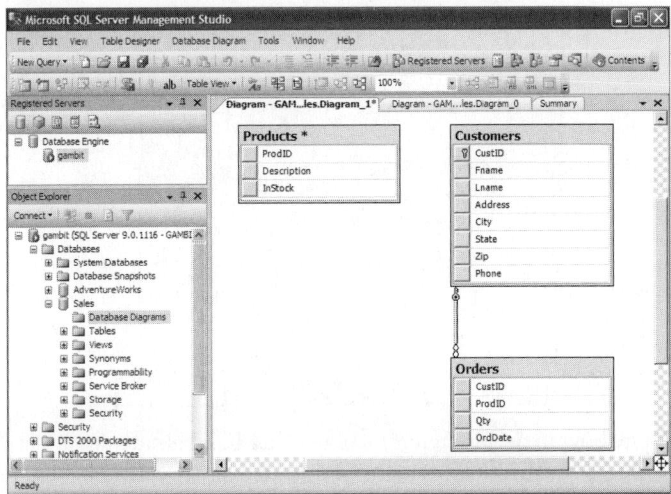

NOTE A database diagram is a graphic representation of the database schema. The schema is the structure of the database, and it describes things such as the names of columns, datatypes, table relationships, and all other components of the database structure.

Now that you have successfully created a database diagram for the Sales database, let's see what the database diagram can do. In this next set of steps, you are going to create a primary key on the products table and then relate the products and orders tables, all using the database diagram:

1. To create a primary key on the products table, right-click the ProdID column and select Set Primary Key (you may need to enlarge the graphic by increasing the percentage in the zoom drop-down box on the toolbar to see the column names). Notice the little key icon just to the left of the column name.

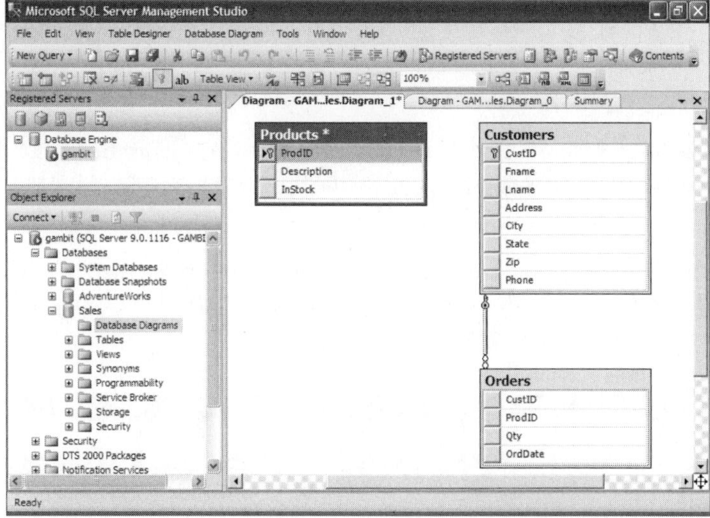

2. To create a foreign-key relationship between the products table and the orders table, hover your mouse pointer over the gray box to the left of the ProdID column in the orders table.

3. Click and drag the mouse to the products table, and drop the icon on the ProdID column.

4. Accept the defaults in the Tables and Columns dialog box by clicking OK.

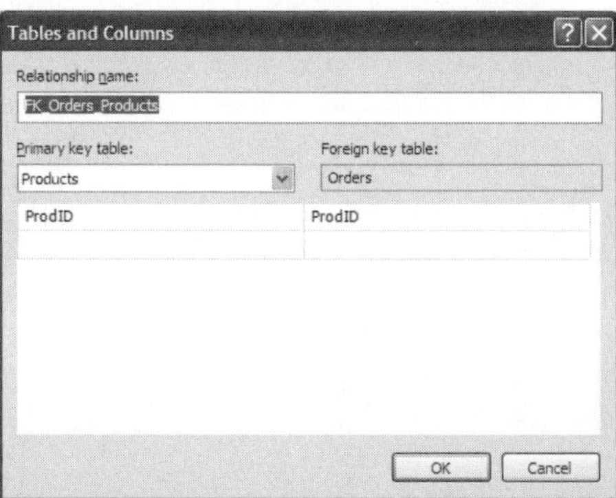

5. Accept the defaults in the Foreign Key Relationship dialog box by clicking OK.

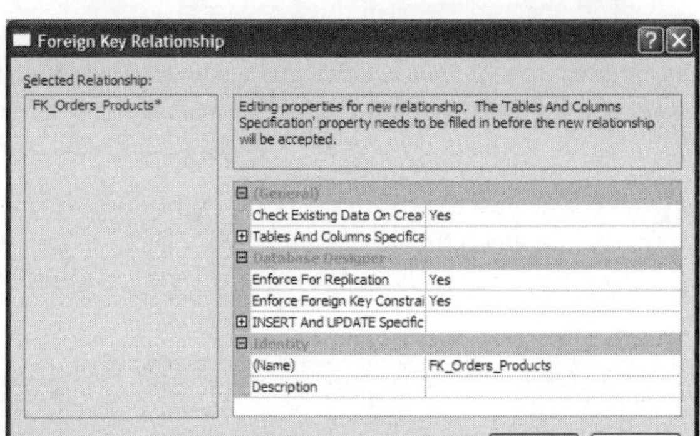

6. Notice the gray line denoting a relationship between the products and orders tables. Close the diagram by clicking the X in the upper-right corner of the screen.

7. When asked to save the diagram, click No.

Now you have a fully functional database diagram that can be used to modify the structure of your tables and create relationships between them. Such diagrams can be very helpful and time-saving when you get to know them.

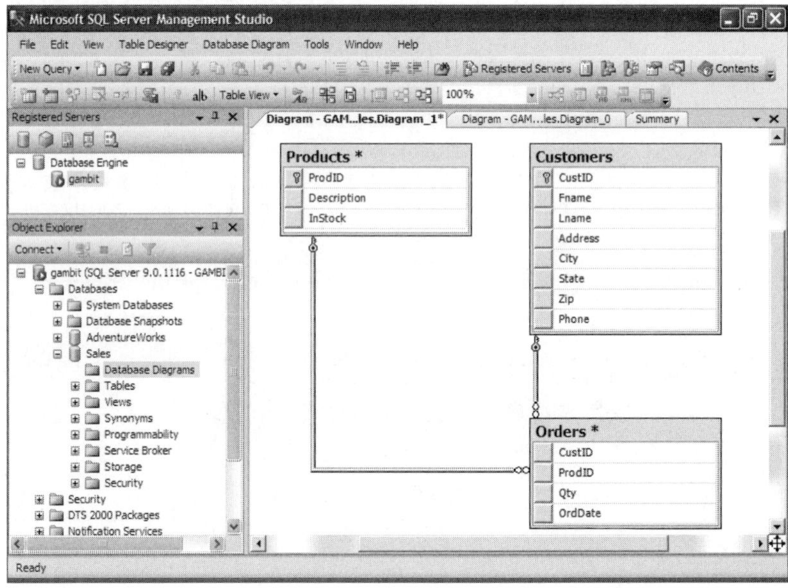

Summary

As you can see, there is a great deal of information involved in creating and managing tables. Here is a brief synopsis of what this chapter covered:

Planning tables In this section, you learned that you must sit down with a pencil and paper and draw out the tables before you create them. You need to decide what the tables will contain, making the tables as specific as possible. You also learned that tables are made up of fields (which contain a specific type of data) and rows (an entity in the table that spans all fields). Each of the fields in the table has a specific datatype that restricts the type of data it can hold—a field with an int datatype can't hold character data, for example. Then you learned that you can create your own datatypes that are just system datatypes with all the required parameters presupplied.

Creating tables In this section, you learned the mechanics of creating the tables in the database—there's not a lot to it, but it's still a very important topic.

Restricting the data In this section, you learned that tables are wide open to just about any kind of data when they're first created. The only restriction is that users can't violate the datatype of a field; other than that, the tables are fair game. To restrict what data your users can enter in a field, you learned how to enforce three types of integrity:

Domain integrity This is the process of restricting what data your users can enter in a field. Check constraints and rules can be used to validate the data that the users try to enter against a list of acceptable data, and defaults can be used to enter data for the user if they forget.

Entity integrity This is the process of making sure that each record in the table is unique in some way. Primary keys are the main way of accomplishing this; they can be used with foreign keys in enforcing referential integrity. Unique constraints are used when there is a field in the table that isn't part of the primary key but that needs to be protected against duplicate values.

Referential integrity This is the process of protecting related data that is stored in separate tables. A foreign key is related to a primary key. Then the data in the primary-key table can't be deleted if there are matching records in the foreign-key table, and records can't be entered in the foreign-key table if there is no corresponding record in the primary-key table. The only way around this behavior is to enable cascading referential integrity, which lets you delete or change records in the primary-key table and have those changes cascade to the foreign-key table.

Using database diagrams Finally you learned that database diagrams are a graphical representation of the schema that can be used to simplify database management and maintenance.

Now that you know how to create tables, you need to know how to speed up the process of extracting the data that will be subsequently stored in them. Toward that end, we'll discuss indexing in the next chapter.

Chapter 12

Indexing

If you wanted to look up *triggers* in this book, how would you go about it? First you would look in the index in the back of the book for the word *triggers*, which is listed alphabetically under the *T* section. Once you located the entry, you would reference the page number next to *triggers* and find the description you needed rather quickly. However, suppose this book had no organization—no index, no table of contents, not even chapters or page numbers. How would you find *triggers* then? You would have to scan the entire book, page by page, until you found what you sought—a painfully slow process. SQL Server tables work much the same way.

When you first create a table and start inserting data, there is no organization to the table whatsoever—information is inserted on a first-come, first-served basis. When you want to find a specific record later, SQL Server has to look through every record in the table to find the record you need. That is called a *table scan*, and it can slow the database server considerably. Because you need fast access to your data, you need to add organization to the tables that contain that data, much like this book is organized with chapters, page numbers, and indexes.

To add organization to tables, you need to understand indexing. In this chapter, we'll discuss the two different types of indexes, clustered and nonclustered, and how they work to accelerate data access. We'll also show you how, when, and where to create these indexes so that they provide the utmost proficiency in data retrieval.

Before you can truly understand how indexes accelerate data access, though, you must understand the index architecture.

Index Architecture

In Chapter 3, "Overview of SQL Server," you learned that SQL Server stores data on the hard disk in 8KB pages inside the database files. By default, these pages and the data they contain aren't organized in any way. To bring order to this chaos, you must create an index. Once you've done so, you have index pages as well as data pages. The data pages contain the information that users have inserted in the tables, and the index pages are used to store a list of all the values in an indexed column (called *key values*) along with a pointer to the location of the record that contains that value in the indexed table. For example, if you have an index on a lastname column, a key value might be Smith 520617—this indicates that the first record with a value of Smith in the lastname field is on extent 52, page 6, record number 17 (an *extent* is a collection of eight contiguous pages in a data file).

There are two types of indexes to create on a table: *clustered* and *nonclustered*. Which type should you use and where? To answer that question accurately, you need to understand how SQL Server stores and accesses data when there is no index in place—this type of table is called a *heap*.

Understanding Heaps

Have you ever been in one of those cities that has streets broken up by canals, highways, and sundry obstructions? Every time you're about to find the address you need, the street ends because of an obstacle of some sort. To continue your search for your destination, you have to refer to your map to find out where the street begins on the other side. The worse the street is broken up, the more often you refer to your map to find the next section of street.

Tables with no clustered index in place, called *heaps*, are a great deal like those broken streets. SQL Server stores tables on disk by allocating one extent (eight contiguous 8KB pages) at a time in the database file. When one extent fills with data, another is allotted. These extents, however, aren't physically next to each other in the database file; they're scattered about much like a street that keeps starting and stopping. That is part of what makes data access on a heap so slow—much like you need to keep accessing your map to find various sections of the street you're on, SQL Server needs to access a map to find various extents of the table it's searching.

Suppose, for instance, that you're searching for a record named Adams in the customers table. That customers table may be quite sizable, so SQL Server needs to find all the extents that belong to that table in the database file before it can even think of searching for Adams. To find those extents, SQL Server must query the sysindexes table.

Don't let the name fool you: Even though this table is generally used to store index information, every table in your database has an entry in the sysindexes table, whether or not the particular table has an index in place. If your table is a heap (such as this customers table), it has a record in the sysindexes table with a value of 0 (zero) in the indid (index identifier) column. Once SQL Server finds the record for the customers table in the sysindexes table and reads a 0 in the indid column, SQL Server looks specifically at the FirstIAM column.

The FirstIAM column tells SQL Server exactly where the first Index Allocation Map (IAM) page is in the database. Much like the street map you use to find various sections of a street, the IAM is what SQL Server must use to find various extents of a heap, as depicted in Figure 12.1. This IAM is the only thing that links pages together in a heap; without the IAM, SQL Server would need to scan every page in the database file to find one table—just like you would have to drive every street in town to find a single address if you had no street map.

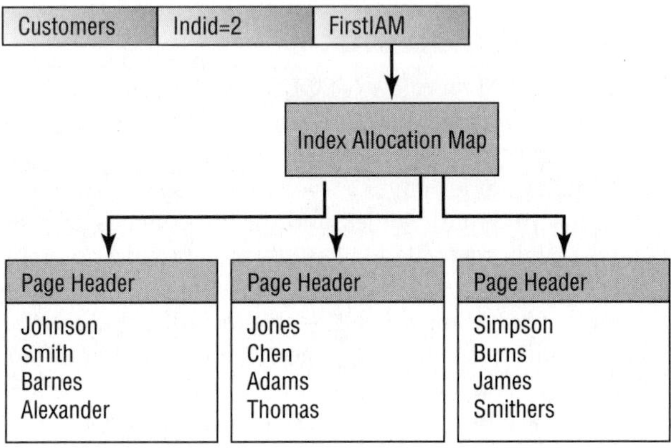

FIGURE 12.1
To find all the pages associated with a table, SQL Server must reference the Index Allocation Map.

Even with this IAM, data access is generally slower than if your table were indexed. Think of it this way: If there were no break in the street on which you were searching for an address, it would be much easier and faster to find your destination. However, because the street is broken up, you must constantly refer to your map to find the next section of street. In the same fashion, SQL Server must constantly refer to the IAM to find the next extent of a table to continue searching for data. This process of scanning the IAM and then scanning each extent of the table for the record needed is called a *table scan*. You can see what a table scan looks like by creating a new query in SQL Server Management Studio:

1. Open SQL Server Management Studio, and connect using Windows Authentication.
2. To force SQL Server to perform a table scan, you need to delete an index. In Object Explorer, expand your server ➤ Databases ➤ AdventureWorks ➤ Tables ➤ HumanResources.EmployeePayHistory ➤ Indexes.
3. Right-click the PK_EmployeePayHistory_EmployeeID_RateChangeDate index, and select Delete.
4. Click OK in the Delete Object dialog box (you'll re-create this index later in the chapter).
5. Click the New Query button, and select New SQL Server Query. Connect using Windows Authentication if requested.
6. Enter the following code on the territories table, which has no index:

```
USE AdventureWorks
SELECT * FROM HumanResources.EmployeePayHistory
```

7. On the Query menu, click Display Estimated Execution Plan. This will show you how SQL Server goes about finding your data.
8. Scroll down to the bottom of the results pane, and hover over the Table Scan icon to view the cost of the scan—this tells you how much CPU time the scan took (in milliseconds).

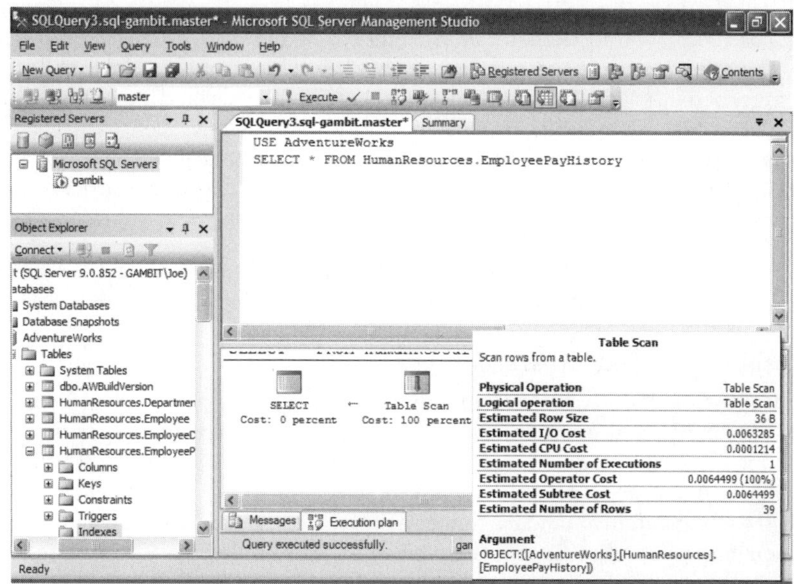

Table scans can slow your system, but they don't always. In fact, table scans can be faster than indexed access if your table is very small (about one extent in size). If you create an index on such a small table, SQL Server must read the index pages and then the table pages. It would be faster just to scan the table and be done with it. So, on small tables, a heap is preferable. On larger tables, though, you need to avoid table scans—to do that, you should understand indexes. We'll start by looking into clustered indexes.

ESTIMATING THE SIZE OF A TABLE IN EXTENTS

This is discussed in more detail in Chapter 11, but here is a brief overview. To estimate the size of a table in extents, do the following:

1. Calculate the size of a record in the table.
2. Divide 8092 by the result from step 1.
3. Divide the number of estimated rows by the result from step 2.
4. Divide the result from step 3 by 8—you'll have the number of extents your table occupies.

Understanding Clustered Indexes

Clustered indexes physically rearrange the data that users insert in your tables. The arrangement of a clustered index on disk can easily be compared to that in a dictionary, because they both use the same storage paradigm. If you needed to look up a word in the dictionary—for example, *satellite*—how would you do it? You would turn right to the *S* section of the dictionary and continue through the alphabetically arranged list until you found the word *satellite.* The process is similar with a clustered index; a clustered index on a lastname column would place *Adams* physically before *Burns* in the database file. This way, SQL Server can more easily pinpoint the exact data pages it wants.

It might help to visualize an index in SQL Server as an upside-down tree. In fact, the index structure is called a *B-tree* (binary-tree) structure. At the top of the B-tree structure, you find the *root page;* it contains information about the location of other pages further down the line called *intermediate-level pages*. These intermediate pages contain yet more key values that can point to still other intermediate-level pages or data pages. The pages at the very bottom of a clustered index, the *leaf pages*, contain the actual data, which is physically arranged on disk to conform to the constraints of the index.

Data access on a clustered index is a little more complex than just looking for letters or numbers in the data pages, though—the way SQL Server accesses the data in this structure is similar to a GPS mapping system in a car.

TIP You can have only one clustered index per table because clustered indexes physically rearrange the data in the indexed table.

ACCESSING DATA WITH A CLUSTERED INDEX

If you've never had the opportunity to drive a car that is equipped with a Global Positioning System (GPS) map guidance system, you're missing quite an interesting experience. The GPS system is a computerized map that is designed to guide you while you're driving. It looks like a small computer screen that rests on a gooseneck pole between the driver and passenger in the front seat, much like a gearshift in a standard transmission car. The interesting thing about this map is that it talks you through the directions—"Turn left one quarter mile ahead," "Turn right at the next intersection," and so on. When it's finished speaking to you, you're at the destination you desire.

In this analogy, the beginning point of your journey is the root page of the clustered index. Each of the twists and turns you take in your journey is an intermediate level of the clustered index, and each one is important in getting to your destination. Finally, the destination in your journey is the leaf level of the index, the data itself. However, because SQL Server doesn't use GPS, what is the map?

When you perform a query on a column that is part of a clustered index (by using a SELECT statement), SQL Server must refer to the sysindexes table where every table has a record. Tables with a clustered index have a value of 1 in the indid column (unlike heaps, which have a value of 0). Once the record has been located, SQL Server looks at the root column, which contains the location of the root page of the clustered index.

When SQL Server locates the root page of the index, it begins to search for your data. If you're searching for *Smith*, for example, SQL Server searches through the entire root page looking for an entry for *Smith*. Since the data you're seeking is toward the bottom of the table, SQL Server most likely won't find *Smith* in the root page. What it will find at the bottom of the root page is a link to the next intermediate page in the chain.

Each page in the clustered index has a pointer, or *link*, to the index page just before it and the index page just after it. Having these links built into the index pages eliminates the need for the IAM pages that heaps require. This speeds up data access because you don't need to keep referring back to the IAM pages—you move right to the next index page in the chain, much like in the GPS analogy where you follow the computer's voice to the next turn in your route.

SQL Server then looks through each intermediate-level page, where it may be redirected to another intermediate-level page or finally to the leaf level. The leaf level in a clustered index is the end destination—the data you requested in your SELECT query. If you've requested one record, that single record found at the leaf level is displayed.

Suppose, though, that you've requested a range of data (for example, *Smith* through *Quincy*). Because the data has been physically rearranged, as soon as SQL Server has located the first value in the search, it can read each subsequent record until it reaches *Quincy*. There is no need to keep referring back to the root and intermediate-level pages to find subsequent data. This makes a clustered index an excellent choice for columns where you're constantly searching for ranges of data or columns with low selectivity. *Selectivity* is the number of duplicate values in a column; low selectivity means that there are many duplicate values in a column. For example a LastName column may contain several hundred records with a value of Smith, which means that it has low selectivity. Whereas a PhoneNumber column should have very few records with duplicate values, meaning that it has high selectivity. The whole process looks a lot like Figure 12.2.

You now know how SQL Server accesses data via a clustered index, but there is more to it than that. Now you need to understand how that data gets there in the first place and what happens if it changes.

Modifying Data with a Clustered Index

To access data on a table with a clustered index, you use a standard SELECT statement—there is nothing special about it. Modifying data with a clustered index is the same—you use standard INSERT, UPDATE, and DELETE statements. What makes this process intriguing is the way SQL Server has to store your data; it must be physically rearranged to conform to the clustered index parameters.

On a heap, the data is inserted at the end of the table, which is the bottom of the last data page. If there is no room on any of the data pages, SQL Server allocates a new extent and starts filling it with data. Because you've told SQL Server to physically rearrange your data by creating a clustered index, SQL Server no longer has the freedom to stuff data wherever there is room. The data must physically be placed in order. To help SQL Server accomplish this, you need to leave a little room at the end of each data page on a clustered index. This blank space is referred to as the *fill factor*.

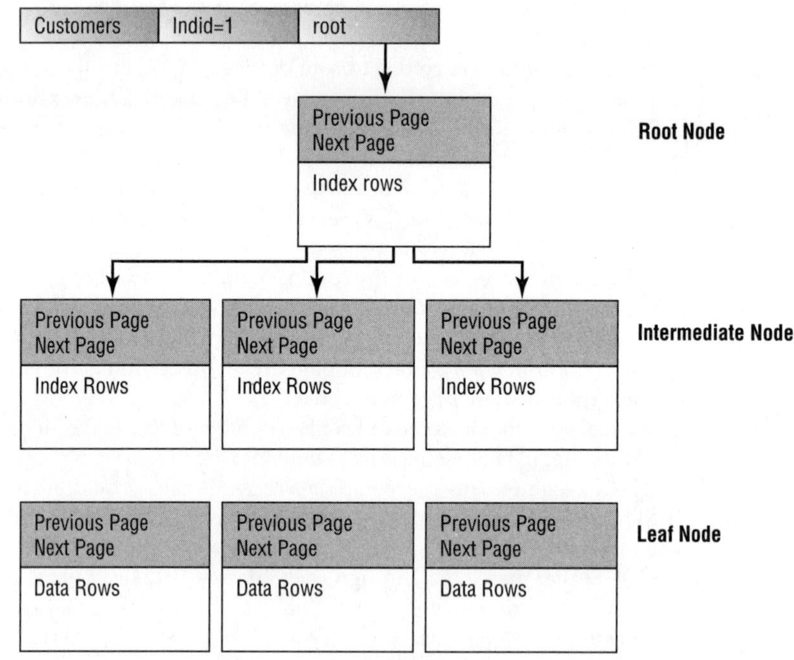

FIGURE 12.2
The data in a table with a clustered index is physically rearranged for ease of location.

Setting the fill factor on a clustered index tells SQL Server to leave blank space at the end of each data page so that there is room to insert new data. For example, suppose you have a clustered index on a lastname column and you want to add a new customer with a last name of *Chen*, which needs to be placed on one of the data pages that contain the *C* data. SQL Server must put this record on the *C* page; with a fill factor specified, you'll have room at the end of the page to insert this new data. Without a fill factor, the *C* page may fill entirely, and there will be no room for *Chen*.

The fill factor is specified when you create the clustered index and can be changed later if you wish. A higher fill factor gives less room, and a lower fill factor gives more room. If you specify a fill factor of 70, for example, the data page is filled with 70 percent data and 30 percent blank space (as shown in Figure 12.3). If you specify 100, the data page is filled to nearly 100 percent, having room for only one record at the bottom of the page (it seems strange, but that's how SQL Server views 100 percent full).

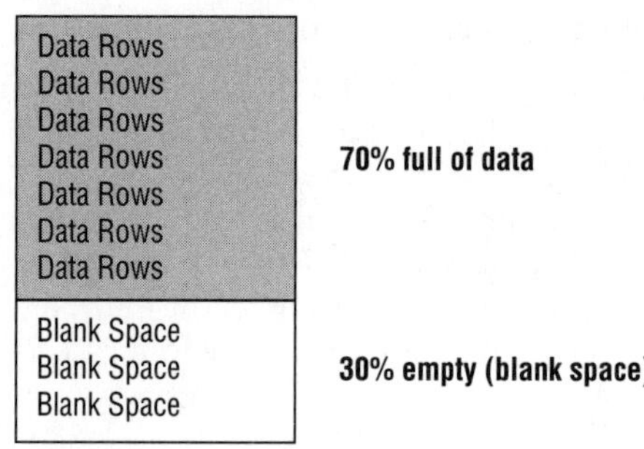

FIGURE 12.3
Set the fill factor to leave blank space for new data in your pages.

SQL Server doesn't automatically maintain the fill factor, though. This means that your data pages can and will fill to capacity eventually. What happens when a data page fills completely?

When you need to insert data into a page that has become completely full, SQL Server performs a *page split*. This means SQL Server takes approximately half the data from the full page and moves it to an empty page, thus creating two half-full pages (or half-empty, depending on how you look at it). Now you have plenty of room for the new data, but there is a new problem with which to contend. Remember that this clustered index is a doubly linked list, each page having a link to the page before it and the page after it. So, when SQL Server splits a page, it must also update the headers at the top of each page to reflect the new location of the data that has been moved. Because this new page can be anywhere in the database file, the links on the pages don't necessarily point to the next physical page on the disk. A link may point to a different extent altogether, which can slow the system.

For example, if you have inserted a new record named *Chen* into the database, but your C page is full, SQL Server will perform a page split. Half the data is moved to a new page to make room for the *Chen* record, but the new page for the data that has been moved isn't in line anymore. Take a look at Figure 12.4 to better understand what can happen.

FIGURE 12.4 Page splits move half the data from a full page to a new page to make room for more data.

Before

page 99 next page 100 Prev Page 98	page 100 next page 101 Prev Page 99	page 101 next page 102 Prev Page 100
Data Data Data Data Data	Data Data Data Data Data	Data Data Data Data Data

After

page 99 next page 100 Prev Page 98	page 100 next page 102 Prev Page 99	page 101 next page 103 Prev Page 102	page 102 next page 101 Prev Page 100
Data Data Data Data Data	Data Data	Data Data Data Data Data	Data Data Data

Notice that before the page split (as shown in Figure 12.4), all the pages were neatly lined up—page 99 pointed to page 100, 100 pointed to 101, and so on. Then after the page split, some of the data had to be moved from page 100 to page 102. Now page 102 comes directly after 100 in the linked list. This means that when you search for data, SQL Server will need to jump from page 99 to page 100, from 100 to 102, from 102 back to 101, and then from 101 to 103. You can see how that might slow the system down, so you need to configure the fill factor to avoid excessive page splits.

The term *excessive* is subjective when discussing page splits, though. In an environment where data is used primarily for reading, such as a decision support services environment, you'll want to use a high fill factor (less free space). This high fill factor will ensure that data is read from fewer pages in the database file. You should use a lower fill factor (more free space) in environments where there is a lot of INSERT traffic. This lower fill factor will cut down on page splits and increase write performance.

Now that you have a better understanding of the inner workings of a clustered index, you're probably ready to create one for each column of your table—but please don't try to do that just yet (even if you want to, you're limited to one clustered index per table). Before you find out where and how to create indexes, you need to learn about nonclustered indexes.

Understanding Nonclustered Indexes

Like its clustered cousin, the *nonclustered index* is a B-tree structure having a root page, intermediate levels, and a leaf level. However, two major differences separate the index types. The first is that the leaf level of the nonclustered index doesn't contain the actual data; it contains pointers to the data that is stored in data pages. The second big difference is that the nonclustered index doesn't physically rearrange the data. It's much like the difference between a dictionary and an index at the back of a topically arranged book.

A clustered index is much like a dictionary in that the data contained therein is physically arranged to meet the constraints of the index. So if you wanted to find *triggers* in a dictionary, you would turn to the *T* section and find your way from there. A nonclustered index is more like the index at the back of a book. If you wanted to find *triggers* in this book, you couldn't turn to the *T* section of the book and look for *triggers* because there is no *T* section to turn to, as there is in a dictionary. Instead you turn to the back of the book and refer to the index, which does have a *T* section. Once you locate *triggers* in the index, you turn to the page number listed to find the information you need. If you're searching for a range of data, you must constantly refer back to the index to find the data you need, because most of the data is contained on different pages. Let's see how this works in a little more detail.

Accessing Data with a Nonclustered Index

Let's return to our map analogy. Most of us have used a paper map at some point to locate a destination. You unfolded it, searched for your destination on the map, and traced out a route to get there. If the route was simple, you may have been able to memorize the directions, but most times you had to refer back to the map constantly to remember where to turn, what street names you were looking for, and so on. Once you finished referring to the map, you were probably at your destination. A nonclustered index is a great deal like this.

When you search for data on a table with a nonclustered index, SQL Server first queries the sysindexes table looking for a record that contains your table name and a value in the indid column between 2 and 251 (0 denotes a heap, and 1 is for a clustered index). Once SQL Server finds this record, it looks at the root column to find the root page of the index (just like it did with a clustered index). Once SQL Server has the location of the root page, it can begin searching for your data.

If you're searching for *Smith,* for example, SQL Server looks through the root page to find *Smith;* if it isn't there, the server finds the highest value in the root page and follows that pointer to the next intermediate-level page. SQL Server keeps following the intermediate-level links until it finds *Smith* in the leaf level. This is another difference between clustered and nonclustered indexes: The leaf level in a nonclustered index doesn't contain the actual data you seek. The leaf level contains a pointer to the data, which is contained in a separate data page—much like the index at the back of a book doesn't have a description of what you're looking for, but refers you to a different page of the book.

If you're searching for a single value, SQL Server needs to search the index only once because the pointer at the leaf level directs SQL Server right to the data. If you're looking for a range of values, though, SQL Server must refer back to the index repeatedly to locate the key value for each record in the range you're trying to find. This means that you should use nonclustered indexes on columns in which you seldom search for ranges of data or columns with high selectivity. As mentioned previously in this chapter selectivity is the number of duplicate values in a column; low selectivity means that a column contains many duplicate values, high selectivity means that there are few duplicate values.

Once SQL Server finds the leaf level it needs, it can use the pointer to find the data page that contains *Smith;* how SQL Server finds the data page depends on whether you have a clustered index in place yet.

If you're searching a nonclustered index that is based on a heap (a table with no clustered index in place), SQL Server uses the pointer in the leaf-level page to jump right to the data page and return your data (as shown in Figure 12.5).

If your table has a clustered index in place, the nonclustered index leaf level doesn't contain a pointer directly to the data; rather it contains a pointer to the clustered index key value, as shown in Figure 12.6. This means that once SQL Server is done searching your nonclustered index, it has to traverse your clustered index as well. Why on Earth would you want to search two indexes to come up with a single value? Wouldn't one index be faster? Not necessarily—the secret lies in updating the data.

FIGURE 12.5
When you're using a nonclustered index on a heap, the leaf page contains a pointer to the data, not the data itself.

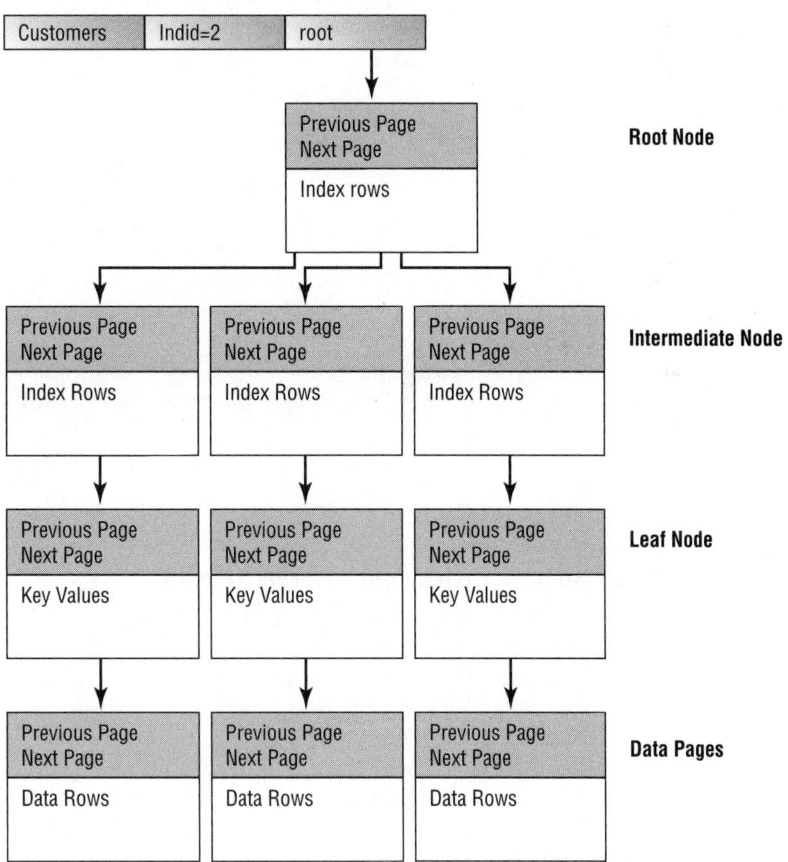

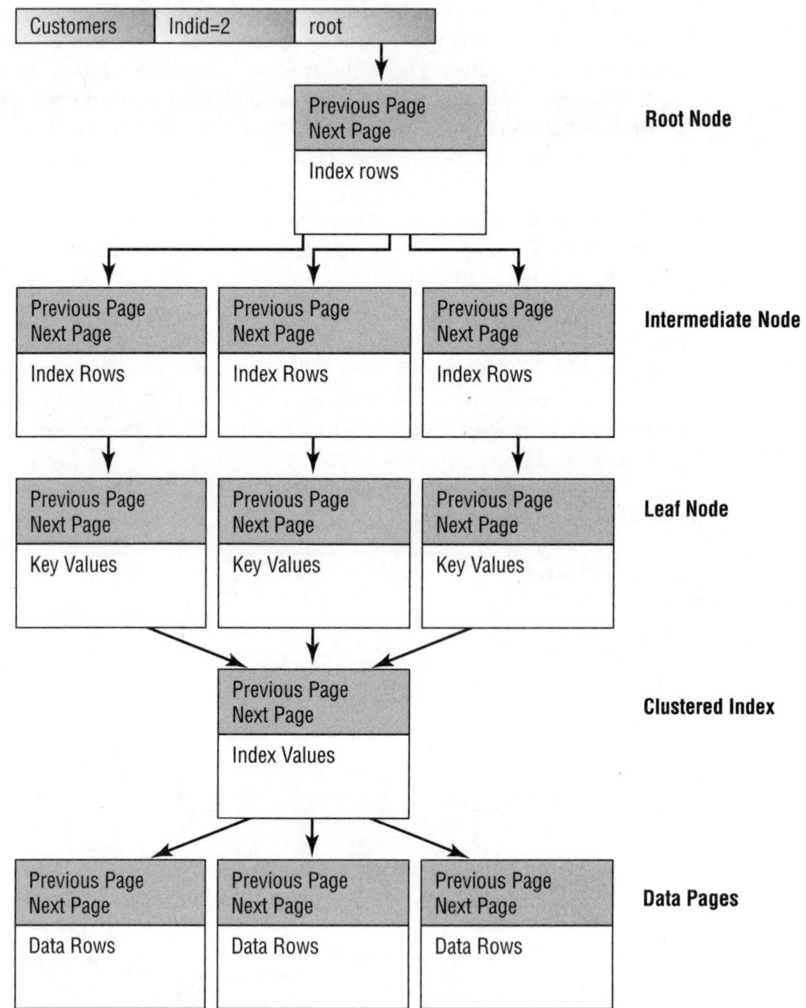

FIGURE 12.6 When you're using a nonclustered index on a clustered index, the leaf page contains a pointer to the clustered index value.

MODIFYING DATA WITH A NONCLUSTERED INDEX

There is nothing special about the commands used to modify data here—you use the standard Transact-SQL statements (`INSERT`, `UPDATE`, and `DELETE`) to accomplish these tasks. The interesting part is how SQL Server stores the data.

When inserting data using a nonclustered index on a heap, SQL Server doesn't have much work to do. It stuffs the data wherever it finds room and adds a new key value that points to the new record of the associated index pages. The process becomes a bit more complex when you throw a clustered index into the equation.

When you insert data into a table with a nonclustered and a clustered index in place, SQL Server physically inserts the data where it belongs in the order of the clustered index and updates the key values of the nonclustered index to point to the key values of the clustered index. When one of the data pages becomes full and you still have more data to insert, a page split occurs: Half the records on the full page are moved to a new page to make room for more data. This process of page splitting is why the key values of the nonclustered index point to the clustered index instead of the data pages themselves.

When you're using a nonclustered index without a clustered index in place, each index page contains key values that point to the data. This pointer contains the location of the extent, and the page and record number of the data being searched for. If a page split occurred and the nonclustered index didn't use clustered index key values, then all the key values for the data that had been moved would be incorrect because all the pointers would be wrong. The entire nonclustered index would need to be rebuilt to reflect the changes. However, because the nonclustered index references the clustered index key values (not the actual data), all the pointers in the nonclustered index will be correct even after a page split has occurred, and the nonclustered index won't need to be rebuilt. That is why you reference the key values of a clustered index in a nonclustered index.

Table 12.1 gives a brief summary of the differences between clustered and nonclustered indexes.

TABLE 12.1: Differences between Clustered and Nonclustered Indexes

CLUSTERED	NONCLUSTERED
Only 1 allowed per table	Up to 249 allowed per table
Physically rearranges the data in the table to conform to the index constraints	Creates a separate list of key values with pointers to the location of the data in the data pages
For use on columns that are frequently searched for ranges of data	For use on columns that are searched for single values
For use on columns with low selectivity	For use on columns with high selectivity

In SQL Server 2005, you can extend nonclustered indexes to include nonkey columns. This is referred to as an index with *included columns*. Including nonkey columns in a nonclustered index can significantly improve performance in queries where all the columns are included in the index. You need to keep a few guidelines in mind:

- Nonkey columns can only be included in nonclustered indexes.
- Columns can't be defined in both the key column and the `INCLUDE` list.
- Column names can't be repeated in the `INCLUDE` list.
- At least one key column must be defined.
- Nonkey columns can't be dropped from a table unless the index is dropped first.
- Text, ntext, and image type columns are not allowed as included columns.
- Column names can't be repeated in the include list.
- A column can't be both a key column and an included column.
- You must have at least one key column defined with a maximum of 16 key columns.
- You can only have up to a maximum of 1023 included columns.

- Nonkey columns can't be dropped from a table unless the index is dropped first.
- The only changes allowed to nonkey columns are:
  - Changing nullability (from NULL to NOT NULL and vice versa)
  - Increasing the length of varbinary, varchar, or nvarchar columns

Now that you know when and where to create both types of indexes, you only need to know how to create them. In the next section, we'll look at the mechanics of creating indexes.

PARTITIONED INDEXES

As we discussed in Chapter 11, "Tables," tables can be partitioned for performance and storage reasons; so can indexes. It's usually best to partition a table and then create an index on the table so that SQL Server can partition the index for you based on the partition function and schema of the table. However, indexes can be partitioned separately. This is useful if:

- The base table isn't partitioned.
- Your index key is unique but doesn't contain the partition column of the table.
- You want the base table to participate in collocated joins with more tables using different join columns.

If you decide that you need to partition your index separately, then you need to keep the following in mind:

- The arguments of the partition function for the table and index must have the same datatype. For example, if your table is partitioned on a datetime column, your index must be partitioned on a datetime column.
- Your table and index must define the same number of partitions.
- The table and index must have the same partition boundaries.

Creating Indexes

After all the work of planning your indexes, creating them is a breeze. We'll look at two methods of creating indexes: through SQL Server Management Studio and by using the Database Tuning Advisor. Let's start with SQL Server Management Studio.

Creating Indexes with SQL Server Management Studio

Back in the heaps section of this chapter, you accessed data by performing a table scan on the HumanResources.EmployeePayHistory table of the AdventureWorks database. Now you're going to change that status by re-creating the index you deleted, using SQL Server Management Studio:

1. Open SQL Server Management Studio, and connect using Windows Authentication.
2. Expand your server in Object Explorer, and then choose Databases ➤ AdventureWorks ➤ Tables ➤ HumanResources.EmployeePayHistory.
3. Right-click Indexes, and select New Index.

4. Limber up your typing fingers, and, in the Index name box, enter **PK_EmployeePayHistory_EmployeeID_RateChangeDate**.
5. Select Clustered for the Index type.
6. Select the Unique check box.
7. Click the Add button next to the Index Key Columns grid.
8. Select the boxes next to the EmployeeID and RateChangeDate columns.

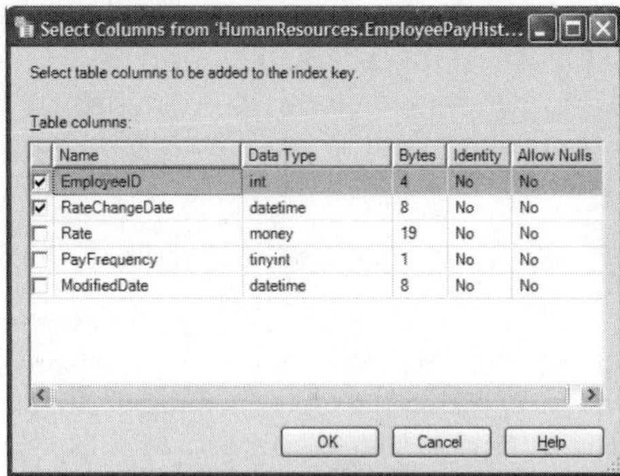

9. Click OK to return to the New Index dialog box.

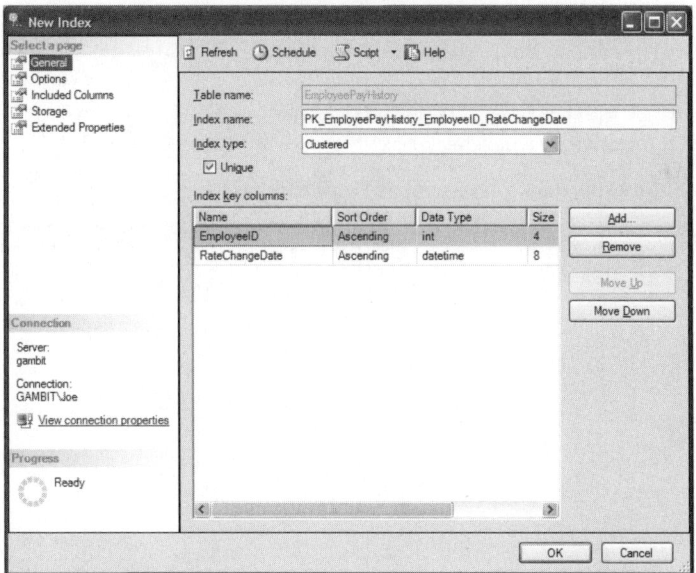

10. Select the Options Page.
11. Select the Set Fill Factor check box, and set the fill factor to 70%.
12. Click OK to create the index.

You can see how easy it is to create an index this way. If you want to make this a nonclustered index, all you need to do is leave the Create As Clustered box unchecked. Nothing to it—the hard part is deciding what to index, as we discussed earlier. As easy as this is, another method is even easier—automatic creation of indexes using the Database Tuning Advisor.

Creating Indexes with the Database Tuning Advisor

SQL Server 2005 comes with an extremely powerful tool called SQL Profiler, whose primary function is monitoring SQL Server. This provides an interesting fringe benefit when it comes to indexing. SQL Profiler specifically monitors everything that happens to the MSSQLServer service, which includes all of the `INSERT`, `UPDATE`, `DELETE`, and `SELECT` statements that are executed against your database. Because SQL Profiler can monitor what your users are doing, it would make sense that SQL Profiler can figure out what columns can be indexed to make these actions faster. Enter the Database Tuning Advisor.

NOTE We'll discuss SQL Profiler in more detail in Chapter 26, "Analysis Services."

When you use SQL Profiler, you generally save all the monitored events to a file on disk. This file is called a *workload*, without which the Database Tuning Advisor can't function. To create the workload, you need to run a *trace* (which is the process of monitoring) to capture standard user traffic throughout the busy part of the day. Here is how to use the Database Tuning Advisor:

1. Open SQL Profiler by choosing Start ➢ Programs ➢ Microsoft SQL Server 2005 and then selecting Profiler.
2. Choose File ➢ New Trace and connect to SQL Server. Once connected you will see the Trace Properties dialog box.
3. For the Trace Name, enter **Index Trace**.
4. Select the Save To File: check box.
5. In the Save As dialog box, enter **c:\index.trc** and click Save.

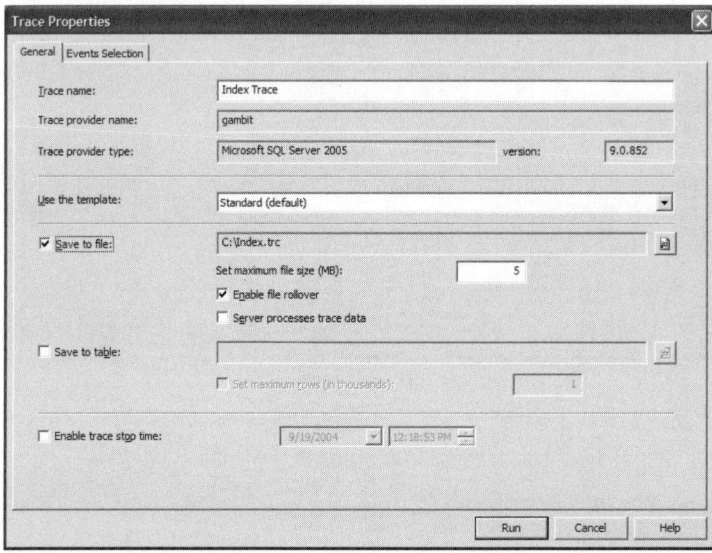

6. Click Run on the Trace Properties dialog box to start the trace.
7. Select Tools ➤ SQL Server Management Studio, and connect using Windows Authentication.
8. Click the New Query button on the toolbar, and select New SQL Server Query. Connect with Windows Authentication if requested.
9. Enter the following code in the query window:

```
USE AdventureWorks
SELECT * FROM HumanResources.Employee
```

10. Execute the query by clicking the !Execute button on the toolbar.
11. Delete the previous query, and enter and execute another query to generate a little more traffic:

```
USE AdventureWorks
SELECT * FROM Sales.SalesOrderHeader
```

12. Switch back to SQL Profiler, and stop the trace by clicking the red button just above the trace window. Notice that the queries you just executed are listed in the trace (there may be quite a bit of information from the system services as well as the SQLServerAgent).

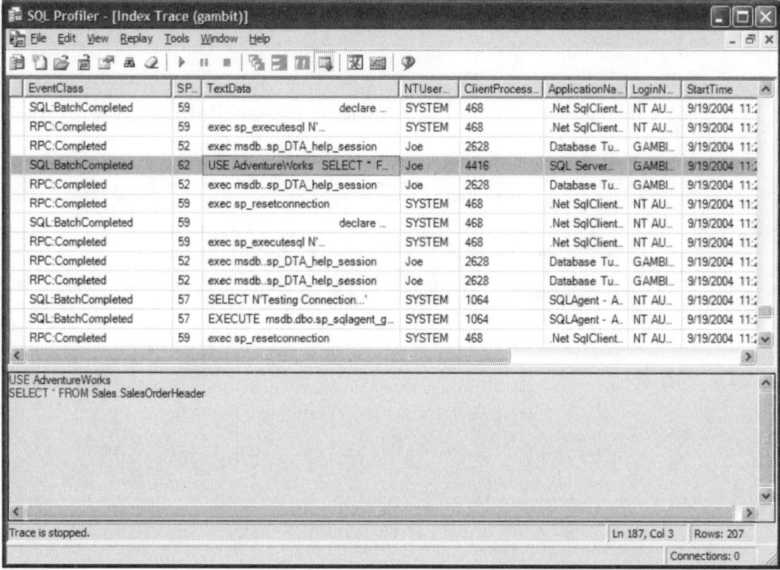

13. Open the Database Tuning Advisor from the Microsoft SQL Server 2005 program group on the Start Menu, and connect using Windows Authentication. A new session will be created for you.
14. In the right pane, make sure the Workload tab is selected, and enter **AdventureWorks Session** in the Session Name box. Notice that the session name in the Session Monitor on the left is changed for you as you type.

15. In the Workload section, leave the File radio button selected, and enter **C:\Index.trc** in the File text box.

16. In the Databases And Tables grid, check the box next to AdventureWorks.

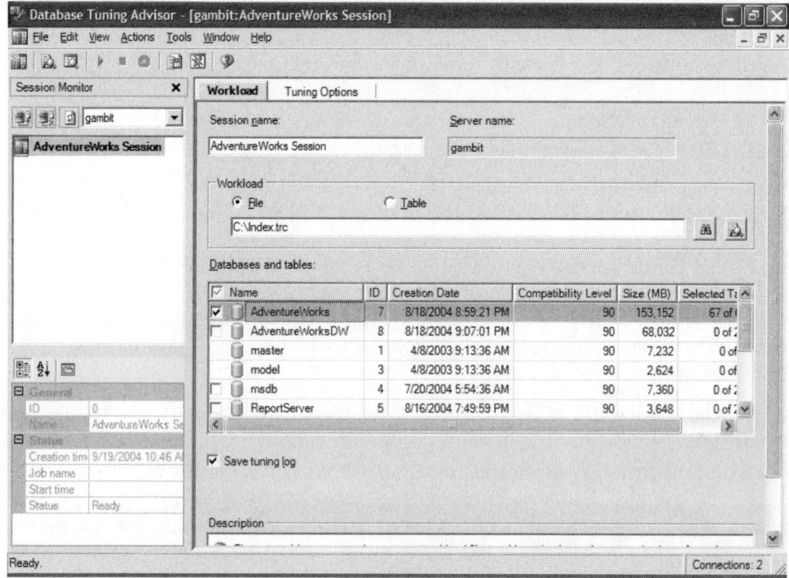

17. In the Selected Tables column, click the down arrow button to see all the tables that are selected.

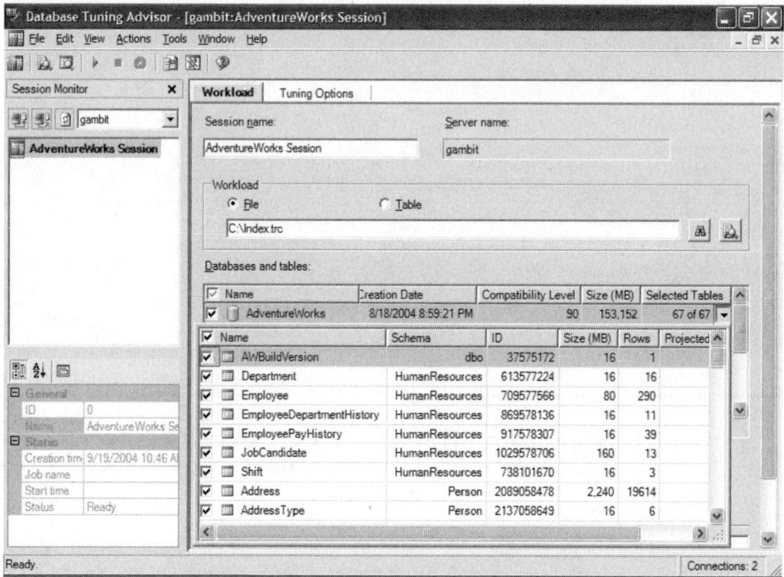

18. Switch to the Tuning Options tab, and note the default settings. Change the Partitioning Strategy To Employ to No Partitioning.

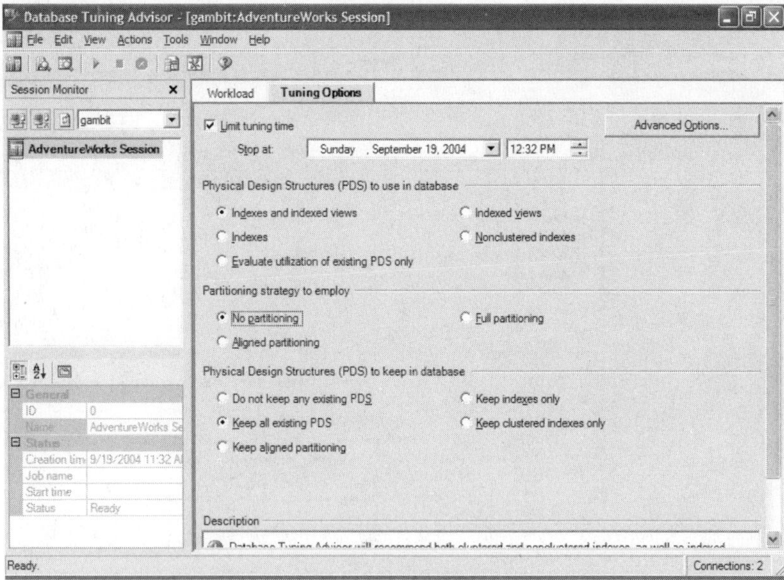

19. Click the Advanced Options button, and again, note (but don't change) the settings.

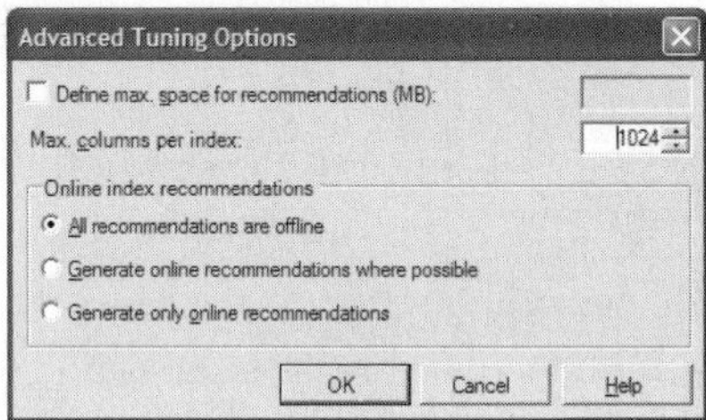

20. Click Cancel to return to the Tuning Options tab.

21. Switch back to the Workload tab.

22. Choose Actions ➤ Start Analysis, and click OK in the Start Analysis dialog box.

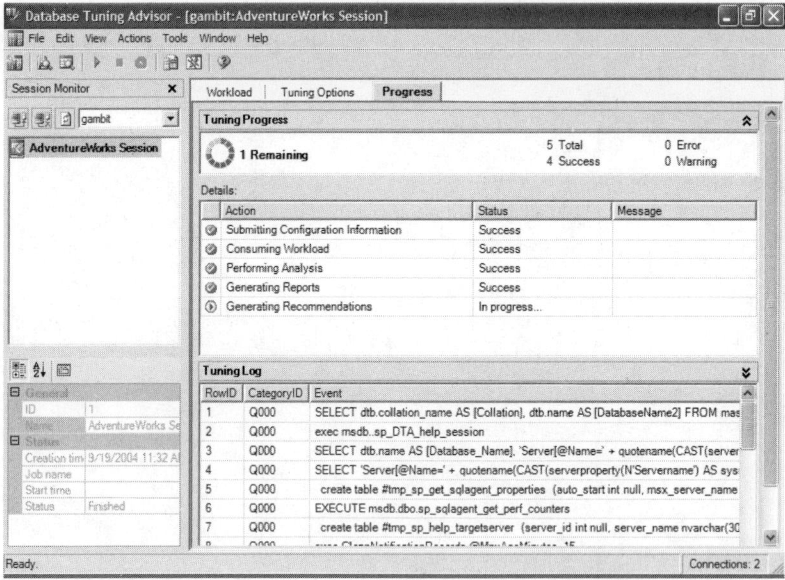

23. When the analysis is complete, you'll be given a list of recommendations (there are no valid recommendations here because the sample database is already tuned).

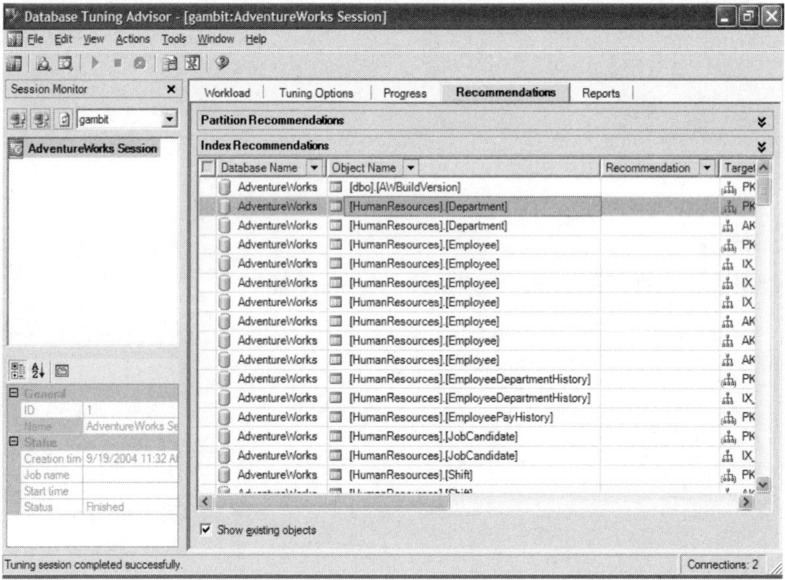

24. Switch to the Reports tab. Select a report from the Select Report drop-down list to see reports of tuning and database statistics.

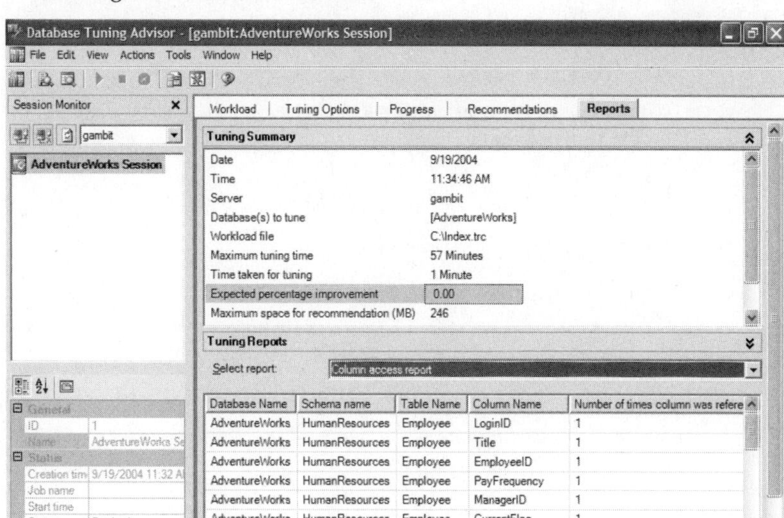

This method, although it may seem a bit time-consuming, can save you a great deal of effort. Because most of the work while creating an index involves deciding what columns to create the index on, you can save yourself the hassle by letting the Database Tuning Advisor decide for you. Of course, this method isn't foolproof, so always double-check it.

Once your indexes have been created, they should be maintained on a regular basis to make certain they're working properly. We'll discuss the process of maintaining indexes and databases in Chapter 16, "Basic Administrative Tasks."

Summary

The first thing you learned in this chapter was how SQL Server accesses and stores data when no index is in place. Without a clustered index, the table is called a heap, and the data is stored on a first-come, first-served basis. When accessing this data, SQL Server must perform a table scan, which means that SQL Server must read every record in the table to find the data you're seeking. This can make data access slow on larger tables; but on smaller tables that are about one extent in size, table scans can be faster than indexing.

Next you learned how to accelerate data access by using indexes. The first index we looked at was the clustered index. This type of index physically rearranges the data in the database file. This property makes the clustered index ideal for columns that are constantly being searched for ranges of data and that have low selectivity, meaning several duplicate values.

Next came nonclustered indexes. These indexes don't physically rearrange the data in the database but rather create pointers to the actual data. This type of index is best suited to high-selectivity tables (very few duplicate values) where single records are desired rather than ranges.

Finally, you learned two different methods of creating indexes. The first method is graphically, through SQL Server Management Studio. The second method is by employing the Database Tuning Advisor. This tool is designed to take the stress of planning the index off of you and place it on SQL Server.

With this newfound knowledge about indexing, you'll be able to speed up data access for your users. However, what if you don't want your users to see all the data in the tables? In the next chapter, we'll show you how to limit the data available to your users by using views.

Chapter 13

Views

It's an interesting challenge to describe views. Microsoft describes a view as either a virtual table or a stored SELECT query, but you might want to try thinking of it as being like a television set. When you watch television, you generally see people engaged in various activities. However, are any of these people actually *inside* your television set? Maybe when you were younger you thought so, but now you know that those people are many miles away in a studio. You're seeing people who aren't really there—you're viewing a representation of them.

Views work in much the same way. *Views* are used to represent the data that is stored in a table, just the way a television set is used to represent people who are in a studio. Of course, there are more advantages to a view than just looking at the data stored in a table; in fact, we'll explore three different ways to use views.

Some of your tables may become quite large, possibly containing thousands of records. Because you most likely don't need to see all that data at once, a view is perfect for returning a small subset of the data in the table.

Many times you'll find that your users want to view data from multiple tables. One method for getting the users the data they need is to create a view that displays data from multiple tables. Then your users can query the view just like a table.

Finally, we'll discuss what it takes to modify data by using a view. However, before we can get into the more advanced topics, you must learn how to create the simplest of views.

Using Views to Partition Tables

In the real world, many companies have extremely large tables that contain hundreds of thousands, if not millions, of records. When your users query such large tables, they usually don't want to see all these millions of records; they want to see only a small portion, or subset, of the available data. You have two ways to return a subset of data: You can use a SELECT query with the WHERE clause specified, or you can use a view.

The SELECT query approach works well for queries that are executed infrequently (called *ad hoc queries*), but this approach can be confusing for users who don't understand Transact-SQL code. For example, if you want to query the AdventureWorks database to see only the firstname, lastname, and phone fields for contacts in the 398 area code, you can execute the following query:

```
USE AdventureWorks
SELECT lastname, firstname, phone from person.contact
WHERE phone LIKE '398%'
```

NOTE For a complete explanation of the % symbol or any part of a SELECT query, refer to Chapter 6.

That query returns a small subset of the data; but how many of your end users understand the code required to get this information? Probably very few. You can therefore write the query into your front-end code, which is the display that your users see (usually in C# or a similar language); but then the query will be sent over the network to the server every time it's accessed, and that eats up network bandwidth. If your users execute this query frequently, you should create a view for them based on the query. Once that view is created, your users can query it just like they would query a table. The only difference between the view and the table is that your view doesn't contain any data—it simply shows the data (much like the television set doesn't contain any people—it just shows you pictures of the people in the studio).

To begin to understand the value of views, you'll create a simple view using the View Assisted Editor.

Creating a View with the View Assisted Editor

Assisted editor is a new term for an old concept, the wizard. Whereas most wizards are several screens in length, assisted editors are usually only one screen, so they can be much faster. In the next series of steps, you'll use the View Assisted Editor to generate a view that displays only those records in a database that have 398 as the first three characters of the phone number:

1. Open SQL Server Management Studio by selecting it from the SQL Server 2005 group under Programs on your Start menu, and connect with Windows Authentication if requested.
2. In Object Explorer, expand your server ➢ Databases ➢ AdventureWorks, and then right-click Views and select New View.
3. In the Add Table dialog box, select Contact (Person) and click Add.
4. Click Close, this brings up the View Assisted Editor.
5. In the Transact-SQL syntax editor text box, under the column grid, type the following:

```
SELECT LastName, FirstName, Phone
FROM Person.Contact
WHERE (Phone LIKE '398 %')
```

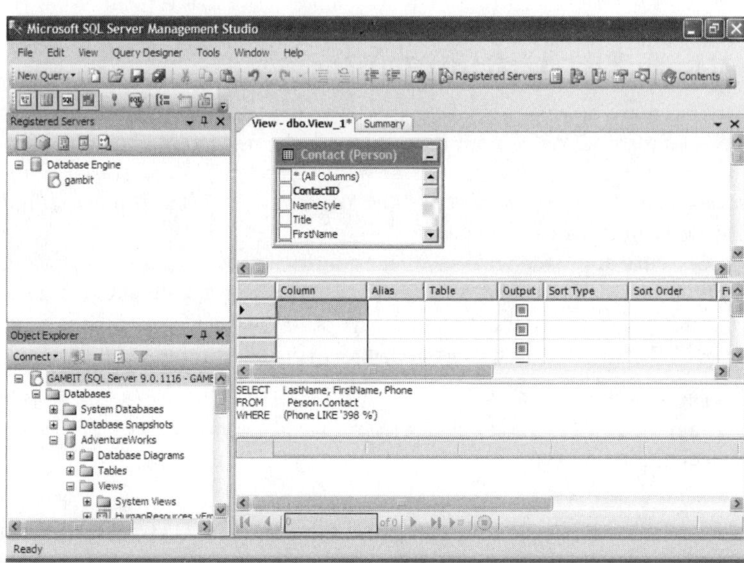

6. Choose File ➢ Save View - dbo.View_1.
7. In the Choose Name dialog box enter Contacts_in_398 and click OK.

Now you'll see a new view called Person.Contacts_in_398 under Views in the AdventureWorks database (you'll see a lot of other views, too—those were created long ago at Microsoft, and we'll get to them later in this chapter). You can test the view to see what it does by querying it just like you would query a table using a SELECT statement:

1. Click the New Query button, and select New SQL Server Query. Connect with Windows Authentication if requested.
2. To test the view, enter and execute the following code:

```
USE AdventureWorks
SELECT * FROM Person.Contacts_in_398
```

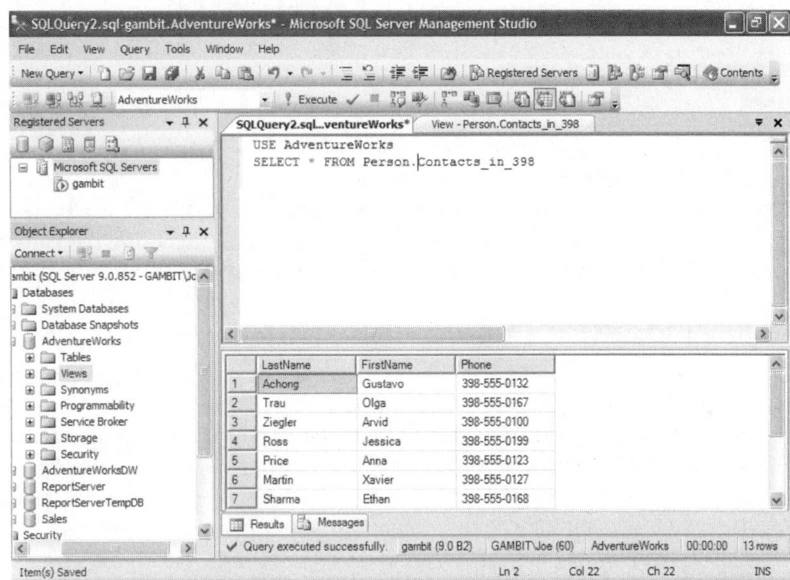

3. To verify that this is exactly the data the SELECT query would have returned, enter and execute the SELECT query on which the view is based:

```
USE AdventureWorks
SELECT lastname, firstname, phone from Person.Contact
WHERE phone LIKE '398%'
```

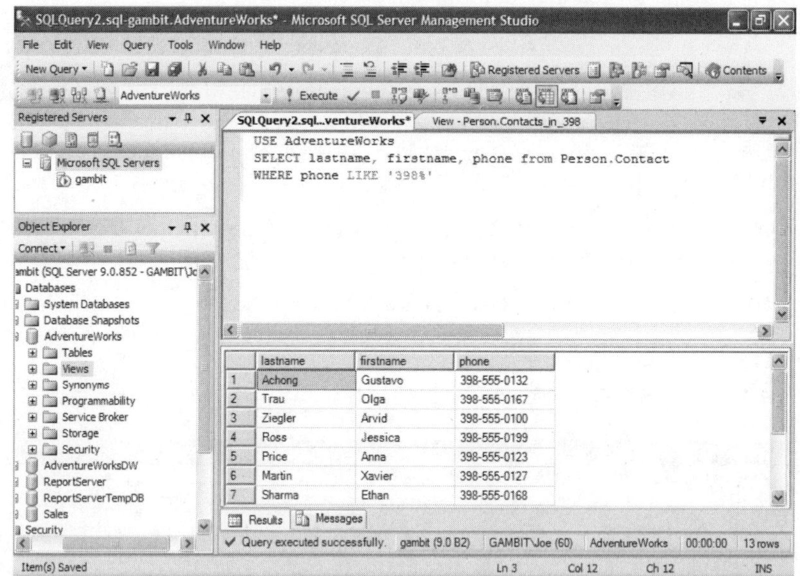

Notice that the view and the SELECT query returned exactly the same results—but which was easier to query? The view was far easier to query because it took less code. However, the requirements for your view may change over time, so you may need to modify the view to reflect those requirements. The next section looks at the process of modifying an existing view.

Modifying a View in the View Assisted Editor

Over time, the requirements for your view may change, or you may have accidentally created the view incorrectly in the assisted editor. Either way, you may need to modify an existing view to display the information you need. For example, suppose that in addition to the first name, last name, and phone number of your contacts, you need to see their title, which is stored in the title field in the Person.Contact table. You must modify the Person.Contacts_in_398 view to accommodate this new requirement by opening the view designer, which is the graphic method for modifying existing views, accessed through SQL Server Management Studio.

Here's how to make the change:

1. Open SQL Server Management Studio (if you're not already there), and expand your server ➤ Databases ➤ AdventureWorks ➤ Views.
2. Right-click the Person.Contacts_in_398 view, and select Modify View to enter the View Assisted Editor.
3. To add the title field to the view, modify the SELECT query so it looks like this:

```
SELECT title, lastname, firstname, phone from Person.Contact
WHERE phone LIKE '398%'
```

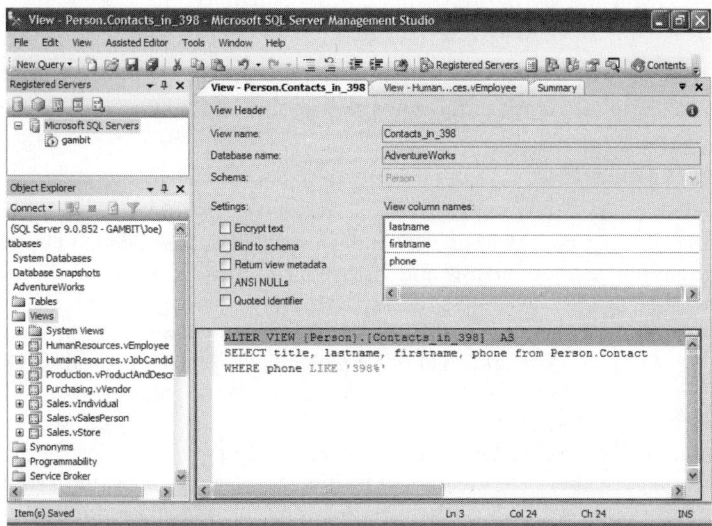

4. Click the Save button on the toolbar.
5. Close the View Assisted Editor by clicking the X button in the upper-right corner of the Assisted Editor.
6. Click the New Query button, and select New SQL Server Query. Connect with Windows Authentication if requested.
7. Enter and execute the following code to test the view:

```
USE AdventureWorks
SELECT * FROM Person.Contacts_in_398
```

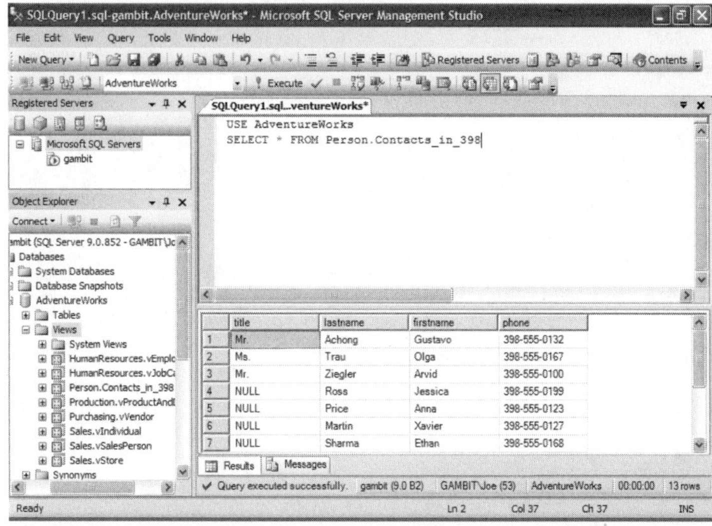

8. Notice that you now see the title field in addition to first name, last name, and phone. At this point, leave the New Query screen open.

Now you have a view that displays all the information you need, but it's a little difficult to read. Let's see how to use aliases to make the data easier to understand for your users.

Using Aliases in a View

As developers, we tend to make the field names that we use in our tables a bit cryptic—we understand them perfectly, but end users usually end up scratching their heads in bewilderment. An example of this might be the firstname and lastname columns in the Person.Contact table—your users are used to seeing these written as two separate words (*first name*, not *firstname*), so the format may throw them off. To make it easier for your users to tell what information is stored in a column just by glancing at it, you can create an alias for the column. An *alias* is used to display a different name for a column to your users, not to change the name of the column itself.

An alias is analogous to a nickname. For example, if your name is Joseph, people may commonly refer to you as Joe—this doesn't legally change your name but gives people an easier way to refer to you in conversation. An alias does the same thing for columns: It gives your users an easier way to refer to them in a result set. Let's see how to do this by creating aliases for the firstname and lastname columns in the Person.Contacts_in_398 view:

1. In Object Explorer, right-click the Person.Contacts_in_398 view in the AdventureWorks database, and select Modify View.

2. In the T-SQL syntax text box, change your SELECT query to look like this:

```
SELECT title as [Title], lastname as [Last Name], firstname as [First Name],
phone as [Phone Number] from Person.Contact
WHERE phone LIKE '398%'
```

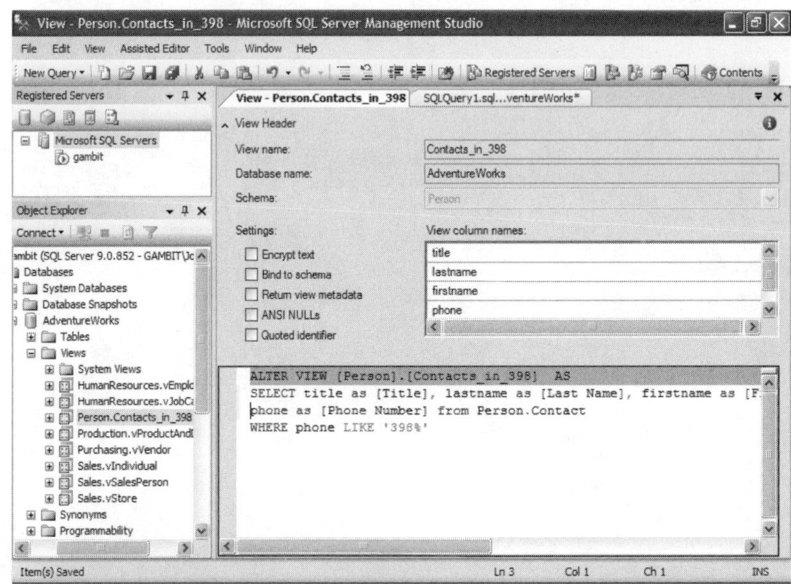

3. Click the Save button (the floppy-disk icon at the top left of the view designer on the toolbar), but don't exit the View Assisted Editor screen.

4. To test the view, switch back to New Query window, and enter and execute the following code:

```
USE AdventureWorks
SELECT * FROM Person.Contacts_in_398
```

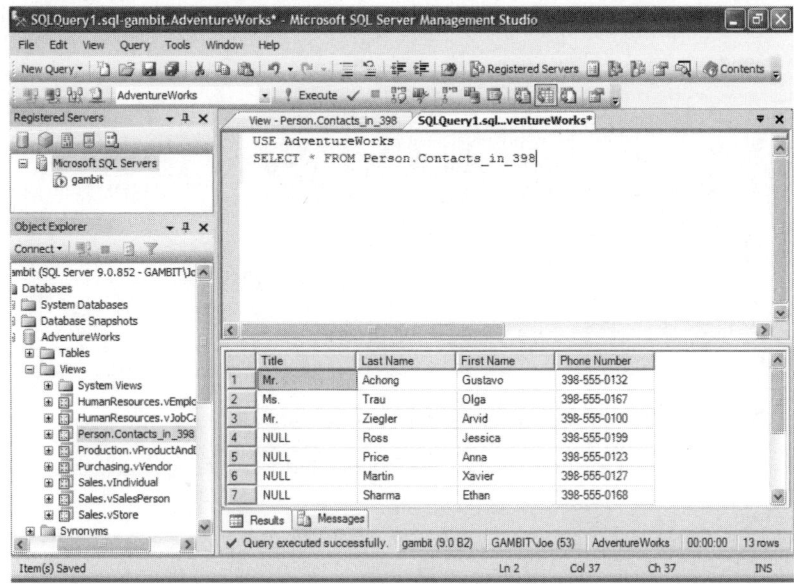

5. Notice that the column names are now a little easier to read. Leave the New Query window open.

Organizing the Result Set

You may have noticed that the result sets you've received from your view so far have had no organization; the records have been randomly displayed. That is because SQL Server stores records in the table on a first-come, first-served basis (unless you have a clustered index, as discussed in Chapter 12, "Indexing"). This makes the result set hard to read, so you need to organize the result set by adding an `ORDER BY` clause to one of the fields in the view. This clause will sort the results of the view in order of the field that has been chosen. In the following series of steps, you'll add some organization to Person.Contacts_in_398 by adding an `ORDER BY` clause to the lastname field:

1. Return to the View Assisted Editor in SQL Server Management Studio, which should still be open from the previous series of steps.

2. In the T-SQL syntax box, modify your code so it looks like this (notice the `TOP` clause):

```
SELECT TOP 100 PERCENT title as [Title], lastname as [Last Name], firstname as
[First Name],
phone as [Phone Number] from Person.Contact
WHERE phone LIKE '398%'
ORDER BY LastName
```

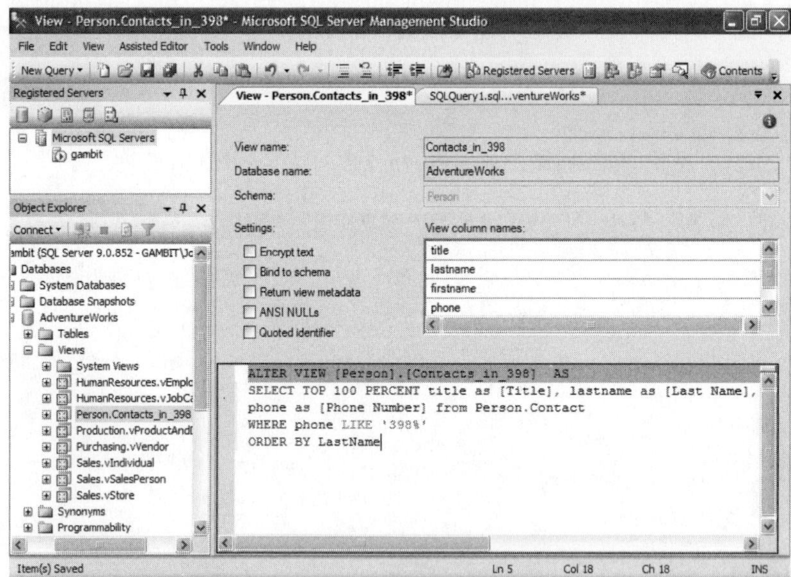

3. Click the Save button, and close the View Assisted Editor.

4. To test the changes, switch to the New Query window, and enter and execute the following code:

```
USE AdventureWorks
SELECT * from Person.Contacts_in_398
```

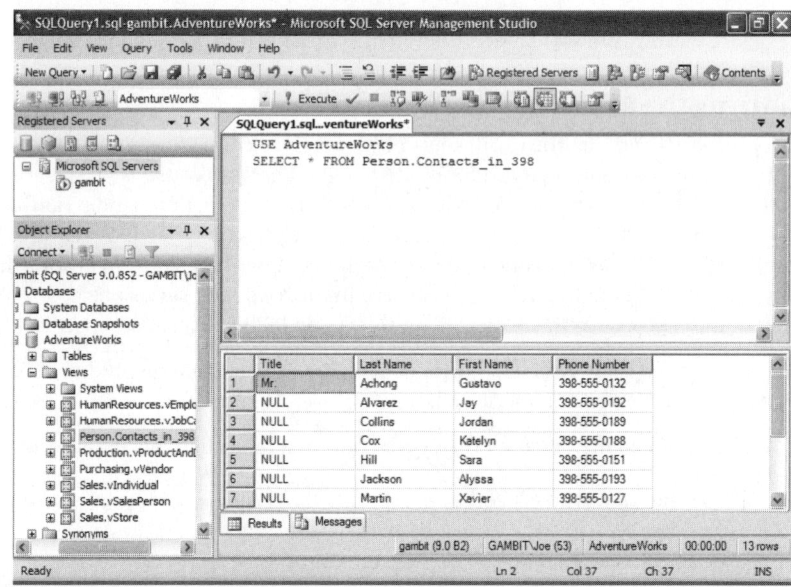

5. Notice that the results are now in order rather than randomly displayed.

Now you have a nice, orderly view of all the employees in the sales department. To get that same result set by using a standard SELECT query, your users would have to execute the following SELECT statement:

```
SELECT TOP 100 PERCENT title as [Title], lastname as [Last Name], firstname as
[First Name],
phone as [Phone Number] from Person.Contact
WHERE phone LIKE '398%'
ORDER BY LastName
```

You can see that views make it much easier to return a small subset of data for your users. Rather than writing the SELECT queries into the front-end code on your users' machines, you can create a view that can be queried much more easily with less code.

That isn't all views are good for, though. They can also come in handy for obtaining result sets based on multiple tables, as you'll see next.

Using Views to Join Tables

In Chapter 4, "Database Design and Normalization," you learned that all your data isn't stored in a single table, because that would make your tables unnecessarily large and hard to manage. To retrieve all the data you need in a result set, you may have to query more than one table at a time by using a SELECT query with a JOIN clause, as discussed in Chapter 6. For example, you could use the following query to see demographic information for all the contacts in the 398 area code, sorted by last name:

```
SELECT TOP 100 PERCENT title as [Title], lastname as [Last Name], firstname as
[First Name],
phone as [Phone Number], i.demographics as [Demographic XML Data] from
Person.Contact c
join Sales.Individual i on c.ContactID = i.ContactID
WHERE phone LIKE '398%'
ORDER BY LastName
```

This query joins the Person.Contact and Sales.Individual tables on a common column (ContactID) to display demographic information for each contact. Although this is a good query, it isn't feasible to store it in the front-end code on the client machines or even to have the users run it manually through SQLCMD because of the excess network bandwidth it would eat up (especially if this is a popular query). It would be far better to turn this into a view that JOINs the two tables.

NOTE The Demographics column in the Sales.Individual table is an xml type column, so the information is returned as XML.

*JOIN*ing Two Tables in a View

If you need to access the amount of product sold on a regular basis, an ad hoc query isn't the way to go because it will generate a great deal of excess network traffic that can otherwise be avoided. By creating a view, you can save that bandwidth and make data retrieval easier for your users. In this series of steps, you'll modify the Person.Contacts_in_398 view to display the demographic information for all contacts in the 398 are code by JOINing the Person.Contact and Sales.Individual tables on the ContactID column they hold in common:

1. Open SQL Server Management Studio, and connect using Windows Authentication if requested.
2. In Object Explorer, expand your server ➤ Databases ➤ AdventureWorks ➤ Views.
3. Right-click Person.Contacts_in_398, and select Modify View to bring up the View Assisted Editor.
4. Modify the code in the T-SQL syntax box so it looks like this:

```
SELECT TOP 100 PERCENT title as [Title], lastname as [Last Name], firstname as
[First Name],
phone as [Phone Number], i.demographics as [Demographic XML Data] from
Person.Contact c
join Sales.Individual i on c.ContactID = i.ContactID
WHERE phone LIKE '398%'
ORDER BY LastName
```

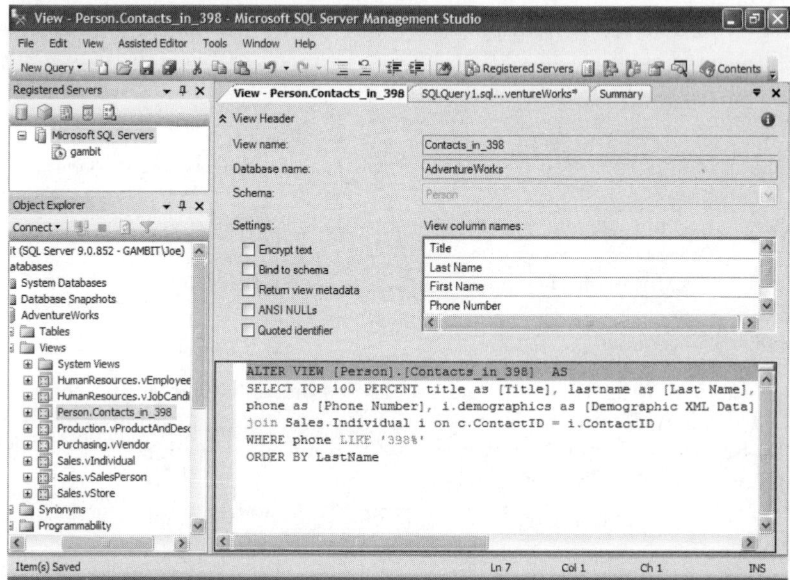

5. Click the Save button on the toolbar.
6. To test the view, open a new SQL Server query, and execute the following code:

```
USE AdventureWorks
SELECT * from Person.Contacts_in_398
```

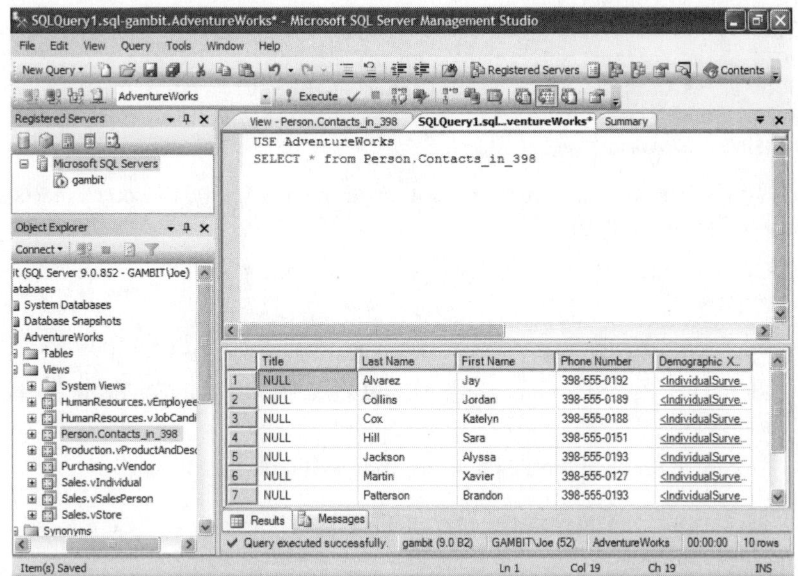

When you compare the SELECT statement from step 4 with the SELECT statement from step 6, you can really see how much better it can be to use a view in place of an ad hoc query. If you wrote the SELECT statement from step 4 in your front-end code (meaning that it's stored on the users' machines), all the lines of that query would need to be sent over the network to the server every time the query is run. Because you turned that query into a view, the only code that traverses the network from the clients to the server is the two lines of code found in step 6. Using views can make data retrieval easier for your users and save network traffic.

Suppose, though, that you need to see what credit card these contacts used to purchase from you in the past. You'll need to make some change to the view by adding another table.

*JOIN*ing Multiple Tables in a View

The data that you need to retrieve from a relational database, such as AdventureWorks, usually isn't contained in a single table. In fact, you quite often need to retrieve data from two, three, or even more tables at a time to have the result set make sense. In the previous section, you added demographic information to the Person.Contacts_in_398 view. Now you need to see what credit cards each of these contacts has used in the past. To display that information, you must add two more tables to the view: Sales.ContactCreditCard and Sales.CreditCard.

You need to add these two tables because of the way they're related to one another. Sales.CreditCard contains information about all the credit cards used on the system, including the credit card name. The Sales.ContactCreditCard table contains three columns: ContactID, CreditCardID, and ModifiedDate. So, to get the name of the credit card used by a contact, you must `JOIN` the Person.Contact table to the Sales.ContactCreditCard table on the ContactID column and then `JOIN` the Sales.ContactCreditCard table to the Sales.CreditCard table on the CreditCardID column:

```
SELECT TOP 100 PERCENT title as [Title], lastname as [Last Name], firstname as
[First Name],
phone as [Phone Number], i.demographics as [Demographic XML Data] , c3.cardtype
as [Card Type]
```

```
FROM Person.Contact c
JOIN Sales.Individual i on c.ContactID = i.ContactID
JOIN Sales.ContactCreditCard c2 on c.ContactID = c2.ContactID
JOIN Sales.CreditCard c3 on c2.CreditCardID = c3.CreditCardID
WHERE phone LIKE '398%'
ORDER BY LastName
```

With the technical details out of the way, you can modify the Person.Contacts_in_398 view to display credit card data:

1. Open SQL Server Management Studio, and connect using Windows Authentication if requested.
2. In Object Explorer, expand your server ➤ Databases ➤ AdventureWorks ➤ Views.
3. Right-click Person.Contacts_in_398, and select Modify View to bring up the View Assisted Editor.
4. Modify the code in the T-SQL syntax box so it looks like this:

```
SELECT TOP 100 PERCENT title as [Title], lastname as [Last Name], firstname as
[First Name],
phone as [Phone Number], i.demographics as [Demographic XML Data] ,
c3.cardtype as [Card Type]
FROM Person.Contact c
JOIN Sales.Individual i on c.ContactID = i.ContactID
JOIN Sales.ContactCreditCard c2 on c.ContactID = c2.ContactID
JOIN Sales.CreditCard c3 on c2.CreditCardID = c3.CreditCardID
WHERE phone LIKE '398%'
ORDER BY LastName
```

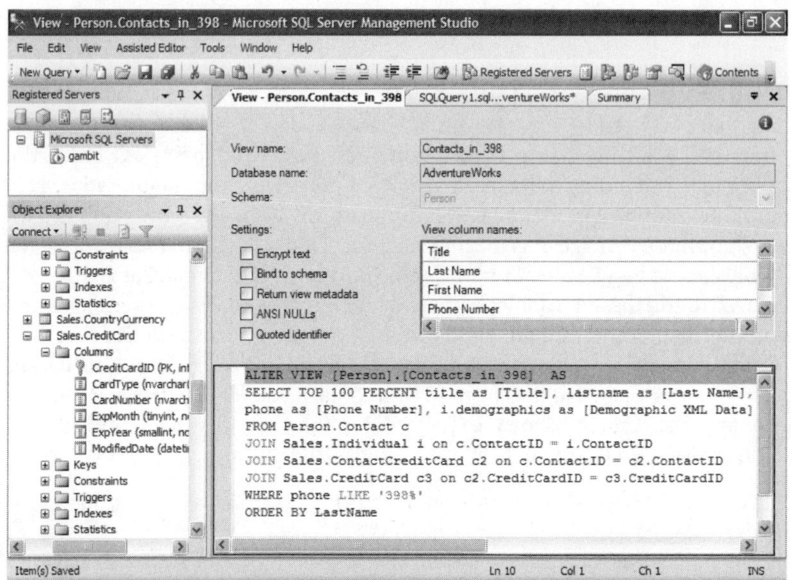

5. Click the Save button on the toolbar.
6. To test the view, open a new SQL Server query, and execute the following code:

```
USE AdventureWorks
SELECT * from Person.Contacts_in_398
```

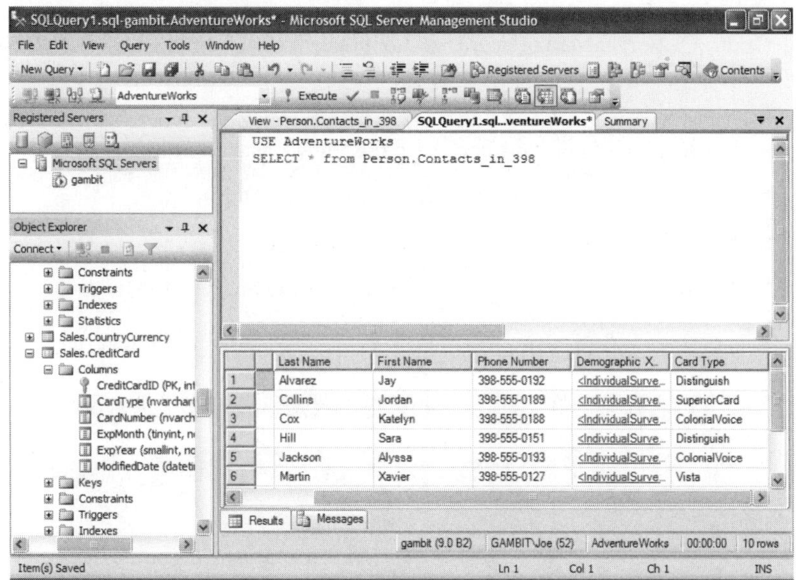

You can see the power and flexibility that a view can give you—but there is even more. Views can be used to enforce security on your data, as well.

Modifying Data through a View

Not only can you use views to retrieve data, but you can also modify data through them—inserting, updating, and deleting records. If you decide to use views to make changes to your data, there are a few points to keep in mind:

- If you use a view to modify data, the modification can affect only one base table at a time. This means that if a view presents data from two tables, you can only write a statement that will update one of those tables—if your statement tries to update both tables, you'll get an error message.
- You can't modify data in a view that uses aggregate functions. *Aggregates* are functions that return a summary value of some kind, such as `SUM()` or `AVG()`. If you try to modify such a view, you'll get an error.
- You saw earlier that views don't necessarily present all the fields in a table; you may see only a few. If you try to insert a record into a view that doesn't show all fields, you could run into a problem. Some of the fields that aren't shown in the view may not accept null values, but you can't insert a value into those fields if they aren't represented in the view. Because you can't insert values in those fields and they don't allow null values, your insert will fail. You can still use such a view for `UPDATE`s and `DELETE`s, though.

NOTE To overcome these limitations, you need to use `INSTEAD OF` triggers, which are discussed in Chapter 15 "Using Triggers."

To modify data through a view, you need to create a view that will allow you to modify data. You don't have one yet, because the view you've been working on thus far doesn't contain enough columns from any of its base tables to allow modifications; so, you need to create a simpler view. Let's begin:

1. Open SQL Server Management Studio by selecting it from the SQL Server 2005 group under Programs on your Start menu, and connect with Windows Authentication if requested.
2. In Object Explorer, expand your server ➤ Databases ➤ AdventureWorks, right-click Views, and select New View. This brings up the View Assisted Editor.
3. In the View Name box, enter **Update_Product_Location**.
4. Select Production from the Schema drop-down list.
5. In the Transact-SQL syntax editor text box, under AS, type the following:

```
SELECT Name, CostRate, Availability from Production.Location
```

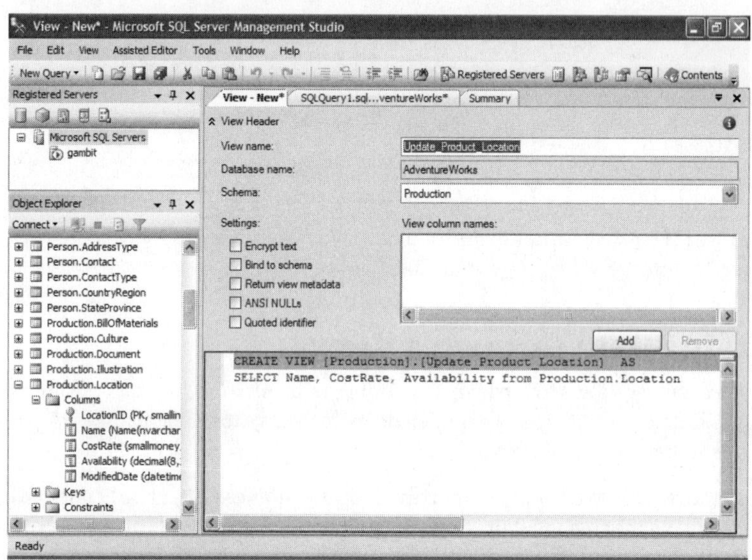

6. Choose File ➤ Save View - New.

Now that you have a view to work with, you can test it to make sure it's exactly what you need; then you can update data with it. Here's how:

1. Open a new SQL Server Query by clicking the New Query button.
2. Enter and execute the following code to test the view:

```
USE AdventureWorks
SELECT * from Production.Update_Product_Location
```

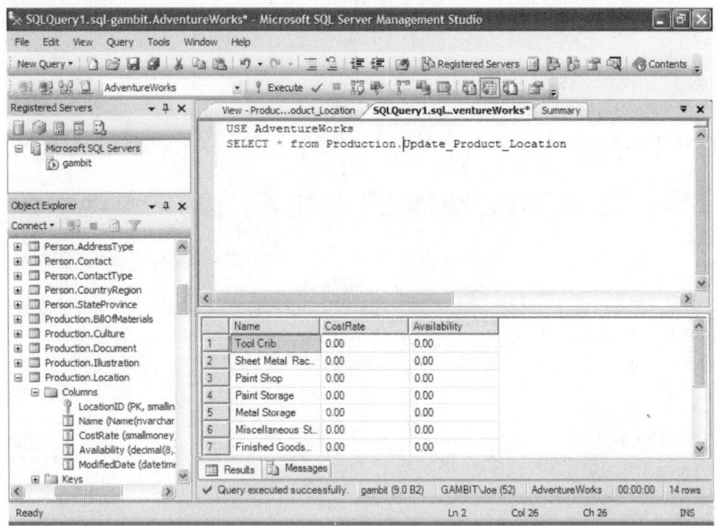

3. Now that you're sure the view is working the way you want, you'll create a new record. Open a new SQL Server query, and then enter and execute the following code:

```
USE AdventureWorks
INSERT Production.Update_Product_Location
VALUES ('Update Test Tool',55.00,10)
```

4. To verify that the record was inserted and that you can see it in the view, execute the following code in the query window:

```
USE AdventureWorks
Select * from Production.Update_Product_Location
where Name = 'Update Test Tool'
```

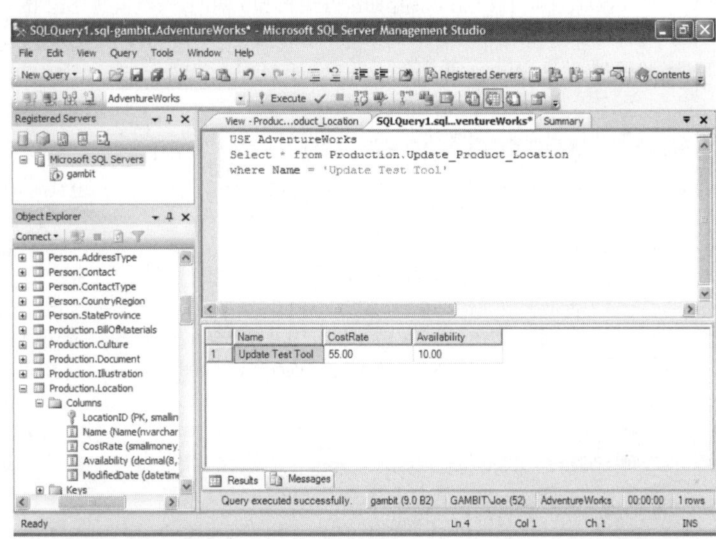

5. To view the data as it was inserted into the base table, enter and execute the following code in the query window:

```
USE AdventureWorks
SELECT * FROM Production.Location
WHERE Name = 'Update Test Tool'
```

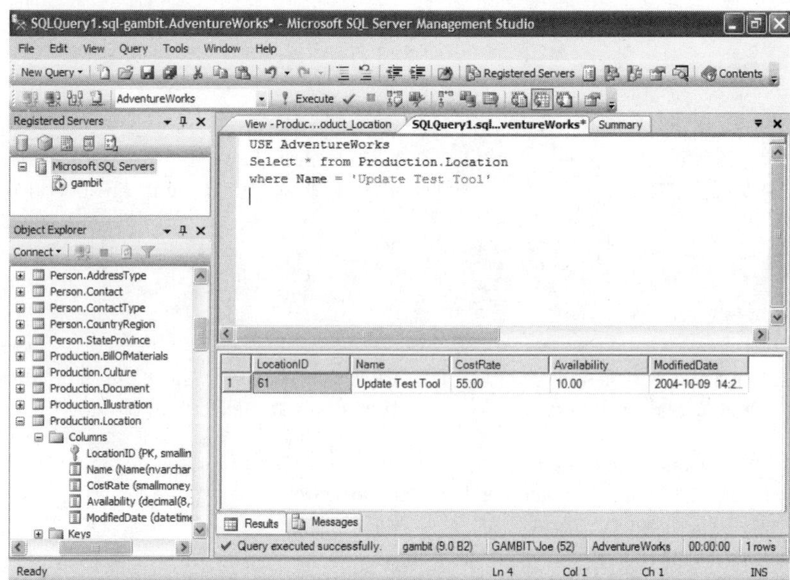

When you look at the result set from the Production.Update_Product_Location view, you should see only three columns, all filled in. When you look at the base table, though, you'll see five columns, all filled in. When you modified the view, you only inserted values for the three columns that were available—SQL Server populated the remaining two columns in the base table because they have default constraints applied, as discussed in Chapter 11, "Tables."

The views you've created so far have returned fairly simple result sets; but in the real world, your views will be more complex and will require a lot of resources to return a result set. To optimize this process, you may want to consider using indexed views.

Working with Indexed Views

The views you've created thus far in this chapter have returned simple result sets that haven't been taxing on system resources. In reality, you'll use queries that require a lot of calculating and data manipulation; such complex queries can tax your system resources and thus slow your system. One way around this bottleneck is to use indexed views.

As we discussed in Chapter 12, an *index* is a list of all the values in a specific column of one of your tables that SQL Server can reference to speed up data access. One type of index is called a *clustered index*; it physically rearranges the data in a table so that the data conforms to the parameters of the index. A clustered index works a great deal like a dictionary, which physically arranges words so that you can skip right to them. To make data access faster on a complex view, you can create a clustered index on the view.

When you create a clustered index on a view, the result set returned by the view is stored in the database the same way a table with a clustered index is stored, meaning that the result set of the view is stored as an entirely separate object in the database and doesn't have to be regenerated (or materialized) every time someone runs a SELECT query against it. However, don't jump in and start creating clustered indexes on all your views just yet; there are a few considerations to discuss first.

NOTE For a complete discussion of indexes, please look into Chapter 12.

Considerations

There are definite benefits to using indexes on complex views, the first being performance. Every time a view is queried, SQL Server must materialize the view. *Materialization* is the process of performing all the JOINs and calculations necessary to return a result set to the user. If the view is complex (requires a large number of calculations and JOINs), indexing it can speed up access because the result set will never need to be materialized—it will exist in the database as a separate object, and SQL Server can call it up whenever it's queried.

Another advantage to indexing a view is the way the query optimizer treats indexed views. The *query optimizer* is the component in SQL Server that analyzes your queries, compares them with available indexes, and decides which index will return a result set the fastest. Once you've indexed a view, the query optimizer considers this view in all future queries no matter what you're querying. This means that queries on other tables may benefit from the index you create on the view.

The bad part about indexing a view is the overhead it incurs on the system. First, indexed views take up disk space because they're stored as separate objects in the database that look just like tables with a clustered index. Because clustered indexes store the actual data rather than just a pointer to the data in the base tables, they require extra disk space. For example, if you create a view that displays the firstname, lastname, and extension columns from the employees table and subsequently place a clustered index on that view, the firstname, lastname, and extension columns will be duplicated in the database.

Another consideration is the way the indexed view is updated. When you first create an indexed view, it's based on the data that exists at the time of the indexing. When you update the tables the view is based on, though, the indexed view is immediately updated to reflect the changes to the base table. This means that if you create an indexed view on a table and then make changes to the records in that table, SQL Server will automatically update the view at the same time. So if you have an indexed view on a table, the modifications are doubled and so is the system overhead.

If you decide that your database would benefit from an indexed view, the tables and view itself must adhere to a few restrictions:

- The ANSI_NULLS and QUOTED_IDENTIFIER options must be turned on when the view is created. To do this, use the sp_dboption stored procedure:

```
Sp_dboption 'ANSI_NULLS', TRUE
Sp_dboption 'QUOTED_IDENTIFIER', TRUE
```

- The ANSI_NULLS option must have been turned on during the creation of all the tables that are referenced by the view.
- The view can't reference other views, only tables.
- Any user-defined function's data access property must be NO SQL and external access property must be NO.

- All the tables referenced by the view must be in the same database as the view and must have the same owner as the view.
- The view must be created with the SCHEMABINDING option. This option prohibits the schema of the base tables from being changed (adding or dropping a column, for instance). If the tables can be changed, the indexed view may be rendered useless. To change the tables, you must first drop the indexed view.
- Any user-defined functions referenced in the view must have been created with the SCHEMABINDING option as well.
- All objects in the view must be referenced by their two-part names: *owner.object*. No one-, three-, or four-part names are allowed.
- There are two types of functions in SQL Server: *Deterministic* functions return the same value each time they're invoked with the same arguments. *Nondeterministic* functions return different values when they're invoked with the same arguments. DATEADD, for example, returns the same result each time you execute it with the same arguments. GETDATE, however, returns a different value each time you execute it with the same arguments, making it nondeterministic. Any functions referenced in an indexed view must be deterministic.
- The SELECT statement that is used to create the view must follow these restrictions:
  - Column names must be explicitly stated in the SELECT statement; you can't use * or *tablename*.* to access columns.
  - You may not reference a column twice in the SELECT statement unless all or all but one reference to the column is made in a complex expression. For example, the following is illegal:

    ```
    SELECT qty, orderid, qty
    ```

    However, the following is legal:

    ```
    SELECT qty, orderid, SUM(qty)
    ```

  - You may not use a derived table that comes from using a SELECT statement encased in parentheses in the FROM clause of a SELECT statement.
  - You can't use ROWSET, UNION, TOP, ORDER BY, DISTINCT, COUNT(*), COMPUTE, or COMPUTE BY.
  - Subqueries and outer or self JOINs can't be used.
  - The AVG, MAX, MIN, STDEV, STDEVP, VAR, and VARP aggregate functions aren't allowed in the SELECT statement. If you need the functionality they provide, consider replacing them with either SUM() or COUNT_BIG().
  - A SUM() that references a nullable expression isn't allowed.
  - A CLS user-defined aggregate function.
  - CONTAINS and FREETEXT aren't allowed in the SELECT statement.

- If you don't have a GROUP BY clause in your SELECT statement, you can't use any aggregate function. For a better understanding of GROUP BY, see Chapter 6.
- If you use GROUP BY, you can't use HAVING, ROLLUP, or CUBE, and you must use COUNT_BIG() in the select list.

TIP All the aggregate and string functions in SQL Server 2005 are considered deterministic.

That is an abundance of restrictions, but each one is necessary to keep the indexed view functioning. With all the considerations out of the way, let's see how to create indexed views.

Creating Indexed Views

In Chapter 12, we told you that the mechanics of creating indexes on tables and creating indexes on views are no different. To prove that a complex view runs faster when it's indexed, though, you must first see how fast it runs without an index in place. In this series of steps, you'll create a complex view similar to Person.Contacts_in_398 and note how much system resource it takes to run:

1. Open SQL Server Management Studio, and connect using Windows Authentication if requested.
2. Click the New Query button, and select New SQL Server Query. Connect using Windows Authentication if requested.
3. Create a view similar to Person.Contacts_in_398 but without the XML column and ORDER BY and TOP clauses. Add the ContactID field and SCHEMABINDING so that the view can be indexed on the ContactID field, which is unique. To do all this, enter and execute the following code:

```
SET QUOTED_IDENTIFIER ON
go
CREATE VIEW [Person].[Indexed_Contacts_in_398] WITH SCHEMABINDING
AS
SELECT c.ContactID, title as [Title], lastname as [Last Name], firstname as
[First Name],
phone as [Phone Number], c3.cardtype as [Card Type]
FROM Person.Contact c
JOIN Sales.ContactCreditCard c2 on c.ContactID = c2.ContactID
JOIN Sales.CreditCard c3 on c2.CreditCardID = c3.CreditCardID
WHERE phone LIKE '398%'
```

4. To test the Person.Indexed_Contacts_in_398 view and see how much IO (input/output resources) it consumes on the system, enter and execute the following query:

```
USE [AdventureWorks]
SET STATISTICS IO ON
SELECT * FROM  Person.Indexed_Contacts_in_398
```

5. When you click the Messages tab at the bottom of the screen, you should see something similar to the following (logical reads tells you how many pages were read from memory):

```
(12 row(s) affected)
Table 'CreditCard'. Scan count 0, logical reads 20, physical reads 0, read-ahead
reads 0, lob logical reads 0, lob physical reads 0, lob read-ahead reads 0.
Table 'ContactCreditCard'. Scan count 10, logical reads 20, physical reads 0,
read-ahead reads 0, lob logical reads 0, lob physical reads 0, lob read-ahead
reads 0.
Table 'Worktable'. Scan count 0, logical reads 0, physical reads 0, read-ahead
reads 0, lob logical reads 0, lob physical reads 0, lob read-ahead reads 0.
Table 'Contact'. Scan count 1, logical reads 558, physical reads 0, read-ahead
reads 0, lob logical reads 0, lob physical reads 0, lob read-ahead reads 0.
```

Now you're ready to create an index on the Person.Indexed_Contacts_in_398 view. Let's create an index on the ContactID column, because it's unique:

1. Choose Query ➤ New Query With Current Connection to open a new query.
2. Enter and execute the following code to create the index:

```
USE [AdventureWorks]
CREATE UNIQUE CLUSTERED INDEX
Cl_Indexed_View on Person.Indexed_Contacts_in_398(ContactID)
```

3. To test the indexed view, you'll execute the same code you used to test the original view in step 4 of the last series of steps:

```
USE [AdventureWorks]
SET STATISTICS IO ON
SELECT * FROM Person.Indexed_Contacts_in_398
```

4. You should see the following results in the Messages tab of the query window:

```
(12 row(s) affected)
Table 'Indexed_Contacts_in_398'. Scan count 1, logical reads 3, physical reads
0, read-ahead reads 0, lob logical reads 0, lob physical reads 0, lob read-
ahead reads 0.
```

Notice that the results you saw after the index was created are the same as the results from before the index was created. This is the case because this query isn't too complex and therefore doesn't benefit from having an index created. However, it does give a simple method for demonstrating the mechanics of creating a clustered index on a view. In the real world, this process will be much more complex, so weigh the benefits carefully before implementing this solution.

One small problem you may have noticed with the queries so far is that they return a static result set. For example, the last view returned only the customers who have a phone number in the 398 area code. Under this paradigm, you would need to create a separate view for every area code on Earth. It's a good thing you have inline functions to help out with parameters.

Enhancing Indexed Views with Inline User-Defined Functions

User-defined functions work a great deal like views in that they return a result set; the beauty of *inline user-defined functions* is that they accept parameters, whereas views (indexed or not) don't. A good example of when you might want to use parameters is the view you created in the previous section, which returned all the customers in the 398 area code. If you wanted to see specific area codes in your view, you could create a separate view for each area code. There's a better way: Create an inline function.

In this next series of steps, you'll create an inline function that can show you the customers in your customers table who live in any country:

1. Open a new SQL Server query in SQL Server Management Studio. Enter and execute the following code to create a user-defined inline function that displays customers from any country:

```
USE AdventureWorks
GO
CREATE FUNCTION fn_Contact_Area (@Area char(3))
RETURNS TABLE
AS
RETURN (
   SELECT title as [Title], lastname as [Last Name], firstname as [First
Name],
   phone as [Phone Number], i.demographics as [Demographic XML Data] ,
c3.cardtype as [Card Type]
   FROM Person.Contact c
   JOIN Sales.Individual i on c.ContactID = i.ContactID
   JOIN Sales.ContactCreditCard c2 on c.ContactID = c2.ContactID
   JOIN Sales.CreditCard c3 on c2.CreditCardID = c3.CreditCardID
   WHERE phone LIKE @Area + '%'
      )
```

2. To test the function, click the New Query button, and enter and execute the following query:

```
USE AdventureWorks
SELECT * from fn_Contact_Area('208')
```

Notice that with the user-defined inline function, you can select whatever area code you want by passing the function a parameter (in this case, `'208'`). Inline user-defined functions should prove to be a very useful tool.

Now that you can create various types of views and use them to manage your user data, you're ready for a slightly more advanced topic to aid you in managing system data: using distributed partitioned views.

Using Distributed Partitioned Views

Another useful tool in SQL Server 2005 is the distributed partitioned view. *Distributed partitioned views* make tables on multiple servers look like one table. This feature is valuable when you have massive tables in your databases and need the processing power of multiple servers to make the databases function efficiently.

A normal view is made up of one or more tables in a single database on a single server. When these tables become extremely large (depending on your hardware), you can partition them by splitting them up and assigning them to multiple servers. The tables are then referred to as *member tables*, and the databases that contain them are called *member databases*. All the servers that participate are called a *federation* of servers. This situation looks a lot like Figure 13.1.

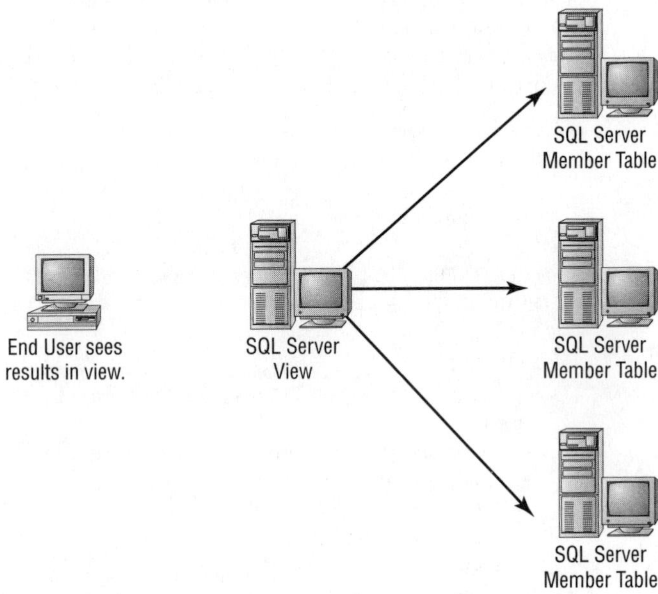

FIGURE 13.1
Distributed partitioned views are useful for extremely large tables that need to scale.

TIP You may have used local partitioned views in previous versions of SQL Server, but these are included only for backward compatibility.

Another tool that you can use to make working with SQL Server easier is the information schema view.

Using Information Schema Views

Suppose that you need to know the names of all the tables in your database for an application you're working on. You have two methods to get this information using Transact-SQL code. The first is to use system stored procedures, specifically `sp_tables`. This method doesn't always produce an accurate result, though, because you're looking only for table names; and `sp_tables` returns anything that can be used in a SELECT statement, including views.

NOTE We'll discuss stored procedures in Chapter 14. They're used to store queries on the server so the queries don't need to be stored on the client machines.

To get a more accurate result, you can query the *information schema* views. These are special views that Microsoft has implemented to comply with the American National Standards Institutes (ANSI) SQL-92 standard for SQL Server database servers and to make it easier for you to read system information. Here is a list of all the available information schema views in each and every database:

CHECK_CONSTRAINTS This gives a list of each check constraint owner by the current database user as well as the exact syntax of the constraint. It's based on the sysobjects and syscomments system tables.

COLUMN_DOMAIN_USAGE This view lists all the columns in the database that have a user-defined datatype. It's based on the sysobjects, syscolumns, and systypes system tables.

COLUMN_PRIVILEGES This tells you what columns in what tables the current user has been granted permissions on and what permissions have been granted. It's based on the sysprotects, sysobjects, and syscolumns system tables.

COLUMNS This view gives extensive detail about each column that is accessible to the current user in the database. It's based on the sp_datatype_info (from master), systypes, syscolumns, syscomments, sysconfigures, and syscharsets system tables.

CONSTRAINT_COLUMN_USAGE This returns each column owned by the current database user that has a constraint defined on it. It's based on the sysobjects, syscolumns, and systypes system tables.

CONSTRAINT_TABLE_USAGE Using this view returns a list of all tables in the database that have constraints applied. It's based on the sysobjects system table and isn't as detailed as the `TABLE_CONSTRAINTS` view.

DOMAIN_CONSTRAINTS This returns all the user-defined datatypes that are accessible to the current user in the database that have a rule bound to them. It's based on the sysobjects and systypes system tables.

DOMAINS This returns all the user-defined datatypes in the database that are accessible by the current user. It's based on the spt_datatype_info (from the master database), systypes, syscomments, sysconfigures, and syscharsets system tables.

KEY_COLUMN_USAGE Use this view to display each column in the database that is defined as a primary, foreign, or unique key. It's based on the spt_values (from master), sysobjects, syscolumns, sysreferences, and sysindexes system tables.

PARAMETERS This view returns information about parameters used in user-defined functions or stored procedures that are accessible to the current user. For functions, this view also displays information about return values.

REFERENTIAL_CONSTRAINTS This returns all the foreign-key constraints in the database. It's based on the sysreferences, sysindexes, and sysobjects system tables.

ROUTINE_COLUMNS Use this view to retrieve information about columns returned by table-valued functions.

ROUTINES This returns information about the functions and stored procedures accessible to the current user.

SCHEMATA This returns all the databases in which the current user has permissions. It's based on the sysdatabases, sysconfigures, and syscharsets system tables.

TABLE_CONSTRAINTS This returns a row for each table in the current database that has a constraint defined on it. It's based on the sysobjects system table and contains more detail than the `CONSTRAINT_TABLE_USAGE` view.

TABLE_PRIVILEGES This has one row for each table privilege that has been granted to or by the current user. It's based on the sysprotects and sysobjects system tables.

TABLES This returns one row for each table in the database on which the current user has permissions. It's based on the sysobjects system table.

VIEW_COLUMN_USAGE This view tells the current user which columns in the database they own are used in views. It's based on the sysobjects and sysdepends system tables.

VIEW_TABLE_USAGE This tells the current user which tables they own are currently used as base tables for a view. It's based on the sysobjects and sysdepends system tables.

VIEWS This returns one row for each view in the database that is accessible by the current user. It's based on the sysobjects and syscomments system tables.

Now that you know what you have to work with, how do you work with it? Suppose, for example, that you're writing a `SELECT` query that requires a `JOIN` to return all the information you need, but you can't remember the names of the columns defined as primary and foreign keys in the tables with which you're working. You could open SQL Server Management Studio and dig around for a while to find this information, or you can do the following:

1. Open a new SQL Server query in SQL Server Management Studio.
2. To find the names of all the columns that have primary and foreign keys defined, enter and execute the following code:

```
USE AdventureWorks
SELECT constraint_name, column_name
FROM information_schema.key_column_usage
```

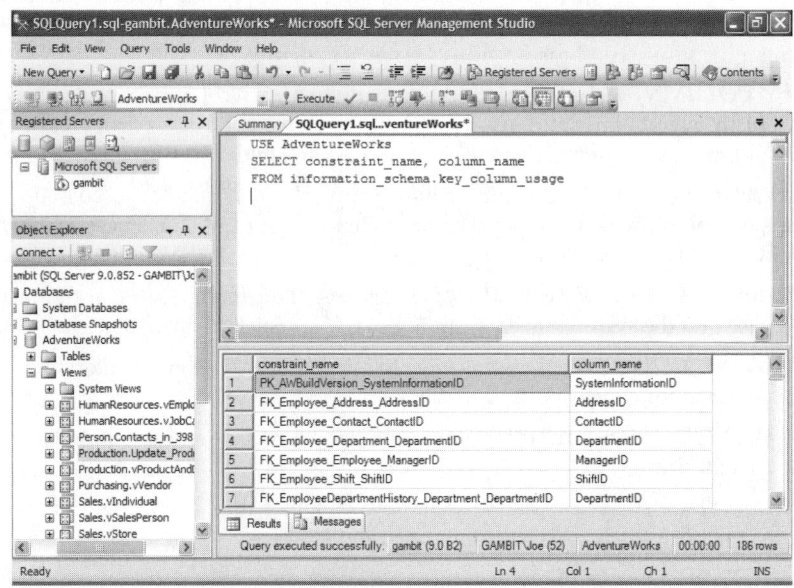

3. Notice that each column is listed as well as its corresponding constraint. To return this same information, you would have to query the spt_values, sysobjects, syscolumns, sysreferences, and sysindexes system tables.

The other information schema views will prove just as useful in your quest to write efficient programs. As you work with SQL Server, there will be times when you need information from the system tables (called *metadata*) but you can't remember what it is. If you can't find the information you need in the information schema views, you can look to their parent, the catalog views.

Using Catalog Views

New to SQL Server 2005, *catalog views* are the most general interface to access system metadata. In fact, all catalog metadata that is available to users is accessed through the catalog views. Here are a few of the more common ones:

Sys.Configurations This displays information about how the various server configuration options are set, such as the number of user connections and available locks.

Sys.Data_spaces Use this to find information about the filegroups and partition schemes available for use.

Sys.Databases This contains a row for each database on the server. Using this view, you can find the state of a database, the compatibility level, the owner, the recovery model, and every other option that can be set on the database.

Sys.Database_files This view returns a row for each file in a particular database and shows you options like the physical name, state, and size of the file.

Sys.Backup_devices This gives you information about all the backup devices available on the system.

Sys.Server_principals Use this view to find information about the security principals (logins, groups, roles, and so on) at the server level. For an in-depth discussion of security, see Chapter 18, "Security and SQL Server 2005."

Sys.Columns This returns one row per column for each object in the database that has columns. You can use this to find information such as the column name, datatype, and max_length.

Sys.Indexes This returns a row for each heap or index for tabular objects in the database, like tables or indexed views. With this you can find index names, types, uniqueness, fill factor, and so on.

Sys.Tables Use this to find information about any user-defined tables in the database.

Sys.Views This returns information about all the user-defined views in the database.

Of course, this is just a small sampling of the catalog views available, but you get the idea. The catalog views are a very useful tool for finding metadata. Let's query one of the more commonly used catalog views to get a feel for it:

1. Open a new SQL Server query in SQL Server Management Studio.

2. To find the names of all the columns that have primary and foreign keys defined, enter and execute the following code:

```
USE AdventureWorks
SELECT * FROM Sys.Tables
```

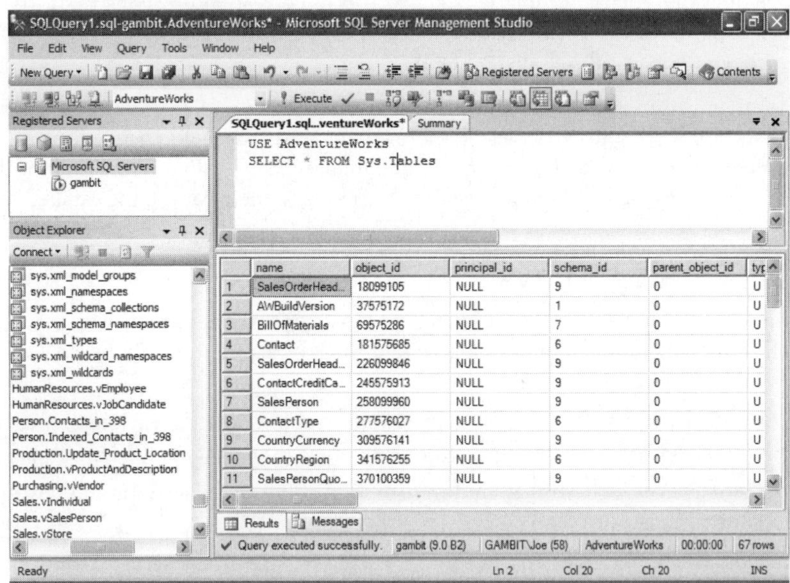

3. Notice that each table is listed along with an array of metadata such as the creation date and table type.

Summary

At the beginning of this chapter, you learned what a view is. Much like a television set doesn't actually contain people, your view doesn't actually contain any data—it's just another means of seeing the data in the table.

You learned how to create the simplest of views: the single table view. By using the View Assisted Editor, you created a simple view and tested it. Then, to modify and further enhance the view, you made changes by adding columns, aliases, and `ORDER BY` clauses.

Next you delved into the murky depths of multiple-table views, creating a view that referenced two tables. To make the view more useful, you entered the View Assisted Editor and added two more tables—bringing the total to four—and tested the view.

After you had a couple of views under your belt, you learned how to use views to modify data. Don't forget that there are a few caveats to modifying data through a view:

- You can't modify more than one table at a time through a view.
- If your view is based on aggregate functions, you can't use it to modify data.
- If your view is based on a table that contains fields that don't allow null values, yet your view doesn't display those fields, you won't be able to insert new data. You can update and delete data, though.

Next you discovered that you can index views. Doing so is particularly useful if your view is very complex, because it can take a while to materialize. If you create an index on the view, SQL Server won't need to materialize it every time someone queries it, because the result set is stored in the database the same way a table with a clustered index is stored. Just remember that there are many caveats to creating and maintaining indexed views—don't create them unless you absolutely need them. You also learned that inline user-defined functions can come in handy when you're querying data, because they accept parameters and views don't.

Then you learned about information schema views. These are designed to help you in your quest for metadata. They return such information as what tables have constraints applied or what columns are used in view definitions. Information schema views will make your development cycles move much more quickly once you start working with these views regularly.

Finally, you learned about the new catalog views. The basis for the information schema views, the catalog views can be used to return metadata for any object on the server.

Now that you have a better understanding of how to view your data, let's see how to improve the process of modifying data by using stored procedures.

Chapter 14

Stored Procedures

Two of a database user's most important concerns are speed and efficiency. Without both of these, your users would spend most of their time engaging in the fine art of thumb-twiddling. So the question arises: How can you give your users the speed and efficiency they need and deserve? Here we'll look at a tool that can assist you in this task.

This tool, designed primarily to enhance data retrieval, is the stored procedure. We'll look at user-defined stored procedures as well as system stored procedures and extended stored procedures.

Understanding Stored Procedures

A *stored procedure* is a query that is stored in a database on SQL Server rather than being stored in the front-end code (usually C# or a similar language) on the client machine. Why would you want to store queries in the database on your server? There are three very good reasons related to performance, compiling, and management.

How do stored procedures increase performance? Think of the queries that you have been executing throughout this book. A query that displays all the products in the Production.Product table in the AdventureWorks database that were made available for sale after January 1, 2003 would look as follows, for example:

```
USE AdventureWorks
SELECT Name, Color, ListPrice, SellStartDate
FROM Production.Product
WHERE SellStartDate > '1/1/2003'
ORDER BY SellStartDate, Name
```

Although this query doesn't seem too large (at five lines of text), imagine having 5,000 users on your network executing the same query all day long, sending it from their machines to the server over the network. That adds up to a lot of network traffic, which can cause congestion. Network congestion occurs when there is too much network traffic for the networking components to handle. Some of that traffic is lost and must be re-sent, so it's actually sent twice—which can slow down your network (and therefore your users) noticeably.

To relieve congestion and keep your network running at full speed, you need to lessen the amount of code that is sent from your client machines to the server over the network and thereby change the amount of traffic generated on the network. All you need to do to accomplish this is store the code on the server, rather than on the client, by turning the query into a stored procedure. Once you have created this stored procedure, the only code your users need to send over the network to get their data is the following:

```
EXEC stored_procedure_name
```

Another advantage that stored procedures have over ad hoc queries involves compiling. When SQL Server compiles a query, it reads the query, looks at such things as JOINs and WHERE clauses, and compares that query with all the available indexes to see which index (if any) would return data to the user fastest. Once SQL Server determines which indexes will function best, it creates an execution plan (which is a set of instructions for SQL Server on how to run the query) and stores that plan in memory. Ad hoc queries must be compiled nearly every time they're run, whereas stored procedures are precompiled. This means that stored procedures have gone through the compilation process and have a plan waiting in memory, so they execute faster than ad hoc queries.

TIP When an ad hoc query is run, SQL Server stores the execution plan in memory as long as there is room. So, an ad hoc query may not need to be compiled every single time it's executed.

NOTE For a discussion of JOINs and WHERE clauses, please see Chapter 6, "SELECT Queries." For a discussion of indexes, refer to Chapter 12.

Stored procedures offer another advantage: They can make database management easier. For example, if you need to make modifications to an existing query, and that query is stored on the users' machines, you must make those changes on all of the users' machines. If you store the query centrally on the server, as a stored procedure, you need to make the changes only once, at the server. This can save you a great deal of time and effort.

This doesn't mean that stored procedures should be used for every query that will ever be passed to your server. If a query will be run only infrequently (an ad hoc query), there is no real need to create a stored procedure on the server to contain it. If your users will run your query regularly, you should consider creating a user-defined stored procedure to contain it. Let's see how to do that now.

NOTE You can also use stored procedures to secure your databases. More on how to do that in Chapter 18, "Security and SQL Server 2005."

Understanding User-Defined Stored Procedures

Because of the performance and management benefits that stored procedures offer, it's important that you understand how to create and use them. Let's start by creating a basic stored procedure that returns a simple result set. Then we'll work with more advanced options.

Basic Stored Procedures

The easiest stored procedure to create and use is one that returns a simple result set without requiring any parameters (which we'll talk about later in this chapter), much like the query that was mentioned at the outset of this chapter. In fact, you're going to turn that query into a stored procedure in the next series of steps. This stored procedure is designed to retrieve all the products in the Production

.Product table in the AdventureWorks database that became available for sale after January 1, 2003. Let's see how it's done:

1. Open SQL Server Management Studio. In Object Explorer, expand your server ➤ Databases ➤ AdventureWorks ➤ Programmability.
2. Right-click the Stored Procedures icon, and select New Stored Procedure to bring up the Stored Procedure Assisted Editor.
3. In the Name text box, enter **Show_Products**.
4. In the Schema drop-down list box, select Production.
5. Leave Execute as CALLER; this tells SQL Server to impersonate the caller when it runs the procedure.
6. In the Transact-SQL syntax box, change the code to look like this:

```
SELECT Name, Color, ListPrice, SellStartDate
FROM Production.Product
WHERE SellStartDate > '1/1/2003'
ORDER BY SellStartDate, Name
```

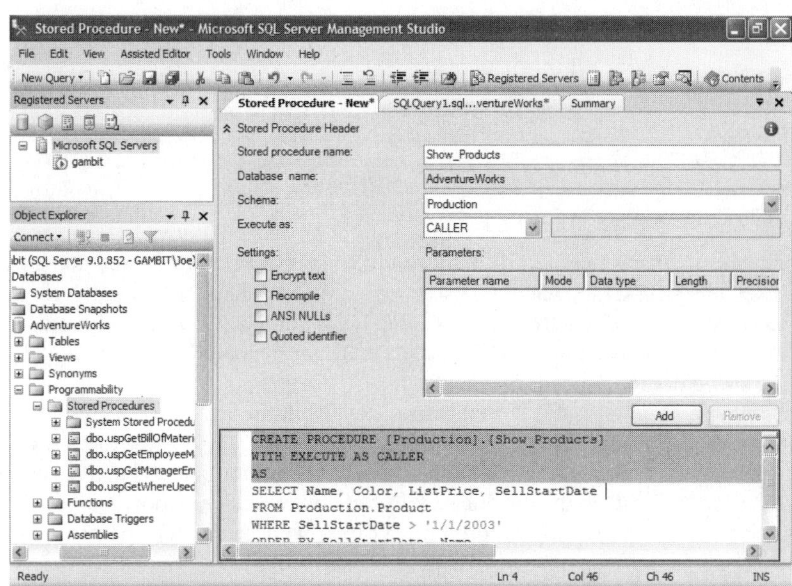

7. Click the Save button on the toolbar to create the procedure.

8. To test the new procedure, open a new SQL Server query and execute the following code in the query window:

```
USE AdventureWorks
EXEC Production.Show_Products
```

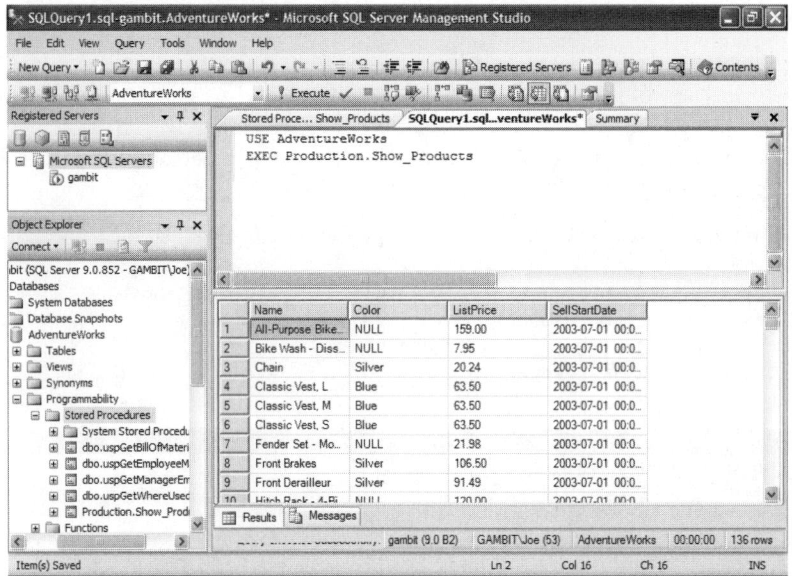

9. Close the query window.

That wasn't so hard, was it? All you needed to do was add `Create Procedure` *`procedure_name`* `WITH EXECUTE AS CALLER AS` to the front of a standard SELECT statement. Now, when your users need to see all the products that began selling before January 1, 2003, they can send only that one line of code (`EXEC Production.Show_Products`) over the network, as opposed to the five lines of code it took before the procedure was created.

The only problem with this stored procedure is that the values are all static. So, if your users need to see all the products that began selling after January 1, 1998, this stored procedure does them no good—they must create an ad hoc query. Another solution would be to create a separate stored procedure for each date in the products table, but you can imagine how tedious that would be. The best solution is to create a single stored procedure that accepts input parameters.

Using Input Parameters

Input parameters in stored procedures are placeholders for data that the user needs to enter. Technically, input parameters are memory variables because they're stored in memory and the contents can change (they're variable). For example, in the previous stored procedure, you could have used an input parameter in place of the static value `'1/1/2003'`; then the users could enter whatever date they wanted. To illustrate the point, let's modify the `Production.Show_Products` stored procedure to accept input from your users (this will show you not only how to use input parameters, but also how to modify an existing stored procedure):

1. Open SQL Server Management Studio. In Object Explorer, expand your server ➢ Databases ➢ AdventureWorks ➢ Programmability ➢ Stored Procedures.
2. Right-click the `Production.Show_Products` stored procedure, and select Modify to bring up the Stored Procedure Assisted Editor.
3. Under the Parameters list box, click the Add button.
4. Use the following information to create your parameter

   Parameter Name: `@Date`

   Mode: In

   Datatype: datetime
5. Modify the query in the T_SQL syntax box to use the new parameter by making it look like this:

```
SELECT Name, Color, ListPrice, SellStartDate
FROM Production.Product
WHERE SellStartDate > @Date
ORDER BY SellStartDate, Name
```

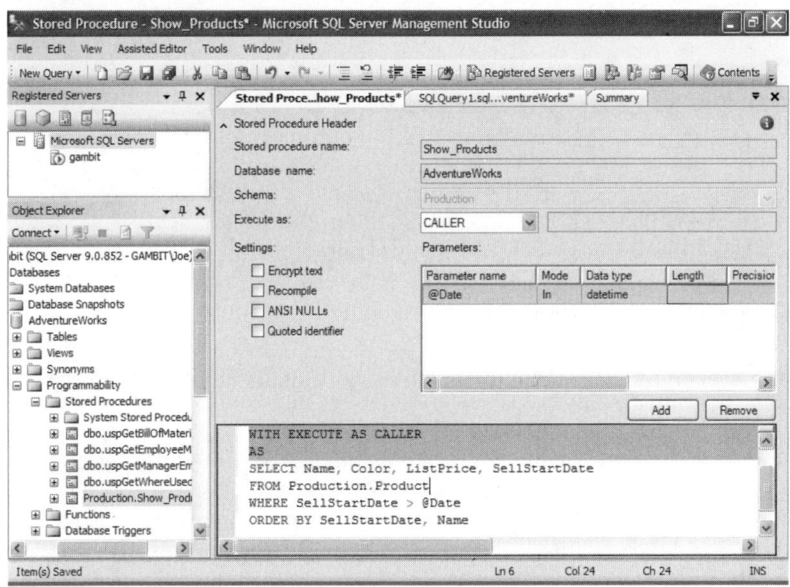

6. Click the Save button on the toolbar to save the changes.

Now that you have modified the `Production.Show_Products` stored procedure to accept input parameters from the user, you're ready to test the new functionality:

1. To test the changes, open a new SQL Server query and execute the following code:

```
USE AdventureWorks
EXEC Production.Show_Products '1/1/1998'
```

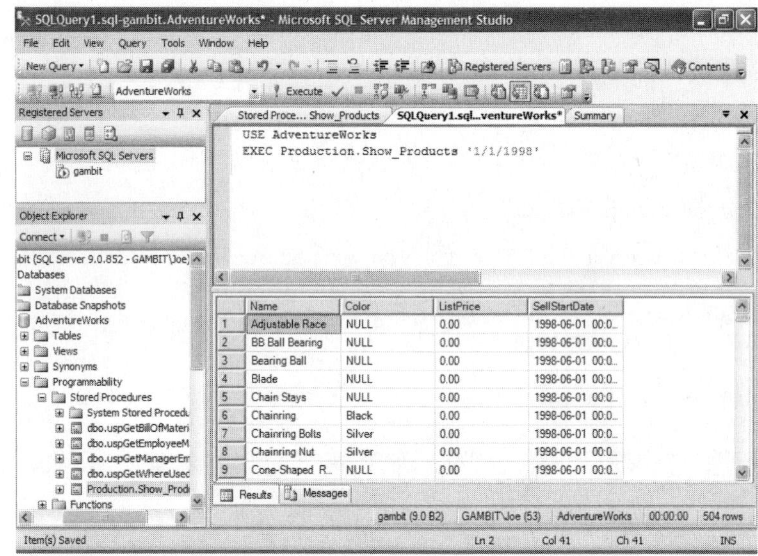

2. Try it with a different date:

```
USE AdventureWorks
EXEC Production.Show_Products '7/1/2000'
```

3. Close the Query Window.

NOTE Memory variables are discussed in more detail in Chapter 5, "Transact-SQL Overview and Basics."

Did you notice what you did with the previous stored procedure? Instead of forcing the users to search only for January 1, 2003, you gave them the flexibility to search for any date by adding a variable (`@Date`) to the beginning of the stored procedure. In this case, `@Date` was replaced by January 1, 1998 and then by July 1, 2000. However, what happens if the user accidentally forgets to type a date, or they want to see January 1, 2003 most of the time and other dates only occasionally? In that instance, you can provide a default value for the input parameter:

1. Open SQL Server Management Studio. In Object Explorer, expand your server ➢ Databases ➢ AdventureWorks ➢ Programmability ➢ Stored Procedures.
2. Right-click the `Production.Show_Products` stored procedure, and select Modify to bring up the Stored Procedure Assisted Editor.

3. In the Parameters list box, in the Default column of the `@Date` parameter, type **'1/1/2003'**.

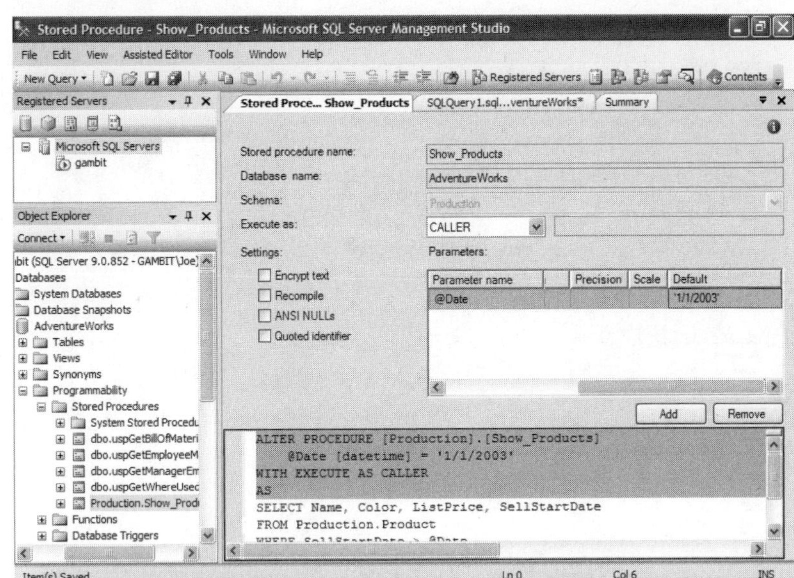

4. Click the Save button on the toolbar to save the changes.

5. To test the changes, open a new SQL Server query and execute the following code.

```
USE AdventureWorks
EXEC Production.Show_Products
```

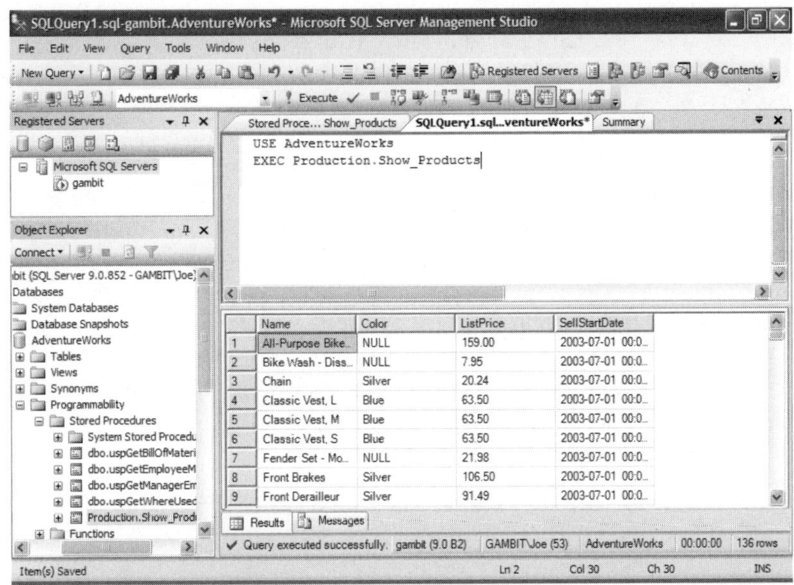

6. Try it with a different date to make sure you can still use input parameters:

```
USE AdventureWorks
EXEC Production.Show_Products '1/1/1998'
```

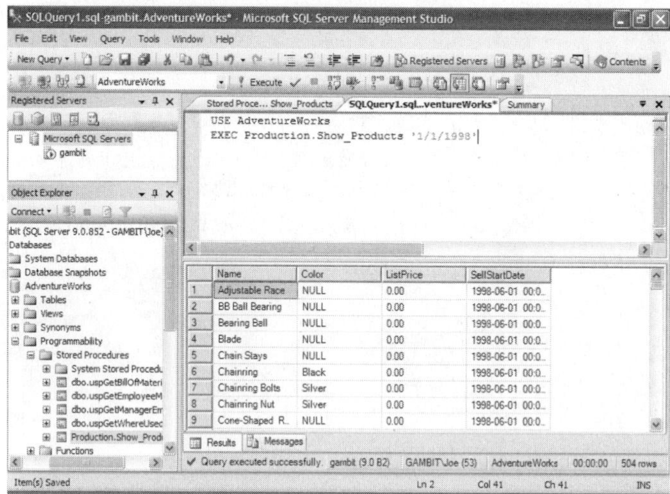

7. Close the query window.

Did you see what you did? In the second line of code, you told SQL Server that if the user forgets to enter a value for the input parameter, SQL Server should assume that they meant 1/1/2003 by adding the `@Date datetime = '1/1/2003'` code. However, if the user does enter a parameter, as you did in step 6, SQL Server uses that value, instead.

You're now starting to see the true potential of stored procedures, but there is more. Suppose that your users don't want to see a result set from the query they enter—maybe they need to see the result of a mathematical calculation. You'll encounter this a lot in financial and accounting departments (they're always doing math, for some reason). To accommodate such folks, you can create a stored procedure that uses both input and output parameters.

Using Output Parameters

An *output parameter* is an input parameter in reverse. With the input parameter, you supply a value for the stored procedure to use. With an output parameter, the stored procedure returns a value for use in further queries. The output parameter is even created in the same space as the input parameters, right between the procedure name and AS sections of the code; the only difference in creating an output parameter is that it's defined with the word OUTPUT immediately afterward (as you'll soon see). Let's create a simple calculator stored procedure to see what an output parameter can do:

1. Open SQL Server Management Studio. In Object Explorer, expand your server ➢ Databases ➢ AdventureWorks ➢ Programmability.
2. Right-click the Stored Procedures icon, and select New Stored Procedure to bring up the Stored Procedure Assisted Editor.
3. In the Name text box, enter **Calc**.
4. In the Schema drop-down list box, select Production.

5. Leave Execute as CALLER; this tells SQL Server to impersonate the caller when it runs the procedure.
6. Under the Parameters list box, click the Add button.
7. Use the following information to create your first input parameter:

   Parameter Name: `@first`

   Mode: In

   Datatype: int
8. Under the Parameters list box, click the Add button.
9. Use the following information to create your second input parameter:

   Parameter Name: `@sec`

   Mode: In

   Datatype: int
10. Under the Parameters list box, click the Add button.
11. Use the following information to create your output parameter:

    Parameter Name: `@ret`

    Mode: Out

    Datatype: int
12. In the Transact-SQL syntax box, change the code to look like this:

```
SET @ret = @first + @sec
```

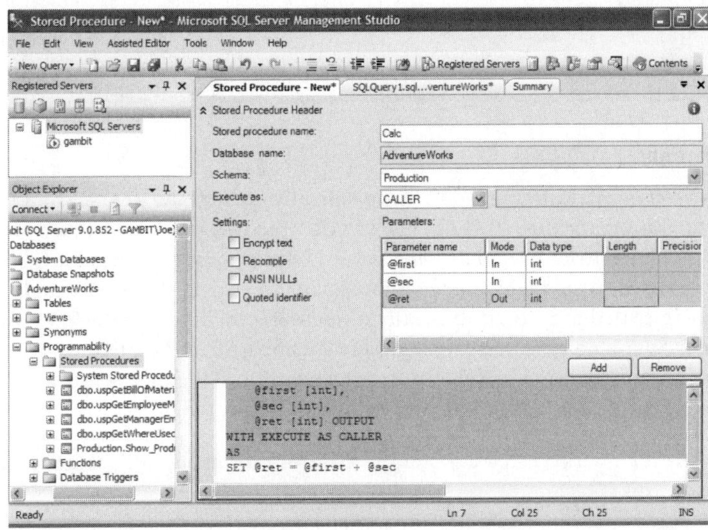

13. Click the Save button on the toolbar to save the procedure.

With the procedure in place, you're ready to test. To get the output parameter back from the stored procedure, you must have a place to put the parameter; so when you execute the query, you must specify both input parameters (one and two) as well as a place to store the output parameter when it's returned:

1. To test the changes, open a new SQL Server query and execute the following code (notice that the `@answer` variable is specifically designated to hold the result returned by the `@ret` output parameter in the stored procedure):

```
USE AdventureWorks
DECLARE @answer int
EXEC Production.Calc 1, 2, @answer OUTPUT
SELECT 'The answer is:',@answer
```

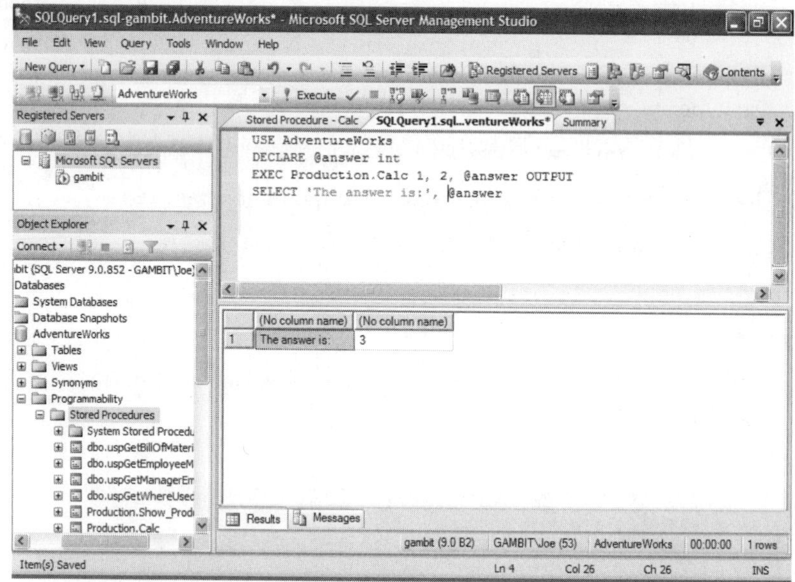

2. Close the query window.

Again, did you see what happened? You specifically created the `@ret` parameter to return a value to the program that called it. Next, before you executed the stored procedure, you created a variable to hold the output parameter that would be returned, by using the `DECLARE @answer` code (DECLARE is used to create memory variables). After creating a variable to hold the output parameter, you executed the stored procedure and instructed it to put the `@ret` value into the `@answer` memory variable, and you displayed it by using a SELECT statement. It's a lot like a relay race, where one runner hands a baton to the next runner until the race is finished. In this instance, the `@ret` variable is handing a value to the `@answer` variable, which is then displayed for the user.

NOTE For more information about CLR store procedures, see Chapter 19, "Integrating SQL Server with Microsoft .NET."

Now that you know how to create and use stored procedures, you need to understand how to keep them running fast. Let's look in a little more in depth at how they work and how to optimize them.

Common Language Runtime Stored Procedures

In SQL Server 2005, you have the ability to write stored procedures in languages other than Transact-SQL. In fact, you can write stored procedures in any Common Language Runtime (CLR) compliant language, such as Visual C#, Visual Basic .NET, Managed Visual C++, and so on. These are called *external stored procedures.*

CLR programming is out of the scope of this book, but here are some basics to keep in mind when you're designing CLR procedures:

- Your methods must be declared as `PUBLIC STATIC`, and they can only return void or int.
- If your method returns an int datatype, then SQL Server will treat it as an exit code (0 for success, 1 for failure).
- If you need to return a value other than int, use the `SqlContext.GetPipe()` method to construct a `SqlPipe` object.
- If you need to return a text message, use the `Send` method of the `SqlPipe` object, `SqlPipe.Send(`*`string`*`)`.
- To return tabular results, use one of the overloads of the `Execute` method of the `SqlPipe` object, `SqlContext.GetPipe.Execute(`*`cmd_string`*`)`.

Once you have designed and compiled a CLR procedure, you need to create the procedure in SQL server using the `CREATE PROCEDURE` command using the `WITH EXTERNAL` clause, like this:

```
CREATE ASSEMBLY CLR_Stored_Proc
FROM '\\MachineName\ CLR_Stored_Proc\bin\Debug\CLR_Stored_Proc.dll'
GO
CREATE PROCEDURE New_CLR_Proc
(
    @CustID int,
    @CsutName nvarchar(255),
    @CustAddress nvarchar(255)
)
AS EXTERNAL NAME CLRStoredProc.CustomerImport.ImportNameAddress
GO
```

Optimizing Stored Procedures

To optimize a stored procedure, it's best for you to understand a little more about how SQL Server executes queries. When SQL Server first executes a query (any query, not just stored procedures), it compiles the query first. The compiling process is just SQL Server peering inside your query to see what you're trying to accomplish. Specifically, SQL Server looks at what tables you're `JOIN`ing and what columns you have specified in the `WHERE` clause of your query. Once the server has this knowledge, it can develop an *execution plan,* which is a map of what indexes would return data fastest. Once the execution plan has been devised, SQL Server stores it in *procedure cache,* which is an area of RAM that has been specifically apportioned for this purpose. Now, whenever you run the same query again or a very similar query, SQL Server doesn't need to create another execution plan to get your data; it uses the execution plan that has been stored in the procedure cache.

This can cause a problem for you at times, though. For instance, you may need to change the structure (or schema) of your database, adding a new table or columns to an existing table. If this kind of change occurs, SQL Server automatically recompiles your stored procedures to use the changes in the structure. The only time the stored procedure won't be recompiled is if you create a new index; in that instance, you must recompile the stored procedure manually so that SQL Server can create an execution plan that takes advantage of the new index.

Or, suppose you have a stored procedure that uses widely varied input parameters every time you run it. Some of those parameters may affect the JOIN or WHERE clause statements in the stored procedure, and because SQL Server uses those parameters to create an execution plan, it may not be wise to use the same execution plan every time the stored procedure is run—you may want to recompile it. You have two ways to force SQL Server to recompile your stored procedure; the first is by creating it with the WITH RECOMPILE statement.

WITH RECOMPILE forces SQL Server to create a new execution plan each and every time you execute the stored procedure; it's the best way to create a stored procedure that has input parameters that change drastically every time you use it (and affect the JOIN and WHERE clauses in the stored procedure). For example, if you want to recompile the Production.Show_Products stored procedure every time you run it, the code to create it will look as follows:

```
CREATE PROCEDURE [Production].[Show_Products]
   @Date [datetime] = '1/1/2003'
WITH RECOMPILE, EXECUTE AS CALLER
AS
SELECT Name, Color, ListPrice, SellStartDate
FROM Production.Product
WHERE SellStartDate > @Date
ORDER BY SellStartDate, Name
```

The WITH RECOMPILE option tells SQL Server to create a new execution plan every time the stored procedure is executed and not store that execution plan in cache. That can be tedious and slow if you need to change the execution plan only occasionally, though. If that is the case, you should use the second method for recompiling a stored procedure: the EXECUTE...WITH RECOMPILE statement. EXECUTE...WITH RECOMPILE tells SQL Server to create a new execution plan just this one time, not every time the statement is executed. If you use this statement, the code used to create the stored procedure doesn't change; but when you execute the stored procedure, it looks like this:

```
EXEC Production.Show_Products WITH RECOMPILE
```

By using these RECOMPILE statements, you can keep your stored procedures running fast. However, thus far, you haven't secured them from prying eyes—let's do that now.

Securing Your Stored Procedures

When you create a stored procedure, you're just creating a query that is stored on the server rather than on the client machines. These stored procedures are contained in the syscomments system table in each database and are completely accessible by default. This means that by executing a simple SELECT query against the syscomments table in the database where the stored procedure was created, your users can see all the code used to create the procedure. This may not be desirable, because one of the main uses of a stored procedure is to remove the user from the complexity and structure of the underlying tables—and, as we'll discuss in Chapter 18, "Security and SQL Server 2005," stored procedures are used for securing tables as well. By reading the definition of the stored procedure right from syscomments, the users will bypass that security; in other words, they will be hacking. To avoid that, you should create stored procedures using the `WITH ENCRYPTION` statement.

`WITH ENCRYPTION` is designed to keep prying eyes out of definitions stored in the syscomments table—not just for stored procedures, but for everything stored there (views, triggers, and so on). In the following exercise, you'll execute a `SELECT` query against the syscomments table in the pubs database to find out what is stored there and, therefore, what your users could see:

1. Open a new SQL Server query in SQL Server Management Studio, and log in using Windows Authentication (unless you need to use SQL Server Authentication).

2. Enter the following code, and execute it by clicking the Execute on the toolbar (you have to join the sysobjects table because the name is stored there—only the ID is stored in syscomments):

```
USE AdventureWorks
SELECT ob.name, com.text
FROM syscomments com
JOIN sysobjects ob
ON ob.id = com.id
WHERE ob.name = 'Show_Products'
```

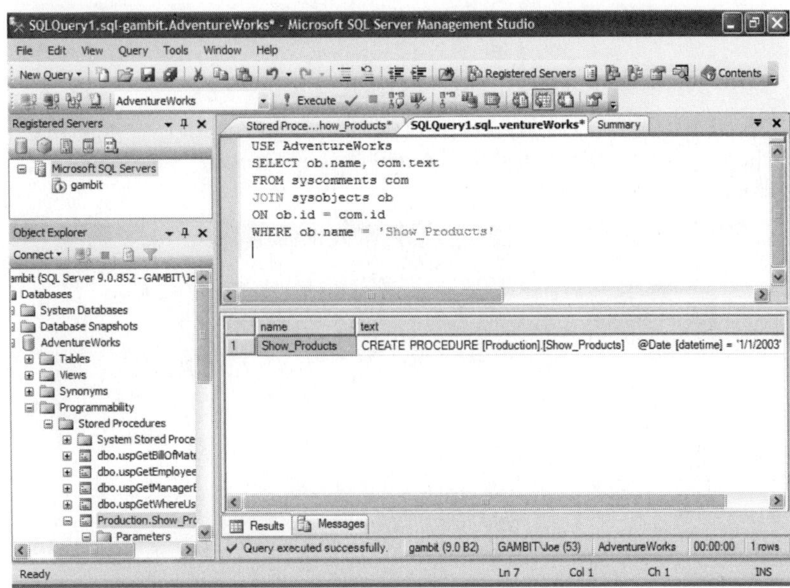

3. Notice in the result set that you can read the code used to create and run the stored procedure.

4. To encrypt it, open SQL Server Management Studio. In Object Explorer, expand your server ➤ Databases ➤ AdventureWorks ➤ Programmability ➤ Stored Procedures.

5. Right-click the `Production.Show_Products` stored procedure, and select Modify to bring up the Stored Procedure Assisted Editor.

6. To encrypt the stored procedure, select the Encrypt Text check box.

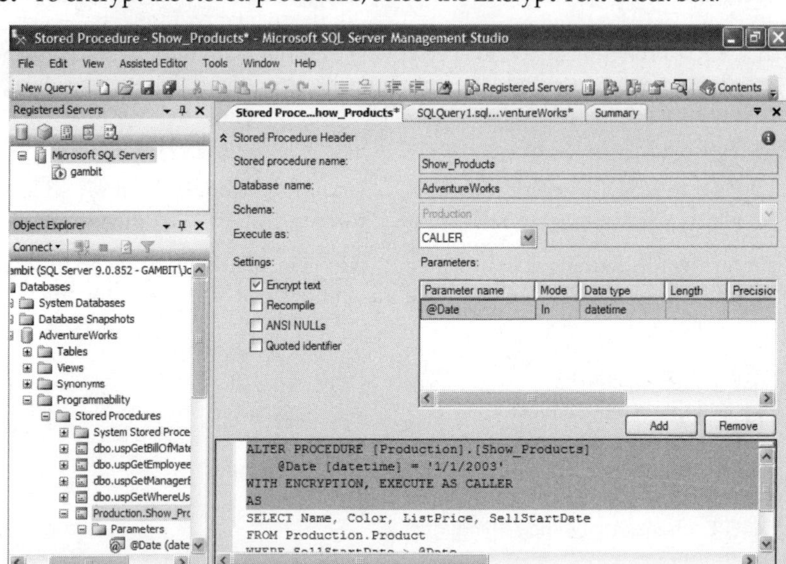

7. Click the Save button on the toolbar to apply the changes.

8. To verify that it has been encrypted, double-click `Production.Show_Products` to bring up the properties again. You should receive an error message stating that the body of the object is encrypted.

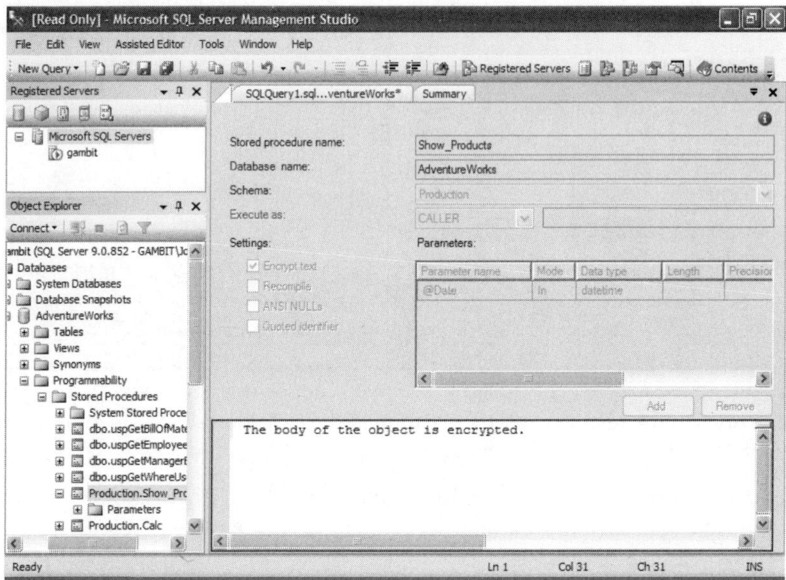

9. Open a new SQL Server query, and execute the query from step 2 again; notice that this time you can't read the text from syscomments, because it's now a null value.

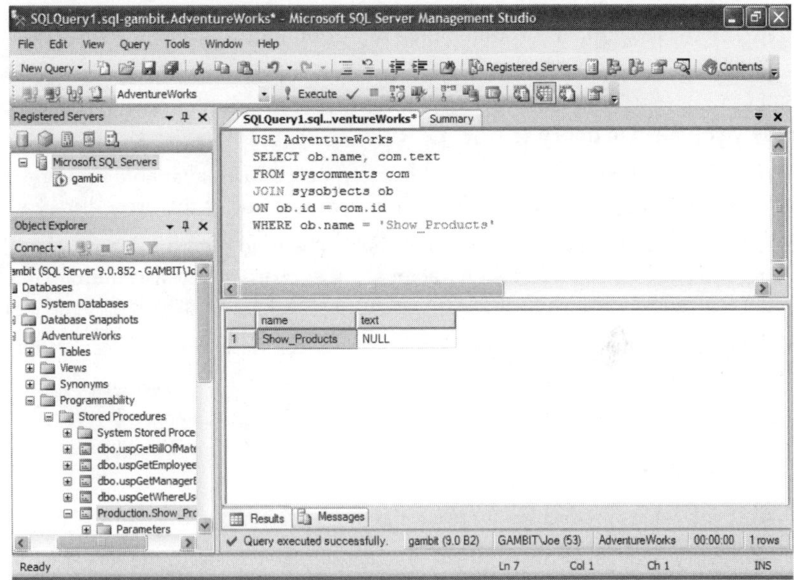

10. Close the query window.

WARNING Once you create an object, such as a stored procedure, using `WITH ENCRYPTION`, you can't decrypt the object. Make sure you're finished modifying the object for a while before encrypting and store the source code in a secure location in case you need to change it later.

User-defined stored procedures (the ones you make yourself) are a very powerful tool, but they aren't the only stored procedures with which you have to work. Microsoft has given you a batch of ready-made stored procedures that are designed to help you work with system tables. These are called *system* and *extended stored procedures*.

System and Extended Stored Procedures

Microsoft has started using the term *metadata* quite a bit these days; it means information about information. When the term is applied to SQL Server, it means information about objects on the server, such as how big a database file is or what permissions a user has. When you want to change or read such system information, you can open the system tables directly and start fiddling with the data inside; but that usually turns out badly because most of the values in the system tables aren't designed to be understood by mere mortal humans (most of the values in these tables are numeric and not easily decoded). A much better way (and the supported way) to change or read the system information is by using system stored procedures.

Using System Stored Procedures

Every time you add a database, add a login (which is used to grant access to SQL Server), create an index, or add or modify any object on the server, you're making changes to the system tables, which is where SQL Server stores information about your objects. The information stored in these system tables is mostly numeric data, which is difficult to read, let alone modify, directly. That is why Microsoft has given you scores of stored procedures (about 1230) to help with the task of modifying system tables. They're all stored in the master and msdb databases, and most begin with the characters *sp_*. Here is a synopsis of some of the more common system stored procedures:

sp_tables This stored procedure shows you any object that can be used in the `FROM` clause of a `SELECT` query. It's useful if you have forgotten or just don't know the exact name of the table or view you need to query.

sp_stored_procedures This lists all the stored procedures available for your use. Again, it's useful if you have forgotten or just don't know the name of the procedure you need.

sp_server_info Using this procedure is the best way to determine how your SQL Server was configured at setup, such as the character set or sort order that was defined at install, what version of SQL Server you're running (for example, desktop or standard), and so on.

sp_databases This lists all the available databases on the server. It can be useful for finding database names.

sp_start_job This is used to start an automation job in SQL Server. It's very handy for jobs that are scheduled on demand. We'll discuss jobs and automation in Chapter 17, "Automating Administration."

sp_stop_job This procedure stops a job that has been started.

sp_addlogin This procedure is used to add a standard login to the server to allow users access to the server as a whole. It's very useful for creating a script that will regenerate user logins in the event of a system crash. We'll discuss security and logins in Chapter 18.

sp_grantlogin This is used to grant access on SQL Server to a Windows account. This should be combined with the `sp_addlogin` account to create a script to re-create user accounts in the event of a disaster.

sp_setapprole An account role in SQL Server (as you'll see in Chapter 18) is used to make sure that only approved applications are used to access your database. This stored procedure activates the application role so that the user can access the database with the permissions that are granted to the application role.

sp_password As you'll see in Chapter 18, there is a difference between standard and Windows NT login accounts. This stored procedure is used to change passwords for standard, and only standard, logins.

sp_configure Several global configuration options can be set to change the way SQL Server behaves. For example, you can tell the server whether to allow updates to system tables directly or how much system memory to use. The `sp_configure` stored procedure can be used to change such options. The available options are listed here:

- `Ad Hoc Distributed Queries`
- `affinity I/O mask`
- `affinity mask`
- `Agent XPs`
- `allow updates`
- `awe enabled`
- `blocked process threshold`
- `c2 audit mode`
- `clr enabled`
- `cost threshold for parallelism`
- `cross db ownership chaining`
- `cursor threshold`

- `default full-text language`
- `default language`
- `default trace enabled`
- `disallow results from triggers`
- `fill factor`
- `index create memory`
- `in-doubt xact resolution`
- `lightweight pooling`
- `locks`
- `max degree of parallelism`
- `max full-text crawl range`
- `max server memory`
- `max text repl size`
- `max worker threads`
- `media retention`
- `min memory per query`
- `min server memory`
- `nested triggers`
- `network packet size`
- `Ole Automation Procedures`
- `open objects`
- `ph_timeout`
- `precompute rank`
- `priority boost`
- `query governor cost limit`
- `query wait`
- `recovery interval`
- `remote access`
- `remote admin connections`
- `remote login timeout`
- `remote proc trans`
- `remote query timeout`
- `Replication XPs`
- `RPC parameter data validation`
- `scan for startup procs`
- `server trigger recursion`
- `set working set size`
- `show advanced options`
- `SMO and DMO XPs`
- `Database Mail XPs`
- `SQL Mail XPs`
- `transform noise words`
- `two digit year cutoff`
- `user connections`
- `User Instance Timeout`
- `user instances enabled`
- `user options`
- `Web Assistant Procedures`
- `xp_cmdshell`

sp_attach_db All the databases on your SQL Server have a record in the sysdatabases system table in the master database. This record tells SQL Server where the database is on disk, how big it is, and so on. If you were to lose your master database and (heaven forbid) not have a good backup, you would need to run this stored procedure to re-create the records in sysdatabases for each of the databases on your server.

sp_processmail SQL Server is capable of not only sending but also receiving and responding to e-mail. When SQL Mail is configured (which you'll learn how to do in Chapter 17), you can send a query via e-mail to the MSSQLServer service. When you run this stored procedure, the MSSQLServer service reads the query in the e-mail and sends back the result set.

sp_monitor This stored procedure gives a quick snapshot of how your server is doing—how busy the processor is, how much RAM is in use, and so on.

sp_who You can't perform some administrative tasks, such as renaming or restoring a database, if someone is using it at the time. To find out who is using a database on the server so that you can disconnect them, use this stored procedure.

sp_rename This changes the name of any object in the database.

sp_renamedb This changes the name of the database itself.

sp_help This can be used to find information about any object in the database. It returns properties such as created date, column names, foreign-key constraints, and so on.

sp_helptext This is used to display the actual text that was used to create an object in the database. This information is read from the syscomments table.

sp_help* Many other stored procedures have `sp_help` as the first few characters. All of them are designed to give you specific information about a type of object in the database.

These system stored procedures are used like any other stored procedure. Let's look at an example:

1. Open SQL Server Management Studio from the SQL Server 2005 group under Programs on the Start menu, and log in with Windows NT Authentication (unless you must use SQL Server Authentication).

2. To use `sp_help` to get information about the Production.Product table in the AdventureWorks database, open a new SQL Server query and execute the following code:

```
USE AdventureWorks
EXEC sp_help 'Production.Product'
```

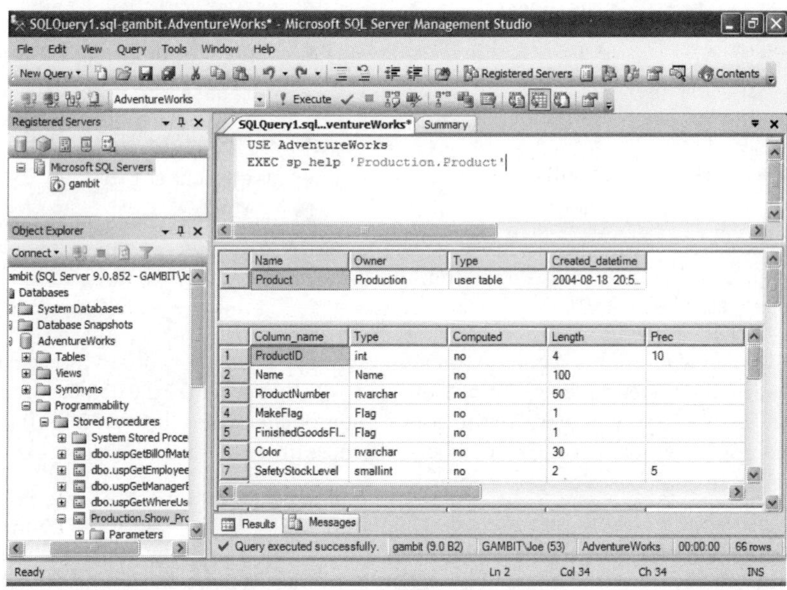

3. To see how your SQL Server is faring at the moment, use the `sp_monitor` stored procedure:

```
EXEC sp_monitor
```

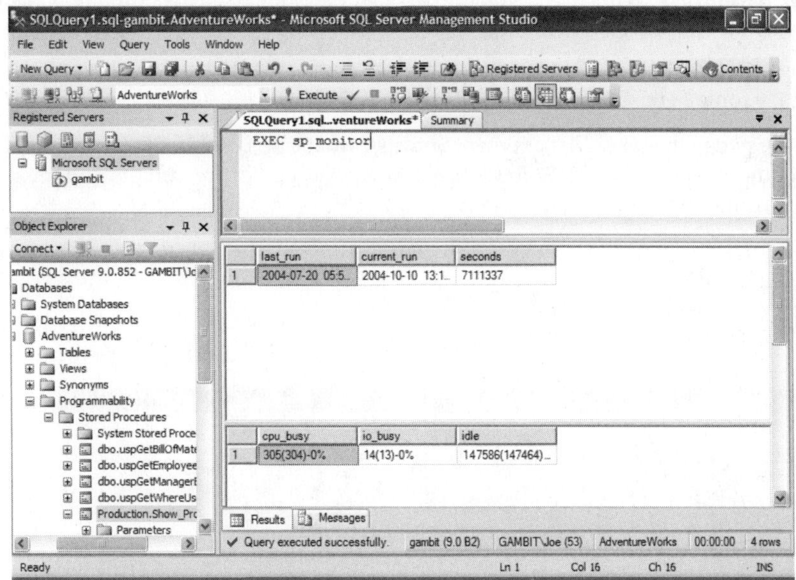

4. Close the query window.

Using Extended Stored Procedures

Extended stored procedures do just what their name implies: They extend the capabilities of SQL Server so that it can do things a database server would not ordinarily be capable of doing. For example, you wouldn't expect a database server to be able to execute a command from the command prompt; but thanks to an extended stored procedure that comes with SQL Server (xp_cmdshell), SQL Server can do just that.

Extended stored procedures are C++ code saved in and executed from a Dynamic Link Library (DLL). Most of the extended stored procedures are executed with other system stored procedures, so you won't use them very often by themselves, but here is a short list of the ones you may use:

xp_cmdshell This stored procedure is used to run programs that are ordinarily run from the command shell, such as the dir command or md (make directory). It comes in very handy when you need to have SQL Server create a directory for automatically archiving Bulk Copy Program (BCP) files or something of that nature.

xp_fileexist This procedure can be used to test for the existence of a file and, if that file exists, to do something (such as BCP) with it. The following code shows you how to test for the existence of the autoexec.bat file. If @ret equals 1, the file exists; if it equals 0, the file doesn't exist. This isn't documented in Books Online or on the Microsoft website, so we'll give you the syntax here. The second line declares a variable to hold an output parameter, the third line calls the procedure with an output parameter, and the fourth line displays the output (note that this must be done in the master database):

```
USE Master
DECLARE @ret int
EXEC xp_fileexist 'c:\autoexec.bat', @ret output
SELECT @ret
```

xp_fixeddrives This shows you the drive letters of the fixed disks and how many megabytes of available space are on each one.

Again, each of these extended stored procedures is executed just like a regular stored procedure. Let's try some here:

1. Open SQL Server Management Studio from the SQL Server 2005 group under Programs on the Start menu, and log in with Windows Authentication (unless you must use SQL Server Authentication).

2. To use `xp_cmdshell` to get a directory listing of your C drive, enter and execute the following code:

```
EXEC xp_cmdshell 'dir c:'
```

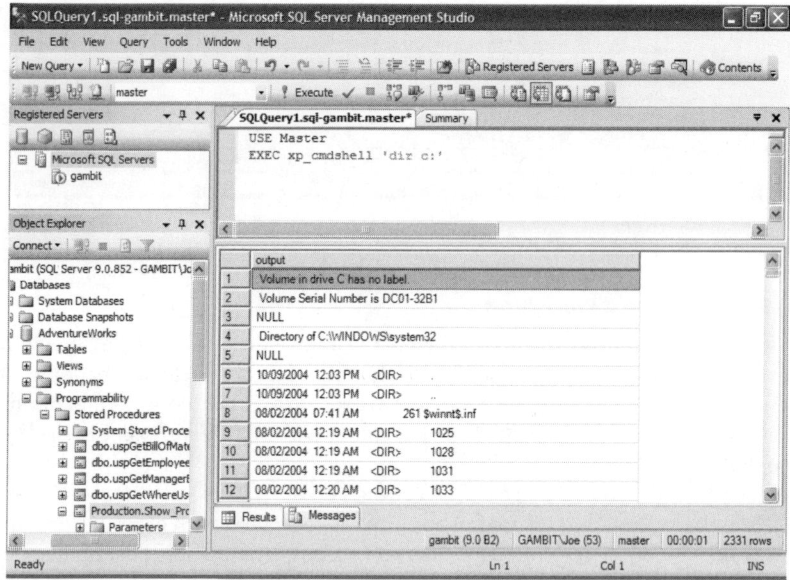

3. To see whether you have a file named `autoexec.bat` on your C drive, enter and execute the following code (it will return a 1 if the file exists):

```
DECLARE @ret int
EXEC xp_fileexist 'c:\autoexec.bat', @ret output
SELECT @ret
```

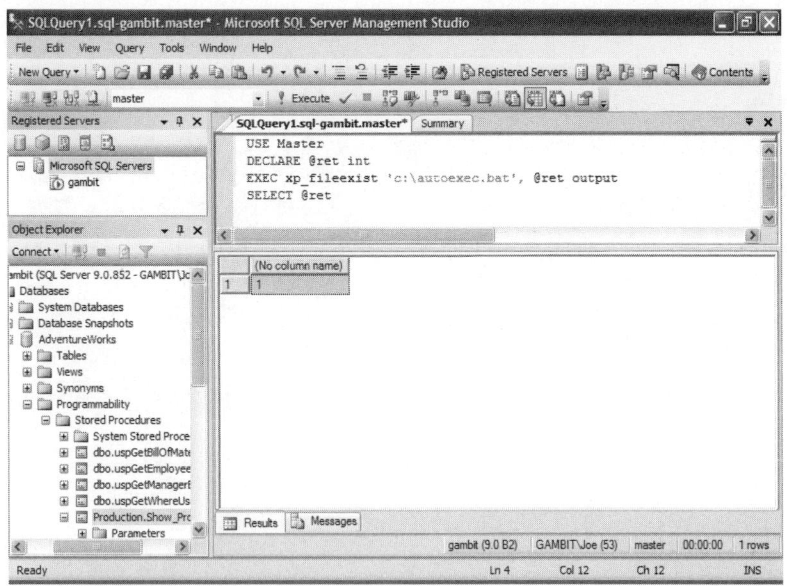

4. Close SQL Server Management Studio.

Summary

In this chapter, you learned all about stored procedures. We first discussed what they are—a collection of Transact-SQL statements (usually a query) that is stored centrally on the server waiting to be executed by users. The advantage to storing them centrally is that when your users execute them, they aren't sending hundreds of lines of code over the network and thus bogging it down—they're sending only one line of code: `EXEC` *`stored_procedure`*. These stored procedures are also easier to manage than dispersed code because when you need to make a change to the code, you have to do it only at the server rather than running around to each client machine.

After learning what stored procedures are, you found out how to create them. We explained how to create a simple stored procedure that returns a result set to the user using static parameters that can't be changed. Next you learned how to allow users to control the information they get back by using input and output parameters.

Then, we discussed how to optimize some stored procedures by recompiling them when necessary. You learned that all stored procedures have a record associated with them in the syscomments table that contains all the text used to create and execute the procedure. To secure this code, you can encrypt the entry in syscomments with the `WITH ENCRYPTION` clause.

After that, you discovered the power of system and extended stored procedures. The system stored procedures are the easiest and best way to modify system data, and the extended stored procedures are used for extending the abilities of SQL Server beyond those of a normal database server.

Now that you have stored procedures under your belt, you can make access to your data faster and more efficient. However, you still need to be able to control what the users are putting in those databases. In the next chapter, we'll introduce you to one method of controlling that data: using triggers.

Chapter 15

Using Triggers

As a database administrator or developer, you want to be able to control what data your users are inserting, updating, or deleting in your tables. For example, you may not want a user to be able to delete a customer account from one table if there is a pending sale for that account in another table. For that type of control, a simple foreign-key relationship works fine.

Another example would be when you want your users to insert and update data but not delete it. In that instance, you need to modify the security settings on your server to deny delete permissions to your users for that one table (we'll discuss permissions in Chapter 18, "Security and SQL Server 2005").

Suppose, though, that you have a credit limit column in your customers table and that you don't want users to be able to increase the credit limit past $10,000 without management approval. Or suppose that you want to automatically notify a manager every time a customer is deleted from a database so the manager can ask the person who deleted the account for details. Maybe you want to know when a user has inserted a new customer so you can track the user's sales and give them a big, fat bonus later. In each of these examples, you can't use the simple permissions or foreign-key relationships—you need to use triggers.

In this chapter, we're going to discuss all four types of triggers: `INSERT`, `UPDATE`, `DELETE`, and `INSTEAD OF`. You'll see not only how they work, but also how you can use them to enforce complex business logic on your databases. We'll begin by providing a basic understanding of triggers.

Understanding Triggers

A *trigger* is a collection of SQL statements that looks and acts a great deal like a stored procedure (which we discussed in Chapter 14). The only real difference between the two is that a trigger can't be called with the `EXEC` (short for execute) command; triggers are activated (or fired) when a user executes a Transact-SQL statement. Data Manipulation Language (DML) triggers fire on `INSERT`, `UPDATE`, and/or `DELETE` statements; and Data Definition Language (DDL) triggers fire on `CREATE`, `ALTER`, and/or `DROP` statements (more on DDL triggers later in this chapter). For example, suppose you've defined an `INSERT` trigger on a customer information table stating that your users can't add a new customer from outside the United States. As soon as any user tries to insert a new customer, the `INSERT` trigger executes and determines whether the record passes the criteria set forth in the trigger. If the record passes, the insert is completed; if the record doesn't pass, the record isn't inserted.

SQL Server is able to block data modifications if they don't pass your stringent criteria because triggers are considered transactions. A *transaction* (as discussed in Chapter 8, "Topics in Advanced Transact-SQL") is a block of Transact-SQL code that SQL Server treats as a unit. Code is grouped into a transaction by means of a `BEGIN TRAN` statement at the beginning of the code and a `COMMIT` statement at the end; these statements can be placed either by the user (an *explicit* transaction) or by SQL Server (an *implicit* transaction). Because a trigger is seen as a transaction, you need to add only the `ROLLBACK` command to the appropriate spot in the code if you don't want to let a record pass the trigger. The ROLLBACK command causes the server to stop processing the modification and disallow the transaction, forgetting that it ever took place (this is true of all types of triggers).

To go one step further, you can send an error message to the user who tried to violate the trigger by using the RAISERROR() command. If you want to get really fancy, you can even tell on them and have the error message sent to a manager.

In this sense, triggers can be thought of as database watchdogs. If you've never seen a watchdog in action, it may help to visualize it. A watchdog is generally used to guard animals out in the pasture—cows, sheep, horses, and so on. The watchdog quietly sits and waits, doing nothing, until something happens—such as a predator approaching the flock. As soon as that predator comes up, the watchdog springs into action, barking, chasing, and attacking until the predator has been vanquished. Triggers act in the same way, waiting quietly on the database server until a user tries to modify data, and then springing into action to enforce your business logic.

Of course, there are other ways to enforce business logic For example, you learned about foreign-key relationships in Chapter 4, "Database Design and Normalization." With a foreign-key relationship in place between a customers table and an orders table, you can keep your users from deleting a customer with a pending order. You can also prevent a user from inserting an order for a customer who doesn't exist in the customers table.

You'll also learn about permissions in Chapter 18, where you'll find that you can deny users the permission to insert, update, or delete. If, for example, you deny insert permission to some of your users, those users can't insert any records at all. The same goes for the update and delete permissions—if any of these are denied, the action doesn't take place. If any of these permissions are granted, the users can do whatever they would like with very little inhibition.

These methods are great for implementing simple business logic, such as *marketing can't delete, but they can insert* or *customers can't be deleted if they have a pending order.* Most companies have business logic that is a great deal more complex than that. They may, for example, have a business rule that states *sales can't update a user's credit limit to exceed $10,000 without management approval* or *a user may not delete a customer with a credit limit above $10,000.* These are very common business rules that can't be implemented by using the foreign-key relationships or permissions on a table. Only by using triggers can you properly enforce this complex business logic. Let's start that process now, by working with INSERT triggers.

Working with *INSERT* Triggers

INSERT triggers can be used to modify, or even disallow, a record being inserted. A good example of how to use an INSERT trigger involves keeping users from adding certain types of records, such as customers with a credit limit over $10,000. Another example is adding data to the record being inserted, perhaps adding the date the record was created or the name of the user inserting the record. You can even use an INSERT trigger to cascade changes to other tables in your database. For example, suppose you have two databases: a contact manager database and a human resources database. Many companies keep the same information in both databases because they want to have employee information listed as a contact as well. An INSERT trigger (as well as UPDATE and DELETE triggers) can cascade updates in one database to the other to keep all information in both databases current.

INSERT triggers fire (are executed) every time someone tries to create a new record in a table using the INSERT command. As soon as a user tries to insert a new record into a table, SQL Server copies the new record into a table in the database called the *trigger table* and a special table stored in memory called the *inserted table*. As shown in Figure 15.1, this means that your new record exists in two tables, the trigger table and the inserted table. The records in the inserted table should exactly match the records in the trigger table.

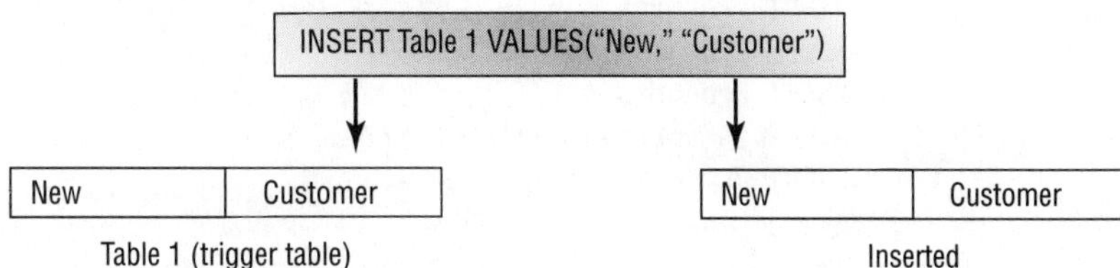

FIGURE 15.1
SQL Server places newly created records in the trigger table and the inserted table.

Inserted is a valuable table when you need to cascade changes to other tables throughout the database. For example, suppose you have a database that contains customer, order detail, and product inventory information. Every time you sell an order to a customer, you need to subtract the total of the order from the inventory in the products table to keep the inventory current. There are two ways to do this. First, you could store the amount of product sold to the customer in a *memory variable* (which is a temporary storage area created in memory) and update the products table with a second UPDATE statement; but that requires extra code, which can slow the system and therefore isn't a clean solution. The second way involves using the logical inserted table. The value that you need is being stored in two places, the trigger table and the inserted table, so you can pull the value from inserted and apply it to order details. This means you can write code into your INSERT trigger to automatically subtract data from the products table based on values in the inserted table. The code would resemble something as follows:

```
UPDATE p
SET p.instock = (p.instock - i.qty)
FROM Products p JOIN inserted I
ON p.prodid = i.prodid
```

To create this trigger and see how it works, you must meet a few prerequisites. First, you'll need the sales database you created in Chapter 11, "Tables." If you don't have that database, refer to Chapter 11 to create it. Next, you'll fill the tables with some values:

1. Open SQL Server Management Studio by selecting it from the SQL Server 2005 group in Programs on the Start menu, and log in using either Windows or SQL Server Authentication.

2. You need to enter some customers to sell products to. Open a new SQL Server query window, and enter and execute the following code to populate the customers table with customer information (if these values exist in your table from a previous chapter, you can skip this step; to verify this, run the query SELECT * FROM customers):

```
USE Sales
INSERT customers
VALUES ('Gary','McKee','111 Main','Palm Springs','CA','94312',' 7605551212')
INSERT customers
VALUES ('Tom', 'Smith', '609 Georgia', 'Fresno', 'CA', '33045', '5105551212')
INSERT customers
VALUES ('Shane', 'Travis', '806 Star', 'Phoenix', 'AZ', '85202', '6021112222')
```

3. You need some products to sell. To populate the products table with product and inventory information, enter and execute the following code:

```
INSERT Products
VALUES ('Giant Wheel of Brie', 200)
```

```
INSERT Products
VALUES ('Wool Blankets', 545)
INSERT Products
VALUES ('Espresso Beans', 1527)
INSERT Products
VALUES ('Notepads', 2098)
```

4. Close the query window.

Now that you've populated the tables in the sales database with data, you're ready to create a trigger that will automatically update the instock column of the products table based on the amount of product sold to a customer. To do that, you'll create an `INSERT` trigger on the orders table, because when you sell something to a customer, you insert a new record in the orders table:

1. Open SQL Server Management Studio by selecting it from the SQL Server 2005 group under Programs on the Start menu, and expand your server ➤ Databases ➤ Sales ➤ Tables ➤ dbo.Orders.
2. Right-click the Triggers folder, and select New Trigger.
3. In the Name box, enter **InvUpdate**.
4. Deselect the Update and Delete check boxes under DML Events.
5. In the Transact-SQL Syntax box, insert the following code to complete the trigger:

```
UPDATE p
SET p.instock = (p.instock - i.qty)
FROM Products p JOIN inserted i
ON p.prodid = i.prodid
```

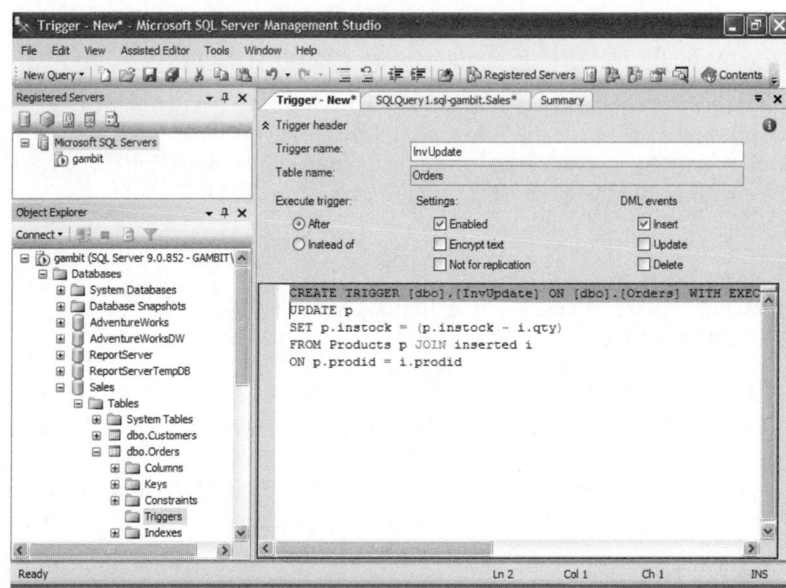

6. Click the Save button to create the trigger.

With the INSERT trigger in place on the orders table, you can test the trigger. In the following series of steps, you'll create a new record in the orders table (thereby simulating an order by a customer) to cause the INSERT trigger to fire. This should reduce the instock amount in the products table:

1. Open a new SQL Server query, and execute the following code to verify the instock quantity for item 1 (it should be 200):

```
USE Sales
SELECT prodid, instock
FROM Products
```

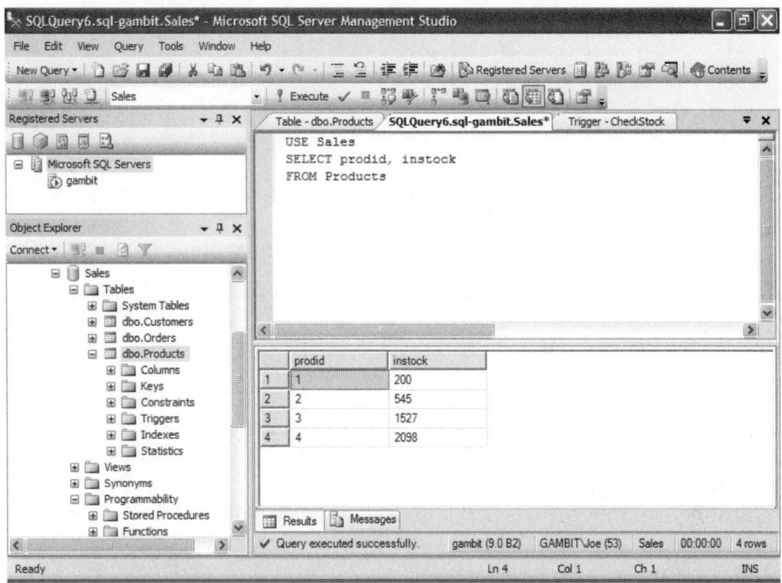

2. To cause the INSERT trigger to fire, you need to insert a new record in the orders table. To do this, select Query ➤ New Query With Current Connection, and enter and execute the following code, which assumes that you're selling 15 count of product number 1 to customer ID 1 on today's date (GETDATE() is used to return today's date):

```
USE Sales
INSERT Orders
VALUES (1,1,15,getdate())
```

3. To verify that the INSERT trigger fired and removed 15 from the instock column of the products table, click the New Query button, and enter and execute the following code:

```
USE Sales
SELECT prodid, instock
FROM Products
```

4. Notice that the exact quantity you sold customer number 1 (qty 15) was subtracted from the total instock quantity of prodid 1. You now have 185 instead of 200.

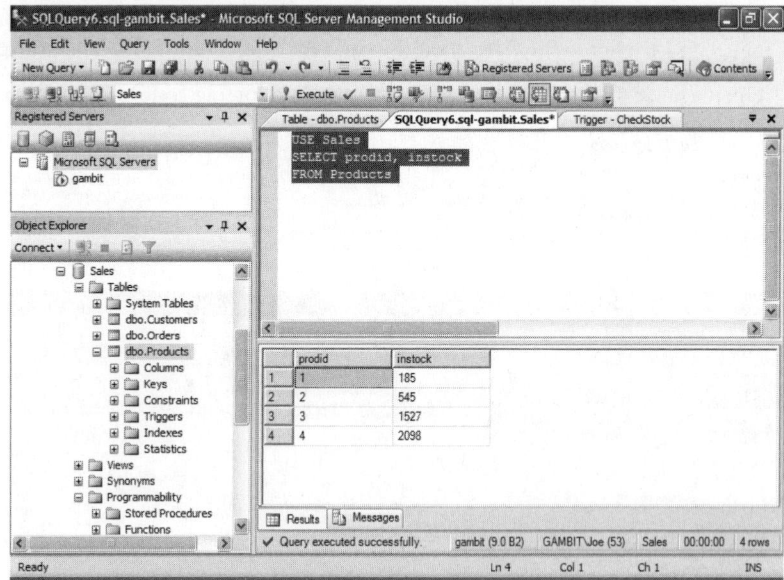

5. Close the query windows.

Did you see what happened here? You created an INSERT trigger that referenced the logical inserted table. Whenever you insert a new record in the orders table now, the corresponding record in the products table will be updated to subtract the quantity of the order from the quantity on hand in the instock column of the products table.

The next type of trigger that we'll look into is just as powerful. Let's delve into DELETE triggers.

Working with *DELETE* Triggers

DELETE triggers are used for restricting the data that your users can remove from a database. For example, you may not want your users to be able to remove clients from the customers table who have at least $10,000 in credit. Going even further, you may want your users to be able to delete such customers, but you want an e-mail to be sent to management every time a user deletes one of these customers so the manager knows who deleted the customer and when.

Ordinarily, when a user executes a DELETE statement, SQL Server removes the record from the table, and the record is never heard from again. That behavior changes when a DELETE trigger is added to the table. With a DELETE trigger in place, SQL Server moves the record being deleted to a logical table in memory called *deleted*; the records aren't entirely gone, and you can still reference them in your code. This comes in handy for complex business logic.

TIP **The special deleted table can easily be compared to the Recycle Bin in the Windows operating system, where deleted files are moved before they're deleted from the system. The biggest difference is that the deleted table is automatically purged of records after a transaction is complete, whereas the Recycle Bin must be purged manually.**

Suppose you want to keep your users from deleting customers who have more than $10,000 in credit with your company. Without a DELETE trigger in place, a user could successfully delete any record they wanted, regardless of the amount of credit the customer had. With a DELETE trigger in place, however, SQL Server places the record in question in the deleted table, so you can still reference the credit limit column and base the success of the transaction on the value therein.

To get a firsthand look at how this type of trigger functions, let's create a DELETE trigger designed to prevent your users from deleting customers who live in Arizona (the code would be much the same for restricting users from deleting someone with a high credit limit):

1. Open SQL Server Management Studio by selecting it from the SQL Server 2005 group under Programs on the Start menu, and expand your server ➢ Databases ➢ Sales ➢ Tables ➢ dbo.Customers.
2. Right-click the Triggers folder, and select New Trigger.
3. In the Name box, enter **AZDel**.
4. Deselect the Insert and Update check boxes under DML Events.
5. In the Transact-SQL Syntax box, insert the following code to complete the trigger (the ROLLBACK statement is used to cancel the transaction if the customer lives in Arizona):

```
IF (SELECT state FROM deleted) = 'AZ'
 BEGIN
 PRINT 'Cannot remove customers from AZ'
 PRINT 'Transaction has been cancelled'
 ROLLBACK
 END
```

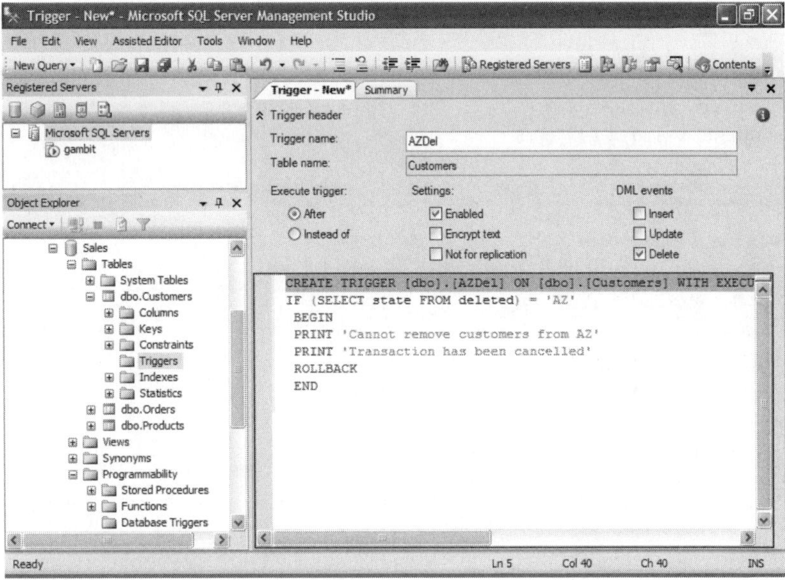

6. Click the Save button to create the trigger.

With the trigger in place, you can try to delete a customer who lives in Arizona to test the trigger:

1. Open a new SQL Server query, and execute the following code to verify that you have customers from Arizona (for example, Shane Travis should be in AZ):

```
USE Sales
SELECT * FROM customers
```

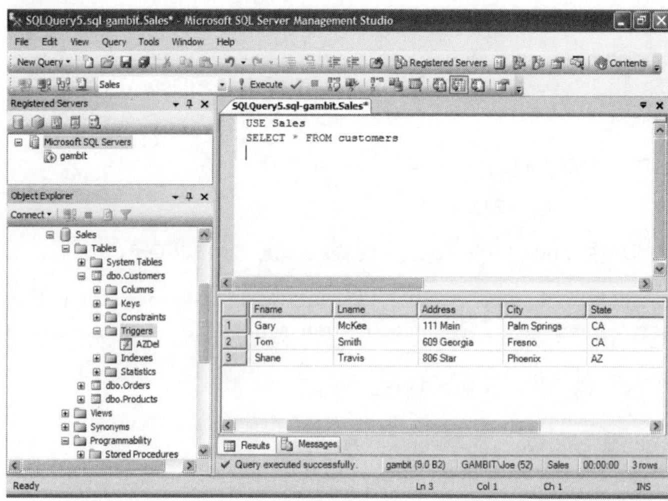

2. To cause the DELETE trigger to fire, try to delete Shane from the customers table. To do this, select New Query With Current Connection from the Query menu, and enter and execute the following code (you should see an error message upon execution):

```
USE Sales
DELETE from customers
WHERE lname = 'Travis'
```

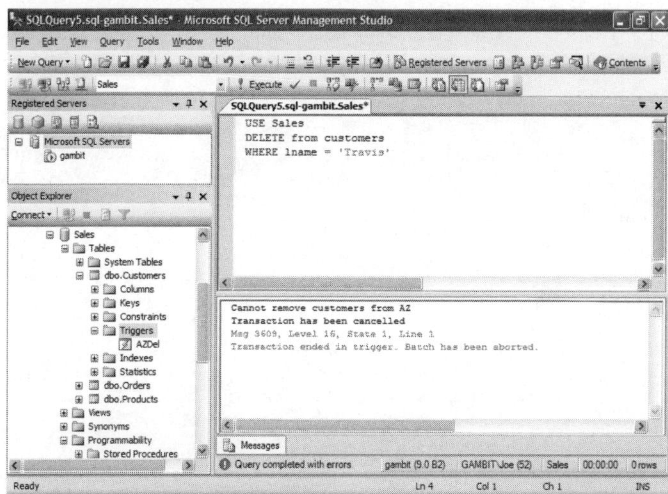

3. To verify that Shane has not been deleted, enter and execute the following code (you should still see Shane):

```
USE Sales
SELECT * FROM customers
```

4. Once you've verified that Shane is still a customer, close the query window.

Again, did you notice what you did? You created a DELETE trigger that used the logical deleted table to make certain that you weren't trying to delete a customer from the great state of Arizona—if you did try to delete such a customer, you would be met with denial in the form of an error message (generated by the PRINT statement you entered in the trigger code).

Now that you're armed with an understanding of the inner workings of INSERT and DELETE triggers, UPDATE triggers will be easier to comprehend.

Working with *UPDATE* Triggers

It stands to reason that UPDATE triggers are used to restrict UPDATE statements issued by your users. These types of triggers are specifically designed to restrict the existing data that your users can modify. Again, a good example is the credit limit scenario we've been using throughout this chapter. Since you've already established that you may not want your users to insert or delete clients who have a large amount of credit, you probably also don't want your users to modify an existing customer who has a large amount of credit. Or, you may want your users to be able to increase credit limits, but you want a message to be sent to management so they know which user has increased or decreased a credit limit and can get details from the user later. That is what an UPDATE trigger is designed to do—intercept data modifications and verify them.

The method that the UPDATE trigger uses is a combination of the methods used by the INSERT and DELETE triggers. Remember that the INSERT trigger uses the inserted table, and that a DELETE trigger uses the deleted table—the UPDATE trigger uses both tables. This is because an UPDATE action is actually two separate actions: a delete followed by an insert. First the existing data is deleted, and then the new data is inserted; it appears to the user that the existing data has been modified, when in fact it has been completely removed and replaced. This works out to your advantage.

If a user wants to modify a customer's credit limit to exceed $10,000, without a trigger in place, the credit limit column will be changed without any intervention. With an UPDATE trigger in place, SQL Server will place the existing record in the deleted table and the new record (the one above $10,000) in the inserted table. Now you can compare the two tables (inserted and deleted) to see whether the transaction should be completed.

In fact, the way your sales database sits, it could benefit from an UPDATE trigger. Right now there is no way to keep your users from overselling a product; they could sell a product even after you ran out, and the instock column of the products table would be taken down into negative numbers. That would look really bad in front of your valued customers, so you want to be able to tell them that you're out of stock on an item rather than overselling. Let's create a trigger that checks the InStock column in the products table to verify that you have stock on items before allowing an order to be placed:

1. Open SQL Server Management Studio by selecting it from the SQL Server 2005 group under Programs on the Start menu, and expand your server ➢ Databases ➢ Sales ➢ Tables ➢ dbo.Products.

2. Right-click the Triggers folder, and select New Trigger.
3. In the Name box, enter **CheckStock**.
4. Deselect the Insert and Delete check boxes under DML Events.
5. In the Transact-SQL Syntax box, insert the following code to complete the trigger:

```
IF (SELECT InStock from inserted) < 0
 BEGIN
 PRINT 'Cannot oversell Products'
 PRINT 'Transaction has been cancelled'
 ROLLBACK
 END
```

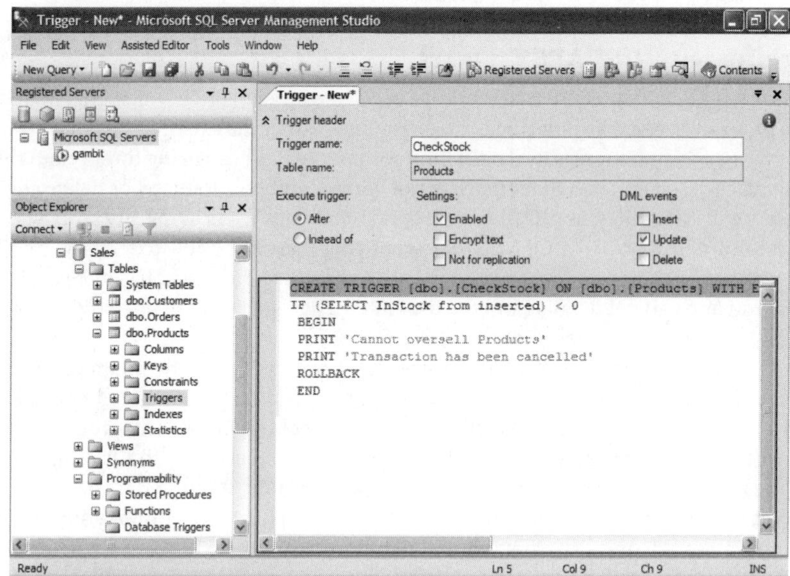

6. Click the Save button to create the trigger.

Now that you have an `UPDATE` trigger in place, you can test it by trying to oversell one of your products. You'll do this by updating one of the records in the products table directly:

1. Open a new SQL Server query, and execute the following code to verify the quantity in stock on available products (prodid 2 should have 545 in stock currently):

```
USE Sales
SELECT prodid, instock FROM Products
```

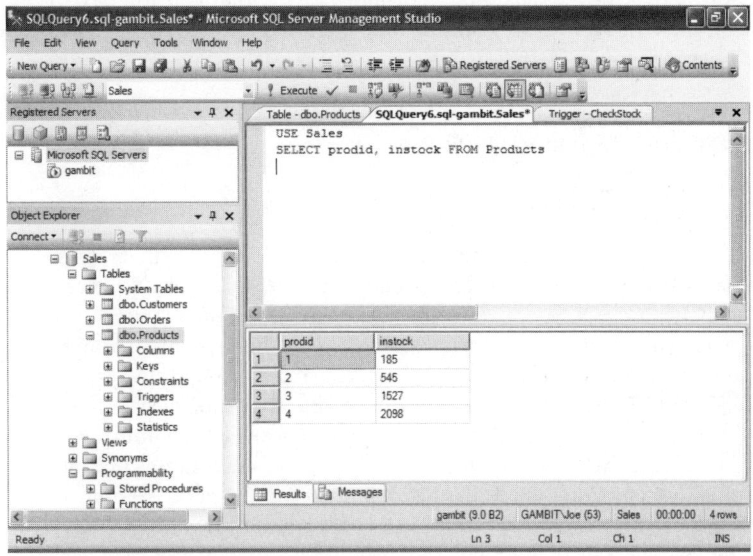

2. To cause the UPDATE trigger to fire, you'll try to sell 600 units of product ID 2 (wool blankets) to a customer. Open a new SQL Server query, and enter and execute the following code (you should see an error message upon execution):

```
USE Sales
UPDATE Products
SET InStock = (Instock - 600)
WHERE prodid = 2
```

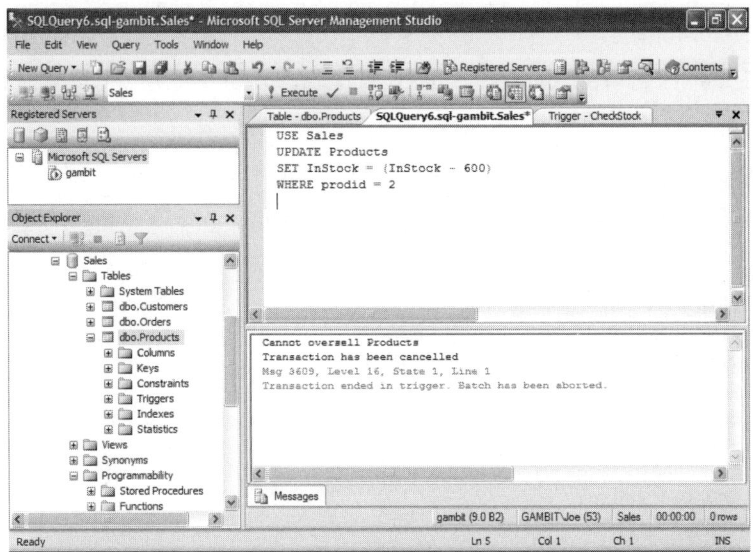

3. To verify that the transaction was disallowed and that you still have 545 wool blankets in stock, click the New Query button, and enter and execute the following code (you should still see 545 of prodid 2):

```
USE Sales
SELECT prodid, instock FROM Products
```

4. Close the query window.

Look a little closer at what you did: You created an UPDATE trigger that references the inserted table to verify that you aren't trying to insert a value that is less than zero. You need to check only the inserted table because SQL Server performs any necessary mathematical functions before inserting your data, which means that SQL Server subtracted 600 (the new value) from 545 (the existing value) before inserting the data in the table. This means the inserted table always holds the new value you need to verify. UPDATE triggers are a powerful tool, but they can be even more useful with the IF UPDATE statement, which is used to check for updates to a single column.

It may be the case that you don't mind having most of the columns in a table updated, but there is one column that you don't want changed for any reason. A good example might be a human resources database that contains various pieces of personnel information, such as names, addresses, pay rates, and social security numbers. Most of this information is subject to change, but the social security number is set for life and should not be updated for any reason (unless, of course, it was entered incorrectly in the first place). The IF UPDATE statement can be used to check for modifications to that one column and disallow them specifically.

Let's create an UPDATE trigger using the IF UPDATE statement to get a better understanding of this process. In this trigger, you'll disallow changes to the phone number field in the customers database. Be aware that this isn't a real-world example, because phone numbers do change from time to time, but it should get the point across:

1. Open SQL Server Management Studio by selecting it from the SQL Server 2005 group under Programs on the Start menu, and expand your server ➤ Databases ➤ Sales ➤ Tables ➤ dbo.Customers.

2. Right-click the Triggers folder, and select New Trigger.

3. In the Name box, enter **CheckPN**.

4. Deselect the Insert and Delete check boxes under DML Events.

5. In the Transact-SQL Syntax box, insert the following code to complete the trigger:

```
IF UPDATE(phone)
 BEGIN
 PRINT 'Cannot change phone numbers'
 PRINT 'Transaction has been cancelled'
 ROLLBACK
 END
```

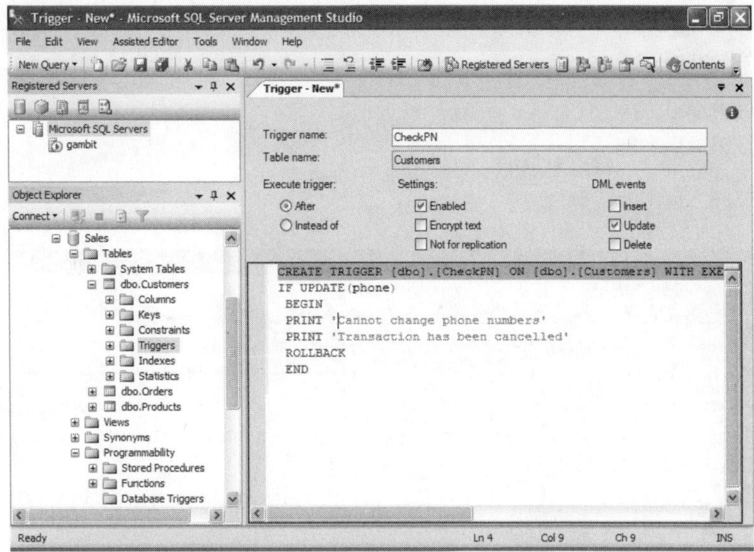

6. Click the Save button to create the trigger.

With the `IF UPDATE` trigger in place, you can test it. In the next series of steps, you'll try to update a customer's phone number to fire the trigger:

1. Open a new SQL Server query, and execute the following code to verify the phone numbers in the customers table (Tom Smith's should be 510-555-1212):

```
USE Sales
SELECT fname, lname, phone FROM customers
```

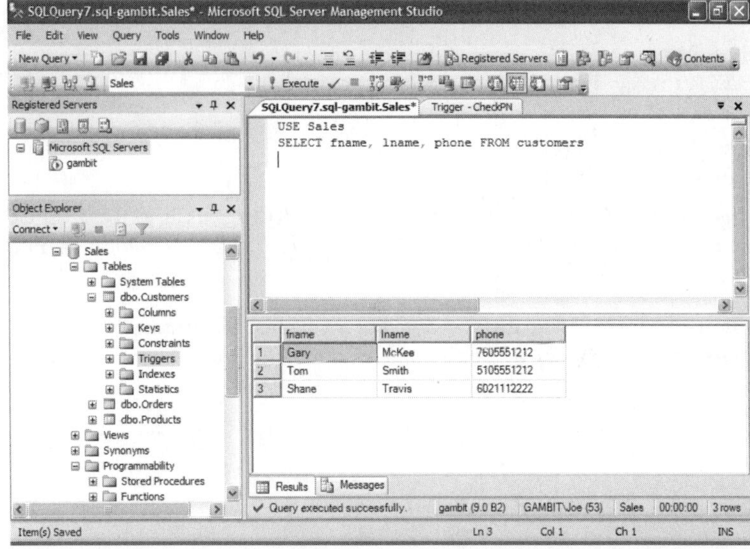

2. To cause the UPDATE trigger to fire, you'll try to modify Tom Smith's phone number. Open a new SQL Server query, and enter and execute the following code (you should be greeted with an error message):

```
USE Sales
UPDATE customers
SET phone = '8881234567'
WHERE lname = 'Smith'
```

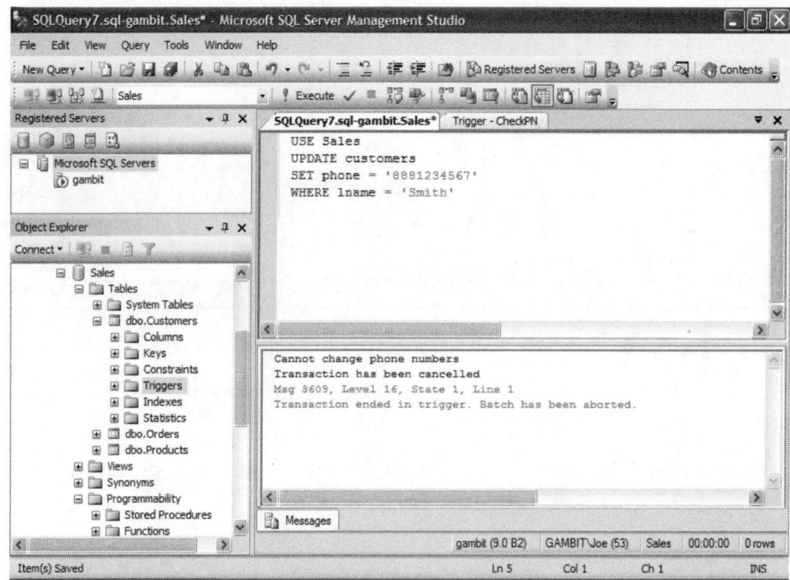

3. To verify that the transaction was disallowed, enter and execute the following code:

```
USE Sales
SELECT fname, lname, phone FROM customers
```

4. Close Query Analyzer.

NOTE The IF UPDATE statement can be used in INSERT triggers as well as in UPDATE triggers. Just don't try to use IF UPDATE in a DELETE trigger, because specific columns aren't changed by a DELETE statement.

Notice how you were able to instruct SQL Server to check for modifications on a specific column. Now, if anyone tries to change a phone number, they will be disallowed. Of course, the IF UPDATE statement is much more powerful than that; if you use your imagination, you'll find a great number of tasks for which this statement can prove useful.

Another type of trigger that will prove helpful is the INSTEAD OF trigger. Let's look at it now.

Working with *INSTEAD OF* Triggers

In Chapter 13, we discussed views, which are used to display the data stored in your tables in various ways. Views can be used to display only a few of the columns in a table, only a subset of the rows in a table, or data from more than one table at a time. This works out great when you just want to see the data, but there can be problems when you try to modify data through a view.

Because views may not display all the columns in a table, data modification statements can fail. For example, suppose you have a customers table like the one in your sales database that contains customer information such as name, address, city, state, zip code, and so on. Then suppose that you have created a view that displays all the columns except the city field. If you try to update the customers table through the new view, the update will fail because the city field (which is a required field) isn't available through the view. Using an INSTEAD OF trigger can make this type of update successful.

In the following series of steps, you'll create an INSTEAD OF trigger that can insert into a table a value that isn't available through a view. To accomplish this, you'll first create a view that doesn't display the city column (which is a required column for updates), and then you'll try to update through this column. Next you'll create an INSTEAD OF trigger that can insert the missing value for you, after which you'll try the insert again. Here we go:

1. You need to create a view that doesn't display the city column. To create a view that displays only customers from Phoenix, open a new SQL Server query in SQL Server Management Studio, and enter and execute the following code:

```
USE Sales
GO
CREATE VIEW PHX_Customers AS
SELECT fname, lname, address, state, zip, phone
FROM Customers
WHERE City = 'Phoenix'
```

2. To verify that the view displays only the columns you want, click the New Query button, and enter and execute the following query:

```
USE Sales
SELECT * FROM PHX_Customers
```

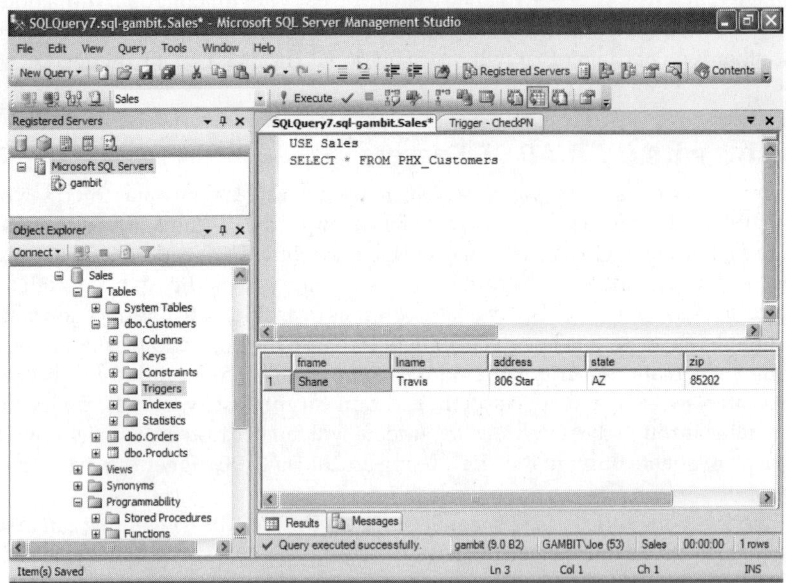

3. Try to insert a new customer through the view. To do so, select Query ➤ New Query With Current Connection, and enter and execute the following code:

```
USE Sales
INSERT PHX_Customers
VALUES ('Timothy', 'Calunod', '123 Third', 'CA', '95023', '9252221212')
```

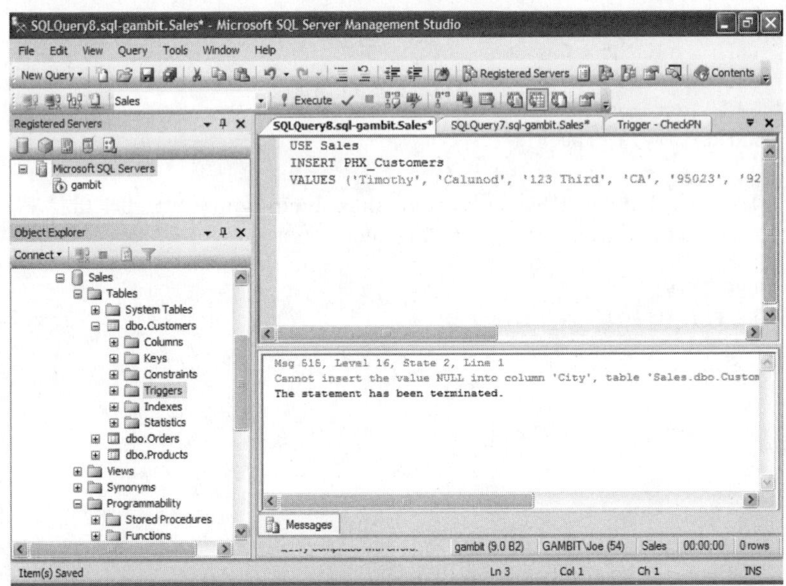

Now you have a view that you know you can't insert new records through, because the view doesn't include the city field, which is required to be populated in the customers table. In the next series of steps, you'll create an `INSTEAD OF` trigger that inserts the missing value for you when you insert through the view:

1. In Object Explorer, expand the Views folder under the Sales database, and then right-click Triggers and select New Trigger.
2. In the Name box, enter **Add_City**.
3. Notice that the Execute Trigger option is set to Instead Of (the only available option).
4. Deselect the Update and Delete check boxes under DML Events.
5. In the Transact-SQL Syntax box, insert the following code to complete the trigger:

```
DECLARE
 @FNAME VARCHAR(20),
 @LNAME VARCHAR(20),
 @ADDR VARCHAR(50),
 @CITY VARCHAR(20),
 @STATE STATE,
 @ZIP CHAR(5),
 @PHONE CHAR(10)

SET @CITY = 'Phoenix'

SET @FNAME = (SELECT FNAME FROM INSERTED)
SET @LNAME = (SELECT LNAME FROM INSERTED)
SET @ADDR = (SELECT ADDRESS FROM INSERTED)
SET @STATE = (SELECT STATE FROM INSERTED)
SET @ZIP = (SELECT ZIP FROM INSERTED)
SET @PHONE = (SELECT PHONE FROM INSERTED)

INSERT CUSTOMERS
VALUES(@FNAME, @LNAME, @ADDR, @CITY, @STATE, @ZIP, @PHONE)
```

6. Click the Save button to create the new trigger.
7. To test the trigger, enter and execute the same code from step 3 in the last series:

```
USE Sales
INSERT PHX_Customers
VALUES ('Timothy', 'Calunod', '123 Third', 'CA', '95023', '9252221212')
```

8. To verify that the data was inserted into the customers table and that the city column was populated, select Query ➤ New Query With Current Connection, and enter and execute the following query:

```
USE Sales
SELECT * FROM Customers
```

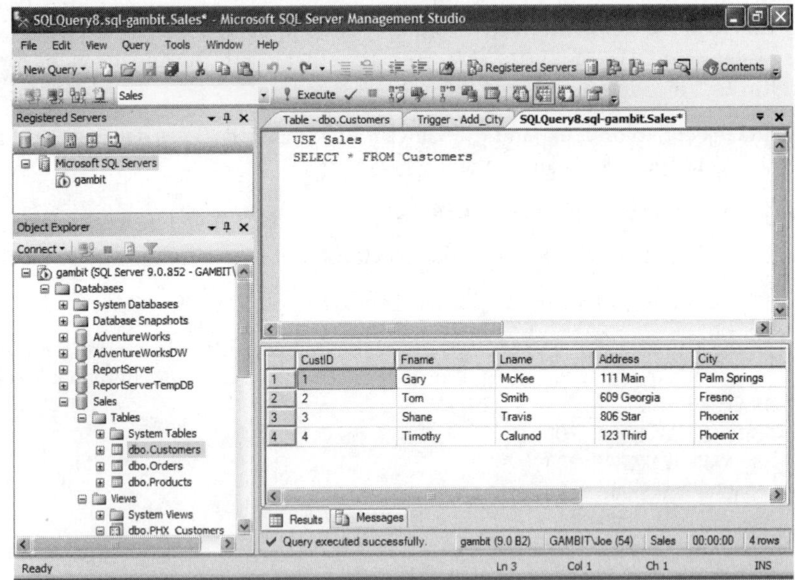

9. Close the query window.

In the first series of steps, you created a view that doesn't display the city column. Next you tried to insert a new record using the PHX_Customers view, which failed because you were unable to insert the required city value through the view. Next you created a trigger, which read all the values that you needed to insert from the inserted table and stored them in memory variables, and you created a memory variable to hold the missing city value. After filling the memory variables, all you had to do was insert the record into the customers table using the values stored in the memory variables you created—and *voilà*, you had a new customer record.

With a firm grasp of the basics of how triggers function, you're ready to look into some slightly more advanced topics.

Advanced Considerations

As with anything you do with SQL Server, there are more advanced topics to be considered when working with triggers. For example, `INSERT`, `UPDATE`, and `DELETE` triggers can be combined into one trigger for ease of management. Also, instead of using the `PRINT` statement to send errors (as you've been doing), there is a more advanced method—the `RAISERROR()` function. Finally, you need to understand recursive triggers, which occur when a trigger on one table performs an action that sets off the trigger on another table. Let's start by looking at how to combine `INSERT`, `UPDATE`, and `DELETE` triggers into one trigger.

Combining Trigger Types

Suppose you need to make certain that no one messes with your clients who have a credit limit over $10,000. Those customers should not be inserted, updated, or deleted by anyone except management, no matter what. Since you know how to create `INSERT`, `UPDATE`, and `DELETE` triggers at this point, you may think you need to use three separate triggers to keep this sort of thing from happening, but take heart—it's much simpler than that.

The three types of triggers you've just discovered can be combined into one trigger. You can combine any of the three types in any fashion: You can have an INSERT, UPDATE trigger; an UPDATE, DELETE trigger; or an INSERT, DELETE trigger; or all three can be lumped together to ease the administrative control over your triggers. When you combine the types, they work the same as they would by themselves; they just accomplish more.

Take a look at this example, where you'll modify the AZDel trigger to disallow updates and deletes of customers from Arizona:

1. Open SQL Server Management Studio by selecting it from the SQL Server 2005 group under Programs on the Start menu, and expand your server ➤ Databases ➤ Sales ➤ Tables ➤ dbo.Customers ➤ Triggers.
2. Right-click the AZDel trigger, and select Modify.
3. In the right pane, select the Update check box under DML Events (click Yes if you're asked to remove any comments in the header).

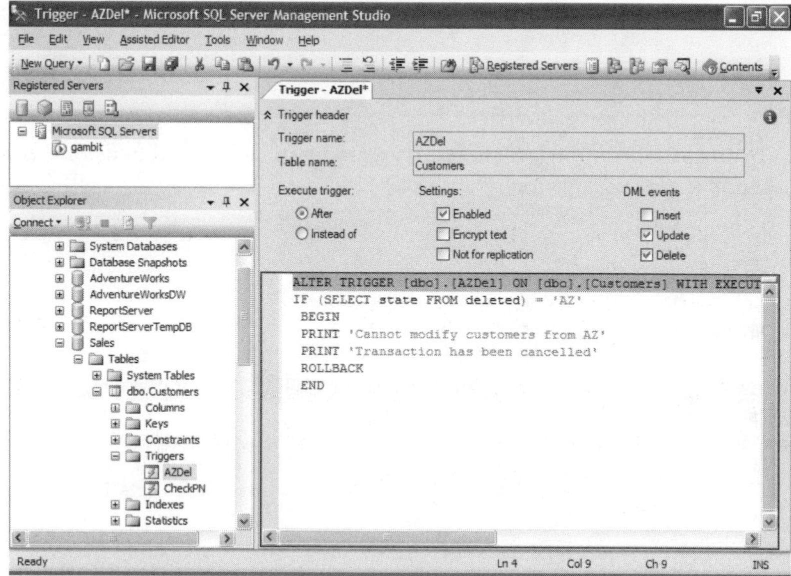

4. Click the Save button to save your modifications.
5. To test the trigger, open a new SQL Server query and enter and execute the following code to verify that you have customers from Arizona (among others, Shane Travis should be in AZ):

```
USE Sales
SELECT * FROM customers
```

6. To cause the DELETE trigger to fire, try to delete Shane from the customers table (you should see an error message upon execution):

```
USE Sales
DELETE from customers
WHERE lname = 'Travis'
```

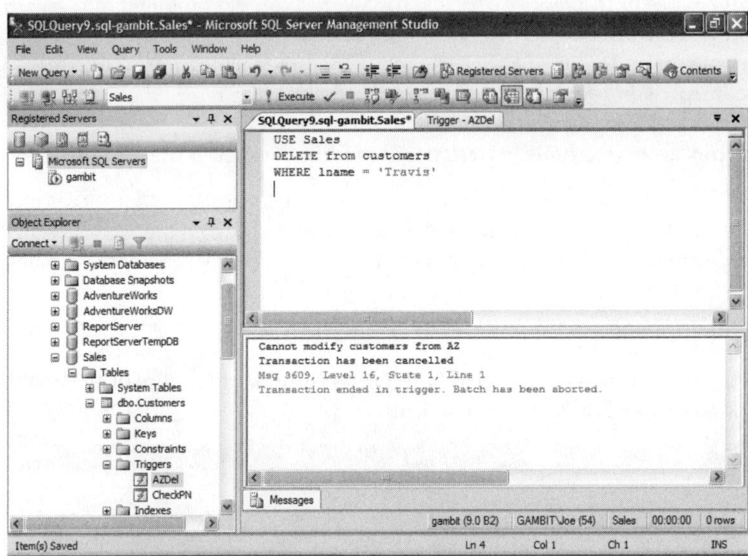

7. To cause the UPDATE trigger to fire, try to update Shane from the customers table (you should see an error message upon execution):

```
USE Sales
UPDATE customers
SET fname = 'John'
WHERE lname = 'Travis'
```

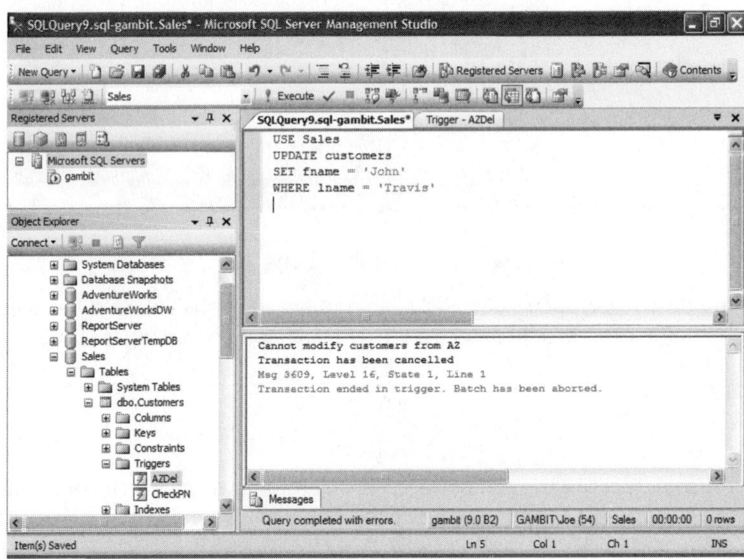

8. Close the query window.

Because you're able to combine triggers, you need to use only this single combined trigger instead of two triggers (one DELETE and one UPDATE). Combining triggers will make your job as a database guru much easier when you get used to it. Something else that will make your job easier is the ability to display meaningful errors when a trigger is violated.

Reporting Errors with *RAISERROR()*

So far, you have been using the PRINT statement to display error messages to your users when they violate a trigger. This approach works OK, but it's limited in what it can do. For example, you can't use PRINT to send an alert to management if someone deletes a customer, because PRINT isn't designed to send messages to anyone other than the person issuing the offending command. For more control, you need to use RAISERROR(), because it's designed to help send error messages to anyone.

To make RAISERROR() really shine, you need a full understanding of alerts and operators; with both of those in place, there is no limit to what a trigger can do (we'll discuss alerts and operators in Chapter 17, "Automating Administration"). For now, though, you need to get used to using RAISERROR() to send messages to your end users. The syntax for the RAISERROR() command looks as follows:

```
RAISERROR('Message', severity, state)
```

The *'Message'* parameter is the text you want the user to see on the screen when they violate the trigger. In Chapter 17, you'll replace this text with an error number that can be used to fire an alert to send an e-mail. The *severity* parameter tells the system how serious this error is; you'll most likely use severity 10, which is informational. The state parameter is used just in case this particular error can be raised from more than one place in the trigger. For example, if this error could be raised at the beginning, you would set the state to 1; in the middle, it would be state 2; and so on.

NOTE Errors can be set to several severity levels, ranging from 1 (reserved by SQL Server) to 25 (the most critical of errors).

Let's modify the AZDel trigger to use RAISERROR() instead of PRINT to report errors to users:

1. Open SQL Server Management Studio by selecting it from the SQL Server 2005 group under Programs on the Start menu, and expand your server ➤ Databases ➤ Sales ➤ Tables ➤ dbo.Customers ➤ Triggers.

2. Right-click the AZDel trigger, and select Modify.

3. Change the code in the Transact-SQL syntax box to look as follows:

```
IF (SELECT state FROM deleted) = 'AZ'
 BEGIN
 RAISERROR('Cannot modify customers from AZ', 10, 1)
 ROLLBACK
 END
```

4. Click the Save button to modify the trigger.

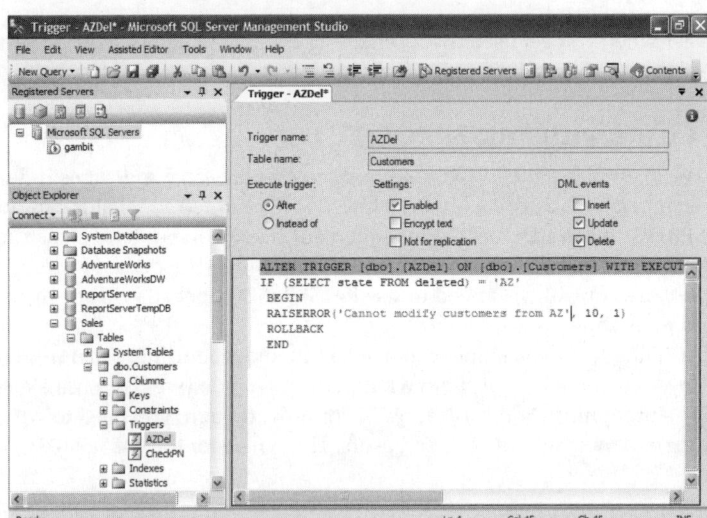

5. To test the trigger, open a new SQL Server query.

6. To cause the RAISERROR() statement to fire, try to delete Shane from the customers table again (you should see an error message upon execution):

```
USE Sales
DELETE FROM customers
WHERE lname = 'Travis'
```

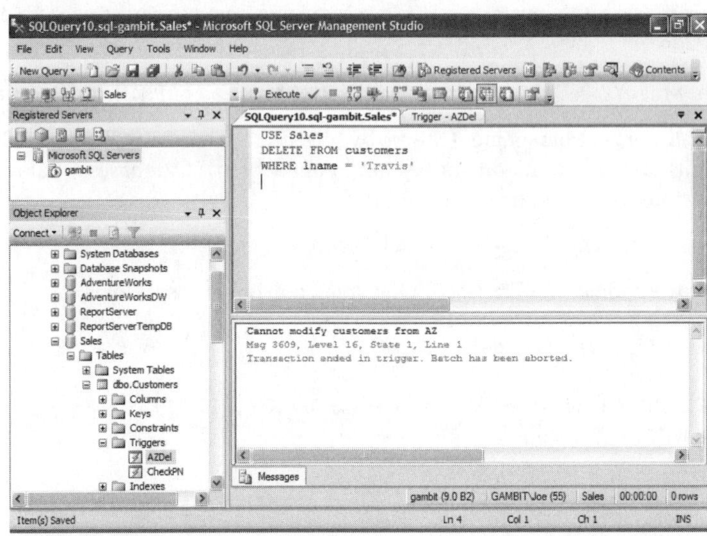

7. Close the query window.

You were able to display the same error message before with the PRINT statement, but now you'll be ready to use the more advanced features of alerts, something that PRINT statements can't do.

There is one final, advanced topic that you need to be aware of when working with triggers. They can be recursive if you let them.

Recursive Triggers

As you've seen throughout the chapter, triggers can exist on every table in the database. Those triggers can also contain code that updates other tables; you saw that in the `INSERT` trigger at the outset. Here's the dilemma, though: A trigger that updates other tables can cause triggers on other tables to fire. This is called a *recursive trigger*.

A good example of a recursive trigger is the `INSERT` trigger you saw at the outset of the chapter. When you insert a new record in the orders table in your sales database, the `INSERT` trigger on the orders table fires and updates the InStock column of the products table, subtracting the amount sold from the amount on hand. There is also an `UPDATE` trigger on the products table that fires every time the table is updated to make sure that you aren't taking the InStock column below zero and thus overselling the product. This means the `INSERT` trigger on the orders table can cause the `UPDATE` trigger on the products table to fire, meaning it's a recursive trigger.

If you were to try the scenario presented right now, it wouldn't work; Microsoft is trying to save you from yourself, so recursive triggers are disabled by default. Recursive triggers are very complex, and you need to understand your tables and triggers thoroughly before enabling recursive triggers. You must be familiar with two important issues when you enable recursive triggers on your database:

- All the triggers together are considered one big transaction. A `ROLLBACK` command used anywhere, in any of the triggers, will cancel all the data input. All the data will be erased, and nothing will be put in any of the tables.
- Triggers can be recursive up to only 16 levels. This means that if trigger 16 in the chain fires off a seventeenth trigger, it's like issuing a `ROLLBACK` command: Everything will be erased.

That being said, let's turn on and test recursive triggers on your sales database:

1. Open SQL Server Management Studio, and expand your server ➤ Databases.
2. Right-click the sales database, and select Properties.
3. On the Options page, change Recursive Triggers Enabled to True.

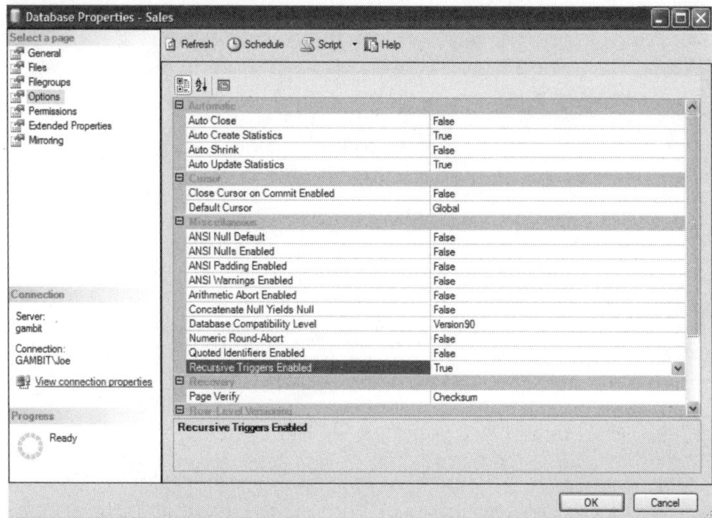

4. Click OK to apply the change.
5. To fire the trigger on the orders database and have it in turn fire the trigger on the products database, open a new SQL Server query and enter and execute the following code, which will add an order for customer 1, prodid 2, qty 600 sold today (note that this will fail because you're trying to oversell the product):

```
USE Sales
INSERT Orders
VALUES (1,2,600,getdate())
```

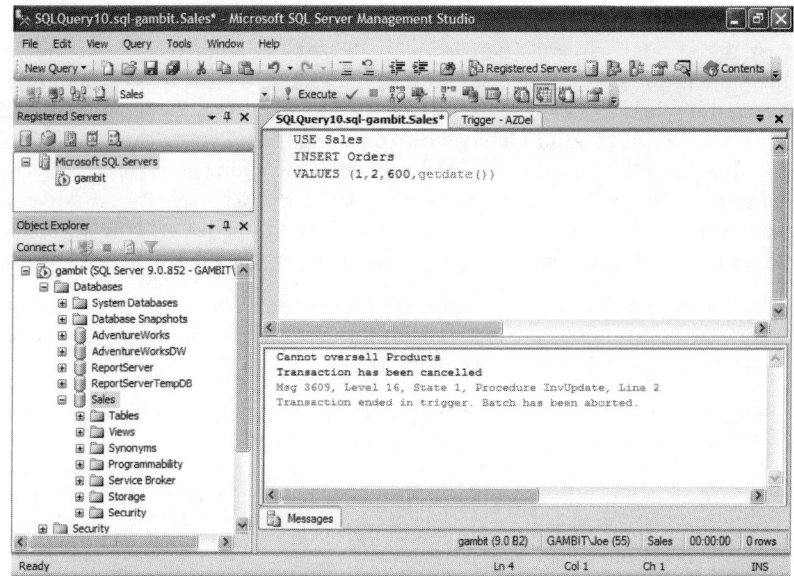

6. To verify that the entire transaction was rolled back, check for an order placed today for 600 of prodid 2 (you should not see the order, because it has been rolled back):

```
USE Sales
SELECT * from Orders
```

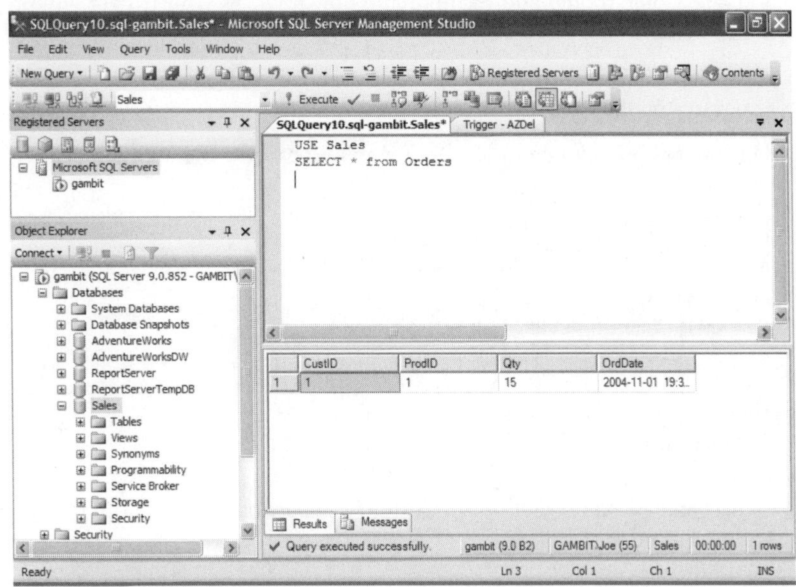

7. Close the query window.

Notice what you did: You inserted a new record into the orders table that fired the `INSERT` trigger on the orders table. That `INSERT` trigger tried to update the products table, which in turn fired the `UPDATE` trigger on the products table. That `UPDATE` trigger figured out that you were trying to oversell the product and rolled back the entire transaction, leaving you with nothing but an error message. When used properly, this technique can be a useful tool; when used improperly, it can be very detrimental. Get to know your database before you turn on this feature.

Using DDL Triggers

Like Data Manipulation Language triggers, Data Definition Language (DDL) triggers fire in response to an event. The big difference between DDL and DML triggers is the event that fires them. DDL triggers don't fire in response to `INSERT`, `UPDATE`, and `DELETE` statements; instead, they fire on `CREATE`, `ALTER`, and `DROP` statements—any statement that modifies the structure of the database.

This new type of trigger can come in very handy if you want to control who gets to modify the structure of a database and how they get to modify it, or even if you just want to track changes to the schema. For example, suppose you have a temporary contract employee working on a sensitive database, and you want to make sure they can't drop columns without telling you first. You can create a DDL trigger to prevent it from happening. Or, you can allow the contractor to drop columns all they want, and use a DDL trigger to log the changes to a table.

Let's create a DDL trigger and see firsthand how it works. This trigger will prevent you from dropping or altering tables in the sales database:

1. Open SQL Server Management Studio by selecting it from the SQL Server 2005 group under Programs on the Start menu.
2. Open a new SQL Server query, and enter and execute the following code:

```
USE Sales
GO
CREATE TRIGGER CantDropCustomers
ON DATABASE
FOR DROP_TABLE, ALTER_TABLE
AS
   PRINT 'You must disable Trigger " CantDropCustomers" to drop or alter
tables!'
   ROLLBACK ;
```

3. Select Query ➤ New Query With Current Connection, and test your new trigger by entering and executing this code:

```
DROP_TABLE Products
```

4. You should see an error message telling you that you can't drop tables because they're protected by your new trigger.

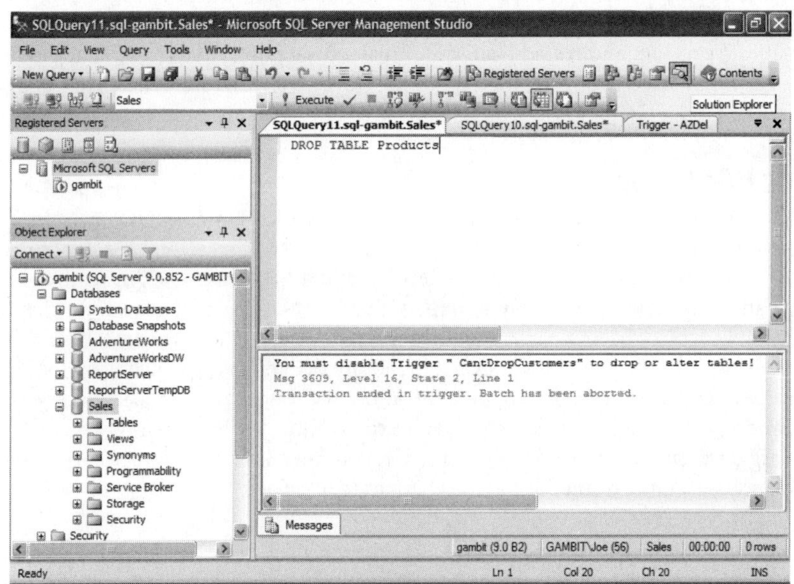

5. Close SQL Server Management Studio.

Summary

There was a lot of information to assimilate in this chapter, information that will make your job, and therefore your life, easier.

The first thing you learned is what a trigger is and how it functions. Triggers are data watchdogs that fire when a user attempts to perform an `INSERT`, `UPDATE`, or `DELETE` action. These three types of triggers can be combined in any form, and each trigger is considered an implicit transaction because SQL Server places a `BEGIN TRAN` at the beginning of the transaction and a corresponding `COMMIT` statement at the end. To keep track of the data being inserted or removed, triggers use the logical deleted and inserted tables.

You got to create some triggers, starting with each type separately and then combining two of the types (`DELETE` and `UPDATE`). We then discussed how to better control data modification through a view using the `INSTEAD OF` trigger. This special type of trigger is used to replace the action that an `INSERT`, `UPDATE`, or `DELETE` trigger might take so that the data in a view's base tables will be preserved.

After that, you discovered that the `PRINT` statement isn't the cleanest way to return error messages to users, so you worked with the `RAISERROR()` statement, which we'll discuss in more detail in Chapter 17.

Then, you learned that triggers can cause each other to fire. These are referred to as recursive triggers; they can be a powerful ally or a powerful foe, so use them wisely.

Finally we talked about the new DDL triggers. Using these triggers, you can protect your database schema from accidental or malicious updates by intercepting Data Definition Language statements.

Now that you understand the power of the trigger, you're ready to move forward. In the next chapter, we'll look at some necessary procedures for maintaining your databases.

Part 4

Administering SQL Server

In this section:

Chapter 16

Basic Administrative Tasks

If you buy a brand-new car, how long do you think it will continue to run without any maintenance? It may last a few months, maybe even a year, before it finally breaks down and quits functioning altogether. If you want to keep your car running in top shape for years to come, you have to perform regular maintenance, such as changing the oil, rotating the tires, and so on. SQL Server is no different; you must perform regular maintenance if you want to keep your server in top running condition.

The first maintenance task we'll explore is probably the most important: You must perform regular backups. Without a backup strategy, you can—no, you will—lose data. Therefore you'll want to pay close attention as we discuss each of the four types of backup (full, differential, transaction log, and filegroup) and how to use each one.

Another important topic that we'll cover is how to read the SQL Server error logs and what to do with the information you find there. SQL Server keeps its own error logs apart from the Windows NT logs that you may be used to reading in Event Viewer, so this section of the book will serve you well.

Finally, we'll delve into the depths of index maintenance. You created indexes in Chapter 12 ("Indexing"); now you need to know how to keep them running by performing regular maintenance on them. We'll start by looking into backups.

Backing Up Your Data

A *backup* is a copy of your data that is stored somewhere other than the hard drive of your computer, usually on some type of tape (a lot like the kind you listen to); but a backup can also be stored on a hard drive on another computer connected over a local area network (LAN). Why would you want to keep a copy of your data in two places? There are many reasons.

The first reason for keeping a backup is the possibility of hardware failure. Computer hardware has a Mean Time Between Failures (MTBF) that is measured in hours. This means that every 40,000 hours or so, a piece of hardware is going to fail, and there is little you can do about it. True, you could implement fault tolerance by providing duplicate hardware, but that isn't a complete guarantee against data loss. If you don't want to lose your data when a hard disk goes bad, it's best to back up.

Another reason is the potential for natural disaster. No matter how much redundant hardware you have in place, it isn't likely to survive the wrath of a tornado, hurricane, earthquake, flood, or fire. To thwart the wrath of the elements, you need to back up your data.

A final reason is provoked by all the injustice in today's world. Many employees are angry with their boss or their company in general, and the only way they see to get revenge is by destroying or maliciously updating sensitive data. This is the worst kind of data loss, and the only way to recover from it is by having a viable backup.

Now that you have some very good reasons to back up your data, you need to know how to do it. We'll look into four different types of backup that you can perform to protect your data. But first, you need to know how the backup process works.

How Backups Work

Some things are common to all types of backup. For instance, you may wonder when you'll be able to get your users off the database long enough to perform a backup. Stop wondering—all backups in SQL Server are *online backups*, which means your users can access the database while you're backing it up. How is this possible? Because SQL Server uses *transaction logs*.

In Chapter 3, "Overview of SQL Server," you learned that SQL Server issues checkpoints on databases to copy committed transactions from the transaction log to the database. The transaction log is a lot like a diary. In a diary, you put a date next to everything that happens to you. It might look as follows:

11-21-05	Bought a car
11-22-05	Drove new car to show off
11-23-05	Drove car into tree
11-24-05	Started looking for new car

Much like a diary, a transaction log puts a log sequence number (LSN) next to each line of the log. A transaction log would look as follows:

147	Begin Tran 1
148	Update Tran 1
149	Begin Tran 2
150	Update Tran 2
151	Commit Tran 1
152	Checkpoint
153	Update Tran 2
154	Commit Tran 2

When a backup is started, SQL Server records the current LSN. Once the backup is complete, SQL Server backs up all the entries in the transaction log from the LSN it recorded at the start of the backup to the current LSN. Here's an example of how it works:

1. SQL Server checkpoints the data and records the LSN of the oldest open transaction (in this case, 149 Begin Tran 2, because it wasn't committed before the checkpoint).
2. SQL Server backs up all the pages of the database that contain data (no need to back up the empty ones).
3. SQL Server grabs all the parts of the transaction log that were recorded during the backup process—that is, all the lines of the transaction log with an LSN higher than the LSN recorded at the start of the backup session (in this case, 149 and above). This way, your users can still do whatever they want with the database while it's being backed up.

To perform any type of backup, you need a place to store it. The medium that you'll use to store a backup is called a *backup device*. Let's see how to create it now.

Creating a Backup Device

Backups are stored on a physical backup media, which can be a tape drive or a hard disk (local or over a network connection). SQL Server isn't aware of the various forms of media attached to your server, so you must inform SQL Server where to store the backups. That is what a backup device is for; it's a representation of the backup media. You can create two types of backup devices: permanent and temporary.

Temporary backup devices are created on the fly when you perform the backup. They're useful for making a copy of a database to send to another office so that they have a complete copy of your data. Or, you may want to consider using a temporary backup device to make a copy of your database for permanent offsite storage (usually for archiving).

NOTE Although it's true that you could use replication (discussed in Chapter 27, "Notification Services") to copy a database to a remote site, backing up to a temporary backup device may be faster if your remote site is connected via a slow wide area network (WAN) link (such as 56K Frame Relay).

Permanent backup devices can be used over and over again; you can even append data to them, making them the perfect device for regularly scheduled backups. Permanent backup devices are created before the backup is performed and, like temporary devices, can be created on a local hard disk, on a remote hard disk over a LAN, or on a local tape drive. Let's create a permanent backup device now:

1. Open SQL Server Management Studio by selecting it from the SQL Server 2005 group under Programs on the Start menu. Expand your server and then Management.
2. Right-click Backup Devices in Object Explorer, and select New Backup Device.
3. In the Device Name box of the Backup Device dialog box, enter **AdvWorksFull**. Notice that the filename and path are filled in for you; make sure you have enough free space on the drive that SQL Server has selected.

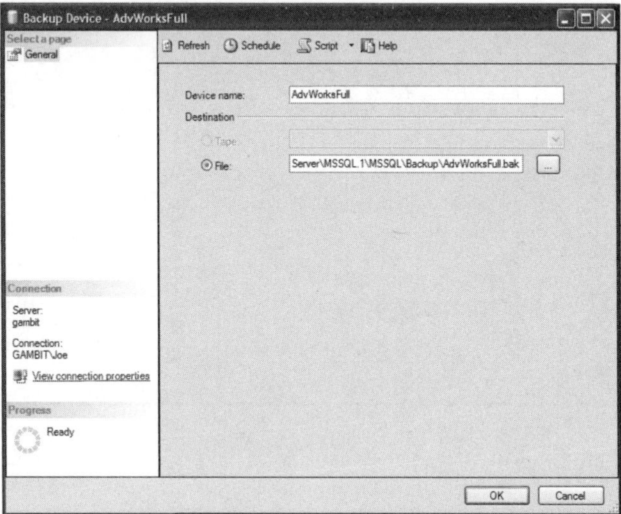

4. Click OK to create the device.

If you go to Windows Explorer and search for a file named `AdvWorksFull.bak` right now, don't be too surprised if you don't find it. SQL Server hasn't created a file yet; it simply added a record to the sysdevices table in the master database telling SQL Server where to create the backup file the first time you perform a backup to the device.

TIP If you're using a tape drive as a backup medium, it must be physically attached to the SQL Server machine. The only way around this requirement is to use a third-party backup solution.

Performing a Full Backup

Just as the name implies, a *full backup* is a backup of the entire database. It backs up the database files, the locations of those files, and portions of the transaction log (from the LSN recorded at the start of the backup to the LSN at the end of the backup). This is the first type of backup you need to perform in any backup strategy because all the other backup types depend on the existence of a full backup. This means you can't perform a differential or transaction log backup if you have never performed a full backup.

To create your *baseline* (which is what the full backup is called in a backup strategy), let's back up the AdventureWorks database to the permanent backup device you created in the previous section of this chapter:

1. Open SQL Server Management Studio. Expand your server and then Databases.
2. Right-click AdventureWorks, and select Properties.
3. On the Files page, change the Recovery Model to Full so you can perform a transaction log backup later.

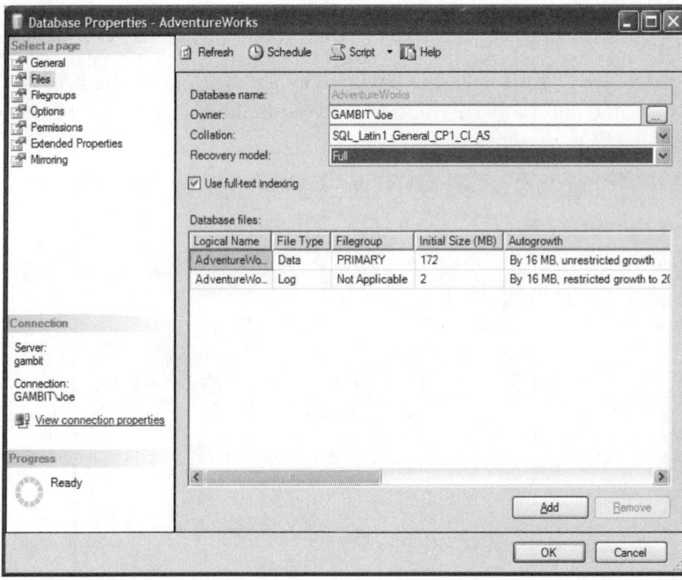

4. Click OK to apply the changes.

5. Right-click AdventureWorks under Databases, point to Tasks, and click Back Up.
6. In the Backup dialog box, make sure AdventureWorks is the selected database to back up and the Backup Type is Full.
7. Leave the default name in the Name box. In the Description box, type **Full Backup of AdventureWorks**.
8. Under Destination, a disk device may already be listed. If so, select the device and click Remove.
9. Under Destination, click Add.
10. In the Select Backup Destination box, click Backup Device, select AdvWorksFull, and click OK.

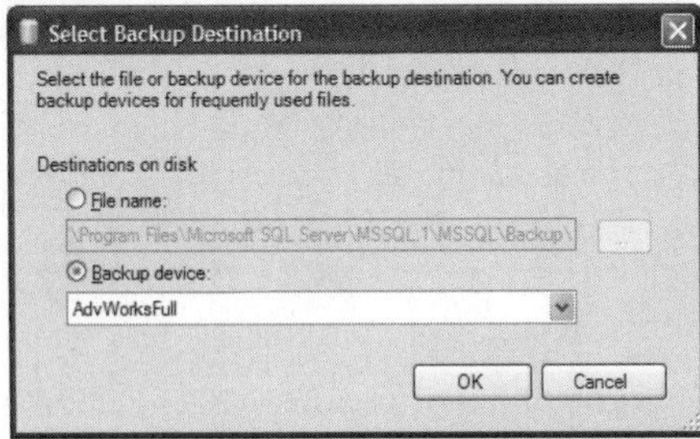

11. You should now have a backup device listed under Destination. Switch to the Options page.

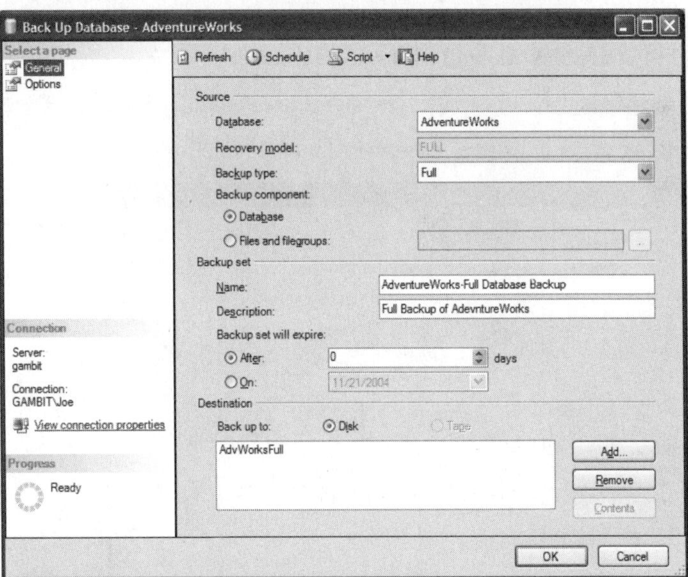

12. On the Options page, select Overwrite All Existing Backup Sets. This option initializes a brand-new device or overwrites an existing one.

13. Select Verify Backup When Finished to check the actual database against the backup copy and be sure they match after the backup is complete.

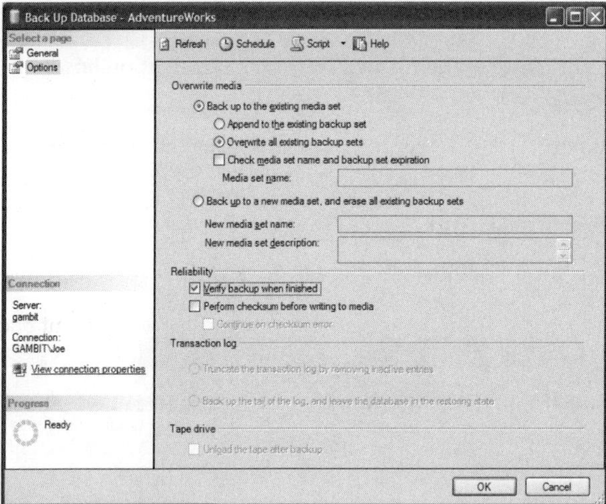

14. Click OK to start the backup.

You now have a full backup of the AdventureWorks database. Let's look inside the AdvWorks-Full device to make sure the backup is there:

1. In SQL Server Management Studio, expand Backup Devices under Management in Object Explorer.
2. Right-click AdvWorksFull, and select Properties.
3. On the Media Contents page, you should see the full backup of AdventureWorks.
4. Click OK to get back to SQL Server Management Studio.

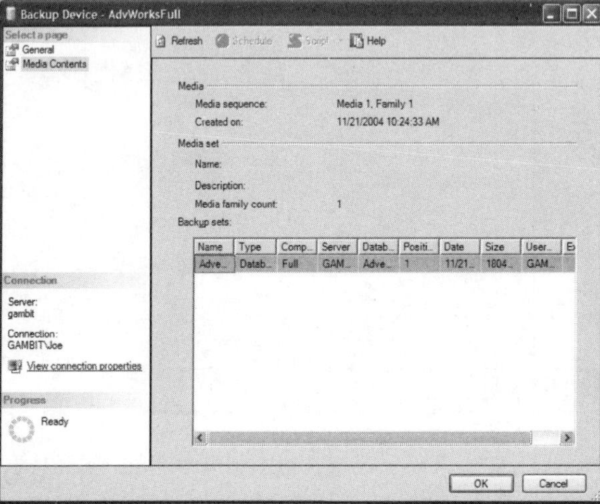

Now that you have a full backup in place, you can start performing other types of backups. Let's look at differential backups next.

Performing Differential Backups

Differential backups are designed to record all the changes made to a database since the last full backup was performed. Thus if you perform a full backup on Monday and a differential backup on Tuesday, the differential will record all the changes to the database since the full backup on Monday. Another differential backup on Wednesday would record all the changes made since the full backup on Monday. The differential backup gets a little bigger each time it's performed, but it's still a great deal smaller than the full backup; so, a differential is faster than a full backup.

SQL Server figures out which pages in the backup have changed by reading the last LSN of the last full backup and comparing it with the data pages in the database. If SQL Server finds any updated data pages, it backs up the entire extent (eight contiguous pages) of data, rather than just the page that changed.

Performing a differential backup follows almost the same process as a full backup. Let's perform a differential backup on the AdventureWorks database to the permanent backup device you created earlier:

1. Open SQL Server Management Studio. Expand your server and then Databases.
2. Right-click AdventureWorks, point to Tasks, and select Back Up.
3. In the Backup dialog box, make sure AdventureWorks is the selected database to back up and the Backup Type is Differential.
4. Leave the default name in the Name box. In the Description box, type **Differential Backup of AdventureWorks**.
5. Under Destination, make sure the AdvWorksFull device is listed.

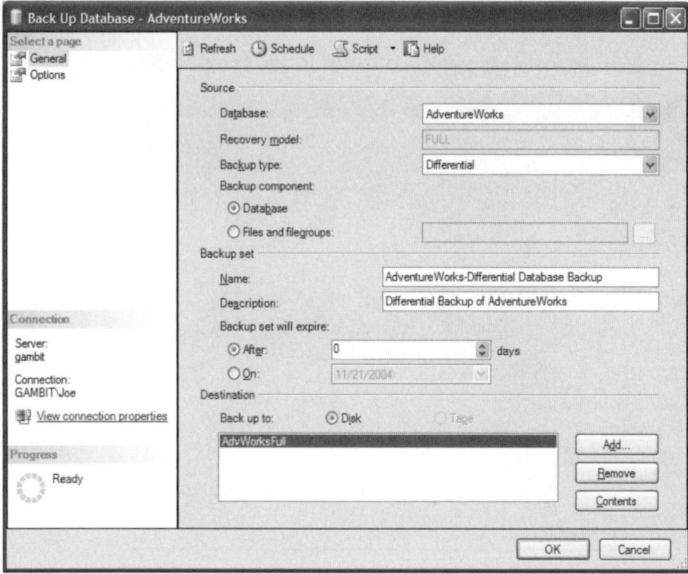

6. On the Options page, make sure Append To The Existing Backup Set is selected so that you don't overwrite your existing full backup.

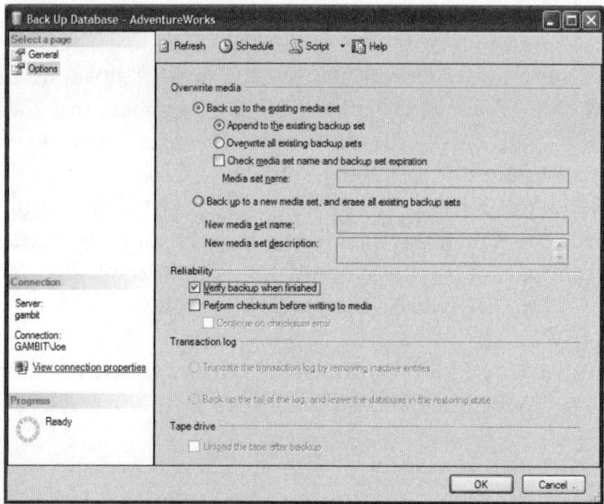

7. On the Options tab, select Verify Backup When Finished.
8. Click OK to start the backup.

Now you need to verify that the differential and full backups are on the AdvWorksFull device where they should be:

1. In SQL Server Management Studio, expand Backup Devices under Management in Object Explorer.
2. Right-click AdvWorksFull, and select Properties.
3. On the Media Contents page, you should see the differential backup of AdventureWorks.

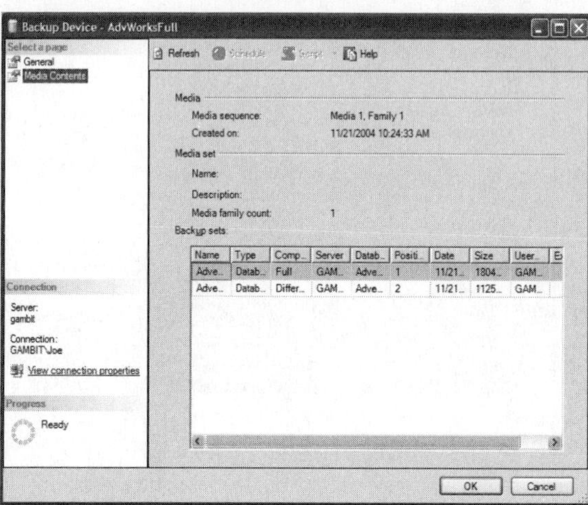

Name	Type	Comp...	Server	Datab...	Positi...	Date	Size	User...
Adve...	Datab...	Full	GAM...	Adve...	1	11/21...	1804...	GAM...
Adve...	Datab...	Differ...	GAM...	Adve...	2	11/21...	1125...	GAM...

4. Click OK to get back to SQL Server Management Studio.

Performing only full and differential backups isn't enough. If you don't perform transaction log backups, your database could stop functioning.

Performing Transaction Log Backups

Although they rely on the existence of a full backup, *transaction log backups* don't back up the database itself. This type of backup only records sections of the transaction log, specifically since the last transaction log backup. It's easier to understand the role of the transaction log backup if you think of the transaction log the way SQL Server does: as a separate object. Then it makes sense that SQL Server requires a backup of the database as well as the log.

In addition to the fact that a transaction log is an entity unto itself, there is another important reason to back it up. When a database is configured to use the Full or Bulk-Logged recovery model, a transaction log backup is the only type of backup that clears old transactions out of the transaction log; full and differential backups can only clear the log when the database being backed up is configured to use the Simple recovery model. Therefore, if you were to perform only full and differential backups on most production databases, the transaction log would eventually fill to 100 percent capacity, and your users would be locked out of the database.

WARNING **When a transaction log becomes 100 percent full, users are denied access to the database until an administrator clears the transaction log. The best way around this is to perform regular transaction log backups.**

Performing a transaction log backup doesn't involve a lot of steps, so let's go through them. In this section, you'll perform a transaction log backup on the AdventureWorks database using the backup device created earlier in this chapter:

1. Open SQL Server Management Studio. Expand your server and then Databases.
2. Right-click AdventureWorks, point to Tasks, and select Back Up.
3. In the Backup dialog box, make sure AdventureWorks is the selected database to back up and the Backup Type is Transaction Log.
4. Leave the default name in the Name box. In the Description box, type **Transaction Log Backup of AdventureWorks**.
5. Under Destination, make sure the AdvWorksFull device is listed.

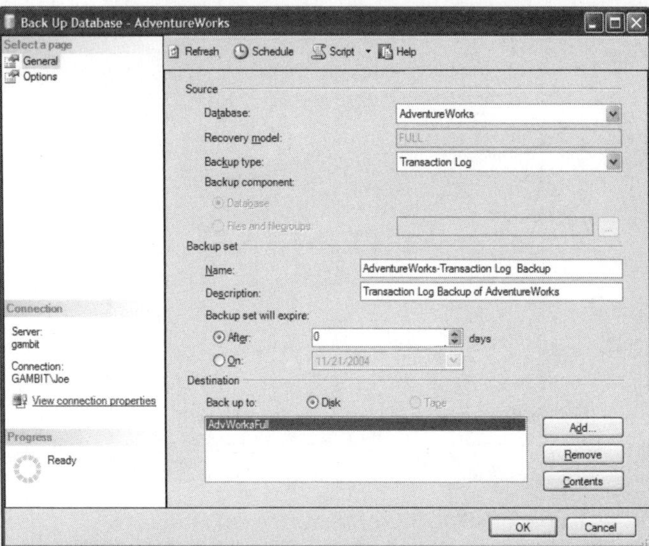

6. On the Options page, make sure Append To The Existing Backup Set is selected so that you don't overwrite your existing full backup.

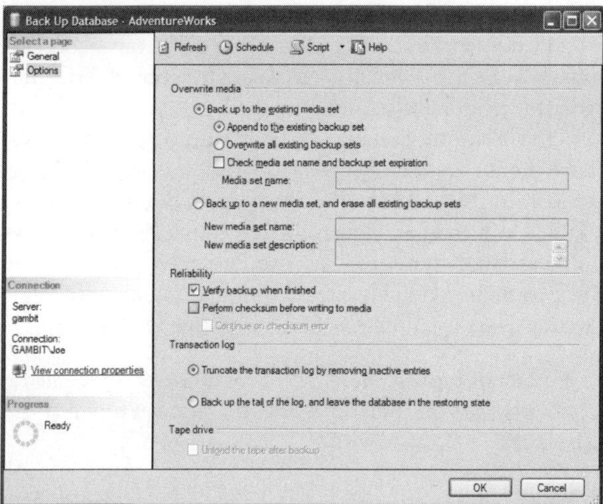

7. On the Options page, select Verify Backup When Finished.
8. Click OK to start the backup.

It's again prudent for you to manually verify that you did not accidentally overwrite the full and differential backups that were stored in your backup device:

1. In SQL Server Management Studio, expand Backup Devices under Management in Object Explorer.
2. Right-click AdvWorksFull, and select Properties.
3. On the Media Contents page, you should see the transaction log backup of AdventureWorks.

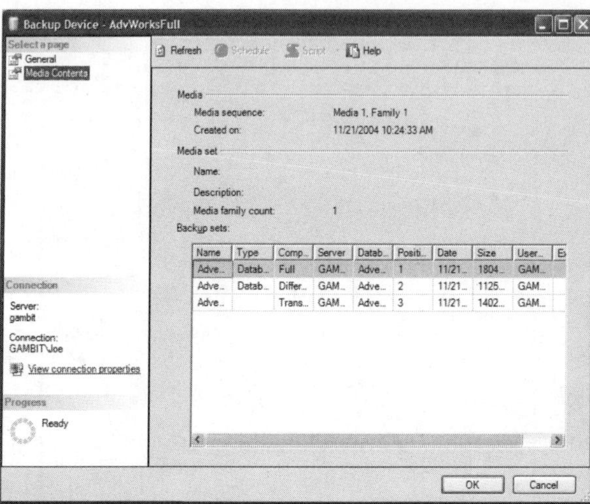

4. Click OK to get back to SQL Server Management Studio.

Full, differential, and transaction log backups are great for small to large databases, but there is another type of backup specially designed for very large databases that are usually terabytes in size. Let's look into filegroup backups to see how they can be used in such a scenario.

Performing Filegroup Backups

A growing number of companies have databases that are reaching the terabyte range. For good reason, these are known as *very large databases* (VLDBs). Imagine trying to perform a backup of a 2TB database on a nightly, or even weekly, basis. Even if you have purchased the latest, greatest hardware, you're looking at a very long backup time. Microsoft knows you don't want to wait that long for a backup to finish, so it gives you a way to back up small sections of the database at a time: a *filegroup backup*.

We discussed filegroups in Chapters 3 and 10 ("Databases"), so we won't rehash much detail here. A *filegroup* is a way of storing a database on more than one file, and it gives you the ability to control on which of those files your objects (such as tables or indexes) are stored. This way, a database isn't limited to being contained on one hard disk; it can be spread out across many hard disks and thus can grow quite large. Using a filegroup backup, you can back up one or more of those files at a time rather than the entire database all at once.

However, you need to be aware of a caveat when using filegroup backups to accelerate the backup process for VLDBs. Filegroups can also be used to expedite data access by placing tables on one file and the corresponding indexes on another file. Although this speeds up data access, it can slow the backup process because you must back up tables and indexes as a single unit, as shown in Figure 16.1. This means that if the tables and indexes are stored on separate files, the files must be backed up as a single unit; you can't back up the tables one night and the associated indexes the next.

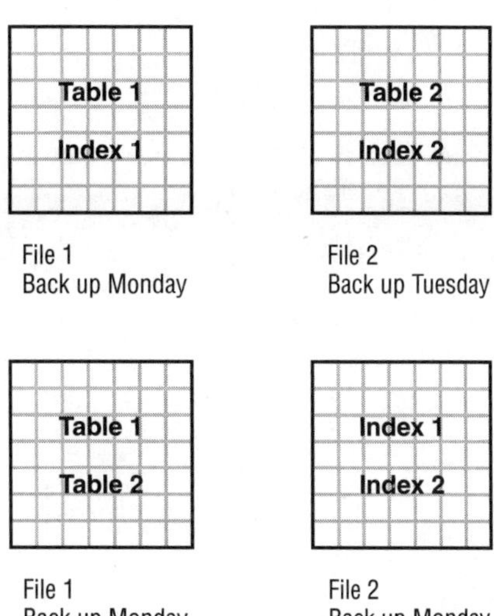

FIGURE 16.1 Tables and indexes must be backed up as a single unit if they're stored on separate files.

To perform a filegroup backup, you need to create a filegroup. Let's add a file to the Sales database you created in Chapter 10:

1. Open SQL Server Management Studio. Expand your server and then Databases.
2. Right-click the Sales database, and select Properties.

3. On the Filegroups page, click the Add button. In the Name text box, enter **Secondary**.

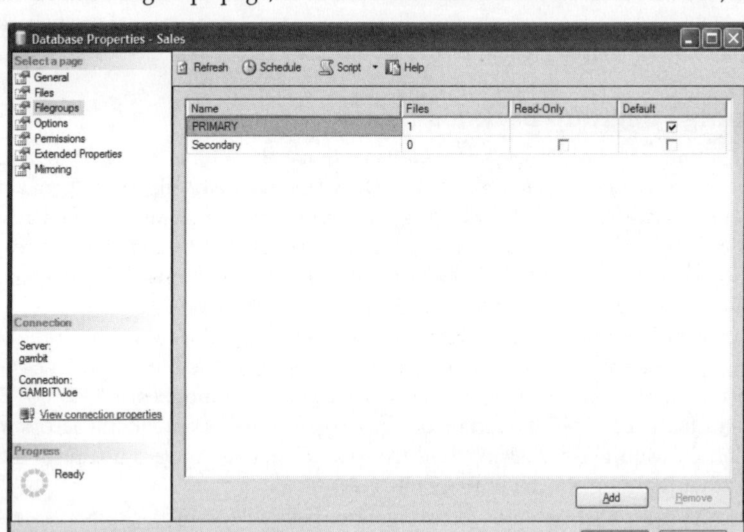

4. On the Files page, click the Add button and enter this information:
   - Name: Sales_Data_2
   - File Type: Data
   - Filegroup: Secondary
   - Initial Size: 5
5. Click OK to create the new file on the Secondary filegroup.

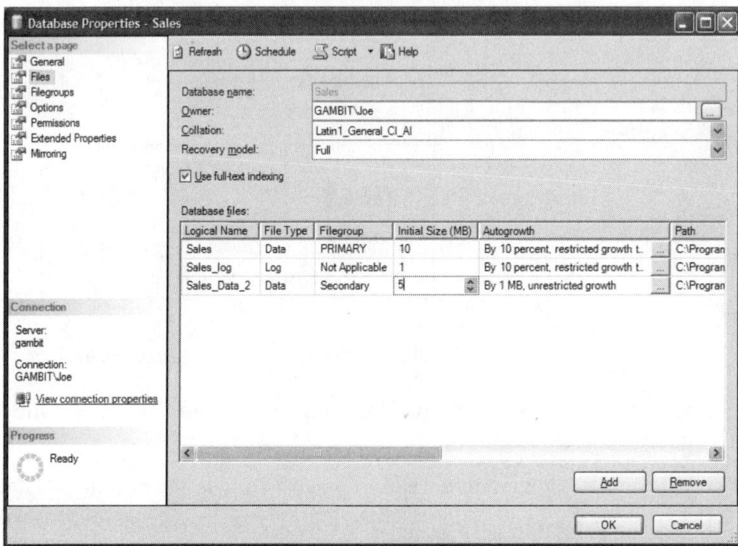

Now you need to add a table to that filegroup and create a record in it so that you'll be able to test the restore process later in this chapter:

1. In SQL Server Management Studio, expand the Sales database, right-click Tables, and select New Table.
2. Under Column Name in the first row, enter **Emp_Name**.
3. Next to Emp_Name, select varchar as the datatype. Leave the default length of 50.
4. Just below Emp_Name in the second row, type **Emp_Number** as the column name with a type of varchar. Leave the default length of 50.

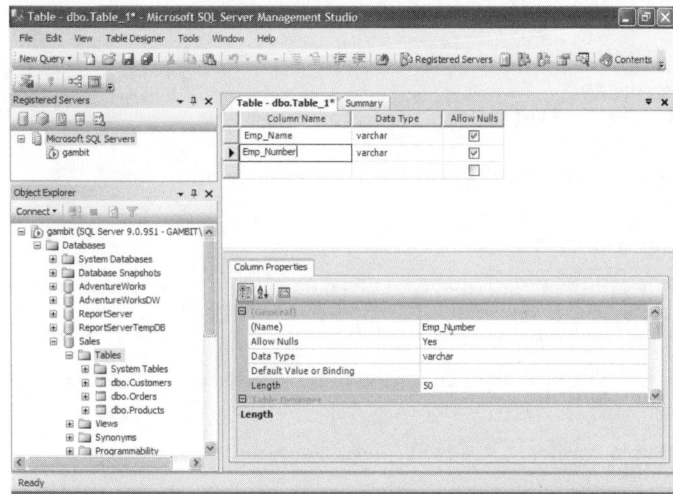

5. Select View ➤ Properties Window.
6. Expand the Regular Data Space Specification section, and change the Filegroup Or Partition Scheme Name setting to Secondary.

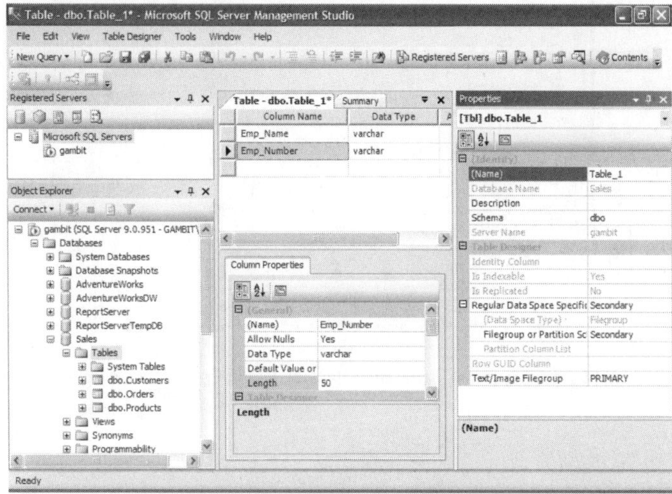

7. Click the Save button to create the new table (it looks like a floppy disk on the toolbar), and enter **Employees** for the table name.
8. Close the table designer by clicking the X in the upper-right corner of the window.

Now you need to add some data to the new table so that you'll have something to restore from the backup you're about to make:

1. Click the New Query button, and Select New SQL Server Query in SQL Server Management Studio.
2. To add records to the Employees table, enter and execute the following code (note that the second value is arbitrary):

```
USE Sales
INSERT Employees
VALUES('Tim Hsu', 'VA1765FR')
INSERT Employees
VALUES('Sue Hernandez', 'FQ9187GL')
```

3. Close the query window.

With a second filegroup in place that contains data, you can perform a filegroup backup:

1. Right-click the Sales database in Object Explorer, point to Tasks, and select Back Up.
2. In the Backup dialog box, make sure Sales is the selected database to back up and the Backup Type is Full.
3. Under Backup component, select Files And Filegroups.
4. In the Select Files And Filegroups dialog, check the box next to Secondary and click OK (notice that the box next to Sales_Data_2 is automatically checked).

5. Leave the default name in the Name box. In the Description box, type **Filegroup Backup of Sales**.

6. Under Destination, make sure the AdvWorksFull device is the only one listed.

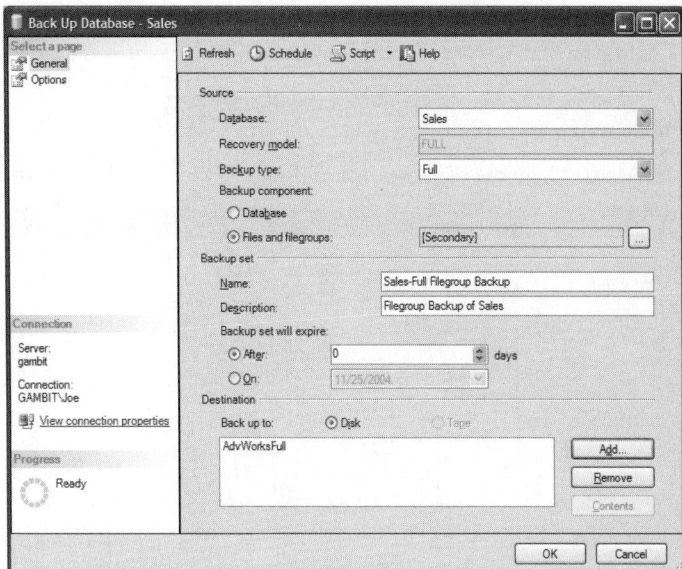

7. On the Options tab, make sure Append To The Existing Backup Set is selected so that you don't overwrite your existing backups.

8. On the Options tab, select Verify Backup When Finished.

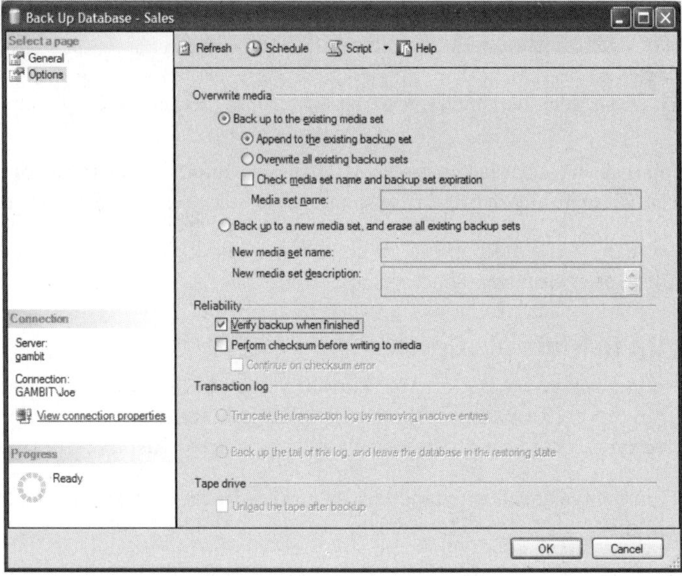

9. Click OK to start the backup.

Now that you have backed up a single file of the Sales database, let's verify that it made it to the backup device:

1. In SQL Server Management Studio, expand Backup Devices under Management in Object Explorer.
2. Right-click AdvWorksFull, and select Properties.
3. On the Media Contents page, you should see the filegroup backup of Sales.

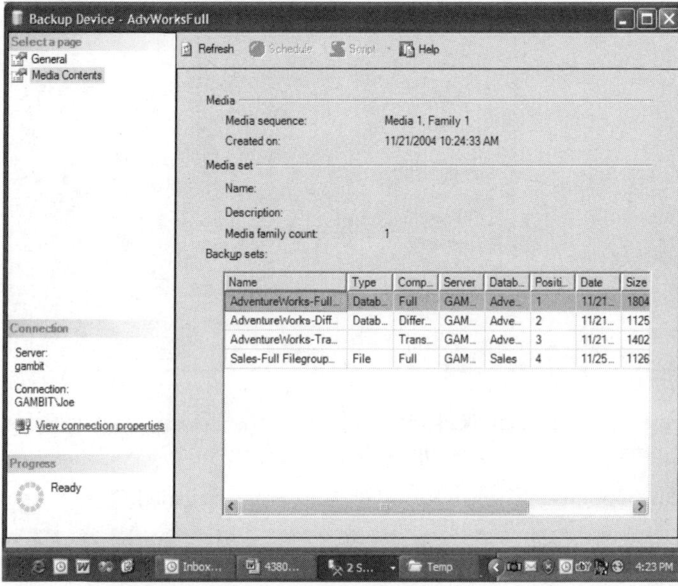

4. Click Close, and then click OK to get back to SQL Server Management Studio.

NOTE You could have backed up the Sales database to another backup device named Sales; we had you back it up to an existing device so that the exercise would move along faster.

That takes care of the mechanics of all four types of backup. Next, let's look at a technique to make the backups even faster—backing up to multiple devices.

Backing Up to Multiple Devices

Thus far you've seen how to perform backups to a single backup device. If you really want to speed things up, you can perform backups to multiple devices at the same time. This type of backup can be performed on the hard disk, network, or local tape drive, just like a normal backup.

NOTE If you want to do this with tape devices, you need more than one local tape drive in the SQL Server machine.

This type of backup uses multiple devices in parallel and writes the data in stripes across the media. What does that mean? You may expect that you fill one device to capacity and then move on to the next, but that isn't what happens. The data is *striped* across all the media at the same time, which means all the devices are written to at once; this is why it's faster to use multiple devices for backup operations

There is just one small drawback: Once you combine backup devices, they can't be used separately. As shown in Figure 16.2, if you back up AdventureWorks to three devices (BD1, BD2, and BD3), you can't back up another database to just BD3; you must use all three devices for the backup. The three devices are now considered part of a media set and can't be used separately without losing all the backups stored on the set.

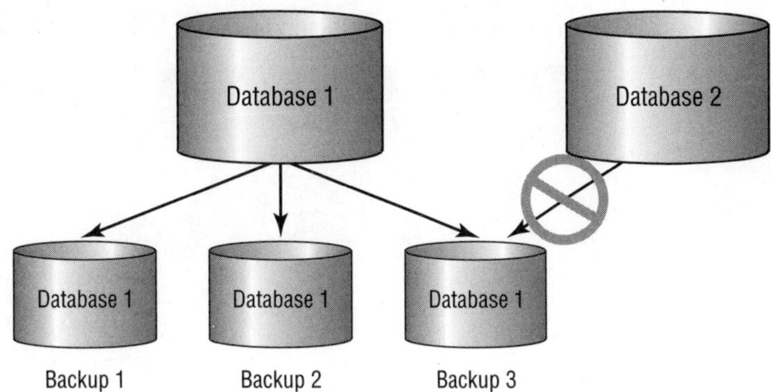

FIGURE 16.2 The backup devices in a media set can't be used for individual backups.

NOTE You can separate the files in a media set by formatting the files in the set, but by doing so you render the entire set useless—you should format all the devices in the set.

To perform a backup with multiple devices, you need to create two more backup devices and then perform a backup. Let's do that now:

1. Open SQL Server Management Studio by selecting it from the SQL Server 2005 group under Programs on the Start menu. Expand your server and then Management.
2. Right-click Backup Devices in Object Explorer, and select New Backup Device.
3. In the Name box of the Backup Device dialog box, enter **PSDev1**. Notice that the filename and path are filled in for you; make sure you have enough free space on the drive that SQL Server has selected.
4. Click OK to create the device.
5. Right-click Backup Devices in Object Explorer, and select New Backup Device.
6. In the Name box of the Backup Device dialog box, enter **PSDev2**. Again, notice that the filename and path are filled in for you.
7. Click OK to create the device.

Now that you have multiple devices, you can perform a parallel striped backup. In this instance, you're going to perform a full backup of the Model database:

1. Right-click Model under System Databases, point to Tasks, and click Back Up.
2. In the Backup dialog box, make sure Model is the selected database to back up and the Backup Type is Full.

3. Leave the default name in the Name box. In the Description box, type **Full Backup of Model**.
4. Under Destination, a disk device may already be listed. If so, select the device and click Remove.
5. Under Destination, click Add.
6. In the Select Backup Destination box, click Backup Device, select PSDev1, and click OK.
7. Under Destination, click Add.
8. In the Select Backup Destination box, click Backup Device, select PSDev2, and click OK.

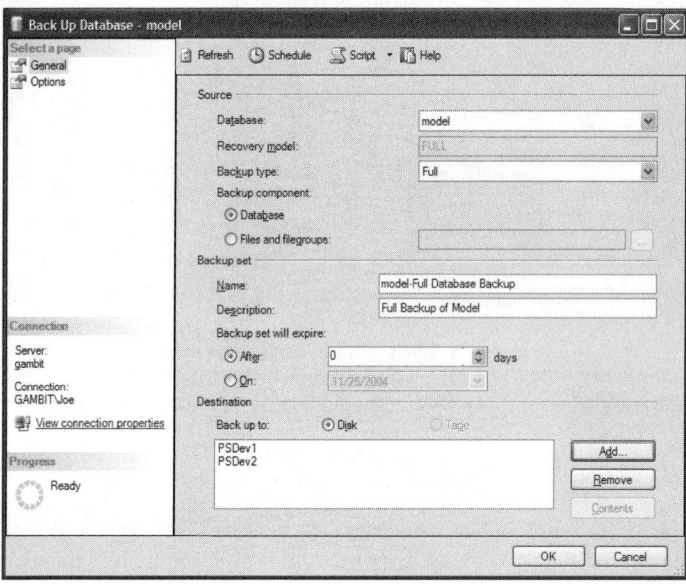

9. On the Options page, select Overwrite All Existing Backup Sets. This option initializes a brand-new device or overwrites an existing one.
10. Check Verify Backup When Finished to check the actual database against the backup copy and be sure they match after the backup is complete.
11. Click OK to start the backup.

Next, you can verify that the backup is on the two devices you specified:

1. In SQL Server Management Studio, expand Management and then Backup Devices.
2. Right-click PSDev1 or PSDev2 (it doesn't matter which), and select Properties.
3. In the Properties dialog box, you should see the Model backup on the Media Contents page. You should also note that the Media Family Count property is 2, denoting that this is part of a multiple device backup.

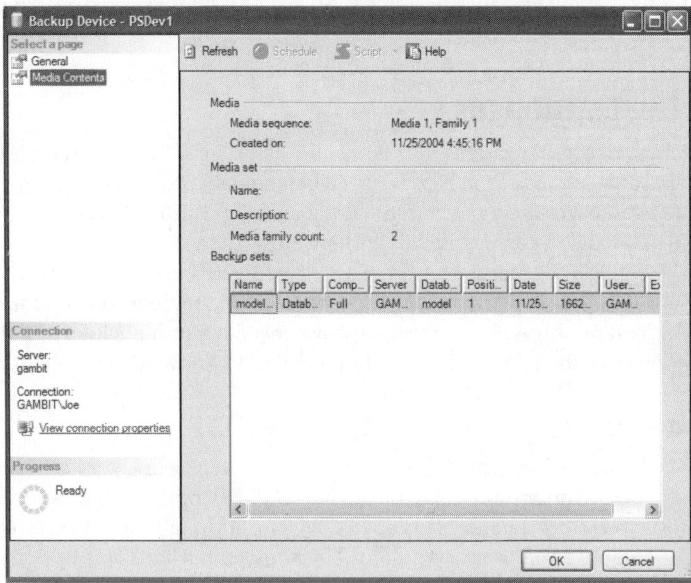

4. Click OK to get back to SQL Server Management Studio.

Knowing how to perform the various types of backups is extremely important, but it's useless if you don't know how to restore. Let's look at the restoration process next.

TIP By using the Transact-SQL backup statement, you can set a password for a backup set or media set to protect your data. If a password is set, users must have the password to back up and restore data from the protected backup or media set.

Advanced Backup Options

You can use a couple of slightly more advanced options to help with your database backups.

Copy Only Backups Sometimes you'll need to make a special backup of a database outside of your normal backup scheme. For instance, you may need to send a copy of your database to an off-site archive for safekeeping. To do this without throwing off the rest of your backups, you can create a *copy-only backup* that backs up the database without affecting the logs or database in any way. You do so using the COPY_ONLY option of the BACKUP statement.

Partial Full and Differential Backups A *partial backup* is a special type of backup that can only be used with filegroups. It only backs up the PRIMARY filegroup and all read/write filegroups. Read-only filegroups aren't backed up. You only need to back up read-only filegroups occasionally, because they don't change; thus partial backups can make backups faster. To perform a partial backup, use the READ_WRITE_FILEGROUPS option of the BACKUP statement.

NOTE Another way to back up a database is to copy it to another server with the Copy Database Wizard, which we'll discuss later in this chapter.

Restoring Databases

One of the most depressing sights you'll see as a database administrator is a downed database. Such a database is easy to spot in SQL Server Management Studio because SQL Server displays the word *Shutdown* in parentheses next to the database in question. This means something bad happened to the database; a corrupt disk is a likely culprit.

Suspect or corrupt databases aren't the only reasons to perform restores, though. You may, for example, need to send a copy of one of your databases to the home office or to a child office for synchronization. You may also need to recover from mistaken or malicious updates to the data. These reasons, and many others, make it important for you to know how to perform restores.

Standard Restores

Restoring a database doesn't involve a lot of steps, but there is one very important setting you need to understand before undertaking the task. The `RECOVERY` option, when set incorrectly, can thwart all your efforts to restore a database. The `RECOVERY` option tells SQL Server that you're finished restoring the database and that users should be allowed back in. This option should be used only on the last file of the restore process.

For example, if you performed a full backup, then a differential backup, and then a transaction log backup, you would need to restore all three of them to bring the database back to a consistent state. If you specify the `RECOVERY` option when restoring the differential backup, SQL Server won't allow you to restore any other backups; you have told SQL Server in effect that you're done restoring and it should let everyone start using the database again. If you have more than one file to restore, you need to specify `NORECOVERY` on all restores except the last one.

SQL Server also remembers where the original files were located when you backed them up. Thus if you backed up files from the D drive, SQL Server will restore them to the D drive. This is great unless your D drive has failed and you need to move your database to the E drive. You'll also run into this problem if you have backed up a database on a server at the home office and need to restore the database to a server at a child office. In this instance, you need to use the `MOVE...TO` option. `MOVE...TO` lets you back up a database in one location and move it to another location.

Finally, before SQL Server will allow you to restore a database, SQL Server performs a safety check to make sure you aren't accidentally restoring the wrong database. The first thing SQL Server does is compare the database name that is being restored with the name of the database recorded in the backup device. If the two are different, SQL Server won't perform the restore. Thus if you have a database on the server named Accounting and you're trying to restore from a backup device that has a backup of a database named Acctg, SQL Server won't perform the restore. This is a lifesaver, unless you're trying to overwrite the existing database with the database from the backup. If that is the case, you need to specify the `REPLACE` option, which is designed to override the safety check.

With all that said, you're ready to restore a database. First, let's make one of the databases suspect so that you can see exactly what SQL Server does to restore it. Specifically, let's blow away AdventureWorks:

1. Open the SQL Server Computer Manager from the Start menu.
2. Expand Services, and select SQL Server.

3. Right-click SQL Server in the right pane, and click Stop. You'll be asked whether you wish to stop the SQLServerAgent service as well; click Yes.
4. Find the file `AdventureWorks_Data.mdf` (usually in `C:\Program Files\Microsoft SQL Server\MSSQL.1\MSSQL\Data\`).
5. Rename the file `AdventureWorks_Data.old`.
6. Find the file `AdventureWorks_Log.ldf`, and rename it `AdventureWorks_Log.old`.
7. From the Computer Manager, restart the SQL Agent and SQL Server services.
8. Open SQL Server Management Studio, and expand databases under your server name. AdventureWorks should be marked Shutdown.

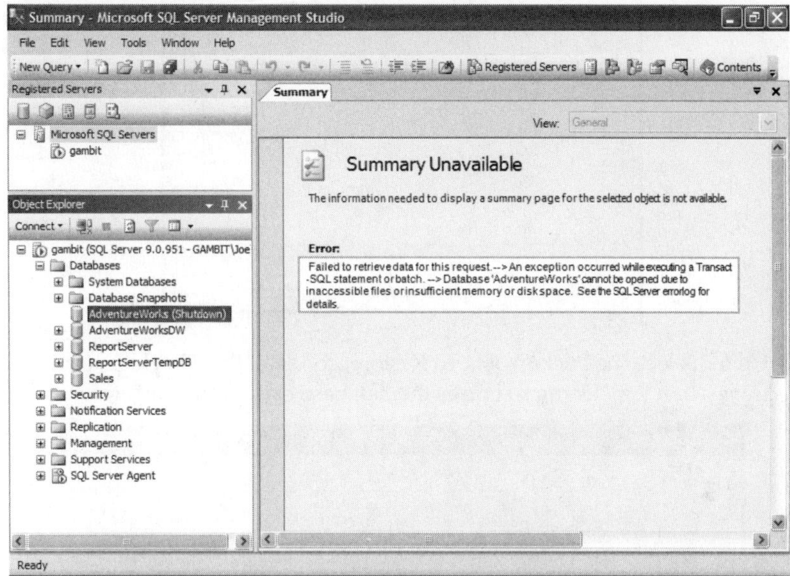

NOTE You had to stop all the SQL Server services because while they're running, all the databases are considered open files—you wouldn't be able to work with them outside of SQL Server.

Now that you have a suspect database on your hands, you can restore it:

1. Right-click Databases, and select Restore Database.
2. In the Restore Database dialog box, select AdventureWorks from the To Database drop-down list box.
3. Under Source For Restore, select From Device. Click the ellipsis button (…) next to the text box to select a device.
4. In the Specify Backup dialog, select Backup Device from the Backup Media drop-down list box, and click Add.

5. In the Select Backup Device dialog, select AdvWorksFull and click OK.

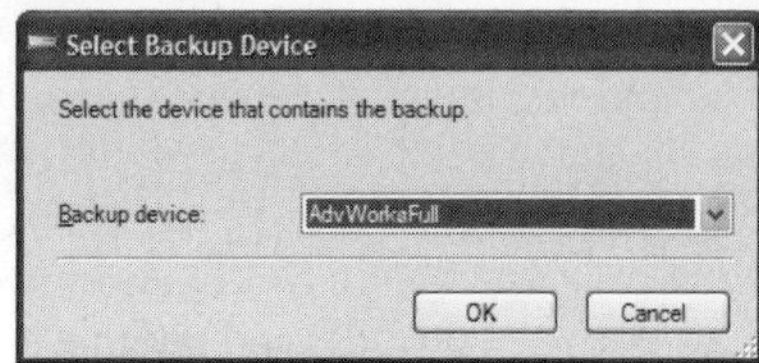

6. Click OK to close the Specify Backup dialog box.

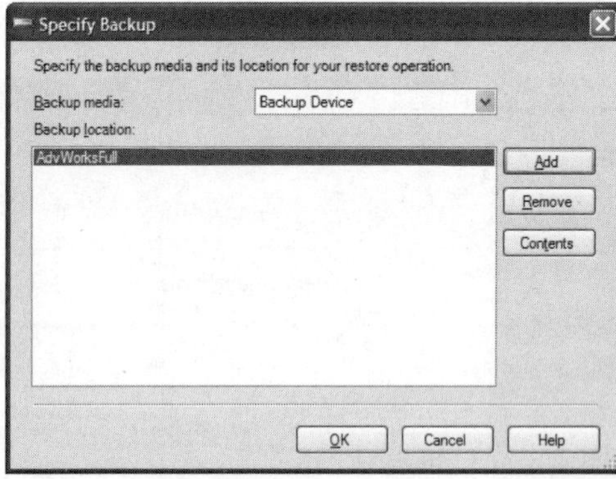

7. Under Select The Backup Sets To Restore, check all three backups (full, differential, and transaction log). Doing so brings the database back to the most recent state.

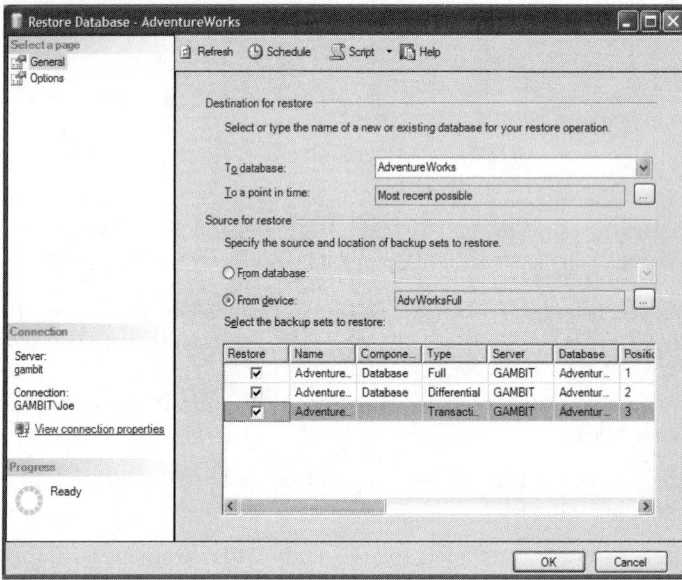

8. On the Options page, make sure the RESTORE WITH RECOVERY option is selected, because you have no more backups to restore.

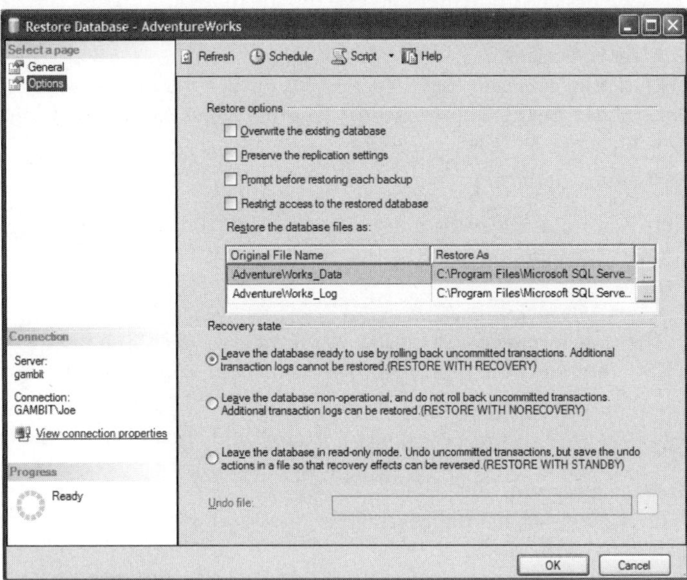

9. Click OK to begin the restore process.
10. In SQL Server Management Studio, right-click Database and click Refresh.
11. Expand Databases, and you should see AdventureWorks back to normal.

This type of restore is very useful if the entire database becomes corrupt and you need to restore the whole thing. However, what if only a few records are bad, and you need to get back to the state the database was in just a few hours ago?

Point-in-Time Restores

You'll usually get requests to bring the data back to a previous state at the end of the month, when accounting closes out the monthly books. Most often the request sounds as follows: "We forgot to carry a one; can you bring the data back to yesterday at about 2:00?" At this point you remember that accounting signs your paycheck and you're delighted to help them in any way you can; so you tell them you can do it. "How is this possible?" you may ask. If you're performing transaction log backups, you can perform a *point-in-time restore.*

In addition to stamping each transaction in the transaction log with an LSN, SQL Server stamps them all with a time. That time, combined with the `STOPAT` clause of the `restore` statement, makes it possible for you to bring the data back to a previous state. You need to keep two things in mind while using this process. First, it doesn't work with full or differential backups, only transaction log backups. Second, you'll lose any changes that were made to your entire database after the `STOPAT` time. For instance, if you restore your database to the state it was in yesterday at 2:00 p.m., everything that was changed from yesterday at 2:00 p.m. until the time you restore the database will be lost and must be reinserted. Other than that, the point-in-time restore is a useful and powerful tool. Let's use it on AdventureWorks:

1. You need to add a record that will survive the restore. Open a new SQL Server query in SQL Server Management Studio by clicking the New Query button on the toolbar.

2. To create a new record, enter and execute the following code:

```
USE AdventureWorks
INSERT HumanResources.Shift(Name, StartTime, EndTime, ModifiedDate)
VALUES('Test Shift 1',getdate()+1,getdate()+2,getdate())
```

3. Note the time right now.

4. Wait two minutes, clear the query window, and then enter a new record using the following code:

```
USE AdventureWorks
INSERT HumanResources.Shift(Name, StartTime, EndTime, ModifiedDate)
VALUES('Test Shift 2',getdate()+1,getdate()+2,getdate())
```

5. To see both records, clear the query window, and enter and execute the following code:

```
USE AdventureWorks
SELECT * FROM HumanResources.Shift
```

6. To perform a point-in-time restore, you must perform a transaction log backup. Open SQL Server Management Studio. Expand your server and then Databases.

7. In Object Explorer, right-click AdventureWorks, point to Tasks, and select Back Up.

8. In the Backup dialog box, make sure AdventureWorks is the selected database to back up and the Backup Type is Transaction Log.

9. Leave the default name in the Name box. In the Description box, type **Point-in-time Backup of AdventureWorks**.

10. Under Destination, make sure the AdvWorksFull device is listed.

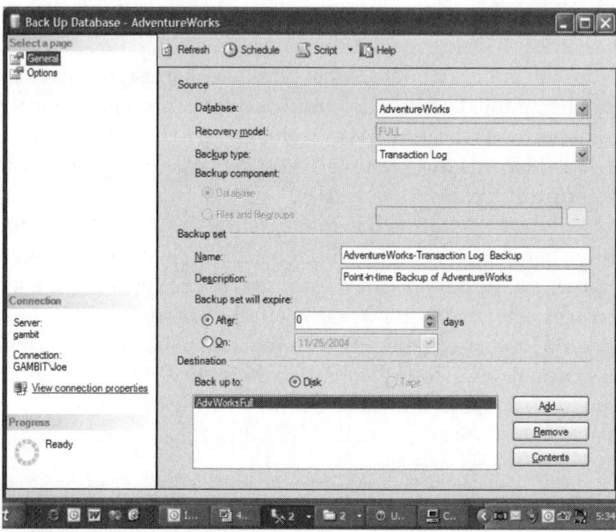

11. On the Options page, make sure Append To The Existing Backup Set is selected so that you don't overwrite your existing full backup.
12. On the Options page, select Verify Backup When Finished.
13. Click OK to start the backup.

You have created two new records and performed a transaction log backup. Now you're ready to roll the database back to the point in time just before you added the second record, to test the functionality of the point-in-time restore:

1. Open SQL Server Management Studio. Expand your server and then Databases.
2. Right-click AdventureWorks, point to Tasks, move to Restore, and select Database.
3. Click the ellipsis button next to the To A Point In Time text box.
4. In the Point In Time Restore dialog box, enter the time from step 3 of the previous series of steps and click OK.

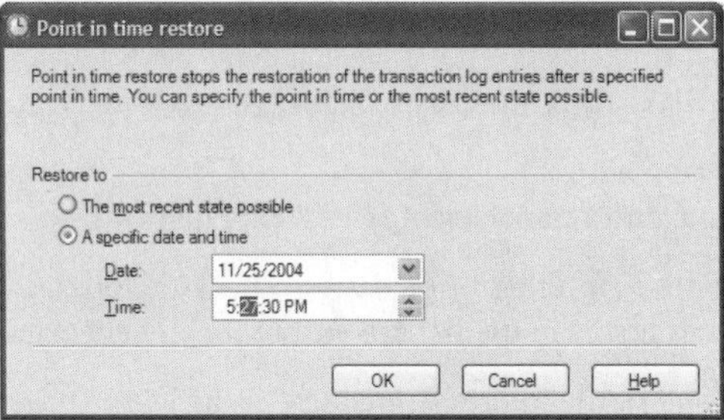

5. Make sure you're restoring from the AdvWorksFull device, select all the available backups in the device, and click OK to perform the restore.

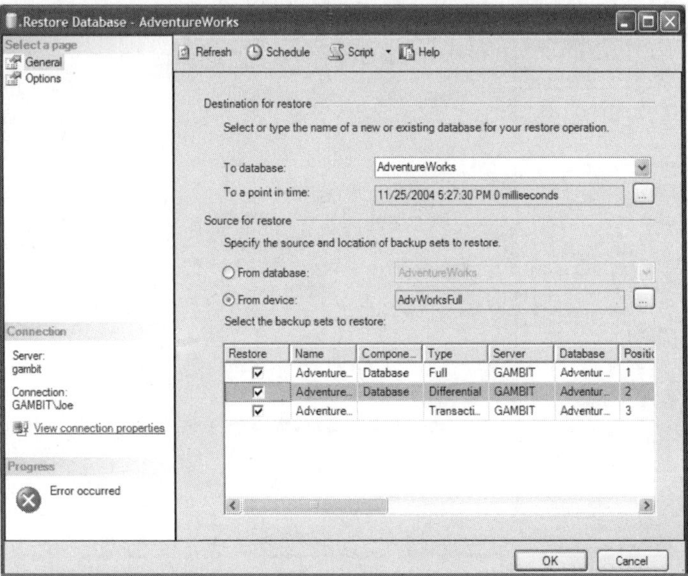

6. To test the restore, open a new SQL Server Query in SQL Server Management Studio, and enter and execute the following code:

```
USE AdventureWorks
SELECT * FROM HumanResources.Shift
```

7. Notice that Test Shift 2 is no longer there, but Test Shift 1 remains.

There is another type of restore that will come in handy for VLDBs; piecemeal restores.

Piecemeal Restores

Piecemeal restores are used to restore the primary filegroup and (optionally) some secondary filegroups and make them accessible to users. Remaining secondary filegroups can be restored later if needed.

Earlier in this chapter, you added a filegroup to the Sales database; then you added a table to that filegroup, created some records in it, and backed up the secondary filegroup. You need to back up the primary filegroup before you can perform a piecemeal restore, though, so let's perform another backup:

1. Right-click the Sales database in Object Explorer, point to Tasks, and select Back Up.
2. In the Backup dialog box, make sure Sales is the selected database to back up and the Backup Type is Full.
3. Under Backup Component, select Files And Filegroups.
4. In the Select Files And Filegroups dialog, check the box next to Sales and click OK (notice that all the other boxes in the list are automatically checked for you).
5. Leave the default name in the Name box. In the Description box, type **Piecemeal Backup of Sales**.
6. Under Destination, make sure the AdvWorksFull device is the only one listed.

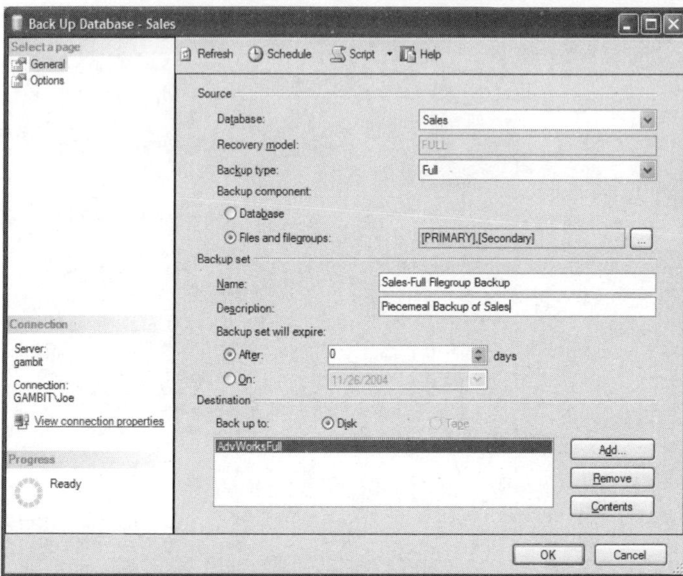

7. On the Options page, make sure Append To The Existing Backup Set is selected so that you don't overwrite your existing backups.
8. On the Options tab, select Verify Backup When Finished.
9. Click OK to start the backup.

Now you're ready to perform a partial restore of the Sales database to a new database that you'll call sales_part, to see how piecemeal restores work:

1. Open a new SQL Server query in SQL Server Management Studio by clicking the New Query button.
2. Enter and execute the following code to restore the sales database to a new database named sales_part:

```
RESTORE DATABASE sales_part
  FILEGROUP = 'PRIMARY'
  FROM DISK='C:\Program Files\Microsoft SQL
Server\MSSQL.1\MSSQL\Backup\AdvWorksFull.bak'
  WITH FILE=6,RECOVERY,PARTIAL,
  MOVE 'sales' TO 'C:\sales2.pri',
  MOVE 'sales_log' TO 'c:\sales2.log'
```

3. To test the restore, enter and execute the following code:

```
USE sales_Part
SELECT * FROM Employees
```

4. This code should fail because the filegroup containing the Employees table wasn't restored. Enter and execute this code:

```
USE Sales_Part
SELECT * FROM Customers
```

5. Close the query window.

This demonstrates the capabilities of the piecemeal restore process. You can use it to restore the primary and, optionally, other filegroups to the same or another database to make the data accessible to users. Remaining filegroups can be restored later.

With the mechanics of backing up and restoring under your belt, you're ready for a discussion of theory. You need to know not only how but when to use each of these types of backups. You need to devise a viable backup strategy.

Devising a Backup Strategy

Referring to the analogy at the outset of this chapter, if you were an ace mechanic and could fix every part of a car, your skills would serve you no purpose if you didn't know how to drive. You could work on the mechanics of the vehicle all day long, but you could never drive the car anywhere. This principle holds true with anything you do, including backing up data in SQL Server. If you understand the mechanics but not the theory, you can't do anything valuable with your product; therefore you need a backup strategy.

A *backup strategy* is a plan that details when to use which type of backup. For example, you could use only full backup, or full with differential, or any other valid combination. Your challenge is to figure out which one is right for your environment. Here, we'll look at the pros and cons of each available strategy.

Full Backups Only

If you have a relatively small database, you can perform just full backups with no other type; but you need to understand what we mean by a *relatively small database*. When you're speaking of backups, the size of a database is relative to the speed of the backup medium. For example, a 200MB database is fairly small, but if you have an older tape drive that isn't capable of backing up a 200MB database overnight, you won't want to perform full backups on the tape drive every night. On the other hand, if you have a set of hardware that is capable of a 1GB backup in a few hours, you can consider a full-backups-only strategy. We can't tell you what to do in every situation; we can only present the principles that govern what you should do.

The disadvantage of a full-only strategy is that it gives a comparatively slow backup when compared with other strategies. For example, if you perform a full backup every night on a 100MB database, you're (obviously) backing up 100MB every night. If you're using differential with full, you aren't backing up the entire 100MB every night.

The major advantage of a full-only strategy is that the restore process is faster than with other strategies, because it uses only one tape. For instance, if you perform a full backup every night and the database fails on Thursday, all you need to restore is the full backup from Wednesday night, using only one tape. In the same scenario (as you'll see), the other strategies take more time because you have more tapes from which to restore.

One other disadvantage of a full-only strategy involves the transaction log. As we discussed earlier in this chapter, the transaction log is cleared only when a transaction log backup is performed. With a full-only strategy, your transaction log is in danger of filling up and locking your users out of the database. You can do two things to avoid this problem. First, you can set the Truncate Log On Checkpoint option on the database, which instructs SQL Server to completely empty the log every time it writes to the database from the log (a process called *checkpointing*). This isn't the best solution, though; you'll lose up-to-the-minute recoverability because the latest transactions will be deleted every time the server checkpoints. If your database crashes, you can restore it only to the time of the last full backup.

Another, cleaner option is to perform the full backup and, immediately afterward, perform a transaction log backup with the `TRUNCATE_ONLY` clause. With this clause, the log won't be backed up, just emptied. Then, if your database crashes, you can perform a transaction log backup with the `NO_TRUNCATE` clause. The `NO_TRUNCATE` clause tells SQL Server not to erase what's in the log already so that its contents can be used in the restore process. This approach gives you up-to-the-minute recoverability as well as a clean transaction log.

TIP The first thing you should do in the event of any database failure is use the `NO_TRUNCATE` option with the transaction log backup to save the orphaned log.

Full with Differential Backups

If your database is too large to perform a full backup every night, you may want to consider adding differentials to the strategy. A full/differential strategy provides a faster backup than full alone. With a full-only backup strategy, you're backing up the entire database every time you perform a backup. As shown in Figure 16.3, with a full/differential strategy, you're backing up only the changes made to the database since the last full backup, which is faster than backing up the whole thing.

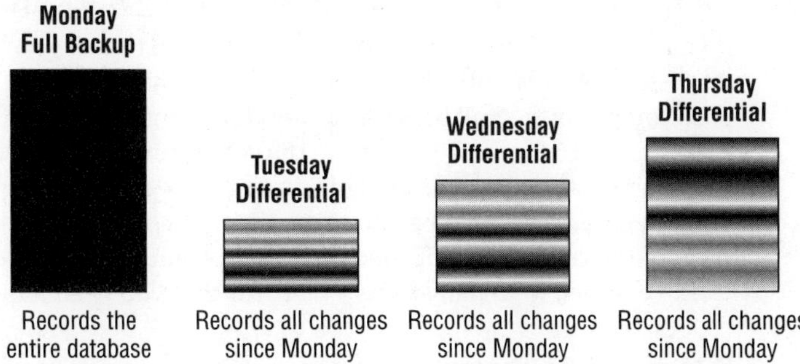

FIGURE 16.3 Differential backups are faster than full backups because they record only the changes to the database since the last full backup.

The major disadvantage of the full/differential strategy is that the restore process is slower than with the full-only strategy, because full/differential requires you to restore more backups. Suppose you perform a full backup on Monday night and differentials the rest of the week, and your database crashes on Wednesday. To bring the database back to a consistent state, you'll need to restore the full backup from Monday and the differential from Tuesday. If your database crashes on Thursday, you'll need to restore the backups from Monday and Wednesday. If it crashes on Friday, you'll restore the full backup from Monday and the differential from Thursday.

The only other disadvantage to be aware of is that differential backups don't clear the transaction log. If you opt for this method, you should clear the transaction log manually by backing up the transaction log with the `TRUNCATE_ONLY` clause.

Full with Transaction Log Backups

Another method to consider, regardless of whether your database is huge, is full/transaction. This method offers several advantages. First, it's the best method to keep your transaction logs clean, because this is the only type of backup that purges old transactions from your transaction logs.

This method also makes for a very fast backup process. For example, you can perform a full backup on Monday and transaction log backups three or four times a day during the week. This is possible because SQL Server performs online backups, and transaction log backups are usually small and quick (your users should barely notice).

Transaction log backups are also the only type of backup that gives you point-in-time restore capability. "How often will I use that?" you may ask. If you have any people in your company who aren't perfect, you'll probably use this capability quite a bit, so it's best to have it when you need it.

The disadvantage of this strategy is that the restore process is a little slower than with full alone or full/differential. This is the case because there are more backups to restore, and any time you add more work to the process, it gets slower. For instance, suppose you perform a full backup on Monday and transaction log backups three times a day (at 10:00 a.m., 2:00 p.m., and 6:00 p.m.) throughout the week. If your database crashes on Tuesday at 3:00 p.m., you'll need to restore only the full backup from Monday and the transaction log backups from Tuesday at 10:00 a.m. and 2:00 p.m. However, if your database crashes on Thursday at 3:00 p.m., you'll need to restore the full backup from Monday as well as all the transaction log backups made on Tuesday, Wednesday, and Thursday before the crash. So although this type of backup may have blinding speed, it involves a lengthy restore process. It may be better to combine all three types of backups.

Full, Differential, and Transaction Log Backups

If you combine all three types of backups, you get the best of all worlds. The backup and restore processes are still relatively fast, and you have the advantage of point-in-time restore as well. Suppose you perform a full backup on Monday, transaction log backups every four hours (10:00 a.m., 2:00 p.m., and 6:00 p.m.) throughout the day during the week, and differential backups every night. If your database crashes at any time during the week, all you need to restore is the full backup from Monday, the differential backup from the night before, and the transaction log backups up to the point of the crash. This approach is nice, fast, and simple. However, none of these combinations work very well for a monstrous VLDB; for that you need a filegroup backup.

Filegroup Backups

We discussed the mechanics of the filegroup backup earlier in this chapter, so you know they're designed to back up small chunks of the database at a time rather than the whole thing all at once. This may come in handy, for example, with a 700GB database contained in three files in three separate filegroups. You can perform a full backup once per month and then back up one filegroup per week during the week. Every day, you perform transaction log backups for maximum recoverability.

Suppose the disk containing the third file of your database crashes. With the other backup strategies we have discussed, you would need to restore the full backup first and then the other backups. With filegroup backups, you don't need to restore the full backup first (thank goodness). All you need to restore is the backup of the filegroup that failed and the transaction log backups that occurred after the filegroup was backed up. If you backed up your third filegroup on Wednesday and then it fails on Friday, you'll restore the filegroup backup from Wednesday and the transaction log backups from Thursday and Friday up to the point of the crash.

NOTE SQL Server is fully capable of determining which transactions belong to each filegroup. When you restore the transaction log, SQL Server applies only the transactions that belong to the failed group.

Whew! Backups are a big chunk of information to assimilate, but they're very important. Now you're ready for the next phase of administration and maintenance: maintaining the indexes on your databases.

Maintaining Indexes

In Chapter 12, you learned that you need indexes on most SQL Server tables to speed up access to the data. Without these indexes, SQL Server would need to perform table scans, reading every record in the table, to find any amount of data. You can use two types of indexes to speed up access to the data: *clustered* and *nonclustered*. You may remember that clustered indexes physically rearrange the data in the table, whereas nonclustered indexes are more like the index at the back of a book, maintaining pointers to the data in the table. No matter which type of indexes you use, you must perform maintenance on them to make sure they're performing at peak efficiency.

The first thing you need to watch for in an index (especially a clustered index) is *page splitting*. As described in Chapter 12, a page split is caused when a page of data fills to 100 percent and more data must be added to it. For example, suppose you have a clustered index based on last name, and the page containing the last names starting with *A* is 100 percent full. You now need to add a new customer with the last name of Addams. SQL Server will try to add the name to the page that contains the rest of the last names that start with *A*, but it will fail because there is no more room on the page. Realizing that you may need to add more records of this type later, the server takes half the records on the page and puts them on a new page. The server then links the new page to the page before it and the page after it in the page chain.

Page splitting has a few disadvantages. First, the new page that is created is out of order. Instead of going from one page to the next when looking for data, SQL Server has to jump around the database looking for the next page it needs. This is referred to as *fragmentation*. Not only that, but the server also has to take the time to delete half the records on the full page and rewrite them on a new page.

Surprisingly, page splitting offers an advantage in an online transaction processing (OLTP) environment. A lot of writing and updating go on in an OLTP environment, and they can use all the extra free space that page splitting provides. For the most part, though, you'll find that you need to recover from the effects of page splitting by rebuilding the index. Before you do that, you need to ascertain whether your index is fragmented badly enough to warrant reconstruction. The way to determine this is by querying DM_DB_INDEX_PHYSICAL_STATS.

Understanding *DM_DB_INDEX_PHYSICAL_STATS*

To overcome the effects of database fragmentation, you need to either reorganize or completely rebuild the indexes on the tables. That is time-consuming, so you should do it only when needed. The only way to tell whether your indexes need reconstruction is to perform DM_DB_INDEX_PHYSICAL_STATS.

TIP In previous versions of SQL Server, you would have used DBCC SHOWCONTIG to find index fragmentation, but that approach is now deprecated.

You can get information from DM_DB_INDEX_PHYSICAL_STATS using a simple SELECT query. Here is the syntax:

```
sys.dm_db_index_physical_stats
(
    { '[ database_name . [ schema_name ] . | schema_name ] table_name'
      | NULL
      | DEFAULT
    }
    , { 'index_name' | NULL | DEFAULT | '*' }
    , { partition_id | NULL | DEFAULT | 0 }
    , { 'mode' | NULL | DEFAULT }
)
```

Here is what the arguments stand for:

- database_name is the name of the database as a string.
- schema_name is the name of the schema as a string.
- table_name is the name of the table as a string. This can also be DEFAULT or NULL, which return all tables and views in the database.
- Index_name is the name of a specific index as a string. This can also be DEFAULT, NULL, or *. DEFAULT and NULL return only the base table, which can be a clustered index or a heap. The * returns all indexes on the table.
- Partition_id is the number of the partition you want to query if the database is partitioned. DEFAULT, NULL, and 0 return all partitions; any other non-negative value returns data for a specific partition.

- mode is the scan-level mode to use on the database. Valid values are DEFAULT, NULL, LIMITED, SAMPLED, and DETAILED. The default value is LIMITED.

When queried, DM_DB_INDEX_PHYSICAL_STATS returns a table with the columns listed in Table 16.1.

TABLE 16.1: DM_DB_INDEX_PHYSICAL_STATS Return Columns

Column Name	Datatype	Description
TableName	nvarchar	Name of the table or indexed view.
IndexName	nvarchar	Name of the index.
PartitionNumber	int	Partition number for the table or index. If the table or index isn't partitioned, this value is 1.
IndexType	nvarchar	Description of the index or allocation unit type. Possible values are heap, clustered index, nonclustered index, large object (LOB) data, or row-overflow object.
Depth	Int	Number of index levels, including the leaf level. This value is 1 for heaps, row-overflow, and LOB objects.
AvgFragmentation	Float	Logical fragmentation percentage. This value is 0 for heaps, row-overflow, and LOB objects.
Fragments	Bigint	Number of fragments in the index. This value is 0 for heaps, row-overflow, and LOB objects.
AvgFragmentSize	Float	Average number of fragments in one fragment of an index. This value is 0 for heaps, row-overflow, and LOB objects.
Pages	Bigint	Total number of data pages.
AvgPageFullness	Float	Average percent of page fullness. This value is null in LIMITED scan mode.
Records	Bigint	Total number of records in the index leaf level. This value is 0 for heaps, row-overflow, and LOB objects and null in LIMITED scan mode.
GhostRecords	Bigint	Number of ghost records that have been released by a snapshot isolation transaction. This value is null in LIMITED scan mode.
VersionGhostRecords	Bigint	Number of ghost records retained by an outstanding snapshot isolation transaction. This value is null in LIMITED scan mode.
MinimumRecordSize	Int	Minimum record size in the index leaf level. This value is null in LIMITED scan mode.
MaximumRecordSize	Int	Maximum record size in the index leaf level. This value is null in LIMITED scan mode.

TABLE 16.1: DM_DB_INDEX_PHYSICAL_STATS Return Columns *(CONTINUED)*

COLUMN NAME	DATATYPE	DESCRIPTION
AverageRecordSize	Int	Average record size in the index leaf level. This value is null in LIMITED scan mode.
ForwardedRecords	Int	Number of forwarded records in a heap. This value is null in LIMITED scan mode and 0 for any object other than a heap.

The scan modes each have advantages and disadvantages, as listed in Table 16.2.

TABLE 16.2: Scan Modes

MODE	DESCRIPTION	ADVANTAGES	DISADVANTAGES
Limited	Reads only parent-level pages.	This is the fastest mode. It's accurate, and it allows concurrent access during the scan.	Only a subset of statistics is calculated.
Sampled	Parent-level pages are read, and indexes with fewer than 10,000 pages are scanned at 100%. Otherwise they're scanned at 1% and 2% simultaneously. If the difference between the two is close, then the 2% scan is reported; otherwise a 10% sample is performed.	This mode is faster than a detailed scan. It calculates all statistics and allows concurrent access during the scan.	Calculated statistics may not be 100% accurate.
Detailed	Parent-level pages and all leaf-level pages are read.	This mode calculates all statistics based on all available data.	This is the slowest mode, and data modification is prohibited during the scan.

If you want to find the fragmentation on the Sales.SalesOrderDetail table in the AdventureWorks database, the query might look like this:

```
USE AdventureWorks;
SELECT IndexName, AvgFragmentation
FROM sys.dm_db_index_physical_stats ('Sales.SalesOrderDetail', DEFAULT, DEFAULT,
'DETAILED');
```

This query gives you the index names in the Sales.SalesOrderDetail table and the corresponding amount of fragmentation. Using this data, you can decide whether to reorganize or rebuild your indexes.

Reorganizing and Rebuilding Indexes

If the amount of fragmentation on your index is less than 30 percent, you should reorganize your index; anything higher requires a rebuild. To reorganize an index, use the `ALTER INDEX REORGANIZE` statement, which replaces the `DBCC INDEXDEFRAG` function. Here is what it looks like if you want to reorganize the PK_Product_ProductPhotoID index on the Production.ProductPhoto table in the AdventureWorks database:

```
USE AdventureWorks
ALTER INDEX PK_ProductPhoto_ProductPhotoID
ON Production.ProductPhoto
REORGANIZE
```

There are two effective ways to rebuild indexes on a table. One way is to use the `CREATE INDEX` statement with the `DROP_EXISTING` option. To reconstruct an index that is being used as a primary key, you use `ALTER INDEX REBUILD`, which is also used to repair corrupt indexes and rebuild multiple indexes at once.

Let's reconstruct the indexes on the Production.Product table in the AdventureWorks database:

1. Open a new SQL Server query in SQL Server Management Studio.
2. Enter and execute the following code to reconstruct the index on the Production. Product table:

   ```
   USE AdventureWorks;
   ALTER INDEX ALL
   ON Production.Product
   REBUILD WITH (FILLFACTOR = 80, ONLINE = ON,
                 STATISTICS_NORECOMPUTE = ON);
   ```

3. Query the `DM_DB_INDEX_PHYSICAL_STATS` statement to see whether the fragmentation is gone:

   ```
   USE AdventureWorks;
   SELECT IndexName, AvgFragmentation
   FROM sys.dm_db_index_physical_stats ('Production.Product', DEFAULT, DEFAULT,
   'DETAILED');
   ```

4. You should see 0 percent fragmentation.

Now you know not only how to keep your databases free from threat of annihilation by backing them up but also how to keep them running quickly by rebuilding the indexes when necessary. But one important piece of the administrative burden is still missing: You must be able to read the SQL Server error logs to keep the system running in top shape.

Reading the Logs

When you go to the doctor's office with a health problem, the doctor asks a series of questions to find out what the problem is and how best to fix it. This is a much more effective approach than guessing what might be wrong and applying the wrong fix. You're the doctor when it comes to fixing a SQL Server, and you need to know how to ask the server questions rather than just guessing and applying the wrong fix. You can ask SQL Server questions about "where it hurts" by reading the error logs.

SQL Server generates a new error log every time the server is restarted, and it keeps an archive of the previous six error logs to use in trend tracking over time. These error logs can be viewed in SQL Server Management Studio under Management or with a common text editor such as Notepad (if you want to use a text editor, you'll find the error logs in the `\Errorlog` directory of your SQL Server directory). No matter how you want to do it, you need to set a schedule for viewing the error logs on a regular basis. Let's look at the error logs with SQL Server Management Studio:

1. Open SQL Server Management Studio. Expand your server and then Management.
2. Under Management, expand SQL Server Logs.
3. Under Logs, right-click Current, and select View SQL Server Log.
4. In the contents pane (the right pane), scroll through and notice all the log entries.

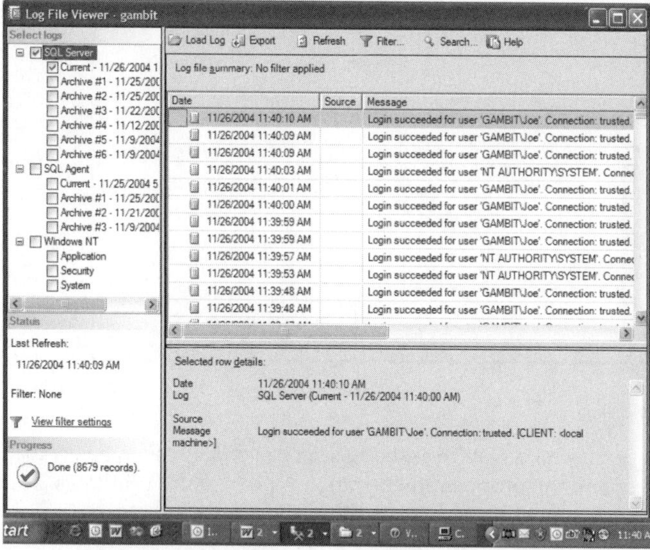

When you're reading these logs, you're usually looking for problem words such as *failed*, *problem*, or *unable*. Nothing jumps out and says, "Hey fix this," so you have to develop a trained eye and keep watch for subtle problems that may crop up.

One final tool that will come in handy is the Copy Database Wizard.

Copying Databases

One of the handiest tools in the SQL Server arsenal is the Copy Database Wizard. This wizard is designed to copy or move a database and all its associated objects to another server. Why would you want to do that? There are a few good reasons:

- If you're upgrading your server, the Copy Database Wizard is a quick way to move your data to the new system.
- The wizard can be used to create a backup copy of the database on another server, ready to use in case of emergency.
- Developers can copy an existing database and use the copy to make changes without endangering the live database.

The Copy Database Wizard will prove to be a valuable tool in your administrative functions, so let's see how to use it. In this example, you'll make a copy of the Sales database:

1. Open SQL Server Management Studio by selecting it from the Microsoft SQL Server group under Programs on the Start menu.
2. Right-click your server, point to Launch Wizard, and select Copy Database. You'll be presented with the welcome screen.

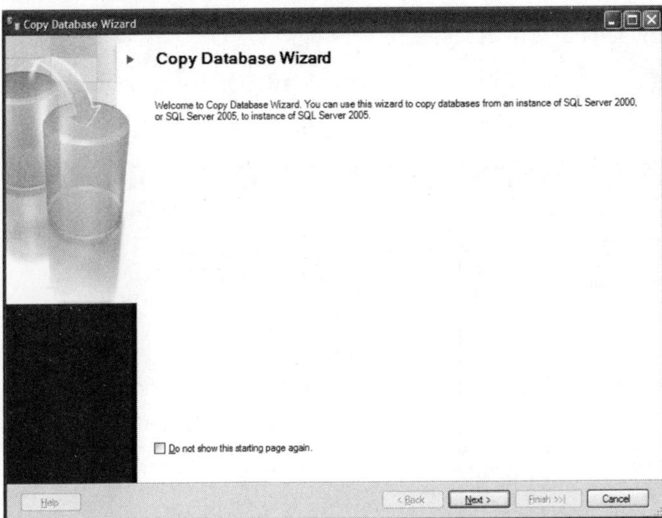

3. Click Next.
4. On the second screen, you're asked to select a source server. Select the default instance of your server and the proper authentication type (usually Windows Authentication), and click Next.

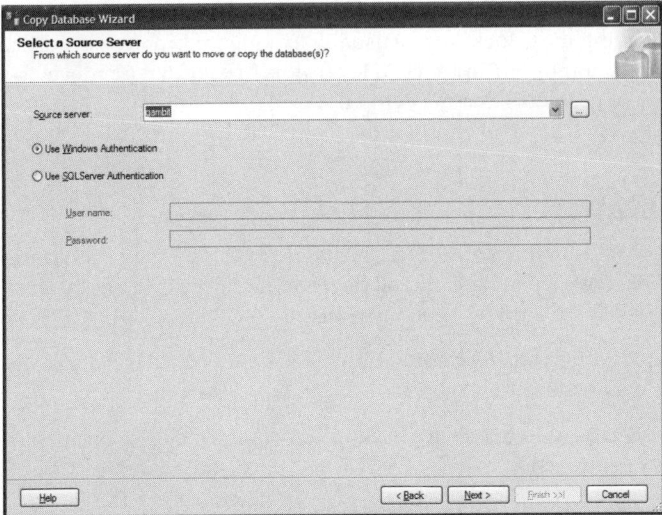

5. On the next screen, you need to select a destination. Choose the (local) instance of the server. Choose the appropriate type of security, and click Next.

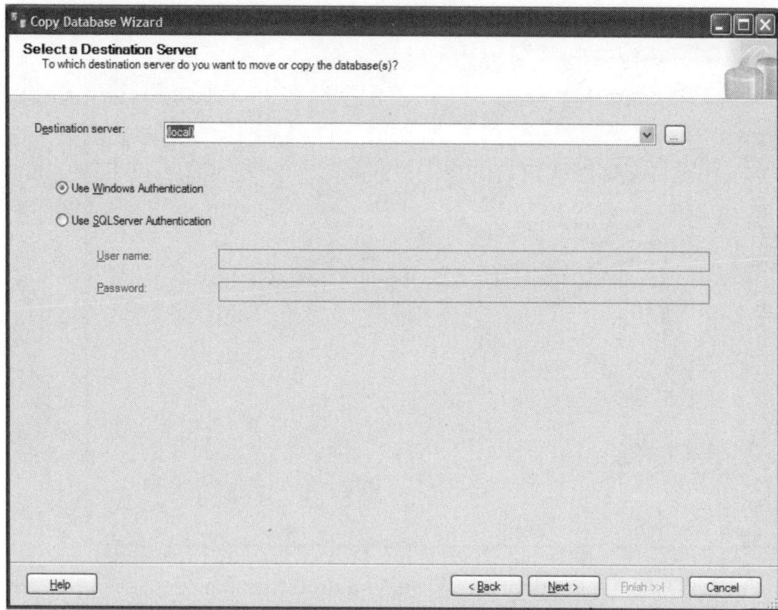

6. Next, you're asked which mode you would like to use. You need flexibility to make a copy on the same server, so select the Use The SQL Management Object Transfer Method option and click Next.

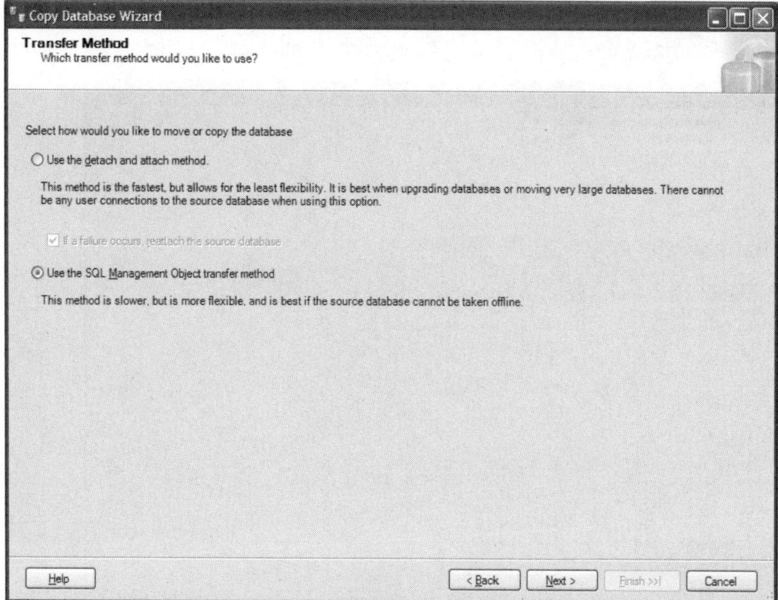

7. Next you're asked which database you would like to move or copy. Check the Copy box next to Sales, and click Next.

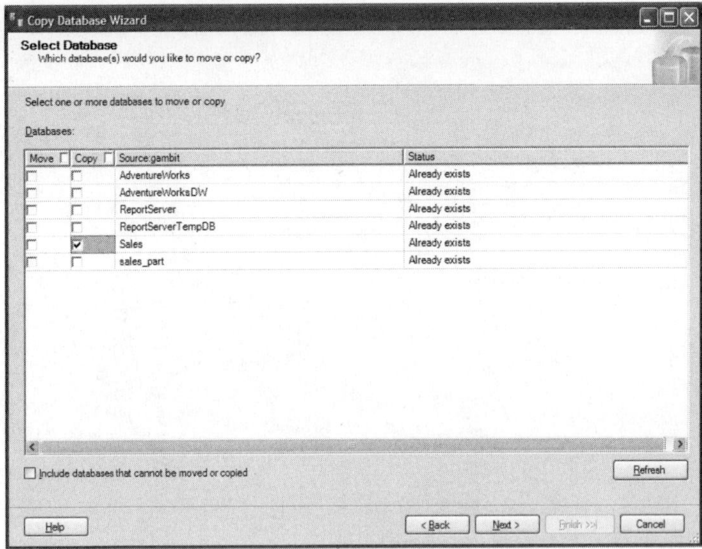

8. On the Database Destination screen, you need to make a few changes:

   - Change the destination database name to Sales_copy.
   - Change Sales.mdf to Sales_copy.mdf by clicking the ellipsis button next to the filename.
   - Change Sales_Data_2.ndf to Sales_Data_2_copy.ndf by clicking the ellipsis button next to the filename.
   - Change Sales_1.ldf to Sales_1_copy.ldf by clicking the ellipsis button next to the filename.

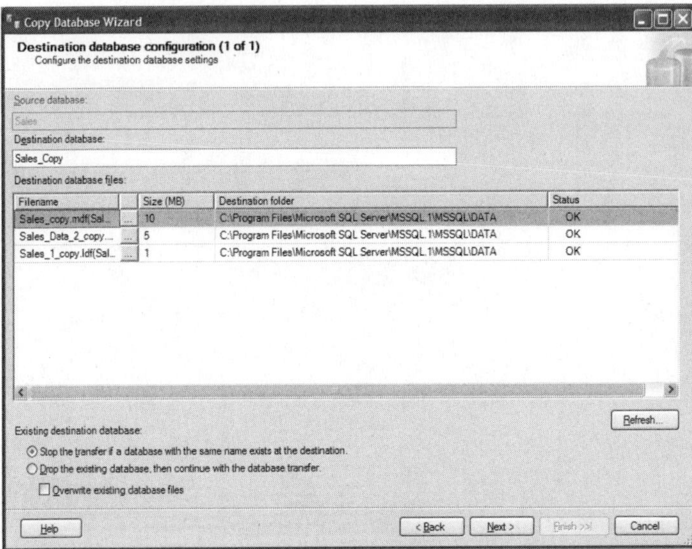

9. Click Next. You're now given the option to change the name of the package that will be created. This option only matters if you plan to save the package and execute it later. Accept the defaults, and click Next.

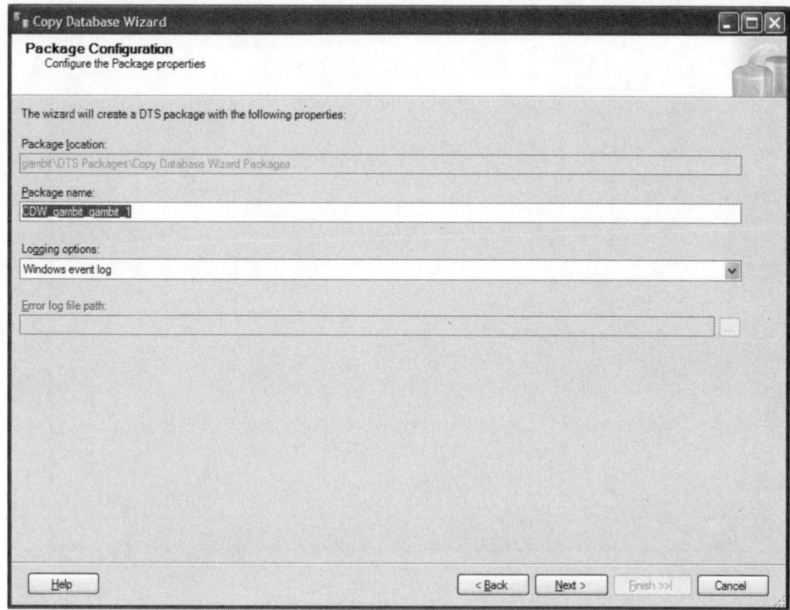

10. On the next screen, you're asked when you would like to run the DTS job that is created by the wizard. Select Run Immediately, and click Next.

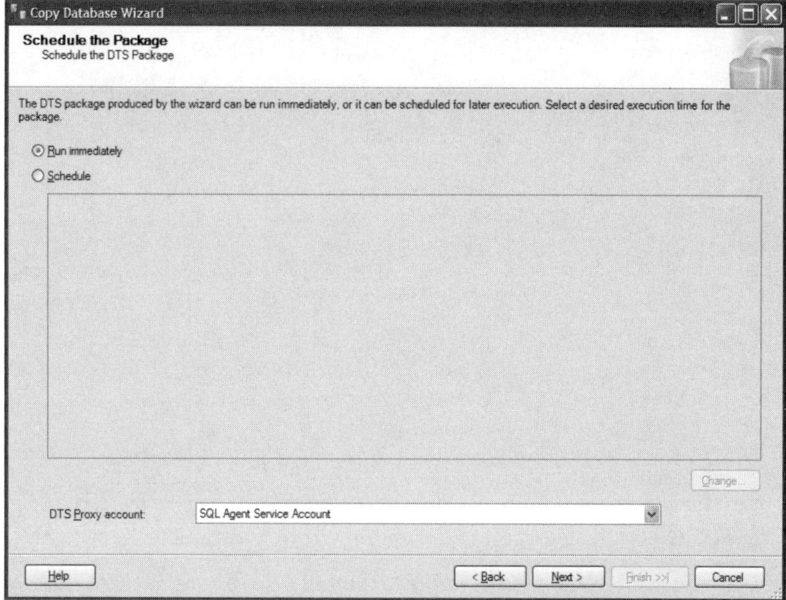

11. The final screen presents you with a summary of the choices you've made. Click Finish to copy the Sales database.

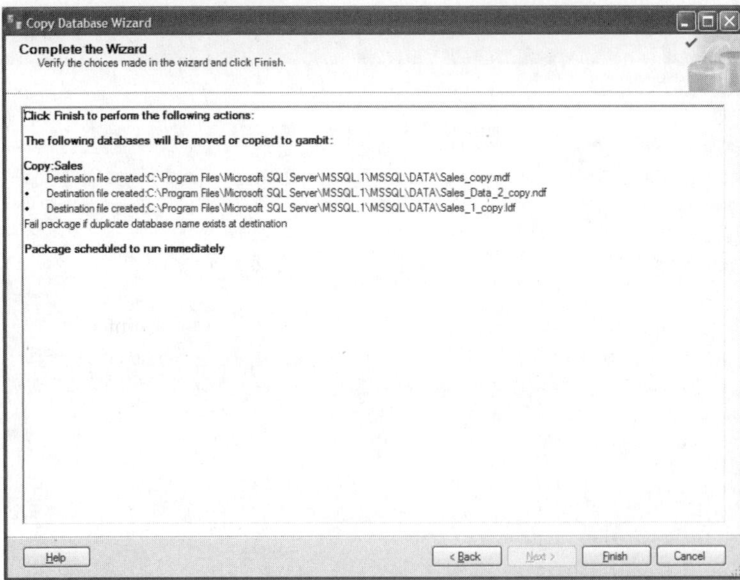

12. You'll see the Log Detail screen, which shows you each section of the job as it's executed. Clicking the Report button (after the job is competed) shows each step of the job and its outcome.

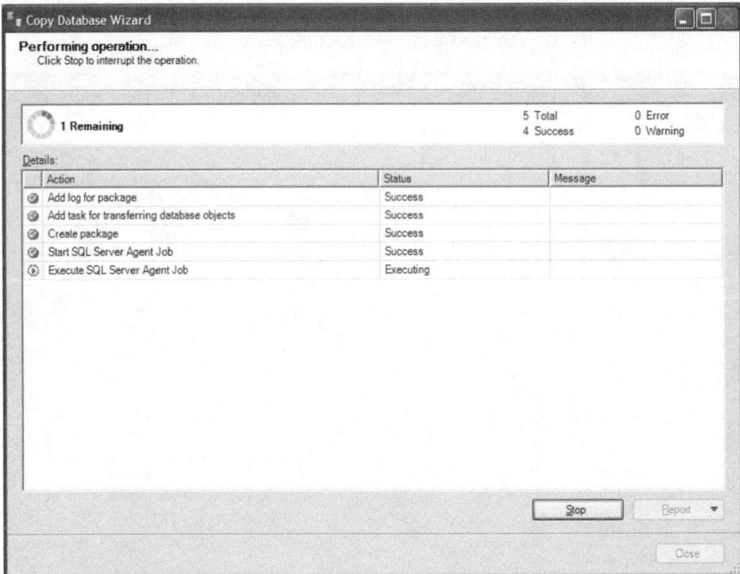

13. Click Close on the Performing Operation screen to complete the wizard.

The Copy Database Wizard is a simple tool that makes a complex task much easier.

Summary

In this chapter, we talked about how to administer and maintain your databases so that they will always run in top condition.

The first topic was backups. There are many reasons to back up data: natural disaster, hardware malfunction, even people with malicious intent. If you perform regular backups, you can overcome these problems.

You can use four types of backups to help thwart the evils that would claim your data. First is the full backup, the basis of all other backups, which makes a copy of the entire database. Next, the differential backup grabs all the changes made to the database since the last full backup. The transaction log backup is very useful for a quick backup strategy, point-in-time restores, and clearing the transaction log on a periodic basis. Finally, the filegroup backup makes backups of small chunks of very large databases.

After discussing backups, we hashed out the fine points of index maintenance. It's very important to keep your indexes up to snuff so that data access is always fast. To do so, use `SYS.DM_DB_INDEX_PHYSICAL_STATS` to determine fragmentation, and then use `ALTER INDEX REORGANIZE`, `ALTER INDEX REBUILD` or `CREATE INDEX` with the `DROP_EXISTING` option to reconstruct fragmented indexes.

Next, we looked at the importance of monitoring the SQL Server event logs as well as the mechanics of doing so. Finally, we discussed the Copy Database Wizard.

Now that you know you need to perform all these tasks, probably on a nightly or weekly basis, wouldn't it be nice if you could have someone else do it for you? In the next chapter, we'll discuss automation; you'll learn how to make SQL Server do a lot of your work, including backups.

Chapter 17

Automating Administration

Throughout this book, we have discussed administrative activities that would best be performed during off-hours. These activities include backing up databases, creating large databases, reconstructing indexes—the list goes on. Most of these activities need to be performed on a regular basis, not just once. For example, you'll need to back up at frequent intervals. Because most administrators would rather not have to stand at the SQL Server to start the task in question, SQL Server has the built-in capability to automate tasks.

The first thing we need to discuss is the basics of how automation works in SQL Server. We'll explain some of the basic concepts of automation and how the SQL Server Agent service plays a part.

After we discuss the basics of automation, we'll examine SQLiMail, SQL Server 2005's new mail-processing functionality. It's essential to configure SQLiMail because SQL Server is capable of sending you e-mail when there is a problem as long as e-mail is configured properly.

Next we'll explain how to configure operators. An *operator* is a person who is able to receive messages from SQL Server via e-mail, pager, or Net Send. Configuring an operator tells SQL Server whom to contact and when they're available.

After you have operators in place, you can start creating jobs, the heart of automation. *Jobs* are the activities that you need to administer, such as database backups or index reconstruction. We'll discuss each part of a job, the steps required to complete the job, and the schedules that tell SQL Server when to run the job. We'll also go over the process of creating multiserver jobs, which can be created on one server and run on multiple servers over a network.

Next we'll discuss how to configure alerts, which are used to warn you of problems or events that have occurred on the server. Not only will we explain how to configure standard SQL Server alerts, but we'll also discuss the methods for creating your own user-defined alerts to cover any possible event that may occur on your server.

After all this, we'll discuss the Database Maintenance Wizard. This special wizard is designed to automate all the standard database maintenance procedures such as backups, index reconstruction, transaction log backup, and so on.

We'll start this chapter with a discussion of the basics of automation.

Automation Basics

Nearly any administrative task you can think of can be automated through SQL Server. True, that may sound like an exaggeration, but look at the things that you can automate:

- Any Transact-SQL code
- Scripting languages such as VBScript or JavaScript
- Operating system commands
- Replication tasks (which you'll learn about in Chapter 25 "Replication")

Some popular tasks to automate using this functionality are as follows:

- Database backups
- Index reconstruction
- Database creation (for very large databases, or VLDBs)
- Report generation

Because this functionality is so powerful, it's easy to see why you need to use SQL Server's automation capabilities. However, before you start to use this functionality, you need to know how it works.

At the heart of SQL Server's automation capability is the SQL Server Agent service (also referred to as the *agent*). Automation and replication are the sole functions of that service. The service uses three subcomponents to accomplish its automation tasks: alerts, operators, and jobs.

Alerts An *alert* is an error message or event that occurs in SQL Server and is recorded in the Windows Application log. Alerts can be sent to users via e-mail, pager, or Net Send. If an error message isn't written to the Windows application log, an alert is never fired off.

Operators When an alert is fired, it can be sent to a user. Users who need to receive these messages are known in SQL Server as *operators*. Operators are used to configure who receives alerts and when they're available to receive these messages.

Jobs A *job* is a series of steps that define the task to be automated. It also defines schedules, which dictate when the task is to be executed. Such tasks can be run one time or on a recurring basis.

These three components work together to complete the tapestry of administration. Here is an example of what may happen:

1. A user defines a job that is specified to run at a certain time.
2. When the job runs, it fails and thus writes an error message to the Windows event log.
3. When the SQL Server Agent service reads the Windows event log, the agent finds the error message that the failed job wrote and compares it to the sysalerts table in the MSDB database.
4. When the agent finds a match, it fires an alert.
5. The alert, when fired, can send an e-mail, pager message, or Net Send message to an operator.
6. The alert can also be configured to run another job, designed to repair the problem that caused the alert.

For any of this to function, though, the SQL Server Agent service must be properly configured. To begin with, the agent must be running for automation to work. There are three ways to verify this: First, you can open SQL Server Management Studio and notice the SQL Server Agent icon—if it's a red circle with an X, the service is stopped; if it's a green arrow, the service is started. (You can start the service by right-clicking the icon and selecting Start.) You can also check and change the state of the service by using the SQL Computer Manager or by using the Services applet in Control Panel.

Not only should the agent be running, but it's also best to have it log on with a domain account as opposed to a local system account, because using the local system account won't allow you to work with other SQL Servers on your network. This means you can't perform multiserver jobs (discussed later in this chapter), carry out replication (discussed in Chapter 25), or use SQL Server's e-mail capabilities. To make sure the agent is logging on with a domain account, open the Services applet in Control Panel (if you're using Windows 2000 or 2003, you'll find it in Administrative Tools under Programs on the Start menu), double-click the SQL Server Agent service, and select a domain account by clicking the ellipsis box next to This Account.

Once all of this is in place, you're nearly ready to begin working with automation. First, you should configure SQL Server to send e-mail using SQLiMail.

Configuring SQLiMail

New to SQL Server 2005, SQLiMail is used to send e-mail for the SQL Server services. Previous versions of SQL Server had SQLMail and SQLAgentMail, both of which used MAPI and required a MAPI client (commonly Outlook) to be installed on the server. SQLiMail doesn't use MAPI; it uses the standard Simple Mail Transfer Protocol (SMTP) and therefore doesn't require a MAPI client to be installed.

This new method is better for a number of reasons. First, the application that handles the mail (`SQLiMail90.exe`) runs as a separate process, so if a problem occurs, SQL Server is unaffected. You can also specify more than one mail server, so if one mail server goes down, SQLiMail can still process mail.

SQLiMail is also scalable because it processes mail in the background. When you make a request to send mail, SQLiMail adds a request to the Service Broker queue, which allows the request to be handled asynchronously, and even saves the request if the server goes down before it can be handled (see Chapter 29 for more on the Service Broker). Also, multiple copies of SQLiMail can run at once, and you can have multiple mail profiles and mail host databases on the same server (more on this later in this section).

To top it off, SQLiMail is more secure and easier to manage than its predecessors. It has granular control so you can limit which users are allowed to send mail. You can also specify what file extensions are allowed and disallowed as attachments, as well as the maximum size of those attachments. Everything SQLiMail does is logged in the Windows application log, and sent messages are retained in the mailhost database for auditing.

This all sounds great, but how do you use it? First you need an SMTP mail server somewhere on the network with a mail account configured for the SQL Server Agent service account. Setting up and configuring an SMTP server is out of the scope of this book, but if you have an e-mail account with your Internet Service Provider (ISP), you can use that. Then you can configure SQLiMail using the configuration wizard. Let's configure MSDB as a mailhost database now:

1. Open SQL Server Management Studio, and connect to your server.
2. Expand Management in Object Explorer, right-click SQLiMail, and select Configure SQLiMail.
3. On the Welcome Screen, click Next.

4. On the Select Configuration Task page, select Set Up SQLiMail By Performing The Following Tasks and click Next.

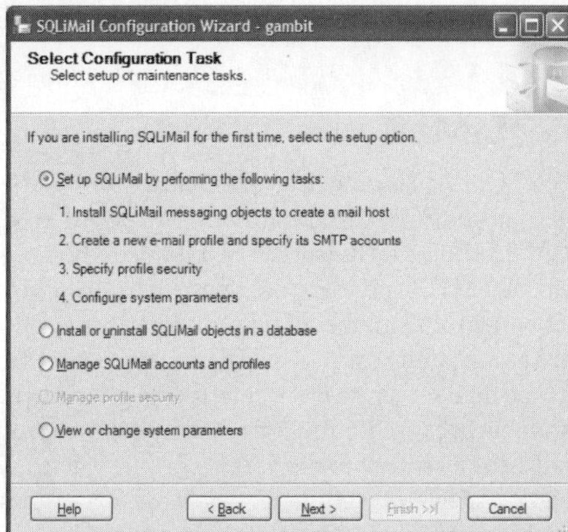

5. On the Install Messaging Objects screen, select the msdb database and click Next.

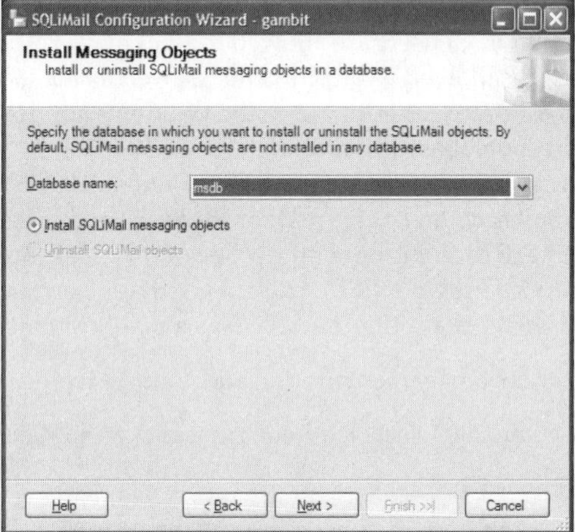

6. On the New Profile screen, create a mail profile and associate it with a mail server account:

   A. Enter **SQLAgentProfile** in the Profile name box.

   B. Under SMTP Accounts, click Add.

   C. In the Account Name box, enter **Mail Provider Account 1**.

D. In the description, enter **E-mail account information**.

E. Fill in your Outgoing Mail Server information using the information provided by your ISP or network administrator.

F. If your e-mail server requires you to log on, select the SMTP Server Requires Authentication check box and enter your logon information.

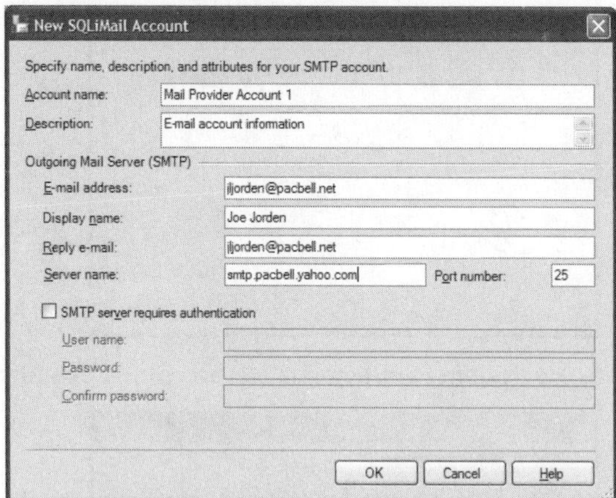

G. Click OK to return to the wizard. Your account should now be listed under SMTP Accounts.

7. Click Next.

8. On the Manage Profile Security page, select the Public check box next to the mail profile you just created to make it accessible to all users. Set the Default Profile setting to Yes, and click Next.

9. On the Configure System Parameters page, accept the defaults and click Next.

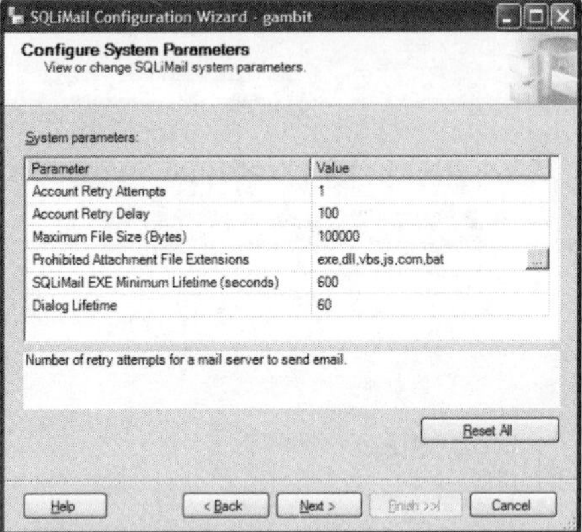

10. On the Complete the Wizard page, review all your settings and click Finish.

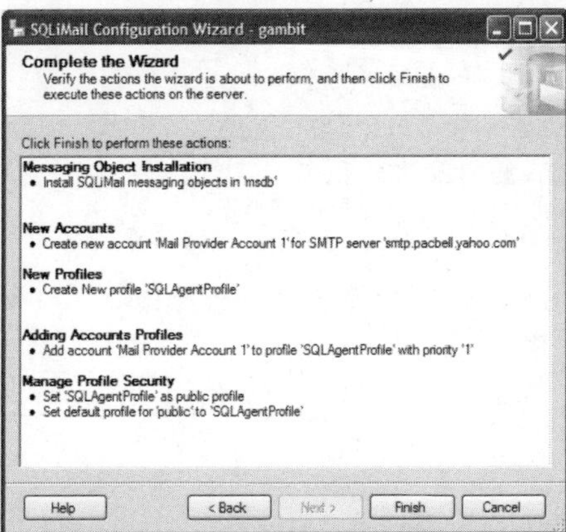

11. When the system is finished setting up SQLiMail, click Close.

SQLiMail Configuration Wizard - gambit

Configuring...
Click Stop to interrupt the operation.

Success — 5 Total, 5 Success, 0 Error, 0 Warning

Details:

Action	Status	Message
Install SQLiMail messaging objects in 'msdb'	Success	
Create new account 'Mail Provider Accou...	Success	
Create New profile 'SQLAgentProfile'	Success	
Add account 'Mail Provider Account 1' to ...	Success	
Set 'SQLAgentProfile' as public profile	Success	

Stop　Report　Close

Now you need to configure the SQL Server Agent to use the mail profile you just created:

1. In Object Explorer, right-click SQL Server Agent and select Properties.
2. On the Alert System page, select the Enable mail profile check box.
3. Select SQLiMail from the Mail system drop-down list.
4. Select SQLAgentProfile from the Mail profile drop-down list.

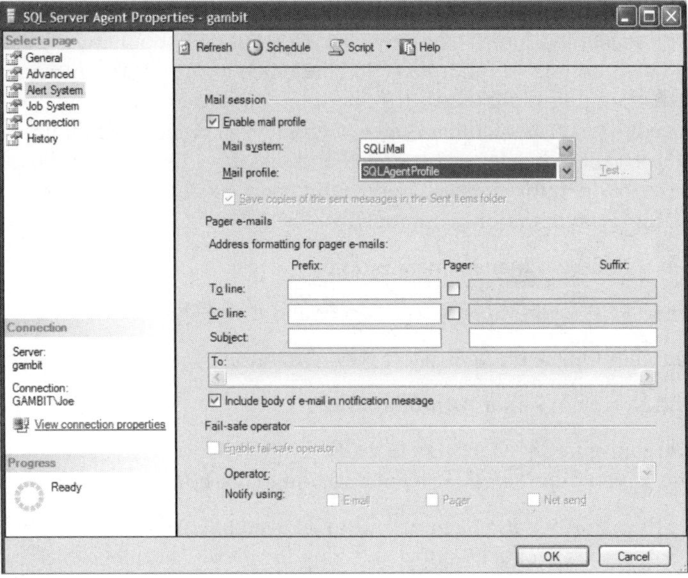

5. Click OK.
6. From SQL Computer Manager, stop and restart the SQL Server Agent service.

You can run the configuration wizard again at any time to make changes to the SQLiMail configuration. For example, you may want to:

- Create a new SQLiMail database.
- Add or remove accounts or profiles.
- Manage profile security by marking them as public or private.
- View or change system parameters.
- Uninstall SQLiMail.

With SQLiMail successfully configured, you can create operators that receive e-mail from SQL Server.

TIP Internet Information Services comes with a built-in SMTP server that you can use with SQLiMail.

Creating Operators

Several settings need to be configured for SQL Server to be able to contact you when there are problems. Such settings include whom to contact, when contacts are available, how those people should be contacted (via e-mail, pager, or Net Send), and what problems should they be alerted about. An *operator* is the object used in SQL Server to configure all these settings.

NOTE Net Send messages are messages sent from a source machine to a destination machine that pop up on the user's screen in a dialog box over all the open applications.

Suppose, for example, that several people in your company need to be alerted when a problem occurs with SQL Server, and each of them needs to be alerted for different problems and in various ways. Your database administrator may need to be alerted about any administration issues (for example, a failed backup or full transaction log) via e-mail and pager. Your developers may need to be alerted to programming issues (for example, deadlocks) via e-mail. Perhaps managers in your company need to know about other issues, such as a user deleting a customer from a customer database, and they want to be alerted by a Net Send message. You can handle these types of users by creating separate operators for each and configuring the desired settings.

Let's configure an operator to demonstrate:

1. Open SQL Server Management Studio.
2. In Object Explorer, expand your server and then SQL Server Agent.
3. Right-click Operators, and select New Operator.
4. In the Name box, enter **Administrator**.
5. If you configured your system to use SQLiMail Mail, enter your e-mail address as the e-mail name. If you didn't configure your system to use e-mail, skip this step.
6. Type the name of your machine in the Net Send box. You can find it by right-clicking the My Computer icon on the Desktop, selecting Properties, and then clicking the Network Identification tab. The computer name is the first section of the full computer name (before the first period). For instance, if the full computer name is `instructor.domain.com`, the computer name is `instructor`.

7. If you carry a pager that is capable of receiving e-mail, you can enter your pager's e-mail address in the Pager E-mail Name box.

8. At the bottom of the screen, you can select the days and times this operator is available for notification. If a day is checked, the operator will be notified on that day between the start and end times noted under Start Time and End Time. For now, leave this set to Always Active.

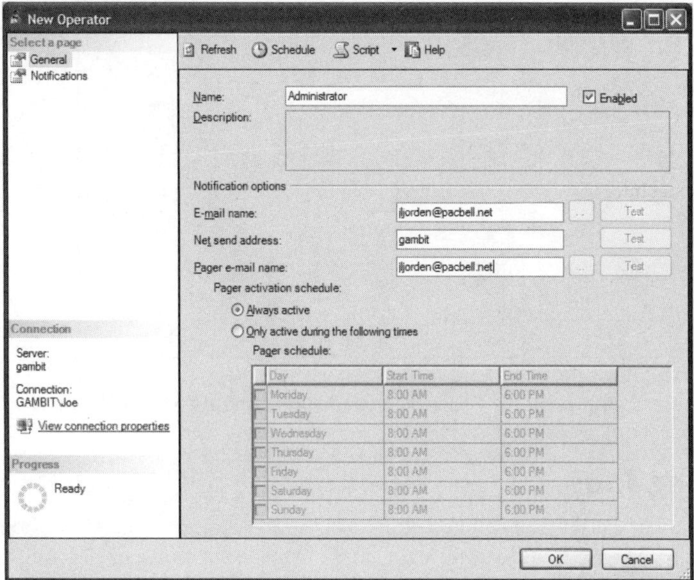

9. To test the operator, click the Test button next to each of the three notification methods. The e-mail and pager tests both send an e-mail, and the Net Send test causes a dialog box to pop up on your screen.

10. We'll discuss the Notifications tab later; for now, click OK to create the operator.

Because operators can be made active at different times, it's possible to accidentally leave a small period of time uncovered. If an error occurs in that window of time, no operator will receive the alert, because none are on duty. To avoid such a problem, you should create a fail-safe operator, which is designed to receive alerts when no one is scheduled to be on duty. Here is how to create one:

1. In SQL Server Management Studio, right-click the SQL Server Agent icon in Object Explorer, and select Properties.

2. On the Alert System page, select the Enable Fail-safe Operator check box.

3. Select Administrator in the Operator drop-down list.

4. Select the check box next to Net Send so that you'll receive Net Send messages as a fail-safe operator.

5. Click OK to apply the changes.

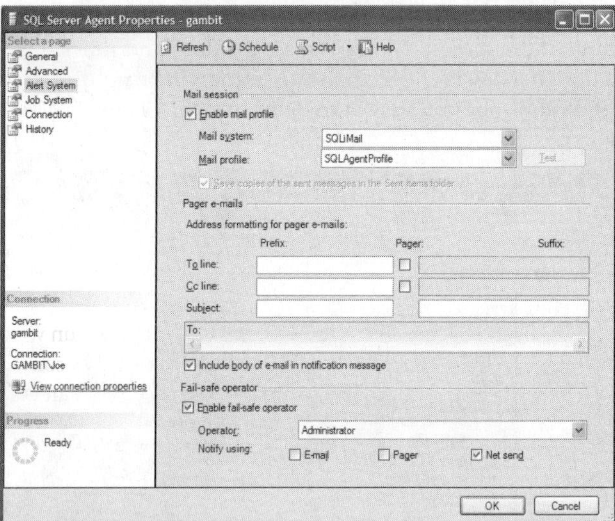

With an operator in place, you're ready to start creating jobs to automate tasks.

Creating Jobs

A *job* is a series of tasks that can be automated to run whenever you need them to. It may be easier to think of it as being like cleaning your house. Most of us think of cleaning our house as one big job that needs to be done, but it's really a series of smaller tasks such as dusting the furniture, vacuuming the carpet, doing the dishes, and so on. Some of these steps need to be accomplished in succession (for example, dusting before vacuuming); others can happen any time (for example, the dishes don't need to be done before you can wash the windows).

Any job on SQL Server works in much the same way. Take, for example, a job that creates a database. This isn't just one big job with one step to accomplish before you're finished; several steps should take place. Step one creates the database. The next step backs up the newly created database, because it's in a vulnerable state until it's backed up. After the database has been backed up, you can create tables in it and then perhaps import data into those tables from text files. Each of these tasks is a separate step that needs to be completed before the next can be started, but not all jobs are that way.

By controlling the flow of the steps, you can build error correction into your jobs. For example, in the create-database job, each step has simple logic that states *on success go to the next step; on failure quit the job.* If the hard disk turns out to be full, the job stops. If you create a step at the end of the job that is designed to clear up hard-disk space, you can create logic that states *if step one fails, go to step five; if step five succeeds, go back to step one.* With the steps in place, you're ready to tell SQL Server when to start the job.

To tell SQL Server when to run a job, you need to create schedules, and you have a lot of flexibility there. If a job creates a database, it wouldn't make much sense to run the job more than once, so you create a single schedule that activates the job after hours. If you're creating a job that is designed to perform transaction log backups, you want a different schedule; you may want to perform these backups every two hours during the day (from 9:00 a.m. to 6:00 p.m.) and then every three hours at night (from 6:00 p.m. to 9:00 a.m.). In this instance, you need to create two schedules: one that is active from 9:00 a.m. to 6:00 p.m. and activates the job every two hours, and another that is active from 6:00 p.m. to 9:00 a.m. and activates the job every three hours. If you think that's fancy, you'll love the next part.

Not only can you schedule jobs to activate at certain times of the day, but you can also schedule them to activate only on certain days of the week (for example, every Tuesday), or you can schedule them to run only on certain days of the month (for example, every third Monday). Jobs can be scheduled to run every time the SQL Server Agent service starts up, and they can even be scheduled to run every time the processor becomes idle.

Schedules can be set to expire after a certain amount of time, so if you know you're going to be done with a job after a few weeks, you can set it to expire—it will automatically be disabled (not deleted, just shut off).

You also have the capacity to be notified about the outcome of a job. When you create a job, you can add an operator to the job that's notified on success, on failure, or on completion (regardless of whether the job failed or succeeded). This comes in very handy when the job you're running is critical to your server or application.

With the ability to change the logical flow of steps, schedule jobs to run whenever you want, and have jobs notify you on completion, you can see how complex jobs can become. With this complexity in mind, it's always a good idea to sit down with pencil and paper and plan your jobs before creating them; doing so will make your work easier in the long run.

SQL Server uses two types of jobs: local and multiserver. Let's look at each of these, starting with local jobs.

Creating Local Server Jobs

Local jobs are standard jobs with a series of steps and schedules. They're designed to run on the machine where they're created (hence the name *local jobs*). To demonstrate local jobs, let's schedule one that creates a new database and then backs it up:

1. Open SQL Server Management Studio by selecting it from the SQL Server 2005 group under Programs on the Start menu.
2. Expand your server in Object Explorer, and then expand SQL Server Agent.
3. Right-click Jobs, and select New Job.
4. In the Name box, type **Create Test Database** (leave the rest of the boxes on this page with the default settings).

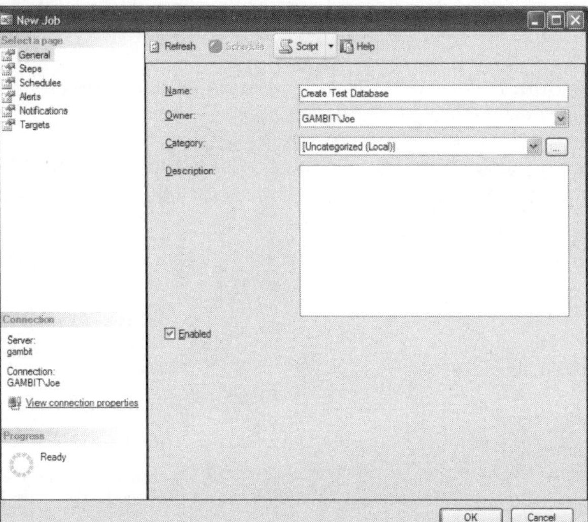

5. Go to the Steps page, and click the New button to create a new step.
6. In the Step Name box, type **Create Database**.
7. Leave the type as Transact-SQL, and enter the following code to create a database named Test on the C: drive:

```
CREATE DATABASE TEST ON
PRIMARY (NAME=test_dat,
FILENAME='c:\test.mdf',
SIZE=10MB,
MAXSIZE=15,
FILEGROWTH=10%)
```

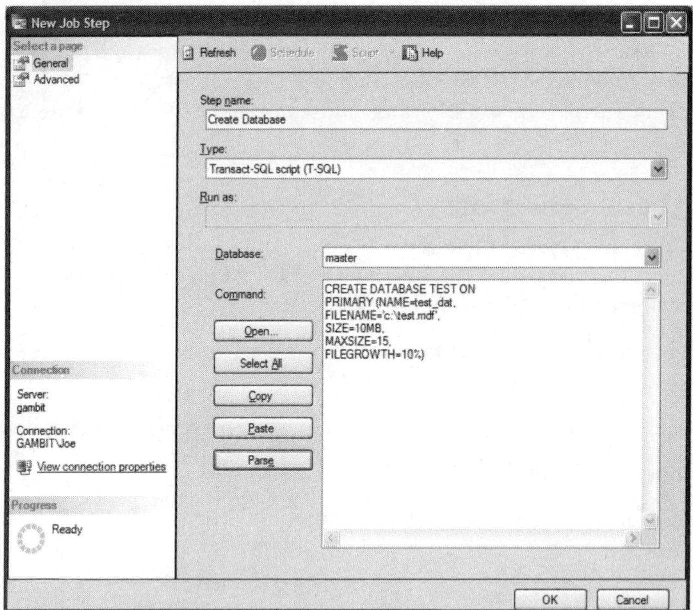

8. Click the Parse button to verify that you entered the code correctly, and then move to the Advanced page.
9. On the Advanced page, verify that Action To Take If Job Succeeds is set to Go To The Next Step and that Action To Take If Job Fails is set to Quit The Job Reporting Failure. Click OK.

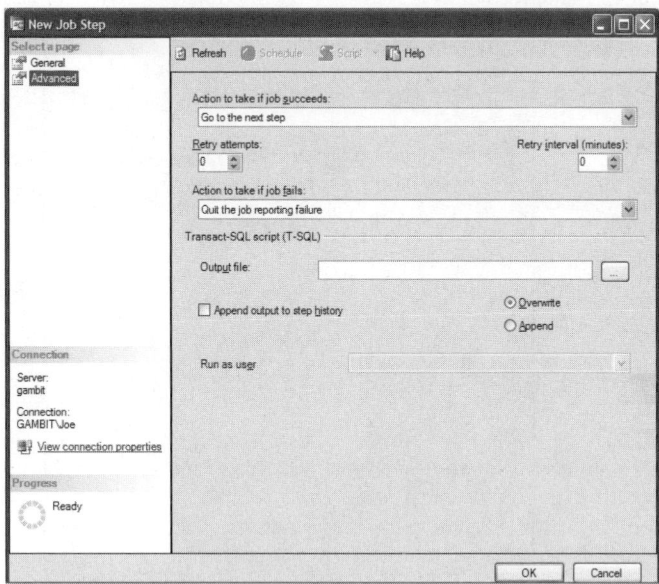

10. To create the second step of the job, click the New button.
11. In the Name box, enter **Backup Test**.
12. Leave the Type as Transact-SQL Script, and enter the following code to back up the database once it's created:

```
EXEC sp_addumpdevice 'disk', 'Test_Backup',     'c:\Test_Backup.dat'
BACKUP DATABASE TEST TO Test_Backup
```

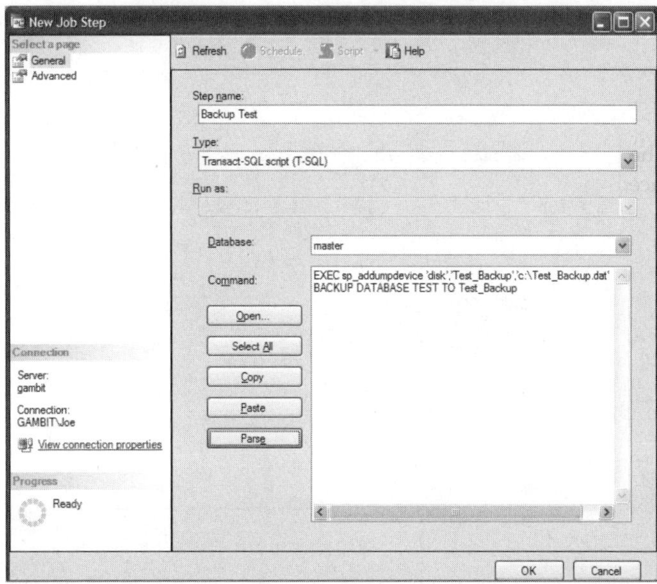

13. Click OK to create the step.

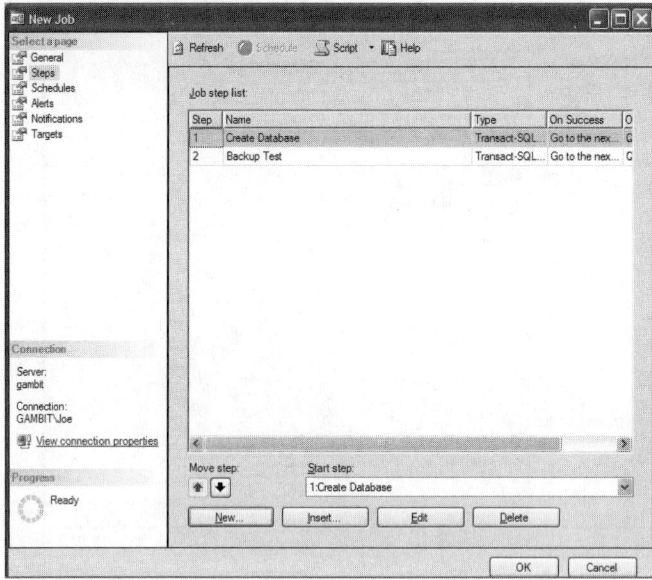

14. Move to the Schedules page, and click the New button to create a schedule that will instruct SQL Server when to fire the job.

15. In the Name box, type **Create and Backup Database**.

16. Under Schedule Type, select One Time. Set the time to be 5 minutes from the time displayed in the system tray (the indented part of the Start bar, usually at the bottom right of your screen).

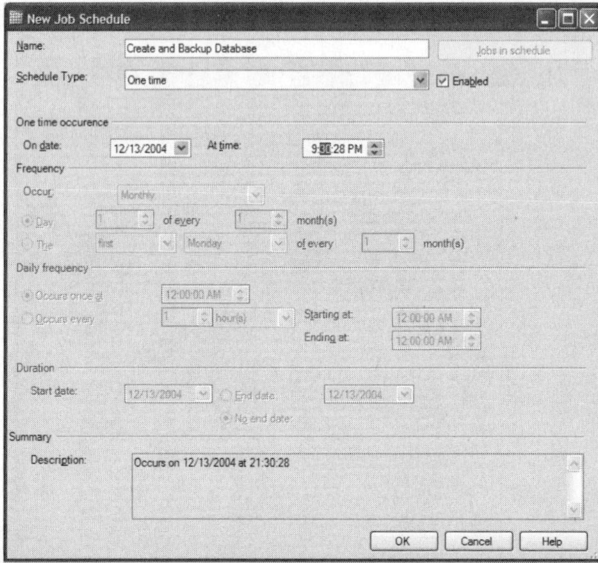

17. Click OK to create the schedule, and move to the Notifications tab.

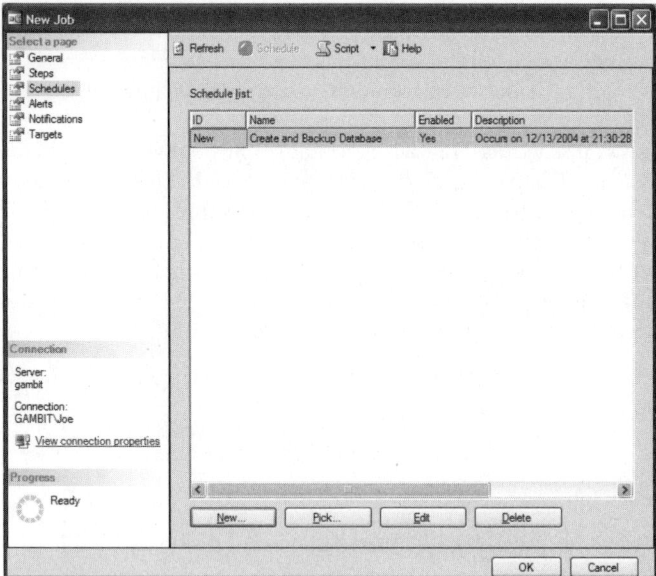

18. On the Notifications tab, select the check boxes next to E-Mail (if you configured SQLiMail earlier) and Net Send, choosing Administrator as the operator to notify. Next to each, select When The Job Completes from the list box (this will notify you no matter what the outcome of the job is).

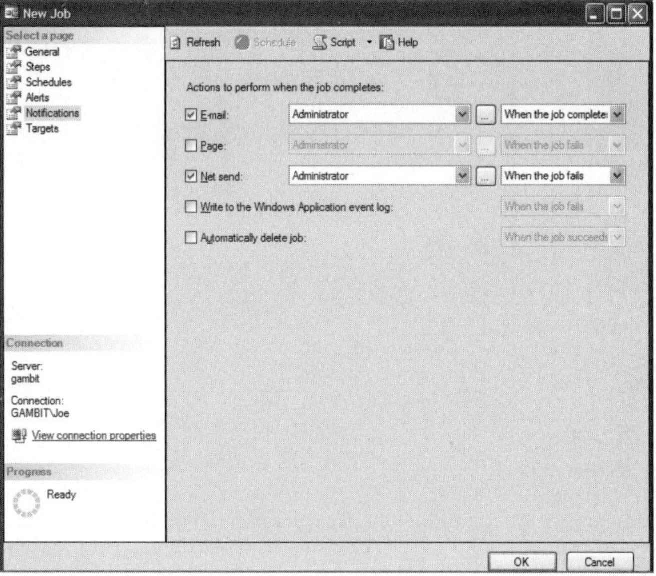

19. Click OK to create the job. Wait until the time set in step 16 to verify completion. You should see a message pop up on your screen, notifying you of completion.

What just happened? You created a job with two steps; the first step created a new database named Test, and the second step backed up the database to a new backup device. This job was scheduled to run only one time and notify you of completion (whether or not it was a success). The two steps in this job were Transact-SQL type jobs, which means they were standard Transact-SQL statements, much like you've been using throughout this book. You can run any Transact-SQL statement in this fashion, but that's not all.

Not only can you schedule Transact-SQL statements, but you can also schedule any active scripting language: VBScript, JavaScript, Perl, and so forth. This frees you from the boundaries of Transact-SQL, because the scripting languages have features that SQL Server doesn't implement. For example, you can't directly access the file structure on the hard disk using Transact-SQL (to create a new text file, for example), but you can with a scripting language. Listing all the advantages of scripting languages goes beyond the scope of this book; but to demonstrate how SQL Server schedules such tasks, let's create a job that prints a statement:

1. Open SQL Server Management Studio by selecting it from the SQL Server 2005 group under Programs on the Start menu.
2. Expand your server, and then expand SQL Server Agent.
3. Right-click Jobs, and select New Job.
4. In the Name box, type **VBTest** (leave the rest of the boxes on this tab with the default settings).

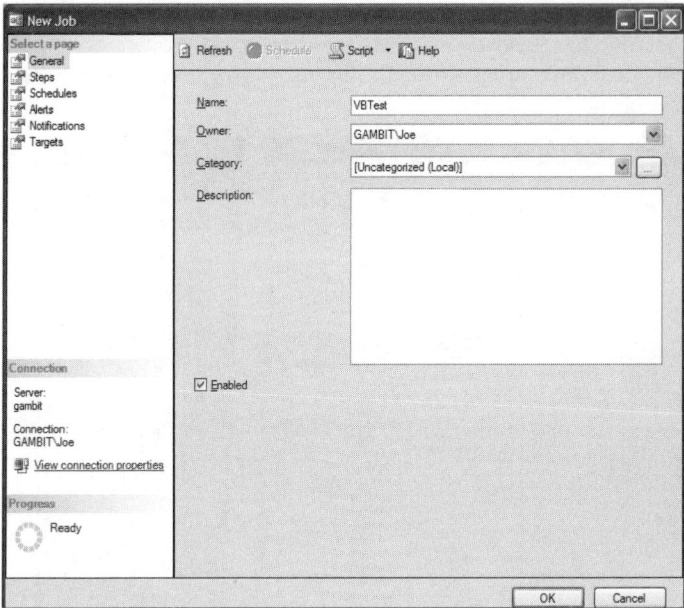

5. Go to the Steps page, and click the New button to create a new step.
6. In the Step Name box, type **Print**.
7. Choose ActiveX Script as the Type, and then select the VBScript radio button.

8. Enter the following code in the Command box:

```
sub main()
 Print "Your job was successful"
end sub
```

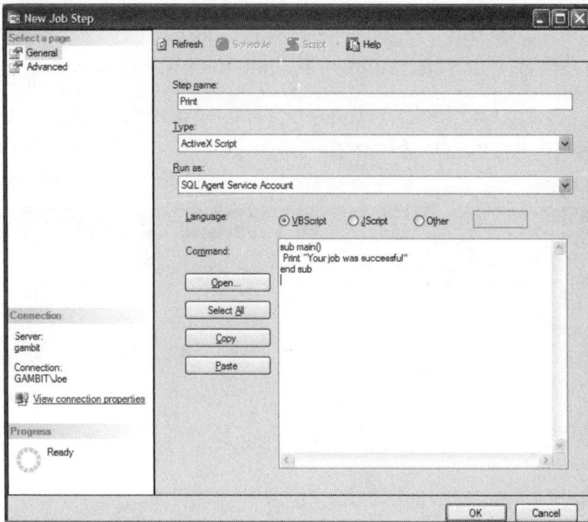

9. Click OK.
10. Move to the Schedules page, and click the New button.
11. In the Name box, type **Run Print**.
12. Under Schedule Type, select One Time, and set the time to be 5 minutes from the time displayed in the system tray (the indented part of the Start bar, usually at the bottom right of your screen).

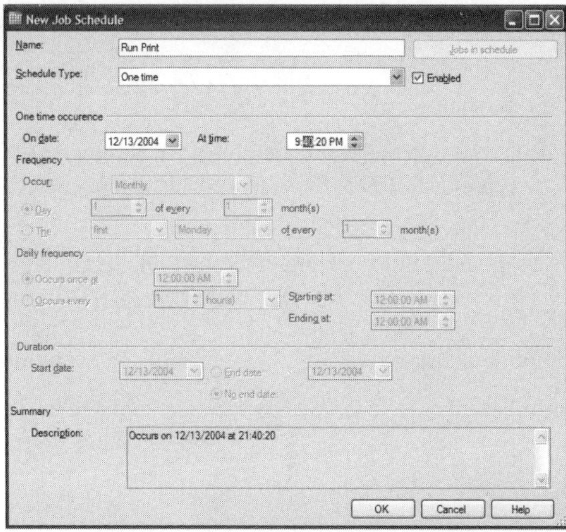

13. Click OK to create the job, and wait until the time set in step 12 to verify completion.

Now that you've created a VBScript job, you need to know whether it ran successfully. True, you could set a notification for yourself, but there is another way to verify the status of a job. SQL Server keeps track of the job's history, when it was activated, whether it succeeded or failed, and even the status of each step of each job. To verify whether your VBScript job succeeded, let's check the job's history:

1. In SQL Server Management Studio, right-click the VBTest job, and select View Job History.
2. To show the status of each step of the job, click the plus sign icon next to the step.
3. Select the Print step, and look for the text *Your job was successful* at the bottom of the dialog box in the Errors and/or Messages box. This is the text generated by the VBScript function.

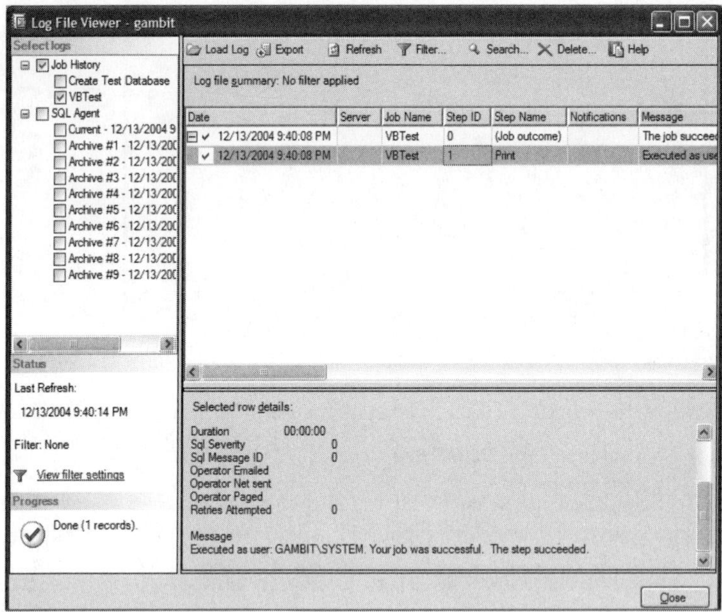

4. Click Close to exit the dialog box.

The history of each job is stored in the MSDB database. By default, 1,000 lines of total history can be stored, and each job can take up to 100 of those records. If you need to change those defaults, follow these steps:

1. In SQL Server Management Studio, right-click the SQL Server Agent and select Properties.
2. Select the History page.
3. To change the amount of data saved for all jobs, modify the Maximum Job History Log Size.
4. To change the number of rows that each job can take, change the Maximum Job History Rows Per Job.

5. To have the agent automatically clear the history, select the Automatically Remove Agent History check box.

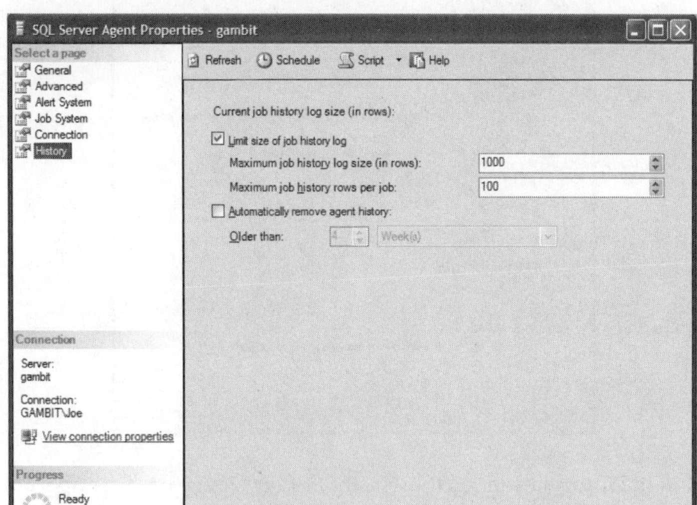

6. Click OK when you have made the necessary changes.

It's not hard to see the value of creating local jobs on SQL Server, but there is more. Multiserver jobs are designed to make automation easier across multiple servers.

Creating Multiserver Jobs

A growing number of companies have multiple database servers. Each of these servers require jobs; some are unique to the server, but many are repetitive, each server having the same job. One way to solve this problem is to create local jobs on each server separately, but this process is time consuming and hard to manage. A better way to make this happen is to create multiserver jobs.

A *multiserver job* is a job that is created once, on one server, and downloaded to other servers over the network where the job is run. To create multiserver jobs, you must first designate two types of servers: a master and targets. The *master server* (or MSX) is where the multiserver jobs are created and managed. The *target servers* poll the master server at regular intervals for jobs (you'll see how to change this a little later in the chapter), download those jobs, and then run them at the scheduled time. This is done using the Master Server Wizard; let's run it now.

NOTE **To perform this series of steps, you'll need to have a second instance of SQL Server running on your machine.**

1. Open SQL Server Management Studio from the SQL Server 2005 group under Programs on the Start menu.

2. Expand the default instance of your server in Object Explorer.

3. Right-click the SQL Server Agent, and select Multiserver Administration and Make This a Master. Doing so starts the Master Server Wizard.

4. On the opening screen of the wizard, click Next.

5. Fill in the information for the Master Server Operator. This operator will receive notification of multiserver jobs. If you configured e-mail support earlier, enter your own e-mail address as the E-mail Address and your machine name as the Net Send Address and click Next.

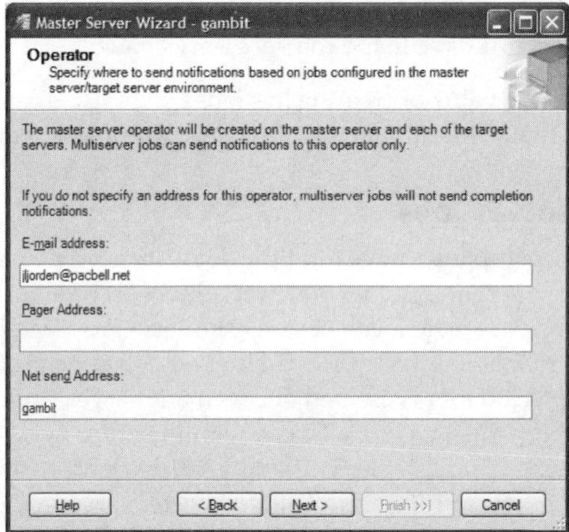

6. In the Target Servers dialog box select *servername\second_instance* in the Registered Servers list and click the > button to add it to the Target Servers list. Doing so enlists this as a target server (it will now accept jobs from the master server). Click Next to continue.

7. On the Checking Server Compatibility screen, click Close (if there were errors, you'll need to fix them before you can continue).

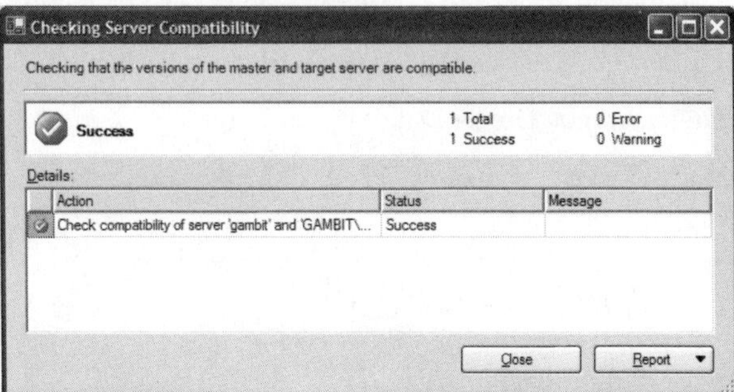

8. On the Master Server Login Credentials screen, allow the wizard to create an account if necessary by leaving the check box selected. Click Next.

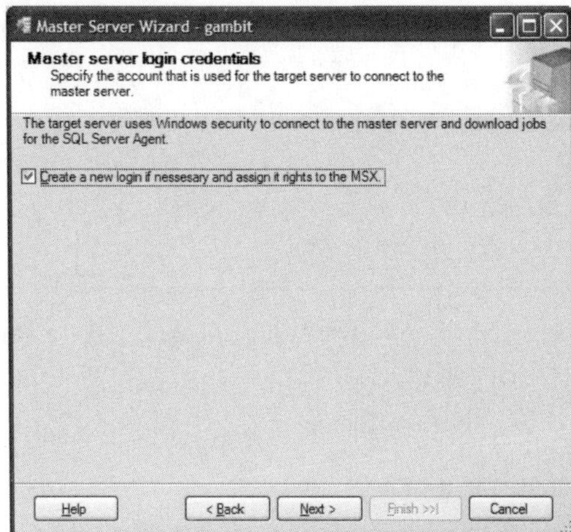

9. On the final screen, click Finish to create the master server and enlist the target.

Now that you have created a master server and enlisted a target server, let's create a job on the master that will run on the target and notify the Master Server Operator (you) when it's complete:

1. Under SQL Server Agent on the Master server, right-click Jobs and select New Job.
2. In the Name box, type **Create Database on Target**.

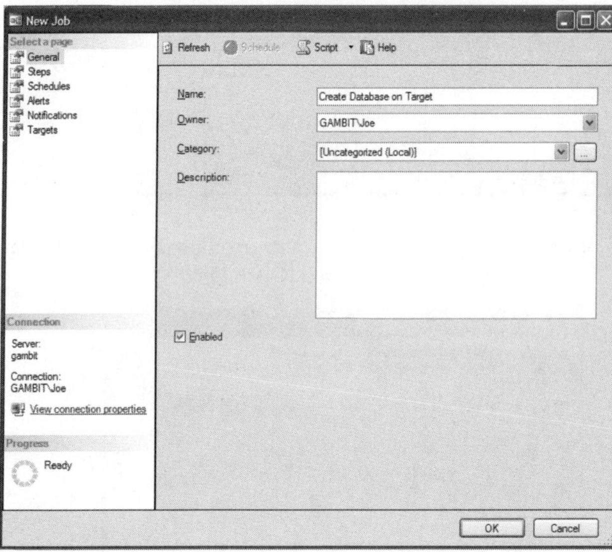

3. On the Steps page, click the New button and enter **Create Target Database** in the Name box.
4. Leave the Type as Transact-SQL Script, and enter the following code to create a database named TARGET on the C: drive:

```
CREATE DATABASE TARGET ON
PRIMARY (NAME=target_dat,
```

```
FILENAME='c:\target.mdf',
SIZE=10MB,
MAXSIZE=15,
FILEGROWTH=10%)
```

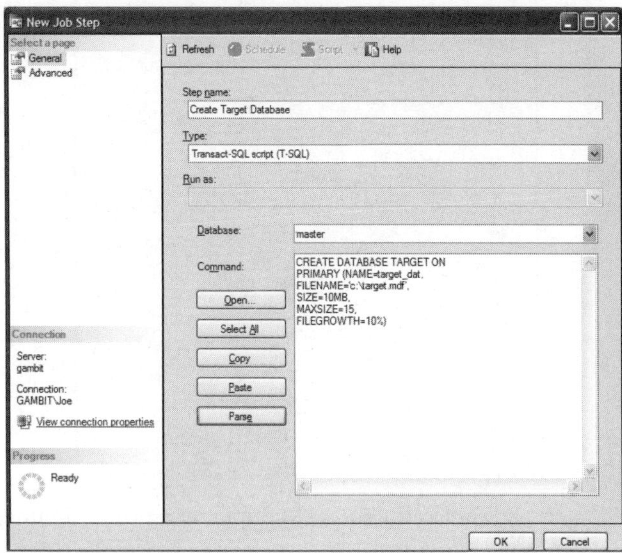

5. Click OK to create the step.
6. On the Schedules page, click the New button to create a new schedule.
7. In the Name box, enter **Create Target Database**.
8. Select One Time for the Schedule Type, and set the time to be 10 minutes from the time listed in the system tray. Click OK to create the schedule.

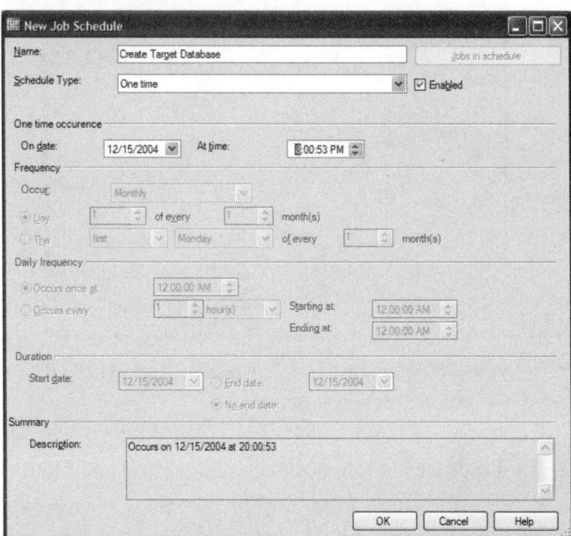

9. On the Notifications page, select the check box next to Net Send, and select MSXOperator and When The Job Completes from the drop-down lists.

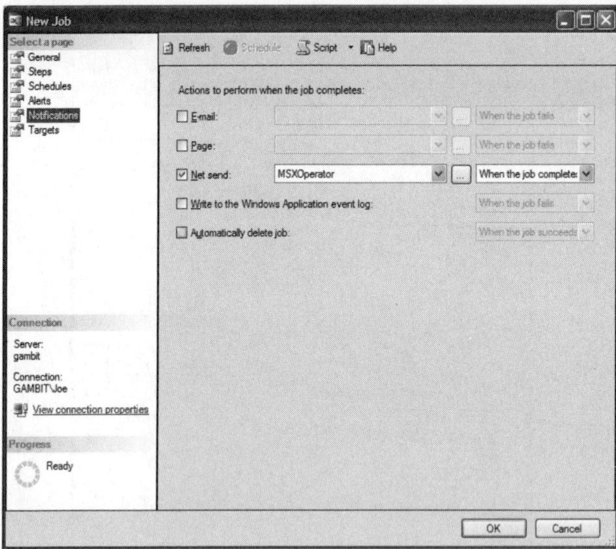

10. 10. On the Targets page, select the Target Multiple Servers radio button, and select the check box next to your target server instance.

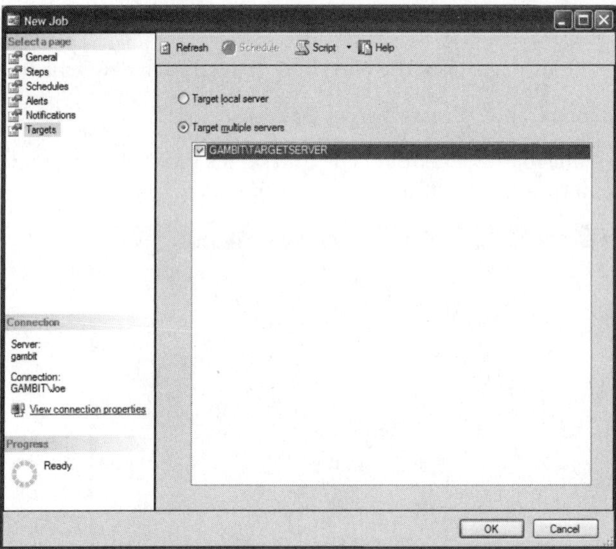

11. Click OK to create the job. Wait until the time specified in step 8, and then check for the new database named Target on the target server.

NOTE After you create a multiserver job, SQL Server adds Local and Multi-Server folders under the Jobs folder.

Notice what you did: You created a job on the master server that was then downloaded to the target server, where it was executed and created the target database. But how did the job get to the target server? The targets are configured to poll the master server for jobs every 60 seconds by default. This may be overkill in most environments, so you need to know how to configure that setting. You also need to be able to force a server to poll the master if you can't wait for the polling interval to pass. All of this is done using the `sp_post_msx_operation` stored procedure. The syntax to synchronize the clock on a target named Second looks like this:

```
sp_post_msx_operation @operation='SYNC-TIME', @object_type='server', @specific_
target_server='Second'
```

The code to change the polling interval on the Second server to 5 minutes (600 seconds) would look like this:

```
sp_post_msx_operation @operation='SET-POLL', @object_type='server', @specific_
target_server='Second', @value='600'
```

Now that you know how to create jobs to automate tasks on SQL Server, you're ready to enhance your system even further. Let's look at the process for creating alerts, which can automatically fix errors for you.

Creating Alerts

An alert is fired when an event (usually a problem) occurs on SQL Server; some examples are a full transaction log or incorrect syntax in a query. These alerts can then be sent to an operator so that they can be tended to. Alerts are based on one of three things: an error number, an error severity level, or a performance counter.

All the errors that can occur in SQL Server are numbered (there are about 3,000 of them). Even with so many errors listed, there aren't enough. For example, suppose you want to fire an alert when a user deletes a customer from your customers database. SQL Server doesn't have an alert with the structure of your database or your users' names; therefore you have the ability to create new error numbers and generate an alert for such proprietary things. Alerts can be created to fire on any valid error number.

Each error in SQL Server also has an associated severity level, stating how serious the error is. Alerts can be generated by severity level. Table 17.1 lists the more common levels.

TABLE 17.1: Severity Levels of Errors

LEVEL	DESCRIPTION
10	This is an informational message caused by mistakes in the information that was entered by the user. It isn't serious.
11–16	These are all errors that can be corrected by the user.
17	These errors are generated when the server runs out of resources, such as memory or hard-disk space.
18	A nonfatal internal error has occurred. The statement will finish, and the user connection will be maintained.

TABLE 17.1: Severity Levels of Errors *(CONTINUED)*

LEVEL	DESCRIPTION
19	A nonconfigurable internal limit has been reached. Any statement that causes this will be terminated.
20	A single process in the current database has suffered a problem, but the database itself is unscathed.
21	All processes in the current database are affected by the problem, but the database is undamaged.
22	The table or index that is being used is probably damaged. You should run DBCC to try to repair the object. (Alternatively, the problem may be in the data cache, which means a simple restart may suffice.)
23	This message usually means the entire database has been damaged somehow, and you should check the integrity of your hardware.
24	Your hardware has failed. You'll probably need to get new hardware and reload the database from backup.

Alerts can also be generated from performance counters. These are the exact same counters that you would see in Performance Monitor, and they come in very handy for correcting performance issues such as a full (or nearly full) transaction log. You can also generate alerts based on Windows Management Instrumentation (WMI) events. You'll see these in more detail later in the chapter. To start, let's create some alerts using the errors and severity levels that are built into SQL Server.

Event Alerts Based on Standard Errors

Standard alerts are based on the error messages or severity levels that are built into SQL Server. To create an alert based on one of these events, the error must be written to the Windows event log, because the SQL Server Agent reads errors from there. Once the SQL Server Agent has read the event log and detected a new error, the agent searches through the MSDB database looking for a matching alert. When the agent finds one, the alert is fired; it can in turn notify an operator, execute a job, or both.

You'll create one of those alerts here—the one that fires from an error number (alerts based on severity work the same, except they're based on the severity of an error, not the number). Then, to fire that alert, you'll use the `RAISERROR()` command, which is designed specifically for the purpose of firing alerts. Let's begin by creating an alert based on error number 1 that sends a Net Send notification to an operator:

1. Open SQL Server Management Studio, expand your server, and then expand SQL Server Agent.
2. Right-click Alerts, and select New Alert.
3. In the Name box, enter **Number Alert**.
4. Select SQL Server Event Alert from the Type list.
5. Select <all databases> from the Database Name list.

6. Because you can't manually fire errors below 13000, you'll use error number 14599, but you need to modify it so it's written to the event log every time it fires. To do that, select the Error Number radio button, and enter **14599** in the error number text box. Click the ellipsis (…) button next to the error number text box.

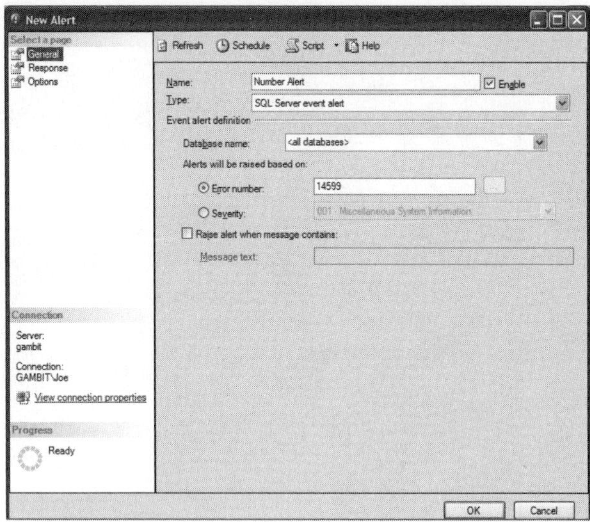

7. In the Manage SQL Server Messages dialog box that pops up, leave the text boxes blank and click the Find button to locate all messages.
8. Select error number 14599 in the subsequent list, and click Edit.
9. In the Edit dialog box, select the Always Write To Windows Eventlog check box, and click OK.
10. On the Response page, select the Notify Operators check box and select the Net Send check box next to Administrator.

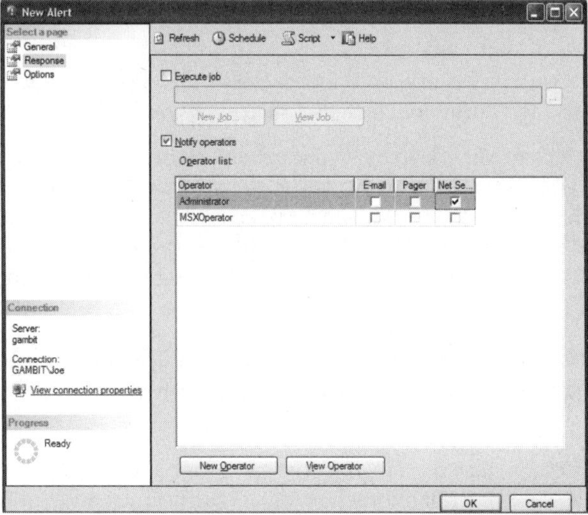

11. On the Options page, select the Net Send check box under Include Error Alert Text In, and click OK.

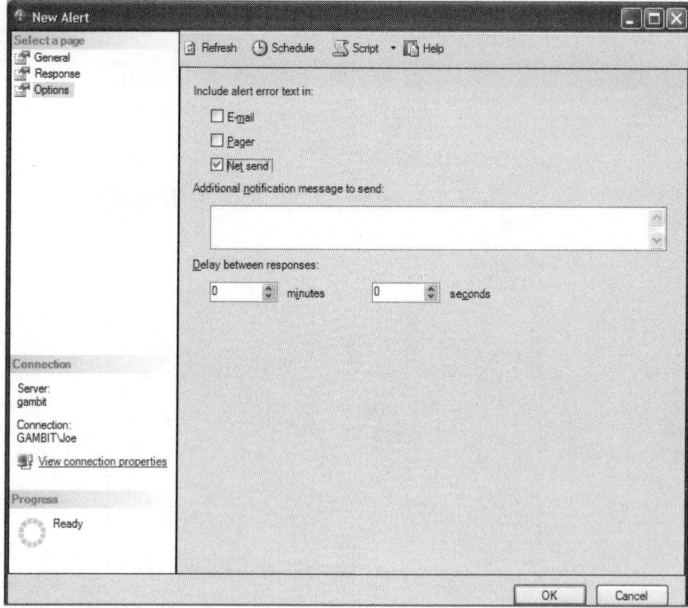

Now that you have an alert that is designed to fire whenever error number 14599 occurs, let's generate error number 14599 using the `RAISERROR()` command:

1. Open a new SQL Server Query by clicking the New Query button in SQL Server Management Studio.
2. Enter and execute the following code to fire off the error:

```
RAISERROR(14599,10,1)
```

3. When the Net Send message pops up, note the detail it gives you, including the error number, description, and additional text, and then click OK.

Let's break down this process, step by step. First you created an alert based on error number 14599; but since that error wasn't originally configured to be written to the Windows event log, you had to modify it so that it would be written there (if an error isn't written to the event log, its alerts will never fire). Then you configured the alert to notify an operator (you) via a Net Send message whenever the alert fires. After that, you used the `RAISERROR()` command to force the alert to fire and send you notification.

TIP Several alerts have been created for you, all of which have *Demo* in their name. These are real errors that you need to be alerted to, so set notification on them and remove the word *Demo* from the names.

Many alerts are fired because of problems that can be repaired using minimal Transact-SQL code (a good example of this is a full transaction log). Because you would probably rather see a message that states "There was a problem, and it's fixed" rather than "There's a problem; come and fix it yourself," you can configure alerts to execute jobs to fix the problems that caused the alerts to fire. Let's modify your existing alert to do just that:

1. In SQL Server Management Studio, expand Alerts under SQL Server Agent.
2. Right-click Number Alert, and select Properties.
3. Select the Response page.
4. Select the Execute Job check box, and enter **VBTest** in the job name box.

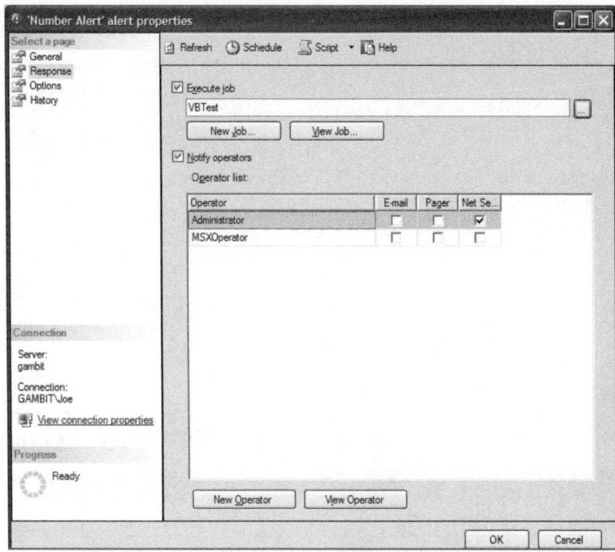

5. Click OK to apply the changes.

Now that you've modified the alert, let's fire it off again and watch it run your VBTest job:

1. Open a new SQL Server Query by clicking the New Query button in SQL Server Management Studio.
2. Enter and execute the following code to fire off the error:

```
RAISERROR(14599,10,1)
```

3. When the Net Send message pops up, note the message at the bottom stating that the VBTest job has run, and then click OK.

Creating alerts based on built-in errors isn't so rough, is it? Even though SQL Server includes nearly 3,700 such errors, there aren't enough to cover all your needs. Therefore, you need to know how to create custom error messages on which to base your alerts.

Event Alerts Based on Custom Errors

Having 3,700 errors may seem like an awful lot, but they don't cover every situation for which you might need an alert. For example, suppose you have a sales department that allows customers to order on credit, and you need to keep track of those credit lines. Your sales managers probably want to be notified whenever a customer with good credit is deleted or the customer's credit limit is decreased, or they may want to know when a customer's credit is raised above a $10,000 limit. In any event, these error messages don't exist in SQL Server by default; you must create the error message before you can use it to fire an alert.

You're allowed to create as many error messages as you want in SQL Server, starting with error number 50001 (this is the starting number for all user-defined errors). Let's create an alert based on a user-defined error and fire it off with the `RAISERROR()` command:

1. Open a new SQL Server Query by clicking the New Query button in SQL Server Management Studio.
2. Enter and execute the following code to create the new error:

```
USE master
GO
EXEC sp_addmessage @msgnum=50001, @severity=10,
   @msgtext=N' This is a custom error.', @with_log='TRUE'
GO
```

3. In Object Explorer, expand your server, and then expand SQL Server Agent.
4. Right-click Alerts, and select New Alert.
5. In the Name box, enter **Custom Alert**.
6. Select the Error Number radio button, and enter **50001** in the error number text box.

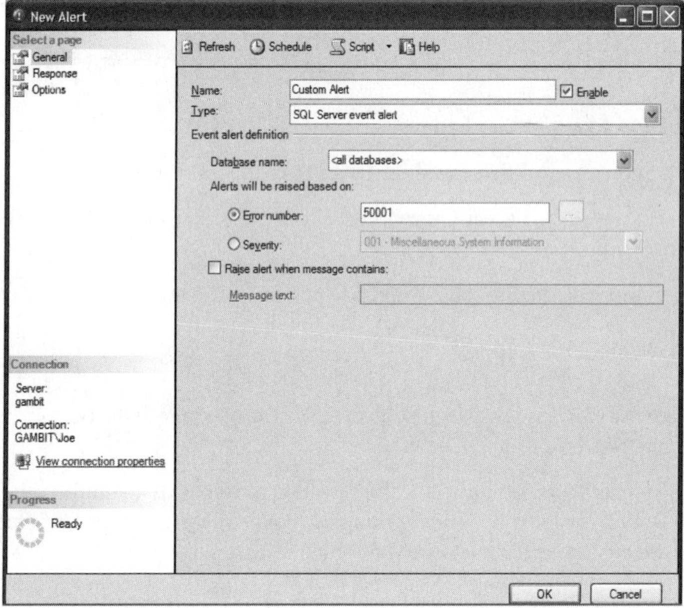

7. On the Response page, select the Notify Operators check box and select the Net Send check box next to Administrator.

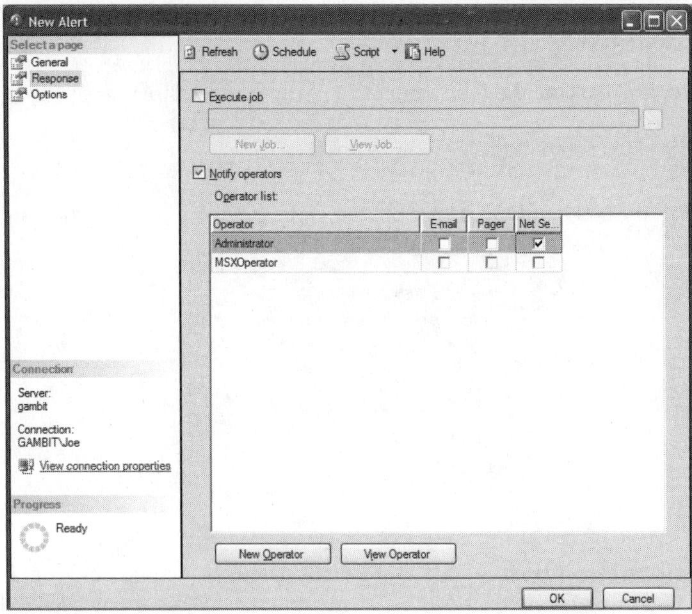

8. On the Options page, select the Net Send check box and click OK to create the alert.

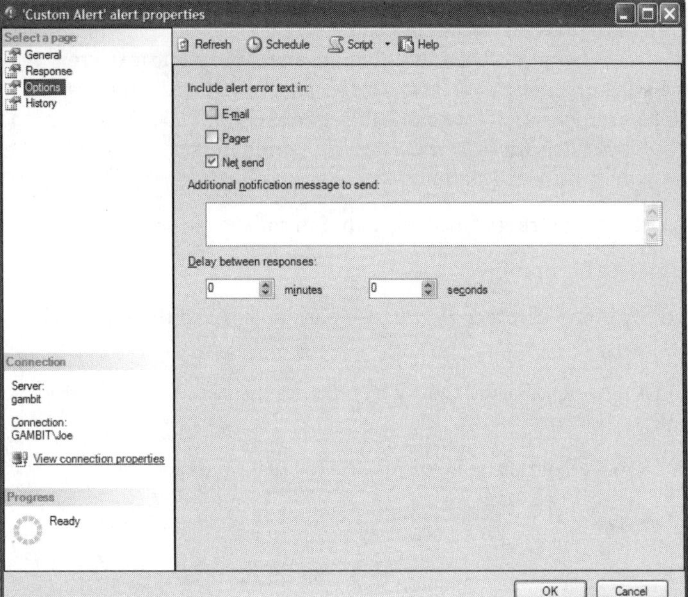

Now that you have an alert based on an error message of your own design, let's test it by using the RAISERROR() command:

1. Open a new SQL Server Query by clicking the New Query button in SQL Server Management Studio.

2. Enter and execute the following code to fire off the error:

```
RAISERROR(50001,10,1)
```

3. When the Net Send message pops up, note the detail it gives you, and then click OK.

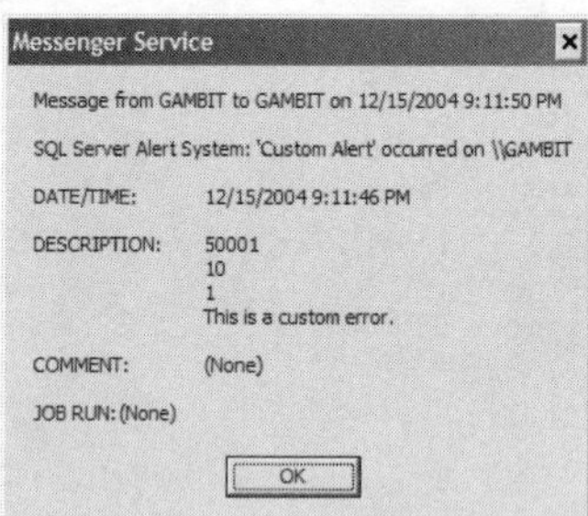

The alert you just created is good, but isn't as useful as it could be. What if you need an alert to tell a manager in a customer service department that a customer has been deleted? If you employ the method used in the last series of steps, you'll have a bland, slightly informative message stating that a customer has been deleted. If you use parameters in your error message, though, you can make the text much more meaningful.

A *parameter* is a placeholder for information that is supplied when the error is fired. For example, *A customer has been deleted* always displays the same static text every time the error occurs; but if you use a parameter such as *Customer %ls has been deleted*, you can use the RAISERROR() command with a parameter that looks like this—RAISERROR(50001,10,1,'Bob Smith')—to create the result *Customer Bob Smith has been deleted*. Parameters can be more useful than static text; the parameters you can use are as follows:

- %ls and %s for strings (such as 'Bob Smith')
- %ld and %d for numbers

Let's modify your customer alert to use parameters and then fire it off using the RAISERROR() command:

1. Open a new SQL Server Query by clicking the New Query button in SQL Server Management Studio.

2. Enter and execute the following code to create the new error:

```
USE master
GO
EXEC sp_addmessage @msgnum=50001, @severity=10,
@msgtext=N' This is a custom error by %ls', @with_log='TRUE',
@replace='replace'
GO
```

3. To fire the error off, enter and execute the following code:

```
RAISERROR(50001,10,1,'SQL Guru')
```

4. When the Net Send message pops up, note that the description now contains the text *SQL Guru*, which replaced the `%ls` in the message text.

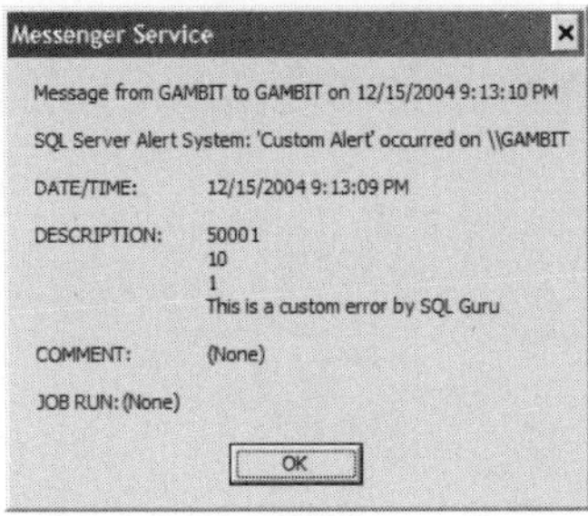

5. Click OK to close the Net Send message.

Now you have a better understanding of alerts that are based on error messages, both standard and custom, but there is more. In SQL Server 2005, you can create alerts that are designed to repair problems before they even become problems; these are known as performance alerts.

Performance Alerts

Event alerts are great for tending to a problem after it has occurred, but not all problems can wait that long. Some problems need to be discovered before they can cause damage to your system. This is done using a *performance alert*.

Performance alerts are based on the same performance counters that you may have seen in the Windows Performance Monitor program. These counters provide statistics about various components of SQL Server and then act on them. A good example of when to use such an alert would be with a full transaction log error.

When a transaction log fills to 100 percent, no users can access the database, so they can't work. Some companies lose substantial amounts of money every hour their users aren't working, and it could take some time before you can bring the database to a useable state by clearing the transaction log. Therefore, you should find the problem before it happens by clearing the transaction log when it reaches a certain percentage, say 80 percent.

To demonstrate the capability of performance alerts, you're going to create an alert that isn't something you're likely to see in the real world. In this example, you'll create an alert that fires off when the transaction log for the AdventureWorks database is less than 100 percent full. On your own systems, you would want to set this to fire off when the log is about 70 percent full and then fire a job that will back up (and thus clear) the transaction log. Let's create that now:

1. Open SQL Server Management Studio, expand your server, and then expand SQL Server Agent.

2. Right-click Alerts, and select New Alert.

3. In the Name box, enter **Performance Alert**.

4. In the Type list, select SQL Server Performance Condition Alert.

5. In the Object box, select SQLServer:Databases.
6. In the Counter box, select Percent Log Used.
7. In the Instance box, select AdventureWorks.
8. Make sure that Alert If Counter is set to Falls Below.
9. In the Value box, type **100**.

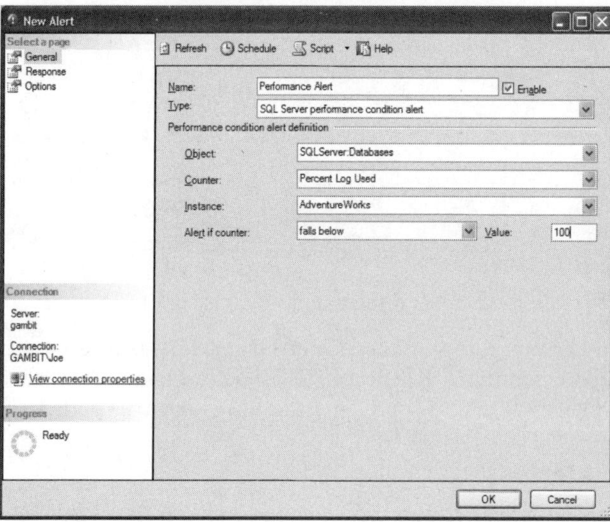

10. Select the Response tab, select the Notify Operators check box, and select the Net Send check box next to your operator name.
11. Click OK to create the alert.
12. When the Net Send message pops up, note the detail that is provided and click OK to close the message.

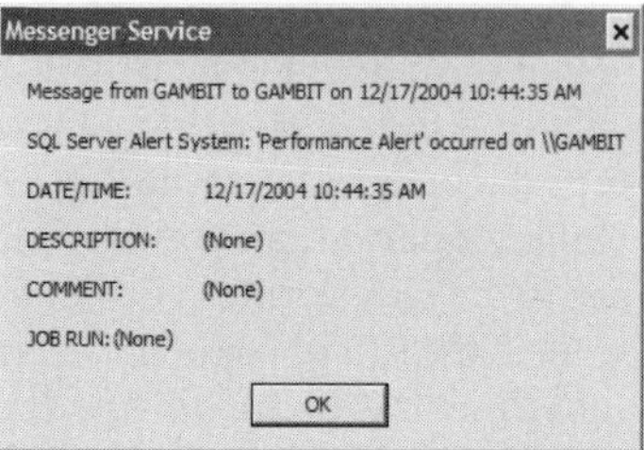

Because you probably don't want that error popping up every few minutes, you need to disable it now:

1. In SQL Server Management Studio, under Alerts In SQL Server Agent, double-click the Performance Alert to expose its properties.
2. Deselect the Enable check box and click OK to apply the changes.

There is also a new type of alert in SQL Server 2005 that is sure to come in handy: WMI alerts.

WMI Alerts

Windows Management Instrumentation (WMI) is Microsoft's implementation of Web-Based Enterprise Management, which is an industry initiative to make systems easier to manage by exposing managed components like systems, applications, and networks as a set of common objects. SQL Server has been updated to work with WMI and respond to WMI events. But with all of the technobabble out of the way, what does that mean to you?

Using WMI alerts, you can respond to events that you couldn't even see before. For example, you can create an alert to fire off when an `ALTER LOGIN` command is issued. This can be very useful for managing security. You can create an alert to fire when a `CREATE TABLE` command is run, so you can keep track of storage on your database. The only limitation is your imagination—and you need to know how to create WMI alerts. Let's create a WMI alert that fires when a DDL statement like `CREATE TABLE` is issued on the AdventureWorks database:

1. Open SQL Server Management Studio, expand your server, and then expand SQL Server Agent.
2. Right-click Alerts, and select New Alert.
3. In the Name box, enter **WMI Alert**.
4. In the Type list, select WMI Event Alert.
5. Make sure the Namespace is `\\.\root\Microsoft\SqlServer\ServerEvents\MSSQLSERVER`.
6. Enter this query in the query box:

```
SELECT * FROM DDL_DATABASE_LEVEL_EVENTS
WHERE DatabaseName = 'AdventureWorks'
```

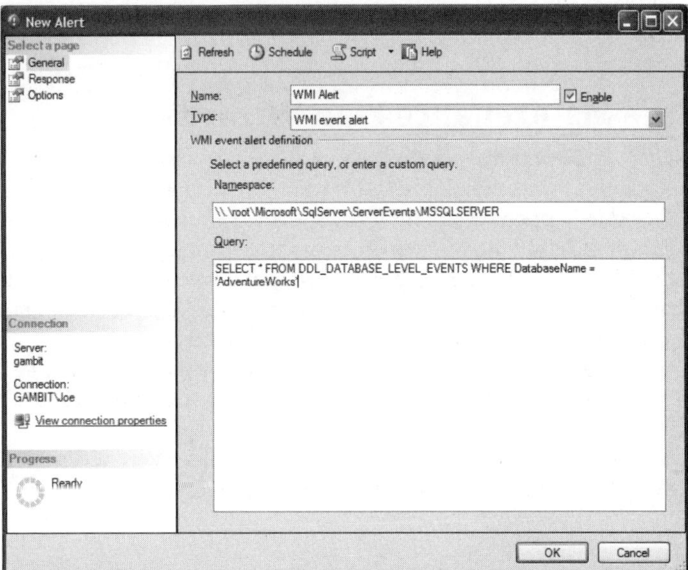

7. Select the Response tab, select the Notify Operators check box, and select the Net Send check box next to your operator name.
8. On the Options page, select the Net Send check box under Include Alert Error Text In, and Click OK to create the alert.
9. Open a new SQL Server query in SQL Server Management Studio by clicking the New Query button.
10. Enter and execute the following code to fire the new alert:

```
USE AdventureWorks
ALTER TABLE Person.Address ADD WMI_Test_Column VARCHAR(20) NULL
```

11. When the Net Send message pops up, note the detail that is provided and click OK to close the message.
12. To get the AdventureWorks database back to normal, execute this command (note that the WMI alert will fire again):

```
USE AdventureWorks
ALTER TABLE Person.Address DROP COLUMN WMI_Test_Column
```

13. To disable the alert, open it, deselect the Enable check box, and click OK.

NOTE If you've read Chapter 15 ("Using Triggers), then you've probably noticed that WMI alerts are very similar to DDL triggers. That's because they use the same WMI technology.

Now that you understand the concepts of operators, jobs, and alerts, you're ready to learn an easy way to use them to manage your databases. Let's look at the Database Maintenance Plan Wizard.

Using the Maintenance Plan Wizard

Many tasks need to be performed to keep your databases running at peak performance at all times. Such things as index reorganization, database file size reduction, and database and transaction log backups all need to happen on a regular basis to keep your server running smoothly. The trick is that most of these tasks should happen off-hours. "No problem," you may respond. "I'll just create jobs for them." That is the proper response, but you'll have to create a number of jobs for each of your databases to keep them all up to par. To avoid all the labor of creating multiple jobs for multiple databases, use the Database Maintenance Plan Wizard.

The wizard is designed to create jobs for all the standard maintenance tasks that need to be performed on a database at regular intervals. The best way to describe it is to take you through it step by step, so here goes.

In SQL Server Management Studio, right-click your server, and select Maintenance Plan from the Launch Wizard menu—you'll see a welcome screen, as shown in Figure 17.1. Click the Next button.

FIGURE 17.1
The welcome screen is the first thing you see when you enter the Maintenance Plan Wizard.

On the second screen that pops up, you're asked what you would like to name the plan and what server you would like to include in your maintenance plan; you may select any server that is registered in SQL Server Management Studio. Enter **Maintenance Plan 1** in the Name box, enter a description if you'd like, select your local server, and click Next (see Figure 17.2).

FIGURE 17.2
You can execute a maintenance plan on local or remote servers.

In the Select Maintenance Tasks screen (shown in Figure 17.3), you're asked how you would like to handle data optimization:

- Check database integrity
- Shrink database
- Defragment indexes
- Re-index
- Update statistics

- History cleanup
- Launch SQL Server Agent job
- Backup database (Full)
- Backup database (Differential)
- Backup database (Transaction Log)

In this case, accept the defaults, and click Next.

FIGURE 17.3
You can be very selective about the optimization tasks you perform.

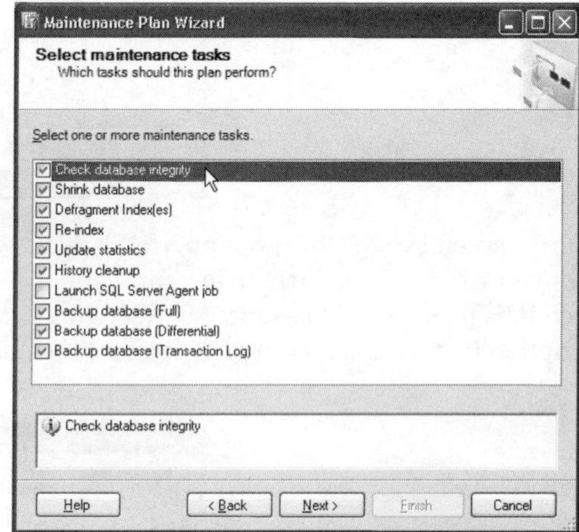

On the next screen (Figure 17.4), you can set the order in which these tasks are performed. Leave the default, and click Next.

FIGURE 17.4
You can also set the order in which the optimization tasks are performed.

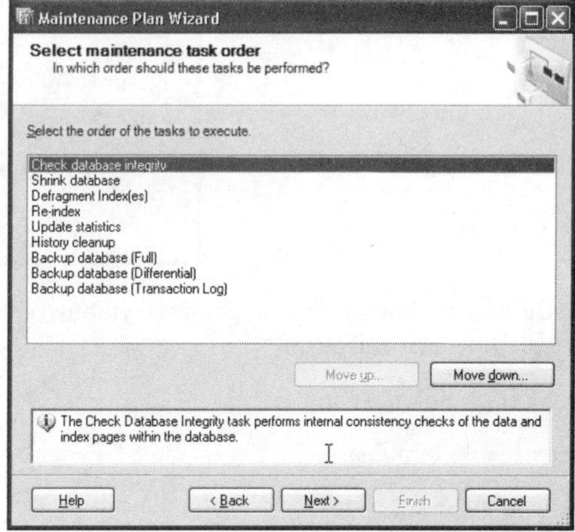

The next screen allows you to select the databases you want to include in your maintenance plan. When you click the drop-down list, you're presented with several choices as shown in Figure 17.5:

All Databases This encompasses all databases on the server in the same plan.

All System Databases This choice affects only the master, model, and MSDB databases.

All User Databases This affects all databases (including AdventureWorks) except the system databases.

These Databases This choice allows you to be selective about which databases to include in your plan.

In this instance, select All Databases, and click Next.

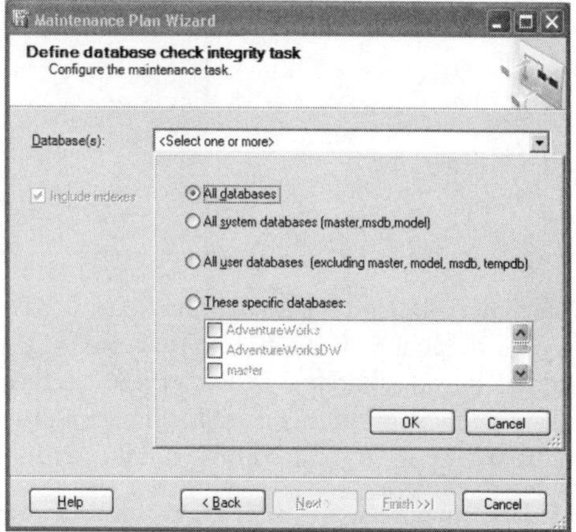

FIGURE 17.5
You can be very selective about the databases included in your maintenance plan.

On the Define Shrink Database Task page (Figure 17.6), you can define how a database should be shrunk when it gets too large. You can define when to shrink it, how much to shrink it, and whether to keep the free space or give it back to Windows. From the drop-down list, select All Databases, and then click Next.

FIGURE 17.6
You can control how and when the databases should be shrunk.

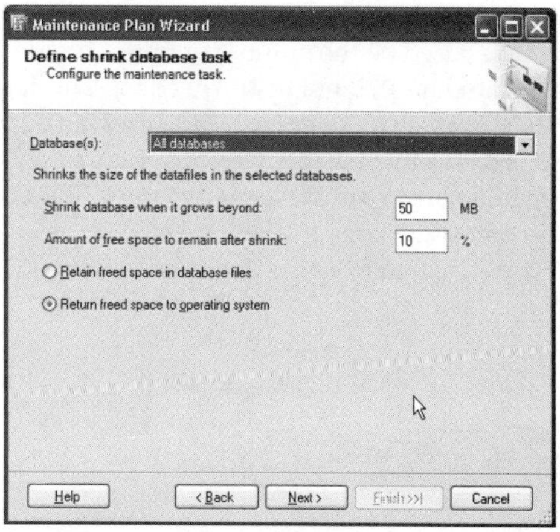

On the Define Defragment Index Task page (Figure 17.7), you can select which objects in which databases you want to defragment indexes for. For example, you can defragment indexes on just the Person.Contact table in the AdventureWorks database, or you can defragment all indexes on all tables in every database, or any option in between. In this case, select All Databases from the Databases drop-down list, and click Next.

FIGURE 17.7
You have very granular control over index defragmentation.

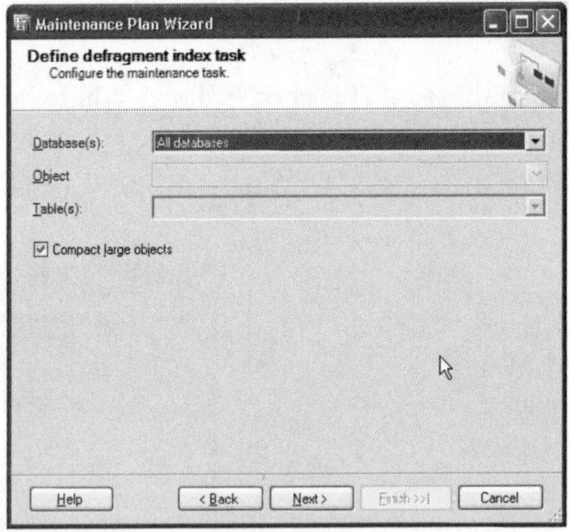

As shown in Figure 17.8, the Define Re-index Task page gives you a number of options for reindexing your databases. But what do they mean? The smallest unit of storage in a SQL Server database is an 8KB unit called a *page*. Each page can be created with a small amount of free space at the end (called a *fill factor*) that is used for inserting new data into the page. This option is used to restore the free space to pages in the database file. This task has two primary options:

- Reorganize Pages With The Original Amount Of Free Space regenerates pages with their original fill factor.
- Change Free Space Per Page Percentage To creates a new fill factor. If you set this to 10, for example, your pages will contain 10 percent free space.

Again select All Databases, accept the defaults, and click Next.

Next comes the Define Update Statistics Task page, shown in Figure 17.9. The query optimizer uses statistics to determine which index (if any) should be used to return results from a query. The statistics are based on the number of times a value appears in a column; and because the values in a column can change, the statistics need to be updated to reflect those changes. This option updates those statistics. Again, select All Databases, and click Next.

Next is the Define History Cleanup Task page, shown in Figure 17.10. All the tasks performed by the maintenance plan are logged in the MSDB database. This list is referred to as the *history*, and it can become quite large if it isn't pruned occasionally. On this screen, you can set when and how the history is cleared from the database so you can keep it in check. Again, accept the defaults, and click Next.

FIGURE 17.8
You also have very granular control over reindexing.

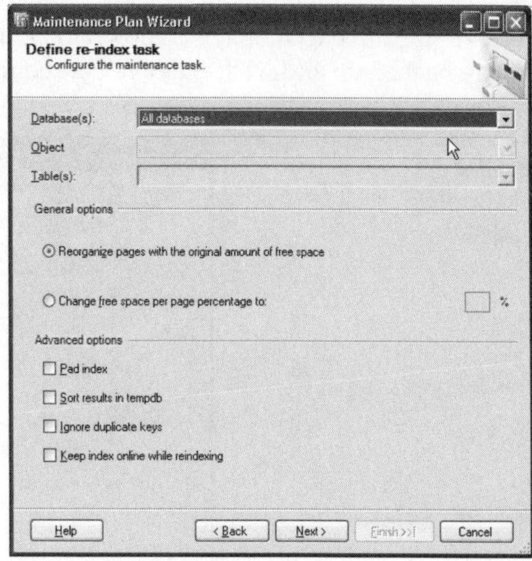

FIGURE 17.9
The database maintenance plan can update statistics for you.

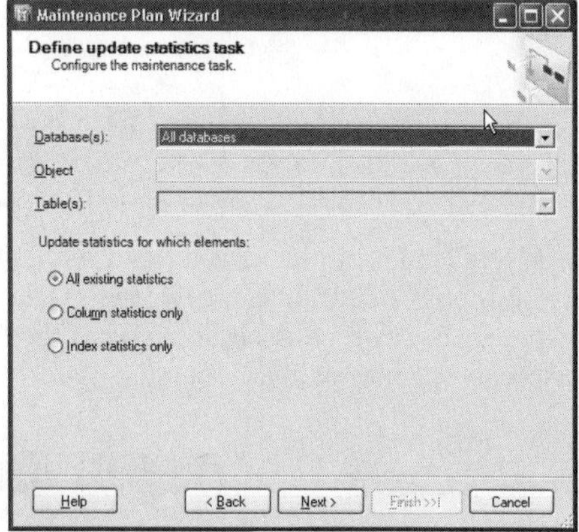

FIGURE 17.10
Use the maintenance plan to keep the history tables small.

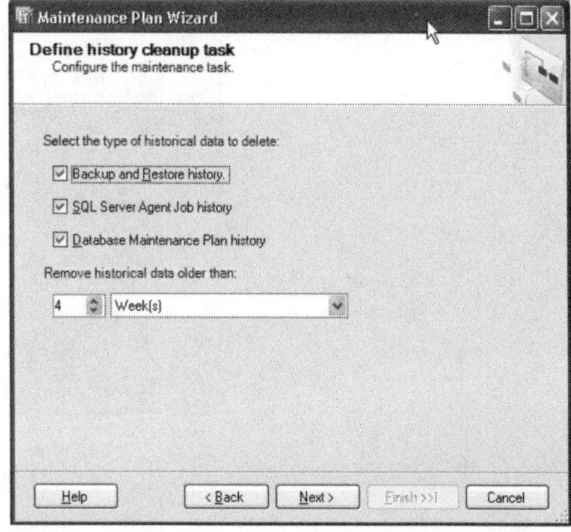

The next three screens allow you to control how full, differential, and transaction log backups are performed (the full backup page is shown in Figure 17.11). On this page, you can select which databases are backed up and where they're backed up to. Accept the defaults, and click Next.

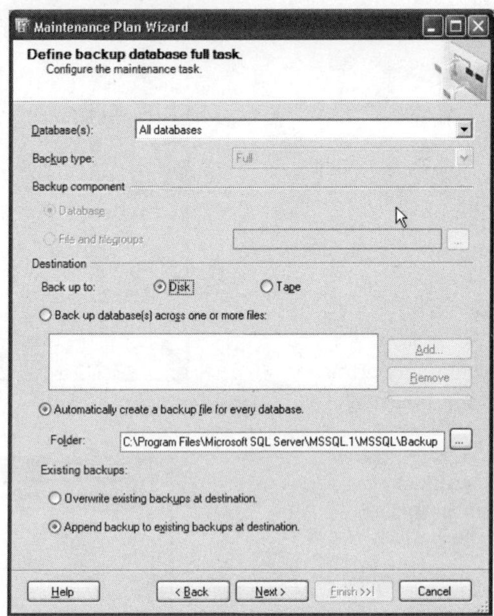

FIGURE 17.11 You can define what to back up and where to store the backup files.

On the Select Plan Properties screen (Figure 17.12), you can schedule the maintenance plan to run automatically or on demand. It's usually best to schedule the plan to run automatically so you don't have to be there to fire it off yourself, so create a schedule for the job by clicking the Create button. You can also select an operator to alert when the plan runs. When you're finished, click Next.

FIGURE 17.12 Schedule the plan to run at the most appropriate time.

On the Select Report Options page (Figure 17.13), you can write a report to a text file every time the job runs, and you can e-mail the report to an operator. In this case, write a report to `c:\report.txt`, and click Next.

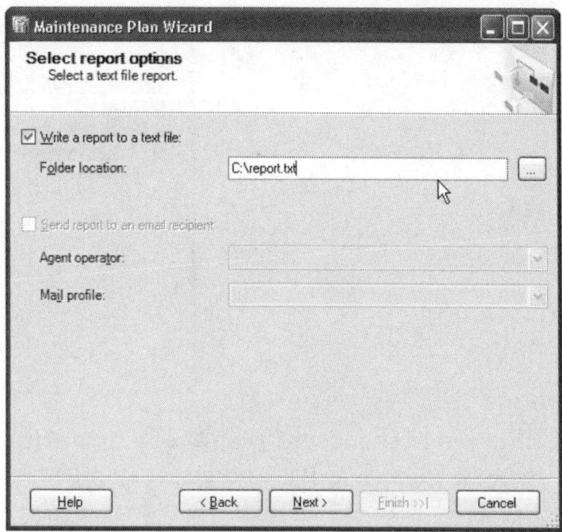

FIGURE 17.13
You can define what to back up and where to store the backup files.

As shown in Figure 17.14, on the next page you can view a summary of the tasks to perform. Click Finish to create the maintenance plan.

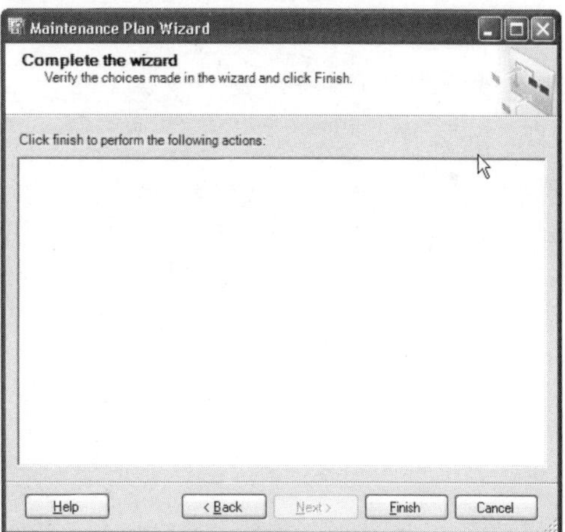

FIGURE 17.14
The summary screen displays a synopsis of the plan you're about to create.

Once SQL Server is finished creating the maintenance plan, you can click Close (see Figure 17.15).

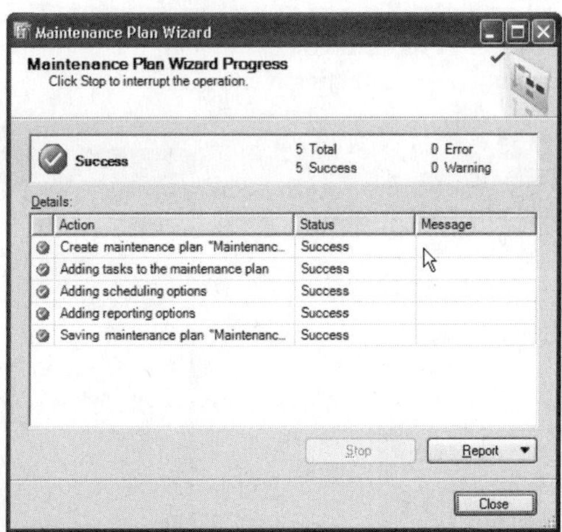

FIGURE 17.15
Success! You have a maintenance plan.

If you need to change the plan at any time after you've created it, all you need to do is expand Maintenance Plans, which is under Management, right-click the plan, and select Modify. As shown in Figure 17.16, you can change any aspect of your maintenance plan from the Properties dialog box. You'll probably want to read up on SQL Integration Services in Chapter 22 before making too many changes, because this is an Integration Services job.

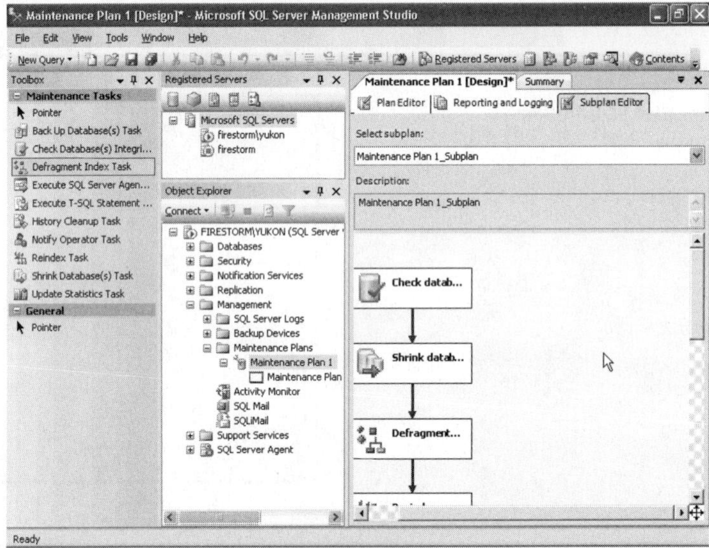

FIGURE 17.16
You can change any aspect of your plan by bringing up its properties in SQL Server Management Studio.

To view the history of the plan, right-click it, and select Maintenance Plan History. This option displays everything the plan has accomplished recently.

As you can see, maintenance plans are very helpful in keeping your database running smoothly and efficiently. Now you don't have to worry about staying late to run maintenance jobs or which task should be completed first. The plan does it all for you.

Summary

That was a lot of ground to cover, but it will save you a lot of time and effort in server administration and reporting. We discussed a number of topics in this chapter, including:

Automation basics In this section, you learned that automation includes three main components: operators, jobs, and alerts. Operators are the individuals who are notified when a problem needs attention; they can be notified via e-mail, pager, or Net Send messages. Jobs are series of tasks and schedules that can be automated to activate at any time; they can include Transact-SQL code, command executive code, or scripting language code.

Configuring mail support To configure mail support, you learned that you first need create a MailHost database and add a profile and an account. When these are in place, you can start sending e-mail. If you want to send mail to operators you need to make MSDB a MailHost database.

Creating operators In this section, you learned how to create operators and configure them to receive e-mail, pager, or Net Send messages. You can also configure them to be available only at certain times of the day by setting their availability.

Creating jobs In this section, you learned how to create local server jobs and then multiserver jobs:

- Local server jobs run only on the local system, and they can be configured to run any type of code at any time. They can be configured to inform an operator when they complete, when they succeed, or when they fail.
- Multiserver jobs are created on a central machine (called the MSX or master) and then distributed to multiple remote machines (called targets), where they're executed. These jobs come in very handy in a multiple-server environment.

Creating alerts Alerts are used to notify an operator when an error has occurred. Not all errors fire an event, though—only those that are written to the Windows event log and have an alert configured fire an alert that notifies someone. In this section, you learned how to create alerts that are based on the standard error messages that come with SQL Server as well as how to create your own custom error messages that can be used for any purpose. We then discussed how to create and use performance alerts to stop problems before they start. You also learned how to create WMI alerts so you can be notified when server events occur such as `CREATE TABLE` or other DDL statements.

Using the Database Maintenance Plan Wizard Many tasks need to be performed on your server to keep it running smoothly and efficiently. You need to back up databases and transaction logs, reorganize index and data pages inside the database files, and check for database integrity regularly. Rather than try to remember to do all of that and the order to do it in, use the Database Maintenance Plan Wizard to automate these processes for you.

Now that you know how to automate the tasks on your system, you need to learn how to secure your system as well. Let's peer into the depths of SQL Server security in the next chapter.

Chapter 18

Security and SQL Server 2005

Protecting information—guarding access to an organization's data—is much like protecting a physical structure. For example, imagine that you own a business and the building that houses it. You don't want the general public to gain access to your building—only your employees should have access. However, you also need restrictions on the areas to which your employees have access. Because only accountants should have access to the accounting department, and almost no one should have access to your office, you must put various security systems in place.

Protecting SQL Server (your "building") holds true to this concept: No one gets in unless they're granted access, and once users are inside, various security systems keep prying eyes out of sensitive areas. In this chapter, we'll discuss the methods used to apply security to SQL Server.

Understanding Security Modes

To continue our analogy, for your employees to gain access to the building, they need some sort of key, whether a metal key or an electronic access card. For your users to gain access to SQL Server, you need to give them a key as well. The type of key you give them largely depends on the type of lock—authentication mode—you use.

An *authentication mode* is how SQL Server processes usernames and passwords. SQL Server 2005 provides two such modes: Windows Authentication mode and Mixed mode.

Windows Authentication Mode

With this mode, a user can sit down at their computer, log on to the Windows domain, and gain access to SQL Server using the Kerberos security protocol. Although an in-depth discussion of Kerberos is beyond the scope of this book, here is a brief overview of how this security protocol works:

1. When the user logs on, Windows performs a DNS lookup to locate a Key Distribution Center (KDC).
2. The user's machine logs on to the domain.
3. The KDC issues a special security token called a Ticket Granting Ticket (TGT) to the user.
4. To access the SQL Server, the user's machine presents the TGT to the SQL Server; if the ticket is accepted, the user is allowed access.

It may be easier to think of Kerberos security as a trip to the carnival. If you've ever been to a carnival and seen all the rides, you probably know that to get on one of those rides, you need a ticket. You must buy that ticket from a counter at the gate of the carnival. Once you have tickets in hand, you can give them to the ride operators and enjoy yourself on the rides.

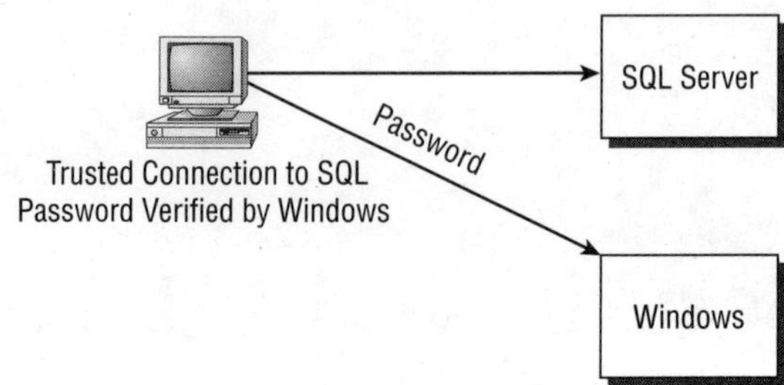

FIGURE 18.1
Using a trusted connection, SQL Server trusts Windows to verify user passwords.

In Kerberos security, the services, such as SQL Server, would be considered the rides that you want to access; but to use the services, you need to present a ticket. The ticket you present is the TGT that you received from the KDC at logon time, so you can think of the KDC as the counter at the carnival that sells the tickets. Once you have this TGT, you can access any services to which you've been given permission, including SQL Server 2005.

The main advantage of Windows Authentication mode is that users don't have to remember multiple usernames and passwords. That vastly increases security, because there is less danger of users writing down their passwords and storing them in an unsafe place (such as a sticky note on their monitor). This mode also gives you tighter reign over security, because you can apply Windows password policies, which do such things as expire passwords, require a minimum length for passwords, keep a history of passwords, and so on.

One of the disadvantages is that only users with Windows accounts can open a trusted connection to SQL Server. This means that someone like a Novell client can't use Windows Authentication mode because they don't have a Windows account. If it turns out that you have such clients, you'll need to implement Mixed mode.

Mixed Mode

Mixed mode allows both Windows Authentication and SQL Server Authentication. SQL Server Authentication works as follows:

1. The user logs on to their network, Windows or otherwise.
2. The user opens a *nontrusted* (see Figure 18.2) connection to SQL Server using a username and password other than those used to gain network access. It's called a nontrusted connection because SQL Server doesn't trust the operating system to verify the user's password.
3. SQL Server matches the username and password entered by the user to an entry in the Syslogins table.

The primary advantage is that anyone can gain access to SQL Server using Mixed mode. Mac users, Novell users, Banyan Vines users, and the like can gain access. You could also consider this to be a second layer of security, because if someone hacks into the network in Mixed mode, it doesn't mean they have automatically hacked into SQL Server at the same time.

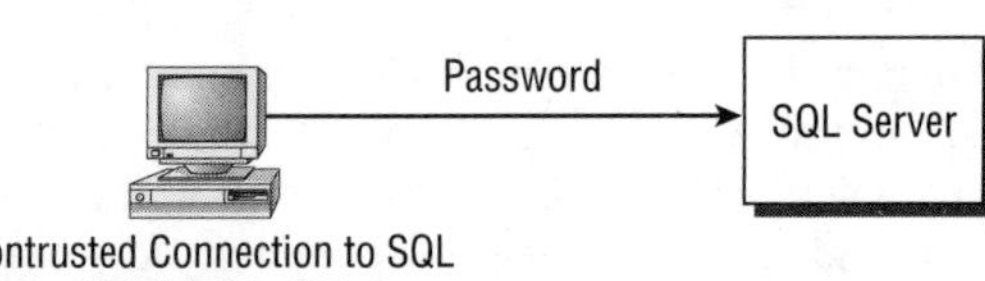

FIGURE 18.2
With a nontrusted connection, SQL Server verifies user passwords itself.

Ironically, multiple passwords can be a problem as well as an advantage. Consider that users will have one username and password to log on to the network and a completely separate username and password to gain access to SQL Server. When users have multiple sets of credentials, they tend to write them down and thus breach the security system you have worked so hard to set up.

Setting the Authentication Mode

As an administrator, you'll probably set the authentication mode no more than once: at installation time. The only other time you might need to change the authentication mode would be if changes were made to your network. For example, if you set your SQL Server to Windows Authentication mode and needed to include Macintosh clients, you would need to change to Mixed mode.

It's interesting to note that although most things in SQL Server can be done through either SQL Server Management Studio or Transact-SQL (T-SQL), setting the authentication mode is one of the rare things that can be done only through SQL Server Management Studio. The next series of steps takes you through setting the authentication mode:

1. Open SQL Server Management Studio by selecting it from the SQL Server 2005 group under Programs on the Start menu, and then right-click your server in Object Explorer, and select Properties.
2. Select the Security page.
3. In the Server Authentication section, select SQL Server And Windows Authentication Mode. Doing so sets you to Mixed mode for the rest of the exercises.

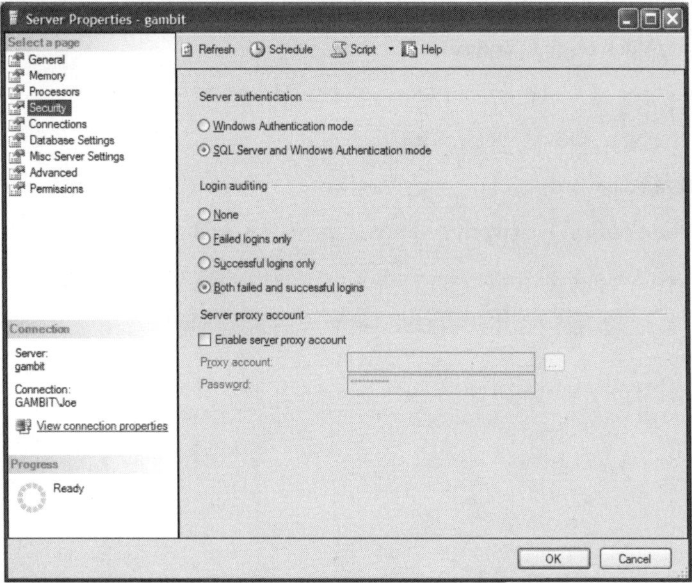

4. Click OK to close the Server Properties dialog box.

Now that you've set the proper authentication mode, it's time to move forward and give your users a key to your building with SQL Server logins.

SQL Server Logins

Once you've decided what type of lock (authentication mode) to use on your building, you can start handing out keys so that your employees can gain access. A real key gives your employees access to the building as a whole but to none of the resources (such as filing cabinets) inside. In the same way, a SQL Server key—a *login*—gives your users access to SQL Server as a whole but not to the resources (such as databases) inside. If you're a member of the sysadmin or securityadmin fixed server role (discussed later in this chapter), you can create one of two types of logins: standard logins (such as the metal key in our analogy) and Windows logins (such as the newer electronic access card).

Standard Logins

You learned earlier in this chapter that only clients with a Windows account can make trusted connections to SQL Server (where SQL Server trusts Windows to validate the user's password). If the user (such as a Macintosh or Novell client) for whom you're creating a login can't make a trusted connection, you must create a standard login for them. In the next series of steps, you'll create two standard logins that will be used later in the chapter.

NOTE Although you can create standard logins in Windows Authentication mode, you won't be able to use them. If you try, SQL Server will ignore you and use your Windows credentials instead.

1. Open SQL Server Management Studio, and expand your server by clicking the + sign next to the icon named after your server.
2. Expand Security, and expand Logins.
3. Right-click Logins, and select New Login.
4. Select the SQL Server Authentication radio button.
5. In the Name box, type **SmithB**.
6. In the Password text box, type **Password1** (remember, passwords are case sensitive).
7. In the Confirm Password text box, type **Password1** again.
8. Under Defaults, select AdventureWorks as the default database.

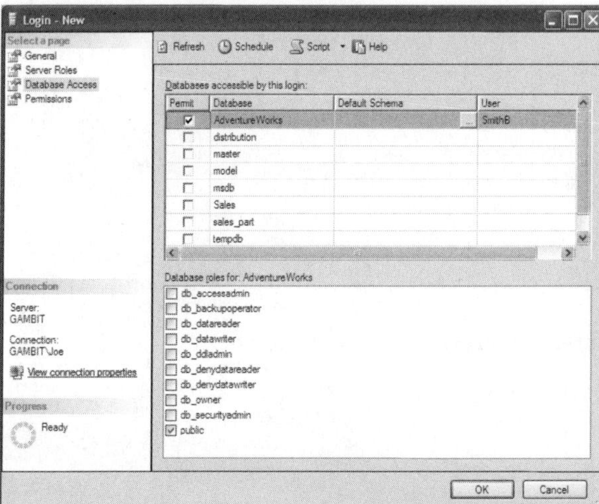

9. On the Database Access page, select the Permit check box next to AdventureWorks to give your user access to the default database.

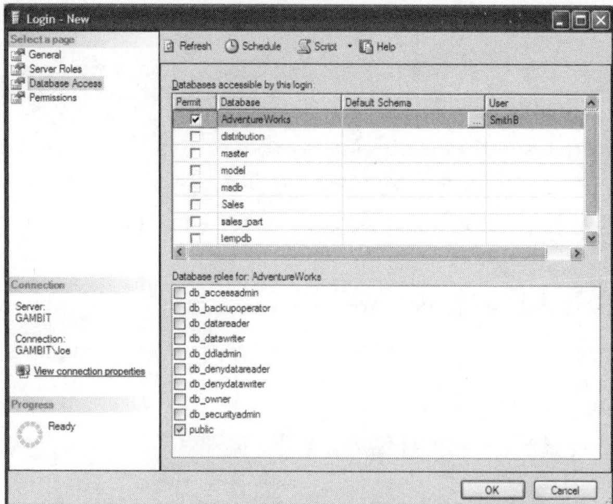

10. Click OK, and notice your new Standard type login in the contents pane.

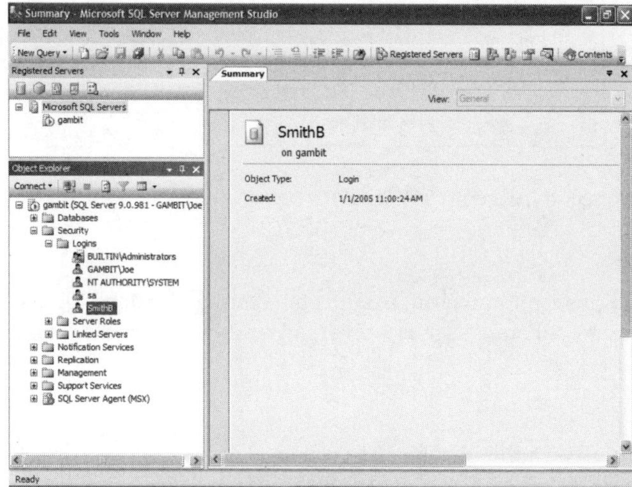

11. Right-click Logins, and select New Login.

12. Select the SQL Server authentication radio button.

13. In the Name box, type **GibsonH**.

14. In the Password text box, type **Password1**.

15. In the Confirm Password text box, type **Password1**.

16. Under Defaults, select AdventureWorks as the default database.

17. Don't select the Permit check box next to AdventureWorks on the Database Access page. You'll create a database user account later in this chapter.
18. Click OK to create your new login.
19. A dialog box will pop up informing you that GibsonH has no access to the selected default database. We will grant that later so click OK to continue.

Now you're ready to test your new logins to make sure they work. Let's do that with the SmithB login:

1. Open a new SQL Server Query by clicking the New Query button in SQL Server Management Studio.
2. Select SQL Server Authentication from the Authentication drop-down list.
3. In the Login Name box, type **SmithB**.
4. In the Password box, type **Password1**.

5. Click OK to connect to AdventureWorks.

Windows Logins

Creating Windows logins isn't much different from creating standard logins. Although standard logins apply to only one user, however, a Windows login can be mapped to one of the following:

- A single user
- A Windows group an administrator has created
- A Windows *built-in* group (for example, Administrators)

Before you create a Windows login, you must decide to which of these three you want to map it. Generally you'll map to a group that you've created. Doing so will help you a great deal in later administration. For example, suppose you have an Accounting database to which all 50 of your accountants require access. You could create a separate login for each of them, which would require you to manage 50 SQL Server logins. On the other hand, if you create a Windows group for these 50 accountants and map your SQL Server login to this group, you'll have only 1 SQL Server login to manage.

The first step in creating Windows logins is to create user accounts in the operating system. In this next set of instructions, you'll create some user accounts and groups:

1. Open Active Directory Users and Computers, and select Action ➤ Create New ➤ User. (Active Directory Users and Computers is located in the Administrative Tools group under Programs on the Start menu.)
2. Create six new users with the criteria from the following list:

Username	Description	Password	Must Change	Never Expires
MorrisL	IT	Password1	Deselect	Select
RosmanD	Administration	Password1	Unselect	Select
JohnsonK	Accounting	Password1	Deselect	Select
JonesB	Accounting	Password1	Deselect	Select
ChenJ	Sales	Password1	Deselect	Select
SamuelsR	Sales	Password1	Deselect	Select

3. While in Active Directory Users and Computers, create a Domain Local Security group called Accounting.
4. Add the new users you just created whose Description value is Accounting.
5. While still in Active Directory Users and Computers, create a Domain Local Security group named Sales.
6. Add all the users whose Description value is Sales.
7. Open Local Security Policy from the Administrative Tools group under Programs on the Start menu.
8. Expand Local Policies, and click User Rights Assignment.
9. Double-click the Log On Locally right, and click Add.
10. Select the Everyone group, click Add, click OK, and then click OK again (on a production machine this is not a best practice, this is only for this exercise).
11. Close the Local Policies tool, and open SQL Server Management Studio.

TIP If you do not have access to a domain you can do all of this in Computer Management under Local Users and Groups.

With your user accounts and groups created, you're ready to create SQL Server logins that map to these accounts:

1. Open SQL Server Management Studio, and expand your server by clicking the + sign next to the icon named after your server.
2. Expand Security, and expand Logins.

3. Right-click Logins, and select New Login.
4. In the Login Name box, type ***Sqldomain*\Accounting** (the name of the Local group created earlier).
5. Under Defaults, select AdventureWorks as the default database.

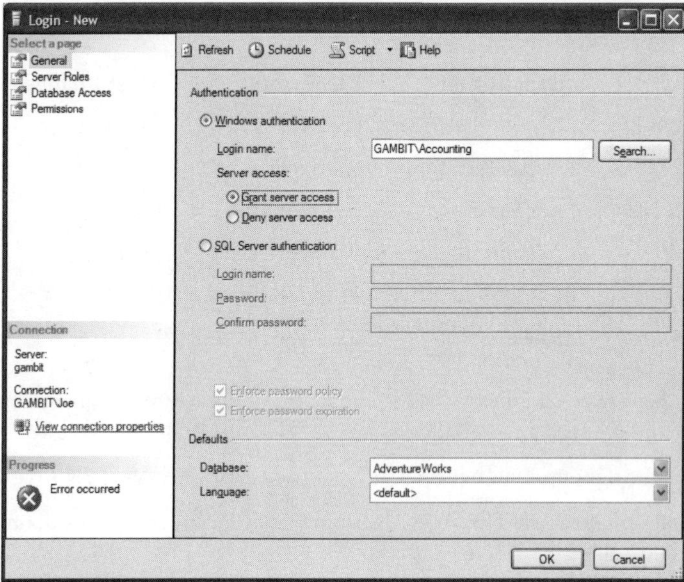

6. On the Database Access page, select the Permit check box next to AdventureWorks to give your user access to the default database.
7. Click OK to create the login.
8. Right-click Logins, and select New Login.
9. In the Login name box, type ***Sqldomain*\Sales** (the name of the Local group created earlier).
10. Under Defaults, select AdventureWorks as the default database.
11. On the Database Access page, select the Permit check box next to AdventureWorks to give your user access to the default database.
12. Click OK to create the login.
13. Right-click Logins, and select New Login.
14. Fill in the Login Name field with ***Sqldomain*\RosmanD**.

15. Under Defaults, select AdventureWorks as the default database.

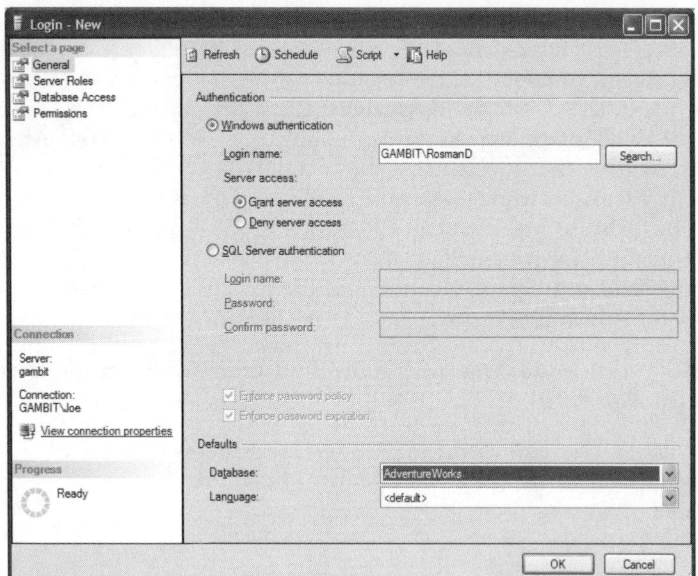

16. On the Database Access page, select the Permit check box next to AdventureWorks to give your user access to the default database.
17. Click OK to create the login.
18. Right-click Logins, and select New Login.
19. Fill in the Login name field with ***Sqldomain*\MorrisL**.
20. Under Defaults, select AdventureWorks as the default database.
21. On the Database Access page, select the Permit check box next to AdventureWorks to give your user access to the default database.
22. Click OK to create the login.

Now that you have some Windows group and user logins to work with, let's test them. First you'll log in as a member of one of the groups you created, and then you'll log in as a specific user:

1. Log off Windows, and log back on as JonesB.
2. Open a new SQL Server query in SQL Server Management Studio, and select Windows Authentication from the Authentication drop-down list.
3. Close SQL Server Management Studio, log off Windows, and log back on as RosmanD.
4. Open a new SQL Server query in SQL Server Management Studio, and select Windows Authentication from the Authentication drop-down list.

Items Common to All Logins

You may have noticed that some things are common to all the logins you created.

The first is the default database. When a user first logs in to SQL Server, they connect to the default database. If you don't set the default database, it is master—which isn't the best place for your users to get started. You should change that to a different database—for example, an Accounting database if you're working with an accounting user. You can also set a default language, which won't need frequent changing, because the default is the server's language. A different language can be set here for users who require it.

In all types of logins, you can grant database access at create time. On the Database Access page of the SQL Server Management Studio New Login dialog box, all you need to do is select the database to which this login requires access; doing so automatically creates a database user account, like you did for the AdventureWorks database in the last set of exercises.

WARNING **If you create a Windows login using `sp_grantlogin`, you can't set the default database or language.**

In addition, you can add users to a fixed server role at the time you create them; you do this on the Server Roles tab in SQL Server Management Studio. Fixed server roles—limitations on access—are discussed next.

Fixed Server Roles

Back to our analogy: As the owner, when you walk into your building, you're allowed to do whatever you want (after all, you own it). When members of the accounting department walk in, however, they're limited in what they can do. For example, they aren't allowed to take keys away from other workers, but they may be allowed to do other administrative tasks, such as signing checks.

That is what *fixed server roles* are used for—to limit the amount of administrative access that a user has once logged in to SQL Server. Some users may be allowed to do whatever they want, whereas other users may only be able to manage security. You can assign users any of eight server roles. The following list starts at the highest level and describes the administrative access granted:

Sysadmin Members of the sysadmin role have the authority to perform any task in SQL Server. Be careful whom you assign to this role, because people who are unfamiliar with SQL Server can accidentally create serious problems. This role is only for the database administrators (DBAs).

Serveradmin These users can set server-wide configuration options, such as how much memory SQL Server can use or how much information to send over the network in a single frame. They can also shut down the server. If you make your assistant DBAs members of this role, you can relieve yourself of some of the administrative burden.

Setupadmin Members here can install replication and manage extended stored procedures (these are used to perform actions not native to SQL Server). Give this role to the assistant DBAs as well.

Securityadmin These users manage security issues such as creating and deleting logins, reading the audit logs, and granting users permission to create databases. This too is a good role for assistant DBAs.

Processadmin SQL Server is capable of multitasking; that is, it can do more than one thing at a time by executing multiple processes. For instance, SQL Server might spawn one process for writing to cache and another for reading from cache. A member of the processadmin group can end (or *kill*, as it's called in SQL Server) a process. This is another good role for assistant DBAs and developers. Developers especially need to kill processes that may have been triggered by an improperly designed query or stored procedure.

Dbcreator These users can create and make changes to databases. This may be a good role for assistant DBAs as well as developers (who should be warned against creating unnecessary databases and wasting server space).

Diskadmin These users manage files on disk. They do things such as mirroring databases and adding backup devices. Assistant DBAs should be members of this role.

Bulkadmin Members of this role can execute the `BULK INSERT` statement, which allows them to import data into SQL Server databases from text files. Assistant DBAs should be members of this role.

Now, let's apply this knowledge by assigning some users to fixed server roles, thereby limiting their administrative authority:

1. Open SQL Server Management Studio by selecting it from the SQL Server 2005 group under Programs on the Start menu, expand Security, and expand Server Roles.
2. Double-click Sysadmin Server Role Properties.
3. Click Add, click Browse, select the check box next to *SqlDomain*\MorrisL, click OK, and then OK again.

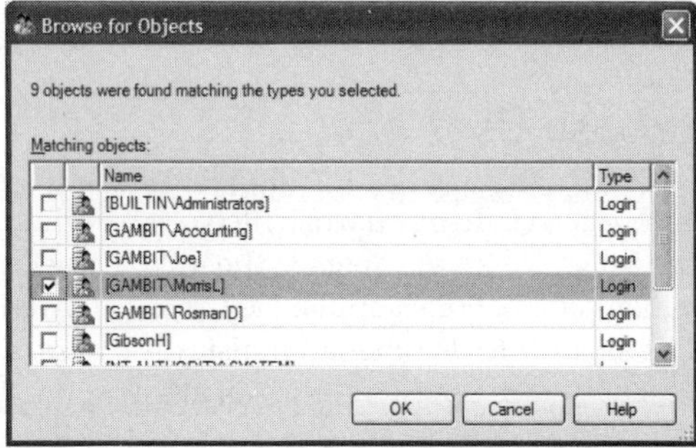

4. MorrisL should now appear in the Role Members list.

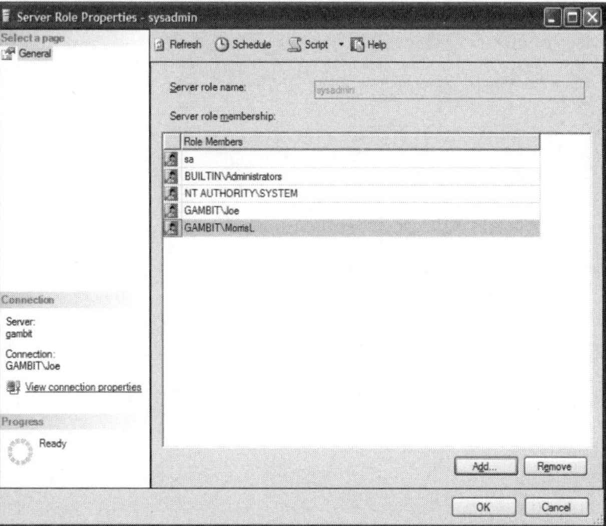

5. Click OK to exit the Server Role Properties dialog box.
6. Double-click Serveradmin Server Role Properties.
7. Click Add, enter *SqlDomain*\GibsonH, and click OK.
8. Click OK to exit the Server Role Properties dialog box.

TIP If you don't want users to have any administrative authority, don't assign them to a server role. This limits them to being normal users.

TIP Builtin\Administrators is automatically made a member of the sysadmin server role, giving SQL Server administrative rights to all of your Windows administrators. Because not all of your Windows administrators should have these rights, you may want to create a SQLAdmins group in Windows, add your SQL Server administrators to that group, and make the group a member of the sysadmin role. Afterward you should remove Builtin\Administrators from the sysadmin role.

You're ready to grant your users access to the databases that reside on your SQL Server by creating database user accounts.

Creating Database User Accounts

Now that your employees have access to your building as well as the proper administrative access once they're inside, they need access to other resources to do their work. For example, if you want to give your accounting department access to the accounting files, you need to give them a new key—one to the file cabinet. Your employees now have two keys, one for the front door and one for the file cabinet.

In much the same way, you need to give users access to databases once they have logged in to SQL Server. You do so by creating database user accounts and then assigning permissions to those user accounts (permissions are discussed later). Once this process is complete, your SQL Server users also have more than one key, one for the front door (the login) and one for each file cabinet (database) to which they need access. In the next set of steps, you'll give users access to the AdventureWorks database by creating database user accounts:

1. Open SQL Server Management Studio, and expand your server.
2. Expand Databases by clicking the + sign next to the icon.
3. Expand the AdventureWorks database.
4. Expand Security, and click the Users icon.
5. Right-click Users, and select New Database User.
6. Click the ellipsis button next to the Login Name box, and click Browse. View all the available names; note that only logins you've already created are available.
7. Select the check box next to GibsonH, and click OK twice.

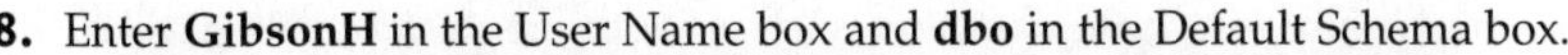

8. Enter **GibsonH** in the User Name box and **dbo** in the Default Schema box.

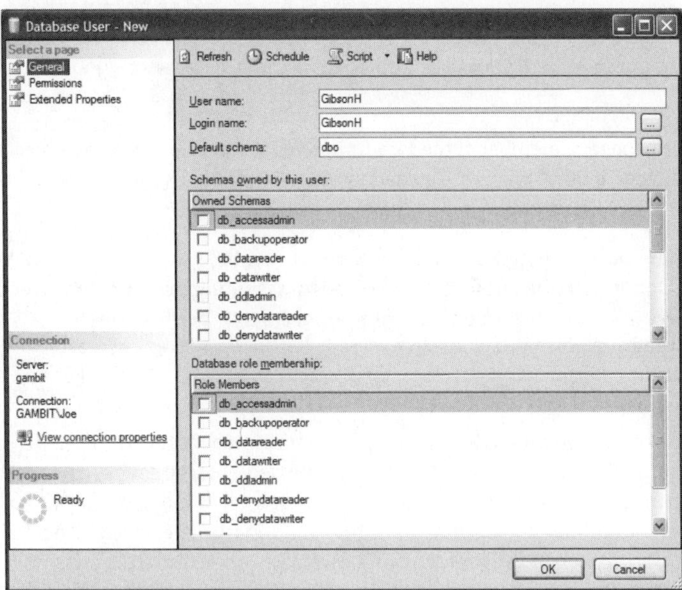

9. Click OK to create the GibsonH database user account.

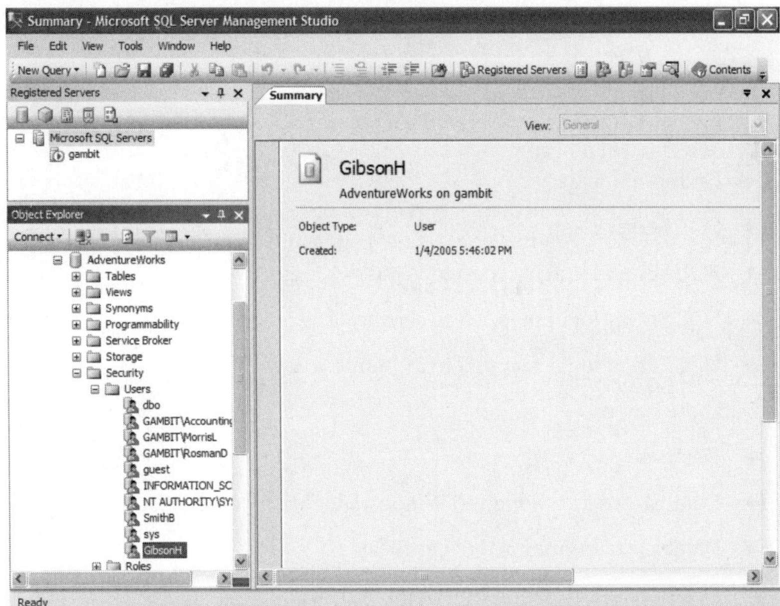

You may have noticed that two user accounts already exist in your databases when they are first created: DBO and Guest. Members of the sysadmin fixed server role automatically become the database owner (DBO) user in every database on the system. In this way, they can perform all the necessary administrative functions in the databases, such as adding users and creating tables. *Guest user* is a catch-all database user account for people who have a SQL Server login but not a user account in the database. These users can log in to the server as themselves and access any database where they don't have a user account. The guest account should be limited in function, because anybody with a SQL Server login can use it.

NOTE Whenever a member of the sysadmin fixed server role creates an object (such as a table), it isn't owned by that login. It's owned by the DBO. If GibsonH created a table, it wouldn't be referred to as GibsonH.table but as dbo.table instead.

Now that you've created user accounts for everyone, you need to restrict what those users are capable of doing with the database. You do so by assigning permissions directly to the users or adding the users to a database role with a predefined set of permissions.

Understanding Permissions

To continue our business analogy, it would be unthinkable for the sales department to go over to the accounting department and start writing themselves large checks. In most businesses today, the sales department doesn't have permission to even look at the checkbook. To take the analogy one step further, not all the people in the accounting department have full access to the checkbook; some have permission to only read from it, whereas others have permission to write checks from it.

You see the same situation in SQL Server. Not all your users should be able to access the accounting or human resources databases, because they contain sensitive information. Even users who are allowed in to these sensitive databases should not necessarily be given full access.

Any object that SQL Server regulates access to is referred to as a *securable*. Securables can fall under three scopes:

- Server scope
  - Server
  - Endpoint
  - SQL Server login
  - SQL Server login mapped to Windows login
  - SQL Server login mapped to certificate
  - SQL Server login mapped to asymmetric key
- Database scope
  - Database users
  - Database users mapped to Windows login
  - Database users mapped to certificate
  - Database users mapped to asymmetric key
  - Database roles
  - Application roles
  - Assemblies

- Message type
- Service contract
- Service
- Fulltext catalog
- DDL events
- Schema

- Schema scope
  - Table
  - View
  - Function
  - Procedure
  - Queue
  - Type
  - Rule
  - Default
  - Synonym
  - Aggregate

All of these objects are secured by applying permissions.

Statement Permissions

In your building, do you allow the contractors who constructed it to come in and use your files, copiers, and various other resources? No, you gave them permission to construct the building initially and make renovations over time—but not to use the files and other such resources inside.

In SQL Server, this constraint is akin to granting the contractors *statement permissions*. Statement permissions have nothing to do with the actual data; they allow users to create the structure that holds the data. It's important not to grant these permissions haphazardly, because doing so can lead to such problems as *broken ownership chains* (discussed later) and wasted server resources. It's best to restrict statement permissions to DBAs, assistant DBAs, and developers. The next set of instructions demonstrate the mechanics of applying the following statement permissions:

- Create Database
- Create Table
- Create View
- Create Procedure
- Create Index
- Create Rule
- Create Default

NOTE When you create a new database, a record is added to the sysdatabases system table, which is stored in the master database. Therefore the Create Database statement can be granted on only the master database.

1. To prepare SQL Server for the following exercises, you need to remove all permissions from the public role, because the existing permissions will interfere with your work. Open a new SQL Server query in SQL Server Management Studio, and execute the following query:

```
USE AdventureWorks
REVOKE ALL from public
```

2. Close the query window, and don't save the changes.
3. In Object Explorer, expand your server, and then expand Databases.
4. Right-click the AdventureWorks database, and select Properties.
5. In the Properties dialog box, select the Permissions page.
6. Grant RosmanD the Create Table permission by selecting the Allow check box next to Create Table.
7. Grant Accounting the permission to Backup Database and Backup Log.
8. If the Guest user has any permissions granted, remove them by deselecting each check box. Click OK to apply your changes.

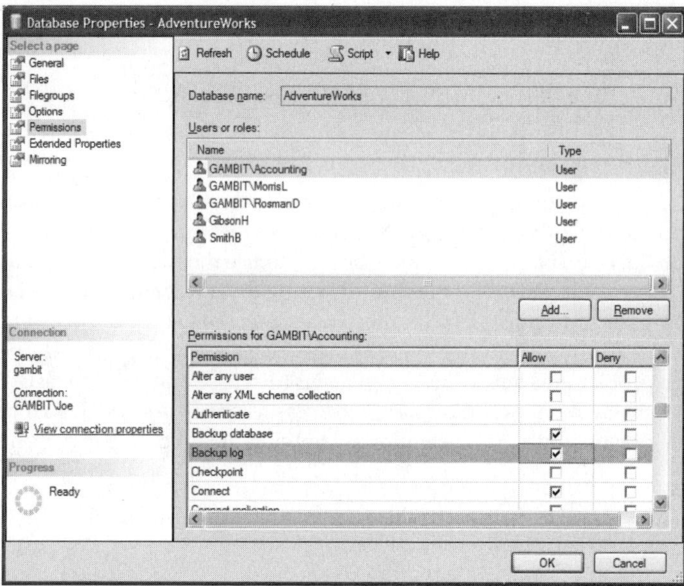

9. Log off Windows, and log back on as JonesB.

10. Open a new SQL Server query in SQL Server Management Studio, connect using Windows Authentication, and type the following query:

```
USE AdventureWorks
CREATE TABLE Statement1
(column1    varchar(5)     not null,
column2    varchar(10)    not null)
```

11. From the Query pull-down menu, select Execute Query. Notice that the query is unsuccessful because JonesB (a member of the Accounting group) doesn't have permission to create a table.

12. Close SQL Server Management Studio, log off Windows, and log back on as RosmanD.

13. Open a new SQL Server query in SQL Server Management Studio, and enter and execute the code from step 10 again. This time it's successful, because RosmanD has permission to create tables.

Object Permissions

Once the structure exists to hold the data, you need to give users permission to start working with the data in the databases, which is accomplished by granting *object permissions* to your users. Using object permissions, you can control who is allowed to read from, write to, or otherwise manipulate your data. The 12 object permissions are listed here for you:

Control This permission gives the principal ownership-like capabilities on the object and all objects under it in the hierarchy. For example, if you grant a user Control permission on the database, then they have Control permission on all the objects in the database, such as tables and views.

Alter This permission allows users to `CREATE`, `ALTER`, or `DROP` the securable and any object under it in the hierarchy. The only property they can't change is ownership.

Take Ownership This allows the user to take ownership of an object.

Impersonate This permission allows one login or user to impersonate another.

Create As the name implies, this permission lets a user create objects.

View Definition This permission allows users to see the T-SQL syntax that was used to create the object being secured.

Select When granted, this permission allows users to read data from the table or view. When granted at the column level, it lets users read from a single column.

Insert This permission allows users to insert new rows into a table.

Update This permission lets users modify existing data in a table but not add new rows to or delete existing rows from a table. When this permission is granted on a column, users can modify data in that single column.

Delete This permission allows users to remove rows from a table.

References Tables can be linked together on a common column with a foreign-key relationship, which is designed to protect data across tables. When two tables are linked with a foreign key, this permission allows the user to select data from the primary table without having Select permission on the foreign table.

Execute This permission allows users to execute the stored procedure where the permission is applied.

Let's get some hands-on experience with applying and testing object permissions in this next set of steps:

1. Open SQL Server Management Studio, expand your server, expand Databases, expand AdventureWorks, and then expand Tables.
2. Right-click Person.Address, and select Properties.
3. On the Permissions page, add ***Sqldomain*\Sales** and **SmithB** under Users Or Roles.
4. Grant Sales Select permission by clicking the Allow check box next to Select.
5. Grant SmithB Select permission by selecting the Allow check box next to Select.
6. If the Guest user has any permissions granted, remove them by clicking each one until all checkboxes are clear.

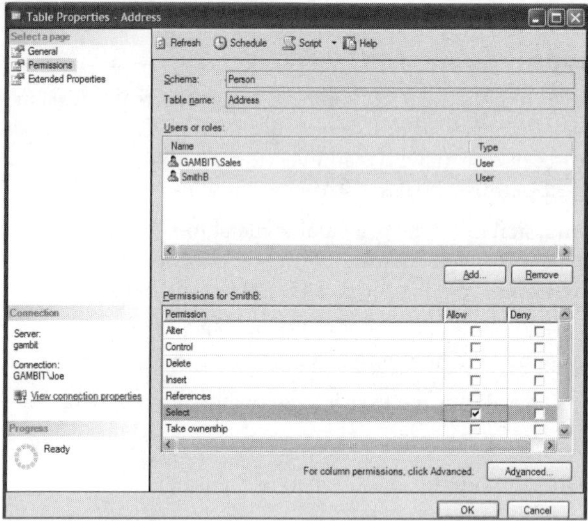

7. Click OK, and close SQL Server Management Studio.
8. Log off Windows, and log back on as JonesB.
9. Open a new SQL Server query in SQL Server Management Studio, and connect using Windows Authentication.
10. Execute the following query (it fails because Accounting doesn't have Select permission):

```
USE AdventureWorks
SELECT * FROM authors
```

11. Close SQL Server Management Studio, and repeat steps 8 through 10 for ChenJ. The query succeeds this time because Sales (of which ChenJ is a member) has Select permission.
12. Log off Windows, and log back in as yourself.

Although granting permissions to single users is useful from time to time, it's better, faster, and easier to apply permissions *en masse.* This requires understanding database roles.

Database Roles

Continuing our business analogy, your accountants need to write corporate checks. You could give them permission to do so in one of two ways. First, you could give each of the accountants their own checkbook drawn from a single account with permission to write checks from it. That would be an accounting nightmare—trying to keep track of all the checks that had been written during the month. The better way to accomplish this is to get one corporate account with one checkbook and give the accountants as a group permission to write checks from that one book.

In SQL Server, when several users need permission to access a database, it's much easier to give them all permissions as a group rather than try to manage each user separately. That is what database roles are for—granting permissions to groups of database users, rather than granting permissions to each database user separately. There are three types of database roles to consider: fixed, custom, and application.

Fixed Database Roles

Fixed database roles have permissions already applied; that is, all you have to do is add users to these roles, and the users inherit the associated permissions. (This is different from custom database roles, as you'll see later.) Several fixed database roles in SQL Server can be used to grant permissions:

db_owner Members of this role can do everything the members of the other roles can do as well as some administrative functions.

db_accessadmin These users have the authority to say who gets access to the database by adding or removing users.

db_datareader Members here can read data from any table in the database.

db_datawriter These users can add, change, and delete data from all the tables in the database.

db_ddladmin Data Definition Language (DDL) administrators can issue all DDL commands; this allows them to create, modify, or change database objects without viewing the data inside.

db_securityadmin Members here can add and remove users from database roles, and manage statement and object permissions.

db_backupoperator These users can back up the database.

db_denydatareader Members can't read the data in the database, but they can make schema changes (for example, adding a column to a table).

db_denydatawriter These users can't make changes to the data in the database, but they're allowed to read the data.

Public The purpose of this group is to grant users a default set of permissions in the database. All database users automatically join this group and can't be removed.

WARNING Because all database users are automatically members of the Public database role, you need to be cautious about the permissions that are assigned to the role.

It's time to limit the administrative authority of your users once they gain access to the database by adding them to fixed database roles:

1. Open SQL Server Management Studio, expand your server, expand Databases, and then expand AdventureWorks.

2. Expand Security, then Roles, and then Database Roles.

3. Right-click db_denydatawriter, and select Properties.
4. Click Add.
5. Type **SmithB** in the Enter Object Names To Select box, and click OK.

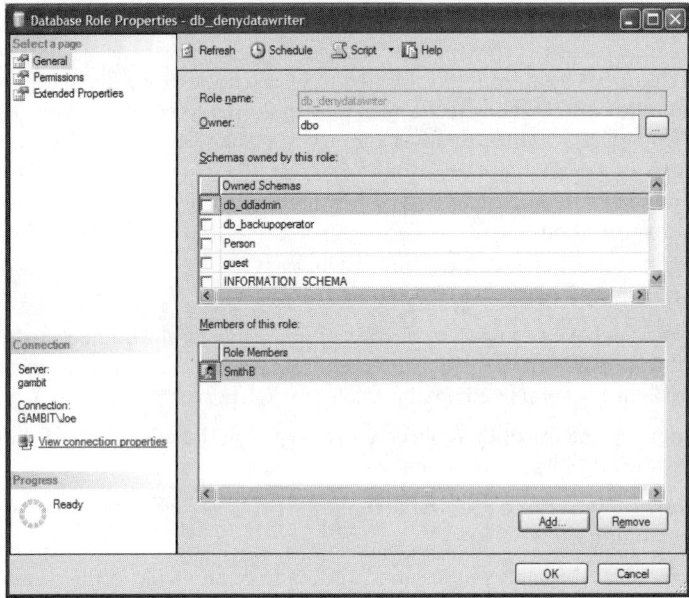

6. Click OK again to go back to SQL Server Management Studio.
7. Right-click db_denydatareader, and select Properties.
8. Click Add.
9. Type **GibsonH** in the Enter Object Names To Select box, and click OK.
10. Open a new SQL Server query in SQL Server Management Studio, and connect using SQL Server Authentication.
11. In the User Name box, type **SmithB**; in the Password box, type **Password1**.
12. The following query tries to update information in the Authors table; it fails because SmithB is a member of the db_denydatawriter role:

```
INSERT INTO HumanResources.Department (DepartmentID, Name, GroupName,
ModifiedDate) values (200, 'Test','TestGroup',GetDate())
```

13. Close the query window.

Fixed database roles cover many—but not all—of the situations that require permissions to be assigned to users. That is why you need to understand custom database roles.

Custom Database Roles

There will, of course, be times when the fixed database roles don't meet your security needs. You may have several users who need Select, Update, and Execute permissions in your database and nothing more. Because none of the fixed database roles give that set of permissions, you need to create a *custom database role*. When you create this new role, you assign permissions to it and then assign users to the role; the users inherit whatever permissions you assign to that role. That is different from the fixed database roles, where you don't need to assign permissions, but just add users. The next set of instructions explain how to create a custom database role.

NOTE You can make your custom database roles members of other database roles. This is referred to as *nesting roles*.

1. Open SQL Server Management Studio, expand your server, expand Databases, and then expand AdventureWorks.
2. Expand Security and then Roles.
3. Right-click Database Roles, and select New Database Role.
4. In the Role Name box, type **SelectOnly**, and enter **dbo** in the Owner box.
5. Add ***Sqldomain*\RosmanD** to the Role Members list.

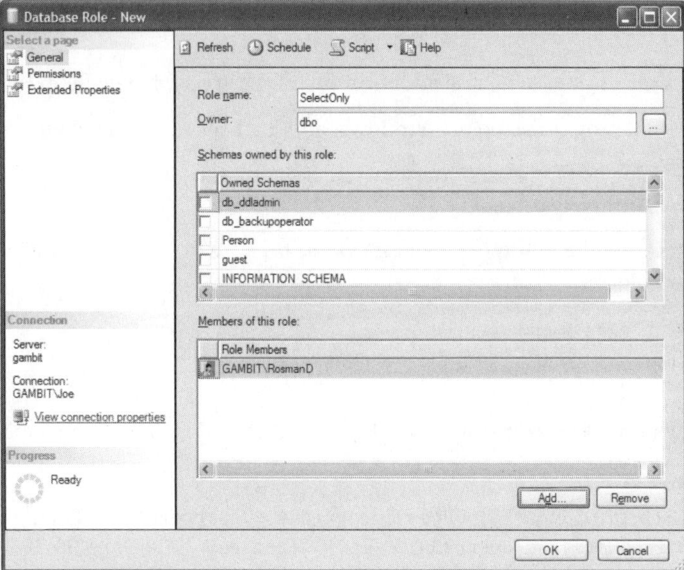

6. On the Permissions page, click Add Objects, select the Specific Objects radio button, and click OK.
7. Click the Objects Type button, select Tables, and click OK.
8. Click Browse, select the HumanResources.Department check box, and click OK.

9. In the Permissions For HumanResources.Department list, select the Allow check box next to Select, and click OK.

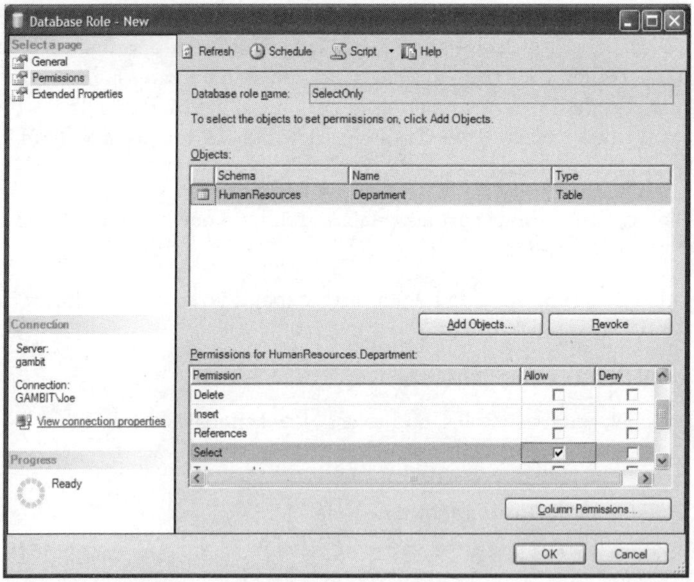

10. Click OK to create the role and return to SQL Server Management Studio.

11. Close all programs, log off Windows, and log back on as RosmanD.

12. Open a new SQL Server Query in SQL Server Management Studio, and connect using Windows Authentication.

13. Notice that the following query succeeds because RosmanD is a member of the new SelectOnly role:

```
USE AdventureWorks
SELECT * FROM HumanResources.Department
```

14. Now notice the failure of the next query because RosmanD is a member of a role that is allowed to select only:

```
INSERT INTO HumanResources.Department (DepartmentID, Name, GroupName,
ModifiedDate) values (200, 'Test','TestGroup',GetDate())
```

15. Close all programs, log off Windows, and log back on as yourself.

The final database role—the application role—grants you a great deal of authority over which applications can be used to work with the data in your databases.

Application Roles

Suppose that your human resources department uses a custom program to access their database and that you don't want them using any other program for fear of damaging the data. You can set this level of security by using an *application role*. With this special role, your users can't access data using just their SQL Server login and database account; they must use the proper application. Here is how it works:

1. Create an application role and assign it permissions.
2. Users open the approved application and are logged in to SQL Server.
3. To enable the application role, the application executes the sp_setapprole stored procedure (which is written into the application at design time).

Once the application role is enabled, SQL Server no longer sees users as themselves; it sees users as the application, and grants them application role permissions. Let's create and test an application role now:

1. Open SQL Server Management Studio, and expand Databases, then AdventureWorks, and then Security.
2. Right-click Application Roles, and select New Application Role.
3. In the Role Name box, type **EntAppRole**.
4. Enter **dbo** in the Default Schema box.
5. In the Password and Confirm Password boxes, type **Password1**.

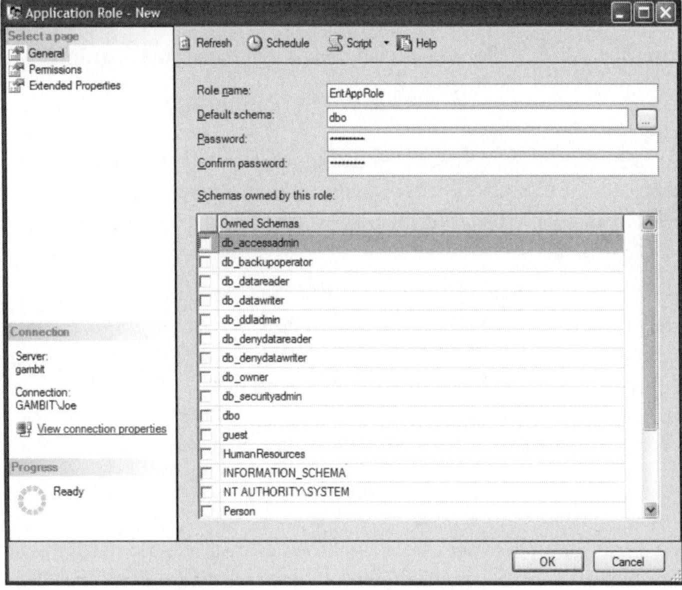

6. On the Permissions page, click Add Objects, select the Specific Objects radio button, and click OK.
7. Click the Objects Type button, select Tables, and click OK.
8. Click Browse, select the HumanResources.Department check box, and click OK.

9. In the Permissions For HumanResources.Department list, select the Allow check box next to Select, and click OK.
10. Open a new SQL Server query in SQL Server Management Studio, and connect using SQL Authentication with GibsonH as the username and Password1 as the password.
11. Notice that the following query fails because GibsonH has been denied Select permissions due to membership in the db_denydatareader database role:

```
USE AdventureWorks
SELECT * FROM HumanResources.Departments
```

12. To activate the application role, execute the following query:

```
sp_setapprole @rolename='EntAppRole', @password='Password1'
```

13. Clear the query window, and don't save the changes; repeat step 11 without opening a new query, and notice that the query is successful this time. This is because SQL Server now sees you as EntAppRole, which has Select permission.
14. Close the query window.

Permission States

All the permissions in SQL Server can exist in one of three states: granted, revoked, or denied.

Grant

Granting allows users to use a specific permission. For instance, if you grant SmithB Select permission on a table, they can read the data within. You know a permission has been granted when the Allow check box is selected next to the permission in the permissions list.

Revoke

A *revoked* permission isn't specifically granted, but a user can inherit the permission if it has been granted to another role of which they are a member. That is, if you revoke the Select permission from SmithB, they can't use it. If, however, they are a member of a role that has been granted Select permission, SmithB can read the data just as if they had the Select permission. A permission is revoked when neither Allow or Deny boxes are selected next to a permission.

Deny

If you *deny* a permission, the user doesn't get the permission—no matter what. If you deny SmithB Select permission on a table, even if they're a member of a role with Select permission, they can't read the data. You know a permission has been denied when the Deny check box is selected next to the permission in the permissions list.

In the following series of steps, you'll get some hands-on experience with changing the states of permissions and witnessing the effects:

1. Open SQL Server Management Studio, and expand your server, then Databases, then AdventureWorks, and then Security.

2. Expand Users, right-click SmithB, and select Properties.
3. On the Permissions page, click Add Objects, select the Specific Objects radio button, and click OK.
4. Click the Objects Type button, select Tables, and click OK.
5. Click Browse, select the HumanResources.Department check box, and click OK.
6. In the Permissions For HumanResources.Department list, select the Allow check box next to Select, and click OK.

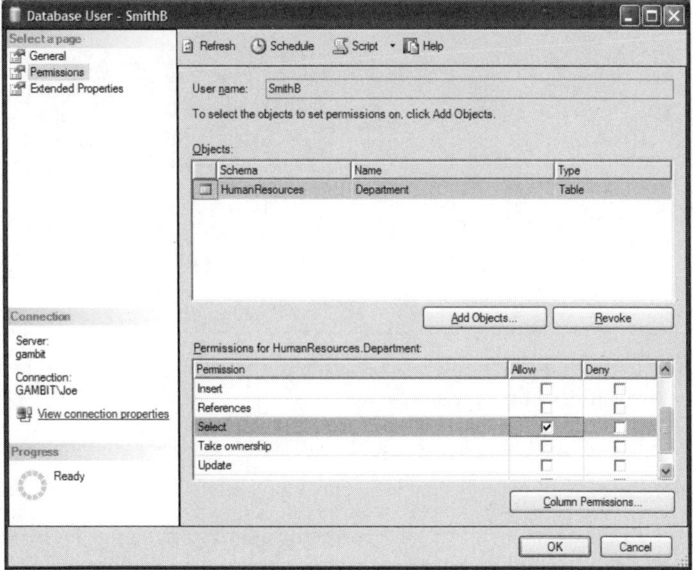

7. Open a new SQL Server Query, and connect as SmithB using SQL Server Authentication.
8. Execute the following query. It's successful because SmithB has Select permission on the HumanResources.Department table:

```
USE AdventureWorks
SELECT * FROM HumanResources.Department
```

9. Right-click SmithB under Users in the AdventureWorks database, and select Properties.
10. On the Permissions page, click Add Objects, select the Specific Objects radio button, and click OK.
11. Click the Objects Type button, select Tables, and click OK.
12. Click Browse, select the HumanResources.Department check box, and click OK.

13. In the Permissions For HumanResources.Department list, deselect the Allow check box next to Select, and click OK.

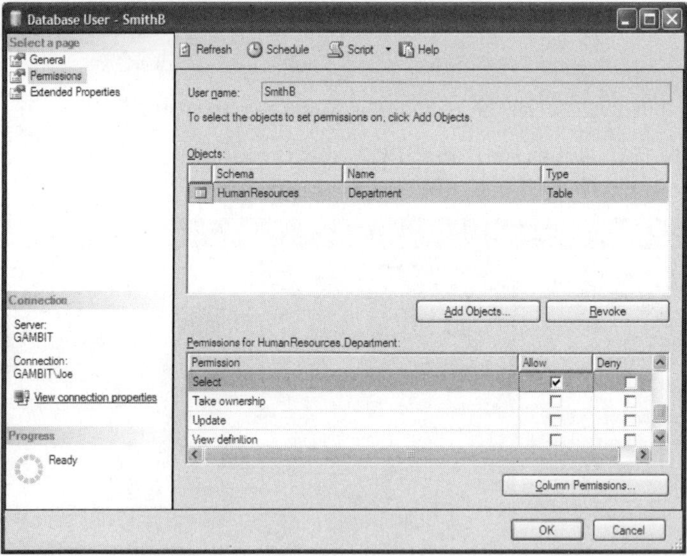

14. Return to the query window, and execute the query in step 8. It fails because SmithB doesn't have explicit Select permission.

15. Right-click SmithB under Users in the AdventureWorks database, and select Properties.

16. Under Role Membership, select the check box next to the db_datareader role.

17. Return to the query window, and rerun the query from step 8. Now it's successful, because SmithB has inherited the Select permission from the db_datareader role and doesn't need to have it explicitly applied.

18. Right-click SmithB under Users in the AdventureWorks database, and select Properties.

19. On the Permissions page, click Add Objects, select the Specific Objects radio button, and click OK.

20. Click the Objects Type button, select Tables, and click OK.

21. Click Browse, select the HumanResources.Department check box, and click OK.

22. In the Permissions For HumanResources.Department list, select the Deny check box next to Select, and click OK.

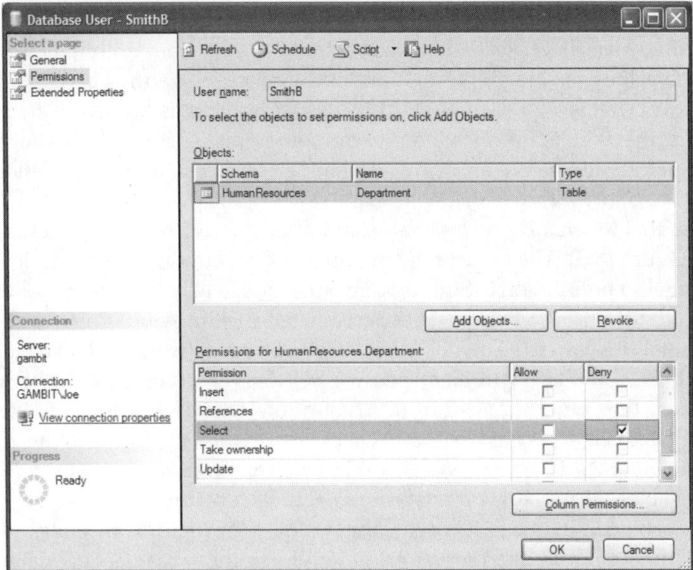

23. Return to the query window, and again run the query from step 8. It fails this time because you've specifically denied SmithB access; therefore they can no longer inherit the Select permission from the db_datareader role.

24. Right-click SmithB under Users in the AdventureWorks database, and select Properties.

25. On the Permissions page, click Add Objects, select the Specific Objects radio button, and click OK.

26. Click the Objects Type button, select Tables, and click OK.

27. Click Browse, select the HumanResources.Department check box, and click OK.

28. Under Role Membership, deselect the check box next to the db_datareader role.

29. In the Permissions For HumanResources.Department list, deselect the Deny check box next to Select, and click OK.

With a better understanding of how and where permissions are applied, let's look into one of the problems generated when permissions are applied improperly: the broken ownership chain.

Ownership Chains

In the physical world, people own objects that they can do with as they please, including lending or giving them to others. SQL Server understands this concept of ownership. When a user creates an object, they own that object and can do whatever they want with it. For example, if RosmanD creates a table, they can assign permissions as they choose, granting access only to those users they deem worthy. That is a good thing until you consider what is known as an *ownership chain*.

An object that is on loan still belongs to the owner; the person who has borrowed it must ask the owner for permission before allowing another person to use it. Acting without such permission would be like a *broken ownership chain*.

Suppose that RosmanD creates a table and grants permissions on that table to Accounting (as shown in Figure 18.3). Then one of the members of Accounting creates a view based on that table and grants Select permission to SmithB. Can SmithB select the data from that view? No, because the ownership chain has been broken. SQL Server checks permissions on an underlying object (in this case, the table) only when the owner changes. Therefore, if RosmanD had created both the table and the view, there would be no problem, because SQL Server would check only the permissions on the view. Because the owner changed from Accounting (who owned the view) to RosmanD (who owned the table), SQL Server needed to check the permissions on both the view and the table.

How can you avoid broken ownership chains? The first way that may come to mind is to make everyone who needs to create objects a member of the sysadmin fixed server role; then everything they create is owned by the DBO user rather than by the login. For example, because MorrisL is a member of the sysadmin fixed server role, everything they create in any database is owned by the DBO, not MorrisL. Although this is technically possible, it's a poor method because it grants a great deal of administrative privilege over the server to people who don't need such privilege.

A much better way to avoid broken ownership chains is to make all the users who need to create objects members of either the db_owner or db_ddladmin fixed database role. Then, if they need to create objects, they can specify the owner as DBO (for example, `'create table dbo.table_name'`). This way, the DBO owns all objects in the database, and because the ownership never changes, SQL Server never needs to check any underlying permissions.

FIGURE 18.3
When objects that rely on each other have different owners, it's called a broken ownership chain.

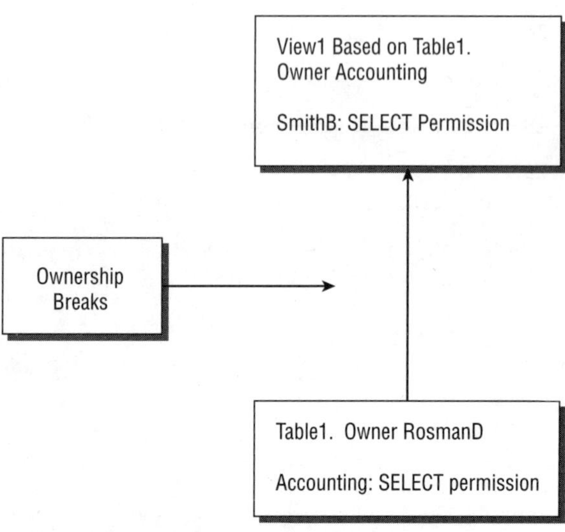

WARNING Don't forget that members of the db_owner role can do whatever they like with a database, whereas db_ddladmins have limited authority. Therefore, you may want to use db_ddladmin in most instances.

TIP When a db_owner or db_ddladmin member creates an object as another user, it can be any database user, not just the DBO.

Now you have a good understanding of local security, but what if you have to access data on more than one server? Let's look at how to implement security in a distributed environment.

N-Tier Security

Let's return to our business analogy: Your business is prospering, and you have expanded into two buildings. Your employees need access to resources in both buildings, which means you need to give your users a key to the new place.

You have the same concerns when your resources are spread across multiple SQL Servers; your users may need access to resources on multiple, or *n* number of, servers. This is especially true of something called a *distributed query* (see Figure 18.4), which returns result sets from databases on multiple servers. Although you may wonder why you would want to perform distributed queries when you can replicate the data between servers (replication is discussed in Chapter 27), there are practical reasons for doing the former. Don't forget that because SQL Server is designed to store terabytes of data, some of your databases may grow to several hundred megabytes in size—and you don't want to replicate several hundred megabytes under normal circumstances.

FIGURE 18.4
A distributed query involves data from more than one server.

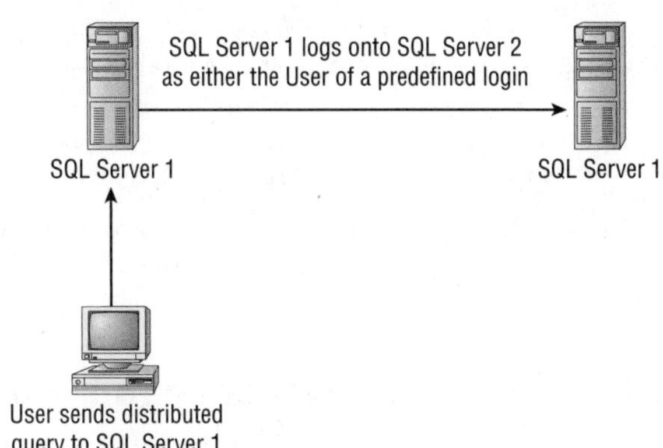
SQL Server 1 logs onto SQL Server 2
as either the User of a predefined login
SQL Server 1
SQL Server 1
User sends distributed
query to SQL Server 1

The first step in configuring your server to perform distributed queries is to inform SQL Server that it will be talking to other database servers by running the `sp_addlinkedserver` stored procedure. The procedure to link to a server named AccountingSQL looks something like this:

```
sp_addlinkedserver @server='AccountingSQL', @provider='SQL Server'
```

Your users can then run distributed queries by specifying two different servers in the query. The query `select * from SQLServer.AdventureWorks.dbo.authors, AccountingSQL.AdventureWorks.dbo.employees` accesses data from both the SQLServer server (the server the user is logged in to, or the sending server) and the AccountingSQL server (the remote server) in the same result set.

The security issue here is that the sending server must log in to the remote server on behalf of the user to gain access to the data. SQL Server can use one of two methods to send this security information: security account delegation or linked server login mapping. If your users have logged in using Windows Authentication, and all the servers in the query are capable of understanding Windows domain security, you can use *account delegation*. Here's how it works:

1. If the servers are in different domains, you must make certain that the appropriate Windows trust relationships are in place. The remote server's domain must trust the sending server's domain. If you're using only Windows domains, the trust relationships are automatically created for you.
2. Add a Windows login to the sending server for the user to log in with.
3. Add the same account to the remote server.
4. Create a user account for the login in the remote server's database, and assign permissions.
5. When the user executes the distributed query, SQL Server sends the user's Windows security credentials to the remote server, allowing access.

If you have users who access SQL Server with standard logins, or if some of the servers don't participate in Windows domain security, you'll need to add a *linked login*. Here's how to do it:

1. On the remote server, create a standard login and assign the necessary permissions.
2. On the sending server, map a local login to the remote login using the `sp_addlinkedsrvlogin` stored procedure. To map all local logins to the remote login RemUser, type the following:

```
sp_addlinkedsrvlogin @rmtsrvname='AccountingSQL', @useself=FALSE,
@locallogin=NULL, @rmtuser='RemUser', @rmtpassword='Password1'
```

3. When a user executes a distributed query, the sending server logs in to the AccountingSQL (remote) server as RemUser with a password of *Password1*.

Considering all the work you've put into your security system up to this point, you want to be sure that no one bypasses it somehow. Using SQL Profiler, you can monitor your security system; let's see how.

Monitoring SQL Server Logins with SQL Profiler

Most people have at one time or another had to pass through a security checkpoint. At that checkpoint, a security guard sat, watching monitors and searching packages. Why was the guard there? Because you can have the most advanced security system in the world, but without someone keeping watch, it will eventually fail. A thief would simply need to probe the system systematically for weak spots and, once they were found, take advantage of them to break in. With the guard watching, this becomes a great deal more difficult.

The same is true for SQL Server. You can't simply put a security system in place and then leave it. You must keep watch, just like the security guard, to make certain no one is probing for weak spots and attempting to break in. This task of keeping watch has been delegated to SQL Profiler.

NOTE SQL Profiler is discussed in more detail in Chapter 26.

SQL Profiler is used to track and record activity on the SQL Server, by performing a trace (as you'll see a little later in this section). A *trace* is a record of the data captured about events, which can be a stored in a database table, a trace log file that can be opened and read in SQL Profiler, or both. Two types of traces exist: shared and private. *Shared traces* are viewable by anyone, whereas *private traces* are viewable only by the user who created them (or the owner of the trace). Although your security trace should be private, your optimization and troubleshooting traces can be shared.

The actions that are monitored on the server are known as *events*, and those events are logically grouped together in *event classes*. Not all of these events are concerned with security; in fact, most of them have to do with optimization and troubleshooting. The following sections list the classes and events that are important from a security standpoint.

Event Class Errors and Warnings

Loginfailed This tells you if someone has tried to log in unsuccessfully. If you notice someone repeatedly failing to log in, then either the user forgot their password or someone is trying to hack in using that account.

Event Class Server

ServiceControl This monitors SQL Server starts, stops, and pauses. If you note a stop or pause and you're the only administrator, then there is a problem with the server itself—or someone has hacked in with an administrative account.

Event Class Objects

Object:Deleted This tells you if an object, such as a table or view, has been deleted. From a security standpoint, this is after the fact, because the damage may have already been done. By monitoring this event, however, you can catch the culprit if something is improperly deleted.

Let's see how to use SQL Profiler to monitor failed logins in this next series of steps:

1. Open SQL Profiler by selecting it from the SQL Server 2005 group under Programs on the Start menu.
2. Choose File ➤ New Trace, and connect using Windows Authentication.
3. In the Trace Name box, type **Security**.
4. Select Blank as the template to use.
5. Select the Save To File check box, and click OK to select the default filename.
6. Select the Save To Table check box, connect using Windows Authentication, and use the following criteria to fill in the subsequent dialog box:

```
Database: AdventureWorks
Owner: dbo
Table: Security
```

7. Click OK to return to the previous dialog box.

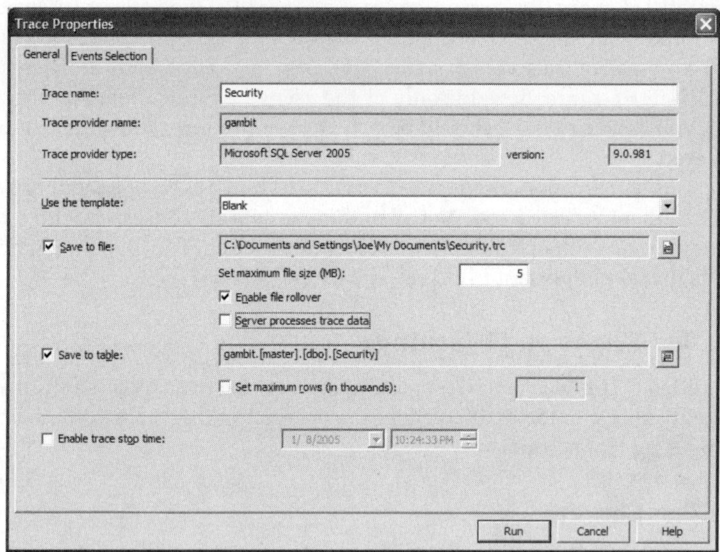

8. Select the Events Selection tab.

9. In the Select The Server Event Classes To Trace box, expand Security Audit. Select the Audit Login Failed check box.

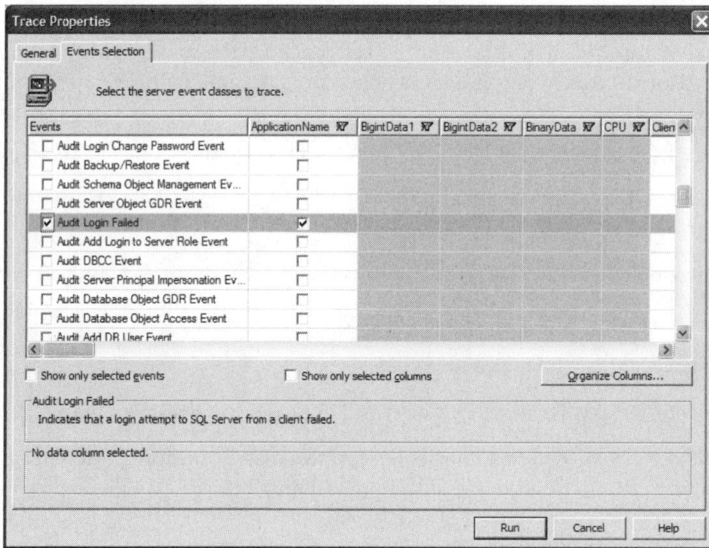

10. Click Run to start the trace.

11. To test the trace, leave SQL Profiler open, and open a new SQL Server query in SQL Server Management Studio. Connect using SQL Authentication with username SmithB and password *coconut*. This will fail because you've supplied the wrong password.

12. Return to SQL Profiler, and notice that a login failure has been recorded for user SmithB.

13. Go back to SQL Server Management Studio, and log in as SmithB with a password of *Password1*. This will succeed because you've entered the correct password.

14. Close SQL Server Management Studio, and return to SQL Profiler. Notice that there is no successful login record for SmithB, because you're monitoring only failed logins.

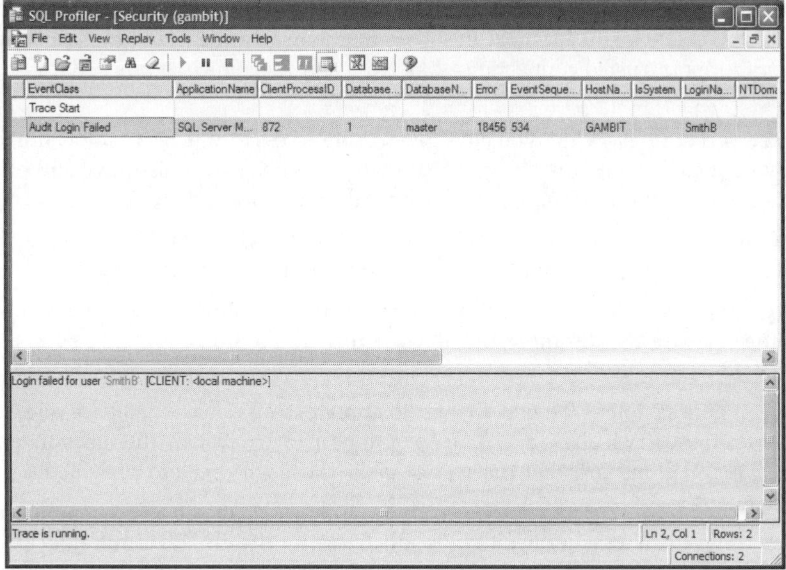

15. Select File ➤ Stop Trace, and then select File ➤ Close.

16. Choose File ➤ Open ➤ Trace File.

17. Open the `Security.trc` file and notice that all the events just recorded have been saved for later viewing.

18. Close SQL Profiler, open a new SQL Server query in SQL Server Management Studio, and log in using Windows Authentication.

19. To view the data in the Security table that SQL Profiler created, execute the following query:

```
USE AdventureWorks
SELECT * FROM security
```

20. Close SQL Profiler and SQL Server Management Studio.

Creating a Security Plan

Suppose you have just been hired as database administrator for AlsoRann Inc., a small company that relies heavily on its SQL Server. A great deal of the data on the SQL Server is proprietary and therefore must be secured. You realize, however, that jumping right in and randomly applying permissions to databases is going to result in a mess—if not a disaster—so you take a more logical approach: You develop a security plan.

Creating a good security plan is always the first step in applying security to any type of system. Here are a few things you should consider in your plan:

Type of users If all your users support trusted connections, you can use Windows accounts. If you have the authority to create groups in Windows, you may be able to create Windows groups and then create logins for those groups rather than creating individual accounts. If not all your users support trusted connections (like Novell or Macintosh), you need to use Mixed mode authentication and create some standard logins.

Fixed server roles Once you have given users access to SQL Server, how much administrative power, if any, should they be given? If your users need administrative authority, add them to one of the fixed server roles; if not, there is no need to add them.

Database access Once your users are logged in, to which databases do they have access? It's highly unlikely that every user needs a user account in every database.

Type of access Once the user has a database user account, how much authority do they have in the database? For example, can all users read and write, or is there a subset of users who are allowed to only read?

Group permissions It's usually best to apply permissions to database roles and then add users to those roles. There are some exceptions in every system, though; you may need to apply some permissions directly to users, especially those who need to be denied access to a resource.

Object creation Figure out who needs the authority to create objects, such as tables and views, and group them together in either the db_owner or the db_ddladmin role. Doing this allows users to create objects as the DBO instead of as themselves. In this way, you can avoid broken ownership chains.

Public role permissions Remember that all database user accounts are members of the Public role and can't be removed. Whatever permission the Public role has are given to your users. Limit the permissions on the Public group.

Guest access Do you want users with no database user account to be able to access databases through a guest account? For some databases, such as a catalog, this may be acceptable. In general, however, this can be considered a security risk and should not be used on all databases.

Table 18.1 shows the employees of AlsoRann Inc. and their security needs.

TABLE 18.1: The Employees of AlsoRann Inc.

NAME	NT GROUP	DEPARTMENT	NETWORK	ADMIN	PERMISSIONS
SmithB	N/A	Service	Novell	None	Read, no Write
GibsonH	N/A	Development	Novell	Server Configuration	Write, Create, no Read

TABLE 18.1: The Employees of AlsoRann Inc. *(CONTINUED)*

NAME	NT GROUP	DEPARTMENT	NETWORK	ADMIN	PERMISSIONS
RosmanD	None	Administration	Windows	None	Select, Insert, Update
MorrisL	None	IT	Windows	All	All
JohnsonK	Accounting	Accounting	Windows	None	Read, Write
JonesB	Accounting	Accounting	Windows	None	Read, Write
ChenJ	Sales	Sales	Windows	None	Read, Update
SamuelsR	Sales	Sales	Windows	None	Read, Update

The first thing you may notice is that there are two Novell network users. This means you need to create at least two standard logins and implement Mixed mode authentication.

The next thing to notice is that some of the users—specifically, Accounting and Sales—are already grouped together in Windows. Rather than create accounts for each individual member of these departments, you can instead add a Windows Group login for the whole lot of them. Because RosmanD and MorrisL aren't members of a Windows group, they need Windows User logins.

Next, look at the administrative rights that each user needs over the system. Because GibsonH needs to be able to configure server settings such as memory use, they should be added to the serveradmin fixed server role. Because MorrisL needs full administrative access to the entire system, they should be added to the sysadmin fixed server role.

To make our example easier to comprehend, we have given AlsoRann only one database. Look at the permissions that everyone needs on that database. As a customer service rep, SmithB needs permission to read the data but not to write any data; the db_denydatawriter fixed database role fits those needs well.

As a developer, GibsonH needs permission to create objects in the database, but they should not be able to read the data. Make GibsonH a member of the db_ddladmin role so that they can create objects as DBO and avoid broken ownership chains. We could have made GibsonH a member of the db_owner group and achieved the same effect, but then they would have been able to do whatever they wanted in the database, including reading the data.

RosmanD needs to be able to select, insert, and update data, but they should not be able to delete any data. No fixed database role grants these three permissions together. You could apply all these permissions directly to RosmanD, but what if you hire more people who need the same permissions? It might be a better idea to create a custom database role; grant that role the Select, Insert, and Update permissions; and make RosmanD a member of that role. The same is true of the Sales group, which needs permission to read and update; they require a custom role.

For Accounting, it will be easiest just to add them to the db_datareader and db_datawriter roles; that way, they will receive permissions to read and write to the database. MorrisL doesn't need to be a member of any role; because they're a member of the sysadmin fixed server role, they're automatically considered the DBO in every database on the server.

In the real world, of course, a security plan isn't going to be nearly this simple. You'll have hundreds, if not thousands, of users to deal with from a variety of networks, each needing different permissions. To sum up, although developing a security plan is probably more work than the actual implementation, you can't do without it.

Summary

SQL Server 2005 has a sophisticated security system that allows you to carefully implement your security plan. SQL Server can operate in Mixed security mode, which means that Windows users and groups can be given access directly to SQL Server, or separate, unique accounts can be created that reside only in SQL Server. If SQL Server is running in Windows Authentication mode, every user must first connect with a preauthorized Windows account.

This chapter examined the processes of creating and managing logins, groups, and users. You learned how to create a Standard login and a Windows User or Group login using SQL Server Management Studio or T-SQL, and when each type is appropriate. If you have a well-designed security plan that incorporates growth, managing your user base can be a painless task.

To limit administrative access to SQL Server at the server level, you learned that you can add users to a fixed server role. To limit access in a specific database, you can add users to a database role, and if one of the fixed database roles isn't to your liking, you can create your own. You can even go so far as to limit access to specific applications by creating an application role.

Each database in SQL Server 2005 has its own independent permissions. We looked at the two types of user permissions: statement permissions, which are used to create or change the data structure, and object permissions, which manipulate data. Remember that statement permissions can't be granted to other users.

The next section in this chapter described the database hierarchy. We looked at the permissions available to the most powerful users—the sysadmins—down through the lower-level database users.

You then learned about chains of ownership. These are created when you grant permissions to others on objects you own. Adding more users who create dependent objects creates broken ownership chains, which can become complex and tricky to work with. You learned how to predict the permissions available to users at different locations within these ownership chains. You also learned that to avoid the broken ownership chains, you can add your users to either the db_owner or the db_ddladmin database role and have your users create objects as the DBO.

Permissions can be granted to database users as well as database roles. When a user is added to a role, they inherit the permissions of the role, including the Public role, of which everyone is a member. The only exception is when the user has been denied permission, because Deny takes precedence over any other right, no matter the level at which the permission was granted.

We then looked at remote and linked servers and at how security needs to be set up to make remote queries work. We finished with a look at *n*-tier security and applications.

Now that you have a better understanding of security and administration in general, you're ready to begin learning about programming with SQL Server. Let's start in the next chapter by learning about ADO.

Part 5

Development with SQL Server

In this section:

Chapter 19

Integrating SQL Server with Microsoft .NET

For many years, T-SQL has been the only practical programming language for SQL Server. If you wanted SQL Server itself to run your code, you had to write the code in either T-SQL or C++. The latter choice, using C++ to create extended stored procedures, was beyond the capabilities of many DBAs and developers.

One of the biggest changes in SQL Server 2005 is the easing of this restriction. SQL Server 2005 is intimately tied to Microsoft's .NET Common Language Runtime (CLR), and it can execute code written in any CLR language. That means you can now write stored procedures, triggers, user-defined functions, and user-defined types in an array of languages including Visual Basic, C#, and many others. In this chapter, we'll show you how.

Understanding .NET and the CLR

The Common Language Runtime is one of the core parts of Microsoft's .NET programming initiative, which is several years old. SQL Server now functions as a CLR host, allowing you to leverage much of .NET from within SQL Server. To understand what this means, you need to know something about .NET. In this section, we'll describe some of the features and innovations that are the underpinnings of the .NET Framework:

- The Common Language Runtime (CLR)
- Managed execution
- The Common Type System (CTS)
- Cross-language interoperability
- The .NET Framework class library
- Namespaces
- Assemblies
- Application domains
- Security

The Common Language Runtime

The Common Language Runtime (CLR) is the core of the .NET Framework. All code written in the .NET languages is executed via the CLR. In that respect, the CLR is similar to previous runtimes such as the Visual Basic runtime. Visual Basic code is executed via the Visual Basic runtime, which translates the VB language into low-level Windows API calls.

The CLR is a much more active component of applications than the VB runtime is. In fact, the CLR takes such an active role in the execution of code that code written for the CLR is referred to as *managed code*. That's because the CLR provides services, in addition to executing code. For example, the CLR takes care of all memory management and garbage collection (reusing memory occupied by objects that are no longer in use) for .NET applications.

The CLR is responsible for enforcing various rules that are designed to make .NET applications robust. These include constraints on datatypes, memory usage, and application security. Because all of this management is taking place in the CLR, it's impossible for even poorly written .NET code to contain many common types of errors. For example, memory leaks (where an object is instantiated and never destroyed) are impossible in managed code. And this protection comes at no cost to the developer: You don't have to write a single line of code to be assured that your application won't contain memory leaks.

NOTE Although memory leaks are impossible, there's no guarantee when the .NET garbage collector will be called to dispose of unwanted objects. If you create many .NET objects in a short period of time on a busy server, these objects could tie up memory for a long time after you're done with them.

Managed Execution

The entire process of turning your source code into an application that can be run by the CLR is referred to as *managed execution*. This process consists of four steps, and it needs to be performed whether the code will be a stand-alone application or a CLR stored procedure called from SQL Server:

1. Create your program's source code using a specialized development environment such as Visual Studio or a general-purpose tool such as a text editor.
2. Use a .NET compiler to turn the source code into a form known as Microsoft Intermediate Language (MSIL). MSIL files typically have the file extension `.dll` or `.exe`; they look like executable files to the operating system, although they can't run without the CLR. The MSIL format is independent of any particular operating system or hardware architecture. No matter which language you use for the source code, it always compiles to MSIL.
3. When you run a .NET executable, the .NET Framework uses a just-in-time (JIT) compiler to translate the MSIL instructions into actual hardware-specific instructions that can be executed by your computer's CPU.
4. The CLR passes the compiled code to the CPU, monitoring its execution to perform management services such as memory management, security checking, and versioning support.

Figure 19.1 shows the managed execution process schematically.

As Figure 19.1 shows, the MSIL version of your application contains information other than the code to perform the application's functions. This *metadata* is a separate section of the MSIL file that describes the contents of the file. The CLR uses the metadata to ensure proper operation of the code. For example, the metadata contains descriptions of the datatypes exposed by your application; the CLR can use these descriptions to make sure it properly interoperates with other applications. The metadata also provides information to SQL Server about which operations are safe to execute within a SQL Server procedure.

FIGURE 19.1
The managed execution process

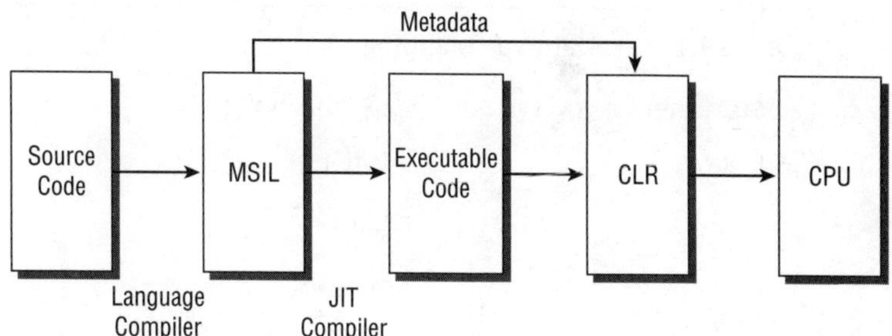

The Common Type System

The CLR defines the Common Type System (CTS). At its most basic level, you can think of the CTS as defining all the datatypes that managed code is allowed to use. It also defines rules for creating, persisting, using, and binding to types.

Because the CTS includes rules for creating new types, you're not limited to a small set of datatypes. In particular, you can define your own values (for example, Visual Basic .NET enumerations) or your own classes such that they will be acceptable to the CTS. As long as you're using a .NET language, the operation of defining CTS-acceptable types is transparent. The compiler will take care of following the CTS rules.

The CTS manages many categories of types, including these:

- Built-in value types such as byte or Int32 (a 32-bit signed integer)
- User-defined value types (for example, you could write code to define a complex number type)
- Enumerations
- Pointers
- Classes from the .NET Framework class library
- User-defined classes
- Arrays
- Delegates (pointers to functions)
- Interfaces

All types managed by the CTS are guaranteed to be *type safe*. That means the CLR and CTS ensure that an instance of a type can't overwrite memory that doesn't belong to it.

To write .NET code that interoperates with SQL Server, you need to understand the mapping between SQL Server datatypes and .NET datatypes. Table 19.1 lists the SQL Server datatypes and their equivalent .NET datatypes. Each .NET language (such as C# or Visual Basic) also implements its own datatypes on top of these generic .NET datatypes.

Cross-Language Interoperability

Because the CLR manages all .NET code, regardless of the language it's written in, the .NET Framework is an ideal environment for cross-language interoperability. That is, code written in one .NET

TABLE 19.1: Datatype Mapping

SQL SERVER DATATYPE	.NET DATATYPE
Binary	Byte[]
Bigint	Int64
Bit	Boolean
Char	None
Cursor	None
Datetime	DateTime
Decimal	Decimal
Float	Double
Image	None
Int	Int32
Money	Decimal
Nchar	String, Char[]
Nchar(1)	Char
Ntext	None
Numeric	Decimal
Nvarchar	String, Char[]
Nvarchar(1)	Char
Real	Single
Smalldatetime	DateTime
Smallint	Int16
Smallmoney	Decimal
SQL_variant	Object
Table	ISQLResultSet
Text	None

TABLE 19.1: Datatype Mapping *(CONTINUED)*

SQL SERVER DATATYPE	.NET DATATYPE
Tinyint	Byte
Uniqueidentifier	Guid
Timestamp	None
Varbinary	Byte[]
Varchar	None
Xml	None

language can be easily used from another .NET language. This interoperability is pervasive. For example, you can define a class in VB .NET and then call the methods of that class, or even derive a new class from the original class, in C# code.

The key to interoperability is the metadata contained in MSIL files. Because this metadata is standardized across all .NET languages, a component written in one language can use the metadata to figure out the proper way to call a component written in another language. This metadata is also what makes it possible for the CLR hosted within SQL server to run MSIL code as part of a T-SQL batch.

However, not every .NET language can use all the features of the CLR. For example, the CTS defines a 64-bit unsigned integer datatype, but not all languages allow you to define variables using that type. To ease this problem, .NET defines the Common Language Specification (CLS). The CLS is a set of rules that dictates a minimum core set of .NET constructs that every .NET language must support. If you write components that conform to the CLS, you can be sure they will be usable by components written in other .NET languages.

The .NET Framework Class Library

The other major component of the .NET Framework, besides the CLR, is the .NET Framework class library. A *class library* is a set of predefined classes that can be used to access common functionality. By supplying a class library, the .NET Framework keeps developers from having to "reinvent the wheel" in many cases.

The .NET Framework class library is exceptionally rich, containing several hundred classes. These classes encapsulate functionality such as the following:

- Defining data with the CLR datatypes
- Defining data structures including lists, queues, and hash tables
- Installing software
- Debugging applications
- Globalizing software
- Reading and writing data

- Interoperating with unmanaged code
- Managing threads
- Handling security

WARNING If you're not comfortable with concepts such as classes, objects, properties, and methods, you'll need to remedy this before you start working with .NET.

Namespaces

Classes within the .NET Framework class library are arranged in *namespaces*, groups of objects that perform similar functions. Namespaces also contain other .NET entities such as structures, enumerations, delegates, and interfaces. Namespaces, in turn, are arranged into a hierarchy. For example, one class you'll see used in ADO.NET code is named `System.Data.SqlClient.SqlConnection`. An object instantiated from this class represents a single connection to a SQL Server database. This is the `SqlConnection` class within the `System.Data.SqlClient` namespace (a collection of classes dealing with access to OLE DB data), which is, in turn, contained within the `System.Data` namespace (a collection of classes dealing with data access), which is, in turn, contained within the `System` namespace (the root namespace for almost all of the .NET Framework class library namespaces).

The .NET Framework class library contains nearly 100 namespaces. A complete listing would be exhausting and (because such a listing already appears in the .NET Framework SDK documentation) pointless. Table 19.2 lists some of the important .NET namespaces.

TABLE 19.2: Selected .NET Framework Namespaces

NAMESPACE	CONTENT
`System.Collections`	Abstract data structures including lists, hash tables, queues, and dictionaries
`System.Data`	The root namespace for the ADO.NET classes
`System.Data.Common`	Classes shared by all .NET data providers
`System.Data.OleDb`	The OLE DB .NET data provider
`System.Data.SqlClient`	The SQL Server .NET data provider
`System.Data.SqlTypes`	Implementations of the SQL Server native datatypes
`System.Diagnostics`	Debugging and tracing aids
`System.DirectoryServices`	An interface to the Windows Active Directory
`System.Drawing.Printing`	Printer functionality
`System.Globalization`	Classes useful in globalizing an application
`System.IO`	Classes for reading and writing streams and files
`System.Messaging`	Inter-application messaging support

TABLE 19.2: Selected .NET Framework Namespaces *(CONTINUED)*

NAMESPACE	CONTENT
`System.Net`	Network protocol support
`System.Resources`	Resource file support
`System.Runtime.Remoting`	Support for distributed applications
`System.Runtime.Serialization`	Support for saving objects to files or streams
`System.Security`	Security and permissions functionality
`System.Web`	Support for communication with web browsers
`System.Windows.Forms`	Stand-alone user interface components
`System.XML`	Classes for using XML

Assemblies

.NET groups code into units called *assemblies*. An assembly can consist of a single file or of components distributed across multiple files. In all cases, there is one file that contains the *assembly manifest*, part of the metadata that lists the contents of the assembly.

When you're writing .NET code, you can designate which files will go into an assembly and which other assemblies a particular assembly is designed to work with. The CLR uses assemblies as a fundamental unit of management in many respects:

- Permissions are requested and granted on an assembly as a whole.
- A type retains its identity within an assembly. That is, if you declare a type named CustomType within an assembly, that type will be identical in all files contained in the assembly. But different assemblies may contain two different types named CustomType.
- The assembly manifest specifies which types may be used by code outside the assembly.
- Version tracking is done on the assembly level. An assembly can specify the version of another assembly that it requires, but it can't specify a version for an individual file within an assembly.
- Assemblies are deployed as a unit. When an application requests code contained in an assembly, it must install the entire assembly. SQL Server includes T-SQL commands to load assemblies.

.NET also allows *side-by-side* assemblies. That is, you can have two versions of the same assembly installed on the same computer, and different applications can use them simultaneously.

Application Domains

Application domains provide a second level of code grouping in .NET. An application domain is composed of a group of assemblies loaded together. The CLR enforces isolation between application domains, such that code running in one application domain can't directly manipulate objects in another application domain.

NOTE The CLR provides services for allowing cross-domain calls. You can manipulate objects across application domain boundaries by copying them between application domains or by constructing a proxy to forward the calls.

Application domains are not the same as Windows processes. On the Windows level, all the code within a single application (such as Internet Explorer) runs in a single operating system process. But on the .NET level, multiple application domains can be contained within a single process. This allows, for example, several .NET-developed controls to be used on the same ASP.NET web page without any risk that one will corrupt the other. In SQL Server, a single instance of the CLR can host code for multiple processes by placing each process's code within its own application domain.

Security

.NET is the first Microsoft development environment designed with serious attention to security. It's a fact of life that security holes have become more critical as more applications are connected to the Internet, where a wide variety of people with bad intentions can attempt to exploit any gaps.

The .NET Framework implements both *code access security* and *role-based security*. Code access security is designed to protect the operating system from malicious code by granting permissions to resources based on the source of the code and the operations the code is attempting to perform. You can mark classes and their members within your application to deny unknown code from using those resources.

Role-based security allows you to grant or deny access to resources based on credentials supplied by users. In role-based security, a user's identity determines the roles to which the user belongs, and permissions are granted to roles. The user's identity can be determined either by their Windows login credentials or by a custom scheme used only by your application.

Using .NET Code in SQL Server

You can use SQL Server data from applications written in .NET, but the integration between SQL Server and .NET goes far beyond that sort of arm's-length use. (We'll cover the .NET APIs for retrieving data from SQL Server in Chapter 20, "ADO.NET and SQL Server.") Beginning with SQL Server 2005, a copy of the CLR runs inside of SQL Server; this is referred to as *hosting* the CLR in SQL Server. This gives SQL Server the ability to execute four different types of .NET procedures:

- Scalar-valued user-defined functions
- Table-valued user-defined functions
- User-defined procedures
- User-defined triggers

You can also define new SQL Server types in .NET code.

CLR Hosting in SQL Server

When you write a stand-alone .NET application and run it, the CLR uses the basic services of the operating system. For example, when the application requires memory, the CLR requests that memory from the operating system.

When the CLR is hosted in SQL Server, the situation is fundamentally different. In this case, SQL Server, not the underlying operating system, provides basic services to the CLR:

- Threads are provided by the SQL Server scheduler. This means SQL Server can detect deadlocks involving .NET code and preempt long-running threads.
- The CLR gets its memory allocations from SQL Server. This means SQL Server can keep .NET code within the overall memory limits you've set for SQL Server, and SQL Server and the CLR won't compete for memory.
- The CLR depends on SQL Server to provide synchronization services, so that different threads can be efficiently scheduled.

Figure 19.2 provides a schematic look at the way.NET code interfaces with SQL Server. As you'll see later in this chapter, this complexity is largely transparent to the developer. After you've created and hooked up .NET code for SQL Server, it can be easily integrated with T-SQL code in a single batch.

FIGURE 19.2
Hosting the CLR in SQL Server

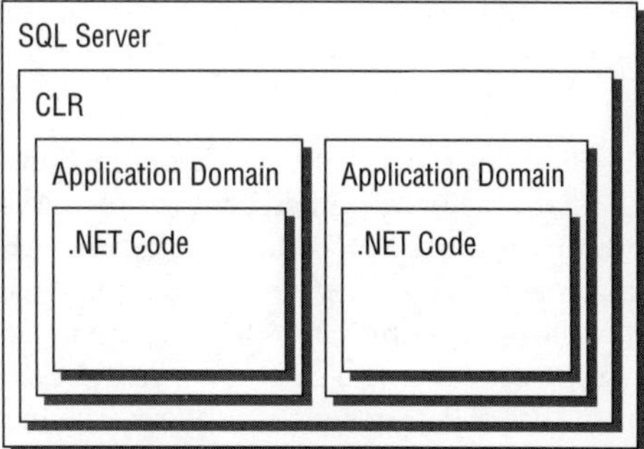

Writing CLR User-Defined Functions

With the basic theory out of the way, it's time to get down to some practice. The easiest way to use .NET code within SQL Server is to create a user-defined function in a .NET language, which can then be called just like a T-SQL user-defined function. You can build three types of user-defined functions in the CLR:

- Scalar-valued user-defined functions (which return a single value)
- Table-valued user-defined functions (which return an entire table)
- User-defined aggregate functions (which behave similarly to built-in aggregates such as `SUM` and `MIN`)

We'll show you how to create scalar-valued and table-valued user-defined functions. You're less likely to need to build your own aggregate functions; if you do, the details are in Books Online.

WRITING SCALAR-VALUED USER-DEFINED FUNCTIONS

A scalar-valued user-defined function returns a single scalar type such as an integer or a string. The function can have zero or more inputs. Such functions are implemented in .NET code as static methods of a class. A static method is one that can be called without creating an instance of the class. For example, here's the Visual Basic .NET code for a class that exposes two static functions (the Shared keyword declares a class member in Visual Basic .NET to be static):

```
Imports Microsoft.SqlServer.Server

Namespace Conversions
    Public Class Mass
        <SqlFunction(DataAccess:=DataAccessKind.None)> _
        Public Shared Function PoundsToKg( _
         ByVal Pounds As Double) As Double
            PoundsToKg = 0.4536 * Pounds
        End Function

        <SqlFunction(DataAccess:=DataAccessKind.None)> _
        Public Shared Function KgToPounds( _
         ByVal Kilograms As Double) As Double
            KgToPounds = 2.205 * Kilograms
        End Function
    End Class
End Namespace
```

As the first step toward making these functions callable from SQL Server, we saved this code in a Visual Basic class library named Conversions. We set the assembly name to Conversions and the root namespace to an empty string (you can make both of these settings in the Assembly section of the project's property pages if you're using Visual Studio .NET 2003 to build the code or the Application section of the project's property pages if you're using Visual Studio 2005). Compiling this assembly will give you code that you can call from SQL Server, but there's more work to do first.

Note the use of the SqlFunction *attribute* in angle brackets before each function declaration. Such attributes provide metadata to SQL Server. In this case, the SqlFunction attribute tells SQL Server to use the functions as user-defined functions, and the inclusion of the DataAccessKind.None value indicates that the function doesn't call back to the SQL Server database for any data. SQL Server can optimize the way it calls the function, knowing that it won't need to supply additional data.

COMPILING .NET CODE

To try any of the examples in this chapter, you'll need to be able to compile .NET code. There are two basic ways you can go about this.

The easiest solution is to use Visual Studio, Microsoft's integrated development environment (IDE) for .NET applications. Visual Studio comes in a variety of editions, from low-cost hobbyist versions through expensive versions aimed at the enterprise market. You can get more details about Visual Studio by visiting http://msdn.microsoft.com/vstudio/.

Alternatively, you can download the latest free .NET Framework Software Development Kit (SDK) from http://msdn.microsoft.com/netframework/ and use any text editor to create your source code files. The .NET Framework SDK includes tools for compiling .NET code as well as the entire .NET Framework class library. This is a superset of the .NET runtime, which is installed with SQL Server. If you decide to go this route, you should also check out the free SharpDevelop IDE, which can make developing .NET code much easier than writing it in a text editor. You can find SharpDevelop at www.icsharpcode.net/OpenSource/SD/.

The next step is to tell SQL Server that these functions exist and that it's allowed to call them. SQL Server won't execute code in arbitrary .NET assemblies, as a security measure. Starting with SQL Server 2005, T-SQL extensions handle this task. First you need to register the assembly, using the `CREATE ASSEMBLY` statement:

```
CREATE ASSEMBLY Conversions
FROM 'C:\Conversions\bin\Conversions.dll'
```

Registering the assembly makes the assembly available to SQL Server but doesn't expose any of the assembly's contents. In the case of user-defined functions, you need to call the `CREATE FUNCTION` statement once for each function in the assembly:

```
CREATE FUNCTION PoundsToKg(@Pounds FLOAT)
RETURNS FLOAT
AS EXTERNAL NAME Conversions.[Conversions.Mass].PoundsToKg
GO
CREATE FUNCTION KgToPounds(@Kilograms FLOAT)
RETURNS FLOAT
AS EXTERNAL NAME Conversions.[Conversions.Mass].KgToPounds
GO
```

The `CREATE FUNCTION` statement associates the CLR functions with SQL Server functions. The SQL Server functions don't have to have the same name as the CLR functions they call, although in this case they do. The `EXTERNAL NAME` clause specifies which function to use; it's in the format *`Assembly.Class.Method`*. The *`Assembly`* here is the name registered with the *`CREATE ASSEMBLY`* statement, and the *`Class`* is the full class including any namespace information (`Conversions.Mass` in this example).

TIP **If you need to get rid of a CLR function or assembly, you can use the corresponding `DROP FUNCTION` and `DROP ASSEMBLY` statements.**

All that remains is to call the functions. To do so, you use the same syntax you'd use for user-defined functions in T-SQL, always prefixing the function name with the owner name. Here's an example:

```
SELECT dbo.PoundsToKg(50), dbo.KgToPounds(40)
```

Figure 19.3 shows the result of executing this statement in SQL Server Management Studio.

FIGURE 19.3
Calling CLR user-defined functions

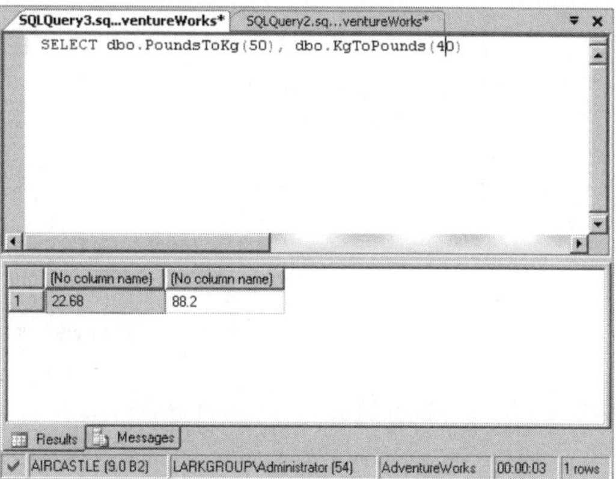

As you can see, the integration of the CLR with SQL Server is tight enough that you can't tell, simply by reading the SQL statement, whether the function is written in T-SQL or some CLR language.

Of course, implementing these simple conversion functions in Visual Basic, while a good demonstration of how to hook everything up, doesn't make a lot of sense. SQL Server is capable of doing multiplication itself, and implementing these functions in T-SQL would involve less overhead. But you can do many things with the .NET languages that are difficult or impossible in T-SQL. Here are a few reasons you might call .NET code from SQL Server:

- To work with system resources such as the event log, WMI, or performance counters that are difficult to access from T-SQL
- To use advanced .NET Framework classes such as the cryptographic functions
- To perform complex mathematical calculations, possibly using a third-party math library
- To move SQL Server data to web pages or disk files in a format that SQL Server itself has difficulty creating

WRITING TABLE-VALUED USER-DEFINED FUNCTIONS

A table-valued user-defined function returns an entire table rather than a single scalar value. To create such a function in a .NET language, you must implement the `IEnumerable` interface. This allows you a great deal of flexibility: all .NET arrays and collections implement this interface, so you can return practically anything to SQL Server as a table-valued user-defined function. You must decorate the function with an attribute that specifies a second procedure that SQL Server can use to translate individual rows into SQL Server data types, as you'll see in Listing 19.1.

To demonstrate the process of creating a table-valued user-defined function, we've created one to return a conversion table from feet to meters. Listing 19.1 includes all the code for the class in the Visual Basic class library.

LISTING 19.1: `Conversions.Length` Class

```
Imports Microsoft.SqlServer.Server
Imports System.Data.Sql
Imports System.Data.SqlTypes
Imports System.Runtime.InteropServices

Namespace Conversions

    Public Class Equivalent
        Public Feet As Double
        Public Meters As Double
    End Class

    Public Class Length

        ' Return a table of twenty rows, two columns
        ' First column is length in feet, second
        ' is equivalent in meters.
        <SqlFunction(FillRowMethodName:="FillRow")> _
```

```
        Public Shared Function InitMethod() As IEnumerable
            Dim LengthArray(19) As Equivalent
            For i As Integer = 0 To 19
                LengthArray(i) = New Equivalent
                LengthArray(i).Feet = 3.28 * CDbl(i)
                LengthArray(i).Meters = CDbl(i)
            Next
            Return LengthArray
        End Function

        ' Interpret one row from the returned array into SQL columns
        Public Shared Sub FillRow(ByVal obj As Object, _
         <Out()> ByRef Feet As SqlDouble, _
         <Out()> ByRef Meters As SqlDouble)
            Dim LengthEntry As Equivalent
            LengthEntry = CType(obj, Equivalent)
            Feet = LengthEntry.Feet
            Meters = LengthEntry.Meters
        End Sub
    End Class
```

End NamespaceTo use this function, you must first compile the assembly and register it with the CREATE ASSEMBLY statement. Then you use CREATE FUNCTION to register the function itself:

```
CREATE FUNCTION BuildLengthTable()
RETURNS TABLE
(Feet FLOAT, Meters FLOAT)
AS
EXTERNAL NAME Conversions.[Conversions.Length].InitMethod
```

In this case, CREATE FUNCTION must include a description of the table. After you register the function, you can call it like any other table-valued user-defined function. For example, you can select all the data from the function:

```
SELECT * FROM dbo.BuildLengthTable()
```

Figure 19.4 shows the result.

Writing CLR Stored Procedures

CLR stored procedures are very similar to CLR functions but with a few more sophisticated capabilities:

- CLR stored procedures can have a return value.
- CLR stored procedures can have output parameters.
- CLR stored procedures can return messages to the client.
- CLR stored procedures can invoke DDL and DML statements.

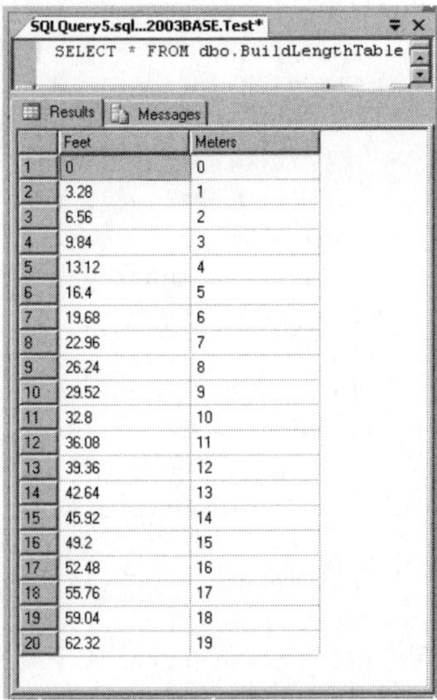

	Feet	Meters
1	0	0
2	3.28	1
3	6.56	2
4	9.84	3
5	13.12	4
6	16.4	5
7	19.68	6
8	22.96	7
9	26.24	8
10	29.52	9
11	32.8	10
12	36.08	11
13	39.36	12
14	42.64	13
15	45.92	14
16	49.2	15
17	52.48	16
18	55.76	17
19	59.04	18
20	62.32	19

FIGURE 19.4
Calling a CLR table-valued user-defined function

Messages and invoking statements depend on the `SqlClient` namespace. We'll discuss these capabilities in the section "Using the *Sql* Namespace" later in the chapter. In this section, we'll demonstrate the use of return values and output parameters. To create a stored procedure in a .NET language, you write a static function and decorate it with the `SqlProcedure` attribute:

```
Imports System.Data.Sql
Imports Microsoft.SqlServer.Server

Namespace Conversions
    Public Class Temperature
        <SqlProcedure()> _
        Public Shared Function KelvinToCelsius( _
         ByVal Kelvin As Double, ByRef Celsius As Double) As Integer
            ' Temperature must be above OK
            If Kelvin <= 0 Then
                Return 0
            Else
                Celsius = Kelvin - 273.15
                Return 1
            End If
        End Function
    End Class
End Namespace
```

Registering a stored procedure uses the familiar `CREATE PROCEDURE` statement with the new `EXTERNAL NAME` clause:

```
CREATE PROCEDURE KelvinToCelsius
  @Kelvin FLOAT,
  @Celsius FLOAT OUTPUT
AS EXTERNAL NAME Conversions.[Conversions.Temperature].KelvinToCelsius
```

In this case, the `@Celsius` parameter is treated as an output parameter. The return value of the stored procedure is given by the integer value of the function in the .NET code.

TIP If you're following along with the examples in this chapter and creating all of the code in a single assembly, you'll need to drop and recreate the assembly in SQL Server each time you modify the code.

Writing CLR Triggers

You can also use .NET code to create triggers. The CLR supports both Data Manipulation Language (DML) and Data Definition Language (DDL) triggers. Triggers are represented by static functions with no return type; you can (but aren't required to) apply the `SqlTrigger` attribute to DML triggers only. Triggers can use a special class named `SqlTriggerContext` to obtain the `INSERTED` and `DELETED` tables, determine which columns were modified in an `UPDATE` statement, or get details about DDL operations that fired a trigger.

For example, here's the skeleton of a trigger that determines whether it was called in response to an `INSERT`, `UPDATE`, or `DELETE`, and that knows which columns were updated:

```
Imports System.Data.Sql
Imports System.Data.SqlServer
Imports Microsoft.SqlServer.Server

Namespace Conversions
    Public Class Triggers
        Public Shared Sub TriggerSkeleton()
            ' Retrieve the trigger context
            Dim tc As SqlTriggerContext = _
             SqlContext.GetTriggerContext
            Select Case tc.TriggerAction
                Case TriggerAction.Insert
                    ' INSERT statement
                Case TriggerAction.Delete
                    ' DELETE statement
                Case TriggerAction.Update
                    ' UPDATE statement
                    Dim ColumnsUpdated As Boolean() = _
                     tc.ColumnsUpdated
                    For Each b As Boolean In ColumnsUpdated
                        If b Then
                            ' Corresponding column
                            ' was updated
                        End If
                    Next
            End Select
        End Sub
    End Class
End Namespace
```

The `SqlContext.GetTriggerContext` method is a static method supplied by SQL Server. Your code can call this method to get the context of the trigger that invoked the code. You can then use the properties of the `TriggerContext` object to find out more about the trigger, such as the columns that were updated.

NOTE For this code to work, you need to reference `sqlaccess.dll`, which contains the `System.Data.SqlServer` namespace. This library is installed in the `BINN` subdirectory when you install SQL Server.

To attach this trigger to actions, you use the `CREATE TRIGGER` statement:

```
CREATE TRIGGER TriggerSkeleton
ON MyTable
FOR DELETE, INSERT, UPDATE
AS EXTERNAL NAME Conversions.[Conversions.Triggers].TriggerSkeleton
```

Writing CLR User-Defined Types

Unlike the other CLR objects, which are .NET implementations of familiar SQL Server objects, user-defined types represent something brand new for SQL Server. You can extend the list of SQL Server datatypes by writing your own user-defined type. The code to do so can be involved, but the end result is a new type that you can use alongside int, float, and the other built-in types.

User-defined types are .NET classes subject to some restrictions:

- They must be decorated with the `SqlUserDefinedType` attribute.
- They must be decorated with the `Serializable` attribute.
- They must implement the `INullable` interface.
- They must contain public static `Parse` and `ToString` methods to convert from and to a string representation of the type.
- They must expose data elements as public fields or public properties.

In this section, we'll show you the code for creating and using a simple user-defined type. Listing 19.2 demonstrates how you can declare a complex number type, consisting of a real part and an imaginary part, in Visual Basic code.

LISTING 19.2: Defining the Complex Type

```
Imports System
Imports System.Data.Sql
Imports System.Data.SqlTypes
Imports System.Runtime.Serialization
Imports Microsoft.SqlServer.Server

<Serializable(), _
 SqlUserDefinedTypeAttribute(Format.Native)> _
Public Structure Complex

    Implements INullable
    Private is_Null As Boolean
    Private m_Real As Double
    Private m_Imaginary As Double
```

```
' Track whether this instance is a null
Public ReadOnly Property IsNull() As Boolean _
   Implements INullable.IsNull
    Get
        Return (is_Null)
    End Get
End Property

' Return a string representation
Public Overrides Function ToString() As String
    If Me.IsNull Then
        Return "NULL"
    Else
        Return m_Real & "," & m_Imaginary
    End If
End Function

' Convert string representation to an instance
Public Shared Function Parse(ByVal s As SqlString) _
 As Complex
    If s.IsNull Then
        Return Nothing
    Else

        'Parse input string here to separate out parts
        Dim c As New Complex()
        Dim str As String = Convert.ToString(s)
        Dim parts() As String = str.Split(",")
        c.Real = parts(0)
        c.Imaginary = parts(1)
        Return (c)
    End If
End Function

' Return a null instance
Public Shared ReadOnly Property Null() As Complex
    Get
        Dim c As New Complex
        c.is_Null = True
        Return (c)
    End Get
End Property

' Real part
Public Property Real() As Double
    Get
        Return (m_Real)
    End Get
    Set(ByVal Value As Double)
```

```
            m_Real = Value
        End Set
    End Property

    ' Imaginary part
    Public Property Imaginary() As Double
        Get
            Return (m_Imaginary)
        End Get
        Set(ByVal Value As Double)
            m_Imaginary = Value
        End Set
    End Property

    ' Add this instance to another
    Public Function AddTo( _
     ByVal c As Complex) As Complex
        Dim res As New Complex
        res.Real = m_Real + c.Real
        res.Imaginary = m_Imaginary + _
         c.Imaginary
        Return res
    End Function

End Structure
```

In addition to the required code scaffolding, this type definition also includes an AddTo method. In practice, you'd probably define many different methods in a type like this, but one will suffice to show you the syntax.

Registering a user-defined type is easy; once you register the containing assembly, you call CREATE TYPE. We'll assume that the Complex type is in the Conversions assembly:

```
CREATE TYPE Complex
EXTERNAL NAME Conversions.Complex
```

Note that for types, the external name is the assembly name and the class or structure name.

Once you've registered the type, you can use it just like a built-in type. For example, you can create a table using the type as the datatype for a column:

```
CREATE TABLE ComplexTest
 (ID int IDENTITY(1,1) PRIMARY KEY,
 C Complex)
```

With the table in place, you can insert data. To get a new instance of the Complex type, use the CAST or CONVERT statement to convert the string representation into an instance of the type. These functions both call into the Parse function in your type's code.

```
INSERT INTO ComplexTest(C)
VALUES(CAST('1,1' AS Complex))
GO
```

```
INSERT INTO ComplexTest(C)
VALUES(CAST('-1,-1' AS Complex))
GO
INSERT INTO ComplexTest(C)
VALUES(CAST('0,0' AS Complex))
GO
```

You can also use CAST or CONVERT to get type instances in other SQL statements where they're needed. For example, you could use them in an UPDATE statement to specify new values for the Complex column.

To retrieve data, you could use a simple SELECT statement:

```
SELECT ID, C FROM ComplexTest
GO
```

However, as Figure 19.5 shows, the results may not be what you expect, because this statement tries to return the actual data storage format , which SQL Server can't display.

That's where the ToString method in the class comes in. To get back human-readable details from a user-defined type, specify ToString, as in the following example:

```
SELECT ID, C.ToString() AS Complex
FROM ComplexTest
```

Figure 19.6 shows the results of this statement.

FIGURE 19.5
Raw data from a CLR type

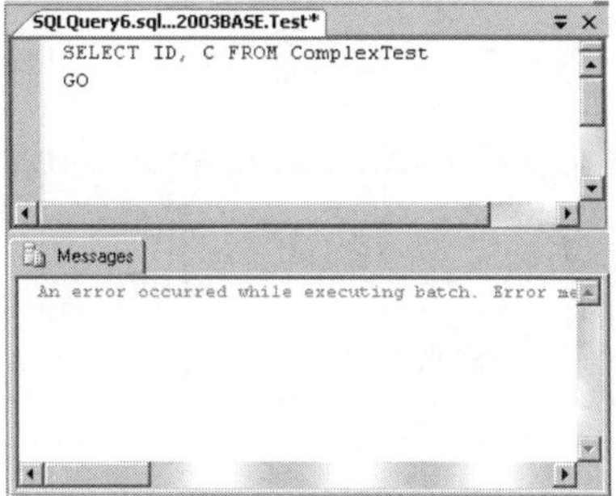

FIGURE 19.6
Formatted data from a CLR type

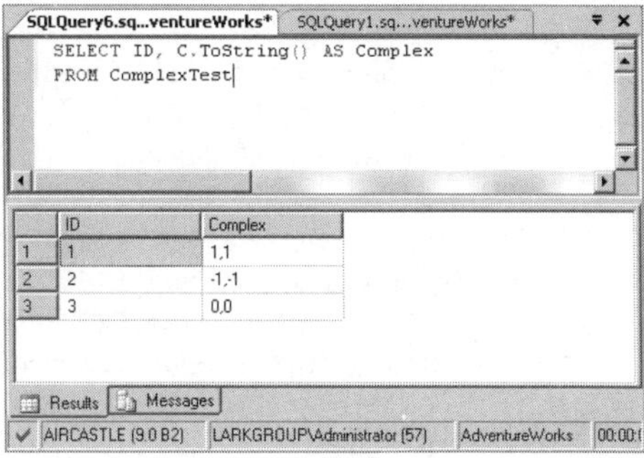

Because you control the ToString method, you can have any representation you like for the CLR type. For example, it would be easy to do the additional string processing to represent the complex types according to the pattern 3i+2j. You do, however, need to remember to change the Parse method to match.

Finally, you can call any public method from the class by appending the method name to a column of the appropriate datatype. With the class as presented, this SQL would add 1,1 to each row in the table:

```
SELECT ID,
C.AddTo(CAST('1,1' AS Complex)).ToString() AS NewComplex
FROM ComplexTest
```

Using the *Sql* Namespace

When you install SQL Server, it includes a .NET assembly containing the System.Data.Sql namespace. You already saw an example of this namespace when we built a CLR trigger; the System.Data.Sql namespace provides the SqlTriggerContext object. This namespace is also known as the *in-process managed provider*. This is a new ADO-NET provider whose task it is to communicate from the CLR back to SQL Server. It doesn't communicate with just any SQL Server (.NET includes the existing System.Data.SqlClient namespace for that purpose). Instead, when you load CLR code into SQL Server (by using CREATE ASSEMBLY), the in-process managed provider lets you connect directly to the server that hosts the code. You can use this provider to retrieve data from the server or to send data to the server.

NOTE For an overview of ADO.NET data providers, see Chapter 20.

Using the In-Process Managed Provider

To show you how the in-process managed provider works, here's a user-defined function that uses data from the server instance that calls the function:

```
Imports System.Data.SqlServer
Imports System.Data.Sql
Imports Microsoft.SqlServer.Server

Namespace AWExtras
    Public Class Production
        <SqlFunction(DataAccess:=DataAccessKind.Read)> _
         Public Shared Function InventoryTotal _
         (ByVal ProductID As Integer) As Double
            ' Create a SqlCommand to the hosting database
            Dim cmd As SqlCommand = SqlContext.GetCommand
            cmd.CommandType = CommandType.Text
            cmd.CommandText = "SELECT SUM(StandardCost*Quantity) " & _
             "AS InventoryValue FROM Production.Product " & _
             "INNER JOIN Production.ProductInventory " & _
             "ON Production.Product.ProductID = " & _
             "Production.ProductInventory.ProductID() " & _
             "WHERE(Production.Product.ProductID = " & _
            CStr(ProductID) & ") " & _
             "GROUP BY Production.Product.ProductID"
```

```
            ' Execute the command and return the result
            InventoryTotal = CDbl(cmd.ExecuteScalar())
        End Function
    End Class
End Namespace
```

This code starts its work with the `SqlContext` object, which you can think of as a `SqlConnection` that points directly back to the hosting database. In this case, we've used the `SqlContext` to acquire a `SqlCommand`, which then executes a SELECT statement to compute the aggregate total of inventory for a specific product. The results of the statement are used as the return value of the function. Here are the SQL statements to register the assembly and the function:

```
CREATE ASSEMBLY AWExtras
FROM 'C:\AWExtras\bin\AWExtras.dll'
GO
CREATE FUNCTION InventoryTotal(@ProductID int)
RETURNS float
AS EXTERNAL NAME AWExtras.[AWExtras.Production].InventoryTotal
GO
```

After you register the function, you can execute such statements as `SELECT dbo.InventoryTotal(775)`, which returns the total inventory value for product number 775 in the AdventureWorks database.

Using the *SqlPipe* Object

The second important object in the `Sql` namespace is the `SqlPipe` object. This is the key to sending data back to SQL Server directly from your CLR code (rather than as the return value for a function). You can think of the `SqlPipe` object as analogous to the ASP.NET `Response` object. Anything you drop in the `SqlPipe` comes out the other end in the calling T-SQL code. For example, when you're writing a CLR stored procedure, you can use a `SqlPipe` object to transmit results back to the server. Here's an example that you could also include within the Production class:

```
<SqlProcedure()> _
Public Shared Sub SuggestProductNames()
    ' Generate some random names
    Dim a() As String = {"Shiny ", "Red ", "Titanium "}
    Dim b() As String = {"Rotary ", "Sonic ", "Polished "}
    Dim c() As String = {"Wheels", "Calipers", "Frame"}
    Dim Products(5) As String
    For i As Integer = 0 To 4
        Products(i) = a(Int(Rnd(1) * 3)) & _
         b(Int(Rnd(1) * 3)) & c(Int(Rnd(1) * 3))
    Next
    ' Get the pipe back to the hosting database
    Dim sp As SqlPipe = SqlContext.GetPipe
    ' Convert the data into rows and send it back
    ' First define the column schema
    Dim colschema() As SqlMetaData = _
    {New SqlMetaData("SuggestedName", _
     SqlDbType.NVarChar, 50)}
    ' Then define the table schema
```

```
        Dim tableschema As SqlMetaData = _
         New SqlMetaData("row", SqlDbType.Row, colschema)
        Dim newrec As SqlDataRecord
        ' Start sending records
        newrec = SqlContext.GetConnection.CreateRecord(tableschema)
        newrec.SetSqlString(0, Products(0))
        sp.SendResultsStart(newrec, True)
        ' Send the remaining records
        For i As Integer = 1 To 4
            newrec = SqlContext.GetConnection.CreateRecord(tableschema)
            newrec.SetSqlString(0, Products(i))
            sp.SendResultsRow(newrec)
        Next
        ' Tell the server we're done
        sp.SendResultsEnd()
    End Sub
```

This code first uses string-processing and random number functions to make up random product names. Then it gets the `SqlPipe` object from the `SqlContext` object, giving the code a pipeline back to the calling database. The remaining code constructs a synthetic table and sends it back. The `SqlMetaData` objects are used to define the column and row structure of the table. The next step is to use the `CreateRecord` method to create rows, one at a time, and send them back down the `SqlPipe`. In this example, we're using the `SendResultsStart`, `SendResultsRow`, and `SendResultsEnd` method of the `SqlPipe` to send a result set back over the pipe, one row at a time. Figure 19.7 shows the result.

The `SqlPipe` class also has a number of other methods available. The most useful is the `Send` method, which can accept a `SqlDataReader`, an object that implements `ISqlRecord`, a `SqlError` object, or a simple string. This lets you send back result sets, errors, or messages to the calling code.

FIGURE 19.7
Result set created in CLR code

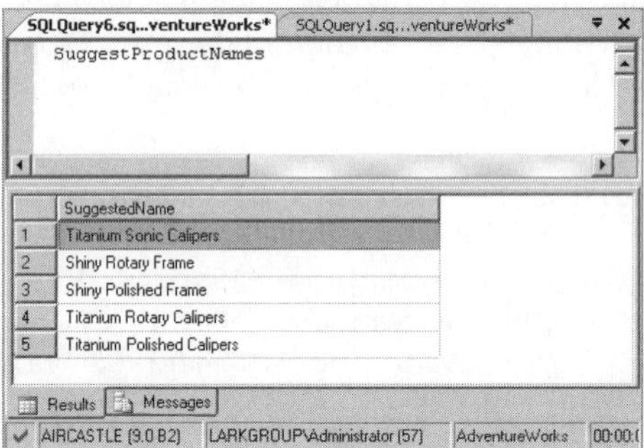

Summary

In this chapter, you learned how SQL Server 2005 tightly interacts with the .NET Common Language Runtime. After a rundown of the CLR architecture, we showed you how to create objects such as user-defined functions, triggers, stored procedures, and datatypes using the CLR and .NET languages. You also learned about the `System.Data.Sql` namespace and the objects it contains to help integrate .NET and SQL Server. These capabilities open new horizons for SQL Server development.

In the next chapter, we'll look at another aspect of SQL Server and .NET: using ADO.NET to retrieve and manipulate SQL Server data from an external .NET application.

Chapter 20

ADO.NET and SQL Server

In most applications involving SQL Server, not all of the development is done on the server itself. This is the essence of client-server computing: Work is partitioned between a central server and distributed clients. In order to view and modify server-side data from a client application, you use a client data access library.

Over the years, Microsoft has released a number of client data access libraries that can use SQL Server data, including DB-Lib, Data Access Objects (DAO), Remote Data Objects (RDO), and ActiveX Data Objects (ADO). Although all of these libraries are still in use, they're no longer undergoing active development. Instead, Microsoft recommends that all new client applications use ADO.NET to interact with the server.

NOTE ADO.NET is not an acronym; it's just the name of the technology.

ADO.NET is the only client data access library that we're going to cover in this book. Even if you've used another library for that purpose in the past, you should consider migrating to ADO.NET (which requires migrating your client code to a .NET language) to take advantage of current advances in the state of the art. In this chapter, we'll start by describing the ADO.NET object model and then look at what you can do with ADO.NET.

NOTE There's much more to ADO.NET than we can cover here. For a more in-depth look, see *Mastering C# Database Programming* by Jason Price (Sybex, 2003) or *Mastering Visual Basic .NET Database Programming* by Evangelos Petroutsos and Asli Bilgin (Sybex, 2003).

ADO.NET Namespaces and Classes

ADO.NET consists of dozens of classes spread over several .NET namespaces. For our purposes, three of these namespaces are important:

System.Data This namespace contains classes that represent data in memory. These classes are independent of the source of the data. That is, you use the same classes whether the data comes from SQL Server, Access, or an XML file. The most important of these classes is the `DataSet`.

System.Data.SqlClient This namespace contains classes that connect directly to SQL Server. These classes act directly on data in a SQL Server database and server to hook the `System.Data` classes up to a SQL Server database.

System.Data.SqlTypes This namespace contains classes whose scope and semantics match those of the native SQL Server datatypes. For example, any value in a SQL Server money column can be represented by an instance of the `System.Data.SqlTypes.SqlMoney` class.

Figure 20.1 shows schematically how these namespaces and some of their classes fit together.

FIGURE 20.1
ADO.NET objects

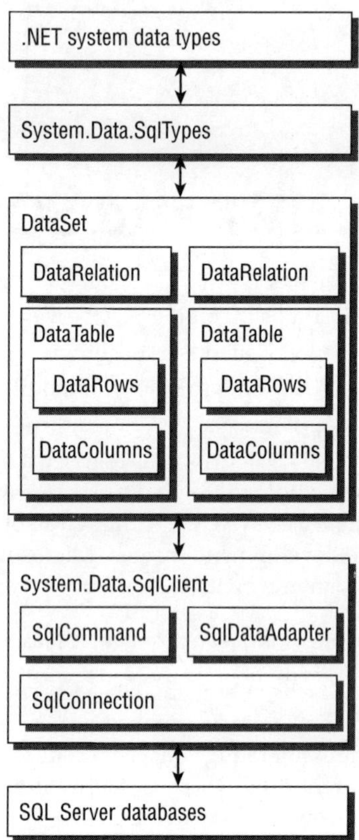

System.Data.SqlClient is an example of an ADO.NET *data provider*. Other data providers provide access to other types of data. For example, System.Data.OracleClient works with Oracle databases, and System.Data.OleDb works with other OLE DB data sources. We won't discuss these other providers, but their classes work in an analogous fashion to those in the SqlClient namespace; so, the knowledge you gain from working with SQL Server will help you use these other namespaces when you need them.

Understanding *DataSets*

The key class in the System.Data namespace is the DataSet. The easiest way to think of this class is that it can represent an entire relational database in memory. A DataSet can contain multiple DataTable objects, and the relations between these DataTable objects can be specified by DataRelation objects. Other objects allow you to enforce unique constraints and foreign key constraints between DataTable objects.

Within a DataTable, you can also drill down to individual DataRow objects. The DataRow object is the lowest level of detail, giving access to data stored in the DataSet. Alternatively, you can use DataColumn objects to retrieve column-level metadata about a DataTable.

DataSets are designed for use in disconnected scenarios. That is, their data remains valid even if the connection to the original database is severed. You can also serialize (that is, convert) a DataSet (and all of its constituent objects) to XML for easy transport between components. It's possible to create complex data movement scenarios such as this one:

1. Fill a `DataSet` on a client machine by connecting to SQL Server.
2. Disconnect the `DataSet` from the SQL Server.
3. Use XML to send the `DataSet` to another client machine across the Internet.
4. Edit the data in the `DataSet` on the second client machine.
5. Send the `DataSet`, again as XML, back to the original client.
6. Reconnect to the database.
7. Commit the changes that were made while the `DataSet` was disconnected.

Understanding the SQL Server Data Provider

The SQL Server data provider includes three key classes that work directly with SQL Server:

SqlConnection This class represents a connection to a single SQL Server. `SqlConnection` implements connection pooling, which helps keep server load under control while making connections available quickly to clients.

SqlCommand This class represents a T-SQL statement or a stored procedure. You can use `SqlCommand` to manipulate data directly in the SQL Server database.

SqlDataAdapter This class provides a two-way pipeline between the database and a `DataSet`. `SqlDataAdapter` can both retrieve data from the database and commit changes back to the database.

Understanding SQL Types

SQL Server datatypes don't necessarily match the native .NET datatypes. For example, the Money datatype in SQL Server takes on exact values in the range from –922,337,203,685,477.5808 to +922,337,203,685,477.5807. Representing this exact range in a .NET system type is impossible; nothing matches exactly. But the `System.Data.SqlTypes.SqlMoney` class takes on this exact range of values, which means you can easily use `SqlMoney` to move values back and forth to a database.

There's another difference between the SQL types and the .NET system datatypes. The SQL types are all nullable, so they can also represent null values in your database. .NET system types, such as `Int32` or `Double`, can't take null as a value.

The SQL types are also equipped with a rich set of mathematical and conversion functions to allow you to move data from them to the .NET system datatypes.

Making and Managing Connections

The first step to working with SQL Server from .NET code is to connect to the database. To do this, you need to instantiate a `SqlConnection` object and then call its Open method.

Building Connection Strings

The easiest way to create a connection to a SQL Server database using ADO.NET is to instantiate a `SqlConnection` object using a constructor that takes a connection string. Listing 20.1 shows how this is done.

COMPILING .NET CODE

The code examples in this chapter use the C# language, which was introduced by Microsoft in 2002 as part of the original .NET release. Even if you don't know C#, its similarities to C, C++, and Java make it pretty easy for most developers to read.

We haven't used Visual Studio .NET for most of our examples, so you won't need to have a copy of that tool to work with them. Instead, you can download the free .NET Framework SDK from `http://msdn.microsoft.com/netframework/`. The SDK includes the entire framework as well as command-line compilers for both C# and Visual Basic .NET.

To use the C# command-line compiler, select Start ➢ Programs ➢ Microsoft .NET Framework SDK ➢ .NET Framework SDK Command Prompt. Then call the csc compiler, followed by the name of the source file. For example, to compile the example in the file `20-1.cs`, you'd enter this command line:

```
csc 20-1.cs
```

LISTING 20.1: Connecting to a SQL Server Database

```
using System;
using System.Text;
using System.Data;
using System.Data.SqlClient;

namespace Chapter_20
{
    class _20_1
    {
        static void Main(string[] args)
        {
            string connStr =
                "Initial Catalog=AdventureWorks;" +
                "Data Source=(local);Integrated Security=SSPI;";
            SqlConnection con =
                new SqlConnection(connStr);
            con.Open();
            Console.WriteLine(con.ConnectionString);
            Console.ReadLine();
        }
    }
}
```

As you can see, a `SqlConnection` connection string is a set of *keyword=value* pairs separated by semicolons. Table 20.1 shows the keywords you can use in a `SqlConnection` connection string.

TABLE 20.1: `SqlConnection` connection string keywords

KEYWORD	DESCRIPTION
`Application Name`	Application name supplied to SQL Server. Defaults to .NET SqlClient Data Provider.
`AttachDBFileName` or `Initial File Name`	Name of a file to attach as a database. You must also include the `Database` keyword in the connection string.
`Connect Timeout` or `Connection Timeout`	Number of seconds to wait for a connection. Defaults to 15 seconds.
`Connection Lifetime`	Number of seconds that a connection can last in the pool.
`Connection Reset`	Determines whether connections are reset when removed from the pool. Setting this to `false` prevents extra round trips when working with SQL Server 7.0.
`Current Language`	SQL Server language to use.
`Data Source` or `Server` or `Address` or `Addr` or `Network Address`	The name or IP address of the SQL Server.
`Encrypt`	If set to `yes` or `true`, uses SSL encryption for all data between the client and the server. Defaults to `false`.
`Enlist`	If set to `true` (the default), connections are automatically enlisted in the transaction context of the calling thread.
`Initial Catalog` or `Database`	Name of the database to use.
`Integrated Security` or `Trusted Connection`	If set to true, yes, or sspi, uses integrated Windows authentication. If set to false or no, uses SQL Server accounts for authentication, which is the default.
`Max Pool Size`	Maximum number of connections that will be saved in the pool. The default is 100.
`Min Pool Size`	Minimum number of connections to maintain in the pool. The default is 0.
`Network Library` or `Net`	Name of the network library to use.
`Packet Size`	Size (in bytes) of packets used to communicate with SQL Server. Defaults to 8192.
`Password` or `Pwd`	Password to use when connecting.
`Persist Security Info`	If set to `true`, saves passwords in the connection string after connecting. Defaults to `false`.

TABLE 20.1: `SqlConnection` connection string keywords *(CONTINUED)*

KEYWORD	DESCRIPTION
`Pooling`	Setting this to `false` turns off connection pooling. Defaults to `true`.
`User ID`	SQL Server user account to use when connecting.
`Workstation ID`	Name of the workstation to send to SQL Server. Defaults to the local computer name.

Handling Connection Pooling

Connecting to a database is a relatively expensive operation. SQL Server must verify the security context of the connection, allocate a thread for it to operate in, and so on. To speed up operations, the `SqlClient` namespace implements *connection pooling*. When you tell your .NET application that you're finished with a `SqlConnection` object, .NET doesn't immediately tear it down and release the resources. Instead, it saves the connection in a pool for future use. When you ask for another connection, one can be returned much more quickly from the pool than it could be built from scratch.

The SQL Server data provider maintains one connection pool for each unique connection string in the application. When you open the first connection for a particular connection string, the provider creates the connection pool. If you've specified a minimum pool size, the provider also instantiates that many connections. Each time you open a connection, the provider checks to see whether a connection is available in the pool. If so, that connection is returned immediately. If not, and the pool contains fewer than the maximum number of connections, the provider creates a new connection. If the pool is full, and no connections are available, requests for new connections are queued until one becomes available.

When connections reach their specified lifetime, the data provider removes them from the connection pool. Invalid connections are also removed (for example, a connection to a server which has since been removed from the network), but the provider won't do this until it discovers, by trying to connect, that the connection is invalid.

TIP To make connection pooling work efficiently, you should return connections to the pool as soon as you're finished with them. You can do this by calling the `Close` or `Dispose` method of the `SqlConnection` object.

Using the *SqlCommand* Object

The `SqlCommand` object represents a single T-SQL statement or stored procedure. Depending on the underlying statement, you may or may not get results back from the `SqlCommand` object. The `SqlCommand` object includes full support for both input and output parameters.

Executing a Query

Listing 20.2 shows code to execute a query in a SQL Server database using the `SqlCommand` object.

LISTING 20.2: Using the SqlCommand Object

```
using System;
using System.Text;
using System.Data;
using System.Data.SqlClient;

namespace Chapter_20
{
    class _20_2
    {
        static void Main(string[] args)
        {
            string connStr =
                "Initial Catalog=AdventureWorks;" +
                "Data Source=(local);Integrated Security=SSPI;";
            SqlConnection con =
                new SqlConnection(connStr);
            SqlCommand cmd =
                new SqlCommand("UPDATE Person.Contact SET " +
                "MiddleName = 'Alfred' WHERE ContactID = 1", con);
            con.Open();
            cmd.ExecuteNonQuery();
            con.Close();
        }
    }
}
```

This particular piece of code uses a constructor for the SqlCommand object that takes two parameters: a SQL string to be executed and a connection over which to execute the command. To execute the command, you have to first open the associated connection and then call the ExecuteNonQuery method of the SqlCommand object. After that, the code closes the connection to return it to the pool.

Although there's no indication in the code that the SQL statement worked, you can verify its effects by using SQL Server Management Studio to inspect the table, as shown in Figure 20.2.

Using Parameters

You can also use a SqlCommand object to execute a SQL Server stored procedure. Here the use of the SqlParameter object is critical. This object represents a single parameter to a stored procedure and can be used for both input and output parameters. For example, suppose you create the following stored procedure in the AdventureWorks database:

```
CREATE PROC procGetName
  @ContactID int,
  @Name nvarchar(100) OUTPUT
AS
  SELECT @Name = FirstName + ' ' + LastName
  FROM Person.Contact
  WHERE ContactID = @ContactID
```

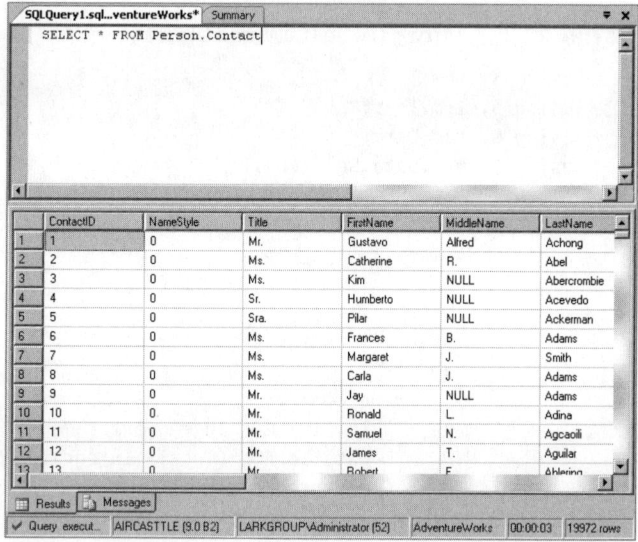

FIGURE 20.2
Data altered by a SqlCommand object

You can then use the code shown in Listing 20.3 to execute the stored procedure and display the contents of the output parameter.

LISTING 20.3: Using a SqlCommand with Parameters

```
using System;
using System.Text;
using System.Data;
using System.Data.SqlClient;

namespace Chapter_20
{
    class _20_3
    {
        static void Main(string[] args)
        {
            string connStr =
                "Initial Catalog=AdventureWorks;" +
                "Data Source=(local);Integrated Security=SSPI;";
            SqlConnection con =
                new SqlConnection(connStr);
            SqlCommand cmd =
                new SqlCommand();
            cmd.Connection = con;
            cmd.CommandText = "procGetName";
            cmd.CommandType = CommandType.StoredProcedure;
            SqlParameter par=
                new SqlParameter("@ContactID", SqlDbType.Int);
            par.Value = 16;
```

```
            cmd.Parameters.Add(par);
            par =
                new SqlParameter("@Name", SqlDbType.NVarChar, 100);
            par.Direction = ParameterDirection.Output;
            cmd.Parameters.Add(par);
            con.Open();
            cmd.ExecuteNonQuery();
            Console.WriteLine(cmd.Parameters["@Name"].Value);
            con.Close();
            Console.ReadLine();
        }
    }
}
```

This code defines two `SqlParameter` objects, each constructed by specifying its name and datatype (and, in the case of the one with a variable size, its size). Note that the names match the names of the parameters in the stored procedure. The code sets the `Value` property of the input parameter and uses the `Direction` property to mark the other object as being an output parameter. After you execute the query, the returned value can be read from the `Value` property of the output parameter.

Retrieving a Single Value

The `SqlCommand` object also supplies a method designed to simplify retrieving a single value from the database. The `ExecuteScalar` method returns the value from the first column of the first row of any result set constructed by the query. Listing 20.4 shows an example.

LISTING 20.4: Using the `ExecuteScalar` Method

```
using System;
using System.Text;
using System.Data;
using System.Data.SqlClient;

namespace Chapter_20
{
    class _20_4
    {
        static void Main(string[] args)
        {
            string connStr =
                "Initial Catalog=AdventureWorks;" +
                "Data Source=(local);Integrated Security=SSPI;";
            SqlConnection con =
                new SqlConnection(connStr);
            SqlCommand cmd =
                new SqlCommand("SELECT FirstName FROM "
                + "Person.Contact WHERE ContactID = 16");
            cmd.Connection = con;
```

```
                con.Open();
                string FirstName = cmd.ExecuteScalar().ToString();
                Console.WriteLine(FirstName.ToString());
                con.Close();
                Console.ReadLine();
            }
        }
    }
```

Note that anything beyond the first column and first row of results is discarded when you use this method.

Using the *SqlDataReader* Object

The SqlCommand object is useful for executing queries and stored procedures, but it falls short when you want to work with all the data in a table. For that purpose, you can turn to the SqlDataReader object. The SqlDataReader object provides what is sometimes called a *firehose cursor* from a SQL Server statement that returns data. This is a set of records that is optimized for quick retrieval. The data returned by the SqlDataReader can be read only once, from the start of the results to the end, and is always read-only.

NOTE If you're familiar with classic ADO, the SqlDataReader is the equivalent of a forward-only, read-only Recordset.

Opening a *SqlDataReader*

The first step in using the SqlDataReader is to open it. You can't instantiate a SqlDataReader directly using the new keyword. Instead, you must use the ExecuteReader method of a SqlCommand object, as shown in Listing 20.5.

LISTING 20.5: Opening a SqlDataReader

```
using System;
using System.Text;
using System.Data;
using System.Data.SqlClient;

namespace Chapter_20
{
    class _20_5
    {
        static void Main(string[] args)
        {
            string connStr =
                "Initial Catalog=AdventureWorks;" +
                "Data Source=(local);Integrated Security=SSPI;";
            SqlConnection con =
                new SqlConnection(connStr);
```

```
            SqlCommand cmd =
                new SqlCommand("SELECT * FROM Person.Contact");
            cmd.Connection = con;
            con.Open();
            SqlDataReader dr = cmd.ExecuteReader();
            Console.WriteLine(dr.HasRows);
            dr.Close();
            con.Close();
            Console.ReadLine();
        }
    }
}
```

Assuming the text of the `SqlCommand` object is a statement that returns rows, you can use the `ExecuteReader` method to take those rows and present them to the `SqlDataReader`. As you'll see in the next section, this enables the `SqlDataReader` to retrieve the specified data. In this case, the code is only calling the `HasRows` property, which returns `true` if the `SqlDataReader` contains any data.

WARNING With previous versions of SQL Server, the `SqlDataReader` was a blocking object; while you had one open, you couldn't perform any other operations that used the underlying `SqlConnection` object. With SQL Server 2005, a new feature called Multiple Active RecordSets (MARS) removes this limitation. It's still a good idea to close objects that you're not using so their resources can be released.

Retrieving Data

Retrieving data from a `SqlDataReader` is a two-step process (after you've instantiated the object). First, you call the `Read` method to load the next row into the `SqlDataReader`. Then, you call one or more of the `Get` methods to return data. Listing 20.6 shows an example.

LISTING 20.6: Retrieving Data with a `SqlDataReader`

```
using System;
using System.Text;
using System.Data;
using System.Data.SqlClient;

namespace Chapter_20
{
    class _20_6
    {
        static void Main(string[] args)
        {
            string connStr =
                "Initial Catalog=AdventureWorks;" +
                "Data Source=(local);Integrated Security=SSPI;";
            SqlConnection con =
                new SqlConnection(connStr);
```

```
                SqlCommand cmd =
                    new SqlCommand("SELECT * FROM Person.Contact");
                cmd.Connection = con;
                con.Open();
                SqlDataReader dr = cmd.ExecuteReader();
                dr.Read();
                Console.WriteLine(dr.GetString(5));
                while (dr.Read())
                {
                    Console.WriteLine(dr.GetString(5));
                }
                dr.Close();
                con.Close();
                Console.ReadLine();
            }
        }
    }
```

The Read method returns true as long as there is data in the SqlDataReader after the read operation is performed. With data loaded into the SqlDataReader, this example uses the GetString method to get some of the data back out. The numeric parameter to this method is the zero-based column number containing the data; in the case of the Person.Contact table, the sixth column contains the last name of the contact. Figure 20.3 shows the tail end of the data returned by running this procedure.

FIGURE 20.3
Data from a SqlDataReader

GetString is only one of many methods for returning data contained in a SqlDataReader object. Table 20.2 shows the various methods you can choose from for this purpose.

TABLE 20.2: Data retrieval methods of SqlDataReader

METHOD	RETURNS
GetBoolean	Boolean value
GetByte	Single byte
GetBytes	Stream of bytes, optionally starting at an offset

TABLE 20.2: Data retrieval methods of SqlDataReader *(CONTINUED)*

METHOD	RETURNS
GetChar	Single character
GetChars	Array of characters, optionally starting at an offset
GetDateTime	DateTime object
GetDecimal	Decimal object
GetDouble	Double value
GetFloat	Float value
GetGuid	GUID value
GetInt16	16-bit integer value
GetInt32	32-bit integer value
GetInt64	64-bit integer value
GetSqlBinary	SqlBinary object
GetSqlBoolean	SqlBoolean object
GetSqlByte	SqlByte object
GetSqlDateTime	SqlDateTime object
GetSqlDouble	SqlDouble object
GetSqlGuid	SqlGuid object
GetSqlInt16	SqlInt16 object
GetSqlInt32	SqlInt32 object
GetSqlInt64	SqlInt64 object
GetSqlMoney	SqlMoney object
GetSqlSingle	SqlSingle object
GetSqlString	SqlString object
GetSqlValue	Object representing a SQL variant
GetString	String value
GetValue	Data in its native format

Note that for almost all these datatypes, you can choose between methods that automatically perform the conversion to .NET system types (such as `GetInt16`) and methods that return classes from the `System.Data.SqlTypes` namespace (such as `GetSqlInt16`). If you're retrieving the data to use it with other SQL Server procedures, you'll probably want to keep it in the native SQL type; otherwise, the automatic conversion is useful.

Using the *DataSet* and *SqlDataAdapter* Objects

A `SqlDataReader` is useful (and fast) when you just want to read data from a SQL Server database, but it doesn't let you modify any of the data you read. For that purpose, you need to work with the `SqlDataAdapter` and `DataSet` objects. The overall process usually goes like this:

1. Create a `SqlDataAdapter` that can work with the data of interest.
2. Use the Fill method of the `SqlDataAdapter` to load data into the `DataSet`.
3. Add, edit, or delete data in the `DataSet`.
4. Use the `Update` method of the `SqlDataAdapter` to send changes back to the database.

As you can see, changing data in the `DataSet` doesn't make any changes to the database. The `DataSet` itself is a generic, in-memory, disconnected representation of data. Only when you use the `SqlDataAdapter` (or another data adapter from one of the other namespaces) does the `DataSet` interact with stored data.

Setting Up the *SqlDataAdapter*

The `SqlDataAdapter` class is responsible for moving data from the database to a `DataSet` and then moving changes back to the database. But it doesn't do this by magic. Instead, you must set four properties of the `SqlDataAdapter` to configure it:

SelectCommand This property specifies a `SqlCommand` object that can be used to retrieve records from the database.

DeleteCommand This property specifies a `SqlCommand` object that can be used to delete records from the database.

InsertCommand This property specifies a `SqlCommand` object that can be used to add records to the database.

UpdateCommand This property specifies a `SqlCommand` object that can be used to update existing records in the database.

Listing 20.7 shows how you can set up a `SqlDataAdapter` to deal with a single database table.

LISTING 20.7: Setting Up a `SqlDataAdapter`

```
using System;
using System.Text;
using System.Data;
using System.Data.SqlClient;

namespace Chapter_20
{
```

```
    class _20_7
    {
        static void Main(string[] args)
        {
            string connStr =
                "Initial Catalog=AdventureWorks;" +
                "Data Source=(local);Integrated Security=SSPI;";
            SqlConnection con =
                new SqlConnection(connStr);
            SqlDataAdapter da = new SqlDataAdapter();
            // Set up the SqlDataAdapter
            SqlCommand cmdS = new SqlCommand("SELECT UnitMeasureCode, " +
                "Name FROM Production.UnitMeasure", con);
            da.SelectCommand = cmdS;
            SqlCommand cmdI = new SqlCommand("INSERT INTO " +
                "Production.UnitMeasure(UnitMeasureCode, Name) " +
                "VALUES (@UnitMeasureCode, @Name)", con);
            cmdI.Parameters.Add(new SqlParameter("@UnitMeasureCode",
                SqlDbType.NChar, 3, "UnitMeasureCode"));
            cmdI.Parameters.Add(new SqlParameter("@Name",
                SqlDbType.NVarChar, 50, "Name"));
            da.InsertCommand = cmdI;
            SqlCommand cmdU = new SqlCommand("UPDATE " +
                "Production.UnitMeasure SET UnitMeasureCode = " +
                "@UnitMeasureCode, Name = @Name WHERE " +
                "UnitMeasureCode = @Original_UnitMeasureCode", con);
            cmdU.Parameters.Add(new SqlParameter("@UnitMeasureCode",
                SqlDbType.NChar, 3, "UnitMeasureCode"));
            cmdU.Parameters.Add(new SqlParameter("@Name",
                SqlDbType.NVarChar, 50, "Name"));
            cmdU.Parameters.Add(
                new SqlParameter("@Original_UnitMeasureCode",
                SqlDbType.NChar, 3, ParameterDirection.Input,
                false, 0, 0, "UnitMeasureCode",
                DataRowVersion.Original, null));
            da.UpdateCommand = cmdU;
            SqlCommand cmdD = new SqlCommand("DELETE FROM " +
                "Production.UnitMeasure WHERE " +
                "UnitMeasureCode = @UnitMeasureCode", con);
            cmdD.Parameters.Add(new SqlParameter("@UnitMeasureCode",
                SqlDbType.NChar, 3, ParameterDirection.Input,
                false, 0, 0, "UnitMeasureCode",
                DataRowVersion.Original, null));
            da.DeleteCommand = cmdD;
        }
    }
}
```

The important things to note in this code are two new constructors for `SqlParameter` objects that directly tie them to columns in the resulting `DataSet`. The first of these accepts the parameter name, datatype, size, and source column name:

```
cmdu.Parameters.Add(new SqlParameter("@Name",
    SqlDbType.NVarChar, 50, "Name"));
```

The second constructor accepts the parameter name, datatype, size, nullability, precision, scale, column name, row version, and default value:

```
cmdD.Parameters.Add(new SqlParameter("@UnitMeasureCode",
    SqlDbType.NChar, 3, ParameterDirection.Input,
    false, 0, 0, "UnitMeasureCode",
    DataRowVersion.Original, null));
```

Thus, even if the value in a column has changed, you can use the original value as a parameter to a stored procedure. The `DataRowVersion` enumeration also lets you specify the current, default, or proposed value of a column.

This example only sets up the `SqlDataAdapter` object. Now, it's time to do something with it.

Filling the DataSet

After you've set up a `SqlDataAdapter`, you can call its `Fill` method to transfer data from the database to a `DataSet`. Listing 20.8 shows this process as well as a simple method to dump the contents of a `DataSet`.

LISTING 20.8: Filling a `DataSet`

```
using System;
using System.Text;
using System.Data;
using System.Data.SqlClient;

namespace Chapter_20
{
    class _20_8
    {
        static void Main(string[] args)
        {
            string connStr =
                "Initial Catalog=AdventureWorks;" +
                "Data Source=(local);Integrated Security=SSPI;";
            SqlConnection con =
                new SqlConnection(connStr);
            SqlDataAdapter da = new SqlDataAdapter();
            // Set up the SqlDataAdapter
            SqlCommand cmdS = new SqlCommand("SELECT UnitMeasureCode, " +
                "Name FROM Production.UnitMeasure", con);
            da.SelectCommand = cmdS;
            SqlCommand cmdI = new SqlCommand("INSERT INTO " +
                "Production.UnitMeasure(UnitMeasureCode, Name) " +
```

```
                "VALUES (@UnitMeasureCode, @Name)", con);
            cmdI.Parameters.Add(new SqlParameter("@UnitMeasureCode",
                SqlDbType.NChar, 3, "UnitMeasureCode"));
            cmdI.Parameters.Add(new SqlParameter("@Name",
                SqlDbType.NVarChar, 50, "Name"));
            da.InsertCommand = cmdI;
            SqlCommand cmdU = new SqlCommand("UPDATE " +
                "Production.UnitMeasure SET UnitMeasureCode = " +
                "@UnitMeasureCode, Name = @Name WHERE " +
                "UnitMeasureCode = @Original_UnitMeasureCode", con);
            cmdU.Parameters.Add(new SqlParameter("@UnitMeasureCode",
                SqlDbType.NChar, 3, "UnitMeasureCode"));
            cmdU.Parameters.Add(new SqlParameter("@Name",
                SqlDbType.NVarChar, 50, "Name"));
            cmdU.Parameters.Add(
                new SqlParameter("@Original_UnitMeasureCode",
                SqlDbType.NChar, 3, ParameterDirection.Input,
                false, 0, 0, "UnitMeasureCode",
                DataRowVersion.Original, null));
            da.UpdateCommand = cmdU;
            SqlCommand cmdD = new SqlCommand("DELETE FROM " +
                "Production.UnitMeasure WHERE UnitMeasureCode = " +
                "@UnitMeasureCode", con);
            cmdD.Parameters.Add(new SqlParameter("@UnitMeasureCode",
                SqlDbType.NChar, 3, ParameterDirection.Input,
                false, 0, 0, "UnitMeasureCode",
                DataRowVersion.Original, null));
            da.DeleteCommand = cmdD;

            // Fill the DatSet
            DataSet ds = new DataSet();
            da.Fill(ds, "Production.UnitMeasure");
            foreach (DataTable dt in ds.Tables )
            {
                Console.WriteLine("Table: " + dt.TableName);
                foreach(DataRow dr in dt.Rows )
                {
                    for (int i = 0; i < dt.Columns.Count; i++)
                    {
                        Console.Write(dr[i] + "  ");
                    }
                    Console.WriteLine();
                }
            }
            Console.ReadLine();
        }
    }
}
```

You need to specify the DataSet variable and the name that should be used for the table within the DataSet. After you've filled the DataSet, you can use a mix of foreach and for loops to visit every item in every DataRow in every DataTable within the DataSet. Figure 20.4 shows the tail end of the output from this example.

FIGURE 20.4
Data from a DataSet

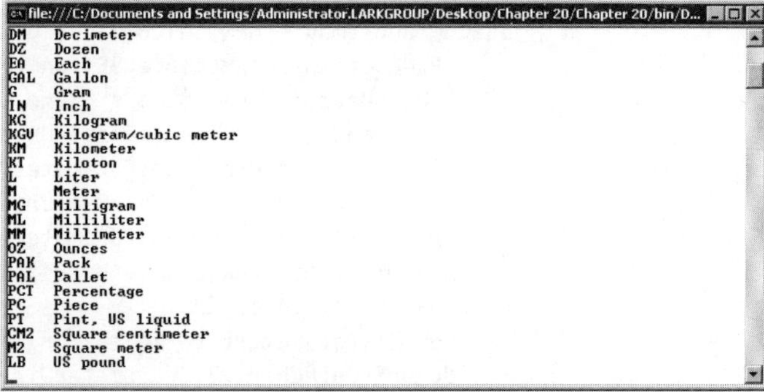

TIP You don't have to call the Connection.Open or Connection.Close method when you're using the SqlDataAdapter to fill a DataSet. The SqlDataAdapter class handles connection management on its own.

Modifying the *DataSet*

After you've loaded data into a DataSet, you're free to modify it. If you've worked with earlier Microsoft data access APIs, such as Data Access Objects (DAO) or ActiveX Data Objects (ADO), you may expect a fair amount of complexity here. But you'd be wrong. Microsoft has done a great job of simplifying data access with ADO.NET, and data modification is one place where this simplification really shows.

EDITING DATA

To edit data in a DataSet, you locate the appropriate item in a DataRow and change it. Listing 20.9 shows an example.

LISTING 20.9: Editing Data in a DataSet

```
using System;
using System.Text;
using System.Data;
using System.Data.SqlClient;

namespace Chapter_20
{
    class _20_9
    {
        static void Main(string[] args)
        {
            string connStr =
```

```
    "Initial Catalog=AdventureWorks;" +
    "Data Source=(local);Integrated Security=SSPI;";
SqlConnection con =
    new SqlConnection(connStr);
SqlDataAdapter da = new SqlDataAdapter();
// Set up the SqlDataAdapter
SqlCommand cmdS = new SqlCommand("SELECT UnitMeasureCode, " +
    "Name FROM Production.UnitMeasure", con);
da.SelectCommand = cmdS;
SqlCommand cmdI = new SqlCommand("INSERT INTO " +
    "Production.UnitMeasure(UnitMeasureCode, Name) " +
    "VALUES (@UnitMeasureCode, @Name)", con);
cmdI.Parameters.Add(new SqlParameter("@UnitMeasureCode",
    SqlDbType.NChar, 3, "UnitMeasureCode"));
cmdI.Parameters.Add(new SqlParameter("@Name",
    SqlDbType.NVarChar, 50, "Name"));
da.InsertCommand = cmdI;
SqlCommand cmdU = new SqlCommand("UPDATE " +
    "Production.UnitMeasure SET UnitMeasureCode = " +
    "@UnitMeasureCode, Name = @Name WHERE " +
    "UnitMeasureCode = @Original_UnitMeasureCode", con);
cmdU.Parameters.Add(new SqlParameter("@UnitMeasureCode",
    SqlDbType.NChar, 3, "UnitMeasureCode"));
cmdU.Parameters.Add(new SqlParameter("@Name",
    SqlDbType.NVarChar, 50, "Name"));
cmdU.Parameters.Add(
                new SqlParameter("@Original_UnitMeasureCode",
    SqlDbType.NChar, 3, ParameterDirection.Input,
    false, 0, 0,
                "UnitMeasureCode", DataRowVersion.Original, null));
da.UpdateCommand = cmdU;
SqlCommand cmdD = new SqlCommand("DELETE FROM " +
    "Production.UnitMeasure WHERE UnitMeasureCode = " +
                "@UnitMeasureCode", con);
cmdD.Parameters.Add(new SqlParameter("@UnitMeasureCode",
    SqlDbType.NChar, 3, ParameterDirection.Input,
    false, 0, 0,
                "UnitMeasureCode", DataRowVersion.Original, null));
da.DeleteCommand = cmdD;

// Fill the DatSet
DataSet ds = new DataSet();
da.Fill(ds, "Production.UnitMeasure");

// Print the contents of the fourth row
DataRow dr = ds.Tables[0].Rows[3];
Console.WriteLine("Original: " + dr[0] + " " + dr[1]);

// Now change them
```

```
                dr[0] = "BKT";
                dr[1] = "Bucket";

                // Print the changed contents
                Console.WriteLine("Edited: " + dr[0] + " " + dr[1]);
                Console.ReadLine();
            }
        }
    }
```

To change data in a DataSet, you change the value of the desired element. In this case, the procedure writes new data to both the first and second columns in the fourth row of the data (as it is for other .NET collections, the numbering is zero-based). Figure 20.5 shows the output.

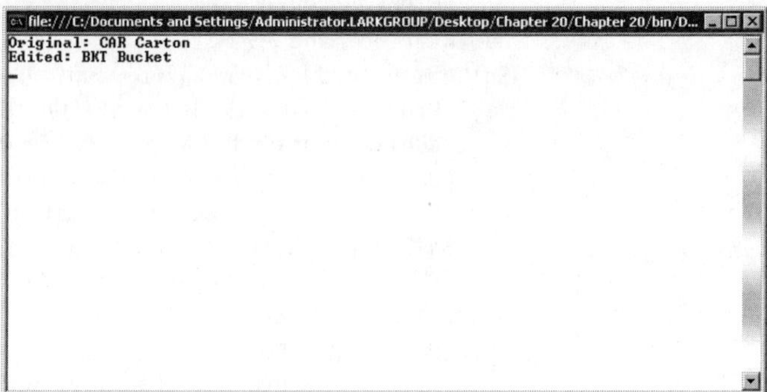

FIGURE 20.5 Editing data in a DataSet

NOTE If you run the procedure a second time, you'll see that the changes you made don't persist: The data retrieved from the database is still there when you re-run the procedure. You'll learn how to save your changes in the section "Updating the Database," later in this chapter.

ADDING NEW DATA

A DataSet is a collection of DataTable objects, each of which is a collection of DataRow objects. To add new data to a DataSet, you create a new DataRow and add it to the appropriate DataTable. Listing 20.10 shows the pattern for this operation.

LISTING 20.10: Adding Data to a DataSet

```
using System;
using System.Text;
using System.Data;
using System.Data.SqlClient;

namespace Chapter_20
{
    class _20_10
    {
```

```
static void Main(string[] args)
{
    string connStr =
        "Initial Catalog=AdventureWorks;" +
        "Data Source=(local);Integrated Security=SSPI;";
    SqlConnection con =
        new SqlConnection(connStr);
    SqlDataAdapter da = new SqlDataAdapter();
    // Set up the SqlDataAdapter
    SqlCommand cmdS = new SqlCommand("SELECT UnitMeasureCode, " +
        "Name FROM Production.UnitMeasure", con);
    da.SelectCommand = cmdS;
    SqlCommand cmdI = new SqlCommand("INSERT INTO " +
        "Production.UnitMeasure(UnitMeasureCode, Name) " +
        "VALUES (@UnitMeasureCode, @Name)", con);
    cmdI.Parameters.Add(new SqlParameter("@UnitMeasureCode",
        SqlDbType.NChar, 3, "UnitMeasureCode"));
    cmdI.Parameters.Add(new SqlParameter("@Name",
        SqlDbType.NVarChar, 50, "Name"));
    da.InsertCommand = cmdI;
    SqlCommand cmdU = new SqlCommand("UPDATE " +
        "Production.UnitMeasure SET UnitMeasureCode = " +
        "@UnitMeasureCode, Name = @Name WHERE " +
        "UnitMeasureCode = @Original_UnitMeasureCode", con);
    cmdU.Parameters.Add(new SqlParameter("@UnitMeasureCode",
        SqlDbType.NChar, 3, "UnitMeasureCode"));
    cmdU.Parameters.Add(new SqlParameter("@Name",
        SqlDbType.NVarChar, 50, "Name"));
    cmdU.Parameters.Add(
        new SqlParameter("@Original_UnitMeasureCode",
        SqlDbType.NChar, 3, ParameterDirection.Input,
        false, 0, 0, "UnitMeasureCode",
        DataRowVersion.Original, null));
    da.UpdateCommand = cmdU;
    SqlCommand cmdD = new SqlCommand("DELETE FROM " +
        "Production.UnitMeasure WHERE UnitMeasureCode = " +
        "@UnitMeasureCode", con);
    cmdD.Parameters.Add(new SqlParameter("@UnitMeasureCode",
        SqlDbType.NChar, 3, ParameterDirection.Input,
        false, 0, 0, "UnitMeasureCode",
        DataRowVersion.Original, null));
    da.DeleteCommand = cmdD;

    // Fill the DatSet
    DataSet ds = new DataSet();
    da.Fill(ds, "Production.UnitMeasure");

    // How many rows in the first table?
    Console.WriteLine("The table has " +
```

```
                ds.Tables[0].Rows.Count + " rows");

                // Add a new row
                DataRow dr = ds.Tables[0].NewRow();

                // Fill in some data
                dr[0] = "BKT";
                dr[1] = "Bucket";

                // Add it back to the table
                ds.Tables[0].Rows.Add(dr);

                // Print the new rowcount
                Console.WriteLine("The table has " +
                ds.Tables[0].Rows.Count + " rows");
                Console.ReadLine();
            }
        }
    }
```

The NewRow method of the DataTable object returns a DataRow object that matches the schema of the DataTable. You can then fill in data for the new row and use the Add method of the DataTable's Rows collection to make the row a part of the DataTable.

Deleting Data

Finally, deleting data requires a single method call, as shown in Listing 20.11. In this case, we're adding a DataRow and then removing it immediately.

Listing 20.11: Deleting Data from a DataSet

```
using System;
using System.Text;
using System.Data;
using System.Data.SqlClient;

namespace Chapter_20
{
    class _20_11
    {
        static void Main(string[] args)
        {
            string connStr =
                "Initial Catalog=AdventureWorks;" +
                "Data Source=(local);Integrated Security=SSPI;";
            SqlConnection con =
                new SqlConnection(connStr);
            SqlDataAdapter da = new SqlDataAdapter();
```

```
// Set up the SqlDataAdapter
SqlCommand cmdS = new SqlCommand("SELECT UnitMeasureCode, " +
    "Name FROM Production.UnitMeasure", con);
da.SelectCommand = cmdS;
SqlCommand cmdI = new SqlCommand("INSERT INTO " +
    "Production.UnitMeasure(UnitMeasureCode, Name) " +
    "VALUES (@UnitMeasureCode, @Name)", con);
cmdI.Parameters.Add(new SqlParameter("@UnitMeasureCode",
    SqlDbType.NChar, 3, "UnitMeasureCode"));
cmdI.Parameters.Add(new SqlParameter("@Name",
    SqlDbType.NVarChar, 50, "Name"));
da.InsertCommand = cmdI;
SqlCommand cmdU = new SqlCommand("UPDATE " +
    "Production.UnitMeasure SET UnitMeasureCode = " +
    "@UnitMeasureCode, Name = @Name WHERE " +
    "UnitMeasureCode = @Original_UnitMeasureCode", con);
cmdU.Parameters.Add(new SqlParameter("@UnitMeasureCode",
    SqlDbType.NChar, 3, "UnitMeasureCode"));
cmdU.Parameters.Add(new SqlParameter("@Name",
    SqlDbType.NVarChar, 50, "Name"));
cmdU.Parameters.Add(
    new SqlParameter("@Original_UnitMeasureCode",
    SqlDbType.NChar, 3, ParameterDirection.Input,
    false, 0, 0, "UnitMeasureCode",
    DataRowVersion.Original, null));
da.UpdateCommand = cmdU;
SqlCommand cmdD = new SqlCommand("DELETE FROM " +
    "Production.UnitMeasure WHERE UnitMeasureCode = " +
    "@UnitMeasureCode", con);
cmdD.Parameters.Add(new SqlParameter("@UnitMeasureCode",
    SqlDbType.NChar, 3, ParameterDirection.Input,
    false, 0, 0, "UnitMeasureCode",
    DataRowVersion.Original, null));
da.DeleteCommand = cmdD;

// Fill the DatSet
DataSet ds = new DataSet();
da.Fill(ds, "Production.UnitMeasure");

// How many rows in the first table?
Console.WriteLine("The table has " +
    ds.Tables[0].Rows.Count + " rows");

// Add a new row
DataRow dr = ds.Tables[0].NewRow();

// Fill in some data
dr[0] = "BKT";
dr[1] = "Bucket";
```

```
                // Add it back to the table
                ds.Tables[0].Rows.Add(dr);

                // Print the new rowcount
                Console.WriteLine("The table has " +
                    ds.Tables[0].Rows.Count + " rows");

                // Now delete the last row in the table
                ds.Tables[0].Rows[ds.Tables[0].Rows.Count - 1].Delete();

                // Print the new rowcount
                Console.WriteLine("The table has " +
                    ds.Tables[0].Rows.Count + " rows");

                Console.ReadLine();
            }
        }
    }
```

The `Delete` method of the `Rows` collection does the job here.

Updating the Database

Now you know how to make changes to the data in a `DataSet`—but how do you get those changes back to the database? The answer is to call the `Update` method of the corresponding `SqlDataAdapter`, like this:

```
da.Update(ds, "Production.UnitMeasure");
```

The `Update` method takes the same parameters as the original `Fill` method. This method then takes all the changes in the `DataSet` and writes them back to the database:

- For each deleted row, it calls the query specified by the `DeleteCommand` property of the `SqlDataAdapter`.
- For each added row, it calls the query specified by the `InsertCommand` property of the `SqlDataAdapter`.
- For each edited row, it calls the query specified by the `UpdateCommand` property of the `SqlDataAdapter`.

If you neglect to provide one of the necessary `SqlCommand` objects, the corresponding changes to the database won't be made. Note that the `DataSet` doesn't have to be connected to a database for its entire lifetime: You can use a `SqlDataAdapter` to fill a `DataSet`, ship the `DataSet` to another computer via XML, persist changes to a serialized XML file, send the file back to the original computer via floppy disk, and reconstitute the `DataSet` object. Even in this convoluted scenario, you can call the `Update` method to write changes back to the database.

A User Interface Example

To put all the pieces together, we've designed the simple form shown in Figure 20.6.

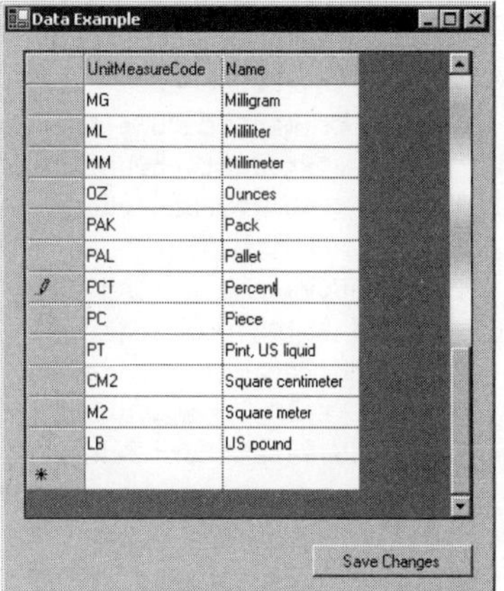

FIGURE 20.6
Editing SQL Server data via ADO.NET and Windows forms

This form, built with Visual Studio 2005, takes a `DataSet` and displays it on a DataGridView control. The DataGridView handles all the user interface interactions. Its built-in functionality includes the following:

- Click in any cell and type to edit existing values.
- Click the selector to the left of a row and then press Delete to delete a row.
- Click in the empty row at the end of the grid and type to create a new row.

The code for this form is similar to what you've seen in the last several listings. Listing 20.12 shows the code that's run when you load the form.

LISTING 20.12: Loading Data to the User Interface

```
SqlDataAdapter da = new SqlDataAdapter();

private void Form1_Load(object sender, EventArgs e)
{
    string connStr =
        "Initial Catalog=AdventureWorks;" +
        "Data Source=(local);Integrated Security=SSPI;";
    SqlConnection con =
        new SqlConnection(connStr);
    // Set up the SqlDataAdapter
    SqlCommand cmdS = new SqlCommand("SELECT UnitMeasureCode, " +
        "Name FROM Production.UnitMeasure", con);
    da.SelectCommand = cmdS;
    SqlCommand cmdI = new SqlCommand("INSERT INTO " +
        "Production.UnitMeasure(UnitMeasureCode, Name) " +
        "VALUES (@UnitMeasureCode, @Name)", con);
    cmdI.Parameters.Add(new SqlParameter("@UnitMeasureCode",
        SqlDbType.NChar, 3, "UnitMeasureCode"));
```

```
            cmdI.Parameters.Add(new SqlParameter("@Name",
                SqlDbType.NVarChar, 50, "Name"));
            da.InsertCommand = cmdI;
            SqlCommand cmdU = new SqlCommand("UPDATE " +
                "Production.UnitMeasure SET UnitMeasureCode = " +
                "@UnitMeasureCode, Name = @Name WHERE " +
                "UnitMeasureCode = @Original_UnitMeasureCode", con);
            cmdU.Parameters.Add(new SqlParameter("@UnitMeasureCode",
                SqlDbType.NChar, 3, "UnitMeasureCode"));
            cmdU.Parameters.Add(new SqlParameter("@Name",
                SqlDbType.NVarChar, 50, "Name"));
            cmdU.Parameters.Add(
                new SqlParameter("@Original_UnitMeasureCode",
                SqlDbType.NChar, 3, ParameterDirection.Input,
                false, 0, 0, "UnitMeasureCode",
                DataRowVersion.Original, null));
            da.UpdateCommand = cmdU;
            SqlCommand cmdD = new SqlCommand("DELETE FROM " +
                "Production.UnitMeasure WHERE UnitMeasureCode = " +
                "@UnitMeasureCode", con);
            cmdD.Parameters.Add(new SqlParameter("@UnitMeasureCode",
                SqlDbType.NChar, 3, ParameterDirection.Input,
                false, 0, 0, "UnitMeasureCode",
                DataRowVersion.Original, null));
            da.DeleteCommand = cmdD;

            // Fill the DatSet
            DataSet ds = new DataSet();
            da.Fill(ds, "UnitMeasure");

            // And show it on the UI
            dgvUnitMeasure.DataSource = ds;
            dgvUnitMeasure.DataMember = "UnitMeasure";
        }
```

Note that the SqlDataAdapter object is defined at the class level so that it remains in scope even when the load code has finished running. After filling the DataSet, the code displays it on the user interface by setting the DataSource and DataMember properties of the DataGridView control. The user is then free to edit, add, or delete data as they wish. Clicking the Save Changes button calls the Update method of the SqlDataAdapter, handing back the DataSet that the DataGridView is using as its DataSource:

```
private void btnSaveChanges_Click(object sender, EventArgs e)
{
    da.Update((DataSet)dgvUnitMeasure.DataSource, "UnitMeasure");
}
```

Summary

In this chapter, you learned how to use ADO.NET to access data from SQL Server 2005. After an introduction to the basic ADO.NET namespaces and classes, we showed you how to use the `SqlCommand` object to execute T-SQL statements and retrieve single pieces of data. We then examined the `SqlDataReader`, which is ideal for retrieving data quickly, and the more flexible `DataSet`, which provides a means for holding data in memory and editing it.

In the next chapter, we'll move on to a different programming topic: SQL Management Objects (SMO) and Replication Management Objects (RMO). These APIs provide objects that you can use to manage SQL Server from your own code.

Chapter 21

SMO and RMO Programming

ADO.NET, which you learned about in the previous chapter, can provide your applications with programmatic access to the data stored on a SQL Server. By retrieving metadata for tables and columns, ADO.NET can even provide some access to the schema information on a SQL Server.

However, there's more to a SQL Server than just data and schema information. Think about all of the activities you can perform within SQL Server Management Studio. For example:

- Creating new logins and roles
- Linking servers and listing the tables from linked servers
- Monitoring alerts
- Setting up replication

Of course, we could name many more SQL Server activities. Management Studio provides a rich, object-oriented environment for managing nearly all facets of SQL Server operations. However, what do you do if you'd like to make it possible for users to perform some of those operations without introducing them to the power and danger of using Management Studio directly?

The answer is that you write a specialized application that communicates with SQL Server via an object library. SQL Server ships with several object libraries that are useful for this type of task. In particular, you can use SQL Management Objects (SMO) for general-purpose SQL Server management, and Replication Management Objects (RMO) for handling replication-related tasks. In this chapter, we'll look at these two object libraries.

What Is SMO?

As we've already mentioned, SMO stands for *SQL Management Objects.* The name gives you two clues about this particular library:

- It contains a number of objects specific to SQL Server.
- It's aimed at management, rather than data, functions.

You should turn to the SMO object library when you want to do in code something that you could do easily from Management Studio. In fact, Management Studio itself uses SMO to perform most of its functions, and SMO was originally designed for this purpose. The SQL Server team went on to document the objects in this library, though, so it's available to everyone as a supported part of SQL Server.

NOTE SMO is a replacement for an older library named SQL Server Distributed Management Objects (DMO). DMO shipped with SQL Server 7.0 and SQL Server 2000. Most of the object names in SMO are compatible with those in SQL-DMO, and much SMO code is similar to SQL-DMO code. However, SMO is a .NET library while the older SQL-DMO was a COM library, so you'll need to change programming environments if you're upgrading older code.

There are times when SMO is not the best solution. In particular, if you want to work with the data stored on a SQL Server, you should look at ADO.NET or another data-access library (such as the older classic ADO) instead of SMO. Although SMO can execute arbitrary SQL statements on a server, it's not really designed for this purpose.

SMO can be overwhelming the first time you see it, because it contains a wide variety of objects with hundreds of methods and properties. In this chapter, we'll introduce the most important of these objects and give you some examples of their use. For a full list of SMO objects, methods, and properties, refer to the SQL Management Objects book in SQL Server Books Online.

The SMO Object Model

Although we've only demonstrated ADO.NET with SQL Server, the ADO.NET objects can be used with a variety of databases. That is, those objects can be used with any data source on your computer. In contrast, the SMO objects are designed specifically and only for use with SQL Server. It shouldn't surprise you then that the SMO object model closely mimics the way that things are arranged in Management Studio

To cover the full range of operations that you can perform from Management Studio, SMO includes a lot of objects. Some of these are so obscure that you'll very seldom need them. For example, the `RemoteServiceBinding` object represents a single remote binding for Service Broker. To keep this chapter manageable, we won't try to cover every single object in depth. Rather, we'll introduce all of the objects first to give you an overview, and then drill down into some of the more interesting and useful objects.

The Major SMO Objects

Object hierarchies are commonly presented as diagrams showing the relationships between objects. For example, Figure 20.1 (in the previous chapter) took this approach to showing you the ADO.NET object model. However, the SMO object model is so large that any diagram would take many pages. Instead, we've compiled Table 21.1, which lists some of the major SMO objects. This table should give you a sense of the things that you can manage with SMO.

TABLE 21.1: SMO Objects

OBJECT	REPRESENTS
Alert	An alert
Backup	A backup operation
BackupDevice	A backup device
Check	A check constraint

TABLE 21.1: SMO Objects *(CONTINUED)*

OBJECT	REPRESENTS
Column	A column in a table or other object
ConfigProperty	A configuration option
Configuration	The configuration of the entire SQL Server
Database	A database
DatabaseActiveDirectory	The Active Directory information for a database
DatabaseOptions	Database-wide settings
DatabaseRole	A security role
Default	A default constraint
ForeignKey	A foreign key constraint
FullTextCatalog	A full-text catalog
FullTextIndex	A single full-text index
Index	An index
Information	Nonconfigurable server information (such as the SQL Server version)
Job	A SQL Server Agent job
LinkedServer	A linked server
Login	A SQL Server login
Operator	A SQL Server Agent operator
Parameter	A parameter to a stored procedure or user-defined function
RegisteredServer	A server registered with Management Studio
Restore	A restore operation
Server	An instance of SQL Server
ServerGroup	A group of servers in Management Studio
ServiceBroker	The Service Broker for a database
Settings	Server-level configurable settings
SqlAssembly	.NET assembly used by SQL Server

TABLE 21.1: SMO Objects *(CONTINUED)*

OBJECT	REPRESENTS
SqlMail	The SQL Mail service
StoredProcedure	A stored procedure
Table	A table
Trigger	A trigger
User	A user
View	A view

TIP Many of the objects listed in Table 21.1 are grouped into a corresponding collection. For example, there's a `ColumnCollection` object that contains a collection of `Column` objects.

As you can see, most of the names of objects are what you'd expect from experience with Management Studio. For example, each database in SQL Server Enterprise Manager contains a node listing full-text catalogs, and sure enough, SMO includes a `FullTextCatalogs` collection.

The Server Object

The `Server` object represents a SQL Server. As such, it's the obvious object with which much SMO code starts. Most of the other objects that you'll be concerned with are descendants of the Server `object`. This means that you can retrieve them using properties of the Server object. For example, once you've instantiated a `Server` object and connected it to a particular server, you can use the `Databases` property of the `Server` object to determine how many databases are hosted on the server, and then retrieve an individual `Database` object referring to a particular database. Listing 21.1 shows a code sample to perform these tasks.

LISTING 21.1: Working with the Server object

```
using System;
using System.Text;
using Microsoft.SqlServer.Management.Smo;

namespace Chapter_21
{
    class _21_1
    {
        static void Main(string[] args)
        {
            Server s = new Server("(local)");
            Console.WriteLine(s.Databases.Count);
```

```
                Database d = s.Databases["AdventureWorks"];
                Console.WriteLine(d.Name);
                Console.ReadLine();
            }
        }
    }
```

In this example, s is a Server object, which is instantiated to point at the SQL Server on the same computer where the code is running. After creating the Server object, the code retrieves the number of databases on the server, and then assigns a particular database to a new Database object.

NOTE All of the sample code in this chapter was written using C#. You can compile it using Visual Studio .NET 2005, or the command-line csc compiler from the .NET Framework SDK. You need to set references to the Microsoft.SqlServer.ConnectionInfo and Microsoft.SqlServer.Smo libraries as well. Of course, because SMO is implemented as a set of .NET libraries, you can also use the objects, methods, and properties that it exposes from any .NET language.

You can also use the Server object to perform operations that affect an entire server. For example, you could use properties and methods of this object to drop a database, set server-wide options, or manipulate the default timeout for SQL Server logins.

NOTE In the following pages, we'll list the properties, methods, and events of the Server object. These lists will give you an overview of the tasks that you can perform directly with this object.

PROPERTIES

Table 21.2 lists the properties of the Server object. Although in general we're not going to list all the properties of objects in this chapter, we wanted to give you a feel for the richness of the SMO object model.

TABLE 21.2: Properties of the Server Object

PROPERTY	DESCRIPTION
ActiveDirectory	Retrieves the ActiveDirectory object for this server
BackupDevices	Retrieves the BackupDeviceCollection for this server
Configuration	Retrieves the Configuration object for this server
Databases	Retrieves the DatabaseCollection for this server
DefaultTextMode	Specifies whether the default text mode is set for this server
EndPoints	Retrieves the EndPointCollection for this server
Events	Retrieves the ServerEvents object for this server
FullTextService	Retrieves the FullTextService object for this server

TABLE 21.2: Properties of the Server Object *(CONTINUED)*

PROPERTY	DESCRIPTION
Information	Retrieves the Information object for this server
InstanceName	The name of this instance
JobServer	Retrieves the JobServer object for this server
Languages	Retrieves the LanguageCollection for this server
LinkedServers	Retrieves the LinkedServerCollection for this server
Logins	Retrieves the LoginCollection for this server
Mail	Retrieves the SqlMail object for this server
Name	The name of the server
ProxyAccount	Retrieves the ServerProxyAccount object for this server
Properties	Retrieves a collection of Property objects for this server
ReplicationServer	Retrieves the replication service for this server
Roles	Retrieves the ServerRoleCollection for this server
Settings	Retrieves the Settings object for this server
State	Retrieves the current state of the server
SystemDataTypes	Retrieves the SystemDataTypeCollection for this server
SystemMessages	Retrieves the SystemMessageCollection for this server
Triggers	Retrieves the ServerDdlTriggerCollection for this server
UserDefinedMessages	Retrieves the UserDefinedMessageCollection for this server
UserOptions	Retrieves the UserOptions object for this server

As you can see, the properties of the `Server` object are almost entirely concerned with returning other objects. Even things you might expect to find directly attached to the `Server` object, such as properties representing its configuration, are pushed down to subsidiary objects.

METHODS

Table 21.3 lists the public methods of the Server object.

TABLE 21.3: Public Methods of the Server Object

METHOD	DESCRIPTION
Alter	Commits property changes
AttachDatabase	Attaches an existing database
CompareURN	Compares two Uniform ResourceNames
DeleteBackupHistory	Deletes the backup history
Deny	Denies permissions, similar to the T-SQL DENY keyword
DetachDatabase	Detaches a database
DetachedDatabaseInfo	Returns information about a detached database file
EnumAvailableMedia	Creates a DataTable listing the media available to SQL Server
EnumCollations	Creates DataTable listing the collations supported by this instance
EnumDatabaseMirrorWitnessRoles	Creates a DataTable listing mirror witness roles for the server or a database
EnumDetachedDatabaseFiles	Creates a DataTable listing detached database files
EnumDetachedLogFiles	Creates a DataTable listing detached log files
EnumDirectories	Creates a DataTable listing directories relative to a specified path
EnumErrorLogs	Creates a DataTable listing error logs
EnumLocks	Creates a DataTable listing current locks
EnumMembers	Creates a DataTable listing members of roles
EnumObjectPermissions	Creates a DataTable listing the permissions on a specific object
EnumPerformanceCounters	Creates a DataTable listing SQL Server performance counters
EnumProcesses	Creates a DataTable listing processes that are running on the server computer
EnumServerAttributes	Creates a DataTable listing server attributes
EnumServerPermissions	Creates a DataTable listing the permissions on the server
EnumStartupProcedures	Creates a DataTable listing startup procedures
EnumWindowsDomainGroups	Creates a DataTable listing groups in the current Windows domain
EnumWindowsGroupInfo	Creates a DataTable listing information about a Windows group

TABLE 21.3: Public Methods of the Server Object *(CONTINUED)*

METHOD	DESCRIPTION
EnumWindowsUserInfo	Creates a DataTable listing information about a Windows user
GetActiveDbConnectionCount	Returns the number of active connections for a particular database
GetDefaultInitFields	Returns the default values used when a specified object is initialized
GetPropertyNames	Gets the names of all properties for a specified object
GetSmoObject	Gets an object from its URN
Grant	Grants permissions, similar to the T-SQL GRANT keyword
IsDetachedPrimaryFile	Verifies whether a specified file is a detached primary file
IsWindowsGroupMember	Verifies whether a user is in a specified Windows group
KillAllProcesses	Kills all processes associated with a specified database
KillDatabase	Drops all connections to a database and deletes the database
KillProcess	Stops a process on the server
ReadErrorLog	Creates a DataTable with the contents of an error log
Refresh	Updates the properties of the Server object
Revoke	Revokes permissions, similar to the T-SQL REVOKE keyword
SetDefaultInitFields	Sets a list of properties to initialize when an object is fetched

Note that although methods and properties can both return information to the user, there are differences between them. SMO uses methods for three distinct situations:

- When the Server object is being told to perform an action (such as dropping a database)
- When retrieving information requires supplying other information (such as checking whether a user ID belongs to a particular Windows group)
- When the return value consists of multiple pieces of information (such as the list of all detached database files on a system)

These rules for distinguishing methods from properties are consistent across all the SMO objects.

EVENTS

Table 21.4 lists the events that the Server object makes available. All of these events are available at the level of the Server object, but in fact they're supplied by the `ServerConnection` object.

TABLE 21.4: Events Related to the Server Object

EVENT	OCCURS WHEN...
InfoMessage	An information message is returned by the server
RemoteLoginFailed	An attempt to connect to a remote server fails
ServerMessage	A success-with-information message is returned by the server
StateChange	The server enters a new state
StatementExecuted	SMO submits a T-SQL batch to be executed

To use these events, you need to instantiate a `ServerConnection` object and then work with a `Server` object derived from it. Listing 21.2 shows an example.

LISTING 21.2: Subscribing to a SQL Server event with SMO

```
using System;
using System.Text;
using Microsoft.SqlServer.Management.Common;
using Microsoft.SqlServer.Management.Smo;

namespace Chapter_21
{
    class _21_2
    {
        protected static void OnStatement(object sender,
            StatementEventArgs args)
        {
            Console.WriteLine(args.SqlStatement);
        }

        static void Main(string[] args)
        {
            ServerConnection sc = new ServerConnection("(local)");
            sc.StatementExecuted +=
               new StatementEventHandler(OnStatement);
            Server s = new Server(sc);
            // Do other work with the server
            // derived from this connection
            Console.ReadLine();
        }
    }
}
```

The Configuration Object

The `Configuration` object and its child objects (which are all of the type ConfigProperty) are another important part of the SMO object model. With these objects, you can retrieve or set the same configuration options for a server that you can set with the `sp_configure` stored procedure or the configuration options of Management Studio.

The Configuration object itself has a variety of properties, each of which corresponds to something that you can configure—for example, MaxServerMemory and PriorityBoost. Each of these properties returns a ConfigProperty object. The properties of the ConfigProperty object include:

DisplayName The name of the option

Description A lengthier description of the option

ConfigValue The current value of the option

Minimum The minimum allowed value of the option

Maximum The maximum allowed value of the option

RunningValue The value currently used by the server (this can differ from the ConfigValue property if the ConfigValue property has been changed and the change has not yet been committed to the server)

You'll see an example of using the Configuration and ConfigProperty objects later in this chapter in the section "Changing a Configuration Option."

The Database Object

One of the principle objects in the SMO object model is the Database object. This object represents an entire database, and it provides a way to both manipulate database-wide properties and get to other objects stored in the database. Table 21.5 shows some of the principle properties (P) and methods (M) of the Database object. This is not an exhaustive listing. For the full details of these objects, refer to the SMO reference in SQL Server Books Online.

TABLE 21.5: Selected Details of the Database Object

NAME	TYPE	DESCRIPTION
ActiveConnections	P	Number of active connections in the database
Alter	M	Updates database property changes
CheckCatalog	M	Checks the integrity of the database catalog
Checkpoint	M	Forces a write of dirty pages to the disk
Create	M	Creates a new database
DatabaseOptions	P	Returns the DatabaseOptions object for the database
DataSpaceUsage	P	Gets the space used by data in the database
ExecuteNonQuery	M	Executes a T-SQL batch in this database

TABLE 21.5: Selected Details of the Database Object *(CONTINUED)*

NAME	TYPE	DESCRIPTION
ExecuteWithResults	M	Executes a batch and return results
GetTransactionCount	M	Gets the number of open transactions in the database
IsFullTextEnabled	P	Returns true if the database has full-text search enabled
LastBackupDate	P	Date and time when the database was last backed up
Owner	P	Returns the name of the database owner
Parent	P	Returns the Server object that is the parent of this database
PrimaryFilePath	P	Gets the path and filename of the primary database file
Rename	M	Renames the database
Script	M	Generates a T-SQL script to recreate the database
SetOffline	M	Takes the database offline
SetOnline	M	Returns the database to online status
StoredProcedures	P	Returns the StoredProcedureCollection for the database
Tables	P	Returns the TableCollection for the database
Views	P	Returns the ViewCollection for the database

You'll see one use for the Database object in the section "Creating a Database" later in this chapter.

The DatabaseOptions Object

The `DatabaseOptions` object is SMO's way of allowing you to set the overall options that control a database. Each Database object has one `DatabaseOptions` object as a child. As you change the properties of this object, SQL Server changes the options of the referenced database to match. The properties of this object include:

AnsiNullDefault True to enable SQL-92 null behavior

AutoClose True to close the database when the last user exits

AutoCreateStatistics True to automatically create statistics as required

AutoShrink True to periodically attempt to shrink the database

AutoUpdateStatistics True to automatically update statistics as required

CloseCursorsOnCommitEnabled True to close cursors when changes are committed

ConcatenateNullYieldsNull True to propagate nulls in string concatenation

LocalCursorsDefault True to give cursors created in a batch local scope

QuotedIdentifiersEnabled True to allow quoted delimiters

ReadOnly True to make the database read-only

RecursiveTriggersEnabled True to allow triggers to fire other triggers

You'll see an example of using the `DatabaseOptions` object later in the chapter in the section "Changing a Configuration Option."

The StoredProcedure Object

The `StoredProcedure` object, as you can probably guess by now, represents a single SQL Server stored procedure. This can be either a system stored procedure or a user-defined stored procedure. You can use the methods and properties of this object to create stored procedures, set their properties, execute them, and so on.

Table 21.6 shows the methods (M) and properties (P) of the StoredProcedure object. This is a complete list, because this object does not have the overwhelming complexity of some of the other objects that represent larger parts of SQL Server.

TABLE 21.6: Details of the StoredProcedure Object

NAME	TYPE	DESCRIPTION
Alter	M	Assigns new text to the stored procedure
AnsiNullsStatus	M	True when this stored procedure refers to a table defined with ANSI null behavior
AssemblyName	P	Name of any .NET assembly that this stored procedure depends on
ChangeSchema	M	Changes the schema of the stored procedure
ClassName	p	Class containing this stored procedure
Create	M	Creates a new stored procedure
CreateDate	P	Date and time this stored procedure was created
DateLastModified	P	Date and time this stored procedure was modified
Deny	M	Denies permission to a specific user
Drop	M	Drops the stored procedure
EnumObjectPermissions	M	Returns a list of permissions for this stored procedure
Events	M	Gets the events for this stored procedure
ExecutionContextPrincipal	P	Returns the execution context for this stored procedure
ExtendedProperties	P	Returns the ExtendedPropertyCollection for this stored procedure

TABLE 21.6: Details of the StoredProcedure Object *(CONTINUED)*

NAME	TYPE	DESCRIPTION
ForReplication	p	True if this stored procedure is marked for replication
Grant	M	Grants permissions to a specific user
ID	P	Unique identifier that SQL Server uses to track this stored procedure
IsEncrypted	P	True if this stored procedure is encrypted
IsObjectDirty	M	True if there are unsaved changes
IsSystemObject	M	True if this is a system stored procedure
MarkDropped	M	Notifies other sessions that this stored procedure will be dropped
MethodName	P	Method Name for the stored procedure
NumberedStoredProcedures	P	Gets the NumberedStoredProcedureCollection for this stored procedure
Parameters	P	Gets the ParameterCollection for this stored procedure
Parent	P	Gets the Database containing this stored procedure
ProcedureType	P	Gets the procedure type
QuotedIdentifierStatus	P	True if this stored procedure depends on a table that uses quoted identifiers
Recompile	P	True if the stored procedure should be recompiled before execution
Revoke	M	Reverses the effect of `Grant` or `Deny`
Script	M	Generates a T-SQL script for this stored procedure
Startup	P	True if this stored procedure runs at server startup
SystemObject	P	True if this is a system stored procedure
TextBody	P	Actual T-SQL text of the stored procedure
TextHeader	P	The stored procedure header
TextMode	P	True if the text header is editable

You'll learn more about the StoredProcedure object in the section "Creating and Executing a Stored Procedure" later in this chapter.

The Table Object

The `Table` object represents a single table within a database. Child objects of the `Table` object let you work with all the other things that go into a table: columns, indexes, keys, constraints, and so on. Figure 21.1 shows some of the other objects that are descendants of the `Table` object. Later in this chapter, in the section "Creating a Table," you'll see how to use some of these objects together in code.

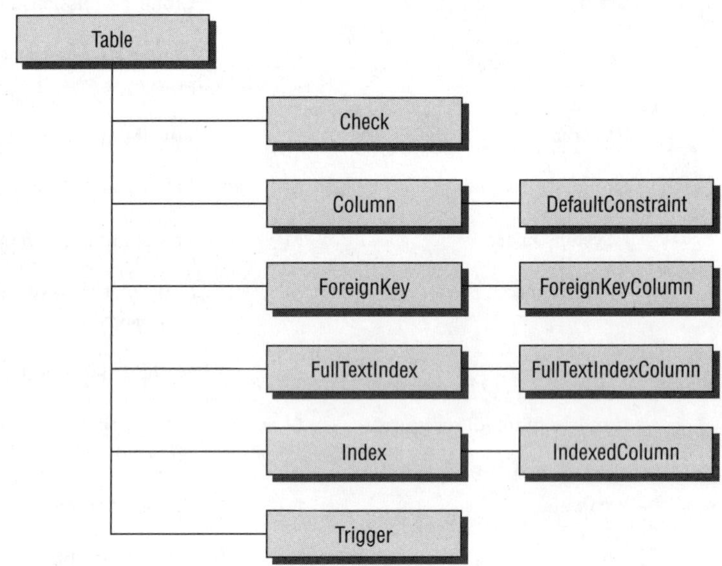

FIGURE 21.1
The Table object and its descendants

The Table object is quite complex, with many methods and properties. Table 21.7 lists some of the more important methods (M) and properties (P) of this object.

TABLE 21.7: Selected Details of the Table Object

NAME	TYPE	DESCRIPTION
AnsiNullsStatus	P	True if the table uses ANSI null handling
DataSpaceUsed	P	Actual storage space used (in KB) for the table's data
EnumForeignKeys	M	Lists all the foreign keys derived from this table
ForeignKeys	P	Returns the ForeignKeyCollection for this table
HasClusteredIndex	P	True if the table has a clustered index
HasIndex	P	True if the table has any index
RebuildIndexes	M	Rebuilds the indexes for the table

TABLE 21.7: Selected Details of the Table Object *(CONTINUED)*

NAME	TYPE	DESCRIPTION
Replicated	P	True if the table is replicated
RowCount	P	Number of rows stored in the table
TruncateData	M	Deletes all rows from the table without logging

The Column Object

The Column object is a subsidiary of the Table object. The Table object contains a Columns collection, which in turn contains one Column object for each column in the table. Of course, you can use the Columns collection to iterate through all of the columns in a table, as shown in Listing 21.3.

LISTING 21.3: Listing the columns in a table

```
using System;
using System.Text;
using Microsoft.SqlServer.Management.Smo;

namespace Chapter_21
{
    class _21_3
    {
        static void Main(string[] args)
        {
            Server s = new Server("(local)");
            Database d = s.Databases["AdventureWorks"];
            // Retrieve the first table in the database
            Table t = d.Tables[0];
            // And iterate over its columns
            foreach (Column c in t.Columns)
                Console.WriteLine(c.Name);
            Console.ReadLine();
        }
    }
}
```

You'll probably find yourself using the properties of the Column object more than its methods. This is common as you get to the more specific objects. In code, you can use properties to describe these objects, but manipulating objects via methods is normally left to the larger objects.

Table 21.8 shows some of the methods (M) and properties (P) of the Column object.

TABLE 21.8: Selected Details of the Column Object

NAME	TYPE	DESCRIPTION
BindDefault	M	Associates a default with this column
Collation	P	Collation for this column
Computed	P	True if this is a computed column
ComputedText	P	T-SQL statement used to generate the value of a computed column
DataType	P	Name of the datatype for this column
Identity	P	True if this is an identity column
IdentityIncrement	P	Increment for an identity column
IdentitySeed	P	Starting value for an identity column
InPrimaryKey	P	True if this column is part of the primary key
Nullable	P	True if the column is nullable

The Alert Object

Not all of the objects within SMO are directly related to data. A good example of one of these helper objects is the `Alert` object. The `Alert` object corresponds to a single SQL Server alert. If you're working in Management Studio, you'll find alerts in the Alerts folder under the SQL Server Agent node.

NOTE Alerts are covered in more detail in Chapter 17, "Automating Administration."

You can use the Alert object to create a new alert or modify the properties of an existing alert. Table 21.9 shows some of the methods (M) and properties (P) of the Alert object.

TABLE 21.9: Selected Details of the Alert Object

NAME	TYPE	DESCRIPTION
CategoryName	P	Category that this alert belongs to
DatabaseName	P	Database that this alert monitors
EnumNotifications	M	Lists all the notifications for this alert
IsEnabled	P	True if this alert is active
JobName	P	Job to run when this alert is activated
MessageID	P	Error number that activates this alert
Severity	P	Error severity that activates this alert

Sample SMO Code

Now that you have some idea that SMO objects exist, and know the sort of properties and methods that they implement, it's time to see some examples of their use. In this section, we'll show you seven techniques that are representative of the kinds of things you can do with SMO:

- Creating and connecting a Server object
- Creating a database
- Changing a configuration option
- Creating a table
- Dropping a table
- Creating and executing a stored procedure
- Creating an alert

However, before we dig into the code, we'd like to talk just a bit about *why* you would write this sort of application. SMO is mainly useful for two sorts of programs: general-purpose management utilities and limited-use utilities that are safe for users.

Some developers make their living enhancing and extending applications like SQL Server. Suppose, for example, you have an idea for a better way to design tables. Perhaps instead of the standard grid metaphor, you're envisioning a drag-and-drop environment, where you can grab predefined fields and stick them together to form tables. Well, once your application has progressed to the point where the user interface works, you'll need to tell SQL Server what objects to create and which properties to assign to those objects. SMO is the obvious choice for this interface to SQL Server because it encompasses all of the things one normally needs to do with objects.

On the other end of the spectrum, you might have users who occasionally need to perform an administrative task on your SQL Server. Perhaps the personnel department is responsible for adding new hires in a specific job position to the list of authorized SQL Server operators. You wouldn't necessarily want to train your personnel people in the complete use of Management Studio. Instead, you could use SMO in conjunction with Visual Basic to create a specialized front-end program that could be used only for creating operators. Using SMO with Visual Basic would be easier to train your personnel folks to use and safer for the server.

We hope that those two illustrations, combined with the code in the rest of the chapter, will inspire you to use SMO in your own applications.

Creating and Connecting a Server Object

Before you can do anything else with SMO, you need to establish a connection to the SQL Server with which you want to work. How you do this depends on your local security settings. You've already seen the simplest possible way to do this, using integrated security to the local SQL Server:

```
Server s = new Server("(local)");
```

Connecting to a different server with integrated security is just as easy:

```
Server s = new Server("ServerName");
```

If you're not using integrated security, things get a bit more complicated. In this case, you need to use the ServerConnection object to log in:

```
Server s = new Server();
ServerConnection sc = s.ConnectionContext;
sc.LoginSecure = false;
sc.Login = "UserName";
sc.Password = "Password";
```

Here the LoginSecure property tells the ServerConnection object (which, you'll note, is retrieved from the ConnectionContext property of the Server object) to use a SQL Server login rather than a Windows login. From there, you can set the name of the login and the password. Of course, you can also use this method with a remote server by supplying the server name.

Creating a Database

SMO is well suited for the creation of new objects. For example, you can use SMO to create a database entirely through code, without using the UI or explicitly executing a CREATE DATABASE statement. In fact, SMO has gone a long way to simplify the database creation process, compared to SQL-DMO. With SQL-DMO, you needed to specify filenames and file groups, create the database, and then append it to the databases collection of the server. With SMO, the entire process has been reduced to two lines of code, as shown in Listing 21.4.

LISTING 21.4: Creating a new database

```
using System;
using System.Text;
using Microsoft.SqlServer.Management.Common;
using Microsoft.SqlServer.Management.Smo;

namespace Chapter_21
{
    class _21_4
    {
        static void Main(string[] args)
        {
            Server s = new Server("(local)");
            // Create a new database
            Database d = new Database(s, "NewDatabase");
            d.Create();
        }
    }
}
```

TIP If you need control over the details of file placement, you can still get it by working with the DataFile and FileGroup objects. But you're not required to do so.

That's all you need to do to create a new database with SMO. As with any other method of creating a new database, the database will initially be a copy of the model database. You could use SMO to add tables, views, stored procedures, and other objects to the new database.

Changing a Configuration Option

As you already know, you can set several configuration options for a database, controlling such things as whether nulls are handled according to ANSI rules or whether the database closes automatically when the last user logs out. You can set these options in code using the SMO DatabaseOptions object.

For example, suppose you're planning to execute a query via code, and that this query depends on the `CONCAT_NULL_YIELDS_NULL` database option being set. To be positive that the query will succeed, you'll need to check that the option is on first. Listing 21.5 shows the way to do that with SMO.

LISTING 21.5: Changing a configuration option

```
using System;
using System.Text;
using Microsoft.SqlServer.Management.Common;
using Microsoft.SqlServer.Management.Smo;

namespace Chapter_21
{
    class _21_5
    {
        static void Main(string[] args)
        {
            Server s = new Server("(local)");
            // Retrieve the AdventureWorks database
            Database d = s.Databases["AdventureWorks"];
            // Get the options object
            DatabaseOptions dopt = d.DatabaseOptions;
            if (!dopt.ConcatenateNullYieldsNull)
            {
                dopt.ConcatenateNullYieldsNull = true;
                dopt.Alter();
            }
        }
    }
}
```

You can use the same technique to set any of the database options; they're all implemented as properties of the DatabaseOptions object. The section on the DatabaseOptions object earlier in this chapter lists all of the applicable properties.

Creating a Table

Creating objects is simple with SMO. There's a general pattern used to build up objects:

1. Create the new object.

2. Set the object's properties.

3. Add the object to the appropriate collection.

When creating a new table with SMO, this pattern repeats several times, because to create the table, you must create the columns of the table. Here's a code sample illustrating table creation. It starts, of course, by connecting to a server. It also retrieves the particular database in which this table will be stored:

```
Server s = new Server("(local)");
// Retrieve the AdventureWorks database
Database d = s.Databases["AdventureWorks"];
```

Next the code instantiates the `Table` object and assigns a name to it. This requires only a single statement:

```
// Make a new table
Table t = new Table(d, "TestTable");
```

The table is created with an empty `Columns` collection. If you tried to add the table to the database at this point, you'd receive an error, because a table must have at least one column. To add a column to the table, you create a `Column` object, set its properties, and add it to the `Table` object's Columns collection:

```
// Add a column
Column c = new Column(t, "CustomerID");
c.Identity = true;
c.IdentitySeed = 1;
c.IdentityIncrement = 1;
c.DataType = DataType.Int;
c.Nullable = false;
t.Columns.Add(c);
```

Once the `Column` object has been added to the collection, it's a permanent part of the table. You can reuse the same `Column` object to add more columns to the table:

```
// Add some more columns
c = new Column(t, "CustomerName");
c.DataType = DataType.VarChar(50);
c.Nullable = false;
t.Columns.Add(c);

c = new Column(t, "ContactName");
c.DataType = DataType.VarChar(50);
c.Nullable = true;
t.Columns.Add(c);
```

Finally, when you're done creating the table and are ready to save it back to the database, you call its `Alter` method to commit the changes:

```
// And create the table
t.Create();
```

Dropping a Table

Dropping a table is even easier than creating it. You just need to call the Drop method of the Table object:

```
Server s = new Server("(local)");
// Retrieve the AdventureWorks database
Database d = s.Databases["AdventureWorks"];
// Get the table
Table t = d.Tables["TestTable"];
// And drop it
t.Drop();
```

Creating and Executing a Stored Procedure

As you can probably guess by now, creating a stored procedure involves creating an object, setting its properties, and adding it to the appropriate collection. Listing 21.6 shows an example.

LISTING 21.6: Creating a stored procedure

```
using System;
using System.Text;
using Microsoft.SqlServer.Management.Common;
using Microsoft.SqlServer.Management.Smo;

namespace Chapter_21
{
    class _21_6
    {
        static void Main(string[] args)
        {
            Server s = new Server("(local)");
            // Retrieve the AdventureWorks database
            Database d = s.Databases["AdventureWorks"];

            // Create a new stored procedure in the database
            StoredProcedure sp =
                new StoredProcedure(d, "procInsertCust");

            // Define and add the parameters
            StoredProcedureParameter spp1 =
                new StoredProcedureParameter(sp,
                "@CustName", DataType.VarChar(50));
            sp.Parameters.Add(spp1);
            StoredProcedureParameter spp2 =
                new StoredProcedureParameter(sp,
                "@ContactName", DataType.VarChar(50));
            sp.Parameters.Add(spp2);

            // And define the body of the procedure
```

```
                sp.TextBody = "INSERT INTO TestTable " +
                    "(CustomerName, ContactName) " +
                    "VALUES (@CustName, @ContactName)";

                // Finally, save it to the database
                sp.Create();
            }
        }
    }
```

Note that information is supplied to the stored procedure three different ways. First, the name of the stored procedure is contained in the original statement that creates the `StoredProcedure` object. Second, the parameters to the stored procedure are supplied as `StoredProcedureParameter` objects, which must be appended to the appropriate collection. Finally, the body of the stored procedure is the TextBody property of the `StoredProcedure` object. Listing 21.7 shows the corresponding SQL script for this stored procedure so you can see how all of the parts fit together.

LISTING 21.7: SQL script for a stored procedure

```
CREATE PROCEDURE [dbo].[procInsertCust]
    @CustName [varchar](50),
    @ContactName [varchar](50)
AS
INSERT INTO TestTable
    (CustomerName, ContactName)
    VALUES (@CustName, @ContactName)
```

You might expect executing a stored procedure to be a method of the `StoredProcedure` object. However, you'd be wrong. If you need to execute a stored procedure via SMO, you can use the `ExecuteNonQuery` method of the Database object:

```
Server s = new Server("(local)");
// Retrieve the AdventureWorks database
Database d = s.Databases["AdventureWorks"];
d.ExecuteNonQuery("procInsertCust \"Microsoft\", \"Bill Gates\"");
```

NOTE If you ran the code to drop `TestTable`, you'll need to re-create it before you can execute the stored procedure.

Creating an Alert

As a final example, let's look at creating an object that's not directly associated with data. Even though an alert is substantially different from a table or a stored procedure, creating an alert follows the same pattern as the other examples we've examined, as you can see in Listing 21.8.

LISTING 21.8: Creating an alert

```
using System;
using System.Text;
using Microsoft.SqlServer.Management.Common;
using Microsoft.SqlServer.Management.Smo;
using Microsoft.SqlServer.Management.Smo.Agent;

namespace Chapter_21
{
    class _21_8
    {
        static void Main(string[] args)
        {
            Server s = new Server("(local)");
            // Create a new alert
            Alert a = new Alert(s.JobServer, "Full AdventureWorks");

            // Associate the alert with a particular error
            a.MessageID = 9002;
            a.DatabaseName = "AdventureWorks";

            // And add it to the job list
            a.Create();
        }
    }
}
```

NOTE Error 9002 is the SQL Server error that indicates a full database.

Note that this code fragment will create the alert, but won't assign any response to it. You could follow a similar pattern to create an `Operator` object and then use the `AddNotification` method of the `Alert` object to cause that operator to be notified when and if this alert happened.

Using RMO

Like SMO, Replication Management Objects (RMO) provide a set of objects implemented in managed code. The RMO objects are devoted specifically to the tasks of replication administration, monitoring, and synchronization. Using RMO, you can perform such tasks as:

- Configuring publishing and distribution servers
- Enable and disable publishing
- Create publications and articles
- Delete publications and articles
- Manage a replication topology
- Synchronize subscriptions

NOTE To use RMO, you'll first need to have a good grasp of the fundamentals of replication itself. See Chapter 25, "Replication," for more details.

Like SMO, RMO provides a large number of objects, so that you can manipulate every aspect of replication programmatically. It would take an entire book to dig into the RMO object model in depth, so we'll just show you a few examples to give you a feeling for what you can do with these objects. For example, Listing 21.9 shows how you can use RMO to create a new article.

LISTING 21.9: Creating an article

```
using Microsoft.SqlServer.Management.Common;
using Microsoft.SqlServer.Replication;

namespace Chapter_21
{
    class _21_9
    {
        static void Main(string[] args)
        {
            // Connect to the publishing server
            ServerConnection sc = new ServerConnection("(local)");
            sc.Connect();

            // Set up a new transactional article
            TransArticle ta = new TransArticle();
            ta.ConnectionContext = sc;
            ta.Name = "TestArticle";
            ta.DatabaseName = "AdventureWorks";
            ta.SourceObjectName = "TestTable";
            ta.SourceObjectOwner = "dbo";
            ta.PublicationName = "AWPublication";
            ta.Type = ArticleOptions.LogBased;

            // Create the article.
            ta.Create();
        }
    }
}
```

NOTE There are a number of assumptions here: that the publishing and distribution servers already exist, and that there's already a publication named AWPublication for this article to be added to.

TIP You'll need to set a reference to `Microsoft.SqlServer.Rmo.dll` to run any RMO code.

As you can see, RMO follows the same broad patterns as SMO: create a SQL Server object by creating a new .NET object, setting its properties appropriately, and then calling the `Create` method. You can use similar code to create a new publication.

As a second example, here's how you can synchronize a pull subscription programmatically, assuming that the local database is a subscriber:

```
// Connect to the subscribing server
ServerConnection sc = new ServerConnection("(local)");
sc.Connect();

// Create the pull subscription
TransPullSubscription tps =
    new TransPullSubscription();
tps.ConnectionContext = sc;
tps.DatabaseName = "AdventureWorks";
tps.PublisherName = "MyPublishingServer";
tps.PublicationDBName = "AdventureWorks";
tps.PublicationName = "AWPublication";

// And do the synchronization
tps.SynchronizeWithJob();
```

Summary

In this chapter, you learned the basics about SMO, the Server Management Objects library, and RMO, the Replication Management Objects library. After a brief introduction to the extensive list of objects provided by this library, you saw a few of the most important objects:

- The Server object represents an entire SQL Server.
- The Configuration object lets you set configuration options affecting an entire server.
- The Database object represents a SQL Server database.
- The DatabaseOptions object lets you set options in an individual database.
- The StoredProcedure object represents a single stored procedure.
- The Table object represents a single table.
- The Column object represents a column within a table.
- The Alert object represents a SQL Server Agent alert.

After learning about the objects, you saw examples of them in code. The basic SMO object-creation pattern of creating an object, setting its properties, and then saving it was demonstrated several times, along with some examples of replication programming.

Next we'll introduce another major SQL Server component, SQL Server Integration Services. With SQL Server Integration Services, you can programmatically control complex jobs that move data around and integrate SQL Server with other data sources.

Chapter 22

Integration Services

Microsoft SQL Server is designed to help you manage data throughout your enterprise, whether or not that data is stored in a SQL Server database. In this chapter, we'll take a look at a key piece of this enterprise orientation, SQL Server Integration Services (SSIS), which provides tools and utilities to help you manage data.

What Is Integration Services?

Back in the old days SQL Server 7.0 and 2000 shipped with something called Data Transformation services, or DTS. DTS was a flexible tool for moving and transforming data from a variety of OLE DB data sources. It was one of the most useful tools in all of SQL Server.

Despite its well-deserved reputation DTS had important shortcomings. It needed better scalability for one. Also DTS packages weren't easily transportable between systems—meaning that packages designed to perform a transfer from SQL Server system A couldn't be reused to perform the same transfer from another system with any ease. DTS also lacked high quality error handling and logging, and wasn't very easily managed.

SQL Server 2005's Integration Services (SSIS) has been designed from the ground up to be an enterprise ETL platform for Windows that could match any stand-alone enterprise-level Business Intelligence (BI) ETL products. It's important to remember that while SSIS is DTS's successor, that's the extent of the resemblance—this is a very different product.

SSIS was written using managed .NET code and provides an all-new architecture. SSIS includes a new graphic designer and a greatly enhanced selection of data transfer tasks and transformations. Integration Services, like the old DTS, supports 100 percent of the source and target destination, meaning it can independently connect to both the source and destination data sources without requiring that either data source be a SQL Server system.

SSIS is a complete workflow engine, and has split the old DTS unified workflow into control and dataflow components that are independent of one another, enabling a lot more power in what you can do in control flow. Microsoft claims that SSIS is seven times faster than DTS, primarily because of advanced data flow architectures that enable concurrent processing and distributable execution.

Within SSIS, Business Intelligence Developer Studio (BIDS) is the primary tool for designing and modifying packages. BIDS includes a wizard-driven Package Designer, or if you prefer you can invoke the Import/Export wizard. SQL Server Management Studio allows you to easily administer packages and is of particular value to DBAs.

We'll look at these and the other tools for using SSIS in this chapter, starting with the various ways to create, configure, and deploy Packages. But first let's quickly review SSIS installation basics.

SSIS Installation Facts

SSIS is included only in the Enterprise, Developer, and Standard editions of SQL Server 2005. It is not part of the Workgroup or Express edition. SSIS is not installed by default when you install SQL Server 2005, but must be selected. One of the nicer aspects of SSIS is that you can either install it on the same system as SQL Server 2005 or on a dedicated SSIS-only system.

The advantage to installing it alone is if you use a lot of packages, you can offload processing to a different platform, therefore saving stress on the on the primary database system.

SSIS Service

SSIS includes the SQL Server Integration Services service, a Windows service that is used to manage Integration Services packages from within Management Studio. The service is installed by default when you install the SSIS and is set to start automatically. As with any other Windows Service, you can pause or stop Integration Services, as well as change the startup type to automatic, manual, or disabled through the Services snap-in in Microsoft Management Console (MMC) snap-in.

When running, the Integration Services service allows you to do the following from Management Studio:

- Start and stop remote and locally stored packages.
- Monitor remote and locally running packages.
- Import and export packages.
- Manage package storage.
- Customize storage folders.
- Stop running packages when the service is stopped.
- View the Windows Event log.
- Connect to multiple Integration Services servers.

If you only want to design and execute Integration Services packages, Integration Services does not have to be running. You can continue to run packages using the SQL Server Import and Export Wizard, the SSIS Designer, Package Execution Utility, and the `dtexec` command prompt utility. However, it must be active in order to list and monitor packages using Management Studio, as well as monitor packages stored in the package store. The package store can be either the msdb database in an instance of SQL Server 2005 or designated folders in the file system.

Business Intelligence Development Studio

Business Intelligence Development Studio (BIDS) is a new addition in SQL Server 2005. The new studio is the environment in which you'll be developing business intelligence solutions (in other words, data manipulation) such as cubes, data sources, data source views, reports, and data transformation packages. All projects are developed in the context of a solution. A solution is really a container that can include multiple Data Transformation projects as well as Analysis Services and Report projects. A solution is also server independent. The key to understanding solutions is to think of them holistically, rather than as a diffuse entity.

By default BIDS displays four windows:

- Designer for creating and modifying business intelligence objects. The designer provides a code view and a design view of an object.
- Solution Explorer for managing the projects in the solution.
- Properties window for viewing and modifying the properties of an object.
- Toolbox window for listing the controls that are available to a business intelligence project.

BIDS also includes templates for the following project types that you'll typically use to develop business intelligence solutions:

- Analysis Services Projects
- Import Analysis Services 9.0 Database
- Integration Services Project
- Report Server Project Wizard
- Report Model Project
- Report Server Project

Before creating our first solution using SSIS, let's spend a few moments poking around and getting to know this new studio a little better.

Designer Window

Of the four main windows in BIDS, the designer window is by far the most important and the one you will come to know best. It also provides you a graphical view of the object. Depending on which of the business intelligence component types you're working with, you'll be presented with a different designer that's custom built to meet the needs of that particular component. For example, in the Data Source View Designer, which is included in all project types, you can edit the schema and change properties for an existing data source view. The SSIS Designer enables you to create SSIS packages, and the Report Designer is used, you guessed it, to create and preview reports.

The code window, which is usually accessed as a tab in the designer window, displays the XML code that defines the object. In BIDS, the code and designer views of an object can be opened at the same time.

Designer Windows can display both the design view (Figure 22.1) and the code view (Figure 22.2) as two tabs on the designer window.

FIGURE 22.1
Design view of a typical integration services package

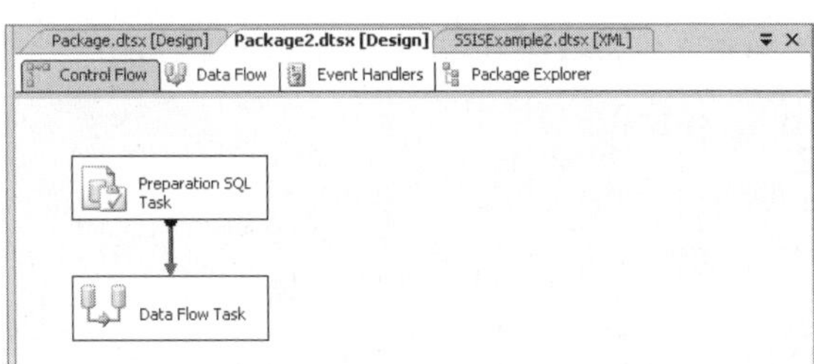

FIGURE 22.2
Code view of a typical integration services package

Solution Explorer

Solution Explorer bears considerable resemblance in appearance to Object Explorer that you have been using in Management Studio. The projects that are available and their associated files are presented in an organized fashion, allowing you ready access to the contents and the commands that are applicable. A small toolbar lets you implement common commands for an item that you select in the treeview. To access Solution Explorer, select Solution Explorer on the View menu.

For example, in an Analysis Services Project, the Tree View (Figure 26.3) is the same for every project. At the top of the tree is a Solution Node, under which are various projects. Each project has the same set of folders though obvioudly the folder and node names will vary depending on the type of solution.

- Data Sources
- Data Source Views
- Cubes
- Dimensions
- Mining Models
- Roles
- Assemblies
- Miscellaneous

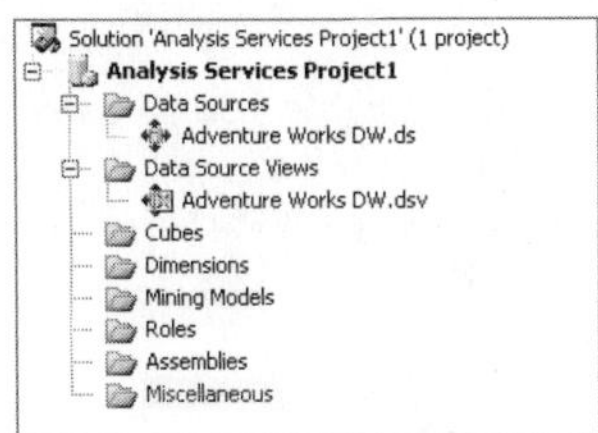

FIGURE 22.3 Solution Explorer view of an Analysis Services Solution

As you will see as you work through this and future chapters, right-clicking on folders and the files and objects contained within them allows you easy access to standard commands and operations.

Note that if a project is shown in bold font it serves as the Startup Project for running and debugging purposes. By default the first project in a solution is the designated startup project but you can change that. If there is more than one startup project, then the solution node is shown in bold font. Startup projects run automatically when you start the Visual Studio debugger.

You can also select multiple items in a single project or multiple items spanning several projects. This enables you to perform batch operations. When you select multiple items, the available commands are the combination of the commands that exist in all the selected items. You can also use multiple selection functionality to help determine or edit the intersecting properties of two or more solution items.

Properties Window

The Properties Window (Figure 26.4) allows you to view and change any design-time properties and events of the selected object. You can also use the Properties window to edit and view file, project, and solution properties. If you can't see it, you can open the Properties Window via the View menu. Grayed out items are read only.

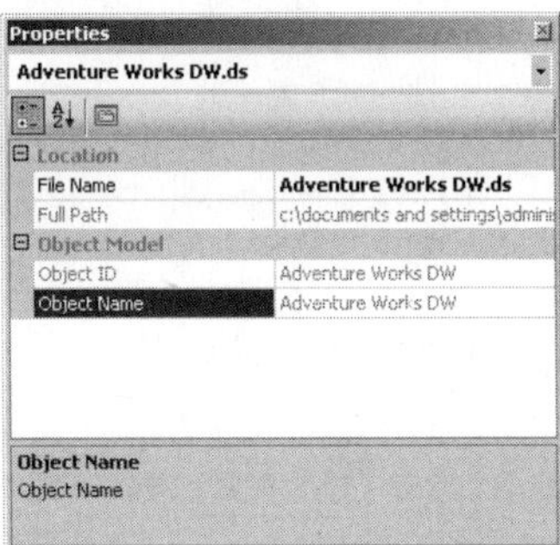

FIGURE 22.4 Typical Properties Window

Toolbox

The Toolbox, as the name suggests, displays tools and other items for use in projects. There is always a General tab present, additional displays Control Flow Items, Maintenance Tasks, and Report Items. These options change depending on the designer or editor in use.

Other Windows

BIDS provides additional windows that enable you to work with breakpoints, display error and status messages, manage tasks, and list search results.

Breakpoints open via the Debug Menu. Choose Windows and then select Breakpoints. The breakpoint list has three columns:

- Name
- Condition
- Hit Count

In addition you can add the following columns via the Columns button:

- Language
- Function
- File
- Address
- Data
- Program

Open the Error List window from the View menu or Ctrl-E. This window enables you to review error messages for the current solution. The Error List window allows you to identify and locate problems detected as you edit or compile the solution. Additionally you double-click any IntelliSense communication to open the appropriate editor, moving the insertion point to the chosen location.

The Output window, accessed via the View Menu or Ctrl-Alt-O displays status messages for features in the integrated development environment (IDE). In addition, some IDE features can deliver content to special Output Window panes. Output from external tools such as .bat or .com files, normally displayed in a DOS window, is also available.

The Task List window is used to keep track of the steps and duties assigned in the building of the solution. To display the Task List window, select View ➤ Task List. Alternatively you can use the keyboard shortcut Ctrl-+-T. In Task List you can review IntelliSense content, enter user notes, sort and filter task lists, and create new tasks.

In the Find Results windows you can display matches for text searches through the Find in Files dialog box. You access either the Find Results 1 or Find Results 2 window from the View menu.

Creating and Designing Packages

A package is an organized collection of components—the unit of execution for an SSIS transfer operation, the sine qua non by which SSIS functions and lets you manipulate data.

In its simplest form, a package contains the source target and destinations for data. It can include any transformations as well as any component (e.g., tasks) that define the work flow or the sequence of actions to be performed by SSIS.

Now that you've got a good handle on what a package is and what it's used for, we're going to show you how you can create a very simple package in SSIS. Later on we'll review how to configure, deploy, and manage packages.

First things first though.

Creating a Project

Before you can create a package you need to have a project to place it in. A project is simply a container that holds related files. For example, the files required to create a specific ETL solution—including the package, data source, and data source view definitions—are all part of one project.

Projects are, in turn, stored in a solution. You can create a solution first and then add an Integration Services project to it. Or you can create the project and if a solution doesn't exist, BIDS will create one for you. A solution can contain multiple projects of different types.

Packages are developed within the project.

The Integration Services project manages the object definitions of data sources, data source views, and packages. The files for data sources, data source views, and packages are stored in separate folders within an Integration Services project.

The steps to create a project include the following:

1. Click the Start Menu. Select Programs ➢ Microsoft SQL Server 2005 ➢ SQL Server Business Intelligence Development Studio (BIDS).
2. Select File ➢ New ➢ Project, which opens the BIDS project dialog box shown in Figure 22.5.

FIGURE 22.5
New project dialog box

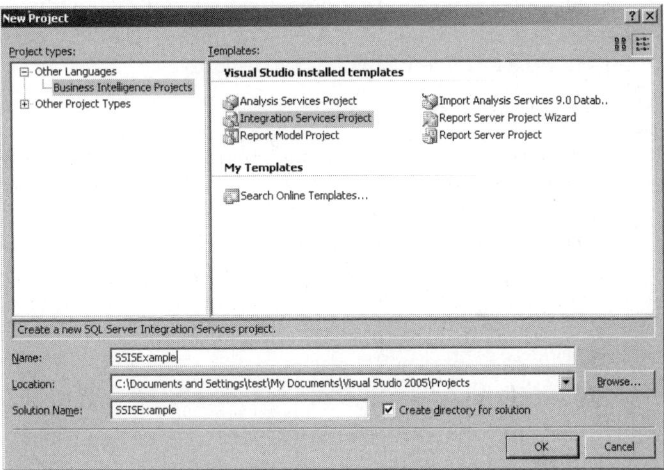

3. Next, select Integration Services Project as the project template and specify the name of the project as SSISExample as shown in Figure 22.5. Accept the remaining values and click OK. The project is created.

You'll notice in Figure 22.6 that your new project consists of four virtual folders, each with a different purpose:

Data Sources Folder Contains project-level data sources that can be referenced by multiple packages.

Data Source Views Contains data source views, which are built on data sources and can be referenced by sources, transformations, and destinations. For more information, see Data Source View (SSIS).

SSIS Packages As the name implies, this is where the packages for the project are stored.

Miscellaneous A grab bag folder for files other than source, data source view, or package files.

FIGURE 22.6
SSIS project folder tree

A quick note on files in SSIS projects. Whenever you add a new or existing project to a solution, BIDS creates project files with the ext,ensions `.dtproj`,`.dtproj.user`, and `.database`.

The `*.dtproj` file holds information about project configurations, data sources and packages. The `*.dtproj.user` file contains user specified preferences for working with the project. Finally, the `*.database` file contains information that BIDS needs to open the Integration Services project.

Containers

Before we start talking about packages in earnest, you should be familiar with another new construct that Microsoft has added to SSIS, called *containers*. The primary purpose for Integration Services containers is to add structure and flow control to packages and services to tasks. Containers group related tasks and support repeating control flows in packages to execute repeated tasks or to provide scope for variables. Containers can include other containers in addition to tasks.

In a package, containers can be used to:

- Repeat tasks.
- Group tasks and containers that need to succeed or fail in concert with one another.

Integration Services provides four types of containers for building packages:

Foreach Loop Container Runs a control flow repeatedly by using an enumerator.

For Loop Container Runs a control flow repeatedly by testing a condition.

Sequence Container Groups tasks and containers into control flows that are subsets of the package control flow.

Task Host Container Provides services to a single task.

Packages and event handlers are also types of containers. Containers include control flows that are made up of executables and precedence constraints. Containers may use event handlers, and variables. The task host container is an exception: because the task host container encapsulates a single task, it does not use precedence constraints.

Executables Executables are container-level tasks and any containers within the container. An executable can be one of the tasks and containers that SSIS provides or a custom task.

Precedence Constraints Precedence constraints link containers and tasks within the same parent container into an ordered control flow. Think of them as the SSIS traffic cop.

Event Handlers Event handlers, at the container level, respond to events raised by the container or the objects it includes. You will see how to use event handlers within packages later in the chapter.

Variables Variables that are used in containers include the container-level system variables that Integration Services provides and the user-defined variables that the container uses.

Now that we've got all the bits and pieces in place and have scratched the surface of some of the key elements, let's get busy creating some packages.

Creating Packages with the Import/Export Wizard

Now that you've seen how simple it is to create a project, let's take a look at the various ways you can create a package. The simplest and most common method is to use the Import and Export Wizard. Like all Wizards, it helps you through the design process one step at a time by asking questions. In this case, the end result of running the wizard is a SSIS package that will perform a single transfer operation between two databases. Second, you can choose to work with the SSIS Package Designer. The designer doesn't offer the hand-holding of the wizards, but it allows you the flexibility to combine multiple SSIS tasks and create a workflow using those tasks.

You can also use the wizard and the SSIS Designer together. Once you've used the wizard to create the package and copied the data you can open and edit the saved package using the SSIS Designer. You can also use the Designer to add tasks, transformations, and event-driven logic.

The Import and Export Wizard offers the simplest method of building a Microsoft SSIS package. The wizard can copy data to and from a variety of data sources, including:

- Microsoft SQL Server
- Flat files
- Microsoft Office Access
- Microsoft Office Excel
- Other OLE DB providers

In addition, you can use ADO.NET providers, though only as sources. There are four ways to start the Import Export Wizard.

1. Click the Start Menu. Select Programs ➢ Microsoft SQL Server 2005 ➢ Business Intelligence Development Studio (BIDS).
2. If no Integration Services Project exists, select File ➢ New ➢ Project, and then create a new project as described above. If a project already exists, select the project.
3. Right-click the SSIS Packages folder, and then click SSIS Import and Export Wizard.

OR

1. Click the Start Menu. Select Programs ➢ Microsoft SQL Server 2005 ➢ Business Intelligence Development Studio (BIDS).
2. If no Integration Services Project exists, select File ➢ New ➢ Project, and then create a new project as described above. If a project already exists, select the project.
3. Select Project from the menu and click SSIS Import and Export Wizard.

OR

1. Click the Start Menu. Select Programs ➢ Microsoft SQL Server 2005 ➢ SQL Server Management Studio, and connect to the Database Engine server type.
2. Expand the Databases folder and select and right-click a database.
3. Select Tasks, and then click Import Data or Export data.

OR

1. From the command prompt, type **C:\Program Files\Microsoft SQL Server\90\Tools\Binn\VSSHell\Common7\IDE\DTSWizard.exe**.

Whichever way you choose will launch the Import Export Wizard and the first screen you'll see is the splash screen as shown in Figure 22.7.

FIGURE 22.7
Import and Export Wizard splash screen

1. From the splash screen, click Next.
2. The Choose a Data Source panel, shown in Figure 22.8 consists of three parts. At the very top you can select the source for the data. This combo box allows you to choose any OLE DB provider that's installed on your system as the data source. For example, you can choose to copy data from a SQL Server database (the default), a Microsoft Access database, Microsoft Excel spreadsheet, or an Oracle database, just to name a few.

The appearance of this panel will change depending on what data source you select. For example, if you choose SQL Native Client as the Data source, you will need to choose a server, supply authentication information, and choose a database. On the other hand, if you choose to use a Microsoft Access data source, the frame's controls change to prompt you for only the filename, username, and password to use when opening the Access database.

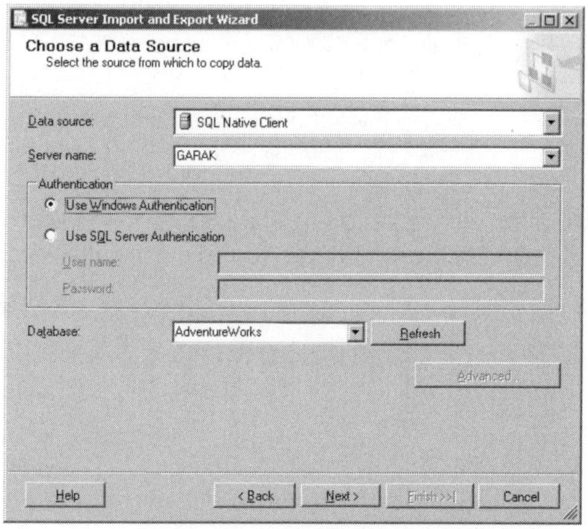

FIGURE 22.8
Choose a Data Source panel in the Import and Export Wizard.

1. After you choose a data source, in this example we are using the AdventureWorks database and click Next, the wizard shows the Choose a Destination panel. This panel is an exact copy (except for the caption) of the Choose a Data Source panel. Once again, you can choose any OLE DB database as the target for your SSIS operation. You can also opt to create a new SQL Database and specify the database properties.
2. To create a new database, click the New button next to the database text window, name the new databases SSISExample, accept the defaults and click OK. The new database is created, and you are returned to the Choose a Destination screen, with the new SSISExample database appearing as shown in Figure 22.9.

FIGURE 22.9
Choose a Destination panel in the Import and Export Wizard.

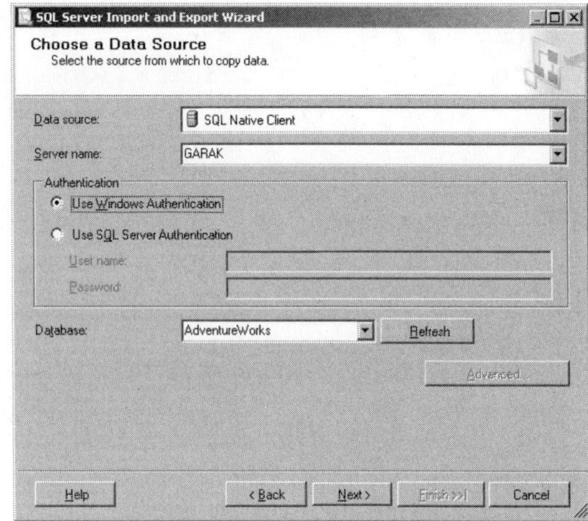

3. Click next to open the Specify Table Copy or Query panel, shown in Figure 22.10.

FIGURE 22.10
Specify Table Copy or Query panel in the Import and Export Wizard.

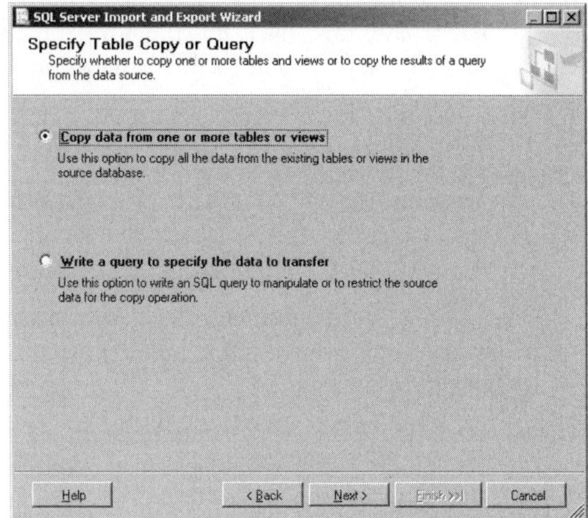

There are two choices on this panel. If you want to move entire tables from the source to the destination, choose "Copy data from one or more tables or views" from the Source Database. Note that you can still use this option to copy a partial table if you've defined a view in the source that includes only the data of interest. Alternatively, to define the data to be copied using a SQL statement, choose "Write a query to specify the data to transfer."

4. The next panel in the wizard depends on your choice in the Specify Table Copy or Query panel. If you chose to copy tables and views, and specified the AdventureWorks database, you'll see the Select Source Tables and Views panel, shown in Figure 22.11.

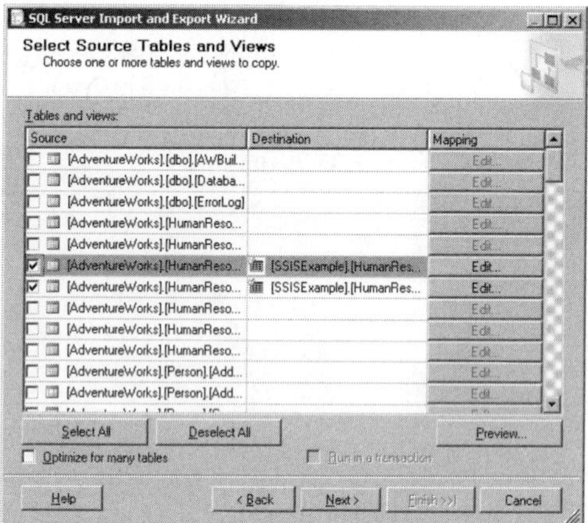

FIGURE 22.11
Select Source Tables and Views panel in the DTS Wizard.

This panel lets you perform a number of operations related to selecting data:

- To include a table or view in the data to be transferred, check the check box to the left of the table or view's name.
- To specify a destination table for the data, select it from the drop-down list in the Destination column. This list includes all of the tables in the destination database. It will default to a table of the same name as any selected source table, if possible.
- To see the data in a source table, select the table and click the Preview button. SQL Server will display a dialog box containing up to 100 rows from this table.

5. To customize the way that the data is transferred from the source to the destination, select the source and destination tables, and click the Edit button in the Mapping column. This opens the Column Mappings dialog box, shown in Figure 22.12.

The Column Mappings dialog box allows you to customize the way that data is moved from the source database to the destination database. For any table, you can use this dialog box to perform these actions:

- To decide whether to create the destination column from scratch, delete rows from the destination table, or append rows to the destination table, and choose the appropriate option on the Column Mappings tab.
- To change which source column is mapped to which destination column, choose a source column from the drop-down list in the Mappings section of the Column Mappings tab.

- To create primary or foreign keys on the destination table, select Create Destination Table on the Column Mappings tab and then check the appropriate boxes on the Constraints tab.
- To customize the CREATE TABLE statement used to create the destination table, select Edit SQL and then modify the SQL statement.

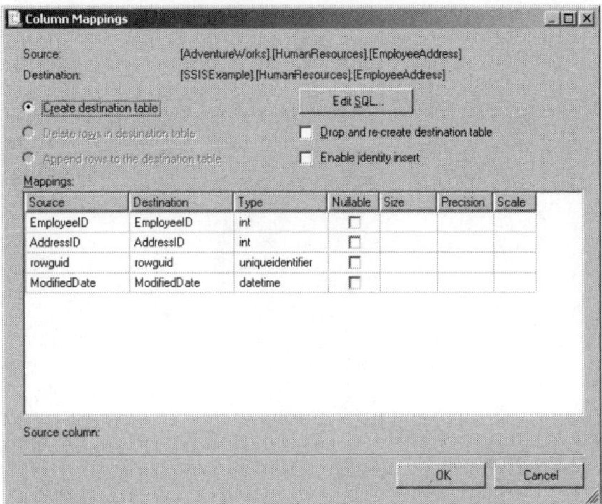

FIGURE 22.12 Column Mappings dialog box

Once you've finished amending the columns and tables—naturally within the limits of the datatype and innate properties of the source and destination—return to the Select Source Tables and Views. If you want to see what the data looks like, click Preview.

6. Click Next to open the Complete the Wizard panel and review the settings as shown in Figure 22.13. Notice in the third bullet item that because we started the Import and Export Wizard by right-clicking on the SSIS Packages folder in the SSISExample Project, the package we've created will be saved to that folder with the not very imaginative name `Package1.dtsx`.

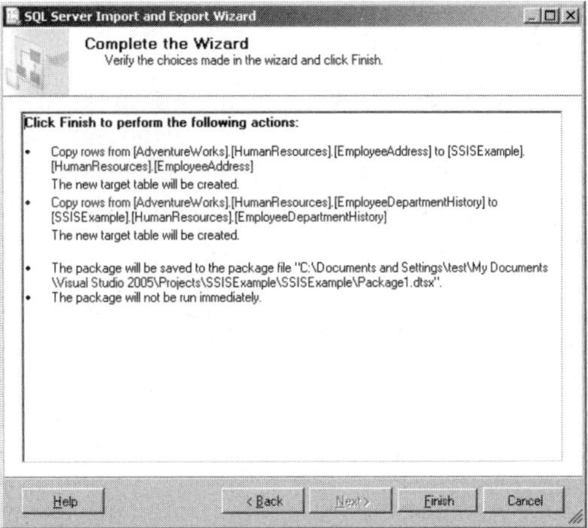

FIGURE 22.13 Complete the wizard information panel.

7. Click Finish. If you've been following along, the package appears in the SSIS Packages folder as `Package1.dtsx` and a graphic of the package's processes appear in the Control Flow window of the SSIS Designer as shown in Figure 22.14.

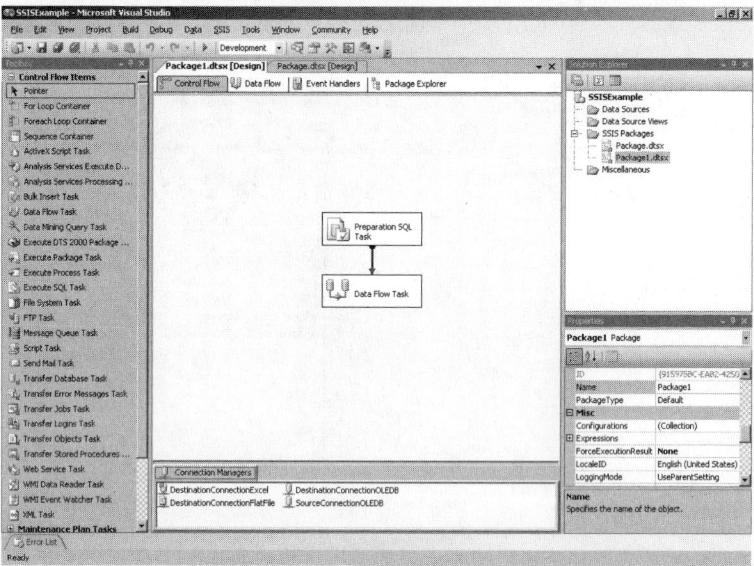

FIGURE 22.14
SSIS Designer showing new package

8. Close the project and exit BIDS.

Congratulations! You've built your first SSIS package!

Creating Packages with SSIS Designer

SSIS Designer is a graphical tool for creating packages. It includes separate design surfaces for building a control flow, data flows, and event handlers in packages. You can also access the dialog boxes, windows, and wizards that allow you to add advanced functions and features to packages.

The five main tabs of the SSIS Designer work surface are Control Flow, Data Flow, Event Handler, Package Explorer, and Execution Results. You'll become very familiar with the first three of these tabs and the views they provide in the rest of this chapter. As the name implies, the Execution Results tab opens a window that shows the results of any operation you run. The last tab, Package Explorer, is another new SSIS and provides a hierarchical tree view of the package that's displayed in the designer.

Before we move onto designing a package, one quick note about SSIS Designer and Integration Services service—the service that manages and monitors packages. The Integration Services service does not have to be running to create or modify packages in SSIS Designer. However, if you stop the service while SSIS Designer is open, you will no longer be able to open the dialog boxes that SSIS Designer provides and will have to close SSIS designer, exit, and then reopen BIDS, the Integration Services project, and the package.

With that said, let's create a new package using SSIS Designer. For the sake of clarity we're going to make a simple package that transfers data from one table to another in the AdventureWorks database. In fact it's really just a variation on the one we made with the Import and Export Wizard.

1. From the Windows taskbar, select Start ➢ Programs ➢ Microsoft SQL Server 2005 ➢ Business Intelligence Development Studio.
2. Select the SSISExample project you created earlier. Or if you prefer Click File ➢ New ➢ Project and create a new Integration Services Project.
3. In the Solution Explorer pane, right-click the SSISExample project and then select Add ➢ New Item from the pop-up menu.
4. From the Add New Item—SSISExample dialog box, select the New SSIS Package template. Enter `SSISExample2.dtsx` in the name text box, as shown in Figure 22.15, and then click Add.

FIGURE 22.15
Select a New SSIS Package template.

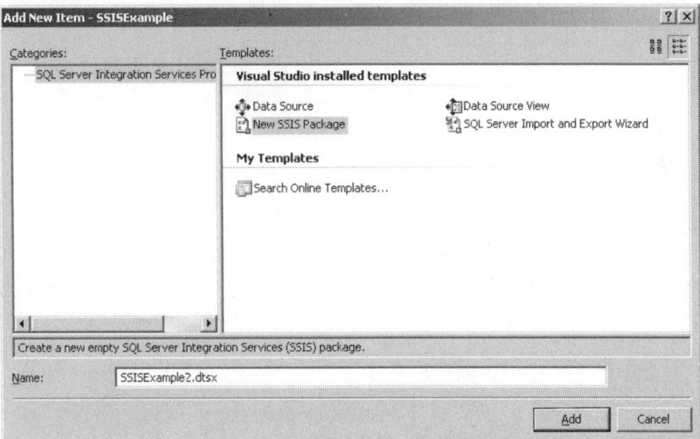

5. In the Solution Explorer, expand the SSISExample folder, right-click the Data Sources folder, and then select New Data Source from the context menu to start the Data Source Wizard. On the Welcome to the Data Source Wizard page, click Next.
6. On the "Select how to define the connection" page, click the New button.
7. In the Connection Manager dialog box, in the Select or enter a server name drop-down list, type ***localhost*** or select the server you want to use, as shown in Figure 22.16.
8. Under Log on to the server, select Use Windows Authentication. In the Select or enter a database name on the drop-down list, select AdventureWorks, and then click OK.
9. In the Data Source Wizard dialog box, click Next.
10. In the Completing the wizard page, review the Connection string properties, and then click Finish.

NOTE The benefit of using data sources is that you can reference them across multiple packages. In a package, you have the option to create connections to the data source or point to the data source directly.

FIGURE 22.16
Connection Manager

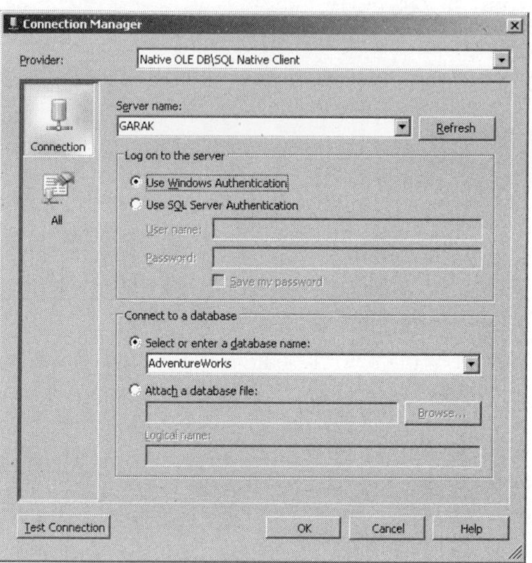

11. To create a new connection from a data source, right-click on the Connection Manager box, in the lower center part of the BIDS screen. Select New OLE DB Connection.

12. In the Select Data Connection dialog box shown in Figure 22.17, highlight the `localhost.AdventureWorks` data connection, and then click OK. This adds a new connection that points to the AdventureWorks data source, which can be used across package tasks.

13. Confirm that you've selected the Control Flow tab (found at the top of the design surface).

14. Select View ➤ Toolbox to open the Toolbox window if it is not visible.

FIGURE 22.17
Data Connection dialog box

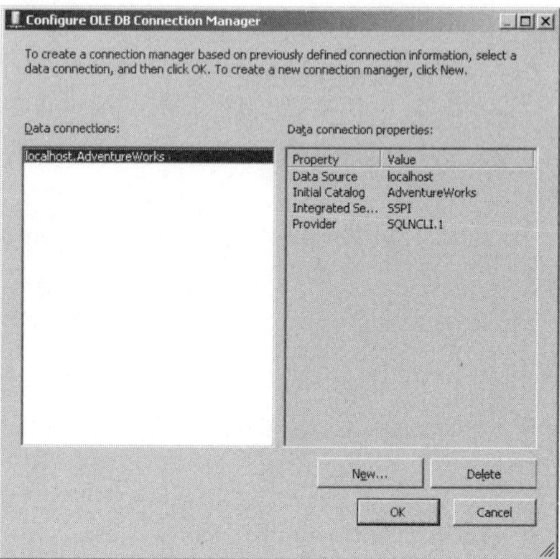

INSERTING CONTROL FLOW TASKS

1. In the Control Flow Items list of the Toolbox are shown the three different types of Control Flow Containers as well as a list of Control Flow Tasks. We'll come back to the containers later.

One of the key differences between creating packages with the Import and Export Wizard and the SSIS Designer is that the designer allows you to add tasks to the package. A *task* is a piece of functionality the server can perform. Tasks obviously add immense flexibility to SSIS packages. SQL Server 2005 provides 25 different control flow tasks.

ActiveX Script task The ActiveX Script task executes an ActiveX script that performs a specified action.

Analysis Services Execute DDL Task Executes T-SQL DDL statements. See Chapter 26 for more information on Analysis Services.

Analysis Services Processing Task The Analysis Services Processing task allows SSIS to refresh the data in a Microsoft Analysis Server cube.

Bulk Insert Task The Bulk Insert task uses the BULK INSERT facility of SQL Server to quickly move external data into a table. This is the fastest way to load data to SQL Server. However, you can't do any data transformations or validation within a Bulk Insert task, which makes it unsuitable if the data isn't already in the exact correct format.

Data Flow Task Copies and transforms data between data sources

Data Mining Query Task The Data Mining Query task enables SSIS to run a query to extract results from a Microsoft Analysis Server Data Mining model.

Execute DTS 2000 Package Task The Execute DTS 2000 Package task runs packages that were developed by using the SQL Server 2000 tools. By using this task, you can include SQL Server 2000 DTS packages in SQL Server 2005 data transformation solutions. A package can include both Execute Package tasks and Execute DTS 2000 Package tasks, because each type of task uses a different version of the runtime engine.

Execute Package Task The Execute Package task allows one SSIS package to call another SSIS package as a subroutine. This task also allows you to treat the called package as part of a transaction, so that you can commit or roll back the results of multiple packages as a unit.

Execute Process Task The Execute Process task tells SSIS to launch an external program, batch file, or script. You can also provide a timeout period and any command-line parameters that the external program requires.

Execute SQL Task The Execute SQL task can send a SQL statement to any connection in the SSIS package for execution.

File System Task The File System task performs operations on files and directories in the file system. The File System task allows a package to create, move, or delete directories and files. It can also be used to set file and directory attributes.

File Transfer Protocol Task The FTP task allows you to move a file or group of files from one location to another. You can move files from either an Internet FTP server or a directory, and post files to an FTP server or directory. This task is most useful for bringing in files from outside your organization that you want to include in a data warehouse.

Message Queue Task The Message Queue task allows a SSIS package to send a message via Microsoft Message Queue (MSMQ). This task is designed to allow different servers within an organization to coordinate operations without needing to be constantly in touch with one another.

Script Task The Script task executes scripts written in VB.NET using the Microsoft Visual Studio for Applications (VSA) environment. The code is custom Microsoft Visual Basic .NET code that is compiled and executed at package runtime.

Send Mail Task The Send Mail task sends e-mail as part of a SSIS package. You can use this, in conjunction with the workflow features of SSIS, to notify an operator of the success or failure of a package or send messages in response to an event that the package raises at runtime. For example, the task can notify a database administrator about the success or failure of the FTP task.

Transfer Databases Task The Transfer Databases task allows SSIS to move or copy entire databases from one SQL Server to another.

Transfer Error Messages Task The Transfer Error Messages task copies error messages from one SQL Server to another. You can use this task to collect all error messages generated in the course of executing a SSIS package to a single location.

Transfer Jobs Task The Transfer Jobs task transfers jobs from the msdb database on one SQL Server to another SQL Server.

Transfer Logins Task The Transfer Logins task transfers logins from one SQL Server to another.

Transfer Objects Task The Transfer SQL Server Objects task moves entire objects from one SQL Server to another. This task can move the same types of objects that the SSIS Wizard can move when working in native SQL Server mode.

Transfer Master Stored Procedures Task The Transfer Master Stored Procedures task allows SSIS to copy stored procedures from the master database on one SQL Server to another.

Web Service Task The Web Service task executes a Web service method. The Web Service task can be used to write to a variable the values that a Web service method returns. Additionally it can be used to write the value that a Web service returns to a file.

WMI Data Reader Task The WMI Data Reader task runs queries using the Windows Management Instrumentation (WMI) Query Language that return information from WMI about a computer system. For example, you can use this task to query the Windows event logs on a local or remote computer and write the information to a file or variable. Similarly you can get information about hardware, software applications, and what versions are installed.

WMI Event Watcher Task The WMI Event Watcher task monitors for a WMI event using a Management Instrumentation Query Language (WQL) event query to specify events of interest. Typically you would use this task to run a package that deletes files when the available memory on a server drops below a specified percentage or to look for installation of an application and then run a package that uses the application.

XML Task The XML task accesses data in XML documents or applies operations to the documents using Extensible Stylesheet Language Transformations (XSLT) style sheets and XPath expressions.

As you'll see later, Data WorkFlow and Maintenance Tasks are built-in. In addition to the built-in tasks, SSIS can also use custom tasks created by independent developers. Creating a custom task is an advanced topic beyond the scope of this book.

Although each type of task has its own properties, the general process of inserting a task into a DTS package is the same in all cases. Either select the task from the Task menu or locate the icon for the task in the Task toolbar and click it (or click and drag it to the design surface). In any case, a Properties dialog box will pop up to prompt you for the necessary information to complete the task. For example, Figure 22.18 shows the Properties dialog for a Data Flow task, which as you'll recall copies and transforms data between two data sources.

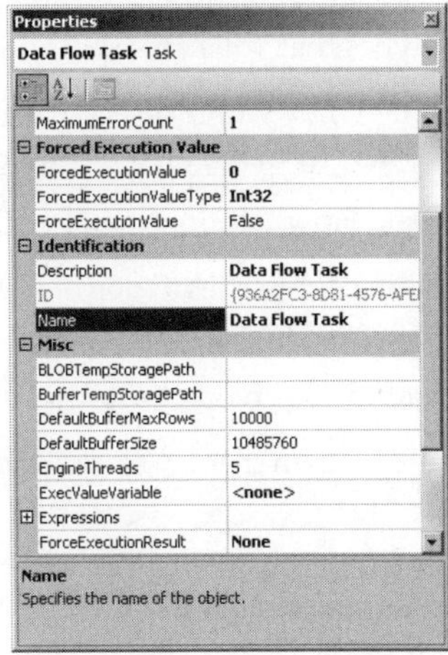

FIGURE 22.18
Data Flow task properties sheet

Since this a very simple example, the only task that we'll insert is the Data Flow task. However, you should feel free to experiment moving the various tasks into the Control Flow Editor and viewing their individual properties.

1. From the Control Flow Items list, drag and drop a Data Flow task onto the Control Flow Editor. The designer should look like Figure 22.19.

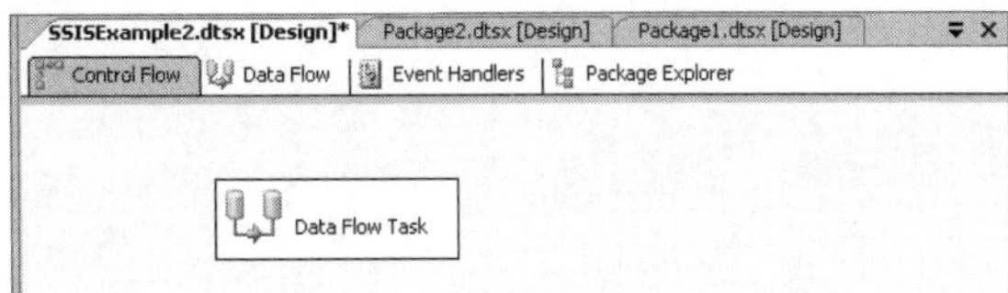

FIGURE 22.19
Control Flow Editor panel

2. In the Control Flow Editor, double-click the Data Flow task, which also selects the Data Flow tab and opens the Data Flow Editor.

SELECTING DATA FLOW SOURCE

Notice that the contents of the toolbox have changed to items that you use to work with the data flow. The toolbox is divided into three groups: Data Flow Sources, Data Flow Transformations, and Data Flow Destinations.

The six basic types of Data Flow Sources are:

- DataReader Source
- Excel Source
- Flat File Source
- OLE DB Source
- Raw File Source
- XML Source

Each of these has its own properties and in many instances, such as the OLE DB source, will have its own list of types that you can select and modify.

1. Add an OLE DB Source object by selecting and then dragging and dropping an OLE DB Source object from the toolbox and onto the Data Flow Editor.
2. In the Data Flow Editor, double-click the OLE DB Source object.
3. In the Source Properties dialog box, in the Connection drop-down list, verify that `localhost.AdventureWorks` is selected.
4. In the Data access mode drop-down, select Table or view.
5. In the drop-down menu, select `[HumanResources].[Employee]` as in Figure 22.20.

FIGURE 22.20
OLE DB Source Editor

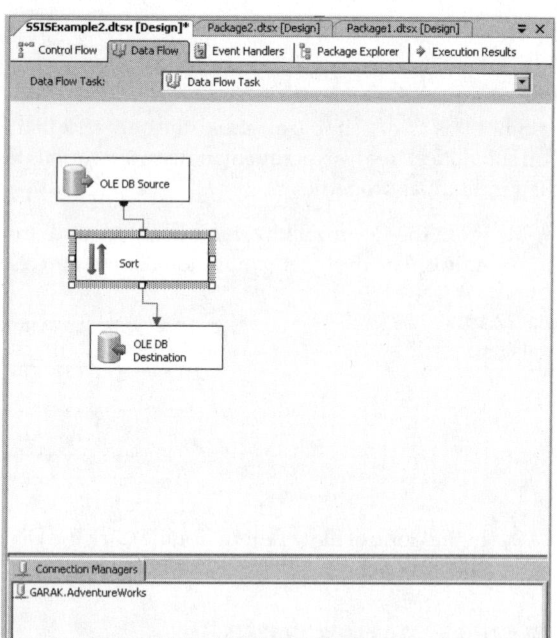

INSERTING TRANSFORMATIONS IN A DATA FLOW

SSIS transformations control what happens to data when it's moved from the source to the destination. You can choose from any of a large number of built-in transformations, or custom transformations you define yourself. Creating custom transformations is another advanced topic outside the scope of this book. There are the 28 built-in standard transformations:

Aggregate Transformation Performs aggregations such as the transformation that performs aggregations such as AVERAGE, SUM, and COUNT.

Audit Transformation Provides information about the environment, such as names of the package, computer, and operator that can be added to the data flow.

Character Map Transformation Applies string functions to character data.

Conditional Split Transformation Evaluates data and routes it to different outputs.

Copy Column Transformation Creates new output columns by copying input columns.

Data Conversion Transformation Converts the datatype of an input column to a different output datatype.

Data Mining Query Transformation Runs data mining prediction queries.

Derived Column Transformation Creates an output column from the results of expressions.

Export Column Transformation Inserts data from a data flow into a file.

Fuzzy Grouping Transformation Standardizes values in input column data.

Fuzzy Lookup Transformation Looks up values in a reference table using a fuzzy match.

Import Column Transformation Reads data from a file and adds it to a data flow.

Lookup Transformation Looks up values in a reference table using an exact match.

Merge Transformation Merges two sorted data sets.

Merge Join Transformation Joins two data sets using a FULL, LEFT, or INNER join.

Multicast Transformation Distributes the input data to multiple outputs.

OLE DB Command Transformation Runs SQL commands for each row in a data flow.

Percentage Sampling Transformation Makes a sample data set using a percentage that specifies the sample size.

Pivot Transformation Pivots the input data according to an input column value.

Row Count Transformation Counts the input rows and stores the count in a variable.

Row Sampling Transformation Creates a sample data set by specifying the number of rows in the sample.

Script Component Transformation Uses script to extract, transform, or load data.

Slowly Changing Dimension Transformation Coordinates updating and inserting rows into OLAP dimensions.

Sort Transformation Sorts input data and copies the sorted data to the transformation output.

Term Extraction Transformation Extracts terms from text.

Term Lookup Transformation Looks up terms in a reference table and counts terms extracted from text.

Union All Transformation Merges multiple data sets.

Unpivot Transformation Unpivots input data according to an input column value.

For simplicity's sake, let's add a Sort transformation to our package and then configure it to sort on the employee's birth date.

1. Expand the Data Flow Transformations folder. Drag the Sort Transformation object onto the Data Flow Editor.
2. In the Data Flow Editor, click the OLE DB Source object, and drag and drop the green data flow arrow onto the Sort Transformation box.
3. Double-click the Sort object to open the Sort Transformation Editor. Select BirthDate to sort the list of employees by age. Set Sort Type to ascending, as shown in Figure 22.21. As you will notice, you can control a number of aspects of the Sort Transformation, or, for that matter any transformation in this phase.

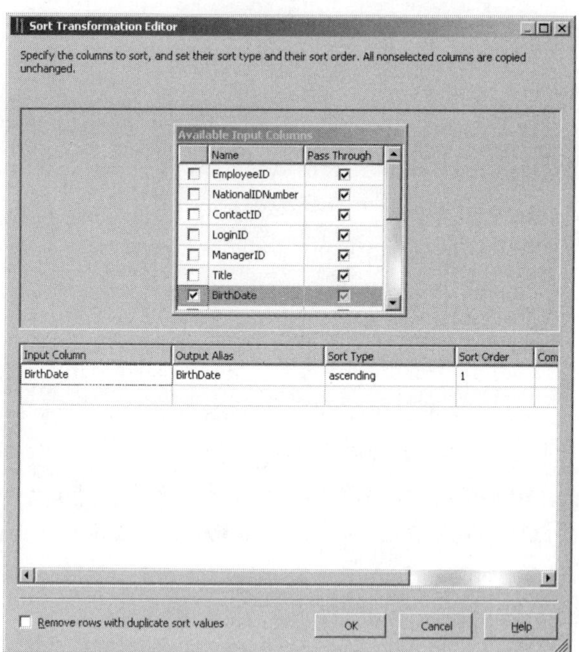

FIGURE 22.21
Sort Transformation Editor page

4. Click OK to return to the Data Flow Editor.

SELECTING DATA FLOW DESTINATION

Of course the data has to have a place to go. As you should have guessed by now, there are a large number of Data Flow Destinations—11 in all:

Data Mining Model Training Trains data mining models.

DataReader Destination Exposes the data in a data flow by using the ADO.NET DataReader interface.

Dimension Processing Loads and processes an SQL Server 2005 Analysis Services dimension.

Excel Destination Writes data to an Excel file.

Flat File Destination Writes data to a flat file.

OLE DB Destination Loads data using an OLE DB provider.

Partition Processing Loads and processes an Analysis Services partition.

Raw File Destination Writes raw data to a file.

Recordset Destination Creates an ADO recordset.

SQL Server Destination Bulk inserts data into a SQL Server 2005 table or view.

SQL Server Mobile Destination Inserts rows into a SQL Server Mobile database.

To specify a destination for the data, continue working in the Data Flow Editor.

1. In the Toolbox, in the Data Flow Items list, drag and drop an OLE DB Destination object onto the Data Flow Editor.

2. In the Data Flow Editor, click the Sort object, and drag and drop the green data flow arrow onto the OLE DB Destination object.
3. In the Data Flow Editor, double-click the OLE DB Destination object.
4. In the OLE DB Destination Editor dialog box, in the Connection drop-down list, verify that `locahost.AdventureWorks` is selected.
5. In the Name of the table or the view drop-down list, click the New button. Edit the `CREATE TABLE` statement so the name of the destination table is [dbo].[SSISExample2].
6. Click the Mappings tab, to verify the source-to-destination column mappings.
7. Click OK. The Data Flow window should resemble the one shown in Figure 22.22, with an OLE DB source object, a Sort transformation, and an OLE DB Destination.
8. Select the File ➤ Save All menu item.

FIGURE 22.22
Data Flow pane

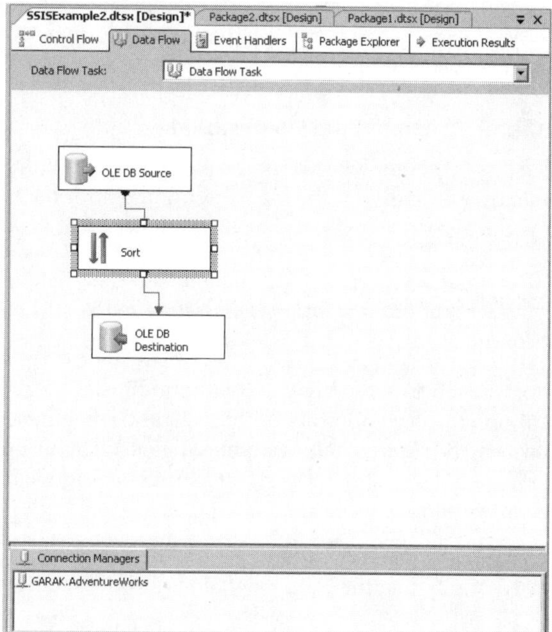

Congratulations! You've successfully created a package using SSIS Designer. For the time being leave the designer open to your current project, while we digress a bit on the ways you can save a SSIS package. Then, we'll talk about how to run a package.

Saving Packages

In BIDS, packages created with SSIS Designer are saved to the file system as XML files with the extension `.dtsx files`. You can also save copies of the package in the msdb database in SQL Server 2005 or to the package store. The package store represents the folders in the file system location that the Integration Services service manages.

If you save a package to the file system, you can later use Integration Services service to import the package to SQL Server or the package store.

To save a package to the file system, do the following:

1. In Business Intelligence Development Studio, open the SSIS project that contains the package you want to save to a file.
2. In Solution Explorer, click the package you want to save.
3. On the File menu, click Save Selected Items.

Running Packages

Once you've created a package, you will almost certainly want to run it. That is, after all, why you created it in the first place. You may need to run the package immediately, or you may want the package to run at a specified time.

A package in SSIS can be run in a number of ways. Packages can be run from the SSIS Designer; through the SSIS `dtexec` utility, from within Management Studio or as a step in a SQL Server Agent job.

We'll examine each of these methods, starting with BIDS, where the package you created is patiently waiting to run.

Running Packages in SSIS Designer

The most common way to run packages is from within the SSIS Designer component of BIDS, primarily because it is the ideal environment for package development, debugging, and testing. If you run a package from the SSIS Designer, it always runs immediately.

TIP When a solution has multiple projects, set the project that contains the package that you want to run as the startup project before you run the package.

While a package is running, the SSIS Designer displays the progress of package execution on the Progress tab. You can view the start and finish time of the package and its tasks and containers, in addition to information about the tasks and containers in the package that failed. After the package finishes, the runtime information remains available on the Execution Results tab.

As you'll see later in the chapter, SSIS packages can be enabled for logging, allowing you to record runtime information in log files.

To run the SSISExample2 package that you just created, return to the still open SSIS Designer.

1. Verify that the Data Flow tab is selected at the top of the designer.
2. In the Solution Explorer, right-click the `SSISExample2.dtsx` package, and then click Execute Package. While the package executes, notice how the colors change:
    - Gray means waiting to execute.
    - Yellow means currently executing.
    - Green means success.
    - Red indicates failure.

    Also note the number of records that have been processed and loaded. Figure 22.23 shows the completed flow.

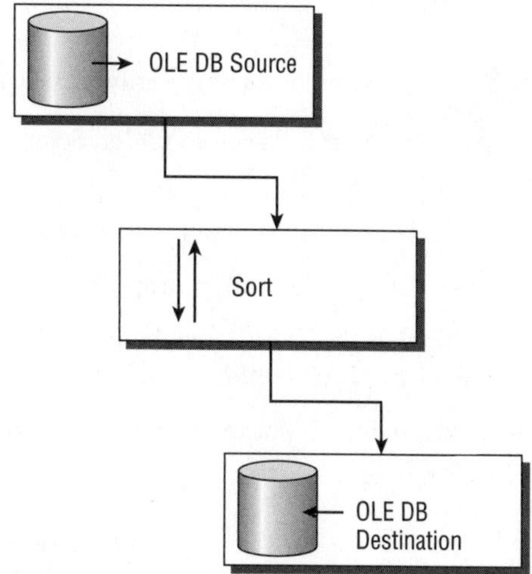

FIGURE 22.23
After successful completion, the objects are green and the diagram includes the number of affected rows.

3. When the package finishes its execution, select Debug ➤ Stop Debugging, or click the link below the pane to return to Design mode.

RUNNING PACKAGES USING DTEXEC UTILITY

The DTEXEC command prompt utility can be used to run SSIS packages, as well as configuring them (using DTEXEC as a configuration tool will not be covered in this book).

The DTEXEC utility provides access to all the package configuration and execution features, such as connections, properties, variables, logging, and progress indicators. The DTEXEC utility gives you the ability to load packages from three sources: a Microsoft SQL Server database, the SSIS service, and the file system.

1. Open a Command Prompt window.
2. Type **DTEXEC /** followed by the DTS, SQL, or File option and the package path, including the package name.
3. If the package encryption level is EncryptSensitiveWithPassword or EncryptAllWithPassword, use the Decrypt option to provide the password. If no password is included, DTEXEC will prompt for the password.
4. Add any additional command-line options you want.
5. Press Enter.

RUNNING PACKAGES USING MANAGEMENT STUDIO

Before you can run a package from within Management Studio you have to import it.

Import a Package

To import a package, do the following:

1. Open Management Studio.
2. On the View menu, click Object Explorer.

3. In Object Explorer, click Connect ➢ Integration Services.

WARNING If you cannot connect, verify that the Integration Services service is started.

4. Expand the Stored Packages folder. Select MSDB and right-click the folder.
5. Select Import Package to open the Import Package. In this example, we're going to import the SSISExample2 package we created earlier.
6. In the Package Information drop-down box, select File System.
7. Click on the ellipsis button next to the Package path text box and navigate to the `SSISExample2.dtsx` file.
8. Accept the default package name, in this case SSISExample2. The dialog should resemble Figure 22.24.

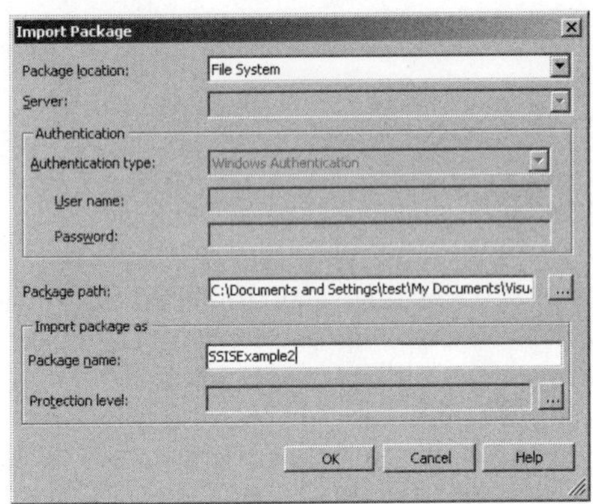

FIGURE 22.24
The Import Package dialog box

9. Click OK. The package is imported.

Run the Package

1. To run the package, right-click on the package and select Run Package from the context menu, the Execute Package Utility appears (Figure 22.25).
2. You can use the Execute Package Utility to configure a number of settings, including Configurations, Command Files, Connection Managers, Execution Options, Reporting, Logging, Set Values, Verification, and Command Line, some of which we will discuss in greater detail later. Once you have made your selections, click the Execute button.
3. The Package Execution Progress pane appears and shows the progress (Figure 22.26).
4. When the Package Execution completes, click Close twice.

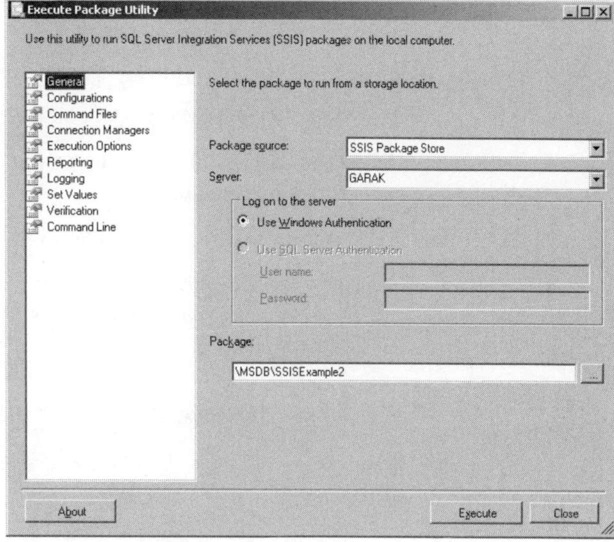

FIGURE 22.25
Execute Package Utility

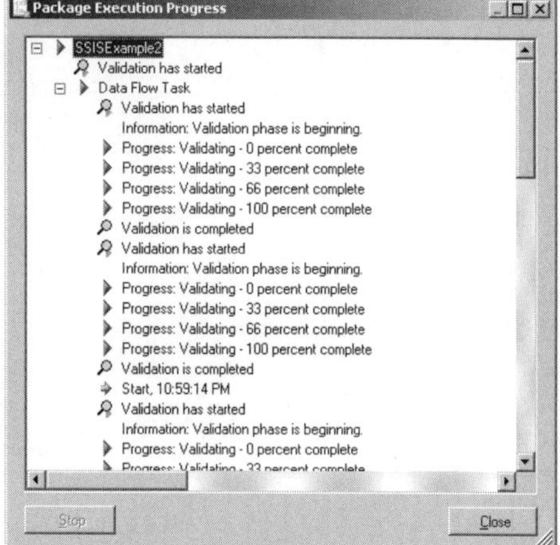

FIGURE 22.26
Package Execution Progress

RUNNING PACKAGES AS A SCHEDULED SQL SERVER AGENT JOB

As you know from earlier chapters, you can schedule events to run in SQL Server 2005 by creating a SQL Server Agent Job in Management Studio.

You may want to run packages only at certain times or on a routine basis. Follow these steps:

1. In Management Studio, open the instance of SQL Server in which you want to create a job or the instance that contains the job to which you want to add a step. In this example we'll create a new job.
2. Expand SQL Server Agent, right-click Jobs, and then click New Job.

3. On the General page, as shown in Figure 22.27, provide a job name, select an owner and job category, and, if you want, add a job description.
4. Select Enabled to make the job available for scheduling.
5. Click Steps, and then click New.
6. In the step name text box type, **SSISExampleStep**. In the Type list, select SQL Server Integration Services package execution.
7. In the Run as list, select the proxy account with the credentials that the job will use.
8. On the General tab, select the package source as SQL Server, the server as *localhost*, specify the SSISExample2 package stored in SQL Server, provide the server name, and select the authentication mode to use.

FIGURE 22.27
New Job Step window

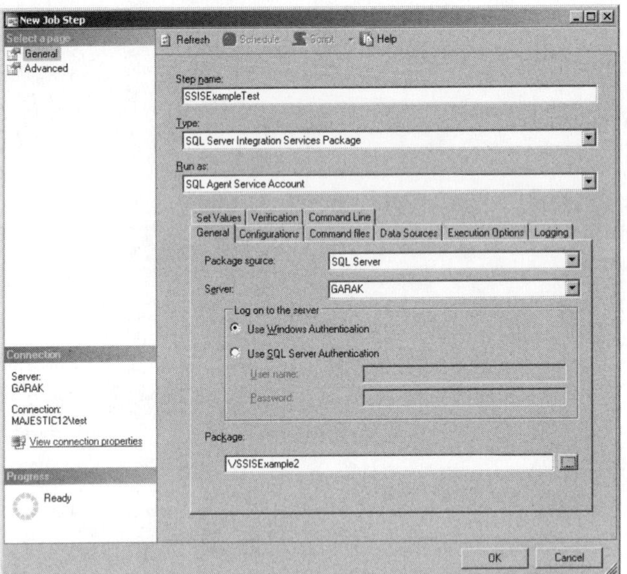

9. You can specify a number of additional settings under the remaining tabs. When ready, click OK.
10. To schedule the job to run, select Schedules. Click the New button. Specify a name, type of recurrence, and other options. Once you're satisfied, click OK twice to exit.

The package will run as specified.

Other Design Operations

As you will have already noticed, the entire package design environment is extremely rich and varied. Among the built-in tasks, built-in transformations, data sources, and destinations, as well as all their configurable variables, there are literally millions, if not billions of permutations.

In addition to the very small number we've viewed creating and running the simple example packages, SSIS Designer offers a number of additional capabilities.

IMPLEMENT LOGGING

SSIS has logging capabilities and can write log entries when runtime events occur. You can enable logging on the package only, or you can choose to enable logging on any task or container that the package includes. Integration Services supports a diverse set of logging providers, and gives you the ability to create custom log providers. In SSIS Designer, you define the logging options by using the Configure SSIS Logs dialog box.

1. In BIDS, open the Integration Services project that contains the package you want.
2. On the SSIS menu, click Logging.
3. Select a log provider in the Provider type list, and then click Add.
4. In the Configuration column, select a connection manager or click `<New connection>` to create a new connection manager of the appropriate type for the log provider you select:
   - For Text File, use a File connection manager.
   - For SQL Server Profiler, use a File connection manager.
   - For SQL Server, use an OLE DB connection manager.
   - For Microsoft Windows Event Log, do nothing. SSIS automatically creates the log.
   - For XML File, use a File connection manager.

   Repeat the above for each log to use in the package.

NOTE A package can use more than one log of each type.

5. If you want to, you can mark "select the package-level" check box, select the logs to use for package-level logging, and then click the Details tab. On the Details tab (Figure 22.28), you can select to either log all events or select individual events. Alternatively you can click Advanced, then select which information to log. By default, all information is logged.

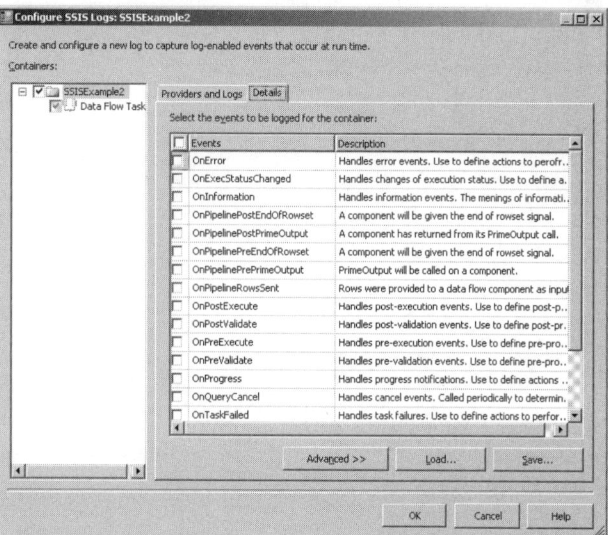

FIGURE 22.28
Configure SSIS Logs Details window

6. On the Details tab, click Save. The Save As dialog box appears. Locate the folder in which to save the logging configuration, type a filename for the new log, and then click Save.
7. Click OK.
8. Click Save Selected Items on the File menu to save the updated package.

CHECKPOINTS

Checkpoints allow SSIS to restart failed packages from the point of failure rather than rerunning the whole package. Configuring a package to use checkpoints causes it to write information about package execution to a checkpoint file. When the failed package is rerun, the checkpoint file is examined to determine where to restart the package. If the package runs successfully, the checkpoint file is deleted, and then re-created the next time the package is run.

1. In BIDS, open the Integration Services project that contains the package you want to configure.
2. In Solution Explorer, double-click the package.
3. Click the Control Flow tab, then right-click anywhere in the background of the control flow design surface, and click Properties.
4. Set the SaveCheckpoints property to True as shown in Figure 22.29.
5. Type the name of the checkpoint file in the CheckpointFileName property.
6. Set the CheckpointUsage property. Setting it to Always means to always restart the package from the checkpoint. IfExists is used if you want to restart the package only when the checkpoint file is available.

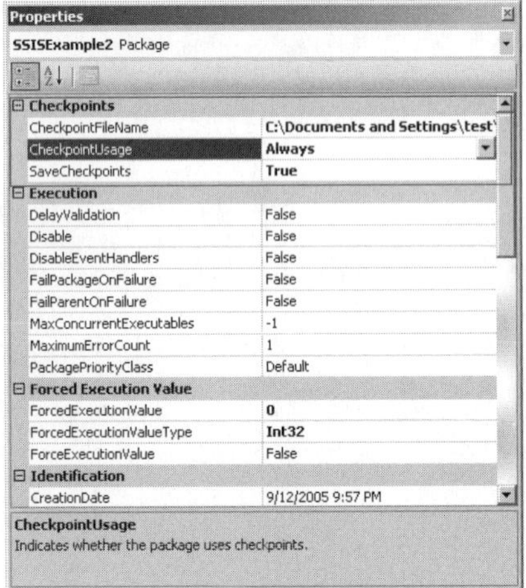

FIGURE 22.29
Package properties page showing checkpoints

7. To configure the tasks and containers from which the package can restart, right-click the desired task or container and click Properties.
8. Set the FailPackageOnFailure property to True for each selected task and container.
9. Click Save Selected Items on the File menu to save the updated package.

VARIABLES

SSIS introduces being able to use variables with packages. Variables can be used to provide communication among objects in the package, and between parent and child packages. Variables can also be used in expressions and scripts.

The two types of variables are system and user defined. *System variables* are provided by SSIS. Whenever you create a new package, add a container or a task to the package, or create an event handler, SSIS automatically includes a set of system variables, containing such information as the computer name where the package is running and the time the package began running. All system variables are read only.

User-defined variables are defined by the user and can be employed in a variety of ways including in scripts; in the expressions used by the For Loop container, the Derived Column transformation, the Conditional Split transformation; and precedence constraints as well as property expressions that update property values.

To add a variable to a package, do the following:

1. In BIDS, select the Integration Services package you want to work with. Then, in Solution Explorer, double-click the package to open it.
2. To define the scope of the variable, do one of the following:
    - If setting the scope of the package, click anywhere on the design surface of the Control Flow tab.
    - If setting the scope to an event handler, select an executable and an event handler on the design surface of the Event Handler tab.
    - If setting the scope of a task or a container, open the Control Flow or Event Handler design surface and click the task or container you want to work with.
3. On the SSIS menu, click Variables to open the Variables window as shown in Figure 22.30.
4. In the Variables window, click the Add Variable icon. The new variable is added to the list. You can modify value by selecting from the column you want to change.

FIGURE 22.30
Variables window

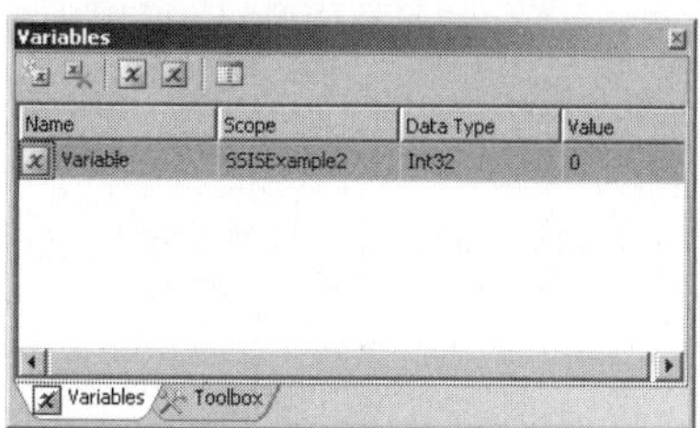

5. To save the updated package, click Save Selected Items on the File menu.

EXPRESSIONS

An expression is a combination of symbols—identifiers, literals, functions, and operators—that yields a single data value. Simple expressions can be a single constant, variable, or function, though usually they are quite complex and use multiple operators and functions as well as referencing any number of columns and variables. In SSIS, expressions can be used to define conditions for case statements, create and update values in data columns, assign values to variables, update or populate properties at runtime, define constraints in precedence constraints, and provide the expressions used by the For Loop container.

Only the following elements can use expressions:

- Conditional Split transformation
- Derived Column transformation
- Variables
- Precedence constraints (but the expressions must evaluate to true or false)
- For Loop container

Expressions can also be used to update the values of properties of packages, containers such as the For Loop and Foreach Loop, tasks, connection managers, log providers, and Foreach enumerators. For example, using a property expression, the string `"Localhost.AdventureWorks"` can be assigned to the ConnectionName property of the Execute SQL task.

The expression builder—available in the Conditional Split Transformation Editor, Derived Column Transformation Editor dialog boxes, and the Expression Builder dialog boxes—is a graphical tool for building expressions.

For example, to create an expression in the Derived Column Transformation, do the following:

1. In BIDS, open the Integration Services project that contains the package you want, then in Solution Explorer, double-click the package to open it.
2. In the SSIS Designer, click the Control Flow tab, and then click the Data Flow task with the data flow where you want to implement an expression.
3. Click the Data Flow tab, and drag the Derived Column transformation from the Toolbox to the design surface.
4. Drag the green connector from the source or a transformation to the Derived Column transformation.
5. Double-click the transformation to open its dialog box.
6. In the left pane, expand Variables to access system and user-defined variables, and expand Columns to access the transformation input columns.
7. In the right pane, expand Mathematical Functions, String Functions, Date/Time Functions, NULL Functions, Type Casts, and Operators to access the functions, the casts, and the operators that the expression grammar provides.
8. In the Derived Column Transformation Editor dialog box, as shown in Figure 22.31, drag variables, columns, functions, operators, and casts to the Expression column. You can also type an expression directly in the Expression column.
9. Click OK to exit the dialog box.

NOTE If the expression is not valid, an alert appears describing the syntax errors in the expression.

10. To save the updated package, click Save Selected Items on the File menu.

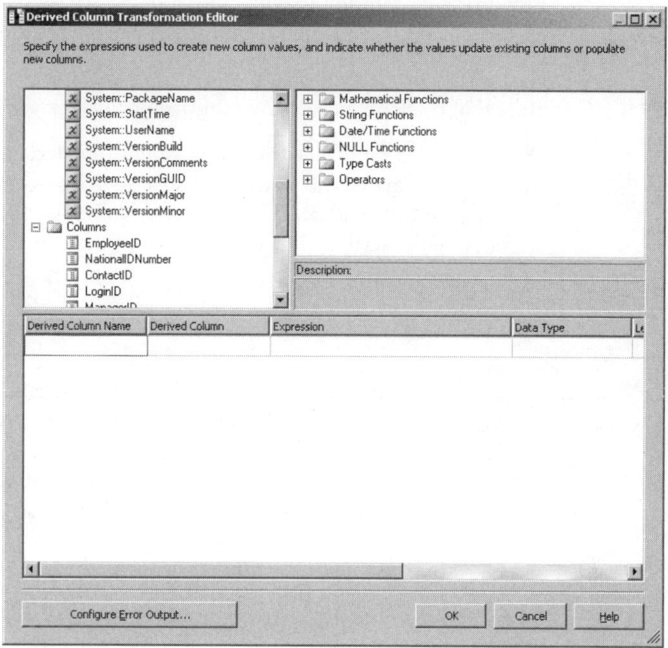

FIGURE 22.31 Derived Column Transformation Editor

PROPERTY EXPRESSIONS

Property expressions allow you to dynamically update a property value at runtime. For example, a property expression can update the *To* line that a Send Mail task uses with an e-mail address that is stored in a variable.

Another way to use property expressions is to customize configurations for each deployed instance of a package. This makes it possible to dynamically update package properties for different environments.

NOTE Property expressions are not available for properties of data flow components.

Property expressions can use system or user-defined variables. A property can use only one property expression and a property expression can apply only to one property. However, you can build multiple identical property expressions and assign them to different properties.

To create a property expression

1. In BIDS, open the Integration Services project that contains the package you want, then in Solution Explorer, double-click the package to open it.
2. If the item is a task or a loop, double-click the item, and then click Expressions in the editor.
3. Right-click the item and then click Properties. Click the Expressions ellipsis (…).
4. In the Property Expressions Editor, select a property in the Property list, and then do one of the following:
   - Type an expression in the Expression column and click OK.
   - Click the ellipsis (…) in the expression row of the property.

5. In Expression Builder, expand Variables to access system and user-defined variables.
6. In the right pane, expand Mathematical Functions, String Functions, Date/Time Functions, NULL Functions, Type Casts, and Operators to access the functions, the casts, and the operators that the SSIS expression language provides.
7. Drag variables, columns, functions, operators, and casts to the Expression box or type the expression in the box. If you click Evaluate Expression, you can view the evaluation result of the expression and make any necessary changes. If the expression is not valid, an alert appears that describes the syntax errors in the expression.
8. Click OK.

QUERIES

The Execute SQL task, the OLE DB source, the OLE DB destination, and the Lookup transformation can use queries. These SQL statements can create, update, and delete database objects and data; run stored procedures; and perform `SELECT` statements.

The source of the SQL statement can be a direct input, a file connection, or a variable. If you want to use a direct input, the SSIS Designer provides Query Builder, a graphical tool for creating SQL queries.

Using Query Builder offers the following advantages:

- Query Builder allows you to compose your query visually and a text pane that displays the SQL text of your query. You can work in either the graphical or text panes. Query Builder synchronizes the views so the query text and graphical representation always match.
- If you add more than one table to your query, Query Builder automatically determines how the tables are related and constructs the appropriate `JOIN` command.
- You can use T-SQL `SELECT` statements to return data, or to create queries that update, add, or delete records in a database.
- You can execute your query, then view and edit results immediately.

If you don't want to use Query Builder, you can provide direct input by typing the query in the task or data flow component dialog box or the Properties window.

Event Handlers

The ability to raise and handle events is another new feature introduced with SSIS. So before leaving the whole topic of package design, we need turn back a bit and look at Package Event Handlers.

Event handling lets packages respond to events that containers and tasks might raise at runtime. These events can be fired by package elements to signal different states, including error conditions, when a task has started, when a task completes, or a change in variable status

You can create custom event handlers that respond to these events by running a workflow when the event is raised. For example, you can create an event handler that sends an e-mail message when a task fails.

An event handler is similar to a package. Like a package, an event handler can provide scope for variables and includes a control flow and, optionally, data flows. You can build event handlers for packages, the Foreach Loop container, the For Loop container, the Sequence container, and all tasks.

You create event handlers by using the design surface of the Event Handlers tab in the SSIS Designer. Let's see how to add an event handler to the SSISExample2 package we created earlier.

1. In BIDS, open the SSISExample project. In Solution Explorer, double-click the SSISExample2 package to open it.
2. Click the Event Handlers tab.
3. In the Executables list, select the executable for which you want to create an event handler.
4. In the Event Handler list, select the event handler you want to build.
5. Click the link on the design surface of the Event Handler tab.
6. Add the Send Mail task. If you want, you can add more than one item and connect them using a precedence constraint by dragging the constraint from one control flow item to another.
7. Configure the Send Mail task by double-clicking on the tab and making the necessary settings. An example is shown in Figure 22.32.

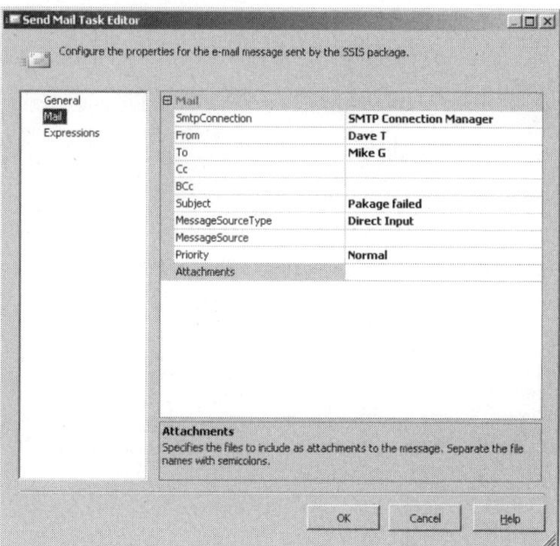

FIGURE 22.32
Send Mail Task Editor

8. On the File menu, click Save Selected Items to save the package. Now, if there is an error when the package executes, an e-mail will be sent from Dave T's account to Mike G with the subject "Package Failed."

Deploying Packages

Now that you have created packages, run them to make sure they worked, and saved them, you need to deploy them to make them available. Happily SSIS makes it simple to deploy packages to any computer and comes complete with a box full of tools and wizards you can use for this purpose.

SSIS packages can be deployed using a deployment utility, the import and export package features in Management Studio, or by saving a copy of the package. However, only the deployment utility can deploy multiple packages, including the package dependencies (e.g., configurations) and the files that contain supporting information (e.g., documentation).

Configurations

Before you build a deployment utility for the packages, you can create package configurations that update properties of package elements at runtime. These configurations are automatically included when you deploy the packages.

Package configurations are used for updating values of properties at runtime. For example, you can update the values of variables or the connection strings of connection managers.

Configurations make packages more flexible. For example you can use configurations to make it easier to move packages from development to production environments; and configurations can help set values when you deploy packages to a number of different servers.

SSIS supports several different places to store package configurations, also called Configuration types:

- XML configuration file
- Environment variable
- Registry entry
- Parent package variable
- SQL Server table

NOTE The SQL Server table and XML configuration file can include multiple configurations.

Each configuration is a property/value pair. The configurations are obviously included when you create a package deployment utility. When you install the packages, the configurations can be updated as a step in the package installation.

Creating a package configuration is easy, as you'll see in this example using our SSISExample project and the SSISExample2 package.

1. In BIDS, open the SSISExample project. In Solution Explorer, double-click the SSISExample2 package to open it.
2. In the SSIS Designer, click the Control Flow, Data Flow, Event Handler, or Package Explorer tab.
3. On the SSIS menu, click Package Configurations.
4. In the Package Configuration Organizer dialog box, select Enable package configurations, and then click Add.
5. On the welcome page of the Package Configuration Wizard page (Figure 22.33), click Next
6. On the Select Configuration Type page, specify the configuration type—in this case XML configuration file—and then set the properties that are relevant to the configuration type. Here you will specify the Configuration file as `SSISExampleXMLConfig.xml` and click Next.
7. On the Select Objects to Export page, select the properties of package objects to include in the configuration by clicking the boxes. Click Next.
8. On the Completing the Wizard page, type the name of the configuration, and then click Finish.
9. View the configuration in the Package Configuration Organizer dialog box as shown in Figure 22.34.

FIGURE 22.33
Package Configuration Wizard welcome screen

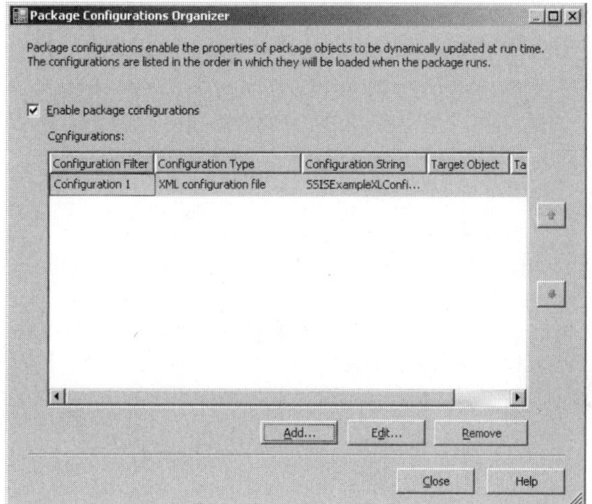

FIGURE 22.34
Package Configuration Organizer

10. Click Close to complete the wizard.

Congratulations. You've learned the steps necessary to create a configuration that will be deployed with your package when the package runs.

Creating a Deployment Utility

As mentioned earlier packages can be "deployed" using a deployment utility, the import and export package features in Management Studio, or by saving a copy of the package. However, these are very limited deployments and, in view of the changes to SSIS, barely deserve to be called a deployment. Only the deployment utility can deploy multiple packages, including the package dependencies (e.g., configurations) and the files that contain supporting information (e.g., documentation).

The package deployment process has two main steps. The first is to build a deployment utility for the Integration Services project. This deployment utility contains the packages you want to deploy.

The second step is to run the Package Installation Wizard to install the packages to the file system or to an instance of SQL Server 2005.

The deployment utility is really just the folder that contains the files you need to deploy the packages in a project on a target server. The deployment utility is created on the source computer where the project is stored.

The first step in creating a deployment utility is to configure the build process to create a deployment utility, and then to build the project. When you build the project, all packages and package configurations in the project are automatically included. If you want to include additional files, such as a readme file, in the deployment, place the files in the project's Miscellaneous folder of the Integration Services project. When the project is built, these files are also automatically included.

You can configure each project deployment differently by setting the properties on the deployment utility to customize the way the packages in the project will be deployed. To access the properties of a project, right-click the project and click Properties. The following deployment utility properties can be configured:

AllowConfigurationChange Specifies whether configurations can be updated during deployment.

CreateDeploymentUtility Specifies whether a package deployment utility is created when the project is built. This property must be True to create a deployment utility.

DeploymentOutputPath The location, relative to the Integration Services project, of the deployment utility.

When you build an Integration Services project, a manifest file, `SSISDeploymentManifest.xml`, is created and added, together with copies of the project packages and package dependencies, to the `bin\Deployment` folder in the project, or to the location specified in the DeploymentOutputPath property. The manifest file lists the packages, the package configurations, and any miscellaneous files in the project.

Now we'll create a deployment utility with our reliable SSISExample2 project.

1. In BIDS, open the SSISExample project. In Solution Explorer, double-click the SSISExample2 package to open it.
2. Right-click the SSISExample project and click Properties.
3. In the SSIS Example Property Pages dialog box, click Deployment Utility as shown in Figure 22.35.
4. To update package configurations when packages are deployed, set AllowConfigurationChanges to True.
5. Set CreateDeploymentUtility to True. You can also set the location of the deployment utility. Click OK.
6. In Solution Explorer, right-click the project, and then click Build.
7. View the build progress and any build errors in the Output window. If the Deployment Utility is successfully built, Build succeeded appears in the bottom status bar.

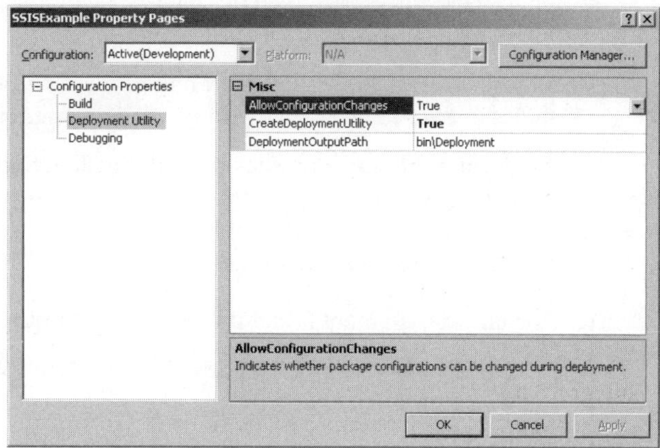

FIGURE 22.35
Deployment Utility Properties page

Installing Packages

Now that you have the deployment utility built, the next step is to install the packages by copying the deployment folder to the destination computer. The path was already specified in the Deployment-OutputPath property of the Integration Services project for which you just created the deployment utility. The default path is `bin\Deployment`, relative to the Integration Services project.

The easiest and most common way to install packages to the file system or to SQL Server is to invoke Package Installation Wizard, which guides you through the steps to install packages to the file system or to SQL Server. One thing you should remember is that file-based dependencies for packages are always installed to the file system no matter what method you've chosen. If you install the package to the file system, the dependencies are installed in the same folder as the one that you specified for the package. If you are installing to SQL Server, you can specify the folder in which to store the file-based dependencies.

Another nice feature of Package Installation Wizard is that if the package includes configurations you want to modify for use on the destination computer, you can update the values of the properties while using the wizard.

NOTE In addition to installing packages by using the Package Installation Wizard, you can copy and move packages by using the `DTUTIL` command-line utility.

WARNING Before you can run the Package Installation Wizard you must copy the deployment folder, created when you built a deployment utility, to the target computer.

To Deploy Packages to the File System

1. Open the deployment folder on the target computer.
2. Double-click the manifest file, `SSISExample2.SSISDeploymentManifest`, to start the Package Installation Wizard.
3. On the Deploy SSIS Packages page, select the File system deployment option. You can also choose Validate packages after installation to validate the packages on the target server.

4. On the Select Installation Folder page, specify the folder in which to install packages and package dependencies.
5. If the package includes configurations, you can edit updatable configurations by updating values in the Value list on the Configure Packages page.
6. If you elected to validate packages after installation, view the validation results of the deployed packages.

To Deploy Packages to SQL Server

1. Open the deployment folder on the target computer.
2. Double-click the manifest file, `SSISExample2.SSISDeploymentManifest`, to start the Package Installation Wizard.
3. On the Deploy SSIS Packages page, select the SQL Server deployment option. You can also choose Validate packages after installation to validate the packages on the target server.
4. On the Specify Target SQL Server page, specify the instance of SQL Server to install the packages to and select an authentication mode. If you select SQL Server Authentication, you will have to provide a username and a password.
5. On the Select Installation Folder page, specify the folder for the package dependencies that will be installed in the file system.
6. If the package includes configurations, you can edit configurations by updating values in the Value list on the Configure Packages page.
7. If you elected to validate packages after installation, view the validation results of the deployed packages.

Migrating DTS 2000 Packages

SSIS provides several options for keeping all of the work that you did using SQL Server 2000 Data Transformation Services (DTS). Options include migrating DTS packages to the SQL Server 2005 format, running DTS packages by using the SQL Server 2000 DTS runtime, or integrating DTS packages into SSIS using the Execute DTS 2000 Package Task.

Migrating DTS packages into the SSIS format is— as you might expect—wizard-driven and generally straightforward. When you use Package Migration Wizard one of the nicer benefits is that it leaves the original DTS packages intact and unchanged, just in case.

Tasks That Will Migrate:

- Execute SQL Task
- Bulk Insert Task
- FTP Task
- Execute Process Task
- Send Mail Task
- Copy Server Objects Task
- Execute Package Task

Items That Won't Migrate:

- ActiveX Script Task
- Dynamic Properties Task
- Analysis Services DTS Processing Task

Items That Must Be Manually Converted:

- Custom Tasks
- Copy Database Wizard Task
- Data Driven Query Task
- Data Pump
- Parallel Data Pump
- Transform Data Task

If all the tasks in the package can be mapped to new tasks in SSIS, the structure of the migrated package is very similar to the structure of the DTS package. Of course, if tasks do not map directly to SSIS tasks, the migration will change the package structure.

Other package elements such as precedence constraints, connections, and variables are migrated to the equivalent element in SQL Server 2005. Package passwords are not migrated with packages migrated as SSIS packages. However, SSIS supports package passwords in DTS packages and in the Execute DTS 2000 Package task.

You can migrate DTS packages that are stored in a SQL Server 2000 msdb database, in Meta Data Services, or in structured storage files. The packages can be migrated to the file system as `.dtsx` files or to the SQL Server 2005 msdb database.

Using the Package Migration Wizard

You can run the Package Migration Wizard from Management Studio and BIDS.

Running the Package Migration Wizard from Management Studio

1. Click Start ➤ Programs ➤ Microsoft SQL Server 2005 ➤ SQL Server Management Studio.
2. In the Connect to Server dialog box, select Database Engine in the Server type list, and then click Connect.
3. Expand the Management ➤ Legacy ➤ Data Transformation Packages folder, right-click the folder and select Migration Wizard.

Running the Package Migration Wizard from BIDS

1. Click Start ➤ All Programs ➤ Microsoft SQL Server 2005 ➤ Business Intelligence Development Studio.
2. Click File ➤ Open, and locate the Integration Services project from which you want to run the wizard.
3. Right-click the SSIS Packages folder and then click Migrate DTS 2000 Packages.

You should make a habit of opening all migrated packages and checking for any issues, especially validation failures. Always remember that even if migration is not a practical option you can still run any DTS package in SSIS.

Managing Packages

You manage and administer packages from Management Studio by connecting to the Integration Services. Once you've connected to Integration Services, you'll see two top-level folders, Running Packages and Stored Packages.

Monitoring Running Packages

The Running Packages folder lists the packages that currently are running on the server. This is a read only folder, contains no subfolders, and is not extensible. If no packages are currently running, the folder is empty.

If you want to view information about a single running package, click the package. Information such as the version and description of the package is displayed on the Summary page. If you're interested in all of the Running Packages, click the Running Packages folder. Information such as the execution duration of running packages will also appear on the Summary page.

TIP Refresh the folder to display the most current information.

You can stop a running package from the Running Packages folder by right-clicking the package and then clicking Stop.

Managing Package Stores

The Stored Packages folder lists all the packages that are saved in the package stores that are registered with the Integration Services service. The package stores are either folders in the file system or a SQL Server database

When it starts, the Stored Packages folder contains two folders by default: File System and MSDB. The File System folder lists the packages are saved to the file system in the folders specified in the configuration file for the Integration Services service. The default folder is the Packages folder, located in `%Program Files%\Microsoft SQL Server\90\DTS`. The MSDB folder lists packages saved to the SQL Server msdb database on the server.

You can add custom folders to the root package store folder (by default these are File and MSDB). Custom folders can reflect the way you want to organize packages, be it by function, name, or some other criterion. You can also add custom subfolders to custom folders, thus creating a file hierarchy that meets your business needs. Obviously all custom folders can be deleted or renamed. You cannot rename or delete the File and MSDB folders unless you update the root folders specified in the Integration Services Service configuration file, a topic not covered in this book.

Importing and Exporting Packages

Integration Services packages can be saved to either to the msdb database or to the file system. You can copy a package from one storage type to the other by using the import or export feature that Integration Services provides. You can also import a package to the same storage type using a different name to create a copy of a package. The `DTUTIL` command-line utility can also be used to import and export packages.

Earlier, while discussing how to run a package from within Management Studio, we learned viewed how to import a package in Management Studio. Exporting packages isn't very difficult. Also, as you'll recall, importing and exporting packages is a simplistic way of deploying them.

To export a package:

1. Open SQL Server Management Studio and connect to Integration Services.
2. In Object Explorer, expand the Stored Packages folder.
3. Expand the subfolders to locate the package you want to export.
4. Right-click the package, click Export, and then select either the SQL Server option (MSDB) or the File System option, then complete the appropriate variables. Figure 22.36 shows the dialog for exporting a package to the file system.

FIGURE 22.36
Export Package

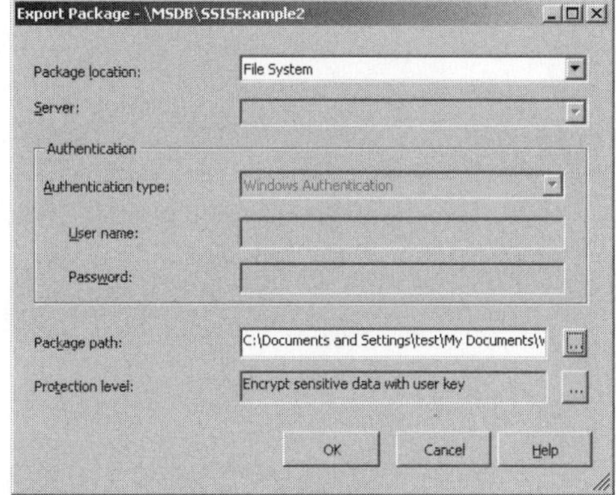

5. To update the protection level of the package, click the browse button (…) and choose a different protection level by using the Package Protection Level dialog box. If the "Encrypt sensitive data with password or the Encrypt all data with password" option is selected, you'll need to type and confirm a password.
6. Click OK to complete the export.

Summary

In this chapter, you learned about SQL Server Integration Services (SSIS). Integration Services provides a very flexible OLE DB–based method for moving data between different data sources and manipulating it while it's being moved. SSIS also provides a number of other capabilities that let you integrate it into a workflow solution.

You learned about the two main ways to create packages, the Import and Export Wizard and the SSIS Package Designer. You've also reviewed the many ways you can design and configure packages and taken a look at the many options available to you as you create packages. Finally you've learned some of the ways you can use Management Studio to help you manage packages for maximum effect.

In the next chapters, we'll see how to use Locking in SQL Server applications with the Internet, starting with the Web Assistant.

Part 6

Advanced Topics

In this section:

Chapter 23

Locking

One of the key features of SQL Server 2005 is that it's been designed from the start to support many users of the same database at the same time. It's this support that leads to the need for *locking*. Locking refers to the ability of the database server to reserve resources such as rows of data or pages of an index for the use of one particular user at a time. In this chapter, we'll explore the reasons why locking is necessary in multiuser databases and see the details of SQL Server's locking implementation.

Why Locking?

It may seem counterintuitive that a multiuser database would require the ability to lock users out of their data. Wouldn't it make more sense to just let everyone get to the data, so they can get their business done as fast as possible and let the next person use the data? Unfortunately, this doesn't work, because working with data often takes many operations that require everything stay consistent. In this section, we'll discuss the specific problems that locking solves:

- Lost updates
- Uncommitted dependencies
- Inconsistent analysis
- Phantom reads

We'll also take a look at concurrency, and explain the difference between optimistic and pessimistic concurrency.

Lost Updates

One of the classic database problems is the *lost update*. Suppose Joe is on the phone with the Accounting Department of XYZ Corporation, and Mary, who is entering changes of address for customers, happens to find a change of address card for XYZ Corporation at roughly the same time. Both Joe and Mary display the record for XYZ from the Customers table on their computers at the same time. Joe comes to an agreement to raise XYZ's credit limit, makes the change on his computer, and saves the change back to the SQL Server database. A few minutes later, Mary finishes updating XYZ's address and saves her changes. Unfortunately, her computer didn't know about the new credit limit (it had read the original credit limit before Joe raised it), so Joe's change is overwritten without a trace.

A lost update can happen any time two independent transactions select the same row in a table and then update it based on the data that they originally selected. One way to solve this problem is to lock out the second update. In the example above, if Mary was unable to save changes without first retrieving the changes that Joe made, both the new credit limit and the new address would end up in the Customers table.

Uncommitted Dependencies

Uncommitted dependencies are sometimes called *dirty reads*. This problem happens when a record is read while it's still being updated, but before the updates are final. For example, suppose Mary is entering a change of address for XYZ Corporation through a program that saves each changed field as it's entered. She enters a wrong street address, then catches herself and goes back to correct it. However, before she can enter the correct address, Mark prints out an address label for the company. Even though Mary puts the correct data in before leaving the company's record, Mark has read the wrong data from the table.

One way to avoid the problem of dirty reads is to lock data while it's being written, so no one else can read it before the changes are final.

Inconsistent Analysis

The *inconsistent analysis* problem is related to the uncommitted dependencies problem. Inconsistent analysis is caused by *nonrepeatable reads*, which can happen when data is being read by one process while the data's being written by another process.

Suppose Betty is updating the monthly sales figures for each of the company's divisions by entering new numbers into a row of the Sales table. Even though she puts all the changes on her screen to be saved at once, it takes SQL Server a little time to write the changes to the database. If Roger runs a query to total the monthly sales for the entire company while this data is being saved, the total will include some old data and some new data. If he runs the query again a moment later, it will include all new data and give a different answer. Thus, the original read was nonrepeatable.

Inconsistent analysis can be avoided if reads are not allowed while data is being written.

Phantom Reads

The final major problem that locking can help solve is the problem of *phantom reads*. These occur when an application thinks it has a stable set of data, but other applications are inserting rows into the data. Suppose Roger retrieves a query that includes all of the sales for March. If he asks for sales for March 15 twice in a row, he should get the same answer. However, if Mildred was inserting data for March 15, and Roger's application read the new data, he might get a different answer the second time. The new data is called phantom data, because it appeared mysteriously even though it wasn't originally present in the data that was retrieved.

Phantom reads can be avoided if some processes are locked out of inserting data into a set of data that another process is using.

Optimistic and Pessimistic Concurrency

There are two broad strategies for locking in the world of databases. These are referred to as *concurrency control methods* because they control when users can work with resources that other users are also manipulating.

With *optimistic concurrency control*, the server makes the assumption that resource conflicts are unlikely. In this case, resources (for example, a row in a table) are locked only while a change is about to be saved. This minimizes the amount of time that resources are locked. However, it increases the chance that another user will make a change in a resource before you can. For example, you might discover when trying to save a change that the data in the table is not the data that you originally read, and need to read the new data and make your change again.

With *pessimistic concurrency control*, resources are locked when they are required and are kept locked throughout a transaction. This avoids many of the problems of optimistic concurrency control, but raises the possibility of deadlocks between processes. We'll discuss deadlocks later in the chapter.

In almost all situations, SQL Server uses pessimistic concurrency control. It's possible to use optimistic concurrency control by opening tables with a cursor instead of a query. Chapter 8, "Topics in Advanced T-SQL," covers the use of cursors in T-SQL. You can also use optimistic concurrency by specifying one of the snapshot isolation levels in T-SQL statements. We'll discuss this method later in this chapter.

Isolation Levels

The ANSI SQL standard defines four different isolation levels for transactions. These levels specify a transaction's tolerance of incorrect data. From lowest to highest, the four isolation levels are as follows:

- Read Uncommitted
- Read Committed
- Repeatable Read
- Serializable

A lower isolation level increases concurrency and decreases waiting for other transactions, but increases the chance of reading incorrect data. A higher isolation level decreases concurrency and increases waiting for other transactions, but decreases the chance of reading incorrect data.

With the highest level of isolation, transactions are completely serialized, which means that they are completely independent of one another. If a set of transactions is serialized, the transactions can be executed in any order, and the database will always end up in the same state.

The default isolation level for SQL Server transactions is Read Committed, but as you'll see later in this chapter, you can adjust this default for particular transactions.

NOTE For a discussion of the properties that define transactions and the T-SQL statements that manage transactions, see Chapter 8.

SQL Server also supports two additional levels of isolation beyond the ones specified by the ANSI standard. These two levels, Read Committed (Snapshot) and Snapshot, use row versioning for optimistic concurrency. Table 23.1 shows which database problems can still occur with each isolation level. A "yes" entry in the table means that the specified problem can occur.

TABLE 23.1: Isolation Levels and Database Problems

ISOLATION LEVEL	LOST UPDATES	DIRTY READS	NONREPEATABLE READS	PHANTOM READS
Read Uncommitted	Yes	Yes	Yes	Yes
Read Committed (Locking)	Yes	No	Yes	Yes
Read Committed (Snapshot)	Yes	No	Yes	Yes
Repeatable Read	No	No	No	Yes

TABLE 23.1: Isolation Levels and Database Problems *(CONTINUED)*

ISOLATION LEVEL	LOST UPDATES	DIRTY READS	NONREPEATABLE READS	PHANTOM READS
Snapshot	No	No	No	No
Serializable	No	No	No	No

Locking Mechanics

To understand the way that SQL Server manages locks and properly interpret the display of locking information in SQL Server Enterprise Manager, you need to understand a few technical concepts. In this section, we'll cover the basics of these concepts, including locking granularity, locking modes, lock escalation, and dynamic locking.

Locking Granularity

Locking granularity refers to the size of the resources being locked at any given time. For example, if a user is going to make a change to a single row in a table, it might make sense to lock just that row. However, if that same user were to make changes to multiple rows in a single transaction, it could make more sense for SQL Server to lock the entire table. The table locking has higher granularity than the row locking.

SQL Server 2005 can provide locks on nine levels of granularity:

RID RID stands for row ID. A RID lock applies a lock to a single row in a table.

Key Sometimes locks are applied to indexes rather than directly to tables. A key lock locks a single row within an index.

Page A single data page or index page contains 8KB of data.

Extent Internally, SQL Server organizes pages into groups of eight similar pages (either data pages or index pages) called extents. An extent lock thus locks 64KB of data.

HOBT HOBT stands for Heap or B-Tree. This is a special lock that protects an index or data pages in a table that does not have a clustered index.

Allocation Unit An allocation unit lock can lock a particular type of data within a table, such as all regular data, all large object data, or all variable length data.

Table A table lock locks an entire table.

File A file lock locks an entire database file.

DB Under exceptional circumstances, SQL Server may lock an entire database. For example, when a database is placed into single-user mode for maintenance, a DB lock may be used to prevent other users from entering the database.

The smaller the lock granularity, the higher the concurrency is in the database. For example, if you lock a single row rather than an entire table, other users can work with other rows in the same table. The trade-off is that smaller lock granularity generally means more system resources are devoted to tracking locks and lock conflicts. In addition to these lock types, there is also a Metadata lock that prevents altering the metadata (schema) of a table. This doesn't fit into the hierarchy of increasing amounts of data listed above.

Locking Modes

All locks are not created equal. SQL Server recognizes that some operations need complete and absolute access to data, while others merely want to signal that they might change the data. To provide more flexible locking behavior and lower the overall resource use of locking, SQL Server provides the following types of locks (each type has an abbreviation that is used in SQL Server Enterprise Manager):

Shared (S) Shared locks are used to ensure that a resource can be read. No transaction can modify the data in a resource while a shared lock is being held on that resource by any other transaction.

Update (U) Update locks signal that a transaction intends to modify a resource. An update lock must be upgraded to an exclusive lock before the transaction actually makes the modification. Only one transaction at a time can hold an update lock on a particular resource. This limit helps prevent deadlocking (discussed in more detail later in the chapter).

Exclusive (X) If a transaction has an exclusive lock on a resource, no other transaction can read or modify the data in that resource. This makes it safe for the transaction holding the lock to modify the data itself.

Bulk Update (BU) SQL Server places bulk update locks on a table when bulkcopying data into the table, if the `TABLOCK` hint is specified as part of the bulkcopy operation or the table lock on bulk load option is set with `sp_tableoption`. Bulk update locks allow any process to bulkcopy data into the table, but do not allow any other processes to use the data in the table.

Key Range A key range lock locks the range of rows read by a single query that uses the serializable isolation level. It ensures that other transactions cannot insert rows into that range of rows. Key range locks come in several different varieties depending on which operations the query is performing.

Later in the chapter, you'll see how to use locking hints in T-SQL to specify the exact lock mode that should be used for a particular operation.

One of the factors that determines whether a lock can be granted on a resource is whether another lock already exists on the resource. Here are the major rules that SQL Server applies to determine whether a lock can be granted:

- If an X lock exists on a resource, no other lock can be granted on that resource.
- If a U lock exists on a resource, an S lock can be granted on that resource.
- If an S lock exists on a resource, an S or U lock can be granted on that resource.
- If a BU lock exists on a resource, a BU lock can be granted on that resource.
- Key range locks are generally incompatible with other locks.

Lock Escalation

SQL Server continuously monitors lock usage to strike a balance between granularity of locks and resources devoted to locking. If a large number of locks on a resource with lesser granularity are acquired by a single transaction, SQL Server might escalate these locks to fewer locks with higher granularity.

For example, suppose a process begins requesting rows from a table to read. SQL Server places shared locks on the RIDs involved. If the transaction reads most of the rows on a data page, SQL Server discards the shared locks for the RIDs and places a shared lock on the page itself instead. If the transaction continues to read rows, SQL Server eventually places the shared lock at the table level and discards the locks at the page and RID level.

The goal is to balance the number of locks that need to be monitored against the need to keep data as available to other processes as possible. SQL Server maintains its own dynamic lock escalation thresholds, and you can neither see nor change these thresholds. However, it's important to understand that sometimes you might get more locking than you thought you asked for, due to lock escalation.

Dynamic Locking

SQL Server locking is dynamic. What this means to you as an application developer is that you almost never have to worry about locking. As part of generating the execution plan for a query, SQL Server determines the type of locks to place when that query is executed. This includes both the locking mode and the locking granularity. Lock escalation is also part of the dynamic locking strategy SQL Server employs.

Dynamic locking is designed to make life easier for database administrators and users alike. Administrators don't need to constantly monitor locks (although, as you'll see in the next section, it is possible to do so), nor do they need to manually establish lock escalation thresholds. Users don't need to specify a locking mode for queries (though they can use locking hints to do so in special situations).

SQL Server's dynamic locking is usually oriented toward performance. By using the most appropriate level of locks for a particular operation (table locks, page locks, or row locks), SQL Server can minimize the overhead associated with locking and so improve overall performance.

Viewing Current Locks

As a database administrator, you may find that you need to investigate the locks that are in use on your server. Perhaps users are complaining of poor performance, and you suspect that some application is claiming more locks than it really needs. Or perhaps a resource is locked, and you can't figure out what process owns the lock. Fortunately, SQL Server provides several tools that you can use to see what's going on with SQL Server locking. In this section, we'll demonstrate the use of the `sys.dm_tran_locks` dynamic management view and show you how to use SQL Server Enterprise Manager to view locking activity.

Using *sys.dm_tran_locks*

If you want a quick snapshot of locking activity within SQL Server, you can query the `sys.dm_tran_locks` dynamic management view in Management Studio. By default, any user with VIEW SERVER STATE permission can query `sys.dm_tran_locks`.

The result set from `sys.dm_tran_locks` includes these columns:

resource_type The type of resource being locked This can be DATABASE, FILE, PAGE, KEY, EXTENT, RID, APPLICATION, OBJECT, METADATA, HOBT, or ALLOCATION_UNIT.

resource_subtype Some resources have subtypes; in such cases, this column includes additional identifying information for the subtype.

resource_database_id The SQL Server database ID for the database containing the lock. To see the database IDs on your server matched to database names, you can execute **SELECT * FROM master.sysdatabases**.

resource_description Additional textual identifying information for the resource.

resource_associated_entity_id The SQL Server object ID for the object being locked. You can retrieve the name of the object by executing **SELECT object_name(*ObjId*)**.

resource_lock_partition ID of the partition if this is a partitioned resource; zero otherwise.

request_mode The lock mode.

request_type Always LOCK.

Status The lock request status. GRANTED indicates that the lock was granted, WAIT indicates that the lock is blocked by a lock held by another process, and CONVERT shows that a lock is trying to change modes (e.g., shared to update) but that the change is blocked by a lock held by another process.

request_reference_count The number of times this resource has been locked.

request_lifetime For internal user only.

request_session_id Session ID that owns this resource.

request_exec_context_id Execution context ID that owns this resource.

request_request_id Batch ID that owns this resource.

request_owner_type This can be TRANSACTION, CURSOR, SESSION, SHARED_TRANSACTION_WORKSPACE, or EXCLUSIVE_TRANSACTION_WORKSPACE.

request_owner_id If this request is owned by a transaction, this is the transaction ID.

request_owner_guid If this request is owned by a distributed transaction this is the MSDTC identifier for the transaction.

request_owner_lockspace_id For internal use only

lock_owner_address Memory address of the data space that tracks this request.

There are two primary uses for the sys.dm_tran_locks view. First, you might think there's a deadlock problem on your server and need to see all the locks on the server. If the sys.dm_tran_locks output contains many locks with a status of WAIT or CONVERT, you should suspect a deadlock.

Second, sys.dm_tran_locks can help you see the actual locks placed by a particular SQL statement, because you can retrieve the locks for a particular process. For example, consider this T-SQL batch:

```
USE AdventureWorks
BEGIN TRANSACTION
INSERT INTO Production.Location ([Name], CostRate, Availability)
 VALUES ('Dump', 0.00, 1)
SELECT * FROM sys.dm_tran_locks WHERE request_session_id = @@spid
ROLLBACK TRANSACTION
```

After setting the database to use, this batch first begins a transaction, because locks are held for the duration of the current transaction. By holding the transaction open, you can examine the locks before SQL Server releases them. The next statement (the INSERT) is the one that will actually acquire the locks. The next statement is the form of sys.dm_tran_locks to show the locks for the current transaction. The @@spid system variable retrieves the session ID for the current transaction. Finally, the batch rolls back the transaction so that no actual change is made to the database.

Figure 23.1 shows the result of running this batch. As you can see, even a single SQL statement might need to lock many resources to properly execute. In the case of an INSERT statement, the indexes for the table must all be locked to insert the new row.

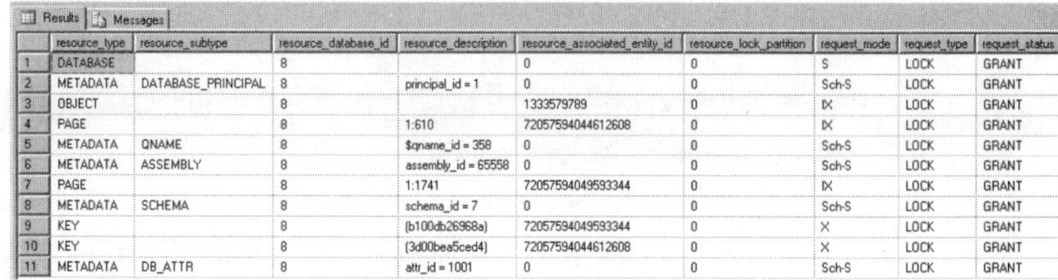

	resource_type	resource_subtype	resource_database_id	resource_description	resource_associated_entity_id	resource_lock_partition	request_mode	request_type	request_status
1	DATABASE		8		0	0	S	LOCK	GRANT
2	METADATA	DATABASE_PRINCIPAL	8	principal_id = 1	0	0	Sch-S	LOCK	GRANT
3	OBJECT		8		1333579789	0	IX	LOCK	GRANT
4	PAGE		8	1:610	72057594044612608	0	IX	LOCK	GRANT
5	METADATA	QNAME	8	$qname_id = 358	0	0	Sch-S	LOCK	GRANT
6	METADATA	ASSEMBLY	8	assembly_id = 65558	0	0	Sch-S	LOCK	GRANT
7	PAGE		8	1:1741	72057594049593344	0	IX	LOCK	GRANT
8	METADATA	SCHEMA	8	schema_id = 7	0	0	Sch-S	LOCK	GRANT
9	KEY		8	(b100db26968a)	72057594049593344	0	X	LOCK	GRANT
10	KEY		8	(3d00bea5ced4)	72057594044612608	0	X	LOCK	GRANT
11	METADATA	DB_ATTR	8	attr_id = 1001	0	0	Sch-S	LOCK	GRANT

FIGURE 23.1
Using sys.dm_tran_locks to investigate locks

Using Management Studio

You can also use Management Studio to display locking information. Of course, all of the information that Management Studio will display is also available via sys.dm_tran_locks and other T-SQL statements, but you may find the graphical view in Management Studio more convenient. The locking information in Management Studio is displayed in a separate Activity Monitor window. To open this window, expand the Management node in Management Studio to find the Activity Monitor node, and double-click the Activity Monitor node. You can view three types of information in Activity Monitor:

- Process Info
- Locks By Process
- Locks By Object

Figure 23.2 shows some of this information on a test server.

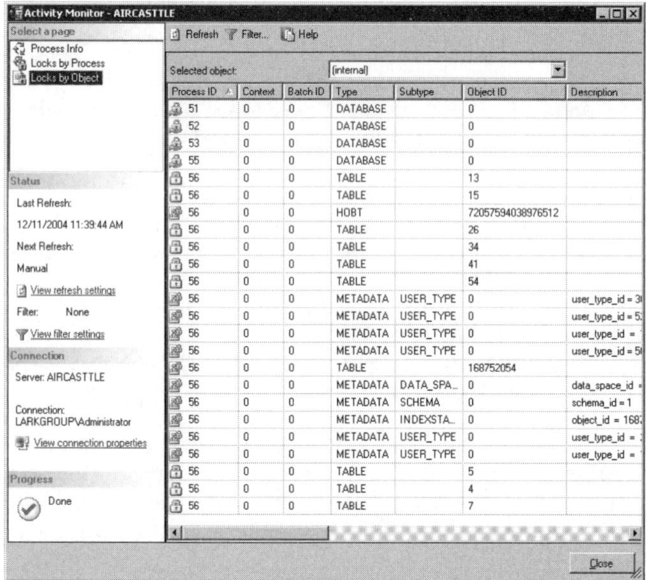

Process ID	Context	Batch ID	Type	Subtype	Object ID	Description
51	0	0	DATABASE		0	
52	0	0	DATABASE		0	
53	0	0	DATABASE		0	
55	0	0	DATABASE		0	
56	0	0	TABLE		13	
56	0	0	TABLE		15	
56	0	0	HOBT		72057594038976512	
56	0	0	TABLE		26	
56	0	0	TABLE		34	
56	0	0	TABLE		41	
56	0	0	TABLE		54	
56	0	0	METADATA	USER_TYPE	0	user_type_id = 3
56	0	0	METADATA	USER_TYPE	0	user_type_id = 5
56	0	0	METADATA	USER_TYPE	0	user_type_id =
56	0	0	METADATA	USER_TYPE	0	user_type_id = 5
56	0	0	TABLE		168752054	
56	0	0	METADATA	DATA_SPA...	0	data_space_id =
56	0	0	METADATA	SCHEMA	0	schema_id = 1
56	0	0	METADATA	INDEXSTA...	0	object_id = 168
56	0	0	METADATA	USER_TYPE	0	user_type_id =
56	0	0	METADATA	USER_TYPE	0	user_type_id =
56	0	0	TABLE		5	
56	0	0	TABLE		4	
56	0	0	TABLE		7	

FIGURE 23.2
Displaying lock information in Activity Monitor

The Process Info node displays the following information for each process currently running on the server:

Process ID The process ID assigned to the process by SQL Server. This column also displays an icon that indicates the current status of the process.

User The SQL Server user who owns the process.

Database The database containing the data that the process is using.

Status Either Background, Sleeping, or Runnable. Background processes are generally automatic jobs that require no user intervention. Sleeping processes are awaiting a command. Runnable processes are actively manipulating data.

Open Transactions The number of open transactions that are a part of the process.

Command The most recent SQL Server command executed by the process.

Application The application name (if any) that the process has registered with SQL Server.

Wait Time The amount of time, in milliseconds, that the process has been waiting for another process to complete.

Wait Type Shows whether a process is waiting for another process to complete.

Resource The name of the resource (if any) for which the process is waiting.

CPU The number of milliseconds of CPU time that the process has used.

Physical IO The number of physical input or output operations that the process has performed.

Memory Usage The number of kilobytes of memory the process is using.

Login Time The date and time that the process connected to SQL Server.

Last Batch The date and time that the process last sent a command to SQL Server.

Host The server where the process is running.

Net Library The network library being used for connection to SQL Server by the process.

Net Address The physical network address of the process.

Blocked By The process ID (if any) of another process that is blocking this process.

Blocking The `spid` (if any) of another process that is being blocked by this process.

Execution Context Every subthread in the same process will have an identical execution context ID.

The Locks By Process node displays a combo box that lets you select any process currently holding locks on the server. When you select a process, Activity Manager displays the following information:

Object The object being locked.

Lock Type The type of object being locked. This can be DB (database), FIL (file), IDX (index), PAG (page), KEY (key), TAB (table), EXT (extent), or RID (row identifier).

Lock Mode The locking mode of the lock.

Lock Status GRANT, CNVT, or WAIT.

Request Owner Either Sess for a session lock or Xact for a transaction lock.

Index The index (if any) being locked.

Resource The resource (if any) being locked.

Process ID The SQL Server process ID of the process holding this lock.

The Locks By Object displays a combo box that lets you choose any object that is currently locked on the server. When you select an object, Activity Manager displays the following information:

Process ID The SQL Server process ID of the process holding this lock.

Lock Type The type of object being locked. This can be DB (database), FIL (file), IDX (index), PAG (page), KEY (key), TAB (table), EXT (extent), or RID (row identifier).

Lock Mode The locking mode of the lock.

Lock Status GRANT, CNVT, or WAIT.

Request Owner Either Sess for a session lock or Xact for a transaction lock.

Index The index (if any) being locked.

Resource The resource (if any) being locked.

Object The object being locked.

Deadlocks

It's possible for one process to block another process from acquiring a lock that the second process needs to succeed. For example, suppose that one application launches this batch:

```
BEGIN TRANSACTION
UPDATE Production.Location SET CostRate = CostRate * 1.1
COMMIT TRANSACTION
```

A moment later (before the first process commits its transaction), a second process launches this batch:

```
BEGIN TRANSACTION
UPDATE Production.Location SET CostRate = CostRate * 2
COMMIT TRANSACTION
```

Assuming that nothing else is happening on the server at the time, the first process will ask for and receive an exclusive lock on the Products table. The second process will also ask for an exclusive lock on the Products table, but because only one process can have an exclusive lock on a table at a time, SQL Server won't grant this lock. Instead, the second process's lock request will be placed in the WAIT state by SQL Server. When the first update finishes, the second process will be given its lock and can complete its update.

Blocking is a normal consequence of locking resources. In this case, both processes are able to complete their work. SQL Server uses locking to ensure that they do their work in an orderly fashion.

A *deadlock* is a situation in which multiple processes simultaneously require locks that are being held by other processes. For example, suppose the first transaction is as follows:

```
BEGIN TRANSACTION
UPDATE Production.Location SET CostRate = CostRate * 1.1
UPDATE Production.Product SET ReorderPoint = ReorderPoint * 2
COMMIT TRANSACTION
```

At the same time, a second application submits this batch:

```
BEGIN TRANSACTION
UPDATE Production.Product SET ReorderPoint = ReorderPoint + 1
UPDATE Production.Location SET CostRate = CostRate * 2
COMMIT TRANSACTION
```

If the timing is just right (or, depending on your point of view, just wrong), these batches lead to this sequence of events:

1. The first application submits batch #1.
2. The second application submits batch #2.
3. The first application asks for and receives an exclusive lock on the Production.Location table.
4. The second application asks for and receives an exclusive lock on the Production.Products table.
5. The first application asks for a lock on the Production.Products table, and this lock request is placed in the WAIT state, because the second application has a lock on the Production .Products table already.
6. The second application asks for a lock on the Production.Location table, and this lock request is placed in the WAIT state, because the first application has a lock on the Production.Location table already.

That's a deadlock. Neither application can complete its transaction, because each is waiting for the other to release a lock. If something isn't done about this situation, the locks will persist forever, and both applications will be hung.

Deadlocks need not involve only two applications. It's possible to have a chain of applications involving three or more transactions where each is waiting for a lock held by one of the others to be released, and all the applications are mutually deadlocked.

SQL Server is designed to detect and eliminate deadlocks automatically. The server periodically scans all processes to see which ones are waiting for lock requests to be fulfilled. If a single process is waiting during two successive scans, SQL Server starts a more detailed search for deadlock chains.

If it finds that a deadlock situation exists, SQL Server automatically resolves the deadlock. It does this by determining which transaction would be least expensive for SQL Server to undo and designating that transaction as the deadlock victim. SQL Server then automatically rolls back all the work that was performed by that transaction and returns error 1205: "Your transaction (process *spid*) was deadlocked with another process and has been chosen as the deadlock victim. Rerun your transaction."

If you like, you can tell SQL Server that your transaction should be preferentially chosen as the deadlock victim even if it's not the least expensive transaction to roll back. You can do this by issuing the following statement in your batch:

```
SET DEADLOCK_PRIORITY LOW
```

To minimize the chance of deadlocks in your own applications, follow these rules:

- Always access objects in the same order. For example, if the second transaction in the deadlock example above had updated the Production.Location table before the Production.Products table, the deadlock would not have been possible. One of the processes would have locked and then released both tables, freeing the other process to do the same.
- Keep transactions short. Remember that locks are always held for the duration of a transaction. The longer your application keeps a lock on an object and the more objects that it locks, the greater the chance that it will get into a deadlock situation with another application. One consequence of this rule is that you should not lock an object and then wait for user input. Hundreds or thousands of other processes could try to use the object while the user is thinking, because computers work so much more quickly than people do.

- Use T-SQL to customize the locking behavior of your application to use the lowest possible isolation level and to hold only necessary locks. We'll cover the ways in which you can customize locking behavior in the next section.

Customizing Locking Behavior

Although SQL Server does an excellent job of handling locks automatically and transparently to the application developer, it's not perfect for every application. Sometimes you'll want to customize the locking behavior that SQL Server uses for your applications. You can do this in four ways:

- By marking a transaction as a preferential deadlock victim
- By setting a lock timeout
- By setting a transaction isolation level
- By supplying a locking hint

We covered the use of `SET DEADLOCK_PRIORITY LOW` to mark a transaction as a preferential deadlock victim earlier in the chapter. In this section, we'll look at the other ways that you can customize locking behavior in your applications.

Setting the Lock Timeout

By default, there is no lock timeout for SQL Server transactions. That is, if a transaction is blocked (not deadlocked) waiting for another transaction to release a lock, the blocked transaction will wait forever. This is not always the best possible behavior, though it does maximize the chance of the blocked transaction being completed eventually.

If you like, you can set a lock timeout within a transaction. To do this, use the following T-SQL statement:

```
SET LOCK_TIMEOUT timeout_period
```

The lock timeout period is supplied in milliseconds. For example, to set a 2-second lock timeout, you could execute the following statement:

```
SET LOCK_TIMEOUT 2000
```

SQL Server also supplies a global variable `@@lock_timeout` that allows an application to retrieve the current lock timeout. Figure 23.3 shows the use of both `SET LOCK_TIMEOUT` and `@@lock_timeout` within a T-SQL batch.

TIP If there is currently no timeout set (that is, if applications will wait indefinitely for a lock), `@@lock_timeout` returns –1.

Setting the Transaction Isolation Level

As we mentioned earlier in the chapter, SQL Server defaults to the Read Committed transaction isolation level. If your application requires a different transaction isolation level, you can change it for the current session with the `SET TRANSACTION ISOLATION LEVEL` statement:

```
SET TRANSACTION ISOLATION LEVEL
 { READ UNCOMMITTED
```

```
    | READ COMMITTED
    | REPEATABLE READ
    | SNAPSHOT
    | SERIALIZABLE
}
```

FIGURE 23.3
Setting a lock timeout

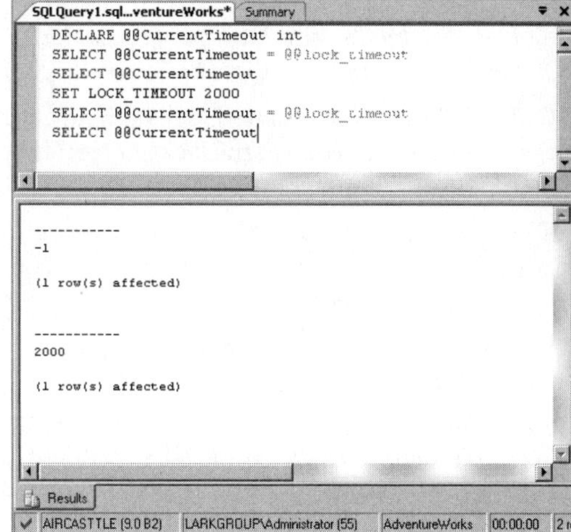

Each of the choices within this SQL statement sets the corresponding transaction isolation level as defined in the SQL standard. Technically, here's how each one works:

READ UNCOMMITTED The session doesn't issue shared locks or honor exclusive locks when it's reading data. It's possible to read uncommitted (dirty) data from this session. Rows can appear and disappear during the course of a transaction.

READ COMMITTED This is the default transaction isolation level for SQL Server. Shared locks are held while data is being read to avoid dirty reads. Other transactions can still change the data, so nonrepeatable reads and phantom data are possible with this level of transaction isolation.

REPEATABLE READ The session issues exclusive locks for all data that it reads, so other users can't change this data during the course of a transaction. However, the table itself isn't locked, so other users can insert new rows, resulting in phantom data.

SNAPSHOT Specifies that the data for the session will be the transactionally consistent version of the data that existed at the start of the session. The effect is as if the session gets a snapshot of the data to work with, and other sessions are not allowed to modify the snapshot. The ALLOW_SNAPSHOT_ISOLATION database option must be set to ON before you can start a transaction that uses the SNAPSHOT isolation level.

SERIALIZABLE The session issues a range lock on all of the data that it reads. A *range lock* is a special type of exclusive lock that not only locks the existing data, but also prevents new data from being inserted. This isolation level makes sure that data is unchanged while this session is working with it, but this level poses the most chance of concurrency issues and deadlocks with other sessions.

To view the current transaction isolation level for a session, issue the `DBCC USEROPTIONS` statement.

WARNING Transaction isolation levels are set per session, not per transaction. If you set the transaction isolation level to REPEATABLE READ or SERIALIZABLE for a transaction, you should explicitly return it to READ COMMITTED at the end of the transaction.

Locking Hints

If you need control over locking for an individual SQL statement rather than for an entire connection, you can use a table-level locking hint. Locking hints can be used in `SELECT`, `UPDATE`, `INSERT`, and `DELETE` statements. Refer to Chapters 6 and 7 for the full syntax details of these statements.

SQL Server 2005 supports these table-level locking hints:

HOLDLOCK Holds a shared lock until an entire transaction is completed. Normally shared locks are released as soon as the locked object is no longer required. This is the equivalent of the SERIALIZABLE transaction isolation level.

NOLOCK The statement does not issue shared locks and does not honor exclusive locks when reading data. This hint allows dirty reads. It is the equivalent of the READ UNCOMMITTED transaction isolation level.

PAGLOCK Forces the use of multiple page locks where ordinarily a single table lock would be used instead.

READCOMMITTED Uses the READ COMMITTED transaction isolation level for this statement. The database uses locks or row versioning, according to whether the READ_COMMITTED _SNAPSHOT database option is on.

READCOMMITTEDLOCK Uses the READ COMMITTED transaction isolation level for this statement. The database always uses locks.

READPAST Tells SQL Server to skip any locked rows to complete this statement. This hint works only at the READ COMMITTED isolation level and skips only RID locks, not page, extent, or table locks. The locked rows are simply ignored in the result of the statement.

READUNCOMMITTED Uses the READ UNCOMMITTED transaction isolation level for this statement.

REPEATABLEREAD Uses the REPEATABLE READ transaction isolation level for this statement.

ROWLOCK Forces the use of multiple row locks where ordinarily page or table locks would be used.

SERIALIZABLE Uses the SERIALIZABLE transaction isolation level for this statement.

TABLOCK Forces the use of table-level locks rather than row- or page-level locks.

TABLOCKX Forces the use of an exclusive table-level lock. This lock blocks all other transactions from using this table for the duration of the transaction.

UPDLOCK Forces the use of update rather than shared locks when reading a table. This hint decreases concurrency, but it ensures that you can later update data without other users having changed the data in the interim.

XLOCK Specifies that the transaction should take and hold exclusive locks on all data it uses until the transaction is committed.

Application Locks

SQL Server 2000 added a new type of lock to those supported in previous versions, the *application lock.* An application lock is a lock created by client code (for example, a T-SQL batch or a Visual Basic application) rather than by SQL Server itself. Application locks allow you to use SQL Server to manage resource contention issues between multiple clients, even when the resources themselves are not managed by SQL Server.

Why would you want to use an application lock rather than writing your own locking code in your application? The SQL Server lock manager is thoroughly tested code that's been designed to support thousands of users. When you use the SQL Server lock manager, you can be sure that your application's locking is using the same locking rules with which you're already familiar. As an added bonus, you get deadlock detection and the ability to monitor locks with SQL Server Enterprise Manager.

In this section, we'll look at the two stored procedures that handle application locking: `sp_getapplock` and `sp_releaseapplock`.

sp_getapplock

To create an application lock, your code should call the `sp_getapplock` stored procedure:

```
sp_getapplock [@Resource =] 'resource_name',
 [@LockMode =] 'lock_mode'
 [,[@LockOwner =] 'lock_owner']
 [,[@LockTimeout =] 'value']
[,[@DbPrincipal =] 'database_principal]
```

This stored procedure takes five arguments:

@Resource An arbitrary resource name. It's up to the application to come up with this name and ensure that it's unique. That is, if two applications request a lock on resource *wombat*, SQL Server will assume that they're talking about the same resource. Resource names can be up to 255 Unicode characters long.

@LockMode Can be Shared, Update, Exclusive, IntentExclusive, or IntentShared.

@LockOwner Either Transaction (the default) or Session.

@LockTimeout Timeout value in milliseconds. If you set this to zero, an attempt to set a lock that can't be granted immediately will return an error rather than waiting for the lock.

@DbPrincipal A user, role, or application role. The caller of the function must be in `@DbPrincipal`, or `dbo`, to execute the stored procedure.

Just like any other lock, an application lock is associated with a particular database. So, suppose your application was working with data from the AdventureWorks sample database and a text file named `suppliers.txt`. To lock that file exclusively, you could call `sp_getapplock` as follows:

```
USE AdventureWorks
sp_getapplock @Resource = 'suppliers.txt',
 @LockMode = 'Exclusive'
```

The return value from sp_getapplock depends on what happens inside the lock manager. This stored procedure can return these values:

0 Lock was granted.

1 Lock was granted after releasing other incompatible locks.

–1 Request timed out.

–2 Request was cancelled.

–3 Request was chosen as a deadlock victim.

–999 Invalid parameters were supplied.

If you supply a value of Transaction for the @LockOwner parameter, or do not supply a value for this parameter at all, locks are released when your code commits or rolls back the transaction. If you supply a value of Session for this parameter, SQL Server releases any outstanding locks when you log out.

sp_releaseapplock

To release an application lock, your code should call the sp_releaseapplock stored procedure:

```
sp_releaseapplock [@Resource =] 'resource_name'
 [,[@LockOwner =] 'lock_owner']
[,[@DBPrincipal =] 'database_principal]
```

Both the resource_name and the lock_owner parameters must match those in the call to sp_getapplock that created the lock (though the database principal may differ). If you omit the @LockOwner parameter, it defaults to Transaction (so you only need to supply this parameter to release a Session lock).

This stored procedure returns 0 if the lock was successfully released and –999 if there was any error in releasing the lock. Normally, an error here would mean that what you were trying to release doesn't actually exist.

To release the application lock that was created with the call to sp_getapplock in the previous section, you could use the following T-SQL:

```
USE pubs
sp_releaseapplock @Resource = 'authors.txt'
```

Summary

In this chapter, you learned about SQL Server locking. You saw why locking is necessary to preserve data integrity and learned about the mechanics of SQL Server locking. You learned how to view the current locks on a SQL Server, how to prevent deadlocks, and how to customize SQL Server's locking behavior. You also saw how you can use SQL Server's own lock manager to handle locking semantics for objects within your applications.

In the next chapter, we'll explore the other possibilities besides altering locking behavior for optimizing the performance of your SQL Server applications.

Chapter 24

Monitoring and Optimizing SQL Server 2005

Imagine for a moment that you are the chief operating officer of a sizable company. It is your job to make sure that the company runs smoothly and that everything gets done efficiently. How will you do this? You could just guess at it, randomly assigning tasks and then assuming that they are going to be done. Imagine the chaos that would ensue if you were to use this approach. Nothing would get done. Some departments would have too much to do, others would have nothing to do—and your company would go bankrupt.

A better approach would be to ask for reports from the various department managers and base your decisions on those reports. You might discover, for instance, that the accounting department has too much work and could use some help. Based on this report, you could hire more accountants. You might find that the production department has very little to do because the sales department has not been doing a good job; based on this report, you could motivate sales to get to work so that production would have something to do.

Now, instead of being in charge of the entire company's operations, you are in charge of your SQL Server. Here too, you need to make certain that everything is getting done efficiently. Again, you could just guess at this and randomly assign tasks, but that is an invitation to disaster. You need to get reports from your department managers: in this case, the CPU, the disk subsystem, the database engine, and so on. Once you have these reports, you can assign tasks and resources accordingly.

Most system administrators don't perform monitoring and optimization functions because they believe they don't have the time. Most of their time is spent on firefighting—that is, troubleshooting problems that have cropped up. It's safe to say that if the system administrators had taken the time to monitor and optimize the systems, those problems might never have arisen in the first place. That makes monitoring and optimization *proactive* troubleshooting, not *reactive*, as is the norm.

In this chapter, we discuss the various methods and tools for getting the reports you need from your SQL Server. As is best with monitoring and tuning, we'll start at the bottom and work our way up; we'll discuss the tools (System Monitor, the Management Studio Query Editor, and SQL Profiler) and then move on to repairs.

Using System Monitor

To ensure that your company functions properly, you need to make certain that the very foundation of the company is doing its job. You need a management group that works well together and gets things done—a group where each member pulls their own share of the load.

With SQL Server, this management group is the computer system itself. SQL Server cannot function properly if it does not have available system resources such as memory, processor power, fast disks, and a reliable network subsystem. If these systems do not work together, the overall system will not function properly. For example, if the memory is being overused, the disk subsystem slows down, because the memory has to write to the pagefile (which is on the disk) far too often. To keep such things from happening, you need to get reports from the subsystems; you can do this using System Monitor.

System Monitor comes with Windows and is located in the Administrative Tools folder on the Start menu (it is labeled Performance). Four views are available for your use:

Graph This view displays a graph of system performance. As values change, the graph will spike or dip accordingly.

Report The report view looks like what you might get on a piece of paper, except that the values here change with system use.

Alert With alert view, you can tell System Monitor to warn you when something bad is looming on the horizon, perhaps when CPU use is almost—but not quite yet—too high. This type of warning gives you time to fix potential problems before they become actual problems.

Log This is for record keeping. With log view, you can monitor your system over a time period and view the information later, as opposed to viewing it in real time (the default).

With each of these views, you monitor objects and counters. An *object* is a part of the system, such as the processor or the physical memory. A *counter* displays the statistical information about how much that object is being used. For example, the % Processor Time counter under the Processor object will tell you how much time your processor spends working. Table 24.1 lists common counters and their recommended values.

TABLE 24.1: Common Counters and Values in System Monitor

OBJECT	COUNTER	RECOMMENDED VALUE	USE
Processor	% Processor Time	Less than 75%	The amount of time the processor spends working.
Memory	Pages/Sec	Fewer than 5	The number of times per second that data had to be moved from RAM to disk and vice versa.
Memory	Available Bytes	More than 4MB	The amount of physical RAM available. This number should be low, because NT uses as much RAM as it can grab for file cache.
Memory	Committed Bytes	Less than physical RAM	The amount of RAM committed to use.
Disk	% Disk Time	Less than 50%	The amount of time that the disk is busy reading or writing.
Network Segment	% Network Utilization	Less than 30%	The amount of network bandwidth being used.

WARNING To see the Network Segment: % Network Utilization, you must install the Network Monitor Agent in Control Panel ➢ Network ➢ Services tab.

Now let's get some practice with System Monitor:

1. Log in to Windows as Administrator.
2. From the Start menu, select Programs ➢ Administrative Tools ➢ Performance. Notice that the graph is already populated with counters.
3. On the toolbar click the Add button (it looks like a + sign) to bring up the Add Counters dialog box.

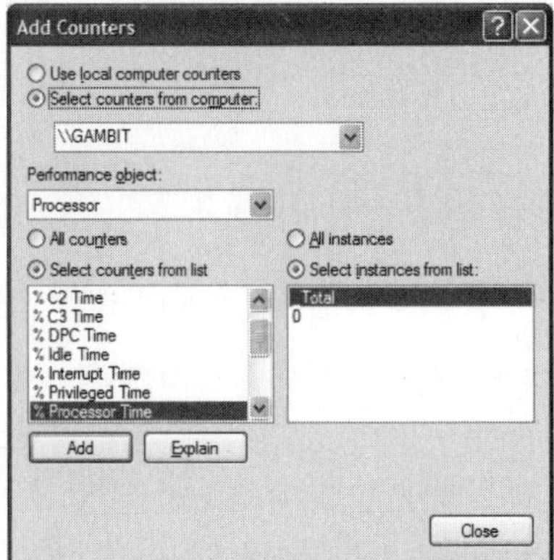

4. In the Performance object box, select Memory.
5. In the Counter box, select Available Bytes and click Add.
6. Click Close and notice the graph being created on the screen.

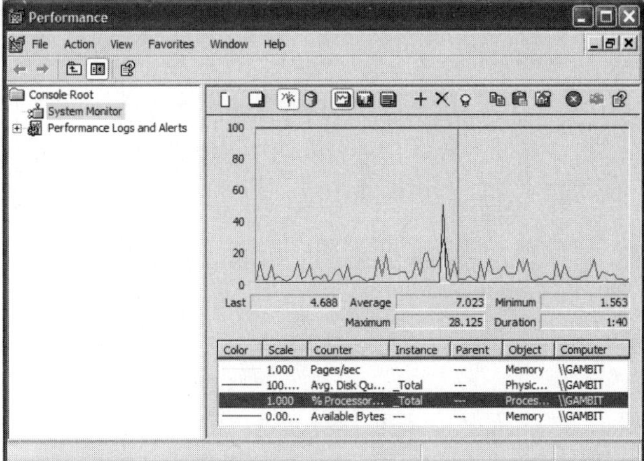

7. Press Ctrl+H and notice the current counter turns white. This makes the chart easier to read.

8. On the toolbar, click the View Report button (it looks like a sheet of paper) and notice how the same data appears in Report view.

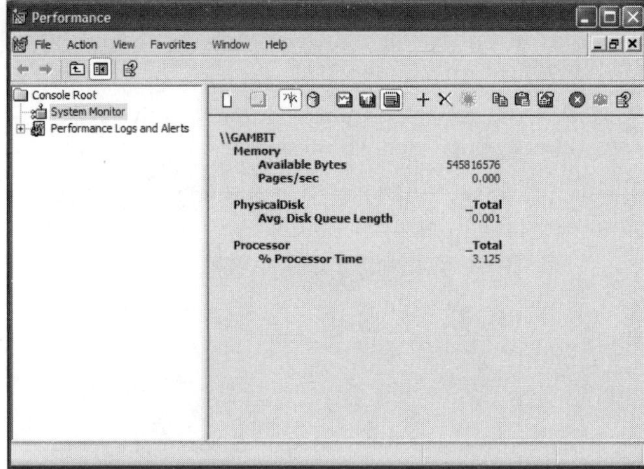

9. In the left pane, expand Performance Logs and Alerts, right-click Alerts, and select New Alert Settings.
10. Enter **`Test Alert`** in the Name box and click OK.
11. In the Alert Settings dialog, enter **`Test Alert`** in the Comment field.
12. Click Add.
13. Select the Processor object and the % Processor Time counter and click Add, then click Close.
14. Select Under from the "Alert when value is" drop-down list, enter 70 for the Limit, and click OK. This will generate an alert if the processor is not busy 70 percent of the time. In the real world, this would be set to over 70 percent, thus warning you just before it becomes a serious problem.
15. Click OK to create the alert.

16. To view the alerts, open Event Viewer and look for them in the Application log.

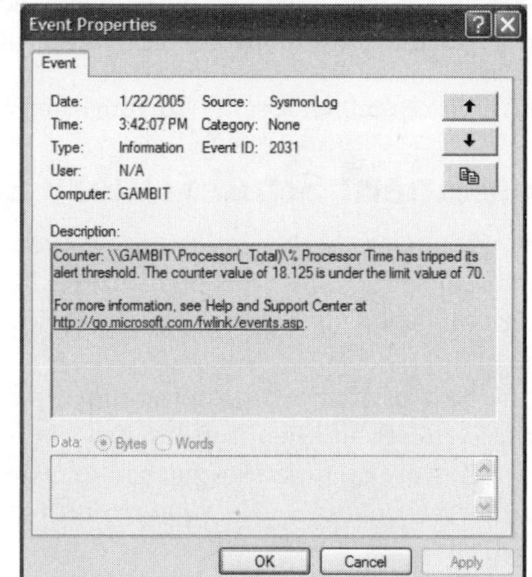

17. Watch the alerts generated for a short time, then select the alert and press the Delete key on the keyboard.
18. Exit System Monitor.

You can monitor SQL Server as well as Windows objects using System Monitor, because SQL Server provides its own objects and counters. The process for monitoring SQL Server is the same as it is with Windows—you just add different objects and counters. The SQL Server counters that you will be using most often are listed in Table 24.2.

TABLE 24.2: Most Frequently Used SQL Server Performance Monitor Counters

OBJECT	COUNTER	USE
SqlServer:Buffer Manager	Buffer Cache Hit Ratio	How much data is being retrieved from cache instead of disk.
SqlServer:Buffer Manager	Page Reads/Sec	Number of data pages that are read from disk each second.
SqlServer:Buffer Manager	Page Writes/Sec	Number of data pages that are written to disk each second.
SqlServer:General Statistics	User Connections	Number of user connections. Each of these will take some RAM.
SQLServer:Memory Manager	Total Server Memory (KB)	Total amount of memory that SQL Server has been dynamically assigned.
SQLServer:SQL Statistics	SQL Compilations/Sec	Number of compiles per second.

Now that the system resources are working together, you can start creating queries. Rather than just randomly creating queries and hoping they work quickly, let's see how you can create queries and start the optimization process at the same time using the Management Studio Query Editor.

NOTE If you found any resource problems, some fixes are listed at the end of this chapter.

Using the Management Studio Query Editor

To return to our analogy, if you were in charge of a corporation, you would need employees to do the work and make your business run. How do you hire them? You cannot just select people off the street and offer them jobs; you need to be sure they are qualified, so you interview prospective candidates before hiring them.

In SQL Server, you can think of queries as your employees, because queries are used to get the data out of the database and present it to your users. Just as you would interview prospective employees to see whether they are qualified to get their jobs done efficiently, you need to "interview" a query to see whether it is qualified to be used in production. The tool for this job is the Management Studio Query Editor.

Up to this point in the book, you have been using the Management Studio Query Editor to enter queries and see results, but it is capable of doing more. It is used not only to enter queries, but also to analyze them, to see how many resources they consume, and to see how fast they run. The Management Studio Query Editor accomplishes these feats by timing each step of the execution; this includes parsing the command you typed in and checking for errors, loading the data into memory, performing the query on the data, and more. If you would like to see a graphic representation of everything SQL Server is doing with your query, you can tell the Management Studio Query Editor to display an execution plan. This will display a series of icons that lead you through the execution process.

This next series of instructions shows you how to analyze a query using Query Editor:

1. From the Start menu, choose Programs ➢ SQL Server 2005 ➢ SQL Server Management Studio and connect using either Windows or SQL authentication.

2. Click the New Query button and select SQL Server Query to open the query editor. Connect using either Windows or SQL authentication.

3. From the Query menu, select Query Options.

4. On the Advanced page, check Set Statistics Time, which displays the amount of CPU time used by the query, and Set Statistics IO, which displays the amount of disk I/O used by the query. Click OK to apply the options and return to Query Editor.

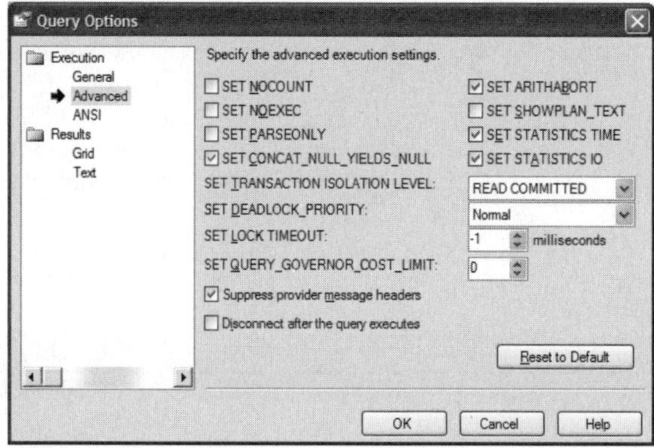

5. From the Query menu, select Include Actual Execution Plan to see a graphic representation of how SQL Server executes your query after it is executed.
6. On the query window toolbar, select AdventureWorks in the DB list box to set AdventureWorks as the default database.
7. In the query window, enter and execute the following query:

```
SELECT * FROM Person.Address
```

8. At the bottom of the screen, select the Messages tab, and notice the Execution and Parse and Compile times, then click Execution Plan just below the results pane (see Figure 24.1).

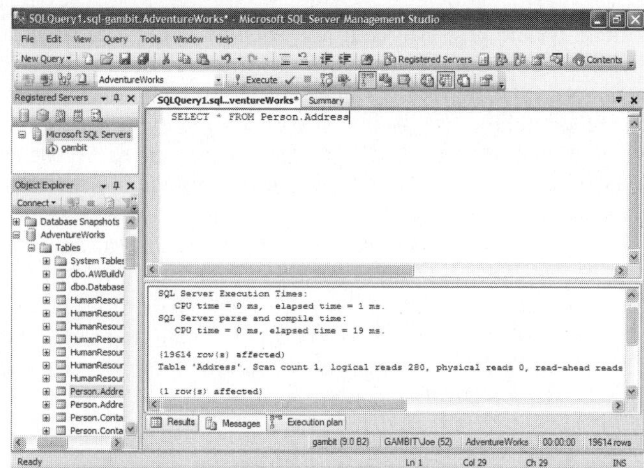

FIGURE 24.1
Execution times in the results pane

9. In the Execution Plan pane, hold your mouse pointer over each icon in turn; notice that they come with tooltips to help you better understand each step of execution (see Figure 24.2).

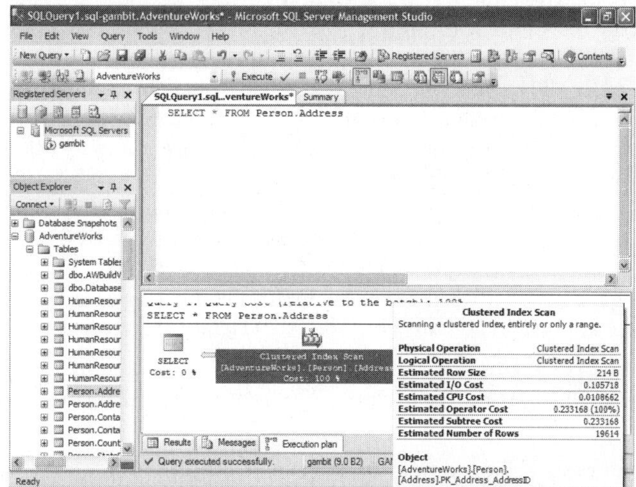

FIGURE 24.2
The Execution Plan pane with tooltips

10. Close Query Editor.

TIP By entering a query and selecting Display Estimated Execution Plan from the query menu, you can see how SQL Server plans to execute the plan without actually executing it. This can be very useful for potentially long-running queries.

So what did all of those numbers mean? In the messages pane that you see in Figure 24.1, you see several lines that read SQL Server Execution Times; these tell you how much time the SQL Server spent executing the actual command (in milliseconds). The Parse and Compile times tell you how much time (in milliseconds) SQL Server spent checking your query for syntax errors and breaking it up into smaller chunks for processing.

The line toward the middle of the messages window tells you how much time SQL Server spent using resources on the hard disk. The scan count tells you how many tables (or indexes) of which SQL Server needed to read every single record. Logical reads tell you how many data pages came from memory, and physical reads tell you how many data pages came from the hard disk itself. Read-ahead reads happen when SQL Server tries to anticipate the next record that you will ask for and thus reads ahead to try to load that data into memory.

All of these text messages that you are seeing in Figure 24.1 also show up in the graphic execution plan seen in Figure 24.2. The graphic plan is much easier to read and displays more information than the text messages. For example, when you hover the mouse over one of the icons (which is how you got the tooltip seen in Figure 24.2), you will see a great deal of information, which tells you exactly how much CPU time and disk I/O was required to perform a specific step of the execution of a query.

Once the analysis is complete, you will have a better idea of how to build your queries and optimize them for speed (which we'll discuss later in the chapter), but you will not yet have the full picture. To get a full understanding of how your queries respond to everyday use, you need to monitor them under stress—which is why we have SQL Profiler.

Monitoring with SQL Profiler

In running a company, once you have the management team working in harmony, you can focus your attention on the rest of the workforce. In this analogy, Query Editor would be like interviewing prospective employees; you want to be sure they have the appropriate qualifications, can fit in with the rest of the team, and will do their fair share of the work before you hire them. Like new employees, new queries need to be monitored regularly (with queries, on a day-to-day basis).

Profiler allows you to monitor and record what is happening inside the database engine. This is accomplished by performing a *trace*, which is a record of data that has been captured about events. Traces are stored in a table, a trace log file, or both, and can be either shared (viewable by everyone) or private (viewable only by the owner).

The actions you will be monitoring, called *events*, are anything that happens to the database engine, such as a failed login or a completed query. These events are logically grouped into *event classes* in Profiler so that they will be easier for you to find and work with. Some of these events are useful for maintaining security, and some are useful for troubleshooting problems, but most of these events are used for monitoring and optimization. The event classes that are available to you are as follows:

Cursors A cursor is an object that is used to work with multiple rows of data by moving through them one row at a time. This event class is used to monitor events that are generated by cursor usage.

Database This is a collection of events that monitor automatic changes in size for data and log files.

Errors and Warnings The events in this class are used to monitor errors and warnings such as a failed login or syntax errors.

Locks When users access data, that data is locked so that other users cannot modify data that someone else is reading. This class of events is used to monitor the locks placed on your data.

Objects Monitor this class of events to see when objects (such as tables, views, or indexes) are opened, closed, or modified in some way.

Performance This collection of events displays Showplan event classes as well as event classes produced by Data Manipulation operators.

Scans Tables and indexes can be scanned, which means that SQL Server must read through every single entry in the object to find the data for which you are looking. The events in this class are used to monitor such object scans.

Security Audit These events are used to monitor security. Such things as failed logins, password changes, and role changes are contained in this category.

Server This category contains classes that are used to monitor server control and memory change events.

Sessions When a user connects to SQL Server, that user is said to have started a session with the server. This event class is used to monitor user sessions.

Stored Procedures A stored procedure is a collection of Transact-SQL code that is stored on the server, ready to be executed. This event class is used to monitor events that are triggered by the use of stored procedures.

Transactions A *transaction* is a group of Transact-SQL commands that are viewed as a unit, meaning that they must all be applied to the database together or none of them are applied. This event class is used to monitor SQL Server transactions (including anything that happens to a transaction log where transactions are recorded) as well as transactions that go through the Distributed Transaction Coordinator.

TSQL This event class is used to monitor any Transact-SQL commands that are passed from the client to the database server.

User Configurable If the other events in Profiler do not meet your needs, you can create your own event to monitor with these user-configurable events. This comes in especially handy for custom applications that you may create.

OLEDB OLEDB is an interface that programmers can use to connect to SQL Server. This event class can be used to monitor OLEDB-specific events.

Broker The Service Broker is a new component in SQL Server 2005 that provides asynchronous message queuing and delivery. The Broker event class is useful for monitoring event generated by the Service Broker.

Full text Full text indexing gives you flexibility in querying SQL Server by letting you search for phrases, word variations, weighted results, and so on. These indexes are controlled by a separate service (msftesql). Using this event class you can monitor events generated by the full text index service and its indexes.

Deprecation Over the years, many commands have been deprecated in SQL Server. One such example is the `DUMP` statement, which was used in earlier versions of SQL Server to back up databases and logs, but is no longer a valid command. The Deprecation event class helps you track down procedures and programs that are using deprecated functions and commands and update them.

Progress Report This class of events helps you monitor progress of long-running commands, like online index operations.

When you create a trace, it is based on a *trace template*. A template is a predefined trace definition that can be used to create a trace by itself, or you can modify it to fit your needs. You can choose from several templates:

Blank This template has no configuration at all. It is a blank slate that you can use to create a completely unique trace definition.

SP_Counts This can be used to see how many stored procedures are started, what database ID they are called from, and which SPID (server process id) called the stored procedure.

Standard This template records logins and logouts, existing connections (at the time of the trace), completed Remote Procedure Calls (RPCs), and completed Transact-SQL batches.

TSQL This records the same events as the Standard template except that this template displays only the EventClass, TextData, SPID, and StartTime data columns. This is useful for tracking what queries are being run, when they are being run, and who is running them.

TSQL_Duration This is designed to track what queries are being executed and how long those queries take. This is especially useful for finding queries and stored procedures with poor performance.

TSQL_Grouped This template is used to discover what applications are being used to connect to SQL Server and who is using those applications. This template tracks queries that are being run and groups them by Application name, then Windows user-name, then SQL Server username, and then Process ID.

TSQL_Replay Trace files can be replayed against a server, meaning that every action in a trace file can be executed as if it were coming from a user. This template is especially useful for replaying against a server to find the cause of a crash or some other unexpected event.

TSQL_SPs This template is used to find out who is running stored procedures and what those stored procedures do.

Tuning This is used specifically for creating a trace file for the Database Tuning Advisor, which we will discuss later in this chapter.

Let's get some hands-on experience creating a trace in Profiler by creating a trace that monitors the opening and closing of objects:

1. From the Start menu, go to the Microsoft SQL Server menu under Programs and click Profiler.
2. From the File menu, select New, then click Trace to bring up the Trace Properties dialog box.
3. Connect to your default server instance using the proper authentication.
4. In the Trace name box, type **`Monitor`**.
5. Use the TSQL_Replay template (we'll replay this later).
6. Check the Save To File check box, and click OK to accept the default name and location. Leave the "Enable file rollover" box checked and the Server Processes trace data box unchecked.

NOTE When the Server Processes trace data box is checked, SQL Server processes the trace. This can slow server performance, but no events are missed. If the box is unchecked, the client processes the trace data. This results in faster performance, but some events may be missed under a heavy server load.

7. Check the Save To Table check box, log in to your default server instance, and fill in the following:
   - Database: AdventureWorks
   - Owner: dbo
   - Table: Monitor

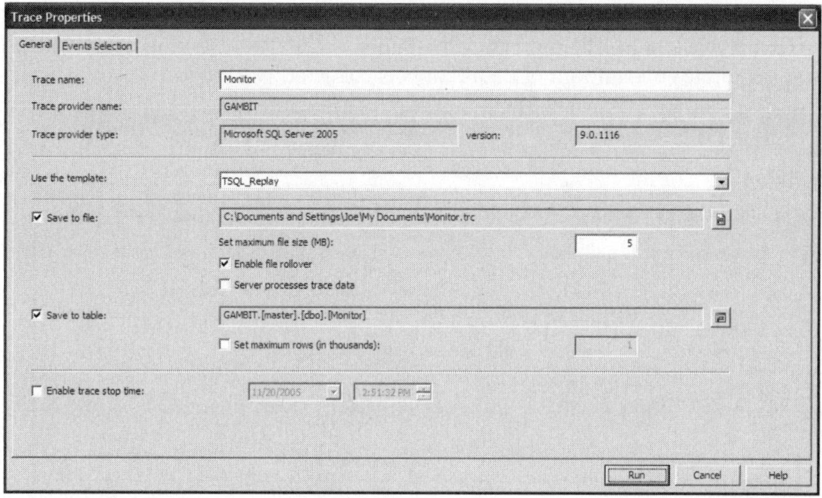

8. Click the Events Selection tab.
9. In the Events grid, expand Security Audit (if it is not already expanded) and check the box to the left of Audit Database Object Access Event. This will monitor the opening and closing of objects, such as tables.

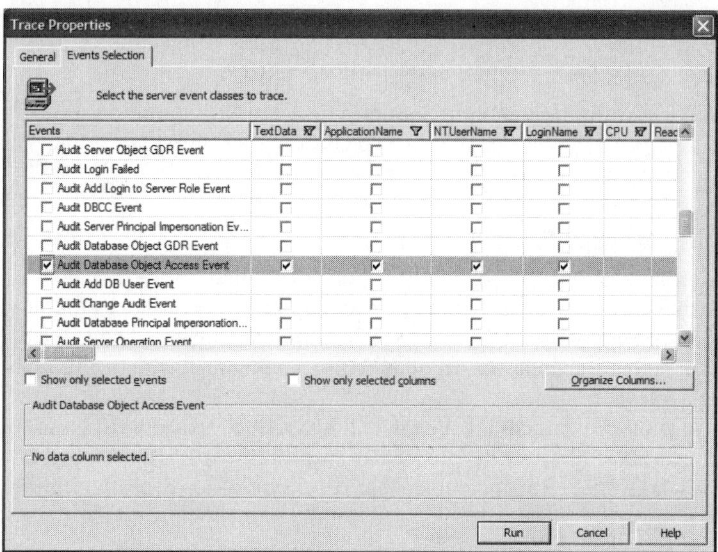

10. Click Run to start the trace.
11. Leave Profiler running and open a new SQL Server query in Management Studio.
12. Execute the following query:

```
USE AdventureWorks
SELECT * FROM Person.Contact
```

13. Switch back to Profiler and click the Pause button (double blue lines). In the Profiler window, notice the amount of data that was collected.

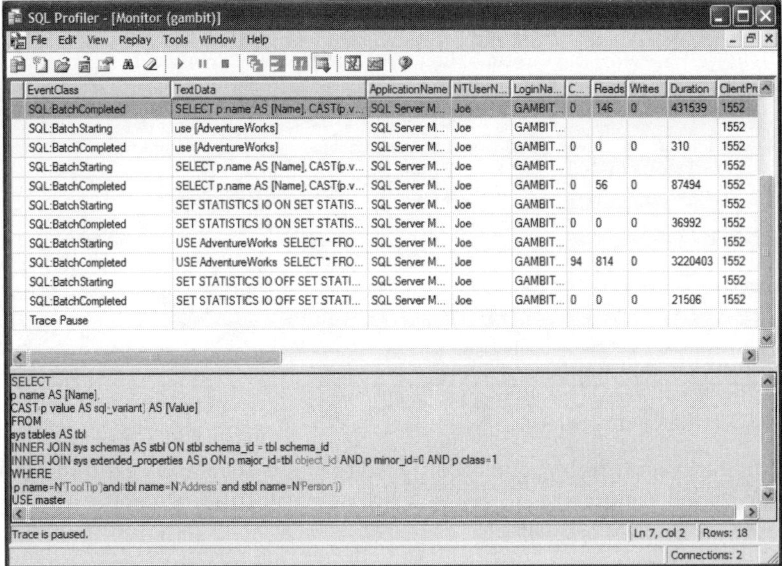

14. Close Profiler and Management Studio.

If you look toward the end of the results in the trace, you should see the SELECT query that you executed in step 12. Once a trace has been recorded, everything in the trace can be executed as if it were coming from a user. This is a process called *replaying*.

Replaying a Trace File

When a detective is trying to solve a crime, one of the first things they do is re-create the action as closely as they can. This helps them find specific details that cannot be found any other way. When something bad happens to SQL Server (such as a server crash), you need to be able to re-create the circumstances that led up to the event as closely as possible, which you can do with Profiler by replaying a trace.

Loading your saved traces into Profiler allows you to replay them against the server and, in this way, figure out exactly where the problem occurred. An especially nice touch is that you don't have to play the whole trace all at once; you can take it step-by-step to see exactly where the problem lies, and you can even play the saved traces against a different server so that you don't crash your production server in the process. Let's try this out in the next series of instructions:

1. Open Profiler; from the File menu, select Open and Trace File.
2. In the Open dialog box, select Monitor and click OK.
3. On the toolbar in the trace window, click the Execute One Step button (a blue arrow pointing to a gray line). This will execute a single step at a time.
4. Log in to your default instance of SQL Server.
5. On the Replay Configuration dialog box that comes up next, you can choose to create an output filename, which will store all error messages and output for later review. Leave this blank.
6. Under Basic Replay Options, you can opt to enable debugging by replaying events in the order they were recorded or disable debugging by replaying multiple events at the same time. Select the option to replay events in the order they were recorded, enable debugging, and click Start.

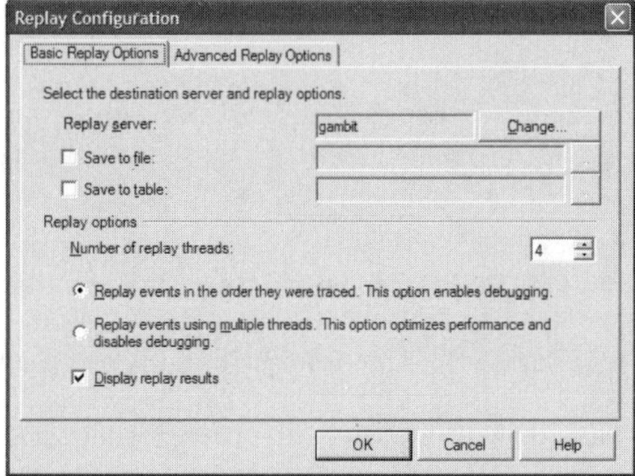

7. Scroll down and select the first line you find that contains `SQL:BatchCompleted`.
8. On the toolbar, click the Run To Cursor button (an arrow pointing to double braces). This will execute all steps between the current position and the event you have selected.
9. Click the Start Execution button (a yellow arrow) to finish replaying the trace. There is an interval between steps, because you selected the Maintain Interval check box earlier.
10. Close Profiler.

The Profiler is a wonderful tool for monitoring database activity and reporting problems, but that is not all it can do. Profiler comes with yet another wizard that will help you even further to improve the performance of your queries—the Database Tuning Advisor.

Using the Database Tuning Advisor

If one musical instrument in an orchestra is out of tune, the entire symphony sounds bad, and the performance is ruined. In the same way, if even one SQL Server database were out of tune, it could slow down the entire system. Perhaps an index was created using the wrong columns, or maybe users have started querying different data over time, which would require the creation of new indexes. If any of this is true, your databases need tuning.

The one thing you need before you can run the Database Tuning Advisor is a *workload.* You get this by running and saving a trace in Profiler (usually by creating a trace with the Tuning template). It is best to get this workload during times of peak database activity to make sure that you give the Advisor an accurate load. First, we need to create a workload file that we can use with the Advisor:

1. From the Start menu, go to the Microsoft SQL Server menu under Programs and click Profiler.
2. From the File menu, select New, and then click Trace to bring up the Trace Properties dialog box.
3. Connect to your default server instance using the proper authentication.
4. In the Trace name box, type **`Tuning`**.
5. Use the Tuning template.
6. Check the Save To File check box, and click OK to accept the default name and location. Leave the "Enable file rollover" box checked and the Server Processes trace data box unchecked.
7. Click Run to start the trace.
8. Leave Profiler running and open a new SQL Server query in Management Studio.
9. Execute the following query:

```
USE AdventureWorks
SELECT TOP 100 PERCENT title as [Title], lastname as [Last Name], firstname as
[First Name],
phone as [Phone Number], i.demographics as [Demographic XML Data] from
Person.Contact c
join Sales.Individual i on c.ContactID = i.ContactID
```

10. Switch back to Profiler and click the Stop button (red box) and close Profiler.

The next series of steps will show you how to run the Database Tuning Advisor using the workload file you just created:

1. Open the Database Tuning Advisor from the Microsoft SQL Server 2005 menu on the Start Menu.
2. Connect to your server using the appropriate authentication method. This will create a new session in the Advisor.
3. In the Session name box enter **`Tuning Session`**.
4. In the Workload section, click the browse button (it looks like a pair of binoculars) and locate the `Tuning.trc` trace file created earlier.

5. In the Databases and tables grid, check the box next to AdventureWorks.

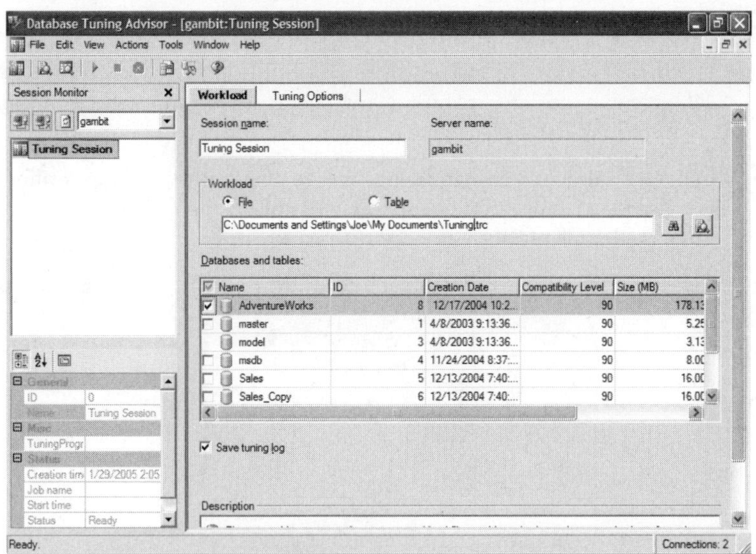

6. Switch to the Tuning Options tab. From here you can instruct the Advisor what physical changes to make to the database; specifically you can have the advisor create new indexes (clustered and non-clustered) and partition the database.
7. Leave the "Limit tuning time" option checked and set for the default time; this prevents the Advisor from taking too much system resources.
8. Leave the default options for PDS options to use in database, Partitioning strategy to employ, and PDS to keep in database.

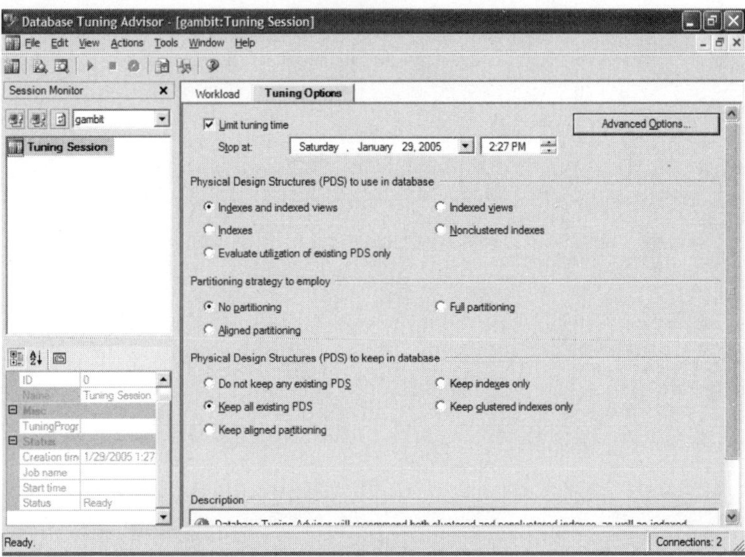

9. Click the Advanced Options button. From here you can set these options:
   - "Define max. space for recommendations" sets the maximum amount of space used by recommended physical performance structures.
   - "All recommendations are offline" will generate recommendations that may require you to take the database offline to implement the change.
   - "Generate online recommendations where possible" will return online recommendations even if a faster offline method is possible. If there is no online method, then an offline method is recommended.
   - "Generate only online recommendations" will only return online recommendations.

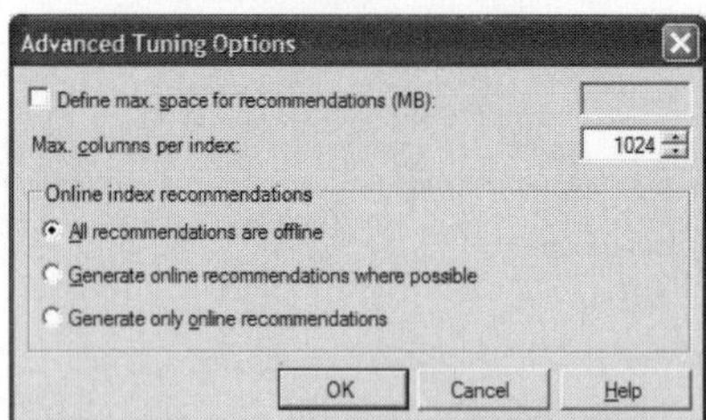

10. Click Cancel to return to the Advisor.
11. From the Actions menu, select Start Analysis.
12. On the Start Analysis dialog box, select Start now and click OK.

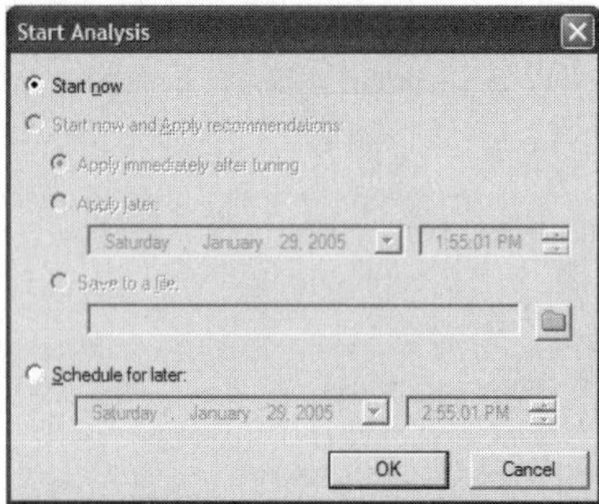

13. You should see a progress status screen during the analysis phase.

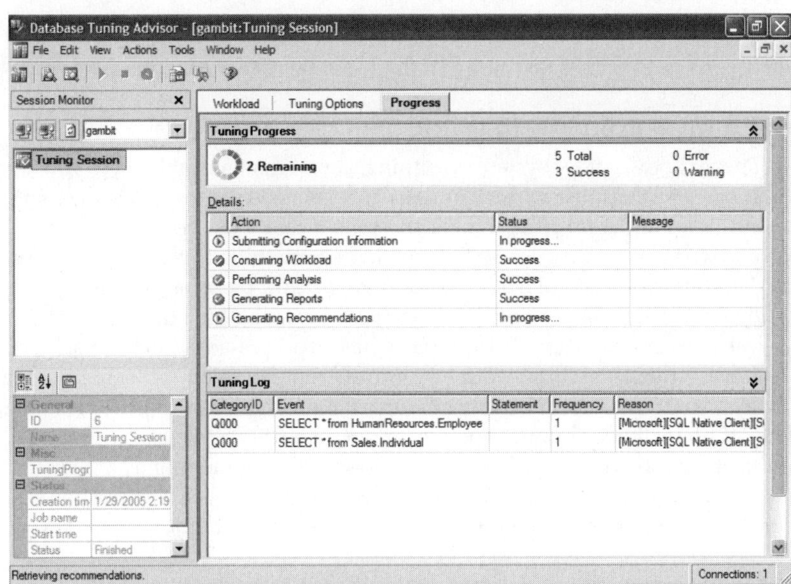

14. After analysis is complete, you will be taken to the recommendations screen, you probably won't see any recommendations for this small workload file though.

15. You can also check the reports screen for more detailed information on the analysis process.

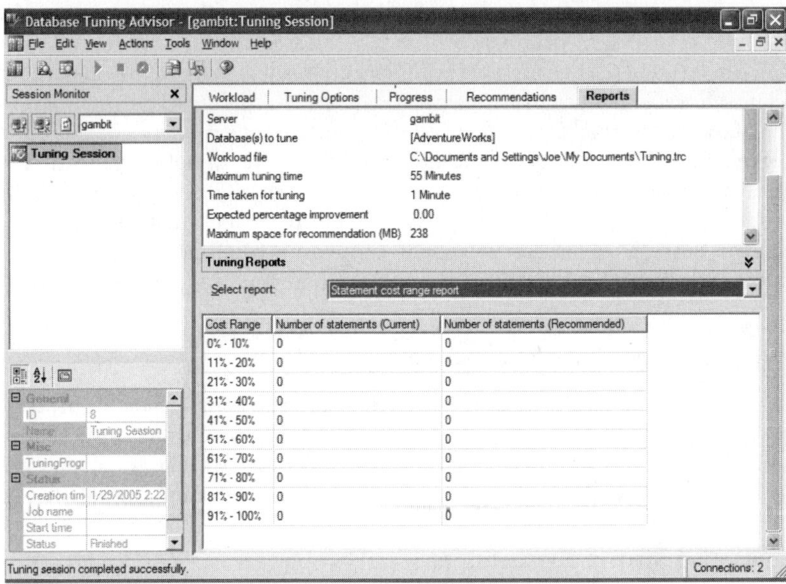

16. Close the Database Tuning Advisor.

Tips and Techniques

If you want the best results from SQL Server's monitoring tools, you need to know and use the proper techniques. If you don't, the end result will not be what you are hoping for—or what you need.

Setting a Measurement Baseline

You will never know if your system is running slower than normal unless you know what normal is, which is what a *measurement baseline* does: It shows you the resources (memory, CPU, etc.) SQL Server consumes under normal circumstances. You create the measurement baseline before putting your system into production so that you have something to compare your readings to later on.

The first thing you need to create an accurate measurement baseline is a test network with just your SQL Server and one or two client machines. You limit the number of machines involved because all networks have broadcast traffic, which is processed by all the machines on the network. This broadcast traffic can throw your counts off—sometimes a little, sometimes quite a bit. You may instead want to consider shutting down as many machines as possible and generating your baseline off-hours if your budget does not allow for a test network.

You can then start your baseline. The Windows counters mentioned at the outset of this chapter as well as the preset SQL Server counters should provide an accurate baseline with which you can compare future readings. Then you can move to the next technique.

Data Archiving and Trend Tracking

Although the consequences of throwing away your SQL Server monitoring records are not quite as severe as facing an IRS auditor without records and receipts, you still need to save, or *archive*, your records. One of the primary reasons to do so is to back up requests for additional equipment. For example, if you ask for funds to buy more memory for the SQL Server, but don't bring any proof that the system needs the RAM, you are probably not going to get the money. If you bring a few months' worth of reports, however, and say, "After tracking SQL Server for a time, we've found this…" management may be far more willing to give you the money you need. Using archived data in such fashion is known as *trend tracking*.

One of the most valuable functions of using your archived data for trend tracking is proactive troubleshooting—that is, anticipating and avoiding problems before they arise. Suppose you added 50 new users to your network about three months ago and are about to do it again. If you archived your data from that period, you would be able to recall what those 50 users did to the performance of the SQL Server, and you could compensate for it. On the other hand, if you threw that data away, you might be in for a nasty surprise when your system unexpectedly slows to a crawl.

Optimization Techniques

SQL Server can dynamically adjust most of its settings to compensate for problems. It can adjust memory use, threads spawned, and a host of other settings. In some cases, unfortunately, those dynamic adjustments may not be enough—you may need to make some manual changes.

We'll look at a few specific areas that may require your personal attention.

Queries and Stored Procedures

The first thing to ask yourself when you are getting slow response times is whether you could be using a stored procedure instead of a local query. Stored procedures differ from local code in two ways: They are stored on the SQL Server, so they do not need to be transmitted over the network, which causes congestion. In addition, stored procedures are precompiled on the server; this saves system resources, because local code must be compiled once it gets to the system.

Overall, stored procedures are the way to go, but if you need to use local queries, you should consider how they are written, because poorly constructed queries can wreak havoc on your system. If, for example, you have a query that is returning every row of a table when only half of that is required, you should consider rewriting the query. Improper use of WHERE clauses can also slow your queries down. Make sure that your WHERE clauses reference indexed columns for optimal performance.

Tempdb

Is your tempdb big enough to handle the load that your queries put on it? Think of tempdb as a scratchpad for SQL Server; when queries are performed, SQL Server uses this scratchpad to make notes about the result set. If tempdb runs out of room to make these notes, system response time can slow down. Tempdb should be between 25 and 40 percent of the size of your largest database (e.g., if your largest database is 100MB, tempdb should be 25 to 40MB).

Query Governor

Right out of the box, SQL Server will run any query you tell it to, even if that query is poorly written. You can change that by using the Query Governor. This is not a separate tool, but is part of the database engine and is controlled by the Query Governor Cost Limit. This setting tells SQL Server not to run queries longer than *x* (where *x* is a value higher than zero). If, for example, the Query Governor Cost Limit is set to 2, any query that is estimated to take longer than 2 seconds would not be allowed to run. SQL Server can estimate the running time of a query because SQL Server keeps statistics about the number and composition of records in tables and indexes. The Query Governor Cost Limit can be set by using the command `sp_configure 'query governor cost limit', '1'` (the 1 in this code can be higher). The Cost Limit can also be set on the Server Settings tab of the Server Properties page in Enterprise Manager.

NOTE If the Query Governor Cost Limit is set to zero (the default), all queries will be allowed to run.

Setting Trace Flags

A *trace flag* is used to temporarily alter a particular SQL Server behavior. Much like a light switch can be used to turn off a light and then turn it back on again, a trace flag can be used to turn off (or on) a behavior in SQL Server. Trace flags are enabled with DBCC TRACEON and turned off with DBCC TRACEOFF. The command to enable trace flag 1204 would look like this: `DBCC TRACEON(1204)`. Table 24.3 lists some of the trace flags available to you.

TABLE 24.3: Uses of Trace Flags

TRACE FLAG	USE
107	This instructs the server to interpret numbers with a decimal point as type float instead of decimal.
240	This trace flag prints version information for extended stored procedure dynamic link libraries. If you write your own extended stored procedures, this trace flag will prove useful in troubleshooting.

TABLE 24.3: Uses of Trace Flags *(CONTINUED)*

TRACE FLAG	USE
1204	This will tell you what type of locks are involved in a deadlock and what commands are affected.
1205	This flag returns even more detailed information about the commands affected by a deadlock.
1704	This will print information when temporary tables are created or dropped.
2528	This trace flag disables parallel checking of objects by the DBCC CHECKDB, DBCC CHECKFILEGROUP, and DBCC CHECKTABLE commands. If you know that the server load is going to increase while these commands are running, you may want to turn these trace flags on so that SQL Server checks only a single object at a time and therefore places less load on the server. Under ordinary circumstances, though, you should let SQL Server decide on the degree of parallelism.
3205	This will turn off hardware compression for backups to tape drives.
3604	When turning on or off trace flags, this flag will send output to the client.
3605	When turning on or off trace flags, this flag will send output to the error log.
7505	This enables 6.x handling of return codes when a call to dbcursorfetchx causes the cursor position to follow the end of the cursor set.

Max Async I/O

It should go without saying that SQL Server needs to be able to write to disk, because that's where the database files are stored—but is it writing to disk fast enough? If you have multiple hard disks connected to a single controller, multiple hard disks connected to multiple controllers, or a RAID system involving striping, the answer is probably no. The maximum number of asynchronous input/output (Max Async I/O) threads by default in SQL Server is 32. This means that SQL Server can have 32 outstanding read and 32 outstanding write requests at a time. Thus, if SQL Server needs to write some data to disk, SQL Server can send up to 32 small chunks of that data to disk at a time. If you have a powerful disk subsystem, you will want to increase the Max Async I/O setting.

The value to which you increase this setting depends on your hardware, so if you increase the setting, you must then monitor the server. Specifically, you will need to monitor the Physical Disk: Average Disk Queue Performance Monitor counter, which should be less than two (note that any queue should be less than two). If you adjust Max Async I/O and the Average Disk Queue counter goes above two, you have set Max Async I/O too high and will need to decrease it.

NOTE You will need to divide the Average Disk Queue counter by the number of physical drives to get an accurate count. That is, if you have three hard disks and a counter value of six, you would divide six by three—which tells you that the counter value for each disk is two.

LazyWriter

LazyWriter is a SQL Server process that moves information from the data cache in memory to a file on disk. If LazyWriter can't keep enough free space in the data cache for new requests, performance slows down. To make sure this does not happen, monitor the SQL Server: Buffer Manager – Free Buffers Performance Monitor counter. LazyWriter tries to keep this counter level above zero; if it dips or hits zero, you have a problem, probably with your disk subsystem. To verify this, you need to check the Physical Disk: Average Disk Queue Performance Monitor counter and verify that it is not more than two per physical disk (see above). If the queue is too high, LazyWriter will not be able to move data efficiently from memory to disk, and the free buffers will drop.

RAID

RAID (Redundant Array of Inexpensive Disks) is used to protect your data and speed up your system. In a system without RAID, data that is written to disk is written to that one disk. In a system with RAID, that same data would be written across multiple disks, providing fault tolerance and improved I/O. Some forms of RAID can be implemented inexpensively in Windows, but this uses such system resources as processor and memory. If you have the budget for it, you might consider getting a separate RAID controller or Storage Area Network (SAN) device that will take the processing burden off Windows. Here are the most common types of RAID:

RAID 0 Stripe Set This provides I/O improvement, but not fault tolerance.

RAID 1 Mirroring This provides fault tolerance and read-time improvement. This can also be implemented as duplexing, which is a mirror that has separate controllers for each disk.

RAID 0+1 Mirrored Stripe Set This is a stripe set without parity that is duplicated on another set of disks. This requires a third-party controller, because Windows NT does not support this level of RAID natively.

RAID 5 Stripe Set with Parity This provides fault tolerance and improved I/O.

Adding Memory

Windows Server operating systems can support large amounts of memory. The 2003 Standard Edition supports 4GB of RAM, Enterprise Edition supports 32GB, and Datacenter supports up to 64GB of RAM. This is great news for SQL Server because, like most server products, it likes lots of RAM. Another feature to consider is Address Windowing Extensions, or AWE for short. Without going into too much detail, AWE allows applications quick access to memory in excess of 4GB while still using 32-bit pointers to the memory. This means the SQL Server 2005 can use a huge memory cache if AWE is enabled. To enable AWE for SQL Server, run sp_configure, and set AWE enabled to 1, then restart SQL Server.

Manually Configuring Memory Use

Although SQL Server can dynamically assign itself memory, it is not always best to let it do so. A good example of this is when you need to run another BackOffice program, such as Exchange, on the same system as SQL Server. If SQL Server is not constrained, it will take so much memory that there will be none left for Exchange. The relevant constraint is the *max server memory* setting; by adjusting it, you can stop SQL Server from taking too much RAM. If, for example, you set it to 102,400—100 × 1024 (the size of a megabyte)—SQL Server will never use more than 100MB of RAM.

You could also set *min server memory*, which tells SQL Server to never use less than the set amount; this should be used in conjunction with *set working size*. Windows uses virtual memory, which means that data that is in memory and has not been accessed for a while can be stored on disk. The *set working size* option stops Windows from moving SQL Server data from RAM to disk, even if SQL Server is idle. This can improve SQL Server's performance, because data will never need to be retrieved from disk (which is about 100 times slower than RAM). If you decide to use this option, you should set *min server memory* and *max server memory* to the same size, and then change the *set working size* option to 1.

Summary

This chapter has stressed the importance of monitoring and optimization. Monitoring allows you to find potential problems before your users find them; without it, you have no way of knowing how well your system is performing.

Performance Monitor can be used to monitor both Windows NT and SQL Server. Some of the more important counters to watch are Physical Disk: Average Disk Queue (which should be less than two) and SQLServer:Buffer Manager: Buffer Cache Hit Ratio (which should be as high as possible).

Query Editor allows you to see how a query will affect your system before you place the query in production. The Profiler is used to monitor queries after they have been placed in general use; it is also useful for monitoring security and user activity. Once you have used Profiler to log information about query use to a trace file, you can run the Database Tuning Advisor to optimize your indexes.

Once you have created all logs and traces, you need to archive them. The various log files can be used later for budget justification and trend tracking.

This chapter also presented some tips for repairing a slow-running system. You can change the Max Async I/O setting if your disk is not working hard enough to support the rest of the system, and you may need to upgrade your disk subsystem if the SQL Server: Buffer Manager - Free Buffers Performance Monitor counter hits zero. RAID can also speed up your SQL Server. If you can afford a separate controller, you should get one to take some of the burden off Windows. If you can't afford one, you can use Windows RAID level 1 for fault tolerance and speed.

Now that you know how to optimize your server and keep it running at peak performance, it will be much easier to perform all of the tasks on your SQL Server. This is especially true of the next topic that we will discuss—replication.

Chapter 25

Replication

For one reason or another, companies may have more than one database system, especially in larger companies with more than one location or multiple departments that keep their own servers. Regardless of the reason, many of these servers need to have copies of each other's databases. For example, if you have two servers for your human resources department (one in New York and one in Singapore), you may need to keep a copy of each database on each server so that all of your human resources personnel can see the same data. The best way to copy this data is through replication.

Replication is designed specifically for the task of copying data and other objects (such as views, stored procedures, and triggers) between servers and making certain that those copies stay up-to-date. In this chapter, we look into the inner workings of replication. First we discuss some terminology that is used to describe the various parts of replication. After you have an understanding of the terms, we can discuss the roles that SQL Servers play in the replication process. Next we move into the types and models of replication, and finally we replicate. Let's get started.

Understanding Replication

The sole purpose of replication is to copy data between servers. There are several good reasons for doing so:

- If your company has multiple locations, you may need to move the data closer to the people who are using it.
- If multiple people want to work on the same data at the same time, replication is a good way of giving them that access.
- Replication can separate the functions of reading from writing data. This is especially true in OLTP (online transaction processing) environments where reading data can place quite a load on the system.
- Some sites may have different methods and rules for handling data (perhaps the site is a sister or child company). Replication can be used to give these sites the freedom of setting their own rules for dealing with data.
- Mobile sales users can install SQL Server 2005 on a laptop, where they might keep a copy of an inventory database. These users can keep their local copy of the database current by dialing in to the network and replicating.

You may be able to come up with even more reasons to use replication in your company, but to do so, you need to understand the publisher/subscriber concept.

The Publisher/Subscriber Metaphor

Microsoft uses the publisher/subscriber metaphor to make replication easier to understand and implement. It works a lot like a newspaper or magazine publisher. The newspaper has information that people around the city want to read; therefore the newspaper publishes this data and has news carriers distribute it to the people who have subscribed. As shown in Figure 25.1, SQL Server replication works much the same in that it too has a publisher, a distributor, and a subscriber:

Publisher In SQL Server terminology, the publisher is the server with the original copy of the data that others need—much like the newspaper publisher has the original data that needs to be printed and distributed.

Distributor Much like the newspaper needs carriers to distribute the newspaper to the people who have subscribed, SQL Servers need special servers called distributors to collect data from publishers to distribute to subscribers.

Subscriber A subscriber is a server that requires a copy of the data that is stored on the publisher. The subscriber is akin to the people who need to read the news, so they subscribe to the newspaper.

NOTE A SQL Server can be any combination of these three roles.

The analogy goes even further: All of the information is not just lumped together in a giant scroll and dropped on the doorstep—it is broken up into various publications and articles so that it is easier to find the information you want to read. SQL Server replication follows suit:

Article An article is just data from a table that needs to be replicated. Of course, you probably do not need to replicate all of the data from the table, so you don't have to. Articles can be horizontally partitioned, which means that not all records in the table are published, and they can be vertically partitioned, which means that not all columns need be published.

Publication A publication is a collection of articles and is the basis for subscriptions. A subscription can consist of a single article or multiple articles, but you must subscribe to a publication as opposed to a single article.

Now that you know the three roles that SQL Servers can play in replication and that data is replicated as articles that are stored in publications, you need to know the types of repliction.

FIGURE 25.1
SQL Server can publish, distribute, or subscribe to publications in replication.

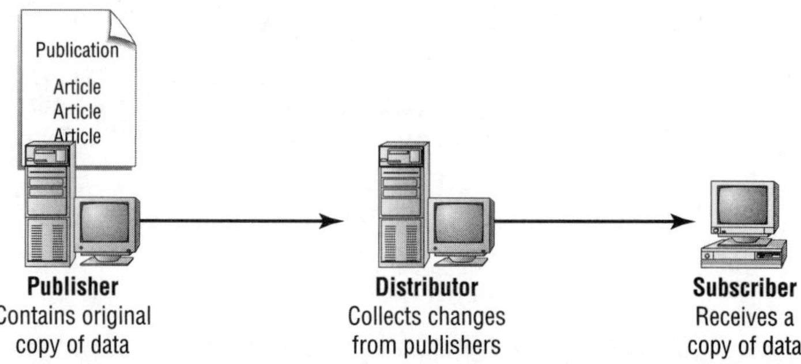

Replication Types

It is important to control how publications are distributed to subscribers. If the newspaper company does not control distribution, for example, many people may not get the paper when they need it, or other people may get the paper for free. In SQL Server, you need to control distribution of publications so that the data gets to the subscribers when it is needed.

There are three basic types of replication: Transactional, Snapshot, and Merge, which we will discuss in more detail below. There are some key factors to consider when choosing a replication type:

Autonomy Autonomy is the amount of independence that your subscribers have over the data they receive. Some servers may need a read-only copy of the data, while others may need to be able to make changes to the data they receive.

Latency This refers to how long a subscriber can go without getting a fresh copy of data from the server. Some servers may be able to go for weeks without getting new data from the publisher, while other instances may require a very short wait time.

Consistency Possibly the most popular form of replication is transactional replication, where transactions are read from the transaction log of the publisher, moved through the distributor, and applied to the database on the subscriber. This is where transactional consistency comes in. Some subscribers may need all of the transactions in the same order they were applied to the server, while other subscribers may need only some of the transactions.

Once these factors have been considered, you are ready to choose the replication type that will work best for you.

Background: Distributed Transactions

Before looking at the various flavors of transactional replication, a brief bit of background and review of distributed transactions is in order.

In some instances, multiple servers may need the same transaction at the exact same time, as in a bank, for example. Suppose that the bank has multiple servers for storing customer account data, each server storing a copy of the same data and all servers can modify the data in question. Now suppose that a customer comes to an automatic teller machine and withdraws money from their account. The action of withdrawing money is a simple Transact-SQL transaction that removes money from the customer's checking account record, but remember that more than one server holds this data. If the transaction makes it to only one of the bank's servers, the customer could go to ATMs all over town and withdraw enough money to retire on, and the bank would have a very hard time stopping them.

To avoid such a scenario, you need to get the exact same transaction to all of the subscribers at the same time. If the transaction is not applied to all of the servers, it is not applied to any of the servers. This type of replication is called *distributed transactions* or *two-phase commit (2PC)*. Technically this is not a form of replication; 2PC uses the Microsoft Distributed Transaction Coordinator and is controlled by the way the Transact-SQL is written. A normal, single-server transaction looks like this:

```
BEGIN TRAN
TSQL CODE
COMMIT TRAN
```

A distributed transaction looks like this:

```
BEGIN DISTRIBUTED TRAN
TSQL CODE
COMMIT TRAN
```

Using distributed transactions will apply the same transaction to all required servers at once or to none of them at all. This means that this type of replication has very low autonomy, low latency, and high consistency.

Transactional Replication

In transactional replication, the individual transactions are replicated. Transactional replication is preferable when data modifications are to be replicated immediately, or when transactions have to be atomic (either all or none applied). Also, with transactional replication, a primary key is required as each transaction is replicated individually. As described below there are three key types of transactional replication: standard, with updating subscribers, and peer-to-peer.

Standard Transactional Replication

All data modifications made to a SQL Server database are considered transactions, whether or not they have an explicit `BEGIN TRAN` command and corresponding `COMMIT TRAN` (if the `BEGIN…COMMIT` is not there, SQL Server assumes it). All of these transactions are stored in a transaction log that is associated with the database. With *transactional* replication, each of the transactions in the transaction log can be replicated. The transactions are marked for replication in the log (because not all transactions may be replicated), then they are copied to the distributor, where they are stored in the distribution database until they are copied to the subscribers via the Distribution Agent.

The only real drawback is that subscribers to a transactional publication must treat the data as read only, meaning that users cannot make changes to the data they receive. Think of it as being like a subscription to a newspaper—if you see a typo in an ad in the paper, you can't change it with a pen and expect the change to do any good. No one else can see your change, and you will just get the same typo in the paper the next day. So, transactional replication has high consistency, low autonomy, and middle-of-the-road latency. For these reasons, transactional replication is usually used in server-to-server environments.

Transactional Replication with Updating Subscribers

This type of replication is almost exactly like transactional replication, with one major difference: The subscribers can modify the data they receive. You can think of this type of replication as a mix of 2PC and transactional replication in that it uses the Distributed Transaction Coordinator and distributed transactions to accomplish its task.

The two types of updatable subscriptions are *immediate* and *queued*. Immediate updating means that the data is updated immediately. For this sort of update to occur at the subscriber, the publisher and subscriber must be connected. In queued updating, the publisher and subscriber do not have to be connected to update data at the subscribers and updates can be made while either is offline.

When data are updated at a subscriber, the update is sent to the publisher when next connected. The publisher then sends the data to other subscribers as they become available. Immediate updating is done using 2PC. When queued updating is used, the transactions can be applied whenever network connectivity is available between the publisher and the subscriber.

Because the updates are sent asynchronously (meaning not at the same time) to the publisher, the same data may have been updated by the publisher or another subscriber, resulting in conflicts occurring when applying updates. All conflicts are detected and resolved through a conflict resolution policy defined when the publication is created.

Updatable subscriptions can be enabled through Management Studio's New Publication Wizard or through a stored procedure. Publications created through the wizard have both immediate and queued updating enabled by default. If creating a publication through a stored procedure you can enable one or both options. You always have the option in both methods to switch update modes.

Peer-to-Peer Transactional Replication

Transactional replication uses also peer-to-peer replication to support updating data by subscribers. This method is designed for applications (as opposed to another SQL Server) that might modify the data at any of the databases participating in replication. An example is an online shopping application that modifies a database with each order or purchase (e.g., updating the mailing lists, changing the inventory, etc.).

A key difference between standard (read-only) transactional replication or transactional replication with updating subscriptions and peer-to-peer transactional replication is that the latter is not hierarchical. Instead all the nodes are peers and each node publishes and subscribes to the same schema and data. Hence, each node contains identical schema and data.

SNAPSHOT REPLICATION

While transactional replication copies only data changes to subscribers, *snapshot replication* copies entire publications to subscribers every time it replicates. In essence, it takes a snapshot of the data and sends it to the subscriber every time it replicates. This is useful for servers that need a read-only copy of the data and do not require updates very often—in fact, they could wait for days or even weeks for updated data.

A good example of where to use this type of replication is in a department store chain that has a catalog database. The headquarters keeps and publishes the master copy of the database where changes are made. The subscribers can wait for updates to this catalog for a few days if necessary.

The data on the subscriber should be treated as read only here as well, because all of the data is going to be overwritten anyway each time replication occurs. This type of replication is said to have high latency, high autonomy, and high consistency.

Snapshots are created using the Snapshot Agent and stored in a snapshot folder on the publisher. Snapshot Agent runs under SQL Server Agent at the distributor and can be administered through Management Studio.

NOTE **Snapshot replication is principally used to establish the initial set of data and database objects for merge and transactional publications.**

MERGE REPLICATION

By far, this is the most complex type of replication to work with, but also the most flexible. *Merge replication* allows changes to be made to the data at the publisher as well as at all of the subscribers. These changes are then replicated to all other subscribers until finally your systems reach convergence, the blessed state at which all of your servers have the same data. Because of its flexibility, merge replication is typically used in server-to-client environments.

The biggest problem with merge replication is known as a *conflict*. This problem occurs when more than one user modifies the same record on their copy of the database at the same time. For example, if a user in Florida modifies record 25 in a table at the same time that a user in New York modifies record 25 in their own copy of the table, a conflict will occur on record 25 when replication takes place because the same record has been modified in two different places, and therefore SQL Server has two values from which to choose. Conflict resolution priority is specified through the New Subscription Wizard or in Management Studio. You can also use Management Studio's Replication Conflict Viewer tool to examine and resolves conflicts (you will see how to set later in this chapter). If you can figure out how to apply the SQL Server methodology to resolve conflicts throughout the world, you will likely receive the Nobel Peace Prize as well.

Merge replication works by adding triggers and system tables to the databases on all of the servers involved in the replication process. When a change is made at any of the servers, the trigger fires off and stores the modified data in one of the new system tables, where it will reside until replication occurs. This type of replication has the highest autonomy, highest latency, and lowest transactional consistency.

But how does all of this occur? What is the driving force behind replication? Let's look at the four agents that make replication run.

Replication Agents

Any of the types of subscriptions listed in the last section can be either push or pull subscriptions. A *push subscription* is configured and controlled at the publisher. This method of subscription is like the catalogs that you receive in the mail—the publisher decides when you get updates because the publisher knows when changes have been made to the information inside the catalog. The same is true of a push subscription in replication—the publisher decides when changes will be sent to the subscribers.

Pull subscriptions are more like a magazine subscription. You write to the publisher of the magazine and request a subscription—the magazine is not automatically sent to you. Pull subscriptions work much the same in that the subscriber requests a subscription from the publisher—the subscription is not sent unless the subscriber asks for it.

With either method of replication, five agents are used to move the data from the publisher to the distributor and finally to the subscriber:

Log Reader Agent This agent is used primarily in transactional replication. It reads the transaction log of the published database on the publisher and looks for transactions that have been marked for replication. When it finds such a transaction, the log reader agent copies the transaction to the distribution server, where it is stored in the distribution database until it is moved to the subscribers. This agent runs on the distributor in both push and pull subscriptions. To start the Log Reader agent, enter `logread.exe` on the command line.

Distribution Agent This agent moves the snapshot (for snapshot and transactional replication) and the transactions in the distribution database tables to the subscribers. In a push subscription, this agent runs on the distributor, but in a pull subscription, it runs on the subscriber. Therefore, if you have a large number of subscribers, you may want to consider using a pull subscription method to lighten the load on the distribution server. To start the Distribution Agent, enter `distrib.exe` on the command line.

Snapshot Agent The name of this agent would lead you to suspect it worked only with snapshot replication, but it works with all three types of replications. This agent makes a copy of the publication on the publisher and either copies it to the distributor, where it is stored in the distribution working folder (\\ **`distribution_server\Program Files\Microsoft SQL Server\MSSQL$(instance)\REPLDATA`**), or places it on removable disk (such as a CD-ROM or Zip drive) until it can be copied to the subscriber. With snapshot replication, this agent runs every time replication occurs; with the other types of replication, this agent runs on a less frequent basis and is used to make sure that the subscribers have a current copy of the publication, including the most up-to-date structure for the data. This agent runs on the distributor in either a push or a pull subscription. Snapshot Agent runs under SQL Server Agent at the distributor and can be administered through Management Studio. You can also invoke the Snapshot Agent from the command line using `snapshot.exe`.

Merge Agent This agent controls merge replication. It takes changes from all of the subscribers, as well as the publisher, and merges the changes with all other subscribers involved in replication. This agent runs on the distributor in a push subscription and on the subscriber in a pull subscription. To invoke from the command line, enter `replmerg.exe`.

Queue Reader Agent This agent, which is used with snapshot and transactional publications that allow queued updating, reads the messages in a SQL Server queue or a Microsoft Message Queue. It then applies the relevant message to the publisher. To start the Queue Reader Agent, enter `qrdrsvc.exe` on the command line. Once you have selected the type of replication you need, you can pick the physical model to go with it.

Replication Models

SQL Server can play three roles in replication: publisher, distributor, and subscriber. Before you can successfully implement replication, you need to know where to place these servers in your scheme. Microsoft has a few standard replication models that should make it easier for you to decide where to put your servers.

Single Publisher, Multiple Subscribers

In this scenario, there is a single, central publishing server where the original copy of the data is stored and several subscribers that need copies of the data. This model lends itself well to transactional or snapshot replication.

A good example of when to use this is if you have a catalog database that is maintained at company headquarters and your satellite offices need a copy of the catalog database. The database at headquarters could be published, and your satellite offices would subscribe to the publication. If you have a large number of subscribers, you could create a pull subscription so that the load is removed from the distribution server, making replication faster. Figure 25.2 should help you visualize this concept.

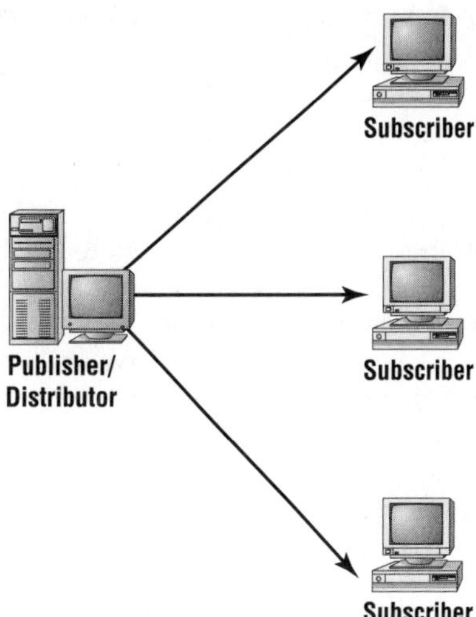

FIGURE 25.2
Several servers can subscribe to a single publisher.

MULTIPLE PUBLISHERS, SINGLE SUBSCRIBER

This model has a single server that subscribes to publications from multiple servers. As shown in Figure 25.3, this lends itself to the following scenario.

Suppose that you work for a company that sells auto parts and you need to keep track of the inventory at all of the regional offices. The servers at all of the regional offices can publish their inventory databases, and the server at company headquarters can subscribe to those subscriptions. Now the folks at company headquarters will know when a regional office is running low on supplies, because headquarters has a copy of everyone's inventory database.

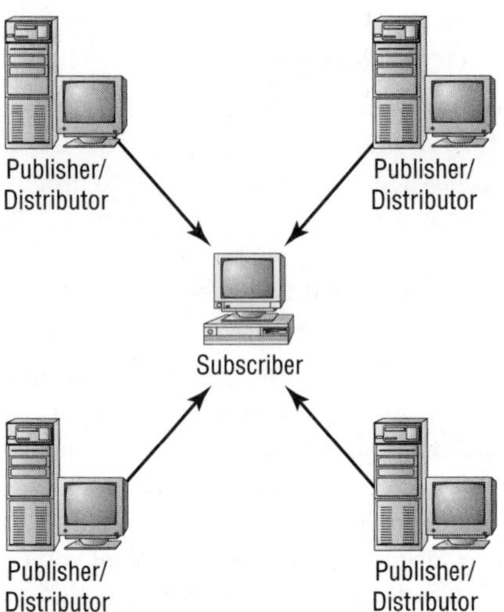

FIGURE 25.3
A single server can also subscribe to multiple publishers.

MULTIPLE PUBLISHERS, MULTIPLE SUBSCRIBERS

In this model, each server is a publisher, and each server is a subscriber (see Figure 25.4). You may instantly think that this lends itself to merge replication, but that is not always the case. This model can lend itself to other types of replication as well.

For example, suppose that you work at a company that rents videos. Each video store needs to know what the other video stores have in stock so that when a customer wants a specific video, they can be instantly directed to a video store that has a copy of the desired video. To accomplish this, each video store would need to publish a copy of their video inventory, and each store would need to subscribe to the other stores' publications. In this way, the proprietors of the video store would know what the other video stores have in stock. If this is accomplished using transactional replication, there will be very little latency, because the publication would be updated every time a transaction takes place.

REMOTE DISTRIBUTOR

In many instances, the publishing server also serves as the distributor, and this works fine. However, there are instances when it is advantageous to devote a server to the task of distribution. Take the following scenario, for example (as shown in Figure 25.5).

Many international companies need data replicated to all of their subsidiaries overseas. A company with headquarters in New York may need to have data replicated to London, Frankfurt, and

Rome, for example. If the server in New York is both the publisher and the distributor, the process of replication would involve three very expensive long-distance calls: one to each of the three subscribers. If you place a distributor in London, though, the publisher in New York would need to make only one call, to the distributor in London. The distributor would then make connections to the other European servers and therefore save money on long-distance calls between servers.

HETEROGENEOUS REPLICATION

Not all replication takes place between SQL Servers. Sometimes you need to have duplicate data on a Sybase, Oracle, or other database server. *Heterogeneous replication* is the process of replicating data from SQL Server to another type of database system and vice versa in the case of an Oracle database. The only requirement for the subscriber in this case is that it must be OLE-DB compliant. If the target is OLE-DB compliant, it can be the recipient of a push subscription from SQL Server.

FIGURE 25.4
Servers can both publish and subscribe to one another.

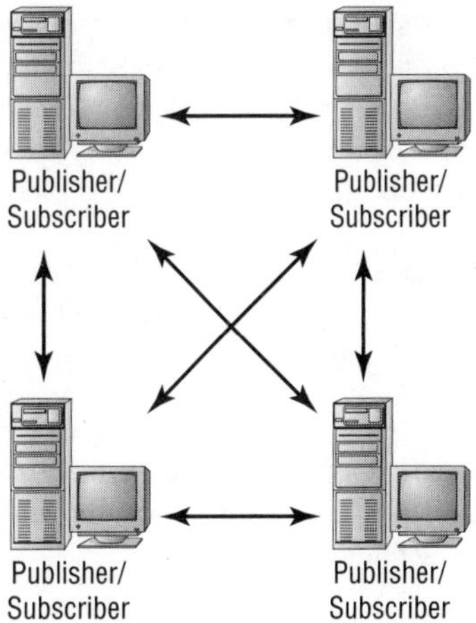

FIGURE 25.5
A server can be dedicated to the task of distribution.

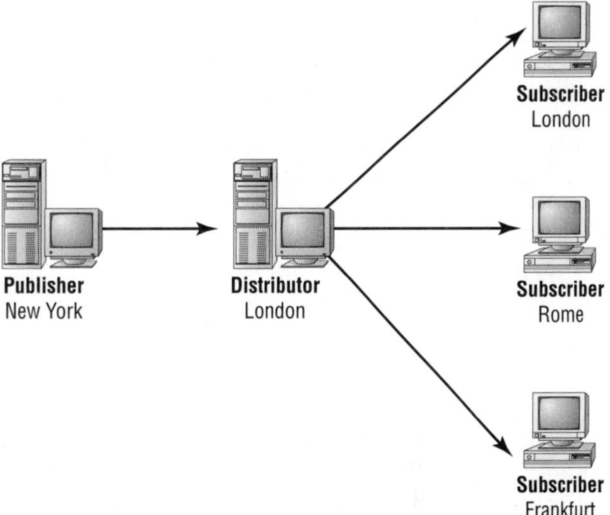

NOTE Oracle is a fully supported publisher in SQL Server 2005 for transactional and snapshot replication, but not for merge replication. Creating and using an Oracle publisher is essentially the same as creating and using a SQL Server publisher.

Heterogeneous replication can provide a means of integrating data by either using Oracle as a source of data to be replicated to SQL Server, IBM, Oracle, and Sybase databases or using SQL Server as the data source.

Transactional replication has heterogeneous replication features, which make it best suited of the three types of replication in these instances.

With a thorough understanding of the terminology, the types, and the models of replication, you are ready to start setting it up. Let's replicate, shall we?

Setting Up Replication

There are a few steps to setting up and configuring replication. First, you need a distributor to collect changes from the publishers and copy them to the subscribers. Then, you need a publisher on which to create articles and publications. Finally, you need a subscriber to accept these publications.

The distributor will have a lot of work to do, especially if it is servicing more than one publisher and more than one subscriber, so give it plenty of RAM. Also, all of the changes from the publishers are stored in one of two places: For transactional replication, all of the changes are stored in the distribution database; for other types, the changes are stored in the distribution working directory (`\\distribution_server\Program Files\Microsoft SQL Server\MSSQL$(instance)\MSSQL\REPLDATA`), so make sure you have enough disk space to handle all of the changes that will be flowing through the system.

NOTE The distribution database stores changes and history for transactional replication; for all other types, the distribution database merely stores history—changes are stored in the distribution working folder.

WARNING Because only administrators have access to the C$ share on any given server, the account used by the SQLServerAgent service needs to be an administrator on the distribution server, or replication will fail.

Once the distributor is ready to go, you can proceed with replication. The first step is to configure the distributor, which we will do now.

NOTE For the exercises in this chapter, you will need to have two instances of SQL Server running. For details on how to install a second instance of SQL Server 2005, refer to the Books On Line documentation.

NOTE A note on nomenclature. SERVER refers to the default instance of SQL Server "Garak" in the exercises and graphics. SECOND refers to the second instance of SQL Server. It appears as Garak\Second in the graphics.

1. Open Management Studio by selecting it from the SQL Server 2005 program group under Programs on the Start menu.

2. Select your default instance of SQL Server (SERVER) and then in Object Explorer right-click the Replication node and select Configure Distribution. This starts the Configure Distribution Wizard. Click Next.

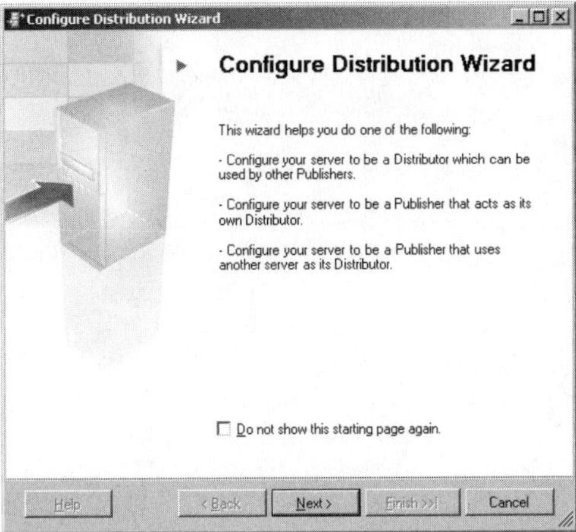

3. On the second screen, you are asked to select a distributor; this is where the distribution database and distribution working folder reside. You will work with the local server, so check the radio button labeled "'SERVER' will act as its own Distributor; SQL Server will create a distribution database and log." Click Next.

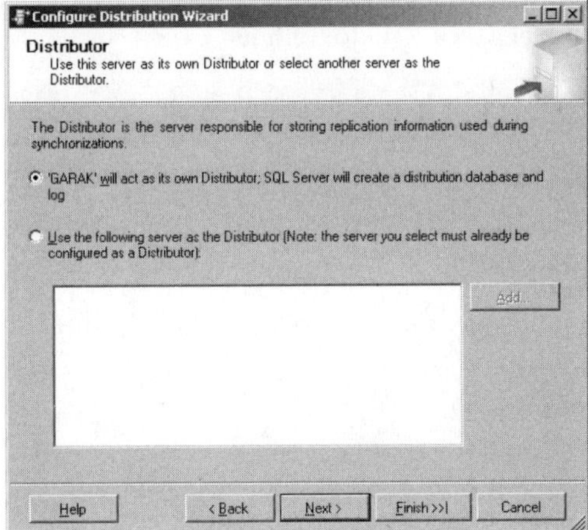

4. If you have not configured SQL Server Agent to start automatically, a dialog box will appear and ask you whether or not to start SQL Server Agent automatically. Normally you would

select "Yes, configure the SQL Server Agent service to start automatically." Note that this dialog will not appear if you have previously configured SQL Server Agent to start automatically.

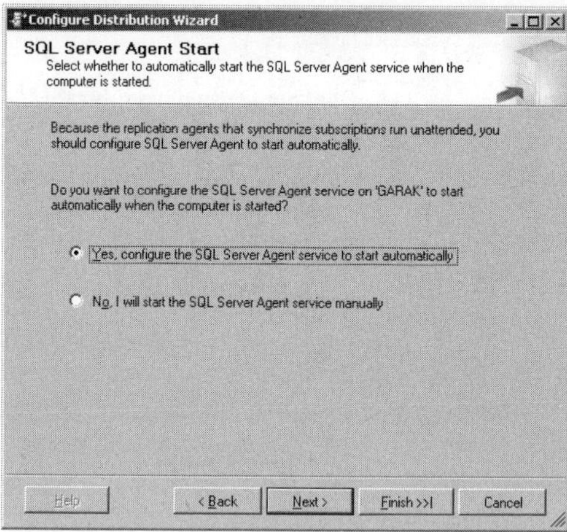

5. The next screen asks you to specify the root location where snapshots from publishers that use this distributor will be stored. You need to specify a network path to refer to the snapshot folder in order for Distribution and Merge agents to access the snapshots of their publications. You also need to use a network path to refer to the snapshot folder to support both push and pull subscriptions. Create a network share on the local computer and refer to it in the text. For example, in the root of C create a folder named *repldata*, and enter **\\SERVER\ReplData** in the Snaphost folder. Click Next to continue.

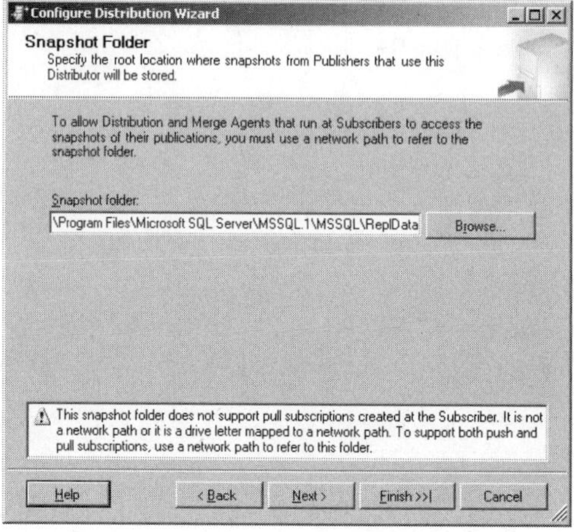

WARNING If you have not enabled the SQL Server Agent service configuration will fail. The SQL Server Agent Service is disabled by default. In order to enable it you must use the Surafce Area Configuration Wizard accessible through Start ➢ Programs ➢ Microsoft SQL Server ➢ Configuration Tools ➢ SQL Server Surface Area Configuration.

6. On the next screen, you need to provide information about the distribution database: its name, data file location, and transaction log location. It is best to have the data file and transaction log on different physical hard disks for recoverability, but for this exercise, accept all of the defaults and click Next to continue.

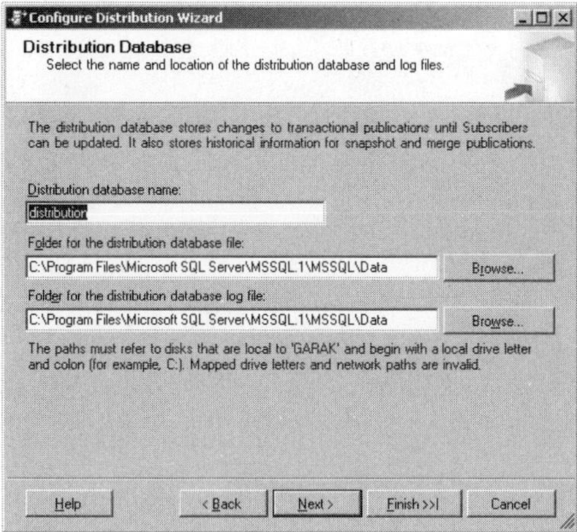

7. The next screen allows you to enable publishers. Enabling a publisher means that it is allowed to use this server as a distributor. This keeps unauthorized servers from bogging down your distributor. In this case, select both the SERVER and SECOND servers. Click Next.

WARNING If the SECOND server does not appear in the list, click the Add button and Select Add SQL Publisher. Then connect to the SECOND server. Once you have done so the SECOND server will appear in this list.

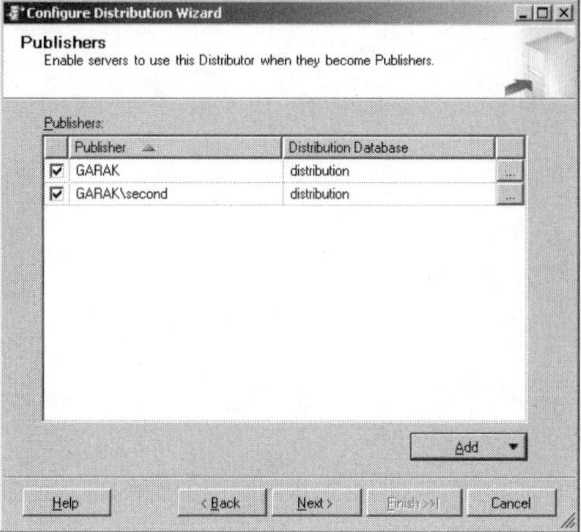

8. The next screen prompts you to specify the password to be used by a remote publisher when it automatically connects to the distributor to perform replication administration. You should enter a strong password that meets or exceeds the password policy for the domain. Click Next to move to the Wizard Actions page.

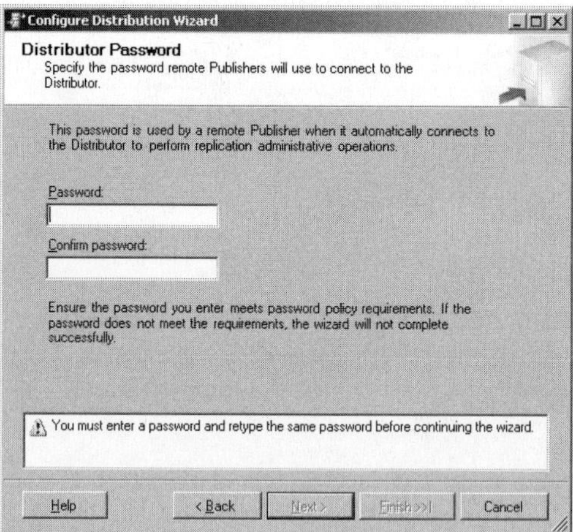

9. On the Wizards Action screen, you are asked to specify what happens at the completion of the wizard. You can select "Configure distribution" or "Generate a script file with steps to configure distribution" or both or neither. For now leave the window as is. Click Next.

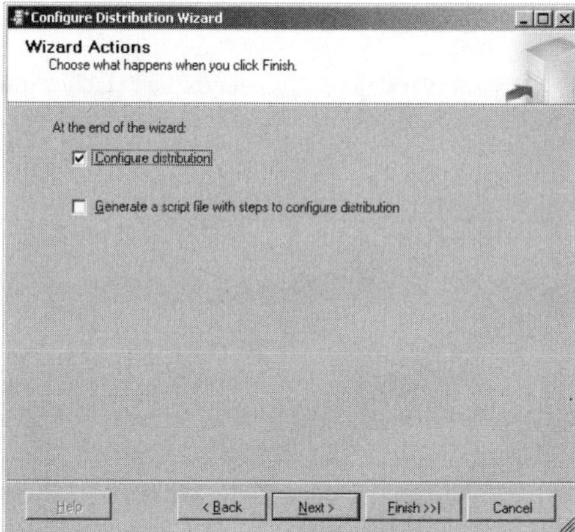

10. On the Complete the Wizard screen, review the choices you have made and if they are correct, click Finish.

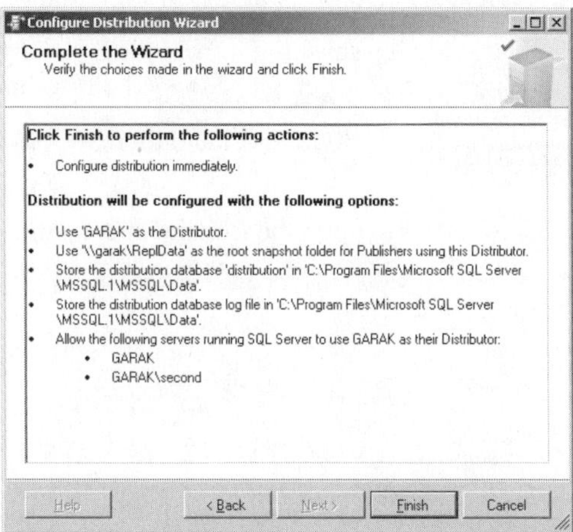

11. The Configuring Windows screen opens. SQL Server displays a list of tasks that are being performed while it configures replication, after which it will inform you of success. Note that any publishers you designated in step 6 have been enabled. You can click the Report button to view, save, copy the report to the clipboard, or send the report as an e-mail message. Click Close to complete the wizard.

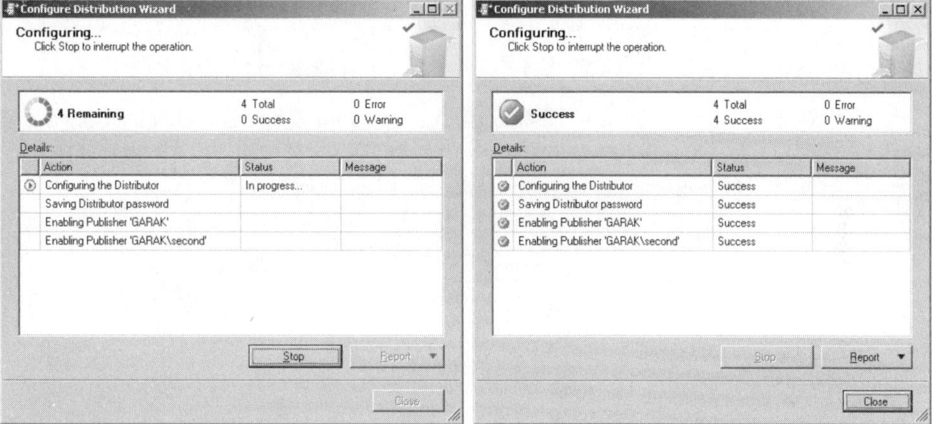

Enabling a Database for Replication

Before you can create publications on a database, the database must be enabled for replication by a person in the sysadmin fixed server role. Enabling a database for replication allows the creation of one or more publications on the database by a user in db_owner fixed database role for that database.

A database is usually enabled when a publication is successfully created using the New Publication Wizard (described in the next section) by a sysadmin.

Enabling a database can also be done explicitly through Management Studio.

1. Open Management Studio by selecting it from the SQL Server 2005 program group under Programs on the Start menu (you must be logged on as a user with sysadmin role).
2. Select your default instance of SQL Server and then in Object Explorer select and right-click the Replication folder.
3. Select Publisher Properties to open the General sheet of the Publisher properties page.

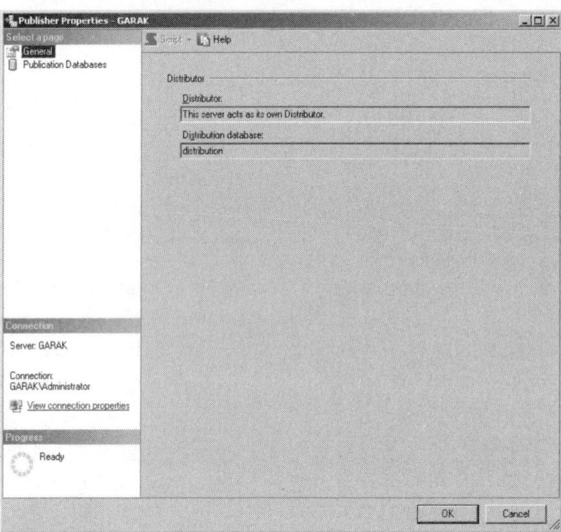

4. Select Publication Databases. A new window opens with a list of available databases and two columns of check boxes marked Transactional and Merge.

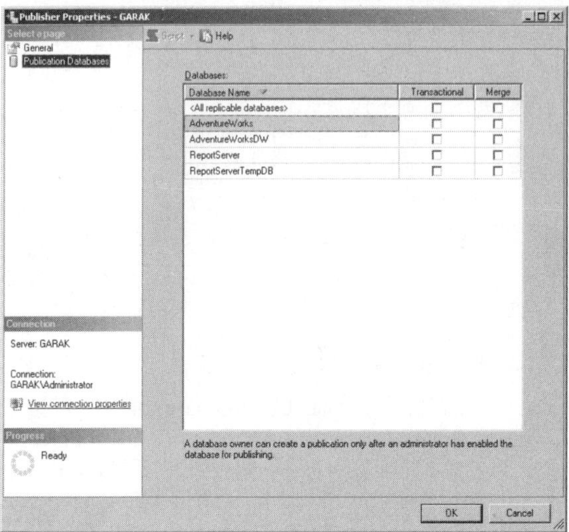

5. Select the Transactional and/or Merge check box for each database you want to replicate. You must select Transactional to enable the database for snapshot replication. In this example we are enabling the AdventureWorks sample database. Click OK.

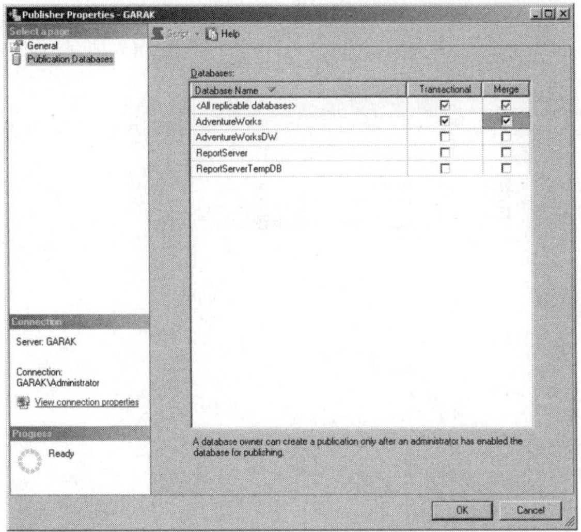

WARNING Enabling a database does not publish the database

Creating and Subscribing to a Snapshot Publication

In this section, you are going to configure a snapshot publication on the AdventureWorks database. Then, you will have the SECOND server subscribe to the publication. Finally, you will test replication by adding a new record to the published article.

Creating a Snapshot Publication

1. If you are not in Management Studio, open it by selecting it from the SQL Server 2005 group under Programs on the Start menu.
2. Click your default server (not SECOND) in Object Explorer, then expand the folders.
3. Expand the Replication node. Right-click the Local Publications folder. Select New Publication to open the New Publication Wizard. Click Next to open the next screen.

4. On the Publication Database screen of the wizard, you are presented with a list of databases on the server. Select AdventureWorks by highlighting it and click Next to move to the next screen.

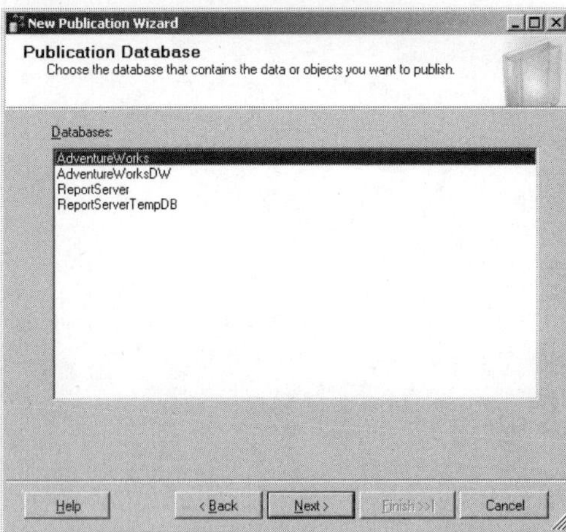

5. In the Publication Type screen there is a list of the four types of publications supported in SQL Server 2005. The lower pane provides a brief description of each type of publication. Select Snapshot Publication by highlighting it and click Next.

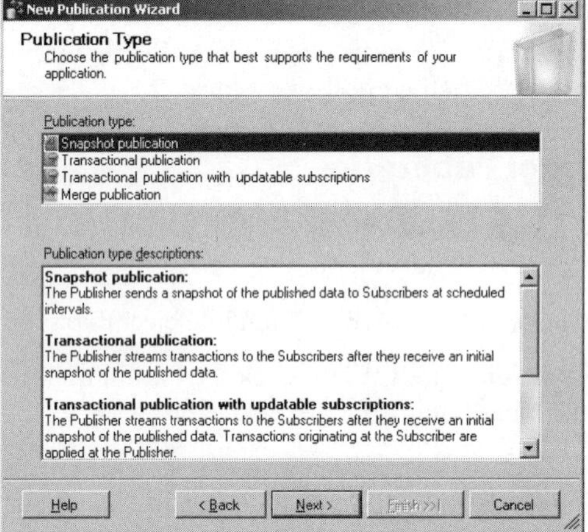

6. In the Articles screen you are asked to select which objects you wish to publish. Expand Tables and select the box next to Address (Person) to enable it for publication. Note that by expanding the Address (Person) folder you can also select/deselect columns within the table for publication as well. (Deselecting or removing columns from the article is referred to as vertical partitioning.) Click Next.

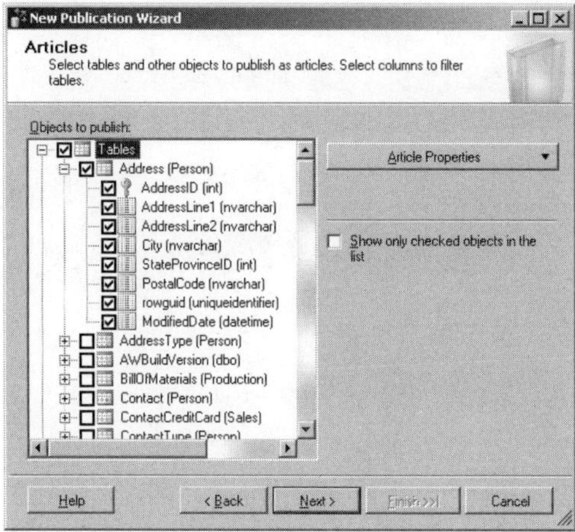

NOTE By clicking the Article Properties button you can set the properties of the highlighted article or all the articles of that type of database object.

7. On the next screen, you need to decide whether you will add filters to exclude unwanted rows. In this instance, you will not add filters but simply click Next.

NOTE Excluding rows in an article from replication by filtering is referred to as *horizontal partitioning*.

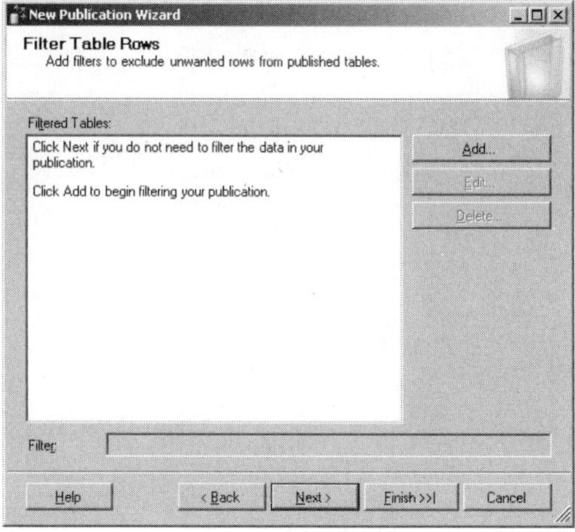

8. The next screen asks you to specify when to run the Snapshot Agent. You can either run it immediately or schedule it to run at specified times. If you intend to change the snapshot properties, you should not run the Snapshot Agent until after you change the publication

properties. Check the box labeled "Create a snapshot immediately and keep the snapshot available to initialize subscriptions." Click Next.

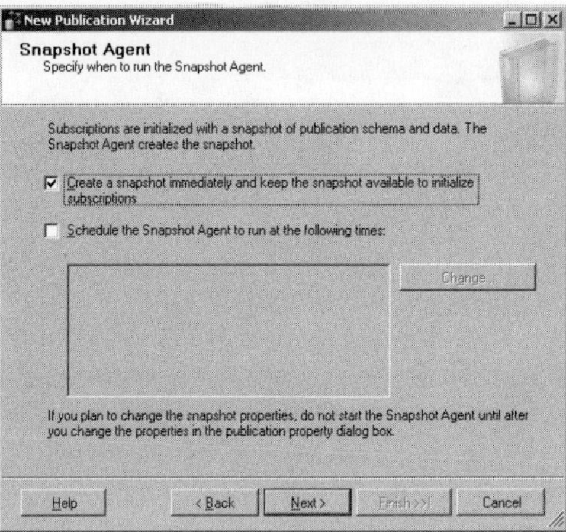

9. On the next screen, you are asked to provide the account under which the agent involved in this type of publication will run. Since this is a snaphot publication you are asked to provide this information for the Snapshot Agent. Click the button labeled Security Settings to open the Snapshot Agent Security window.

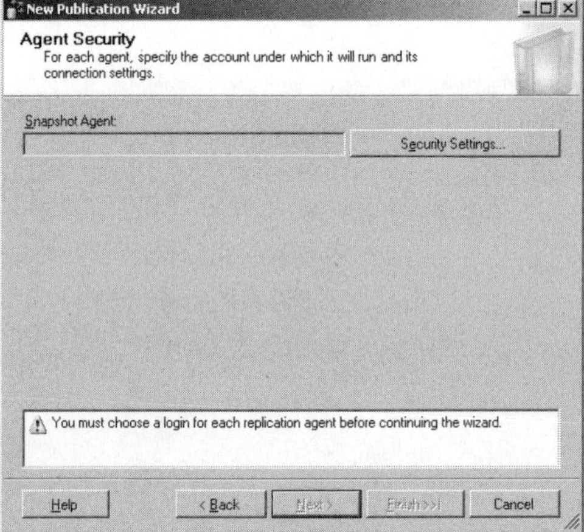

10. In this window, specify the account to be used and whether you will connect to the publisher by impersonating the process account or using a specified SQL Server login. In this example we are using a domain account with administrator privileges.

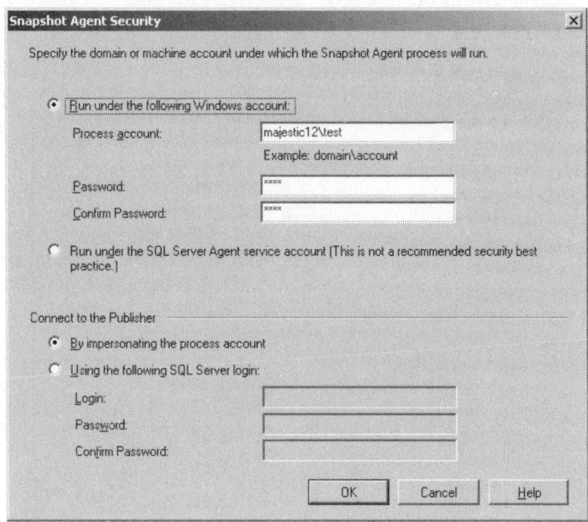

11. Click OK. On the Agent Security window click Next.
12. On the next screen, you need to choose what happens when you click Finish. You can either opt to create the publication immediately, generate a script file with the steps to create the publication, both, or neither. Leave the default setting of "Create the publication immediately" checked and click Next.

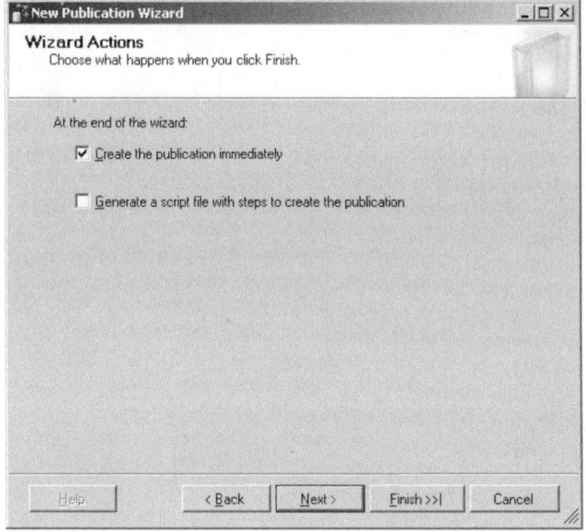

13. The next window asks you to provide a name for the publication. In this example we will use **SnapshotPublicationExercise**. Review the list of actions in the lower dialog box to confirm the settings and then click Finish.

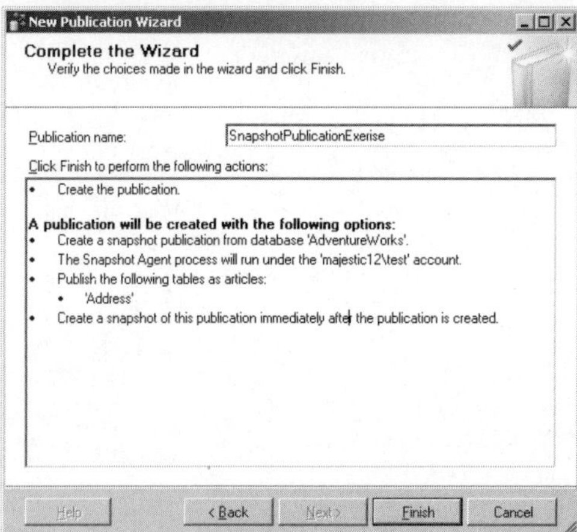

14. The Creating Publication window opens and the publication is created. Once the publication is completed, you are informed of the successful creation of the publication. Click Close to complete the wizard.

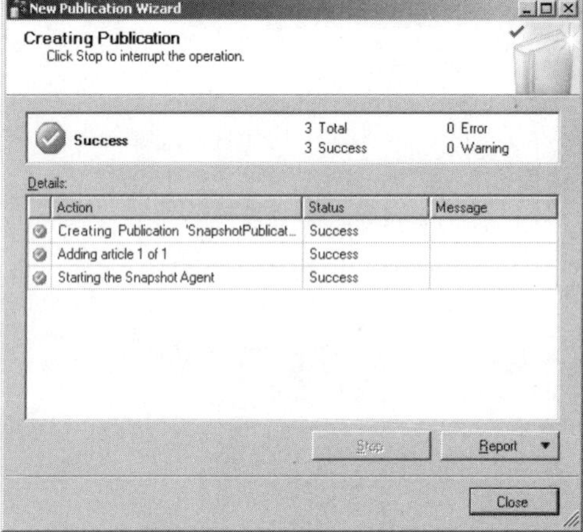

15. Confirm that the new publication can be located in the Local Publications folder under Replication in Object Explorer where you should see a pink book icon. (Typically when you click Close, you will be taken to this folder.) This is the icon used for a snapshot publication (other types are different colors). Notice that right-clicking on the publication gives you ready access to a number of options, including creating a new subscription, creating a new publication, generating scripts, reinitializing all subscriptions, generating a snapshot, and a means of accessing the property sheet. You can also delete the publication or refresh the view. As you learned in Chapter 9, one of the more powerful features of Management Studio

is that its design makes it possible to successfully manage or initiate relevant tasks from this type of pop-up menu.

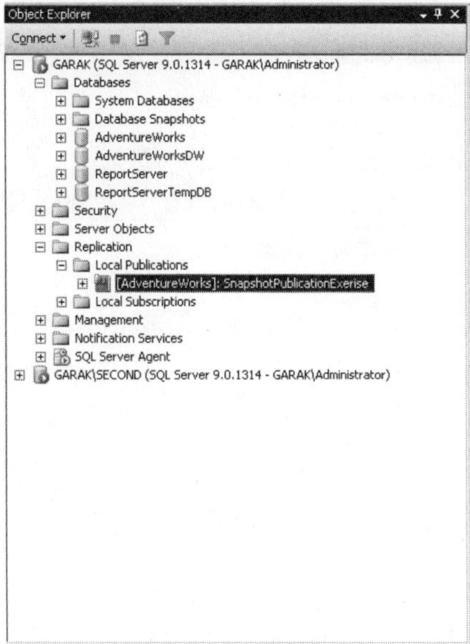

Creating a Snapshot Subscription

You can launch the Subscription wizard any number of ways. You can right-click on an existing publication and select New Subscriptions. Alternatively you can open the Replication node in Object Explorer and select Subscriptions at This Server, right-click, and double-click the New Subscriptions option. In this exercise you are going to use the latter method to create a push subscription.

1. Open the SECOND server instance, expand the folders, expand the Replication node and right-click the Local Subscriptions folder. From the menu, click New Subscriptions to launch the New Subscription Wizard. Click Next on the opening screen.

2. On the Publication sheet you will need to select the publisher where the publication can be found. If not already connected, you will need to select the Server and connect. In this case connect to SERVER and select the SnapshotPublicationExercise. Click Next.

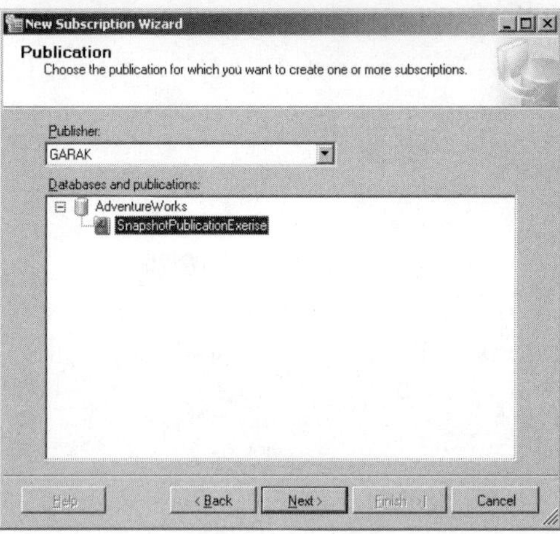

3. The next page asks you where to run the Distribution Agent. You can opt to run the agent either at the distributor (a push subscription) or at its subscriber (a pull subscription). If you want a mix of agents running subscriptions at different locales (and as different types), you will need to run the wizard more than once. In this example, confirm that the radio button next to "Run all agents at the Distributor, SERVER (push subscriptions)" is marked and click Next.

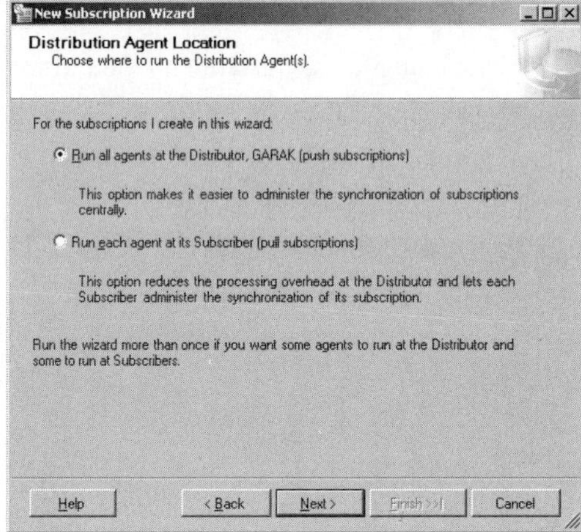

4. You are now asked to choose the Subscriber and specify the subscription database. Mark the box by SECOND and in the column marked Subscription Database, select `<New database>` from the drop-down menu.

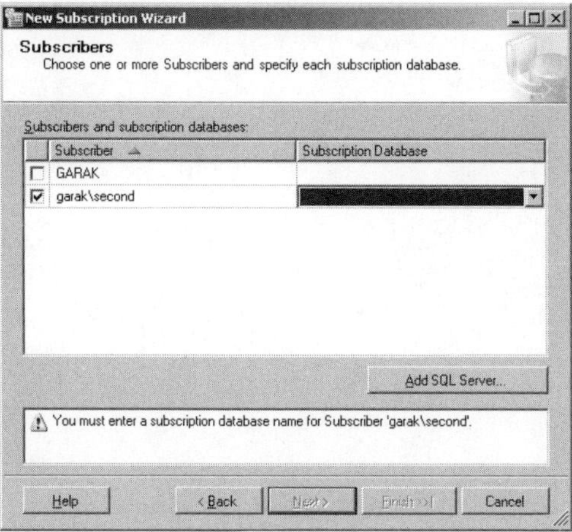

5. A new window opens. In the Database Name box type **ReplicationExercises**. Accept the rest of the defaults.

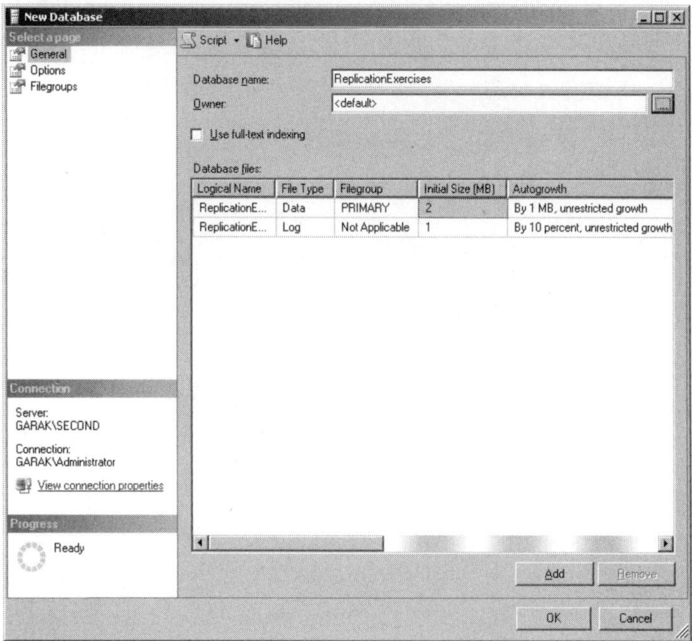

6. Click OK to return to the Subscribers screen and click Next.

7. On the Distribution Agent Security screen you will specify the account and connection options for the Distribution Agent. To do so, click the ellipsis at the far right of the row containing SECOND.

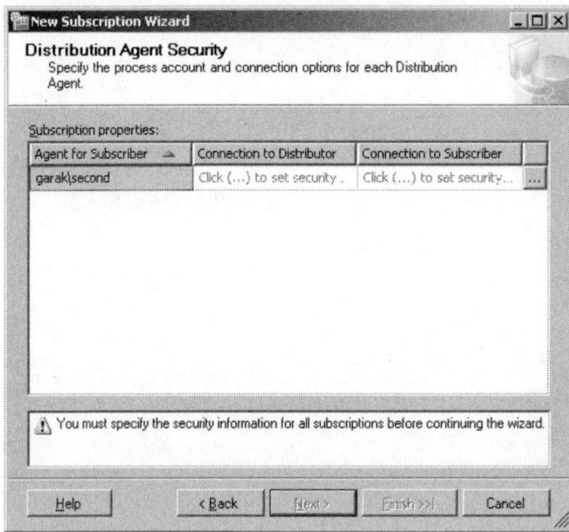

8. On the Distribution Agent Security page specify a process account consisting of a domain or machine account under which the process will run during synchronization. You can also specify the account used to connect to both the distributor and the subscriber.

   In this example we are using a domain account that has administrator privileges.

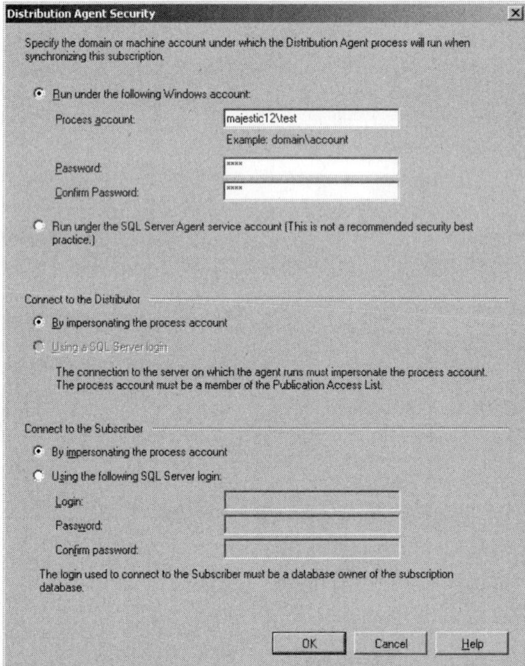

9. After you have done so, click OK to return to the Distribution Agent Security window. Note that the connection methods have been added. Click Next.

10. On the Synchronization Schedule sheet, either you can set the schedule for synchronization using a preset schedule or you can define one yourself. Continuously means that the server will check for updates and pull them over whenever there is a change in the data. The Agent Schedule option allows you to pick a specific time for updating, and the Run On Demand Only option will instruct SQL Server not to replicate changes automatically—you will need to start replication yourself. In this exercise select Run On Demand Only. Click Next.

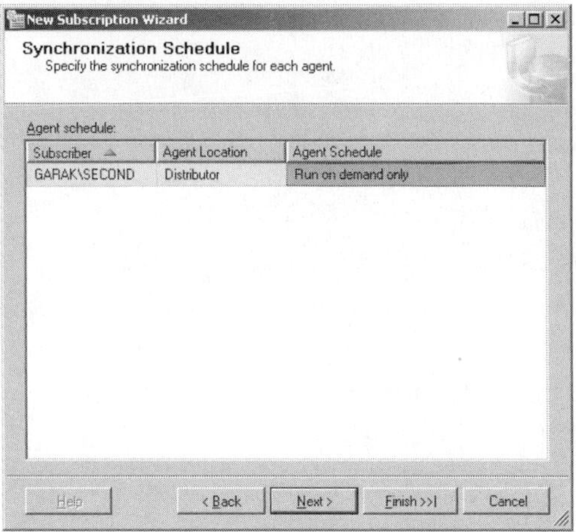

11. The next window asks you when to initialize the subscription with a snapshot of the publication data and schema. For the purposes of this exercise accept the default value Immediately. Click Next.

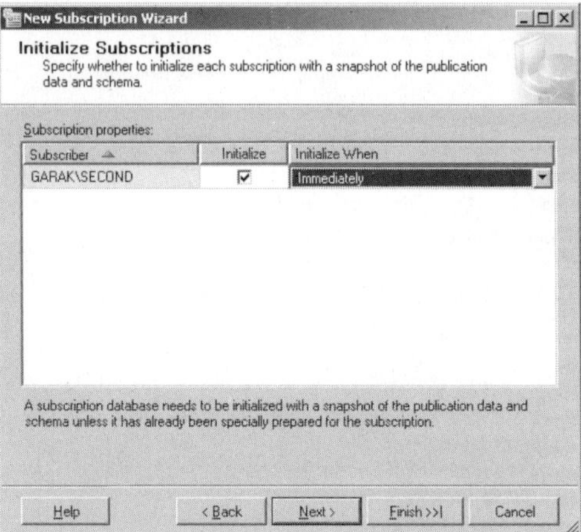

12. You are then asked to choose what happens when you click Finish. Just like when you created the Publication, you can create the subscription immediately, generate a script file that contains the step to create the subscription, or both. Accept the default and click Next.

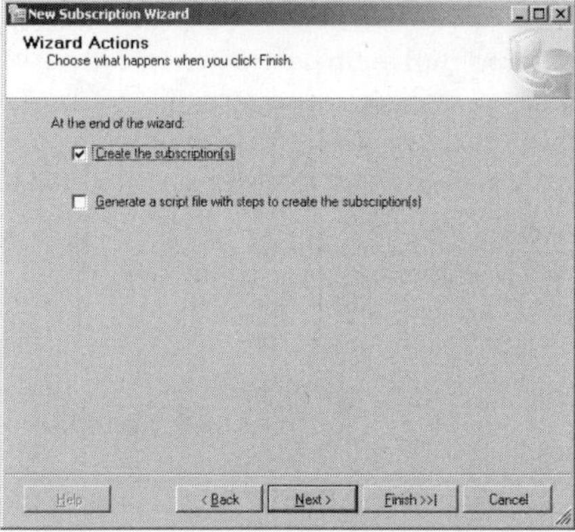

13. The next window provides you with a summary of the actions you have opted for in the wizard. If you are satisfied with the values and options, click Finish to create the subscription.

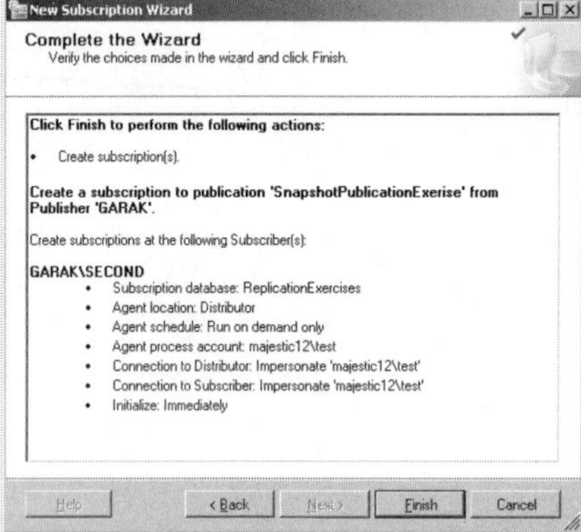

14. The wizard then creates the specified subscription and starts the synchronization agent. When completed a Success message appears in the window. Click Close to exit the wizard.

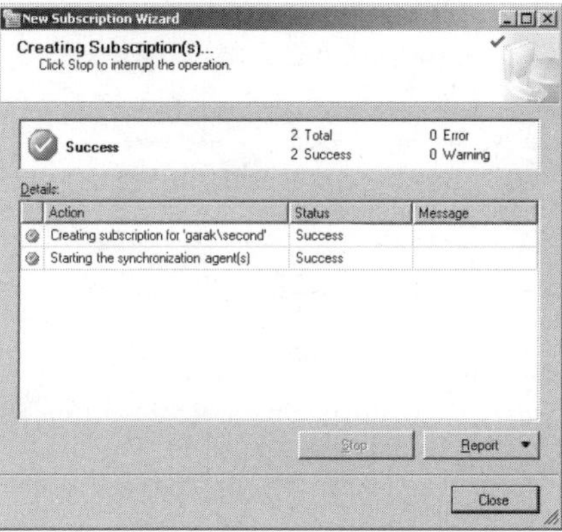

15. To confirm that the subscription has been created, go to SERVER, open Object Explorer and then the Replication node. Click the Local Publications folder and expand the SnapshotPublicationExercise:AdventureWorks publication and note the new subscription SECOND .ReplicationExercises. (You may need to refresh the folder view.)

    Notice that when you open the SECOND instance, expand the Replication node, and then open the Local Subscriptions folder, you will also find a subscription labeled In 'ReplicationExercises' to 'SERVER:AdventureWorks:SnapshotPublicationExercise'. In the SECOND Databases folder you should also see the new database ReplicationExercises that was created while making the new subscription.

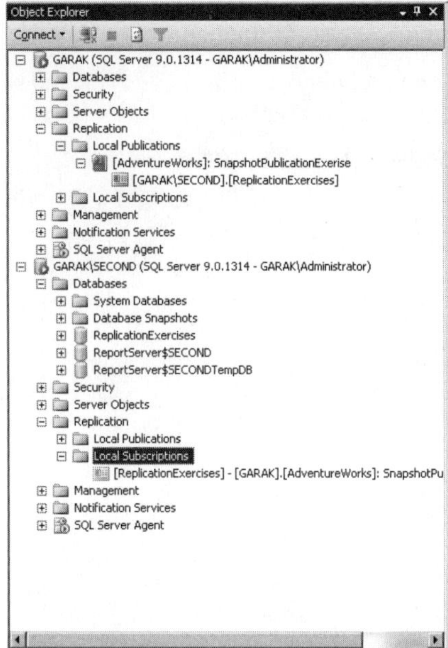

Testing Snapshot Replication

Now that we have created a publication and a push subscription, let's test the new arrangement to make sure replication actually occurs by pushing the subscription to the SECOND server instance. To do that we need to create some changes in the AdventureWorks database's Employee Table.

1. Close any open dialog boxes and return to Management Studio.
2. Right-click the default SERVER and select New Query.
3. Enter and execute the following code to change the data in the Address table of the AdventureWorks database.

```
USE Adventureworks
INSERT Person.Address (AddressLine1, AddressLine2, City, StateProvinceId,
PostalCode)
VALUES ('Suite 1121', '920 9th Street', 'Dhahran', '80', '31311')
```

4. Confirm that a new record has been added by executing the following code:

```
USE AdventureWorks
SELECT * FROM Person.Address
```

5. Scroll to the bottom of the table and confirm that the new row data you created has been added to the end of the table. These changes need to be "pushed" to the ReplicationExercises subscription on SECOND.

6. To do so, right-click SERVER in Object Explorer and click Connect. Then expand the Replication node on SERVER. Expand the Local Publications folder and right-click the SnapshotPublicationExercise. In the pop-up menu, select Launch Replication Monitor.

7. After the Replication Monitor opens, open SERVER and select .[AdventureWorks]: SnapshotPublicationExercise. Right-click and select Generate Snapshot from the pop-up menu.

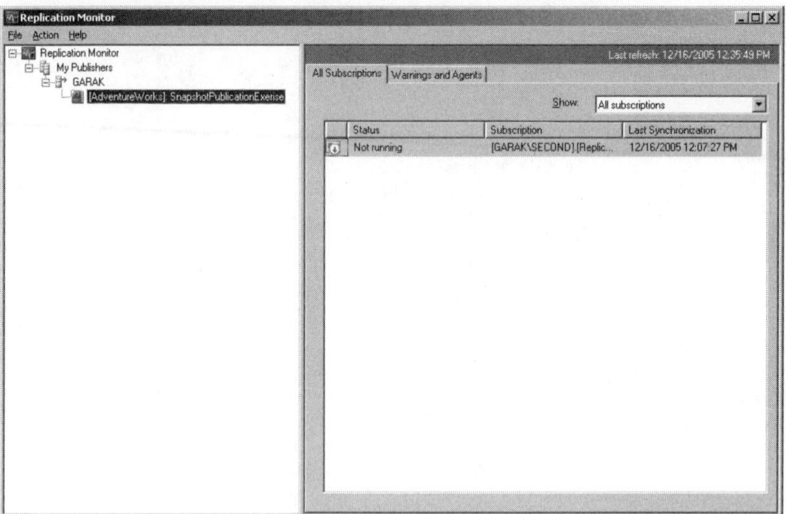

OR

You can also generate a snapshot by right-clicking SERVER in Object Explorer and clicking Connect. Expand the Replication node on SERVER. Expand the Local Publications folder and right-click the SnapshotPublicationExercise. In the pop-up menu, select View Snapshot Agent Status.

In the View Snapshot Agent Status window, click Start. A new snapshot is generated.

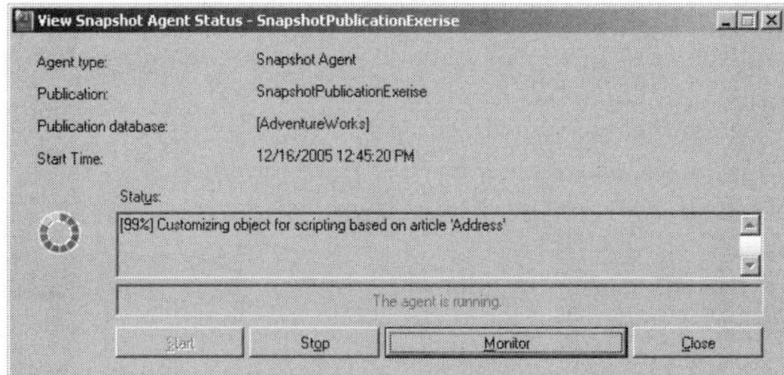

TIP You can access Replication Monitor from within the View Snapshot Agent Status window by clicking the Monitor button.

8. Right-click the subscription and select View Synchronization Status. In the View Synchronization Status window, click Start to begin synchronization and replication. When completed, Click Close.

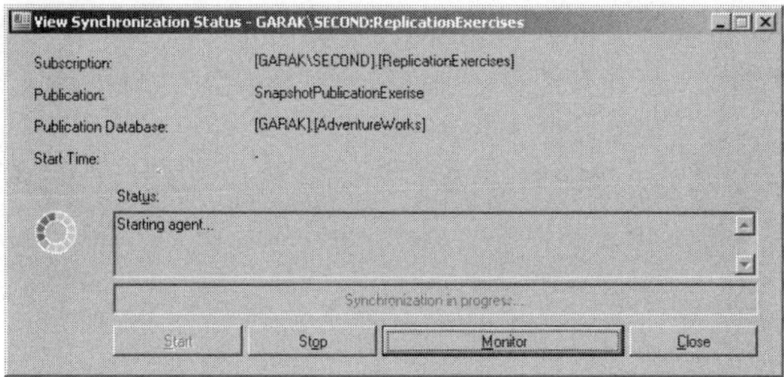

OR

Right-click the subscription and select Replication Monitor. Open SERVER and select .[AdventureWorks]: SnapshotPublicationExercise. Right-click the [SECOND]:Replication-Exercises subscription and select Start Syncronizing to begin synchronization and replication.

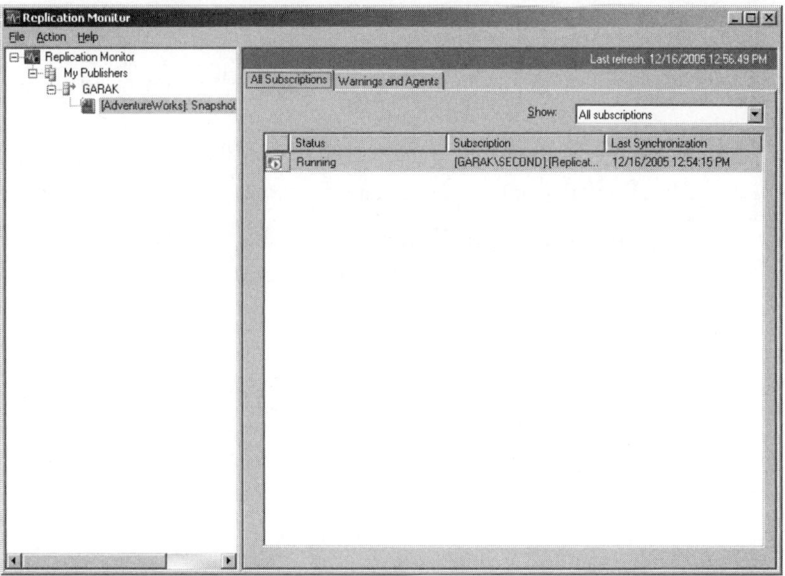

9. To confirm replication has occurred, connect to SECOND. Click the New Query button on the toolbar (or right-click SECOND and select New Query).

10. In the Query window enter and execute the following code:

```
USE ReplicationExercises
SELECT * FROM Address
```

11. Scroll to the bottom of the table and you should see the new record added.

With that, you have successfully created a snapshot publication and subscription as well as replicated changes via a push subscription. We move on to transactional replication.

Creating and Subscribing to a Transactional Publication

Now we're going to configure a "standard" (without updatable subscriptions) transactional publication on the AdventureWorks database. Then, you will have the SECOND server subscribe to the publication. Finally, you will test replication by adding a new record to the published article.

Creating a Transactional Publication

You will probably notice that with Management Studio there isn't really all that much difference between creating a snapshot and a transactional publication. However, "the devil is in the details" as the saying goes and you need to pay careful attention to the differences when they occur.

1. If you are not in Management Studio, open it by selecting it from the SQL Server 2005 group under Programs on the Start menu.

2. Click your default SERVER (not SECOND) in Object Explorer, and expand the Replication folder.

3. Right-click the Local Publications folder and select New Publication to open the New Publication Wizard. Click Next to open the next screen.

4. On the Publication Database screen of the wizard, you are presented with a list of databases on the SERVER. Select AdventureWorks by highlighting it and click Next to move to the next screen.

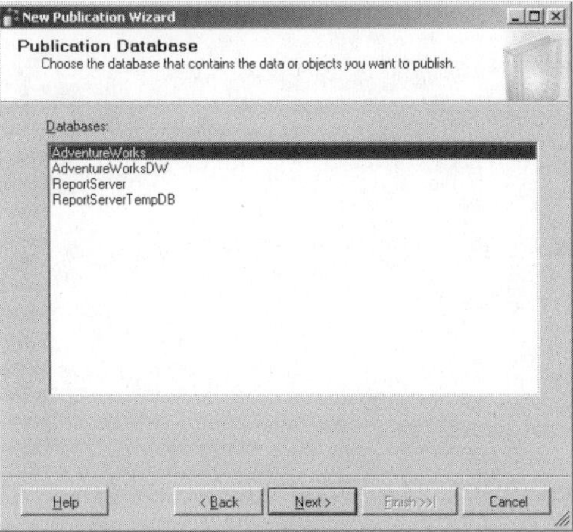

5. In the Publication Type screen there is a list of the four types of publications supported in SQL Server 2005. The lower pane provides a brief description of each type of publication. Select Transactional publication by highlighting it and click Next.

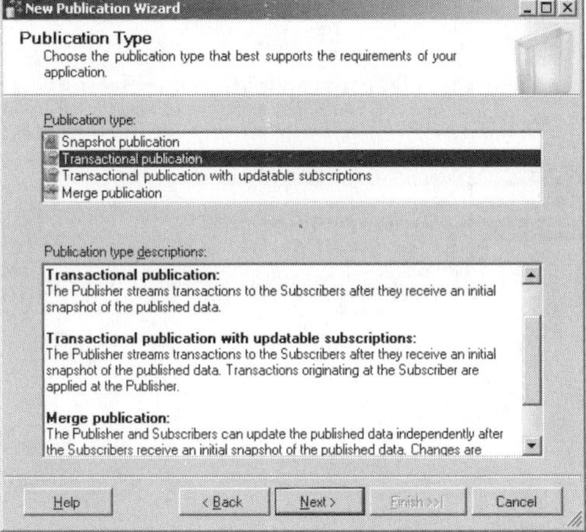

6. In the Articles screen you are asked to select which objects you wish to publish. Expand Tables and select the box next to CreditCard to enable it for publication. Note that by expanding the CreditCard folder you can also select/deselect variables within the table for

publication as well. (Deselecting or removing columns from the article is referred to as vertical partitioning.) Click Next.

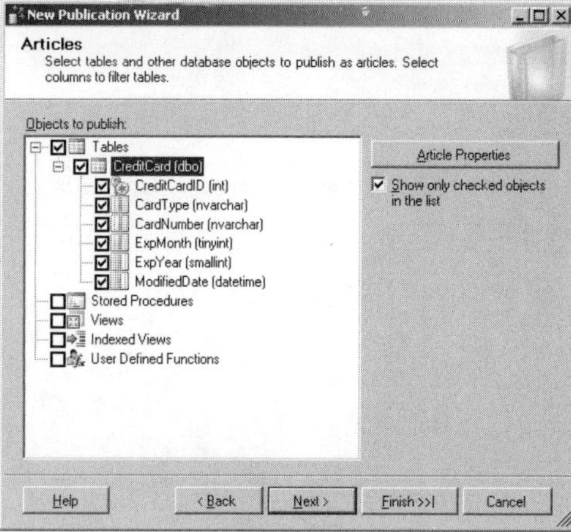

NOTE By clicking the Article Properties button you can set the properties of the highlighted article or all the articles of that type of database object.

7. On the next screen, you need to decide whether you will add filters to exclude unwanted rows. In this instance, you will not add filters but simply click Next.

NOTE Excluding rows in an article from replication by filtering is referred to as *horizontal partitioning.*

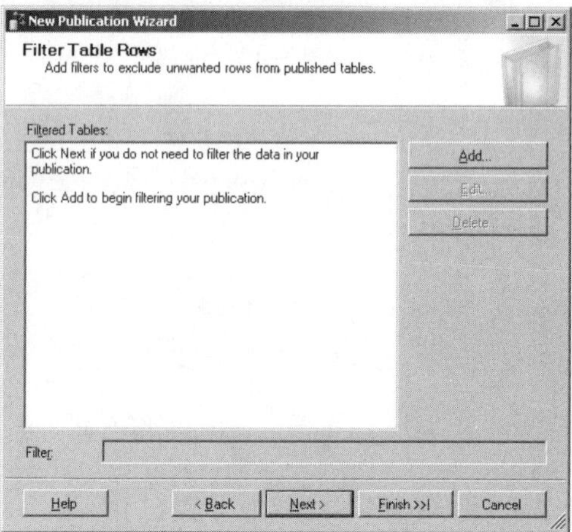

8. The next screen asks you to specify when to run the Snapshot Agent. You can either run it immediately or schedule it to run at specified times. If you intend to change the snapshot properties, you should not run the Snapshot Agent until after you change the publication properties. Select "Create a snapshot immediately and keep the snapshot available to initialize subscriptions." Click Next.

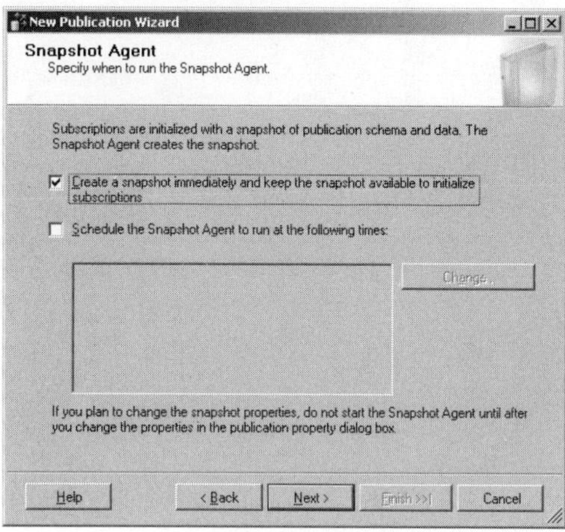

9. On the next screen, you are asked to provide the account under which the agent involved in this type of publication will run. Since this is a snapshot publication you are asked to provide this information for the Snapshot Agent. Click the button labeled Security Settings to open the Snapshot Agent Security window.

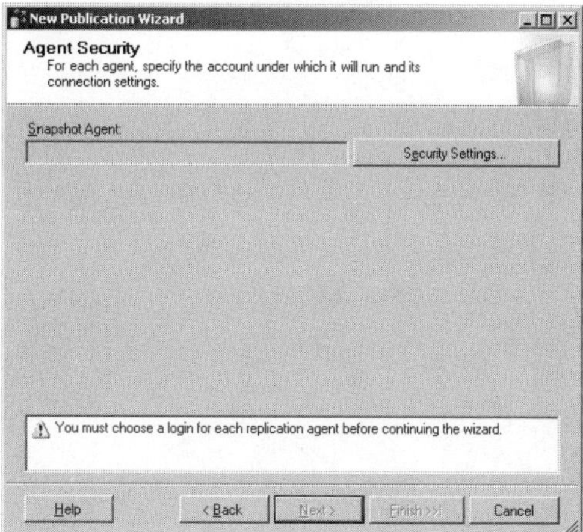

10. In this window, specify the account to be used and whether you will connect to the publisher by impersonating the process account or using a specified SQL Server login. In this example we are using a domain account with administrator privileges.

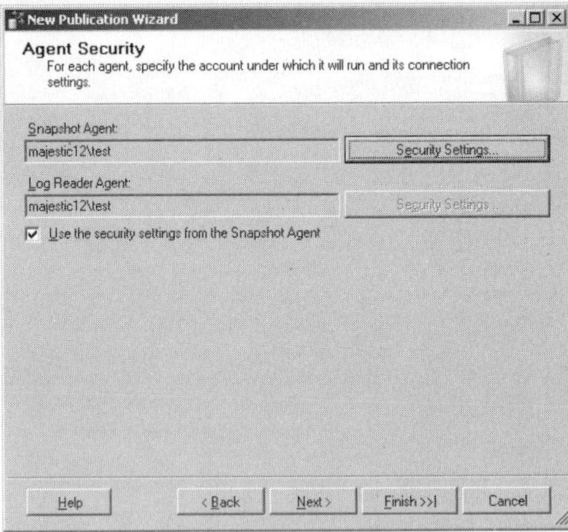

11. Click OK. On the Agent Security window click Next.

    On the next screen, you need to choose what happens when you click Finish. You can either opt to create publication immediately, generate a script file with the steps to create the publication, both, or neither. Leave the default setting of "Create the publication immediately" checked and click Next.

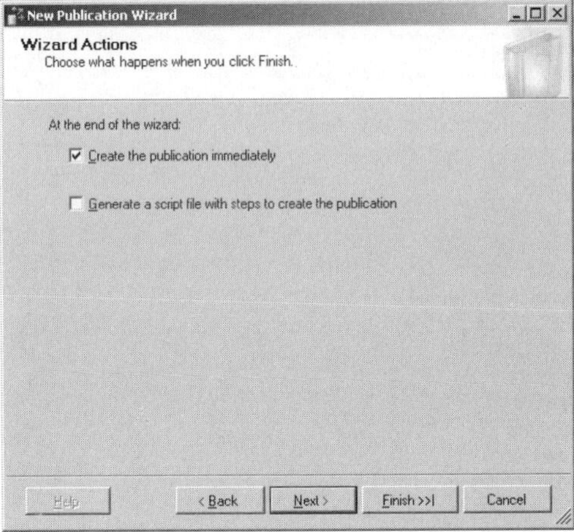

12. The next window asks you to provide a name for the publication. In this example we will use TransactionalPublicationExercise. Review the list of actions in the lower dialog box to confirm the settings and then click Finish.

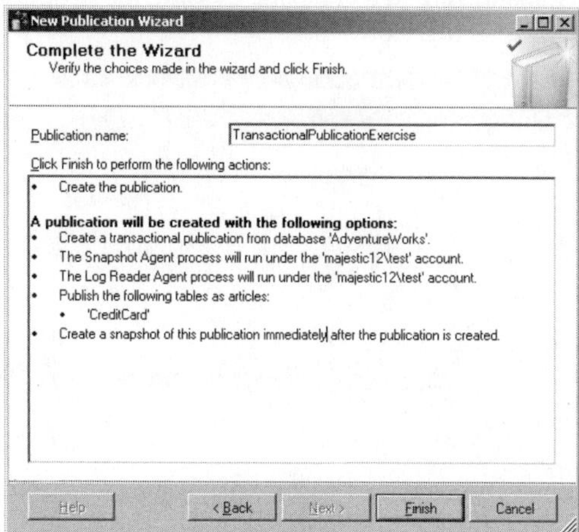

13. The Creating Publication window opens and the publication is created. Once the publication is completed, you are informed of the successful creation of the publication. Click Close to complete the wizard.

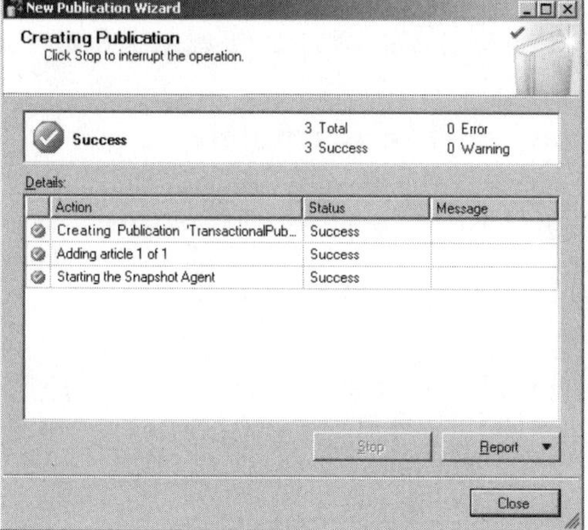

14. Confirm that the new publication can be located in the Publications folder of Object Explorer where you should see a blue book icon. This is the icon used for transactional replication (other types are different colors). Notice that right-clicking on the publication gives you ready access to a number of options, including creating a new subscription, creating a new publication, generating scripts, validating a subscription, reinitializing all subscriptions,

generating a snapshot, and a means of accessing the property sheet. You can also delete the publication or refresh the view.

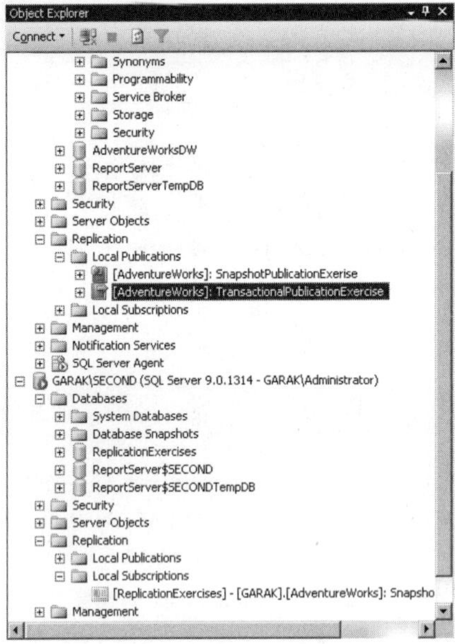

Creating a Transactional Subscription

As explained earlier, you can launch the Subscription Wizard any number of ways. You can right-click an existing publication and select New Subscriptions. Alternatively you can open the Replication node in Object Explorer and select Local Subscriptions, right-click, and double-click the New Subscriptions option at either the publisher or the subscriber. In this exercise you are going to use the latter method from the publisher.

1. Open the default SERVER instance, expand the folders, expand the Replication node, and right-click the Local Subscriptions folder. From the menu click New Subscriptions to launch the New Subscription Wizard. Click Next on the opening screen.

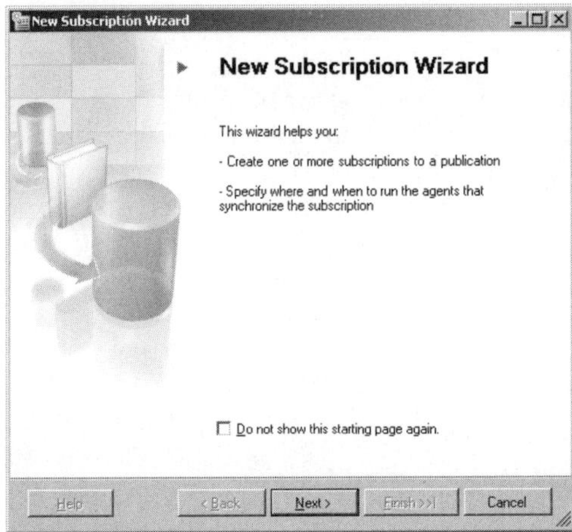

2. On the Publication sheet you will need to select the publisher where the publication can be found. If not already connected, you will need to select the server and connect. In this case connect to SERVER and select the TransactionalPublicationExercise. Click Next.

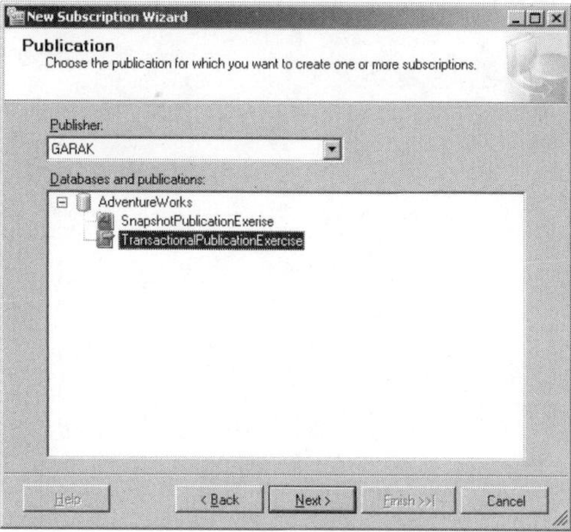

3. The next page asks you where to run the Distribution Agent. You can opt to run the agent either at the distributor (a push subscription) or at its subscriber (a pull subscription). If you want a mix of agents running subscriptions at different locales (and as different types), you will need to run the wizard more than once. In this example, confirm that the radio button next to "Run all agents at the Distributor, SERVER (push subscriptions)" is marked and click Next.

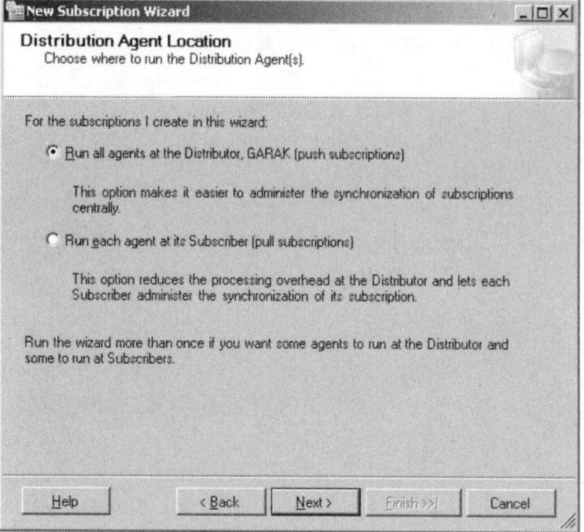

4. You are now asked to choose the subscriber and specify the subscription database. (If SECOND does not appear in the list you will need to click the Add Subscriber button and connect to SECOND). Mark the box by SECOND. In the column marked Subscription Database, select ReplicationExercises (created in the previous subscription) database from the drop-down menu. If you do not have a subscription database already available, you will have to

create one as outlined in steps 5–6 under the "Creating a Snapshot Subscription" section earlier in this chapter.

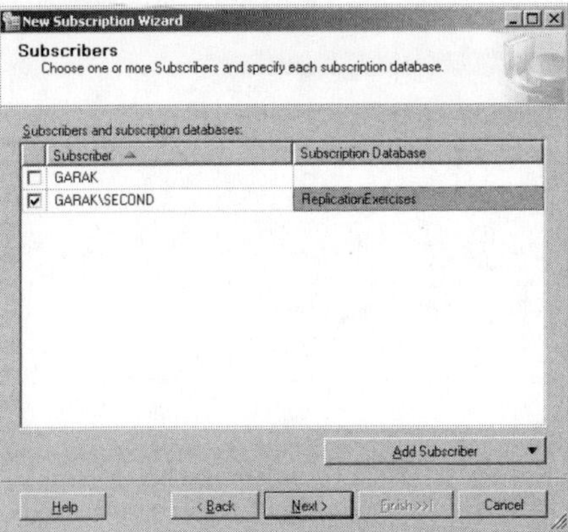

5. On the Distribution Agent Security screen you will specify the account and connection options for the Distribution Agent. To do so, click the ellipsis at the far right of the row containing SECOND.
6. On the Distribution Agent Security Agent, specify a process account consisting of a domain or machine account under which the process will run during synchronization. You can also specify the account used to connect to both the distributor and the subscriber.

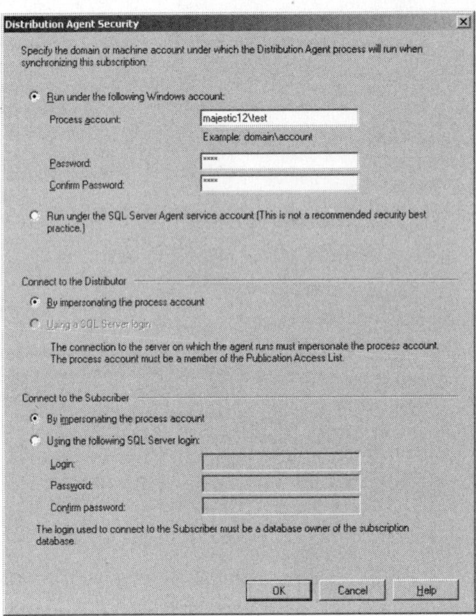

7. Click OK to return to the Distribution Agent Security window. Note that the connection methods have been added. Click Next.

8. On the Synchronization Schedule sheet, either you can set the schedule for synchronization using a preset schedule or you can define one yourself. The default of Run Continuously means that the server will check for updates and pull them over whenever there is a change in the data. Leave the current setting of Run Continuously. Click Next.

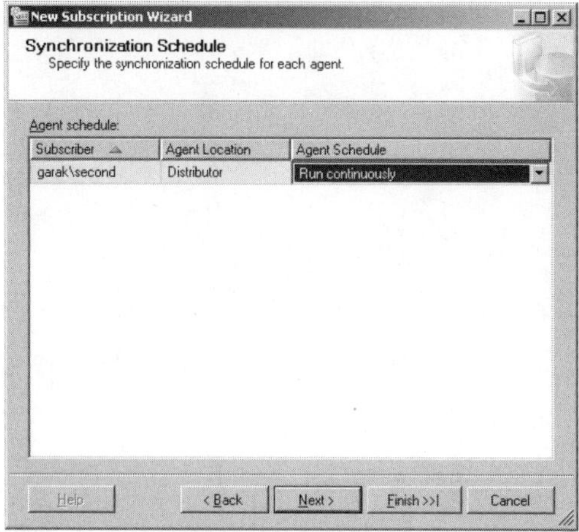

9. The next window asks you when to initialize the subscription with a snapshot of the publication data and schema. For the purposes of this exercise, accept the default value, Immediately. Click Next.

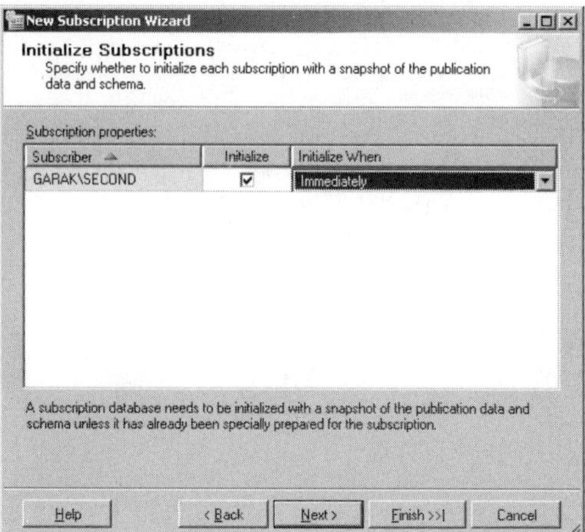

10. You are then asked to choose what happens when you click Finish. As when you created the publication, you are can create the subscription immediately, generate a script file that contains the step to create the subscription, or both. Accept the default to create the subscription immediately and click Next.

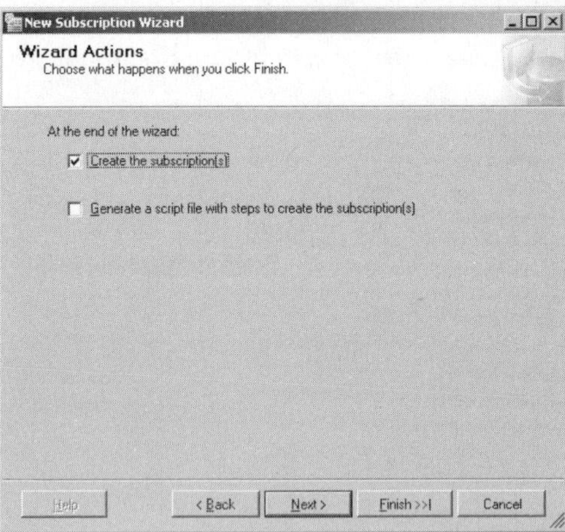

11. The next window provides you with a summary of the actions you have opted for in the wizard. If you are satisfied with the values and options, click Finish to create the subscription.

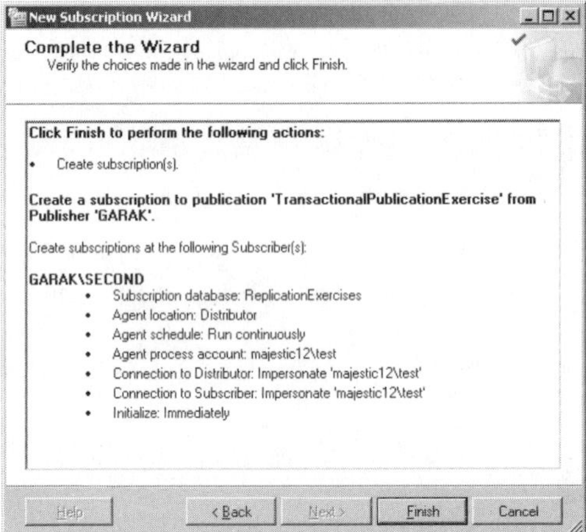

12. The wizard then creates the specified subscription and starts the synchronization agent(s). When completed a Success message appears in the window. Click Close to exit the wizard.

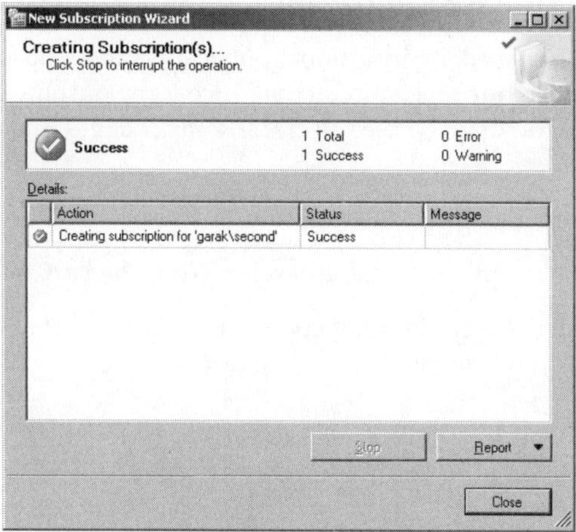

13. To confirm that the subscription has been created, go to SERVER and open Object Explorer and then the Replication node. Right-click the Local Publications folder and expand the [AdventureWorks]: TransactionalPublicationExercise publication and note the new subscription SECOND: ReplicationExercises. Notice that when you open the SECOND instance, expand the Replication folder, then open the Local Subscriptions folder, you will also find a subscription labeled [Replication-Exercises]-[SERVER].[AdventureWorks]: Transactional-PublicationExercise You may need to right-click the Local Subscriptions folder and select Refresh if the subscription is not immediately present.

Testing Transactional Replication

Now that we have created a transactional publication and a push subscription, let's test the new arrangement to make sure replication actually occurs by pushing the subscription to the SECOND server instance. To do that, we need to create some changes in the AdventureWorks database's document table.

1. Close any open dialog boxes and return to Management Studio.
2. Right-click the default SERVER and select New Query. Connect if prompted.
3. Enter and execute the following code to change the data in the document table of the AdventureWorks database.

```
USE AdventureWorks
INSERT Sales.CreditCard (CardType,CardNumber, ExpMonth,ExpYear)
VALUES ('TazzieCharge', '00966506839735', '11', '2010')
```

4. Confirm that a new record has been added by executing the following code:

```
USE AdventureWorks
SELECT * FROM Sales.CreditCard
```

5. Scroll to the bottom of the table and confirm that the new row data you created has been added to the end of the table.

   Because you previously set synchronization scheduling on the subscription to "Run Continuously," the push occurs immediately. To confirm that the changes have been replicated to the ReplicationExercises database's CreditCard table, do the following.

6. Right-click SECOND. Click the New Query button on the toolbar (or right-click SECOND and select New Query). Connect to SECOND when prompted.
7. In the Query window enter and execute the following code:

```
USE ReplicationExercises
SELECT * FROM Sales.CreditCard
```

8. Scroll to the bottom of the table and you will see the new record added.

	CreditCardID	CardType	CardNumber	ExpMonth	ExpYear	ModifiedDat
19...	19228	Vista	11117061659942	5	2007	2004-05-04
19...	19229	Vista	11113316231269	8	2006	2003-10-26
19...	19230	Distinguish	55555952112799	4	2005	2004-02-27
19...	19231	SuperiorCard	33338727611909	9	2007	2003-09-10
19...	19232	Distinguish	55551883899215	1	2006	2003-08-19
19...	19233	SuperiorCard	33335458414079	1	2005	2003-12-03
19...	19234	Vista	11114074915665	1	2007	2003-10-31
19...	19235	ColonialVoice	77774511327745	1	2006	2003-06-01
19...	19236	Vista	11112645284978	10	2008	2004-02-21
19...	19237	SuperiorCard	33336254511031	5	2005	2004-07-21
19...	19238	TazzieCharge	966506839735	11	2010	2004-11-08

Congratulations, you have successfully created a transactional publication and push subscription. But what if you want to allow the subscriber to update the information it receives and to send it back to the publisher? To do that, you need to create a transactional publication with updatable subscriptions.

Creating and Subscribing to a Transactional Publication with Updatable Subscriptions

This type of replication is almost exactly like transactional replication, with one major difference: The subscribers can modify the data they receive. You can think of this type of replication as a mix of 2PC and transactional replication in that it uses the Distributed Transaction Coordinator and distributed transactions to accomplish its task.

In this exercise we are going to be ambitious and create a transactional publication with updatable subscriptions, use vertical partitioning while creating the article, create a pull subscription, and test and use the updatable nature of the subscription to make a change to the table on the subscriber that will be replicated to the publisher. Hold onto your hats and make sure to pay attention. We're only going to do this once.

Creating a Transactional Publication with Updatable Subscriptions

You may have already decided that there wasn't going to be much difference between setting up a transactional publication and a transactional publication with updatable subscriptions. Think again. This type of publication is quite different and involves several different steps than creating either a snapshot or transactional publication.

1. If you are not in Management Studio, open it by selecting Start ➢ Programs ➢ Microsoft SQL Server 2005 ➢ SQL Server Management Studio.
2. Click your default server (not SECOND) in Object Explorer, expand the folders, and open the Replication folder.
3. Right-click the Local Publications folder and select New Publication to open the New Publication Wizard. Click Next to move to the next screen.

4. On the Publication Database screen of the wizard, you are presented with a list of databases on the Server. Select AdventureWorks by highlighting it and click Next to move to the next screen.

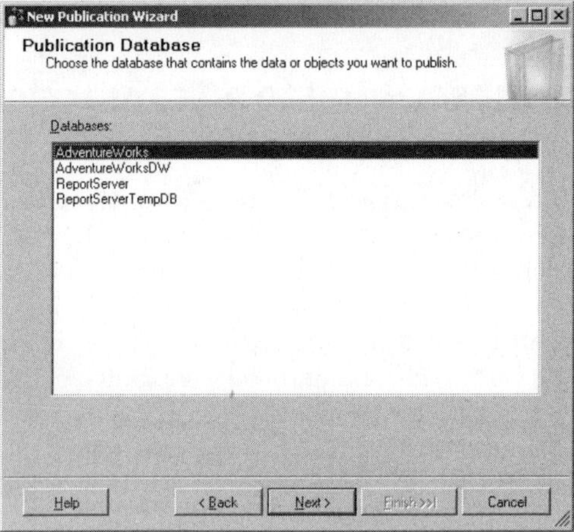

5. In the Publication Type screen there is a list of the four types of publications supported in SQL Server 2005. The lower pane provides a brief description of each type of publication. Select "Transactional publication with updatable subscriptions" and then click Next.

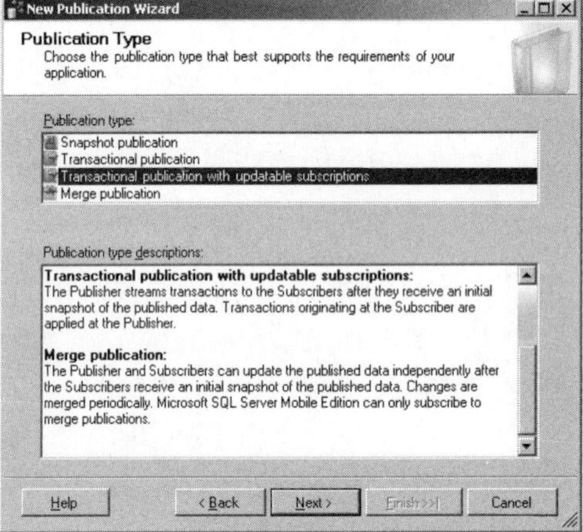

6. In the Articles screen you are asked to select which objects you wish to publish. Expand Tables and select the box next to Vendor to enable it for publication. Note that by expanding the Vendor folder you can also select/deselect columns within the table for publication as well. (Deselecting or removing columns from the article is referred to as vertical partitioning.) Deselect the column ModifiedDate to create a vertical partition.

You can also select the "Show only checked objects in the list" check box to limit the clutter in the view to the objects you select. Click Next.

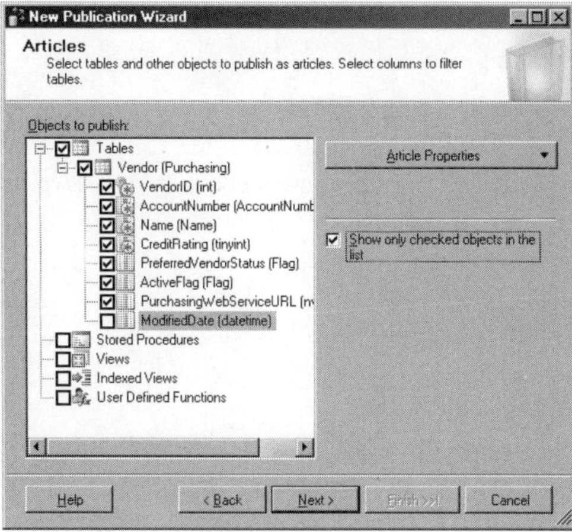

NOTE By clicking the Article Properties button you can set the properties of the highlighted article or all the articles of that type of database object.

7. On the next screen you are presented with a summary of key issues that may or may not affect your application and require changes. In this case the wizard provides a warning that a uniqueidentifier column will be added to the table since it does not already have one. This will result in an increase in the size of the table and causes any INSERT statement not using column lists to fail. Click Next.

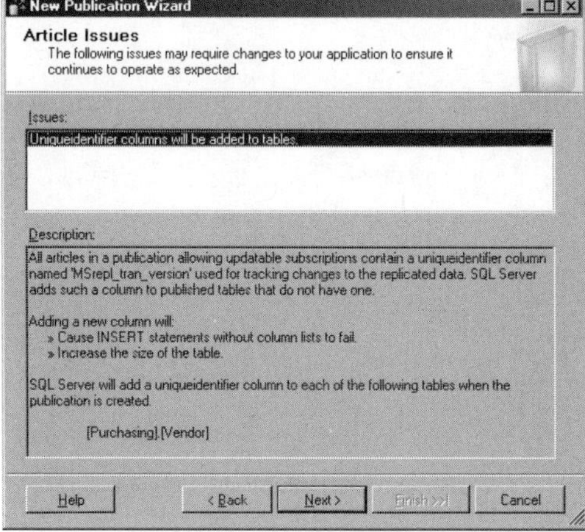

8. On the next screen, you need to decide whether you will add filters to exclude unwanted rows. In this instance, you will not add filters but simply click Next.

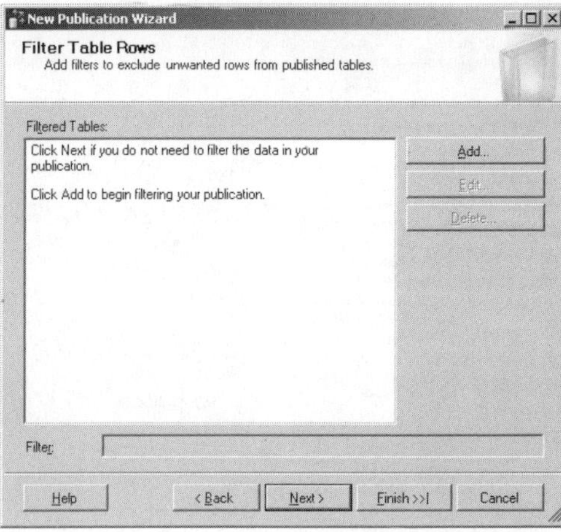

NOTE Excluding rows in an article from replication by filtering is referred to as *horizontal partitioning.*

9. The next screen asks you to specify when to run the Snapshot Agent. You can either run it immediately or schedule it to run at specified times. If you intend to change the snapshot properties, you should not run the Snapshot Agent until after you change the publication properties. Keep the default value of "Create a snapshot immediately and keep the snapshot available to initialize subscriptions." Click Next.

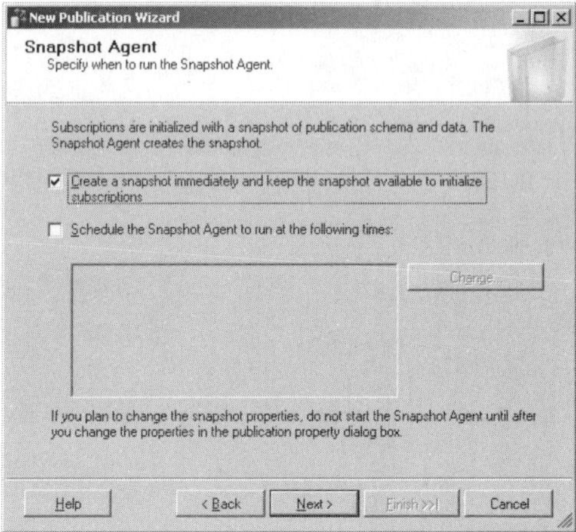

10. You are now asked to provide the account under which the Snapshot Agent, Log Reader Agent, and Queue Reader Agent will run. A box allows you use the same security settings for both the Snapshot Agent and Log Reader Agent. Click the button labeled Security Settings to open the Snapshot Agent Security window.

11. In this window, specify the account to be used and whether you will connect to the publisher by impersonating the process account or using a specified SQL Server login. In this case we are using an domain account with administrator privileges. Click OK.

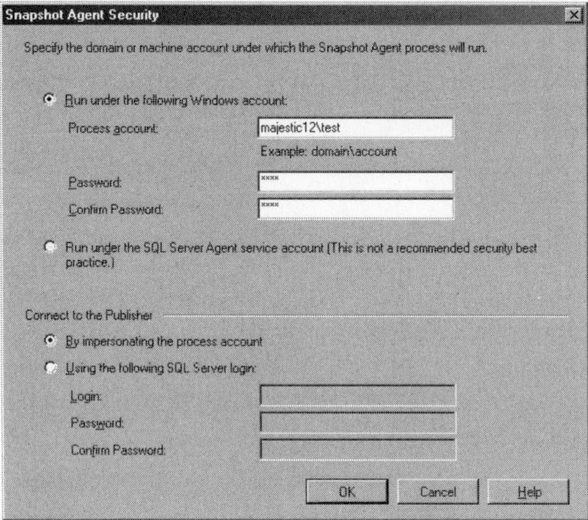

12. Open the Security Settings tab for Queue Reader Agent and specify the account to be used to run the agent and what authentication method you will use to connect to the Server. In this case we are using a domain account with administrator privileges. Click OK. On the Agent Security window click Next.

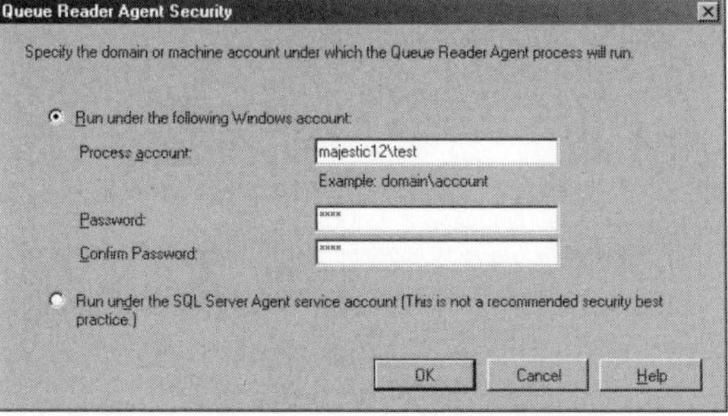

13. On the next screen, you need to choose what happens when you click Finish. You can either opt to create publication immediately, generate a script file with the steps to create

the publication, both, or neither. Leave the default setting of "Create the publication immediately" checked and Click Next.

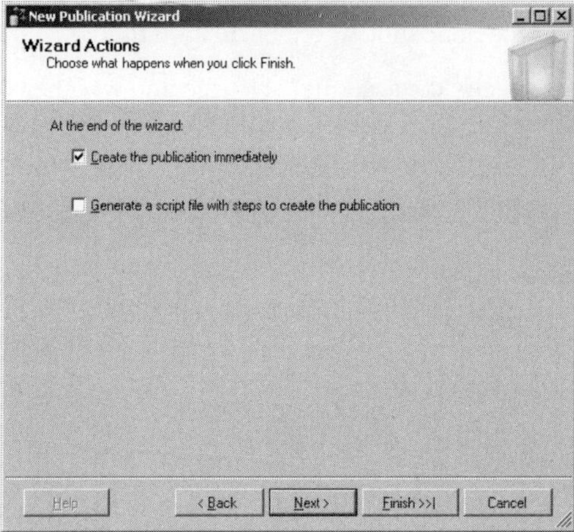

14. The next window asks you to provide a name for the publication. In this example we will use TransRepUpdPubExercise. Review the list of actions in the lower dialog box to confirm the settings and then click Finish.

15. The Creating Publication window opens and the publication is created. Once the publication is completed, you are informed of the successful creation of the publication. Click Close to complete the wizard.

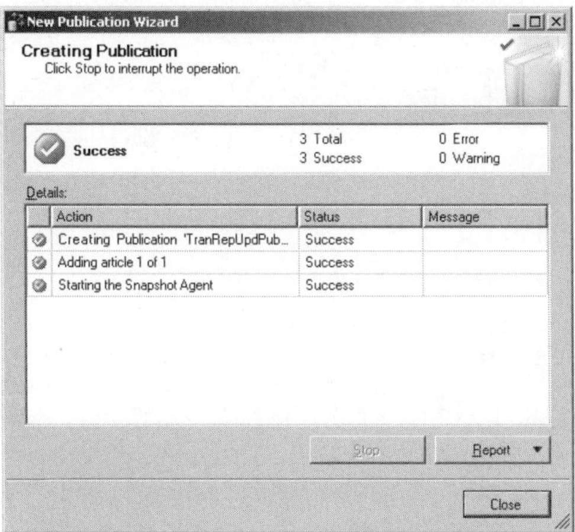

16. Confirm that the new publication can be located in the Publications folder of Object Explorer where you should see a blue book icon. This is the icon used for transactional replication (other types are different colors). Notice that right-clicking on the publication gives you ready access to a number of options, including creating a new subscription, creating a new publication, generating scripts, validating a subscription, reinitializing all subscriptions, generating a snapshot, and a means of accessing the property sheet. You can also delete the publication or refresh the view.

Creating a Transactional Updatable Subscription

As explained earlier, you can launch the Subscription Wizard any number of ways. You can right-click on an existing publication and select new subscriptions. Alternatively you can open the Replication node in Object Explorer and select Local, right-click, and double-click the New Subscriptions option at either the publisher or the subscriber. In this exercise you are going to use the latter method from the publisher.

Before Beginning: A Note on Security

When you configure an immediate updating subscription, you need to specify an account at the subscriber that is used to make connections to the publisher. These connections are then used by the triggers that fire at the subscriber and propagate changes to the publisher. There are three options available for the type of connection:

- A linked server that replication creates: the connection is made with the credentials you specify at configuration time.
- A linked server that replication creates: the connection is made with the credentials of the user making the change at the subscriber.
- A linked server or remote server that you have already defined.

For this example we will use the latter option by registering SERVER in the systable of SECOND. The simplest way to do so this is to call and execute the stored procedure AddLinkedServer. To do so right-click SECOND and select New Query.

In the open window type the following code:

```
EXECUTE sp_addlinkedserver
@server = 'SERVER'
```

Where SERVER is the name of the publisher.

CREATING THE SUBSCRIPTION

1. Open the default SERVER instance, expand the folders, expand the Replication node, open Local Publications, and right-click the [AdventureWorks]:TranRepUpdPubExercise publication. From the menu, click New Subscriptions to launch the New Subscription Wizard. Click Next on the opening screen.

2. On the Publication sheet you will need to select the publisher where the publication can be found. If not already connected you will need to select the Server and connect. In this case connect to SERVER and select TransRepUpdPubExercise. Click Next.

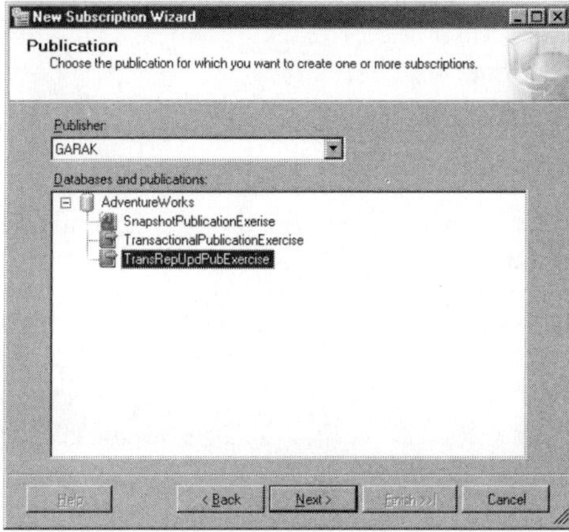

3. The next page asks you where to run the Distribution Agent. You can opt to run the agent either at the distributor (a push subscription) or at its subscriber (a pull subscription). If you want a mix of agents running subscriptions at different locales (and as different types), you will need to run the wizard more than once. In this example, confirm that the radio button next to "Run each agent at its Subscriber (pull subscriptions)" is marked and click Next.

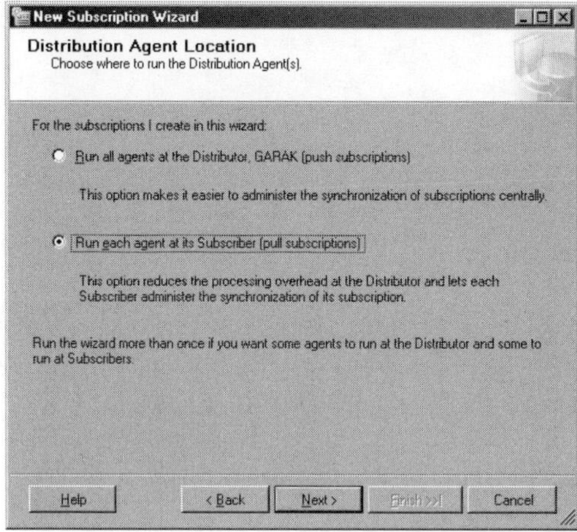

4. You are now asked to choose the subscriber and specify the subscription database. Mark the box by SECOND. If SECOND does not appear in the list you will need to click the Add Subscriber button and connect to SECOND. In the column marked Subscription Database, select ReplicationExercises database (created in the snapshot subscription exercise) from the drop-down menu. If you do not have a subscription database already available, you will have to create one as outlined in steps 5–6 under the "Creating a Snapshot Subscription" section earlier in this chapter.

5. On the Distribution Agent Security screen you will specify the account and connection options for the Distribution Agent. To do so, click the ellipsis at the far right of the row containing SECOND.

6. On the Distribution Agent Security Agent screen, specify a process account consisting of a domain or machine account under which the process will run during synchronization. You can also specify the account used to connect to both the distributor and the subscriber.

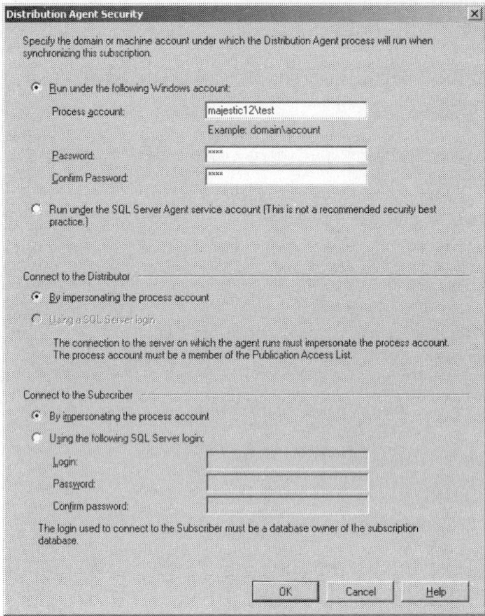

7. Click OK to return to the Distribution Agent Security window. Note that the connection methods have been added. Click Next.

8. On the Synchronization Schedule sheet, either you can set the schedule for synchronization using a preset schedule or you can define one yourself. The default of Run Continuously means that the server will check for updates and pull them over whenever there is a change in the data. Leave the current setting of Run Continuously. Click Next.

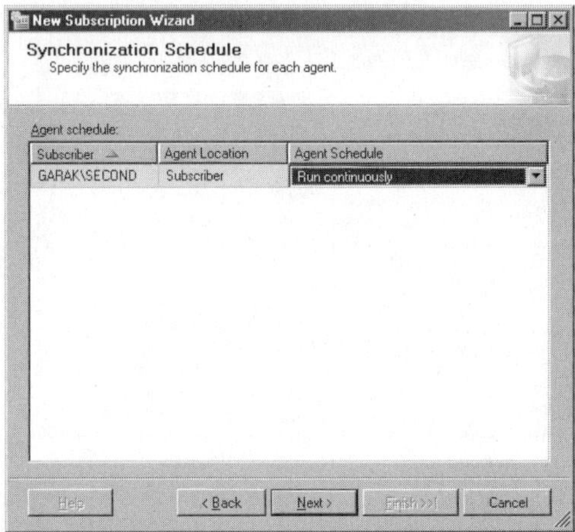

9. The next window gives you the opportunity to choose when changes are committed at the publisher. You can opt for either simultaneously committing changes or queuing changes to be committed when possible.

   - *Simultaneously commit changes* creates an immediate updating subscription. Subscribers make changes to their local copy of the data, and those changes are sent back to the publisher using the Microsoft Distributed Transaction Coordinator. Both publisher and subscriber must have a reliable connection to each other.
   - *Queue changes and commit when possible* establishes a queued updating subscription. This is similar to immediately updating subscriptions inasmuch as it allows users to make changes to the replicated copy of the data. Unlike immediate updating, though, these changes can be stored at an intermediate host until they can be transmitted. This is very useful when clients need to be able to make changes to the data, but they have an unreliable network connection.

   Accept the default value Simultaneously Commit Changes. Click Next.

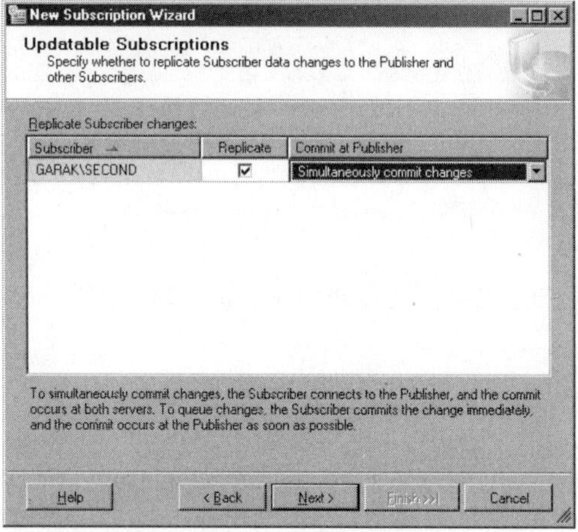

10. On the Login for Updatable Subscriptions page, select "Use a linked server or remote server that you have already defined." This will cause the wizard to use the SERVER connection created before you started the exercise.

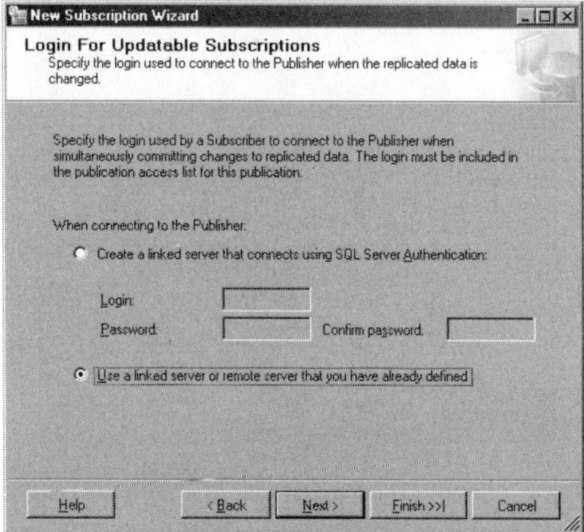

11. On the Initialize Subscriptions window, accept the default value "Immediately" for when to initialize the subscription with a snapshot of the publication data and schema.

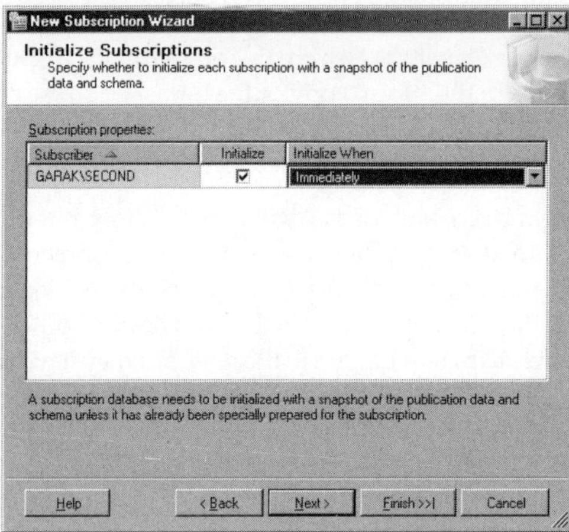

12. On the next screen, you need to choose what happens when you click Finish. You can opt to either create subscription immediately, generate a script file with the steps to create the subscription, both, or neither. Leave the default setting of Create the Subscription(s) checked and click Next.

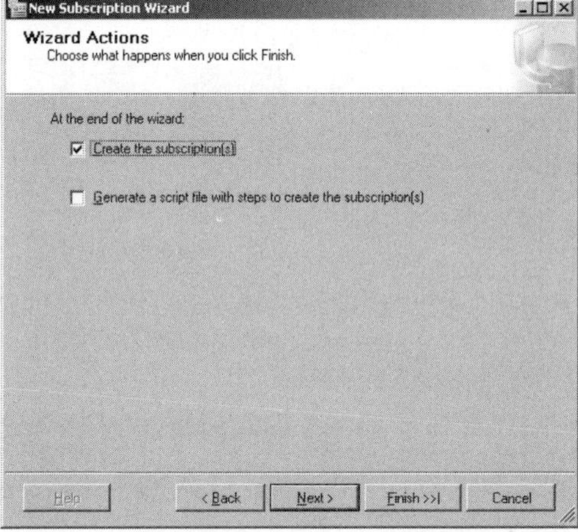

13. The next window provides you with a summary of the actions you have opted for in the wizard. If you are satisfied with the values and options, click Finish to create the subscription.

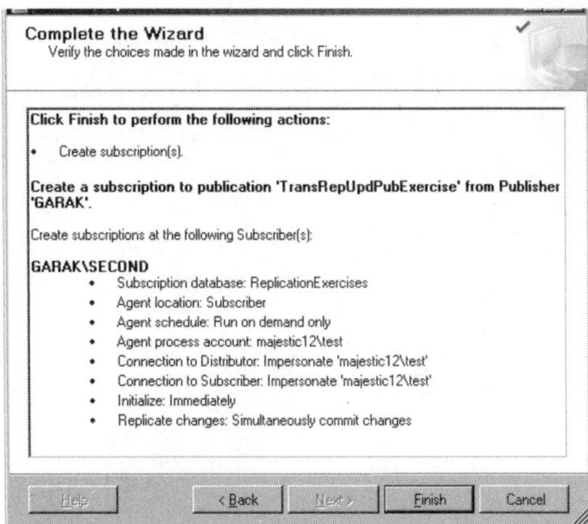

14. The wizard then creates the specified subscription and starts the synchronization agent(s). When completed a Success message appears in the window. Click Close to exit the wizard.

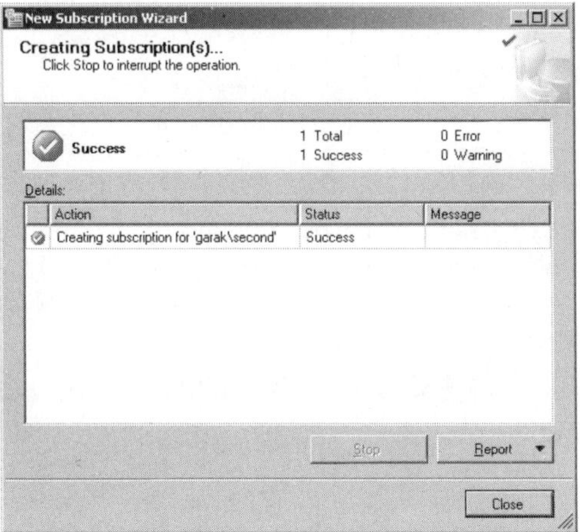

15. To confirm that the subscription has been created, go to SERVER and open Object Explorer and then the Replication node. Right-click the Local Publications folder and expand the [AdventureWorks]:TransRepUpdPubExercise publication and note the new subscription [SECOND]: ReplicationExercises. (You may need to refresh the publication first by right-clicking on the folder and selecting Refresh from the pop-up menu.)

Open the SECOND instance; expand the Replication node, then expand the Local Subscriptions folder to find a subscription labeled [ReplicationExercises]-[SERVER].[Adventureworks]:Trans-RepUpdPubExercise. You will also find two new tables in the Replication_Exercises database.

One is the article, Purchasing.Vendor, and the other is a table of conflict information, Purchasing.conflict_TransRepUpdPubExercises_Vendor.

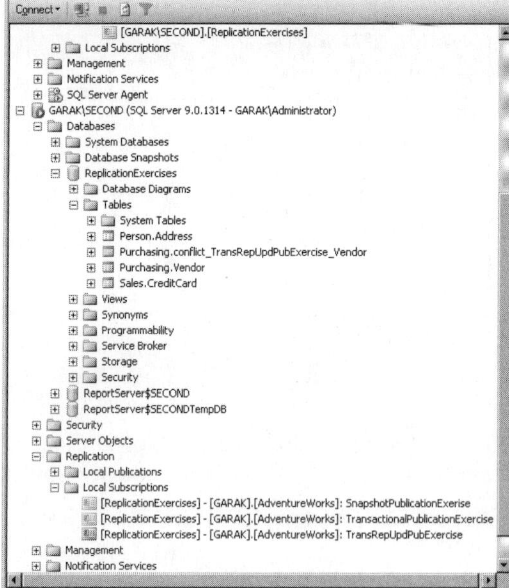

Testing Transactional Replication with Update Subscriptions

Now that we have created a transactional publication with updatable subscriptions and a pull subscription, let's test the new arrangement to make sure replication actually occurs by pulling the subscription to the SECOND server instance. To do that we need to create some changes in the AdventureWorks database's Vendor table.

1. Close any open dialog boxes and return to Management Studio.
2. Right-click the default SERVER and select New Query. Connect if prompted.
3. Enter and execute the following code to change the data in the Vendor table of the AdventureWorks database.

```
USE AdventureWorks
INSERT Vendor
(AccountNumber,Name,CreditRating,PreferredVendorStatus,ActiveFlag,PurchasingWe
bServiceURL)
VALUES ('TUTHILL0901','Waves on George', '1','3','1','www.trevallyn.com')
```

4. Confirm that the new record has been added by executing the following code:

```
USE Adventureworks
SELECT * FROM Purchasing.Vendor
```

5. Scroll to the bottom of the table and confirm that the new row data you created has been added to the end of the table.

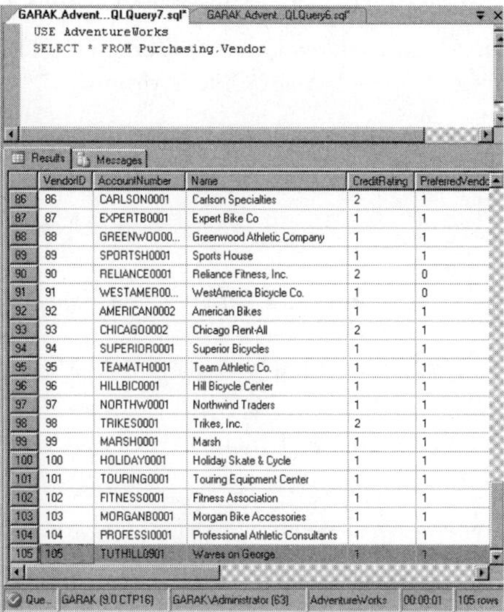

Because you previously set synchronization scheduling on the subscription to Run Continuously, the pull occurs immediately. To confirm that the changes have been replicated to the ReplicationExercises database's Vendor table, do the following.

6. Right-click SECOND. Click the New Query button on the toolbar (or right-click SECOND and select New Query). Connect to SECOND when prompted.
7. In the Query Window enter and execute the following code:

```
USE ReplicationExercises
SELECT * FROM Purchasing.Vendor
```

8. Scroll to the bottom of the table and you will see the new record added.

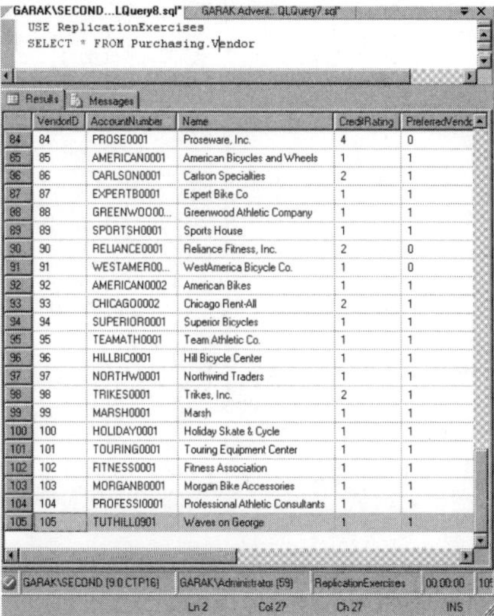

Now let's see what happens when we make a change to the database on the subscriber.

9. Right-click SECOND. Click the New Query button on the toolbar (or right-click SECOND and select New Query). Connect to SECOND if prompted.

10. In the Query window enter and execute the following code to change the data in the Vendor table of the ReplicationExercises database.

```
USE ReplicationExercises
INSERT Purchasing.Vendor
(AccountNumber,Name,CreditRating,PreferredVendorStatus,ActiveFlag,PurchasingWe
bServiceURL)
VALUES ('MAASH0001','Maashingaidze Widgets','1','2','1', 'www.maashwidgets.com')
```

11. To confirm that the changes have been made to the ReplicationExercises database's Vendor table, do the following:

    In the Query window enter and execute the following code:

```
USE ReplicationExercises
SELECT * FROM Purchasing.Vendor
```

    Scroll to the bottom of the table and you will see the new record added.

12. To prove that the update worked, connect to SERVER, and in a new query window create and execute the following code:

```
USE Adventureworks
SELECT * FROM ReplicationExercises
```

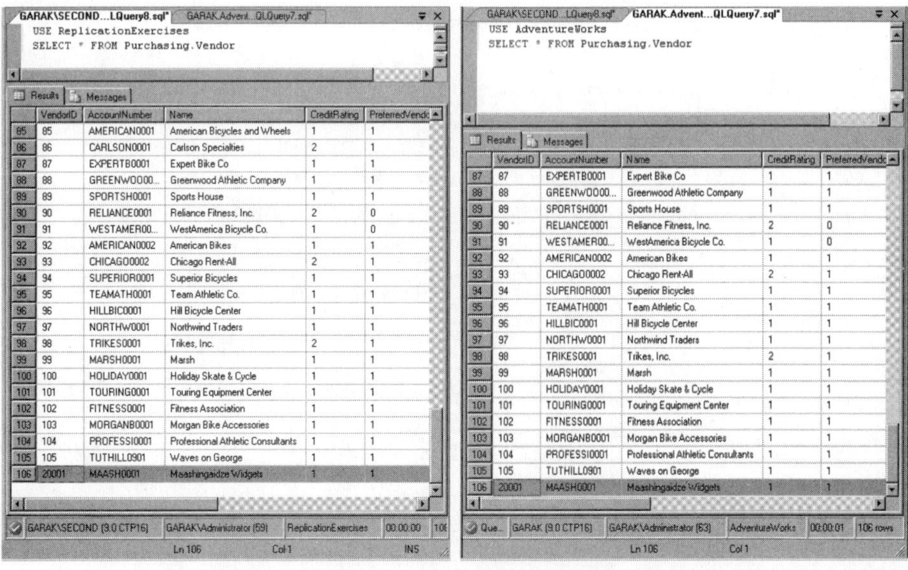

	VendorID	AccountNumber	Name	CreditRating	PreferredVendc
85	85	AMERICAN0001	American Bicycles and Wheels	1	1
86	86	CARLSON0001	Carlson Specialties	2	1
87	87	EXPERTB0001	Expert Bike Co	1	1
88	88	GREENWOO00...	Greenwood Athletic Company	1	1
89	89	SPORTSH0001	Sports House	1	1
90	90	RELIANCE0001	Reliance Fitness, Inc.	2	0
91	91	WESTAMER00...	WestAmerica Bicycle Co.	1	0
92	92	AMERICAN0002	American Bikes	1	1
93	93	CHICAGO0002	Chicago Rent-All	2	1
94	94	SUPERIOR0001	Superior Bicycles	1	1
95	95	TEAMATH0001	Team Athletic Co.	1	1
96	96	HILLBIC0001	Hill Bicycle Center	1	1
97	97	NORTHW0001	Northwind Traders	1	1
98	98	TRIKES0001	Trikes, Inc.	2	1
99	99	MARSH0001	Marsh	1	1
100	100	HOLIDAY0001	Holiday Skate & Cycle	1	1
101	101	TOURING0001	Touring Equipment Center	1	1
102	102	FITNESS0001	Fitness Association	1	1
103	103	MORGANB0001	Morgan Bike Accessories	1	1
104	104	PROFESSI0001	Professional Athletic Consultants	1	1
105	105	TUTHILL0901	Waves on George	1	1
106	20001	MAASH0001	Maashingaidze Widgets	1	1

	VendorID	AccountNumber	Name	CreditRating	PreferredVendc
87	87	EXPERTB0001	Expert Bike Co	1	1
88	88	GREENWOO00...	Greenwood Athletic Company	1	1
89	89	SPORTSH0001	Sports House	1	1
90	90	RELIANCE0001	Reliance Fitness, Inc.	2	0
91	91	WESTAMER00...	WestAmerica Bicycle Co.	1	0
92	92	AMERICAN0002	American Bikes	1	1
93	93	CHICAGO0002	Chicago Rent-All	2	1
94	94	SUPERIOR0001	Superior Bicycles	1	1
95	95	TEAMATH0001	Team Athletic Co.	1	1
96	96	HILLBIC0001	Hill Bicycle Center	1	1
97	97	NORTHW0001	Northwind Traders	1	1
98	98	TRIKES0001	Trikes, Inc.	2	1
99	99	MARSH0001	Marsh	1	1
100	100	HOLIDAY0001	Holiday Skate & Cycle	1	1
101	101	TOURING0001	Touring Equipment Center	1	1
102	102	FITNESS0001	Fitness Association	1	1
103	103	MORGANB0001	Morgan Bike Accessories	1	1
104	104	PROFESSI0001	Professional Athletic Consultants	1	1
105	105	TUTHILL0901	Waves on George	1	1
106	20001	MAASH0001	Maashingaidze Widgets	1	1

Congratulations, you have now successfully completed creating a transactional publication with updatable subscriptions and a pull subscription. You have also successfully updated the subscriber's copy of the database table and replicated it to the publisher, where it can be replicated to other subscribers.

Creating and Subscribing to a Merge Publication

Merge replication is used when the publisher and all subscribers need to be able to make changes to their local copy of the data and have those changes replicated to all other subscribers in the replication topology. To demonstrate how this works, you will configure a merge publication on the AdventureWorks database. Then, you will have the SECOND server subscribe to the publication. Finally, you will modify the same record in both databases and see how to deal with the subsequent conflict.

NOTE Microsoft SQL Server Mobile Edition can only subscribe to merge publications.

Creating a Merge Publication

The creation of a merge publication involves several steps that differ from creating either a snapshot or transactional publication.

1. If you are not in Management Studio, open it by selecting it from the SQL Server 2005 group under Programs on the Start menu.
2. Click your default server (not SECOND) in Object Explorer and expand the folders, then open the Replication folder.
3. Right-click the Local Publications folder and select New Publication to open the New Publication Wizard. Click Next to move to the next screen.
4. On the Publication Database screen of the wizard, you are presented with a list of databases on the SERVER. Select AdventureWorks by highlighting it and click Next to move to the next screen.
5. In the Publication Type screen there is a list of the four types of publications supported in SQL Server 2005. The lower pane provides a brief description of each type of publication. Select Merge Publication and then click Next.

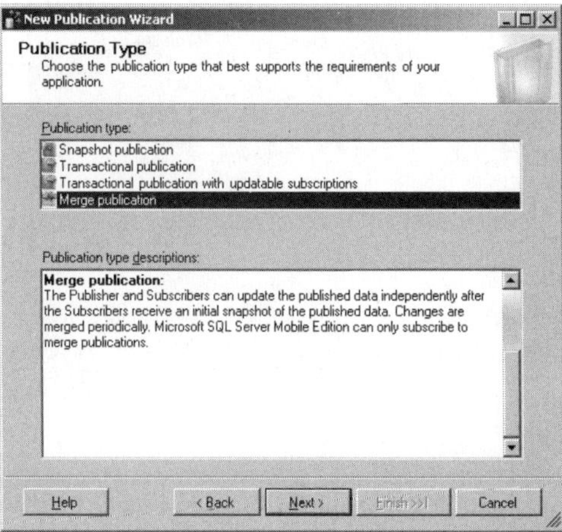

6. You are next asked to specify the SQL Server versions that will be used by subscribers to this publication. Select SQL Server 2005.

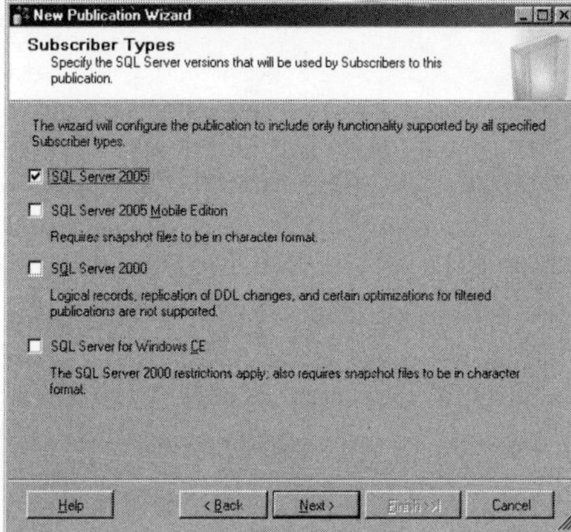

7. In the Articles screen you are asked to select which objects you wish to publish. Expand Tables and select the box next to the CountryRegion (Person) table to enable it for publication. Note that there are several columns marked with a green asterisk in a circle. These denote columns that must be published (and cannot be deselected). These include columns that:

   - Are primary keys
   - Are part of a foreign key constraint
   - Do not have the IDENTITY property set, do not allow nulls, and have no default value
   - Are rowguides (columns required in merge publications)

   You can also select the "Show only checked objects in the list" check box to limit the clutter in the view to the objects you select. Click Next.

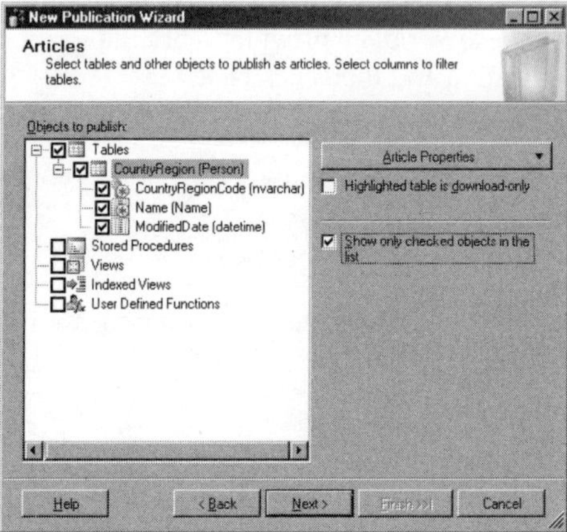

NOTE By clicking the Article Properties button you can set the properties of the highlighted article or all the articles of that type of database object.

8. If you right-click on an article, a pop-up menu gives you access to windows where you can set additional properties. Select "Set properties of this Table Article" to open the Article Properties window. While this window is available in other types of publications, the options are very limited. This is not the case in merge publications. The Article Properties dialog box has two tabs. Under the Properties tab you have access to a number of additional setting related to how objects will be copied to the subscriber, properties of the destination object, identification, range management, and merging changes.

   Under the Resolver tab you can determine how conflicts are resolved. If you choose to use the default resolver, the conflicts are resolved based on preset priority settings for the subscriber or the first change written to the publisher, depending on the type of subscription used. You also have the option to use a custom resolver. This is where you will also add any input that is required by the resolver. Another option is to allow the subscriber to resolve conflicts if it is going to use on-demand synchronization (specified when the subscription is created). Use resolve conflicts interactively using the Interactive Resolver.

   Leave the settings as you find them and click OK to close the Properties sheet and click Next to move to the Article Issues screen.

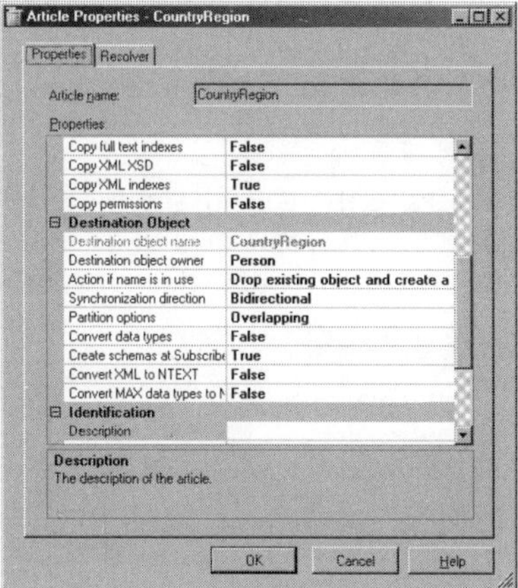

9. On the next screen you receive an informational page informing you about changes that need to be made. In this case SQL Server will add both a uniqueidentifier column with a unique index and the ROWGUIDCOL property to the Sales.CreditCard table. Click Next.

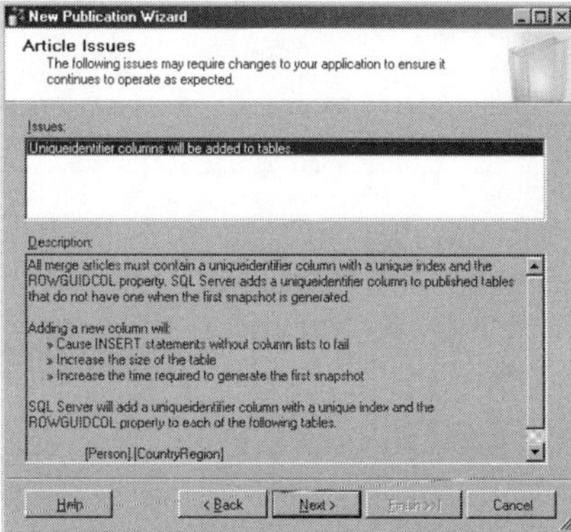

10. On the next screen, you need to decide whether you will add filters to exclude unwanted rows. In this instance, you will not add filters but simply click Next.

NOTE Excluding rows in an article from replication by filtering is referred to as *horizontal partitioning.*

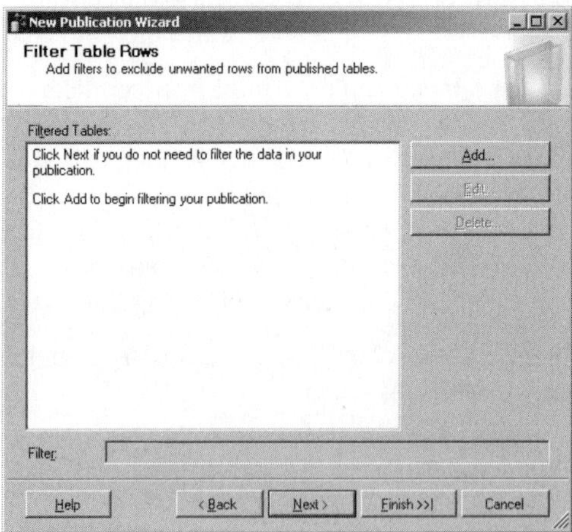

11. The next screen asks you to specify when to run the Snapshot Agent. You can either run it immediately or schedule it to run at specified times or both. This is done to make sure the subscriber is always up-to-date. Accept the default values and click Next.

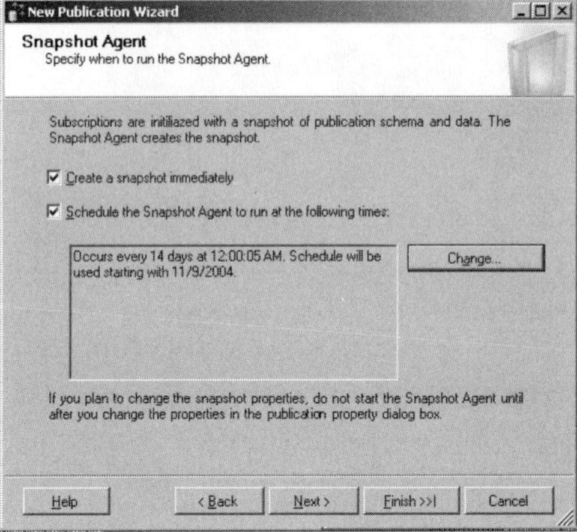

12. You are now asked to provide the account under which the Snapshot Agent will run. Click the button labeled Security Settings to open the Snapshot Agent Security window. In this window, specify the account to be used and whether you will connect to the publisher by impersonating the process account or using a specified SQL Server login. In this instance we will use a domain account. Click OK. Then click Next on the Agent Security window.

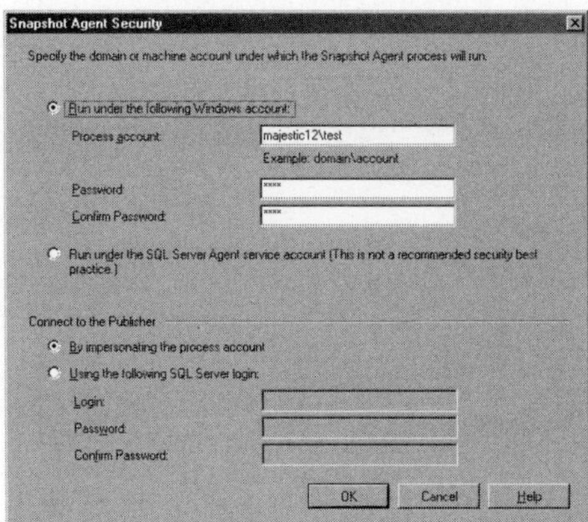

13. On the next screen, you need to choose what happens when you click Finish. You can opt to either create publication immediately, generate a script file with the steps to create the publication, both, or neither. Leave the default setting of Create the Subscription(s) checked and click Next.

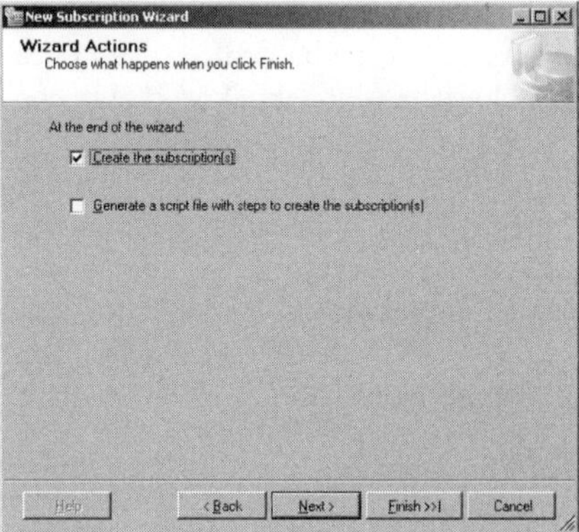

14. The next window asks you to provide a name for the publication. In this example we will use MergeExercise. Review the list of actions in the lower dialog box to confirm the settings and then click Finish.

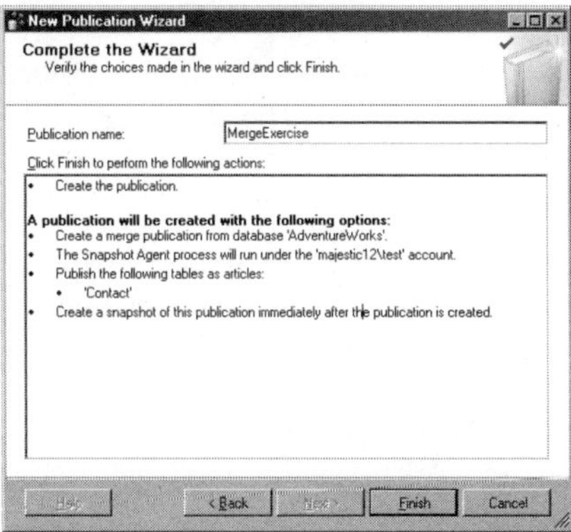

15. The Creating Publication window opens and the publication is created. Once the publication is completed, you are informed of the successful creation of the publication. Click Close to complete the wizard.

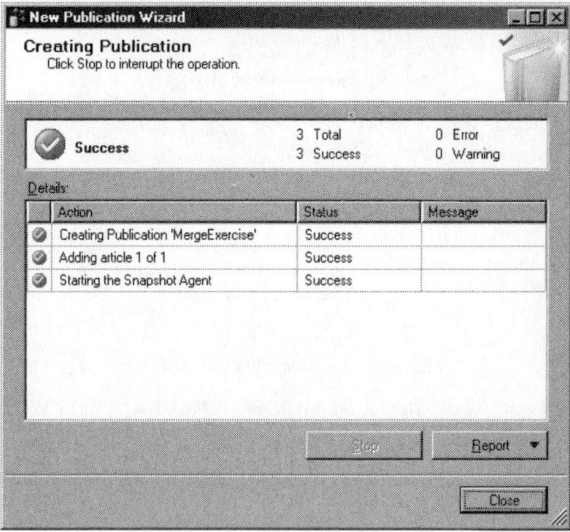

16. Confirm that the new publication can be located in the Local Publications folder of Object Explorer where you should see a yellow book icon with converging green and blue arrows. This is the icon used for merge replication (other types are different colors). Notice that right-clicking on the publication gives you ready access to a number of options, including creating a new subscription, creating a new publication, generating scripts, validating a subscription, reinitializing all subscriptions, generating a snapshot, and a means of accessing the property sheet. You can also delete the publication or refresh the view.

Creating a Merge Subscription

As explained earlier, you can launch the Subscription Wizard any number of ways. You can right-click on an existing publication and select New Subscriptions. Alternatively you can open the Replication node in Object Explorer and select Local Subscriptions, right-click, and double-click the New Subscriptions option at either the publisher or the subscriber.

1. Open SERVER, expand the Replication and Local Publications folder, right-click on the AdventureWorks: MergeExercise publication and select New Subscriptions from the menu. The New Subscription Wizard begins. Click Next.

2. On the Publication sheet you will need to select the publisher where the publication can be found. If not already connected, you will need to select the SERVER and connect. In this case connect to SERVER and select the MergeExercise publication. Click Next.

3. The next page asks you where to run the Distribution Agent. You can opt to run the agent either at the distributor (a push subscription) or at its subscriber (a pull subscription). Most merge subscriptions are pull subscriptions because merge subscribers are normally offline. In this example, confirm that the radio button next to "Run each agent at its Subscriber (pull subscriptions)" is marked and click Next.

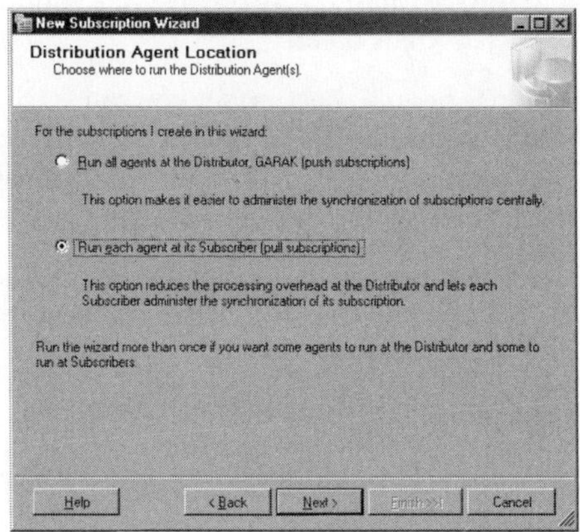

4. You are now asked to choose the subscriber and specify the subscription database. Mark the box by SECOND. (If SECOND is not listed, click the Add SQL Server Subscriber button and connect to SECOND.) In the column marked Subscription Database, select ReplicationExercises database (created in the snapshot subscription exercise) from the drop-down menu. If you do not have a subscription database already available, you will have to create one as outlined in steps 5–6 under the "Creating a Snapshot Subscription" section earlier in this chapter.

5. On the Distribution Agent Security screen you will specify the account and connection options for the Distribution Agent. To do so, click the ellipsis at the far right of the row containing SECOND.

6. On the Distribution Agent Security screen, specify a process account consisting of a domain or machine account under which the process will run during synchronization. You can also specify the account used to connect to both the distributor and the subscriber. In this example we are using a domain account.

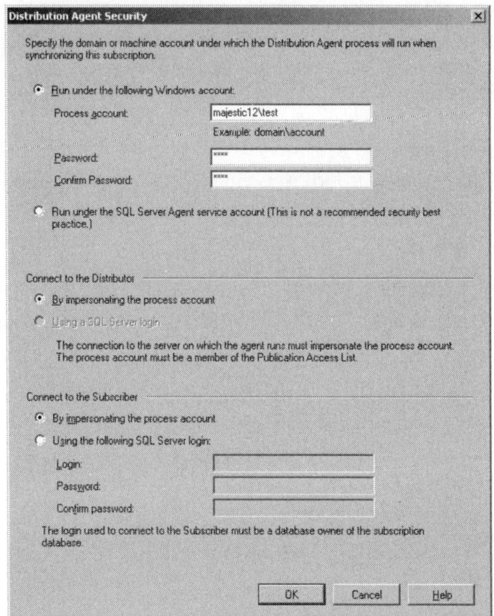

7. Click OK to return to the Distribution Agent Security window. Note that the connection methods have been added. Click Next.

8. On the Synchronization Schedule sheet, either you can set the schedule for synchronization using a preset schedule or you can define one yourself. The default "Run on demand only" will instruct SQL Server not to replicate changes automatically—you will need to start replication yourself. In this exercise set the value to Run Continuously. Click Next.

9. On the Initialize Subscriptions window, accept the default value of Immediately for when to initialize the subscription with a snapshot of the publication data and schema.

10. On the next screen, you need to choose the subscription type, Server or Client. In SQL Server 2000 these were called global and local.

    Merge replication is normally used in server-to-client environments. Subscribers with a server subscription can (1) republish data to other subscribers, (2) act as alternate synchronization partners, and (3) resolve conflicts according to a priority you set. In this exercise, set the Subscription Type to Server and accept the default Priority for Conflict Resolution of 75.00 and click Next.

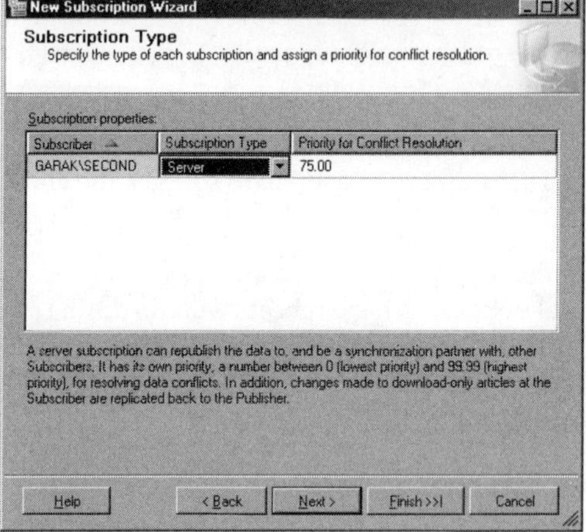

11. On the next screen, you need to choose what happens when you click Finish. You can either opt to create subscription immediately, generate a script file with the steps to create the subscription, both, or neither. Leave the default setting of "Create the subscription(s)" checked and click Next.

12. The next window provides you with a summary of the actions you have opted for in the wizard. If you are satisfied with the values and options, click Finish to create the subscription.

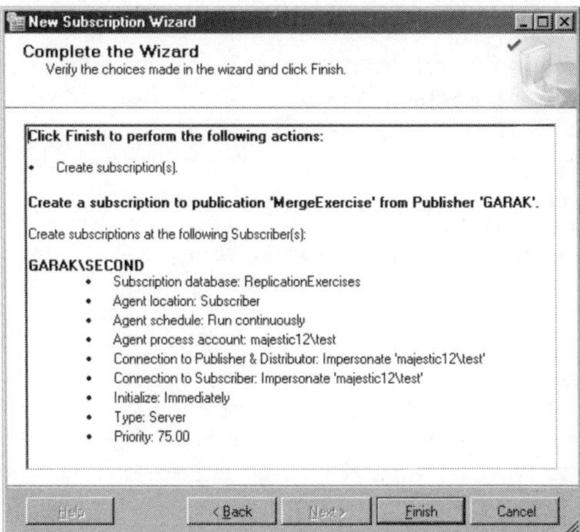

13. The wizard then creates the specified subscription and starts the synchronization agent. When completed a Success message appears in the window. Click Close to exit the wizard.

14. To confirm that the subscription has been created, go to SERVER and open Object Explorer and then open the Replication folder, then the Local Publications folder. Expand the [AdventureWorks]:MergeExercise publication and note the new subscription [SECOND].[ReplicationExercises]. (You may need to refresh the publication first by right-clicking on the folder.)

    Open the SECOND instance, expand the Replication node, then expand Local Subscriptions to find a subscription labeled [ReplicationExercises]-[SERVER].[AdventureWorks]:MergeExercise. You will also find a new table consisting of the article (i.e. Person.Contact) in the ReplicationExercises database.

Testing Merge Replication

Now that we have created a merge publication with updatable subscriptions and a push subscription, let's test the new arrangement to make sure replication actually occurs and to test how conflicts are resolved by pulling the subscription to the SECOND server instance. To do that, we need to create some changes in the AdventureWorks database's Vendor table.

1. Close any open dialog boxes and return to Management Studio.

2. Right-click the default SERVER and select New Query. Connect if prompted.

3. Enter and execute the following code to change the data in the CreditCard table of the AdventureWorks database.

```
USE AdventureWorks
INSERT Person.CountryRegion (CountryRegionCode,Name)
VALUES  ('AC', "Alpha Centauri')
```

4. Because you previously set synchronization scheduling on the subscription to Run Continuously, the pull occurs immediately. Confirm that new record has been added by checking both the ReplicationExercises and AdventureWorks databases by creating and executing the following code on the relevant server.

   On SERVER:

```
USE AdventureWorks
SELECT * FROM Person.CountryRegion
```

   ON SECOND:

```
USE ReplicationExercises
SELECT * FROM Person.CountryRegion
```

5. Scroll to the top of each table and confirm that the new row data you created has been added to the table.

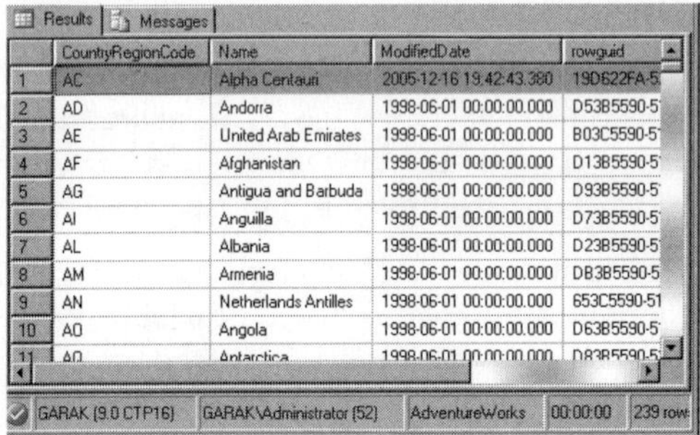

	CountryRegionCode	Name	ModifiedDate	rowguid
1	AC	Alpha Centauri	2005-12-16 19:42:43.380	19D622FA-5
2	AD	Andorra	1998-06-01 00:00:00.000	D53B5590-5
3	AE	United Arab Emirates	1998-06-01 00:00:00.000	B03C5590-5
4	AF	Afghanistan	1998-06-01 00:00:00.000	D13B5590-5
5	AG	Antigua and Barbuda	1998-06-01 00:00:00.000	D93B5590-5
6	AI	Anguilla	1998-06-01 00:00:00.000	D73B5590-5
7	AL	Albania	1998-06-01 00:00:00.000	D23B5590-5
8	AM	Armenia	1998-06-01 00:00:00.000	DB3B5590-5
9	AN	Netherlands Antilles	1998-06-01 00:00:00.000	653C5590-51
10	AO	Angola	1998-06-01 00:00:00.000	D63B5590-5
11	AQ	Antarctica	1998-06-01 00:00:00.000	D83B5590-5

Testing Conflict Resolution

With a working merge publication in place and a pull subscription running, you can make a change to the same record on both servers at the same time and see which change applies. In the next series of steps, you will open two new queries, one connected to each instance of SQL Server, and test the replication of data:

1. Open the first query by right-clicking on SERVER and select New Query.
2. Enter the following code but *do not* execute it yet:

```
USE AdventureWorks
UPDATE Person.CountryRegion
SET Name = 'Alfalfa Centauri'
WHERE CountryRegionCode = 'AC'
```

3. Open the second query by right-clicking on SECOND and selecting New Query. Connect if prompted. Enter the following code, but *do not* execute it yet. This will change the exact same data on the subscriber as was changed on the publisher:

```
USE ReplicationExercises
UPDATE Person.CountryRegion
SET Name= 'Aleph Centauri'
WHERE CountryRegionCode = 'AC'
```

4. Execute the query in the SECOND copy of Query Analyzer.
5. Switch to the query connected to SERVER and execute the query.
6. Wait for about 5 minutes (to give the server time to replicate), switch to the query connected to SECOND, then enter and execute the following code to see whether the change replicated:

```
USE ReplicationExercises
SELECT * FROM Person.CountryRegion
WHERE CountryRegionCode = 'AC'
```

7. When you see the value of *Alfalfa Centauri* in the query connected to SECOND, close both copies of Query Analyzer—replication was successful.

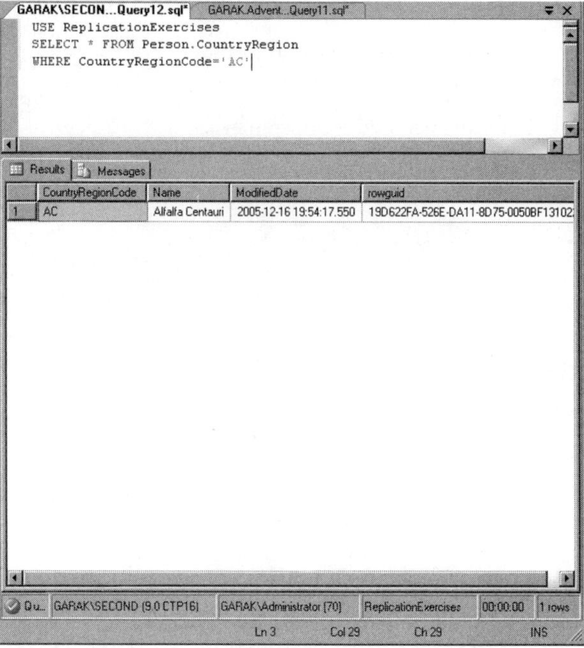

Now you have a major problem though; notice that the subscriber now contains the value that was entered at the publisher through the query connected to SERVER rather than the value that was entered at the subscriber. This is referred to as a *conflict* and can be rectified in Management Studio.

There are two types of conflict resolution.

In the *default method* as used here, resolutions are settled and applied *immediately* according to a preset set of criteria (either built-in or custom-defined). In this case the conflict resolver is priority-based since it is between servers. In a client subscriptions, the first change written to the publisher wins.

In *interactive conflict resolution* you must resolve all conflicts manually during on-demand synchronization. You also have the option to edit the conflicting data. You can configure Management Studio to use interactive conflict resolution in a number of ways:

- In the Resolver tab of the Article properties window when the publication is created
- In the Resolver Table of the Publication properties page after the publication is created
- Through the Subscription Properties pages on the subscriber

We will use the default method in this exercise based on the settings you made when setting up the MergeExercise publication.

8. In Management Studio, expand the default server and select AdventureWorks under Databases.
9. Expand the Replication and Publications folders. Right-click the [AdventureWorks]:Merge-Exercise publication.
10. Select View Conflicts from the pop-up menu.
11. The Select Conflict Table dialog box opens. Select CountryRegion(1) and click OK.

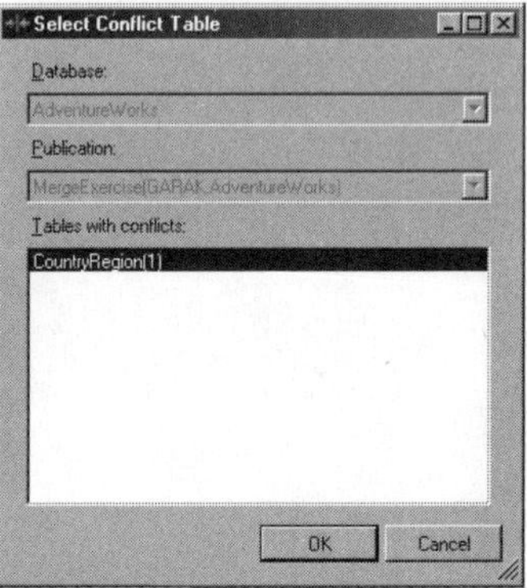

12. The Replication Conflict Viewer opens, allowing you to see the rows that have conflicts. The winner is the server that had the highest priority set when you created the subscription.

A list of conflicts and the losers is displayed n the center pane. In the lower pane you are provided details of the conflicts.

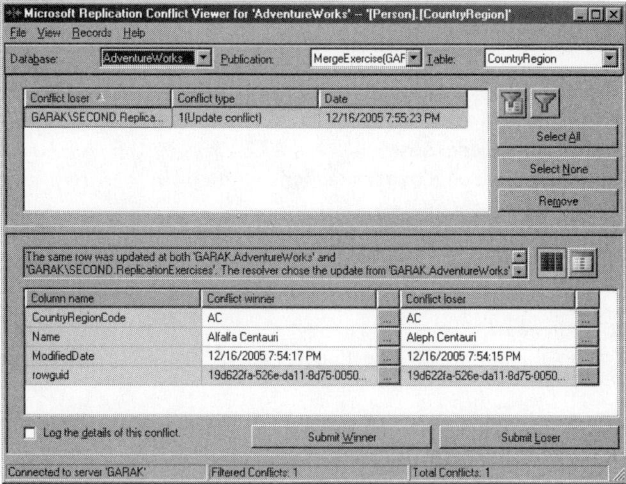

13. Notice the ellipsis at the end of each column value. Clicking it opens a separate window where you can edit the values in that column. Values and columns that can't be changed are grayed out.

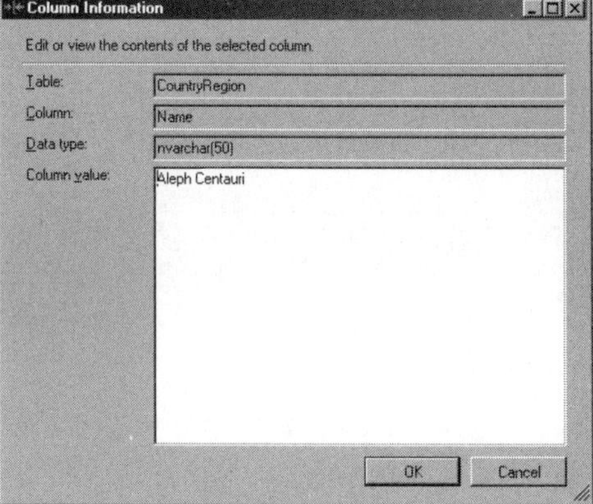

14. There are two buttons to choose from at the bottom of the dialog box.

   - Submit Winner will make the change from the winning server permanent.
   - Submit Loser will overwrite the automatically resolved data with that displayed under Conflict Loser.
   - Note that to apply different data from that entered at either instance, you can simply edit either the winner or the loser through the Column Information window and apply that value via the Submit Winner or Submit Loser button.

15. In this instance we will apply the data from the ReplicationsExercises database on SECOND as the winner. To do so click the Submit Loser button.

16. Once complete, close the Replication Conflict Viewer and switch to the query connected to SECOND.

17. Enter and execute the following to make sure the second update is still there:

```
USE ReplicationExercises
SELECT * FROM Person.CountryRegion
WHERE CountryRegionCode = 'AC'
```

18. Now switch to the query connected to SERVER, and enter and execute the following code:

```
USE AdventureWorks
SELECT * FROM Person.CountryRegion WHERE CountryRegionCode = 'AC'
```

Notice that the database was updated with the data from the second database that you selected to make permanent in the Replication Conflict Viewer.

19. Close Management Studio.

You've been busy and should be pleased with yourself. You have successfully created a merge publication and subscription that allow users on both the subscriber and publisher to update the same data at the same time. When you updated the same data on both servers at once (the AC CountryRegionCode record), the server with the highest priority (SERVER) tentatively won the conflict. To make sure that the right data is in the databases after a conflict, you then opened the Microsoft Replication Conflict Viewer and told SQL Server which data to keep in the databases, opting in this instance to side with the underdog and save the subscriber's entry.

Now you have successfully created snapshot, transactional, transactional with updatable subscriptions, and merge publications. You have both pushed and pulled them to the subscribers. You have resolved conflicts and explored myriad details that help you understand how replication is accomplished. However, what happens if replication stops working? That is why you have Replication Monitor.

Using Replication Monitor

Either a philosopher or a frustrated office worker once said, we are all at the mercy of our machines. This is especially true regarding replication, because the process spans so many machines. If one of these machines has a problem or a network link breaks down, replication will stop. As a SQL Server DBA, you will need to be able to find the cause of these problems and bring replication back online. That is what Replication Monitor is for.

Replication Monitor is found in Management Studio and any instance of SQL Server, whether it is a distributor, publisher, or subscriber on the distributor machine. Replication Monitor is designed to assess the overall health of the replication topology as well as provide information on the performance of publishers and subscribers so you can detect problems and improve performance.

Let's get some hands-on experience working with the Replication Monitor tools:

1. Open Management Studio by selecting it from the SQL Server 2005 group under Programs on your Start menu.
2. On SERVER, right-click the Replication folder and select Launch Replication Monitor. (Note that you can Monitor Replication from any instance of SQL Server regardless of its role.)
3. If this is the first time you are opening Replication Monitor, you will be asked to add a publisher to monitor by either clicking the link in the right pane, using the action menu, or right-clicking the My Publishers node and selecting Add Publisher.

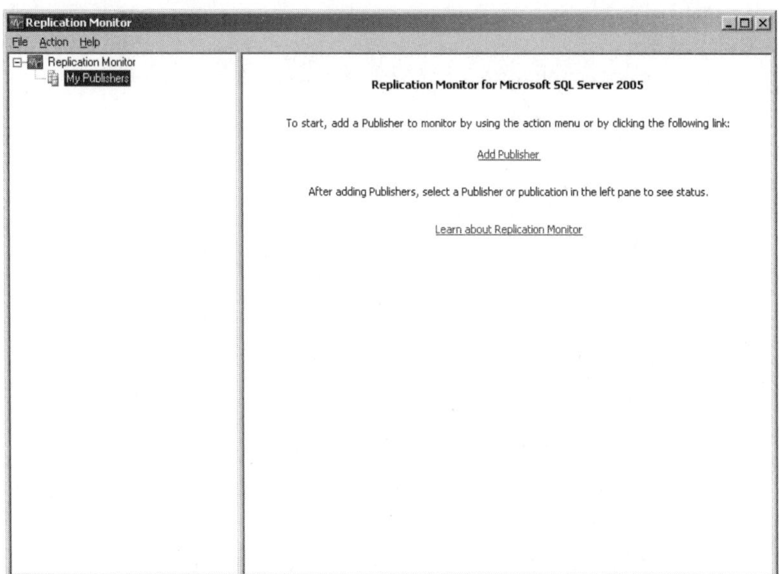

NOTE You can also access Replication Monitor by right-clicking a publication and selecting Launch Replication Monitor.

4. Choose one of these methods and launch the Add Publisher window if necessary.

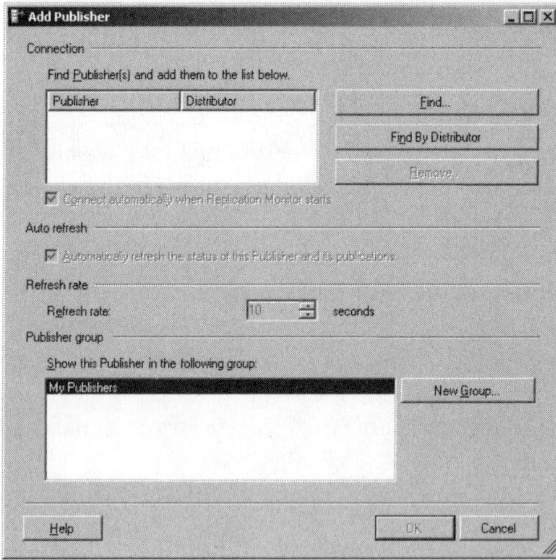

5. The first thing to do is locate a publisher to be monitored. You can find a publisher either by using the Find button to connect to a specific distributor or by clicking the Find by Distributor button to connect to a distributor and its list of publishers. Click Find and select SERVER.

6. Selecting the publisher in the pane gives you access to other options on the page including whether to connect automatically when Replication Monitor is started, whether to automatically refresh the status of the publisher and the refresh rate, and whether or not to place the publisher in a group. Note that this group is solely for administrative purposes to make finding and organizing your publisher easier in Replication Monitor. It has no effect outside the context of Replication Monitor. Accept the defaults and click OK.

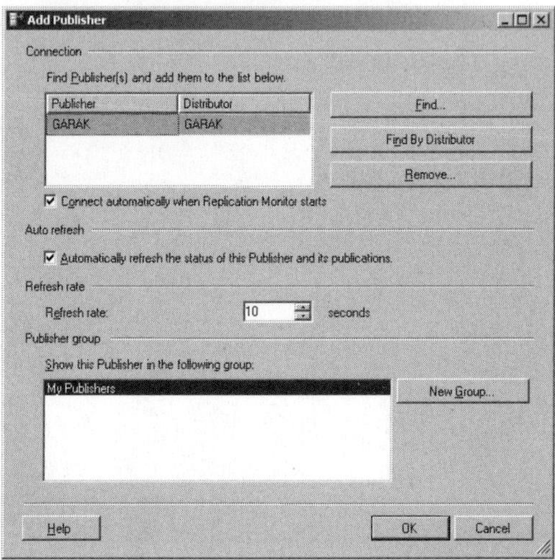

7. In the left pane of Replication Monitor notice that SERVER has been added to the MyPublishers folder. Expand it to reveal the [AdventureWorks].MergeExercise publication from the previous exercises (others may appear depending on whether or not you deleted them at the conclusion of the exercise or not—it's not necessary that they be there).

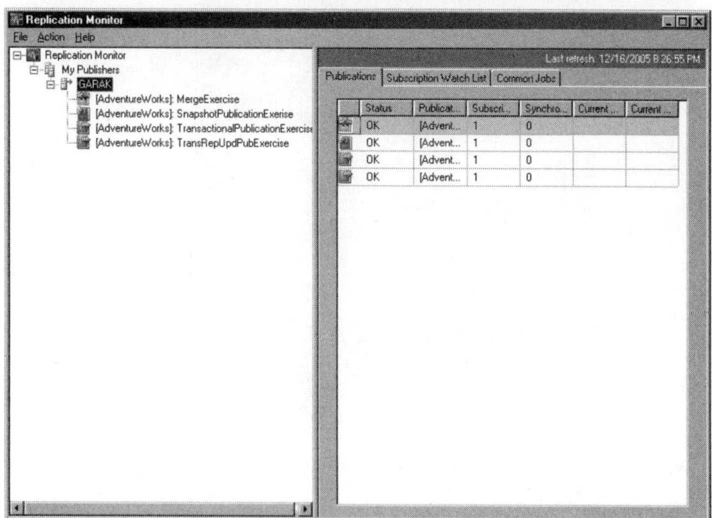

8. Right-click the publisher SERVER and select Agent Profiles. This will bring up the Properties sheet. Scroll through each of the agent pages and notice all of the profiles associated with each agent. Notice as well that you can set the default values for all new agents of that type. You can also set performance profiles values and apply them to all existing agents by clicking the Change Existing Agents button in the lower right of the page. Select the Merge Agents page.

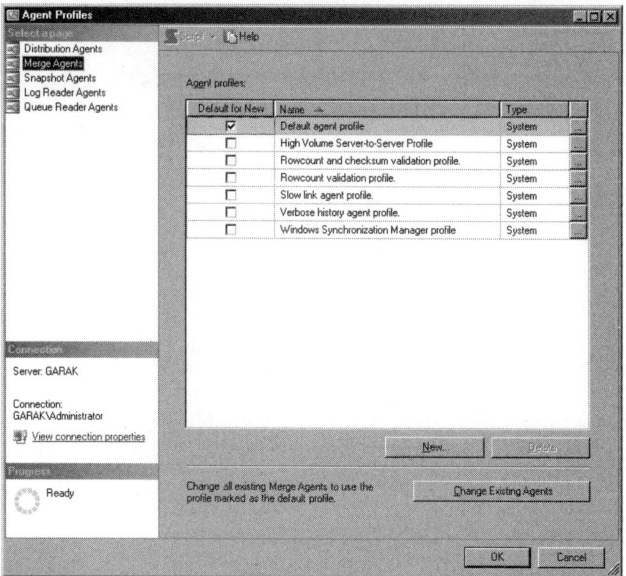

9. Notice that each profile has an ellipsis to the far right (to the right of the Type column). Click the one next to Default Agent Profile. The Properties sheet opens. Notice all of the options that are available and then click Close.

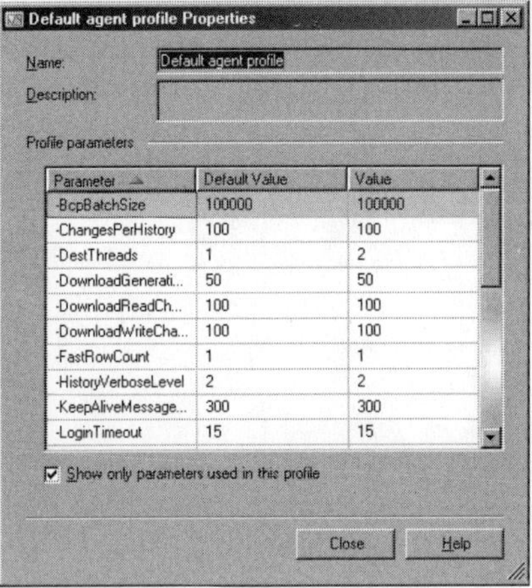

10. On the Agent Profiles page, click Cancel.

11. On the Replication Monitor main page, expand SERVER and select the [Adventure-Works].MergeExercise publication. In the right pane you will be shown a list of subscriptions associated with the publication. There are two tabs, All Subscriptions and Warnings and Agents.

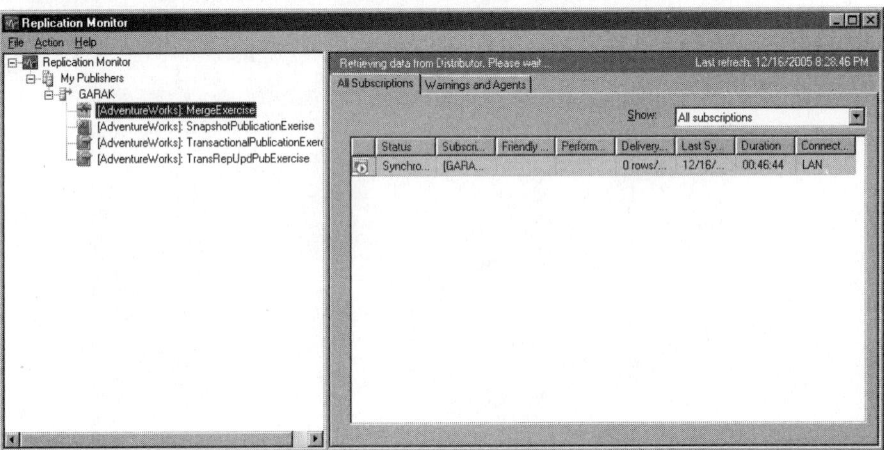

12. Under the Warnings and Agents tab you can enable and set a threshold related to the type of subscription, in this case a merge subscription. View the options and settings and then click the All Subscriptions tab.

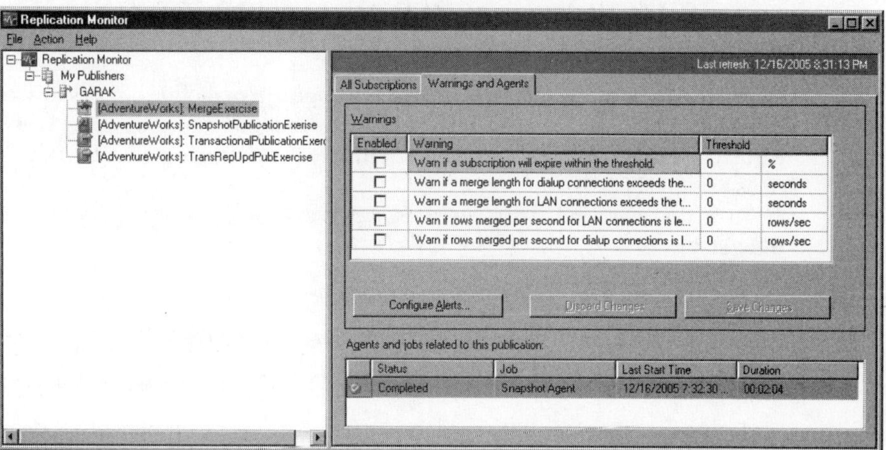

13. Select and right-click the subscription created for the MergeExercise publication. Click View to see the synchronization history of this subscription and the articles processed. You can also view errors.

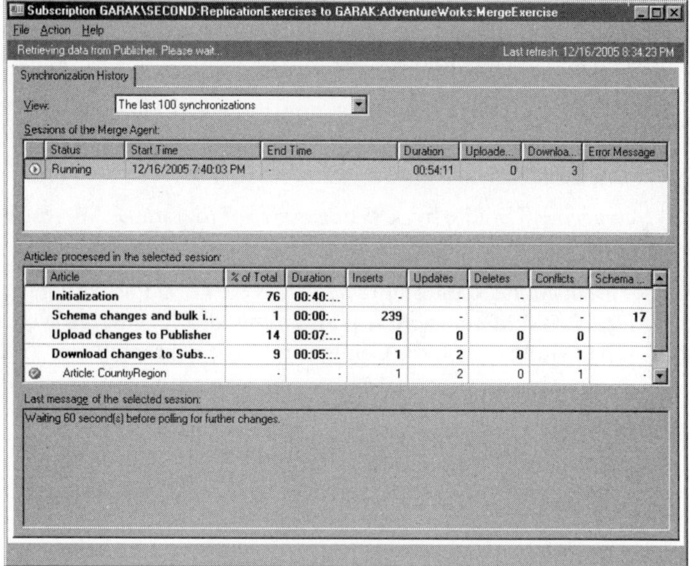

14. Now that you're familiar with Replication Monitor and its features, go ahead and close all the open windows.

Configuring Web Synchronization for Pull Subscriptions to Merge Replications

With the growth of the Internet and the development of mobile devices to access SQL databases on an intermittent basis, the need for web synchronization became obvious. Web synchronization uses a Microsoft Internet Information Server (IIS) to synchronize pull subscriptions to merge publications using HTTP.

To do this you need to first install SQL Server Connectivity components on the IIS by following these steps:

1. Log on to the IIS server as an administrator.
2. Launch the SQL Server Installation Wizard from the SQL Server 2005 installation disk.
3. On the Components to Install page of the SQL Server Installation Wizard, click Advanced.
4. On the Feature Selection page, expand the Client Components node.
5. Click Connectivity Components, and then click "Entire feature will be installed on local hard drive."
6. Complete the wizard, and then restart the computer.

WARNING **Certificate Services must be installed on the server and a certificate installed on the website to set up web synchronization.**

Once that is done you will need to set up web synchronization on SQL Server. Remember, you can only use web synchronization for a merge publication and the connecting system must be using a pull subscription.

7. Open Management Studio by selecting Start ➢ Programs ➢ Microsoft SQL Server ➢ SQL Server Management Studio.
8. On SERVER open the Replication node, then the Local Publications folder and select the [AdventureWorks].MergeExercise publication. Select Configure Web Synchronization from the pop-up menu to launch the Configure Web Synchronization Wizard.

9. The next window asks you which type of server to use: SQL Server or SQL Mobile Edition. Select SQL Server. Click Next.

10. On the Web Server page, select the IIS Server that will synchronize subscriptions (SERVER). Then, select "Create a new virtual directory." Expand the Web Sites and then SERVER, and click Default Web Site. Click Next.

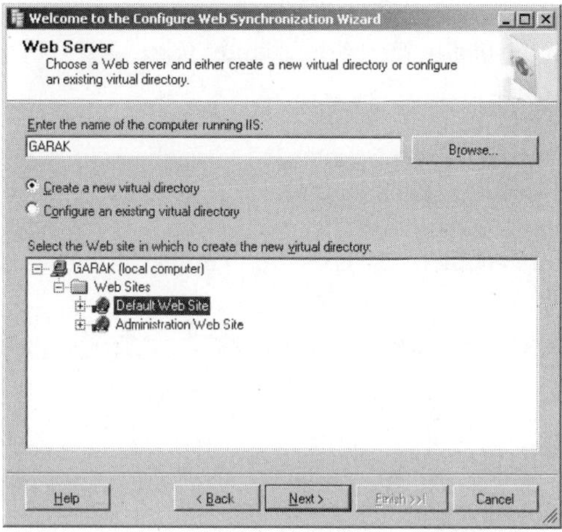

WARNING If you do not have a certificate installed on the selected website, clicking Next will generate an error and you will be unable to continue.

11. On the next page enter an alias for the virtual directory in the Alias box. For this example we will use WebSyncExercise. Enter a path for the virtual directory to use in the Path box: `C:\Inetpub\wwwroot\WebSyncExercise`. Click Next.

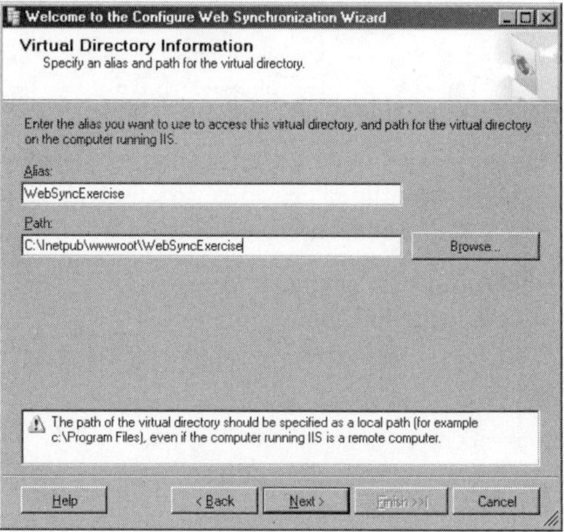

12. Two dialog boxes open and ask whether you want to create a new folder and to copy the SQL Server Isapi.dll. Click Yes to both.

13. On the Authenticated Access window, clear all boxes except Basic Authentication. Enter the domain of the IIS server in the Default domain box. Click Next.

14. On the Directory Access page click Add. Then add the accounts that *subscribers* will use to make connections to the IIS server. You *must* specify these account(s) on the Web Server Information page on the New Subscription Wizard when you run it. Click OK and then click Next.

15. Now enter the network path of the snapshot share you created when setting up the snapshot publication at the beginning of the chapter (e.g., `\\SERVER\repldata`). Click Next.

16. Review your options and click Finish.

17. Next, configure the [AdventureWorks].MergeExercise publication to allow web synchronization by right-clicking on the publication and selecting Properties from the pop-up menu. On the FTP Snapshot and Internet page, check the box next to "Allow Subscribers to synchronize by connecting to a Web server." Enter the address of the Web server to which subscribers should connect. Click OK.

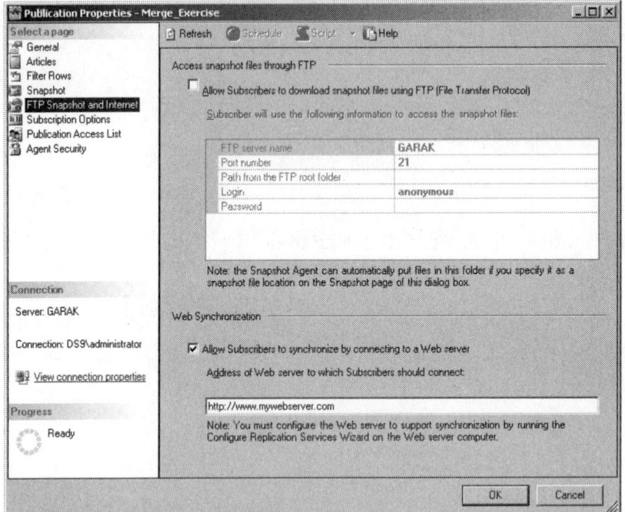

18. Configure a pull subscription to use web synchronization by running the New Subscription Wizard. Follow the steps outlined previously for the pull subscription under the section above labeled "Creating a Merge Subscription" until you come to the Web Synchronization page.

19. On the Web Synchronization page mark the check box next to Use Web Synchronization (in this example we are using SECOND).

20. On the Web Server Information page, accept the default address used on the publisher or enter the FQDN of another server. You can only choose the type of authentication that was enabled on the IIS server through either the Configure Web Synchronization Wizard or IIS Manager. Microsoft recommends using Basic Authentication. SSL is required for both types. Click Next and complete the wizard.

NOTE It is recommended that the subscription type be set to client for a web synchronized subscription.

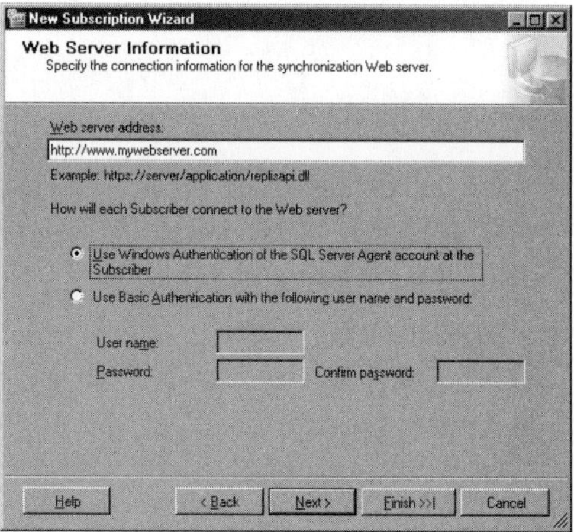

Congratulations, you have now successfully configured a merge publication for web synchronization with a pull subscription. Take a break, you earned it.

Whew! That was a lot of information, but with it, you are ready to get your databases next to your users by using replication.

Summary

We covered a lot of ground in this chapter. You learned all of the terminology and components necessary to run replication and the mechanics of setting it up.

First, you learned what replication is for—getting data next to your users. This may be necessary because the users are too far away from the data, they need their own copy for reporting purposes, or a variety of reasons that we didn't even consider.

Next, we covered the terminology you need to know to get replication running. The publisher/subscriber metaphor was used to describe how replication works. The publisher contains the original copy of the data; the subscriber receives a copy of the data; and the distributor is used to collect the changes from the publisher and copy them to the subscriber.

There are several types of replication available; which one you use depends on a few factors: latency, autonomy, and consistency. You need to decide how fast, how often, and how accurate the subscribers need copies of the data before you can choose a type, and then you can select from transactional, merge, or snapshot replication. You can also configure transactional publications to use updatable subscriptions, which allow for greater autonomy.

Next we hashed out the mechanics of actually setting up all three primary types of replication: snapshot, transactional (including standard and with updatable subscriptions), and merge. After that, we looked into the uses and mechanics of Replication Monitor. Lastly we took a broad overview of the role of web synchronization in replication.

Now we are ready to discuss the online analytical processing (OLAP) services that come with SQL Server 2000.

Chapter 26

Analysis Services

Most of this book has focused on getting data into a SQL Server database and then later getting the same data out of the database. You might create, for example, an application that takes sales orders from customers. Later on you could run queries to retrieve the orders and fulfill them. This pattern of activity, where individual actions deal with small pieces of the database, is sometimes called online transaction processing, or OLTP.

However, databases have another use, particularly after they collect a lot of data. Suppose your organization has taken 10 million sales orders and you want to look for patterns in the data. Perhaps people in Maine tend to buy more products in blue packages. That's a fact that you could use to your marketing advantage, if only you knew about it.

This sort of high-level aggregation of data, looking for patterns and summarizing what's in a database, is called *online analytical processing*, or OLAP. Microsoft SQL Server 2005 includes a separate program called Microsoft SQL Server 2005 Analysis Services. Analysis Services makes it possible to perform OLAP-based analysis on SQL Server and other OLE DB databases.

In this chapter, you'll learn the basic concepts of OLAP and then see how it's implemented in Analysis Services. We'll also show you how to use OLAP from a client application to help retrieve aggregated information on your data.

NOTE We don't try to cover all the details of Analysis Services or Analysis Server in this book. This chapter provides an introduction to this complex product; for more details, you should refer to Books Online and to the excellent set of tutorials included with the product.

Understanding OLAP

The basic idea of OLAP is fairly simple. Suppose you have a *lot* of data—say, 10 billion rows of Web site tracking information, with the users' IP addresses, what they clicked, when they clicked it, which browser they were using, and so on. Now suppose you want to know how many people clicked a particular banner ad during March and April of 2005. You *could* write a fairly simple query to get the information you want. The catch is that it would probably take a very long time for SQL Server to churn through all that information.

And what if the data was not in a single SQL Server table, but scattered around various databases throughout your organization? Distributed heterogeneous queries are neat, but even slower.

What if, after seeing the monthly numbers, you wanted to drill down to weekly or daily numbers? That would be even more time consuming and require writing even more queries.

That's where OLAP comes in. The basic idea is to trade off increased storage space now for speed of querying later. SQL Server 2005 includes within it Microsoft SQL Server 2005 Analysis Services, which is designed to make this trade-off.

One additional note, even though OLAP is closely associated with data warehousing, they are not the same. Data warehouses, that is, databases that are deliberately structured to be queried and analyzed, do employ similar techniques and employ similar terminology but that resemblance should not be mistaken for being the same. For example OLAP techniques can be directly applied to operational data. Similarly data warehouses can be used without an OLAP implementation.

Later in the chapter, you'll see how you can use Analysis Services to extract summary information from your data. First, though, you need to familiarize yourself with a new vocabulary.

Analysis Services Terminology

In this section, we'll introduce you to the key concepts and terms of Analysis Services. These include:

- Cube
- Dimension
- Measure
- Fact table
- Dimension table
- Level
- MOLAP
- ROLAP
- HOLAP
- Partition
- Virtual cube

Cubes and Their Parts

The basic unit of storage and analysis in Analysis Services is the cube. A *cube* is a collection of data that's been aggregated along multiple dimensions to make querying happen quickly. For example, a cube of sales data might be aggregated along a store's dimension and a customer's dimension, making the cube fast when you ask questions concerning sales by store or sales to a class of customer.

Cubes are ordered into dimensions and measures. *Dimensions* come from dimension tables, while *measures* come from fact tables.

A *dimension table* contains hierarchical data by which you'd like to summarize. Examples would be a customer table, which you could group by country, state, and city; or an orders table, where you might want to group detail information by year, month, week, and day of receipt.

Each cube has one or more dimensions, each based on one or more dimension tables. A dimension represents a category for analyzing business data: geographical region or time in the examples above. Typically, a dimension has a natural hierarchy so that lower results can be rolled up into higher results: cities aggregated into states, or state totals into country totals. Each type of summary that can be retrieved from a single dimension is called a *level*, so you speak of a city level or a state level in a geographic dimension.

A *fact table* contains the basic information that you wish to summarize. This might be order detail information, payroll records, batting averages, or anything else that's amenable to summing and averaging. Any table that you've used with a Sum or Avg function in a totals query is a good bet to be a fact table.

Each cube can contain one or more measures, each based on a column in a fact table (or a calculated expression), that you'd like to analyze. A cube containing batting average data would let you look at total hits for two particular teams over three consecutive years, for example.

Of course, fact tables and dimension tables are related, which is hardly surprising, given that you use the dimension tables to group information from the fact table. There are two basic OLAP schemas for relating these tables. In a *star schema*, every dimension table is related directly to the fact table. In a *snowflake schema*, some dimension tables are related indirectly to the fact table. For example, if your cube includes tblOrderDetails as a fact table, with tblCustomers and tblOrders as dimension tables, and tblCustomers is related to tblOrders, which in turn is related to tblOrderDetails, then you're dealing with a snowflake schema.

NOTE There are additional schema types besides the star and snowflake schemas, including parent-child schemas and data-mining schemas. However, the star and snowflake schemas are the most common types in normal cubes.

MOLAP, ROLAP, and HOLAP

Analysis Services offers three different ways to make the trade-off between size and speed: multidimensional OLAP (MOLAP), relational OLAP (ROLAP), and hybrid OLAP (HOLAP) storage settings.

MOLAP copies all of the data and all of the aggregates to the analysis server, where they are stored in an optimized multidimensional format. MOLAP gives the best query performance of the three types, because everything is right there when it's queried. On the other hand, it also takes up the most space and requires the most time to prepare. MOLAP has five subtypes: low latency, medium latency, scheduled, automatic, and standard. Differences among them relate to the relative value each type places on between query performance and the availability of the most current data.

ROLAP storage leaves the original data in the relational tables where it's already stored. ROLAP uses a separate set of relational tables to store and retrieve the aggregate data that the server uses to calculate cubes. ROLAP is the best bet for large data sets that are infrequently queried, because it minimizes up-front processing time and storage requirements.

HOLAP, as you might guess, is a hybrid of these two approaches. The original data remains in relational tables, but aggregations are stored on the server in the optimized multidimensional format. HOLAP is intermediate between ROLAP and MOLAP in speed and storage requirements.

Partitions and Virtual Cubes

You can divide a single cube into multiple *partitions*. Different partitions can be stored in different ways. In fact it is good practice to configure storage differently for different partitions in a large measure group. For example, you might store geographic dimensions in ROLAP format and time dimensions in a MOLAP format in the same cube. The partitions of a single cube do not even need to be stored on a single server, so you can take older or less frequently used data and move it to a separate server.

Just as partitions are a subset of cubes, *virtual cubes* are a superset of cubes. Virtual cubes let you retrieve information across multiple cubes. For example, if you have a cube of batting information and a cube of pitching information, you could build a virtual cube that would let you analyze the effects of pitching statistics on batting averages.

Using Analysis Services

In this section, we'll look at the actual steps involved in using SQL Server 2005 Analysis Services to analyze your data. To do this, we'll use the AdventureWorks Data Warehouse (DW) sample data that ships with SQL Server 2005.

Business Intelligence Development Studio

As you learned earlier in Chapter 22, Business Intelligence Development Studio (BIDS) is a useful tool for building Analysis Services Solutions and Projects, (as well as other types of projects and solutions).

BIDS comes with two pre-existing Analysis Services related templates, as shown in Figure 26.1, Analysis Services Project and Import Analysis Services 9.0 Database Wizard. The latter allows you to read the contents of an existing Analysis Services database and create a project based on it.

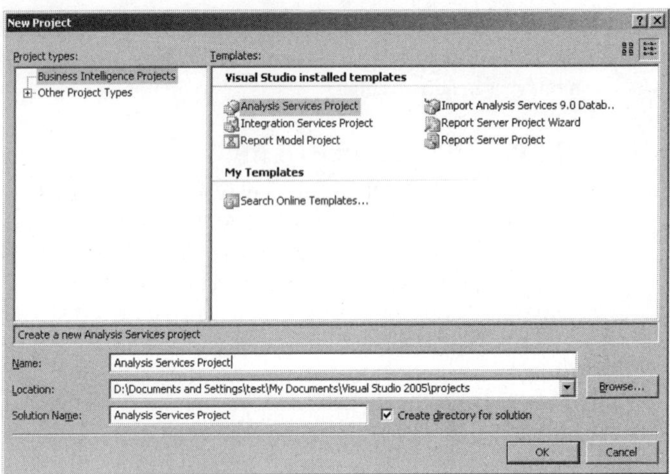

FIGURE 26.1 Business Intelligence Development Studio New Projects pane.

Management Studio

Before moving on to adding a database, let's take a brief overview of the role that Management Studio plays in Analysis Services. As previously mentioned, BIDS is designed for developing applications in the form or solutions and projects, and constructs such as cubes, dimensions and data sources.

Management Studio, on the other hand, is actually designed for the administration and development of database objects. In terms of Analysis Services, Management Studio's function is to administer and configure existing objects. Similarly it is used when you are applying a solution that uses SQL Server database objects. In other words, as a rule of thumb in Analysis Services, you use BIDS to create and develop and Management Studio to administer.

Like all rules of thumb the above is not quite accurate since both Management Studio and BIDS provide projects organized into solutions. In Management Studio these Analysis Services activities are saved as Analysis Server scripts, while in BIDS they are saved as Analysis Server projects. You should open any project with the same tool that created it.

Creating an Analysis Services Project

Finally let's get down to business and open BIDS to create a new Analysis Services project. The project we're going to create is based on the AdventureWorks Data Warehouse (DW) sample database that ships with SQL Server 2005. We'll also be using the standard project template for Analysis Services to create this project. So get out your pencils and let's go build ourselves something.

1. Click Start ➢ All Programs ➢ Microsoft SQL Server 2005 ➢ Business Intelligence Development Studio to open it. Note that the default view is, from left to right, a tab for the Toolbox, an open space for the Designer/Code Window; Solution Explorer, and the Properties windows.

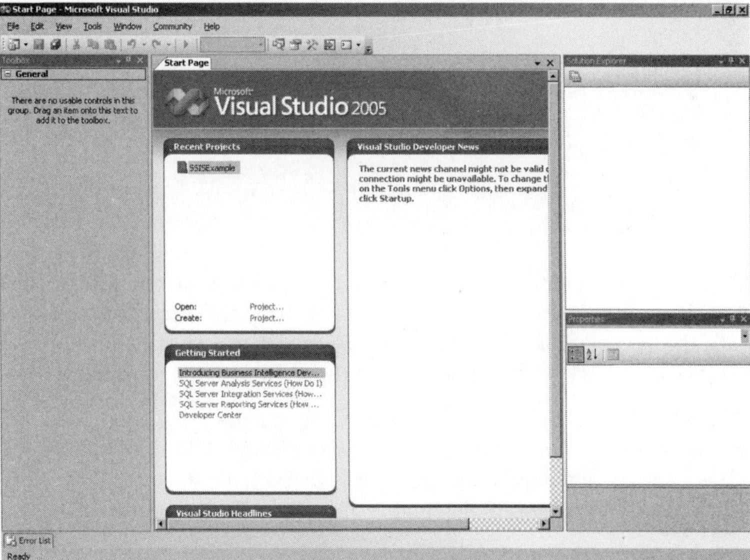

2. Select File menu ➢ New ➢ Project.

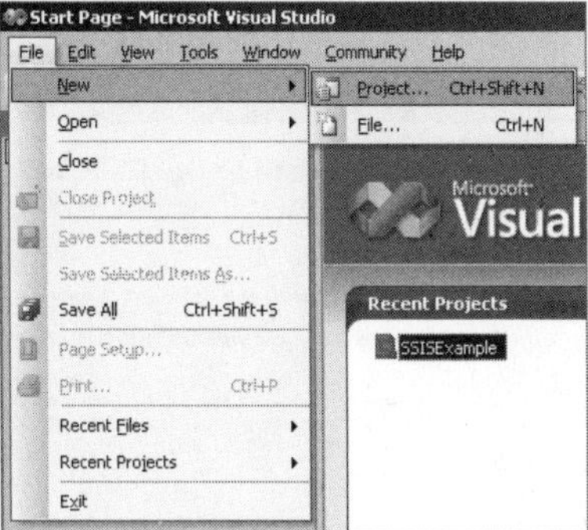

3. As mentioned above, BIDS has templates for a number of different project types from preconfigured templates. Highlight the Analysis Services Project template and name it

AdventureWorksExercise (note this changes the Solution name as well). Accept the default location and click OK.

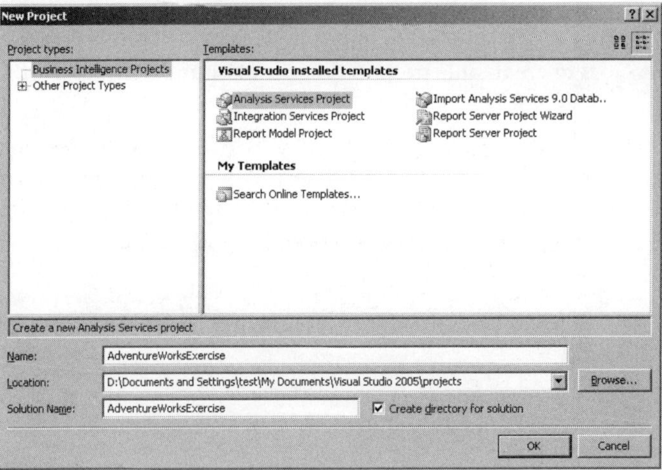

4. After a few moments, the view returns to BIDS but now you will see that Solution Explorer contains the AdventureWorksExercise Solution. The solution contains the project AdventureWorksExercise. However, as you probably have noticed, the eight folders of the project are empty—what's a project without data? Time to go get some.

5. The first step is to define the data source that will be used to extract data and metadata. For this exercise you will be using the AdventureWorksDW database. This database should already be present in your instance of SQL Server. If not, you will have to use the installation procedure to add the sample database to your SQL Server instance.

NOTE In more elaborate projects you will probably define multiple data sources.

6. In Solution Explorer, right-click the Data Sources folder and select New Data Source to start the Data Source Wizard.

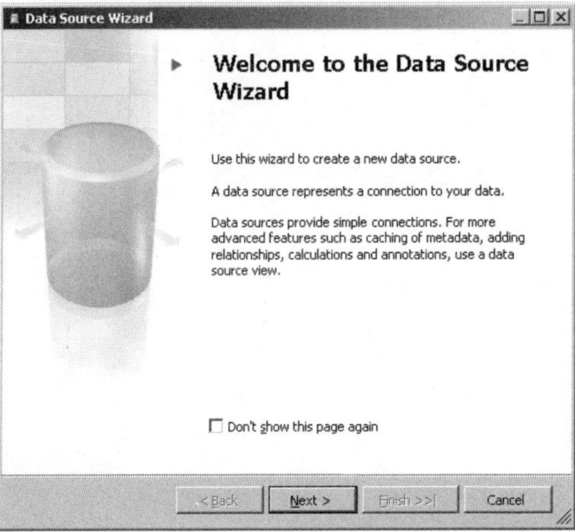

7. Click Next. On the "Select how to define the connection" page you are asked to define the data source based on an existing or new connection. Alternatively you can define a data source based on a previously defined data source in the current solution. You can also select one from another Analysis Services project if you desire. Click New to open the Connection Manager dialog box.

8. In the Provider list box, select SQLClient Data Provider. In the Select Or Enter A Server Name list box type **`localhost`**. Then select the radio button next to Use Windows Authentication. In Item 3, Select Or Enter A Database Name, select AdventureWorksDW from the drop-down list. Click OK.

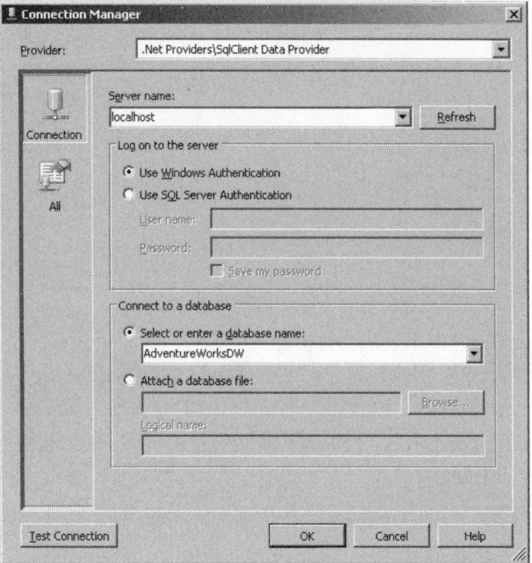

9. Click Next to move to the Impersonation Information page. Specify the credentials that will be used to connect to the data source.

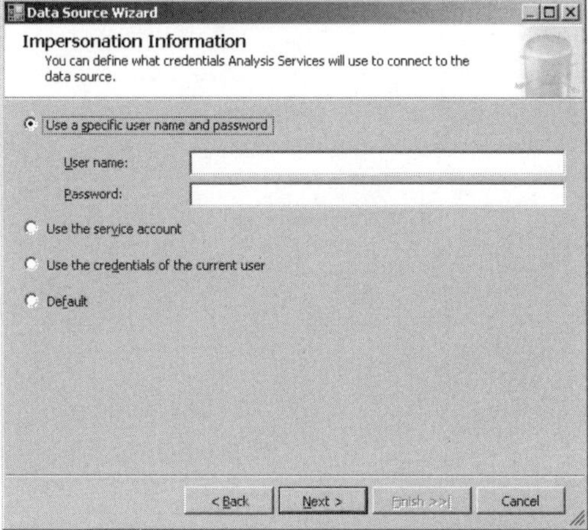

10. Click Finish to open the Completing the Wizard page. Confirm the settings are as you want them and then click Finish to create the new data source. Notice that the new data source appears in the Data Sources folder of the AdventureWorks Exercise. An icon with four blue arrows pointing outward from a database symbol is used to indicate a data source.

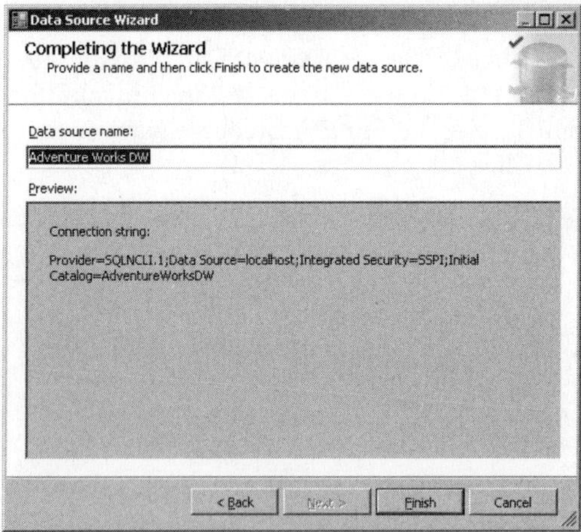

11. Now that you've defined a data source, the next step in the process is to define a data source view. A data source view provides a single unified view of the metadata; this view is then used by a variety of tools and applications to access the data. Right-click the Data Source Views folder and select New Data Source view to launch the Data Source View Wizard. Click Next.

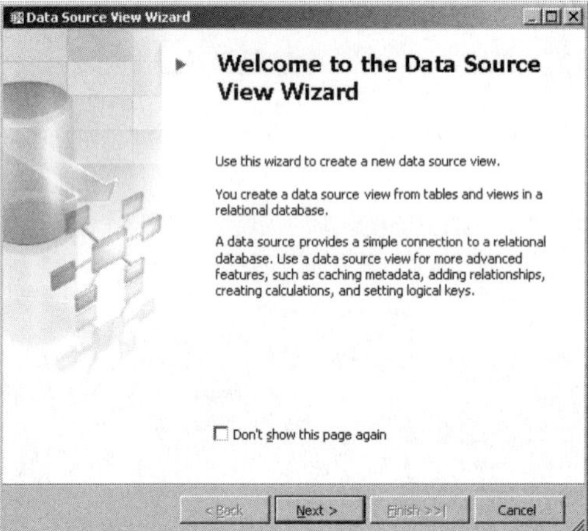

12. In the Select a Data Source window, select Adventure Works DW. Note that you can also launch the Data Source Wizard form this window by clicking the New Data Source button. Click Next.

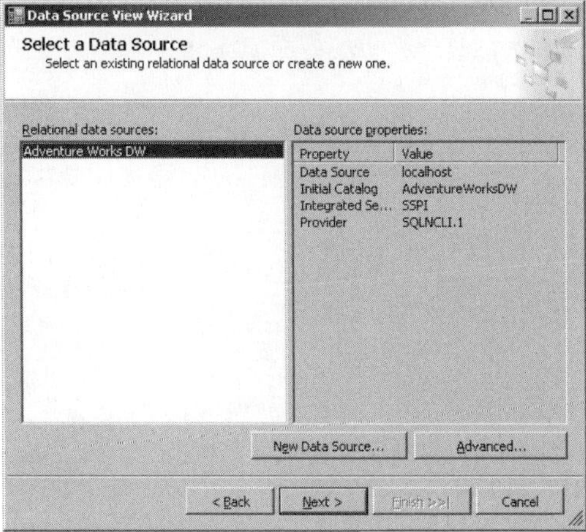

13. In the Select Tables and Views page, select the FactInternetSales table and click the > button. Then select the Add Related Tables button to also include all the tables with a relationship to FactFinance. Normally you might be more selective or apply the filters, but let's make this exercise an easy one. Click Next.

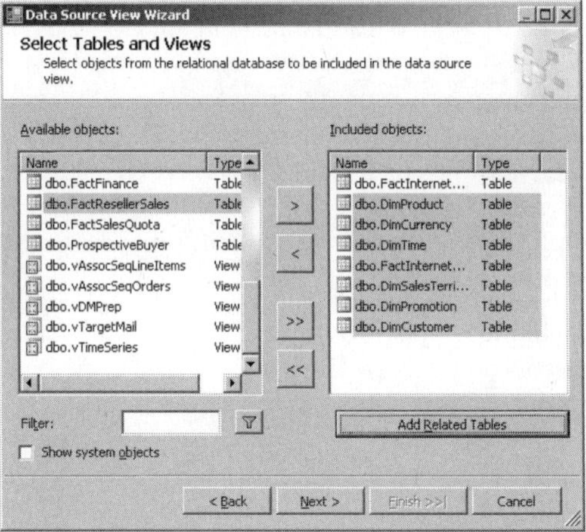

14. On the Completing the Wizard page, you are given the option to provide a name for the view and to review your other selections. Accept the default name and click Finish to complete the wizard. Notice that the Solution Explorer is now populated with a file in the Data Source folder. Notice also that the Designer Window is now populated with a diagram of the

data source, a list of tables. A new Diagram Organizer pane allows you to create new diagrams of the relationships among tables.

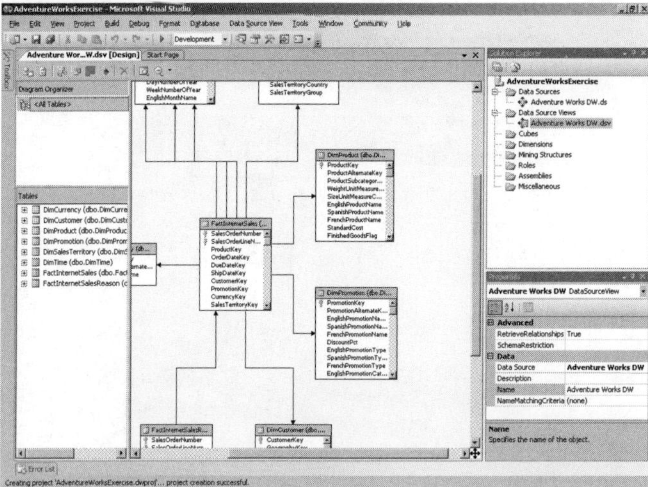

Congratulations! You have successfully added a data source and a data source view based on the AdventureWorks DW.

Creating a Cube

After you've created the data source and data source view, the next step is to define an Analysis Services cube based on the data source view. There are two ways to define a cube. The first is to define the dimensions independent of any cube and, once that has been done, define a cube (or more than one cube) based on those dimensions.

The second manner, and the one used here, is to create the cube, defining it and its dimensions by using the Cube Wizard. This is the preferred method for simple cubes. You would follow the first method for complex applications involving multiple cubes that contain a large number of different database dimensions.

1. In the Solution Explorer window, right-click the Cubes folder under the AdventureWorksExercise project and select New Cube, to open the Cube Wizard.

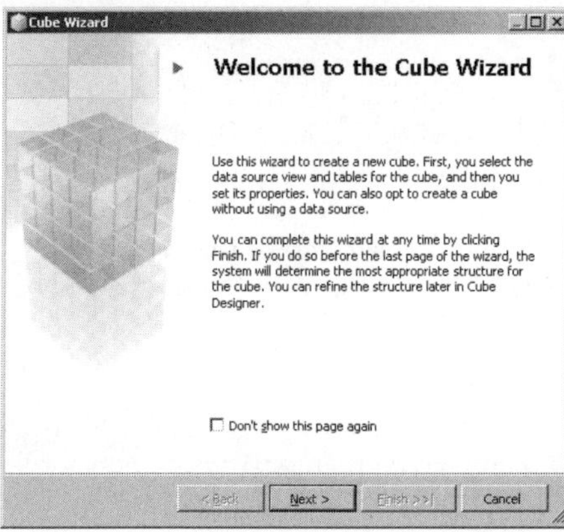

2. Click Next to open the Select Build Method window. Note that the default value is to build the cube with a data source. Ensure that the "Auto Build" check box is marked and that "Create attributes and hierarchies" appears in the drop-down list.

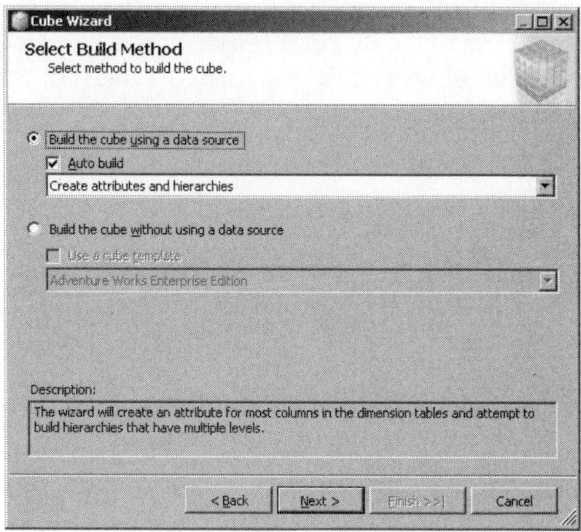

3. Click Next. On the Select Data Source View page, you can see the Adventure Works DW data source view. If multiple data source views been created, they would also have appeared here, but since only one was created, select the Adventure Works DW. Clicking Finish here causes the wizard to define the cube with the assistance of Auto Build. For now though we will click Next in order to view and make any necessary changes to IntelliCube's selections.

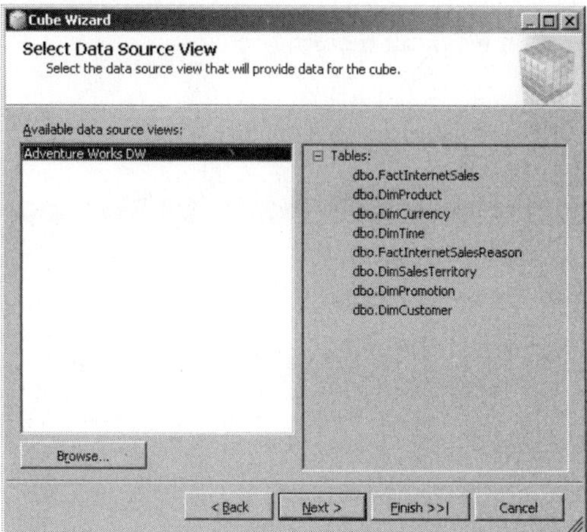

4. Clicking Next opens the Detecting Fact and Dimensions Table. Cube Wizard does a scan of the tables in the data source view to identify the fact and dimension tables.

5. Click Next. The Identify Fact and Dimension Tables window shows the selection of fact and dimension tables as determined by IntelliCube. In this case it has identified two of the tables as a fact table and the remaining as dimension tables. Fact tables contain the measures you are interested in. Dimensions contain the information about the measures. For example, a

fact table might have the number of houses available, while a dimensions table would contain the number of rooms or the color of the house. You can override these selections, although this is rarely necessary. Every fact and dimension table must have a relationship between them or you will receive an error. It's also possible for a table to be both a fact and a dimension table. Finally, you can specify a time dimension table, and use it to associate time properties with columns in the designated dimension table. This association is required for time-based MDX calculations (e.g., YTD).

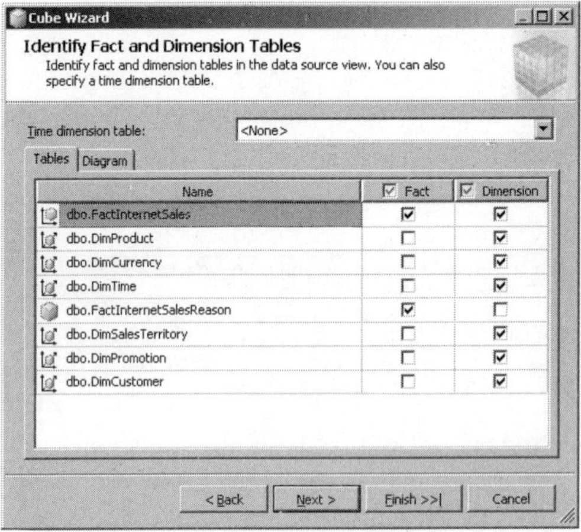

6. Click Next to move to the Select Measures window. Here you select those columns within the fact table that contain the data to be aggregated. These columns must be numeric for this exercise to accept the default measures.

WARNING You should not choose any of the foreign keys in the table as measures; these fields will be used to relate the fact table to the dimension tables.

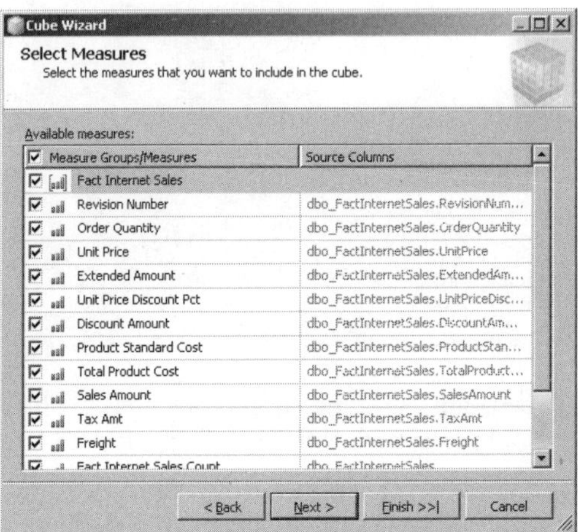

7. Click Next to open the Detecting Hierarchies window. On this page, IntelliCube scans the dimensions and detects the hierarchies by sampling records in each column to establish if a many-to-one (hierarchical) relationship exists among them.

8. Click Next. The Review New Dimensions page appears, showing the structures of the detected dimensions. You can expand the dimension nodes to reveal attributes and hierarchies nodes, which you can also expand. If necessary, you can expand the nodes and clear the check boxes to remove columns from the dimension.

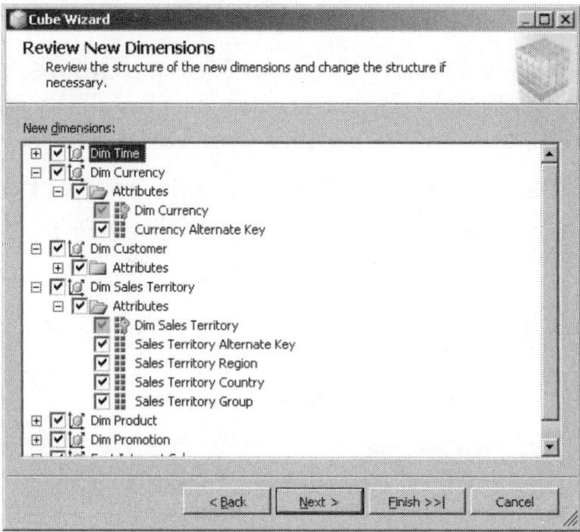

9. Click Next. On the Completing the Wizard page, you can review the dimensions, measures, measure groups, hierarchies, and attributes in the Preview pane.

10. Click Finish to create the cube. The new cube appears in the Cubes folder and related dimensions appear in the Dimensions folder of the AdventureWorksExercise project. Also the cube appears in the cube designer window. You should also notice that the data source view designer is still open on another tab in BIDS.

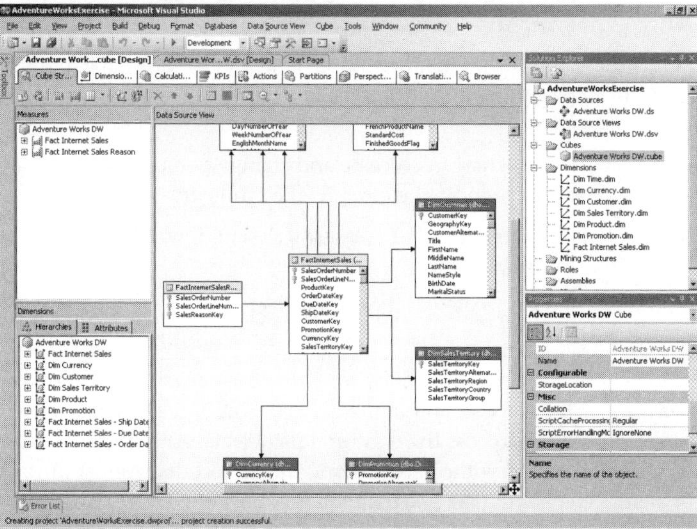

Using Cube Designer

The Cube Designer tool provides you with the ability to edit and modify the properties of a cube. As you can see in Figure 26.2 the Cube Designer comes with nine tabs that provide you with different view of the cube as follows:

Cube Structure View is used to modify the architecture of the cube.

Dimension Usage View is used to define the relationships and granularity between dimensions and groups. This is valuable with multiple fact tables where you may have to specify whether measures apply to one or more dimensions.

If you select a dimensions table listed under Measure Groups and click on the ellipsis button, you can define the relationship type and select the granularity attribute. Clicking the Advanced key on the Define Relationship page allows you edit bindings.

Note that right-clicking any object opens a pop-up menu from which you can add Cube Dimension, define Default Relationship, create a New Linked Object, and open the Properties sheet, as well as cut, copy, paste, delete, and rename actions.

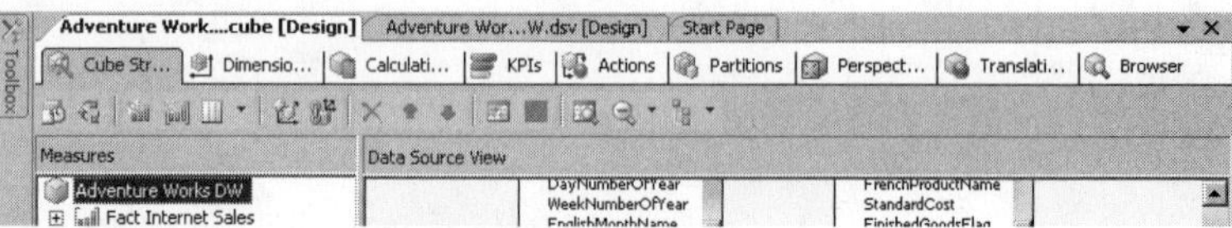

FIGURE 26.2 Cube Designer comes with nine tabs, providing different views.

Calculations View is used to create new calculations, reorder and review existing calculations, and do a step-by-step debug of the any calculations. You can also use this view to define members and measures based on existing values.

KPIs View (Key Performance Indicators) is where you can create or modify KPIs in the selected cube. KPIs determine information about a value, such as whether the defined value exceeds or falls short of a goal or whether a trending is improving or worsening for a value.

Actions View is used to create or edit actions such as drill through or reporting. An action is anything that provides client applications with context-sensitive information, commands, and end user accessible reports.

Partitions View allow you to store parts of cube in different locations with differing properties such as an aggregation definition. The Partitions View is used to create or edit partitions for the selected cube.

Perspectives View is where you create and change perspectives—which are a defined subset of a cube that basically reduces the perceived complexity of the cube.

Translations View manages (and creates) translated names for cube objects. Examples include month or product names.

Browser View is used to view data in the selected cube.

Deploying a Cube

The only way you can view the data in the new cube and its objects is to deploy the project to an Analysis Server and then process the cube and its objects. Although it is true that a lot of the cube and metadata can be edited without deploying the project or establishing a connection to an Analysis Server, being able to actually see the data is extremely helpful in editing it. For example you may want to view the sorted data in a dimensions table to determine whether you need to make changes to the sort order or apply other parameters.

Deploying a cube is very simple. In Solution Explorer right-click the AdventureWorksExercise project. In the pop-up menu select Deploy. The Output Window opens and displays the instructions, while the Deployment Progress window, as shown in Figure 26.3, offers a detailed description of the deployment.

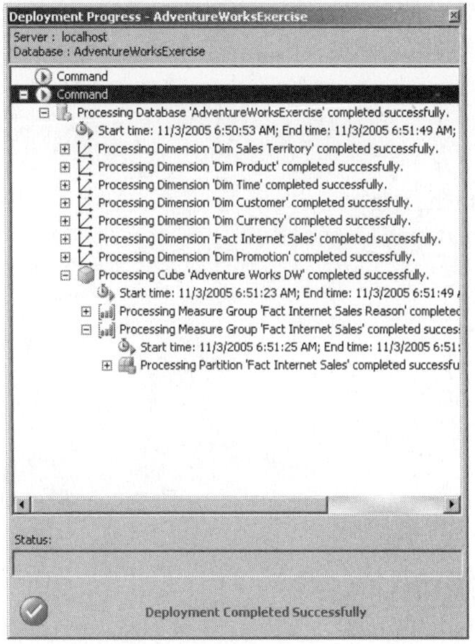

FIGURE 26.3
The Deployment Progress window shows a detailed description of actions taken during deployment.

Processing a Cube

So far you've created a simple cube and deployed it. Now you're ready to process the cube. Processing a cube makes Analysis Services create the precalculated aggregations that hold the data from the cube. Basically when you tell Analysis Services to process a cube, you are asking it to process some or all of the partitions within all of the measure groups of the selected cube—and of course any unprocessed dimensions that are participating in the cube. To process a cube simply right-click it in Solution Explorer and select Process. (You can also right-click the cube in Analysis Server under Management Studio.)

The Process Cube page will open. You are asked to select the Object, Type, and Process Option, which define the method you are going to use.

If you're creating the cube for the first time you should choose Process Full. Other options include:

- Process Default
- Process Data
- Process Structure
- Process Index
- Process Incremental
- Unprocess

Note that Process Incremental is exactly the same as Process Full when applied to an unprocessed partition.

When you click Run, the cube processing begins and displays a status window, Process Progress (Figure 26.4), which shows exactly what steps the processing is taking. When the process is finished, you can close this window and the Process Cube page to return to BIDS.

FIGURE 26.4
Processing a cube

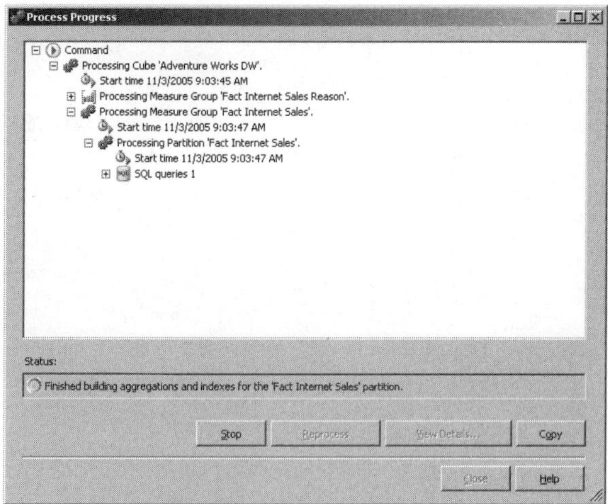

Browsing the Cube

After the cube has been processed, you can finally use it to analyze data. Remember, that's why you created the cube in the first place. From within BIDS a cube's data can be viewed in several ways, but for now let's make it simple:

1. Select the cube in the Cubes folder of Solution Explorer, right-click and select Browse from the pop-up menu, which opens the Browser windows in Cube Designer.

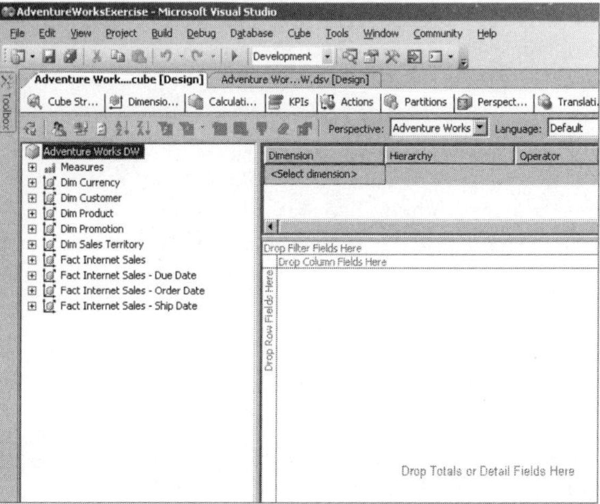

2. In the leftmost pane (called the Metadata pane), expand the Measures folder, then the Fact Internet Sales folder. Then drag and drop the Sales Amount measure to the Drop Totals or Detail Fields Here area.

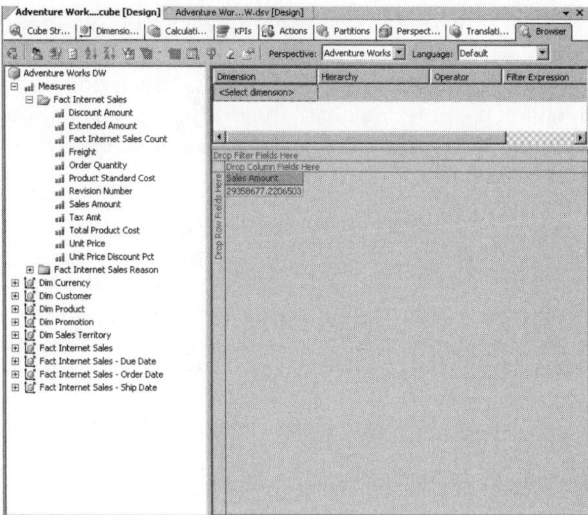

3. In the Metadata pane click on the Dim Currency dimension and expand it. Select the Dim Currency, then drag and drop it to the Drop Column Fields Here area. Now open the Dim Product dimension, expand it, select Model Name, then drag and drop in the Drop Row Fields Here area.

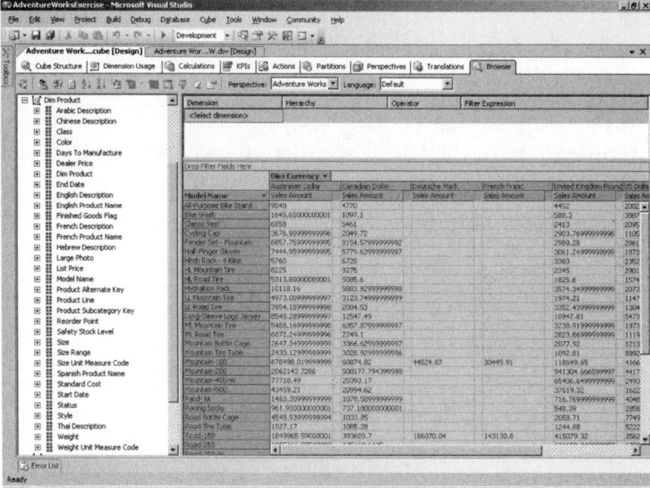

4. As you can see, you have a cross-tabulation of sales by item by currency. You can further manipulate the data:

   - To filter the data that is displayed, drag items to Drop Filter Fields Here.
   - Click the triangle to the right of the field name, and then clear the check boxes next to the levels and members that you do not want to display.

- Right-clicking the measure in the Drop Totals or Detail Fields Here provides you with other options for viewing the data. Selecting the Show As option also allows you specify both actual numbers and percentages.

As you can see, the cube browser is very flexible. This flexibility in turn demonstrates the flexibility of data cubes themselves. Any given piece of data in a cube—for example, the amount derived from sales of HL Mountain Tires in Australian dollars could have been derived from the original SQL Server database by writing a particular query. What Analysis Services does for you, though, is make the results of all similar queries available at one time, without additional processing.

Using Dimension Wizard

Creating dimensions is a common task in Analysis Services and there are a variety of ways to do so. One way, as you have seen, is by using Cube Wizard to quickly create all the dimensions in a cube when you create the cube. But what if you want to create a dimension at other times? The quickest and most painless way to create a dimension in BIDS is by using the Dimension Wizard.

There are several dimension-creating scenarios:

- A standard dimension based on an existing data source view
- A standard dimension without an existing data source view
- A time dimension based on a time dimension table
- A server time dimension based on a date range to create a dimension
- A linked dimension

In this chapter we'll look at how to create all of these.

CREATING A STANDARD DIMENSION USING AN EXISTING DATA SOURCE VIEW

1. In Solution Explorer, right-click the Dimensions folder and select New Dimension from the pop-up menu, to open the Dimension Wizard..

2. Click Next. In the Select Build Method window you are presented with the option to build the dimension either with or without a data source. Make sure the radio button next to "Build the dimension using a data source" is selected. Choosing this option means that the dimensions structure will be based on dimension tables, their columns, and any existing relations between columns in the table. Mark the check box "Auto Build" to create attributes columns in the dimension tables and build multiple level hierarchies. Accept the default value Create Attributes and Hierarchies and click Next.

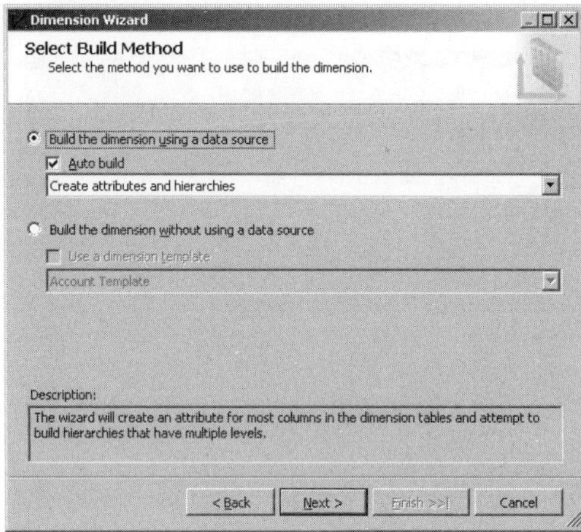

3. The next step is to specify the data source view to use. Select Adventure Works DW. To display schema for a data source view, click the Browse button.

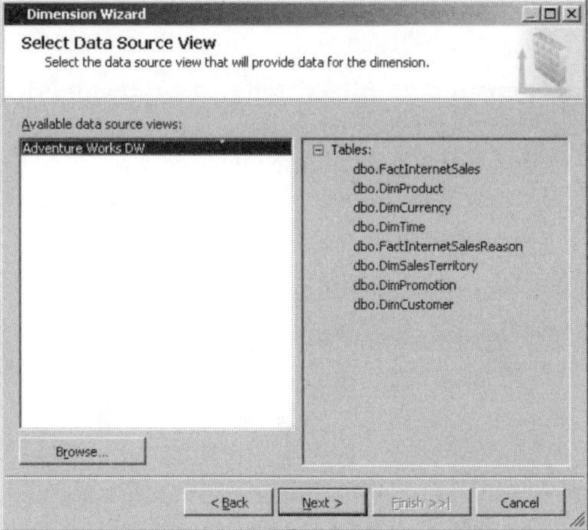

You can base a dimension table on five primary types of schema:

Star Schema Used when the dimension information is contained in a single table.

Snowflake Schema Used when the dimension information is spread across multiple tables. For instance, you might have a products table and a products_category table, and want to aggregate a dimension consisting of product and category.

Parent-Child Used when you have a table containing multiple levels of information, usually with a self-join. For example, you might have a regions table where each region can be related to a parent region in the same table.

Virtual Dimension Used when a dimension is based on properties of another dimension.

Mining Model Used to create a data-mining dimension using data prediction.

For the simple example in this chapter, the dimension is represented with a basic star schema, that is, the dimension consists of information from a single table related directly to the fact table.

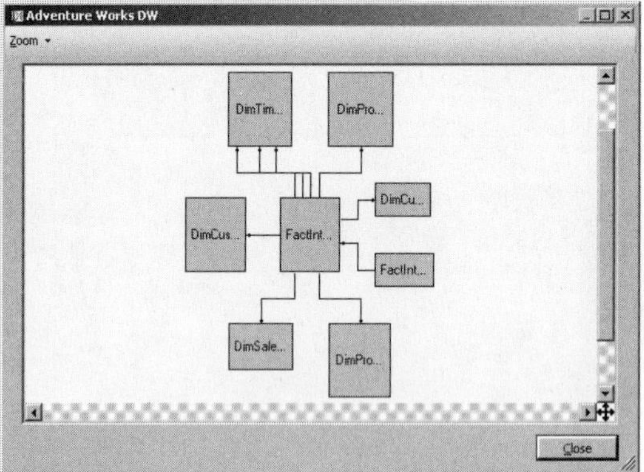

4. Click Next to go the Select the Dimension Type panel. Three types of dimensions are available:

   Standard Dimension A dimension that aggregates data according to anything other than time and date.

   Time Dimension A dimension that aggregates data by time and date based on the values in the table where the attributes are bound to the columns of a dimension tables.

   Server Time Dimension A dimension that aggregates data by time and date based on a range. The data for this type of dimension is created and stored on the server rather than coming from a table in the data source view. Attributes of this type of dimension have time attribute bindings that define the attributes according to specified time periods, for example months, week, days, or years.

   Select Standard Dimension and click Next.

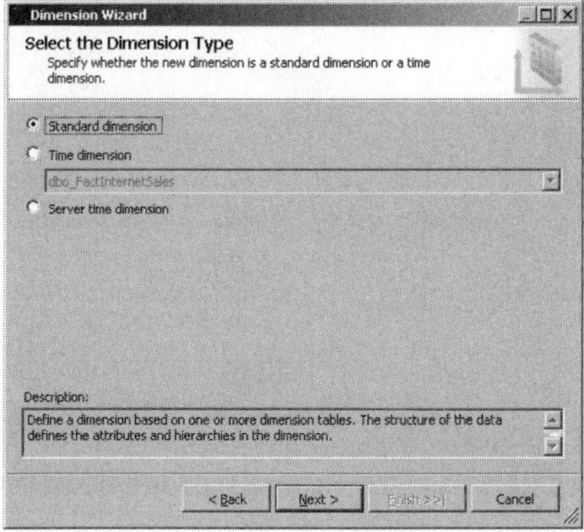

5. Clicking Next opens the Select the Main Dimension Table page. The records in the main table typically correspond to the leaf members of the dimension. For example, you would specify an employee table for an employees dimension. You will also specify one or more key columns that uniquely identify the main table records. For this exercise select dbo.FactInternetSales table and accept the designation of SalesOrderNumber and SalesOrderLineNumber as key columns.

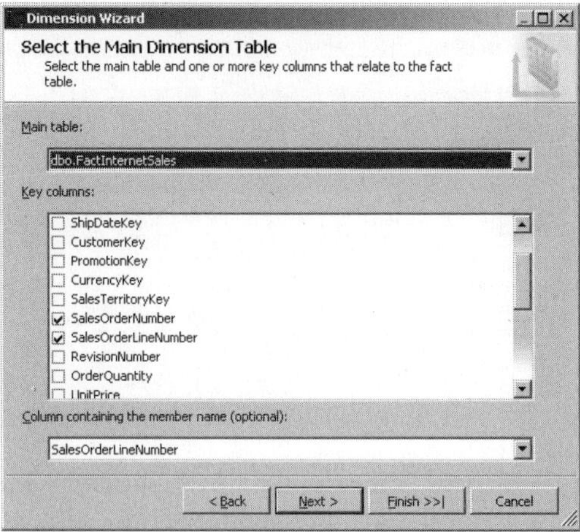

6. Click Next to open the Select Related Tables window. Here is where you can review the list of tables that are directly or indirectly related to the main dimension table. You can select which related table you wish to include in the schema for the dimension. Any selected table's columns can be added as attributes to the dimension. In this example select dbo .DimProduct and dbo.DimCustomer

7. After you select the related tables and click Next, you can choose the columns to use as dimension attributes. As you can see, every column in all of the selected tables is available for selection or removal from the dimension. For each attribute in the list you can also specify the name, the key column, and the name column. For this example, go through the list

and only leave the following attributes marked: English Product Name, Color, Model Name, English Description, First Name, Last Name, Marital Status, English Occupation, and Currency Name. Click Next.

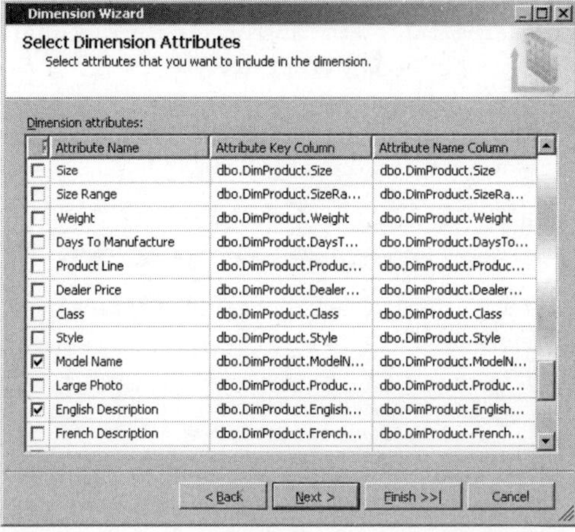

8. On the Specify Dimension Type page, you can specify the types of information contained by the dimension. You can also identify standard attributes for the specified dimension type. It also sets the Type property for the dimension and for any attributes you may identify as standard types for the dimension. Dimension types include:

   - Accounts
   - BillofMaterials
   - Channel
   - Currency
   - Customers
   - Geography
   - Organization
   - Products
   - Promotion
   - Quantitative
   - Rates
   - Regular
   - Scenario
   - Time

As you might expect this page can be a very powerful tool for customization of your table as well as a means of assigning standard attribute types for any existing dimensions. For this exercise, simply accept the default value of Regular and click Next.

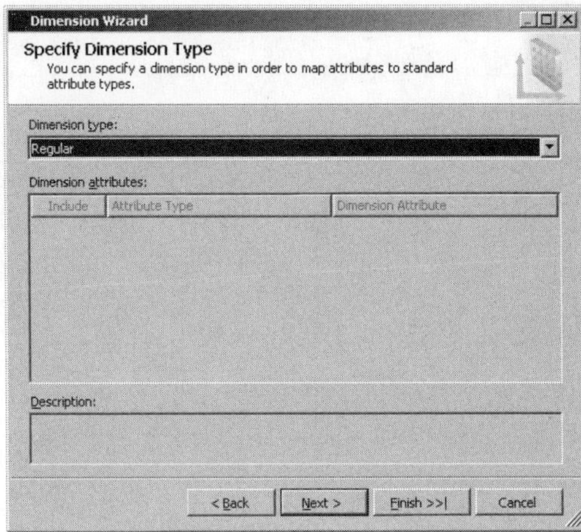

9. As soon as you open the Detecting Hierarchies window, Dimension Wizard scans the new dimension for relationships and creates any necessary hierarchies. In this simple example there are none, so click Next. On the Review New Hierarchies page, click Next.

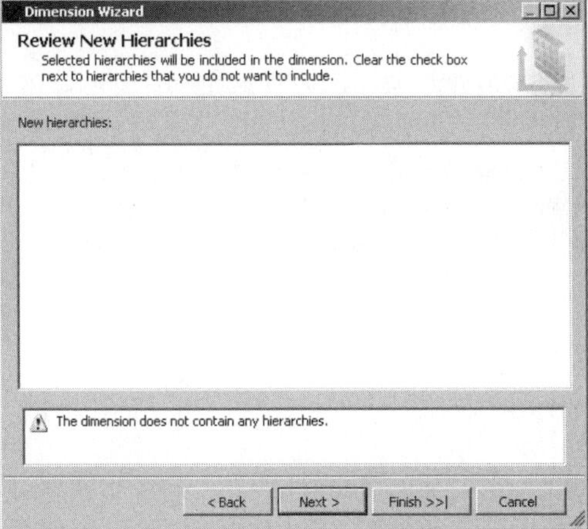

10. On the Completing the Wizard Page, rename the Dimension Dim AdventureWorksExercise and click Finish to complete the wizard and create the dimensions. While not required, it is good practice to preface the names of different table types with descriptive prefixes, such as

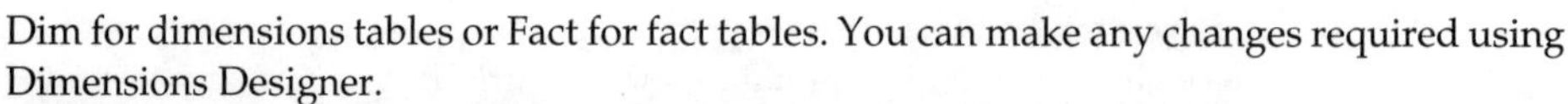

Dim for dimensions tables or Fact for fact tables. You can make any changes required using Dimensions Designer.

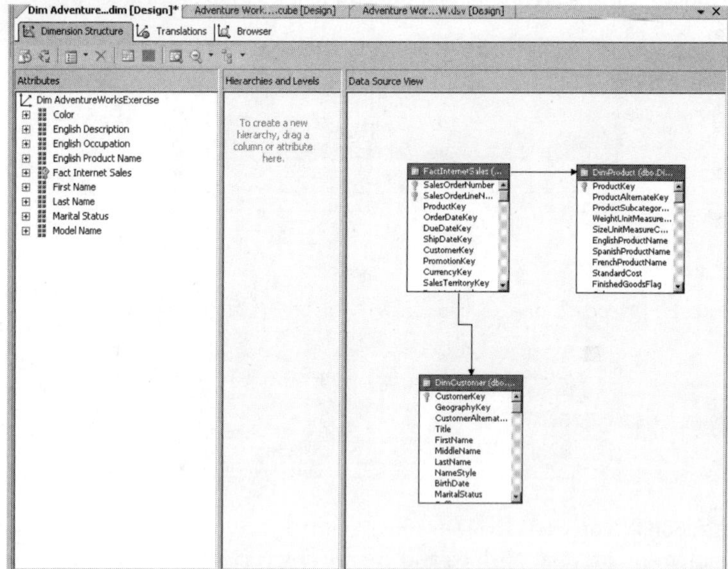

Creating a Standard Dimension without Using an Existing Data Source View

1. In Solution Explorer, right-click the Dimensions folder and select New Dimension from the pop-up menu to start the New Dimension Wizard.
2. Click Next. In the Select Build Method you are presented with the option to build the dimension either with or without using a data source. Mark the radio button next to "Build the dimension without using a data source." Selecting the "Use a dimension template" check box provides you access to several templates you can use to use to build common dimension types:
   - Account
   - Customer
   - Date
   - Department
   - Destination Currency
   - Employee
   - Geography
   - Internet Sales Order Detail
   - Organization
   - Product
   - Promotion
   - Reseller Sales Order Detail

- Reseller
- Sales Channel
- Sales Detail
- Sales Summary Order Details
- Sales Territory
- Scenario
- Source Currency
- Warehouse

For the purposes of this exercise, select the Customer Template.

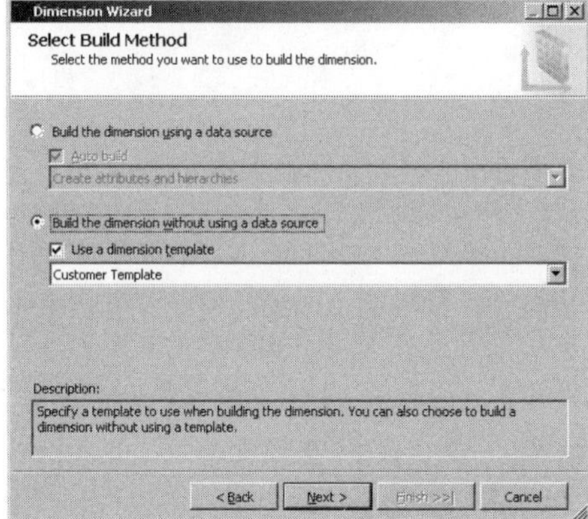

3. Click Next to go the Specify Dimension Type panel. The Dimension type is already grayed out because of your selection of the Customer Template in the previous step. From the list of typical dimension attributes, you can select the ones you want in your new dimension by marking or clearing the check box. You can edit the dimension attribute name by selecting it in the Dimension Attribute column. Accept all the defaults and click Next.

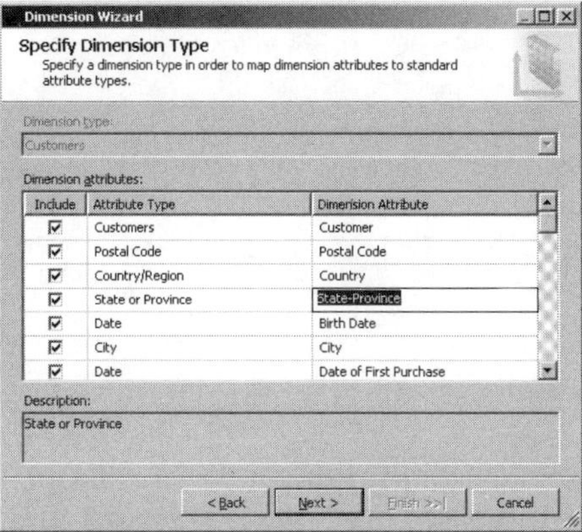

4. In the Specify Dimension Key and Type window, you designate the key attribute for the dimension. If you did not select any attributes to be included in the table, the wizard automatically creates a key attribute by combining the dimension name and "ID." For now, just accept the default key attribute Customer. You are also asked to specify whether this is a changing dimension. Members of a changing dimension move over time to different locations within the hierarchy. Selecting this box allows Analysis Services to track these changes. Leave the box unmarked and click Next.

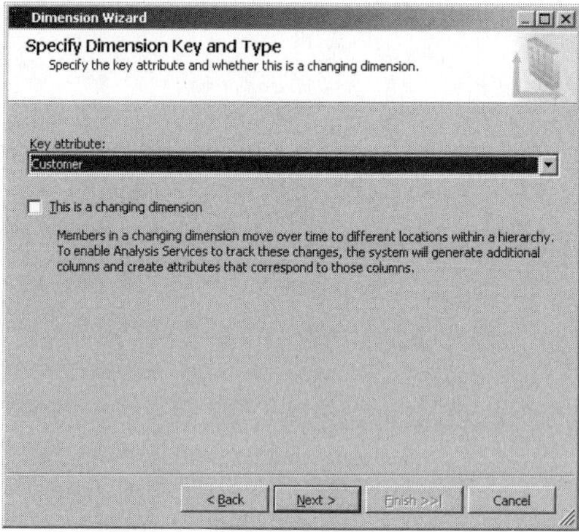

5. On the Completing the Wizard page, review the settings. Also rename the new table Dim CustomerExercise and then click Finish.

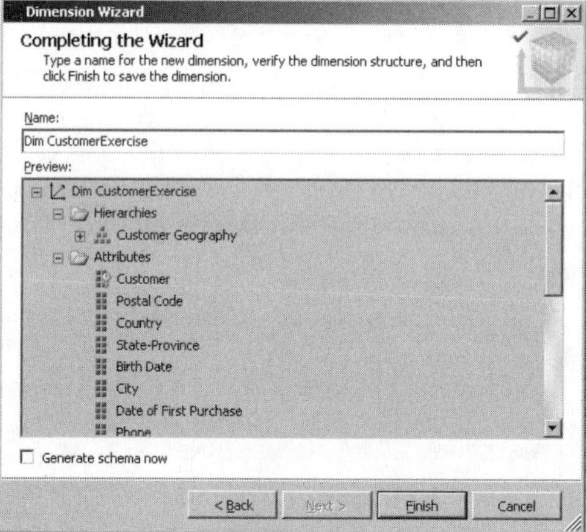

CREATING A TIME DIMENSION

As you learned above, a time dimension is based either on a table in the data source view or on a date range. That means its really is not much different from a standard dimension since its attributes are bound to columns of a dimension table just like any other standard dimension. A range-based time dimension is normally used when there is no separate time table to define time periods. In that case the attributes will have time-attribute bindings, which define the attributes according to specified time periods (such as years, months, weeks, and days). Because the data for a range-based time dimension is created and stored on the server rather than coming from any table in the data source, a range-based time dimension is called a server time dimension.

In this exercise we create a time dimension without using a data source view.

1. In Solution Explorer, right-click the Dimensions folder and select New Dimension from the pop-up menu to launch the Dimension Wizard. On the splash screen, click Next.
2. On the Select Build Method page, select "Build the dimension using a data source" radio button. Make sure the Auto Build check box is marked. Click Next.

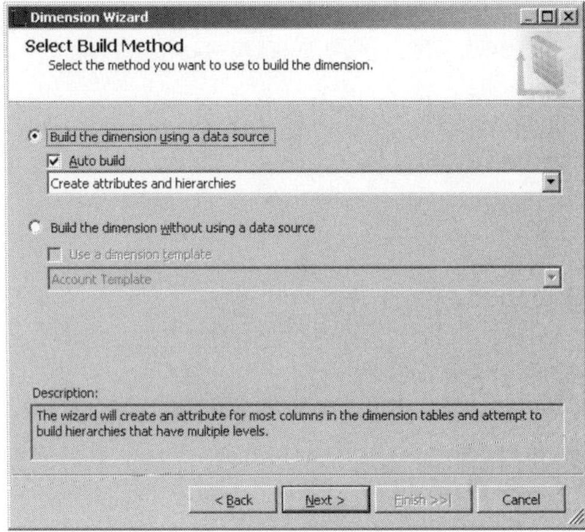

3. On the Select Data Source View page, select Adventure Works DW. Click Next.
4. On the Select the Dimension Type page, mark the radio button next to Time Dimension and select dbo_DimProduct.

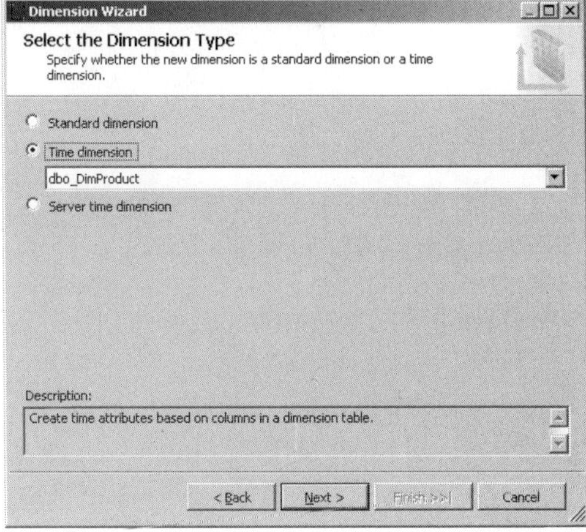

5. Click Next. Here you specify the columns that define the time period. Select Date and use the drop-down box to select StartDate. Select Undefined Time and use the drop down box to select EndDate. These associations that you establish are used by the wizard to recommend hierarchies and set the Type property for corresponding attributes in the new time dimension.

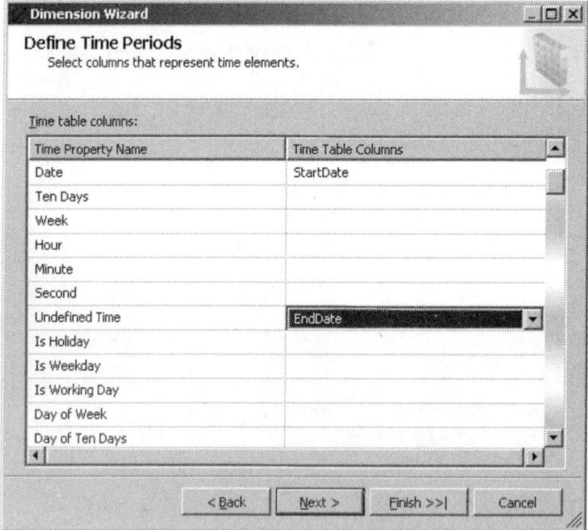

6. Click Next to move to the Review New Hierarchies page. Click Next.

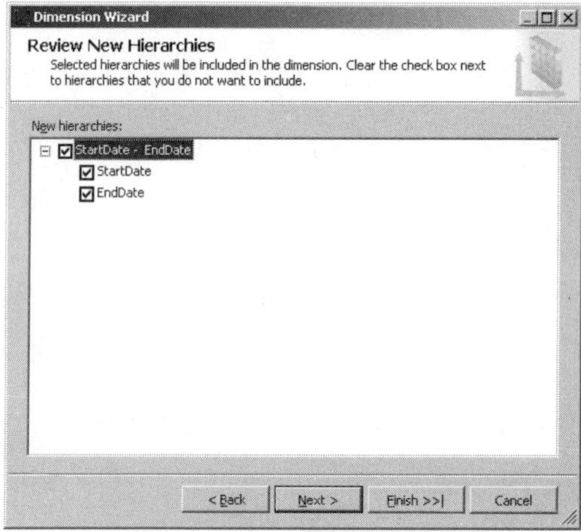

7. On the Finishing the Wizard page, name the time dimension Dim ProductExample and click Finish.

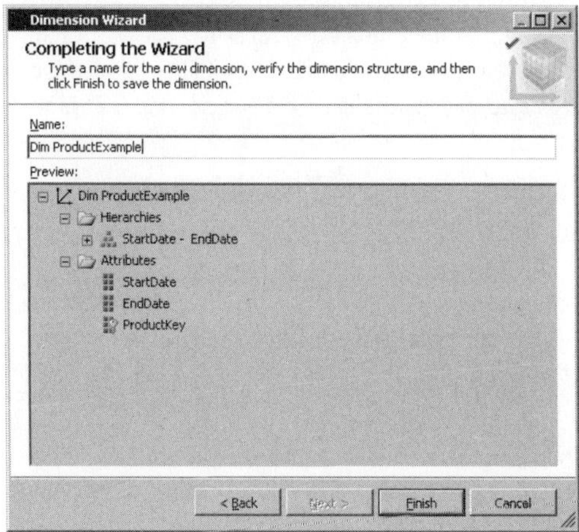

CREATING A SERVER TIME DIMENSION

You can create a time dimension without using a data source by creating either a standard time dimension or server time dimensions. The wizard follows similar steps for each type.

1. In Solution Explorer, right-click the Dimensions folder and select New Dimension from the pop-up menu. Click Next on the Dimension Wizard splash page.
2. On the Select Build Method page, select "Build the dimension without using a data source" radio button. Do not select the "Use a dimension template" button. Click Next.

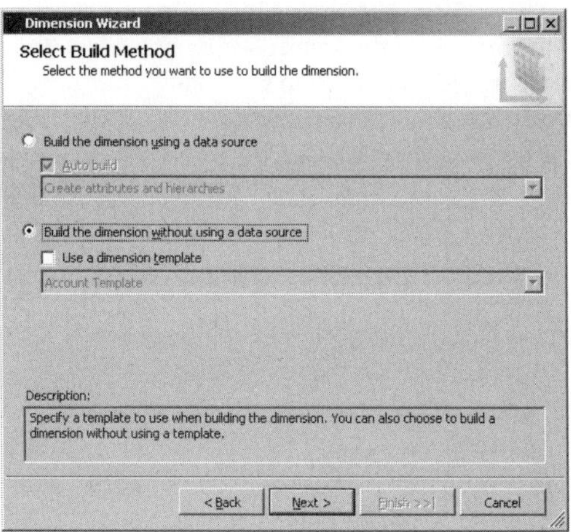

3. On the Select the Dimension Type page, mark the radio button next to Server Time Dimension.

   A time dimension table has columns that define specific time periods (such as year, quarter, and month). If you are creating a standard time dimension without using an existing data source, Analysis Services will generate the table automatically.

However, if you have chosen to create a server time dimension, then you specify the time periods as well as the start and end dates for the dimension. The wizard uses the specified time periods to create the time attributes. When you process the dimension, Analysis Services generates and stores the data on the server that is required to support the specified dates and periods.

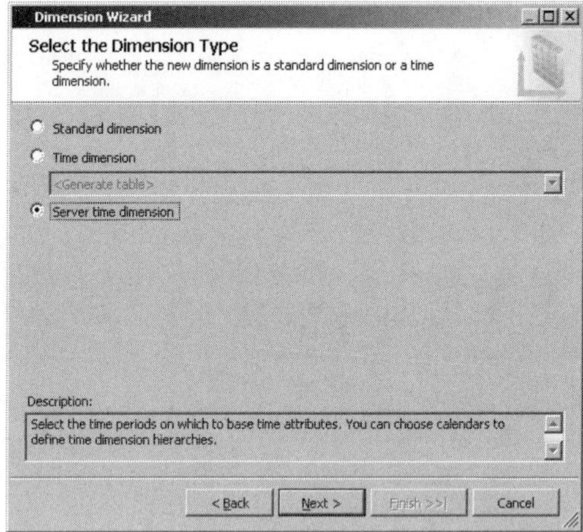

4. In the next window you specify the columns that define the time period. When creating a server time dimension you specify the range of dates you want to include in the dimension. Here the default values are for January 1, 2002, to December 31, 2005. Any transactions outside the range either do not appear or appear as unknown members in the dimension, depending on the UnknownMemberVisible property setting for the dimension. You can also change the first day of the week used by your data (the default is Sunday). You can also select the time periods that apply to the data. You can use any of the choices, but must always select the Date time period since the Date attribute is the key attribute for this dimension and must be used. Select both Date and Month. Next to Language For The Member Names, you can use the drop-down box to select the language to label members of the dimension. Click Next.

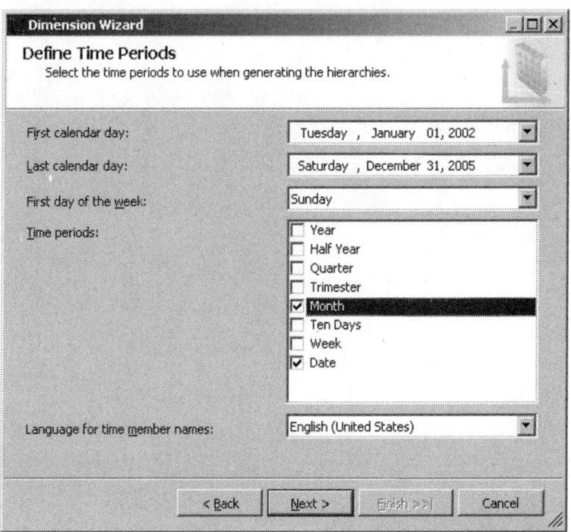

5. On the Select Calendars page you can add to the automatically created 12-month Gregorian calendar from any of the following: Fiscal Calendar; Reporting Or Marketing Calendar; Manufacturing Calendar; and ISO 8601 Calendar. Select Fiscal Calendar. Note that you can specify the star day and month as well as the Fiscal Calendar naming convention. Click Next.

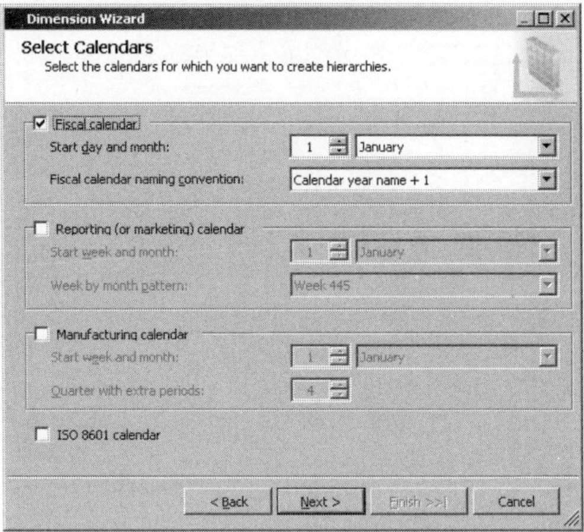

6. Depending on which time periods you select in the Define Time Periods page of the wizard, the calendar selections you just made will determine attributes that are created in the dimension. For example, if you select the Day and Month time periods on the Define Time Periods page of the wizard and the Fiscal Calendar on this previous page, the Fiscal Month, Fiscal Day, Fiscal Day Of Month attributes are created for the fiscal calendar. These will be shown in the Completing The Wizard page. Notice that calendar-specific hierarchies have also been created. Finally, review the attributes and hierarchies created by the wizard and name the time dimension, in this case call it Dim TimeExercise2. Click Finish to complete the wizard and create the dimension. After you complete the dimension, you can make changes to it using Dimension Designer (Figure 26.5).

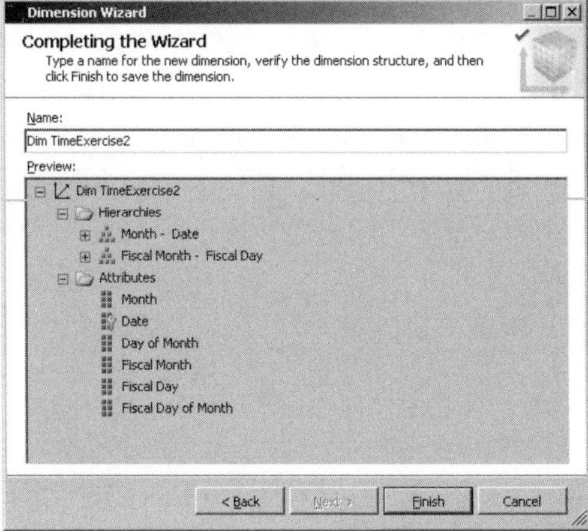

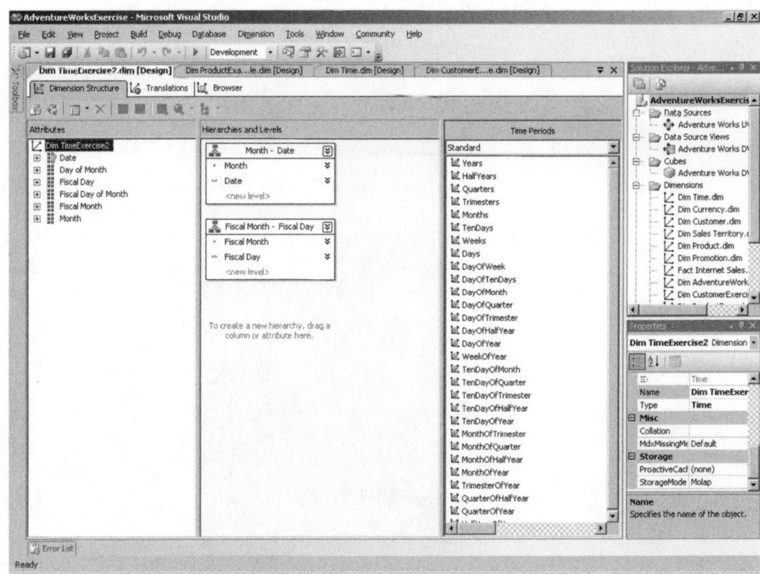

FIGURE 26.5
The Dim TimeExercise2 Server Dimension table in Dimension Structure view

CREATING LINKED DIMENSIONS

Linked dimensions are an advanced topic outside the scope of this chapter, but the concept is an important one that we'll touch on here.

Linked dimensions, as well as linked measures, replace virtual and linked cubes that were used in previous versions of Analysis Services. When you import an Analysis Services database created in a previous version, dimensions in the virtual cube that were based on dimensions in another database become linked dimensions in a nonvirtual cube, while the virtual cube's measure groups become linked measures in the new cube version.

Basically a linked dimension is one that is based on a dimension stored in another database that is located either on the same server or on a completely different server. The advantage to linked dimensions is that you can create and maintain a dimension on a single database while still making it available to users of many databases.

NOTE Dimension writeback is not supported for a linked dimension.

NOTE Linked dimensions cannot be modified except by modifying the source dimension.

1. To start the Linked Object wizard, right-click the Dimension folder and then select New Linked Dimension from the pop-up menu. The wizard leads you through the steps necessary to create a linked dimension. Click Next.

2. On the Select the Data Source page, choose the "Analysis Services data sources" source or create a new one using the New Data Source wizard that can be launched from within the Linked Object Wizard.
3. On the Select Objects page, specify the objects to link to or import from the list of available objects. You cannot link to linked dimension in the remote database.
4. The next to the last step is to review the Completing the Linked Object Wizard page. If you link a dimension that has the same name as an existing dimension, the wizard automatically appends an ordinal number. Clicking Finish cause the wizard to complete and the dimension is added to the Dimensions folder.
5. Remember that you cannot change the structure of a linked dimension so it can't be seen in the Dimension Builder view. After processing the linked dimension you can view it with the Browser view as well as create a translation for the name and rename it.

Data Mining

Although consolidating data into cubes is a good first step in analysis, it doesn't answer all of the questions that you might ask. For example, aggregated data by itself won't spot patterns. Suppose you have millions of rows of sales data and want to know whether particular stores do better for female shoppers than others, or whether a particular product promotion actually correlates well with increased sales. You can get at some of these answers by constructing cubes and drilling down, but to find patterns, a better answer is data mining.

Data mining is an automatic process that looks at the data in a cube and searches for patterns. This pattern search can be based on a variety of algorithms; as the developer, you can specify the factors that are important to you.

BEFORE YOU START

Creating a mining model is straightforward process, but like so many things it is most successful if you follow an old carpenter's adage. Whenever a carpenter is about to work with a particularly fine piece of wood, he or she will "measure twice, cut once." In other words the steps and planning you use prior to creating the model determine the success of the solution and effectiveness of the model.

The approach you take to planning your model should follow these steps:

Problem Definition This may sound obvious but it is often the aspect of model development that gets the least attention. Just like the carpenter has to know the type of project before selecting the wood to use for it, before beginning to make a model you need to thoroughly understand the problem you are trying to solve. You also need to have a thorough understanding of the data including its limitations and you need to state the final objective. The sorts of questions you should be asking follow:

- What attribute am I trying to predict?
- What sorts of relationships are being looked at?
- How is the data distributed?
- How are columns or tables related to each other?
- Is this model for prediction or just to look for patterns and associations?

Data Preparation Once the problem is defined, you can begin the process of finding and collecting raw data. These data can be, and in the real word usually are, scattered all over the enterprise. Your principal task in this stage is to gather all the data related to the problem and work it into consistent and usable format—sometimes referred to as "cleaning the data." This step can include making sure that data errors are eliminated or corrected. You should ensure that everyone is using the same standard or that conversions between them exist to allow for a meaningful comparison. If you are trying to compare the salaries in New York with those in London, you need to make sure that the two currencies are normalized.

Know Thy Data If you don't understand the structure of your data set, how can you know what to ask? How can you be sure which columns to add? If you try to build models without knowing the data, it will turn into an exercise in futility.

Building and Validating the Model A model that doesn't work isn't worth the time it takes to deploy. The best approach is to randomly separate the original data set into training (model-building) and testing (validation) data sets. The training data is used to build the model. Building prediction queries and running them against the testing data set then tests the accuracy. Since you already know the outcome of the predictions because the data come from the same set used to train the model, you can assess whether or not the model's accuracy falls within acceptable parameters.

Deploy the Model Once you have a model with acceptable levels of effectiveness, you deploy it into a production environment. This is *not* the end of the process, only the beginning. The models are now being used in decision-making process and, as more data comes into the company, it also means that the model must be updated. Basically the minute you deploy the model it starts to become obsolete. To overcome this problem, you need to develop a process to reprocess the models to assure and enhance their effectiveness.

USING THE DATA MINING WIZARD

Building a full data set and going through the entire process described above is entirely beyond the scope of this book. In fact, an effective explanation of the process would require an entire book. But you should be familiar with the steps necessary to create a new mining structure and a new mining model. The distinction between the two is basic. A mining structure is a data structure based on information derived from analysis of OLAP or relational data. A mining model is used to make predictions. In this simple exercise the goal is to familiarize you with the Data Mining Wizard. In a real world scenario you would, as explained earlier, need to devote much preparation and examination to the task.

1. In Solution Explorer, right-click the Mining Structure folder and select New Mining Structure to launch the Data Mining Wizard. Click Next.

2. In the Select the Definition Method page, you can specify using either an existing relational database or a data warehouse to define the mining structure. Accept the default "From existing relational database or data warehouse" to define the mining structure based on tables and columns from an existing relational database. Click Next.

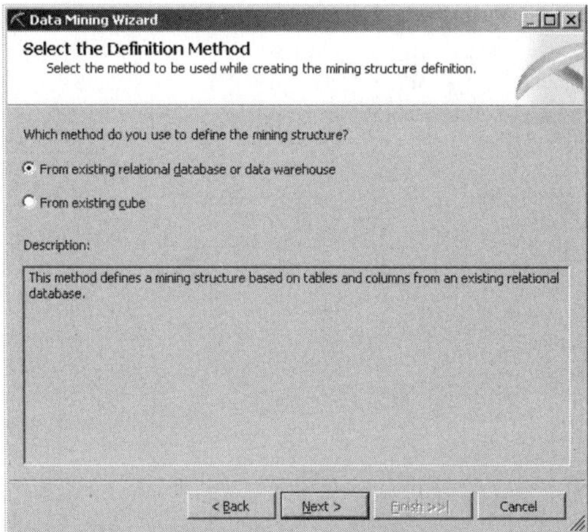

3. In the Select the Data Mining Technique, you are asked to choose from among the following options.

   Microsoft Association Rules Association Rules look for items that are likely to appear together in transactions and can be used to predict the presence of an item based on the presence of others in the transaction.

   Microsoft Clustering Clustering looks for natural groupings of data. This is most useful if you just want to see factors that tend to occur together.

   Microsoft Decision Trees Decision Trees let you make predictions and create virtual dimensions from the analysis results.

   Microsoft Linear Regression Uses linear regression statistic based on existing data to predict outcome

   Microsoft Logistic Regression Uses logistic regression statistic based on existing data to predict outcome

   Microsoft Naïve Bayes Naïve Bayes is a classification algorithm that works well for predictive modeling as long as the attributes are discrete or discretized. All input attributes are assumed to be independent given the predictable attribute.

   Microsoft Neural Network Neural Network can be best used to classify discrete attributes as well as the regression of continuous attributes when you are interested in predicting multiple attributes.

   Microsoft Sequence Clustering Sequence Clustering allows you to predict the likely ordering of events in a sequence based on known characteristics.

   Microsoft Time Series Time Series allows you predict future time-related events based on discovered or known patterns.

   In this example, accept the default value Microsoft Decision Trees. Click Next.

4. On the Select The Data Source View page select the AdventureWorks DW view. Normally, of course, you would have spent considerably more time in preparing the model, but this will do for the current exercise. Click Next.

5. In the Specify Table Types window, select DimCustomer as the Case Table. In this simple exercise, we will not use any nested tables. A table can only be a nested table if it has a many-to-one relationship with the case table.

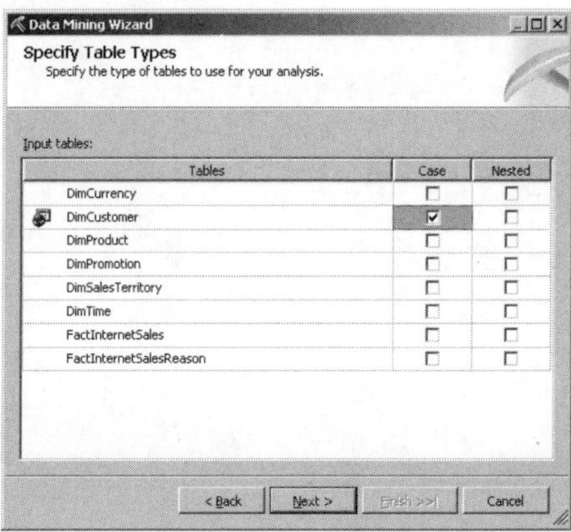

6. On the Specify The Training Data window, you will identify the columns to be used in this analysis and specify whether they are Key, Input, or Predictable. In this case we'll select BirthDate as the predictable attribute to see what other factors correlate with it. When the check box for Predictable next to BirthDate is marked, the Suggest button becomes active. Click the Button to see the suggested related columns and their correlations score. For this exercise, remove the following check marks: MiddleName, French Occupation, Spanish Occupation, English Occupation, Gender, and HouseOwner Flag.

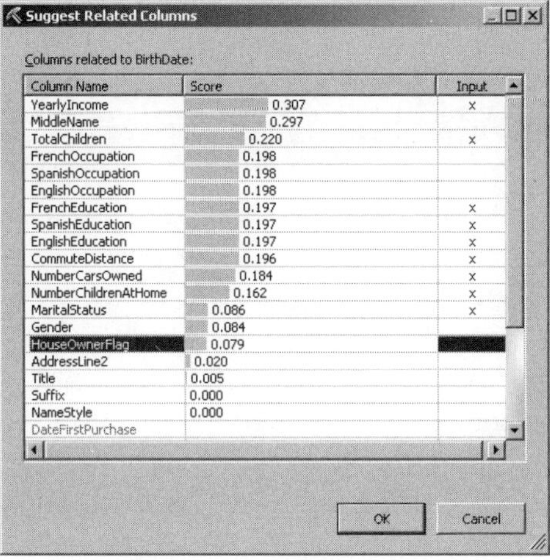

Click OK. Note that suggested input values are marked as such in the Specify Training Data window. Click Next.

7. In the Specify Columns' Content And Data Type page you can alter the content or datatype for any of the selected columns. Make no changes and click Next.

8. On the Completing The Wizard page, give the new Mining Structure the name Mining CustomerExercise. Click Finish to complete the wizard and create the mining structure.

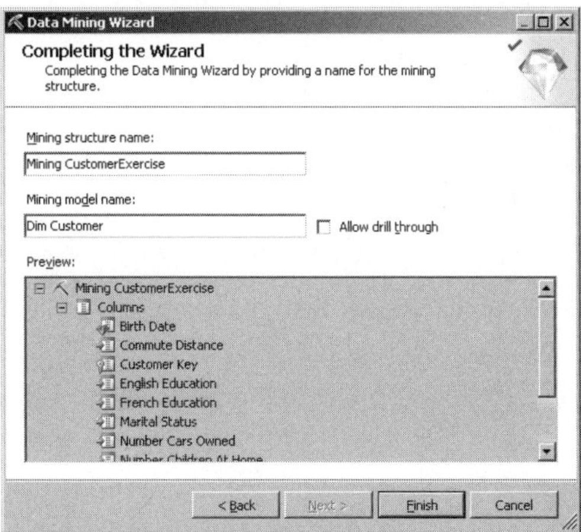

9. Upon completion you should process the model by right-clicking and selecting Process. You may first be asked to process the project. After the model has been processed, you can open Designer view and Mining and look at it. Figure 26.6 shows a data-mining model open in the Mining Model Viewer. The different shadings used in the model indicate how strongly the input data correlates with the factor being predicted as shown in the Node Legend pane.

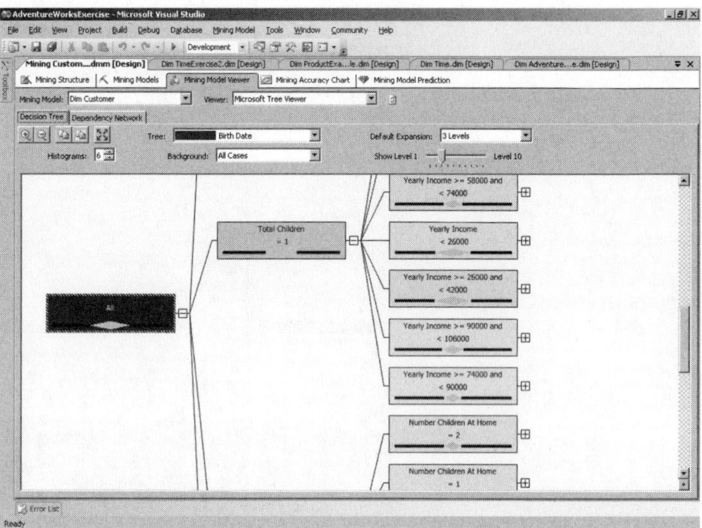

FIGURE 26.6
Viewing a data-mining structure

Deploying Analysis Services

After you've completed the development of your Analysis Services project in BIDS, tested it in your test environment, worked out the kinks, and smoothed out the wrinkles, you should congratulate yourself. You also better deploy into the production environment if you plan on keeping your job.

PLANNING THE DEPLOYMENT

Deployment into the production environment requires some planning, and as we've discussed above, it's always worth taking a few moments to assess and plan the deployment before actually carrying it out. Remember "measure twice, cut once."

This chapter is not the place for a detailed discussion on planning a deployment but you must consider the following questions:

- Does the destination server have the necessary hardware and software resources?
- How will other related but non–Analysis Services objects, such as DTS, reports, or schemas be deployed?
- How will availability be assured if there are hardware or software failures?

- What needs to be deployed and when? How many updates? How frequently?
- What sort of scalability considerations need to be taken into account?
- What about security?

Remember that the above list is far from exhaustive. Plan, assess, replan, and reassess before you start the deployment. And keep up a routine process of continuous reassessment. It will save you time and resources in the end.

The last thing you have to decide is which tool to use to deploy the Analysis Services database onto an Analysis server in a production environment. Analysis Services comes with three tools to perform this task:

- XML Script
- The Analysis Services Deployment Wizard
- The Synchronize Database Wizard

In this exercise you will use the Analysis Services Deployment Wizard, but first let's briefly touch on the other two methods.

Using an XML Script

In the first method, using an XML script, you use Management Studio to generate an XML script of the metadata of an existing Analysis Services database and then execute that script on another server to recreate the initial database. This is done through use of the `CREATE TO` option in the Script Database command.

The resulting script can then be run on another computer to recreate the schema (metadata) of the database. One caveat—because the script generates the entire database only there is no way to incrementally update already deployed objects when using this method. Nor, when using the Script Database As command, can you modify specific properties (e.g., the database name, security settings, etc.) when generating the script, though you can do so manually after the script has been generated or in the deployed database after the script has been run.

Using the Synchronize Database Wizard

This wizard, which is run from within Management Studio, is used to synchronize the metadata and data between any two Analysis Services databases by copying both from the source server to the destination server.

The wizard can also be used to deploy a database from a staging to a production server. Another use is to synchronize a database already on a production server with changes made to a database on a staging server. This means you can perform all cube and dimension processing on a staging server while users can still query the resources on the production server. As soon as the synchronization is complete, the users are automatically switched to the new data and metadata. It can also create a script to be run at a later time to synchronize the databases.

You invoke the Synchronize Database Wizard from within Management Studio by connecting to an instance of Analysis Server, right-clicking the Database folder, and selecting Synchronize.

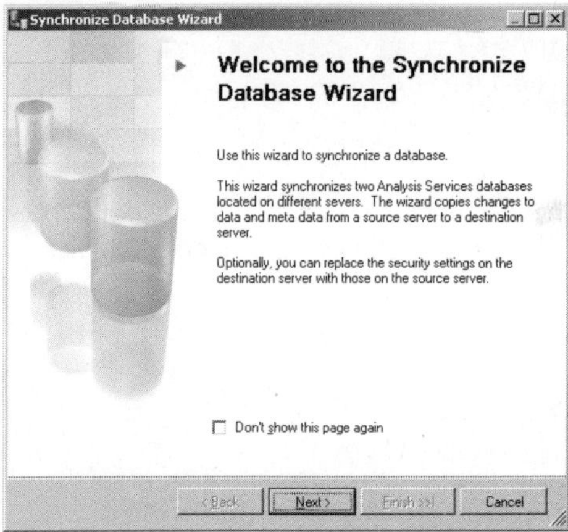

USING THE ANALYSIS SERVICES DEPLOYMENT WIZARD

There are two ways to run the wizard. The first is from the command prompt, using the `Microsoft.AnalysisServices.Deployment.exe` file found in the `C:\ Program Files\ Microsoft SQL Server\90\Tools\Binn\VSShell\Common7\IDE` folder. By using the `/A` switch you can specify answer file mode.

In answer file mode you can modify the input files originally built in when the Analysis Services project was created in BIDS.

Using the `/S` switch will run the wizard in silent mode. Output mode, called for with the `/O` switch, causes the wizard to generate an XMLA deployment script for later execution based on the input files.

While there may be good reasons to use the command prompt method, the easiest method is by invoking the wizard interactively. To use the wizard interactively do the following:

1. Select Start ➢ Programs ➢ Microsoft SQL Server 2005 ➢ Analysis Services ➢ Deployment Wizard to launch the Analysis Services Deployment Wizard.

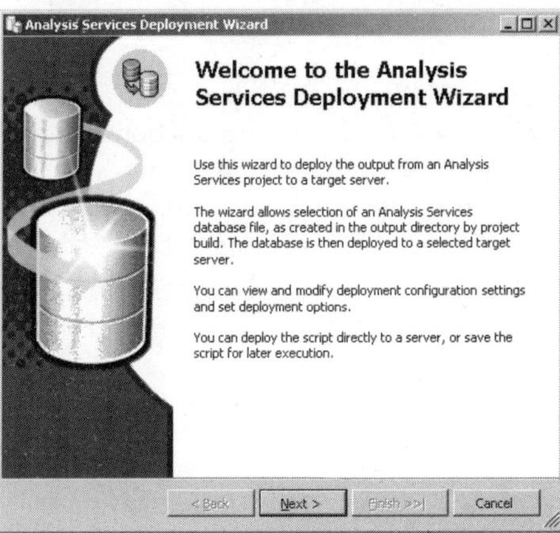

2. In the next window specify the path to the *.asdatabase file you wish to use. In this case use the AdventureWorks Exercise example at C:\Documents and Settings\%*username*%\My Documents\Visual Studio 2005\Projects\AdventureWorksExercise\AdventureWorksExercise\bin\AdventureWorksExercise.asdatabase. Click Next.

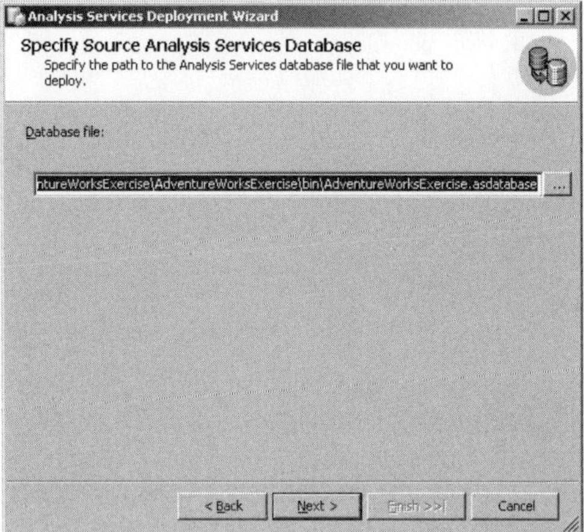

3. In the Installation Target window specify a target server and database to which to deploy the Analysis Services database. If the database doesn't exist it will be created. Otherwise it will be overwritten. Specify `localhost` as the server and AdventureWorksExercise as the database. Click Next.

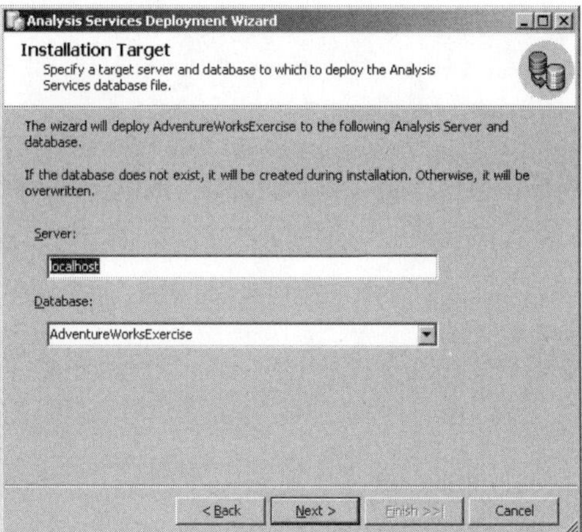

4. Now you are asked to specify options for partitions and roles to determine how any existing partitions, security roles, permissions, and role members are handled during deployment. Accept the default values and click Next.

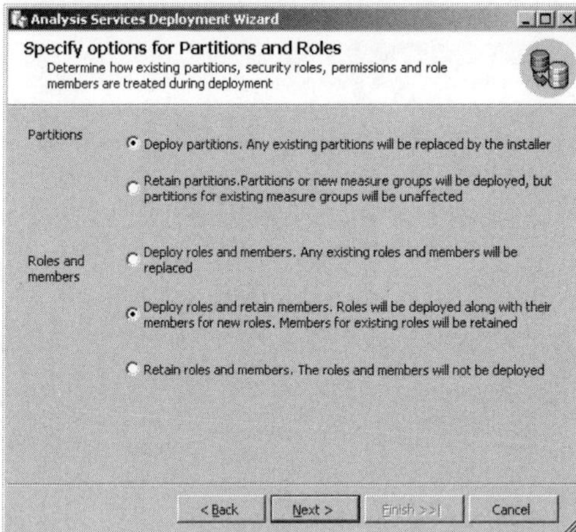

5. Next you are given the option to set the configuration properties for each of the objects. Since this is a new deployment, make no changes and click Next.

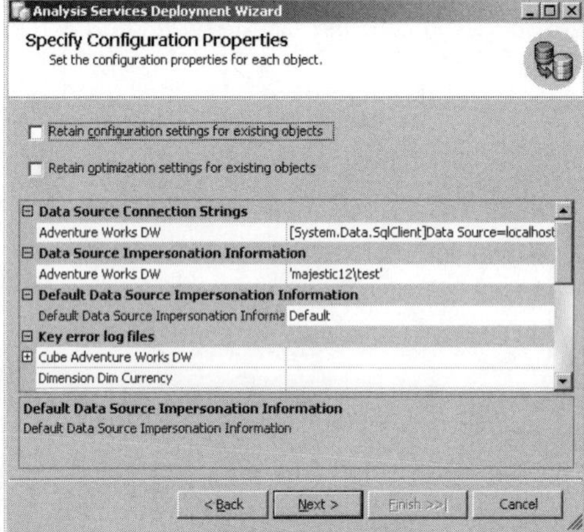

6. In the Select Processing Options windows, accept Default Processing as the way for the objects in the database to be processed. If you mark the "Include all processing in a single transaction" check box, everything is done and written to as a single transaction. Click Next.

7. Now you are asked to confirm that deployment should proceed. If you mark the "Create deployment script" check box, it will generate the XMLA script file and write it to the specified location for later use or review.

8. Click Next. If you marked the "Create deployment" check box, the wizard creates and saves the script file to a designated location and the deployment is completed with the idea that you will invoke the script later.

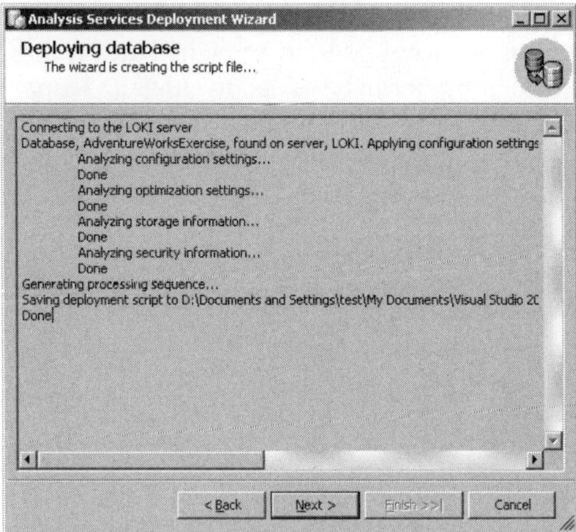

9. If you left the box unmarked, then deployment takes place as soon as you click Next. You can keep track of the progress in the dialog windows. As soon as the database is deployed, click Next to open the Deployment Complete window. Click Finish to close the wizard.

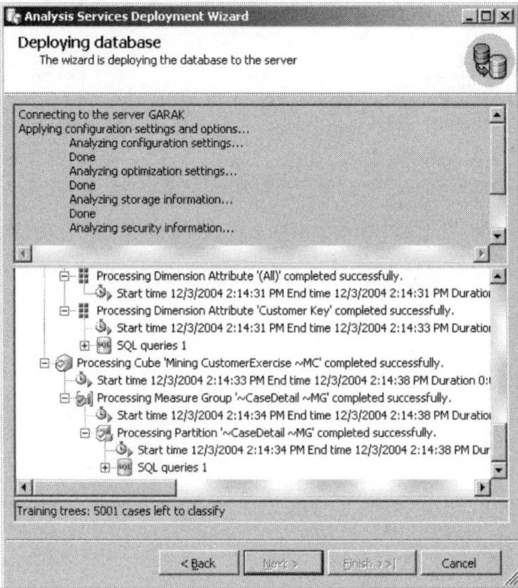

Creating an Analysis Services Project in SQL Server Management Studio

While we have primarily focused on using and creating Analysis Service projects through BIDS, Management Studio provides a way to design and test Transact-SQL queries, MDX queries, and XML for Analysis scripts interactively.

You create an Analysis Services project in Management Studio by using a template from the Management Studio Projects group. It can be added to either an empty solution or an existing solution.

To create a new project in an empty solution, select File ➤ New ➤ Project to open the Projects Group. Select Analysis Server Scripts, and name it AnalysisServicesProjectExample in the Name box. Click OK to create the new project and the solution.

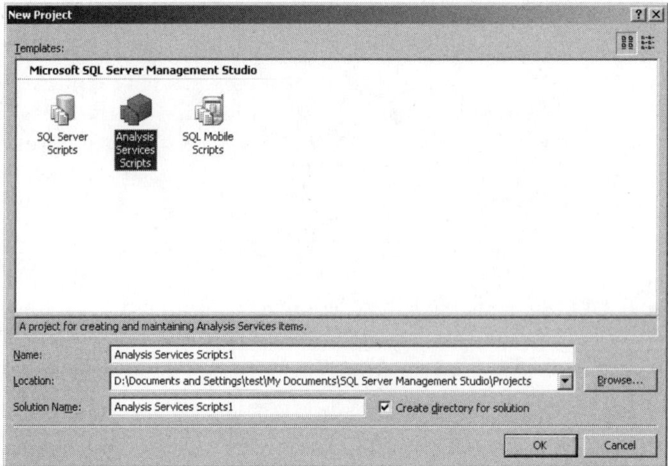

A new solution is created in Solution Explorer, along with the new project AnalysisServices-ProjectExample.

Three folders serving as object containers are created:

- Connections, which contains the connection strings for Analysis Service connections
- Queries, which contains scripts for MDX and XMLA queries
- Miscellaneous, which contains all other file types that might be used in the solution

Summary

In this chapter, you learned about online analytical processing (OLAP) and the tools that SQL Server 2000 provides to do this sort of analysis. The primary tool is Microsoft SQL Server 2000 Analysis Services, a full-featured OLAP analysis product. You learned the basic terminology of OLAP and saw how to use Business Intelligence Development Studio to develop basic application. You created, browsed, and processed cubes, and familiarized yourself with the different types of dimensions. You also learned the various ways to deploy an Analysis Services project and how to create one from within Management Studio.

And that's only the tip of the deep and expansive iceberg of Analysis Services capabilities.

In the next chapter, we'll introduce a new product debuting in SQL Server 2005, Notification Services, which is used to develop and deploy applications that generate and send personalized timely messages to a wide variety of devices.

Chapter 27

Notification Services

Microsoft SQL Server Notification Services was not included as a part of SQL Server 2000 but introduced in 2003 as a free add-on and labeled version 2.0. In SQL Server 2005 it is included as part of the package.

As the name suggests Notification Services is the intended platform for developing and deploying applications that generate and send notifications to users based on what they would like to be notified about. To put it in simpler terms, Notification Services are services that check whether any event has occurred on the specified data or if any user has subscribed to be notified when that event occurs, and sends the notification to that user. Integrating a technology like Notification Services into SQL Server 2005 is a logical move and an elegant design decision. This is because nearly all notifications are based on data changes (or additions), such as stock price reaching a search threshold.

The notifications, as you will see, are personalized, timely messages that can be sent to a wide variety of devices. For example, a user might want to be notified by e-mail/SMS or when stock prices of a particular company rise or fall below a predetermined mark. Or a user might want his or her cell phone to play a tune or send a message about flight delays or special fares.

A notification can be generated and sent to the user when the triggering event occurs. Or, a notification can be generated and sent on a predetermined schedule specified by the user through his or her subscriptions.

Notifications can be sent to a wide variety of devices such as a cell phone, personal digital assistant (PDA), Microsoft Windows Messenger, or e-mail account, to name only a few. Because these sorts of devices are usually in the possession of the user on a continuous basis, notifications are perfect for sending high-priority or time critical information.

There are literally thousands of situations where we would want to be informed of changing circumstances. Notification Services is intended to make it possible for you to easily set them up and implement them.

Architecture

Notification Services architecture is simple and deceptively flexible so that you no longer have the pains of implementing features for notifications such as polling events, scheduling, formatting, and delivery. These features are already built in to Notification Services for easy integration and development.

Before going further in this discussion of Notification Services, you should be familiar with the follow key concepts and the terms associated with them.

- An *event* is a piece of information that subscribers are interested in or an action that occurred affecting the specified data.
- A *subscriber* is person or application that receives notifications when an event occurs.

- A *subscription* is a specified request by a subscriber that describes when and what he or she wants to be notified (e.g., a subscriber specifies that he or she wants to be notified when a stock price drops 5 percent).
- A *notification* is a message that contains information related to a subscription. A notification might contain a message about the final score of a ball game or a stock or that an opening has occurred in the boss's schedule.

How It Works: The Simple View

How this all works is fairly simple as you can see in Figure 27.1; subscribers create subscription data (which can be added using SMOs) to a Notification Services application. Events are populated to an events table with the help of event providers via direct or indirect collection. Once events are populated into the events table, the Notification Services, (which can be configured to a schedule or immediate operation), begins processing rules. The rules, which are part of the subscription, are checked by the generator checks to see if any events match them. If matches are found, Notification Services creates notifications and fills the notifications table. Once notifications arrive in notifications table, Notification Services processes each notification, formats it, and sends it using the specified channel, either immediately or at a scheduled time based on the configuration. The steps are broken down as follows:

- Subscribers create subscriptions related to the application.
- The application collects events.
- Notification Services, using Transact-SQL queries, matches subscriptions to events.
- When an event and subscription match, Notification Services generates a notification.
- Notification Services then formats the notification and sends it to a delivery service.

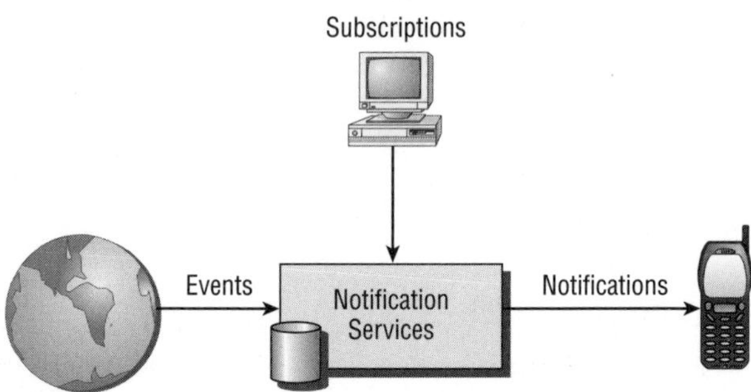

FIGURE 27.1 Simplified diagram of how a notification occurs

How It Works: The Detailed View

Now that you've got the super high-level picture, let's drill down to more detail. The better you understand the process, the easier it will be in the long run.

As we've seen, a Notification Services application collects events and subscriptions, generates notifications, and then distributes the notifications to external delivery services, such as a Simple Mail Transfer Protocol (SMTP) server, a cell phone, or another channel.

To do that, Notification Services stores subscriber and subscription data in one or more SQL Server databases. Subscription management objects—part of the Notification Services API—can be used to create a custom subscription management application to manage subscriber and subscription data.

Using event providers, Notification Services now gathers and stores event data in the application's database. For example, the file system watcher event provider monitors a directory for XML event data. Using this event provider, you can drop XML event files in the directory. The event provider reads the XML events and submits them to the application database. Later in this chapter we'll use that process to generate an event. Event providers can be run by the event provider host component, or can run independently of Notification Services.

Next, the generator matches subscriptions and events and generates notifications. The generator runs on the interval defined for the application. You, the developer, write Transact-SQL queries that determine how subscriptions are evaluated and what information goes into the notifications.

The distributor formats notifications and sends them to subscribers using one or more delivery services. The application developer specifies the transformation from raw data to a formatted notification using a content formatter such as XSLT.

The Notification Services platform uses the NS$*instance_name* service to run notification applications. This service, the primary component of the Notification Services engine, runs the three internal functions: the event provider, the generator, and the distributor.

Figure 27.2 shows how Notification Services implements this architecture.

Subscription Management Architecture

To be able to send you a copy of a magazine you order, a publisher needs to know who you are, what magazine you want, and where to send the magazine. In much the same way, before notifications can be sent, a Notification Services application needs to know about the subscribers, what data the subscribers need to have, and where to send the information. Magazines use circulation departments to handle this process; in SQL Server, Notifications Services uses subscription management to handle this subscriber, subscription, and subscriber device data.

FIGURE 27.2
How a notification occurs

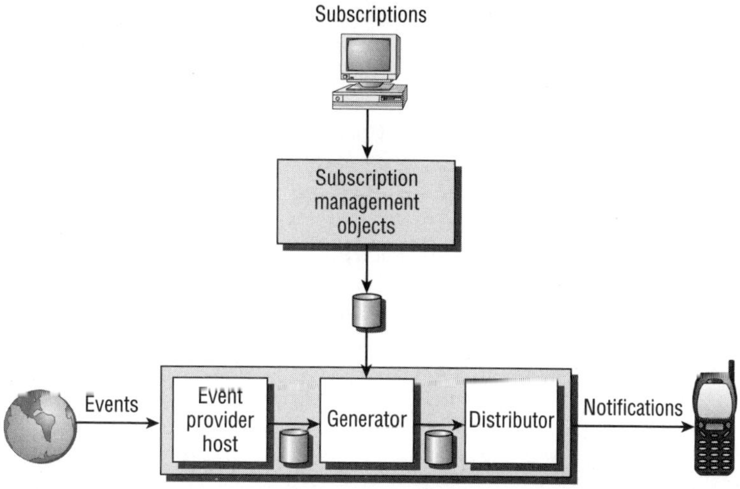

Subscriptions
Subscription management objects
Events
Event provider host
Generator
Distributor
Notifications

The application developer writes a custom subscription management application to handle subscription management. This application, which can be either a Web application or standard Microsoft Windows application, writes the subscriber, subscription, and subscriber device data to the proper databases. The developer uses subscription management objects to handle them.

Notification Services also stores both subscriber and subscriber device data in a central Notification Services database. Subscription data is stored in application-specific databases. This storage architecture allows all applications to share any global subscriber data while at the same time segregating storing the subscriptions for each application.

When a Notification Services application is running, the application uses the subscription data to generate notifications and then uses the subscriber data to format and distribute the notification, as seen in Figure 27.3.

FIGURE 27.3
How a subscription management application uses subscription management objects to communicate with Notification Services

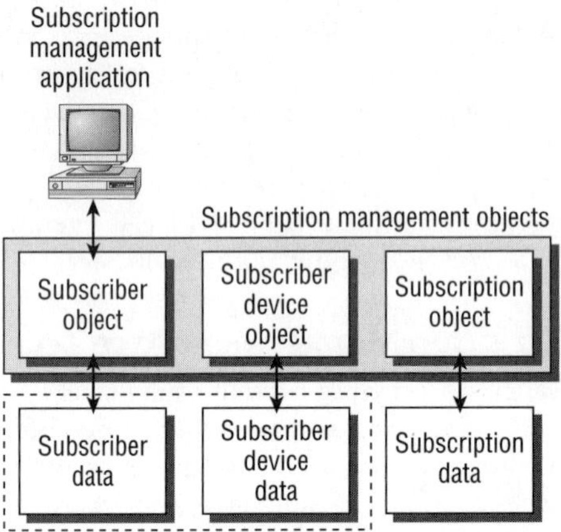

Event Collection Architecture

Event collection involves obtaining event data from one or more sources such as XML files, applications, or databases. This information is then given to a notification application, which assesses and then decides whether to generate a notification. In Notification Services, event collection is handled by *event providers*.

Every application will use one or more different event providers to collect events. Each event provider submits data to the application using one of the four event APIs: a managed API, a COM API that uses the managed API, an XML API, and a SQL Server API.

The managed API uses the Event and EventCollector objects to submit single events. Then, using the names of the fields in an event table, an application submits an event object to the event collector, which then writes the data to the event table. The COM API uses COM interop to expose the event classes as COM interfaces.

The XML API provides a way to bulk-load XML data. The XML event provider collects an XML document or stream from an event source and submits the data to the XMLLoader, which then writes the events to the event table.

The SQL Server API uses stored procedures to load event data from database objects. Two typical ways of using the SQL Server event provider are to invoke the provider using a stored procedure and to run a query according to a schedule. The event provider receives a result set and writes it to the event table using the API stored procedures.

You have the option to create your own custom event providers using any of the APIs just listed. Another, easier method is to use the one of the standard event providers supplied with Notification Services. These event providers can pick up XML data from a watched folder, can query SQL Server databases, and can query Analysis Services cubes.

An event provider is either hosted or non-hosted. Hosted event providers run within Notification Services by a component called the event provider host. The event provider host runs using the same schedule as the generator component; the schedule is defined in the application definition file.

Non-hosted event providers run as external applications and submit events on their own schedule. For example, an event provider hosted by Internet Information Services (IIS) that exposes a Web method for submitting events is a non-hosted event provider. Note as well that an event provider hosted inside a process you write is also a non-hosted event provider.

Notification Services Programming Framework

Notification Services uses a programming framework that facilitates quick application development. Developers really only have one primary, albeit critical, task in terms of application development, and that is to create the application definition file (ADF). Typically all the developer has to do is worry about the ADF, but note that while not covered here, additional tasks may be required, depending on your application.

If you plan on building a notification application using the standard components, follow these steps:

Define the application in the ADF. The ADF contains information about the events, event providers, subscriptions, notifications, and application settings. The ADF allows you to define the structure of data, queries used to process data, how notifications are formatted and delivered, and operational parameters for your application. As mentioned above, additional tasks may be required based on entries in the ADF. For example, if you plan to use the file system watcher event provider, you will have to create an XML Schema definition language (XSD) file defining the XML event schema. If you opt to use XSLT to format notifications, you would have to create XSLT files to convert the notification data into a readable message.

Create a subscription management application using the Notification Services API. The Notification Services API provides a number of classes (for managed code) and interfaces (for unmanaged code) to simplify the collection and submission of subscriber and subscription data.

With those two pieces complete, you're ready to test and deploy the application. To do so:

1. Configure an instance of Notification Services by creating a configuration file. An instance is a named configuration of Notification Services that hosts one or more applications. The configuration file defines the name of the instance, names the applications hosted by the instance, and configures databases, protocols, and delivery channels for the instance.

2. Create, register and enable an instance of Notification Services by using the NSControl Create command to create the instance and then use NSControl Register to register it. NSControl Create creates the instance and application databases. NSControl Register registers the instance and can optionally be used to create the NS$*instance_name* service that runs the Notification Services engine and the performance counters used to monitor the instance.

3. Activate the subscription management application.

TIP As you will see later in this chapter, you can use Management Studio to easily do all of these tasks, thus saving yourself extra work.

Notification Services Components

The purpose of a Notification Services Application is to generate notifications for delivery to subscribers. A Notification Services application runs on a platform based on the Notification Services engine and SQL Server. Many applications also use IIS to host their subscription management application or custom event providers, although this is not required and is not provided as part of Notification Services.

A Notification Services application is composed of six primary components:

- The Notification Services platform, consisting of the Notification Services engine (which contains the provider host, generator, and distributor components) and the Notification Services SQL Server databases. The platform stores system data and provides functions for notification generation and distribution.
- Two metadata files: the configuration file, which describes the configuration information for a Notification Services instance, and the ADF, which defines the data and structure of a Notification Services application. When NSControl Create runs, it uses these files to set up the Notification Services instance and applications, including the SQL Server tables and other objects.
- The subscription management application, which manages subscriber and subscription information, and adds, updates, and deletes it in Notification Services.
- One or more event providers, which gather event data and submit it to Notification Services.
- One or more content formatters, which take raw notification data after it has been generated and format it appropriately for display on the target device.
- One or more delivery protocols, which create a notification message and then route the message to the external delivery service that delivers the message to the target device.

Notification Services uses database processing to manage large volumes of data, subscriptions, events, and notifications.

Configuration Considerations in Development

Before you begin planning and developing a notification application you should be aware of the four most common configurations. Each has its own advantages and disadvantages, and understanding them will help you plan effectively depending on the solution you are being asked to provide:

In a *single -server* configuration, all components—including SQL Server, the Notification Services Engine and the Web server component for the subscription management application—run on one server, normally a 2-CPU or 4-CPU server. You should consider this for small Notification Services applications that operate within an intranet. It is not recommended for Internet applications, primarily because placing the Web server and the database on the same server raises serious security issues.

In an *remote database server configuration*, everything is split across two servers for security and performance improvement. The SQL Server database and all Notification Services engine components (the provider host, generator, and distributor) run on one server, which is typically a 2-CPU or 4-CPU server. The other server acts as the Web server for the subscription management application. You should think of using this one for small Internet applications when you need to put subscription management applications on a Web server outside an enterprise firewall. You can also find it useful for medium-sized intranet applications in cases when you need resources for the application that exceed the capabilities of a single server. Resources needed for the application would be too much for a single server.

For large intranet applications and medium-to-large Internet applications, the most common configuration is a *scale-out* configuration. The components are split among at least three servers—one to run SQL Serve, another with the Notification Services engine components, and one or more Web servers for the subscription management application.

Finally, if you are concerned about availability you can use SQL Server failover clustering in a configuration called a *high-availability configuration.* This configuration allows several servers to be associated, so that the database can failover from one server to another if an error occurs. Additionally the Notification Services engine components, which run on a separate server, have an additional backup server available for failover of these application functions. This configuration is recommended for large intranet applications and medium-to-large Internet applications that require high availability.

Creating an Application: Overview

Even though most of the time you will be able to make use of samples packaged with SQL Server and other available code samples to help you in your application development, you should be aware of the basic principles in developing a Notification Services application. In the next few sections you will be looking at a high-level overview of the required steps to application development.

When developing a Notification Services application you will normally follow these steps:

1. When necessary, create a configuration file to define the Notification Services instance that will host the application.
2. Design the application by creating an ADF to define the application.
3. Specify one or more event classes. Note that each event class corresponds to a particular kind of event used by the application.
4. Specify one or more notification classes.
5. Specify one or more subscription classes. Specifying a subscription class involves creating rules by writing T-SQL statements to either generate notifications or update chronicle tables.
6. Create one or more notification generation rules (in a subscription class in an ADF) that will match your event data with your subscription data to produce notifications.
7. Build the application using the nscontrol utility. You can do this either through Management Studio, or by running the nscontrol directly from the command line. This utility takes all of the information specified in the ADF, and sets up the SQL Server database and tables needed for the application. For example, an event table is created for each event class you define, and a subscription table is created for each subscription class you define.
8. Write some simple scripts to test your notification generation rules and make sure they are producing notifications as expected. For this step, you can use the `NoOp.xslt` file with the standard XSLT content formatter and the standard file delivery protocol to easily produce the notifications.

9. Create or modify a subscription management application to submit information about subscribers, subscriber devices, and subscriptions to the system with the Notification Services APIs.
10. Define an event provider using either one of the standard event providers included with Notification Services, or by developing a custom event provider tailored to your specific needs. Optionally you can create one or more XSLT files for use by the standard XSLT content formatter or use a custom content formatter you have created to meet your specific business needs.
11. Finalize the application settings in the ADF, to optimize application performance and manage system resource consumption.
12. Finally, test and, if successful, deploy the application.

NOTE If you want you can develop a custom delivery protocol tailored to your specific needs.

Creating an Instance Configuration File

In addition to the ADF, each instance of Notification Services is defined by a configuration file that contains information about the instance, the instance's applications with pointers to the application definitions, and information about delivery channels and protocols. When you deploy the instance, the data in the configuration file is used to create an instance database.

NOTE The configuration file must conform to the `ConfigurationFileSchema.xsd` schema, which is in the Notification Services XML Schemas folder.

Each instance of Notification Services has a configuration file. This file contains information about the instance, general information about the instance's applications, and information about delivery channels and protocols.

`<NotificationServicesInstance>` is the top-level node.

You can hard code configuration file values for each element of the configuration file, or you can use parameters. If you use parameters in the configuration file, you can define default values for the parameters in the `<ParameterDefaults>` node.

`Use <Version>` node for specifying the configuration file version number consists of four elements: `<Major>`, `<Minor>`, `<Build>`, and `<Revision>`.

`Use <History>` node for keeping a history of your configuration file consists of four elements: `<CreationsDate>`, `<CreationTime>`, `<LastModifiedDate>`, and `<LastModifiedTime>`.

`<InstanceName>` is used to define a unique name for the instance. The instance name is used as follows: the instance database is named *instance_name*NSMain, and application database names are a concatenation of *instance_name* and *application_name*. As you will see the application name is defined in the `<Application>` node and the Windows service that runs the instance of Notification Services is named NS$*instance_name*.

Within the configuration file, you must use the `<SqlServerSystem>` element to specify which instance of SQL Server 2005 stores instance and application data.

NOTE In a default instance the value is the name of the computer that hosts the SQL Server 2005 databases. For a named instance of SQL Server, the `<SqlServerSystem>` value must be in the form `computer\instance_name`.

The `<Database>` node is optional. If not specified the database engine creates the instance database using the model database as a template, which may not be the best fit for your uses unless you have modified the model database.

The <Applications> node contains all <Application> nodes as elements. Each <Application> element has a set of child elements that define application settings, such as the application name, a base directory path that points to application files, and application parameters that are passed into the application definition file.

In the <Protocols> node specify custom protocols supported by the instance. Notification Services supplies two standard protocols: SMTP and File. If applications use these protocols, you do not need to define the protocols in the <Protocols> section of the configuration file. Custom protocols require use of this node. Each custom protocol should have a name, a class name, and an assembly name.

<DeliveryChannels> specifies one or more delivery channels (which are instances of a delivery protocol). The <DeliveryChannel> node can provide information such as server names, usernames, and passwords. The <EncryptArguments> element is used to encrypt arguments for delivery channels and event providers that are stored in the instance database and application databases. You turn argument encryption on by setting the value in the <EncryptArguments> element to true. (By default, the value is false.)

NOTE If you turn on argument encryption, you must provide an encryption key when you run NSControl Create and when you run NSControl Register.

Sample Instance Configuration File

```
<?xml version="1.0" encoding="utf-8"?>
<!--Microsoft Notification Services "Configuration File"-->

<NotificationServicesInstance xmlns:ns="http://www.microsoft.com/
MicrosoftNotificationServices/ConfigurationFileSchema" xmlns="http://
www.microsoft.com/MicrosoftNotificationServices/ConfigurationFileSchema"
xmlns:xsi="http://www.w3.org/2001/XMLSchema-instance" xsi:schemaLocation="http://
www.microsoft.com/MicrosoftNotificationServices/ConfigurationFileSchema http://
localhost/NotificationServices/ConfigurationFileSchema.xsd">

<!--Default Parameters-->
<ParameterDefaults>
    <Parameter>
        <Name>BaseDirectoryPath</Name>
        <Value>
        C:\Program Files\Notification Services\%InstanceName%
        </Value>
    </Parameter>
    <Parameter>
        <Name>System</Name>
        <Value>MyServer</Value>
    </Parameter>
```

```
</ParameterDefaults>

<!--Version-->
<Version>
    <Major>2</Major>
    <Minor>0</Minor>
    <Build>162</Build>
    <Revision>1</Revision>
</Version>

<!--History-->
<History>
    <CreationDate>2001-09-22</CreationDate>
    <CreationTime>10:30:00</CreationTime>
    <LastModifiedDate>2002-4-22</LastModifiedDate>
    <LastModifiedTime>22:30:00</LastModifiedTime>
</History>

<!--Instance Name-->
<InstanceName>%InstanceName%</InstanceName>

<!--SQL Server machine name-->
<SqlServerSystem>%System%</SqlServerSystem>

<!--Database-->
<Database>
    <NamedFileGroup>
        <FileGroupName>primary</FileGroupName>
        <FileSpec>
            <LogicalName>PrimaryFG1</LogicalName>
            <FileName>%BaseDirectoryPath%\Primary.mdf</FileName>
            <Size>10MB</Size>
            <MaxSize>14MB</MaxSize>
            <GrowthIncrement>15%</GrowthIncrement>
        </FileSpec>
    </NamedFileGroup>
    <NamedFileGroup>
        <FileGroupName>MyFileGroup</FileGroupName>
```

```
        <FileSpec>
            <LogicalName>MyLogicalName</LogicalName>
            <FileName>%BaseDirectoryPath%\MyLogicalName.mdf</FileName>
            <Size>55MB</Size>
            <MaxSize>100MB</MaxSize>
            <GrowthIncrement>15%</GrowthIncrement>
        </FileSpec>
    </NamedFileGroup>
    <NamedFileGroup>
        <FileGroupName>MyDefault2</FileGroupName>
        <FileSpec>
            <LogicalName>MyLogicalDefault2</LogicalName>
            <FileName>%BaseDirectoryPath%\MyDefault2.mdf</FileName>
            <Size>1MB</Size>
            <MaxSize>3MB</MaxSize>
            <GrowthIncrement>15%</GrowthIncrement>
        </FileSpec>
    </NamedFileGroup>
</Database>

<!--Applications-->
<Applications>
    <Application>
        <ApplicationName>Stock</ApplicationName>
        <BaseDirectoryPath>
        %BaseDirectoryPath%\Stock
        </BaseDirectoryPath>
        <ApplicationDefinitionFilePath>
        StockADF.xml
        </ApplicationDefinitionFilePath>
        <Parameters>
            <Parameter>
                <Name>DBSystem</Name>
                <Value>%System%</Value>
            </Parameter>
            <Parameter>
                <Name>NSSystem</Name>
                <Value>%System%</Value>
```

```
            </Parameter>
        </Parameters>
    </Application>
</Applications>

<!--Protocols-->
<Protocols>
    <Protocol>
        <ProtocolName>SMS</ProtocolName>
        <ClassName>Protocols.SMSProtocol</ClassName>
        <AssemblyName>SMS.dll</AssemblyName>
    </Protocol>
</Protocols>

<!--Delivery Channels-->
<DeliveryChannels>
    <DeliveryChannel>
        <DeliveryChannelName>EmailChannel</DeliveryChannelName>
        <ProtocolName>SMTP</ProtocolName>
        <Arguments>
            <Argument>
                <Name>User</Name>
                <Value>%User%</Value>
            </Argument>
            <Argument>
                <Name>Pwd</Name>
                <Value>%Pwd%</Value>
            </Argument>
        </Arguments>
    </DeliveryChannel>
    <DeliveryChannel>
        <DeliveryChannelName>CustomSMSChannel</DeliveryChannelName>
        <ProtocolName>SMS</ProtocolName>
        <Arguments>
            <Argument>
                <Name>User</Name>
                <Value>%User%</Value>
            </Argument>
```

```
            <Argument>
                <Name>Pwd</Name>
                <Value>%Pwd%</Value>
            </Argument>
        </Arguments>
    </DeliveryChannel>
</DeliveryChannels>

<!--Argument Encryption Flag -->
<EncryptArguments>false</EncryptArguments>

</NotificationServicesInstance>
```

Creating an Application Definition File

An application definition file is required for every notification application. The ADF stores all the metadata used to define the application, including the structures of event subscriptions the application accepts as input and the framework of the notifications. The ADF will also set the instructions on how the designated application is supposed to function.

Basically you set four major subsets of settings and metadata: application settings, event metadata, subscription metadata, and notification metadata. A discussion of each follows

Application Settings

Application settings are written to specify such items as the computers that host Notification Services when processing occurs (either on demand or schedule). The application setting will also document key metadata about the ADF, including its modification setting.

This information is contained in several sections of the ADF. The Application Settings section contains the following nodes:

- `<Parameter Defaults>` is used to define application parameters. Note that you can define parameters in the configuration file as well and those definitions take precedence over those defined in the ADF.
- `<Version>` allows you to track version information and has four required child elements: `<Major>`, `<Minor>`, `<Build>`, and `<Revision>`.
- `<History>` allows you to see when the ADF was created and last modified. It has four required child elements: `<CreationDate>`, `<LastModifiedDate>`, `<CreationTime>`, and `<LastModified Time>`.
- `<Database>` is used if you want to create your application database using settings other than SQL Server defaults. In the absence of this node, the SQL Server defaults are used. If you choose not to specify application database information, the `<Database>` node must be excluded from the ADF. There are four optional child elements: `<NamedFileGroup>`, `<LogFile>`, `<DefaultFileGroup>`, and `<CollationName>`.

- `<Generator>` settings determine which server hosts the generator and the number of threads the generator can use when processing applications.
- `<Distributor>` contains the settings for which server hosts a distributor, how frequently it runs, and how many threads it can use when processing work items.
- `<ApplicationExecution Settings>` are used to maintain execution information about the application. It consists of 10 optional child elements:

  `<QuantumDuration>`

  `<ChronicleQuantumLimit>`

  `<SubscriptionQuantumLimit>`

  `<ProcessEventsInOrder>`

  `<PerformanceQueryInterval>`

  `<EventThrottle>`

  `<SubscriptionThrottle>`

  `<NotificationThrottle>`

  `<DistributorLogging>`

  `<Vacuum>`

Event Metadata

Notification Services requires that each event your application accepts must be defined. To do this you document them as event classes in the ADF. When the notification application is set up using NSControl Create, the event class information is used to implement SQL Server objects (like tables and indexes) that will manage the data for this event class.

You must also use the ADF to document any event providers that your application uses.

You do all of this by creating an event class in the ADF. You can define one or more event classes for each application you develop.

Event class information is stored in the `/EventClasses/EventClass` section of the ADF. You must create one `<EventClass>` node for each event class that you require.

You define an event class by doing the following:

1. Name your event class.
2. Define the fields in your event class. The event providers use the definitions to validate their event data. Additionally these fields are used to provide the schema for the event table in SQL Server that stores the event data.
3. If you wish you can take the option to specify the SQL Server filegroup where the event table should be created. If you don't specify one, it is automatically created on in the default filegroup for the application database.

4. If you want to index your event table, provide T-SQL statements to create one or more indexes on your event table.
5. If you plan to make use of event chronicle tables in the application, define a chronicle rule and associate it with this event class. You will also need to define one or more event chronicle tables associated with this event class.

NOTE The Notification Services stored procedure `NSDiagnosticEventClass` can be used to gather information about an event class.

To define an event provider:

1. Name the event provider.
2. If you are defining a hosted event provider, whether standard or custom, you must document the class name of your event provider. *This step is not required for non-hosted event providers.*
3. If you are defining a custom-hosted event provider, record the assembly name of your event provider. *This step is not required for non-hosted event providers or standard event providers.*
4. If you are defining a hosted event provider, identify the server that runs the provider function of Notification Services. *This step is not required for non-hosted event providers.*
5. If defining a scheduled event provider, define the schedule for your event provider. This step is required only for scheduled hosted event providers. *This step is not required for event-driven or non-hosted event providers.*
6. If defining a hosted event provider that requires arguments, define the arguments that should be passed to your event provider each time it is initialized. *This step is unnecessary for event providers that do not require any arguments, or for non-hosted event providers.*

NOTE The Notification Services stored procedures `NSDiagnosticEventProvider` and `NSEventBatchDetails` can be used to gather information about an event provider and submitted events.

Standard Event Providers

Notification Services comes with two built-in standard event providers that help you develop and deploy Notification Services applications rapidly:

File System Watcher Event Provider: monitors an operating system directory, and is triggered when an XML file is added to the directory. It reads the file contents into memory, and then writes the event information to the event table via the EventLoader.

SQL Server Event Provider: uses either (1) developer-defined T-SQL query that polls a database table for changes or additions to its data. Notification Services–provided stored procedures are then used to create events based on this new or updated data, and to write these events to the event table. Or (2) a static or dynamic MDX query to gather data from an Analysis Services cube and submit the data as events to an application.

Subscription Metadata

Subscriptions determine what notifications subscribers receive and when. In addition, subscriptions can store information about the target devices for the notifications. For instance, a subscriber can have news alerts sent to his or her instant messaging service during the day, and have traffic alerts sent to a cell phone during commuting hours.

As explained earlier, you develop a subscription management application as a component of your Notification Services system to collect subscriber, subscription, and subscriber device information. You define the types of subscriptions your Notification Services application will accept by creating subscription classes in your ADF. You can define one or more subscription classes for each Notification Services application you develop.

Follow these steps to define a subscription class:

1. Name your subscription class.
2. Define the fields that make up your subscription class. These fields will validate any subscription data supplied by a subscription management application. Notification Services also uses them to create the SQL Server subscription table to hold the subscription data. SQL Server table creation occurs when the application is added to Notification Services by the system administrator, using the NSControl Create or NSControl Update command.
3. You can designate the SQL Server filegroup for the subscription table if you don't want to use the default value, which is the same filegroup as the application database.
4. To index your subscription table (an option), provide the T-SQL statements needed to create one or more indexes on your subscription table.
5. There will be an `<EventRules>` node if you define the event rules associated with this subscription class. Note that there must be at least one notification generation rule defined in either the `<EventRules>` or the `<ScheduledRules>` node to generate notifications.
6. A `<ScheduledRules>` node is present if you want to define the scheduled rules associated with this subscription class. You must have at least one notification generation rule defined in either the `<EventRules>` or the `<ScheduledRules>` node if you want to generate notifications.
7. If you want or need subscription chronicle tables in your application, define one or more subscription chronicle tables associated with this subscription class. The subscription chronicle tables store subscription data for use in your application.

NOTE You create one `<SubscriptionClass>` node for each subscription class that you have defined.

Notification Metadata

As you should be aware of by now, the whole point to Notification Services is to create notifications based on the subscriptions and events that are entered into the system. It does this by using a notification generation rule, which matches subscription information to event data.

A subscription class, as you saw above, is capable of providing both event-driven and scheduled subscriptions. You must create rules to handle either or both of these types of subscriptions, depending on your application, when you create your subscription class. Whether a particular subscription is event-driven or scheduled also determines when notifications for that subscription are generated and delivered, and what table is used to provide the event data used in the notification generation rule.

Notification generation populates the notification table with raw data. After the generator function completes, the batches are made available for formatting by the distributor function. Notification formatting aggregates the notification data, which is composed of notification fields and recipient information, and then formats this data appropriately for its destination device and specified locale.

In addition, you need to specify the channel by which the formatted notification is delivered. All of this information is defined in the Notification Class section of the ADF.

To define a notification class do the following:

1. Name your notification class.
2. Define the fields in your notification class. These fields provide the data that can be sent to your subscribers and are used to create the SQL Server notification table that stores the notification data.
3. You can designate the SQL Server filegroup for the notification table if you don't want to use the default value, which is the same filegroup as the application database.
4. Declare to the content formatter that this notification class is to use. (The content formatter takes the raw notification data and formats it appropriately for display.)
5. Indicate whether this notification class uses digest delivery. Digest delivery means that all notifications for the same subscriber that are generated by one execution of the notification generation rule are grouped and handled as a single notification.
6. If you are using Notification Services Enterprise Edition, indicate whether this notification class uses multicast delivery. Multicast delivery means that all notifications that share identical data and are in the same distributor work item are formatted just once, and then this formatted data is sent out to all subscribers.
7. If you are using Notification Services Enterprise Edition, specify a notification batch size for notifications of this class.
8. Specify one or more delivery protocols to use for notification delivery. This consists of specifying header or other notification-specific information required for messages created by this delivery protocol.
9. Specify an expiration age for notifications of this class.

Deploying and Managing Notification Services with Management Studio

As you will have noticed we have covered a lot of material on Notification Services, nearly all of which has to do with development. But for Notification Services to be of any value, you must successfully deploy all of its components. The simplest way to deploy it is through Management Studio. SQL Server 2005 Notification Services includes a set of sample application that we will use to illustrate the various steps. In our example here we use the Stock sample, which provides event-driven and scheduled subscriptions. The Notification Services samples are installed by default to `C:\Program Files\Microsoft SQL Server\90\Tools\Samples\1033\Engine\Notifcation Services`.

NOTE Before running the sample make sure that you have installed Notification Services.

1. From the Start ➢ Programs ➢ Microsoft SQL Server 2005 ➢ SQL Server Management Studio. When prompted connect to an instance of SQL Server 2005.
2. In Object Explorer, right-click the Notification Services folder and select New Notification Services Instance to open the dialog box.

3. Click the Browse button and select the `appConfig.xml` file in the Stock sample's root folder: `C:\Program Files\Microsoft SQL Server\90\ \Samples\\ \Notification Services\ Stock\InstanceConfig.xml`.

4. In the Parameters box, enter `C:\Program Files\Microsoft SQL Server\90\Samples\ Notification Services\Stock\InstanceConfig.xml` in the SampleDirectory field.

5. In NotificationServicesHost, enter your local server name (in this example we will use one named GARAK).

6. In the box marked SqlServer, enter the name of the SQL Server instance (again GARAK in this example).

7. Mark the box next to "Enable instance after it is created" and click OK.

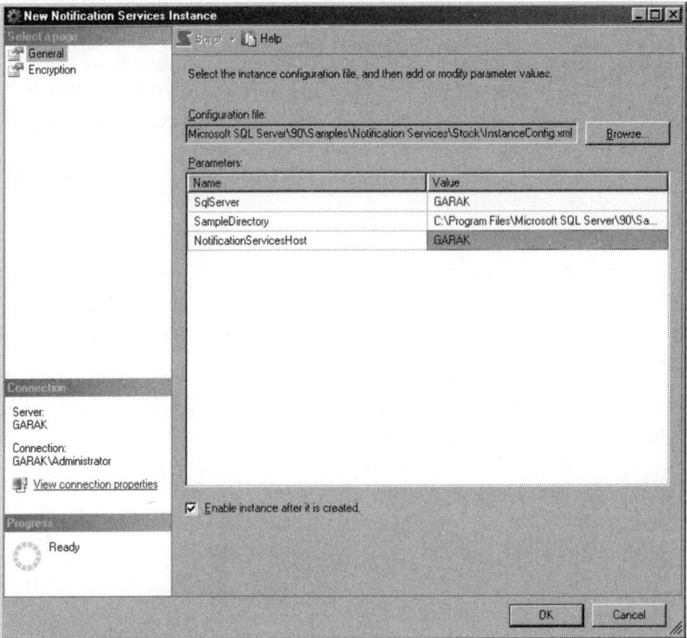

8. After the instance has been successfully created, click the Close button.

9. Now that the Notification Services instance has been created and enabled, you need to register the instance of Notification Services and create the Windows service needed to run Notification Services. Open the Notification Services folder, right-click StockInstance, point to Tasks, and then select Register.

10. In the Register dialog box, select the Create Windows service check box. This is the Windows service that runs the instance of Notification Services on this computer.

11. Under Service Logon, enter a Windows account and password. This must be a local, domain, or built-in Windows account that is a member of the Users group on the local computer. This is the Windows account under which the service will run. If you use Windows Authentication to access SQL Server, the Windows service will also use this account to connect to SQL Server. (Microsoft recommends using Windows Authentication.)

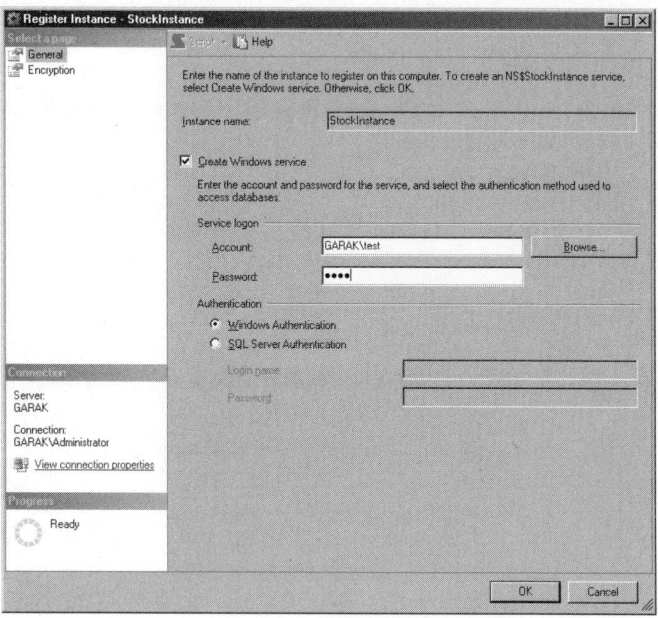

12. Click OK. When Notification Services has finished registering the instance, click Close.

13. In Object Explorer, expand the Security folder. If you need to create a new database login account for the Windows service, right-click Logins and select New Login and create the Login account. To use Windows authentication, select Windows authentication and enter the same Windows account you specified when registering the instance.

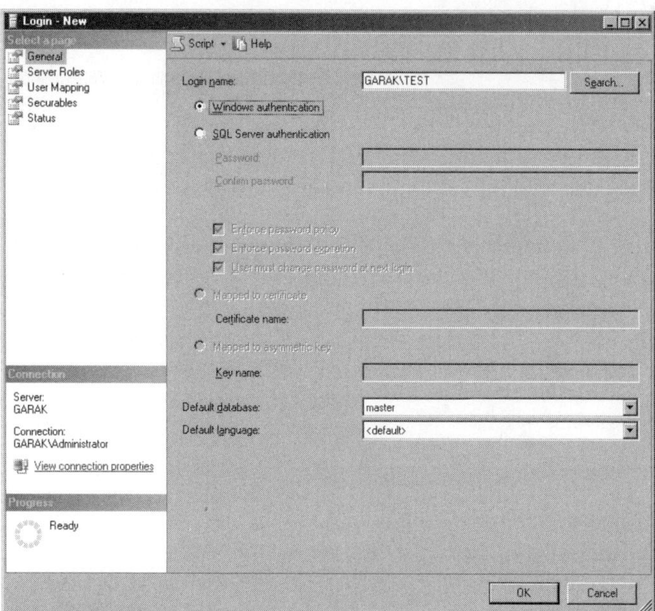

NOTE If the login already exists, simply right-click on the login ID, select properties, and in the Login dialog box select User Mapping. If the login is new, then in the left pane of the Login dialog box, select User Mapping.

14. In the "Users mapped to this login" box, select StockInstanceNSMain by marking the map check box.
15. In the "Database role membership for StockInstanceNSMain" box, select NSRunService.
16. In the "Users mapped to this login" section, select StockInstanceStock by marking the map checkbox.
17. In the "Database roles for StockInstanceStock" box, select NSRunService. Click OK to apply the permissions.

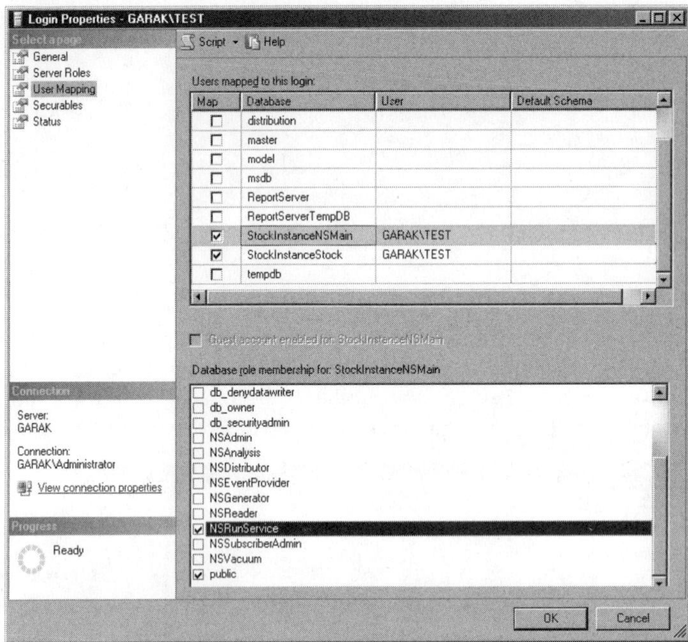

18. Before going any further we need to configure security for the Events folder. To do so, navigate to the Stock sample's Events folder using Windows Explorer. Right-click the Events folder, select Sharing And Security, and then select the Security tab. Click the Add button and add the account used by the Windows service and give the account Read and Modify permissions. Click OK to apply the changes.

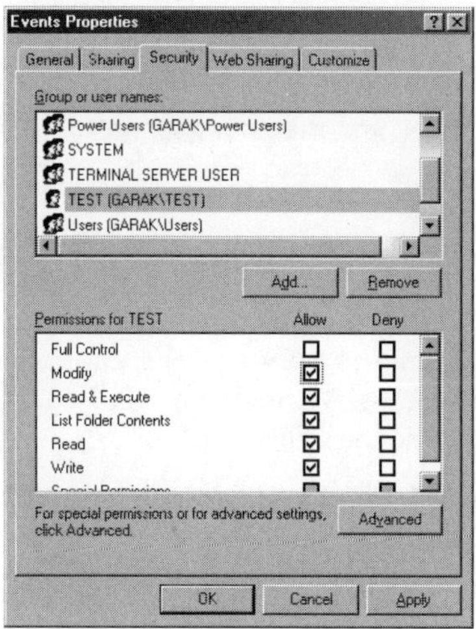

19. Next, navigate to the Stock sample's Notifications folder. Right-click the Notifications folder, select Sharing and Security, and then select the Security tab. Click the Add button and add the account used by the Windows service. In the "Group or user names" box, select the account you just added. In the "Permissions for" box, select Write to add it to the other permissions. Click OK to apply the changes.

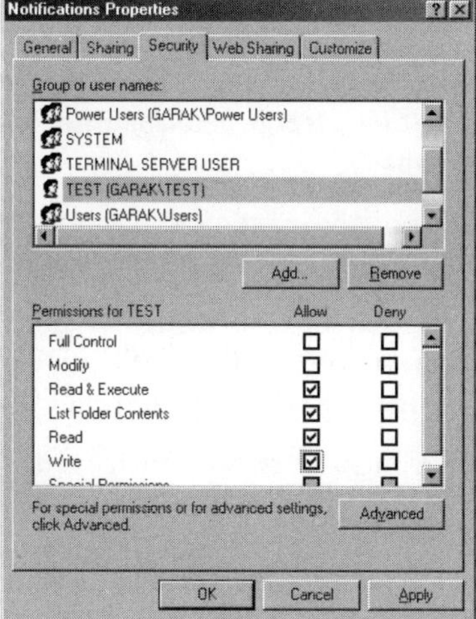

20. In Object Explorer, open the Notification Services folder. Right-click StockInstance and then select Start. (In Windows 2003 Server you will be prompted to confirm that you want to start all Windows Services associated with the instance. Click Yes)

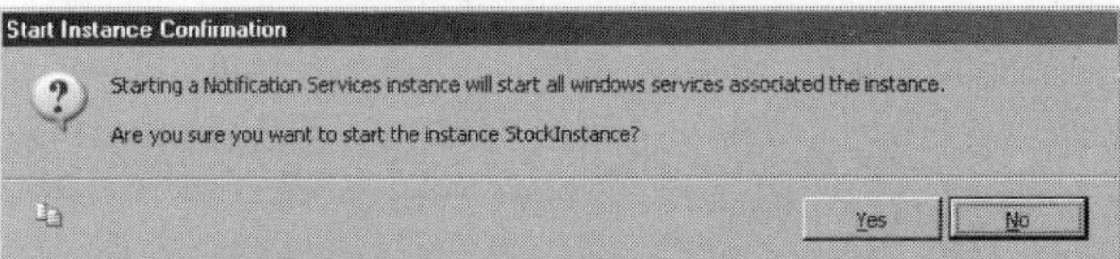

We are going to add subscribers, subscriptions, and events using the Microsoft .NET Framework SDK (optionally you can use Visual Studio 2005), using C# (optionally you can use Visual Basic). To do so you need to do the following:

1. From the Start menu, ➤ Programs ➤ Microsoft .NET Framework SDK v2.0, and then click .NET Framework SDK Command Prompt.
2. To reach the Stock sample's root folder, type the following command for the default location: **`cd C:\Program Files\Microsoft SQL Server\90\Samples\Notification Services\Stock\`**.
3. To build the subscribers project type: **`msbuild /nologo  /verbosity:quiet /property:Configuration=Debug AddSubscribers\cs\AddSubscribers\AddSubscribers.csproj`**.
4. Type the following to run `AddSubscribers.exe`: **`AddSubscribers\cs\AddSubscribers\bin\Debug\AddSubscribers.exe`**.
5. Type the following to build the Subscriptions project :**`msbuild /nologo /verbosity:quiet /property:Configuration=Debug AddSubscriptions\cs\AddSubscriptions\AddSubscriptions.csproj`**.
6. Type the following to run `AddSubscriptions.exe`: **`[C#] AddSubscriptions\cs\AddSubscriptions\bin\Debug\AddSubscriptions.exe`**.
7. Type the following to build the NonHostedEventProvider project: **`msbuild /nologo /verbosity:quiet /property:Configuration=Debug NonHostedEventProvider\vb\NonHostedEventProvider\NonHostedEventProvider.csproj`**.
8. Type the following to run `NonHostedEventProvider.exe`: **`NonHostedEventProvider\cs\NonHostedEventProvider\bin\Debug\NonHostedEventProvider.exe`**.

USING VISUAL STUDIO 2005

If you are using Visual Studio 2005, do the following:

Open the solution file of your choice (`Stock.sln` or `Stock_VB.sln`).

Run the AddSubscribers project to add subscribers.

Run the AddSubscriptions project to add subscriptions.

Run the NonHostedEventProvider project to add one event using a non-hosted provider.

9. To test your sample and generate a notification, in Windows Explorer, navigate to the Stock sample's root folder, and then copy the `EventData.xml` file to the Events subfolder. When you drop the file, the file system watcher event provider will read the data from the file, submit it to the application, and then change the file extension to .done.

NOTE If there is an error when reading or submitting data, the event provider will change the file extension to .err. Look in the Windows Event Viewer for additional details about the error.

10. Give Notification Services about a minute to produce notifications, then navigate to the Stock sample's Notifications folder. You should find a file named `FileNotifications.txt`. This file contains all notifications sent by this application.

Summary

We've covered a lot of ground in this chapter and if you're a bit confused or overwhelmed, don't be too concerned. The key points to keep in mind are that Notification Services is intended to respond to requests by users about changes to the data that they specify. In NS-ese we say that Notification Services sends subscribers notifications of events based on their individual subscriptions. We have also reviewed and determined that the basic simplicity of Notification Services design makes it elegantly suited for maximum flexibility by designers and developers. The new features allow you to send notifications to a variety of devices and even customize those notifications based on the time of day.

We've also looked at the basic architecture and the two main files you will have to be concerned with when developing your own notification applications, the configuration, and applications definition files. Finally, as you will have seen in our walkthough, setting up and deploying an instance of Notification Services is quite simple and involves only a few basic steps.

Chapter 28

Reporting Services

As you've seen, SQL Server 2005 does an excellent job helping you gather, store, analyze, tweak, manipulate, transform, reform, and just about anything else you can think to do with data. If that's all there was to effective use of data and the databases they are stored in, then we'd be done.

However, in order for information to be of any value it needs to shared, typically in the form of a report. If your database is in a business environment, it may contain information on sales, finance, production, delivery, or any of a dozen other areas. This information, sometimes called business intelligence, is important to your organization. And the reality is that if the business intelligence can't be put into a form where it can be given to others who need to know or make decisions based on those data, it's all been a waste of energy.

Ideally you should have a means of making sure that you have the ability to extract and present information from a database in any number of different combinations of format, timing, security, and outputs, with minimal hassle and to the widest possible audience.

That's what SQL Server Reporting Services does. Reporting Services provides an environment in which you can create a number of different types of reports from a number of different data sources. Once completed, you can deploy the reports to a report server, which then makes them available via the Internet in a structured, secure environment. This easy sharing of "business intelligence" with management, coworkers, partners, and customers allows for companywide, nationwide, and global communication. It allows you to use the data from relational and multidimensional sources and create and manage freeform, tabular, matrix, and graphical reports derived from that data. These reports can be based on data from SQL Server, Analysis Services, Oracle, and any .NET data provider (e.g., ODBC). You can create the reports on your own, or use predefined models and data sources.

In this chapter we discuss Reporting Services and how to use them to help you maximize the benefit of your gathered business intelligence.

Uses of Reporting Services

As you have already figured out from the above, Reporting Services can be a valuable tool in any number of instances. In a business environment (or any other environment where databases are in use for that matter), Reporting Services can be used to prepare and distribute information to users who need reports to assist in making decisions as well as assessing threats and opportunities, whether on a routine or ad hoc basis.

Let's look at some examples of what might be required of typical business reports. For the sake of this discussion we'll examine the needs of a mythical health provider, Gideon Healthcare, which operates a chain of hospitals across the Northeast and Midwest United States.

Gideon Healthcare's medical supplies department uses an order-entry system that updates the inventory database every 8 hours. However, the procurement director is concerned that this frequency may not be adequate because of the tendency of large orders or health events to suddenly change the available on-hand stock, creating pressure on the supplies director to maintain proper stock levels. These directors requested a new system that will provide them with an up-to-date report that is sent immediately to their computers following an update to the inventory database during business hours so they can make changes to acquisition orders within an hour of updates as needed. The report should be sent to both directors' computers as soon as possible. Complicating the matter a bit is that Gideon Healthcare's laboratory warehouse in stored in Pennsylvania, while the inventory system is in New Hampshire.

You are also responsible for maintaining information on the manpower status of the company, particularly temporary employees that are used in the various laboratories. This information is updated daily in the database. A report covering manpower utilization and forecasts is printed weekly at corporate headquarters and mailed to each personnel director. The human resources director would like the manpower data to be available to the personnel directors in a timelier manner so that temporary employees can be identified and vacations scheduled efficiently. This report should be accessible over the Internet from anywhere in the country and based on data in the database.

The CEO has her own set of requirements. She instructs you to provide her with information on key aspects of the company—for example, the balance sheet, inventory status, sales, manpower levels, and stock prices—at 8:00 A.M. each day. The information needs to be in a format that is appropriate for printing and sharing with senior management at their daily 9:30 A.M. meeting.

As you can see from these very simple examples, reports might be requested or needed in a virtually unlimited number of ways. In general reports tend to fall into two types. Standard scheduled reports occur regularly in a standard format, on a standard schedule such as that being requested by the CEO. The second type are ad hoc reports that are created as needed. As you will see, Reporting Services includes tools that allow you to create and refine both types of reports, with a high degree of flexibility.

Finally, if you are a developer or advanced user you can use Reporting Services technology to incorporate reporting features in a custom application either through an API and coding or by making using the Report Viewer controls that are included in Visual Studio 2005 when the application doesn't require a report server and its features.

Reporting Overview

Before diving into making reports and using them, it's worth taking a few moments to go over the basics. Understanding these features, terms, and tools before you actually start making reports will help you create better reports and manage Reporting Services more efficiently and effectively.

Reporting Life Cycle

Every report has a reporting life cycle that consists of three separate activities:

Report Authoring This is the first phase and refers to the process of defining the report, its properties, how users interact with it, and its "look and feel."

To create a report, the first step is to connect to a data source and get the data. This can be done by a creating a report model that specifies the data you want to work with or through connection strings and queries. Next, you create the report layout, either through preexisting templates or by creating your own from scratch. Finally, preview the report and, if satisfied, publish the report to a report server.

As you'll see in more detail below, Reporting Services has two primary authoring tools, based on what the report requires and the expertise of the report author. Report Designer runs in Visual Studio and is thus the more flexible and high powered of the two as we'll see below. It's intended for data processing professionals though the Report Wizard automates a large part of the process. Report Builder provides ad hoc reporting from relational data sources and is intended for users who know their data, but aren't necessarily data processing professional.

Report Management Once you've created the reports and published them to a report server, you need to manage them, as well as related items like folders, resources, connections, and so on. Reporting Services allows you to do so from a central location, the report server, with a standardized set of tools—either SQL Server Management Studio or Report Manager. Using these tools you can perform a large number of tasks including:

- Defining security
- Setting properties
- Scheduling activities
- Enabling server features
- Creating shared schedules and shared data sources

Reporting Services allows both users and report server administrators to manage reports. Users do this in My Reports, a personal workspace where they can publish and manage their own reports. Administrators can manage the entire report server folder namespace.

Report Delivery The final activity of the reporting life cycle focuses on delivering reports to the end user either in paper format or by making the report accessible to the user. Reporting Services provides two basic methods for accessing and delivering reports.

On-demand access means that users utilize a report viewing tool (e.g., Report Manager, a SharePoint Web Part, or a browser) to access the report when they want to by searching through a report server folder hierarchy. In the Gideon Healthcare example, you are being asked to set up the manpower report for on-demand access.

The other access is subscription-based. A report server administrator creates a report that is automatically delivered to a destination when an event triggers it. Referring back to the Gideon Healthcare example, subscription-based access is what is being created for the procurement and supplies directors. It is also what is being delivered to the CEO, with the trigger in her case being the time of day. The report can be delivered to an e-mail address or a file share with a notification sent that the report is available.

Viewing reports is available through a number of options including HTML, MHTML, XML, CSV, TIFF, PDF, and Excel.

Key Terms

Before proceeding any further it's also important that we define the key terms that you'll find throughout the rest of this book. In the next section, we'll provide an overview of the various tools available in Reporting Services. You'll probably find that learning the jargon is in some ways more difficult than making use of the technology.

Report Definition This is the blueprint for the report usually created with Report Designer or Report Builder. The report definition contains information about the query, format, and other design elements that need to be provided when the report is run. The definition of the report is specified in XML and stored in a file with an RDL (Report Definition Language) extension.

Published Report After an RDL file is created it is then published to a report server. This can be done by deploying it with Report Designer, saving from Report Builder, or uploading it via either Report Manager or Management Studio. The published report is kept in an intermediate format that makes it readily accessible to report users. Only published reports created and saved in Report Builder can be edited or saved back to the report server.

Rendered Report In order for the published report to be viewed, it has to be processed by a report server. The resulting processed report is called a rendered report and contains data and layout information in a format suitable for viewing. Reports are rendered by opening a published report on the report server or having one rendered and sent to an inbox or file share in response to a subscription. Rendered reports can't be edited or saved back to the report server.

Parameterized Report This report type makes use of input values to complete the report. Reporting Services supports both query parameters, which are used during data processing to select or filter data, and report parameters used during report processing, typically to filter large record sets.

Linked Report These are typically used whenever you want to create additional versions of an existing report. The linked report retains the original's report layout and data source properties but allows for changes in all the other settings of the original report such as security, parameters, subscriptions, and so on.

Report Snapshot As the name implies this type of report contains data captured at a single moment in time. These reports are usually created on a schedule basis and stored on a report server for a variety of purposes such as maintaining report history, creating standardized data sets for highly volatile data, and performance enhancement by running them off hours.

Report Model Used for creating ad hoc reports with Report Builder, the report model provides a user-friendly description of the underlying database. Once created using Model Designer and published to a Report Server, a report model allows users to create their own reports without specialized knowledge of how to build queries, data source connections, security, and other technical aspects of report design. Think of it as a paint-by-numbers tool for users to generate reports.

Folder Hierarchy/Report Server Folder Namespace Used interchangeably, the terms refer to the namespace that identifies all the reports, folder, models, shared data source items, and resources stored and managed on a report server. This namespace is composed of predefined and user-defined virtual folders on a report server, as shown in Figure 28.1. This namespace can be accessed via a web browser or a web-enabled application.

FIGURE 28.1
Report Server Folder Namespace showing predefined folder

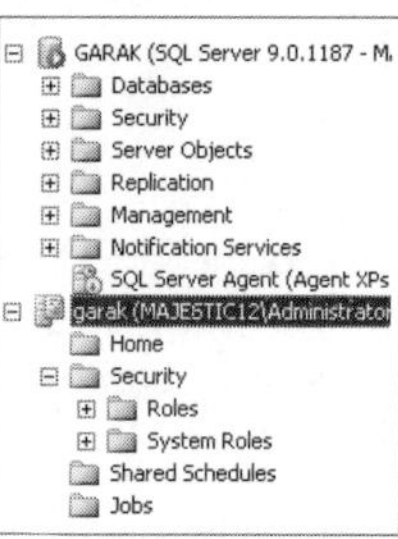

Key Components

In this section, we'll introduce you to the key components and tools of Reporting Services. These include:

- Report Server
- Report Manager
- Report Designer
- Report Builder
- Model Designer
- Reporting Services Configuration Tool
- Report Server Command Prompt Utilities

In addition, Reporting Services includes support of various programmatic interfaces including Windows Management Instrumentation (WMI), Simple Object Access Protocol (SOAP), and URL endpoints.

Report Server A report server is the main processing component of Reporting Services. The principal functions of a report server are to process reports and to make reports available for access either on demand or via subscription. It is also where the various reports are managed and administered.

Report Manager This is a web-based access and management tool that runs in Internet Explorer. Report Manager can be used to administer a report server remotely through HTTP. Report Manager can also be used for report viewing and navigation. Key tasks performed with Report Manager include browsing report server folder, viewing reports and their properties, subscribing to reports, and accessing My Reports folders in the case of an individual user. You can also manage a report server's folder hierarchy and a number of other management and administrative tasks, including creating shared schedules and data-driven subscriptions.

NOTE You can also manage reports by using Management Studio and administer a report server with SQL Server Configuration Manager.

Report Designer Report Designer is based on Visual Studio and accessed through BIDS. Report Designer allows you to create tabular, matrix, or freeform reports; the first two can be created using Report Wizard. Report Designer was intended for use by IT professionals and application developers.

Report Builder Report Builder is an ad hoc reporting tool intended for use by end users who want to generate ad hoc reports simply and effectively without having to understand the data source structure. End users can quickly build and preview reports based on a set of report templates, called a report model. Report Builder employs an easy-to-use drag-and-drop interface. Visual Studio is not needed to author reports, but because Report Builder reports are stored using RDL, they can be edited and modified later using Visual Studio.

Model Designer This tool is used to create the report models used in Report Builder. The Model Designer connects to either a Data Source View in Analysis Server, or to the SQL Server relational database (2005 or 2000) to extract metadata. Only one data source can be currently referenced in a report.

Reporting Services Configuration Tool This tool is used to configure a local or remote report server instance. It must be used to configure a report server installed with the files-only option. The following component tasks can be performed with the Reporting Services Configuration Tool:

- Creating and configuring virtual directories
- Configuring service accounts
- Creating and configuring the report server database
- Managing encryption keys and initializing the report server
- Configuring e-mail delivery

Reporting Services Command Prompt Utilities There are three command-line utilities that can be used to administer a report server.

- The `rsconfig` utility is used to configure a report server connection to the report server database. It also encrypts the connection values.
- The `rskeymgmt` utility is a versatile encryption key management tool that can be used to back up, apply, and re-create symmetric keys. In addition, the tool allows you to attach a shared report server database to a report server instance. The `rs` utility is used to run Visual Basic .NET scripts that operate on report server databases.

Creating Reports

In this section, we'll look at the actual steps involved in using SQL Server 2005 Reporting Services to create, or author a report. To do this, we'll use the AdventureWorks DW sample database that ships with SQL Server. As you have already seen there are two reporting authoring tools, Report Designer and Report Builder.

Using Report Designer

Report Designer has three ways to create report. You can start with a blank report and add your own queries and layout. A second option is to use Report Wizard to automatically create a table or matrix report based on information you provide. Last, you can import an existing report from Microsoft Access. The majority of the time you'll use the Report Wizard for simplicity and ease of use.

Creating a Report with Report Wizard

1. Launch Business Intelligence Development Studio (BIDS) from Start ➢ Programs ➢ Microsoft SQL Server 2005.
2. From the File menu select New ➢ Project to open the New Project dialog box.
3. Confirm that Business Intelligence Projects is selected in the left pane and Report Server Project Wizard is selected in the right pane.
4. In the Name text box type **ReportWizardExample**, accept the default Location and Solution name, and click OK.

   The Report Wizard should start automatically.

TIP If the Report Wizard does not start automatically, you can launch the wizard by opening the Project menu and selecting Add New Item. Alternatively you can right-click the project in Solution Explorer and select Add ➤ New Item from the pop-up menu. Both methods will open the Add New Item dialog box. And then highlight Report Wizard and click Add to launch the Report Wizard.

5. On the Welcome to the Report Wizard window, click Next to go to the Select Data Source dialog box. Select the New data source radio button and make sure the type is set to Microsoft SQL Server. Then click the Edit button to open the Connection Properties dialog.
6. In Server name text box, type **localhost** or use the drop-down button to select a server.
7. Under Log onto the server, confirm the Use Windows Authentication radio button is selected.
8. Under Connect to a Database, in the "Select or enter a database name" select the Adventure-Works DW database. You can use the Test Connection button to confirm you are connected to both the server and the database.

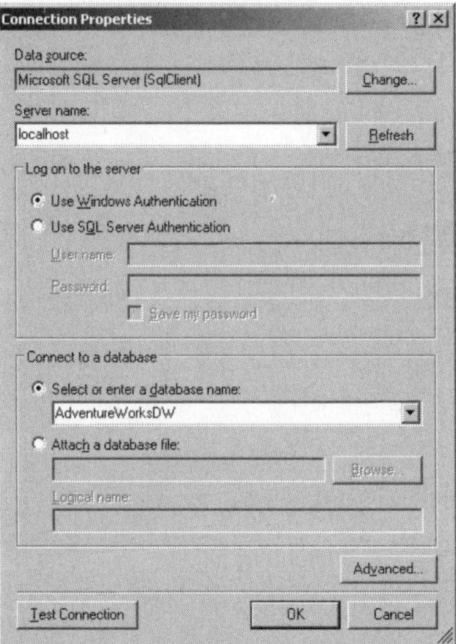

9. Click OK to return to the Select the Data Source dialog box. Confirm that the local server and AdventureWorksDW database are listed in the connection string. Click Next.

10. In the Design the Query dialog box, you can use Query Builder to design a query. In this example you'll use a very simple query to provide information on staff vacation hours and sick hours. To do so enter the following:

```
USE AdventureWorksDW
SELECT FirstName,LastName, DepartmentName,VacationHours, SickLeaveHours FROM
DimEmployee
```

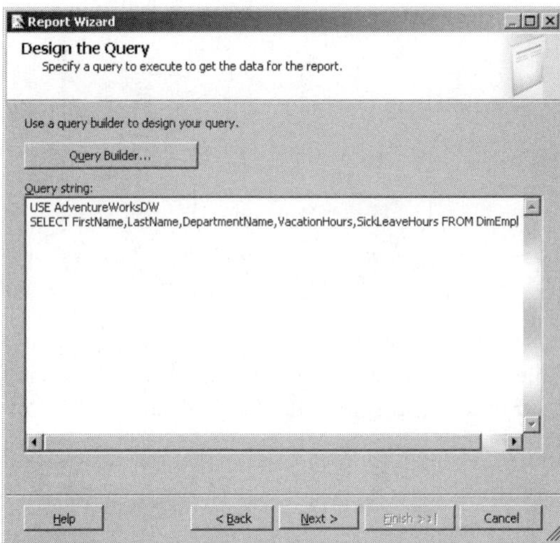

11. Click Next to open the Select the Report Type dialog box. Confirm that the radio button next to Tabular is selected and click Next.

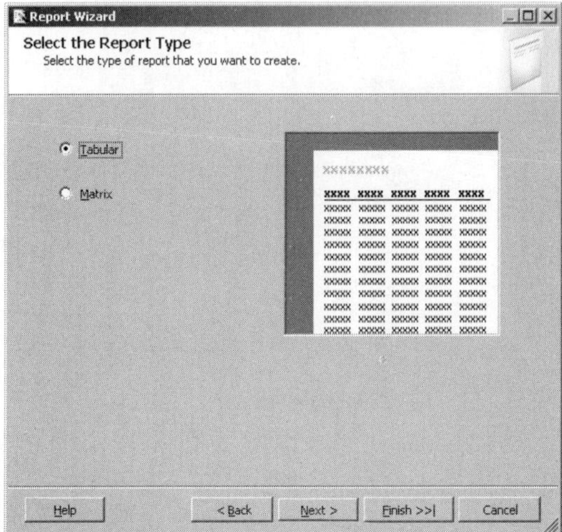

12. In the Design the Table dialog box you will see the five selected fields from the Adventure-WorksDW database in the Available fields box on the left side of the page. You will also see three buttons, Page, Group, and Details, that are used for specifying fields to be added, a fourth button, Remove, is used to remove fields. In this example you want to group employee vacation and sick leave information by department. Highlight the `DepartmentName` field and either click the Group button or drag it into Group box. Add the `FirstName`, `LastName`, `VacationHours`, and `SickLeaveHours` fields into the Details box. You can change the order of fields by highlighting them and dragging them in the list. Rearrange the details displayed in the field list so that `LastName` appears first. Click Next.

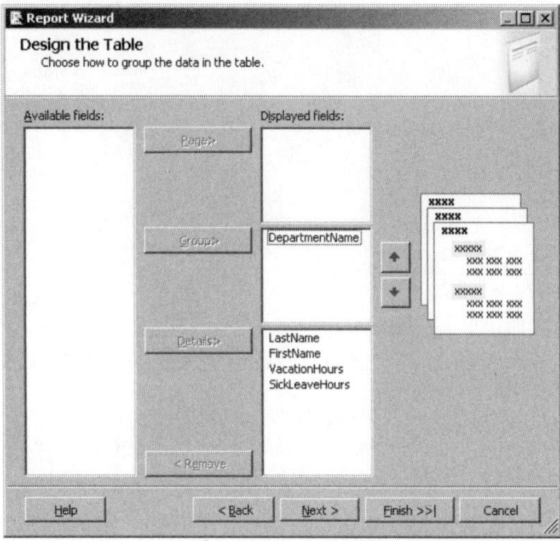

13. In the Choose the Table Layout dialog box, you can choose a variety of options, including whether to allow drilldown and to include subtotals. For this example simply click Next.

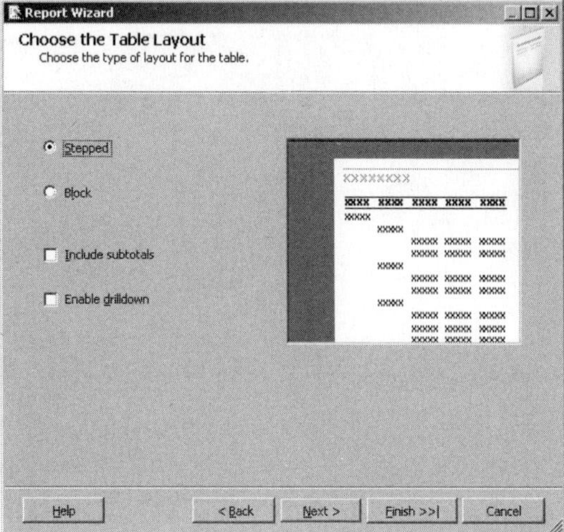

14. In the Choose the Table Style dialog window, select Corporate. Click Next.

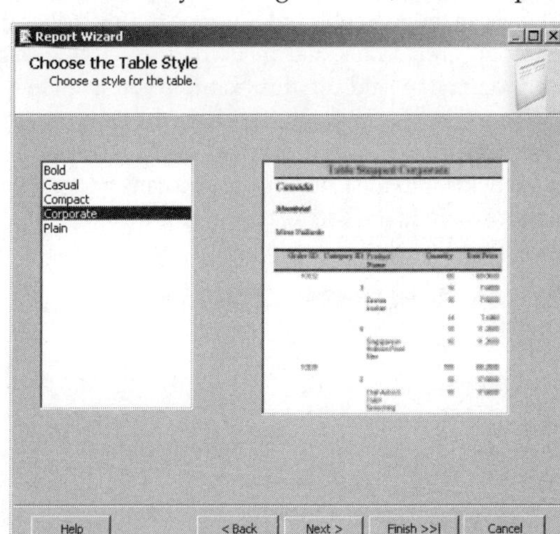

15. In the Choose Deployment Location dialog window, accept the default locations for the report server and deployment folder on the server. Click Next.

16. On the Completing the Wizard page, name the report Available Employee Vacation and Sick Time by Department. Review the contents of the Report Summary to confirm entries are correct. Mark the Preview report check box and press Finish.

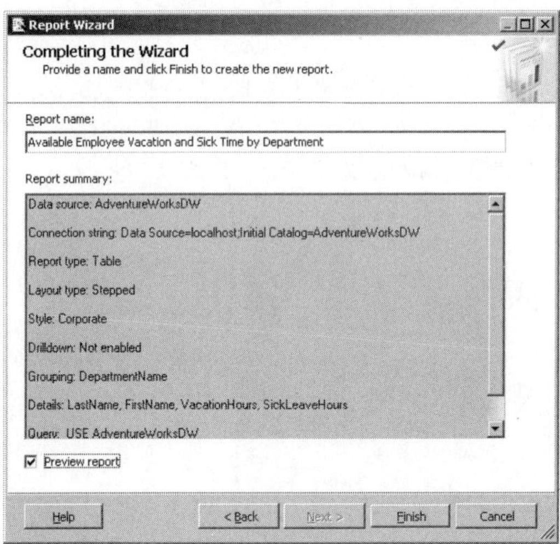

17. After a few moments the report is processed and a preview displayed in BIDS. Note also that the report has been added to the Reports Folder under ReportWizardExample in Solution Explorer.

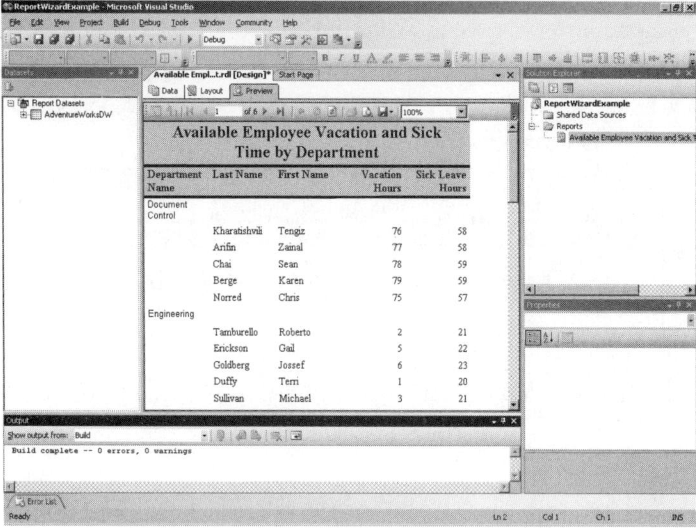

Modifying a Report

Modifying report layouts is very simple with Report Designer. You can make changes to the underlying queries and report layout.

1. Suppose you decide that you would like the Available Vacation Hours report to sort employees by last name as well as group by department. Click on the Data tab to open the Data view. In the Query section add the following line to the end of the query you wrote in step 10: `ORDER BY LastName`. Next re-run the query, then open the preview and note the changes.

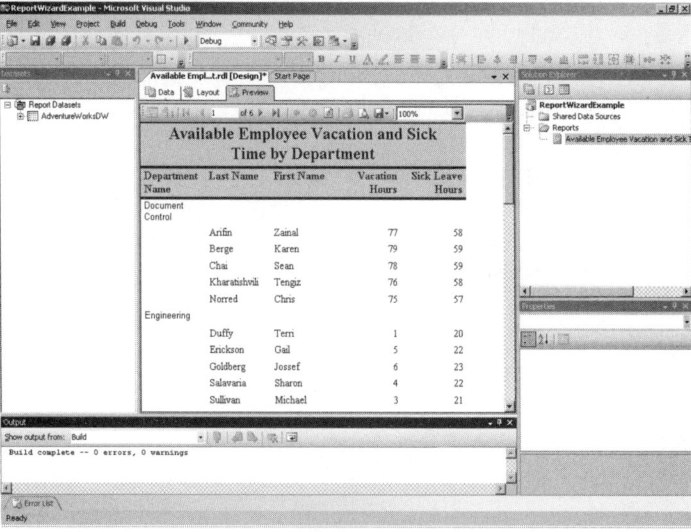

2. Modifying a report layout is also relatively simple. Select the Layout tab and then the Body section of the report. Move the cursor over the table column divider in the bar above `VacationHours` and `SickLeave`. When it changes to a double arrow, drag the column width for the `VacationHours` column so that it shows both Vacation and Hours (about 1.4 inches).

3. Click on Title and change it from Available Employee Vacation and Sick Time by Department to Employee Vacation and Sick Time. When done, the report layout should appear as shown below:

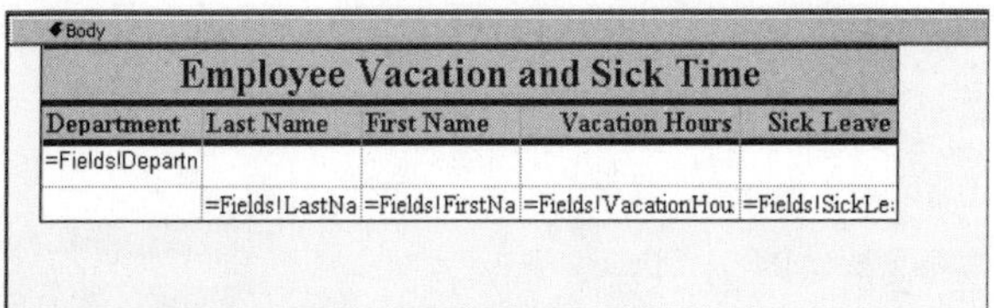

4. You can also use the individual property sheets to adjust and modify individual field and report components. These properties include:

   - Display name
   - Associated tool tips
   - Visibility
   - Navigational elements
   - Font type, size, color, weight, decoration
   - Sorting
   - Actions
   - Placement on the page
   - Alignment
   - Background and foreground colors

In fact there really isn't an element of a report, be it data presentation or aesthetics, that you can't manipulate or modify to meet the user requirements.

Creating a Report Using Report Designer

Although Report Wizard will probably be able to address most of your needs, it has limitations. For example, Report Wizard cannot be used to create freeform reports. In those cases you will need to create reports using Report Designer. You can use this tool to create reports in a number of different formats and elements such as:

- Textboxes
- Tables
- Matrices
- Lists
- Images

- Subreports
- Charts

In this next section, we'll create a simple freeform report using Report Designer.

1. Launch BIDS from Start ➤ Programs ➤ Microsoft SQL Server 2005.
2. From the File menu select New ➤ Project to open the New Project dialog box.
3. Confirm that Business Intelligence Projects is selected in the left pane and Report Server Project is selected in the right pane.
4. In the Name text box, type **ReportProjectExample**, accept the default Location and Solution Name, and click OK.

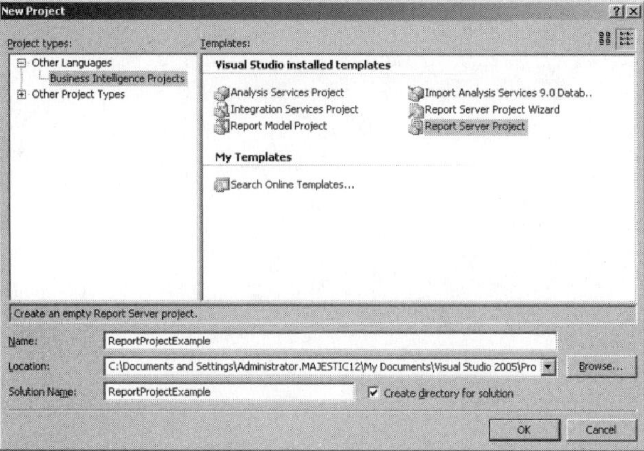

5. In Solution Explorer, right-click ReportProjectExample and select Add ➤ New Item from the pop-up menu.
6. In the Add New Item dialog box, select Report.

WARNING Make sure to select Report, *not* Report Wizard.

7. In the Name text box, enter **ReportProjectExample.rdl** and click Add.

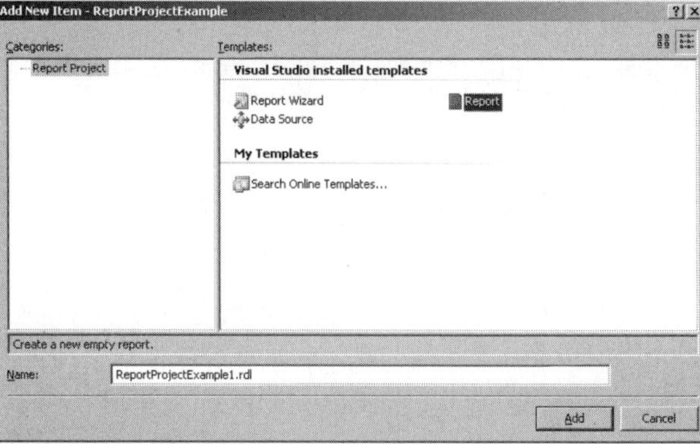

8. In order to create a report there needs to be associated data. We will associate the AdventureWorksDW database with this report. At the top of the Report Designer window, first make sure that the Data tab is selected.

9. In the Dataset drop-down list, select <New Dataset…> to open the Data Source dialog box. Accept the default name and ensure that Microsoft SQL Server is listed under Type. Then, click the Edit button.

10. In Server name text box type **localhost** or use the drop-down button to select a server.

11. Under "Log on to the server," confirm the Use Windows Authentication radio button is selected.

12. Under "Connect to a database" in the "Select or enter a database name," box select the AdventureWorksDW database. You can use the Test Connection button to confirm you are connected to both the server and the database.

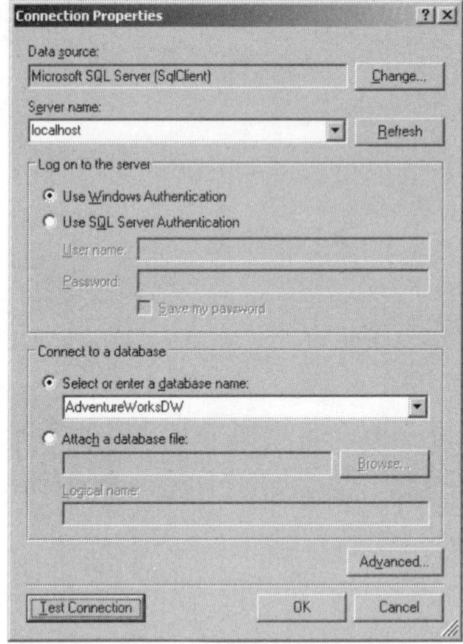

13. Click OK to return to the Select the Data Source dialog box. Confirm that the local server and AdventureWorksDW database are listed in the connection string. Click Next to return to Report Designer.

14. Now you'll create a simple query for the data set. In this case we'll use the same query as we did with the Report Builder Example above:

```
USE AdventureWorksDW
SELECT FirstName,LastName, DepartmentName,VacationHours, SickLeaveHours FROM
DimEmployee
```

15. Now you're ready to create the report layout. In the View pane, click the Layout tab to show the blank report grid in the Layout pane. You can resize the report grid by moving the mouse to a side or bottom edge and clicking and dragging when the pointer changes to a double-headed arrow.

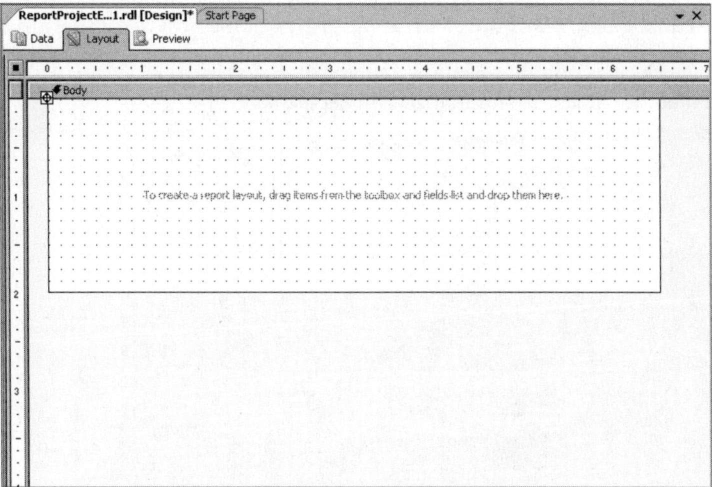

16. Open the Toolbox window by clicking on the Tool icon on the menu or selecting View ➢ Toolbox. Also ensure that the Dataset view is active so that you can access the field. If not you can open it by selecting View ➢ Datasets or pressing the Ctrl-Alt-D keys.

17. In this example you'll create a simple list report showing the total number of vacation and sick leave hours per department. In the Toolbox window, select the List item and double-click it. Then, expand the control so it is the same width as the grid and about eight grid points high.

18. Select the `DepartmentName` field from the Dataset tab and place it on the left side of the layout.

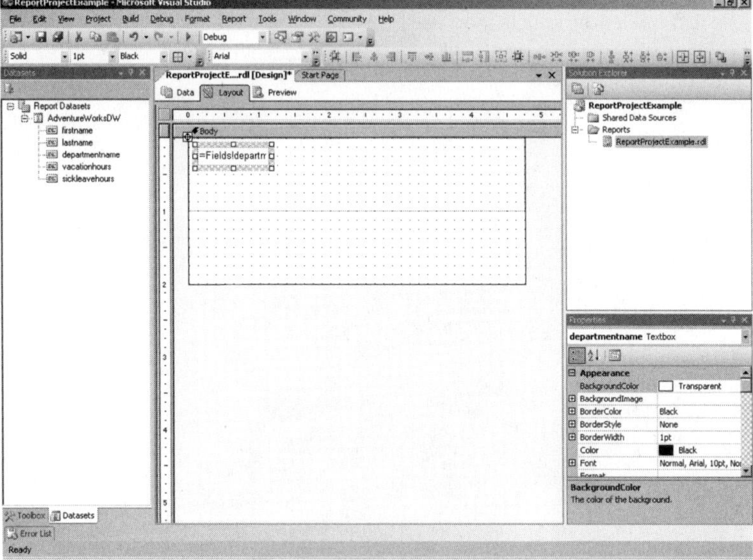

19. Right-click inside the List box. Select Properties from the pop-up menu. In the List Properties dialog box, select the General tab and click the Edit details group button.

20. In the Details Grouping window, in the Expression list, select `=Field!DepartmentName.Value` so that the values are summarized by department.

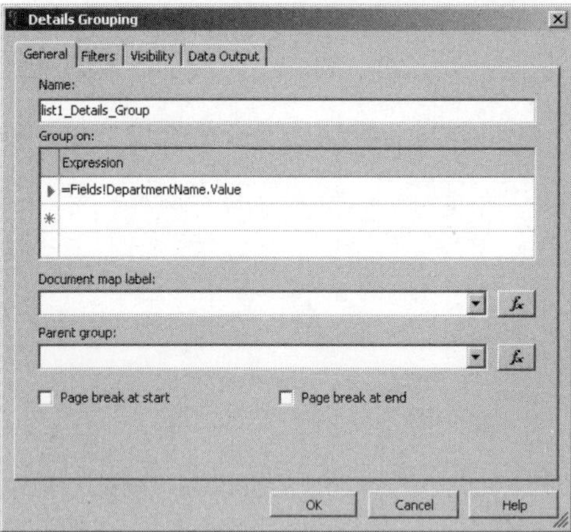

21. Under the Sorting tab, select `=Field!DepartmentName.Value` and Ascending direction to sort the department names alphabetically.

22. Click OK twice to return to the Report Layout window. In the Datasets window select `VacationHours` and then the `SickLeaveHours` and drag them to the right of the DepartmentName box.

23. To change the appearance of the font and basic settings in the DepartmentName text box select the text box and then click on the Properties icon. Expand Font and set FontWeight to Bold.

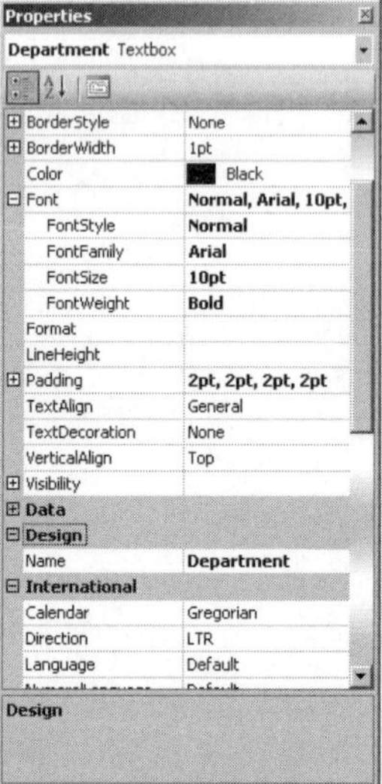

TIP You can also change many, but not all, design properties by selecting the control, right-clicking, and selecting Properties from the pop-up menu.

The Report Layout window should match the following graphic:

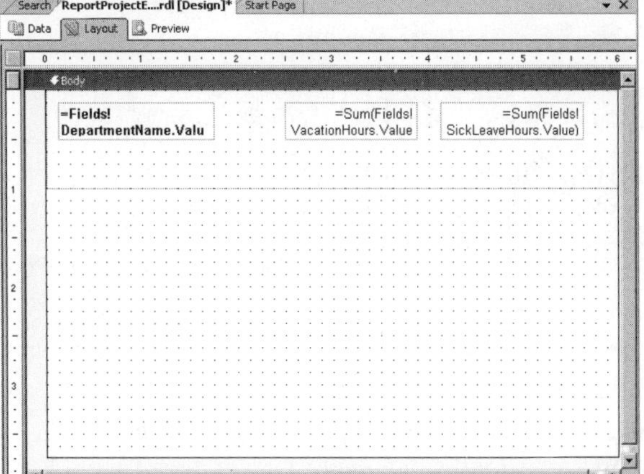

24. Before proceeding further, select File ➤ Save All from the menu.

25. Click on the Preview tab, the results should look like those displayed in the graphic:

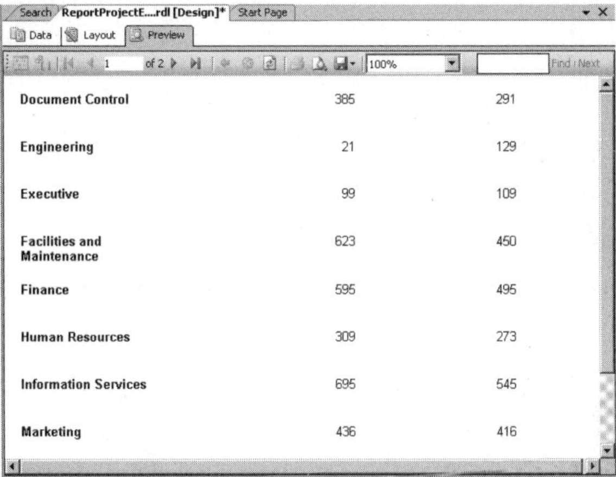

As you can see, the report is lacking many of features you might expect, such as column headings and so forth. Creating and using these elements depends on your needs and how they are reflected in the individual report design. Adding the various design elements is not difficult but a full review of all these features is outside the scope of this book.

Creating a Parameterized Report

You can also add parameters to a report to manipulate the data the report contains. Report parameters can be used to pass values to an underlying query, to pass values to a filter, or as variables for calculating data within the report. You can use parameters to add sorting to a report. Typically the report presents the user with a box to fill in a value when he or she runs the report, but the report can also use an automatically applied default parameter that doesn't require any direct user input. Note that you cannot be in preview mode to complete this exercise.

To add a parameter to the ReportProjectExample report:

1. From the Menu bar, select Report ➢ Report Parameters. Click Add.
2. In the Name box, type **ParameterExample1**.
3. In the Data Type box, you can use the drop-down box to choose from Boolean, DateTime, Integer, Float, and String data. Leave the String setting.
4. Next, type **Text Next to Parameter Text Box** in the Prompt box. When a user runs the report, the text in this field appears next to the parameter text box.
5. Allow the parameter to contain a blank value by selecting Allow blank value.
6. In Available values, select Non-queried. This allows you to provide a static list of values from which the user can choose a value. If you had selected From Query, it would provide a dynamic list from a query.

   The Label property contains the text displayed to the user, while Value is the value passed on to the report server for the parameter. Create three Labels, Example 1, Example 2, and Example 3 and assign them values of 1, 2, and 3 respectively.

NOTE **If From Query is selected, then text boxes for the Dataset, Value field, and Label field are shown instead. The data set used for this option is normally specifically created for the particular report parameter.**

7. In the Default values section, you can select:
   - Non-queried to provide a static default value
   - From Query to provide a dynamic default value from a query
   - None to provide no default value

   If you select either Non-queried or From Query you will be prompted to provide the default values. Select None. Press OK.

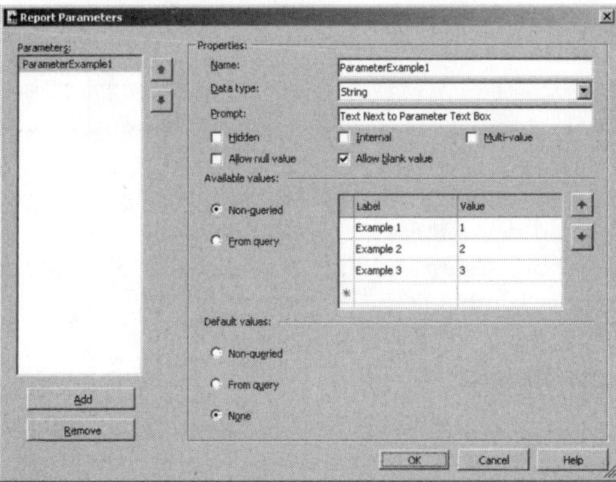

8. Click OK.

Congratulations, you've added a report parameter. Since we won't be using parameters in this report in the rest of the chapter, you'll confirm the presence of the new parameter and then delete it.

1. From the Menu bar select Report ➤ Report Parameters.
2. Confirm that ParameterExample1 appears in the list. Highlight it and press Remove.
3. Click OK.
4. Close BIDS.

NOTE When you create a query that contains a query parameter, a report parameter is automatically created based on the name of the query parameter.

Importing a Microsoft Access Report

Another way to "author" a report using Report Designer is to import one that has already been created inside a Microsoft Access database. In addition to being able to use a report that already exists, imported reports can be modified with Report Designer.

1. Launch BIDS from Start ➤ Programs ➤ Microsoft SQL Server 2005.
2. Open an existing project, or alternatively create a new one into which to import the reports. To create a new project from the File menu, select New ➤ Project to open the New Project dialog box.
3. Select Report Project, give it a name, specify the default Location and Solution name, and then click OK.
4. On the Project menu, point to Import Reports, and then click Microsoft Access. Alternatively, you can right-click the project in Solution Explorer ➤ Import Reports ➤ Microsoft Access.

WARNING The Import Reports option will not appear unless Microsoft Access XP or later is installed on the same computer on which Report Designer is installed.

5. In the Open dialog box, select the Microsoft Access database (.mdb) or project (.adp) that contains the reports, and then click Open. Any errors will appear in the Task List window.
6. Upon completion of the import, the reports form the Microsoft Access database appear in Solution Explorer. The graphic below shows the results of importing reports from the NorthWind database (.mdb) that ships with Microsoft Office 2003 into a report project named AccessImport.

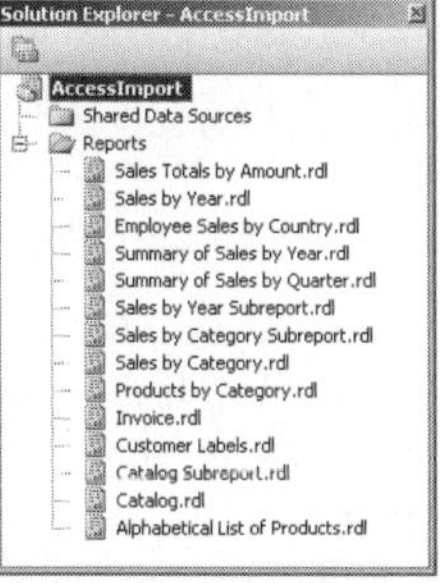

7. Once a report has been added to a project, it can be modified if you wish. It can also be deployed to a report server.

NOTE Reporting Services does not support all Access report objects. Items that are not converted are displayed in the Task List window.

Publishing a Report to a Report Server

Once you're satisfied with the report or the report project, it can be published from BIDS to the Report Server. In fact, the only way a report can be available to end users is by publishing it to a report server.

Publishing a report consists of two distinct steps, build and deploy. When you *build* a report or project, they are built, but not deployed or displayed. This feature is useful if you want to check for errors in the report before placing it on the report server. *Deploying* a report publishes it to the report server.

In this example we will publish the Available Employee Vacation and Sick Time report we created using the Report Wizard by both building it and deploying it to the report server.

1. Launch BIDS from Start ➤ Programs ➤ Microsoft SQL Server 2005. Select the ReportServer-ProjectWizard project or select File ➤ Open ➤ Project/Solution ➤ ReportServerProject Wizard ➤ ReportServerProjectWizard.sln
2. In the Solution Explorer, right-click the ReportWizardExample project and select Properties from the pop-up menu.
3. Set Configuration to Production.
4. Leave the TargetReportFolder value set at ReportWizardExample. You must have publish permissions on the target folder to publish reports to it.
5. In the TargetServerURL, type **http://localhost/reportserver**. Click Apply.

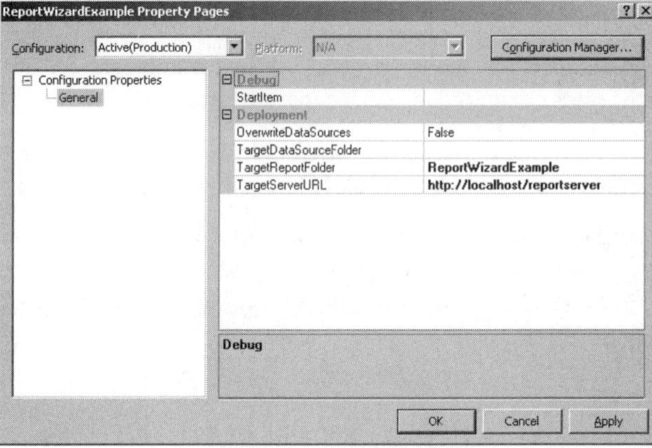

6. Click the Configuration Manager button. Set the Active solution configuration to Production.
7. In the Project contexts box, confirm the Configuration setting for ReportWizardExample is Production. Confirm that Build and Deploy check boxes are marked. If Build only is selected, Report Designer builds the report project and checks for errors before previewing or publishing to a report server. If Deploy is selected, Report Designer will then publish the reports to the report server as defined in deployment properties. If Deploy is not selected, Report Designer displays the report specified in the StartItem property in a local preview window.

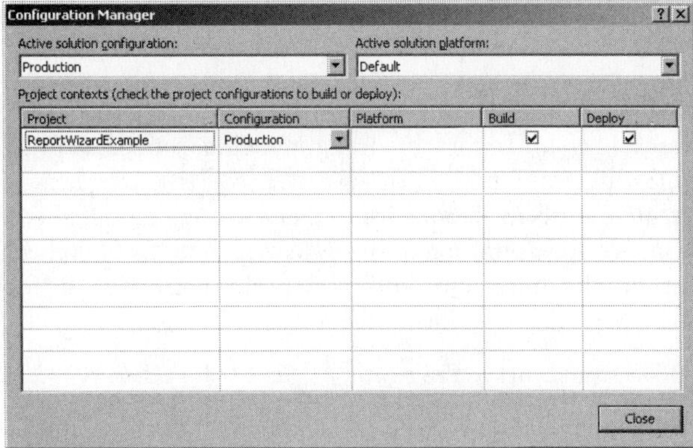

8. Click Close. Click OK.

9. Select Build ➤ Deploy ReportWizardExample from the menu; alternatively you can right-click on the report and select Deploy from the pop-up menu.

10. Status on the deployment will appear in Output window.

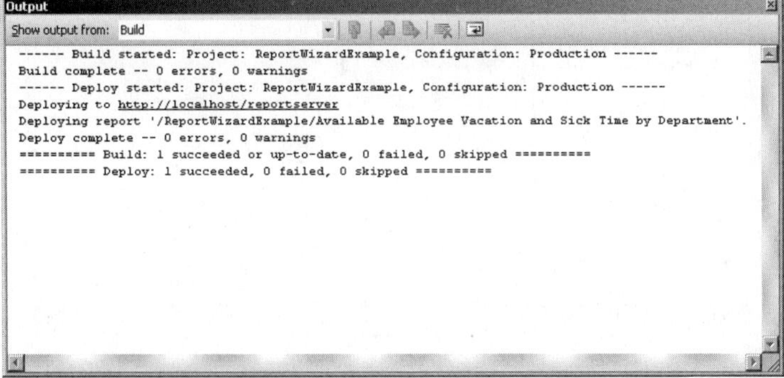

11. Note that once the deployment has completed, the report appears in its own folder in Management Studio in the Object Explorer view of the Report Server as as shown in the graphic. As you will see later in this chapter, the report can also be accessed and viewed through a web browser by you or other end users.

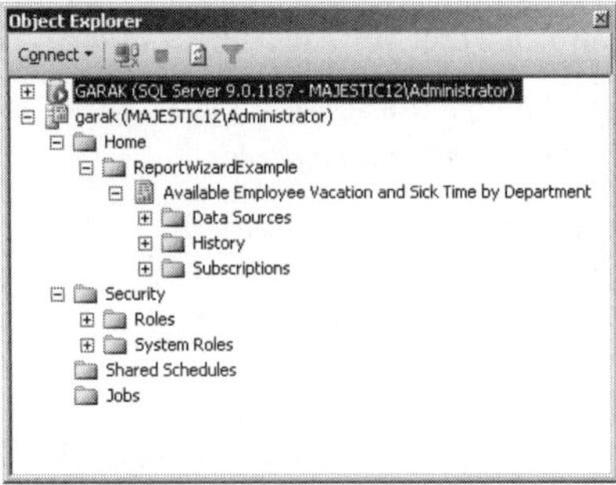

Creating a Report Model

The other tool used in report authoring is Report Builder, which is intended for use by end users who are not necessarily developers or well versed in the underlying data structure, but who are familiar with the data and have a reason to create ad hoc reports.

Typically users will create reports by dragging fields from predefined report models onto a pre-designed report layout template.

In order to create reports in Report Builder, at least one model needs to be available. A report model project contains the definition of the data source (a .ds file), the definition of a data source view (a .dsv file), and the model (an .smdl file). In this section we'll create a report model, called ModelExample.

1. Launch BIDS from Start ➤ Programs ➤ Microsoft SQL Server 2005.
2. From the File menu select New ➤ Project to open the New Project dialog box.
3. Confirm that Business Intelligence Projects is selected in the left pane and Report Model Project is selected in the right pane.
4. In the Name text box type **ModelExample**, accept the default Location and Solution name, and click OK.

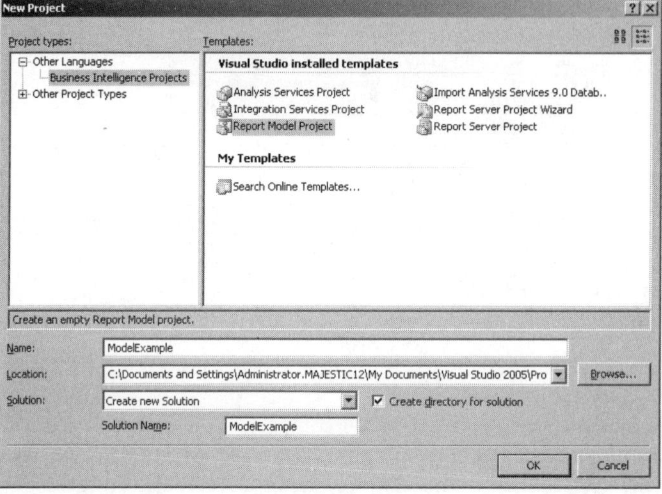

5. The Report Model project template is automatically created and Solution Explorer is populated with Data Sources, Data Sources Views, and Report Model folders.
6. Right-click the Data Sources folder, select Add New Data Source to launch the Data Source Wizard. Click Next on the Welcome screen.
7. In the "Select how to define the connection dialog" box, ensure that the radio button next to "Create a data source based on an existing or new connection" is selected and then click New to open the Connection Manager dialog box.

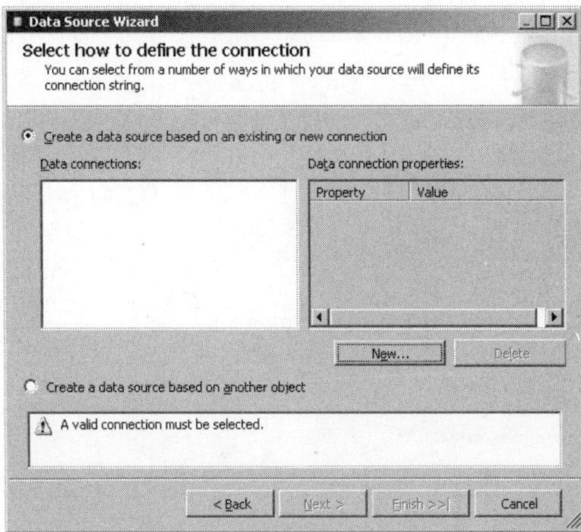

8. Type **localhost** in the Server name text box.

9. In the Connect to a Database section, choose AdventureWorks from the "Select or enter a database" dropdown list.

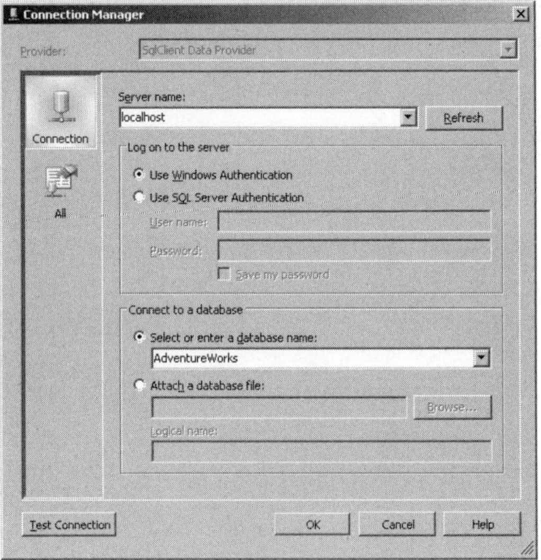

10. Click OK to close Connect to a Database and click Next to go to the Completing the Wizard page. Review the information and accept the default Data source name AdventureWorks. Click Finish.

11. Right-click on the Data Source Views folder and select Add New Data Source View to launch the Data Source View Wizard. Click Next.

12. Select the AdventureWorks data source and then click Next.

13. In the Select Tables and Views dialog box, select Production.Product and Sales.SalesOrderDetail. Click the Add Related Tables button to add the Sales.SpecialOfferProduct and Sales.SalesOrderHeader tables.

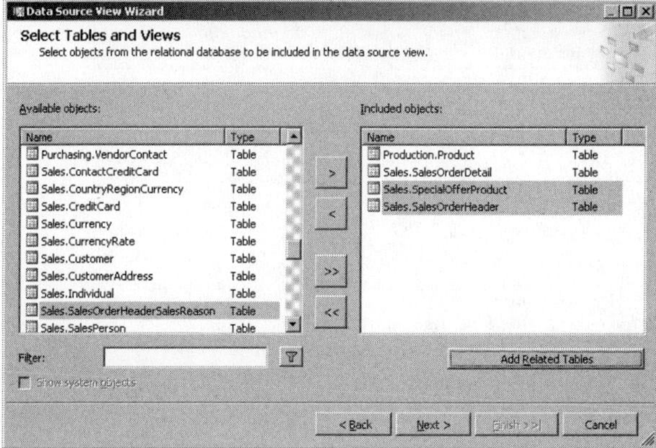

14. Click Next. Accept the default name AdventureWorks and click Finish. The wizard closes and the AdventureWorks data source view file will be created.

15. Right-click on the Report Models folder and select Add New Report Model from the pop-up menu to launch the Report Model Wizard. Click Next.

16. Select the AdventureWorks data source view and click Next.

17. In the "Select Report Model Generation Rules" dialog window, look over the various rules. Note that this is Pass 1 of two passes. In Pass 1 the Report Model Wizard creates objects called entities. Pass 2 refines the model. Accept the defaults and click Next.

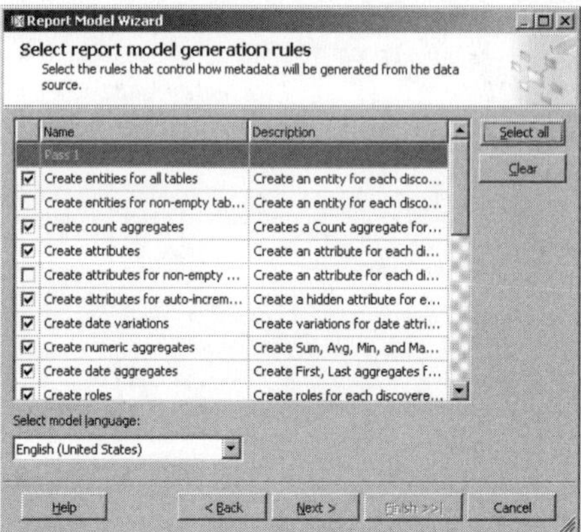

18. Because the Report Model Wizard depends on correct database statistics to generate certain settings within the model, you should select Update statistics before generating. Click Next.

TIP You should always select the Update statistics before generating option whenever you run the Report Model Wizard for the first time or whenever the data source view has changed.

19. In the Completing the Wizard dialog box, name the report model AW ModelExample. The model name is how end users will identify the model. The name should be descriptive enough to make its purpose obvious. Click Run to generate the report model.

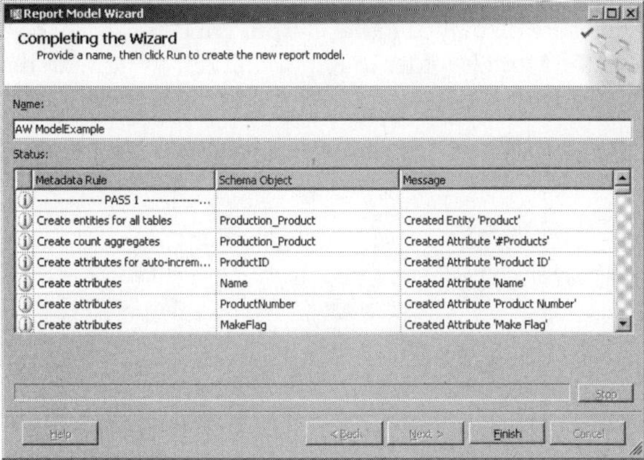

20. Click Finish to close the Report Model Wizard.

Before moving on to the next step, let's take a few moments to review the AW ModelExample report model. Notice that all the entities and folders within the model are now displayed. Selecting an entity displays the list of fields, folders, and roles that are contained within that entity. Selecting a model name, you can right-click to add entities, perspectives, and folders. When an entity is selected, you can right-click to add a folder, source field, expression, and role. You can also change properties (such as sort order) through the Properties dialog box. You can also add and delete roles to an entity and add entities to the report model. You can also delete unwanted entities by right-clicking on the entity and selecting Delete from the pop-up menu.

NOTE Expression based attributes are prefixed with a pound sign (#). While standard attributes are indicated by an "a."

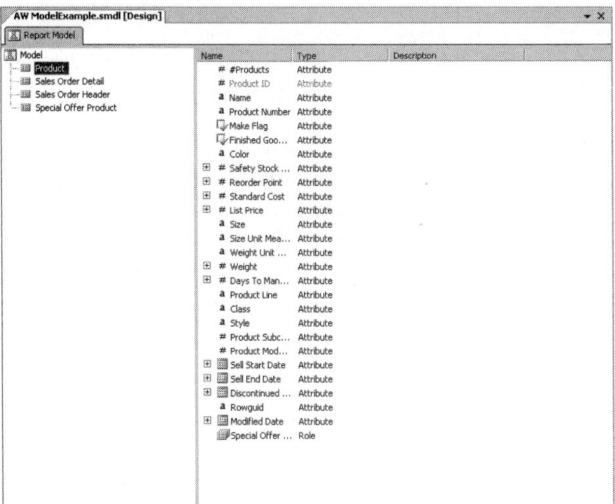

21. As you already know from the previous example, for a report or report model to be accessible to end users it must be published to a report server. Right-click AW ModelExample in Solution Explorer, then select Deploy. The model is then published to the report server using the Target Server URL that you specified when setting up BIDS. If any errors or warnings are encountered, they are displayed in the Output window. Once the model is deployed, it can be found under the Models folder in Report Server, along with the newly created data source used in the model as shown in the following graphic:

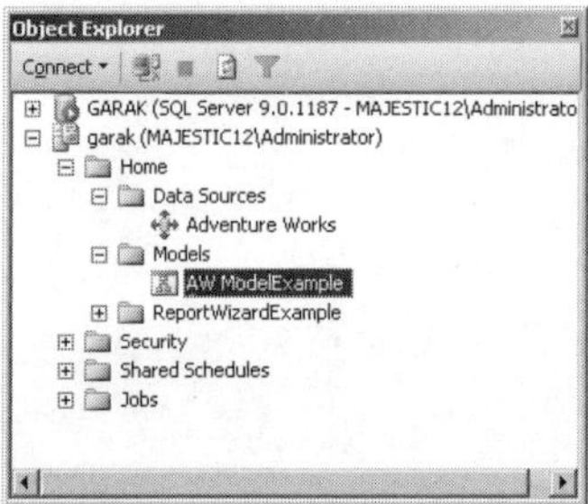

Creating a Report Using Report Builder

Report Builder is a powerful and easy-to-use web-based tool that allows users to create table, matrix, or chart-type reports based on a report model. As you will see, users can select a report layout template that allows them to simply drag and drop relevant fields into the design area. In addition they can filter, group, sort, or modify data by applying formulas. They can also specify parameters. Naturally reports can be formatted using color, fonts, and other design elements. Reports can be saved to the report server or exported as a different file type (e.g., PDF or Excel). Report Builder can be used from any client computer.

In this example, you'll create a simple matrix cross-tabulating sales by product and year.

1. To open Report Builder, you need to launch Report Manager. Open Internet Explorer. In the address bar type **http://<*webservername*>/reports** where ***webservername*** is the name of the report server.

2. Report Manager opens. Select Report Builder. The first time a client invokes Report Builder, relevant files and documentation are downloaded to the client.

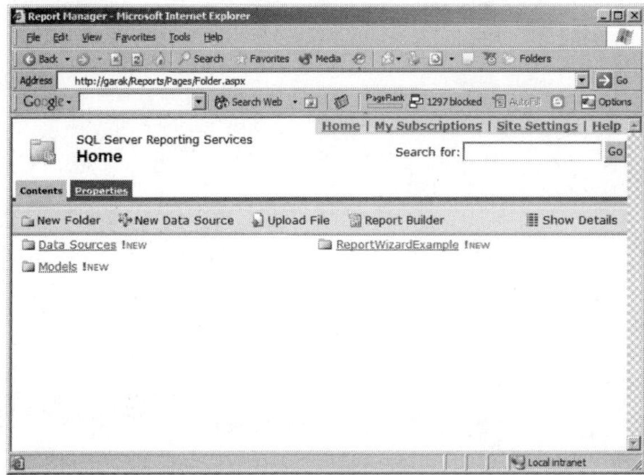

3. After Report Builder opens, select AW ModelExample from the New Report dialog box. Click OK.
4. Select the Matrix layout from the Report Layout pane.
5. Select the Product entity. In the Field pane, select Name and drag it to the Drop Row Groups area on the matrix. Notice that the Explorer Pane has changed to a treeview showing the defined entity roles with the Product entity at the root level and Special Offer as a child, with Sales Order Details and Sales Order as lower level child objects.
6. Click on Sales Order Details and drag the Sum Line Totals aggregate attribute to the Drop totals area on the matrix. Since the values are in currency, right-click the Sum Line Totals field and select Format from the pop-up menu. Under the Number tab, select the currency style. Under the Alignment tab set the Horizontal to Center.
7. Select the Sales Order entity, and expand the Order Date folder. Drag the Order Year attribute to the Drop Column Groups area. Right-click on the number to left of Total and set the Horizontal alignment to center. Add the title Product Sales Orders by Year and adjust the size of the table cells. The table should now resemble the following graphic:

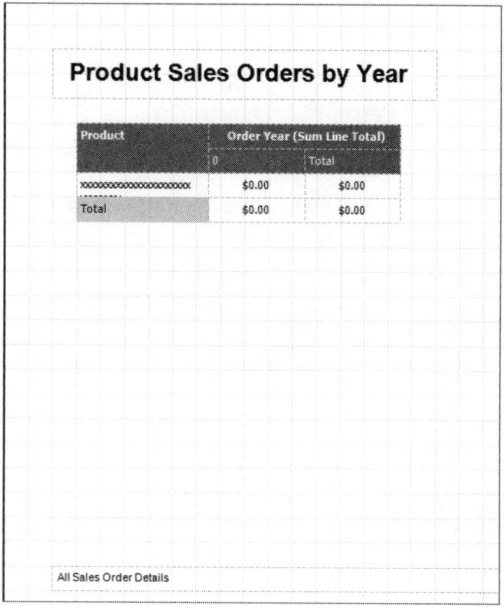

8. On the menu bar, click Run Report.

9. The completed report appears and should resemble that shown in the following graphic:

Product Sales Orders by Year

Product	Order Year (Sum Line Total)				
	2001	2002	2003	2004	Total
All-Purpose Bike Stand			$18,921.00	$20,670.00	$39,591.00
AWC Logo Cap	$2,686.87	$9,387.61	$21,757.10	$17,397.86	$51,229.45
Bike Wash - Dissolver			$9,777.94	$8,629.03	$18,406.97
Cable Lock		$10,084.70	$6,155.52		$16,240.22
Chain			$5,685.93	$3,691.78	$9,377.71
Classic Vest, L			$4,711.70	$8,128.00	$12,839.70
Classic Vest, M			$53,543.08	$36,707.52	$90,250.60
Classic Vest, S			$86,756.00	$69,642.07	$156,398.07
Fender Set - Mountain			$19,408.34	$27,211.24	$46,619.58
Front Brakes			$31,576.61	$18,722.70	$50,299.31
Front Derailleur			$26,903.77	$17,580.50	$44,484.27
Full-Finger Gloves, L		$39,650.11	$30,120.25	$172.85	$69,943.21
Full-Finger Gloves, M		$27,707.73	$20,428.36	$74.08	$48,210.18
Full-Finger Gloves, S		$6,997.76	$4,363.15	$49.39	$11,410.30
Half-Finger Gloves, L		$2,543.20	$11,694.70	$8,674.36	$22,912.26
Half-Finger Gloves, M		$7,927.04	$30,100.37	$16,518.08	$54,545.49
Half-Finger Gloves, S		$3,970.22	$20,097.72	$12,422.61	$36,490.55
Hitch Rack - 4-Bike			$134,868.47	$102,227.69	$237,096.16
HL Bottom Bracket			$22,597.14	$16,984.30	$39,581.44
HL Crankset			$87,145.10	$61,477.48	$148,622.58
HL Fork		$37,488.94	$23,545.67		$61,034.61

10. Report Builder allows you to drill down through the data. As an example click on the name of a product, such as the cable lock. Report Server will generate a new report that lists the details on the selected item.

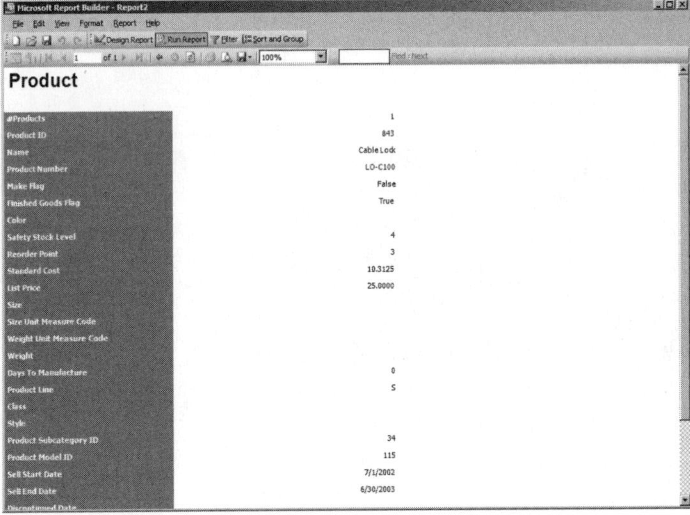

11. To save the ad hoc report (actually you are uploading it to the report catalog), select File ➤ Save As. In the Name text box, type **ProductSalesOrdersByYear**, select the Report Server folder where it will be uploaded and click Save.

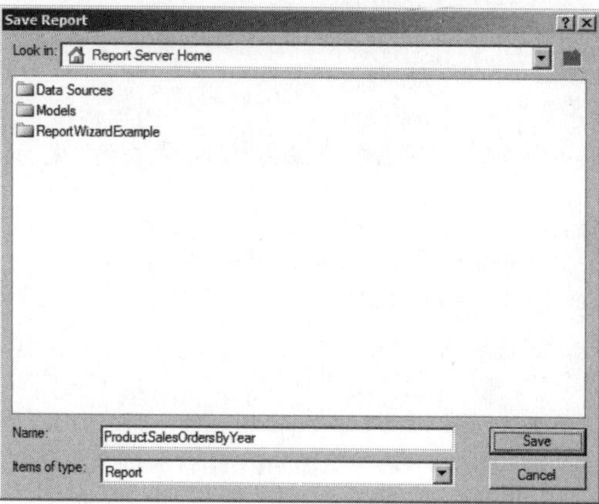

WARNING You cannot create a new folder unless you have sufficient Report Server permissions. Management of folders and the My Folders feature will be discussed later in this chapter.

Report Management

Once you've created and published your report, you'll quickly discover the need to manage and administer both the reports and the report server. Two tools in SQL Server 2005 are designed for working with published reports and other content on the server: Management Studio and Report Manager.

Report Manager allows you to manage a single report server instance using a web-based tool. Management Studio works with one or more report server instances alongside other SQL Server components that are deployed together on the same system. Both have nearly the same functionality. Both allow you to create, delete, secure, and modify items in the same report server folder hierarchy. You can also use these tools to view reports, set distribution schedules, manage report processing, define data connections, and subscriptions, to name only a few.

You've already received a good grounding in the use of Management Studio in Chapter 9 and so we won't be spending much time on how to use it managing reports and the report sever. Instead we'll focus attention on a tool you and your users (assuming they have the proper permissions) can use, Report Manager.

Publishing the Sample Reports

First you'll need some reports to work with. While we could use the reports created earlier in this chapter, let's make use of the sample reports that shipped with SQL Server 2005 instead.

1. Launch BIDS from Start ➤ Programs ➤ Microsoft SQL Server 2005.

2. From the File menu select Open ➤ Project/Solution. The file you want, `AdventureWorksSampleReports.rptproj`, is installed by default at in the folder `C:\Program Files\Microsoft SQL Server\90\Samples\Reporting Services\Report Samples\AdventureWorks Sample Reports`. Click the file and then click Open.

NOTE You need to perform a custom setup of SQL Server 2005 to install these sample files.

3. Click Build ➤ Configuration Manager and set the Active solution configuration to Production or make the change on the standard tool bar as shown below.

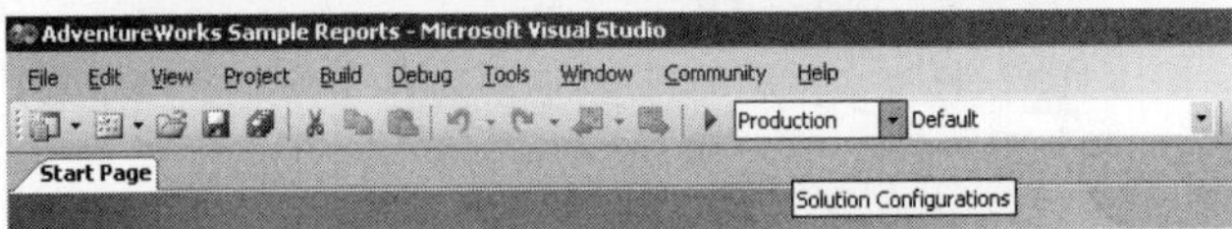

4. From the Debug menu, select Start Debug or press F5 to build and deploy the reports. Once publishing is completed, Internet Explorer opens. You can click a report name to open it in Report Viewer, but let's hold off on that right now.

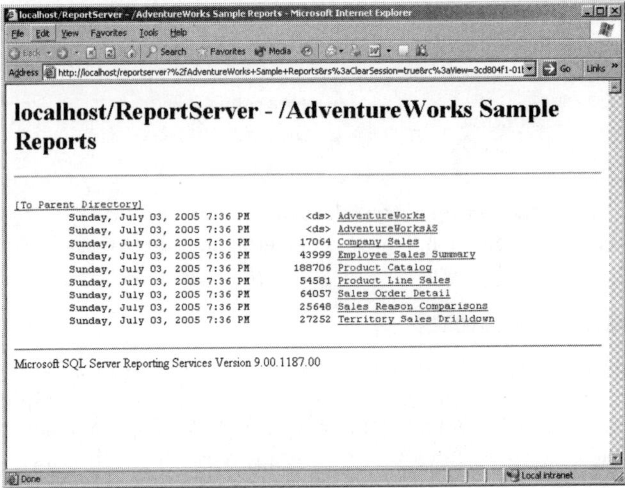

NOTE The AdventureWorks sample reports are configured to publish to the report server on the local computer by default.

5. As you should already know, the reports have also been published to the report server, in this case in a folder labeled AdventureWorks Sample Reports.

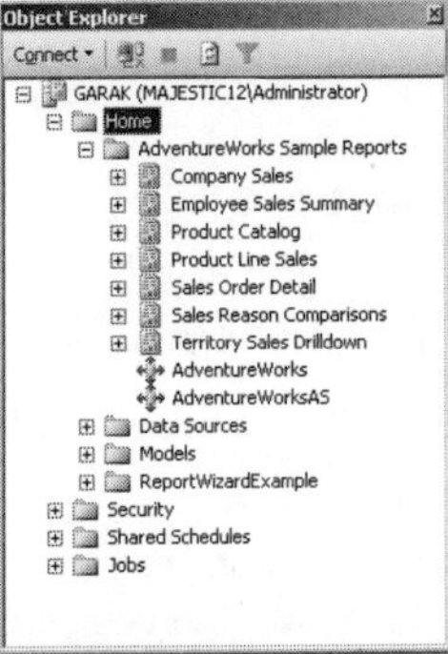

6. Close all open files and programs.

Using Report Manager to Manage Reports

Now we're ready to go. As you'll recall, to launch Report Manager from the Report Builder example above, open Internet Explorer. In the address bar type **http://<*webservername*>/reports** where ***webservername*** is the name of the report server.

The Report Manager home page contains a number of elements you should become familiar with.

In the upper right corner there are four hyperlinks. The first from the left takes you to the Report Manager *Home* page; *My Subscriptions* opens a page where you can manage your report subscriptions; under *Site Settings* you can configure site security, My Reports, logging and access links allowing you to define roles, and manage shared schedules and jobs. *Help* opens a stand-alone Report Manager help file.

Below these hyperlinks is a *Search* box for finding report server contents, such as folders and reports. Note that there are two tabs, *Contents* and *Properties.*

The tool bar has five buttons whose function is self-explanatory:

- New Folder
- New Data Sources
- Upload File
- Report Builder
- Show Details

By default Report Manager opens to the report server Home folder and displays its folders, reports, and other objects. As you'll see shortly you can also choose to enable the My Folders option, in which case the default view for Report Manager will be the user-specific My Folders.

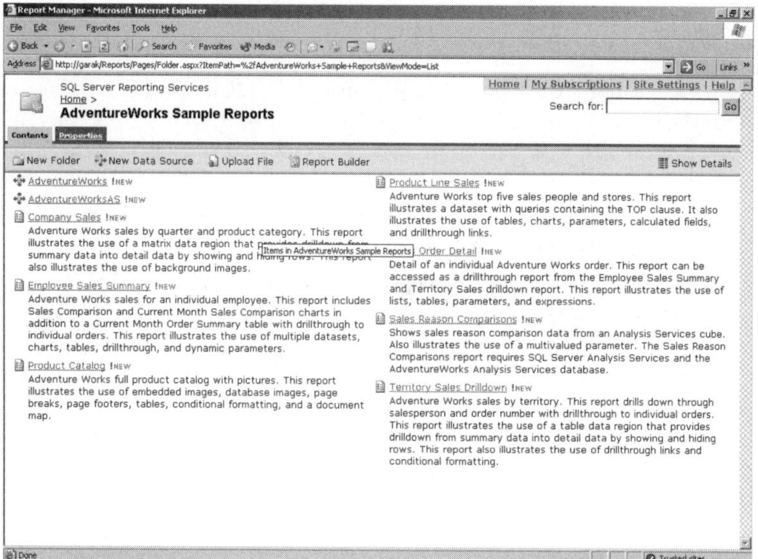

Working with Folders

You can use Report Manager to view, create, modify, and delete folders.

1. To view the contents of a folder, click on the folder name. If you have written annotations or comments, they will also appear.

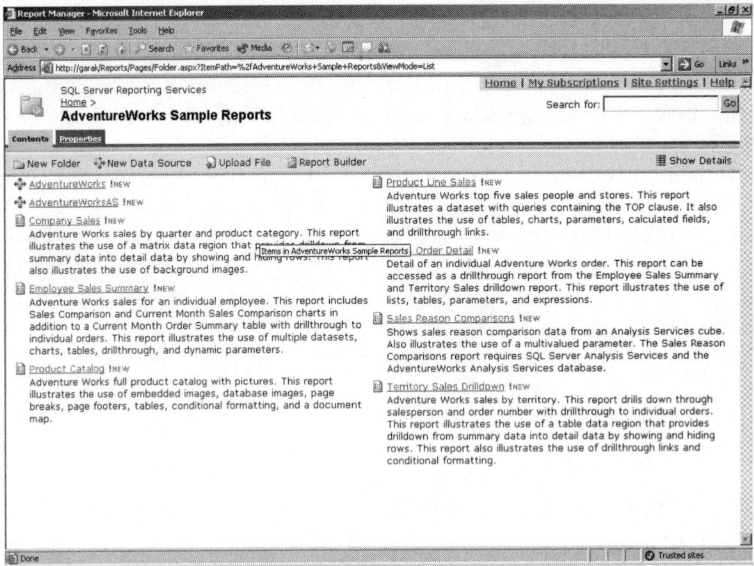

2. To create a folder, navigate to the directory you want the new folder to appear in and click the New Folder button. Enter a name and description. Click OK. Practice by creating a folder called CreateFolderSample.

3. Now let's modify the CreateFolderSample folder. Click to open it, then click the Properties tab. The General properties are displayed. Change the name to CreateFolderExample. In the Description box type **This is an exercise**. Note that you also delete and move the folder using the buttons on this page. Checking the "Hide in list view" box prevents the folder from appearing in Report Manager. Click Apply. Click Home. The modified folder should resemble the one in the following graphic:

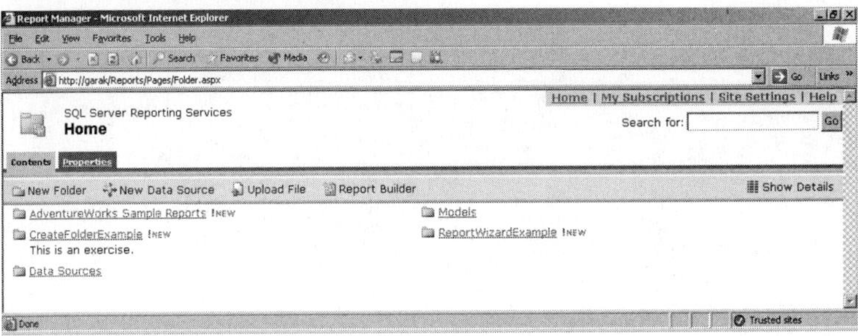

4. To *delete* the CreateFolderExample folder, open it and then click the Properties tab to display the General properties. Click the Delete button. Click OK. The folder has been deleted.

NOTE Remember that changes to folders in Report Manager affect only the virtual folders on the report server and not the underlying content.

My Reports

Reporting Services ships with a feature that allocates each user personal storage in the report server database. This feature allows users to save reports that they own in their own private folder, called My Folders.

The My Reports feature is disabled by default. It is generally considered a good practice to enable My Folders if you want to allow users to control their own information or be able to work with report not intended for public consumption (such as the salary data). Enabling it also cuts downs on administrative overhead since you won't need to create new folders or create and apply security policies for each user on a case-by-case basis. The downside to My Reports is that is does consume server resources that you may not have available.

When you activate My Reports, the report server will create a My Report folder for every domain user who clicks the My Reports link. In addition, in each report that server administrators will see is a Users Folder containing the subfolder for each user.

To enable My Reports:

1. Open Report Manager. Click Site Settings.
2. Mark the check box next to Enable My Reports. Click Apply.

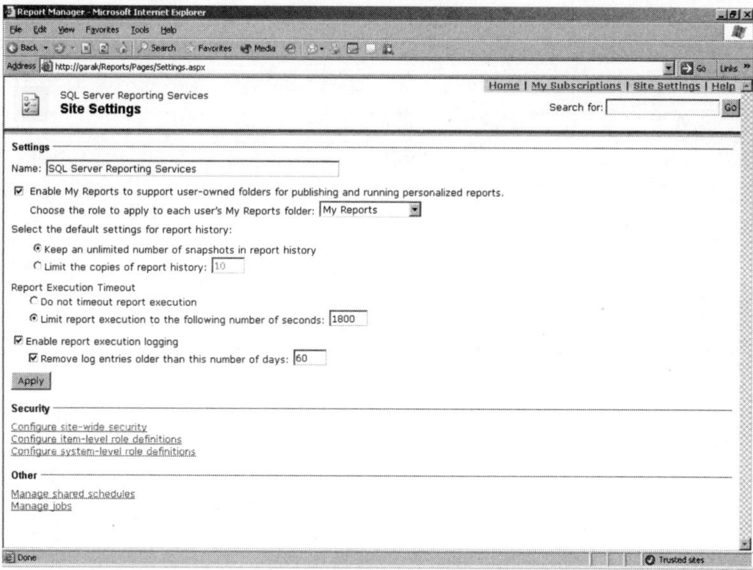

NOTE The My Reports role definition determines what actions and tasks can be performed in the My Reports workspace.

Managing Published Reports

As you've already seen, Report Manager is very easy to use in the manipulation of folders and their contents. That same ease and flexibility applies to working with published reports. In this section you'll use learn how to use Report Manager to:

- View, move, and delete a report
- Configure report properties
- Create a linked report
- Create a parameterized report
- Create a report history by creating report snapshots
- Print a report
- Export a report

VIEWING, MOVING, AND DELETING A REPORT

In order to make use of the information in a published report, you need to be able to view it. You might also decide to move it to a different folder or to delete it entirely.

1. Open Report Manager. Click the AdventureWorks Report folder.
2. Click the Company Sales report and the report opens in a new window.

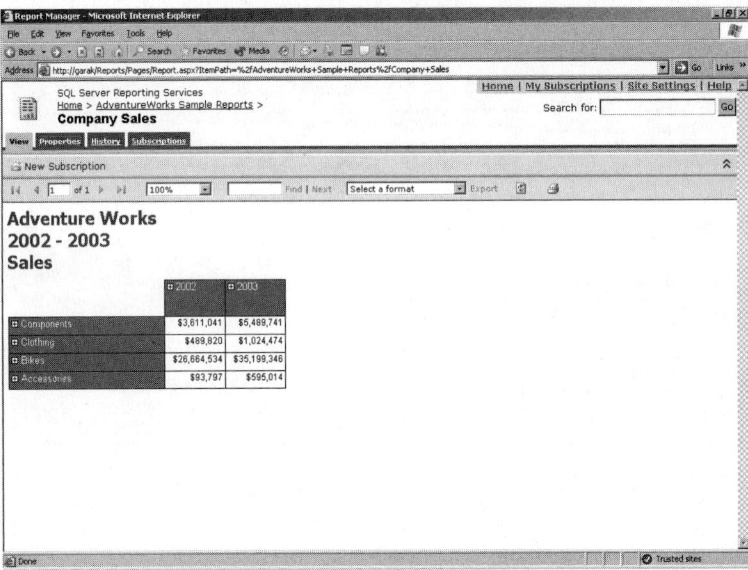

NOTE In addition to Report Manager and Management Studio, you can also view a report through a direct connection to a report server by using a web browser such as Internet Explorer. You can open the report by typing the report's URL address or browse to the report server, and then examine the report server folder hierarchy to select the report you want to view. This is the method that was used to display the sample reports you deployed at the start of this section.

3. To move the report, click the Properties tab. Click the Move button. Highlight My Reports in the tree and click OK. The Company Sales Report is moved to the My Reports folder.

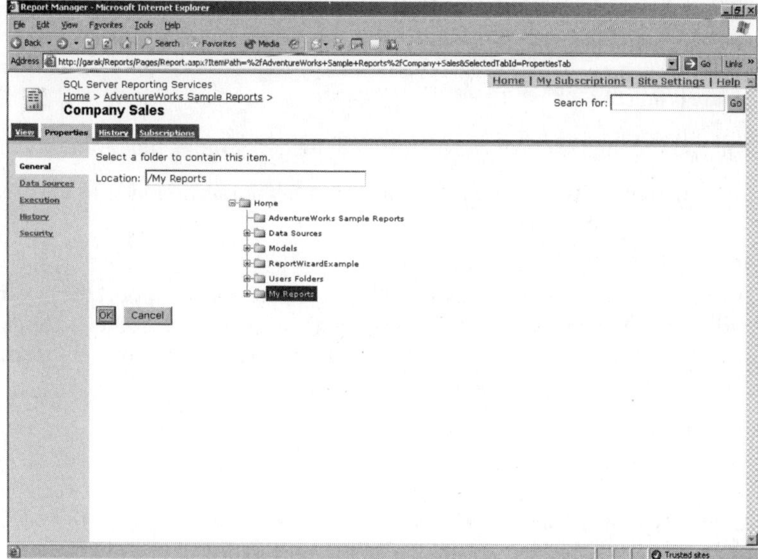

4. After you confirm that Company Sales Report is in the My Reports folder, move it back to the AdventureWorks Sample Reports folder.

5. To delete a report, open the report you want to delete. Click the Properties tab and click the Delete button.

WARNING For the purposes of this chapter, do not delete any reports.

Configuring Report Properties

For every published report you can set or change a variety of properties including the report's name, description, data sources, parameter information, user access, and whether the report runs on demand or on a schedule, as well as other factors.

NOTE If you are using default security, only local administrators can set properties. If using custom role assignments, the user's role assignment must include the task "Manage reports."

Each report has up to six property tabs. General, Data Sources, Execution, History, and Security are present in each report. The sixth, Parameters, appears only in parameterized reports.

General Properties

To access the *General Properties* page, open a report and click the Properties tab. The General Properties page is set to open by default.

- In the Properties section, you can change the report name and add or modify a description.
- Checking the Hide in list view check box allows you prevent the report from showing in the list view (which is also the default page layout).

- In the Report Definition section, you can click Edit if you want to make local modifications to the report definition that are not saved on the report server. Alternatively you can select Update to update the report definition with one from an .rdl file.

WARNING When you update a report definition, you need to reset the data source settings after the update is finished.

- You can use the Delete or Move button to delete or move the report.
- Clicking the Apply button applies any modifications you made to the report.

Creating a Linked Report

Suppose you want to make one or more additional versions of a report that retains the original's layout and data source properties but allows for changes in all the other settings original report such as security, parameters, subscriptions, and so on. These sorts of reports are called *linked reports* and are created through the General Properties tab.

1. Open the report on which you want to base a linked report.
2. Select Properties ➤ General.
3. Click the Create Linked Report button. Specify the new name and optional description. If you want to put the linked report in a different folder, click the Change Location button.

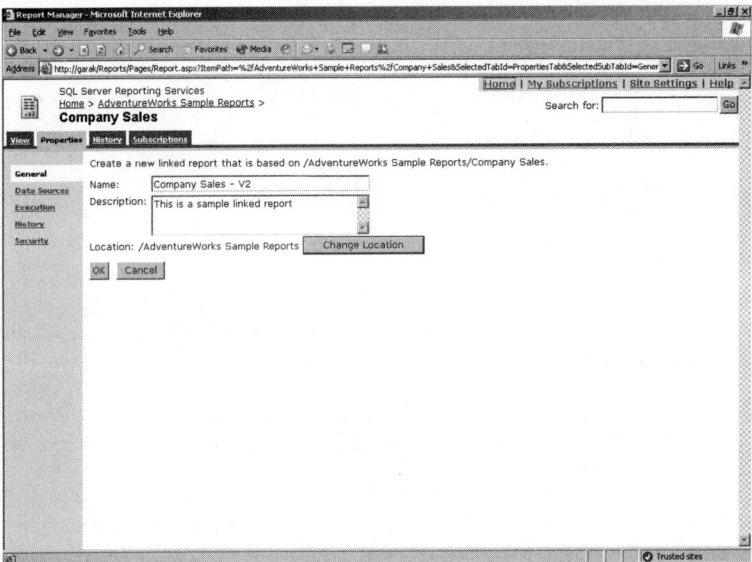

TIP The linked report icon appears as. 

Data Sources Properties

The Data Source Properties contains information specifying the details about the connections contained in the report. Although a single report normally only contains one connection, it can support multiple connections if it contains multiple data sets.

You can use the Data Source Properties page to:

- Switch between a report-specific data source connection and a shared data source.
- Select an existing shared data source.
- Specify credential information.

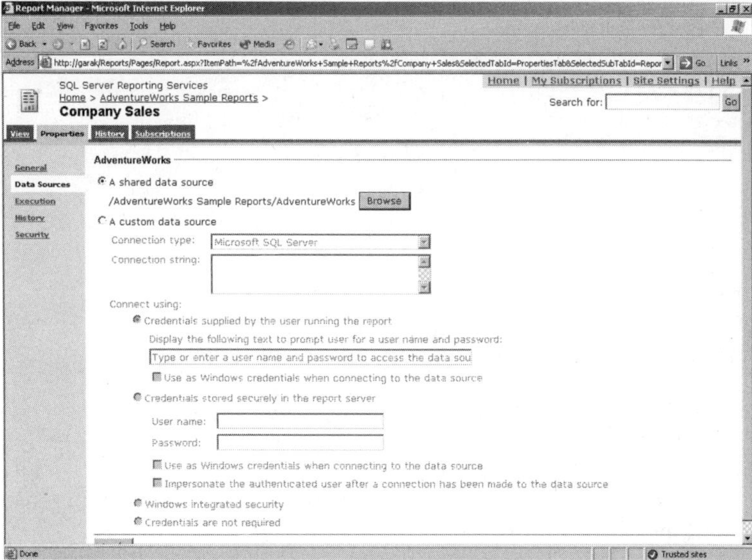

NOTE When you specify credential information, it applies to all users who access the report. For example, if you specified a particular user and password as stored credentials, all users run the report under those credentials.

Execution Properties

The Execution Properties pages contains the information detailing how a report is to be executed when it is run.

You can configure the following tasks:

- Allow users to run the report on demand by selecting "Render this report with the most recent data," and then configure caching options.
- Permit users to process the report as a scheduled snapshot by selecting "Render this report from an execution snapshot." A report snapshot contains data captured at a single moment in time.

NOTE You can specify whether to create a snapshot on a schedule (either report-specific or scheduled) or immediately when you click the Apply button.

- Report execution timeout settings.

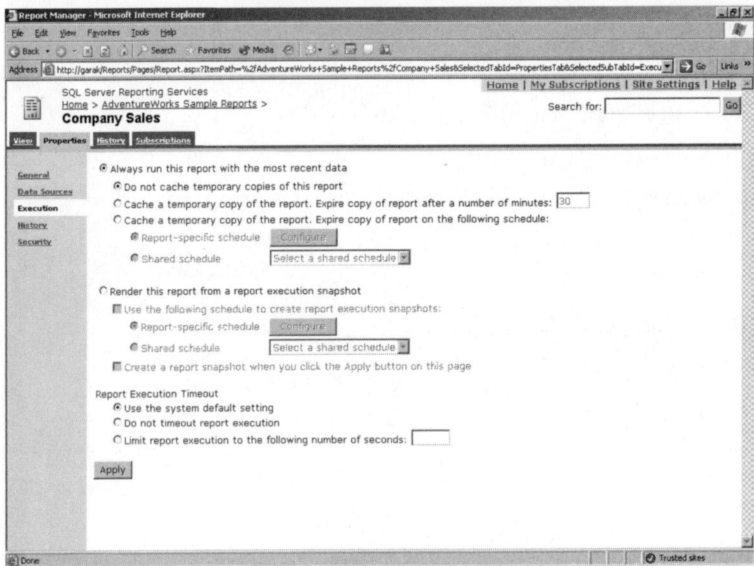

History Properties

You can use the History Properties page to schedule report snapshots to be added to report history and to set limits on the number of report snapshots that are stored in report history.

The following options are available:

- Selecting the "Allow history to be created manually" check box permits you to add snapshots to report history as needed. It also causes the New Snapshot button to appear on the History page.
- To copy a report snapshot to report history, mark the check box next to "Store all report execution snapshots in report history."
- You can opt to use a schedule for snapshots and specify whether it is report-specific or based on a shared schedule by marking "Use the following schedule to add snapshot to report history."
- Finally, you can select the number of snapshots to keep. If you choose "Limit the copies of report history," once the limit is reached older copies are deleted.

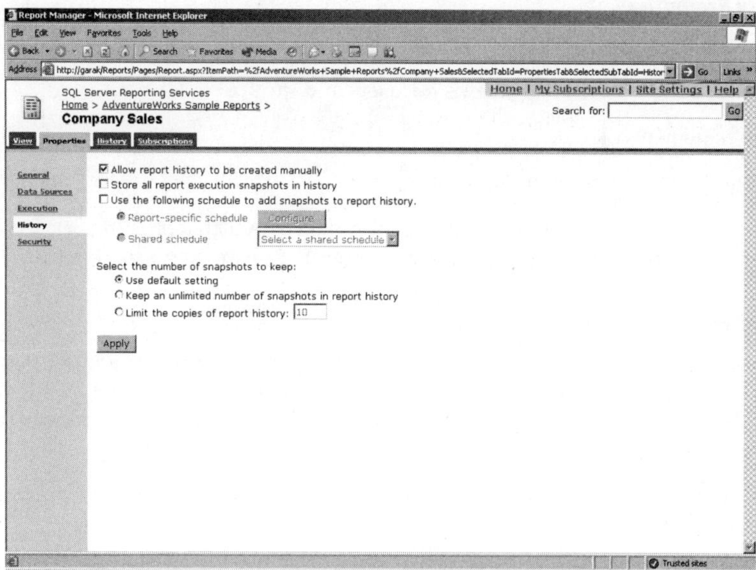

Report History

To view the report history, click the History tab above the view window. If you have marked the radio button next to "Render this report from a report execution snapshot" on the Execution Properties page, the New Snapshot button appears. You can open report snapshots by clicking on them. You can also delete them by marking the check box and pressing the Delete button.

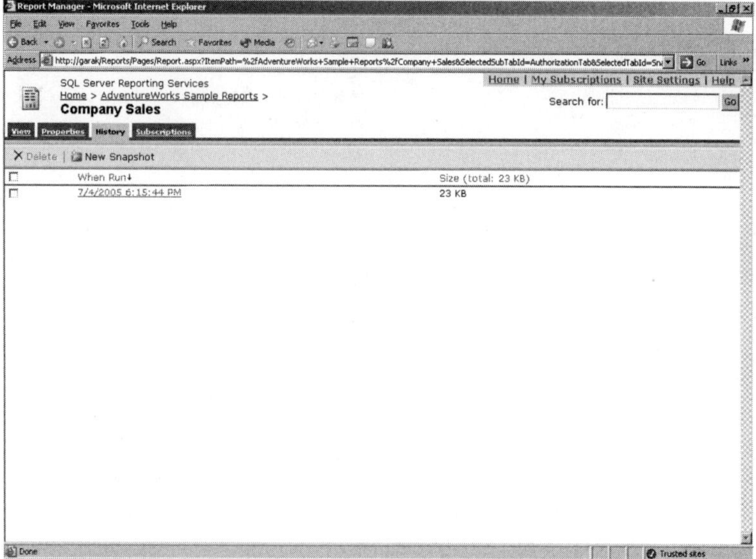

Security Properties

On the Security Properties page you can:

- Edit existing role assignments for users and groups
- Create new role
- Revert setting to parent security

The entire topic of role-based security, the model on which Reporting Services security is based, is covered in another section later in this chapter, Reporting Services Security.

Parameters Properties

The Parameters Properties tab appears only when you access the properties of a parameterized report. Naturally the properties you can set are based on the parameters specified in the report definition. There are also some other limitations and caveats. To see an example of a typical Parameters Properties sheet, do the following:

1. From Report Manager open the Product Lines Sales report in the AdventureWorks Sample Reports folder.
2. Click the Properties tab and select Parameters to open the Parameters Properties page.

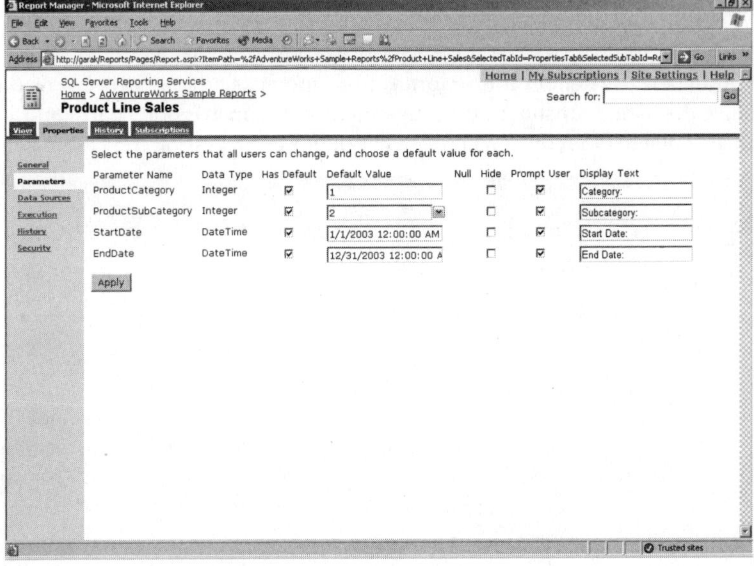

NOTE Not all parameters can be modified in all cases. You can always change the display text and the property that determines whether the parameter is visible to users. However, you cannot always change the default value if the value is derived from a query. In this case, the text string "QueryBased" appears next to the parameter.

3. To set parameter properties, open the Parameters Properties page of the report. You can modify the following properties:

   - Has Default, when unmarked, requires the user to provide a value for the parameter before the report can be processed. If the box is marked, the parameter default value is used.
   - The Default Value property can be a constant or null (if the parameter accepts null values). It cannot be set to an expression.
   - Select the Hide check box if you want to hide the parameter in the report.

NOTE Hiding a parameter does not make it invisible in all situations. Parameters can still be set in subscriptions and through URLs.

WARNING If you hide a parameter, you must provide a default value either in the report definition or on the Parameter Properties page.

   - If Prompt User is marked, then the user is requested to type or select a different valid value for the parameter. Prompt User is enabled whenever Hide is disabled.
   - Use the Display Text to enter the text that appears next to the parameter prompt. You can use this box to enter a label or a set of instructions. This property is enabled when you select Prompt User.

NOTE You cannot delete, rename, reorder, or change the data type of parameters in a published report. In addition, you cannot change the parameter name. To change either of these properties, you must modify the report definition.

Using Management Studio to Manage Reports

In the last section we focused on using the Report Manager tool to conduct management of published reports and their folders. In the section following this one, we'll look at how you can use Report Manager to deliver reports through subscriptions, schedules, printing, and exporting. Before we do that, however, let's look at another report management tool that you're already somewhat familiar with, Management Studio.

The functionality is nearly identical. One key difference is that Management Studio allows you to manage one or more report server instances along with other SQL Server components, such as Analysis Services and Notification Services, deployed together on the same system.

You can, of course, use Management Studio to create, delete, secure, and modify items in the same report server folder hierarchy. You can also use these tools to view reports, set distribution schedules, and manage report processing, data connections, and subscriptions.

Since you're already familiar with Management Studio from Chapter 9, this section will be primarily a high-level view of how to manage published reports with Management Studio.

1. Click Start ➤ Programs ➤ Microsoft SQL Server 2005 ➤ SQL Server Management Studio.
2. Connect to the Report Server by selecting Object Explorer ➤ Connect ➤ Reporting Services.
3. The report server will open and expose the report server folder hierarchy.

4. Expand the Home folder and then expand the AdventureWorks Sample Reports folder.

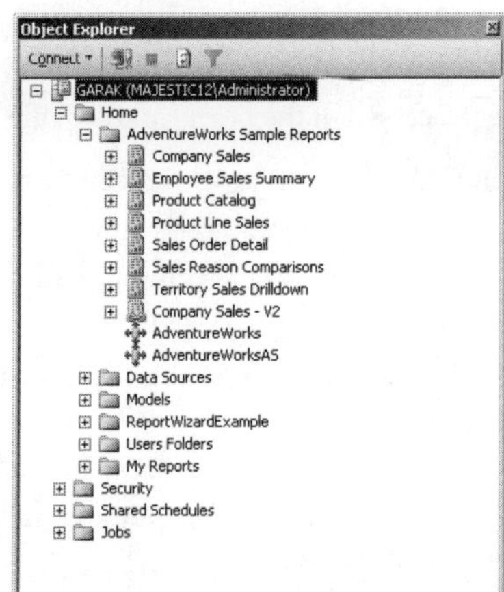

Working with Folders

The report server root has four default folders: Home, Security, Shared Schedules, and Jobs.

Home is the default folder to which reports are published and is automatically populated with the Data Sources and Models subfolders. If you enable the My Reports option, a My Reports folder is automatically generated for each user under the Home folder. In addition, report server administrators will see a folder called Users Folders containing the subfolder for each user.

To manage the folder properties under Home on the Report Server, right-click the folder. You can perform nine tasks from the pop-up menu:

- Create a new folder and set basic properties such as name
- Create a new data source and set the name, description, and connection
- Import a file into the folder
- Move the folder to another part of the tree
- Send a script to a new window, file, or Clipboard
- Rename the folder
- Delete the folder
- Refresh the folder tree
- Open the folder's properties sheet to:
  - Set the name
  - Write description
  - Set permissions
  - Hide/UnHide the folder in list view

NOTE You cannot change the name of the Home folder.

The root Security folder contains two subfolders, Roles and System Roles. Each folder contains a collection of roles. As you will see later in the chapter, roles are a key element of report server security. You can right-click both the Roles and System Roles folders to access menu items that allow you to create a New Role (or System Role), Delete Roles, or Refresh.

The remaining two root folders, Shared Schedules and Jobs, are designed to hold these items. You will be working with Shared Schedules and Jobs later in this chapter.

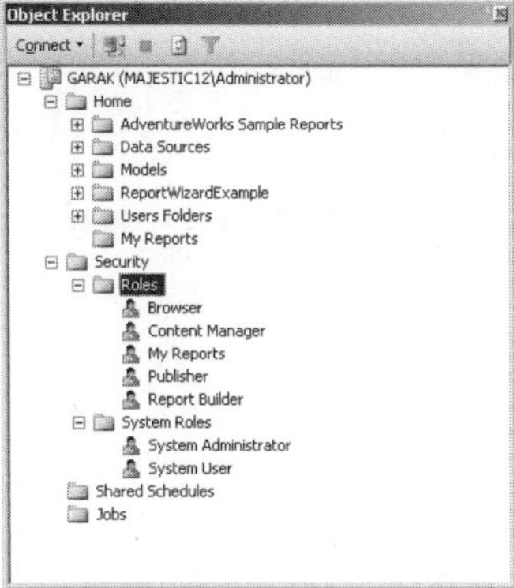

Working with Published Reports

Now that you've seen how you can manipulate folders in Management Studio, let's look at how you can manage and administer reports. If you haven't already done so, select and expand the Home folder, then select AdventureWorks Sample Reports folder, finally expand the Product Line Sales report to reveal three folders: Data Sources, History, and Subscriptions.

Right-click the Product Line Sales folder to open the pop-up menu that contains the following options:

- Edit Report will extract and save a copy of the report definition (.rdl) file where you can edit it.
- View Report will run the report and open it in Report Viewer.

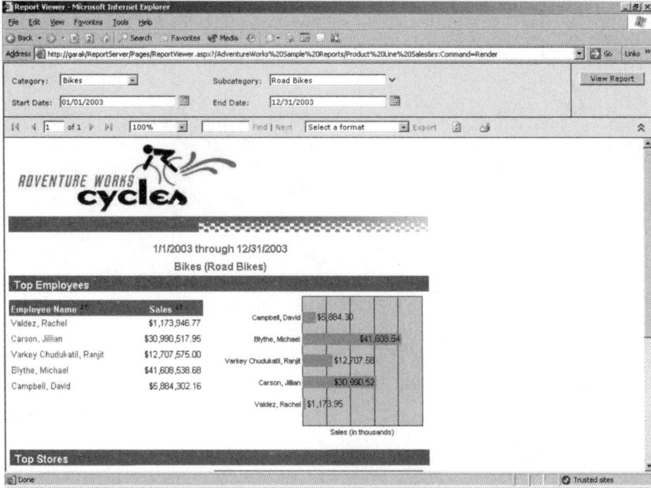

- Replace Report allows you to replace the current rdl with another one.
- New Linked Report creates a new linked report.
- Move moves the report.
- Send script sends a copy of the script to a new window, file, or clipboard.
- Rename allows you to give the report a different name.
- Delete deletes the report.
- Refresh refreshes the report tree.
- Properties opens the Properties sheet for the report.

The Report Properties sheet consists of six pages: General, Parameters, Execution, History, Permissions, and Linked Reports.

- On the General page you can modify the name and description and opt to hide or unhide the report.
- The Parameters properties page allows you to edit the Name, DataType, Has Default, Null, Default Value, Prompt User, and Prompt String attributes. This page only appears when a report includes parameters.
- On the Execution properties page, you can configure how a report is executed when it is run.

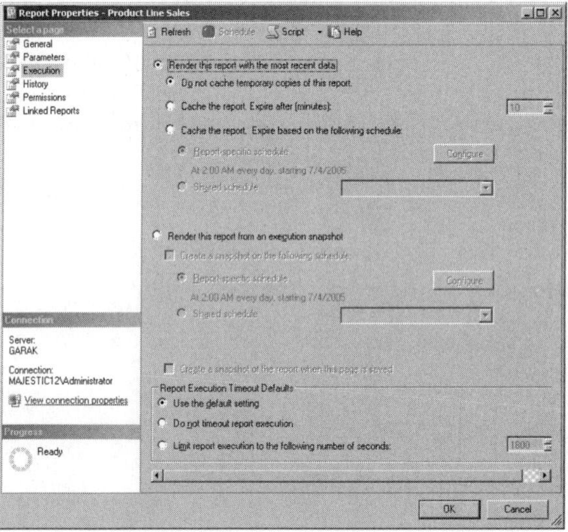

- You can use the History page to configure report history creation options, schedule report snapshots to be added to report history, and set limits on how many report snapshots are stored in report history.
- Use the Permissions page to set security on the report. You can inherit roles from the parent folder or specify roles for each group or user account for the specific report.
- The Linked Reports page displays a list of linked reports. Double-clicking on a linked report opens its properties sheet.

Close the Properties sheet to return to the folder view. make sure the Product Lines Sales Folder is selected and expanded. Now, expand the Data Sources folder. Right-click on the Adventure-Works data source and select the Properties feature that contains information specifying the details about the connections contained in the report. Note that this page is identical to that for Data Source properties in Report Manager.

Click OK to return to the folder view, make sure the Product Lines Sales Folder is selected and expanded.

Click on the History folder and create a new report snapshot by clicking New Snapshot, then click Refresh from the pop-up menu.

Double-click the snapshot to open it in Report Viewer. Alternatively you can right-click the report snapshot and select View Snapshot from the pop-up menu. To remove the snapshot, select Delete.

Make sure the Product Lines Sales Folder is selected and expanded, then right-click on the Subscriptions folder and note the four options on the pop-up menu:

- New Subscription
- New Data Driven Subscription
- Delete All Subscriptions
- Refresh

When a subscription is present, right-clicking on the subscription opens a pop-up menu with the following options:

- New Subscription
- New Data-Driven Subscription
- Delete
- Refresh
- Properties

The Properties option consists of three pages: General, Scheduling, and Parameters. You will learn how to create and configure subscriptions and schedules in the Report Delivery section of this chapter.

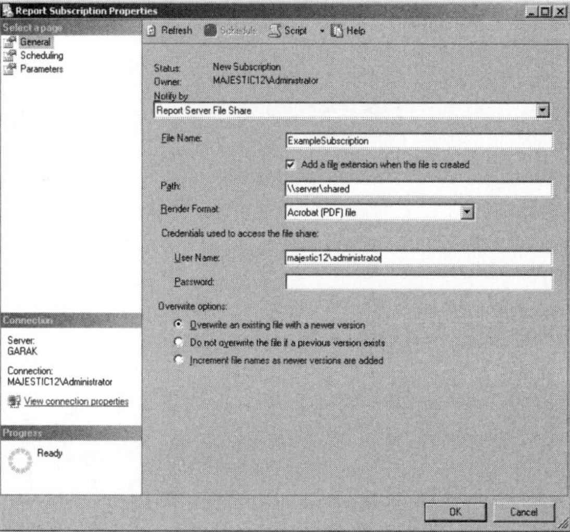

And that's it. As you have seen, you can manage reports and the report server namespace with either Report Manager or Management Studio. Now that you've mastered the art of creating reports and learned how to manage them after they're published, it's time to look at the third and final part of the report life cycle: report delivery.

Report Delivery

In this section you'll learn what a subscription is and how to create one. You'll also learn how to print a report and export them to other formats. As you saw in the earlier sections on managing reports, you can perform these tasks with both Report Manager and Management Studio.

Subscriptions

So far we've only looked at one technology for users to receive reports. They log on to the report server through Report Manager or Management Studio, find the report, and execute it. Alternatively they can invoke Report Builder to create and execute an ad hoc report, which is then delivered to them. These methods are forms of pull technology. Reporting Services also supports push technology for delivering reports. In this type of scenario, Reporting Services executes the report on its own and then sends the competed report to users. This is called a report subscription.

Reporting Services supports two types of subscriptions.

- A *standard subscription* is a request to deliver a particular report to a particular user or group of users. Each standard subscription has one set of report parameters and options for report presentation and delivery. A standard subscription is usually a self-serve operation requiring little technical expertise—the user finds the report he or she wants, then creates the subscription, setting the schedule and delivery options

- A *data-driven subscription* is a bit more complex and typically created by a report server administrator or other person who has expertise in building queries and using parameters. Unlike the standard subscription, presentation, delivery, and parameter values are collected at run time from a data source. You can use data-driven subscriptions, for example, to vary each output for each recipient in a list.

Reporting Services provides support for two delivery options: e-mail and file share. Developers can also create additional delivery extensions to route reports to other locations, but that topic is outside the scope of this book.

The *e-mail delivery option* sends an e-mail to the specified address embedded as either HTML or as an attached document in a variety of formats, including XML, CSV, TIFF, PDF, and Excel. In order to use this option, the report server must be configured for e-mail delivery.

The *file share option* creates a file containing the report in a specified folder on a file share. It can also be used to place the report on a document store managed or indexed by another application such as Microsoft SharePoint Portal Services.

CREATING A STANDARD SUBSCRIPTION WITH FILE SHARE DELIVERY

There are two tools you can use to create a standard subscription, Report Manager and Management Studio.

Using Report Manager

1. Open Report Manager and open the Product Line Sales report in the AdventureWorks Sample Reports folder.
2. Click New Subscription.
3. From the Delivered by drop-down list select Report Server File Share.
4. Type **StandardSubscriptionExample** as the filename.
5. In Path specify the file share you want the report delivered to.
6. In render format, select PDF from the list, or another format if you prefer.
7. Specify the username and password with sufficient permissions to access the file share. These credentials will be used each time the subscription is run.
8. Choose as appropriate from Overwrite options Your choices include Overwrite an existing file with a new version, Do not overwrite the file if a previous user exists and Increment file names as newer versions are added.
9. In the Subscription Processing Options section, mark the radio button next to "When the scheduled report run is complete." Click Select Schedule to open the Schedule Details window.
10. Select Once and enter a time to run the report. Click OK.
11. Accept the values in the Report Parameter Values section and click OK.

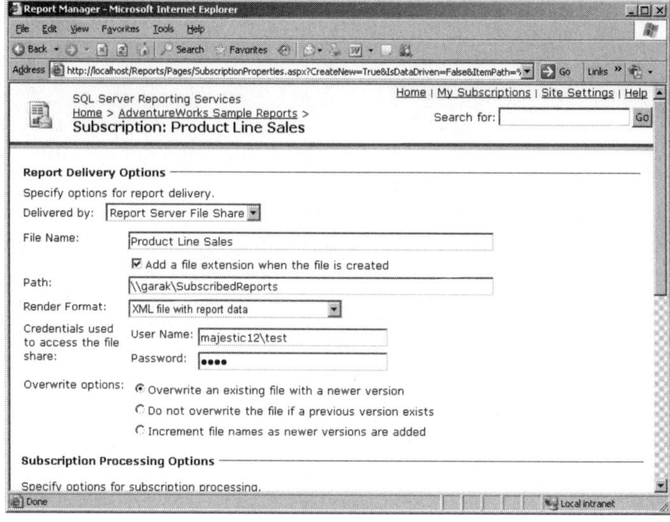

TIP You can access, edit, and delete any subscription you have created by clicking the My Subscriptions tab and selecting the subscription you want to work with.

Using Management Studio

1. Open the Report Server in Management Studio and navigate to Product Line Sales Report under Home/AdventureWorks Sample Reports.
2. Expand the Product Line Sales tree.
3. Right-click the Subscriptions folder and select New Subscription from the pop-up menu.
4. Navigate through the General, Scheduling, and Parameters properties pages and specify the various setting as you would in Report Manager. Click OK.

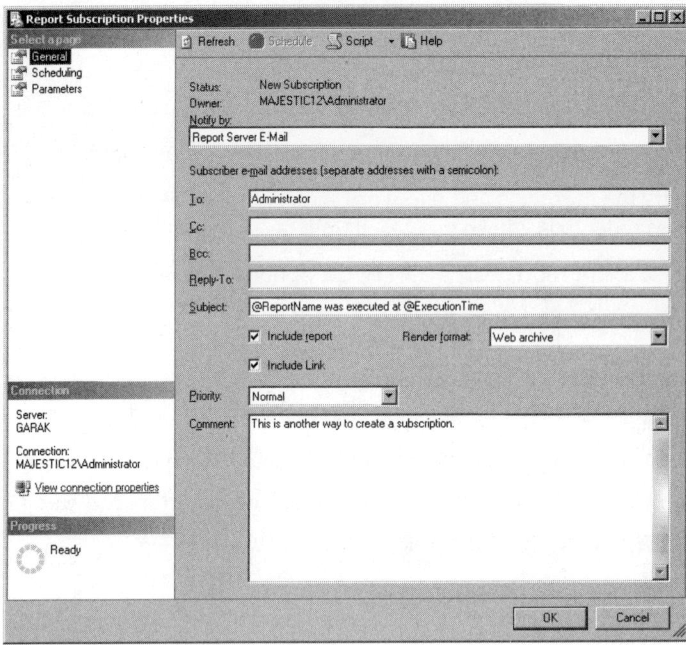

CONFIGURING REPORT SERVER FOR E-MAIL DELIVERY

In order to use the e-mail delivery option, you must have configured the e-mail setting during report server setup. If you did not do so during setup, you will need to use the Report Services Configuration Tool.

1. Click Start ➤ Programs ➤ Microsoft SQL Server 2005 ➤ Configuration Tools ➤ Reporting Services Configuration Tool.
2. Connect to the report server.
3. Select E-mail Settings.

4. Enter a sender address and the name of the SMTP Server.

5. Click Apply to accept the configuration. Any errors will be noted. Click Exit to close the program.

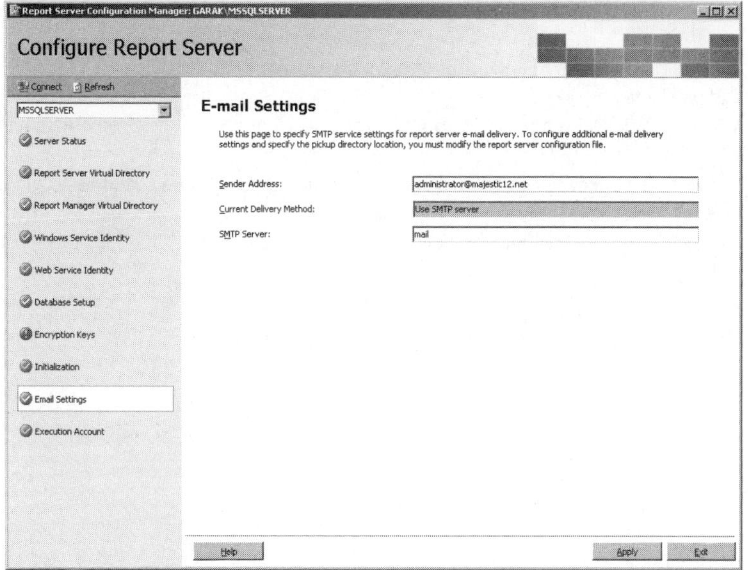

CREATING A DATA-DRIVEN SUBSCRIPTION DELIVERED BY E-MAIL

To create a data-driven subscription, you must know how to write a query or command that gets the data for the subscription. You must also have a data store that contains the source data (i.e., the names of subscribers and the delivery settings associated with each one) to use for the subscription.

WARNING In order to create a data-driven subscription, the report must be configured to use stored credentials or no credentials.

Creating the Recipients Data Store

1. Click Start ➤ Programs ➤ Microsoft SQL Server 2005 ➤ SQL Server Management Studio.

2. Right-click the Database folder and select New Database. Name it Recipients and click OK.

3. Navigate to the Tables folder, right-click, and select New Table.

4. Add five columns: *EmpName*, *Address*, *EmployeeID*, *OutputType*, and *Linked*. For *EmpName* and *Address*, set the data type to varchar(50). For all other columns, use the default data type of nchar(10). Save the table as RecipientInfo.

5. Click New Query on the Management Studio toolbar, and select Database Engine Query.

6. Expand the list of available databases, and select Recipients.

7. In the query window, use the following code to use INSERT INTO to add four rows of data:

```
INSERT INTO Recipients.dbo.RecipientInfo(EmpName, Address, EmployeeID,
OutputType, Linked)
VALUES ('Mike Gunderloy', '<your e-mail address>', '1', 'IMAGE', 'True')

INSERT INTO Recipients.dbo.RecipientInfo (EmpName, Address, EmployeeID,
OutputType, Linked)
VALUES ('Joe Jorden', '<your e-mail address>', '2', 'MHTML', 'True')

INSERT INTO Recipients.dbo.RecipientInfo (EmpName, Address, EmployeeID,
OutputType, Linked)
VALUES ('Dave Tschanz', '<your e-mail address>', '3', 'PDF', 'True')

INSERT INTO Recipients.dbo.RecipientInfo (EmpName, Address, EmployeeID,
OutputType, Linked)
VALUES ('Tom Cirtin', '<your e-mail address>', '4', 'Excel', 'True')
```

WARNING Be sure to replace *<your e-mail address>* with an actual valid e-mail address. You can use the same e-mail address for each row.

8. Click Execute.
9. Confirm the table has four rows of data by using `SELECT * FROM RecipientInfo.`

Creating a Data-Driven Subscription with Report Manager (E-mail Delivery)

1. Open Report Manager and open the Company Sales report in the AdventureWorks Sample Reports folder.
2. Click Subscriptions. Click New Data-Driven Subscription to begin creating the data-driven subscription.
3. Type **Data-Driven Subscription Example.**
4. Select Report Server E-mail in the "Specify how recipients are notified" drop-down box.

NOTE If the Report Server E-mail option does not appear, you will need to configure the Report Server for e-mail delivery as detailed above.

5. Under "Specify a data source that contains recipient information," mark "Specify for this subscription only if it is not already marked." Click Next.
6. Confirm the connection type is set to Microsoft SQL Server.
7. Type **Data Source = localhost;Initial Catalog=Recipients** in the Connection String box.
8. Specify the user credentials for this report—in this case your domain username and password. Click "Use as Windows credentials when connecting to the data source," and then click Next.

9. In the Query pane type **SELECT * FROM RecipientInfo**. Click the Validate button. When the Query is validated, click Next to go to the Specify delivery extension setting for Report Server E-mail page.

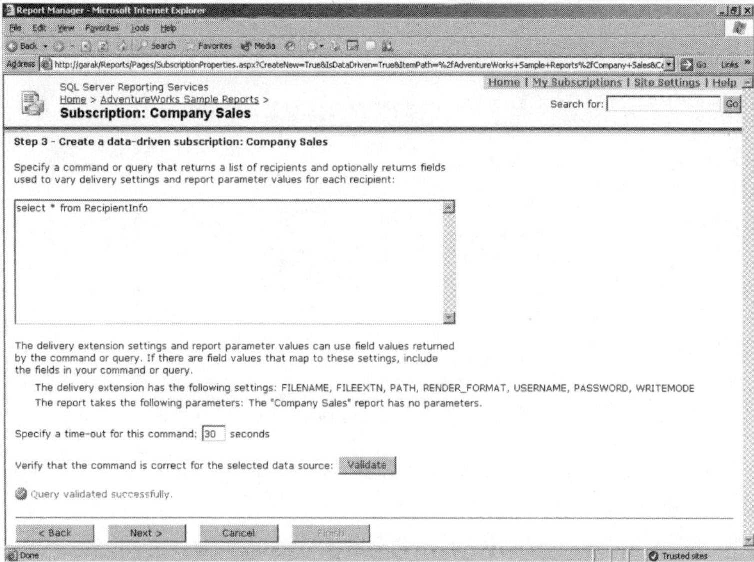

10. In the To option, select "Get the value from the database" and select Address.

11. Accept the no value settings for the CC, BCC, and ReplyTo options.

12. Accept the default value for Include Report. You can opt to send the report and a hyperlink (using the Include Link option), just the report, just a link, or neither.

13. Select "Get the value from the database in the Render Format" option, and select OutputType.

14. Accept the default values for Priority, Subject option, and Comment option.

15. The Include Link option determines whether a link with the report URL is sent. Select "Get the value from the database" and select Linked.

16. Click Next to open the "Specify report parameter values" page.

17. Click Next. Select "On a schedule created for this subscription."

18. Click Next. In the Schedule details section, click once and specify a time.

19. Click Finish to generate the subscription and return to the report's subscription page. From here you can open the subscription for editing as well as delete it.

Creating a Data-Driven Subscription with Management Studio (File Share Delivery)

1. Open the Report Server in Management Studio and navigate to Product Line Sales Report under Home/AdventureWorks Sample Reports.

2. Expand the Company Sales tree.

3. Right-click the Subscriptions folder and Select New Data Subscription from the pop-up menu to start the Data-Driven Subscription Wizard. Click Next.

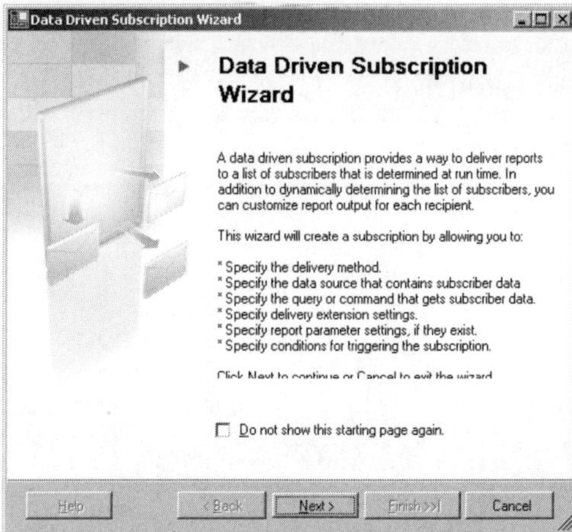

4. Type **Data-Driven Subscription Example2** in the description box. Accept Report Server File Share as the Delivery method. Click Next.

5. On the Delivery Data Source page, select "A custom data source." Type **Data Source = localhost;Initial Catalog=Recipients** in the Connection String box.

6. Select "Credentials stored securely on the report server." Enter your domain username and password. Mark the "Use as Windows credential when connecting to the data source" check box. Click Next to open the Delivery Query page.

7. In the Command text window, type **SELECT * FROM RecipientInfo**. Click the Validate button. When the Query is validated, click Next to go to the Specify delivery extension setting for Report Server E-mail page.

8. On the Extension Setting page, name the `file: Data-Driven Subscription Example2`.

9. In the File Extension field, accept the default value.

10. In the Path field, specify the path to the file share using its UNC name.

11. In Render Format, select Query Results Field from the Setting Source and select OutputType for the setting value.

12. Enter a username with permissions to write to the file share.

13. Enter the password.

14. In the Write mode field, select which option you want to be taken, either OverWrite or Auto-Increment, if a file with the same name is encountered. Click Next.

15. Specify any relevant Parameter Values on this page. The Company Sales report has no user provided parameters. Click Next.

16. Select On a Custom Schedule. In the Type drop-down box, select Once. Specify a Start time and click OK. Click Finish.

Shared Schedules

As you've noticed while working through the examples, each time you had an option to create a schedule for a feature such as a snapshot or a subscription, you've been offered the choice to use a shared schedule.

Shared schedules allow you to use a single schedule definition in multiple places, such as different report, snapshots, and subscriptions. They are particularly useful when a number of events need to use the same timing. For example, you need to run and deliver 10 reports to different managers so that reports arrive in their in-boxes at the start of business on Monday morning.

CREATING A SHARED SCHEDULE WITH REPORT MANAGER

1. Open Report Manager and click Site Settings.

NOTE If the Site Settings option is not available, you don't have the necessary permissions to use them.

2. Click the "Manage shared schedules" link in the Other section.

3. Click New Schedule.

4. In the Schedule name box type **SharedScheduleExample.**

5. In the Schedule Details option, you can set the frequency—days and time the items using this report will run. Set the schedule to run on a weekly basis on Monday and Wednesdays at 7:00 A.M.

6. In the Start and End Dates section you can specify the dates to start and end the schedule. The default values are the date the report is created, with no stop date. Accept these values and click OK.

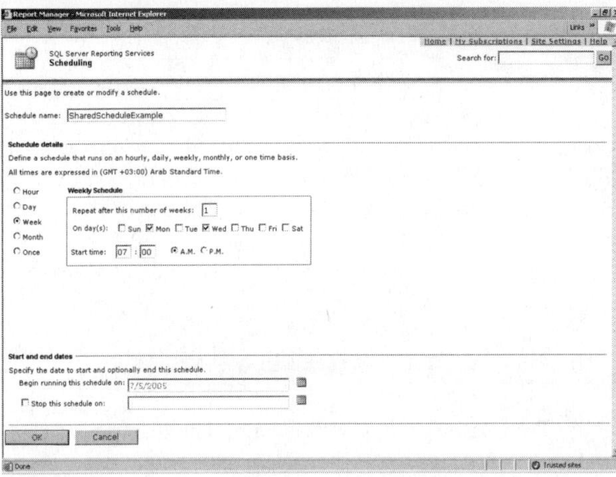

7. The shared schedule appears on the Shared Schedule page, which is accessible from Site Settings ➤ Manage shared schedules. To modify the schedule, click on the schedule you want to change. You can also delete a schedule from this page.

Creating a Shared Schedule with Management Studio

1. Open Management Studio and open a report server.
2. Right-click the Shared Schedules folder. Select New Schedule from the pop-up menu to open the General page of the New Shared Schedule properties box.
3. Type **SharedScheduleExample2** in the Name text box. Choose whatever you like for the frequency and time to run the schedule on.

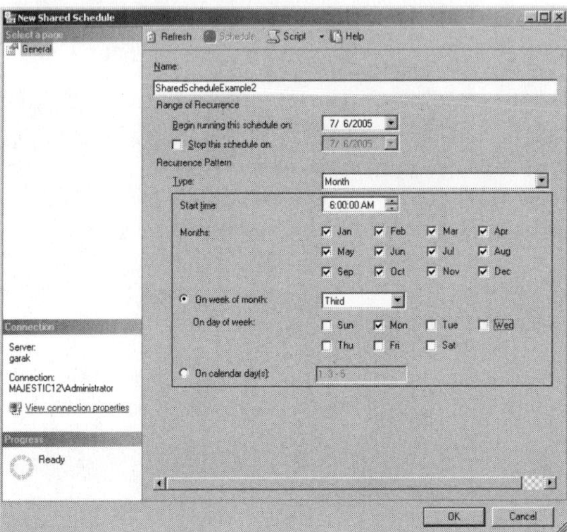

4. Click OK. The new Shared Schedule appears in the folder. To modify an existing shared schedule, right-click the schedule you want to modify, and then click Properties. To delete the shared schedule, right-click on it and select Delete.

Jobs

Scheduled items in Reporting Services actually use the SQL Agent to handle their operations. In fact when you create a schedule, shared or report-specific, you are actually creating a job in the SQL Agent.

There are two types of jobs. User jobs are any that were started by an individual user or subscriptions such as running a report on demand or processing a standard subscription. System jobs are started by the report server independent of a user's invoking them. Examples of system jobs include scheduled snapshots and data-driven subscriptions.

When jobs are executing you can use the Manage Jobs page or folder to view the status of an executing job or to cancel a job.

Opening the Manage Jobs Page with Report Manager

1. Open Report Manager and click Site Settings.
2. Click the Manage jobs link in the Other section.
3. The Manage Jobs page opens and displays any jobs that are actually executing on the server. If no jobs are being run, the page is empty.

Managing Jobs with Management Studio

1. Open Management Studio and open a report server.
2. Click the Jobs folder. Jobs only appear if they are being run.

Printing Reports

In addition to delivery to in-boxes and file shares, another method of report delivery is the old-fashioned way—printing a hard copy. Since all printing is done on the client, the user is provided a standard print dialog box and can control the printers and print options used.

1. Open Report Manager and navigate to the Product Line Sales report, and open it.
2. On the toolbar click the Print icon. The first time you print an HTML report, the report server will attempt to install an ActiveX control that is required for printing. Click Yes.

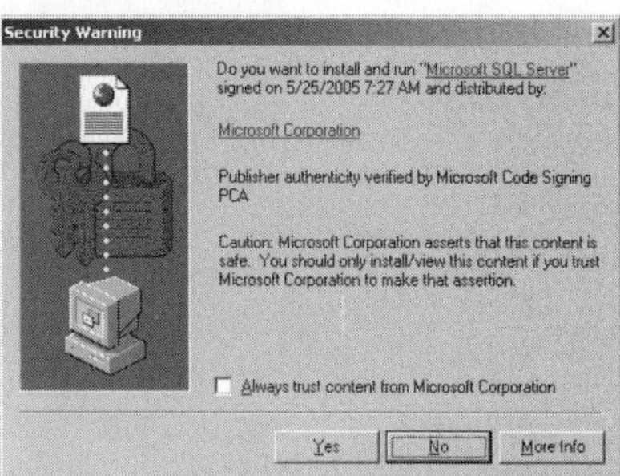

3. In the Print dialog box, select a print device. Click OK.

Exporting a Report

Reporting Services allows you to export a browser-based report to another application. If you export a report you can, of course, work with it inside the application, save it as file in the application, and print the report in the application.

Natively supported export formats include:

- CSV
- Excel
- MHTML (Web Archive)
- PDF
- TIFF
- XML

EXPORTING A REPORT

1. Open Report Manager and navigate to the Product Line Sales report, and open it.
2. On the toolbar select Acrobat (PDF) file in the "Select a format" drop-down list.

NOTE To export a report to another application, the application must be installed on the computer executing the export.

3. Click Export. The report opens in the target application.

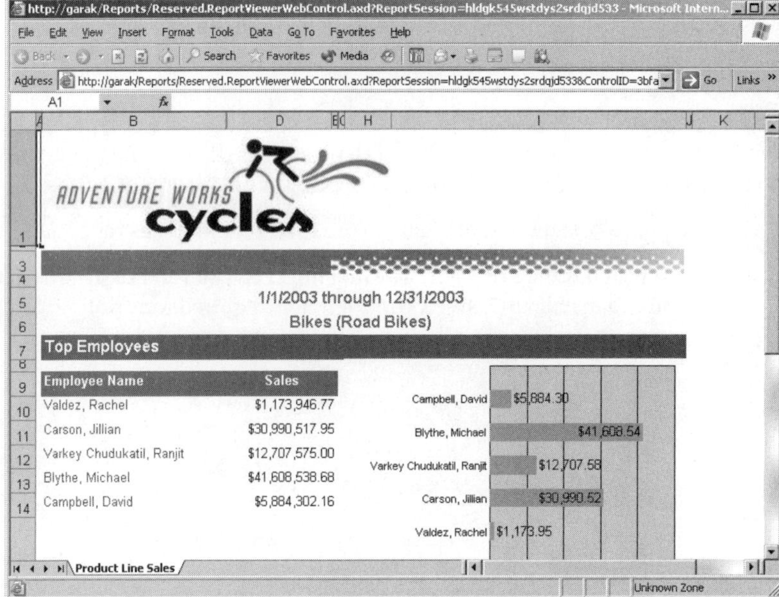

PRINTING A REPORT TO ANOTHER APPLICATION

You can also print a report to another application if you want to make use of the other application's print features.

1. Open Report Manager and navigate to the Product Line Sales report, then open it.
2. On the tool bar select TIFF file and click Export. In the File Download dialog, select Open. The report opens in TIFF format inside the default viewer.

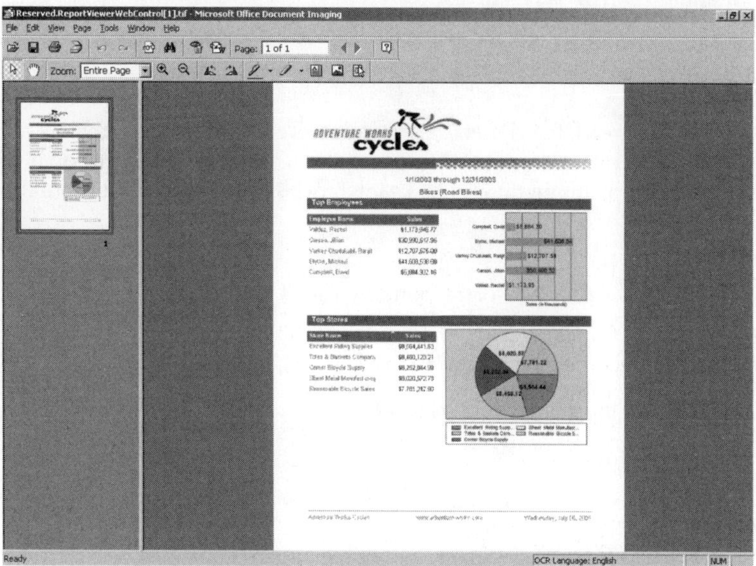

3. Select File ➤ Print, or click the print icon to send the report to a print in the new format.

Reporting Services Security

The reason for securing the reports you have created and published to the report server should be obvious. The reports contain synopses of the information in your database in an understandable format that you may not want to have available to everyone. You may want to limit the ability to view or modify a particular report to certain people. You may want to secure either an individual report or an entire folder of reports, snapshots, and models.

Reporting Services uses Windows authentication and a role-based security model to determine which users or groups can perform operation and access materials and items on a report server.

The actions that users or groups can perform are called *tasks*. There are a total of 25 tasks, such as View Reports, Manage Reports, and Manage Data Sources.

All tasks are predefined. This means you can't modify a task or create your own custom task. There are two types of tasks: *Item-level tasks* can be performed on folders, reports, report models, snapshots, resources, and other items managed by the report server. *System-level tasks* are actions done at the system level, such as managing jobs and shared schedules.

Each task is composed of a set of predefined *permissions* that provide the user with access to specific report server functions. If a user doesn't have the necessary permissions to a function, then it doesn't appear as an option. For example, if a user doesn't have the permission to read a subscription, then he or she won't even see subscription-related pages in Report Manager or items in relevant folders in Management Studio.

Users are granted permissions indirectly as a part of a task. Tasks, in turn, can't work except when assigned to a *role*.

In a role-based security model, all users and groups are assigned to one or more roles. A role determines what tasks the user can perform and in what contexts.

You actually make use of roles in your day-to-day life. As a licensed driver you are able to drive a motor vehicle. Your role of parent allows you to have a say in the upbringing of your children, and to require them to perform certain tasks. As an employee, you have access to the company you work for and certain of its resources.

Let's look at how to use roles.

Roles

As you've already read, the rights to perform tasks are grouped together as roles. Reporting Services contains several predefined roles. In addition, you can make your own role definitions and group together any combinations of tasks for a role that you find most useful for the work at hand.

PREDEFINED ROLE

The predefined roles and their corresponding rights are:

Browser Role Can view and run reports, but cannot create folder or upload new reports. The Browser Role includes the following tasks:

- Manage individual subscriptions
- View folders
- View models
- View reports
- View resources

Content Manager Role Intended for users who need to manage folders, reports, and resources. All members of the local administrators group on the report server computer are automatically assigned to the role. Content Managers can perform any item-level task, but no system-level tasks. The Content Manager Role includes the following tasks:

- Consume reports
- Create linked reports
- Manage all subscriptions
- Manage individual subscriptions
- Manage data sources
- Manage folders
- Manage models
- Manage report history
- Manage reports
- Manage resources

- Manage individual subscriptions
- Set security policies for items
- View data sources
- View folders
- View models
- View reports
- View resources

Report Builder Role The Report Builder Role permits a user to load reports in Report Builder, as well as view and navigate the folder hierarchy. The Report Builder Role includes the following tasks:

- Consume reports
- Manage individual subscriptions
- View folders
- View models
- View reports
- View resources

NOTE To create and modify reports in Report Builder, a user must also have a system role assignment that includes the *Execute report definitions* task.

Publisher Role Publishers can create folder and upload reports, but not change security settings or manage subscriptions and report history. The role is best suited for a user who authors reports in Report Designer and publishes them to a report server. The Publisher Role includes the following tasks:

- Create linked reports
- Manage data sources
- Manage folders
- Manage models
- Manage reports
- Manage resources

My Reports Role The My Reports Role is intended to be used only with the individual user's My Reports folder. This role gives the user the right to do the following on any My Reports folder he or she owns. The My Reports Role includes the following tasks:

- Create linked reports
- Manage data sources
- Manage folders

- Manage individual subscriptions
- Manage reports
- Manage resources
- View data sources
- View folders
- View reports
- View resources

System Administrator Role System administrators have the rights to complete any task necessary to manage the report server. Members of the local administrators group on the report server computer are automatically assigned to System Administrator Role as well as the Content Manager Role. System administrators can:

- Execute report definitions
- Manage jobs
- Manage report server properties
- Manage report server security
- Manage roles
- Manage shared schedules

System User Role System users can view basic information about the report server, but make no modifications. The System User Role also includes the necessary task "Execute report definitions" required to allow the user to create and modify reports in Report Builder. The System User Role includes the following tasks:

- Execute report definitions
- View report server properties
- View shared schedules

Customizing Roles

You can create or modify any role, including predefined roles, by adding or removing tasks from the role definition by using either Report Manager or Management Studio. You can also delete a role. The only caveat is that while role definitions can contain either item-level or system-level tasks, you cannot combine both types in a single role definition.

Create a System-Level Role Definition with Report Manager

1. Open Report Manager and click Site Settings.
2. Select Configure system-level role definitions.
3. Click New Role.
4. Type **SystemLevelRoleExample** in the Name box. Add a description if you wish.

5. Select one or more tasks for the role definition.

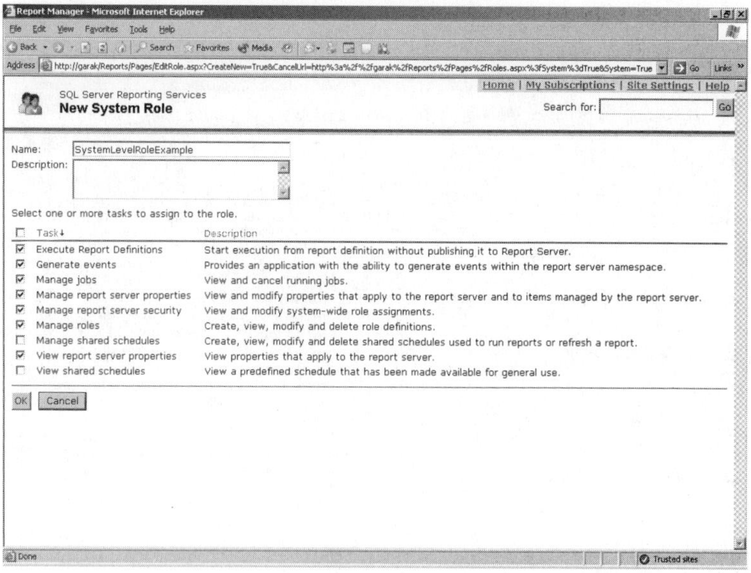

6. Click OK to save the role definition to the report server. Once there it can be used by any user with the permission to create role assignments.

Modify a System-Level Role Definition with Report Manager

1. Open Report Manager and click Site Settings.
2. Select Configure system-level role definitions.
3. Click the `SystemLevelRoleExample` role definition you just created.
4. Modify the task list or the description. Notice that you cannot change the name.
5. If you want to delete the role definition, click the Delete button.
6. Click OK to save the changes in the role definition to the report server. Once there it can be used by any user with the permission to create role assignments.

Create an Item-Level Role Definition with Management Studio

1. Open Management Studio and expand the report server in Object Explorer.
2. Expand the Security folder.
3. Right-click the Roles folder and select New Role to open the New User Role property sheet.
4. In the Name text box, type **Report Analyst.** Add a description if you wish.
5. In the Task Pane, mark the check box next to the tasks you wish members of this role to perform.

6. Click OK. The role definition appears in the Roles folder.

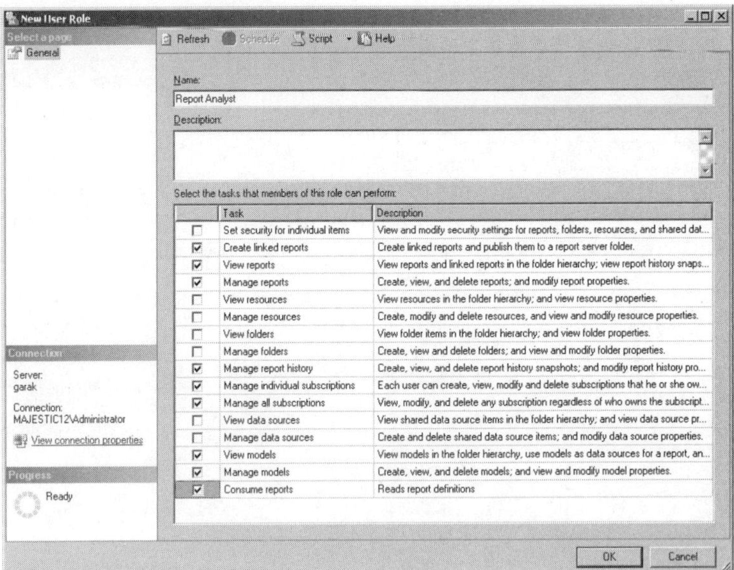

Modify an Item-Level Role Definition with Management Studio

1. Open Management Studio and expand the report server in Object Explorer.
2. Expand the Security folder.
3. Right-click the Roles folder and select the role definition for Report Analyst.
4. Open the User Role Properties by double-clicking Report Analyst or right-clicking it and selecting Properties from the menu
5. In the Task Pane, mark or clear the check boxes next to the tasks you wish to change for this role. You can also modify the description but you cannot change the name.
6. Click OK. The updated role definition is saved to the Roles folder.

You can delete a role definition by navigating to it, right-clicking it, and clicking Delete.

Role Assignments

Roles only become operative when used in a *role assignment*. The role assignment then controls what the user can see and what tasks he or she can perform.

Each role assignment consists of three parts. *Securable items* are the item you want to control access for and include folders, resources, report models, shared data sources, and of course reports. Next, there needs to be a *user or group account* that can be authenticated, usually through Windows security. Last is a *role definition*, which describes the set of tasks the user can perform on the securable items.

By default, all folders (except the Home folder), reports, and other securable items inherit their role assignments from the parent folder.

Managing Role Assignments with Report Manager

You create and modify user and system role assignments using Report Manager as described below:

Create a Role Assignment with Report Manager

1. Open Report Manager and navigate to the Home folder.
2. Select the Properties tab to open the Security page for the Home folder.
3. Click New Role Assignment. Note that you can open the New Role page by clicking the New Role button. This is useful if you don't want to use any of the existing role definitions.
4. In the Group or username text box, type the name of a valid user or group. It must be in the format *DomainName\DomainUserName* or *ComputerName\ComputerUserName* where *DomainName* refers to the domain, *DomainUserName* is a valid user or group in the domain; *ComputerName* is the local computer name, and *ComputerUserName* is a local user or group.
5. Check the check box for the Publisher Role. You can also select multiple roles to apply.

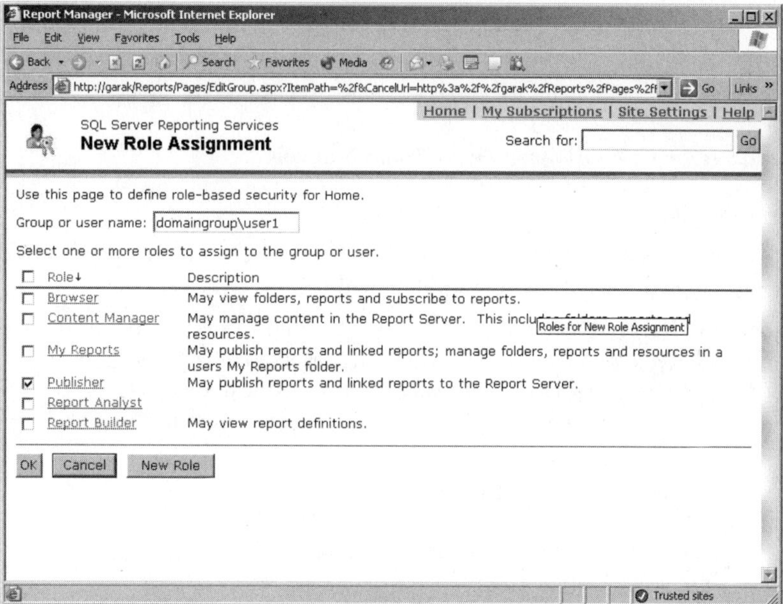

6. Click OK to save the new role assignment and return to the Securities page.

Modify a Role Assignment with Report Manager

1. Open Report Manager and navigate to the Home folder.
2. Select the Properties tab to open the Security page for the Home folder.
3. Click Edit next to the Publisher Role Assignment you created above.
4. On the Edit Role Assignment page, click the Browser check box to add that role.

5. Note that in addition to the Apply button, you can also click New Role. You can also Delete the Role Assignment by clicking the button.

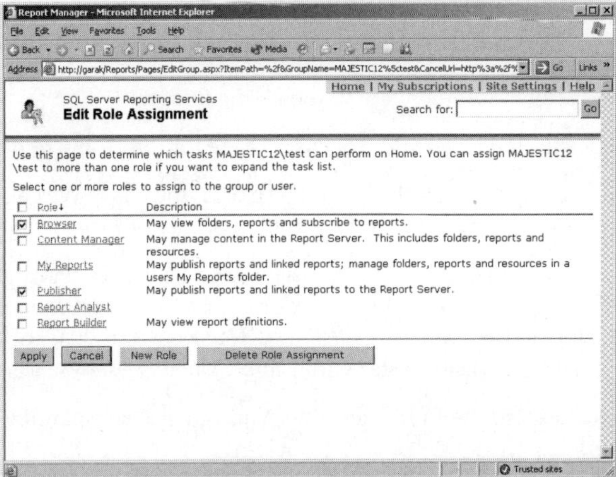

6. Select Apply to save your changes to the report server and return to the Securities. Your new role assignment includes both the Publisher and Browser roles.

Create a System Role Assignment with Report Manager

1. Open Report Manager and click Site Settings.
2. In the Security section, select Configure Sitewide Security to open the System Role Assignments page. Click New Role Assignment.
3. In the Group or Username text box, type the name of a valid user or group you want to assign a system role to. It must be in the format *DomainName\DomainUserName* or *ComputerName\ComputerUserName* where *DomainName* refers to the domain, *DomainUserName* is a valid user or group in the domain; *ComputerName* is the local computer name, and *ComputerUserName* is a local user or group.

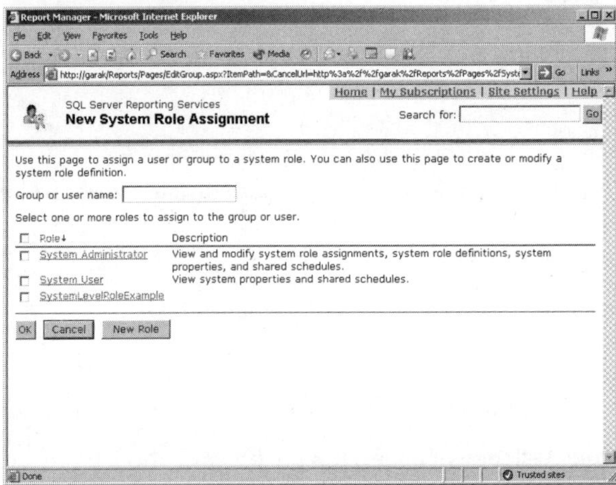

4. Select one or more system role definitions to use.
5. Click OK. The new system role assignments are saved to the report server and you are returned to the System Role Assignments page.

Modify a System Role Assignment with Report Manager

1. Open Report Manager and click Site Settings.
2. In the Security section, select Configure Sitewide Security to open the System Role Assignments page. Click Edit next to the new security role assignment you just created.
3. On the Edit System Role Assignments page, mark or unmark at least one of the roles you used in this role assignment.
4. Click Apply. Note that you can also open the New System Role page by clicking the button or select Delete Role Assignment to remove the role assignment.

MANAGING ROLE ASSIGNMENTS WITH MANAGEMENT STUDIO

You create and modify user and system role assignments using Management Studio as described below:

Create a Role Assignment with Management Studio

1. Open Management Studio and expand the report server in Object Explorer.
2. Right-click Home and select Properties to open to the Permissions page.
3. Click the Add Group or User button to display the Select Users or Groups dialog box.
4. Type the name of a valid user or group you want to assign a role to. It must be in the format *DomainName\DomainUserName* or *ComputerName\ComputerUserName* where *DomainName* refers to the domain, *DomainUserName* is a valid user or group in the domain; *ComputerName* is the local computer name, and *ComputerUserName* is a local user or group.
5. Click OK.
6. Check one or more roles you wish to assign to the user or group. Click OK to save the new role assignment to the report server.

Modify a Role Assignment with Management Studio

1. Open Management Studio and expand the report server in Object Explorer.
2. Right-click Home and select Properties to open to the Permissions page.
3. Select the role assignment you just created and change the roles you assigned by clearing or checking boxes.
4. Click OK.
5. Check one or more roles you wish to assign to the user or group. Click OK to save the new role assignment to the report server. If you want to delete the highlighted role assignment, click Remove.
6. Click OK to save the modifications to the role assignment to the report server.

Create a System Role Assignment with Management Studio

1. Open Management Studio.
2. Right-click the report server and select Properties.
3. Select the Permissions page.

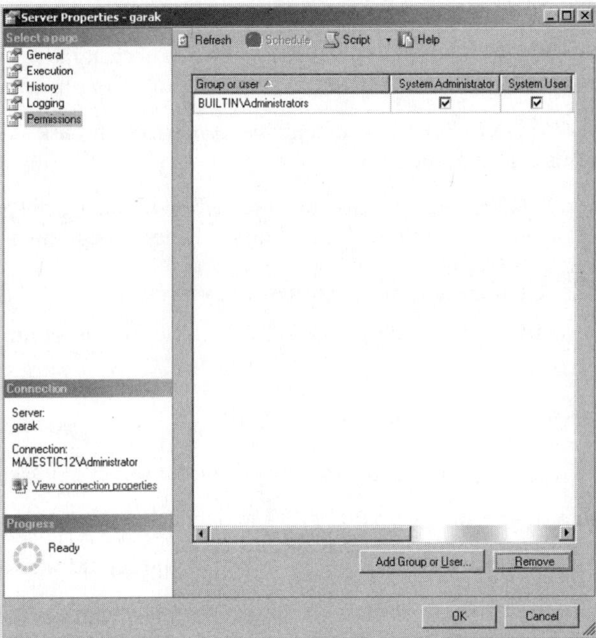

4. Click the Add Group or User button to display the Select Users or Groups dialog box.
5. Type the name of a valid user or group you want to assign a system role to. It must be in the format *DomainName\DomainUserName* or *ComputerName\ComputerUserName* where *DomainName* refers to the domain, *DomainUserName* is a valid user or group in the domain; *ComputerName* is the local computer name, and *ComputerUserName* is a local user or group.
6. Click OK to save the new system role assignment to the report server.

Modify a System Role Assignment with Management Studio

1. Open Management Studio.
2. Right-click the report server and select Properties.
3. Select the Permissions page.
4. Select the role assignment you wish to modify and make changes by selecting or de-selecting the check boxes for the relevant roles. If you wish to delete the role assignment, select it and click the Remove button.
5. Click OK to save the modifications to the system role assignment to the report server.

Report Services Configuration Tool

The Reporting Services Configuration Tool allows you to configure a Reporting Services installation after setup. For example, if you used the files-only option for the report server installation, you need to use this tool to configure the report server so it can be used. If you used the default setup, you can use the configuration tool to verify or modify the server settings.

The Reporting Services Configuration can be used to configure a local or remote report server instance. You must have local system administrator permissions on the report server computer to configure it.

To launch the Report Services Configuration:

1. Click Start ➤ Programs ➤ Microsoft SQL Server 2005 ➤ Configuration Tools ➤ Reporting Services Configuration.
2. Select the Report Server instance you wish to configure. Click Find. Click Connect.

Report Services Configuration Settings

The Reporting Services Configuration Tool offers 10 options to access setting and configuration information. These appear on the left side of the tool. Icons indicate whether the option is configured, not configured, optional, or recommended for configuration.

WARNING It is possible to configure settings that are not valid. Always verify a Reporting Services installation.

Server Status This page provides information on the instance properties including the instance name, the instance ID, whether or not the instance has been initialized, and whether Reporting Services is running. You can use stop the service by clicking the Stop button or clicking the Start button to run the service.

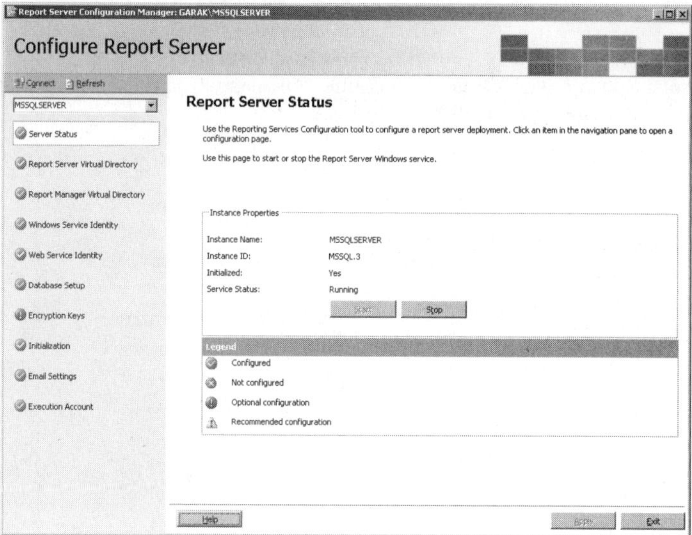

Report Server Virtual Directory This page allows you to specify a virtual directory for the report server. Or you can click the New button to open the Create a New Virtual Directory dialog box.

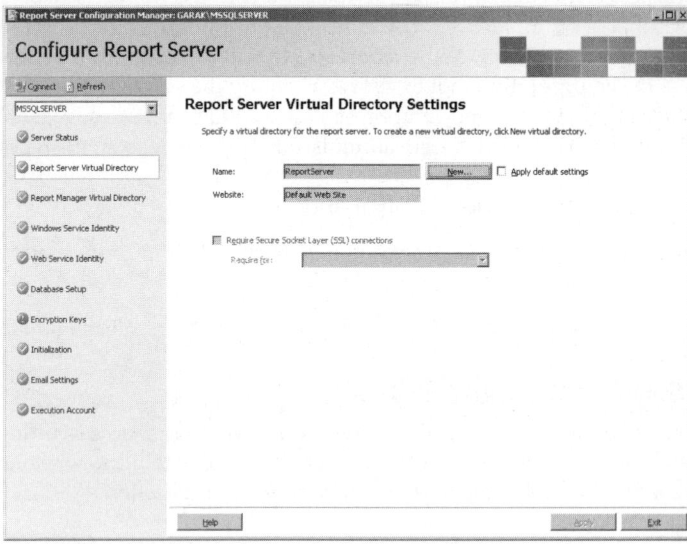

Report Manager Virtual Directory Use this page to specify or create a virtual directory for Report Manager.

Windows Service Identity Use this page to update the Report Server Windows service account. You can specify a Built-in account or Windows account to run the service.

Web Service Identity Here you can specify the application pool to run the Report Server Web service in for both Report Server and Report Manager.

Database Setup On this page you create and configure a connection to a report server database if one doesn't exist. Or you can connect to an existing database by specifying it and providing the proper connection credentials.

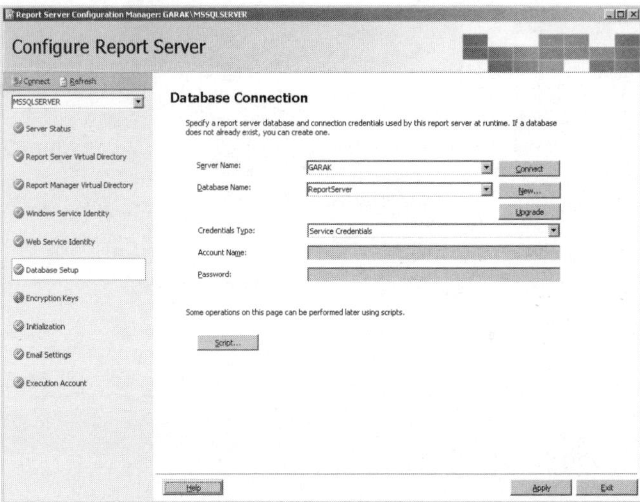

Encryption Keys Reporting Services uses a symmetric key to encrypt and decrypt sensitive data such as credentials, accounts, and connections. On this page you can back up, restore, and re-create encryption keys. If recovery is not possible, you can also delete encrypted values from this page.

Initialization This page can be used to check on the initialization status if a report server and configure a scale-out deployment. You can use button to initialize the server or to remove it.

E-mail Settings As you have seen, report subscriptions can be delivered to electronic mailboxes. In order for this to happen Simple Mail Transport Protocol has to be configured. You can use this page to specify a sender address and which SMTP server to use for e-mail delivery.

Execution Account Set the account and password to be used by the report server to perform unattended operations. Some functionality is lost if you don't specify an account.

Summary

SQL Server 2005 includes a Reporting Services component that is both sophisticated and easy to use.

With Reporting Services you can create custom and defined reports on a scheduled or on-demand basis. End users can use Report Builder to generate reports on an ad hoc basis without extensive technical knowledge. Developers and users in need of more sophisticated reports can use Report Designer and its powerful Report Wizard. You've also reviewed how to create parameterized reports. This chapter examined using Report Designer and its powerful Report Wizard to create reports as well as importing reports from Microsoft Access.

Report Models are the prerequisite to using Report Builder. In this chapter you've learned to create them and apply them to create reports with Report Builder. Since publishing a report is the only way to make it available to users, you've seen how to build and deploy reports as key steps in publishing them to a report server.

Report Manager and Management Studio both allow you to manage published reports and you've looked at how to use both to manage folders as well to view, modify, and delete reports. You learned to set report properties and create snapshots.

You learned about standard and data-driven subscription delivery methods and how to use them to deliver reports to user via e-mail or file share. You also looked at how to create shared schedules and learned about managing jobs. We also looked at how to print reports and export them to different file formats.

Security is a critical aspect of safeguarding data on the report server. In this chapter we learned about the role-based security model employed by Reporting Services and how to use roles and role assignments to safeguard the data.

We finished with a brief overview of the Reporting Services Configuration Tool. And make no mistake, Reporting Services is so robust and all encompassing that in many ways we only scratched the surface of this elegant tool.

Now it's time to turn to the next chapter and learn about another new tool in SQL Server 2005: Service Broker.

Chapter 29

Service Broker

If this is the first time you've heard about Service Broker, rest assured that it has nothing to do with the stock market. Service Broker is another powerful new technology introduced in SQL Server 2005 and targeted primarily at developers.

Service Broker adds guaranteed asynchronous queuing support to SQL Server 2005. Asynchronous queuing provides a high level of scalability to SQL Server 2005 because it allows a program to respond to more requests than the platform may be able to physically handle.

For example, suppose a website was offering the hottest children's book to the market at precisely 12:01 A.M. Now suppose that at that exact moment, 20,000 users simultaneously tried to order books on that server. Unless it was able to use asynchronous queuing, the server would soon be overwhelmed as it tried to launch enough threads to handle all the incoming requests. In that case, all of the requests would be captured in a queue, in the order received. The web server, no longer in danger of being overwhelmed, can now process entries from the queue (in this case, book orders) at its maximum levels of efficiency. So, in a classic case of the total being greater than the sum of its parts, the server would be able to handle a greater number of user connections than would otherwise be possible, thanks to asynchronous queuing.

Asynchronous queuing is already present in your operating system's I/O subsystems as well as the internal operations of the SQL Server 2005 database engine. The addition of Service Broker to SQL Server 2005 brings the capability of handling asynchronous queuing to end-user database applications as well.

In this chapter, you'll learn about the new features provided by the SQL Server Service Broker. You'll get an overview of the new subsystem and learn about its core components. Then, you'll see the basics of how you create Service Broker applications. You'll learn how to create message types and queues and you'll learn how to use new T-SQL commands to enable messaging applications to add messages to a queue as well as receive the messages in the queue. Finally, you'll learn about some of the administrative features found in the Service Broker subsystem.

Understanding Service Broker

As mentioned above, Service Broker is a new feature in SQL Server 2005 that was designed with database developers in mind. The idea was to provide these developers with a tool that assists them to build secure, reliable, and scalable applications. One of the key benefits is that since Service Broker is part of the database engine, administration of the developed application becomes part of the normal administration of the database and doesn't require anything special. In other words, the system-level details of implementing a messaging application are delegated to Service Broker and can be managed independently.

Service Broker adds the ability to perform asynchronous queuing for SQL Server. This new queuing capability is fully transactional. Transactions can incorporate queued events and can be both committed and rolled back. You can access the Service Broker using new SQL statements.

Service Broker can be used both for applications that use a single SQL Server instance and for applications that use more than one instance. In the case of a single SQL Server instance, Service Broker allows database applications using asynchronous programming to radically reduce interactive response time and increase overall throughput.

In addition, queuing applications built using Service Broker can span multiple SQL Server systems and still provide guaranteed message delivery—even to remote queues. The messages that are sent across the queues can be very large, up to 2GB. Service Broker takes care of the mechanics required to break apart the large messages into smaller chunks that are sent across the network and then reassembled at the other end.

NOTE There are both 32-bit and 64-bit versions of Service Broker.

With Service Broker, SQL Server is now a platform for building loosely coupled, asynchronous database applications. Typically large database applications have one or more tables that they use as queues.

The role of a queue is to store messages. When a message arrives, Service Broker inserts it into the queue. Applications communicate with each other by sending and receiving messages from and to Service Broker queues. Once a message is stored in a queue, it is left there until either expiration has elapsed or it has been retrieved.

Using a table as a queue can help improve performance and scalability but maintaining transactional accuracy is difficult. As you will see shortly, Service Broker addresses the complexity of building table queues by implementing queues as built-in database objects. The queue-handling code built into the database kernel handles the locking, ordering, and multithreading processes that cause problems in most homegrown database queues.

To scale out asynchronous database applications, Service Broker includes reliable, transactional messaging between SQL Server instances. Service Broker uses a dialog mechanism that transmits the message between two services exactly once and in order, preventing duplicate messages.

Service Broker also plays a key role in ensuring high availability between services. If, for example, server A is setup to send messages to server B, and a network failure occurs, server A will hold unread messages in the queue until either the expiration has elapsed or server B is again available.

To ensure that an application is always running to process received messages, Service Broker also includes, as you will see below, an activation feature that increases the number of processing stored procedures as the workload increases and that decreases the number of stored procedures as the queue workload decreases or becomes empty.

T-SQL DDL and DML

T-SQL has been enhanced with several new statements that enable the native integration of Service Broker messaging and database procedure. Table 29.1 below summarizes the new DDL statements used to create Service Broker objects.

TABLE 29.1: T-SQL Statements for SQL Server Service Broker Objects

T-SQL DDL	DESCRIPTION
ALTER MESSAGE TYPE	Changes a message type
ALTER QUEUE	Changes a queue

TABLE 29.1: T-SQL Statements for SQL Server Service Broker Objects *(CONTINUED)*

T-SQL DDL	DESCRIPTION
ALTER REMOTE SERVICE BINDING	Changes properties of a remote service binding
ALTER ROUTE	Changes a route
ALTER SERVICE	Changes a service
CREATE CONTRACT	Creates a new contract in a database
CREATE MESSAGE TYPE	Creates a new message type
CREATE QUEUE	Creates a new queue in a database
CREATE REMOTE SERVICE BINDING	Creates a binding that associates a remote service with user credentials
CREATE ROUTE	Creates a new route in a database
CREATE SERVICE	Creates a new service in a database
DROP CONTRACT	Deletes a contract from a database
DROP MESSAGE TYPE	Deletes a message type from a database
DROP QUEUE	Deletes an queue from a database
DROP REMOTE SERVICE BINDING	Deletes a binding from a database
DROP ROUTE	Deletes a route from a database
DROP SERVICE	Deletes a service from a database

In addition to new DDL statements, a new group of T-SQL statements are available that work with messages in a Service Broker application, these Data Manipulation Language (DML) statements are listed in Table 29.2 below.

TABLE 29.2: T-SQL Statements for SQL Server Service Broker Messages

T-SQL DML	DESCRIPTION
BEGIN CONVERSATION TIMER	Starts a timer. When the timer expires, Service Broker puts a message on the queue.
BEGIN DIALOG CONVERSATION	Starts a new dialog.
END CONVERSATION	Ends a conversation used by a dialog. Note that to end a dialog you must end the conversation.

TABLE 29.2: T-SQL Statements for SQL Server Service Broker Messages *(CONTINUED)*

T-SQL DML	DESCRIPTION
GET CONVERSATION GROUP	Provides the conversation group identifier for the next message in a queue. Also locks the conversation group.
GET TRANSMISSION STATUS	Describes the last transmission error for a conversation.
MOVE CONVERSATION	Moves a conversation to a new dialog.
RECEIVE	Receives a message from a queue.
SEND	Sends a message to a queue..

Messaging

We've already talked quite a bit about messaging, which after all is the whole reason for Service Broker. Let's now take a look at some of the key components and attributes of messaging and how they help exchange messages.

Conversations

As you have already surmised, Service Broker is designed around the basic tasks of sending and receiving messages. A *conversation*, as you know from your own real life daily experience, is a reliable ordered exchange of messages. In Service Broker, all conversations are dialogs.

A dialog is a two-way conversation between exactly two endpoints. An endpoint is a source or destination for messages associated with a queue and may receive and send messages. A dialog is always established between initiator and a target. An initiator is the endpoint that issues the `BEGIN DIALOG CONVERSATION` command. The first message always goes from the initiator to the target, but once the conversation begins, any number of messages can be sent in either direction.

Contracts are agreements between two services and two endpoints over which an endpoint, the initiator or target, can send messages of particular message types in a conversation. Each dialog must follow the rules of the contract. Each contract contains one or more message types that can be used during a dialog conversation between two services or, when using the same service, between two endpoints. In addition, each service is defined with one or more contracts.

Contracts are specified either when creating a service or when starting the dialog. Once a service has been created, it is not necessary to specify which contracts that a service can use. Dialogs, on the other hand, have their relevant contracts specified when they're created.

NOTE Monologs, a one-way conversation between a single endpoint and any number of receiver endpoints, are similar to the publish-subscribe messaging model and are not available in SQL Server 2005.

All messages in a dialog are ordered and always delivered in the order they are sent. The order is maintained across single or multiple transactions, input and output thread, and crashes and restarts. Each message also includes a conversation handle that identifies the dialog that is associated with it.

CONVERSATION GROUPS

Another core component, the *conversation group*, is a way of grouping all the dialogs that are used for a particular task. For example all of the transactions required to order the book in our example (at the start of the chapter) can be logically grouped together in a single conversation group. The conversation group is then implemented as a conversation group identifier, which is included as part of all the messages in all the dialogs contained in the conversation group.

The main value to a conversation group is that it provides a locking mechanism for related queues. This lock is used to guarantee message order and manage state across all conversations in the conversation group. This means that when a message is received from any dialog in the conversation group, the group is locked with a lock held by the receiving transaction. For the life of the transaction only the thread that holds the lock can receive messages from any of the dialogs in the conversation group.

NOTE You can lock a conversation group using the `GET CONVERSATION GROUP` command.

What this means in practical terms is that applications don't have to be made resilient to problems that might arise from the simultaneous processing of a single order on multiple threads.

Another important use of a conversation group is to to maintain state across the conversations in a conversation group. If a process involves many messages over time, there is no logic to keep an instance of the application running the whole time. Using the book order example again to illustrate this point the conversation group allows us to store any global state associated with the order processing in the database and retrieve it when the next message associated with the order is received. The conversation group identifier is normally used as the primary key in the state tables.

Asynchronous Queued Transactional Messaging

If you're new to database development, you're probably wondering what exactly the fuss is all about.

Take for example purchasing a book on-line. In an ideal world, you would log onto the Internet, order the book, provide your credit card number, and as soon as the publisher confirmed payment, the book would be shipped to you. But to do it that way is neither the most effective nor the most efficient. That's where *asynchronous queued messaging* comes in.

As you can imagine, queues enable flexible work scheduling, which usually means significant improvements in both performance and scalability. Take the book order entry we just described. The order system needs to process some parts of an order—such as order header, available to promise, and order lines—before you can consider the order complete. But other parts of the order, billing, shipping, and inventory for example, don't have to happen before the system commits the order. If a system can process the parts of the order that can be delayed in a guaranteed but asynchronous manner, your organization can process the core part of the order faster. What this means is the book can be made ready for shipping while the paperwork catches up.

Asynchronous queued messaging also allows parallel activities to be performed more efficiently. For example, the system can check your credit and the availability of the book simultaneously (i.e., "in parallel"), thus improving overall response time. From a systems point of view, queuing can also distribute processing more evenly across systems, providing better load balancing.

A typical Service Broker message processing transaction has the following steps:

1. Begin the transaction.
2. Receive one or more messages from a conversation group.
3. Retrieve the state of the conversation from the state tables.

4. Process the messages and make one or more updates to application data based on the message contents.
5. Send out some Service Broker messages—either responses to incoming messages or messages to other services required to process the incoming message.
6. Read and process more messages for this conversation group, if any are available.
7. Update the conversation state tables with the new state of the conversation.
8. Commit the transaction.

Service Broker supports only *transactional messaging*, because transactional messaging (i.e., messages that are sent and received as transactions) is the only way to ensure that messages are processed exactly once and in order, thereby preventing duplicate messages.

For example, assume your book order is being processed when the order application crashes midway through. When it restarts, how can it tell whether to process the message to bill your credit card that it was processing when it crashed? If the charge was already sent and it reprocesses the message, you may get billed again. Obviously the only safe way to handle this is to make receiving the message part of the same transaction that updates the database. Then, if the system crashes, the database update and the message queue are in the same condition they were before the crash—meaning, no harm, no foul, and you won't have to call your credit card company.

Finally, Service Broker isn't just a messaging system. Although Service Broker's messaging features might be valuable, many Service Broker applications don't require messaging at all. The ability to do asynchronous, queued database actions is useful, even if the database application isn't distributed.

Activation

To ensure that an application is always running to process received messages, Service Broker includes an activation feature. What activation does is enable you to create a stored procedure that is associated with a given input queue. The purpose of this stored procedure is to automatically process messages from that queue. As each new message comes in, the associated stored procedure automatically executes and handles the incoming messages. If the stored procedure encounters an error, it can throw an exception and be automatically recycled.

Service Broker checks the status of the input queue to see how the stored procedure is doing in terms of keeping up with the incoming messages. If there are messages waiting in the queue, Service Broker increases the number of processing stored procedures as the workload increases and decreases the number of stored procedures as the queue workload decreases or becomes inactive.

NOTE Service Broker is part of each database and is enabled by default. You can disable Service Broker for a given database by executing `ALTER DATABASE [Database Name] SET DISABLE_BROKER` or enabling service broker by executing `ALTER DATABASE [Database Name] SET ENABLE_BROKER` respectively.

Message Delivery

By default, Service Broker message delivery is active in a database from the moment it's created. When message delivery has not been activated or turned off, messages stay in the transmission queue.

To activate Service Broker in a database, you simply alter the database to set the ENABLE_BROKER option as in the example below:

```
USE master ;
GO
ALTER DATABASE AdventureWorks SET ENABLE_BROKER ;
GO
```

To prevent Service Broker message delivery to a specific database, deactivate it by altering the database to set the DISABLE_BROKER option, as below:

```
USE master ;
GO
ALTER DATABASE AdventureWorks SET DISABLE_BROKER ;
GO
```

ENDPOINTS AND NETWORKING

While activating Service Broker allows messages to be delivered to the database, it doesn't allow for much in the way of transmission or reception except in the particular instance. In fact Service Broker, by default, does not send or receive messages over the network. To do that, a Service Broker endpoint must be created in order to send and receive messages from outside of the SQL Server instance.

You create a Service Broker endpoint (and activate Service Broker networking) by using a T-SQL statement and specifying the port number and authentication level, for example:

```
USE master;
GO
CREATE ENDPOINT ExampleEndPoint
    STATE = STARTED
    AS TCP ( LISTENER_PORT = 3133 )
    FOR SERVICE_BROKER (AUTHENTICATION = WINDOWS KERBEROS) ;
GO
```

Service Broker will send and receive messages over the network while any Service Broker endpoint is in the STARTED state. To stop this you can either deactivate Service Broker networking or pause Service Broker networking.

Pausing Service Broker prevents Service Broker from transmitting or receiving messages out of the instance, but has no effect on message delivery that occurs within the instance. To pause Service Broker networking, alter all Service Broker endpoints to set the state to STOPPED:

```
USE master;
GO
ALTER ENDPOINT ExampleEndPoint
    STATE = STOPPED ;
GO
```

To resume Service Broker networking, alter the endpoints to set the state to STARTED:

```
USE master;
GO
ALTER ENDPOINT ExampleEndPoint
    STATE = STARTED ;
GO
```

One consideration is that because Service Broker Service will send and receive messages over the network if any Service Broker endpoint is in the STARTED state, the only way to deactivate Service Broker networking is by dropping all of the endpoints:

```
USE master;
GO

DROP ENDPOINT ExampleEndPoint
GO
```

Don't execute the above statement, however, as we're going to need the ExampleEndPoint again.

Message Forwarding

Message forwarding allows a SQL Server instance to accept messages from outside the instance and to send the message along to other instances. Think of it as call forwarding for databases.

Since message forwarding is configured on a Service Broker endpoint, you will need to have already activated Service Broker networking as described above. Once that is done, all you need to do is alter the endpoint and specify the maximum size (in megabytes) for forwarded messages as in the below example:

```
USE master;
GO

ALTER ENDPOINT ExampleEndPoint
    FOR SERVICE_BROKER (MESSAGE_FORWARDING = ENABLED,
                        MESSAGE_FORWARD_SIZE = 15 );
GO
```

To shut off message forwarding, simply alter the endpoint to deactivate it:

```
USE master;
GO

ALTER ENDPOINT ExampleEndPoint
    FOR SERVICE_BROKER (MESSAGE_FORWARDING = DISABLED) ;
GO
```

Message Transport

Service Broker message transport is based on the TCP/IP protocol and bears a strong similarity to the architecture used by TCP/IP and FTP. Service Broker message transport consists of two protocols, the Binary Adjacent Broker protocol (BABP) similar to TCP, and the dialog protocol, which is a higher level protocol like FTP and rides on top of BABP.

BABP provides the basic message transport. Bidirectional and multiplexed, it can handle message transport for multiple dialogs. Its principal role is to send messages across the network as quickly as it can.

The dialog protocol handles end-to-end communication of a dialog and handles message ordering as a one-time-only-in-order delivery system. It also handles sending messages and acknowledging them. It is also responsible for authentication and encryption of messages. Another nice feature of the dialog protocol is that it provides symmetric failure handling, meaning both end nodes are notified of any message delivery failures.

Service Broker Programming

By now you're probably asking yourself how all this translates into practice. Rest assured you're about to learn in this section as you'll see how to create the required Service Broker objects and use them in a very simple application.

Creating a Service Broker Application

Building a Service Broker program can be broken down into the following simple steps:

1. Identifying the required message types and the associated validation.
2. Identifying the various contracts that will be needed and determining the message sequence.
3. Creating the required queues.
4. Creating the required services and binding them to the appropriate queues.
5. Sending messages around and reading them.

The first step in creating a SQL Server Service Broker application is the creation of one or more message types, to describe the messages that will be sent.

```
USE AdventureWorks
CREATE MESSAGE TYPE HelloMessage
VALIDATION = NONE
```

The first parameter is used to name the message type, and the `VALIDATION` keyword indicates that any message type of message body is acceptable.

Once the message type has been created, we need to create a contract that specifies who can send what types of messages:

```
CREATE CONTRACT HelloContract
(HelloMessage SENT BY INITIATOR)
```

The contract also describes the messages that can be received using a particular dialog. The first argument is used to name the contract. The `SENT BY` clause is used to designate which messages are associated with the contract and where those messages come from.

Since communication is between two endpoints, we need to create two queues, one for the sender and one for the receiver:

```
CREATE QUEUE HelloReceiverQueue
CREATE QUEUE HelloSenderQueue
```

If you wanted to use the `ACTIVATION` keyword to automatically fire off a stored procedure to read the contents of the queue, you can revise the code as shown below. However, the stored procedure called for must exist at the time the queue is created otherwise an error is generated. The `MAX_QUEUE_READERS` keyword specifies the maximum number of readers that Service Broker will automatically activate, and the EXECUTE AS option can be used if you want to execute the activated stored procedure under a different user context.

```
CREATE QUEUE HelloReceiverQueue WITH ACTIVATION
(STATUS=ON,
PROCEDURE_NAME = HelloReceiverProc,
MAX_QUEUE_READERS=10,
EXECUTE AS SELF)
```

Since we don't currently have a stored procedure named HelloReceiverProc, make sure the code you're entering for this example reads:

```
CREATE QUEUE HelloReceiverQueue
```

Once the queues are created, you can display the contents by using the SELECT statement, treating the queue as if it were a standard database table. Running the SELECT statement is a good way to check out functionality of any Service Broker application being developed, for example:

```
SELECT * FROM HelloReceiverQueue
```

Now that the queues are made, the next step is to create the required service and bind them to the queues:

```
CREATE SERVICE HelloSenderService
  ON QUEUE HelloSenderQueue (HelloContract)
CREATE SERVICE HelloReceiverService
  ON QUEUE HelloReceiverQueue (HelloContract)
```

As you can see, you create a service using the CREATE SERVICE statement. The first parameter names the service. The ON QUEUE clause identifies the queue associated with the service, and then the contracts that are associated with the service are identified.

If one of the services were located on a remote system, you would also need to create a route. The CREATE ROUTE statement basically provides Service Broker with the system address where the remote service is found.

Now that the necessary Service Broker Objects have been created, you're ready to use them in the application. Begin the conversation between the two services by sending a message:

```
DECLARE @HelloSendDialog UNIQUEIDENTIFIER
DECLARE @message NVARCHAR(100)

BEGIN
  BEGIN TRANSACTION;
  BEGIN DIALOG @HelloSendDialog
        FROM SERVICE HelloSenderService
        TO SERVICE 'HelloReceiverService'
        ON CONTRACT HelloContract
  -- Send a message on the conversation
  SET @message = N'Hello, This is an example';
  SEND  ON CONVERSATION @conversationHandle
        MESSAGE TYPE HelloMessage (@message)
  COMMIT TRANSACTION
```

At the start of this listing, you can see that a variable named HelloSendDialog is created, which contains a unique identifier that will be assigned by a Service Broker dialog.

Next, a transaction is started. As you already know, it's a good idea to wrap all the actions performed by the Service Broker in a transaction so you can commit or roll back any changes to the queues.

The BEGIN DIALOG statement is used to open up a Service Broker dialog. When you declare a dialog, you always need to specify two endpoints. The FROM SERVICE identifies the initiator of the messages, while the TO SERVICE keyword identifies the target endpoint. Here, the sender is named HelloSenderService and the target is named HelloReceiverService. The ON CONTRACT keyword specifies the contract that's used for the dialog.

The two SEND operations, when executed, send two messages to the target service, which will receive those messages and add them to the queue associated with that service. Finally, the transaction is committed.

Since there isn't a stored procedure associated with this simple example, to retrieve a message from the HelloReceiverQueue, execute the following code:

```
RECEIVE CONVERT(NVARCHAR(max), message_body) AS message
 FROM ReceiverQueue
```

As you can see, the syntax for receiving a message is similar to a SELECT statement. A key difference is that a RECEIVE statement reads the message off the queue and deletes it, which is called a *destructive read*. Using the SELECT statement against a queue to see its contents, as described earlier, is *non-destructive* since nothing is deleted.

In the next section, we'll look at how to retrieve messages from a queue via a stored procedure.

Creating a Queue Reading Stored Procedure

Earlier when we were creating the Service Broker application, we made reference to create the target queue, HelloReceiverQueue, upon activation. In that case, an associated stored procedure, HelloReceiverProc, would be automatically started when a message arrives at the queue. The code for the stored procedure is actually quite basic:

```
CREATE PROC HelloReceiverProc
AS
DECLARE @HelloSendDialog UNIQUEIDENTIFIER
DECLARE @message_type_id int
DECLARE @message_body NVARCHAR(1000)
DECLARE @message NVARCHAR(1000)
DECLARE @ResRequestDialog UNIQUEIDENTIFIER
while(1=1)
BEGIN
    BEGIN TRANSACTION
        WAITFOR   (RECEIVE TOP(1)
       @message_type_id = message_type_id,
       @message_body = message_body,
       @ResRequestDialog = conversation_handle
        FROM HelloReceiveQueue), TIMEOUT 200;

       if (@@ROWCOUNT = 0)
       BEGIN
          COMMIT TRANSACTION
```

```
            BREAK
        END

        IF (@message_type_id = 2) -- End dialog message
            BEGIN
                PRINT ' Dialog ended '
                  + cast(@HelloSendDialog as nvarchar(40))
            END
        ELSE
            BEGIN
                BEGIN TRANSACTION
                    BEGIN DIALOG @HelloSendDialog
                    FROM SERVICE HelloSenderService
                        TO SERVICE 'HelloReceiverService'
                        ON CONTRACT HelloContract
                        WITH LIFETIME = 2000;

                    SELECT @message = 'Received:' + @message_body;

                     SEND ON CONVERSATION @HelloSendDialog
                     MESSAGE TYPE HelloMessage (@message);

                     PRINT CONVERT(varchar(30), @message)
                COMMIT TRANSACTION
            END CONVERSATION @HelloSendDialog
    END
    COMMIT TRANSACTION
END
```

The variable to contain the response dialog identification is declared at the top of the stored procedure, followed by three variables that are used to pull back information from the queue that's being read. A loop is then initiated that will read all of the entries from the queue. Inside the loop, a transaction is started and the `RECEIVE` statement is used to receive a message. Here, the `TOP(1)` clause is used to limit the procedure to receiving only a single message at a time, though by eliminating it you could receive all of the messages in the queue. The `RECEIVE` statement populates three variables. The `message_type_id` identifies the type of message, which is typically either a user-defined message or an `End Dialog` message. The `@message_body` variable contains the contents of the actual message, while the `@HelloSendDialog` variable contains a handle that identifies the sending dialog.

The result set is checked to see whether a message was actually received. If not, the last transaction is committed and the procedure is ended. Otherwise, the message type ID is checked to see whether the message is a user message or an End Dialog message. If it's a user message, the contents are processed. First, a dialog is opened to the `HelloSenderService`. This dialog is used to send the message to the `HelloReceiverQueue` and specify the `HelloContract` that restricts the message types that will be allowed.

Once the dialog is opened, the received message is modified by concatenating the string "Received:" with the contents of the message that was received, and then the `SEND` statement is used to send the message to the `HelloReceiverQueue`. Finally, the dialog conversation is ended and the transaction is committed.

Administering Service Broker

Because Service Broker is integrated into the database engine, most administrative tasks are part of the normal administration for the database and Service Broker requires little in the way of administrative overhead. In this section, we'll look at the tasks that are unique to Service Broker.

Managing Applications and Queues

In the case of applications already in production, day-to-day management is part and parcel of normal database maintenance. There are three basic types of non-routine tasks: putting a Service Broker application into production, performing routine maintenance on the application, and removing (uninstalling) the application.

Installing an Application

As you've already seen "installing" an application requires little more than using developer-created installation scripts containing the T-SQL statements creating message types, contracts, queues, services, and stored procedures for the service. In some instances the developer may provide one set of scripts for the target service and a different set of scripts for the initiating service.

The SQL Server administrator reviews and executes the scripts. The administrator also configures the security principals, certificates, remote service bindings, and routes that may be required for the application to work in a production environment.

As part of the installation process, the developer and the administrator should plan and document the procedure to uninstall the application.

Moving an Application

Moving a Service Broker application usually requires moving the database that contains the application to another instance. The database contains the service broker objects, stored procedures, certificates, users, and outgoing routes for the application.

When moving an application it is important to remember to update any services that initiate conversations with the service you are moving. In each database that contains a route for the service you are moving, alter the route (using the `ALTER ROUTE` statement) to use the new network address.

Because endpoints and transport security apply to the instance rather than to a specific database, attaching a database to a new instance does not affect endpoints or transport security for that instance. If your service sends or receives messages over the network, however, make sure that the new instance has an endpoint, and that any transport security for the instance is configured as required by the application.

Starting and Stopping an Application

To temporarily stop a service, alter the queue that the application uses so that the queue status is `OFF`.

```
ALTER QUEUE  HelloSendQueue WITH STATUS = OFF ;
```

When the queue status is `OFF`, Service Broker will not deliver new messages to the queue and will not allow an application to receive messages from the queue, effectively stopping the application and sending an error message to any application that attempts to receive a message.

When a message arrives for a stopped queue, the message is held in the transmission queue for the database until the destination queue becomes available. Service Broker does not consider a message arriving for a stopped queue to be an error, and does not notify the sender. When the queue becomes available, Service Broker delivers the messages in the transmission queue to the service queue. This delivery uses the normal retry logic for messages. Messages are marked delayed in the transmission queue and retried periodically.

Stopping a queue does not reset the conversation timer or the dialog lifetime timer for messages in the queue. If either timer expires while the queue is stopped, Service Broker generates the appropriate messages when the queue starts again.

To restart the application, alter the queue so that the queue status is returned to ON:

```
ALTER QUEUE  HelloSendQueue WITH STATUS = ON ;
```

Once this is executed, if the queue has an activation stored procedure specified and the queue contains messages, once the queue starts, Service Broker immediately starts the activation stored procedure. Because the queue is now available, Service Broker also generates messages for conversation timers and dialog lifetime timers that may have expired while the queue was stopped.

If an application does not use activation, you will need to restart the application using the startup procedure defined for that application.

Backing Up/Restoring Service Broker Applications

Backup and restore procedures for a Service Broker service are integrated with the database in which the service runs. If the service contains components outside the database, such as an external application, these must be backed up and restored separately.

Uninstalling an Application

You should uninstall a Service Broker application when the database continues to be hosted in the same instance, but no longer provides the service that the application implements. Dropping a database drops the Service Broker objects within that database.

The simplest way to uninstall an application is through a series of DROP statements. To uninstall the HelloMessage application from the AdventureWorks database that we created above, execute the following code:

```
USE AdventureWorks
DROP SERVICE HelloSender
DROP SERVICE HelloReceiver
DROP QUEUE HelloSenderQueue
DROP QUEUE HelloReceiverQueue
DROP CONTRACT HelloContract
DROP MESSAGE TYPE HelloMessage
```

Poison Messages

A *poison message* is one that contains information that an application cannot successfully process. A poison message is not necessarily a corrupt message or an invalid request. In fact, Service Broker contains message integrity checks that detect corrupt messages and most applications typically validate the content of a message, discarding any messages that contain an illegal request. Hence, many poison messages were actually valid messages at the time of their creation, but later became impossible to process.

Service Broker comes with automatic poison message detection. When a transaction that contains a RECEIVE statement rolls back five times, Service Broker disables all queues that the transaction received messages from, setting the queue status to OFF. At the same time, it creates a Broker:Queue Disabled event.

It is a good idea to have SQL Server Agent send alerts to an administrator when a queue is disabled. Developers should include the ability to detect when a queue has been disabled by Service Broker in their applications and to inspect the messages in the queue to find the poison message. Once the application identifies the poison message, it sets the queue status to ON and ends the conversation for the message with an error.

While applications should track and remove poison messages automatically without intervention, it may sometimes be necessary to remove a poison message manually.

Manual removal of a poison message can have serious consequences, the most serious of which is interrupting an important conversation. Always make sure to inspect a poison message before removing it from a queue.

The easiest way to see the content of the suspected message is to begin a transaction, receive the message body, display the message body, and then roll back the transaction. Until you are positive that the message in question is a poison message, it is important to roll back the transaction.

Service Broker Security

Applications that send messages between SQL Server instances can use transport security, dialog security, or both. Both types of security provide different protections.

Dialog security provides end-to-end encryption and authorization for conversations between specific services. In other words, the message is encrypted when it is first sent from a dialog, and it is not decrypted until the message reaches its endpoint. The message contents remain encrypted as the message is forwarded across any intermediate hops.

When dialogs are created, they can be secured using the WITH ENCRYPTION clause. When used, a session key is created and used to encrypt the messages sent using the dialog. To implement dialog security, Service Broker uses certificate-based authentication, where the certificate of the sending user is sent along with the message.

Because of the asynchronous nature of SQL Server Service Broker, the security information is stored in the message headers and retrieved by the receiving service when the message is retrieved. This design enables SQL Server Service Broker applications to avoid the need to establish a connection to authenticate messages.

Dialog security should be used for applications that transmit confidential or sensitive data, or send messages over untrusted networks. Dialog security can also help a participant in the conversation identify the other participant in the conversation.

Transport security prevents unauthorized network connections to Service Broker endpoints and optionally provides point-to-point encryption. This is one means of keeping a database from receiving unwanted messages. Because transport security applies to network connections, transport security automatically applies to all conversations to or from the SQL Server instance. Notice, however, that transport security does not provide end-to-end encryption and does not provide authentication for individual conversations.

System Configuration Options

There are several system configuration options that can be set using the sp_configure system stored procedure to influence the behavior of the Service Broker subsystem. Table 29.3 lists the available sp_configure options for the SQL Server Service Broker.

TABLE 29.3: Options for sp_configure

SP_CONFIGURE PARAMETER	DESCRIPTION
broker tcp listen port	Defines the port that Service Broker uses for network connections. The default value is 4022.
broker authentication mode	Sets type of remote authentication that will be used for connections. A value of 1 means no authentication will be used. A value of 2 means that authentication is supported. A value of 3 means authentication is required. The default value is 3.
broker forwarding size limit	Sets the maximum disk space in MB to store messages to be forwarded. The default value is 10.
broker message forwarding	Sets the type of message forwarding that is allowed. A value of 1 means no forwarding is allowed. A value of 2 allows forwarding with the domain. A value of 3 allows external forwarding. The default value is 1.

Service Broker Catalog Views

SQL Server 2005 supplies several new system views that enable you to retrieve information about Service Broker objects and their current statuses. Table 29.4 lists the Service Broker catalog views.

TABLE 29.4: Service Broker Catalog Views

SYSTEM VIEW	DESCRIPTION
sys.conversation_endpoints	Lists the conversation endpoints that are currently active.
sys.remote_service_bindings	Lists the relationships of the services and the users who will execute the service.
sys.routes	Lists the created routes.
sys.service_contract_message_usages	Lists the relationships between contracts and message types.
sys.service_contract_usages	Lists the relationships between contracts and services.
sys.service_contracts	Lists all contracts that have been created.
sys.service_message_types	Lists message types that have been created. System message types are listed first, user-defined messages types next.
sys.service_queues	Lists the queues that have been created.
sys.services	Lists the created services.

TABLE 29.4: Service Broker Catalog Views *(CONTINUED)*

SYSTEM VIEW	DESCRIPTION
sys.transmission_queue	Lists the messages that are queued to be sent.
sys.conversation_groups	Lists the created conversation groups.
sys.service_broker_endpoints	Lists endpoints created within Service Broker.

Summary

In this chapter we've taken a look at Service Broker, another of the new technologies in SQL Server 2005. As we've seen Service Broker is a powerful tool for developing asynchronous queued database applications.

It does this through asynchronous transactional messaging centered around conversations, which in turn are composed of messages, dialogs, queues, and contracts.

We've looked at the key elements of messaging, including how to activate message delivery, message forwarding, and Service Broker networking. We also learned how to create a simple Service Broker application and a stored procedure for retrieving messages from the service queue.

Finally, we've learned the basics of the small amount of Service Broker administration required, since, because of its tight integration with the database engine, many of Service Broker's management tasks are part and parcel of SQL Server 2005 administration.

Next, we'll turn to troubleshooting SQL Server 2005, perhaps one of the most important parts of any successful database administrator's skill set.

Chapter 30

Troubleshooting

Even though Microsoft has developed one of the best database systems on the market, there will still be problems. These problems may come from hardware failure, user error, or perhaps even SQL Server itself. Regardless of the source of the problem, it is your job to find it and repair it.

Although it is not possible for us to cover every situation you may run into, we are going to discuss some of the more common problems and offer some solutions so that you can get your server up and running as fast as possible. Before we can get into specific areas, though, we need to discuss some troubleshooting methods that cover a broad scope of problems.

General Troubleshooting

Imagine the results if you were to randomly apply fixes to SQL Server in hopes of solving a problem. There would be chaos, and the problem would never be solved. Surprisingly, some people do this because they do not take the time, or do not know how, to find the actual cause of a problem. To fix a problem, the logical first step is determining the cause of the problem, and the best way to do that is by reading the error logs.

Error logs in SQL Server 2005 are stored in two places—the first is the SQL Server error logs. Use the following steps to access the SQL Server 2005 error logs:

1. Open Management Studio from the Microsoft SQL Server menu under Programs on the Start menu.
2. In Object Explorer, expand your server and then expand Management.
3. Under Management, expand SQL Server Logs.
4. Under SQL Server Logs, you should see a current log and up to six archives; double-click the current log to open it.

5. In the log file viewer, you should see a number of messages. Many of these are informational, but some will be error messages. To find the errors, just read the description at the right of each error.

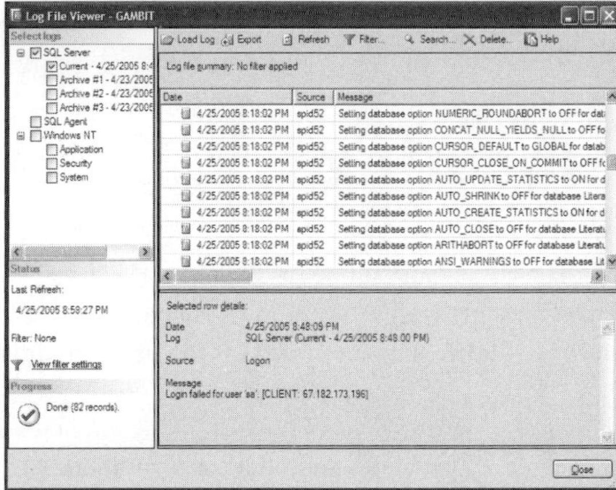

6. Click one of the errors to read more detail in the lower half of the right pane.

7. To view archive logs from here, check the box next to one of the logs.

8. To view Windows event logs, check the box next to an event log.

9. To filter the logs, click on the filter button on the toolbar and enter your filter criteria, then click OK.

The second place you will find SQL Server error messages is in the Windows Application log, which you can access by following these steps:

1. Select Event Viewer from the Administrative Tools group on the Start menu.

2. In the Event Viewer, click the Application Log icon.

3. In the contents pane (on the right), you will see a number of messages. Some of these are for other applications, and a great deal of them are informational. You are primarily interested in yellow or red icons that mention SQL Server in the description.

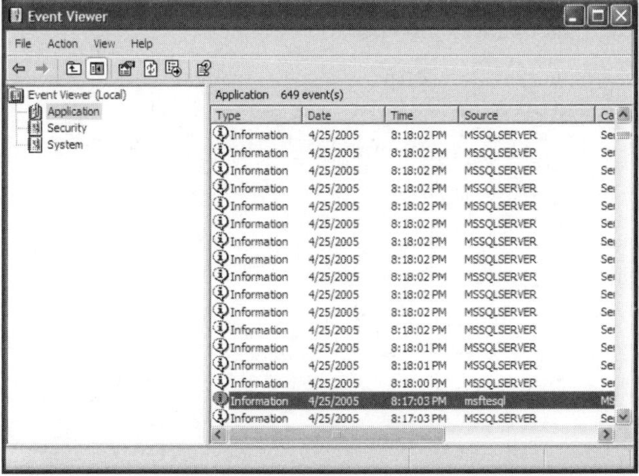

4. Double-click one of the messages to get more detail about it.

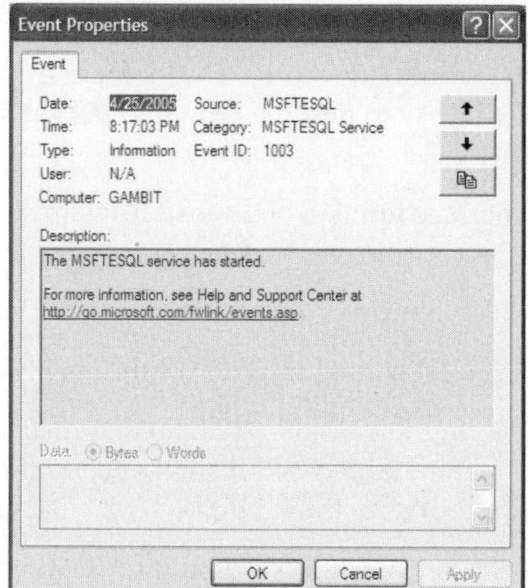

5. Close the Event Viewer.

Because so many people use SQL Server, the chances are good that someone else has had the exact same problem that you are currently experiencing. Therefore, the first thing you should do once you have gleaned information from the error logs is research. You can perform this research a number of places:

- The Microsoft support Web site (at the time of this writing, it is `http://support.microsoft.com`).
- TechNet, which is a library of documents on CD-ROM to which you can subscribe. This is a service from Microsoft, so check with them for current pricing.
- Other Web sites. Scores of Web sites are dedicated to helping support professionals keep their systems up and running—just look for them with a search engine.

Once you have the information you need, you can begin the troubleshooting process. Let's begin with troubleshooting setup.

Troubleshooting Setup

If you run into problems during setup, you can check a few common problems first:

- You must be logged on as an administrator to successfully set up SQL Server.
- Make sure that you have enough disk space to install SQL Server; this is a simple but common problem.
- If you are using a domain account for your services, make sure you have the right password and that the Caps Lock key is not on accidentally (simple, but common).
- If setup cannot read from the CD, make sure it is clean. Fingerprints and other blemishes can interfere with the CD-ROM lasers.

If you are still having problems with setup, you need to read the `%ProgramFiles%\Microsoft SQL Server\90\Setup Bootstrap\LOG\Summary.txt`. This is a special log file that records a summary of all the actions taken during install. Also a number of files contain detailed records for each individual program in the Files subdirectory. The logs in the Files subdirectory have a naming convention that should make it easy to find the right log, `SQLSetup[`*XXXX*`][s]_[`*COMPUTERNAME*`]_[`*PRODUCTNAME*`]_[`*Y*`].log`.

- *XXXXX* = The enumerated number of the install, where the last installation performed has the highest number.
- *COMPUTERNAME* = The computer where setup is being run.
- *PRODUCTNAME* = Product name (the name of the .msi file).
- *Y* = If a Microsoft Windows Installer file (.msi) is installed more than once during a single setup run, this number is added and incremented to the log name. This is mainly seen for Microsoft XML Core Services (MSXML).

So `SQLSetup0001_NYSqlServer_RS.log` would be the first install of Reporting Services on a machine named NYSqlServer, and `SQLSetup0001_ NYSqlServer _NS.log` would be the first install of Notification Services on the NYSqlServer machine.

Once you have SQL Server installed, you may start running into problems with your databases; let's see how to fix them.

Troubleshooting Databases

If you are having trouble accessing a database or a specific object in the database, the first thing to check is permissions. Make certain that the user who is trying to access the data has permission to do so. If permissions are not the problem, you need to check two other areas: database integrity from SQL Server and data file integrity on the hard disk. To check integrity from SQL Server, use DBCC.

Using DBCC

If SQL Server can read the database, but you are having problems accessing parts of the database, you need to verify the integrity of the database using the Database Consistency Checker (DBCC). SQL Server's tool for checking and repairing the logical and physical consistency of a database. DBCC has several options to choose from, depending on the problem at hand:

DBCC CHECKALLOC SQL Server stores data and objects in 8KB pages. Eight contiguous pages are called an extent. Sometimes these pages are not properly allocated; running CHECKALLOC can repair improper allocation of pages.

DBCC CHECKCATALOG This verifies consistency between system tables in a database. Specifically, it checks to make sure that every datatype in the syscolumns table has a corresponding entry in the systypes table and that every table and view in sysobjects has an entry in the syscolumns table.

DBCC CHECKCONSTRAINTS Constraints are used to keep users from entering improper data into the database. If some data makes it past the constraints, you can use CHECKCONSTRAINTS to find the rows that violate the constraint. Once these rows are found, you can remove them.

DBCC CHECKDB This is a superset of CHECKALLOC and CHECKTABLE. It is the safest repair option, because it performs the widest variety of repairs:

- Runs CHECKALLOC
- Runs CHECKTABLE on every table in the database
- Verifies Service Broker data in the database
- Runs CHECKCATALOG
- Validates the contents of all indexed views in the database

DBCC CHECKFILEGROUP This performs the same tests as CHECKDB except that CHECKFILEGROUP is limited to a single filegroup and its related tables.

DBCC CHECKIDENT An identity column contains a numeric value that is incremented with each new record added. If the identity value is thrown off for some reason, CHECKIDENT can repair the identity values.

DBCC CHECKTABLE This performs a physical consistency check on tables and indexed views. The following tests and repairs are made:

- Makes sure that all data and index pages are correctly linked
- Verifies that indexes are in their proper sort order
- Verifies that all pointers are consistent

CHECKALLOC, CHECKDB, and CHECKTABLE have some common options that can be specified to control the way errors are repaired and the amount of data loss that is allowed in the repair process:

REPAIR_ALLOW_DATA_LOSS This is the most comprehensive repair option. It performs all of the checks that the other two options perform, and it adds allocation and deallocation of rows for correcting allocation errors, structural row and page errors, and deletion of corrupted text objects. There is a risk of data loss with this option (as the name implies). To lessen that risk, this option can be performed as a transaction so that the changes made can be rolled back.

Besides this, CHECKDB and CHECKTABLE have another common option:

REPAIR_REBUILD This performs minor, relatively fast repairs such as checking for extra keys in a nonclustered index and some slower repairs such as rebuilding indexes. There is no risk of losing data with this option.

DBCC is run through Query Analyzer. Because CHECKDB is the most commonly used option, let's run it against the AdventureWorks database in the following series of steps:

1. Open SQL Server Management Studio by selecting it from the Microsoft SQL Server group under Programs on the Start menu.
2. Log in using either Windows or SQL Server Authentication.
3. Click the New Query button, select Database Engine Query, and connect using either Windows or SQL Server Authentication.
4. Enter the following command and execute it by clicking the Execute button on the toolbar:

```
DBCC CHECKDB ('AdventureWorks')
```

5. You should see a series of messages that inform you of the results of the tests performed. Read through them and close the new query window.

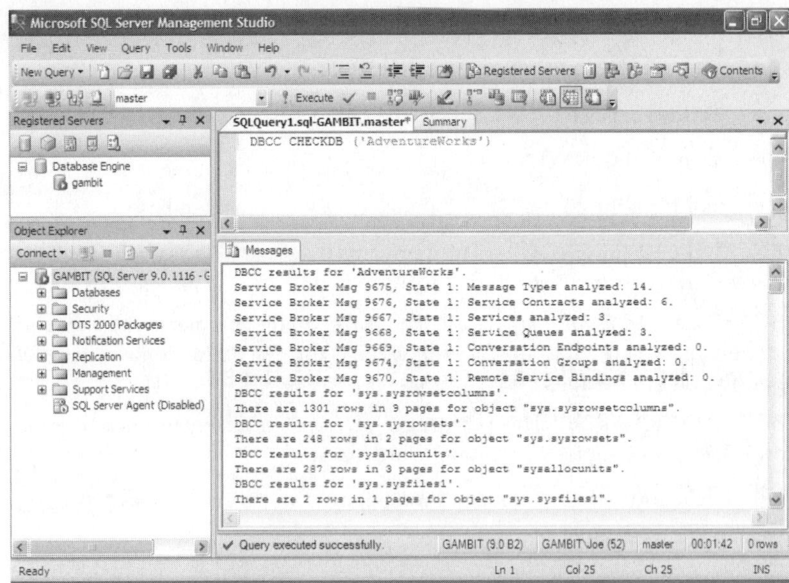

TIP You should create a Database Maintenance Plan that includes repairs and consistency checks. Then you will be sure to run DBCC on a regular basis.

DBCC is great for readable database files, but when SQL Server cannot even read the data files on the hard disk, you have a problem. SQL Server marks the database as shutdown and completely denies access. Therefore, you need to know how to reset a shutdown database.

Repairing Shutdown Databases

A database is shut down when SQL Server cannot read the data files associated with the database from the hard disk. It is easy to spot such a database because the word Shutdown is displayed next to the database in parenthesis. If you try to get information about the database, you receive an error message stating that the database cannot be read from. To repair a shutdown database, you must find out why it has been shut down and fix the problem. A number of problems can cause this to happen:

Incorrect NTFS permissions The service account that the services log on with must have permission to access the database on disk.

Corrupted files on disk Hard disks have moving parts, and they store information magnetically, which means that they are doomed to fail after a period of time. When this happens, your disk starts to develop bad sectors, causing data corruption. If the bad sector happens to contain part of a database file, it may be shut down.

Deleted files If someone accidentally, or purposefully, deletes one of the files associated with a database, it will be shut down.

Renamed files If a file has been renamed, SQL Server will not be able to read it, and the database will be shut down.

Once you have repaired the cause of the problem, you can restart the SQL Server services, and the database should be marked as useable when automatic recovery is complete. If the database is still shut down after you have repaired the problem, you need to use the ALTER DATABASE command to reset the status. For example, to reset the AdventureWorks database you would use this command:

```
ALTER DATABASE AdventureWorks SET ONLINE
```

TIP You may have used the sp_resetstatus stored procedure in previous versions of SQL Server. In SQL Server 2005, sp_resetstatus has been deprecated and should no longer be used.

Another area where you may run into problems is backup and restore. Let's see what we can do to fix these problems.

Troubleshooting Backup and Restores

To start, you cannot modify a database during a backup. This means that you cannot create or delete database files or shrink a database file during a backup. If you try, you will get an error message. Also, you cannot back up a file if it is offline or back up a filegroup if any one of the files is offline.

Another problem that you may run into is restoring a database with a different sort order or collation. This is not allowed and will generate errors (usually 3120 or 3149 in Windows Event Viewer). If you must restore a database with a different sort order or collation, you should install a second instance of SQL Server with the collation and sort order you need, restore the database, and use DTS to transfer the database to the first instance of SQL Server (because DTS can transfer between servers with different sort orders and collations).

If you receive error 3143, you are trying to restore from a tape that has a valid Microsoft tape format, but no SQL Server backup on it. This is possible because Microsoft Backup and SQL Server use the same format. To make sure that you are restoring a valid SQL Server backup, you should issue the RESTORE HEADERONLY command and read the contents of the tape.

If you get error 3227, you are trying to restore a backup from a multiple volume set, and the volume that you are trying to process has already been processed. To correct this problem, insert a tape that has not been restored yet.

Error 3242 means that you are trying to restore from a tape that does not contain a valid Microsoft tape format. This can happen if you use a third-party backup system such as Backup Exec or Legato. To fix this, you should restore the tape from the software that was used to create it.

Transaction log backups must be restored in the order they were backed up. If there is a gap in the order (skipping from backup 1 to backup 3, for example), you will receive error 4305. To avoid this, restore the transaction log backups in the proper order.

When restoring a database, you must specify either the RECOVERY or the NORECOVERY option. These options let SQL Server know whether to allow users back into the database after a restore. If you are on the final restore, select RECOVERY. If you have more backups to restore, use NORECOVERY. If you select RECOVERY and then try to restore another backup, you will receive error 4306.

TIP Descriptions for most error numbers are easily found by performing a search in Books Online.

Another area that will require your attention from time to time is client connectivity.

Troubleshooting Client Connectivity

If a client is having problems connecting to SQL Server, the first thing to do is verify whether the client has a login account on the system. Without an account, a user will be denied access. Assuming that the user has a login account and a database user account for the database they need access to, other areas can be tested.

First, make sure that the client machine can communicate with the server on the network using the `Ping` command. If the `Ping` command works using the machine's address (a TCP/IP example would be 192.168.2.200), try using the remote machine's name to ping (e.g., `ping` *`Server1`*). This will verify that the machine can resolve the remote machine's address to a host name (which is a simpler method of access than an address).

If these two methods work and you still cannot access the server, check to make sure that the client and server have a common network library enabled. SQL Server uses the networking protocols that are installed on your system, but only if the associated network library is enabled. Therefore, if you have the TCP/IP protocol on both your client and server machines, but the TCP/IP network library is not enabled on one of the machines, they will never communicate.

To fix this problem, you need to do one of two things: configure your client to use the same network library as the server or configure the server to use the same network library as the client. To configure the client, use the SQL Native Client Configuration tool in SQL Configuration Manager (as shown in Figure 30.1), found in the Microsoft SQL Server group under Programs on the Start menu. To configure the server, use the SQL Server 2005 Network Configuration tool in the SQL Configuration Manager (as shown in Figure 30.2), also found in the Microsoft SQL Server group under Programs on the Start menu.

FIGURE 30.1
Use the SQL Native Client Configuration tool to configure the network library on the client machine.

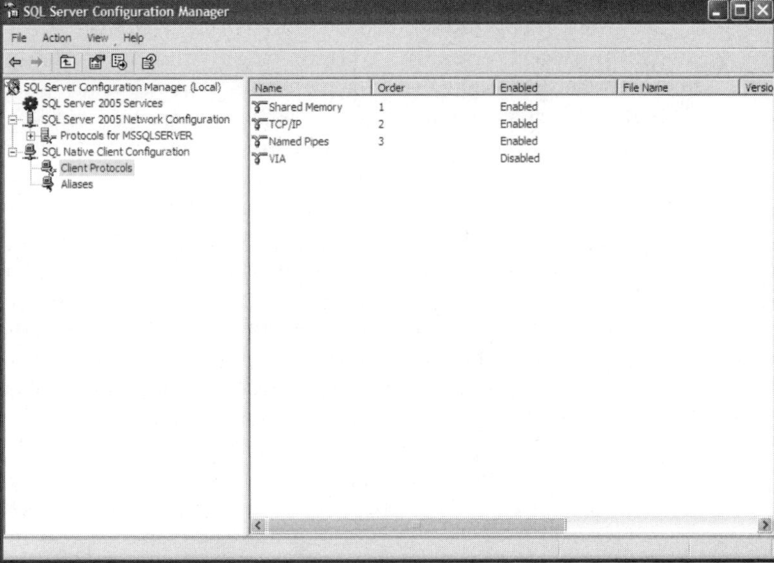

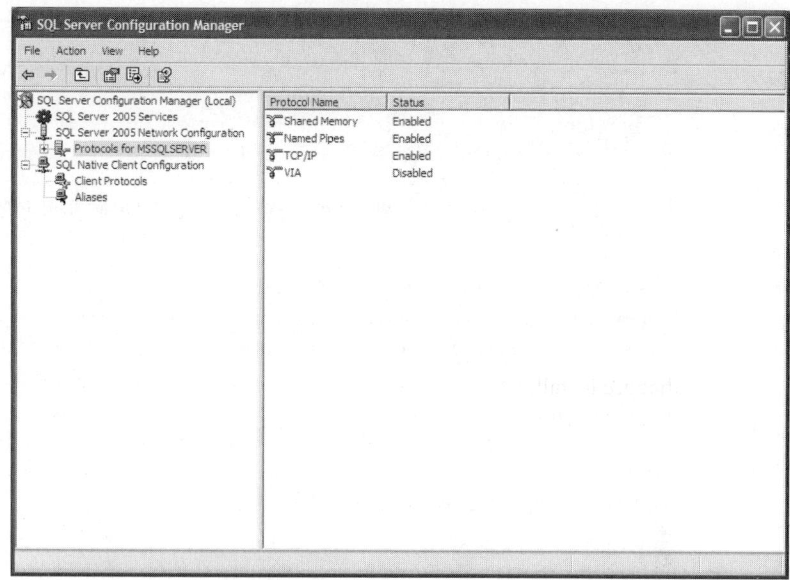

FIGURE 30.2
Use the SQL Server 2005 Network Configuration tool to configure the network library on the server.

NOTE For a complete discussion of the network configuration tools, please see Chapter 3, "Overview of SQL Server."

Replication is another area that will require your attention.

Troubleshooting Replication

Replication is a complex component of SQL Server and therefore is prone to failure from time to time. Several problems could potentially come up. The first place to look when you are having replication problems is on the distributor at the Replication Monitor.

Replication uses a series of agents to transfer data from the publisher to the subscribers: the Log Reader agent, the Distribution agent, the Snapshot agent, the Queue Reader agent, and the Merge agent. If there is a problem with any of these agents, the Replication Monitor on the distributor displays a red X icon on the problem agent. (This is probably the only problem in the computing world where X actually marks the spot.) When you have found the problem agent, you can right-click the agent, and view the history and session details; this should tell you what the problem is. Once you have found the problem, you can diagnose and repair it. There are several areas to look at; the first is security.

Security and Replication

Security is a common cause of replication failure. Such a problem can throw you a curve because it does not show up in the agent history. When an agent starts, it is actually starting a job. When the job is started, SQL Server runs the `xp_logininfo` stored procedure to verify that the account that is trying to start the job has authority to do so. To verify this, SQL Server must query a domain controller. If the domain controller is unavailable, the job will not start, and nothing will be logged in the agent history because the agent never started. To work around this problem, the owner of the job should be either a standard SQL Server login account or a local system account.

Another common security problem is an inability to write to the distribution working folder. Snapshot replication is particularly susceptible to this problem because all of the snapshots are stored there. On a Windows server, the working directory is `\\computer\drive$\MSSQL\Repldata`. This `drive$` share that is used is an administrative share, which means that only administrators can access it. Therefore, if the account used by the SQL Server Agent service is not an administrator on the domain, replication will fail. To fix this, make the account an administrator.

TIP The SQL Server service does not need administrative access; only the SQL Server Agent service does.

Another security-related problem that you may see involves the service account used for the SQL Server Agent service. All of the SQL Server Agent services on all of the servers involved in replication should use the same domain account. If they do not, the distribution server will not be able to connect to the publishers to retrieve data, and it will not be able to connect to the subscribers to write data.

If security is not the problem, you need to look into other areas.

Subscribers Are Not Getting Data

Other problems can keep subscribers from receiving data. If your Distribution agent appears to be working, but none of your subscribers are getting any new data, the problem is likely the Log Reader agent. This is because the Log Reader agent must read changes from the publisher, and then the Distribution agent sends those changes to the subscribers. Therefore, if the Log Reader agent is malfunctioning, the Distribution agent will have nothing to send, and the subscribers will get no new data. To fix this problem, check some things:

- Make sure that the network connection between the distributor and the publisher is up and working.
- Make sure that the SQL Server Agent services on the distributor and publisher are using the same domain account.
- Verify that the transaction log for the distribution database is not full. If it is, the Log Reader will not be able to write changes to the distribution database.

If some of your subscribers are receiving data, but others are not, you have a problem with the distribution process. Do the following:

- Check the agent histories on the distributor—look for error messages that suggest a failing server.
- Make sure that the subscription server is online.
- Check the network connection to the subscription server, especially if it is a WAN connection such as a T1 or analog line.
- Verify that the subscription database is online—check that it is not marked Shutdown, not marked Single or Restricted User, and not marked Read Only.
- Check that the distribution server and subscription servers are using the same domain account for their SQL Server Agent services.

Downed servers can also adversely affect replication. You will need to know what to do if one of the servers in your replication scenario goes down.

Recovering Servers

If one of your subscribers goes down, you will see some errors in the Replication Monitor on your distributor, and your subscriber will be out of synch with the publisher. This is actually not too big of a problem, because SQL Server is good at keeping track of where it left off in replication. If a subscriber goes down, just bring it back online, and it will start replicating again. If it is down for more than 24 hours, you should create a new snapshot for it so that it is completely restored.

If you lose a publisher, your subscribers will not get any new data. However, once again, SQL Server is good about keeping track of where it left off. The Log Reader agent uses pointers in the transaction logs of the publisher's databases to keep track of where it left off, much like you use a bookmark to remember what page you left off in a book. This allows the Log Reader to pick up right where it left off when the publisher comes back online. If you have to restore the published database from a backup, these pointers will be out of synch, and you should create a new snapshot to resynchronize your subscribers.

Losing a distribution server is a little more annoying because replication halts altogether without the distribution server. Like publishers and subscribers, though, the distributor is self-healing. Just bring it back online, and it starts functioning again. The catch is that this has to happen within 24 hours (by default), because there is a fail-safe mechanism in the distribution server that keeps it from replicating old transactions to subscribers. If the distributor is down for longer than this period of time, all of the transactions in the distribution database will time out, and nothing will be replicated. If this happens, just create a new snapshot for all of your subscribers, and you will be up and replicating again.

Another area of SQL Server that may need your attention is jobs and alerts.

Troubleshooting Jobs and Alerts

Jobs are used to automate tasks in SQL Server. Jobs are actually a series of steps that occur, one after the other, to accomplish a task. Alerts are used to warn an administrator of a problem with the server by e-mail, pager, or Net Send message. If jobs are not working, check the following:

- The SQL Server Agent service must be running for jobs to work. If it is not, start it.
- Make sure that the job, each step of the job, and each schedule of the job are enabled.
- Make sure that the owner of the job has all the necessary permissions to run the job.
- Check the logic of your job—make sure all of the steps fire in the correct order.

If your alerts are not firing, check the following:

- Make sure that the alert is enabled.
- Verify that the error message associated with the alert is written to the Windows event log, or it will not fire.
- Because the SQL Server Agent service fires alerts, it must be running.

If your alerts are configured to e-mail or page you when they fire, you need to make sure that e-mail connectivity is functioning. So, let's see how to troubleshoot e-mail connectivity.

Troubleshooting Mail Connectivity

SQL Server has the ability to send e-mail using the new Database Mail functionality. Like any other part of a complex system, it can fail at times. When this happens, there are a few things to check.

First, check to see whether the database in question is a database mail host, because only mail hosts can send mail. A simple query can tell you this:

```
IF EXISTS (SELECT * FROM sys.services
WHERE name = 'iMailResponderService')
PRINT DB_NAME() + N' is a mail host database.' ;
ELSE
PRINT DB_NAME() + N' is not a mail host database.' ;
GO
```

If the database is a mail host and you still cannot send mail, then you need to check the mail profiles. First, check to make sure that the specified mail profile exists in the current database. Second, verify that the user has permission to use the mail profile in question. To check permissions, run the `sysmail_help_principalprofile_sp` stored procedure.

Another problem occurs when you try to send mail, but it never actually gets sent, it just sits in the queue. To troubleshoot this, you need to look in the sysmail_log table in the mailhost database. You should see an entry stating that the external database mail program has been activated. If there is no entry, then you need to see whether the Service Broker is enabled on the mailhost database. You can do that with this code:

```
SELECT is_broker_enabled FROM sys.databases WHERE name = DB_NAME();
```

If it is not enabled (indicated by a value of 0), then you need to activate the service broker in the database. Here is how to activate the service broker in the AdventureWorks database:

```
USE master;
GO
ALTER DATABASE AdventureWorks SET ENABLE_BROKER;
GO
```

If the service broker is already enabled, then you need to check the sysmail_mailitems table for the status of the messages.

- Message status 0 means that the message has not yet been processed by the external database mail program. This can happen when the server falls behind on mail processing due to resource constraints or the SMTP server stops responding.
- Message status 1 means that the external database mail program successfully delivered the message to the SMTP server; further troubleshooting should be done on the SMTP server.
- Message status 2 means that the database mail program could not deliver the message. The most common cause is an incorrect destination e-mail address. The following code shows you how to find the status of e-mails sent from the AdventureWorks database to user RosmanD with a status of 2:

```
USE AdventureWorks;
GO

SELECT items.subject,items.last_mod_date, l.description
```

```
FROM dbo.sysmail_mailitems as items
JOIN dbo.sysmail_log AS l
ON items.mailitem_id = [log].mailitem_id

WHERE items.recipients LIKE '%RosmanD%'  OR
items.copy_recipients LIKE '%RosmanD%' OR
items.blind_copy_recipients LIKE '%RosmanD%'
AND sent_status = 2 ;
GO
```

Now we will look at troubleshooting the services themselves.

Troubleshooting the Services (SQL Server and SQL Server Agent)

If either of the services will not start for some reason, you can check several things to correct the problem:

- Make sure that the account has the logon as a service right on the local computer. This is assigned through Local Security Policy.
- Make sure that the service account is not restricted by logon hours.
- Verify that the password for the service has not expired.
- Make sure that the service account has the following access:
  - Full control over the MSSQL directory
  - Full control over the directory where the system databases are stored

If the service still won't start, you may want to change to another account and test the service.

Summary

Troubleshooting is more of an art form than a science; no hard and fast rules can be made in most cases, only suggestions of where to look, which is what we have presented here—some suggestions of what to do when your server doesn't behave.

First, you found out where to look for error messages so that you can do research. The errors are stored in the SQL Server error logs as well as the Windows Event Viewer Application logs.

Next, you found a few tips in case your server will not even set up. Make sure that you have permission to set up SQL Server and don't forget to check the setup log files for errors.

You learned about database-access troubleshooting. DBCC comes in very handy for repairing database problems when SQL Server can access the data files. If SQL Server cannot access the data files, the database is shut down. When you have diagnosed and repaired the condition that caused the database to be marked suspect, you may need to run `ALTER DATABASE` to change the database back to a useable state.

You learned some tips for troubleshooting the backup and restore process. A number of error messages can pop up when performing these actions, so watch for them. Also, don't try to perform any actions that should not be done while backups are occurring.

Next, you read about client connectivity. Make sure that your clients and servers are using the same networking protocols and that they are either on the same network or have a router in place to connect them. If they still won't connect, make sure that they are using the same network library using SQL Configuration Manager.

You also learned some tips for troubleshooting replication. Replication is one of the most complex parts of the server, so myriad problems can arise. Make sure that your servers have network connectivity, that they are all using the same service account for the SQL Server Agent services, and that the account being used is an administrator.

Jobs and alerts can also cause some problems. Make sure that the SQL Server Agent service is running. For jobs, make sure that the job, each step of the job, and each schedule of the job are enabled. For alerts, make sure that the alert is enabled and that the message associated with the alert is written to the Windows Application log.

Next, you learned how to test for mail connectivity. Make sure the database is set up as a mail host and that a valid profile exists in the database and that users have permission to use the profile. You should also check the sysmail_log and sysmail_mailitems tables for errors and message status.

Finally, you learned some things to do if the services just won't start. Check to make sure that the service accounts have the proper rights and that they are not restricted by logon hours. A service account needs to have a password that never expires, so make sure that the password is still valid.

Appendix

Transact-SQL Reference

Throughout the book, you've seen examples of Transact-SQL (T-SQL) statements. Nearly every SQL Server operation can be performed using T-SQL from a graphical interface such as Query Analyzer or even from the command line using OSQL. This includes operations such as setting up jobs and alerts for which we demonstrated only the Enterprise Manager steps.

In this appendix, we present all the SQL statements that we discussed explicitly in this book. For each statement, we include the entire syntax and a cross-reference to the chapter where that statement is discussed in more depth.

Creating a Database

CREATE DATABASE statement (Chapter 10):

```
CREATE DATABASE database_name
    [ ON
        [ <filespec> [ ,...n ] ]
        [ , <filegroup> [ ,...n ] ]
    ]
[
    [ LOG ON { <filespec> [ ,...n ] } ]
    [ COLLATE collation_name ]
    [ FOR { ATTACH [ WITH <service_broker_option> ]
          | ATTACH_REBUILD_LOG } ]
    [ WITH <external_access_option> ]
]
[;]

<filespec> ::=
[ PRIMARY ]
(
    [ NAME = logical_file_name , ]
    FILENAME = 'os_file_name'
        [ , SIZE = size [ KB | MB | GB | TB ] ]
        [ , MAXSIZE = { max_size [ KB | MB | GB | TB ] | UNLIMITED } ]
        [ , FILEGROWTH = growth_increment [ KB | MB | % ] ]
) [ ,...n ]

<filegroup> ::=
FILEGROUP filegroup_name
    <filespec> [ ,...n ]
```

```
<external_access_option> ::=
    DB_CHAINING { ON | OFF }
  | TRUSTWORTHY { ON | OFF }

<service_broker_option> ::=
    ENABLE_BROKER
  | NEW_BROKER
  | ERROR_BROKER_CONVERSATIONS
```

Cursor Statements

DECLARE CURSOR statement (Chapter 8):

```
DECLARE cursor_name [INSENSITIVE][SCROLL] CURSOR
 FOR select_statement
 [FOR {READ ONLY | UPDATE [OF column_name [,...n]]}]
DECLARE cursor_name CURSOR
 [LOCAL | GLOBAL]
 [FORWARD_ONLY | SCROLL]
 [STATIC | KEYSET | DYNAMIC | FAST_FORWARD]
 [READ_ONLY | SCROLL_LOCKS | OPTIMISTIC]
 [TYPE_WARNING]
 FOR select_statement
 [FOR UPDATE [OF column_name [,...n]]]
```

OPEN statement (Chapter 8):

```
OPEN {[GLOBAL] cursor_name} | cursor_variable_name}
```

FETCH statement (Chapter 8):

```
FETCH
[[ NEXT | PRIOR | FIRST | LAST
  | ABSOLUTE {n | @n_variable}
  | RELATIVE {n | @n_variable}
 ]
 FROM
]
{{[GLOBAL] cursor_name} | @cursor_variable_name}
[INTO @variable_name [,...n]]
```

CLOSE statement (Chapter 8):

```
CLOSE {{[GLOBAL] cursor_name} | cursor_variable_name}
```

DEALLOCATE statement (Chapter 8):

```
DEALLOCATE {{[GLOBAL] cursor_name} | @cursor_variable_name}
```

Database Options

ALTER DATABASE statement (Chapter 5):

```
ALTER DATABASE database_name
SET
{SINGLE_USER | RESTRICTED_USER | MULTI_USER} |
{OFFLINE | ONLINE | EMERGENCY} |
{READ_ONLY | READ_WRITE} |
CURSOR_CLOSE_ON_COMMIT {ON | OFF} |
CURSOR_DEFAULT {LOCAL | GLOBAL} |
AUTO_CLOSE { ON | OFF } |
AUTO_CREATE_STATISTICS { ON | OFF } |
AUTO_SHRINK { ON | OFF } |
AUTO_UPDATE_STATISTICS ON | OFF } |
AUTO_UPDATE_STATISTICS_ASYNC { ON | OFF }
ANSI_NULL_DEFAULT { ON | OFF } |
ANSI_NULLS { ON | OFF } |
ANSI_PADDING { ON | OFF } |
ANSI_WARNINGS { ON | OFF } |
ARITHABORT { ON | OFF } |
CONCAT_NULL_YIELDS_NULL { ON | OFF } |
NUMERIC_ROUNDABORT { ON | OFF } |
QUOTED_IDENTIFIERS { ON | OFF } |
RECURSIVE_TRIGGERS { ON | OFF } |
RECOVERY { FULL | BULK_LOGGED | SIMPLE } |
PAGE_VERIFY { CHECKSUM | TORN_PAGE_DETECTION | NONE }[,...n]
```

sp_dbcmptlevel statement (Chapter 5):

```
sp_dbcmptlevel [[@dbname=] 'database_name']
 [,[@new_cmptlevel=] version]
```

sp_dboption statement (Chapter 5):

```
sp_dboption [[@dbname=] 'database_name']
 [, [@optname=] 'option_name']
 [, [@optvalue=] 'option_value']
```

Deleting Records

DELETE statement (Chapter 7):

```
DELETE
[FROM]
{
 table_name [WITH (table_hint [...n]])
 | view_name
 | OPENQUERY | OPENROWSET | OPENDATASOURCE
}
[FROM table_source]
```

```
[WHERE search_conditions]
[OPTION query_hints]
```

TRUNCATE TABLE statement (Chapter 7):

```
TRUNCATE TABLE table_name
```

Full-Text Search

CONTAINSTABLE statement (Chapter 8):

```
CONTAINSTABLE (table_name, {column_name | *},
 '<search_condition>' [,top_n])

<search_condition>::=
{
 <generation_term> |
 <prefix_term> |
 <proximity_term> |
 <simple_term> |
 <weighted_term>
}
| {(<search_condition>)
 {AND | AND NOT | OR}
 <search_condition> [...n]
 }

<simple_term> ::=
word | "phrase"

<prefix_term> ::=
{"word*" | "phrase*"}

<generation_term> ::=
FORMSOF(INFLECTIONAL | THESAURUS), <simple_term> [,...n])

<proximity_term> ::=
{<simple_term> | <prefix_term> }
{{NEAR | ~} {<simple_term> | <prefix_term>}} [...n]

<weighted_term> ::=
ISABOUT (
{{
  <generation_term> |
  <prefix_term> |
  <proximity_term> |
  <simple_term>
 }
[WEIGHT (weight_value)]
} [,...n])
```

FREETEXTTABLE statement (Chapter 8):

```
FREETEXTTABLE (table_name, {column_name | *},
 'freetext' [, LANGUAGE language_term][,top_n])
```

Inserting Records

INSERT statement (Chapter 7):

```
INSERT [INTO]
{
 table_name [WITH (table_hint [...n])]
 | view_name
 | OPENQUERY | OPENROWSET | OPENDATASOURCE
}
{
 [(column_list)]
 {
  VALUES
  ( { DEFAULT | NULL
    | expression }[,...n] )
  | derived_table
  | execute_statement
 }
}
| DEFAULT VALUES
```

SELECT INTO statement (Chapter 7):

```
SELECT select_list
INTO new_table_name
FROM table_source
[WHERE condition]
 [GROUP BY expression]
HAVING condition]
[ORDER BY expression]
```

Retrieving Records

SELECT statement (Chapter 6):

```
SELECT [ALL | DISTINCT]
 [{TOP integer | TOP integer PERCENT} [WITH TIES]]
 <select_list>
[INTO new_table]
[FROM {<table_source>} [,...n]]
[WHERE search_condition ]
[GROUP BY [ ALL ] group_by_expression [,...n]
        [WITH { CUBE | ROLLUP }]
```

```
[HAVING search_condition]
[ORDER BY { order_by_expression | column_position [ASC | DESC]]
[OPTION ( <query_hint> [ ,...n ])]
```

Rowsets

OPENQUERY statement (Chapter 8):

```
OPENQUERY(linked_server, 'query')
```

OPENROWSET statement (Chapter 8):

```
OPENROWSET ('provider_name',
 'datasource';'user_id';'password',
 'query')
```

OPENDATASOURCE statement (Chapter 8):

```
OPENDATASOURCE(provider_name, connection_string)
```

OPENXML statement (Chapter 8):

```
OPENXML(idoc, rowpattern, [flags])
  [WITH (SchemaDeclaration | TableName)]
```

Transactions

BEGIN TRANSACTION statement (Chapter 8):

```
BEGIN TRANS[ACTION] [transaction_name | @name_variable]
 [WITH MARK ['description']]
```

COMMIT TRANSACTION statement (Chapter 8):

```
COMMIT TRANS[ACTION] [transaction_name | @name_variable]
COMMIT [WORK]
```

ROLLBACK TRANSACTION statement (Chapter 8):

```
ROLLBACK TRANS[ACTION]
 [transaction_name |
 @name_variable |
 savepoint_name |
 @savepoint_variable]
ROLLBACK [WORK]
```

SAVE TRANSACTION statement (Chapter 8):

```
SAVE TRANS[ACTION] {savepoint_name | @savepoint_variable}
```

Updating Records

UPDATE statement (Chapter 7):

```
UPDATE
{
 table_name [WITH (table_hint [...n])]
 | view_name
 | OPENQUERY | OPENROWSET | OPENDATASOURCE
}
SET
{
 column_name = {expression | DEFAULT | NULL}
 | @variable = expression
 | @variable = column = expression
| column_name { .WRITE (expression , @Offset , @Length)
} [,...n]
{
 [FROM {table_source} [,...n]]
 [WHERE search_condition]
}
[OPTION (query_hint [,...n])]
```

User-Defined Functions

CREATE FUNCTION statement (Chapter 5):

```
CREATE FUNCTION [owner_name].function_name
(
 [{@parameter_name data_type [=default_value]} [,...n]]
)
RETURNS data_type
[AS]
{BEGIN function_body END}
```

Index

Note to the Reader: Throughout this index **boldfaced** page numbers indicate primary discussions of a topic. *Italicized* page numbers indicate illustrations.

D

E

F

G

H

I

M

U